THE
PERSONALITY PUZZLE

EIGHTH EDITION

THE
PERSONALITY
PUZZLE
EIGHTH EDITION

DAVID C. FUNDER

University of California, Riverside

W. W. NORTON & COMPANY
New York · London

W. W. Norton & Company has been independent since its founding in 1923, when William Warder Norton and Mary D. Herter Norton first published lectures delivered at the People's Institute, the adult education division of New York City's Cooper Union. The firm soon expanded its program beyond the Institute, publishing books by celebrated academics from America and abroad. By midcentury, the two major pillars of Norton's publishing program—trade books and college texts—were firmly established. In the 1950s, the Norton family transferred control of the company to its employees, and today—with a staff of four hundred and a comparable number of trade, college, and professional titles published each year—W. W. Norton & Company stands as the largest and oldest publishing house owned wholly by its employees.

Editor: Ken Barton
Project Editor: Caitlin Moran
Assistant Editor: Katie Pak
Copy Editor: Rosy Lum
Managing Editor, College: Marian Johnson
Managing Editor, College Digital Media: Kim Yi
Production Manager: Benjamin Reynolds
Media Editor: Kaitlin Coats
Associate Media Editor: Victoria Reuter
Assistant Media Editor: Allison Nicole Smith
Marketing Manager: Ashley Sherwood
Design Director: Rubina Yeh
Design Assistant: Juan Paolo Francisco
Senior Photo Editor: Ted Szczepanski
Director of College Permissions: Megan Schindel
Permissions Specialist: Elizabeth Trammell
Composition: GraphicWorld
Manufacturing: Transcontinental—Beauceville, Quebec

ISBN: 978-0-393-67480-4

W. W. Norton & Company, Inc., 500 Fifth Avenue, New York, NY 10110
wwnorton.com

W. W. Norton & Company Ltd., 15 Carlisle Street, London W1D 3BS

1 2 3 4 5 6 7 8 9 0

For my father

ABOUT THE AUTHOR

David C. Funder is a Distinguished Professor of Psychology and former chair of the department at the University of California, Riverside. Winner of the 2009 Jack Block Award for Distinguished Research in Personality, he is a former editor of the *Journal of Research in Personality*, and a past president of the Association for Research in Personality as well as the Society for Personality and Social Psychology. He is best known for his research on personality judgment and has also published research on delay of gratification, attribution theory, the longitudinal course of personality development, and the psychological assessment of situations. His current research is focusing on the experience of situations in cultures around the world. He has taught personality psychology to undergraduates at Harvey Mudd College, Harvard University, and the University of Illinois, Urbana-Champaign, and continues to teach the course every year at the University of California, Riverside.

Anybody in science, if there are enough anybodies, can find the answer—it's an Easter-egg hunt. That isn't the idea. The idea is: Can you ask the question in such a way as to facilitate the answer?

—GERALD EDELMAN

Even if, ultimately, everything turns out to be connected to everything else, a research program rooted in that realization might well collapse of its own weight.

—HOWARD GARDNER

The first step is to measure whatever can be easily measured. That's OK as far as it goes. The second step is to pretend that whatever cannot be easily measured isn't very important. That's dangerous. The third step is to pretend that whatever cannot easily be measured doesn't exist. That's suicide.

—DANIEL YANKELOVICH

There once was an entomologist who found a bug he couldn't classify—so he stepped on it.

—ERNEST R. HILGARD

Interpretation is the revenge of the intellect upon art.

—SUSAN SONTAG

Of course it is happening inside your head, Harry, but why on earth should that mean it's not real?

—ALBUS DUMBLEDORE
(In *Harry Potter and the Deathly Hallows*, by J. K. Rowling)

CONTENTS IN BRIEF

CONTENTS

PART VII Applications of Personality Psychology   580

PREFACE

IT HAS BEEN A true labor of love to work on this personality textbook through eight editions. Personality psychology has grown and evolved, but my goal has always been the same: to keep the research current, the writing fresh, and, above all, to continue to make the case that *personality psychology is interesting and important*.

How This Book Is Traditional

In many ways, this is a fairly traditional personality textbook. It covers methods, traits, assessment, development, psychoanalysis, behaviorism, motivation, emotion, and cognitive processes. Most personality textbooks are organized around these topics, variously calling them "perspectives," "paradigms," or "domains of knowledge." Here I call them "basic approaches." By any labeling, this range of topics means that the book should fit in easily with just about any typical Personality Psychology syllabus.

"As a matter of fact, I confess to modest hopes—not wildly unfounded, I trust—that my book may resonate beyond the reaches of academe."

How This Book Is Different

But this book is, in other ways, *not* like the others. What would have been the point of writing just more of the same? Read this book, or just flip through the pages, and you will see that it is distinctive in several ways.

1. **Opinions.** This book includes my personal opinions, quite a few of them. An old friend from graduate school wrote a textbook of his own, on a different subject, and happened to see this one. "Wow," he said. "Your publisher lets you state what you think. Mine makes me take out anything they think anybody might disagree with."

   W.W. Norton is a great publisher and gives me a long leash, and I have learned that my friend's experience is more common than my own. But I try not to abuse the privilege. The opinions in this book are professional, not personal. I think I have some credentials and experience that license me (not legally!) to have opinions about psychological issues. I do *not* have any special qualifications to weigh in on politics or morality. Although I have strong opinions about those matters, too, I have tried very hard to leave them out. For example, the debate over abortion is considered in Chapter 13, in the context of a discussion of collectivist versus individualist values. A student once told me that after reading that chapter she couldn't tell what my own position was. Good.

When it comes to my views on professional matters, surely not every instructor (or student) will agree with me on every point. But that's fine. For example, in Chapter 3 I express a rather negative opinion about the use of deception in psychological experiments. I suspect this is a minority position among my colleagues, and perhaps students as well. The ethics of research and experimentation, including this issue, could make for a lively lecture topic or class discussion, focusing on the ways in which my own viewpoint is wrong. I express opinions not in the hope of having the final word on the subject, but in an attempt to stimulate the reader to decide whether he or she agrees with me and to formulate opinions of his or her own. For reasons explained in Chapter 15, this is an excellent way to learn material no matter what the subject.

2. **Respect for Freud.** It is oh-so-fashionable for modern psychologists to trash Freud, all of his works, and even all of psychoanalytic thought. Too often, textbook chapters could even be titled "Why Freud Was Wrong." I don't do this. I find Freudian theory to be a perplexing mixture of wise and even startling insights, strange ideas, and old-fashioned 19th-century sexism. As you can see in Chapters 10 and 11, I seek to emphasize the first of these elements and deemphasize (or ignore) the other two. I have had colleagues ask, How can you teach Freudian theory? It's so boring! To which I answer, Not if you teach it right. (Most years, it's my own students' favorite part of the course.) I have also had colleagues ask, How can you teach Freudian theory? Freud was wrong about so many things! To which I answer, Read Chapter 10. I fixed it.

By the way, orthodox Freudians (there are still a few around) are not especially grateful for what I've done here. They would much rather see a presentation that marches through the entire Freudian canon in chronological order, and includes a detailed apotheosis of *Civilization and Its Discontents* and all of Freud's other major works. There are plenty of places to find presentations like that (my favorite is Gay, 1988). You won't find one here.

3. **Historical perspective.** I am surprised by how many textbooks neglect the history of psychology; in fact, that seems to be a growing trend. I appreciate the urge to present all the latest findings, and, indeed, you will find many new and exciting studies in this book. But that's not enough. How can you understand where you are going if you don't know where you have been? That is one (just one) of the reasons I try to give Freud his due. It is also why this book includes an account of how behaviorism evolved into cognitive social learning theory, how modern positive psychology developed out of existential philosophy and classic humanistic psychology, and how the modern study of personality traits began with Allport and Odbert's famous list of 17,953 ways to describe a person.

4. **Fewer pictures.** Have you already noticed that this textbook doesn't contain as many pictures as most others do? I get complaints. "My college students won't read a book that doesn't have more pictures." Really? Maybe that's true; how sad. But if you would have liked more pictures, blame me, not the publisher. The people marketing this book are all for pictures. But I don't like to have too many, for three reasons:

   a. Pictures are sometimes meaningless window-dressing. I was once leafing through a widely-used personality textbook and noticed a photograph of a student looking thoughtful. The caption read, "Much careful study will be required before a single integrative theory of personality is developed." Someone please tell me the point of that picture.

   b. Pictures can be distracting. This book was written to be *read*, not just looked at. I once replied to someone advising me to have more pictures that John Grisham's books don't have any pictures at all, and yet they sell millions of copies. The response was, "You're not John Grisham." Excellent point! Still, the heart of this book lies in the words, not the illustrations. The words make it worthwhile, or they don't.

   c. One aspect of the kind of pictures commonly seen in textbooks makes me uneasy. Chapter 12 includes a summary of what Carl Rogers said about "conditions of worth," the harm they can do, and the way I think they are promulgated in many typical textbook illustrations. I would rather not do that in a psychology textbook, of all places. Except just once, to illustrate what I'm talking about (see Figure 12.3, in Chapter 12).

5. **More cartoons.** On the other hand, I love well-chosen cartoons. Aaron Javsicas, a former Norton editor, suggested a long time ago that a few *New Yorker* cartoons might liven the book up a bit. You will see that I took this suggestion.[1] But I hope the cartoons are more than just entertaining. I have tried to find ones that underline a point being made in the text. Sometimes the connection is obvious, sometimes perhaps not so much. Trying to figure out why I thought each cartoon was relevant is one way to study for the midterm!

6. **Overall goal.** Probably the most distinctive aspect of this book is its overall goal, which, as I have already said, is to convince the reader of the value of personality psychology. It's fine to cover everything in depth, to include all the latest findings, and even to seek to write in an interesting, engaging manner. Indeed, I did try to do all these things, but they were not my primary aims. To the extent that someone gets through the 600-plus pages of this book and, at the end, concludes that personality psychology is an interesting, important part of science, then I have done what I set out to do. Anything else is gravy.

---

[1] Not all the cartoons are actually from the *New Yorker*; some are from other sources, and a few of my favorites were drawn by my older daughter.

New to the Eighth Edition

Doing a textbook is a strange kind of writing because it's never finished. Every few years, you have to do it again. On the other hand, every few years, you get to do it again. Each edition offers an opportunity not only to update the latest research, but also to seek clearer ways to explain complex ideas and improve the overall organization. And I still continue to find (and attempt to fix) clunky sentences that have somehow survived seven rounds of rewriting and copyediting. Over the editions of this book, some revisions have been major and others have been minor. This one is somewhere in between.

The most significant change in this edition is the addition of a section specifically aimed at demonstrating how personality psychology can be useful. Not everybody realizes that personality is an important applied area of psychology. The new Part VII of this book, called "Applications of Personality Psychology" and the new Chapters 16, 17, and 18 seek to demonstrate how and why. Chapter 16 illustrates how personality psychology can be applied to understanding and improving outcomes in relationships and business, such as choosing the right partner or choosing the right occupation. Chapter 17 summarizes some of the latest developments in understanding personality disorders, and current research on the traits and psychological processes associated with physical health. The final chapter on "What Have We Learned" (called the Epilogue in the Seventh Edition) also tries to highlight some practical lessons drawn from this very long book. I do hope people read this chapter, which I suspect was mostly ignored last time around. Apparently, in the previous edition, about as many people read the Epilogue as read the Preface, and such people are unusual. But they do include you.

Another addition worth noting is new sections on issues of replication and the practice of open science in psychological research (in Chapter 3). These topics have become increasingly prominent lately, and include issues such as publication bias, questionable research practices, *p*-hacking, and ways to increase the reliability of scientific research. No course in any area of psychology is up-to-date without at least some consideration of these issues.

The final major difference between this and the previous edition comes from my continued efforts to improve the way the book is organized. One challenge in maintaining a textbook through eight editions is avoiding book bloat. With every revision, an author is obligated to include the latest findings on each topic, and sometimes add whole new topics that have become important. There is less pressure to take anything out. The result can be a book that gets bigger and bigger until carrying it around can be hazardous to your health (thank goodness for ebooks editions). For this edition, I made an extra effort to remove descriptions of studies that are out-of-date, superseded by newer research, or no longer relevant to current concerns. In particular, I removed quite a bit of material concerning basic principles of behaviorism that are not directly relevant to personality, and old versions of social learning theory that have lesser impact on modern research. This revision allowed me to combine two chapters from the Seventh Edition, on learning and cognitive processes, into a single chapter (Chapter 14) on personality processes.

Pieces of the Personality Puzzle

Pieces of the Personality Puzzle: Readings in Theory and Research (Fifth Edition) is a collection of readings related to the topics covered in this book that my colleague Dan Ozer and I edited several years ago. It is still available as a supplemental text. Selections include original essays by theorists such as Freud, Jung, Erickson, and Allport; classic research articles; and examples of recent empirical research taken from the current research literature. Each article has been edited for clarity and includes explanatory footnotes. Other instructors and I have found that these readings help to provide a firsthand view of the theory and research summarized in *The Personality Puzzle* and can also be the basis of stimulating classroom discussions.

Resources for Instructors

InQuizitive

New for the Eighth Edition of *The Personality Puzzle*, InQuizitive adaptive assessment uses research-proven techniques to improve student learning. Motivating game-like elements engage students in active learning and drive them back into the text when they need to review. Each chapter includes 40–50 questions of varying question types, and each question includes answer-specific feedback to help students grasp course concepts.

Interactive Instructor's Guide

This online repository of teaching assets offers materials for every chapter that both veteran and novice instructors of the course alike will find helpful. Searchable by chapter or asset type, the Interactive Instructor's Guide provides multiple ideas for teaching. The latest version has been revised to coordinate with the addition of new material, research, and updated figures. The Guide also includes links to carefully selected YouTube–style clips and activity ideas that will be continually updated during the life of the edition.

Test Bank

The test bank features approximately 1,700 questions, including 80–100 multiple-choice, 10 matching, and 5 short-answer questions in each chapter. All questions have been updated according to Norton's assessment guidelines to make it easy for instructors to construct quizzes and exams that are meaningful and diagnostic. All questions are classified according to educational objective, student text section, difficulty, and question type. This Norton test bank is available with Exam View Test Generator software, allowing instructors to effortlessly create, administer, and manage assessments. The convenient and intuitive test-generating wizard makes it easy to create customized exams. Other key features include the ability to create paper exams with algorithmically generated variables and to export files directly to your LMS.

Lecture PowerPoints

These text-focused PowerPoints follow the chapter outlines, featuring figures from the text, extra pedagogy notes for the instructor, as well as clicker questions to check students' understanding at the end of each chapter.

Art Slides

All the figures, photos, and tables from the text are offered as JPEGs, both separately and embedded in a PowerPoint set for each chapter. All text art is enhanced for optimal viewing when projected in large classrooms.

Acknowledgments

It is with pleasure that I acknowledge some of the help I have received with this project over the years and editions. First of all, my wife, Patti, has been a source of emotional support, clever ideas, and critical comments throughout the process. Her insights and her skepticism about whether psychology is really a science (she was trained as a cell biologist) continue to keep me on my toes. She also patiently puts up with the foggy state I can go into for weeks and sometimes months while doing this book's periodic revisions.[2] I really and truly could not keep doing this without her. My daughter Morgan has provided some apt hand-drawn illustrations for the book ever since the fifth edition, and contributed some new ones this time around.

Along with Patti, Tiffany Wright (a graduate student at the University of California, Riverside), Chris Langston (a colleague), and Cathy Wick (a former editor at Norton) read the first edition of this book and made many comments and suggestions, most of which I followed. The early encouragement and advice of Paul Rozin was particularly important, and the late Henry Gleitman was also generous. Traci Nagle carefully copyedited the first edition, and a little of the prose she worked so hard on still survives after all these years. Mary N. Babcock made an equally important contribution to the second edition, Anne Hellman to the third, Sarah Mann to the fourth, Susan Middleton to the fifth, Erika Nein to the sixth,

---

[2] She also tolerates the inclusion of the anecdote about one of our early dates in Chapter 10.

Teresa Wilson to the seventh, and Rosy Lum to this edition. Don Fusting, a former Norton editor, used the softest sell in the history of publishing, over a period of years, to convince me to undertake this project in the first place. If not for him, this book would simply not exist.

When Sheri Snavely came on board as editor for the fifth and the sixth and seventh edition, I felt like this book gained a whole new life. I am grateful for her creative ideas, good judgment, collaborative spirit, and most of all for her understanding of and enthusiasm for the distinctive kind of book *The Personality Puzzle* has strived to be. Ken Barton, a long-time friend and helper of the *Puzzle*, picked up the torch for this new edition. He provided valuable advice and guidance—and a bit of restraint here and there—as I prepared this latest revision.

Assistant editor Katie Pak did a terrific job in keeping organized all the various chapters, revised chapters, illustrations, revised illustrations, copyediting, updated references, and all the million other pieces of this book puzzle that flowed across her desk at random times and in no particular order. Also keeping things on track were Benjamin Reynolds, the production manager, and Caitlin Moran, the project editor. Ted Szczepanski, the senior photo editor, helped to track down photographs and other illustrations that, through the vagaries of copyright law and mysteriously disappearing copyright owners, are more difficult to find than they used to be. Kaitlin Coats, Victoria Reuter, and Allison Smith assembled the ever-growing and ever-improving media resources that accompany this edition, for which Erica Baranski, David Condon, Amy Corbett, Gwendolyn Gardiner, Tera Letzring, and Jennifer McDonald contributed terrific new content. Going beyond the call of duty, in the course of working on the ancillary materials, Tera Letzring also discovered some errors in the text that I was very happy to correct, just in time. Finally, there is no point to writing and producing a book if nobody reads it. So I am grateful to Ashley Sherwood and the whole W. W. Norton sales team (who, in a bit of lovable inside jargon, are called "travelers") for their persistent efforts and long journeys to help make this book available to readers across the United States and around the world.

For this and previous editions, I was aided by the wise and knowledgeable advice of the following people:

PREVIOUS EDITIONS

Sarah Angulo, Texas State University, San Marcos

Nicole B. Barenbaum, University of the South

Susan Basow, Lafayette College

Veronica Benet-Martínez, University of California, Riverside

Diane S. Berry, Southern Methodist University

Mia Biran, Miami University (Ohio)

Boris Bizumic, The Australian National University

Dan Boroto, Florida State University

Turhan Canli, State University of New York at Stony Brook

Kimberly Clow, University of Ontario Institute of Technology

Lisa Cothran, University of Tennessee at Chattanooga

Henrik Cronqvist, Claremont McKenna College
Colin DeYoung, University of Minnesota
Brent Donnellan, Michigan State University
Amber Douglas, Mount Holyoke College
Mocha Dryud, Northern Virginia Community College
Peter Ebersole, California State University, Fullerton
Robin Edelstein, University of Michigan
Elizabeth S. Focella, University of Missouri
Jennifer S. McDonald, University of British Columbia
William K. Gabrenya, Florida Institute of Technology
Ian Glendon, Griffith University, Gold Coast Campus
Jeremy Gray, Yale University
Meara M. Habashi, University of Iowa
Christian Hakulinen, University of Helsinki
Cindy Hazan, Cornell University
Robert Hessling, University of Wisconsin–Milwaukee
Shannon Holleran, University of Arizona
Christopher J. Hopwood, Michigan State University
Kazuya Horike, Toyo University
Josh Jackson, Washington University in St. Louis
Alisha Janowsky, University of Central Florida
Wendy Johnson, University of Edinburgh
Daniel N. Jones, University of Texas at El Paso
Joe Kable, University of Pennsylvania
D. Brett King, University of Colorado, Boulder
Scott King, Shenandoah University
Brian Knutson, Stanford University
Zlatan Krizan, Iowa State University
Robert F. Krueger, University of Minnesota
Tera Letzring, Idaho State University
Robin Lewis, California Polytechnic State University
Kenneth Locke, University of Idaho
Brian Marx, Temple University
David Matsumoto, San Francisco State University
Tani McBeth, Portland Community College
Matthias Mehl, University of Arizona
Ricardo Michan, Loyola Marymount University
Joshua Miller, University of Georgia
Dan Molden, Northwestern University
Douglas Mook, University of Virginia
Yozan Mosig, University of Nebraska at Kearney
Denise Newman, University of Virginia
Julie Norem, Wellesley College
Barbara O'Brien, Washington University in St. Louis

Shigehiro Oishi, University of Virginia
Krista Phillips, York University
Aaron L. Pincus, Pennsylvania State University
Janice L. Rank, Portland Community College
Steve Reise, University of California, Los Angeles
Steven Richards, Texas Tech University
Alan Roberts, Indiana University
Brent Roberts, University of Illinois at Urbana-Champaign
Rick Robins, University of California, Davis
Christopher Robinson, University of Alabama at Birmingham
Joseph F. Rychlak, Loyola University of Chicago
Ira Saiger, Yeshiva University
Gerard Saucier, University of Oregon
Alana Saulnier, University of Ontario Institute of Technology
Chloe Schowalter, Hendrix College
Don Sharpsteen, Missouri University of Science and Technology
Phillip Shaver, University of California, Davis
Kennon Sheldon, University of Missouri
Ryne Sherman, Florida Atlantic University
Karen K. Szumlinski, University of California, Santa Barbara
Yohtaro Takano, University of Tokyo
Liz Temple, University of Ballarat
Michele M. Tomarelli, Texas A & M University
Jeanne Tsai, Stanford University
Brian Tschanz, Utah State University
Simine Vazire, Washington University in St. Louis
Drew Westen, Emory University
David Williams, University of Pennsylvania
David Zald, Vanderbilt University
John Zelenski, Carleton University
Marvin Zuckerman, University of Delaware

EIGHTH EDITION

Kevin Bley, UC Davis
Michael Chmielewski, Southern Methodist University
Colin DeYoung, University of Minnesota
Kristen Doran, Delaware Community College
Aleksa Kaurin, Johannes Gutenberg University, Germany
Arthur Mielke, College of Marin
Alan Roberts, Indiana University, Bloomington
Dominic Sagoe, University of Bergen
Claire Siepser
Lyra Stein, Rutgers University
Simine Vazire, UC Davis

Jessica Williamson, Kentucky State University
Betty Witcher, William Peace University
Richie Zweigenhaft, Guilford College
Wiebke Bleidorn, University of California, Davis
Jon Grahe, Pacific Lutheran University
Nicholas Herrera, Long Beach City College
Christopher Hopwood, University of California, Davis
Wade Rowatt, Baylor University
Jana Spain, High Point University
Omri Gillath, The University of Kansas

I also have been gratified by many emails from students. Some of these messages arrive late at night—apparently, the readers of this book and its author keep the same hours. Many include useful questions, suggestions, and corrections that I have incorporated into every edition. Other messages challenged or disagreed with me on key points, and if the people who wrote them look closely at the latest edition, they will see that they too mostly had an effect. But that wasn't even the best part. I can't adequately express how encouraging it is for an author bogged down at one in the morning to have his computer suddenly yield an email that says, "I really enjoyed your book and just wanted to say thanks." Thank *you*.

Finally, I want to acknowledge the very first person who read the first draft of the first edition all the way through. He wrote comments on nearly every page. Usually, they were notations such as "What does this mean?" or "What are you talking about?" These invariably identified places where I had lapsed into incomprehensible jargon or otherwise failed to make sense. Sometimes his comments were just strong expressions of agreement or disagreement. Over the several years that I worked on the first edition, I never once had a conversation with him that did not include the question "How is the book coming along?" and some sort of suggestion that I really ought to be working faster. He looked forward to seeing this book in print and didn't miss it by much. My father, Elvin Funder, died in August 1995, just as I was putting the finishing touches on the first edition. For the second through eighth editions, I have had to imagine what he would say about some of my observations, but even that was helpful. I rededicate this book to him.

David C. Funder
Riverside, California
July, 2019

THE
PERSONALITY PUZZLE

EIGHTH EDITION

THE STUDY OF THE PERSON

> All persons are puzzles until at last we find in some word or act the key to the man, to the woman: straightaway all their past words and actions lie in light before us.
>
> —RALPH WALDO EMERSON

YOU MAY ALREADY HAVE been told that psychology is not what you think it is. Some psychology professors delight in conveying this surprising news to their students on the first day of the term. Maybe you expect psychology to be about what people are thinking and feeling under the surface, these professors expound; maybe you think it is about sexuality, and dreams, and creativity, and aggression, and consciousness, and how people are different from one another, and interesting topics like that. Wrong, they say. Psychology is about the precise manipulation of independent variables for the furtherance of compelling theoretical accounts of well-specified phenomena, such as how many milliseconds it takes to find a circle in a field of squares. If that focus makes psychology boring, well, too bad. Science does not have to be interesting to be valuable.

Fortunately, most personality psychologists do not talk that way. This is because the study of personality comes close to what non-psychologists intuitively expect psychology to be, and addresses the topics most people want to know about (J. Block, 1993; Funder, 1998b). Therefore, personality psychologists have no excuse for being boring. Their field of study includes everything that makes psychology interesting.[1]

---

[1] Thus, if you end up finding this book boring, it is all my fault. There is no reason it should be, given its subject matter.

Specifically, personality psychology addresses how people feel, think, and behave—the three parts of the **psychological triad**. Each is important in its own right, but what you feel, what you think, and what you do are even more interesting in combination, because sometimes they conflict. For example, have you ever experienced a conflict between how you feel and what you think, such as an attraction toward someone you just knew was bad news? Have you ever had a conflict between what you think and what you do, such as intending to do your homework and then going to the beach instead? Have you ever found your behavior conflicting with your feelings, such as doing something that makes you feel guilty (fill in your own example here), and then continuing to do it anyway? If so (and I know the answer is yes), the next question is, why? The answer is far from obvious.

Inconsistencies between feelings, thoughts, and behaviors are common enough to make us suspect that the mind is not a simple place and that even to understand yourself—the person you know best—is not necessarily easy. Personality psychology is important not because it has solved these puzzles of internal consistency and self-knowledge, but because—alone among the sciences and even among the branches of psychology—it regards these puzzles as worth their full attention.

When most people think of psychologists, they think first of the clinical practitioners who treat mental illness and try to help people with a wide range of other personal problems.[2] Personality psychology is not the same as clinical psychology, but the two subfields do overlap. Some of the most important personality psychologists—both historically and in the present day—had clinical training and treated patients (a famous example, of course, is Sigmund Freud). At many colleges and universities, the person who teaches abnormal or clinical psychology also teaches personality psychology. When patterns of personality are extreme, unusual, and cause problems, the two subfields come together in the study of personality disorders. Most important, clinical and personality psychology share the obligation to try to understand whole persons, not just parts of persons, one individual at a time.

In this sense, personality psychology is the largest as well as the smallest subfield of psychology. There are probably fewer doctoral degrees granted in personality psychology than in social, cognitive, developmental, or biological psychology. But personality psychology is closely allied with clinical psychology, which is by far the largest subfield. It also has close relationships with organizational psychology because, as you will see in Chapter 16, personality assessment is useful for understanding vocational interests, occupational success, and leadership. Personality psychology is where the rest of psychology comes together; as you will see, it draws heavily from social, cognitive, developmental, clinical, and biological psychology.

---

[2] This is why nonclinical research psychologists sometimes cringe a little when someone asks them what they do for a living.

It contributes to each of these subfields as well, by showing how each part of psychology fits into the whole picture of what people are really like.

THE GOALS OF PERSONALITY PSYCHOLOGY

~Definition

Personality refers to an individual's characteristic patterns of thought, emotion, and behavior, together with the psychological mechanisms—hidden or not—behind those patterns. This definition gives personality psychology its unique mission to explain whole persons. Of course, personality psychologists may not always succeed at this job. But that is what they are supposed to be doing—putting together the pieces of the puzzle contributed by the other subfields of psychology, as well as by their own research, to assemble an integrated view of whole, functioning individuals in their daily environments.

Basis of Personality Psych

Mission: Impossible

There is only one problem with this mission: It is impossible. In fact, this interesting mission is the source of personality psychology's biggest difficulty. If you try to understand everything about a person at once, you will immediately find yourself completely overwhelmed. Your mind, instead of attaining a broad understanding, may go blank.

The only way out is to choose to limit what you look at. Rather than trying to account for everything at once, you must search for more specific patterns. This search will require you to limit yourself to certain kinds of observations, certain kinds of patterns, and certain ways of thinking about these patterns. A systematic, self-imposed limitation of this sort is what I call a **basic approach** (another commonly used term is *paradigm*). Personality psychology is organized around several different basic approaches.

The most all-encompassing tradition in personality psychology, the **trait approach** (the reference is to personality traits), focuses on the ways that people differ psychologically and how these differences might be conceptualized, measured, and followed over time. This is by far the largest and most dominant approach

"Do you mind if I say something helpful about your personality?"

Five Approaches

Table 1.1	BASIC APPROACHES TO PERSONALITY AND THEIR FOCAL TOPICS
Basic Approach	**Focal Topics**
Trait approach	Conceptualization of individual differences
	Measurement of individual differences
	Consequences of individual differences
	Personality development
	Personality change
Biological approach	Anatomy
	Physiology
	Genetics
	Evolution
Psychoanalytic approach	Unconscious mind
	Internal mental conflict
Phenomenological approach	Conscious awareness and experience
	Free will
	Humanistic psychology
	Cross-cultural psychology
Learning and cognitive approaches	Behaviorism
	Social learning theory
	Cognitive personality psychology

in contemporary personality psychology, and it helps to organize the other approaches, because individual differences are central to pretty much everything.

One specifically focused way to understand individual differences is in terms of the body, concentrating on biological mechanisms such as anatomy, physiology, genetics, even evolution. This is the **biological approach** to personality.

A very different way to understand people is to try to investigate the unconscious mind, and the nature and resolution of internal mental conflict. This is the **psychoanalytic approach**.

Or, one can choose to focus on people's *conscious* experience of the world, their phenomenology, and so follow a **phenomenological approach**. In current research, an emphasis on awareness and experience can lead in one of two directions. The first program of theory and research, called *humanistic psychology*, pursues how conscious awareness can produce such uniquely human attributes as existential anxiety, creativity, and free will—which are important, but of no concern to your dog. The other phenomenological direction emphasizes the degree to which psychology and the very experience of reality might be different

> Existential anxiety, creativity, and free will are important psychological topics, but of no concern to your dog.

in different cultures. Interest in this topic has led to an explosion in recent years of *cross-cultural* personality research.

Yet another way to study the ways people differ from each other is to concentrate on how people change their behavior as a result of rewards, punishments, and other experiences in life, a process called **learning**.[3] Classic *behaviorism* focuses tightly on overt behavior and the ways it can be affected by rewards and punishments. Behaviorism evolved over the years into a related point of view called *social learning*. Social learning theory draws inferences about the ways that mental processes such as observation and self-evaluation determine which behaviors are learned and how they are performed. Over the past couple of decades, social learning theory has, in turn, evolved into an influential and prolific new field of personality research focused on cognitive processes that applies insights and methods derived from the study of perception, memory, and thought. Taken together, behaviorism, social learning theory, and *cognitive personality psychology* comprise the **learning and cognitive processes approaches** to personality.

Competitors or Complements?

The different approaches to personality are often portrayed as competitors, and for good reason. The original, famous champion of each typically made his mark by announcing to the world that his approach finally accounted for everything anybody would ever want to know about human nature, and that all other approaches were pretty much worthless. Sigmund Freud, for one, was vocal in claiming that his version of the psychoanalytic approach was the one true path and even ostracized erstwhile followers, such as Carl Jung, who dared to differ with him on seemingly minor points. B. F. Skinner, with his very different view of human nature, was not much of an improvement in the modesty department. He announced that behaviorism explained everything worth knowing about psychology, and he delighted in denouncing all of the other approaches and their presumptions that people might have traits and thoughts, or even freedom and dignity.

This kind of arrogance is not limited to approaches like psychoanalysis and behaviorism that have been closely associated with famous individual founders. Biologically inclined psychologists have been known to proclaim that everything about personality reduces to a matter of genes, physiology, and brain anatomy. Trait, cognitive, and humanistic psychologists likewise have insisted their approach is the one that covers it all. In fact, major advocates of every basic approach have claimed frequently and insistently not only that their favored approach can explain everything worth explaining, but also that the others are all dead wrong.

---

[3] This narrow use of the term *learning* by behaviorists should not be confused with its broader everyday meaning.

Figure 1.1 **Freud and Skinner** Sigmund Freud and B. F. Skinner had completely different views about human nature, but each insisted that his perspective accounted for everything that was important to know about personality.

Claims like these certainly can help make someone famous, and are perhaps even necessary to attract attention to a point of view. But their rhetorical smoke screen obscures an important fact. It is not obligatory, and I believe it is not helpful, to regard these approaches as mutually exclusive and forever locked in competition. They complement rather than compete with each other because each one addresses a different set of questions about human psychology.

A manager trying to choose a new employee, for instance, must compare individuals to one another; you can't hire everybody, and you can't reject everybody, either. The manager's problem is addressed by the trait approach. When a morally crusading televangelist is arrested for soliciting prostitutes, questions might be raised about his motivation, especially at the unconscious level; a psychoanalytic approach seems necessary here. A parent worried about aspects of a teenager's behavior and how best to make a difference probably could profit from a behavioral approach. A philosopher contemplating the vicissitudes of free will, or even a student considering career plans and wondering about what is really important in life, might find useful insights in the humanistic approach. And so on. Each approach to personality psychology can be useful for handling its own key concerns.

At the same time, each one typically and rather disconcertingly tends to ignore the key concerns of the others (and, as I already mentioned, often denies they are even important). For example, psychoanalysis has a lot to say about the origin of dreams, but contributes next to nothing to understanding behavior change. On the other hand, the principles of behaviorism can be used to teach your dog an amazing variety of tricks but will never explain why she sometimes barks and whines in her sleep.

Distinct Approaches Versus the One Big Theory

By now, the following question may have occurred to you: Why doesn't somebody come up with One Big Theory (you could call it the OBT) that explains everything that the trait, biological, psychoanalytic, humanistic, and learning/cognitive approaches now account for separately? Maybe someday somebody will—and if you become a personality psychologist, it could be you!

In the meantime, you might consider a time-honored principle of engineering: A device that does one thing well tends to be relatively poor at doing anything else. An excellent toaster is completely worthless if what you really need is to make coffee or listen to music. The converse, equally true, is that a device that does many things at the same time will probably do none of them especially well. A combination toaster, coffeemaker, and clock radio—I am sure somewhere there really is such a thing—will probably not be as good at toasting bread, making coffee, or playing music as a more modest appliance that aspires to serve only one of these functions.[4] This principle seems also to be true within psychology, as it describes the inevitable trade-off faced by personality theorists. A theory that accounts for certain things extremely well will probably not explain everything else so well. And a theory that tries to explain almost everything—the OBT—would probably not provide the best explanation for any one thing. Maybe dreams, learning curves, free will, and individual differences in job performance could all be squeezed into one theory, but the result probably wouldn't be pretty.

If you find the welter of approaches to personality confusing, you are in good company. Personality psychologists have worked on this dilemma for decades and still have not come to a solution that satisfies everybody. Some really would like to develop the OBT that explains everything at least fairly well. A surprising number believe that their own currently favored approach *is* the OBT (they are wrong). Others, instead of developing a whole new theory, would like to organize all the current approaches into a single elegant framework (e.g., Mayer, 1998, 2005). Still others, like me, persist in believing that the different basic approaches address different sets of questions, and that each approach generally has the best answers for the questions it has chosen to address.

If you agree with—or at least understand—this final belief, then you will appreciate why this book for the most part considers each basic approach separately. Personality psychology needs to look at people from all of these directions and utilize all of these approaches because different issues—for example, dreams, rates of learning, and individual differences in job performance, as I just mentioned—are best viewed from different perspectives. For the present, I believe it is most useful to teach and apply these approaches one at a time and in their entirety. Perhaps

---

[4] Cell phone cameras, for example, have gotten pretty good, but devices that are *only* cameras are still better, even now.

someday they will become fully integrated. In the meantime, as you will see, each approach has many interesting, important, and useful things to say about the aspects of personality on which it has chosen to focus.

Advantages as Disadvantages and Vice Versa

In the introduction to his novel *Mother Night*, Kurt Vonnegut does his readers the unusual service of telling them the moral of the book they are about to read. "I don't think it's a marvelous moral," he writes, "I just happen to know what it is" (Vonnegut, 1966, p. v). My guess is that he hoped to save hundreds of English classes thousands of hours of trying to figure out what he "meant to say." (I doubt he succeeded.)[5]

As a writer, I do not much resemble Vonnegut (though I wish I did), but I, too, think I know the moral of my book, or at least one of its major themes: In life and in psychology, advantages and disadvantages have a way of being so tightly inter-connected as to be inseparable. *Great strengths are usually great weaknesses, and surprisingly often the opposite is true as well*. Sometimes I enjoy calling this observation **Funder's First Law** (there will be several other such "laws" in this book).[6] This first law applies to fields of research, theories, and individual people.

Personality psychology provides an excellent example of Funder's First Law. As I already noted, personality psychology's biggest advantage over other areas of psychology is that it has a broad mandate to account for the psychology of whole persons and real-life concerns. This mandate makes the study of personality more inclusive, interesting, important, and even more fun than it would be otherwise. But guess what? This mandate is also personality psychology's biggest problem. In the wrong hands it can lead to overinclusive or unfocused research. Even in the best hands, personality psychology can seem to fall far short of what it ought to accomplish. The challenge for a personality psychologist, then, is to maximize the advantages of the field's broad mandate and try to minimize the disadvantages, even though the two are related and perhaps inseparable.

The same is true about the various approaches within personality psychology. Each is good at addressing certain topics and poor at addressing others. Actually, as we have already discussed, each basic approach usually just ignores the topics it is not good at explaining. For example, one reason that behaviorism is so effective at changing behavior is that it ignores the possibility of free will, whereas the phenomenological approach is able to offer a coherent account of free will because it overlooks how rewards and punishments can shape behavior. The strong points

---

[5] For the record, Vonnegut wrote that the moral of his novel is that "we are what we pretend to be, so we must be careful about what we pretend to be" (Vonnegut, 1966, p. v). Come to think of it, this would not be a bad moral for a psychology textbook.

[6] Please don't memorize these laws. They are just my attempt to distill a few of my favorite observations into fortune-cookie-sized sayings.

come with—and are even sometimes a consequence of—the weak points, and vice versa.

This connection between strengths and weaknesses even occurs within individuals. According to one analysis, the personality and ethical "flaws" of several presidents of the United States were precisely the same attributes that allowed them to attain and effectively use power (Berke, 1998). For example, a certain amount of shiftiness—generally considered a character flaw—might enable a president to respond flexibly to changing circumstances. A certain amount of stubbornness—also usually considered a flaw—might enable a president to remain steadfastly committed to important principles. On the other hand, some traits usually considered virtues, such as truthfulness and consistency, might sometimes actually be a handicap in trying to be an effective president. Particular traits can cut both ways as well. Presidents rated as high in *narcissism* (excessive self-regard; see Chapter 6) have tended to be good at public persuasiveness, crisis management, getting votes, and passing legislation. On the other hand, they have also been more likely to be accused of unethical conduct and impeached (Watts et al., 2013).

The same principle applies to other areas of life, such as basketball coaching. Bobby Knight, the longtime coach at Indiana University (and later at Texas Tech), was once described as vulgar, sarcastic, and intimidating—and also, in the same newspaper article, as "loyal, intelligent, charitable, and [a] principled perfectionist who graduates more players than most college basketball coaches" (T. Jones, 2003, p. 6E). Are these two aspects of Knight's character connected? They certainly are, in the sense that they both belong to the same person. A university that hired one of these Bobby Knights got the other one for free. One could speculate that both aspects of this character derived from his passion for perfection, which sometimes led him to constructive behaviors, and sometimes to destructive ones. In any case, everybody's personality comes as a package deal. Personality is coherent; each part stems from and depends on the others (J. Block, 2002).

Figure 1.2 Great Strengths Can Be Great Weaknesses President Nixon's devious nature allowed him to surprise the world with a breakthrough in relations with China, but also led to the Watergate scandal that drove him from office.

You may or may not ever become president or a Big 10 basketball coach yourself, but take a moment and think about your own strongest point. Is it ever a problem for you? Now think about your own weakest point. What are its benefits for you? Given the necessary trade-offs, would you really like to lose all of your weaknesses and keep all of your strengths? Given the way your strengths and weaknesses are interconnected, is this even possible?

Personality psychology is perpetually faced with a similar dilemma. If its scope were narrowed, the field would be more manageable and research would become easier. But then the study of personality would lose much of what makes it distinctive, important, and interesting. Similarly, each basic approach to personality has made a more or less deliberate decision to ignore some aspects of psychology. This is a heavy cost to pay, but so far it seems necessary in order for each approach to make progress in its chosen area.

THE PLAN OF THIS BOOK

This book begins with a brief introduction and an overview of personality psychology that you have almost finished reading. The next two chapters concern how personality psychologists do their research, and will be useful for understanding the chapters that follow. Chapter 2 describes the different kinds of data, or information, that psychologists use to better understand personality, and discusses some of the advantages and disadvantages of each kind. The chapter's goal is to indelibly engrave the following idea into your psyche: *There are no perfect indicators of personality; there are only clues, and clues are always ambiguous*.[7] The chapter also addresses the quality of data (reliability, validity, and generalizability) and basic aspects of research design. Chapter 3 describes the basic methods of personality assessment, including how personality tests are constructed, and explains how to evaluate the strength, or *effect size*, of research findings. It also considers some of the ethical issues evoked by personality assessment, personality research, and scientific research in general.

The second section of this book comprises four chapters that directly address how people differ from one another, the central concern of the trait assessment approach. Chapter 4 discusses the basic question of whether differences between people significantly influence behavior and important life outcomes. (Spoiler Alert: The answer is yes.) Chapter 5 describes research on *personality judgment*—how we all assess personality in our daily lives, and the circumstances under which it is more and less likely to be accurate. Chapter 6 describes how the psychologists have developed personality trait concepts and tried to identify which traits are the

---

[7] This is actually Funder's Second Law, which won't be officially introduced until Chapter 2.

most fundamental, and considers the idea of personality types. In the final chapter in this section, Chapter 7 outlines how and why personality traits develop and also stay the same over the life span, and considers the question of whether personality can be changed, on purpose.

An exciting direction in psychological research is emerging from rapid advances in biology. These discoveries are increasingly applied to the study of personality traits and human nature, and some of that research is surveyed in the third section, which comprises Chapters 8 and 9. Chapter 8 reviews current knowledge about how the architecture and physiology of the nervous system affect behavior and personality. Chapter 9 considers the biological foundations of personality by looking at *behavioral genetics*, which studies how parents might pass on personality traits to their offspring, and *evolutionary psychology*, which addresses the inheritance of personality in a deeper sense, by seeking the origins of human nature in the evolutionary history of the species.

In the fourth section, two chapters consider the psychoanalytic approach, which is closely identified with Freud. Chapter 10 is a basic introduction to psychoanalysis that describes the structure of the mind and psychological development, and offers a critique and evaluation of this perspective. Chapter 11 brings the story of psychoanalysis into the present day, with some consideration of the neo-Freudians (psychoanalysts who came after Freud), object relations theory, attachment theory, and modern research relevant to psychoanalytic ideas.

The fifth section includes two chapters that consider the topics of experience and existence. Chapter 12 describes how the phenomenological aspects of existential philosophy that emphasize individual experience developed into an approach called **humanistic psychology**, which in its modern form considers topics of "positive psychology," including virtue, mindfulness, and happiness. The theme is that an individual's particular worldview or way of experiencing reality is central to his or her personality. Chapter 13 takes this phenomenological point one step further, by considering how individuals' personalities and worldviews—and maybe the whole notion of personality itself—may vary across cultures.

In the sixth section, two chapters describe behaviorism and later approaches to personality that emphasize the processes of learning, motivation, emotion, and cognition that underlie what personality *does*, as opposed to what personality *is*. About 70 years ago, some influential psychologists decided to focus on how people (and animals) behave rather than on what might be going on in the hidden recesses of their minds. The original psychologists who took this approach were the classic behaviorists such as John Watson and B. F. Skinner. Over the later decades of the 20th century, three different derivative theories grew out of behaviorism—theories focused on social interaction and cognitive (mental) processes. Interestingly, all three—the theories of John Dollard and Neal Miller, Julian Rotter, and Albert Bandura—were called "social learning theory." Later, Walter Mischel added a cognitive and phenomenological flavor to social learning theory to produce yet another version, and Carol Dweck elaborated a theory that aims to connect social learning theory with the psychology of personality traits.

At the same time, these theories became increasingly influenced by the rapidly developing field of cognitive psychology. The sixth section of this book describes how some of the concepts and methods of cognitive psychology have been applied to personality, adding insights from the other basic approaches to consider topics including perception, memory, motivation, and emotion. All of these *personality processes*, from learning to cognition and emotion, are summarized in Chapter 14. The collection of thoughts, feelings and knowledge called *the self* is considered in Chapter 15.

As a way of summing up and using what we have learned, the seventh and last section of the book focuses on personality psychology as an applied science, one that can be used for practical aims. Chapter 16 summarizes some of the implications of personality for relationships and business. Chapter 17 addresses the extremes of individual differences that are called the *personality disorders*. With a new edition of the major handbook in psychiatry, the *Diagnostic and Statistical Manual* of the American Psychiatric Association (commonly known as the *DSM*), the approach to personality disorders is in the process of major change. The chapter outlines the differences—and tension—between the old and the new approaches, and the implications for understanding, diagnosis, and treatment. The chapter also considers the implications of personality for physical health, including the startling fact that some personality traits are associated with how long a person can be expected to live. At the end of the journey comes Chapter 18, which offers a brief summary of what I think are the most useful lessons from this book, the ones I hope you will remember long after you finish reading it.

PIGEONHOLING VERSUS APPRECIATION OF INDIVIDUAL DIFFERENCES

Personality psychology tends to emphasize how individuals are different from one another. A critic who wanted to be harsh could even say that personality psychology "pigeonholes" human beings. Some people are uncomfortable with measuring personality or categorizing people into types, perhaps because they find it implausible, undignified, or both.[8]

Other areas of psychology, by contrast, are more likely to treat people as if they were all the same or nearly the same. Not only do the experimental subfields of psychology, such as cognitive and social psychology, tend to ignore how people are

---

[8] As the old saying goes, there are two types of people in the world: those who believe there are two types of people in the world, and those who don't.

different from each other, but also the statistical analyses central to their research literally put individual differences into their "error" terms (see Chapter 2).

But here is yet another example of a potential disadvantage working as an advantage. Although the emphasis of personality psychology often entails categorizing and labeling people, it also leads the field to be extraordinarily sensitive—more than any other area of psychology—to the fact that people really are different. We do not all like the same things, we are not all attracted to the same people (fortunately), and we do not all want to enter the same occupation or pursue the same goals in life (again, fortunately). This fact of individual differences is the starting place for all of personality psychology and gives the field a distinctive and humanistic mission of appreciating the uniqueness of each individual.[9] People are different, and it is necessary as well as natural to wonder how and why.

---

[9] The focus on individual differences is obvious in the trait and psychoanalytic approaches to personality, which concentrate, respectively, on the quantitative measurement of individual differences and on individual psychological case studies. Less obviously, it is also true—even especially true—about behaviorism, which sees the person as the product of a unique learning history and therefore different from anybody else.

WRAPPING IT UP

SUMMARY

The Goals of Personality Psychology

- Personality psychology's unique mission is to address the psychological triad of thought, feeling, and behavior, and to try to explain the functioning of whole individuals. This is an impossible mission, however, so different approaches to personality must limit themselves by emphasizing different psychological topics.

- Personality psychology can be organized into five basic approaches: trait, biological, psychoanalytic, phenomenological, and learning and cognitive processes. Each addresses certain aspects of human psychology quite well and ignores others. The advantages and disadvantages of each approach are probably inseparable.

The Plan of This Book

- This book is grouped into six sections, beginning with a section on research methods and continuing with five sections that survey the basic approaches to personality. It ends with a chapter on the implications of personality for mental health, and then a final summing up.

Pigeonholing Versus Appreciation of Individual Differences

- Sometimes regarded as a field that seeks to pigeonhole people, personality psychology's real mission is to appreciate the ways in which each individual is unique.

KEY TERMS

psychological triad, p. 4
basic approach, p. 5
trait approach, p. 5
biological approach, p. 6
psychoanalytic approach, p. 6
phenomenological approach, p. 6
learning, p. 7
learning and cognitive processes approaches, p. 7
Funder's First Law, p. 10
humanistic psychology, p. 13

THINK ABOUT IT

1. What do we know when we know a person?
2. What is the purpose of psychology? What questions should the science of psychology seek to answer?
3. Why are you taking this course? What do you hope to learn? Of what use do you expect it to be?
4. If you could choose what this course (or book) would be about, what would you ask for? Why?
5. Are psychology textbooks and courses more boring than they should be? If so, why do you think that is? Can something be done about it? Should something be done about it? (Perhaps "boring" just means that a complex topic is being rigorously studied. Do you agree?)
6. Which are more important: answers or questions?

Want to earn a better grade on your test?
Go to **INQUIZITIVE** to learn and review this chapter's content, with personalized feedback along the way.

PART I

THE SCIENCE OF PERSONALITY
Methods and Assessment

A colleague of mine once was choosing what to teach in a general psychology course. She decided to poll her students to find out what they wanted to learn, and listed all the standard topics. One scored so low it wasn't even funny. The all-time least-favorite topic in psychology is . . . research methods. Yet almost every course and every textbook in psychology—including this one, alas—begins with this topic.

Why? The answer is that psychology is a science, meaning that any claim to validity it might have depends on the data upon which it is based. And it is impossible to understand these data without understanding the methods that were used to gather, analyze, and interpret them.[1] But don't worry—methods can be fun. Really! The basic methods of personality research are neither hopelessly obscure nor impossibly technical; and it is only natural that somebody who wants to learn more about psychology should find them interesting and useful.

To see what I mean, let's imagine an acquaintance who claims he can read minds—he has ESP. Are you curious about whether he really can? Maybe not (what *does* it take to pique your interest?). But if you are, then the next question is, how can you find out? You might come up with a few procedures that would test his claim. You could have him guess which playing card you are thinking of, for example. You might even do this several times and keep track of his right and wrong answers. Suddenly, by choosing which questions to ask and how to ask them, you have ventured into the realm of research design. In effect, you have designed an experiment. By writing

---

[1] The word "data" is the plural of "datum," which means a single data point. Thus, for example, one should say "the data are . . ." rather than "the data is . . ." Sometimes I remember to do this.

down the number of right and wrong answers, you have gathered data. And by interpreting the numbers obtained (Do 6 right answers out of 20 qualify as ESP?), you have ventured into the world of statistics! Yet, all you have done is apply good common sense to find out something interesting.

That is what research methods are supposed to do: apply good sense to gather information in order to learn more about questions of interest. The only way to find out something new—about behavior, the mind, or anything else—is to follow a set of procedures that begins with observation (looking at what you want to know about) and ends with data analysis, which means trying to summarize and understand the observations you have recorded.

Chapter 2 presents a detailed account of the kinds of observations that are relevant to understanding personality. All observations are data, and these can be categorized into four basic kinds, called S, I, L, and B data (which, when rearranged, yield the cheerful but misspelled acronym BLIS). The chapter also considers basic issues about the quality of data—their reliability, validity, and generalizability, and *research design,* which is the plan for gathering data.

Chapter 3 introduces *personality assessment,* the class of methods that is most directly relevant to the study of personality. Understanding these methods is critical for understanding the contributions of personality research, and has other important implications. For example, personality tests are often used to select employees. If some people are going to get hired, and others aren't—and this outcome seems inevitable—then the selection needs to be done right. The chapter also addresses how to evaluate research findings, such as the degree to which a personality test can predict behavior. To do this you need to interpret the effect size, or strength, of the result, along with its "replicability," the degree to which you could expect to get the same result if you were to do the study again. Finally, Chapter 3 considers some of the ethical issues that are critically important for psychology and every other branch of science, including the need for research methods to be thoroughly described and the importance of data being openly available for any scientist to examine.

2

PERSONALITY RESEARCH METHODS

PSYCHOLOGY'S EMPHASIS ON METHOD

It is sometimes said that the main thing psychologists know is not content but method. This statement is not usually meant as a compliment. When all is said and done, psychologists do not seem to provide firm answers to questions about the mind and behavior very often. Instead, they offer methods for generating research aimed at these questions. Indeed, sometimes psychologists seem more interested in the research process itself than in the answers their research is supposed to be seeking.

Such a characterization is not entirely fair, but it does contain a kernel of truth. Psychologists, like other scientists, never really expect to reach a final answer to any question. For a researcher, the real thrill is in the chase, and the goal is to continuously improve on tentative answers (hypotheses) rather than to settle anything once and for all.

Another kernel of truth is that, more than any other kind of scientist, psychologists are sensitive and sometimes even self-conscious about research methodology, the way they use statistics, and even about the basic procedures they use to draw inferences from data. Issues like these don't seem to worry physicists and chemists so much. They have fewer debates about methodology, and introductory physics or chemistry textbooks usually do not contain an introspective chapter—like the one you are reading now—on research methods. But no psychology text seems complete without one. Why do you think this is?

Sometimes, the emphasis on methods and process is seen as a sign of weakness, even by psychologists themselves. It's been said that many psychologists suffer from "physics envy." But psychology's self-consciousness about method is one of my favorite things about it. I remember beginning to study chemistry and finding that one of my first assignments was to memorize the periodic table of elements. Where did this table come from, I immediately wanted to know, and why should I believe it? But this was not part of the introductory curriculum. Certain facts were to be memorized and accepted without question. The evidence would come later. This was understandable, I suppose, but it did not seem like much fun.

When I took my first psychology course, the approach was completely different. Although I was somewhat disappointed that the professor did not immediately teach me how to read people's minds (even though I was sure he was reading mine), I was engaged by the approach to knowledge he displayed. Everything was open to question, and almost no "fact" was presented without both a description of the experiment that found it, and a discussion of whether or not the experiment's evidence was persuasive. Some students did not like this approach. Why not just tell us the facts? they complained, like the professor does in chemistry class. But I loved it. It encouraged me to think for myself. Early in the semester, I decided that some of the facts of psychology did not seem all that solidly based. Later on, I even began to imagine some ways in which I could find out more. I was hooked. It could happen to you. Read on.

Scientific Education and Technical Training

Research emphasizes thinking over memorizing because it entails seeking new knowledge, not cataloging facts already known. This distinction is the fundamental difference between scientific education and technical training. By this definition, medical education is technical rather than scientific—it focuses on learning what is known and how to use it. Physicians-in-training do an astonishing amount of sheer memorization, and the last step in medical education is an internship, in which the future doctor shows that she can apply what she has been taught, with actual patients. Scientists-in-training, by contrast, do much less memorization; instead, they are taught to question what is already known and to learn methods to find out more. The last step in scientific education, including in psychology, is the dissertation, a research project in which the future scientist must add something new to the knowledge in her field.

The contrast between technical and scientific approaches applies in many other areas, such as the distinction between pharmacists and pharmacologists, gardeners and botanists, or computer operators and computer scientists. In each case, the issue is not which is "better"; each member of the pair is necessary, and each depends on the other. The biologist goes to a

"Certainly. A party of four at seven-thirty in the name of Dr. Jennings. May I ask whether that is an actual medical degree or merely a Ph.D.?"

physician when sick; most of what the physician knows was discovered by biologists. But they are importantly different. Technical training teaches one to use what is already known; scientific training teaches one to explore the unknown. In science, the exploration of the unknown is called **research.** The essential aspect of research is the gathering of data.

PERSONALITY DATA

Personality is complicated. It is manifested by all of the characteristic ways in which the individual thinks, feels, and behaves—the psychological triad mentioned in Chapter 1. An individual might be deeply afraid of certain things, or attracted to particular kinds of people, or obsessed with accomplishing some highly personal and idiosyncratic goals. The observable aspects of personality are best characterized as clues. The psychologist's task is to piece these clues together, much like pieces of a puzzle, to form a clear and useful portrait of the individual's personality.

In that sense, a psychologist trying to understand an individual's personality is like a detective solving a mystery: Clues may abound, but the trick is to interpret them correctly. A detective arriving on the scene of a burglary finds fingerprints on the windowsill and footprints in the flower bed. These are clues. The detective would be foolish to ignore them. But it might turn out that the fingerprints belong to a careless police officer, and the footprints belong to an innocent gardener. These possibilities are not reasons for the detective to ignore the clues—far from it—but they are reasons to be wary about their meaning.

The situation is similar for a personality psychologist. The psychologist might look at an individual's behavior, test scores, degree of success in daily living, or responses to a laboratory procedure. These are possible clues about personality. The psychologist, like the detective, would be foolish not to gather as many as possible. Also like the detective, the psychologist should maintain a healthy skepticism about the possibility that some or all of them might be misleading.

This brings us to **Funder's Second Law:** *There are no perfect indicators of personality; there are only clues, and clues are always ambiguous.*

> A psychologist trying to understand an individual's personality is like a detective solving a mystery. Clues may abound, but the trick is to interpret them correctly.

"Are you just pissing and moaning, or can you verify what you're saying with data?"

But this skepticism should not go too far. It can sometimes be tempting to conclude that because one kind of clue might be uninformative or misleading, it should be ignored. At different times, various psychologists have argued that self-report questionnaires, demographic data, peers' descriptions of personality, projective personality tests, summaries of clinical cases, or certain laboratory assessment procedures should never be used. The reason given? The method might produce misleading results.

No competent detective would think this way. To ignore a source of data because it might be misleading would be like ignoring the footprints in the garden because they might not belong to the burglar. A much better strategy is to gather all the clues you can with the resources you have. Any of these clues might be misleading; on a bad day, they all might be. But this is no excuse to not gather them. The only alternative to gathering information that might be misleading is to gather no information. That is not progress.

Funder's Third Law, then, is this: *Something beats nothing, two times out of three.*

Four Kinds of Clues

Many years ago, the prominent personality psychologist Henry Murray commented that in order to understand personality, first you have to look at it. This sounds obvious, but like many seemingly obvious statements, when thought about carefully it raises an interesting question. If you want to "look at" personality, what do you look at, exactly?

Four different things. First, and perhaps most obviously, you can see how the person describes herself. Personality psychologists often do exactly this. Second, you can see how other people, who know the person well, describe her. Third, you can see how the person is faring in life. And finally, you can observe what the person does and try to measure her behavior as directly and objectively as possible. These four types of clues can be called S, I, L, and B data. Each method has advantages and disadvantages; all are useful and none is perfect (see **Table 2.1**).[2]

All of sources of data are useful; none is perfect

---

[2] If you have read the writing of other psychologists or even earlier editions of this book, you may notice that these labels keep changing, as do, in subtle ways, the kinds of data to which they refer. Jack Block (J. H. Block & J. Block, 1980) also propounded four types of data, calling them L, O, S, and T. Raymond Cattell (Cattell, 1950, 1965) propounded three types called L, Q, and T. Terri Moffitt (Caspi, 1998; Moffitt, 1991) proposed five types, called S, T, O, R, and I (or STORI). In most respects, Block's L, O, S, and T data match my L, I, S, and B data; Cattell's L, Q, and T data match my L (and I), S, and B data; and Moffitt's T and O match my B, and her R, S, and I match my L, S, and I, respectively. But the definitions are not exactly equivalent across systems. For a detailed typology of B data, see Furr (2009).

Table 2.1	ADVANTAGES AND DISADVANTAGES OF THE MAIN SOURCES OF DATA FOR PERSONALITY

	Advantages	Disadvantages
S Data: Self-Reports	1. Large amount of information 2. Access to thoughts, feelings, and intentions 3. Some S data are true by definition (e.g., self-esteem) 4. Causal force 5. Simple and easy	1. Error 2. Bias 3. Too simple and too easy
I Data: Informants' Reports	1. Large amount of information 2. Real-world basis 3. Common sense 4. Some I data are true by definition (e.g., likeability) 5. Causal force	1. Limited behavioral information 2. Lack of access to private experience 3. Error 4. Bias
L Data: Life Outcomes	1. Objective and verifiable 2. Intrinsic importance 3. Psychological relevance	1. Multi-determination 2. Possible lack of psychological relevance
B Data: Behavioral Observations	1. Wide range of contexts (both real and contrived) 2. Appearance of objectivity	1. Difficult and expensive 2. Uncertain interpretation

ASK THE PERSON DIRECTLY: S DATA If you want to know what a person is like, why not just ask? **S data** are self-judgments. The person simply tells the psychologist (usually by answering a questionnaire) the degree to which he is dominant, or friendly, or conscientious. This might be done on a 9-point scale, where the person checks a number from 1 ("I am not at all dominant") to 9 ("I am very dominant"). Or the procedure might be even simpler: The person reads a statement, such as "I usually dominate the discussions I have with others," and then responds True or False. According to most research, the way people describe themselves by and large matches the way they are described by others (Funder, 1999; McCrae, 1982; D. Watson, 1989). But the principle behind the use of S data is that the world's best expert about your personality is very probably you.

There is nothing the least bit tricky or complicated about S data. The psychologist is not interpreting what the participant says or asking about one thing in order to find out about something else. The questionnaires used to gather S data have what is called **face validity** —they are intended to measure what they seem to measure, on their face.

For instance, right here and now you could make up a face-valid S-data personality questionnaire. How about a new "friendliness" scale? You might include items such as "I really like most people" and "I go to many parties" (to be answered True or False, where a True answer is assumed to reflect friendliness), and "I think people are horrible and mean" (where answering False would raise the friendliness score). In essence, all our new questionnaire really does is ask, over and over in various phrasings, "Are you a friendly person?"

Do we really know ourselves better than anybody else does? Our intuitions would seem to say yes (Vazire & Mehl, 2008). But the truth of the matter is less simple. This is because as a source of information for understanding personality, S data have five advantages and three disadvantages.

Advantage 1: Large Amount of Information   While a few close acquaintances might be with you in many situations in your life, you are present in all of them. In the 1960s, a book called the *Whole Earth Catalog* captured the spirit of the age with cosmic-sounding aphorisms sprinkled through the margins. My favorite read, "Wherever you go, there you are." This saying describes an important advantage of S data. You live your life in many different settings; even your closest acquaintances are with you within one or, at most, a few of them. The only person on earth in a position to know how you act at home, and at school, and at work, and with your enemies, and with your friends, and with your parents is you. This means that the S data you provide can reflect complex aspects of character that no other data source could access.

Advantage 2: Access to Thoughts, Feelings, and Intentions   A second informational advantage of S data is that much, though perhaps not all, of your inner mental life is visible to you, and only you. You know your own fantasies, hopes, dreams, and fears; you directly experience your emotions. Other people can know about these things only if you reveal them, intentionally or not (Spain, Eaton, & Funder, 2000). You also have unique access to your own intentions. The psychological meaning of a behavior often lies in what it was intended to accomplish; other people must infer this intention, whereas your knowledge is more direct.

Advantage 3: Definitional Truth   Some kinds of S data are true by definition—they have to be correct, because they are themselves aspects of the self-view. If you think you have high self-esteem, for example, then you do—it doesn't matter what anyone else thinks.

Advantage 4: Causal Force   S data have a way of creating their own reality. What you will attempt to do depends on what you think you are capable of, and your view of the kind of person you are has important effects on the goals that you set for yourself. This idea—the role of what is sometimes called *self-efficacy*—is considered more fully in Chapter 15. It is also the case that people work hard to bring others to treat them in a manner that confirms their self-conception, a phenomenon called **self-verification** (Swann & Ely, 1984). For example, if you see yourself as a friendly person, or intelligent, or ethical, you might make an extra effort to have other people see you that way, too.

Advantage 5: Simple and Easy   This is a big one. For cost-effectiveness, S data simply cannot be beat. As you will see later in this chapter, other kinds of data require the researcher to recruit informants, look up information in public records, or find some way to observe the participant directly. But to obtain S data, all the researcher has to do is write up a questionnaire that asks, for example, "How friendly are you?" or "How conscientious are you?" Then the psychologist prints up some copies and hands them to everybody within reach. Or, more often, the researcher sets people in front of a computer screen or posts the question-naire on the Internet (Gosling, Vazire, Srivastava, & John, 2004). Either way, the researcher can obtain a great deal of interesting, important information about a lot of people quickly and at little cost. Even 5-year-old children can pro-vide self-judgments that have a surprising degree of validity (though 12-year-olds do better; see Markey, Markey, Tinsley, & Ericksen, 2002; Quartier & Rossier, 2008).

> Even 5-year-old children can provide self-judgments with a surprising degree of validity.

Psychological research operates on a low budget compared with research in the other sciences; the research of many psychologists is "funded" essen-tially by whatever they can cadge from the university's supply closet. Even psy-chologists with government grants have much less money to spend than their counterparts in biology, chemistry, and physics.[3] Sometimes S data are all a psychologist can get.

Disadvantage 1: Bias   Recall that two advantages of S data are that people have unique knowledge of their intentions, and that some self-views of personality are true by definition. The big catch in both of these advantages is that what the person chooses to tell the researcher (or anybody else) about her intentions or self-views might be biased, in at least two ways. First, many of us like to think of ourselves, and tend to describe ourselves, as smarter, kinder, more honest or more psychologically healthy than we really are, and this tendency is particularly strong in certain individuals, such as narcissists (Park & Colvin, 2014). Other people have the reverse tendency and describe themselves more negatively than others do. Interestingly, people actually seem to know whether they are positively

the reverse can be said

---

[3] This discrepancy might make sense (a) if people were easier to understand than cells, chemicals or particles or (b) if it were less important to understand people than cells, chemicals or particles. Is either of these presumptions true?

or negatively biased about themselves, but this knowledge doesn't get rid of the bias (Bollich, Rogers, & Vazire, 2015).

A second potential bias in self-report is that a person always has the option of just clamming up, by keeping some aspects of her intentions and experience private. There is no way to prevent someone from withholding information because of a desire for privacy (in fact, one can sympathize with this desire), but if the person does, the S data she provides will be less than thoroughly accurate. A related concern is "faking," the idea that a person could lie on a personality questionnaire to get the score needed to get a job, for example. However, some writers have pointed out that being able to fake a good score on a personality test requires enough social skill to know what the "right" answers are, and therefore faking is harder than it looks (Hogan & Blickle, 2018). One large study of applicants for a government job showed that when people who were initially rejected for the job after taking a personality test had the opportunity to take the test again, 5.2% changed their scores, but 2.6% changed in the desirable direction and 2.6% changed in the undesirable direction (Hogan, Barrett, & Hogan, 2007)!

Disadvantage 2: Error   Even if an individual were to be completely unbiased in her self-judgment and report, her S-data still could contain errors. For one thing, self-judgment can be especially difficult because of the *fish-and-water effect*, named after the (presumed) fact that fish do not notice they are wet (Kolar, Funder, & Colvin, 1996).[4] A consistently kind or generous person might fail to perceive that her behavior is to any degree unusual—she has been that way for so long, it never occurs to her to act otherwise. In this way, an aspect of her own personality becomes invisible to herself. This kind of process can happen with negative as well as positive traits: You might know people who are so consistently manipulative, domineering, fearful, or rude that they are no longer aware that their behavior is distinctive.

The mind might also work to prevent awareness of certain aspects of the self. Freudians point out that some particularly important memories may be repressed because they are too painful to remember (see Chapter 10). Another factor is lack of insight. The self-judgment of personality, like the judgment of personality more generally, is a complex undertaking that is unlikely to be 100 percent successful (Funder, 1999). And some people just aren't very interested in knowing about themselves. Do you know anybody like this?

Finally, a self-report might be erroneous because the person who provided it was careless. Self-report scales can be long and tedious, and not everybody answers carefully or pays attention all the way to the end. One study found that people who give unreliable S-data because they aren't paying attention are rated by their acquaintances as unconscientious, disagreeable, and introverted, and they also have lower GPA and more class absences (Bowling et al., 2016).

---

[4] I don't actually know whether this is true. There is little research on the self-perception of fishes.

Disadvantage 3: Too Simple and Too Easy   I already mentioned that the single biggest advantage of S data, the one that makes them the most widely used form of data in personality psychology, is that they are so cheap and easy. If you remember Funder's First Law (about advantages being disadvantages), you can guess what is coming next: S data are so cheap and easy that they are probably overused (Funder, 2001; Baumeister, Vohs, & Funder, 2007). According to one analysis, 70 percent of the articles in an important personality journal were based on self-report (Vazire, 2006).

The point is not that there is anything especially wrong with S data; like all the other types, as we shall see, they have advantages and disadvantages. Moreover, Funder's Third Law (about something usually beating nothing) comes into play here; a researcher definitely should gather S data if that is all her resources will allow. The problem is that S data have been used in so many studies, for so long, that it sometimes seems as if researchers have forgotten other kinds of data even exist. But three more kinds of data are relevant to personality psychology, and each has its own special advantages and disadvantages as well.

ASK SOMEBODY WHO KNOWS: I DATA   A second way to learn about an individual's personality is to gather the opinions of the people who know that person well in daily life (Connelly & Ones, 2010). **I data** are judgments by knowledgeable "informants" about general attributes of the individual's personality. Such judgments can be obtained in many ways. Most of my research has focused on college students. To gather information about their personalities, I ask each of them to provide the names and emails of the two people on campus who know him or her the best. We then recruit these people to come to the lab to describe the student's personality, where we ask them questions such as, "On a 9-point scale, how dominant, sociable, aggressive, or shy is your acquaintance?"[5] The numbers yielded by judgments like these constitute I data.

The informants might be the individual's acquaintances from daily life (as in my research), or they could be co-workers or clinical psychologists. The key requirement is that the informants be well-acquainted with the individual they are describing, not that they necessarily have any formal expertise about psychology—usually they do not. Moreover, they may not need it. Usually, close acquaintanceship paired with common sense is enough to allow people to make impressively accurate judgments of each other (Connelly & Ones, 2010; Funder, 1993). Indeed, they may be more accurate than self-judgments, especially when the judgments concern traits that are extremely desirable or extremely undesirable (Vazire & Carlson, 2011). Only when the judgments are of a technical nature (e.g., the diagnosis of a mental disorder) does psychological education become relevant. Even then, acquaintances

---

[5] For obvious reasons, we don't show their answers to the acquaintance.

(handwritten margin note:) (2016) Funder's first Law: States that strengths & weaknesses are so connected that one can't usually exist without the other.

without professional training are typically well aware when someone has psychological problems (Oltmanns & Turkheimer, 2009; Kaurin, Sauerberger, & Funder, 2018).

Another important element of the definition of I data is that they are **judgments.** They derive from somebody observing somebody else in whatever context they happen to have encountered them and then rendering a general opinion (e.g., how dominant the person is) on the basis of such observation. In that sense, I data are judgmental, subjective, and irreducibly human.[6]

I data, or their equivalent, are used frequently in daily life. The ubiquitous "letter of recommendation" that employers and schools often insist on receiving is intended to provide I data—the writer's opinion of the candidate—to the personnel manager or admissions committee.[7] Ordinary gossip is filled with I data because few topics of conversation are more interesting than our evaluations of other people. And the first thing some people do, when invited out on a date, is to ask around: "Do you know anything about him? What's he like?"

As a source of information for understanding personality, I data have five advantages and four disadvantages.

Advantage 1: A Large Amount of Information   A close acquaintance who describes someone's personality is in a position, in principle, to base that description on hundreds of behaviors in dozens of situations. If the informant is a college roommate, she will have observed the "target" of her judgment working, relaxing, interacting with a boyfriend or girlfriend, reacting to an A grade, receiving medical school rejection letters, and so on.

The informational advantage of I data goes beyond the degree of knowledge attained by any single acquaintance. Almost everybody has many acquaintances, which opens the possibility of obtaining more than one judgment of the same person. (This is not possible with S data, of course.) In my research, I try to find at least two acquaintances to judge each of my research participants, and then I average their judgments into a single, aggregate rating. (More would be even better, but two is generally all I can manage.) As we will see later in this chapter, the average of several judgments is much more reliable than the ratings of any single judge, and this fact gives I data a powerful advantage (Hofstee, 1994).

Advantage 2: Real-World Basis   The second advantage of most I data is that they come from observing behavior in the real world. Much of the other information about people that psychologists use does not; psychologists often base

---

[6] Their use is not limited to describing humans, though. I-data personality ratings have been successfully used to assess the personalities of chimpanzees, gorillas, monkeys, hyenas, dogs, cats, donkeys, pigs, rats, guppies, and octopuses (Gosling & John, 1999)!

[7] In many cases, the letter writer is also asked to fill out a form rating the candidate, using numerical scales, on attributes such as ability, integrity, and motivation.

their conclusions on contrived tests of one kind or another, or on observations in carefully constructed and controlled environments (such as experimental laboratories). Because I data derive from behaviors informants have seen in daily social interactions, they enjoy an extra chance of being relevant to aspects of personality that affect important life outcomes. For example, if the people who know you well rate you as highly conscientious, this is probably because they have seen you working hard and being a reliable person. Not surprisingly, then, you are likely to enjoy high academic achievement and career success (Connelly & Ones, 2010).

Advantage 3: Common Sense   A third advantage of I data is that an informant with ordinary common sense will (almost automatically) consider two kinds of context (Funder, 1991). The first is the immediate situation. The psychological meaning of an aggressive behavior can change radically as a function of the situation that prompted it. It makes a difference whether you screamed and yelled at somebody who accidentally bumped you in a crowded elevator or who deliberately rammed your car in a parking lot. And, if you see an acquaintance crying, you will—appropriately—draw different conclusions about his personality depending on whether the crying was caused by the death of a close friend or by the fact that it is raining and your acquaintance was really hoping to play Ultimate Frisbee today.

A second kind of context is provided by the person's other behaviors. Imagine that you see an acquaintance give a lavish gift to her worst enemy. Your interpretation of what this means may (and should) vary depending on whether this acquaintance is someone who, in the past, has been consistently generous, or sneaky and conniving. In the first case, the gift may be a sincere peace offering. In the second case, there are grounds for suspecting a manipulative scheme afoot (Funder, 1991). Or say your acquaintance is upset after an argument with a friend. Your interpretation depends on whether you know this acquaintance to be someone who is easily upset, or someone who is usually disturbed only under extreme circumstances.

Advantage 4: Definitional Truth   Like S data, some kinds of I data are true almost by definition. Take a moment and try to rate yourself on how "charming" you are. Can you? How? It isn't by looking inside yourself—charm only exists in the eyes of other people, and to assess your own charm you can do little other than try to recall whether people have ever told you or reacted to you as if you were charming. If a psychologist wanted to assess this attribute of your personality, he would probably do better to ask your acquaintances than to ask you. The same is true about other traits such as likeability, sense of humor, attractiveness, obnoxiousness, and other aspects of character that reside in the reactions of others. The difficulty we can have in seeing ourselves as others see us may be the reason that I data are generally better than S data for predicting outcomes such as academic

TRY FOR YOURSELF 2.1

S-Data and I-Data Personality Ratings

Self-descriptions (S data) and descriptions of a person by others (I data) can both be valuable sources of information. But the points of view may be different. On the scales below, try rating yourself and then rating someone else you know quite well. Then, if you dare, have the other person do the same to you!

S Data

Instructions: Rate each of the following items according to how well it describes you. Use a scale of 1 to 9, where 1 = "highly uncharacteristic," 5 = "neither characteristic nor uncharacteristic," and 9 = "highly characteristic."

1. Is critical, skeptical, not easily impressed   1 2 3 4 5 6 7 8 9
2. Is a genuinely dependable and responsible person   1 2 3 4 5 6 7 8 9
3. Has a wide range of interests   1 2 3 4 5 6 7 8 9
4. Is a talkative individual   1 2 3 4 5 6 7 8 9
5. Behaves in a giving way to others   1 2 3 4 5 6 7 8 9
6. Is uncomfortable with uncertainty and complexities 1 2 3 4 5 6 7 8 9
7. Is protective of those close to him or her   1 2 3 4 5 6 7 8 9
8. Initiates humor   1 2 3 4 5 6 7 8 9
9. Is calm, relaxed in manner   1 2 3 4 5 6 7 8 9
10. Tends to ruminate and have persistent, preoccupying thoughts   1 2 3 4 5 6 7 8 9

I Data

Instructions: Think of a person you feel you know quite well. Rate each of the following items according to how well it describes this person. Use a scale of 1 to 9, where 1 = "highly uncharacteristic," 5 = "neither characteristic nor uncharacteristic," and 9 = "highly characteristic."

1. Is critical, skeptical, not easily impressed   1 2 3 4 5 6 7 8 9
2. Is a genuinely dependable and responsible person   1 2 3 4 5 6 7 8 9
3. Has a wide range of interests   1 2 3 4 5 6 7 8 9
4. Is a talkative individual   1 2 3 4 5 6 7 8 9
5. Behaves in a giving way to others   1 2 3 4 5 6 7 8 9
6. Is uncomfortable with uncertainty and complexities 1 2 3 4 5 6 7 8 9
7. Is protective of those close to him or her   1 2 3 4 5 6 7 8 9
8. Initiates humor   1 2 3 4 5 6 7 8 9
9. Is calm, relaxed in manner   1 2 3 4 5 6 7 8 9
10. Tends to ruminate and have persistent, preoccupying thoughts   1 2 3 4 5 6 7 8 9

Source: The items come from the California Q-set (J. Block, 1961, 2008) as revised by Bem & Funder (1978). The complete set has 100 items.

achievement and occupational success, both of which depend critically on what others think of us (Connelly & Ones, 2010).

Advantage 5: Causal Force I data reflect the opinions of people who interact with the person every day; they are the person's reputation. And, as one of Shakespeare's characters once noted, reputation is important (see also R. Hogan, 1998). In *Othello*, Cassio laments,

> Reputation, reputation, reputation! O, I have lost my reputation! I have lost the immortal part of myself, and what remains is bestial. My reputation, Iago, my reputation![8]

Shakespear

"Of course. Your reputation precedes you, sir."

Why is reputation so important? The opinions of others greatly affect both your opportunities and *expectancies* (Craik, 2009). If a person who is considering hiring you believes you to be competent and conscientious, you are much more likely to get the job than if that person thought you did not have those qualities. Similarly, someone who believes you to be honest will be more likely to lend you money than someone who believes otherwise. If you impress people who meet you as warm and friendly, you will develop more friendships than if you appear cold and aloof. If someone you wish to date asks around and gets a good report, your chances of romantic success can rise dramatically—the reverse will happen if your acquaintances describe you as creepy. Any or all of these appearances may be false or unfair, but their consequences will nonetheless be important.

Examples

Moreover, there is evidence (considered in Chapter 5) that, to some degree, people become what others expect them to be. If others expect you to be sociable, aloof, or even intelligent, you may tend to become just that! This phenomenon is sometimes called the **expectancy effect** (Rosenthal & Rubin, 1978) and sometimes called **behavioral confirmation** (M. Snyder & Swann, 1978). By either name, it provides another reason to care about what others think of you.

Now consider some drawbacks of I data.

Disadvantage 1: Limited Behavioral Information One disadvantage of I data is the reciprocal of the first advantage. Although an informant might have seen a person's behavior in a large number and variety of situations, he still has not been

---

[8] Iago was unimpressed. He replied, in part, "Reputation is an idle and most false imposition, oft got without merit, and lost without deserving" (*Othello*, act 2, scene 3).

with that person all of the time. There is a good deal that even someone's closest friends do not know. Their knowledge is limited in two ways.

First, there is a sense in which each person lives inside a series of separate compartments, and each compartment contains different people. For instance, much of your life is probably spent at work or at school, and within each of those environments are numerous individuals whom you might see quite frequently there but no place else. When you go home, you see a different group of people; at church or in a club, you see still another group; and so forth. The interesting psychological fact is that, to some degree, you may be a different person in each of these different environments. As William James, one of the first American psychologists, noted long ago,

> Many a youth who is demure enough before his parents and teachers swears and swaggers like a pirate among his "tough" young friends. We do not show ourselves to our children as to our club-companions, to our customers as to the laborers we employ, to our masters and employers as to our intimate friends. (James, 1890, p. 294)

An example of what James was talking about arises when people, whose knowledge of one another has developed in and adapted to one life environment, confront each other in a different environment in which they have developed distinct identities. You may be a conscientious and reliable employee much appreciated by your boss, but you will probably be disconcerted if you suddenly encounter her at a wild Friday night party where you are dancing with a lampshade on your head. (Does anyone actually do this?) At work, seeing your boss is not a problem, but at

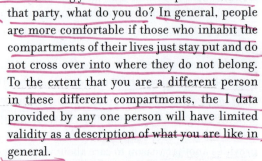

that party, what do you do? In general, people are more comfortable if those who inhabit the compartments of their lives just stay put and do not cross over into where they do not belong. To the extent that you are a different person in these different compartments, the I data provided by any one person will have limited validity as a description of what you are like in general.

Disadvantage 2: Lack of Access to Private Experience   A related limitation is that everybody has an inner mental life, including fantasies, fears, hopes, and dreams. These are important aspects of personality, but they can be reflected in I data only to the extent that they have been revealed to someone else. I data provide a view of personality from the outside;

information about inner psychology must be obtained in some other manner—in most cases via S data (McCrae, 1994; Spain, Eaton, & Funder, 2000; Vazire, 2010)—and in some cases perhaps not at all.

Disadvantage 3: Error   Because informants are only human, their judgments will sometimes be mistaken. I data provided by a close acquaintance can be based on the observation of hundreds of behaviors in dozens of situational contexts. But that is just in principle. As in the case of S data, where it simply is not possible to remember everything you have ever done, no informant can remember everything he has ever seen another person do either.

The behaviors that are most likely to stick in memory are those that are extreme, unusual, or emotionally arousing (Tversky & Kahneman, 1973). An informant judging an acquaintance might tend to forget the ordinary events he has observed but remember vividly the fistfight the acquaintance got involved in (once in four years), or the time she got drunk (for the first and only time), or how she accidentally knocked a bowl of guacamole dip onto the white shag carpeting (perhaps an unusually clumsy act by a normally graceful person). And, according to some psychologists, people have a tendency to take single events like these and imply a general personality trait where none may actually exist (Gilbert & Malone, 1995). Extreme behaviors do deserve extra attention; if you detect signs that a person is dangerous, for example, it is only rational to have this fact influence how you deal with him (Lieder, Griffiths, & Hsu, 2018). However, in most cases, it is the behaviors that a person performs consistently, day in and day out, that are most informative about personality. As a result, the tendency by informants to especially remember the unusual or dramatic may lead to judgments that are less accurate than they could be.

> It is the behaviors that a person performs consistently, day in and day out, that are most informative about personality.

Disadvantage 4: Bias   The term *error* refers to mistakes that occur more or less randomly because memory is not perfect. As with self-reports, the term *bias* refers to something more systematic, such as seeing someone in more positive or negative terms than they really deserve. In other words, personality judgments can be unfair as well as mistaken.

Perhaps an informant does not like, or even detests, the person he was recruited to describe. On the other hand, perhaps he is in love![9] Or, perhaps the informant is in competition for some prize, job, boyfriend, or girlfriend—all quite common situations. The most common problem that arises from letting people choose their own informants—the usual practice in research—may be the "letter of

---

[9] Love is not completely blind, though. People are aware that while they find their romantic partners attractive, others might not share their perception (Solomon & Vazire, 2014).

recommendation effect" (Leising, Erbs, & Fritz, 2010). Just as you would not ask for a letter of recommendation from a professor who thinks you are a poor student, research participants may nominate informants who think well of them, leading to I data that provide a more positive picture than might have been obtained from more neutral parties.

Biases of a more general type are also potentially important. Perhaps the participant is a member of a minority racial group and the informant is racist. Perhaps the informant is sexist, with strong ideas about what all women (or men) are like. If you are studying psychology, you may have experienced another kind of bias. People might have all sorts of ideas about what you must be like based on their knowledge that you are a "psych major." Is there any truth to what they think?

LIFE OUTCOMES: L DATA Have you ever been arrested? Did you graduate from high school? Are you married? How many times have you been hospitalized? Are you employed? What is your annual income? The answers to questions like these constitute **L data**, which are verifiable, concrete, real-life facts that may hold psychological significance. The *L* stands for "life."

L data can be obtained from archival records such as police blotters, medical files, web pages, or questions directly asked of the participant. An advantage of using archival records is that they are not prone to the potential biases of self-report or the judgments of others. But getting access to such data can be tricky and sometimes raises ethical issues. An advantage of directly asking participants is that access is easier and raises fewer ethical issues, because if participants don't want the researcher to know, they don't have to answer. But participants sometimes have faulty memories (exactly how many days did you miss because of illness when you were in elementary school?), and also may distort their reports of some kinds of information (why were you arrested? what is your income?).

L data can be thought of as the results, or "residue," of personality. They reflect how a person has affected her world, including important life outcomes, such as health or occupational success. Or even, consider the condition of your bedroom. Its current state is determined by what you have done in it, which is, in turn, affected by the kind of person you are. One study sent observers into college students' bedrooms to rate them on several dimensions. These ratings were then compared with personality assessments obtained separately. It turns out that people with tidy bedrooms tended to be conscientious, and people whose rooms contained a wide variety of books and magazines tended to be open to experience (Gosling, Ko, Mannarelli, & Morris, 2002; see **Figure 2.1**). Conscientious people make their beds. Curious people read a lot. But a person's degree of extraversion cannot be diagnosed from peeking at her bedroom—the rooms of extraverts and introverts looked about the same.

No matter how L data are gathered, as information about human personality, they have three advantages and one big disadvantage.

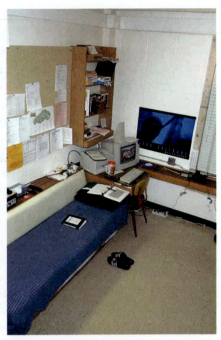

Figure 2.1 **What Your Personal Space Says About You** One example of L data (life-outcome data) that can reveal something about personality is the physical space an individual creates. One of these dorm rooms belongs to someone high in the trait of "conscientiousness"; the other to someone low in this trait. Can you tell which is which? (Of course you can.)

Advantage 1: Objective and Verifiable The first and perhaps most obvious advantage of L data is their specific and objective nature. The number of times someone has been arrested, his income, his marital status, his health status, the number of his Facebook friends and many other psychologically important outcomes are admirably concrete and may even be expressed in exact, numeric form. This kind of precision is rare in psychology.

Advantage 2: Intrinsic Importance An even more important reason L data are important is that often—when they concern outcomes more consequential than the neatness of one's bedroom—they constitute exactly what the psychologist needs to know. The goal of every applied psychologist is to predict, and even have a positive effect on, real-life consequences such as criminal behavior, employment status, success in school, accident-proneness, or the health of her clients.

Advantage 3: Psychological Relevance The third reason L data matter is that in many cases they are strongly affected by, and uniquely informative about, psychological variables. Some people have traits that make them more likely than others to engage in criminal behavior. Some people tend to get in more automobile accidents than others, which is why your rates go up after you file a claim. A certain amount of conscientiousness is necessary to hold a job or to graduate from school (Borman, Hanson, & Hedge, 1997). And, as will be described in Chapter 7, relationship satisfaction, occupational success, and health are all importantly affected by personality.

Disadvantage 1: Multidetermination   However, it is important to keep one important fact in mind. L data have many causes, so trying to establish direct connections between specific attributes of personality and life outcomes is chancy.

[handwritten: outside variables →]

During a recession, many people lose their jobs for reasons that have nothing to do with their degree of conscientiousness or any other psychological attribute. Whether one graduates from school may depend on finances rather than dedication. A messy room may be the result of inconsiderate guests, not the personality of the inhabitant. Health might be affected by behavior and mental outlook, but it is also a function of sanitation, exposure to toxins, and the availability of vaccines, among other factors. Sometimes an accident is just an accident. Even an arrest record doesn't mean much if, as occasionally happens, the person was arrested for a crime she didn't commit.

> Even an arrest record doesn't mean much if the person was arrested for a crime she didn't commit.

This disadvantage has an important implication: If your business is to predict L data from a person's personality, no matter how good you are at it, your chances of success are limited. Even if you (somehow) came to fully understand an individual's psychological makeup, your ability to predict his criminal behavior, employment status, academic success, health, accidents, marriage, or anything else is constrained by the degree to which any of these outcomes is determined by the individual's personality in the first place.

> The ability to predict a life outcome from personality is constrained by the degree to which it is determined by personality in the first place.

This fact needs to be kept in mind more often. Psychologists who have the difficult job of trying to predict L data are often criticized for their limited success, and they are sometimes even harsher in their criticism of themselves. But even in the absolute best case, a psychologist can predict a particular outcome from psychological data only to the degree that the outcome is psychologically caused. L data often are psychologically caused only to a small degree. Therefore, a psychologist who attains any degree of success at predicting criminality, employment, school performance, health, or marriage has accomplished something rather remarkable.

WATCH WHAT THE PERSON DOES: B DATA   The most visible indication of an individual's personality is what she does. Observations of a person's behavior in daily life or in a laboratory produce **B data** (Furr, 2009); the *B*, as you probably already figured out, stands for "behavior."

Figure 2.2 **Naturalistic and Laboratory B Data** Observations of children at play can yield valuable data, whether they are viewed in a natural school situation or a contrived laboratory setting.

The idea of B data is that participants are found, or put, in some sort of a situation, sometimes referred to as a *testing situation*, and then their behavior is directly observed. The situation might be a context in the person's real life (e.g., a student's classroom, an employee's workplace) or a setting that a psychologist has arranged in an experimental laboratory (see **Figure 2.2**). B data also can be derived from certain kinds of personality tests. What all these cases have in common is that the B data derive from the researcher's direct observation and recording of what the participant has done.

NATURAL B DATA The ideal way to collect B data would be to hire a private detective, armed with state-of-the-art surveillance devices and a complete lack of respect for privacy, secretly to follow the participant around night and day. The detective's report would specify in exact detail everything the participant said and did, and with whom. Ideal, but impossible—and probably unethical, too. So, psychologists have to compromise.

One compromise is provided by diary and experience-sampling methods. Research in my own lab has used both. Participants fill out daily diaries that detail what they did that day: how many people they talked to, how many times they told a joke, how much time they spent studying or sleeping, and so on (Spain, 1994). Or, they might report how talkative, confident, or insecure they acted in a situation they experienced the previous day (Sherman, Nave, & Funder, 2010). In a sense, these data are self-reports (S data), but they are not self-judgments; they are reasonably direct indications of what the participant did, described in specific terms close to the time the behavior was performed. But they are a compromise kind of B data because the participant, rather than the psychologist, is the one who actually makes the behavioral observations.

"You're a good listener."

TRY FOR YOURSELF 2.2

What Can L Data Reveal About Personality?

Many kinds of L data are gathered in psychological research. Below are a few examples. On a separate piece of paper, write down the following facts about yourself:

1. Your age.
2. Your gender.
3. The amount of money you earned last month.
4. The number of days of school or work you missed last year because of illness.
5. Your grade point average.
6. The number of miles you travel (driving or otherwise) in an average week.
7. Is your bedroom neat and tidy right now?
8. How much and what kind of food is currently in your kitchen?
9. Have you ever been fired from a job?
10. Are you or have you ever been married?
11. Do you hold a valid passport?
12. How many texts, emails, tweets, or other electronic communications do you receive during an average day?

After you have written your answers, read them over, and answer (to yourself) the following questions:

1. Are any of these answers particularly revealing about the kind of person you are?
2. Are any of these answers completely uninformative about the kind of person you are?
3. Are you certain about your answer to the previous question?
4. If someone who didn't know you read these answers, what conclusions would they draw about you?
5. In what ways would these conclusions be right or wrong?

Experience-sampling methods try to get more directly at what people are doing and feeling moment by moment (Tennen, Affleck, & Armeli, 2005). One early technique was called the "beeper" method (Csikszentmihalyi & Larson, 1992; Spain, 1994) because participants wore radio-controlled pagers that beeped several times a day. The participants then wrote down exactly what they were doing. Technological innovations have updated this procedure; participants carry around handheld computers and enter their reports directly into a database (Feldman-Barrett & Barrett, 2001). Either way, one might suspect that participants would edit what they report, producing sanitized versions of their life events. Based on the reports I have read, I think this is unlikely. At least I hope so! A colleague of mine once did an experience sampling study at his university just after sending his own 18-year-old twin daughters to college in another state. After reading the unvarnished reports of his students' activities, he came very close to summoning his daughters back home.

One useful technique for direct behavioral assessments in real life is the electronically activated recorder (EAR), developed by psychologist Matthias Mehl and his colleagues (Mehl, Pennebaker, Crow, Dabbs, & Price, 2001; Mehl, 2017). The EAR is a digital audio recorder, carried in a research participant's pocket or purse, which samples sounds at preset intervals such as, in one study, for 30 seconds at a time, every 12.5 minutes (Vazire & Mehl, 2008). Afterward, research assistants note what the person was doing during each segment, using categories such as "on the phone," "talking one-on-one," "laughing," "singing," "watching TV," "attending class," and so forth. This technique has some limitations, two of which are that the record is audio only (no pictures) and that for practical reasons the recorder can sample only intermittently during the research participant's day.

But there is more to come, because technology is changing rapidly. Small wearable cameras—only a little larger than lapel pins—are starting to be used. One recent study with 298 participants used cameras that took images every 30 seconds, all day long, producing 254,208 images of 5280 situations (Brown, Blake, & Sherman, 2017). In the face of such massive amounts of data, researchers have had to develop new methods for *ambulatory assessment*, computer-assisted techniques to assess behaviors, thoughts, and feelings during participants' normal daily activities (Fahrenberg, Myrtek, Pawlik, & Perrez, 2007).[10] To share these methods, a Society for Ambulatory Assessment now holds regular conferences.[11]

A relatively new and particularly rich source of real-life B data is social media, such as Facebook and Twitter (Kern et al., 2016). Many people enact a good proportion of their social lives online, and the records of these interactions (which, on the Internet, never go away) can provide a valuable window into their personalities (Gosling, Augustine, Vazire, Holtzman, & Gaddis, 2011). One study found from looking at Facebook profiles it was possible to judge the traits of openness, extraversion, conscientiousness, and agreeableness—but not neuroticism (Back et al., 2010). Another study found that when a Facebook page reflected a large amount of social interaction and prominently displayed an attractive photo of the page's owner, viewers of the page tended to infer—for the most part correctly—that he was relatively narcissistic (Buffardi & Campbell, 2008). And still another study found that friends and romantic partners tend to use and express themselves on Facebook in similar ways (Youyou et al., 2017).

The great thing about B data gathered from real life is that they are realistic; they can describe what people have actually done in their daily lives, including

---

[10] Recording behavior in real-life settings also raises ethical issues, which will be considered in Chapter 3.

[11] Recent conferences have been held in Greifswald (Germany), Ann Arbor, Amsterdam, and Luxembourg. I bet these meeting are a lot of fun but if you decide to attend, be careful how you behave.

Figure 2.3 **Which Avatar Is You?** Research has shown that the avatar you choose to represent yourself may reveal something about your personality.

their virtual, online lives. The disadvantages of naturalistic B data are their considerable difficulty—the EAR method and wearable cameras, in particular, are challenging to use—and the fact that some contexts one might wish to observe, such as how somebody would behave in a crisis, seldom occur under ordinary circumstances. For both of these reasons, B data derived from laboratory contexts remain important.

Laboratory B Data Behavioral observations in the laboratory come in two varieties.

Experiments The first variety is the psychological experiment. A participant is put into a room, something is made to happen, and the psychologist directly observes what the participant then does.[12] The "something" that happens can be dramatic or mundane. The participant might be given a form to fill out, and then suddenly there is a crisis; smoke is pouring under the door. The psychologist, sitting just outside holding a stopwatch, intends to measure how long it will take before the participant goes for help, if she ever does. (Some sit until the smoke is too thick to see through.) If a researcher wanted to assess the participant's latency of response to smoke from naturalistic B data, it would probably take a long time, if ever, before the appropriate situation came along. In an experiment, the psychologist can just make it happen.

Other examples of B data are more mundane, but still interesting. One study asked participants to flip a coin and report how many times it came up heads. Under the honor system, they were paid more money the more heads they reported. Suspiciously, but interestingly, the most heads were reported by people high in the "dark triad" traits of psychopathy, narcissism, and Machiavellianism (Jones & Paulhus, 2017). Another imaginative study asked people to construct computer "avatars" to represent themselves (Kong & Mar, 2015; see **Figure 2.3**). The results showed that their personalities could be accurately judged, to some degree, on the basis of their avatars alone. The properties of these avatars, which included what

[12] By this definition, nearly all data gathered by social and cognitive psychologists are B data, even though those psychologists are ordinarily not accustomed to classifying their data as such. They also do not usually devote much thought to the fact that their technique of data gathering is limited to just one of four possible types.

they wore, whether their eyes were open or closed, and their facial expressions, were rated by research assistants and became B data.

In my own research, I often have participants sit down with partners of the opposite sex and engage in a conversation. This is not a completely bizarre situation compared to what happens in daily life, although it is unusual because the participants know it is an experiment and know it is being video recorded. The purpose is to observe directly aspects of interpersonal behavior and personal style. In other video recorded situations, participants play competitive games, cooperate in building Tinkertoy models, or engage in a group discussion. All of these artificial settings allow direct observation of behaviors that would be difficult to access otherwise. The observations become B data (Funder & Colvin, 1991; Funder, Furr, & Colvin, 2000; Furr & Funder, 2004, 2007).

Physiological Measures   Physiological measures provide another, increasingly important source of laboratory-based B data. These include measures of blood pressure, galvanic skin response (which varies according to moisture on the skin, that is, sweating), heart rate, and even highly complex measures of brain function, such as pictures derived from CT scans or PET scans (which detect blood flow and metabolic activity in the brain; see Chapter 8). All of these can be classified as B data because they are things the participant does—albeit via his autonomic nervous system—and are measured directly in the laboratory. (In principle, these could be measured in real-life settings as well, but the technical obstacles are formidable.)

B data have two advantages and two disadvantages.

Advantage 1: Range of Contexts   Some aspects of personality are regularly manifested in people's ordinary, daily lives. Your sociability is probably evident during many hours every day. But other aspects are hidden or, in a sense, latent. How could you know how you would respond to being alone in a room with smoke pouring under the door unless you were actually confronted with that situation? One important advantage of laboratory B data is that the psychologist does not have to sit around waiting for a situation like this; if people can be enticed into an experiment, the psychologist can make it happen. The variety of B data that can be gathered is limited only by the psychologist's resources, imagination, and ethics.

Advantage 2: Appearance of Objectivity   Probably the most important advantage of B data, and the basis of most of their appeal to scientifically minded psychologists, is this: To the extent that B data are based on direct observation, the psychologist is gathering his own information about personality and does not have to take anyone else's word for it. Perhaps even more importantly, the direct gathering of data makes it possible for the psychologist to devise techniques to increase their precision.

Often the measurement of behavior seems so direct that it is possible to forget that it is just an observation. For example, when a cognitive psychologist measures how long it takes, in milliseconds, for a participant to respond to a visual stimulus flashed on a tachistoscope, this measurement is a behavioral observation. A biological psychologist can take measurements of blood pressure or metabolic activity. Similarly, a social psychologist can measure the degree to which a participant conforms to the opinions of others, or reacts aggressively to an insult. In my laboratory, from the video recordings of my participants' conversations, I can measure how long each one talked, how much each one dominated the interaction, how nervous each one seemed, and so forth (Funder et al., 2000).

Still, even B data are not quite as objective as they might appear because many subjective judgments must be made on the way to deciding which behaviors to observe and how to rate them (Sherman, Nave, & Funder, 2009). Even the definition of behavior can be tricky. Is "arguing with someone" a single behavior? Is "raising one's left arm 2 inches" also a single behavior? How about "completing a painting"? However one chooses to answer these questions, B data have two important, powerful disadvantages.

Disadvantage 1: Difficult and Expensive   Whether in real-life settings or in the laboratory, most kinds of B data are expensive to gather. Experience-sampling methods require major efforts to recruit, instruct, and motivate research participants, and may also need expensive equipment. Laboratory studies require the researcher to set up the testing situation, to recruit participants (and induce them to show up on time), and to code the observational data. This is probably the main reason B data are not used very often compared to the other types (Baumeister et al., 2007). Relatively few psychologists have the necessary resources and want to make the effort.

Disadvantage 2: Uncertain Interpretation   No matter how it is gathered, a bit of B data is just that: a bit of data. It is usually a number, and numbers do not interpret themselves. Worse, when it comes to B data, appearances are often ambiguous or even misleading, making it impossible to be entirely certain what they mean.

For example, consider again the situation in which someone gives you an extravagant gift. Do you immediately conclude that this person is generous, likes you very much, or both? Perhaps, but you are probably sensible enough to consider other possibilities. The conclusion you draw about this behavior will be based on much more than the behavior itself; it depends on the context in which the gift was given and, even more importantly, what else you know about the giver.

The same thing is true of any behavior seen in real life or the laboratory. The person may give a gift or have a sudden intense spike in heart rate or metabolic activity in the prefrontal cortex, or select an avatar with an unhappy expression, or simply sit and wait a long time for a small reward. All these behaviors, and more, can be measured with great precision. But to determine what the behaviors mean, psychologically, requires more information. The most important information is how the B data are associated with the other kinds: S, I, and L data. For example, the reason we know that facial expressions on avatars are informative is that they vary according to the personalities (measured via S data and I data) of the people who choose them.

MIXED TYPES OF DATA It is easy to come up with simple and obvious examples of the four kinds of data. With a little thought, it is almost as easy to come up with confusing or mixed cases.[13] For example, a self-report of your own behaviors during the day is what kind of data? As mentioned earlier, it seems to be a hybrid of B data and S data. Another hybrid between B data and S data is the kind sometimes called *behavioroid*, in which participants report what they think they *would* do under various circumstances. For example, if your neighbor's house suddenly caught on fire, what would you do? The answer to this kind of question can be interesting, but what people think they would do and what they actually do are not always the same (Sweeney & Moyer, 2014). What about a self-report of how many times you have suffered from the flu? This might be regarded as a mixture of L data and S data. What about your parents' report of how healthy you were as a child? This might be a mixture of L data and I data. You can invent many more examples on your own.

The point of the four-way classification offered in this chapter is not to place every kind of data neatly into one and only one category. Rather, the point is to illustrate the types of data that are relevant to personality and to show how they all have both advantages and disadvantages. S, I, L, and B data—and all their possible combinations and mixtures—each provide information missed by the other types, and each raises its own distinctive possibilities for error.

Quality of Data

Alice Waters, the owner of the Chez Panisse restaurant in Berkeley, California, is famous for her passion about ingredients. She insists on personally knowing everybody who supplies her fruits, vegetables, and meats, and frequently visits their farms and ranches. If the ingredients are good, she believes, superb cooking is possible, but if they are bad, you have failed before you started. The ingredients of research are data and, just like in a restaurant, if the ingredients are bad the final product can be no better. We have looked at four basic types of data for personality research: S, I, L, and B data. For each of these—and, indeed, for any type of data in any field—two aspects of quality are paramount: (1) Are the data reliable? (2) Are the data valid? These two questions can be combined into a third question: (3) Are the data *generalizable*?

RELIABILITY In science, the term **reliability** has a technical meaning that is narrower than its everyday usage. The common meaning refers to someone or something that is dependable, such as a person who is always on time or a car that

---

[13] Watch out for these on the midterm.

never breaks down. Reliable data are sort of like that, but more precisely they are measurements that reflect what you are trying to assess and are not affected by anything else. For example, if you found that a personality test taken by the same person gives different scores on different days, you might worry, with good reason, that the test is not very reliable. Probably, in this case, the test score is being overly influenced by things it shouldn't be, which might be anything from the participant's passing mood to the temperature of the room—you may never know. The cumulative effect of such extraneous influences is called **measurement error** (also called *error variance*), and the less there is of such error, the more reliable the measurement.

The influences that are considered extraneous depend on what is being measured. If you are trying to measure a person's mood—a current and presumably temporary **state**—then the fact that he just found out he won the lottery is highly relevant and not extraneous at all. But if you are trying to measure the person's usual, or **trait**, level of emotional experience, then this sudden event is extraneous, the measurement will be misleading, and you might choose to wait for a more ordinary day to administer your questionnaire.

When trying to measure a stable attribute of personality—a trait rather than a state—the question of reliability reduces to this: Can you get the same result more than once? For example, a personality test that, over a long period of time, repeatedly picked out the same individuals as the friendliest in the class would be reliable (although not necessarily valid—that's another matter we will get to shortly). However, a personality test that on one occasion picked out one student as the most friendly, and on another occasion identified a different student as the most friendly, would be unreliable. It could not possibly be a valid measure of a stable trait of friendliness. Instead, it might be a measure of a state or momentary level of friendliness, or (more likely) it might not be a good measure of anything at all.

Reliability is something that can and should be assessed with any measurement, whether it be a personality test, a thermometer reading, a blood-cell count, or the output of a brain scan (Vul, Harris, Winkielman, & Pashler, 2009). This point is not always appreciated. For example, an acquaintance of mine, a research psychologist, once had a vasectomy. As part of the procedure, a sperm count was determined before and after the operation. He asked the physician a question that is natural for a psychologist: "How reliable is a sperm count?" What he meant was, does a man's sperm count vary widely according to time of day, or what he has eaten lately, or his mood? Moreover, does it matter which technician does the count, or does the same result occur regardless? The physician, who apparently was trained technically rather than scientifically, failed to understand the question and even seemed insulted. "Our lab is perfectly reliable," he replied. My acquaintance tried to clarify matters with a follow-up question: "What I mean is, what's the measurement error of a sperm count?" The physician really was insulted now. "We don't make errors," he huffed.

But every measurement includes a certain amount of error. No instrument or technique is perfect. In psychology, at least four things can undermine reliability.

First is low precision. Measurements should be taken as exactly as possible, as carefully as possible. This might seem to go without saying, but every experienced researcher has had the nightmarish experience of discovering that a research assistant wandered away for a drink of water when she was supposed to be timing how long it took a participant to solve a problem, or that an item on a questionnaire was so confusing that participants answered almost at random. Mishaps like this happen surprisingly often; be careful.

Second, the state of the participant might vary for reasons that have nothing to do with what is being studied. Some show up ill, some well; some are happy and others are sad; many college student participants are amazingly short on sleep. One study found that about 3 percent to 9 percent of research subjects[14] are so inattentive that the data they provide are probably not valid (Maniaci & Rogge, 2014). There is not much that researchers can do about this; variations in the state of the participants are a source of error variance or random "noise" in every psychological study.

A third potential pitfall is the state of the experimenter. One would hope that experimenters, at least, would come to the lab well rested and attentive, but alas, this is not always the case. Variation due to the experimenter is almost as inevitable as variation due to the participants; experimenters try to treat all participants the same but, being human, will fail to some extent. Moreover, participants may respond differently to an experimenter, depending on whether the experimenter is male or female, of a different race than the participant, or even depending on how the experimenter is dressed. B. F. Skinner famously got around this problem by having his subjects—rats and pigeons—studied within a mechanically controlled enclosure, the *Skinner box*. But for research with humans, we usually need them to interact with other humans, including research assistants.

A final potential pitfall can come from the environment in which the study is done. Experienced researchers have all sorts of stories that never make it into their reports, involving fire alarms (even sprinklers) that go off in the middle of experiments, noisy arguments that suddenly break out in the room next door, laboratory thermostats gone berserk, and so forth. Events like these are relatively unusual, fortunately, and when they happen, all one can usually do is cancel the study for the day, throw the data out, and hope for better luck tomorrow. But minor variations in the environment are constant and inevitable; noise levels, temperature, the weather, and a million other factors vary constantly and provide another potential source of data unreliability.

---

[14] The term *subject* became passé in psychological research years ago when the *Publication Manual of the American Psychological Association* mandated that the term *participant* be used instead. However, the 2010 edition announced a change in policy: Both terms are again acceptable. Hooray. But you will notice that in this book, I almost always use the term "participant." Once I got in the habit, it was hard to change back.

Table 2.2	RELIABILITY OF PSYCHOLOGICAL MEASUREMENT	
Factors That Undermine Reliability	Low precision
	State of the participant
	State of the experimenter
	Variation in the environment
Techniques to Improve Reliability	Care with research procedure
	Standardized research protocol
	Measure something important
	Aggregation

At least four things can be done to try to enhance reliability (see **Table 2.2**). One, obviously, is just to be careful. Double-check all measurements, have someone proofread (more than once!) the data-entry sheets, and make sure the procedures for scoring data are clearly understood by everyone. A second way to improve reliability is to use a constant, scripted procedure for data gathering.

A third way to enhance reliability in psychological research is to measure something that is important rather than trivial. For example, an attitude about an issue that matters to someone is easy to measure reliably, but if the person doesn't really care (What's your opinion on lumber tariffs?), then the answer doesn't mean much. Experimental procedures that engage participants will yield better data than those that fail to involve them; measurement of big important variables (e.g., the degree of a person's extraversion) will be more reliable than narrow trivial variables (e.g., whether the person is chatting with someone at 1:10 P.M. on a given Saturday).

The fourth and by far the most useful way to enhance the reliability of measurement in any domain is **aggregation,** or averaging. When I was in high school, a science teacher who I now believe was brilliant (I failed to be impressed at the time) provided the class with the best demonstration of aggregation that I have ever seen. He gave each of us a piece of wood cut to the length of 1 meter. We then went outside and measured the distance to the elementary school down the street, about a kilometer (1,000 meters) away. We did this by laying our stick down, then laying it down again against the end of where it was before, and counting how many times we had to do this before we reached the other school.

In each class, the counts varied widely—from about 750 meters to over 1,200 meters, as I recall. The next day, the teacher wrote all the different results on the blackboard. It seemed that the elementary school just would not hold still! To put this observation another way, our individual measurements were unreliable. It was hard to keep lying the meter stick down over and over again with precision, and it was also hard not to lose count of how many times we did it.

But then the teacher did an amazing thing. He took the 35 measurements from the 9:00 A.M. class and averaged them. He got 957 meters. Then he averaged the 35 measurements from the 10:00 A.M. class. He got 959 meters. The 35 measurements from the 11:00 A.M. class averaged 956 meters. As if by magic, the error variance had almost disappeared, and we suddenly had what looked like a stable estimate of the distance.

What had happened? The teacher had taken advantage of the power of aggregation. Each of the mistakes we made in laying our meter sticks down and losing count was essentially random. And over the long haul, random influences tend to cancel one another out. (Random influences, by definition, sum to zero—if they didn't, they wouldn't be random!) While some of us may have been laying our sticks too close together, others were surely laying them too far apart. When all the measurements were averaged, the errors almost completely canceled each other out.

This is a basic and powerful principle, and the **Spearman-Brown formula** in **psychometrics,** the technology of psychological measurement, quantifies how it works (in case you are curious, the exact formula can be found in footnote 9 of Chapter 3). The more error-filled your measurements are, the more of them you need. The "truth" will emerge in there someplace, near the average.

> The more error-filled your measurements are, the more of them you need.

Aggregation is particularly important if your goal is to predict behavior. Personality psychologists once got into a bitter debate (the "consistency controversy"; see Chapter 4) because single behaviors are difficult to predict accurately from personality measurements. This fact caused some critics to conclude that personality didn't exist! However, based on the principle of aggregation, it should be much easier to predict the average of a person's behaviors than single acts. Maybe a friendly person is more friendly at some times than at other times—everyone has bad days. But the average of the person's behaviors over time should be reliably more friendly than the average of an unfriendly person (Epstein, 1979).

VALIDITY Validity is different from reliability. It also is a more slippery concept. **Validity** is the degree to which a measurement actually measures what it is supposed to. The concept is slippery for a couple of reasons.

One reason is that, for a measure to be valid, it must be reliable. But a reliable measure is not necessarily valid. Should I say this again? A measure that is reliable gives the same answer time after time. If the answer is always changing, how can it be the right answer? But even if a measure does give consistent results, that does not necessarily mean it is correct. Maybe it reliably gives the wrong answer (like the clock in my old Toyota, which was correct only twice each day). People who study logic distinguish between what they call *necessary* and *sufficient* conditions. An example is getting a college education: It might be necessary to get a good job, but it is surely not sufficient. In that sense, reliability is a necessary but not a sufficient condition for validity.

A second and even more difficult complication in the idea of validity is that it seems to invoke a notion of ultimate truth. On the one hand, you have ultimate, true reality. On the other hand, you have a measurement. If the measurement matches ultimate, true reality, it is valid. Thus, an IQ measure is valid if it really measures intelligence. A sociability score is valid if it really measures sociability (Borsboom, Mellenbergh, & van Heerden, 2004). But here is the problem: How does anyone know what intelligence or sociability "really" is?

Some years ago, methodologists Lee Cronbach and Paul Meehl (1955) proposed that attributes like intelligence or sociability are best thought of as **constructs.**[15] A construct is something that cannot be directly seen or touched, but which affects and helps to explain things that are visible. A common example is gravity. Nobody has ever seen or touched gravity, but we know it exists from its many effects, which range from causing apples to fall on people's heads to keeping planets in their proper astronomical paths. Nobody has ever seen or touched intelligence either, but it affects many aspects of behavior and performance, including test scores and achievement in real life (G. Park, Lubinski, & Benbow, 2007). This range of implications is what makes intelligence important. An old-time psychologist once said, "Intelligence can be defined as what IQ tests measure." He was wrong.

Personality constructs are the same as gravity or IQ, in this sense. They cannot be seen directly and are known only through their effects. And their importance stems from their wide implications—they are much more than test scores. They are ideas about how behaviors hang together and are affected by a particular attribute of personality. For example, the invisible construct of "sociability" is seen through visible behaviors such as going to parties, smiling at strangers, and posting frequently on Facebook. And the construct implies that these behaviors, and more, should tend to be associated with each other—that somebody who does one of them probably does the others as well. This is because they all are hypothesized to have the same cause: the personality trait of sociability (Borsboom et al., 2004).

However, this hypothesis must be tested, through a process called **construct validation** (Cronbach & Meehl, 1955). For example, you might give participants a sociability test, ask their acquaintances how sociable they are, and count the number of Facebook entries they post and parties they go to in a week. If these four measures are related—if they all tend to pick out the same individuals as being highly sociable—then you might start to believe that each of them has some degree of validity as a measure of sociability. At the same time, you would become more

---

[15] Sometimes the term *hypothetical construct* is used to underline that the existence of the attribute is not known for certain but instead is hypothesized.

confident that the overarching construct makes sense, that sociability is useful for predicting and explaining behavior. Even though you never reach ultimate truth, you can start to reasonably believe you are measuring something real when you can develop a group of different measurements that yield more or less the same result.

GENERALIZABILITY Traditional treatments of psychometrics regarded reliability and validity as distinct. When two measures that were supposed to be "the same" were compared, the degree to which they yielded the same result indicated their reliability. But if the two measures were different, then their relationship would indicate the first (or perhaps the second) measure's degree of validity. For example, if one's score on a friendliness test is pretty much the same as one's score on the same test a month later, this would indicate the test's reliability. But if it also can be used to predict the number of one's Facebook friends, then this fact would indicate the test's validity. Or, alternatively, it could be taken to mean that the number of Facebook friends is a valid measure of friendliness. So, you see that the idea of validity is a bit fuzzy, as is the distinction between measures that should be considered "the same" or "different."

For this reason, modern psychometricians view reliability and validity as aspects of a single, broader concept called **generalizability** (Cronbach, Gleser, Nanda, & Rajaratnam, 1972). The question of generalizability, applied to a measurement or to the results of an experiment, asks the following: To what else does the measurement or the result *generalize*? That is, is the result you get with one test largely equivalent to the result you would get using a different test? Does your result also apply to other kinds of people than the ones you assessed, or does it apply to the same people at other times, or would the same result be found at different times, in different places? All of these questions regard facets of generalizability.

Generalizability Over Participants One important facet is generalizability over participants. Most psychological research is done by university professors, and most participants are college students. (There tend to be a lot of students in the vicinity of professors, and gathering data from anybody else—such as randomly selected members of the community—is more difficult and expensive.) But college students are not very good representatives of the broader population. They are, on average, more affluent, more liberal, healthier, younger, and less likely to belong to ethnic minorities. These facts can make you wonder whether research results found with such students will prove to be true about the national population, let alone the world (Henrich, Heine, & Norenzayan, 2010; D. O. Sears, 1986).

Gender Bias An even more egregious example of conclusions based on a limited sample of humanity comes from the fact that until well into the 1960s, it was fairly routine for American psychological researchers to gather data only from male participants. Some classic studies, such as those by Henry Murray (1938) and Gordon Allport (1937), examined only men. I once had a conversation with a major contributor to personality research during the 1940s and 1950s who admitted frankly that he was embarrassed to have used only male participants. "It is hard to recall why we did that," he said in 1986. "As best as I can remember, it simply never occurred to any of us to include women in the groups we studied."

Since then, the problem may have reversed. There is one particular fact about recruiting participants, rarely mentioned in methods textbooks, that nearly all researchers know from experience: Women are more likely than men to sign up to be in experiments, and once signed up they are more likely to appear at the scheduled time. The difference is not small. From my desk in the psychology department, I used to look directly across the hallway at a sign-up sheet for my research project, which used paid volunteer participants.[16] Because my work needed an exactly equal number of men and women, the sign-up sheet had two separate columns. At any hour of any day, there would be more than twice as many names in the "women" column as in the "men" column, sometimes up to five times as many.

This big difference raises a couple of issues. One is theoretical: Why this difference? One hypothesis could be that college-age women are generally more conscientious and cooperative than men in that age range (which I believe is true), or the difference might go deeper than that. A second issue is that this difference raises a worry about the participants that researchers recruit. It is not so much that samples are unbalanced. Researchers can keep them balanced; in my lab, I simply call all of the men who sign up and about one in three of the women. Rather, the problem is that because men are less likely to volunteer than women, the men in the studies are, by definition, unusual. They are the kind of men who are willing to be in a psychological experiment. Most men aren't, yet researchers generalize from their willing male participants to men in general.[17]

Shows Versus No-Shows   A related limitation of generalizability is that the results of psychological research depend on the people who show up at the laboratory. Anyone who has ever done research knows that a substantial proportion of the participants who sign up never actually appear. The results, in the end, depend on the attributes of the participants who do appear. This fact presents a problem if the two groups are different.

There is not much research on this issue—it is difficult to study no-shows, as you might expect—but there is a little. According to one study, the people who are most likely to appear for a psychological experiment at the scheduled time are those who adhere to standards of "conventional morality" (Tooke & Ickes, 1988). In another, more recent study, 1,442 college freshmen consented to be in a study of personality, but 283 of these never showed up (Pagan, Eaton, Turkheimer, & Oltmanns, 2006). However, the researchers had personality descriptions of everybody from their acquaintances (I-data). It turned out that the freshmen who showed up were more likely to be described as histrionic (emotionally over-expressive), compulsive, self-sacrificing, and needy. The freshmen who never appeared were

---

[16] These days, of course, we sign up participants via the Internet.

[17] It was once suggested to me, quite seriously, that the imbalance could be fixed if we simply paid male participants twice as much as female participants. Does this seem like a good idea to you?

described as relatively narcissistic (self-adoring) and low on assertiveness. It is not clear to me how to put these two studies together, but they do serve as warnings that the people who are included in psychology studies may not always be similar to the many others who aren't.

People who are included in psychology studies may not always be similar to the many others who aren't.

Ethnic and Cultural Diversity   A generalizability issue receiving increased attention concerns the fact that most research is based on a limited subset of the modern population—specifically, the mostly white, middle-class college students referred to earlier. This is a particular issue in the United States, where ethnic diversity is wide, and where minority groups are becoming more assertive about being included in all aspects of society, including psychological research. The pressure is political as well as scientific. One place to see it is in grant application guidelines published by one branch of the U.S. government:

> Applications for grants . . . that involve human subjects are required to include minorities and both genders in study populations. . . . This policy applies to all research involving human subjects and human materials, and applies to males and females of all ages. . . . Assess carefully the feasibility of including the broadest possible representation of minority groups. (Public Health Service, 1991, p. 21)

This set of guidelines addresses the representation of American ethnic minorities in research funded by the U.S. government. As the tone of this directive hints, such representation is difficult. But notice that even if every goal it espouses were to be achieved, the American researchers subject to its edict would still be restricted to studying residents of a modern, Western, capitalist, postindustrial society.[18]

Indeed, Canadian psychologist Joseph Henrich and his colleagues have argued that many conclusions in psychological research are too heavily based on participants who are "WEIRD" in this way, meaning they come from countries that are Western, Educated, Industrialized, Rich, and Democratic (Henrich et al., 2010). The largest part of the research literature is based on participants from the United States, and other leading contributors include Canada, Britain, Germany, Sweden, Australia, and New Zealand—all of which are WEIRD by Henrich's definition. This is a problem, because Henrich presents evidence that people from countries like these are different from denizens of poor, uneducated, preindustrial, autocratic, and Eastern countries[19] on psychological variables ranging from visual perception to moral reasoning.

---

[18] Moreover, an astute reader of a previous edition pointed out that even this diversity prescription is limited to people who identify with one of the traditional genders. It overlooks people who identify as genderqueer, of which there are several varieties (Nestle, Howell, & Wilchins, 2002).

[19] I suppose we could call these "PUPAE" countries, but I doubt the label will stick.

Still, getting the facts straight about members of our own culture in our own time is difficult enough, so we should resist making facile generalizations about members of other cultures—including jumping to conclusions about ways they might be different. To really understand how psychological processes vary around the world will require a vast amount of further research more equally spread across cultures and less concentrated in WEIRD places. Such research is beginning to appear, but we still have much to learn about cross-cultural differences, including how pervasive they really are (see Chapter 13).

> We should resist making facile and simplistic generalizations about members of other cultures—including jumping to conclusions about ways they might be different.

RESEARCH DESIGN

Data gathering must follow a plan, which is the *research design*. No one design is suitable for all topics; according to what one wants to study, different designs may be appropriate, inappropriate, or even impossible. Research designs in psychology (and all of science) come in three basic types: case, experimental, and correlational.

Case Method

The simplest, most obvious, and most widely used way to learn about something is, as Henry Murray advised, just to look at it. According to legend, Isaac Newton was sitting under a tree when an apple hit him on the head, and that got him thinking about gravity. A scientist who keeps her eyes and ears open can find all sorts of phenomena that can stimulate new ideas and insights. The **case method** involves closely studying a particular event or person in order to find out as much as possible.

Whenever an airplane crashes in the United States, the National Transportation Safety Board (NTSB) sends a team and launches an intensive investigation. In January 2000, an Alaska Airlines plane went down off the California coast; after a lengthy analysis, the NTSB concluded this happened because a crucial part, the jackscrew assembly in the plane's tail, had not been properly greased (Alonso-Zaldivar, 2002). This conclusion answered the specific question of why this particular crash happened, and it also had implications for the way other, similar planes should be maintained (i.e., don't forget to grease the jackscrew!). At its best, the case method yields not only explanations of particular events, but also useful lessons and perhaps even scientific principles.

All sciences use the case method. When a volcano erupts, geologists rush to the scene with every instrument they can carry. When a fish previously thought long extinct is pulled from the bottom of the sea, ichthyologists stand in line for a closer look. Medicine has a tradition of "grand rounds" where doctors in training look at individual patients. Even business school classes spend long hours studying examples of companies that succeeded and failed. But the science best known for its use of the case method is psychology, and in particular personality psychology. Sigmund Freud built his famous theory from experiences with patients who offered interesting phobias, weird dreams, and traumatic memories (see Chapter 10). Psychologists who are not psychoanalytically inclined have also used cases; Gordon Allport argued for the importance of studying particular individuals in depth, and even wrote an entire book about one person (Allport, 1965).[20] More recently, psychologist Dan McAdams has argued that it is important to listen to and understand "life narratives," the unique stories individuals construct about themselves (McAdams et al., 2004).

The case method has several advantages. One is that, above all other methods, it is the one that feels like it does justice to the topic. A well-written case study can be like a short story or even a novel; in general, the best thing about a case study is that it describes the whole phenomenon and not just isolated variables.

A second advantage is that a well-chosen case study can be a source of ideas. It can illuminate why planes crash (and perhaps prevent future disasters) and reveal general facts about the inner workings of volcanoes, the body, businesses, and, of course, the human mind. Newton's apple got him thinking about gravity in a whole new direction; nobody suspected that grease on a jackscrew could be so important; and Freud generated an astounding number of ideas just from looking closely at himself and his patients.

A third advantage of the case method is often forgotten: Sometimes, the method is absolutely necessary. A plane goes down; we must at least try to understand why. A patient appears, desperately sick; the physician cannot just say, "More research is needed," and send her away. Psychologists, too, sometimes must deal with particular individuals, in all their wholeness and complexity, and base their efforts on the best understanding they can quickly achieve.

The big disadvantage of the case method is obvious. The degree to which its findings can be generalized is unknown. Each case contains numerous, and perhaps literally thousands, of specific facts and variables. Which of these are crucial, and which are incidental? Once a specific case has suggested an idea, the idea needs to be checked out; for that, the more formal methods of science are required: the **experimental method** and the **correlational method**.

For example, let's say you know someone who has a big exam coming up. It is very important to him, and he studies hard. However, he freaks out while taking the test. Even though he knows the subject matter, he gets a poor grade. Have you ever seen this happen? If you have (I know I have), then this case might cause you to think of a general hypothesis: Anxiety harms test performance. That sounds reasonable, but does this one example prove the hypothesis is true? Not really, but

---

[20] The identity of this person was supposed to be secret. Years later, historians established it was Allport's college roommate's mother.

it was the source of the idea. The next step is to find a way to do research to test this hypothesis. You could do this in either of two ways: with an experiment or a correlational study.

An Experimental and a Correlational Study

The experimental way to examine the relationship between anxiety and test performance would be to get a group of research participants and randomly divide them into two groups. It is important that they be assigned randomly because then you can presume that the two groups are more or less equal in ability, personality, and other factors. If they aren't, then something probably wasn't random. For example, if one group of subjects was recruited by one research assistant and the other group was recruited by another, the experiment is already in deep trouble, because the two assistants might—accidentally or on purpose—tend to recruit different kinds of participants. It is critical to ensure that nothing beyond sheer chance affects whether a participant is assigned to one condition or the other.

Now it's time for the experimental procedure. Do something to one of the groups that you expect will make the members of that group anxious, such as telling them, "Your future success in life depends on your performance on this test" (but see the discussion on ethics and deception in Chapter 3). Tell the other group that the test is "just for practice." Then give both groups something like a 30-item math test. If anxiety hurts performance, then you would expect the participants in the "life depends" group to do worse than the participants in the "practice" group. You might write the results down in a table like **Table 2.3** and display

Table 2.3 | PARTIAL DATA FROM A HYPOTHETICAL EXPERIMENT ON THE EFFECT OF ANXIETY ON TEST PERFORMANCE	
Participants in the High-Anxiety Condition, No. of Correct Answers	**Participants in the Low-Anxiety Condition, No. of Correct Answers**
Sidney = 13	Ralph = 28
Jane = 17	Susan = 22
Kim = 20	Carlos = 24
Bob = 10	Thomas = 20
Patricia = 18	Brian = 19
Etc.	Etc.
Mean = 15	Mean = 25

Note: Participants were assigned randomly to either the low-anxiety or high-anxiety condition, and the average number of correct answers was computed within each group. When all the data were in, the mean for the high-anxiety group was 15 and the mean for the low-anxiety group was 25. These results would typically be plotted as in Figure 2.4.

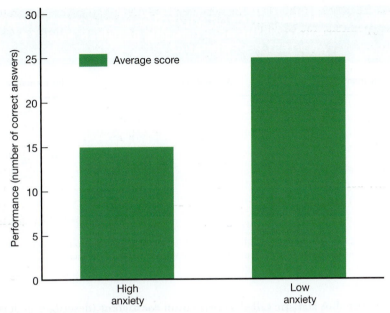

Figure 2.4 Plot of the Results of a Hypothetical Experiment Participants in the high-anxiety condition got an average of 15 out of 30 answers correct on a math test, and participants in the low-anxiety condition got an average of 25 correct.

them on a chart like **Figure 2.4**. In this example, the mean (average) score of the high-anxiety group indeed seems lower than that of the low-anxiety group. You would then do a statistical test, probably one called a t-test in this instance, to see if the difference between the means is larger than one would expect from chance variation alone.

The correlational way to examine the same hypothesis would be to measure the amount of anxiety that your participants bring into the lab naturally, rather than trying to induce anxiety artificially. In this method, everybody is treated the same. There are no experimental groups. Instead, as soon as the participants arrive, you give them a questionnaire asking them to rate how anxious they feel on a scale of 1 to 7. Then you administer the math test. Now the hypothesis would be that if anxiety hurts performance, then those who scored higher on the anxiety measure will score worse on the math test than will those who scored lower on the anxiety measure. The results typically are presented in a table like **Table 2.4** and then in a chart like **Figure 2.5**. Each of the points on the chart, which is called a **scatter plot**, represents an individual participant's pair of scores, one for anxiety (plotted on the horizontal, or x-axis) and one for performance (plotted on the vertical or y-axis). If a line drawn through these points leans in a downward direction from left to right, then the two scores are *negatively correlated*, which means that as one score gets higher, the other gets smaller. In this case, as anxiety gets higher, performance tends to get worse, which is what

| Table 2.4 | PARTIAL DATA FOR A HYPOTHETICAL CORRELATIONAL STUDY OF THE RELATIONSHIP BETWEEN ANXIETY AND TEST PERFORMANCE |||

Participant	Anxiety (x)	Performance (y)
Dave	3	12
Christine	7	3
Mike	2	18
Alex	4	24
Noreen	2	22
Jana	5	15
Etc	. . .	. . .

Note: An anxiety score (denoted x) and a performance score (denoted y) are obtained from each participant. The results are then plotted in a manner similar to that shown in Figure 2.5.

you predicted. A statistic called a **correlation coefficient** (described in detail in Chapter 3) reflects just how strong this trend is. The statistical significance of this correlation can be checked to see whether it is large enough, given the number of participants in the study, to conclude that it would be highly unlikely if the real correlation, in the population, were zero.

Comparing the Experimental and Correlational Methods

The experimental and correlational methods are often discussed as if they were utterly different. I hope this example makes clear that they are not. Both methods attempt to assess the relationship between two variables; in the example just discussed, they were "anxiety" and "test performance." A further, more technical similarity is that the statistics used in the two studies are interchangeable—the t statistic from the experiment can be converted, using simple algebra, into a correlation coefficient (traditionally denoted by r), and vice versa. (Footnote 17 in Chapter 3 gives the exact formula.) The only real difference between the two designs is that in the experimental method, the presumably causal variable—anxiety—is manipulated, whereas in the correlational method, the same variable is measured as it already exists.

This single difference is very important. It gives the experimental method a powerful advantage: the ability to ascertain what causes what. Because the level of anxiety in the experiment was manipulated by the experimenter, and not just measured as it already existed, you know what caused it. The only possible path is anxiety $\rightarrow$ performance. In the correlational study, you can't be so sure. Both variables might be the result of some other, unmeasured factor. For example,

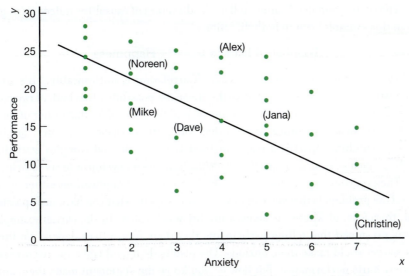

Figure 2.5 **Plot of the Results of a Hypothetical Correlational Study**
Participants who had higher levels of anxiety tended to get lower scores on the math test. The data from the participants represented in Table 2.4 are included, along with others not represented in the table.

perhaps some participants in your correlational study were sick that day, which caused them to feel anxious and perform poorly. Instead of a causal pathway with two variables,

$$\text{Anxiety} \longrightarrow \text{Poor performance}$$

the truth might be more like:

$$\text{Illness} \begin{array}{c} \longrightarrow \text{Anxiety} \\ \longrightarrow \text{Poor performance} \end{array}$$

For obvious reasons, this potential complication with correlational design is called the *third-variable problem*.

A slightly different problem arises in some correlational studies, which is that either of the two correlated variables might actually have caused the other. For example, if one finds a correlation between the number of friends one has and happiness, it might be that having friends makes one happy, or that being happy makes it easier to make friends. Or, in a diagram, the truth of the matter could be either

$$\text{Number of friends} \longrightarrow \text{Happiness}$$

or

$$\text{Happiness} \longrightarrow \text{Number of friends}$$

The correlation itself cannot tell us the direction of causality—indeed, it might (as in this example) run in both directions:

Number of friends ⟵⟶ Happiness

You may have heard the expression "Correlation is not causality." It's true. Correlational studies are informative, but raise the possibility that both of two correlated variables were caused by an unmeasured third variable, that either of them might have caused the other, or even that both of them cause each other. Teasing these possibilities apart is a major methodological task, and complex statistical methods such as *structural equation modeling* have been developed to try to help.

The experimental method is not completely free of complications either, however. One problem is that you can never be sure exactly what you have manipulated and, therefore, of where the actual causality was located. In the earlier example, it was presumed that telling participants that their future lives depend on their test scores would make them anxious. The results then confirmed the hypothesis: Anxiety hurts performance. But how do you know the statement made them anxious? Maybe it made them angry or disgusted at such an obvious lie. If so, then it could have been anger or disgust that hurt their performance. You only know what you manipulated at the visible, operational level—you know what you said to the participants. The psychological variable that you manipulated, however—the one that actually affected behavior—was invisible and can only be inferred. (This difficulty is related to the problem with interpreting B data discussed earlier in this chapter.) You might also recognize this difficulty as another version of the third-variable problem just discussed. Indeed, the third-variable problem affects both correlational and experimental designs, but in different ways.

"Anxiety" manipulation → Unknown psychological result → Poor performance

A second complication with the experimental method is that it can create levels of a variable that are unlikely or even impossible in real life. Assuming the experimental manipulation worked as intended, which in this case seems like a big assumption, how often is your life literally hanging in the balance when you take a math test? Any extrapolation to the levels of anxiety that ordinarily exist during exams could be highly misleading. Moreover, maybe in real-life exams most people are moderately anxious. But in the experiment, two groups were artificially created: One was presumably highly anxious; the other (again, presumably) was not anxious at all. In real life, both groups may be rare. Therefore, the effect of anxiety on performance may be exaggerated. The correlational method, by contrast, assesses levels of anxiety that already exist in the participants. Thus, they are more likely to represent anxiety as it realistically occurs.

This conclusion highlights an important way in which experimental and correlational studies complement each other. An experiment can determine whether one variable *can* affect another, but not how often or how much it actually *does*, in real life. For that, correlational research is required. Also, notice how the correlational study included seven levels of anxiety (one for each point on the anxiety scale), whereas the experimental study included only two (one for each condition). Therefore, the results of the correlational study may be more precise.

A third disadvantage particular to the experimental method is that, unlike correlational studies, experiments often require deception. Correlational studies don't. I will discuss the ethics of deception in Chapter 3.

The final disadvantage of the experimental method is the most important one. Sometimes experiments are simply not possible. For example, if you want to know the effects of child abuse on self-esteem in adulthood, all you can do is try to assess whether people who were abused as children tend to have low self-esteem, which would be a correlational study. The experimental equivalent is not possible. You cannot assemble a group of children and randomly abuse half of them. Moreover, the main thing personality psychologists usually want to know is how personality traits or other stable individual differences affect behavior. But you cannot make half of the participants extraverted and the other half introverted; you must accept the personalities that participants bring into the laboratory.

Many discussions of correlational and experimental designs, including those in many textbooks, conclude that the experimental method is obviously superior. This conclusion is wrong. Experimental and correlational designs both have advantages and disadvantages, as we have seen, and ideally a complete research program would include both.

CONCLUSION

Research is challenging because, by definition, it involves investigating the unknown. But that is also what makes research exciting. It can use many different kinds of data, research designs, and statistical analyses. In the end, the payoff is to learn something nobody ever knew before.

WRAPPING IT UP

SUMMARY

Psychology's Emphasis on Method

- Psychology emphasizes the methods by which knowledge can be obtained. Knowledge about methods is necessary for conducting research, and also for understanding the results of research done by others.

- Science is the seeking of new knowledge, not the cataloging of facts already known. Technical training conveys current knowledge about a subject, so that the knowledge can be applied. Scientific education, by contrast, teaches not only what is known but also how to find out what is not yet known.

Personality Data

- In order to study personality, first you must look at it: All science begins with observation. The observations a scientist makes and expresses as numbers are data.

- For the scientific study of personality, four types of data are available. Each type has advantages and disadvantages.

- S (self-judgment) data comprise a person's assessments of his own personality. The advantages of S data are that each individual has (in principle) a large amount of information about himself; that each individual has unique access to his own thoughts, feelings, and intentions; that some kinds of S data are true by definition (e.g., self-esteem); that S data also have a causal force all their own; and that S data are simple and easy to gather. The disadvantages are that people sometimes make errors or have biases in self-reports, and that S data may be so easy to obtain that psychologists rely on them too much.

- I (informant) data comprise the judgments of knowledgeable acquaintances about the personality traits of the person being studied. The advantages of I data are that there is a large amount of information on which informants' judgments are potentially based; that this information comes from real life; that informants can use common sense; that some kinds of I data are true by definition (e.g., likeability); and that the judgments of people who know the person are important because they affect reputation, opportunities, and expectancies. The disadvantages of I data are that no informant knows everything about another person; that informants' judgments can be subject to random errors, such as forgetting; and that judgments can be systematically biased.

- L (life) data comprise observable life outcomes, such as being arrested, getting sick, or graduating from college. L data have the advantages of being objective and verifiable, as well as being intrinsically important and potentially psychologically relevant, but they have the disadvantages of being determined by many different factors, and sometimes are not even psychologically relevant.

- B (behavioral) data comprise direct observations of a person doing something. Behavior may be observed in the person's real-life environment or an artificial setting constructed in a psychological laboratory. Behaviors can include words spoken, actions performed, and even physiological responses. The advantages of B data are that they can tap into many different kinds of behaviors, including those that might not occur or be easily measured in normal life; and that they are obtained through direct observation, and so are, in that sense, objective. B data have two disadvantages. First, they are difficult and expensive to gather. Second, for all their superficial objectivity, it is still not always clear what they mean psychologically.

- The essence of science is that conclusions should be based on data. Data can vary widely in quality; in personality psychology, the important dimensions of data quality are reliability, validity, and generalizability.

- Reliability refers to the stability or repeatability of measurements. Validity refers to the degree to which a measurement actually measures what it is trying to measure. Generalizability is a broader concept that subsumes both reliability and validity, and refers to the kinds of other measurements to which a given measurement is related.

Research Design

- The plan one uses for gathering psychological data is the research design. The three main methods are case, experimental, and correlational.

- Case studies examine particular phenomena or individuals in detail, and can be an important source of new ideas. To test these ideas, correlational and experimental studies are necessary. Each of the three methods has advantages and disadvantages, but the experimental method is the only one that can be used to determine causality.

KEY TERMS

research, p. 23
Funder's Second Law, p. 23
Funder's Third Law, p. 24
S data, p. 25
face validity, p. 25
self-verification, p. 27
I data, p. 29

THINK ABOUT IT

1. If you wanted to know all about the personality of the person sitting next to you, what would you do?

2. In your opinion, is there anything about another person that is impossible to know? Is there anything that is *unethical* to know?

3. To assess the degree that someone is "sociable" would seem easy to do using S data or I data. How might you assess this trait using L data or B data?

4. Can you think of kinds of observations—data—that you could gather about a person that would fall outside of the BLIS scheme? Which of the four categories comes closest to describing these data?

5. An experimenter gives a subject a set of 10 impossible-to-solve mathematical problems. The experimenter times how long the subject works on the problems before giving up on the task. The minutes-and-seconds measure the experimenter has taken is, of course, B data. The experimenter calls this measure "a real, behavioral measure of persistence." What is right and wrong about this label?

6. People sometimes describe themselves differently than they are described by others (a discrepancy between S data and I data), and they sometimes describe themselves differently from how they act (a discrepancy between S data and B data). Why might this happen? When these kinds of data disagree with each other, which would you tend to believe?

7. Are some kinds of data "privileged" for some kinds of questions? For example, if a person says he is happy (S data), but his acquaintances say he is unhappy (I data), is it possible that the I data could be more valid than the S data? Would it be meaningful to say something like, "He's not as happy as he thinks he is"?

8. If an attribute like "happiness" can most appropriately (or only) be assessed with S data, are there other attributes of personality best (or only) assessable via I data, L data, or B data?

9. Is research done with the predominantly white college students in Western cultures also relevant to members of ethnic minorities or to people who live in other cultures? In what areas would you expect to find the most differences?

10. If you wanted to do research on how alcohol use affects health, would you do experimental studies or correlational studies? What could each kind of study tell you? What would each kind of study *not* be able to tell you? What kinds of studies would be feasible or ethical?

SUGGESTED RESOURCES

American Psychological Association (2010). *Publication Manual of the American Psychological Association* (6th ed.). Washington, DC: American Psychological Association.

This sets the standards that must be followed for all articles in journals published by the American Psychological Association, and most other psychological journals also follow it. The book is full of information and advice on the proper conduct, analysis, and reporting of psychological research. Every aspiring psychologist should have a copy. While the book is not available for free (the Manual is an important source of revenue for APA), a lot of useful and updated information is available, without cost, at www.apastyle.org/manual.

Cronbach, L. J., & Meehl, P. E. (1955). Construct validity in psychological tests. *Psychological Bulletin, 52,* 281–302.

A difficult read, but the classic presentation of how personality psychologists think about the validity of their measurements. One of the most influential methodological articles ever published.

Rosenthal, R., & Rosnow, R. L. (2007). *Essentials of behavioral research: Methods and data analysis* (3rd ed.). New York: McGraw-Hill.

One of the best primers for a beginning researcher. This book includes many topics (such as effect size) not handled well in other methods or statistics texts. You will have to read this book to see what its authors mean by the advice "Think Yiddish, write British."

Want to earn a better grade on your test?
Go to **INQUIZITIVE** to learn and review this chapter's content, with personalized feedback along the way.

3

PERSONALITY ASSESSMENT: EFFECT SIZE, REPLICABILITY, AND OPEN SCIENCE

If something exists, it exists in some quantity, and if it exists in some quantity, it can be measured.

—EDWARD LEE THORNDIKE

ARE YOU MORE OR LESS extraverted than the person sitting next to you? Are you more or less conscientious? To decide who is the most extraverted or conscientious person in the room, or, more broadly, for personality traits to be useful for the scientific understanding of the mind, the prediction of behavior, or for any other purpose, the first step is measurement. The previous chapter considered several methods used by personality research. This chapter begins by more closely considering the methods used for *personality assessment*. But personality assessment—like psychological research more generally—itself needs to be assessed. Evaluating how well "personality tests" predict behavior, as well as evaluating the strength of *any* research result, requires understanding measures of *effect size* and evidence concerning *replicability*. These two topics are addressed in the second part of this chapter. Finally, the third part of this chapter considers the ethics of personality research. Ethical issues include how personality assessments are used, how research participants are treated (and how they must be protected), and the ways in which personality research—and scientific research more generally—is and should be conducted.

PERSONALITY ASSESSMENT

An individual's personality is revealed by characteristic patterns of behavior, thought, or emotional experience that are relatively consistent across time and situations (Allport, 1937). These patterns include motives, intentions, goals, strategies, and subjective representations (the ways in which people perceive and construct their worlds; see Chapter 14). They indicate the degree to which a person desires one goal over another, or thinks the world is changeable as opposed to fixed, or is generally happy, or is optimistic as opposed to pessimistic, or is sexually attracted to members of the same or the opposite sex. All of these variables and many others are relatively stable attributes of individuals. In that sense, they are all personality traits, and any attempt to measure them necessarily entails personality assessment. As a result, assessment is relevant to a broad range of research, including nearly every topic in personality, developmental, and social psychology.

THE BUSINESS OF TESTING

Every year, the American Psychological Association (APA) holds a convention. It's quite an event. Thousands of psychologists take over most of the downtown hotels in a major city such as San Francisco, Boston, or Washington, DC, for a week of meetings, symposia, and cocktail parties. The biggest attraction is always the exhibit hall, where dozens of high-tech, artistically designed booths fill a room that seems to go on for acres. These booths are set up, at great expense, by several kinds of companies. One group is textbook publishers; all the tools of advertising are applied to the task of convincing college professors like me to get their students to read (and buy) books such as the one you are reading right now. Another group is manufacturers of videos and various, sometimes peculiar gadgets for therapy and research. Yet another group is psychological testers. Their booths often distribute free samples that include not only personality and ability tests, but also shopping bags, notebooks, and even beach umbrellas. These freebies prominently display the logo of their corporate sponsor: the Psychological Corporation, Consulting Psychologists Press, the Institute for Personality and Ability Testing, and so on.

You don't have to go to the APA convention to get a free "personality test." On North Michigan Avenue in Chicago, on the Boston Common, at Fisherman's Wharf in San Francisco, and at Covent Garden in London, I have been given brightly colored brochures that ask, in huge letters, "Are you curious about yourself? Free personality test enclosed." Inside is something that looks like a conventional personality test, with 200 questions to be answered True or False. (One item reads, "Having settled an argument out do you continue to feel disgruntled for a while?") But, as it turns out, the test is really a recruitment pitch. If you take it and go for your "free evaluation"—which I do not recommend—you will be told two things. First, you are all messed up. Second, the people who gave you the test have the cure: You need to join a certain "church" that can provide the techniques (and even the strange electrical equipment) needed to pinpoint and fix your problems.

The personality testers at the APA convention and those who hand out free so-called personality tests on North Michigan Avenue have a surprising amount in common. Both seek new customers, and both use all the techniques of advertising, including free samples, to acquire them. The tests they distribute look superficially alike. And both groups exploit a nearly universal desire to know more about personality. The brochure labeled "Are you curious about yourself?" asks a pretty irresistible question. The more staid tests distributed at the APA convention likewise offer an intriguing promise of finding out something about your own or somebody else's personality that might be interesting, important, or useful.

Below the surface, however, they are not the same. The tests peddled at the APA convention are, for the most part, well-validated instruments useful for many purposes. The ones being pushed at tourist destinations around the world are frauds and potentially dangerous. But you cannot tell which is which just by looking at them. You need to know something about how personality tests and assessments are constructed, how they work, and how they can fail. So, let's take a closer look.

"He looks very promising—but let's see how he does on the written test."

PERSONALITY TESTS

One of the most widely used personality tests in the world is the Minnesota Multiphasic Personality Inventory (MMPI).[1] This test was designed for use in the clinical assessment of individuals with psychological difficulties, but it has also been used for many other purposes, such as employment screening. Another widely used test is the California Psychological Inventory (CPI), which is similar to the MMPI in many ways but is designed for use with so-called "normal" or nondisturbed individuals. Others include the Sixteen Personality Factor Questionnaire (16PF); the Strong Vocational Interest Blank (SVIB), used to help people choose suitable careers; the Hogan Personality Inventory (HPI), used by employers for personnel selection; and many more.

Many personality tests, including those just listed, are *omnibus* inventories, which means they measure a wide range of personality traits. The NEO Personality

---

[1] By a tradition of mysterious origin, nearly all personality tests are referred to by their initials, all capital letters, no periods.

Inventory, for instance, measures five broad traits along with 30 subscales or "facets" (Costa & McCrae, 1997).[2]

Others measure just one trait. Tests are available to measure shyness, self-consciousness, self-monitoring, empathy, attributional complexity, nonverbal sensitivity, and so on. No one has done an exact count, but there must be thousands of such tests, and new ones appear every day.

S-Data Versus B-Data Personality Tests

To use the terms introduced in Chapter 2, most personality tests provide S data. They ask you what you are like, so the score you receive amounts to a summary of how you describe yourself. The "self-monitoring" scale asks how closely you watch other people for cues as to how to behave. The "attributional complexity" scale asks about the level of complexity in your thinking about the causes of behavior. The first question on the widely used Stanford Shyness Survey is simply "Do you consider yourself to be a shy person?" The possible responses are "yes" or "no" (Zimbardo, 1977). You can probably guess how this item is scored.

Other personality tests yield B data. The MMPI is a good example. It presents items—such as "I prefer a shower to a bath"—not because the tester is interested in the literal answer, but because answers to this item are informative about some aspect of personality, in this case, empathy. Preferring a shower is the empathic response, for some reason (Hogan, 1969).

Is intelligence a personality trait? Psychologists have differing opinions (what's yours?). Either way, tests of intelligence, or *IQ tests*, also yield B data. Imagine trying to assess intelligence using an S-data test, asking questions such as, "Are you an intelligent person?" and "Are you good at math?" Researchers have actually tried this, but simply asking people whether they are smart turns out to be a poor way to measure intelligence (Furnham, 2001). So, instead, IQ tests ask people questions of varying difficulty, such as reasoning or math problems, that have specific correct answers. These right or wrong answers comprise B data. The more right answers, the higher the IQ score.

> Simply asking people whether they are smart turns out to be a poor way to measure intelligence.

Some experts in assessment have proposed that tests based on (what I call) B data be labeled "performance-based" instruments (McGrath, 2008). These include the IAT, the MMPI, and IQ tests, which were just described. They also include instruments that traditionally have been called "projective" tests.

---

[2] When the test was first introduced, NEO stood for Neuroticism, Extraversion, and Openness. Later versions added Agreeableness and Conscientiousness, but it wasn't renamed OCEAN even though it could (and maybe should) have been (John, 1990).

Projective Tests

THE PROJECTIVE HYPOTHESIS Projective tests were originally based on a theory called the *projective hypothesis* (Frank, 1939). The theory is this: If somebody is asked to describe or interpret a meaningless or ambiguous stimulus—such as an inkblot—her answer cannot come from the stimulus itself, because the stimulus actually does not look like, or mean, anything. The answer must instead come from (be a "projection" of) her needs, feelings, experiences, thought processes, and other hidden aspects of the mind (Murray, 1943). The answer might even reveal something the person does not know about herself. (Notice that this could never happen with S data.)

This is the theory behind the famous Rorschach inkblot (Exner, 1993; Rorschach, 1921). Swiss psychiatrist Hermann Rorschach dropped blots of India ink onto note cards, folded the cards in half, and then unfolded them. The result was a set of symmetric, complex blots.[3] Over the years, uncounted psychiatrists and clinical psychologists have shown these blots to their clients and asked them what they saw.

Of course, the only literally correct answer is "an inkblot," but that is not considered a cooperative response. Instead, the examiner is interested in whether the client will report seeing a cloud, a devil, her father, or whatever. I once heard a clinical psychologist describe a client who reported seeing a "crying St. Bernard." The woman who gave this response was grieving over a boating accident in which she accidentally killed her husband. The psychologist interpreting her response noted that dogs don't cry, but people do, and the traditional role of a St. Bernard is as a rescuer. This interpretation illustrates how whatever the client sees, precisely because it is not actually on the card, may reveal something about the contents of her mind. It also illustrates that the thoughts revealed by the inkblot response might not necessarily be deep, hidden, or mysterious. While it was interesting and probably useful for this therapist to know that his client was still upset about the accident, it wasn't exactly surprising.

Interpretation is sometimes subtler. Consider these two responses to Card I of the Rorschach (which I am not supposed to show you, but you will be able to guess what it looks like). One client said: "This is a butterfly. Its wings are ripped and tattered, and it doesn't have very long to live." Another client responded to the same card by saying: "This is a butterfly. I don't know what to make of these white spaces; I don't know any kind of butterfly with white spots on its wings quite like that. They really shouldn't be there, but I guess its wings are ripped" (McGrath, 2008, p. 471).

Psychologist Robert McGrath (2008) noted that the first response seems to reveal some morbid preoccupations, due to its reference to death and redundant

---

[3] According to legend, Rorschach made many blots in this way but kept only the "best" ones. I've always wondered how he decided which ones they were.

(a)   (b)

Figure 3.1 Two Projective Tests (a) Rorschach inkblot: This picture resembles—but is not—one of the inkblots in Rorschach's famous test. The real blots traditionally are not published so that someone taking the test will see them for the first time. (b) Thematic Apperception Test: The task is to make up stories about a series of pictures like these. Themes in the stories are interpreted as indicating "implicit motives" of which the person might not himself be aware.

use of the words "ripped" and "tattered." The second response seems to reveal a tendency to obsess or overanalyze. This kind of interpretation is difficult to verify, and it stems from the assumption that responses to inkblots reflect the basic way personality operates. Because one client thought the butterfly didn't have long to live, the inference was that she was preoccupied with death; because the other client overanalyzed the Rorschach card, the inference was that he was obsessive in daily life as well.

The same logic has led to the development of numerous other projective tests. The Draw-A-Person test requires the client to draw (you guessed it) a person, and the drawing is interpreted according to what kind of person is drawn (e.g., a man or a woman), which body parts are exaggerated or omitted, and so forth (Machover, 1949). Large eyes might be taken to indicate suspiciousness or paranoia; heavy shading might mean aggressive impulses; and numerous erasures could be a sign of anxiety. The classic Thematic Apperception Test (TAT) asks clients to tell stories about a set of drawings of people and ambiguous events (Morgan & Murray, 1935; Murray, 1943). A more recent version uses pictures that include "a boy in a checked shirt . . . a woman and a man on a trapeze, two men in a workshop, and a young woman working on the [balance] beam" (Brunstein & Maier, 2005,

p. 208). The themes of these stories are used to assess the client's motivational state (McClelland, 1975; Smith, 1992). If a person looks at an ambiguous drawing of two people and thinks they are fighting, for example, this might reveal a need to be aggressive; if the two people are described as in love, this might reflect a need for intimacy; if one is seen as giving orders to the other, this might reflect a need for power.

Projective tests of a sort can even be administered to people "from a distance," without them getting anywhere near a psychologist (Winter, 1991). Psychologists have tried to assess needs and other aspects of personality by analyzing the content of stories, essays, letters, and even political speeches.

The projective hypothesis behind all these tests is an interesting and seemingly reasonable idea, and interpretations of actual responses can be fascinating. A large number of practicing clinicians swear by their efficacy. However, research data on the validity of these tests—the degree to which they actually measure what they are supposed to measure—is scarcer than you might expect (Lilienfeld, Wood, & Garb, 2000).

To again use the terminology introduced in Chapter 2, all projective tests provide B data. They are specific, directly observed responses to particular stimuli, whether inkblots, pictures, or instructions to draw somebody. All the disadvantages of B data therefore apply to projective tests. For one thing, they are expensive. It takes around 45 minutes to administer a single Rorschach and another 1.5 to

TRY FOR YOURSELF 3.1

Two Projective Tests

Instructions: Look at the inkblot in **Figure 3.1a**. On a sheet of paper, write down what it looks like to you—no more than a sentence or two. Then look at the drawing in **Figure 3.1b**. Try to imagine what it depicts, and then write down:

1. Who are the people in the picture?
2. What are they doing right now?
3. What were they doing before this moment?
4. What will happen next?

After you are finished, show the pictures to a friend and, without revealing your own responses, ask him or her to do the same thing. Then, compare your responses. Were they different? Do you think the differences mean anything? Do they reveal anything surprising?

Please note that these are not actual personality tests (the blot is not actually part of the Rorschach, and the picture is not part of the TAT). However, the exercise will give you a general idea of how these tests work.

2 hours to score it (Ball, Archer, & Imhof, 1994). Compare this to the time needed to hand out a pile of questionnaires and run them through a machine. This issue is serious because it would not be enough for projective tests to have some small (and perhaps surprising) degree of validity. For their continued use to make any sense, critics have argued, projective tests should provide extra information that justifies their much greater cost (Lilienfeld et al., 2000).

The even more fundamental difficulty with projective tests is that, perhaps even more than other kinds of B data, a psychologist cannot be sure what they mean. What does it mean when somebody thinks an inkblot looks like a crying dog, or imagines that an ambiguous picture portrays a murder, or draws a person with no ears? Two different interpreters of the same response might come to different conclusions unless a standard scoring system is used (Sundberg, 1977). But of the projective tests, only the TAT is consistently scored according to a well-developed system (McAdams, 1984). While scoring systems have been developed for the Rorschach (Exner, 1993; Klopfer & Davidson, 1962), not everybody uses them, and even then, the training most practitioners get is less than ideal (Guarnaccia, Dill, Sabatino, & Southwick, 2001).

The survival of so many projective tests into the 21st century is something of a mystery. Literature reviews that claim projective tests have some degree of validity generally conclude that other, less expensive techniques work as well or even better (Garb, Florio, & Grove, 1998, 1999; Lilienfeld et al., 2000). Even more disturbing, projective tests of dubious validity, such as ones that ask clients to draw human figures, are sometimes used as evidence in court cases (Lally, 2001).[4] Measurement expert Ann Anastasi wrote several decades ago, "projective techniques present a curious discrepancy between research and practice. When evaluated as psychometric instruments, the large majority make a poor showing. Yet their popularity in clinical use continues unabated" (Anastasi, 1982, p. 564). Her comment remains true today (Camara, Nathan, & Puente, 2000).

Perhaps projective tests endure because some clinical psychologists have fooled themselves. One writer has suggested that these clinicians may lack "a skill that does not come naturally to any of us: disregarding the vivid and compelling data of subjective experience in favor of the often dry and impersonal results of objective research" (Lilienfeld, 1999, p. 38). Perhaps the problem is not that the tests are worthless, but that they have been used inappropriately (Wood, Nezworski, & Garb, 2003). Or, as others have suggested, perhaps the validity of these tests is beside the point. They simply serve a useful, if nonpsychometric, function of "breaking the ice" between client and therapist by giving them something to do during the first visit. Or, just possibly, these instruments have a certain, special

---

[4] This use of projective tests has produced a backlash among people who feel they have been victimized by them. Test stimuli such as inkblots and TAT pictures, which in the past were closely held secrets, are now available on several websites that also offer advice on the best responses.

validity in their application by certain skilled clinicians that cannot be duplicated by other techniques and that has not been fully captured by controlled research.

EVALUATING THE RORSCHACH AND THE TAT While data for the validity of most projective tests is either unpersuasive or simply missing, two widely used tests are held out as exceptions. The Rorschach and the TAT remain in wide use both by researchers and clinicians, and continue to be stoutly defended. So, let's take a closer look at the evidence about these two tests.

According to one survey, 82 percent of clinical psychologists use the Rorschach at least occasionally (Watkins, Campbell, Nieberding, & Hallmark, 1995). The meetings of a major professional society, the Society for Personality Assessment, regularly include research and demonstrations with the Rorschach. It remains clinical psychology's fourth most used test,[5] and continues to be widely taught in clinical graduate programs.

Research indicates that the Rorschach gets best results when it is scored according to one of two specific techniques: either Exner's Comprehensive System (Exner, 1993) or Klopfer's technique (Klopfer & Davidson, 1962). According to a comprehensive review, the correlation coefficient between scores garnered from one of these systems and various criteria relevant to mental health averaged about .33 (Garb et al., 1998).[6] As will be illustrated later in this chapter, this correlation means that a dichotomous (Yes or No) diagnostic decision made using the Rorschach will be correct about 66 percent of the time (assuming that a random decision would be correct 50 percent of the time). Research also suggests that the Rorschach might be particularly valid—and actually somewhat better than the MMPI—for predicting specific outcomes such as suicide, attendance at treatment sessions, or commitment to a mental hospital (Hiller, Rosenthal, Bornstein, Berry, & Brunell-Neuleib, 1999).[7]

The other projective test with some degree of established validity—probably better than the Rorschach—is the TAT (McClelland, 1984). In current research, the test is often administered in a newer, shorter form called the Picture Story Exercise (PSE) (McClelland, Koestner, & Weinberger, 1989). The stimuli for this test are from four to eight (versions vary) drawings or photographs that show scenes such as a ship captain talking to a passenger or two women working in a laboratory. The

---

[5] In case you are curious, the top three are (1) the Wechsler Intelligence Scale for adults, (2) the MMPI, and (3) the Wechsler Intelligence Scale for children (Camara et al., 2000).

[6] The main points the authors of this review intended to make were that the validity of the MMPI is even higher (the parallel $r = .55$ in their analysis), and that, since the MMPI is much cheaper to administer, it should be used instead. At the same time, and perhaps unintentionally, they also provided the most convincing evidence I have seen that the Rorschach does have some degree of validity.

[7] The MMPI was found to be better for predicting psychiatric diagnoses and self-report scores. If you want to see the argument that broke out over these findings, compare the paper by Garb, Wood, Nezworski, Grove, and Stejskal (2001) with the response by Rosenthal, Hiller, Bornstein, Berry, and Brunell-Neuleib (2001). As you can see, many people jumped into the fray.

(a)   (b)   (c)

Figure 3.2 Analyzing Presidential Needs Based on an analysis of their inaugural addresses, psychologist David Winter rated (a) Jimmy Carter as the president of the United States who was highest in need for "achievement," (b) George H. W. Bush as highest in need for "affiliation," and (c) John F. Kennedy as highest in need for "power." (Barack Obama and Donald Trump had not yet been elected; where do you think they would place on these dimensions?)

purpose of the TAT (and PSE) is to measure *implicit motives*, motivations concerning achievement, intimacy, power, and other matters of which the participant might not be fully aware. Studies have shown these motives to be related to complex thinking (cognitive complexity), the experiences one finds most memorable, and other psychological outcomes (Woike, 1995; Woike & Aronoff, 1992).

The methods used to assess motives from the TAT can also be used with other sources of data, including even presidential speeches. The psychologist David Winter (2002) found that presidents who revealed a large need for achievement in their inaugural addresses (e.g., Presidents Wilson, Hoover, Nixon, and Carter) began with a flurry of activity, became frustrated with political obstacles, and ended up achieving little.

Objective Tests

The tests that psychologists call "objective" can be detected at a glance. If a test consists of a list of questions to be answered Yes or No, or True or False, or on a numeric scale, and especially if the test uses a computer-scored answer sheet, then it is an **objective test.** The term comes from the idea that the questions making up the test seem more objective and less open to interpretation than the pictures and blots used in projective tests.

VALIDITY AND SUBJECTIVITY OF TEST ITEMS It is not clear that the term "objective" is really justified (Bornstein, 1999a). Consider the first item of the famous MMPI. The item reads, "I like mechanics magazines," which is to be answered True or False (Wiggins, 1973). The item may seem objective compared with a question like, "What do you see in this inkblot?" But the appearance could be misleading. Does "like" mean interest, fondness, admiration, or tolerance?

Does liking such magazines require that you regularly read them? Are *Popular Mechanics* and *Car and Driver* mechanics magazines? How about *Computer World*? Are only popular magazines included, or does the item also refer to trade journals of professional mechanics or to the research literature produced by professors of mechanical engineering? This item is rather typical. And it illustrates how elusive "objectivity" can be.

It is difficult to escape the conclusion that the items on objective tests, while perhaps not as ambiguous as projective tests, are still not absolutely objective. But maybe that's not such a bad thing. If everybody read and interpreted an item in exactly the same way, then might not everybody also tend to answer the item in the same way? If so, the item would not be very useful for the assessment of individual differences, would it? In some cases, the ambiguity of an objective item may not be a flaw; its interpretation might have to be somewhat subjective in order for responses to imply anything about personality.

Harrison Gough, inventor of the California Psychological Inventory, included on his test a scale called *commonality*, which consists of items that are answered in the same way by at least 95 percent of all people. He included it to detect illiterates pretending they know how to read and individuals trying to sabotage the test. The average score on this scale is about 95 percent, but an illiterate answering at random will score about 50 percent (since it is a true-false scale) and therefore will be immediately identifiable, as will someone who (like one of my former students) answered the CPI by flipping a coin—heads True, tails False.

These are interesting and clever uses for a commonality scale, but its properties are mentioned here to make a different point. Gough reported that when individuals encounter a commonality item—one being "I would fight if someone tried to take my rights away" (keyed True)—they do not say to themselves, "What a dumb, obvious item. I bet everybody answers it the same way." Instead, they say, "At last! A nonambiguous item I really understand!" People enjoy answering the commonality items because they seem clear and easy to answer (J. A. Johnson, 2006).[8] Unfortunately, commonality items are not very useful for personality measurement, because almost everybody responds to them the same way. A certain amount of ambiguity may indeed be necessary (Gough, 1968; J. A. Johnson, 1981).

WHY SO MANY ITEMS? If you look at a typical objective test, one of the first things you will notice is how many questions it asks. The number may be very large. Some of the shorter personality tests have around a dozen items, but most have far more, and a few of the most famous personality tests (such as the MMPI, CPI, and NEO) have hundreds. To complete a test like this can take an hour or more, and a fairly tedious hour at that.

---

[8] Another item from the "commonality" scale reads, "Education is more important than most people think." Almost everybody answers True.

Why so many items? The answer lies in the principle of aggregation that was introduced in Chapter 2. The answer an individual gives to any one question might not be particularly informative; it might vary according to exactly how he interprets it or other extraneous factors. In the terminology used in Chapter 2, a single answer will tend to be unreliable. But if a group of similar questions is asked, the average of the answers ought to be much more stable, or reliable, because random fluctuations tend to cancel each other out.

For this reason, one way to make a personality test more reliable is simply to make it longer. If you add items that measure the trait in question as accurately as the existing items do—something easier said than done, frankly—then the improvement in reliability can be estimated using the Spearman-Brown formula,[9] which was mentioned in Chapter 2. The improvements in reliability can be remarkable. For example, if a 10-item test has a reliability of .60—which would be considered rather poor for an objective test—adding 10 more items can raise the reliability to .75, which would be considered much better. Double the number of items again, to 40, and the reliability increases to .86.

As you will recall from Chapter 2, a reliable test is one that gives close to the same answer time after time. However, you will also recall that, while reliability is necessary for validity, it is no guarantee. The validity of an objective test depends on its content. The crucial task in test construction, then, is to write and select the right questions. That is the topic of the next section.

Methods of Objective Test Construction

Three basic methods are commonly used for constructing objective personality tests: the rational method, the factor analytic method, and the empirical method. Test constructors often employ a mixture of methods, but let's begin by considering the pure application of each.

---

[9] Here is some more specific information for the statistically inclined. The reliability of a test is measured in terms of *Cronbach's alpha* according to the following formula: If n is the number of items in the test, and p is the average correlation among all of the items, then the reliability (alpha, or α) $= np / [1 + p(n - 1)]$ (Cronbach, 1951). The Spearman-Brown formula, just mentioned, predicts the increase in reliability you get when you add equivalent items to a test (W. Brown, 1910; Spearman, 1910). If $k = n_1/n_2$, the fraction by which the number of items is increased, then the reliability of the longer test is estimated by

$$\alpha_{longer\,test} = \frac{k \times \alpha_{shorter\,test}}{1 + (k - 1)\,\alpha_{shorter\,test}}$$

In both formulas, alpha is the predicted correlation between a score on your test and a score on another test of equivalent content and length. Correlation coefficients are explained in detail later in this chapter.

THE RATIONAL METHOD Calling one method of test construction "rational" does not mean the others are irrational. It simply means that the strategy of this approach is to come up with items that seem directly, obviously, and rationally related to what the test developer wishes to measure. An early example of a test constructed this way is one used during World War I. The U.S. Army discovered, not surprisingly, that certain problems arose when individuals who were mentally ill were inducted as soldiers, housed in crowded barracks, and issued weapons. To avoid these problems, the army developed a structured interview comprising a list of questions for a psychiatrist to ask each potential recruit. As the number of inductees increased, this slow process became impractical. There were not enough psychiatrists to go around, nor was there enough time to interview everybody.

To get around these limitations, psychologist R. S. Woodworth (1917) proposed that the questions could be printed on a sheet, and the recruits could check off their answers with a pencil. His list, which became known as the Woodworth Personality Data Sheet (or, inevitably, the WPDS), consisted of 116 questions deemed relevant to potential psychiatric problems. They included "Do you wet your bed?" "Have you ever had fits of dizziness?" and "Are you troubled with dreams about your work?" A recruit who responded Yes to more than a small number of these questions was referred for a more personal examination. Recruits who answered No to all the questions were inducted forthwith into the army.

Woodworth's idea of listing psychiatric symptoms on a questionnaire was not unreasonable, yet his technique raises a variety of problems that can be identified rather easily. For the WPDS to be a valid indicator of psychiatric disturbance—for any rationally constructed, S-data personality test to work—four conditions must hold (Wiggins, 1973).

First, each item must mean the same thing to the person who takes the test as it did to the psychologist who wrote it. For example, in the item from the WPDS, what is "dizziness" exactly? If you have been sitting down for a long time, suddenly stand up, and feel a little bit dizzy, does that count?

Second, the person who completes the form must be able to make an accurate self-assessment. He (only men were being recruited at the time the WPDS was administered) must have a good enough understanding of what each item is asking, as well as the ability to observe it in himself. He must not be so ignorant or psychologically disoriented that he cannot report accurately on these psychological symptoms.

Third, the person who completes the test must be willing to report his self-assessment accurately and without distortion. He must not try to deny his symptoms (in order to get into the army) or to exaggerate them (perhaps in order to stay out of the army). Modern personality tests used for selecting employees can encounter the very same problem in that, rather than responding honestly, people might try give the answers they think will help them get a job (Griffith & Peterson, 2006; Rosse, Stecher, Miller, & Levin, 1998).

Fourth and finally, all of the items on the test must be valid indicators of what the tester is trying to measure—in this case, mental disturbance. Does dizziness really indicate mental illness? What about dreams about work?

For a rationally constructed test to measure an attribute of personality accurately, all four of these conditions must be met. In the case of the WPDS, probably none of them was.[10] In fact, most rationally constructed personality tests fail one or more of these criteria. One might conclude, therefore, that they would hardly ever be used anymore.

Wrong. Up to and including the present day, self-report questionnaires that are little different, in principle, from the WPDS remain the most common form of psychological measurement. Self-tests in popular magazines are also always constructed by the rational method—somebody just thinks up some questions that seem relevant—and they almost always fail at least two or three of the four crucial criteria.

Rationally constructed personality tests appear in psychological journals, too. Such journals present a steady stream of new testing instruments, nearly all of which are developed by the simple technique of thinking up a list of questions. These questions might include measures of health status (How healthy are you?), self-esteem (How good do you feel about yourself?), or goals (What do you want in life?).

For example, research has addressed the differences between college students who follow optimistic or pessimistic strategies in order to motivate themselves to perform academic tasks (such as preparing for an exam). Optimists, as described by this research, motivate themselves to work hard by expecting the best outcome, whereas pessimists motivate themselves by expecting the worst to happen unless they work hard. Both strategies seem to be effective, although optimists may have more pleasant lives (Norem & Cantor, 1986). (These strategies are considered in more detail in Chapter 14.) For the purposes of this chapter, the question is, how are optimists and pessimists identified? The researchers in this study used an eight-item questionnaire that included self-ratings such as "I go into academic situations expecting the worst, even though I know I will probably do OK" (see **Try for Yourself 3.2**).

By the definitions I have been using, this is a rationally constructed, S-data personality test. And, in fact, it seems to work fairly well at identifying students who approach academic life in different ways. So clearly, tests like this can be valid, even though the four criteria for validity raised earlier should always be kept in mind.

---

[10] On the other hand, given how inexpensive it was to administer the WPDS and how expensive it could be to add just one mentally ill person to an armed combat unit, the WPDS may well have been cost-effective.

TRY FOR YOURSELF 3.2

Optimism-Pessimism Test

Instructions: When you answer the following questions, please think about how you prepare for and think about academic situations. Each of the statements below describes how people sometimes think or feel about these kinds of situations. In the blanks beside each statement, please indicate how true it is of you, in academic situations.

1-------2-------3-------4-------5-------6-------7
Not at all   **Very true of me**
true of me

4 ____1. I go into academic situations expecting the worst, even though I know I will probably do OK.

2 ____2. I generally go into academic situations with positive expectations about how I will do. **6**

5 ____3. I carefully consider all possible outcomes before academic situations.

6 ____4. I often worry, in academic situations, that I won't be able to carry through my intentions.

7 ____5. I often think about how I will feel if I do very poorly in academic situations.

2 ____6. I often think about how I will feel if I do very well in academic situations.

4 ____7. I often try to figure out how likely it is that I will do very poorly in academic situations.

7 ____8. I spend a lot of time planning when an academic situation is coming up.

4 ____9. I often try to figure out how likely it is that I will do very well in academic situations.

5 ____10. In academic situations, sometimes I worry more about looking like a fool than doing really well.

4 ____11. Prior to academic situations, I avoid thinking about possible bad outcomes. **4**

6 ____12. Considering what can go wrong in academic situations helps me to prepare.

Scoring Instructions: Add up your answers to items 1, 3, 4, 5, 6, 7, 8, 9, 10, and 12. Reverse-score your answers to items 2 and 11 (that is, convert 1=7, 2=6, 3=5, 4=4, 5=3, 6=2, and 7=1). Then add those scores to the total. In one large sample of people who took this test, the mean was 54.2. Scores do not appear to differ, on average, between women and men or according to age. Scores below 50 would typically be categorized as "strategic optimists"; scores above 60 would be categorized as defensive pessimists.

Source: Adapted from Norem & Prayson (2015).

THE FACTOR ANALYTIC METHOD The factor analytic method of test construction is based on a statistical technique. **Factor analysis** identifies groups of things—which can be anything from songs to test items—that seem to have something in common. The property that ties these things together is called a *factor* (Cattell, 1952).

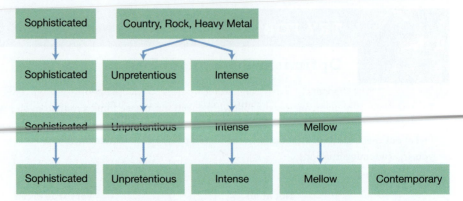

Figure 3.3 A Factor Analysis of Musical Preference Participants rated their preferences for 52 musical clips, and factor analysis revealed that, to a large extent, these preferences were accounted for by five factors listed at the bottom of the figure. The figure also shows that the "unpretentious" and "intense" properties of music characterize the broader description of "country, rock, and heavy metal," and that the "mellow" and "contemporary" factors account for smaller ranges of musical preference. In this display, the width of the boxes reflects the "factor size," or the relative importance of that factor in overall music preference.

Source: Rentfrow, Goldberg & Levitin (2011), p. 1144.

> If you like Farrend's Piano Quintet no. 1 in A Minor, you will probably enjoy "The Way You Look Tonight" by Oscar Peterson, but you won't like "Texas Tornado" by Tracy Lawrence.

One study used factor analysis to study music preference, by asking people to identify pieces that they did and didn't enjoy. The study found that such preferences can be organized in terms of five properties that the researchers labeled "mellow," "unpretentious," "sophisticated," "intense," and "contemporary"[11] (Rentfrow, Goldberg, & Levitin, 2011). So, for example, if you like Farrend's "Piano Quintet no. 1 in A Minor," it turns out that you will probably also enjoy "The Way You Look Tonight" by Oscar Peterson, because both get high scores on the mellow factor. But you probably won't like "Texas Tornado" by Tracy Lawrence, because it has a negative score on that factor; instead, it gets a high score, or "loads," on the second, unpretentious factor.

To use factor analysis to construct a personality test, researchers begin with a list of objective items of the sort discussed earlier. The next step is to administer these items to a large number of participants. Then you and your computer can sit down together and do the factor analysis. The analysis is based on calculating correlation coefficients between each item and each of the other items. The items that

---

[11] If you want to remember these factors, notice that their initials spell MUSIC.

Figure 3.4 Three Questionnaire Items That Measure the Same Factor If these three items are correlated with each other—people who answer True to the first item tend to answer True to the second one and False to the third—they might all "load on," or measure, a common psychological factor.

correlate most highly with each other can be assembled into groups. For example, if a person answers True to the item "I trust strangers," you will find that he is also likely to answer True to "I am careful to turn up when someone expects me" and answer False to "I could stand being a hermit." Such a pattern of likelihood, or co-occurrence, means that these three items are correlated. The next steps are to consider what the items have in common, and then name the factor.

The three correlated items just listed, according to Cattell (1965), are related to the dimension "cool versus warm," with a true-true-false pattern of responses indicating a "warm" personality (see **Figure 3.4**). (Cattell decided on this label simply by considering the content of the items, as you just did.) The factor represented by these items, therefore, is "warm-cool," or, if you prefer to name it by just one pole, "warmth." These three items now can be said to form a "warmth" scale. To measure this dimension in a new participant, you would administer these three items, as well as other items in your original list that correlated highly with them, and discard the rest of the thousands of items you started with.

Factor analysis has been used not only to construct tests, but also to decide how many fundamental traits exist—how many out of the thousands in the dictionary are truly essential. Various analysts have come up with different answers. Cattell (1957) thought there were 16. Eysenck (1976) concluded there are just 3. More recently, prominent psychologists such as Lewis Goldberg (1990), Robert R. McCrae, and Paul Costa (1987) settled on 5; this is the most widely accepted answer at present. These five traits—sometimes called the Big Five—are extraversion, neuroticism, conscientiousness, agreeableness, and openness (see Chapter 6).

> The Big Five traits are extraversion, neuroticism, conscientiousness, agreeableness, and openness.

THE EMPIRICAL METHOD The empirical strategy of test construction is an attempt to allow reality to speak for itself. In its pure form, the empirical approach

B. Smaller

"Give me a hug. I can tell a lot about a man by the way he hugs."

has sometimes been called "dust bowl empiricism." The term refers to the origin of the technique at Midwestern universities (notably Minnesota and Iowa) during the Depression, or dust bowl, years of the 1930s.[12] Intentionally or not, the term also serves as a reminder of how dry this approach is, since it is based strictly on data, not any kind of deeper psychological theory.

Like the factor analytic approach described earlier, the first step of the empirical approach is to gather lots of items. The second step, however, is quite different. For this step, you need to have a sample of participants who have already independently been divided into the groups you are interested in. Occupational groups and diagnostic categories are often used for this purpose. For example, if you wish to measure the aspect of people that makes them good and happy religious ministers, then you need at least two groups of participants—happy, successful ministers and a comparison group. (Ideally, the comparison group would be miserable, incompetent ministers, but typically the researcher will settle for people who are not ministers at all.) Or you might want a test to detect different kinds of psychopathology. For this purpose, you would need groups of people who have been diagnosed as suffering from schizophrenia, depression, hysteria, and so forth. A group of normal people—if you can find them—would also be useful for comparison purposes. Whatever groups you wish to include, their members must be identified before you develop your test.

Then you are ready for the third step: administering your test to your participants.

The fourth step is to compare the answers given by the different groups. If people diagnosed with depression answer a certain group of questions differently from everybody else, those items might form a "depression" scale. Thereafter, new participants who answer questions the same way as people diagnosed with depression did would score high on this scale, and you might suspect that they, too, are depressed. The MMPI, which is the prototypical example of the empirical method of test construction, was built using this strategy. For instance, one item on the depression scale is "I sometimes tease animals," keyed False. This does not mean

---

[12] A severe drought and resulting "dust bowl" afflicted several midwestern states during that period. However, Minnesota and Iowa were not among them.

people who deny teasing animals are depressed! But this answer, on this test, does elevate one's depression score. Or, if successful ministers answer some items in a distinctive way, these items might be combined into a "minister" scale. New participants who score high on this scale, because they answer the way successful ministers do, might be guided to become ministers themselves. The items for the SVIB were selected this way. For example, the percentage of men who reported that they liked "making a speech" was higher for ministers than other groups such as farmers and factory workers, so the item went on the "minister" scale.

This principle can even be used at the individual level. The developers of the MMPI published an atlas, or casebook, of hundreds of individuals who took the test over the years (Hathaway & Meehl, 1951). For each case, the atlas gives the person's scoring pattern and describes his clinical case history. The idea is that a clinical psychologist confronted with a new client can ask the client to take the MMPI, and then look up those individuals in the atlas who scored similarly in the past.

After the items are selected based on the responses of people in the initial groups, the next step is to *cross-validate* that scale by using it to predict behavior, diagnosis, or category membership in new samples of participants. If the cross-validation succeeds, the scale is deemed ready for use.

COMBINATION OF METHODS A surprisingly large number of investigators still use a pure form of the rational method: They ask their participants the questions that seem relevant and hope for the best. The factor analytic approach still has a few adherents. Pure applications of the empirical approach are rare today. The best modern test developers use a combination of all three approaches.

The best way to select items for a personality scale is not haphazardly, but with the intent to sample a particular domain of interest (the rational approach). Factor analysis should then be used to confirm that items that seem similar to each other actually elicit similar responses from real participants (Briggs & Cheek, 1986). Finally, any personality measure is only as good as the other things with which it correlates or that it can predict (the empirical approach). To be worth its salt, any personality scale must show that it can predict what people do, how they are seen by others, and how they fare in life.

EVALUATING ASSESSMENT AND RESEARCH

Psychologists, being human, like to brag. They do this when they describe how well their assessment devices can predict behavior, and also when they talk about the strength of other research findings. Often—probably too often—they use words such as "large," "important," or even "dramatic." Nearly always, they describe their results as "significant." These descriptions can be confusing because there are no rules about how the first three terms can be employed. "Large," "important," and even "dramatic" are just adjectives and can be used at will. However, there are formal and rather strict rules about how the term *significant* can be employed.

Significance Testing

A significant result, in research parlance, is not necessarily large or important, let alone dramatic. But it is a result that would be unlikely to appear if everything were due only to chance. This is important, because in any experimental study the difference between two conditions will almost never[13] turn out to be exactly zero, and in correlational studies an *r* of precisely zero is equally rare. So, how large does the difference between the means of two conditions have to be, or how big does the correlation coefficient need to be, before we will conclude that these are numbers we should take seriously?

The most commonly used method for answering this question is *null-hypothesis significance testing (NHST)*. NHST attempts to answer the question, "What are the chances I would have found this result if nothing were really going on?" The basic procedure is taught in every beginning statistics class. A difference between experimental conditions (in an experimental study) or a correlation coefficient (in a correlational study) that is calculated to be significant at the 5 percent level is different from zero to a degree that, by chance alone, would be expected about 5 percent of the time. A difference or correlation significant at the 1 percent level is different from zero to a degree expected by chance about 1 percent of the time, and so this is traditionally considered a stronger result. Various statistical formulas, some quite complex, are employed to calculate the likelihood that experimental or correlational results would be expected by chance.[14] The more unlikely, the better.

For example, look back at the results in **Figures 2.4** and **2.5**. These findings might be evaluated by calculating the ***p*-level** (probability level) of the difference in means (in the experimental study in Figure 2.4) or of the correlation coefficient (in the correlational study in Figure 2.5). In each case, the *p*-level is the probability that a difference of that size (or larger) would be found, if the actual size of the difference were zero. (This possibility of a zero result is called the *null hypothesis*.) If the result is significant, the common interpretation is that the statistic probably did not arise by chance; its real value, sometimes called the *population value*, is

---

[13]Actually, never.

[14]Another way to determine the chance probability of one's results is with a *randomization test*, which assesses how often the results appear when the data are randomly rearranged (Sherman & Funder, 2009). Because randomization tests do not require the many assumptions required by conventional statistical analyses and are becoming ever more feasible with modern computers, they seem likely to become more widely used in the future.

probably not zero, so the null hypothesis is incorrect, and the result is big enough to take seriously.

This traditional method of statistical data analysis is deeply embedded in the scientific literature and current research practice, and is almost universally taught in beginning statistics classes. But I would not be doing my duty if I failed to warn you that insightful psychologists have been critical of this method for many years (e.g., Rozeboom, 1960), and the frequency and intensity of this criticism have only increased over time (e.g., Cumming, 2012, 2014; Dienes, 2011; Haig, 2005; G. R. Loftus, 1996). Indeed, some psychologists have suggested that conventional significance testing should be banned altogether (Hunter, 1997; F. L. Schmidt, 1996)! That may be going a bit far, but NHST does have some serious problems. This chapter is not the place for an extended discussion, but it might be worth a few words to describe some of the more obvious difficulties (see also Cumming, 2014; Dienes, 2011).

One problem with NHST is that its underlying logic is very difficult to describe precisely, and its interpretation—including the interpretation given in many text-books—is frequently wrong. It is not correct, for example, that the significance level provides the probability that the research (non-null) hypothesis is true. A significance level of .05 is sometimes taken to mean that the probability that the research hypothesis is true is 95%! Nope. You wish. Instead, the significance level gives the probability of getting the result one found if the *null* hypothesis were true. One statistical writer offered the following analogy (Dienes, 2011): The probability that a person is dead, given that a shark has bitten his head off, is 1.0. However, the probability that a person's head was bitten off by a shark, given that he is dead, is much lower. Most people die in less dramatic fashion. The probability of the data given the hypothesis, and of the hypothesis given the data, is not the same thing.[15] And the latter is what we really want to know.

Believe it or not, I really did try to write the preceding paragraph as clearly as I could. But if you found it confusing, you are in good company. One study found that 97 percent of academic psychologists, and even 80 percent of methodology instructors, misunderstood NHST in an important way (Krauss & Wassner, 2002). The most widely used method for interpreting research findings is so confusing that even experts often get it wrong. This cannot be a good thing.

> The probability of the data given the hypothesis, and of the hypothesis given the data, is not the same thing.

A more obvious difficulty with NHST is that the criterion for a significant result is little more than a traditional rule of thumb. Why is a result of $p < .05$ significant, when a result of $p < .06$ is not? There is no real answer, and nobody seems to even know where the standard .05 level came from in the first place (though I strongly

---

[15]However, all other things being equal, they are correlated (Krueger & Heck, 2018).

suspect it has something to do with the fact that we have five fingers on each hand). In fact, an argument broke out recently when some psychologists proposed lowering the .05 threshold to the (seemingly) more stringent level of .005 (Benjamin et al., 2017). Others (including your textbook author) saw little value in replacing one arbitrary threshold with another (Funder, 2017).

Yet another common difficulty is that even experienced researchers too often misinterpret a nonsignificant result to mean "no result." If, for example, the obtained p-level is .06, researchers sometimes conclude that there is no difference between the experimental and control conditions or no relationship between two correlated variables. But actually, the probability is only 6 out of 100 that, if there were no effect, a difference this big would have been found.

This observation leads to one final difficulty with traditional significance tests: The p-level addresses only the probability of one kind of error, conventionally called a **Type I error.** A Type I error involves deciding that one variable has an effect on, or a relationship with, another variable, when really it does not. But there is another kind: A **Type II error** involves deciding that one variable does *not* have an effect on, or relationship with, another variable, when it really *does*. Unfortunately, there is no way to estimate the probability of a Type II error without making extra assumptions (J. Cohen, 1994; Dienes, 2011; Gigerenzer, Hoffrage, & Kleinbolting, 1991).

What a mess. The bottom line is this: When you take a course in psychological statistics, if you haven't done so already, you will have to learn about significance testing and how to do it. Despite its many and widely acknowledged flaws, NHST remains in wide use (S. Krauss & Wassner, 2002). But it is not as useful a technique as it looks at first, and psychological research practice seems to be moving slowly but surely away (Abelson, Cohen, & Rosenthal, 1996; Cumming, 2014; Wilkinson & The Task Force on Statistical Inference, 1999). The p-level at the heart of NHST is not completely useless; it can serve as a rough guide to the strength of one's results (Krueger & Heck, 2018). However, in the future, evaluating research is likely to focus less on statistical significance, and more on considerations such as effect size and replication, the two topics to be considered next.

Effect Size

All scientific findings are not created equal. Some are bigger than others, which raises a question that must be asked about every result: How big is it? Is the effect or the relationship we have found strong enough to matter, or is its size too trivial to care about? Because this is an important question, psychologists who are better analysts of data do not just stop with significance. They move on to calculate a number that will reflect the magnitude, as opposed to the likelihood, of their result. This number is called an **effect size** (Grissom & Kim, 2012).

An effect size is more meaningful than a significance level. Don't take my word for it; the principle is official: The *Publication Manual of the American Psychological Association* (which sets the standards that must be followed by almost all published research in psychology) explicitly says that the probability value associated with statistical significance does not reflect "the magnitude of an effect or the strength of a relationship. For the reader to fully understand the magnitude or importance of a study's findings, it is almost always necessary to include some index of effect size" (American Psychological Association, 2010, p. 34).

Many measures of effect size have been developed, including standardized regression weights (beta coefficients), odds ratios, relative risk ratios, and a statistic called *Cohen's d* (the difference in means divided by the standard deviation). The most commonly used and my personal favorite is the **correlation coefficient.** Despite the name, its use is not limited to correlational studies. As we saw in Chapter 2, the correlation coefficient can be used to describe the strength of either correlational or experimental results (Funder & Ozer, 1983).

CALCULATING CORRELATIONS To calculate a correlation coefficient, in the usual case, you start with two variables, and arrange all of the scores on the two variables into two columns, with each row containing the scores for one participant. These columns are labeled x and y. Traditionally, the variable you think is the cause is put in the x column and the variable you think is the effect is put in the y column. So, in the example considered in Chapter 2, x was "anxiety" and y was "performance." Then you apply a common statistical formula (found in any statistics textbook) to these numbers or, more commonly, you punch the numbers into a computer or maybe even a handheld calculator.[16]

The result is a correlation coefficient (the most common is the *Pearson r*). This is a number that—if you did the calculations right—is somewhere between +1 and –1 (**Figure 3.5**). If two variables are unrelated, the correlation between them will be near zero. If the variables are positively associated—as one goes up, the other tends to go up too, like height and weight—then the correlation coefficient will be greater than zero (i.e., a positive number). If the variables are negatively associated—as one goes up, the other tends to go down, like "anxiety" and "performance"—then the correlation coefficient will be less than zero (i.e., a negative number). Essentially, if two variables are correlated (positively or negatively), this means that one of them can be predicted from the other. For example, back in Chapter 2, Figure 2.5 showed that if I know how anxious you are, then I can predict (to a degree) how well you will do on a math test.

Not everybody knows this, but you can also get a correlation coefficient from experimental studies. For the experiment on test performance, for example, you could just give everybody in the high-anxiety condition a "1" for anxiety and everybody in the low-anxiety condition a "0." These 1s and 0s would go in the x column, and participants' corresponding levels of performance would go in the y

---

[16] Programs to calculate the correlation coefficient are also available online. One easy-to-use calculator can be found at https://www.socscistatistics.com/tests/pearson/.

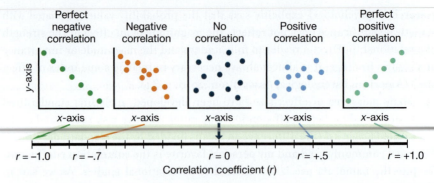

Figure 3.5 Correlation Coefficient The correlation coefficient is a number between −1.0 and 1.0 that indicates the relationship between two variables, traditionally labeled *x* and *y*.

column. There are also formulas to directly convert the statistics usually seen in experimental studies into correlations. For example, the *t* or *F* statistic (used in the analysis of variance) can be directly converted into an *r*.[17] It is good practice to do this conversion whenever possible, because then you can compare the results of correlational and experimental studies using a common metric.

INTERPRETING CORRELATIONS To interpret a correlation coefficient, it is not enough just to assess its statistical significance. An obtained correlation becomes significant in a statistical sense merely by being unlikely to have arisen if the true correlation is zero, which depends almost as much on how many participants you managed (or could afford) to recruit as on how strong the effect really is. Instead, you need to look at the correlation's actual size. Some textbooks provide rules of thumb. One I happen to own says that a correlation (positive or negative) of .6 to .8 is "quite strong," one from .3 to .5 is "weaker but still important," and one from .3 to .2 is "rather weak." I have no idea what these phrases are supposed to mean. Do you?

Another commonly taught way to evaluate correlations is to square them[18], which tells "what percent of the variance the correlation explains." This certainly

---

[17] The most commonly used statistic that reflects a difference between two experimental groups is the *t* (the outcome of a *t*-test). The standard symbol for the commonly used Pearson correlation coefficient is *r*, and n_1 and n_2 refer to the number of participants in the two experimental groups. The experimental *t* can be converted to the correlational *r* using the following formula:

$$r = \sqrt{\frac{t^2}{t^2 + (n_1 + n_2 - 2)}}$$

where n_1 and n_2 are the sizes of the two samples (or experimental groups) being compared.
[18] The reason for doing this has to do with converting variation, which is deviation from the mean, with variance, which is squared deviation from the mean.

sounds like what you need to know, and the calculation is wonderfully easy. For example, a correlation of .30, when squared, yields .09, which means that "only" 9 percent of the variance is explained by the correlation, and the remaining 91 percent is "unexplained." Similarly, a correlation of .40 means that "only" 16 percent of the variance is explained and 84 percent is unexplained. That seems like a lot of unexplaining, and so such correlations are often viewed as small.

Despite the wide popularity of this squaring method (if you have taken a statistics course you were probably taught it), I think it is a *terrible* way to evaluate effect size. The real and perhaps only result of this pseudo-sophisticated maneuver is, misleadingly, to make the correlations typically found in psychological research seem trivial. It is the case that in both correlational research in personality and experimental research in social psychology, the effect sizes expressed in correlations rarely exceed .40. If results like these are considered to "explain" (whatever that means) "16 percent of the variance" (whatever that means), leaving "84 percent unexplained," then we are left with the vague but disturbing conclusion that research has not accomplished much. Yet, this conclusion is not correct (Ozer, 1985).[19] Worse, it is almost impossible to understand. What is really needed is a way to evaluate the size of correlations to help understand the strength and, in some cases, the usefulness of the result obtained.

THE BINOMIAL EFFECT SIZE DISPLAY Rosenthal and Rubin (1982) provided a brilliant technique for demonstrating the size of effect-size correlations. Their method is called the **Binomial Effect Size Display (BESD).** Let's use their favorite example to illustrate how it works.

Assume you are studying 200 participants, all of whom are sick. An experimental drug is given to 100 of them; the other 100 are given nothing. At the end of the study, 100 are alive and 100 are dead. The question is, how much difference did the drug make? Were the 100 people who got the drug more likely to be among the 100 who lived?

Sometimes the answer to this question is reported in the form of a correlation coefficient. For example, you may be told that the correlation between taking the drug and recovering from the illness is .40. If the report stops here (as it often does), you are left with the following questions: What does this mean? Was the effect big or little? If you were to follow the common practice of squaring

---

[19] I have found that many of my colleagues, with PhD's in psychology themselves, resist accepting this fact, because of what they were taught in their first statistics course long ago. All I can do in such cases is urge that they read the Ozer (1985) paper just referenced. To encapsulate the technical argument, "variance" is the sum of squared deviations from the mean; the squaring is a computational convenience but has no other meaning or rationale. However, one consequence is that the variance explained by a correlation is in squared units, not the original units that were measured. To get back to the original units, just leave the correlation unsquared. Then, a correlation of .40 can be seen to explain 40% of the (unsquared) variation, as well as 16% of the (squared) variance.

Table 3.1 | THE BINOMIAL EFFECT SIZE DISPLAY

	Alive	Dead	Total
Drug	70	30	100
No Drug	30	70	100
Total	100	100	200

Life and death outcomes for participants in a hypothetical 200-person drug trial, when the correlation between drug administration and outcome $r = .40$.

Source: Adapted from Rosenthal & Rubin (1982), p. 167.

correlations to yield "variance explained," you might conclude that "84 percent of the variance remains unexplained" (which sounds pretty bad) and decide the drug is nearly worthless.

The BESD provides another way to look at things. Through some simple further calculations, you can move from a report that "the correlation is .40" to a concrete display of what that correlation means in terms of specific outcomes. As shown in **Table 3.1**, a correlation of .40 means that 70 percent of those who got the drug are still alive, whereas only 30 percent of those who did not get the drug are still alive. If the correlation is .30, those figures would be 65 percent and 35 percent, respectively. As Rosenthal and Rubin pointed out, these effects might technically only explain 16 percent or even 9 percent of the variance, but in either case, if you got sick, would you want this drug?

The computational method begins by assuming a correlation of zero, which gives each of the four cells in the table an entry of 50 (i.e., if there is no effect, then 50 participants receiving the drug will live and 50 will die—it does not matter whether they get the treatment or not). Then we take the actual correlation (in the example, .40), remove the decimal to produce a two-digit number (.40 becomes 40), divide by 2 (in this case yielding 20), and add it to the 50 in the upper-left-hand cell (yielding 70). Then we adjust the other three cells by subtraction. Because each row and column must total 100, the four cells, reading clockwise, become 70, 30, 70, and 30.

This technique works with any kind of data. "Alive" and "dead" can be replaced with any kind of dichotomized outcomes—"better-than-average school success" and "worse-than-average school success," for example. The treatment variables could become "taught with new method" and "taught with old method." Or the variables could be "scores above average on school motivation" and "scores below average on school motivation," or any other personality variable (see **Table 3.2**). One can even look at predictors of success for Major League Baseball teams (see **Figure 3.6**).

The BESD shows vividly both how much of an effect an experimental intervention is likely to have, and how well one can predict an outcome from an individual

Table 3.2 | THE BINOMIAL EFFECT SIZE DISPLAY USED TO INTERPRET (HYPOTHETICAL) SCHOOL DATA

	School Performance		
School Motivation	**Above Average**	**Below Average**	**Total**
Above average	50	50	100
Below average	50	50	100
Total	100	100	200

School performance outcomes for 200 students above and below average on school motivation when correlation between the two variables $r = 0$.

	School Performance		
School Motivation	**Above Average**	**Below Average**	**Total**
Above average	65	35	100
Below average	35	65	100
Total	100	100	200

School performance outcomes for 200 students above and below average on school motivation when correlation between the two variables $r = .30$.

measurement of difference. So, when you read—later in this book or in a psychological research article—that one variable is related to another with a correlation of .30 or .40 or whatever, you should construct a BESD in your mind and evaluate the size of the correlation accordingly.

Replication

Beyond the size of a research result, no matter how it is evaluated, lies a second and even more fundamental question: Is the result dependable, something you could expect to find again and again, or did it merely occur by chance? As was discussed above, null hypothesis significance testing (NHST) is typically used to answer this question, but it is not really up to the job. A much better indication of the stability of results is **replication.** In other words, do the study again. Statistical significance is all well and good, but there is nothing quite so persuasive as finding the same result repeatedly, with different participants and in different labs (Asendorpf et al., 2013; Funder et al., 2014).[20]

The principle of replication seems straightforward, but it has led to a remarkable degree of controversy in recent years—not just within psychology, but in many

---

[20] R. A. Fisher, usually credited as the inventor of NHST, wrote "we may say that a phenomenon is experimentally demonstrable when we know how to conduct an experiment that will rarely fail to give us a statistically significant result" (1966, p 14).

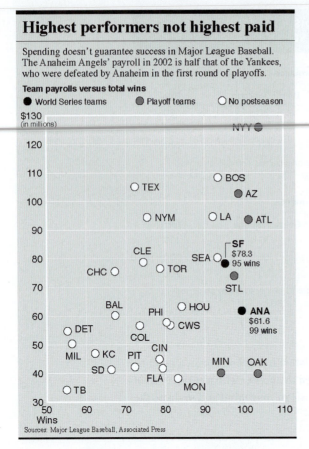

Highest performers not highest paid

Spending doesn't guarantee success in Major League Baseball. The Anaheim Angels' payroll in 2002 is half that of the Yankees, who were defeated by Anaheim in the first round of playoffs.

Team payrolls versus total wins

● World Series teams   ● Playoff teams   ○ No postseason

Sources: Major League Baseball, Associated Press

Figure 3.6 Statistics on the Sports Page An analysis of the relationship between total payrolls of Major League Baseball teams and number of games won during the 2002 season. This chart appeared in the sports section of the *Los Angeles Times*. Notice the conclusion expressed by the headline. Is it valid? The correlation between payroll and games won is .44, which, according to the Binomial Effect Size Display, means that a team that pays above-average salaries has a 72% chance of winning more than half its games, whereas a team that pays below-average salaries has only a 28% chance.

areas of science. One early spark for the controversy was an article, written by a prominent medical researcher and statistician, entitled "Why most published research findings are false" (Ionnadis, 2005). That title certainly got people's attention! The article focused on biomedicine but addressed reasons why findings in many areas of research shouldn't be completely trusted. These include the proliferation of small studies with weak effects, researchers reporting only selected analyses rather than everything they find, and the undeniable fact that researchers are rewarded, with grants and jobs, for studies that get interesting results. Another factor is **publication bias**, the fact that studies with strong results are more likely to be published than studies with weak results—leading to a published literature that makes effects seem stronger than they really are (Polanin, Tanner-Smith, & Hennessy, 2016).

Worries about the truth of published findings spread to psychology a few years later, in a big way, when three things happened almost at once. First, an article in the influential journal *Psychological Science* outlined how researchers could make almost any data set yield significant findings through techniques such as deleting unusual responses, adjusting results to remove the influence of seemingly extraneous factors, and neglecting to report experimental conditions or even whole experiments that fail to get expected results (Simmons, Nelson, & Simonsohn, 2011). Such **questionable research practices (QRP's)** have also become known as *p*-**hacking**, a term which refers to hacking around in one's data until one finds the necessary degree of statistical significance, or *p*-level, that allows one's findings to be published. To demonstrate how this could work, Simmons and his team massaged a real data set to "prove" that listening to the Beatles song "When I'm 64" actually made participants younger!

Coincidentally, at almost exactly the same time, the prominent psychologist Daryl Bem published an article in a major journal purporting to demonstrate a form of ESP called "precognition," reacting to stimuli that are presented *in the future* (Bem, 2011). And then, close on the heels of that stunning event, another well-known psychologist, Diederik Stapel, was exposed for having become famous on the basis of studies in which he, quite literally, faked his data (Bhattacharjee, 2013). The two cases of Bem and Stapel were different because nobody suggested that Bem com-

mitted fraud, but nobody seemed to be able to repeat his findings, either, suggesting that flawed (but common) practices of data analysis were to blame (Wagenmakers, Wetzels, Borsboom, & van der Maas, 2011). For example, it was suggested that Bem might have published only the studies that successfully demonstrated precognition, not the ones that failed. One thing the two cases did have in common was that the work of both researchers had passed through the filters of scientific review that were supposed to ensure that published findings can be trusted.

And this was just the beginning. Before too long, many seemingly well-established findings in psychology were called into question when researchers found that they were unable to repeat them in their own laboratories (Open Science Collaboration, 2015). One example is a study that I described in previous editions of this very book, a study that purported to demonstrate a phenomenon sometimes called "elderly priming" (Anderson, 2015; Bargh, Chen, & Burrows, 1996). College student participants were "primed" with thoughts about old people by having them unscramble words such as "DNIRKWE" (wrinkled), "LDO" (old), and (my favorite) "FALODRI" (Florida). Others were given scrambles of neutral words such as "thirsty," "clean," and "private." The remarkable—even forehead-slapping—finding was that when they walked away from the experiment, participants in the first group moved more slowly down the hallway than participants in the second group! Just being subtly reminded about concepts related to being old, it seemed, is enough to make a person act old.

I reported this fun finding in previous editions because the measurement of walking speed seemed like a great example of B-data, as described in Chapter 2, and also because I thought readers would enjoy learning about it. That was my mistake! The original study was based on just a few participants[21] and later attempts

---

[21]Actually, there were two studies, each with 30 participants, which is a very small number by any standard.

to repeat the finding, some of which used much larger samples, were unable to do so (e.g., Anderson, 2015; Doyen, Klein, Pichon, & Cleeremans, 2012; Pashler, Harris & Coburn, 2011). In retrospect, I should have known better. Not only were the original studies very small, but the finding itself is so remarkable that extra-strong evidence should have been required before I believed it.[22]

The questionable validity of this finding and many others that researchers tried and failed to replicate stimulated lively and sometimes acrimonious exchanges in forums ranging from academic symposia and journal articles to impassioned tweets, blogs, and Facebook posts. At one (low) point, a prominent researcher complained that colleagues attempting to evaluate replicability were no more than "shameless little bullies." But for the most part, cooler heads prevailed, and insults gave way to positive recommendations for how to make research more dependable in the future (Funder et al., 2014; Shrout & Rodgers, 2018). These recommendations include using larger numbers of participants than has been traditional, disclosing all methods, sharing data, and reporting studies that don't work as well as just those that do. The most important recommendation—and one that really should have been followed all along—is to never regard any one study as conclusive proof of anything, no matter who did the study, where it was published, or what its *p*-level was (Donnellan & Lucas, 2018). The key attitude of science is—or should be—that all knowledge is provisional. Scientific conclusions are the best interpretations that can be made based on the evidence at hand. But they are always subject to change.

> Scientific conclusions are the best interpretations that can be made based on the evidence at hand. But they are always subject to change.

ETHICAL ISSUES

Purposes of Personality Testing

According to one wide-ranging survey, the validity of well-developed psychological tests is comparable to that of the most widely used medical tests (Meyer et al., 2001). Still, a further question must be considered: How will test scores be used? The answer has practical and ethical implications (Hanson, 1993).

The most obvious uses for personality tests are those to which they are put by the professional personality testers—the ones who set up the booths at APA conventions—and their customers. The customers are typically organizations such

---

[22] The astronomer Carl Sagan popularized the phrase "extraordinary claims require extraordinary evidence," but he wasn't the first to realize the general idea. David Hume wrote in 1748 that "No testimony is sufficient to establish a miracle, unless the testimony be of such a kind, that its falsehood would be more miraculous than the fact which it endeavors to establish" (Rational Wiki, 2018).

as schools, clinics, corporations, or government agencies that wish to know something about the people they encounter. Sometimes this information is desired so that, regardless of the score obtained, the person who is measured can be helped. For example, schools frequently use tests to measure vocational interests to help their students choose careers. A clinician might administer a test to get an indication of how serious a client's problem is, or to suggest a therapeutic direction.

Sometimes, testing is for the benefit of the tester, not necessarily the person being tested. An employer may test an individual's "integrity" to find out whether he is trustworthy enough to be hired (or even to be retained), or may test to find out about other personality traits deemed relevant to future job performance. The Central Intelligence Agency (CIA) routinely uses personality testing when selecting its agents (D. Waller, 1993).

Reasonable arguments can be made for or against any of these uses. By telling people what kind of occupational group they most resemble, vocational-interest tests provide potentially valuable information to individuals who may not know what they want to do (D. B. Schmidt, Lubinski, & Benbow, 1998). On the other hand, the use of these tests rests on the implicit theory that any given occupation should continue to be populated by individuals like those already in it. For example, if your response profile resembles those obtained from successful mechanics or jet pilots, then perhaps you should consider being a mechanic or a jet pilot. Although this approach seems reasonable, it also could keep occupational fields from evolving and prevent certain individuals (such as women or members of minority groups) from joining fields from which they traditionally have been excluded. For example, an ordinarily socialized American woman may have outlooks or responses that are very different from those of the typical garage mechanic or jet pilot. Does this mean that women should never become mechanics or pilots?

A more general class of objections is aimed at the wide array of personality tests used by many large organizations, including the CIA, major automobile manufacturers, phone companies, and the military. According to one critic, almost any kind of testing can be objected to on two grounds. First, tests are unfair mechanisms through which institutions can control individuals—by rewarding those with the institutionally determined "correct" traits (such as high "conscientiousness") and punishing those with the "wrong" traits (such as low "conscientiousness"). Second, perhaps traits such as "conscientiousness" or even "intelligence" do not matter until and unless they are tested, and in that sense they are invented or "constructed" by the tests themselves (Hanson, 1993). Underlying these two objections seems to be a more general sense, which I think many people share, that there is something undignified or even degrading about submitting oneself to a test and having one's personality described by a set of scores.

All of these objections make sense. Personality tests—along with other kinds of tests such as those measuring intelligence and honesty—and even drug tests do function as a part of society's mechanism for controlling people, by rewarding the "right" kind (those who are intelligent, honest, and don't do drugs) and punishing the "wrong" kind. During the 1930s and 1940s some employers used personality tests to try to screen out job applicants inclined to be pro-union (Zickar, 2001). Does this seem ethical to you?

Still, criticisms that view personality testing as undignified or unethical, when considered, appear rather naïve. These criticisms seem to object to the idea of determining the degree to which somebody is conscientious, or intelligent, or sociable, and then using that determination as the basis of an important decision (such as employment). But if you accept the fact that an employer is not obligated to hire randomly anybody who walks through the door, and that the employer tries to use good sense in deciding who would be the best person to hire (If you were an employer, wouldn't you do that?), then you also must accept that applicants' traits like "conscientiousness," "intelligence," and "sociability" are going to be judged. The only real question is how. One common alternative is for the employer to talk with the prospective employee and try to gauge his conscientiousness by how well his shoes are shined, or his haircut, or some other such clue (Highhouse, 2008). Is this an improvement?

You may argue that you would rather be judged by a person than by a computer scanning a form, regardless of the demonstrated invalidity of the former and validity of the latter (Ones, Viswesvaran, & Schmidt, 1993). Although that is a reasonable position, it is important to be clear about the choice being made. One cannot choose for personality never to be judged—judgments will happen even if all of the tests are burned tomorrow. The only real choice is this: *How* would you prefer to have your personality judged?

As we have seen, the use of personality tests in applied settings raises some important and complex ethical issues. But the ethical issues confronting psychology go beyond personality testing.

"Remember when I said I was going to be honest with you, Jeff? That was a big, fat lie."

Protection of Research Participants

Whenever research involves humans, psychologists (or other researchers, such as medical scientists) need to be concerned about the consequences of what they are doing. Will the research harm the participants? The well-known studies of obedience by Stanley Milgram (1975), in which participants were ordered to give painful shocks to a screaming victim (who was really an unharmed research assistant) would probably not be allowed today by the Institutional Review Boards (IRBs) that must approve almost all research done

Figure 3.7 Was This Experiment Ethical? In the famous Stanford Prison Experiment, participants assigned to act as guards mentally and physically abused the participants assigned to be prisoners.

by university scientists. Likewise, it's hard to imagine a modern IRB that would approve the famous study that set up a mock (but realistic) prison in the basement of the Stanford psychology department, in which participants assigned to be guards mentally and even physically abused the ones assigned to be prisoners (Haney, Banks, & Zimbardo, 1973).

IRBs are also wary of studies that deceive or (let's call it what it is) lie to participants. Quite frequently, psychologists tell their research participants something that is not true.[23] The purpose of such deception usually is to make the research realistic. A participant might be told—falsely—that a test she is taking is a valid measure of IQ or personality, for example. Then the experimenter can assess the participant's reaction when she receives a poor score. Or a participant might be told that another person was described by a "trained psychologist" as both "friendly" and "unsociable" to see how the participant resolves this type of inconsistency. The most common deceptive practice is probably the cover story, in which participants are misinformed about the topic of the study. For example, they might be

---

[23] This is not the same as simply withholding information, as in a double-blind drug trial, in which neither the patient nor the physician knows whether the drug or placebo is being administered. Deception involves knowingly telling a lie.

told the study is examining perceptual acuity, when the actual purpose is to see how long participants are willing to persist at a boring task.

Even today, this kind of deception is allowed by the principles of the American Psychological Association, and by most IRBs, though extra justification for why it's necessary is frequently required. Still, the ethics of deception in research have long been controversial (see, e.g., Baumrind, 1985; Smith & Richardson, 1983) and are not completely settled even now. Fortunately, I suppose, the use of deception is rare in personality research, much of which involves correlation personality measures with behavioral and life outcomes; deception is much more common in the neighboring field of social psychology, but seems less common than it used to be even there.

While deceiving participants may be less of an issue than it was in the past, another is becoming more important: privacy. In particular, the experience-sampling methods that gather real-world B data, described in Chapter 2, offer the possibility of violating the privacy of the people who are participants in the studies, or even bystanders who never agreed to participate. For example, if a participant carries the EAR device or wears a lapel camera all day, the recorded sounds and images not only reveal her own behavior, but also provide information about what other people in the participant's vicinity said and did. The ethical and legal complications are numerous (Robbins, 2017) and some guidelines for using these new methods are beginning to emerge. These include never publishing verbatim quotes that could identify the participant or any other individual, getting consent from everybody who ends up getting recorded (not just the initial participant), and removing all identifying information, such as names, from data files as soon as possible. This is a good start, but privacy issues are bound to become an even more pressing concern as research begins to exploit data available from social media platforms such as Facebook, Twitter, and whatever gets invented next.

The Uses of Psychological Research

A different kind of ethical concern is that psychological research, however it is conducted, might be used for harmful purposes. Just as physicists who develop atomic bombs should worry about what their inventions can do, so too should psychologists be aware of the consequences of what their work might enable.

For example, one field of psychology—behaviorism—has long aimed to develop a technology to control behavior (see Chapter 15). The technology is not yet fully developed, but if it ever is, it will raise deep questions about who decides what behaviors to create and whose behavior should be controlled. The main figure in behaviorism, B. F. Skinner, wrote extensively about these issues (Skinner, 1948, 1971).

....

Who decides what behaviors to create and whose behavior should be controlled?

....

Yet another issue arises when psychologists choose to study racial differences and sex differences. Putting aside whatever purely scientific merits this work might have, it raises a fundamental question about whether its findings are likely to do more harm than good. If some racial group really is lower in intelligence, or if men really are better (or worse) at math than women, are we sure we want to know? The arguments in favor of exploring these issues are that science should study everything, and (on a more applied level) that knowing the basic abilities of a group might help in tailoring educational programs specifically to the needs of its members. The arguments against this research are that such findings are bound to be misused by racists and sexists, and therefore can become tools of oppression themselves, and that knowledge of group characteristics is not really very useful for tailoring programs to individual needs.

When the question is whether or not to study a given topic, psychologists, like other scientists, almost always come down on the side of "yes." After all, ignorance never got anybody very far. Still, there are an infinite number of unanswered questions out there that one could usefully investigate. When a psychologist devotes research time trying to prove that one race is smarter than another, or that one gender is superior to the other in some respect, it is hard not to wish that the researcher had found some other topic equally interesting.

Honesty and Open Science

Honesty is another ethical issue common to all research. The past few years have seen a number of scandals in physics, medicine, and psychology in which researchers fabricated their data; the most spectacular case in psychology involved the Dutch researcher Diederik Stapel, mentioned earlier. Lies cause difficulty in all sectors of life, but they are particularly worrisome in research because science is based on truth and trust. Scientific lies, when they happen, undermine the very foundation of the field. If I report about some data that I have found, you might disagree with my interpretation—that is fine, and in science this happens all the time. Working through disagreements about what data mean is an essential scientific activity. But if you cannot be sure that I really even found the data I report, then there is nothing for us to talk about. Even scientists who vehemently disagree on fundamental issues generally take each other's honesty for granted (contrast this with the situation in politics). If they cannot, then science stops dead in its tracks.

In scientific research, complete honesty is more than simply not faking one's data. A lesson that emerged from the controversies about replication, discussed earlier, is that many problems arise when the reporting of data is incomplete, as opposed to false. For example, it has been a not-uncommon practice for researchers to simply not report studies that didn't "work," i.e., that did not obtain the expected or hoped-for result. And, because of publication bias, few journals are willing to publish negative results in any case. The study failed, the reasoning goes, which means something must have gone wrong. So why would anybody want to hear about it? While this reasoning makes a certain amount of sense, it is also dangerous, because reporting only the studies that work can lead to a misleading picture overall. If 50 attempts to find precognition fail, for example, and one succeeds, then reporting the single success could make it possible to believe that people can see into the future!

A related problem arises when a researcher does not report results concerning all the experimental conditions, variables, or methods in a study. Again, the not-unreasonable tendency is only to report the ones that seem most meaningful, and omit aspects of the study that seem uninformative or confusing. In a more subtle kind of publication bias, reviewers and editors of journals might even encourage authors to focus their reports only on the most "interesting" analyses. But also again, a misleading picture can emerge if a reader of the research does not know what methods were tried or variables were measured that did not yield meaningful results. In short, there is so much flexibility in the ways a typical psychology study can be analyzed that it's easy—much too easy—for researchers to inadvertently "p-hack," which, as mentioned earlier, means that they keep analyzing their data in different ways until they get the statistically significant result that they need (Simmons, Nelson, & Simonsohn, 2011).

The emerging remedy for these problems is a movement towards what is becoming known as **open science,** a set of practices intended to move research closer to the ideals on which science was founded. These practices include fully describing all aspects of all studies, reporting studies that failed as well as those that succeeded, and freely sharing data with other scientists. An institute called the "Center for Open Science" has become the headquarters for many efforts in this direction, offering internet resources for sharing information. At the same time, major scientific organizations such as the American Psychological Association are establishing new guidelines for full disclosure of data and analyses (Appelbaum et al., 2018), and there is even a new organization, the Society for the Improvement of Psychological Science (SIPS) devoted exclusively to promoting these goals.

CONCLUSION

The development of personality tests is one of the most important applications of personality research. But using personality tests in ways that affect people's lives raises a host of important ethical issues, as does the process of psychological research—or any kind of science. Busy researchers don't often spend much time worrying about ethical issues. Their life is complicated enough already. But regardless of what you are doing all day, it is worthwhile to step back once in a while and ask yourself two questions: (1) Why am I doing this? (2) Are these good reasons? This duty extends beyond examining your own actions. As a citizen, it is important to keep close watch on the activities of schools, police departments, doctors, businesses, governments, and, yes, scientists. People usually have good intentions, but nobody can really be trusted to police oneself.

WRAPPING IT UP

SUMMARY

- Any characteristic pattern of behavior, thought, or emotional experience that exhibits relative consistency across time and situations is part of an individual's personality. These patterns include personality traits as well as psychological attributes such as goals, moods, and strategies.

The Business of Testing

- Personality assessment is a frequent activity of industrial and clinical psychologists and researchers. Everybody also assesses the personalities of the people they know in daily life.

- Personality testing is a big business that can have important consequences. But some personality tests are useless or even fraudulent, so it is important to understand how they are constructed and how they are used.

Personality Tests

- An important issue for assessments, whether by psychologists or by laypeople, is the degree to which those assessments are correct. Do they correlate as expected with other assessments of related traits, and can they be used to predict behavior or important life outcomes?

- Some personality tests yield S data and others yield B data, but a more common distinction is between projective tests and objective tests. All projective tests yield B data; most but not all objective tests yield S data.

- Projective tests try to grant insight into personality by presenting participants with ambiguous stimuli and interpreting the participants' open-ended responses. To the extent they are valid—and many are not—they appear to tap into aspects of personality not captured by questionnaire measures.

- The Rorschach test appears to have some degree of validity, but may not offer enough information beyond what can be gained from quicker, easier tests to justify its added expense. The Thematic Apperception Test (TAT) appears to measure aspects of needs (e.g., the need for achievement) that are missed by questionnaire measures.

- Objective tests ask participants specific questions and assess personality on the basis of the participants' choices among predetermined options such as True or False, and Yes or No.

- Objective tests can be constructed by rational, factor analytic, or empirical methods; the state of the art is to combine all three methods.

Evaluating Assessment and Research

- The statistical significance of a result represents the probability that the data would have been obtained if the "null hypothesis" were true, but it is typically misinterpreted as yielding the probability that the substantive (non-null) hypothesis is true. Null-hypothesis significance testing (NHST) has many problems that are increasingly acknowledged. In particular, statistical significance is not the same as the strength or importance of the result.

- A better way to evaluate research than statistical significance is in terms of effect size, which describes numerically the degree to which one variable is related to another. One good measure of effect size is the correlation coefficient, which can be evaluated with the Binomial Effect Size Display (BESD).

- The dependability of a research finding can only be evaluated, ultimately, through replication. This issue came to a head in recent years when some prominent findings were found to not be as well established as psychologists had assumed. No single study can establish the truth of any result, which is why researchers need to repeat and extend findings and always be open to the implications of new data.

Ethical Issues

- Some people are uncomfortable with the practice of personality assessment because they see it as undignified or unfair. However, because people inevitably judge each other's personalities, the real issue is whether personality assessment should be based on informal intuitions or formalized techniques.

- Research must be careful to do nothing to harm participants. Potentials for harm include subjecting people to traumatic experiences, deceiving them, or violating their privacy. The potential for the violation of individuals' privacy is a particular important issue to be aware of for the future.

- Norms of "open science" encourage scientists to fully report all of their research methods and findings, including studies that fail to find the expected or hoped-for result, and to share their data with other scientists.

Conclusion

- As a citizen, it is important to keep close watch on the activities of schools, police departments, doctors, businesses, governments, and, yes, scientists.

KEY TERMS

THINK ABOUT IT

1. If you wanted to understand someone's personality and could ask the person only three questions, what would those questions be? What would the answers reveal?

2. How would you choose someone to be your roommate? Your employee? A date? Would personality traits be relevant to your choice? How would you evaluate those traits?

3. Have you ever taken a personality test? Did the results seem accurate? Were the results useful? Did they tell you anything you did not already know?

4. How many uses can you think of for knowing someone's scores on the MMPI? Are any of these uses unethical?

5. If you were being considered for a job you badly wanted, would you prefer the decision to be based on a personality test score or the employer's subjective judgment of you?

6. If you have taken a statistics course, what does a significance level tell you? What does it not tell you? If we were to stop using significance levels to evaluate research findings, what could we use instead?

7. Let's say we find that you score 4 points higher on a "conscientiousness" test than another person. Alternatively, imagine that women score 4 points higher on the same test, on average, than men do. In either case, is this difference important? What else would we have to know to be able to answer this question?

8. Is deception in psychological research justified? Does it depend on the research question? Does it depend on the specific kind of deception? Does it depend on the kind of informed consent offered by the research participant? Who, if anybody, is harmed by the use of deception in research?

9. Some psychologists research differences between races in intelligence. Let's say members of one race really do have higher IQ scores than members of another race. Consider: Is this the kind of research psychologists should be doing, or is the issue better left alone? Once the research is done, how will the results be used?

10. Repeat question 9, but substitute gender for race.

11. If you found out that the person you had just been talking to was a participant in a research study, and that your own speech and actions had been recorded, would that bother you? Do you think your permission should have been required first?

12. Scientist A manufactures fake data that support his theory and publishes them in a major journal. Scientist B does three studies; two fail to support his theory and one confirms it. He decides only to publish the confirming study. Whose actions harm science more, Scientist A or Scientist B, or are they the same?

13. A scientist works hard to complete a study that includes a lot of difficult-to-obtain data. After she publishes her findings, another scientist says, "I think you maybe analyzed your data wrong. Please show me your data." The first scientist replies, "The data are mine and I worked hard for them. Get your own data." Does she have a point? Can you think of any circumstances in which scientists should not be required to share their data publicly?

14. Scientists often do things that nonscientists do not really understand. How can society make sure that science is used for good rather than evil purposes?

SUGGESTED RESOURCES

Online

Center for Open Science

The Center for Open Science provides many resources to make it easier to do good science. It is where a researcher can "pre-register" a study (state the predictions and planned analyses for a study before it begins), share and access data from other researchers, and share articles that have not been published yet. The website is cos.io.

Society for the Improvement of Psychological Science

This new society, founded in 2016, is already growing to be a major force in psychology. Its purpose is to develop and advocate for improved methods and practices. It holds annual meetings, and its website is improvingpsych.org.

Correlation Calculator

There are many easy ways to calculate a correlation coefficient. This calculator is one of many available online: https://www.socscistatistics.com/tests/pearson/

Philosophy of Psychology Lectures

The late Paul Meehl, a long-time professor at the University of Minnesota, is probably the most respected methodologist in the history of personality psychology.

His ideas about how to connect data with theory provide keen insights into modern controversies, such as issues of replicability and open science, discussed in this chapter. Lectures he gave in one of his graduate-level courses are available online. Although the course is called "Philosophy of Psychology," as he points out in the first lecture the content is really the philosophy of how to do research in psychology (and other fields). You can watch and listen for free at: meehl.umn.edu/recordings/philosophical-psychology-1989

Print

Cumming, G. (2012). *Understanding the new statistics: Effect sizes, confidence intervals and meta-analysis*. New York: Taylor & Francis.

> *The most important of a new generation of statistics textbooks that go beyond conventional null hypothesis significance testing to teach alternative methods for estimating effect sizes and confidence intervals, and cumulating research results over many studies. I expect that the way statistics is taught will change dramatically in the next few years; this book is leading the way. A lot of recent, interesting information on the "new statistics" is available at Cummings' website: thenewstatistics.com/itns.*

Wiggins, J. S. (1973). *Personality and prediction: Principles of personality assessment*. Reading, MA: Addison-Wesley.

> *The classic textbook for personality psychologists, including material of methodological as well as substantive interest. The book is now slightly out of date, but like a true classic, has maintained its interest and value with age.*

Want to earn a better grade on your test?

Go to **INQUIZITIVE** to learn and review this chapter's content, with personalized feedback along the way.

PART II

HOW PEOPLE DIFFER
The Trait Approach

People are different. It is obvious that no two individuals look precisely alike—not even "identical" twins—and it is almost as obvious that no two individuals behave, think, or feel exactly the same way. Everyday language contains many words to describe these differences. Some years ago, the pioneering personality psychologist Gordon Allport sent his loyal assistant, Henry Odbert, to count all the personality-trait words he could find in an unabridged English dictionary. Weeks later, a red-eyed Odbert staggered into Allport's office with the answer: 17,953 (Allport & Odbert, 1936). The words included familiar terms such as *arrogant, shy, trustworthy,* and *conscientious,* along with more obscure entries such as *delitescent, vulnific,* and *earthbred.*[1] The dictionary contains an amazing number and variety of personality traits, because traits are an important part of how people intuitively think and talk about each other.

The trait approach to personality psychology builds on this intuition by translating the natural, informal language of personality into a formal psychology that measures traits and uses them to predict and explain human behavior. The next four chapters focus specifically on the trait approach but, in a broader sense, personality traits are the topic of the entire rest of this book. The *personality trait* is the necessary, basic concept for measuring and understanding individual differences. As you will see, all personality psychologists focus on how people are different from each other, whether these differences are manifested in their genes, the biology of their nervous systems, their unconscious mental processes, or their styles of thinking. All approaches to personality are ways of explaining the stable patterns of cognition and behavior that make one person different from another. Therefore, they all require a way to conceptualize and measure these patterns—and that is where personality traits come in.

[1] Meaning, respectively (and approximately), *secretive, wounding,* and *vulgar.*

But first, we need to address a basic question: Do personality traits even exist? Or, to put the question more reasonably, do they exist *enough* to be important? In particular, can personality measures such as were described in Chapter 3 predict behavior well enough to be truly useful? An argument over this very issue occupied many psychologists for years and continues to arise in one form or another in modern theory and research. As you will learn in Chapter 4, the lessons from this debate have important implications for understanding personality.

Chapter 5 describes how laypersons—nonpsychologists—assess personality in their daily lives without ever using personality tests, and outlines the circumstances under which such everyday assessments are, and are not, likely to be accurate. Chapter 6 describes how personality traits are assessed and used in research. The three basic methods include studying traits one at a time, using long lists of traits all at once, and trying to decide which traits are truly essential. In other words, are all 17,953 personality traits necessary, or can this unwieldy list be boiled down to an essential few? The chapter concludes by considering an alternative to assessing people in terms of traits. Instead, it might be possible to sort people into basic types. As we shall see, the type approach is popular, may be useful for some purposes, but also has serious problems. Finally, Chapter 7 concludes this section on traits with a discussion of personality development, how personality changes and remains the same from youth to old age. It will also address this question: Could you change your personality if you wanted to?

The overall goal of Chapters 4 through 7 is to introduce how personality psychologists seek to understand the ways in which people are psychologically different from each other. As you will learn, knowledge about individual differences is not just interesting; it's useful, too.

4

PERSONS AND SITUATIONS

SOME OF THE WORDS that describe how people differ were invented by psychologists. These include terms such as *neuroticism*, *ego control*, and *self-monitoring*, along with more esoteric labels like *parmia*, *premsia*, and *alexithymia*.[1] But usually, personality research begins with common sense and ordinary words (e.g., Gough, 1995) and, as we saw in Chapter 3, seeks to base the scientific measurement of individual differences on familiar concepts such as sociability, reliability, dominance, nervousness, and cheerfulness (Funder, 1991).

As a result, personality psychology and everyday human observation are in some ways not so different. Both seek to characterize people using similar kinds of terms, and it is even possible to compare one approach to the other. For example, research on accuracy in personality judgment, which will be summarized in Chapter 5, compares everyday judgments that people make of each other to personality assessments based on research and standardized instruments (Funder, 1995, 1999).

THE TRAIT APPROACH

As we begin to consider the trait approach to personality psychology, keep two points in mind. First, almost all research within the trait approach relies on correlational designs (see Chapter 2). If a person scores high on a measure of "dominance," can we accurately predict that she will act in a dominant manner

---

[1] Which mean, respectively (and approximately), *uninhibited*, *sensitive*, and *deficient in emotional understanding*.

(relative to other people) in one or more life situations? As we saw in Chapter 3, the statistical answer is the correlation between the dominance score and some separate indication of the person's dominant behavior.

The second notable aspect of the trait approach is that it focuses exclusively on individual differences. It does not attempt to measure how dominant, sociable, or nervous anybody is in an absolute sense; there is no zero point on any dominance scale or on any measure of any other trait. Instead, the trait approach seeks to measure the degree to which a person might be more or less dominant, sociable, or nervous than someone else. Technically, therefore, trait measurements are made on ordinal rather than ratio scales.[2]

This focus on comparisons is one of the great strengths of the trait approach. It is important to understand and to assess how people differ. But as so often happens (remember Funder's First Law), it must also be considered a weakness: The trait approach, by its very nature, is prone to neglect aspects of psychology common to all people, as well as the ways in which each person is unique. (Other approaches, considered later in this book, do focus on those aspects of human nature.)

The tension between thinking of people in terms of what they share versus how they differ is captured by one of my favorite quotes. In elegant (albeit sexist) phrasing, it reads, "Every man is in certain respects (a) like all other men, (b) like some other men, (c) like no other man" (Kluckhohn & Murray, 1961, p. 53).

What Clyde Kluckhohn and Henry Murray meant, first, is that certain psychological properties and processes are universal. All people have biologically based needs for food, water, and sex, for example. Their second point is that other properties of people differ but in ways that allow individuals to be grouped. People who are consistently cheerful, for instance, might be essentially alike in a way that allows them to be meaningfully distinguished from those who are gloomier (although they might still differ among themselves in other respects). And third, in still other ways, each individual is unique and cannot be meaningfully compared with anyone else. Each person's genetic makeup, past experience, and view of the

---

[2] A measurement is said to lie on an *ordinal scale* when its value reflects a rank order. For example, three racers earn values of 1, 2, and 3 if they place first, second, and third. There is no zero point on this scale (you can't place "oth"), and the numbers 1 and 3 do not imply that the third-place runner was three times slower than the first-place runner. But they do tell you who won and who came in last. A measurement lies on a *ratio scale* if the scale has a true zero point and measurements can be compared in terms of ratios. For example, one runner might go 3 miles an hour, a second runner 2 miles an hour, and a third (rather slow) runner might go 1 mile an hour. These measurements are rational because it is possible to go zero miles an hour (by standing still), and because the first runner can be said to be going 3 times faster than the third runner. Trait measurements are ordinal rather than rational because there is no such thing as "zero dominance," for example, and if one person has a dominance score of 50 and another has a score of 25, this implies the first person is more dominant than the second but not necessarily twice as dominant, whatever that might mean. (See Blanton & Jaccard, 2006, for an interesting discussion of the difficulties in expressing psychological attributes in terms of numbers.)

world are different from those of anyone else who ever lived or ever will (Allport, 1937).

The trait approach comes in at the second, middle level of this analysis, while at the same time (necessarily) neglecting the other two. Because the trait approach is based on the ideas that all "men" are "like some other men" and that it is meaningful and useful to assess broad categories of individual difference, it assumes that in some real sense people *are* their traits. Theorists differ on whether traits simply describe how a person acts, are the sum of everything a person has learned, are biological structures, or combine all of these concepts. But for every trait theorist, these dimensions of individual differences are the building blocks from which personality is constructed.

Which raises a fundamental problem.

"I love the little ways you're identical to everyone else."

PEOPLE ARE INCONSISTENT

You can judge or measure the degree to which someone is shy, conscientious, or dominant, but whatever you conclude the truth to be, there will be numerous exceptions. The individual may act shy with strangers but be warm, open, and friendly with family members. She may be conscientious at work but sloppy and disorganized at home. She may be dominant with people of the same sex but deferential to people of the opposite sex, or vice versa. This kind of inconsistency is seen all the time.

Casual observation, therefore, is enough to confirm that personality traits are not the only factors that control an individual's behavior; situations matter as well. Some situations will make a person act more or less shy, more or less careful, more or less friendly, and more or less dominant. This is because situations vary according to the people who are present and the implicit rules that apply (Price & Bouffard, 1974; Wagerman & Funder, 2007). You act differently at home than you do at work partly because you share your home with your family members but you share your workplace with your coworkers (and perhaps, competitors). You act differently at a party than at a church because some pretty specific, albeit usually implicit, rules of decorum limit acceptable behavior in church. Parties have implicit rules, too, but they offer more leeway (M. Snyder & Ickes, 1985).

If situations are so important, then how important is personality? One possible answer is: not very. Perhaps individuals' behavior is so inconsistent and apt to change according to the situation that there is little use characterizing them in terms of broad personality traits. If this answer is correct, it implies not only that the personality tests considered in Chapter 3 are colossal wastes of time, but also that much of our everyday thinking and talking about people is fundamentally wrong. You should consider the possibility, therefore, that traits do not exist, that people continually change who they are according to the situation, and that everybody is basically the same.

Do you find this idea outrageous? The answer you give may depend on your age and stage in life. When I teach personality psychology to college undergraduates, who are typically 18 to 22 years old, I find that most of them nod and sagely accept the possibility raised in the preceding paragraph. The suggestion that people have few consistent attributes to their personality and change who they are from moment to moment depending on the immediate situation sounds about right to them—or at least it does not immediately strike them as preposterous.

Thus, I was taken aback the first time I presented this same possibility to a night-school class. The course was ostensibly the same as the one I was teaching during the daytime, but the night-school students were, for the most part, adult, working professionals from the metropolitan area, rather than dorm-dwelling 18- to 22-year-olds. These older students had the opposite reaction to the idea that individual differences are not important and that how you act depends on the situation you happen to be in at the moment: "Are you nuts?"

The reason for their different point of view may be that older persons are themselves more consistent than younger ones. Research shows that the stability of the differences between people increases with age: 30-year-olds are more stable across time than are children and adolescents, and people between the ages of about 50 and 70 are the most stable of all (Caspi, Roberts, & Shiner, 2005; McCrae, 2002; see Chapter 7 for more details). Older persons who have embarked on a career track, started families, undertaken adult roles and responsibilities, and established consistent individual identities may find it hard to imagine (or remember) the fluctuating, even erratic, personalities they had when they were younger. In contrast, students who are still financially dependent on their parents, have not yet found spouses or started families, and perhaps have not yet even settled on their career goals, don't find anything unreasonable in the idea that individual differences are unimportant because how you act depends solely on the situation. Indeed, they wonder why anybody would make a fuss. After all, their own personalities are still in the design stage (Roberts, Walton, & Viechtbauer, 2006).

What I am proposing, therefore, is that people differ from each other in the degree to which they have developed a consistent personality (Baumeister & Tice, 1988; Bem & Allen, 1974; M. Snyder & Monson, 1975). This difference might be related to psychological adjustment as well as age: Several studies suggest that the consistency of personality is associated with maturity and general mental health (Asendorpf & van Aken, 1991; Schuerger, Zarrella, & Hotz, 1989). People whose behavior is relatively consistent are less neurotic, more controlled, more mature, and more positive in their relations with others (Donnellan, Conger, & Burzette, 2007; Roberts, Caspi, & Moffitt, 2001; Sherman, Nave, & Funder, 2010).

THE PERSON-SITUATION DEBATE

Whether or not it violates your intuition to claim that behavior is so inconsistent that, for all intents and purposes, personality traits do not exist, an argument about just this point occupied a large number of personality psychologists for more than two decades (or longer—see Cervone, 2005). These psychologists were, and are, the protagonists in the *person-situation debate*, which focuses on this very question: Which is more important for determining what people do: the person or the situation?

To a considerable degree, the debate was triggered by the publication in 1968 of a book by Walter Mischel entitled *Personality and Assessment*.[3] Mischel argued that behavior is too inconsistent from one situation to the next to allow individual differences to be characterized accurately in terms of broad personality traits. Other psychologists—including, not surprisingly, those who were heavily invested in the technology and practice of personality assessment—emphatically disagreed. Thus the person-situation debate began.

The rest of this chapter reviews the basis and resolution of this debate. Ordinarily, arguments among psychologists are one of the things I am trying to spare you in this book. I would rather teach you about psychology than about what psychologists do, much less what they argue about. But I hope to convince you that this one is different. It is not just a tempest in a teapot, as arguments among specialists so often are, nor is it even one of those issues that we can simply settle and then move beyond. Rather, the consistency controversy goes to the heart of how everybody thinks about people and has important implications for understanding individual differences and the bases of important life outcomes.

> Is what a person does utterly dependent on the situation she is in at the time?

There are really three issues here. The first is: Does the personality of an individual transcend the immediate context and provide a consistent guide to her actions, or is what a person does utterly dependent on the situation she is in at the time? Because our everyday intuitions tell us that people have consistent personalities (everybody uses personality-trait terms all day long), this question leads to a second issue: Are common, ordinary intuitions about people fundamentally

---

[3] Ironically, given its title, the book usually is interpreted as arguing that personality does not exist and that useful assessment is impossible.

flawed? The third issue goes even deeper: Why do psychologists continue to argue about the consistency of personality, year after year, decade after decade?

The belief that behavior is largely driven by the situation, and that personality is relatively unimportant, is sometimes called "situationism" (Bowers, 1973). Stripped to its essentials, the situationist argument has three parts:

1. There is an upper limit to how well one can predict what a person will do based on any measurement of that person's personality. This upper limit is a low upper limit.
2. Therefore, situations are more important than personality traits.
3. Therefore, not only is the professional practice of personality assessment a waste of time, but also, everyday intuitions about people are wrong, because people see others as being more consistent across situations than they really are. The "fundamental attribution error" is to believe that personality matters (Ross & Nisbett, 1991).

Strong stuff! But each of these claims wilts a bit under closer scrutiny.

Predictability

THE SITUATIONIST ARGUMENT   The definitive test of the usefulness of a personality trait is whether it can be used to predict behavior. If you know somebody's level or score on a trait, you should be able to forecast what that person will do in the future. Situationists argue that this predictive capacity is severely limited. There is no trait that you can use to predict someone's behavior with enough accuracy to be useful.

"Can I call you back, R.B.? I've got a situation here."

Mischel's book surveyed some of the research concerning the relationships between self-descriptions of personality and direct measurements of behavior, between others' descriptions of personality and direct measurements of behavior, and between one measurement of behavior and another. Or, to use the terms introduced in Chapter 2, Mischel looked at the relationships between S data and B data, between I data and B data, and between B data and other B data. The first two comparisons address the ability of personality-trait judgments to predict behavior; for example, can your self-description or an acquaintance's judgment of your sociability predict how sociable you will act at Friday's party? The third comparison addresses the consistency of behavior across situations; for instance, if you act sociable at Friday's party, will you also be sociable at Tuesday's work meeting?

The data reported in the studies that Mischel reviewed were not, for the most part, taken from real life. Nearly all of the behavioral measurements—the B data—were gathered in laboratory settings. Some studies measured "attitude toward authority" by asking participants for their opinions of photographs of older men, some measured "self-control" by seeing how long children could wait for candy treats provided by the experimenters, and so forth. Only rarely was behavior assessed in more or less natural situations, such as cheating on games at a summer camp. Such naturalistic studies were (and remain) rare, primarily because they are difficult and expensive (see the discussion of B data in Chapter 2). Either way, the critical question is how well a person's behavior in one situation can be predicted either from his behavior in another situation or from his personality-trait scores.

Problems

In psychological research, predictability and consistency are indexed by the correlation coefficient. As you will recall from Chapter 3, this is a number that ranges from +1 to −1, and indexes the association or relationship between two variables, such as a personality score and a behavioral measurement. If the correlation is positive, it means that as one variable increases, so does the other: The higher someone's "sociability" score, the more parties she is likely to attend. If the correlation is negative, it means that as one variable increases, the other decreases: The higher someone's "shyness" score, the fewer parties he is likely to attend. Both positive and negative correlations imply that one variable can be predicted from the other. But if the correlation is near zero, it means the two variables are unrelated; perhaps scores on this particular sociability test have nothing to do with how many parties one attends.

correlation coeffiant

Mischel's original argument was that correlations between personality and behavior, or between behavior in one situation and behavior in another, seldom exceed .30. Another prominent situationist, Richard Nisbett (1980), later revised this estimate upward, to .40. The implication in both cases was that such correlations are small, and that personality traits are therefore unimportant.

This claim concerning the unpredictability of behavior hit the field of personality psychology in the early 1970s with surprisingly devastating force, and continues to echo through the modern research literature. Some personality psychologists, and even more psychologists outside the field of personality, concluded that for all intents and purposes, personality did not exist. This conclusion was based on two premises. The first was that situationists are right, and .40 is the upper limit for the predictability of a given behavior from personality variables or behavior in other situations. The other implicit but necessary premise was that this upper limit is low.

THE RESPONSE It took the representatives of the pro-personality side of this debate a few years to get their rebuttals in line, but when they finally did, they came up with three.

Unfair Literature Review The first counterargument was that Mischel's review of the personality literature, which kicked off the whole controversy, was selective and unfair. After all, the relevant research literature goes back more than 60 years and contains literally thousands of studies. Mischel's review, by contrast, is quite short (only 16 pages [pp. 20–36] of his book, about the length of a typical undergraduate term paper) and concentrates on a few studies that obtained disappointing results rather than on the (perhaps more numerous) studies that obtained more impressive findings.

This is a difficult point to prove or disprove, however. On the one hand, it is obvious that Mischel's review was selective because it is so short. Moreover, he did not exactly go out of his way to find the best studies in the literature; the very first empirical study that Mischel cited (Burwen & Campbell, 1957) was less than exemplary. That study was filled with methodological and empirical flaws (e.g., a number of the participants deliberately sabotaged the research questionnaires), yet still managed to find a bit of evidence in favor of the trait it examined, which was "attitude toward authority." Many of the other studies Mischel cited were little better, and even some of those managed, despite everything, to find evidence for the consistency of personality and behavior (J. Block, 1977).

On the other hand, some studies are bound to find positive results on the basis of chance alone. And although it would be easy to put together a short literature review that looks much more positive than Mischel's, it is not clear how one would prove that such a review was any more fair or less selective. It is extremely difficult to characterize the findings of entire research literatures (see Rosenthal, 1980), and the literature on behavioral consistency is no exception.

I frankly do not know how to establish whether the literature supports consistency with a few exceptions, or whether it supports inconsistency with a few exceptions. So, to move the argument along, let me just "stipulate" (as lawyers say) the Mischel-Nisbett figure: Assume that a correlation of about .40 is the upper limit for how well personality traits can predict behavior, as well as for how consistent behavior is from one situation to another.

We Can Do Better A second counterargument to the situationist critique grants the .40 upper limit, as I just did, but claims that this limit is a result of poor or less than optimal research methodology. The weak findings summarized by Mischel do not imply that personality is unimportant; merely that psychologists can and must do better research.

One way in which research could be improved, according to this counterargument, is for it to move out of the laboratory more often. As I mentioned earlier,

(a)   (b)

Figure 4.1 Personality in the Laboratory and in Real Life Much psychological research is done in controlled laboratory settings. The influence of personality may be more likely to emerge in settings that are a bit more emotionally involving.

nearly all of the behavioral measurements that formed the basis for the situationist critique were made in laboratory situations. Some of these were probably dull and uninvolving. How about behavior in real life? Personality is much more likely to become relevant, it has been argued, in situations that are real, vivid, and important (Allport, 1961). For example, when a person in a laboratory is asked to respond to a picture of an older individual, his personality may or may not become involved (Burwen & Campbell, 1957). But when a person is about to make his first parachute jump, personality plays a more important role in affecting how he feels (Epstein, 1980; Fenz & Epstein, 1967).

A second way research might be improved is to distinguish between people who are and are not predictable from their personality traits. For example, one study asked participants how consistent they were on the trait of "sociability," and found that the behavior of those who said they were consistent was easier to predict accurately than the behavior of those who said they were inconsistent (Bem & Allen, 1974).[4] Research on the trait of self-monitoring suggests that some people, called "high self-monitors," quickly change their behavior according to the situation, whereas "low self-monitors" are more likely to express their personality consistently from one situation to the next (M. Snyder, 1987; see also Chapter 6). Other, related research suggests that people who prefer to be consistent actually are more consistent (Guadagno & Cialdini, 2010; see **Try for Yourself 4.1**). Finally, some behaviors might be more consistent than others. Elements of expressive behavior, such as how much a person gestures or how loudly a person talks, are likely to be

---

[4] Although this was an influential finding and an important idea, Chaplin and Goldberg (1984) provided evidence that the finding is difficult to replicate. Later, Zuckerman et al. (1988) surveyed a broad range of research literature and concluded that this effect of self-rated consistency on behavioral predictability is small but probably real.

TRY FOR YOURSELF 4.1

The Preference for Consistency Scale

Instructions: Rate each of these items using a scale of 1 to 9, where 1 = strongly disagree, 5 = neither agree nor disagree, and 9 = strongly agree.

1. I prefer to be around people whose reactions I can anticipate.   1 2 3 4 5 6 7 8 9
2. It is important to me that my actions are consistent with my beliefs.   1 2 3 4 5 6 7 8 9
3. Even if my attitudes and actions seemed consistent with one another to me, it would bother me if they did not seem consistent in the eyes of others.   1 2 3 4 5 6 7 8 9
4. It is important to me that those who know me can predict what I will do.   1 2 3 4 5 6 7 8 9
5. I want to be described by others as a stable, predictable person.   1 2 3 4 5 6 7 8 9
6. Admirable people are consistent and predictable.   1 2 3 4 5 6 7 8 9
7. The appearance of consistency is an important part of the image I present to the world.   1 2 3 4 5 6 7 8 9
8. It bothers me when someone I depend on is unpredictable.   1 2 3 4 5 6 7 8 9
9. I don't like to appear as if I am inconsistent.   1 2 3 4 5 6 7 8 9
10. I get uncomfortable when I find my behavior contradicts my beliefs.   1 2 3 4 5 6 7 8 9
11. An important requirement for any friend of mine is personal consistency.   1 2 3 4 5 6 7 8 9
12. I typically prefer to do things the same way.   1 2 3 4 5 6 7 8 9
13. I dislike people who are constantly changing their opinions.   1 2 3 4 5 6 7 8 9
14. I want my close friends to be predictable.   1 2 3 4 5 6 7 8 9
15. It is important to me that others view me as a stable person.   1 2 3 4 5 6 7 8 9
16. I make an effort to appear consistent to others.   1 2 3 4 5 6 7 8 9
17. I'm uncomfortable holding two beliefs that are inconsistent.   1 2 3 4 5 6 7 8 9
18. It doesn't bother me much if my actions are inconsistent.   1 2 3 4 5 6 7 8 9

Add up your scores for items 1–17, and then add the reversed score for item 18 (item 1 = 9, 2 = 8, and so forth). Divide the total by 18 to get your average score.

The average score in a large college student sample was 5.43 (sd = 1.19). The interpretation would be that if your score is greater than about 6, you have a strong preference for consistency and are likely to be consistent in your behavior, personality, and attitudes. If your score is lower than about 4, you do not favor consistency and are relatively likely to act inconsistently.

Source: Guadagno & Cialdini (2010), pp. 152–163.

consistent across situations, whereas more goal-directed behaviors, such as trying to impress someone, are more likely to depend on the situation (Funder & Colvin, 1991; see also Allport & Vernon, 1933).

A third possible research improvement is to focus on general behavioral trends instead of single actions. Thus, rather than try to predict whether somebody will act friendly next Tuesday at 3:00 P.M., one is better off trying to predict how friendly that person will behave, on average, over the next year. Do you remember the meter sticks used to illustrate the idea of aggregation in Chapter 2? Just as my fellow high school students and I sometimes placed our sticks too close together, and sometimes too far apart, so, too, do behaviors of a person vary around their average level from occasion to occasion. Sometimes you are a little more aggressive than usual, and sometimes less; sometimes you are more shy than usual, and sometimes less, and so on. This is why your *average* level of aggressive or shy behavior is much more predictable than what you do in any particular moment or place; on average, random variations tend to cancel out (Epstein, 1979; Fishbein & Ajzen, 1974).

The issue is more than just a matter of statistics. It concerns the whole meaning and purpose of personality-trait judgments. When you say that somebody is friendly or conscientious or shy, are you making a prediction of one specific behavior at one specific time, or are you saying something about how you expect the person to act in general, over the long haul (McCrae, 2002)? In most cases, I think, the answer is the latter. When you wish to understand someone, or need to select a roommate or an employee, it is not so critical to know what the person will do at a particular place and time, because that will always depend on specific circumstance at the moment. Rather, you need to know how the person will act, in general, across the various relevant situations of life. You understand that somebody might be late on rare occasions because her car won't start; you know that anybody can have a bad day and be grouchy. But when choosing an employee or a roommate, what you really need to know is: How reliable will the person generally be? Or, how friendly is the person, usually?

These three suggestions—measure behavior in real life, check for variations in consistency, and seek to predict behavioral trends rather than single acts—are all good ideas for improving personality research. However, they represent potential more than reality. To follow any of these suggestions is difficult. Real-life behaviors are not easy to assess (see Chapter 2), individual differences in consistency may be subtle and difficult to measure (Chaplin, 1991), and the prediction of behavioral trends requires, by definition, that the researcher observe many behaviors, not just a few. So, although these suggestions provide good reasons that the situationist critique may underestimate the level of consistency in people's behavior, there is still—after all these years—not enough research to prove that behavioral consistency regularly gets much higher than what is reflected by the correlations around .40 that the situationists now concede.

Besides, both of the first two responses to the situationist critique miss a more basic point, discussed next.

A Correlation of .40 Is Not Small Remember that to be impressed (or depressed) by the situationist critique of personality traits, you must believe two things: (1) A correlation of .40 represents the true upper limit to which one can predict behavior from personality, or see consistency in behavior from one situation to another; and (2) this limit is a *small* upper limit. The discussion so far has concentrated on responses to point 1. But if you were to conclude that a correlation of .40 was not small in the first place (point 2), then the limit would cease to be so worrisome, and the force of the situationist critique would largely dissipate.

Thus, it is critical to evaluate how much predictability a correlation of the size granted by the situationist critique really represents. But to evaluate whether .40 is big or little, or to assess any other statistic, you need a standard of comparison.

Calculations

Two standards are possible: absolute and relative. To evaluate this correlation against an absolute standard, you would calculate how many correct and incorrect predictions of behavior a trait measurement with this degree of validity would yield in a hypothetical context. To evaluate this correlation against a relative standard, you can compare this degree of predictability for personality traits with the accuracy of other methods used to predict behavior (or other outcomes). Let's do both.

An absolute evaluation of a .40 correlation can be obtained from Rosenthal and Rubin's (1982) Binomial Effect Size Display (BESD), which was described in Chapter 3. I won't repeat the description here, but will go straight to the bottom line: According to the BESD, a correlation of .40 means that a prediction of behavior based on a personality-trait score is likely to be accurate 70 percent of the time (assuming a chance accuracy rate of 50 percent).[5] Seventy percent is far from perfect, but it is enough to be useful for many purposes. For instance, an employer choosing who to put through an expensive training program could save large amounts of money by being able to predict with 70 percent accuracy who will or will not be a successful employee at its conclusion.

Let's work through an example. Say a company has 200 employees being considered for further training, but the budget only allows for training 100 of them. Let's further assume that, overall, 50 percent of the company's employees could successfully complete the program. The company picks 100 employees at random and spends $10,000 to train each one. But, as I said, only half of them are successful. So the company has spent a total of $1 million to get 50 successfully trained employees, or $20,000 each.

[5] This figure should not be confused with the "percentage of variance explained" discussed in Chapter 3, which is computed in a different way and has a more obscure interpretation.

Now consider what happens if the company uses a selection test that has been shown to correlate .40 with training success.[6] By selecting the top half of the scorers on this test for training, the company will get 70 successful trainees (instead of 50) out of the 100 who are trained, still at a total cost of $1 million but now at only about $14,300 per successful trainee. In other words, using a test with a .40 validity could save the company $5,700 per successful trainee, or about $400,000. That could pay for a lot of testing.

What about a relative standard? Well, what is the most appropriate basis for comparison when trying to evaluate the predictive ability of personality traits? Situationists, you will recall, believe that the situation, not the person, is all-important in the determination of behavior. To evaluate the ability of personality traits to predict behavior, therefore, it seems appropriate to draw a comparison with the ability of situational variables to predict behavior. That is the topic of the next section.

The Power of the Situation

A key tenet of the situationist position is that personality does not determine behavior—situations do. To evaluate the degree to which a behavior is affected by a personality variable, the routine practice is to correlate a measure of behavior with a measure of personality. But how do you evaluate the degree to which behavior is affected by a situational variable?

This question has received surprisingly little attention over the years, and a technology for assessing situations has only recently begun to be developed (Wagerman & Funder, 2009; Funder, 2016). In the absence of such a technology, the traditional method for estimating the power of situations was rather strange: Determine it by subtraction! If a personality variable correlated .40 with a behavioral measurement and therefore "explained 16 percent of the variance," the remaining 84 percent was assumed to be due to the situation (Mischel, 1968).

Of course, this practice doesn't really make sense, even though it used to be common. I have already protested the needlessly misleading obscurity of the way psychologists talk about "percent of variance" (see Chapter 3). But even if you accept this terminology, it would be just as reasonable to attribute the "missing" variance to other personality variables that you did not measure as it would be to attribute it to situational variables that you also did not measure (Ahadi & Diener, 1989). Moreover, to assign variance by subtraction does not say anything about exactly which aspects of the situation are the ones that matter.

---

[6] This is not an unreasonable number. Ones, Viswesvaran, and Schmidt (1993) reported that, across a large of number of tests and measures of job performance, the predictive validity of some kinds of tests averaged .41. See Chapter 6 for more on the prediction of job performance.

Figure 4.2 A Scud Missile That Missed Its Target Situations, like Scud missiles, can have weak, strong, or unpredictable effects.

It has long seemed remarkable to me that situationists have been willing to claim that situations are important, yet have been seemingly unconcerned with measuring situational variables in a way that indicates precisely how or how much situations affect behavior. After all, not everybody responds to a particular situation in the same way. When situationists claim that situations are important but do not specify what is important about them or to what extent, then, as one trait psychologist pointed out,

> situations turn out to be "powerful" in the same sense as Scud missiles [the erratic weapons used by Iraq during the Persian Gulf Wars] are powerful: They may have huge effects, or no effects, and such effects may occur virtually anywhere, all over the map. (Goldberg, 1992, p. 90)

Moreover, there is no need for situationists to sell themselves so short—to be so vague about what specific aspects of situations can affect behavior. A large and impressive body of psychological research allows the effects of situations to be directly calculated. The data come from nearly every study in experimental social psychology (Aronson, 1972).

In the typical social psychological experiment, two (or more) separate groups of participants are placed, randomly and usually one at a time, into one of two (or

Power of the Situation

social psychology experiment

more) different situations, also called *conditions*. The social psychologist measures what the participants do. If the average behavior of the participants who are placed in one condition turns out to be significantly different (statistically speaking—see Chapter 3) from the average behavior of the participants placed in the other condition, then the experiment is deemed successful.

For instance, you might be interested in the effect of incentives on attitude change. In an experiment, you could ask participants to make a statement they do not believe—for example, that a dull game was really interesting. Then, you could test to see if afterward they come to believe the statement—that the game was not dull after all. Some of your participants could be offered a large incentive (say, $20) to lie and say the dull game was interesting, while the rest are offered a smaller incentive (say, $1). If the two groups of participants change their attitudes about the game to different degrees, then you can conclude that the difference in incentives between the two conditions was the effective cause of this difference in attitudes (although the exact process by which this happened would still be open to question). The differences between the two situations must lead participants to respond differently, and therefore the experiment would demonstrate an effect of a situational variable on behavior (Festinger & Carlsmith, 1959).

The literature of experimental social psychology offers a vast trove of specific examples of situational effects like this. For present purposes, the question is, how large are those effects compared to the effects of personality variables? Perhaps surprisingly, social psychologists historically have paid very little attention to the size of the situational effects they study. They have concentrated on statistical significance, or the degree to which their results would not have been expected by chance. As was discussed in Chapter 3, this is a separate matter from effect size or what one might consider "actual" significance, because even a tiny effect can be highly significant statistically, if one has studied a large enough number of participants.

Personality psychologists, by contrast, have always focused on the magnitude of their ability to predict behavior. The key statistic in personality research, the correlation coefficient, is a measure of effect size and not of statistical significance. Therefore, the "personality coefficient" of .40 is ordinarily not comparable to the effects found in social psychological studies of situational variables, because the two styles of research do not employ a common metric.

Fortunately, this difficulty can be easily remedied. As mentioned in Chapter 2, the experimental statistics used by social psychologists can be converted algebraically into correlations of the sort used by personality psychologists. Some years ago, my colleague Dan Ozer and I did just that (Funder & Ozer, 1983). From the social psychological literature, we chose three prominent examples of the power of situations to shape behavior. We then converted the results of those studies to effect-size correlations.

The first classic study that we chose concerned the "forced compliance" effect demonstrated by Festinger and Carlsmith (1959) in a study similar to the one I just

Table 4.1 | BEHAVIOR AS A FUNCTION OF THE SITUATION

Situational Variable	Behavioral Variable	Effect Size *r*
Incentive	Attitude change	−.36
Hurry	Helping	−.39
Number of bystanders	Helping	−.38
Isolation of victim	Obedience	.42
Proximity of authority figure	Obedience	.36

Sources: Festinger & Carlsmith (1959); Darley & Batson (1967); Darley & Latané (1968); and Milgram (1975). Adapted from Funder & Ozer (1983), p. 110.

described. This study, which found that people who were paid $1 changed their attitude more than those paid $20, was one of the early experimental demonstrations of cognitive dissonance. The effect is a classic of the social psychological literature and perhaps one of the most important and interesting findings in the field. Yet, its statistical size had seldom been reported. Ozer and I performed the simple calculation: The effect of incentive on attitude change following counter-attitudinal advocacy turns out to correspond to a correlation of $r = -.36$. (The correlation has a negative sign because more incentive leads to less change.) This is a direct statistical measure of how strongly rewards can affect attitude change.

A second important program of research in social psychology concerned bystander intervention. John Darley and his colleagues staged several faked but dramatic incidents in which participants came upon apparently distressed individuals lying helplessly in their path (Darley & Batson, 1967; Darley & Latané, 1968). Whether the participants would stop and help turned out to depend, among other things, on whether other people were present and whether the participant was in a hurry. The more people present, the less likely the participant was to stop and help; the correlation indexing the size of this effect was $r = -.38$. Also, the greater the participant's hurry, the less likely the participant was to help; the correlation indexing the size of this effect was $r = -.39$.

The third program of research we reexamined was Stanley Milgram's classic investigation of obedience. In a famous series of studies, Milgram's research assistants ordered participants to give apparently painful and dangerous (but fortunately bogus) electric shocks to an innocent "victim" (Milgram, 1975). If the participants objected, the assistant said, "The experiment requires that you continue."

Milgram identified two variables as relevant to whether a participant would obey this command. The first was the isolation of the victim. When the victim was in the next room and could not be heard protesting, or could be heard only weakly, obedience was more likely than when the victim was right in front of the participant. The correlation that reflects the size of the effect of victim isolation is $r = .42$.

(a)　　　　　　　　　　　　　　(b)

Figure 4.3 The Milgram Obedience Study. Participants were more likely to obey orders to shock an innocent victim if they were physically isolated from him than if they were in the same room; the size of this effect was equivalent to $r = .42$.

The second important variable was the proximity of the experimenter. Obedience was more likely if the research assistant giving the orders was physically present than if he gave orders over the phone or on a tape recorder. The correlation that reflects the size of the effect of experimenter proximity turned out to be $r = .36$.[7]

Recall that the size of the personality coefficient that was supposed to reflect the maximum correlation that can be obtained between personality variables and behavior is about .40. Now, compare that to the effects of situational variables on behavior, as just surveyed: .36, .38, .39, .42, and .36.[8]

One can draw two different conclusions from these results. The little reanalysis by Ozer and me has been summarized by others as implying that neither personality variables *nor* situational variables have much of an effect on behavior. Well, it's nice to be cited, but not so nice to be misunderstood; the weakness of situations or of these experimental effects was *not* the point we were trying to make. Rather, we reanalyzed these particular experiments precisely because, as far as we knew, nobody had ever doubted that each and every one of them demonstrated a powerful, important influence of a situational variable. These experiments are classics of social psychology. They are found in any textbook on the subject and have contributed important insights into social behavior.

We prefer a second conclusion, therefore: These situational variables are important, but many personality variables are important as well. When put on

---

[7] Milgram claimed that personality had little relation to obedience, but a replication years later (which assessed obedience in the context of a fake TV game show) found that people higher on the traits of conscientiousness and agreeableness were more likely to follow "shocking" orders (Bégue et al., 2015).

[8] The negative correlations (the first three) are here listed without a minus sign because evaluation of the size of an effect is independent from its direction.

Table 4.2 | EFFECT SIZES OF SOME IMPORTANT RESEARCH FINDINGS

Finding	Effect Size (r)
People are aggressive when they are in a bad mood.	.41
The higher a person's credibility, the more persuasive s/he will be.	.10
Scarcity increases the value of a commodity.	.12
People attribute failures to bad luck.	.10
People behave as others expect them to behave.	.33
Men are recommended for jobs over women.	.20
Members of a group influence one another.	.33
Married people report higher life satisfaction than others.	.14
People are likely to help others when they are in a good mood.	.26
People usually prefer their own group to other groups.	.35
Boys are more competitive than girls.	.03
Women smile more than men.	.23

Source: Richard et al. (2003), pp. 353–363.

a common scale for comparison, the size of the effects of the person and of the situation are much more similar than many had assumed. Indeed, a wide-ranging literature review concluded that the typical size of a situational effect on behavior, in a social psychological experiment, corresponds to an $r = .21$,[9] noticeably lower than the average of the three studies Dan Ozer and I reanalyzed (Richard et al., 2003). The difference is not surprising. The studies that we chose were classics, after all. And such effect sizes—or smaller—are typical of many other important findings (see **Table 4.2**). Correlations outside the realm of psychology can also be illuminating. For example, consider the correlation between a weather station's elevation above sea level and its average daily temperature. As everyone knows, it tends to be cooler at higher elevations. The actual correlation between these variables is $r = -.34$ (Meyer et al., 2001, p. 132). In this light, calling a correlation of .40 a "personality coefficient" loses a little of its pejorative edge.

Absolute Versus Relative Consistency

There is no doubt that people change their behavior from one situation to the next. This obvious fact has sometimes led to the misunderstanding that personality consistency somehow means "acting the same way all the time." But that's not what it

---

[9] The standard deviation was .15, which means that about two-thirds of social psychological experiments yield an effect size between .06 and .36.

means at all. As was pointed out at the beginning of this chapter, the concept of the personality trait involves *individual differences*. It is individual differences in behavior that are maintained across situations, not how much a behavior is performed. Almost everybody will be more talkative at a party than when standing in line at the Department of Motor Vehicles. But the most talkative person at the party will probably also be the most talkative person at the DMV.

A specific example of how this works is a study my colleague Randy Colvin and I once did (Funder & Colvin, 1991). All the participants appeared at two sessions. At the first session, they were seated with a fellow student of the opposite sex they had never met before, and invited to chat about whatever they wanted while a videotape camera recorded what they did. Later, research assistants rated their behavior from watching the videotapes. A couple of weeks later, the participants returned for a second session and did exactly the same thing, with a different partner. Their behavior was again rated.

Our first analysis of the data simply looked at the average behavior of participants at the two sessions. As you can see in **Table 4.3**, at the second session participants appeared less awkward, less anxious, more interested, more involved, more relaxed, and even more interesting. The reason seems pretty obvious. They weren't so nervous. At the first session they were entering a strange research

Table 4.3	THE EFFECT OF THE SITUATION: BEHAVIORAL DIFFERENCES BETWEEN TWO EXPERIMENTAL SESSIONS	
Behavioral Rating	**Session 1 Mean**	**Session 2 Mean**
Items Higher at Session 1		
Talks at rather than with partner	3.98	3.51
Exhibits an awkward personal style	4.19	3.60
Physical signs of tension and anxiety	5.19	4.66
Shows lack of interest in interaction	3.98	3.55
Keeps partner at a distance	4.81	4.40
Expresses insecurity or sensitivity	4.77	4.49
Behaves in a fearful or timid manner	3.98	3.64
Items Higher at Session 2		
Exhibits social skills	5.94	6.46
Appears relaxed and comfortable	5.56	6.13
Says or does interesting things	5.78	6.08
Expressive in face, voice, or gestures	5.11	5.42

Note: $N = 140$. Behavioral ratings were on a 9-point scale. All the differences are statistically significant at $p < .01$.

Source: Adapted from Funder & Colvin (1991), p. 783.

laboratory for the first time; they didn't know what to expect. By the time of the second session they had been there before, they were more relaxed, and they had a better time. Table 4.3 clearly shows the power of the situation.

 But what about behavioral consistency? We did a second analysis, using exactly the same data. We correlated what participants did at the first session with what they did at the second, one behavior at a time. You can see the results in **Table 4.4**. By any standard—certainly by the standard of the "personality coefficient" mentioned earlier in this chapter—the results are impressive. Behaviors such as speaking in a loud voice, appearing fearful, and laughing—among others—all yielded consistency correlations greater than $r = .60$! And the correlations in Table 4.4 are just a partial list. Indeed, of the 62 consistency correlations we calculated (one for each behavioral rating item), 37 were significant at $p < .001$ (see Chapter 3) and, more importantly, 25 were higher than the .40 revised estimate of the "personality coefficient."

It is important to remember that both Tables 4.3 and 4.4 are from the same data, from the same participants, in the same study. The point of looking at the two tables together is to appreciate how behavioral change and behavioral consistency can and do exist simultaneously (Sauerberger & Funder, 2017). People were less nervous and more socially skilled at the second session than at the first, but the same people who were the *most* nervous and the *most* socially skilled at the first session still were at the second. If you can understand this basic point—and to be

Table 4.4	THE EFFECT OF THE PERSON: CROSS-SITUATIONAL CONSISTENCY BETWEEN TWO EXPERIMENTAL SESSIONS
Behavioral Rating	**Consistency Correlation (r)**
Speaks in a loud voice	.70
Behaves in a fearful or timid manner	.65
Laughs frequently	.63
Is expressive in face, voice, or gestures	.63
Is reserved and unexpressive	.62
Exhibits an awkward interpersonal style	.60
Smiles frequently	.60
Has high enthusiasm and energy level	.59
Speaks quickly	.59
Exhibits social skills	.58
Engages in constant eye contact with partner	.57
Expresses insecurity or sensitivity	.56

Note: $N = 140$. All correlations are significant at $p < .001$. This is a partial list of significant correlations.
Source: Adapted from Funder & Colvin (1991), p. 780.

honest, not even all psychologists do—then you understand the heart of the issue of behavioral consistency.

A more recent study put participants in different situations by having them interact with professional actors portraying people who were dominant, submissive, quarrelsome, and agreeable (Leikas, Lönnqvist, & Verkasalo, 2012). As in the earlier study just summarized, the researchers carefully coded the participants' behavior from video recordings, and calculated the degree to which their behavior was consistent or changed across the different situations. Some of the results are shown in **Table 4.5**.

Notice that almost all of the behaviors were consistent to some degree, and a few of the correlations were quite large. For example, the degree to which a person "gestured" had an average cross-situational consistency correlation of $r = .70$. Other behaviors depended more on the situation. The number of times a

		Proportion of variance	
Outcome variable	Average cross-situational *r*	Person	Situation
Total amount of speaking	.52	.27	.45
Number of speaking turns	.23	.17	.24
Number of questions	.19	.11	.31
Disclosures	−.09	.00	.01
Verbal acknowledgments	.37	.24	.30
No. of "I" words	.14	.12	.06
No. of "you" words	.32	.23	.17
Smiles/laughs	.40	.38	.03
Gestures	.70	.66	.04
Nods	.28	.20	.21
Self-touch	.38	.34	.00
Initiated gazes	.33	.26	.10
Terminated gazes	.31	.22	.11
Mutual gaze frequency	.01	.00	.28
Mutual gaze duration	.33	.19	.28
Posture	.54	.53	.00
Orientation	.63	.60	.03
Micro-level behavior average	.35	.28	.16

Table 4.5 | THE RELATIVE INFLUENCE OF THE PERSON AND THE SITUATION ON SOME EXPERIMENTALLY MEASURED BEHAVIORS

Source: Leikas, Lönnqvist, & Verkasalo (2012), p. 1013.

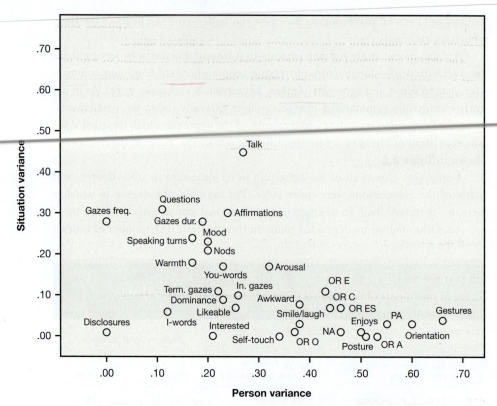

Figure 4.4 Variance in 32 Behaviors Due to Persons and Situations The figure shows that, in general, behaviors with more situation variance had less person variance, and vice versa. The "talk" variable is an interesting exception, because it was affected fairly strongly by both the person and the situation. Abbreviations: OR = observer rated; PA = positive affect; NA = negative affect; Gazes freq. = frequency of mutual gazes; Gazes dur. = duration of mutual gazes; In. gazes = initiated gazes; Term. gazes = terminated gazes; E = extraversion; C = conscientiousness; ES = emotional stability; O = openness; A = agreeableness. Source: Leikas, Lönnqvist, & Verkasalo (2012), p. 1014.

participant gazed into the eyes of his or her partner seemed to depend critically on just who the partner was. And some behaviors were strongly influenced by both the person and the situation. The total amount of talking was quite consistent, but the situation had a strong influence, too.

Another portion of the results of this study is portrayed graphically in **Figure 4.4**. This figure shows clearly that the amount of behavioral variance due to the situation was negatively related to the amount due to the person, as is shown by the general downward slope to the scatter plot (recall Figure 3.5 in the previous chapter). In other words, as the effect of the situation gets stronger, the effect of the person tends to get weaker, and vice versa. But there were exceptions. Both influences were important in determining how much a person talked.

The overall conclusion of this study seems clear, and it is consistent with the other evidence surveyed so far in this chapter: Situations have an important influence on behavior, but people still tend to be consistent. It would probably be going too far to conclude that the data in Table 4.5 and Figure 4.4 show that persons are actually more important than situations, even though the findings do lean in that direction. But there is certainly no indication that situations are so important that personality doesn't matter.

Now we are ready to consider the third part of the situationist argument.

Are Person Perceptions Fundamentally Mistaken?

Recall the situationist argument that the ability of personality variables to predict behavior is limited, if not nonexistent; that situations are much more important; and that people's everyday perceptions of one another, which consist to a large degree of judgments of personality traits, are therefore largely erroneous, or even "fundamentally" mistaken (Ross & Nisbett, 1991). Now that we have dealt carefully with the first two parts of this argument, the third falls of its own weight. The effects of personality on behavior do seem sufficient to be perceived accurately. Despite the situationist critique, our intuitions probably are not that far off base.

Both everyday experience and any fair reading of the research literature make one thing abundantly clear: When it comes to personality, one size does not fit all. Even when they are all in the same situation, some individuals will be more sociable, nervous, talkative, or active than others. And when the situation changes, those differences will still be there (Funder & Colvin, 1991). You may travel the world, but your personality is the baggage you will always have with you.

> You may travel the world, but your personality is the baggage you will always have with you.

The 17,953 trait terms in the English language arose because ideas about personality traits are an important part of Western culture (and perhaps all cultures, as we shall see in Chapter 13). Consider Eskimos and snow: It has long been noted that Eskimo languages have many more words to describe snow than do languages in warmer climes (H. H. Clark & E. V. Clark, 1977; Whorf, 1956).[10] Snow matters

---

[10] This long-standing, famous claim stirred a controversy when linguist Geoffrey Pullum (1991) denied that Eskimos have a particularly large number of words for snow. In response, Cecil Adams (2001), author of the Chicago newspaper column *The Straight Dope*, reported that he was able to find "a couple of dozen terms for snow, ice and related subjects" in an Eskimo dictionary and that Eskimo languages are "synthetic," meaning new words are constructed as the need arises, making it impossible to count how many snow words actually exist. Another observer counted 49 words for snow and ice in West Greenlandic, including *qaniit* (falling snow), *qinuq* (rotten snow), and *sullarniq* (snow blown in a doorway) (Derby, 1994).

a lot to Eskimos; they build shelters from it, they travel across it, and so forth. (Skiers also have a specialized vocabulary for types of snow.) The need to discriminate between many different kinds of snow has led Eskimos to develop words to describe each kind, in order to communicate and think better about this important topic.

The same thing seems to have happened with the language of personality (Leising, Scharloth, Lohse, & Wood, 2014). People are psychologically different, and it is important and interesting to note just how. Words arose to describe these differences—words that make us more sensitive to the differences and that make it possible to talk about them.

The proliferation of trait words is not finished yet; consider the relatively new words *jock*, *nerd*, *preppy*, and *Val*.[11] Personality psychologists are not leaving the language alone either. They have introduced the terms *self-monitoring* and *parmia*, as we have seen, and others such as *private self-consciousness*, *public self-consciousness*, and *threctia* to label aspects of personality that they did not believe existing words described precisely enough (Cattell, 1965).

PERSONALITY AND LIFE

After this survey of the ins and outs of a debate that occupied psychologists for decades, a reader could be forgiven for asking the following rude question: Who cares? Does the existence of personality even matter to anyone other than a personality psychologist who needs something to study? To be sure, the near-resolution of the debate brought about a resurgence of research on topics such as personality processes, personality structure, and the stability and change of personality over time (see Chapters 6 and 7). But what if—shocking thought—you just don't care about personality processes, structure, or stability? Does personality matter, even so?

You knew I was going to say yes. Personality is important on more than just theoretical grounds, and in ways that go beyond what some critics have called a "romantic" conception of human nature (Hofstee & Ten Berge, 2004). Personality affects life outcomes that matter to people, or, as two distinguished psychologists have written, "We assert, without providing evidence, that most people care about their own health and well-being, care about their marital relationships, and care about success and satisfaction in their career" (Ozer & Benet-Martínez, 2006, p. 402).

These writers were exactly right: Who needs evidence to "prove" that the most important outcomes in their lives matter to people? In their article, Ozer and

---

[11] In a bit of regional (California) slang that is already passing out of use, a Val (short for "Valley Girl") is a teenage girl from the San Fernando Valley (just north of Los Angeles), who is stereotyped as being empty headed, materialistic, and boy crazy. More recently, I have heard the term *bro* used to describe a certain type of young male, but I don't really understand it.

Benet-Martínez proceeded to summarize an impressively wide range of research documenting the effects of personality on these outcomes. They organized the traits they surveyed into five large categories (the so-called Big Five to be discussed in Chapter 6), and associated them with individual outcomes such as happiness and long life, interpersonal outcomes such as good relationships and peer acceptance, and what they called "institutional" outcomes, including leadership and career success. Some of their major conclusions are summarized in **Table 4.6**.

As you can see, all five broad traits impact important life outcomes. People who score high on the trait of extraversion tend to be happier than people who score low on this trait. Extraverts also enjoy better psychological health, live longer lives, are more popular, and are seen as better leaders. Agreeable people have healthier hearts than disagreeable people do, are less likely to get arrested, and go further in their careers (I'm guessing those last two outcomes might be related). Conscientious

O.C.E.A.N
explanation

O.C.E.A.N

Table 4.6	LIFE OUTCOMES ASSOCIATED WITH PERSONALITY TRAITS		
	Individual Outcomes	**Interpersonal Outcomes**	**Institutional Outcomes**
Extraversion	Happiness	Peer acceptance	Occupational satisfaction
	Gratitude	Success in dating and relationships	
	Longevity		Community involvement
	Psychological health	Attractiveness	
		Status	Leadership
Agreeableness	Religious involvement	Peer acceptance	Social interests
	Forgiveness	Dating satisfaction	Job attainment
	Humor		Avoidance of criminal behavior
	Heart health		
	Longevity		
	Psychological health		
Conscientiousness	Religious beliefs	Family satisfaction	Job performance
	Good health habits, longevity	Dating satisfaction	Occupational success
			Political conservatism
	Avoidance of drug abuse		Avoidance of criminal behavior
Neuroticism	Unhappiness	Poor family relations	Occupational dissatisfaction
	Poor coping		Criminal behavior
Openness	Forgiveness, inspiration		Artistic interests
			Political liberalism
	Substance abuse		

Source: Adapted from Ozer & Benet-Martínez (2006), p. 415.

OCEAN
Explanation→

people show an even stronger tendency to achieve career success, and conscientiousness is also associated with religious beliefs and better family ties. They also tend to be politically conservative, as opposed to people who score high on measures of openness, who are more likely to be liberal. Neuroticism is associated with a whole host of negative outcomes, including just plain unhappiness.

The reason that personality traits affect so many important outcomes is that they are present throughout life. Moment by moment, people might do any of a wide variety of things for an equally wide variety of reasons. But over time, an energetic and friendly person, for example, will act in ways that are different enough that the effects of thousands of little behaviors accumulate into life outcomes that may be very different from those of a person who is more sedate and aloof. Ozer and Benet-Martínez summarize the implications this way:

> Arguments about whether personality is consistent over time and context . . . have had one . . . unfortunate effect: they have obscured the reasons why proponents of different positions cared about personality in the first place, and first and foremost among these reasons is that personality matters. (Ozer & Benet-Martínez, 2006, p. 416)

PERSONS AND SITUATIONS

So, the evidence is overwhelming that people are psychologically different from one another, that personality traits exist, that people's impressions of each other's personalities are based on reality more than cognitive error, and that personality traits affect important life outcomes. It is important to be aware of this evidence in order to be able to counter the argument, still sometimes heard, that traits are little more than illusions. Having achieved this awareness, it is also important to put the relative role of personality traits and situations into perspective. For any given behavior, at any given time, personality and the situation both matter (Sherman et al., 2015). Personality traits become especially important when the goal is to describe how people act in general, across time, and across situations (Fleeson, 2001).

> For any given behavior, at any given time, personality and the situation both matter.

Interactionism

A sad legacy of the person-situation debate is that many psychologists became used to thinking of the person and the situation as opposing forces—that behavioral consistency and behavioral change cannot coexist. We have seen strong evidence in this chapter that this is not so (see again Tables 4.3, 4.4, and 4.5). It is much more accurate to see persons and situations as constantly interacting to produce behavior together. This is the principle of **interaction-ism** (Funder, 2008).

Persons and situations interact in three major ways (Buss, 1979).[12] First, the effect of a personality variable may depend on the situation, or vice versa. One classic study showed that caffeine had no overall effect on participants' ability to solve some complex cognitive tasks (Revelle et al., 1976). But when personality was taken into account, the results were different. It turned out that after consuming large amounts of caffeine, the performance of introverts got worse, while the performance of extraverts actually got better. This is a classic person-situation interaction: Neither variable has an effect by itself; they work together.

Moreover, situations are not randomly populated: Certain types of people go to or find themselves in different types of situations. This is the second kind of person-situation interaction. A biker bar might be a place where fights reliably break out every Saturday night, but only a certain kind of person would choose to go somewhere like that in the first place.

The third kind of interaction stems from the way people change situations because of what they do in them: The situation in the biker bar changes abruptly once somebody swings that first punch. The process by which people change situations, and then react to those changes, can accelerate quickly. According to one study, when hostile people are allowed to blast noise at each other, they quickly ramp up their level of mutual aggressiveness as one punishes the other, the other punishes back, but even more strongly, and so on up the scale until the situation becomes literally deafening. People lower on hostility were better able to avoid this vicious circle. As the authors of the study noted, "aggressive individuals created a more hostile and aggressive environment for themselves" (C. A. Anderson, Buckley, & Carnagey, 2008).

Persons, Situations, and Values

When I look back on the history of the person-situation debate, I am struck by two things. First, Mischel's argument that personality did not exist impacted the world of psychology with devastating force, even though the original argument in his 1968 book was brief and not very well supported. Second, the controversy persists, albeit less pervasively than before, into the present day. Right now, you could look into the current psychological literature and find, here and there, remarks about how little personality can tell us about behavior, and how much behavior changes according to even minor alterations in situations. The implication of these remarks, still and despite everything, is that what people do is determined almost exclusively by the situations they are in. The fact that this — I'll come out and say

---

[12] In chapter 7, these will be referred to as *person-environment transactions*.

it – *mistaken* view remains so pervasive is the reason that this chapter still appears in this textbook, years after the debate was essentially settled among psychologists familiar with relevant research.

The stubbornly lingering impact of the person-situation debate suggests that deeper issues may be at stake (Funder, 2006). This is just a suspicion, so take it as you will, but I think many psychologists have been eager to accept situationism because the view of human nature it implies is attractive to their philosophical and perhaps even political outlooks. A situationist view of the world, at a superficial level at least, implies that people are free to do whatever they want, rather than having their behavior influenced by their consistent personality. Situationism also implies that everybody is equal to everybody else and that differing outcomes for different people are a function solely of the situations in which they find themselves. Some people get rich and others fall into poverty, some are popular and some are shunned, and, overall, some succeed while others fail. A situationist view implies this is all due to circumstances, and further implies that under the right circumstances anybody could be rich, popular, and successful—a pleasant thought. The alternative view—that people really are different from each other—implies that, even under the best of circumstances, some people have traits that make bad outcomes relatively likely. This does not seem as attractive a prospect.

A situationist view can also—and somewhat paradoxically—help to absolve people from blame. The classic defense offered by Nazi officers for the atrocities they committed during World War II was "I was only following orders." They had a point, and one not so different from excusing criminal behavior on the grounds that the perpetrator suffered from a bad environment. If the situation really can be all powerful, then nothing we do is ever really our fault.

The view from the personality side of the fence is rather different. It begins with the idea that understanding human nature demands more than a one-size-fits-all approach, and it appreciates the unique aspects of every individual. It also offers the possibility that an individual might be able to develop a consistent identity and personal style that allows him to be consistently himself in a way that transcends the moment, rather than being continuously or even helplessly tossed about by situational forces. People who are willing to risk their lives to save others have personalities characterized by dominance, personal growth, and a sense of personal agency and redemption (Dunlop & Walker, 2013). Some of the most inspirational people in history, from Nathan Hale ("I only regret that I have but one life to give for my country") to the unknown hero who stood in front of the procession of tanks during the 1989 crackdown on dissidents in Tiananmen Square in Beijing, are inspirational precisely because they found an inner determinant for their behavior that overrode what would seem to be overwhelmingly powerful incentives to act otherwise. In contrast, while we admire people who are flexible, a person can

Figure 4.5 Does This Behavior Come from the Situation or the Person? As part of a crackdown on protestors in China, the government sent tanks into Tiananmen Square on June 5, 1989. A lone protestor—whose name remains unknown—stopped their advance and became an international hero.

be overly flexible to the point of being manipulative, two faced, untrustworthy—in a word, inconsistent.[13]

So, when psychologists—or nonpsychologists—debate the importance of the person versus the situation, they may really be arguing, implicitly, about their fundamental values. And values like these are deeply held indeed, which may be why the controversy refuses to go away, no matter what the data seem to demand.

Perhaps the resolution of the person-situation debate can help to reconcile this clash. We have seen that people maintain their personalities even as they adapt their behavior to particular situations (Fleeson, 2004; Funder & Colvin, 1991; Roberts & Pomerantz, 2004). Thus, the view of a person as flexibly adaptive to situations *and* generally consistent in personal style are not in conflict after all. If this point ever becomes fully understood and widely accepted, then psychology can

> While we admire people who are flexible, a person can be overly flexible to the point of being manipulative, two faced, untrustworthy—in a word, inconsistent.

---

[13] I'll make a bet here, that your reaction to this sentence can be predicted from the score you earned on **Try for Yourself 4.1**. If you got a high score, you agree. If you got a low score, then you disagree. Was I right?

offer some further lessons: Acknowledging the influence of social conditions on life outcomes does not make personal responsibility irrelevant. Individual freedom can stem from being true to oneself. We do not need to choose between these core values because they do not really conflict. If one result of the person-situation debate is a better understanding of this point, then personality psychology can claim to have provided an important insight into human nature.

PEOPLE ARE DIFFERENT

Late in his career, the eminent Harvard social psychologist Roger Brown wrote,

> As a psychologist,. . . I had thought individual differences in personality were exaggerated. I compared personality psychologists to cultural anthropologists who took pleasure in, and indeed derived status from, the exoticism of their discoveries. I had once presumed to say to Henry A. Murray, Harvard's distinguished personologist: "I think people are all very much the same." Murray's response had been; "Oh you do, do you? Well, you don't know what the hell you're talking about!" And I hadn't. (Brown, 1996, p. 169)

This little exchange captures the person-situation debate in a nutshell. Historically, and even to some extent to the present day, social psychologists

(a)   (b)

Figure 4.6 Murray Versus Brown Personality psychologist Henry Murray (a) once argued with social psychologist Roger Brown (b) about whether everybody was basically the same. Years later, Brown concluded Murray was right: People really are different from each other.

have tended to regard individual differences as being relatively unimportant, while personality psychologists naturally put such differences front and center. After years of believing otherwise, Roger Brown decided personality psychologists were right, and in that decision he finally came to agree with what most nonpsychologists have intuitively believed all along, as well as with the central lesson of the person-situation debate: People are different from each other, and these differences matter.

WRAPPING IT UP

SUMMARY

The Trait Approach

- The trait approach to personality begins by assuming that individuals differ in their characteristic patterns of thought, feeling, and behavior. These patterns are called personality traits.

People Are Inconsistent

- Classifying people according to traits raises an important problem, however: People are inconsistent. Indeed, some psychologists have suggested that people are so inconsistent in their behavior from one situation to the next that it is not worthwhile to characterize them in terms of personality traits. The controversy over this issue is called the person-situation debate.

The Person-Situation Debate

- Situationists, or opponents of the trait approach, argue (1) that according to a review of the personality literature, the ability of traits to predict behavior is extremely limited; (2) that situations are therefore more important than personality traits for determining what people do; and (3) that not only is personality assessment (the measurement of traits) a waste of time, but also many of people's intuitions about each other are fundamentally wrong.

- The rebuttals to the first situationist argument are that a fair review of the literature reveals that the predictability of behavior from traits is better than is sometimes acknowledged; that improved research methods can increase this predictability; and that the putative upper limit for predictability (a correlation of about .40) yields better outcomes than is sometimes recognized.

- The response to the second situationist argument is that many important effects of situations on behavior are no bigger statistically than the documented size of the effects of personality traits on behavior.

- The effect of personality on behavior shows up in relative consistency, the maintenance of individual differences; it does not imply that people act the same way regardless of the situation. Behavioral change and consistency can and often are seen in the same data.

- The evidence in favor of the existence and importance of personality is sufficiently strong as to disconfirm the argument that people's intuitions are fundamentally flawed. People perceive personality traits in themselves and others because such perceptions are often valid and useful.

- The large number of personality-trait terms also implies that traits are a useful way for predicting behavior and understanding personality.

Personality and Life

- A wide-ranging survey of the research literature shows that personality traits affect important life outcomes, including health, longevity, and interpersonal and career success.

Persons and Situations

- Situational variables are best suited for predicting behavior in specific situations, whereas personality traits are more relevant to patterns of behavior that persist across relationship partners, work settings, economic decisions, and other life situations.

- The resolution of the person-situation debate requires recognizing that persons and situations interact to produce behavior together.

- "Interactionism" recognizes that (1) the effect of a person variable may depend on the situation, and vice versa; (2) people with different personalities may choose, or find themselves in, different situations; and (3) situations are affected by the personalities of people who inhabit them.

- The person-situation debate may have been instigated and maintained, in part, because of deeply held philosophical beliefs. Emphasizing the effect of the situation implies personal equality and individual flexibility, along with avoidance of personal blame, whereas emphasizing the person accentuates the importance of self-determination and personal responsibility. The resolution of the debate may imply that these values are not as incompatible as is sometimes assumed.

People Are Different

- The psychological differences among people matter. The business of personality psychology is to describe and measure these differences, and to use them to predict and understand what people do.

KEY TERMS

interactionism, p. 137

THINK ABOUT IT

1. What are the most consistent aspects of the personalities of the people you know? What are the most inconsistent aspects?

2. Do you use personality traits when describing yourself or other people? Or do you describe yourself and others in some other way? What other ways are there?

3. Have you ever misunderstood someone's personality by expecting it to be more consistent than it really is?

4. The next time you talk with your parents, explain the consistency issue to them and ask whether they think people have consistent personality traits. Then do the same with college friends who have not taken this course. Are their answers different? How?

5. What situation are you in right now? Is it determining your behavior? What situation were you in at 10:00 A.M. yesterday? How did it affect the way you felt and acted?

6. What important life outcomes—besides the ones in Table 4.6—do you think might be affected by personality?

7. During the Nuremberg trials after World War II, some participants in wartime atrocities defended themselves by saying they were "only following orders." Is this the same thing as saying that the situation was so strong that their behavior was not determined by their own personal characteristics, so they should not be blamed? What do you think of this defense?

8. Sociologists point out that criminal behavior is much more likely from people who come from crime-prone neighborhoods, low economic levels, and unstable family backgrounds. These are all situational factors. Does this fact imply that crime comes from the situation and not from the person? If so, how can we hold a person responsible for criminal actions?

9. How are the cases described in questions 7 and 8, above, similar to and different from each other?

SUGGESTED RESOURCES

Kenrick, D. T., & Funder, D. C. (1988). Profiting from controversy: Lessons from the person-situation debate. *American Psychologist, 43,* 23–34.

> *A review of the person-situation debate written for a general audience of psychologists (not just for specialists in personality). Kenrick and I attempted to declare the person-situation debate finished; it almost worked.*

Mischel, W. (1968). *Personality and assessment.* New York: Wiley.

> *The book that launched a thousand rebuttals—this is the volume that touched off the person-situation debate. It is well written and, in its key sections, surprisingly brief.*

Ross, L., & Nisbett, R. E. (1991). *The person and the situation: Perspectives of social psychology.* New York: McGraw-Hill.

> *A lively and clearly written exposition of the situationist position. Personally, I disagree with just about everything this book says, but decide for yourself.*

Want to earn a better grade on your test?
Go to **INQUIZITIVE** to learn and review this chapter's content, with personalized feedback along the way.

PERSONALITY JUDGMENT

PERSONALITY ASSESSMENT IS NOT restricted to psychologists. It is practiced by you, your friends, your family—and by me, in my off-duty hours—all day long, every day. Personality traits are a fundamental part of how we think about each other and ourselves, and writings in philosophy and religion indicate that people have been judging personality since at least 1000 B.C. (Mayer, Lin, & Korogodsky, 2011). We choose whom to befriend and whom to avoid on the basis of our personality assessments—will this person be reliable or helpful or honest?—and others make the same judgments and choices about us. We even base our feelings about ourselves partly on our beliefs about our personalities: Am I competent or kind or tough? The judgments we make of one another's personalities and of ourselves are more consequential than those any psychologist will ever make.

Regardless of whether the source of a personality assessment is a psychologist, an acquaintance, or a psychological test, the most important thing to know about that assessment is the degree to which it is right or wrong. As we saw in Chapter 3, psychological tests are evaluated in terms of their validity. Evaluations of amateur judgments generally use the term *accuracy*. But the process of evaluation is fundamentally the same (Funder, 1987, 1995, 1999). The present chapter has two parts. The first part considers how and why the assessments others make of your personality and the assessments you make of others (and yourself) are important. The second part addresses the accuracy of these assessments. To what degree and under what circumstances do everyday judgments of personality agree with each other? To what degree and under what circumstances can they accurately predict behavior? And finally, how is accurate personality judgment possible? How might we become more accurate in knowing other people?

CONSEQUENCES OF EVERYDAY JUDGMENTS OF PERSONALITY

The judgments other people make of your personality reflect a significant part of your social world, so their importance goes beyond their value as accurate (or inaccurate) descriptions. Your reputation among those who know you matters because, as was mentioned during the survey of I data in Chapter 2, it greatly affects both opportunities and expectancies.

Opportunities

Reputation affects opportunities in numerous ways. Since it amounts to what other people think of you, it is an important element of many kinds of interpersonal success—or failure. A potential employer who believes you are smart and reliable is more likely to hire you than someone who doesn't share this opinion, and this will be true whether your reputation on this trait is right or wrong. And the effects of reputation extend far outside the world of work.

> The judgments we make of one another's personalities and of ourselves are more consequential than those any psychologist will ever make.

Consider the case of shyness. Shy people are quite common in American society; one estimate is that about one person in four considers himself to be chronically shy (Zimbardo, 1977). Shy people are often lonely and may deeply wish to have friends and normal interactions with other people, but are so fearful of social involvement that they become isolated. The problem seems particularly acute when dealing with the opposite sex. Because shy people spend a lot of time by themselves, they deny themselves the opportunity to develop normal social skills. When they do venture out, they are so out of practice they may not know how to act (Cheek, 1990). One consequence is that shy people are less likely than the non-shy to ask an opposite-sex person for help. Worse, they actually are less likely to get help if they do ask, apparently because they come off as less warm, confident, and fluent than do individuals who don't suffer from shyness (DePaulo, Dull, Greenberg, & Swaim, 1989).

A particular problem for shy people is that, typically, others do not perceive them as shy. Instead, to most observers, they seem cold and aloof. This is understandable when you consider how shy people often behave. A shy person who lives in your dormitory sees you coming across campus, and you see her. She would actually like to talk to you and perhaps even try to develop a friendship, but she is fearful of rejection or of not knowing quite what to say. (This fear may be realistic, given her lack of social skills.) So, she may pretend not to see you or suddenly reverse course and dodge behind a building to avoid having to talk to you. This kind of behavior, if you notice it, is unlikely to give you a warm, fuzzy feeling deep inside. Instead, there is a good chance that you will feel insulted and even angry. You may be inclined thereafter to avoid *her*.

Thus, shy people generally are not cold and aloof, or at least they do not mean to be. But that is frequently how they are perceived. That perception, in turn, affects the lives of shy people in important negative ways and is part of a cycle that perpetuates shyness. This is just one example of how the judgments of others are an important part of the social world and can have a significant effect on personality and life.

Expectancies

Judgments of others can also affect you through "self-fulfilling prophecies," more technically known as expectancy effects.[1] These effects can affect both intellectual performance and social behavior.

INTELLECTUAL EXPECTANCY EFFECTS The classic demonstration of expectancy effects is the series of studies by Rosenthal and Jacobson (1968). These investigators gave schoolchildren a battery of tests and then told their teachers, falsely, that the tests had identified some of the children as "bloomers" who were likely to show a sharp increase in IQ in the near future. The children were actually selected at random. But when their IQs were tested and compared with those of other children at the end of the school year, the bloomers had actually bloomed! That is, the first-grade children whose teachers expected them to show an increase in IQ actually did, by about 15 points, and the IQs of the second-grade bloomers increased by about 10 points, even though the expectations were introduced randomly.

This pioneering study has come under scrutiny in the years since and one conclusion is that IQ changes of the magnitude it found are probably not realistic (Jussim, 1991). But the general principle that people, and perhaps especially students, to some extent live up or down to what is expected of them seems well-established. The exact process behind this phenomenon has been a matter of controversy. Researchers have proposed at least four different theoretical models (Bellamy, 1975; Braun, 1976; Darley & Fazio, 1980; Rosenthal, 1973b, 1973c). The one that has garnered the most support is a four-factor theory proposed by Robert Rosenthal, one of the original discoverers (M. J. Harris & Rosenthal, 1985).

---

[1] As mentioned in Chapter 2, some psychologists call the expectancy phenomenon "behavioral confirmation."

According to Rosenthal's theory, high-expectancy students perform better because their teachers treat them differently in four ways. The first, *climate*, refers to the way that teachers project a warmer emotional attitude toward the students they expect to do well. The second, *feedback*, refers to the way teachers give feedback that is more differentiated—varying according to the correctness or incorrectness of a student's responses. The third, *input*, refers to the way teachers attempt to teach more material and more difficult material. Finally, the fourth way high-expectancy students are treated differently, called *output*, reflects how teachers give them extra opportunities to show what they have learned. Each of these aspects of teaching leads students to perform better (M. J. Harris & Rosenthal, 1985). This is important research not only because it helps to explain expectancy effects, but also because it demonstrates some of the basic elements of good teaching: It might be better if all students could be treated in the ways that high-expectancy students are treated.

SOCIAL EXPECTANCY EFFECTS A related expectancy effect has been demonstrated in the social rather than the intellectual realm. Mark Snyder and his colleagues (M. Snyder, Tanke, & Berscheid, 1977) performed the following remarkable experiment. Two previously unacquainted college students of the opposite sex were brought to different locations in the psychology building. The experimenter immediately took a picture of the female participant, saying, "You are about to meet someone on the telephone, but before you do this, I need to give him a picture of you so he can visualize who he is talking to." The male participant was not photographed.

The woman's real photograph, just taken, was thrown away. Instead, the experimenter gave the male participant one of two photographs of other female undergraduates who previously had been identified as either highly attractive or less attractive. "This is who you will be meeting on the phone," the male participant was told. The telephone connection was then established, and the two students chatted for several minutes as a tape recorder whirred.

Later, the researchers erased everything that the male student had said. (Remember, he is the one who saw the bogus photograph.) Then they played the edited recording, which contained only the woman's voice, for a new group of students, and asked them to rate, among other things, how warm, humorous, and poised she seemed.

The result: If the man had seen an attractive photograph, the woman was more likely to have behaved in a manner rated as warm, humorous, and poised than when he saw an unattractive photograph. This finding implies that when the male student spoke to a woman he thought to be attractive, his behavior caused her to respond in a warmer and more friendly manner than she would have had he considered her unattractive. Snyder interpreted this effect as another form of self-fulfilling prophecy: Attractive women are expected to be warm and friendly, and are treated in such a manner that they indeed respond that way.[2]

In some ways, this is an even more disconcerting finding than Rosenthal's results concerning IQ. The study suggests that our behavior with other people is influenced by how they expect us to act, sometimes based on superficial cues such as what we look like. Snyder's results imply that, to some extent, we will actually become what other people perceive, or even misperceive, us to be.

EXPECTANCY EFFECTS IN REAL LIFE   Research on expectancy effects is interesting and important, and the two studies just described are classics of the genre. However, there is a further important development in this area of research that I need to tell you about. Psychologist Lee Jussim (1991) asked an important question about expectancy effects that, surprisingly, had seldom been considered: Where do expectancies generally come from?

The usual experiments do not address this question because the expectancies they study are induced experimentally; Rosenthal's teachers believed that some students would improve academically because that is what Rosenthal (falsely) told them that a test predicted. Snyder's male participants expected some women to be warm and friendly because of stereotypes the men held about attractiveness, which Snyder elicited with a misleading photograph.

Jussim suggested that the situation in real life is usually quite different. A teacher who expects a pupil to do well might base this expectation on the pupil's *actual* test results, as well as observations of how the pupil performed in previous classes and reports from other teachers. A male undergraduate who expects a female undergraduate to be warm and charming might base this expectation on how he has seen her act before and what he has been told about her by mutual friends. Moreover, research has shown that, to some degree, physically attractive women really are more socially skillful and likable (Goldman & Lewis, 1977). Therefore, expectancy effects that are utterly false in the lab might be correct to some degree in real life. The self-fulfilling prophecies just described might have the effect of slightly magnifying or even just maintaining behavioral tendencies that the participant has had all along (Jussim & Eccles, 1992).

---

[2] Two complications are worth brief mention. The first is that a slightly different process may lie behind the result. Rather than men directly inducing the women to confirm their expectancies, it may be the case that men are friendlier to attractive women because they are hoping for a date, and colder and more aloof with unattractive women about whom they do not have such hopes. The women then respond in kind. Such a process would technically not be an expectancy effect, although the result would be the same. A related complication concerns the question of whether this effect works the other way around, when female students see pictures of attractive or unattractive men, and the effects on male participants' behavior are examined. A study by Andersen and Bem (1981) addressed this issue. The conclusions were not completely clear, but it did seem that, to some degree, male and female perceivers could both, through what they expected of the other, affect the behavior of opposite-sex targets.

This observation implies that rather than restrict themselves to introducing expectancy effects in the lab, researchers also should study expectancy effects in real life to assess how powerful they are. The studies to date show that expectancy effects are consistently greater than zero, but are they ordinarily strong enough to change a low-IQ child into a high-IQ child, or a cold, aloof person into a warm and friendly one, or vice versa? It is difficult to be sure because, until recently, most research has been more concerned with discovering whether expectancy effects exist than with assessing how important the effects are in relation to other factors that influence behavior.

Two studies suggest that expectancy effects are especially strong when more than one important person in an individual's life holds the expectancy for a long time. When over a period of several years both parents hold the same expectations for an adolescent's alcohol use, the effects on his or her behavior accumulate and increase (Madon, Guyll, Spoth, & Willard, 2004; Madon, Willard, Guyll, Trudeau, & Spoth, 2006). This seems to be especially true, unfortunately, for negative expectancies. When a mother and father both overestimate their child's tendency to abuse alcohol, he or she will have a particularly strong tendency to "live down" to this shared expectation.

Understanding expectancy effects sheds valuable light on the more general question of how people affect each other's performance and social behavior. Rosenthal's research revealed four basic factors that probably ought to be a part of all good teaching. Snyder's research suggests that if you want to be treated in a warm and friendly manner, it might not be a bad idea to expect the best, and act warm and friendly yourself. And parents who do not want their children to become problem drinkers should not begin by assuming the worst.

> When a mother and father both overestimate their child's tendency to abuse alcohol, he or she will have a particularly strong tendency to "live down" to this shared expectation.

THE ACCURACY OF PERSONALITY JUDGMENT

Because people are constantly making personality judgments, and because these judgments are consequential, it would seem important to know when and to what degree these judgments are accurate. It might surprise you, therefore, to learn that for an extended period of time (about 30 years) psychologists went out of their way to avoid researching accuracy. Although research on the accuracy of lay judgments of personality was fairly busy from the 1930s to about 1955, after that the field fell into inactivity, from which it began to emerge only in the mid-1980s (Funder & West, 1993).

There are several reasons why research on accuracy experienced this lengthy hiatus (Funder, 1995; Funder & West, 1993). The most basic reason is that researchers were stymied by a fundamental problem: By what criteria can personality judgments be judged right or wrong (Hastie & Rasinski, 1988; Kruglanski, 1989)? Some psychologists believed this question was unanswerable because any attempt to answer it would simply pit one person's definition of accuracy against another's. Who decides which definition is right?

This point of view was bolstered by the philosophy of **constructivism**, which is widespread throughout modern intellectual life (Stanovich, 1991). Slightly simplified, this philosophy holds that reality, as a concrete entity, does not exist. All that does exist are human ideas, or *constructions*, of reality. This view finally settles the age-old question, "If a tree falls in the forest with no one to hear, does it make a noise?" The constructivist answer: No. A more important implication is that there is no way to regard one interpretation of reality as accurate and another interpretation as inaccurate, because all interpretations are mere "social constructions" (Kruglanski, 1989).

> "If a tree falls in the forest with no one to hear, does it make a noise?" The constructivist answer: No.

This idea—that since there is no reality, judgmental accuracy cannot be assessed meaningfully—is still quite fashionable in certain intellectual circles.[3] Nevertheless, I reject it (Funder, 1995). I find the philosophical outlook of **critical realism** more reasonable. Critical realism holds that the absence of perfect, infallible criteria for determining the truth does not mean that all interpretations of reality are equally correct (Rorer, 1990). Indeed, even psychological researchers who argue that accuracy issues can never be settled (constructivists) still find themselves choosing which research conclusions to believe and not believe—even though their choices might sometimes be wrong. As researchers, they recognize that they must make such choices as reasonably as possible, based on whatever information is at hand or can be gathered. The only alternative is to cease drawing conclusions altogether.

Evaluating a personality judgment is no different. You must gather all the information that might help you determine whether or not the judgment is valid, and then make the best determination you can. The task remains perfectly reasonable, even necessary, though the accuracy of the outcome will always be uncertain (Cook & Campbell, 1979; Cronbach & Meehl, 1955).

Criteria for Accuracy

There is a simpler way to think of this issue. A personality judgment rendered by an acquaintance or a stranger can be thought of as a kind of personality assessment, or even a personality test of the sort considered in Chapter 3. If you think of a personality judgment as a test, then the considerations discussed in the previous two chapters immediately come into play. Assessing the accuracy of a personality

---

[3] Also sometimes in politics, where "alternative facts" battle with objective truth.

Figure 5.1 Are These Really Ducks? What would you need to know to be sure? Or could you ever be sure?

judgment becomes exactly equivalent to assessing the validity of a personality test. And there is a well-developed and widely accepted method for that.

The method is called **convergent validation.** It can be illustrated by the duck test: If it looks like a duck, walks like a duck, swims like a duck, and quacks like a duck, it is very probably—but still not absolutely positively—a duck. (Maybe it's a sophisticated Disney audio-animatronic machine built to resemble a duck, but probably not.) Convergent validation is achieved by assembling diverse pieces of information—such as appearance, walking and swimming style, and quackiness—that "converge" on a common conclusion: It must be a duck. The more items of diverse information that converge, the more confident the conclusion (J. Block, 1989, pp. 236–237).

For personality judgments, the two primary converging criteria are **interjudge agreement** and **behavioral prediction.** If I judge you to be conscientious, and so do your parents, and so do your friends, and so do you, it is likely—though not certain—that you *are* conscientious. Moreover, if my judgment that you are conscientious converges with the subsequent empirical fact that you arrive on time for almost all your class meetings for the next three semesters, and thereby demonstrates **predictive validity,** then my judgment of you is even more probably correct (although 100 percent certainty is never attained).

In sum, psychological research can evaluate personality judgments by asking two questions (Funder, 1987, 1995, 1999): (1) Do the judgments agree with one another? (2) Can they predict behavior? To the degree the answers are Yes, the judgments are probably accurate. So let's use these criteria to evaluate accuracy in various circumstances, beginning at the beginning, with first impressions.

First Impressions

As soon as you meet a person, you start to make judgments of his personality—and he is doing exactly the same thing to you. Neither of you can really help it. Personality judgments are made quickly and almost automatically, with no actual thinking required (Hassin & Trope, 2000). This fact is obviously important; you have no doubt heard the cliché that a person doesn't get a second chance to make a first impression. The impact of first impressions might be why the more "competent-looking" candidate (judged from nothing more than a still photograph) won in more than 70 percent of the 2004 races for the U.S. Senate (Todorov, Mandisodza, Goren, & Hall, 2005; see **Figure 5.2**). Are such first impressions at all accurate? I don't know if the more competent-looking Senate candidates really

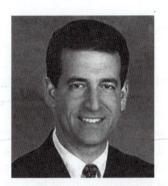 

(a) **Which person is the more competent?**

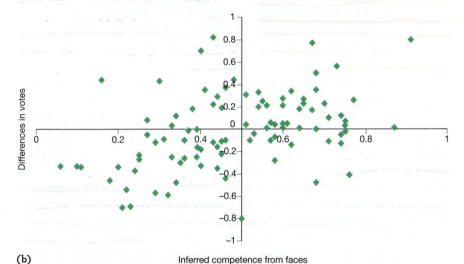

(b)　　　　　　　　　Inferred competence from faces

Figure 5.2 **Voting Preferences as Predicted by Competent Facial Appearance**
The scatter plot (b) shows that candidates in races for the U.S. Senate in 2000, 2002, and 2004 had larger margins of victory over their opponents the more "competent" their faces looked. In the race illustrated (a) the winner was the candidate on the left. Does he look more competent to you?

Source: Todorov, Mandisodza, Goren, & Hall (2005), p. 1624. Figure 1B from A. Todorov, et al. "Inferences of competence from faces predict election outcomes." *Science* 308(5728): 1623–1626. June 2005. Copyright © 2005, American Association for the Advancement of Science. Reprinted with permission from AAAS.

Table 5.1 | ACCURACY OF STRANGERS' JUDGMENT OF PERSONALITY

	Self-Judgment		
Other's Judgment	High	Low	Total
High	65	35	100
Low	35	65	100
Total	100	100	200

Note: These are results of a hypothetical study with 200 participants, where self–other *r* = .30.

were more competent, but there is research that addresses the accuracy of other first impressions.

THE FACE According to one survey, about 75 percent of college undergraduates believe that personality can be judged, to some extent, from facial appearance (Hassin & Trope, 2000). Until recently, most psychologists disagreed (Alley, 1988). Studies assessing whether you could tell anything about personality from, say, the size of someone's nose yielded almost uniformly negative results. More recent studies, however, have begun to focus on what are called *configural* properties of faces, or overall arrangements of features rather than single body parts (Tanaka & Farah, 1993). And when studied in this way, the validity of first impressions seems more promising.

One early study found that after undergraduates sat together in small groups for 15 minutes without talking, their ratings of each other correlated better than *r* = .30 on the traits of "extraversion," "conscientiousness," and "openness to experience" (Passini & Norman, 1966). Referring to the Binomial Effect-Size Display (BESD) described in Chapter 2, this means that rating a stranger in this situation on these three traits is about twice as likely to be right as wrong (see **Table 5.1**). Other, later studies got similar results (Albright, Kenny, & Malloy, 1988; D. Watson, 1989). A glance at someone's face can be enough to make surprisingly accurate judgments of the degree to which someone is dominant or submissive (Berry & Wero, 1993), heterosexual or homosexual (Rule & Ambady, 2008a), or even, in the case of business executives, how much profit his[4] company makes (Rule & Ambady, 2008b).

How is this degree of accuracy possible? Apparently, there really are configural aspects of the face that allow a number of psychological aspects to be judged with a degree of validity. One fascinating study tried to find out what some of those aspects are (Penton-Voak, Pound, Little, & Perrett, 2006). Researchers obtained personality scores from a large sample of participants, and then selected those in

---

[4] All the business executives in this study were male. No surprise.

the top and bottom 10 percent of men and women on five different traits (15 persons in each group). Using a computer imaging program, the 15 faces in each group were averaged into a composite portrait of a generalized—not actual—person who scored high and low on each trait. **Figures 5.3** and **5.4** show the results for the traits of agreeableness, conscientiousness, extraversion, emotional stability (the flip side of neuroticism), and openness. High scorers are in the top row, and low scorers are in the bottom row. Can you tell which trait is which? The participants in the study could, some of the time. On average, they were able to tell apart the high- and low-scoring men on agreeableness and extraversion, but not the other three traits. For women, participants could tell high from low scorers on agreeableness and extraversion.

What do these findings mean? First, they mean that apparently it is possible for people to tell whether a person is high or low in two traits—extraversion and agreeableness—just from looking at the face. In addition, we can do this for emotional stability in men—but (for some reason) not women. Second, the level of accuracy is impressive, and even surprising: The average effect size of the successful discriminations works out to about $r = .80$. However, it is important to remember that these findings come from *averaged* faces of *extreme* scorers—a very artificial situation. What the findings probably mean in practice is that, from looking at someone's face, we are somewhat able to detect accurately the difference between someone who is extremely extraverted and someone who is extremely introverted, or extremely agreeable versus extremely disagreeable. Accurate discrimination in the middle range—where most people are found—is surely more difficult.

Still, the message is that the human face contains far more information about personality than psychologists would have guessed just a few years ago. This fact may be one reason that research has shown that job interviews done over the telephone are not as valid for judging personality as those that are conducted—you know the phrase—"face to face" (Blackman, 2002a, 2002b).

> Job interviews done over the telephone are not as valid for judging personality as those that are conducted face to face.

OTHER VISIBLE SIGNS OF PERSONALITY Visible signs of personality go beyond the face. The degree to which someone dresses fashionably and has a stylish haircut can lead perceivers to infer that she is extraverted, and they are correct more often than not (Borkenau & Liebler, 1993). When a person speaks in a very loud voice, judges are apt to infer that he is extraverted, and that inference is usually accurate, too (Funder & Sneed, 1993; Scherer, 1978). In general, judges will reach more accurate conclusions if the behaviors they observe are closely related to the traits they are judging.

Here's a novel idea for judging someone's personality. Instead of looking at the person, look at her bedroom instead. As we saw in Chapter 2, people whose bedrooms house a variety of reading material are likely to be open to experience, whereas those who carefully make their beds and are otherwise neat tend to be conscientious

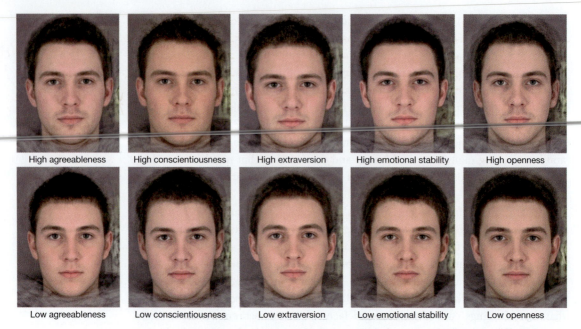

| High agreeableness | High conscientiousness | High extraversion | High emotional stability | High openness |
| Low agreeableness | Low conscientiousness | Low extraversion | Low emotional stability | Low openness |

Figure 5.3 Personality Revealed in the Face: Men These faces are composite portraits of the 10 percent of men who scored highest and lowest on five major personality traits.

(Gosling, 2008b). I don't know whether most people are aware of signs like these, but it does seem to be true that we are often curious to see where someone lives.

People also often assume they can judge a person by the kind of music she listens to. They may be right! When two strangers are in the process of becoming acquaintances and possibly friends, a common topic of conversation is music: which artists and styles each likes, and why. This conversation can yield information about personality (Rentfrow & Gosling, 2006). According to one study, people who enjoy reflective, complex music (New Age) tend to be inventive, imaginative, tolerant, and liberal. People who prefer aggressive and intense music (heavy metal) are more likely to be curious, risk-taking, and physically active. People who like upbeat and conventional music (pop) are relatively cheerful, outgoing, and helpful, but are not very interested in abstract ideas (Rentfrow & Gosling, 2003; see also Zweigenhaft, 2008).

Even the way a person tells a story can reveal something about his personality. In one study, research participants wrote short stories and then other people read them and tried to assess what the writer was like (Küfner, Back, Nestler, & Egloff, 2010). The personality ratings were remarkably accurate. Readers correctly inferred, among other cues, that sophisticated writing and creativity was a sign of openness to experience, and that using words that describe positive emotions and social orientation indicated that the writer tended to be agreeable.

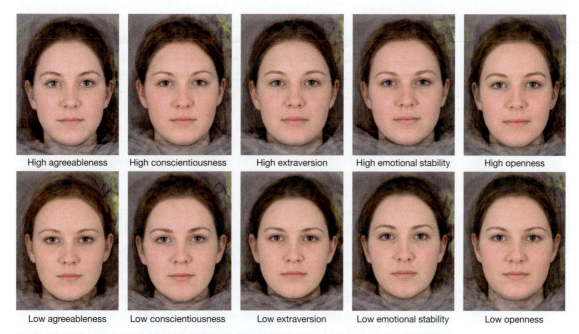

Figure 5.4 **Personality Revealed in the Face: Women** These faces are composite portraits of the 10 percent of women who scored highest and lowest on five major personality traits.

Finally, consider the classic interpersonal cue to personality: the handshake. People often claim to judge others by this cue. One study found that people with a firm handshake tended to be extraverted and emotionally expressive, whereas people with a weak grip were more likely to be shy and anxious (Chaplin et al., 2000). If you were ever taught that a firm handshake is a sign of honesty, however, forget about it. Visit a used-car lot. All the salespeople have firm handshakes.

Moderators of Accuracy

In psychological parlance, a **moderator variable** is one that affects the relationship between two other variables. A moderator of accuracy, therefore, is a variable that changes the correlation between a judgment and its criterion. Research on accuracy has focused primarily on four potential moderators: properties (1) of the judge, (2) of the *target* (the person who is judged), (3) of the trait that is judged, and (4) of the information on which the judgment is based.

THE GOOD JUDGE The oldest question in accuracy research is this: Who is the best judge of personality? Clinical psychologists have long postulated that some people are better at judging personality than others are, and numerous studies tackled this question during the pre-1955 wave of research on accuracy (Taft, 1955). A satisfying answer turned out to be surprisingly difficult. Early studies seemed to show that a good judge in one context or of one trait might not be a good judge in other contexts or with other traits. The only somewhat consistent finding was that highly intelligent and conscientious individuals rendered better judgments—but then again, such individuals are good at nearly any task you give them, so it was not clear that these traits were distinctive to the ability to judge people. Disappointment with this vague conclusion may be one reason why the first wave of accuracy research waned in the mid-1950s (Funder & West, 1993). But the pessimism was probably premature, because the original research was conducted using inadequate methods (Colvin & Bundick, 2001; Cronbach, 1955; Hammond, 1996).

More recent research has renewed the focus on this important topic and begun to ask some important questions. For example, who are the better judges of personality, women or men? The results are mixed. One study gathered personality ratings from strangers who had sat around a table together for a few minutes but not had a chance to speak. In this setting, women were better than men on judging two traits (extraversion and positive emotionality), but not others (Ambady, Hallahan, & Rosenthal, 1995). A further study in which groups including men and women actually had a chance to interact with each other found that women were generally accurate in their overall judgments, but only because they had a more accurate view of what the "normative" or average person is like (Chan, Rogers, Parisotto, & Biesanz, 2011). Women's better understanding of the average person made them appear to be better judges overall.

Another study looked at ratings that college students made after interacting for about 5 minutes and compared the ratings with the students' own self-judgments and with their behavior in three laboratory situations (Kolar, 1996). This study did not find that men and women differed in accuracy, but that the personality correlates of accuracy were different. The most accurate male judges of personality tended to be extraverted, well adjusted, and relatively unconcerned by what other people thought of them. The most accurate female judges tended to be open to new experiences, have a wide range of interests, and value their independence. These results suggest that, for men, accurate personality judgment is part of an outgoing and confident interpersonal style, whereas for women it is more a matter of openness to and interest in other people. Still, the overall conclusion that can be drawn from a large amount of research is that, although the difference is not large, women are better judges of people than men are (Hall, Gunnery & Horgan, 2016).

Either way, the good judge appears to be invested in developing and maintaining interpersonal relationships, a style sometimes called "communion" (Bakan, 1966). One study found that both women and men who put a particular emphasis on interpersonal relationships were more accurate judges of personality (Vogt & Colvin, 2003), and other studies found that accuracy was associated with the related traits of social skill, agreeableness, adjustment, and empathic concern

(Letzring, 2008; Colman, Letzring, & Biesanz, 2017). Moreover, the behavior of people who score high in "attributional complexity"—an ability associated with accurate personality judgment—is generally described as open, positive, expressive, and socially skilled (Fast, Reimer, & Funder, 2008).

Good judges of personality may be more positive in general. People whose typical or "stereotypic" judgments tend to describe others in favorable terms also tend to be more accurate, because most people actually *are* generally honest, friendly, kind, and helpful—which is good to know (Letzring & Funder, 2006). Therefore, the positive outlook on life that is characteristic of people who are psychologically well adjusted can lead them to be better judges of others (Human & Biesanz, 2011b). People who described other people—accurately—in positive terms were themselves described as warm, compassionate, and sympathetic. They tended to *not* be seen as arrogant, anxious, impulsive, or distrustful (Letzring & Funder, 2006). They tend to be more tolerant and responsible (Hall, Andrzejewski, & Yopchick, 2009). Good judges also have greater "cardiac vagal flexibility," which is a measure of heart function that is associated with social sensitivity[5] (Human & Mendes, 2018). (On the flip side, judges characterized by the "dark triad" traits of psychopathy, Machiavellianism (manipulativeness), and sadism[6] tend to judge people both negatively and inaccurately (Rogers, Le, Buckels, Kim & Biesanz, 2018).

Accurate personality judgment may also be a specific, measureable skill. The psychologist Neil Christiansen and his colleagues designed a test to assess "dispositional intelligence," defined as knowledge about how personality is relevant to behavior (see **Table 5.2**). People with higher scores on this test were better able to judge the personalities of individuals who were videotaped answering job interview questions, and also were more accurate judges of the self-reported personalities of their acquaintances. The test was especially accurate at identifying good judges among people who were highly conscientious and agreeable (Christiansen, Wolcott-Burnam, Janovics, Burns, & Quirk, 2005).

Do people know whether they are good judges of personality? The answer appears to be both no and yes (Biesanz et al., 2011). No, because people who describe themselves as good judges, in general, are no better than those who rate themselves as poorer in judgmental ability. But the answer is yes, in another sense. When asked which among several acquaintances they can judge most accurately, most people are mostly correct. In other words, we can usually tell the difference between people who we can and cannot judge accurately.[7] This ability is sometimes called "meta-accuracy" (accuracy about being accurate).

---

[5] In other words, these people have a lot of heart.

[6] The exact term used in the study was "everyday sadism." Really, every day?

[7] People are also pretty good at knowing what other people think of *them* (Carlson & Furr, 2009; Carlson, Vazire, & Furr, 2011).

| Table 5.2 | SAMPLE ITEMS FROM A TEST OF DISPOSITIONAL INTELLIGENCE |

1. Coworkers who tend to express skepticism and cynicism are also likely to:
   a. Have difficulty imagining things
   b. Get upset easily
   c. Dominate most interactions
   d. Exhibit condescending behavior

2. A teacher who has a tendency to discuss philosophical issues is likely to:
   a. Make plans and stick to them
   b. Do things by the book
   c. Come up with bold plans
   d. Prefer to deal with strangers in a formal manner

3. Which of the following situations is most relevant to the trait of *sociability*?
   a. A week after taking a final exam, you go to the professor's office to find out your final grade and you run into a classmate there. While you are both waiting for your grades, your classmate tells you he found the course difficult and is concerned about his performance.
   b. You have just heard that your supervisor received a promotion that he/she has wanted for a long time.
   c. Over the last two years, you have been employed at a job that entails working by yourself. Your boss offers you a chance to do essentially the same thing, but in a group of coworkers.

4. Which of the following situations is most relevant to the trait of *empathy*?
   a. You bump into an athlete you know who was largely responsible for his team losing in a recent game.
   b. Some of your friends have just told you they are planning to go skydiving and have signed up for a free introductory jump.
   c. Over the last two years, you have been employed at a job that entails working by yourself. Your boss offers you a chance to do essentially the same thing, but in a group of coworkers.

ANSWERS: 1 (d); 2 (c); 3 (c); 4 (a). The complete test has 45 items.
Source: Christiansen et al. (2005), pp. 148–149.

Does making an extra effort to be accurate help? Results so far are mixed. In one study, participants who were explicitly instructed to try to get to know one another as well as possible made judgments that were only a little more accurate than those by participants who simply chatted (Letzring, Wells, & Funder, 2006). Another, more recent study found that encouraging judges to try to make correct judgments led them to be more accurate about traits that are distinctive or unusual; at the same time they became less accurate about the traits that nearly everyone has in common—leading to almost no change in accuracy overall (Biesanz & Human, 2010). But another study took the opposite approach, by telling some participants that it was not important to be accurate because the judgment task was just a "warm-up." The result was that judges became less accurate than those who were not demotivated in this way (McLarney-Vesotski, Bernieri, & Rempala, 2011). So a certain amount of trying does seem necessary for accurate judgment.

A final question is: What good is it be a good judge of personality? It is easy to imagine specific cases where it's important to be right, when deciding whether to loan somebody some money or when choosing a roommate, for example. But little research, so far, has investigated the general benefits of being a good judge. One recent study found—perhaps surprisingly—that being a good judge of "distinctive" aspects of personality, of being able to distinguish how people are different from each other, didn't seem very useful. But people who were better "normative" judges of personality, meaning that they correctly understood what most people are like, were more likely to enjoy outcomes such as better interpersonal control, more support from other people, positive emotional experiences, and satisfaction with life (Letzring, 2015). Maybe—and this is just a speculation—it's more important to understand normal people than it is to understand unusual people, because most people are normal!

> Maybe it's more important to understand normal people than it is to understand unusual people, because most people are normal.

THE GOOD TARGET When it comes to accurate judgment, who is being judged might be even more important than who is doing the judging. An intriguing analysis by Lauren Human and Jeremy Biesanz appears to show just that (see **Figure 5.5**). People differ quite a lot in how accurately they can be judged. Everyday experience would seem to bear this out. Some people seem as readable as an open

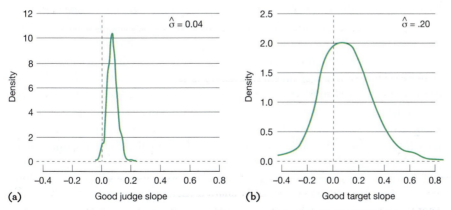

Figure 5.5 Individual Differences in Being a "Good Judge" vs. a "Good Target"
This figure shows the degree of individual differences in the good judge (Panel a) and the good target (Panel b) in a study that had 380 subjects. The $\hat{\sigma}$ (sigma-hat) is an estimate of the degree of variation. The results imply that accuracy depends more on who is being judged than on who does the judging.
Source: Human & Biesanz (2013), p. 249.

book, whereas others seem more closed and enigmatic. Why? Or, as the pioneering personality psychologist Gordon Allport asked in this context, "Who are these people?" (Allport, 1937, p. 443; Colvin, 1993b).

"Judgable" people are those about whom others reach agreement most easily, because they are the ones whose behavior is most predictable from judgments of their personalities (Human et al., 2014). In other words, **judgability** is a matter of "what you see is what you get." The behavior of judgable people is organized coherently; even acquaintances who know them in separate settings describe essentially the same person. Furthermore, the behavior of such people is consistent; what they do in the future can be predicted from what they have done in the past. We could say that these individuals are stable and well organized, or even that they are psychologically well adjusted (Colvin, 1993b; Human et al., 2014).[8] Judgable people also tend to be extraverted and agreeable (Ambady, Hallahan, & Rosenthal, 1995), although there are sometimes disadvantages to being extraverted. Extraverts sometimes just talk too much and listen too little, which can get in the way of them accurately judging the people they are talking with (Cochran, vanDellen, & Haas, 2018).

Theorists have long postulated that it is psychologically healthy to conceal as little as possible from those around you, to exhibit what is sometimes called a "transparent self" (Jourard, 1971). If you exhibit a psychological façade that produces large discrepancies between the person "inside" and the person you display "outside," you may feel isolated from the people around you, which can lead to unhappiness, hostility, and depression. Acting in a way that is contrary to your real personality is a lot of work, and can be psychologically tiring (Gallagher, Fleeson, & Hoyle, 2011). Evidence even suggests that concealing your emotions may be harmful to physical health (D. S. Berry & Pennebaker, 1993; Pennebaker, 1992).

Recent research builds on this theory by pointing out that judgability itself—the "what you see is what you get" factor—is a part of psychological adjustment precisely because it stems from behavioral coherence and consistency.[9] As a result, even new acquaintances of judgable people are able to accurately judge otherwise difficult-to-observe attributes such as "Remains calm in tense situations," "Does a thorough job," and "Has a forgiving nature" (Human & Biesanz, 2011a). This is a pattern with roots that reach into early childhood, and the association between judgability and psychological adjustment appears to be particularly strong among men (Colvin, 1993a).

---

[8] It is reasonable to wonder whether this can go too far. A person who is rigid and inflexible might be judged easily but would not be well adjusted. But remember, from Chapter 4, that "behavioral consistency" means maintaining one's individual distinctiveness, not acting the same way in all situations.

[9] As we shall see in Chapter 17, the reverse pattern of erratic and unpredictable behavior and emotions is a hallmark of the very serious syndrome called "borderline personality disorder."

THE GOOD TRAIT All traits are not created equal—some are much easier to judge accurately than others. For example, more easily observed traits, such as "talkativeness," "sociability," and other traits related to extraversion, are judged with much higher levels of interjudge agreement than are less visible traits, such as cognitive and ruminative styles and habits (Funder & Dobroth, 1987). For example, you are more likely to agree with your acquaintances, and they are more likely to agree with each other, about whether you are talkative than about whether you tend to worry and ruminate. This finding holds true even when the people who judge you are strangers who have observed you for only a few minutes (Funder & Colvin, 1988; see also D. Watson, 1989), or even less (Carney, Colvin, & Hall, 2007). In general, a trait like extraversion, which is reflected by overt behaviors such as high energy and friendliness, is easier to judge than a trait like "emotional stability," which is reflected by anxieties, worries, and other mental states that may not be visible on the outside (S. S. Russell & Zickar, 2005). And behaviors of other people are easier to rate than their beliefs and values (McDonald & Letzring, 2016; Paunonen & Kam, 2014). To find out about less visible, more internal traits like beliefs or tendencies to worry, self-reports (S data; see Chapter 2) are more informative (Vazire, 2010).

This conclusion might seem rather obvious. I once admitted that the main discovery of the study by Kate Dobroth and me is that more-visible traits are easier to see. We needed federal funding to learn that? (Don't worry, our grant was very small.) But the finding does have some interesting implications. One concerns the basis of personality judgments by acquaintances. Some psychologists, reluctant to concede that peer judgments of personality can have any accuracy, have proposed that interjudge agreement is merely the result of conversations judges have with one another or the participants. Thus, these psychologists conclude, peer judgments are not based on the participants' personalities but only on their socially constructed reputations (Kenny, 1991; McClelland, 1972).

This idea might seem plausible, but I doubt it is true. If peers based their personality judgments only on reputation and not on observation, then there would be no reason for observable traits to yield more consistent agreement than unobservable ones. Other people can manufacture a reputation about your ruminativeness just as well as they can about your talkativeness. But while all traits are equally susceptible to being talked about, certain traits are much harder to actually observe. Therefore, the finding that observable traits yield better interjudge agreement implies that peer judgment is based more on direct behavioral observation than on mere reputation (J. M. Clark & Paivio, 1989).

Another investigation addressed a trait the researchers called "sociosexuality," defined as the willingness to engage in sexual relations with minimal acquaintanceship with, or commitment to and from, one's partner (Gangestad, Simpson, DiGeronimo, & Biek, 1992). It seems reasonable to speculate that the accurate perception of this trait may have been important across the history of the human species. According to evolutionary theory, the traits and abilities that make individuals more likely to reproduce are more likely to be present in later generations. (For a more detailed discussion of this issue, see Chapter 9.) A crucial part of reproduction is figuring out who might be interested in mating with you. The hypothesis of this study, therefore, was that, for evolutionary reasons, people should be particularly good at judging this trait as opposed to other traits presumably less important for reproduction.

The study indeed found that individual differences in sociosexuality, as measured by self-report, were detected more accurately by observers than were traits less directly relevant to reproduction, such as "dominance" and "friendliness." Although this finding held true regardless of the sexes of the judge and the target, women judging the sociosexuality of men were especially accurate, and men judging the sociosexuality of other men were even more accurate!

This last finding presents a minor problem for the evolutionary explanation: What would be the reproductive advantage for a man to know the sociosexuality of another man? After thinking about it for a moment, you might be able to answer this question. The problem is, this is a finding evolutionary theory probably would not have predicted. (In case you are wondering, men—probably to their eternal regret—were not particularly good at judging the sociosexuality of women.)

GOOD INFORMATION   The final moderator of judgmental accuracy is the amount and kind of information on which the personality judgment is based.

Amount of Information   Despite findings about first impressions summarized earlier in this chapter, it still seems to be the case that more information is usually better, especially when judging certain traits. One study found that, while traits such as "extraversion," "conscientiousness," and "intelligence" could be judged with some degree of accuracy after only 5 seconds of observation, traits such as "neuroticism" (emotional instability), "openness," and "agreeableness" took considerably longer (Carney et al., 2007). Another study found that people were more accurate in judging each other after interacting twice, compared to just once (Cochran et al., 2018). In a study that examined more extended acquaintanceship, participants were judged both by people who had known them for at least a year and by strangers who had viewed the participants only for about 5 minutes on a videotape. Personality judgments by the close acquaintances agreed much better with the participants' self-judgments than did judgments by strangers (Funder & Colvin, 1988).

But this advantage of longer acquaintanceship did not hold under all circumstances. The videotapes that the strangers watched showed the participant conversing for 5 minutes with a peer of the opposite sex. This video was the sole basis for the strangers' personality judgments. The acquaintances, by contrast, never saw the videotape. Their judgments were based, instead, on their own knowledge of the participant obtained through observations and interactions in daily life over an extended period of time. Interestingly, when the judgments by the strangers and those by the acquaintances were used to try to predict what the participant would do in a separate videotaped interaction with a different opposite-sex peer, the two sets of judgments performed at about the same level of accuracy. That is, the advantage of acquaintances over strangers vanished when the criterion was the ability to predict behavior in a situation similar to one that the strangers had seen but that the acquaintances had not (Colvin & Funder, 1991).

Let me clarify this finding with a personal example. I regularly lecture before 200 or more undergraduates two or three times a week. As a result, a lot of people have seen me lecture but have no way of knowing what kind of person I am in other settings. My wife, on the other hand, has known me well for more than 30 years but has never seen me deliver a lecture (a not uncommon situation among college professors and their spouses). If one of my students and my wife are asked to predict how I will behave in lecture next week, whose predictions will be more accurate? According to Colvin and Funder (1991), the two predictions will be about equally valid. On the other hand, according to Funder and Colvin (1988), if you ask these two people to predict what I will do in any other context, my wife will have a clear advantage.

In our 1991 article, Randy Colvin and I called this phenomenon a *boundary* on the acquaintanceship effect, because we seemed to have found the one circumstance under which strangers could provide personality judgments with a predictive validity equal to those offered by close acquaintances. But this finding may be even more remarkable from a reversed perspective. Even though a close acquaintance—such as a spouse—has never seen you in a particular situation, that person will be able to generalize from observations of you in other situations with sufficient accuracy to predict your behavior in that situation as accurately as someone who has actually seen you in it. From casual observation in daily life, the acquaintances in our study were able to extract information about the participants' personalities that was just as useful in predicting how they would behave under the gaze of a video camera as was strangers' direct observation of behavior in a highly similar situation. The real news of this research may be this ability of close acquaintances to go from their specific experiences to judgments that are generally accurate.

Another study added a further wrinkle to the effect of the quantity of information on accuracy. It turns out that if judges are given more information, this will improve the agreement between their judgments and the target individual's self-judgments, but it does not affect their agreement with each other (Blackman & Funder, 1998). Judges watched a series of videotapes of pairs of people having conversations. Some judges saw only one 5-minute tape, some saw two tapes (for a total of 10 minutes), and so on, up to those who saw six tapes for a total of 30 minutes of observation. Then they tried to describe the personality of one person they watched.

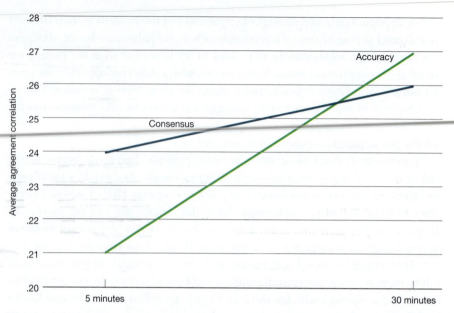

Figure 5.6 Accuracy and Consensus at 5 and 30 Minutes of Acquaintance
Blackman and Funder (1998) evaluated how consensus (interjudge agreement) and accuracy (self–other agreement) changed according to the length of time that judges watched videotapes of the target participants' behavior. The results show that while accuracy improved significantly with longer observation, consensus did not.
Source: Blackman & Funder (1998), p. 177.

The results are illustrated in **Figure 5.6**. Consensus, or the agreement among judges, was almost as good at the beginning as it became by the end; it did not change significantly between the judges who watched 5 minutes versus those who watched 30 minutes of videotape. But accuracy, here indexed by the agreement between their descriptions and the targets' own self-descriptions, did improve both noticeably and significantly.

What caused this difference between consensus and accuracy? The cause seems to be that judges' first impressions of their target agree with each other because they are based on superficial stereotypes and other potentially misleading cues.[10] Because these stereotypes are shared among judges, the judges tend to agree with each other even if they are largely wrong. After observing the target for a period of time, however, judges begin to discard these stereotypes and see the person as he really is. The result is not so much increased agreement among the judges, as it is an improvement in the accuracy of what they agree on (for a related finding, see Biesanz, West, & Millevoi, 2007).

---

[10] I say "potentially" because sometimes stereotypes are correct.

A hypothetical example may clarify these findings. Consider two owners of a garage, Sue and Sally. They need a new mechanic, so they interview an applicant named, say, Luther. Luther's hair is neatly combed, and he arrives on time for his appointment, so they decide he is conscientious and give him the job. Sadly, after a few weeks they realize that he is chronically late for work and leaves his repairs only half done, and that customers are starting to complain about finding beer cans in the backseat. Sue and Sally have a meeting and agree that, contrary to their first impression, Luther is unreliable and must go.

In technical terms, consensus did not change during this sad episode, even though accuracy did. Sue and Sally agreed at the beginning, and they agreed at the end. However, the content of what they agreed about changed dramatically. At the beginning, they agreed about

"When you picked up your car, Mr. Ferguson, after we did the hoses, did you see Luther's shoes?"

an erroneous assumption based on superficial stereotypes; at the end, with the benefit of some actual observations of his performance, they agreed about what Luther was really like. This is the kind of process, I believe, that explains why the accuracy line leans upward in Figure 5.6, even though the consensus line lies almost flat.

Quality of Information Quantity is not the only important variable concerning information. Common experience suggests that sometimes it is possible to learn a lot about someone very quickly, and it is also possible to "know" someone for a long time and learn very little. It appears to depend on the situation and the information that it yields. For example, it can be far more informative to observe a person in a *weak situation*, in which different people do different things, than in a *strong situation*, in which social norms restrict what people do (M. Snyder & Ickes, 1985). This is why behavior at a party is more informative than behavior while riding a bus. At a party, extraverts and introverts act very differently, and it is not difficult to see who is which; on a bus, almost everybody just sits there. This is probably also why, according to some research, unstructured job interviews, where the interviewer and interviewee can talk about whatever comes to mind, are more valid for judging an applicant's personality than are highly structured interviews where the questions are rigidly scripted in advance (Blackman, 2002b).

A common intuition, and one that appears to be correct, is that you learn something extra about a person if you see her in a difficult or emotionally arousing situation. Watching how someone acts in an emergency or how she responds to a letter of acceptance—or rejection—from medical school, or even having a romantic encounter with someone can reveal things about the person that you might not have otherwise suspected. One recent study showed that observing people in a stressful situation—having to make a short speech while being video recorded—led to more accurate judgments of personality than observing them in a situation that was more relaxed (Hirschmüller, Egloff, Schmukle, Nestler, & Back, 2014). By the same token, it is possible to sit next to a person in a class day after day for months and know next to nothing about him. The best situation for judging someone's personality is one that brings out the trait you want to judge. To evaluate a person's approach toward his work, the best thing to do is to observe him working. To evaluate a person's sociability, observations at a party would be more informative (Freeberg, 1969; Landy & Guion, 1970).

One pioneering study evaluated the effect of quality of information using recorded interviews. Participants listened to people being asked either about their thoughts and feelings or about their daily activities, and then tried to describe their personalities through rating a set of 100 traits. It turned out that listening to the thoughts-and-feelings interview "produced more 'accurate' social impressions, or at least impressions that were more in accord with speakers' self-assessments prior to the interviews and with the assessments made by their close friends, than did [listening to] the behavioral . . . interviews" (Andersen, 1984, p. 294). A more recent study found that people who met in an unstructured situation, where they could talk about whatever they wanted, made judgments of each other that were more accurate than judgments by those who met under circumstances that offered less room for idle chitchat (Letzring, Wells, & Funder, 2006). Having a chance to talk is especially important for judging the ways in which people are "distinctive," or different from each other (Letzring & Human, 2014).

The accurate judgment of personality, then, depends on both the quantity and the quality of the information on which it is based. More information is generally better, but it is just as important for the information to be relevant to the traits that one is trying to judge.

The Realistic Accuracy Model

To bring sense and order to the wide range of moderators of accuracy, it is helpful to back up a step and ask how accurate personality judgment is possible in the first place. At least sometimes, people manage to accurately evaluate one or more aspects of the personalities of the people they know. How is this possible? One explanation is in terms of the *Realistic Accuracy Model (RAM)* (Funder, 1995).

THE FOUR STAGES OF RAM In order to get from an attribute of an individual's personality to an accurate judgment of that trait, four things must happen (see

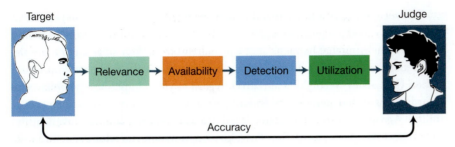

Figure 5.7 **The Realistic Accuracy Model** For an attribute of an individual's personality to be judged accurately, four things must happen: The individual must do something relevant to the attribute; this behavioral information must be available to the judge; the judge must detect this information; and the judge must utilize this information correctly.

Figure 5.7). First, the person being judged must do something *relevant*; that is, informative about the trait to be judged. Second, this information must be *available* to a judge. Third, this judge must *detect* this information. Fourth and finally, the judge must *utilize* this information correctly.

For example, consider an attempt to judge someone's degree of courage. This may not be possible unless a situation comes along that allows a courageous person to reveal this trait. But if the target of judgment encounters a burning building, rushes in, and saves the family inside, then she has done something *relevant*. Next, this behavior must occur in a manner and place that makes it possible for you, as the judge, to observe it. Someone might be doing something extremely courageous right now, right next door, but if you can't see it, you may never know and never have a chance to assess accurately that person's courage. But let's say you happen by just as the target of judgment rescues the last member of the family from the flames. Now the judgment has passed the *availability* hurdle. That is still not enough: Perhaps you were distracted, or you are perceptually impaired (you broke your glasses in all the excitement), or for some other reason you failed to notice the hero. But if you did notice, then the judgment has passed the *detection* hurdle. Finally, you must accurately remember and correctly interpret the relevant, available information that you have detected. If you infer that this rescue means the target person rates high on the trait of courage, then you have passed the *utilization* stage and achieved, at last, an accurate judgment.

This model of accurate personality judgment has several implications. The first and most obvious implication is that accurate personality judgment is difficult. Notice how all four of the hurdles—relevance, availability, detection, and utilization—must be overcome before accurate judgment can be achieved. If the process fails at any step—the person in question never does something relevant, or does it out of sight of the judge, or the judge doesn't notice, or the judge makes an incorrect interpretation—accurate personality judgment will fail.

The second implication is that the moderators of accuracy discussed earlier in this chapter—good judge, good target, good trait, and good information—must be a result of something that happens at one or more of these four stages. For example, a *good judge* is someone who is good at detecting and utilizing behavioral information (McLarney-Vesotski et al., 2011). A *good target* is someone who behaves in accordance with her personality (relevance) in a wide range of situations (availability). A *good trait* is one that is displayed in a wide range of contexts (availability) and is easy to see (detection). Similarly, knowing someone for a long time in a wide range of situations (*good information*) can enhance the range of behaviors a judge sees (availability) and the odds that the judge will begin to notice patterns that emerge (detection).

IMPROVING ACCURACY   A third implication of this model might be the most important of all. According to RAM, the accuracy of personality judgment can be improved in four different ways. Traditionally, efforts to improve accuracy have focused on attempts to get judges to think better, to use good logic and avoid inferential errors. These efforts are worthwhile, but they address only one stage—utilization—out of the four stages of accurate personality judgment. Improvement could be sought at the other stages as well (Funder, 2003).

For example, consider the consequences of being known as a "touchy" person. Someone who easily takes offense will find that people are more cautious or restrained when he is around: They avoid discussing certain topics and doing certain things whenever he is present. As a result, his judgment of these acquaintances will become stymied at the relevance stage—relevant behaviors that otherwise might have been performed in his presence will be suppressed—and he likely will be unable to judge these acquaintances accurately. A boss who blows up at bad news will lead employees to hide their mistakes, thus interfering with the availability of relevant information. As a result, the boss will be clueless about the employees' actual performance and abilities—and maybe even about how well the company is doing.

> A boss who blows up at bad news will lead employees to hide their mistakes.

The situation in which a judgment is made can also affect its accuracy. Meeting someone under tense or distracting circumstances is likely to interfere with the detection of otherwise relevant and available information, again causing accurate judgment to be stymied. People on job interviews or first dates may not always be the most accurate judges of their interviewers or dates.

Can a person be trained to become a better judge of personality? There is surprisingly little research on this topic, but one recent study suggests that answer might just be "yes." Researchers asked participants to watch recordings of job interviews and then rate the candidates' personalities. For example, participants were asked, "For extraversion, what rating did you give the candidate, and why?" Then researchers showed the participants how experts had rated the job candidate's trait, and the reasons for that rating, such as "The experts gave the interviewee a high rating on extraversion because she said she enjoys meeting new people." This procedure was followed for every trait that was rated. The results were that this instruction improved the match between the participants' judgments and two criteria for accuracy: expert ratings, and self-ratings by the candidates themselves (Powell & Bourdage, 2016).

So maybe you can become a better judge of personality by attending to relevant cues, such as the degree to which someone says she enjoys meeting new people. But it involves more than that. You should also try to create an interpersonal environment where other people can be themselves and where they feel free to let you know what is really going on. It may be difficult to avoid situations where tensions and other distractions cause you to miss what is right in front of you. But it might be worth bearing in mind that your judgment in such situations may not be completely reliable, and to try to remember to calm down and be attentive to the other person as well as to your own thoughts, feelings, and goals.

ACCURATE SELF-KNOWLEDGE

As we have seen, making accurate judgments of other people is possible, but also fairly difficult, because of the various problems of bias, incomplete information, and complex inferences. Is knowing yourself any easier? Maybe not. Socrates, among other wise ancient Greeks, advised that it was important to "know thyself." The very existence of this well-known aphorism suggests that knowing yourself is not completely straightforward. And there are good reasons to thinks it's important.

Accurate self-knowledge has long been considered a hallmark of mental health (Jahoda, 1958; Rogers, 1961) for two reasons. First, people who are healthy, secure, and wise enough to see the world as it is, without the need to distort anything, will tend to see themselves more accurately, too. Second, a person with accurate self-knowledge is in a better position to make good decisions on important issues ranging from what occupation to pursue to whom to marry (Vogt & Colvin, 2005). To choose the right major and the right occupation requires accurate knowledge of your own interests and abilities. To choose the right relationship partner, you need to know at least as much about yourself as you do about your partner.

The stages of RAM do not apply just to the judgments you make of others; they are also useful for describing how you judge yourself.

"It's interesting—with each conviction I learn a little bit more about myself."

Accurate self-knowledge requires that you perform behaviors and experience feelings that reveal who you are (*relevance*), that you perceive and become aware of these actions and feelings (*availability* and *detection*), and that you interpret them correctly (*utilization*). In an important sense, you are just one of the people you happen to know, and, to some degree, you come to know yourself the same way you find out about anybody else—by observing what you do and trying to draw appropriate conclusions (Bem, 1972). This is not necessarily easy.

Self-Knowledge Versus Knowledge of Others

Research indicates that, not surprisingly, we have better insight into our personal emotional experience than anyone else does (Spain et al., 2000). But when it comes to overt behavior, the picture is somewhat different. In a study that obtained personality judgments from both the participants and their close acquaintances, the acquaintances' judgments more accurately predicted behavior than did the self-judgments in nearly every comparison (Kolar et al., 1996). For example, acquaintances' judgments of assertiveness correlated more highly with later assertive behavior observed in the laboratory than did self-judgments. The same was true for talkativeness, initiation of humor, feelings of being cheated and victimized by life, and several other characteristics. A more recent study found similar results when self- and others' judgments were used to predict behavior outside the laboratory, in normal daily life. Close acquaintances were as accurate as the self, and the average ratings of two or three acquaintances are sometimes even more accurate (Vazire & Mehl, 2008), especially when it comes to visible, desirable traits like intelligence or charm (Vazire, 2010).

One reason for these surprising findings may be that paying attention to yourself can actually be rather difficult. As you move around all day observing the world from inside your head, you plan your next moves in response to the situations that confront you, one after another. And the only behavior you can observe is what *you* decide to do, not what other people would do in the same situation. In terms of RAM, problems arise at both the relevance and detection stages. But when you view somebody else, from the outside, you are in a better position to compare what she does with what others do, and therefore may be better able to evaluate her personality traits, which, as you will recall from Chapter 4, are relative constructs. Their very essence entails comparing one person with another. If you can see two different people responding to the same situation in two different ways, this is an ideal opportunity to judge differences in their personalities.

For example, imagine you are standing in a long line at an airline counter, and, when it is finally your turn, the clerk is rushed and somewhat rude to you. You do your best to ignore the clerk's behavior, take your boarding pass, and leave. Whatever you learn about yourself from this episode is necessarily limited. Now imagine you get a chance to watch two other people who happen to be ahead of you in line. The first talks to the clerk, shrugs his shoulders, takes his boarding pass, and leaves. The second person begins to talk to the clerk and quickly becomes angry. He turns red in the face and is shaking a finger and raising his voice by the time they finish. Now you are in an excellent position to compare the personalities of these individuals because you saw them react differently to the same stimulus.

One of the great misperceptions many people have about their own behavior is that it is the natural response to the situation and is therefore what anyone would have done (Ross, Greene, & House, 1977). "What else could I do?" you may often hear people ask. Such explanations are somewhat like those of the alcoholic who, after a stressful argument, goes on a bender. The alcoholic might say, "The stress caused me to drink," but of course she forgets that nonalcoholics find other ways to respond to stress. You probably know people who are hostile, deceitful, or unpleasant, who similarly believe they are just responding normally to the situations at hand. The same thing tends to be true of people with personality disorders, who view their symptoms very differently than do the people around them (Thomas, Turkheimer, & Oltmanns, 2003; see Chapter 17). As an outside observer, you see their chronic patterns of behavior, not just the momentary pressures that impinge upon them, and you can also see that other people respond more constructively to similar circumstances (Kolar et al., 1996).

This phenomenon is probably not limited to negative behaviors, although the positive end of the effect has not yet been documented by research. You may know people who are consistently easygoing, kind, diligent, or brave. When asked about their behavior, they seem just as surprised as the alcoholic or hostile person just described: "What else would I do?" they respond. To them, acting in an easygoing, kind, diligent, or brave manner is simply the obvious response to the situations they experience, and they find it hard to imagine acting differently. It takes an outsider's perspective to recognize such behavior as consistent across situations, unusual, and even admirable. Perhaps the tendency to overestimate the influence of situations is more pronounced regarding negative traits such as alcoholism or personality disorders. But I suspect that individuals can be equally blind to their good qualities.[11]

In January 1982, an ice-covered airliner plunged into the Potomac River in Washington, DC, near the heavily traveled Fourteenth Street Bridge. Dozens of onlookers at the scene and thousands of television viewers watched as the

---

[11] Social psychologists identify the *false consensus effect* as the tendency of people to see their own behavior as more common than it really is (see Ross et al., 1977). The present discussion can be compared to research on the *actor-observer effect* (Jones & Nisbett, 1971), which found that people typically see their own behavior as a response to momentary, situational pressures, whereas they see the behavior of others as consistent and as a product of their personality attributes. The present discussion differs from this research by not following the traditional assumption that the actor is correct in thinking his or her behavior is caused by the situation and the observer is wrong in thinking the person was the cause. I suspect that people more often tend to be blind to consistencies in their own behavior, which are better observed from an external perspective (see Funder, 1982; Kolar et al., 1996).

Figure 5.8 Recognition of a Hero Lenny Skutnik, a federal office worker, walked past dozens of bystanders to swim out and rescue a passenger from the frozen Potomac River. A few days later he was honored at President Reagan's State of the Union Address.

handful of survivors clung to bits of floating wreckage amid the ice. Lenny Skutnik, a government clerk passing by on his way home, saw one survivor begin to lose her grip and slip into the water; he kicked off his shoes, tore off his coat, and plunged in, pulling the woman to safety. An instant hero, Skutnik was introduced to the nation later that month by President Reagan during the State of the Union address. But Skutnik was reluctant to take credit, saying that he had simply acted without thinking when he saw someone in need.[12] The critical fact, obvious to everyone but him, was that he acted *differently* from the dozens of others standing on the shore.

More recently, in April of 2010 a French tourist on vacation in New York saw what he at first thought was a doll floating near a pier, and then realized it was a little girl. He immediately jumped in the river to save her, reacting even more quickly than the girl's father nearby. Then, before anyone had a chance to get the tourist's name, he shook off the water and took a cab back to his hotel. It took the media several days to find him back home in Lyon, where he said "Anyone would have done the same thing" (Boyle & Shapiro, 2010).

Author James Brady, who has written about the World War II soldiers who raised the flag on Iwo Jima and other historical topics, has commented that

> it's the observer who sees a hero. . . . I've talked to Medal of Honor winners and everybody says the same thing: "I didn't do anything that anyone else wouldn't do." . . . [A soldier who rescued a companion under fire] didn't see the bullets, he just saw a man that needed his help. It's the people on the outside who see the heroic stuff. It's all in the perspective. (Fisher, 2004)

Occasionally, it might be possible to take an outsider's view on your own behavior. One such occasion might be when you use your memory to survey your past behaviors and see retrospectively how each of your actions fits into a pattern that may have been invisible to you at the time, and how your choices differed from those of others in the same situations. Perhaps Lenny Skutnik realized later how exceptional his behavior was; at the time, he was too focused on someone in need

---

[12] A lesser-known hero of that day was passenger Arland Williams, who refused several times to accept a rescue line while passing it to others. He drowned when the piece of wreckage he was clinging to sank. We don't know what he would have said about his behavior, but my guess is it would have been much the same.

to wonder whether his action was typical, or to contrast it with that of the other people at the scene who were just standing around. In a very different example, when an alcoholic explains the cause of a recent drinking relapse, he is likely to attribute it to a stressful day at work, a fight with a spouse, and so on. But as more time passes, he becomes more likely to view the relapse as part of his chronic pattern of alcoholism (McKay, O'Farrell, Maisto, Connors, & Funder, 1989). Time can give a person perspective.

The purpose of psychotherapy is often to try to gain a broad view of one's own behavior to discover where one's strengths and weaknesses lie. Therapists encourage the client to review past behavior and identify patterns, rather than continuing to see maladaptive behaviors as inevitable responses to momentary pressures. The alcoholic, for example, needs to see his drinking as a chronic and characteristic behavior pattern, not a normal response to situational stress. And then he must find and use the inner strengths that can help overcome this problem.

Improving Self-Knowledge

In what ways can you improve how well you know yourself? There are three basic routes. First, and perhaps most obviously, you can use

Figure 5.9 **No Big Deal Here Either** French tourist Julien Duret jumped into the Hudson River and helped a little girl's father rescue her from drowning. Before anyone could even get his name, he took a cab back to his hotel. The New York *Daily News* eventually found him at home in Lyon. Like Lenny Skutnik, he didn't see how he'd done anything special.

introspection to look into your own mind and understand who you are. Second, you can seek feedback from other people who—if they are honest and they trust you not to be offended—can be an important source of information about what you are really like, including aspects of yourself that might be obvious to everybody but you. Third, you can observe your own behavior and try to draw conclusions from those observations much as anyone else, observing the same behaviors, would do (Bem, 1972).

In terms of RAM, introspection would be included at the fourth and final stage, utilization. The utilization stage emphasizes the importance of accurate memory for and honest evaluation of your behavior, which, as noted previously, might become easier with the passage of time. Seeking to be "mindful," to think about yourself nonevaluatively and to pay close attention to current experience, can also be helpful (Carlson, 2013). The second and third stages, availability and detection, emphasize the information you might be able to get from other people about what you are like. They might simply tell you, thereby making the information obviously available. But you might also have to read subtle, nonverbal indicators of what other people think of you, which makes detection more of an issue.

Some of the most important implications of RAM for self-knowledge lie at the first stage: relevance. As with getting to know another person, you can evaluate yourself only on the basis of what you have observed yourself do, and this is limited by the situations you have experienced and even by restrictions you may have put on yourself. For example, some people test themselves with bungee jumping or mountain climbing, thus allowing themselves to demonstrate attributes they might not otherwise have known they have. I am not really recommending that you go bungee jumping, but it might be worthwhile to consider how you could learn a lot about yourself by going to new places, meeting new people, and trying new things.

Self-knowledge can also be limited by family or culture, rather than by geography. Some families (and some cultural traditions) curb the individual self-expression of young people to a significant degree (see Chapter 14). One's education, occupation, and even spouse may be chosen by others. More commonly, families may exert strong pressures on children to aim for certain educational objectives and follow certain career paths. My university—like many others—has numerous freshman premed students. Strangely, by senior year there are far fewer. In the most difficult kind of case, a student feels pressured by family expectations to be premed, and then in her junior year realizes that she lacks the skills, the interest, or both. It may feel to her as if she has only minutes to decide on a new major, a new occupation, and a new path in life. This will be even more difficult if she has not tried out alternatives—she may have very little basis for understanding her real talents and interests because she was never encouraged to find out what they were.

So, regarding occupational choice, relationship formation, and many other areas, the best advice toward self-knowledge is probably to be yourself. It is not possible to avoid being influenced by the desires and expectations of friends, acquaintances, and family members. But you are most likely to find out what works for you by searching for your interests and testing your abilities. On the basis of accurate self-knowledge, you are most likely to make wise choices about education, occupation, relationship partners, and everything else that matters (see Chapter 15 for more on the importance of the self-concept).

ACCURACY MATTERS

There is no escaping personality assessment. If you somehow manage to evade having your personality judged by tests or by psychologists, you still will find that your personality is judged every hour of every day by your acquaintances, coworkers, friends, and yourself. Furthermore, these judgments will matter just as much as, and probably more than, any that will ever be rendered by tests or psychologists. This is why it matters whether they are accurate. We need to understand others in order to interact with them and make decisions ranging from to whom to lend $10 to whom to marry. When we understand people better, we have better relationships with them (Human, Biesanz et al., 2012; Letzring, 2014; Mast & Hall, 2018). And when we understand ourselves better, we make better life choices. Improving accuracy requires better thinking, but it also depends on our acting in a way that allows other people to be themselves, and also upon giving ourselves permission to be ourselves.

WRAPPING IT UP

SUMMARY

Consequences of Everyday Judgments of Personality

- People judge the personalities of each other and of themselves all the time, and these judgments have important consequences.

- Other people's judgments of an individual can affect that person's opportunities and can create self-fulfilling prophecies or expectancy effects. Therefore, it is important to examine when and how judgments are accurate.

The Accuracy of Personality Judgment

- Research has evaluated the accuracy of personality judgments in terms of consensus and predictive validity. Judgments that agree with judgments from other sources (such as other people) or that are able to predict the target person's behavior are more likely to be accurate than judgments that do not agree with each other or cannot predict behavior.

- First impressions of personality can be surprisingly accurate. Valid information about some attributes of personality can be found in the face, tone of voice, mode of dress, and even the condition of someone's bedroom. However, such judgments are more accurate for some traits than others, and tend to become more accurate with more extended acquaintanceship.

- Research has examined four variables that seem to affect the likelihood of accurate personality judgment: (1) the good judge, or the possibility that some judges are more accurate than others; (2) the good target, or the possibility that some individuals are easier to judge than others; (3) the good trait, or the possibility that some traits are easier to judge accurately than others; and (4) good information, or the possibility that more or better information about the target makes accurate judgment more likely.

- The Realistic Accuracy Model (RAM) of the process of accurate personality judgment describes accuracy as a function of the relevance, availability, detection, and utilization of behavioral cues.

- RAM implies that accurate personality judgment is difficult, helps to explain the four moderators of accuracy, and suggests ways in which one might be able to judge others more accurately.

Accurate Self-Knowledge

- RAM can also be used to explain the basis of self-knowledge, especially at the relevance, detection, and utilization stages.

- Becoming aware of one's own traits may be difficult because some traits are more visible from the outside than from the inside and because our most characteristic behaviors may become invisible to ourselves.

- The most useful way to improve self-knowledge may be to try new things, go new places, meet new people and, above all, allow yourself to be yourself.

Accuracy Matters

- Judgments of personality rendered by ordinary people in daily life, including our judgments of ourselves, are more frequent and more important than those made by psychologists, so it matters whether they are accurate.

KEY TERMS

constructivism, p. 153
critical realism, p. 153
convergent validation, p. 154
interjudge agreement, p. 154
behavioral prediction, p. 154
predictive validity, p. 154
moderator variable, p. 159
judgability, p. 164

THINK ABOUT IT

1. How often do you make judgments of the personalities of other people? When you do, are you usually right or wrong? How can you tell?

2. What did you think about the data on first impressions summarized in this chapter? Have you found that you can judge someone from their facial appearance, tone of voice, or other easily observed clues? What are the potential pitfalls of relying too much on first impressions?

3. Think of a time when you made a personality judgment of someone that turned out to be wrong. What was the cause of your mistake?

4. Have you ever entered the apartment or bedroom of someone you hadn't met yet? Did seeing their living space cause you to make inferences about what kind of person lived there? Were you right? What if someone looked into your bedroom right now? What kind of inferences would they make about you? Would they be right?

5. When people try to judge your personality, is there any aspect they tend to get wrong?

6. When are other people easiest to judge? Does it depend on when or how you met them?

7. What does it really mean to be "accurate" about judging someone's personality? If you think a person is, say, dishonest and the person thinks herself honest, can this kind of discrepancy ever be resolved? How?

8. How well do you think most people know themselves? What aspects of oneself are the hardest to know?

9. Have you taken a course in social psychology? In that course, the topic of this chapter was probably called "person perception" rather than "personality judgment." How else was the topic treated differently?

SUGGESTED RESOURCES

Mast, M.S., & Hall, J.A. (2018). The impact of interpersonal accuracy on behavioral outcomes. *Current Directions in Psychological Science, 27*(5), 309–314.

> *A succinct summary of the correlates and consequences of the ability to judge people accurately.*

Funder, D. C. (1999). *Personality judgment: A realistic approach to person perception.* San Diego: Academic Press.

> *A more detailed, somewhat more technical, and now somewhat out-of-date presentation of personality judgment and the issues concerning accuracy that are covered in this chapter.*

Want to earn a better grade on your test?

Go to **INQUIZITIVE** to learn and review this chapter's content, with personalized feedback along the way.

6

TRAITS AND TYPES
The Big Five and Beyond

TRAITS EXIST (Chapter 4) and can be assessed by psychologists (Chapter 3) as well as by everybody else in daily life (Chapter 5). But what are they really? Let's begin the answer with a reminder of what traits are *not*. They are not the determinants of what people do at all times in all situations; an extravert isn't always extraverted, an agreeable person isn't always agreeable, and an anxious person isn't even always anxious! As was discussed in Chapter 4, what traits characterize best is a person's average behavior over time and across situations. An extraverted person will on average—averaged across everything she does every day for two weeks, for example—behave in a much more active, sociable manner than will an introverted person. But that doesn't mean that the introverted person *never* acts in an active, sociable way; just not so often as an extraverted person (Fleeson & Law, 2015).

The truth of the matter is even subtler than that. There will be times when the introverted person actually acts in a more extraverted manner than the person who is, usually, more extraverted. The same is true of the difference between two people who differ in their level of anxiety; the more anxious person feels that way more often than the less anxious person, but at some times or in some circumstances the person who is classified as less anxious might actually feel more anxiety than the person classified as less anxious, and vice versa. The psychologist Will Fleeson (2001) describes this difference as contrasting "density distributions" of behaviors and states, as illustrated in **Figure 6.1**.

But even though people who differ in extraversion, anxiety, and other traits need not act in accordance with their usual personality all the time, such differences can be and often are large enough to have important effects on how their lives turn out. This is because even small effects of personality on behavior "aggregate" or accumulate over time; as was explained in Chapter 4, personality

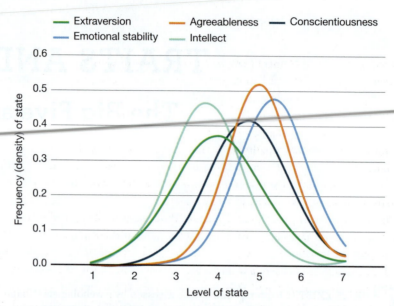

Figure 6.1 **Density Distributions of Behaviors and States** This diagram represents how behaviors and emotional states associated with five personality traits varied for a typical individual over a two-week period. As you can see, extraversion and conscientiousness fluctuated more over time than agreeableness or intellect. However, notice that the expression of all traits spanned almost the entire 7-point scale, which implies that any two people will have overlapping distributions on any given trait. For example, people who are on average high in agreeableness will sometimes (but not very often) be less agreeable than somebody low on agreeableness, and vice versa.

Source: Fleeson, W. (2001). Toward a structure- and process-integrated view of personality: Traits as density distributions of states. *Journal of Personality and Social Psychology, 80,* p. 1016.

> Being just a little bit more conscientious, or a little bit more agreeable, or a little bit more anxious, all day long in everything you do, will lead to consequences that add up over time.

is the baggage you always have with you. It has a sometimes-small but real influence on pretty much everything you do, all day long, every day. Being just a little bit more conscientious, or a little bit more agreeable, or a little bit more anxious, all day long in everything you do, will lead to consequences that add up over time. The result is that different individuals whose traits are only slightly different might end up with very different outcomes in occupational success, relationships, and even health. The purpose of this chapter is to take a closer look at personality traits and types, and how they are studied. The following chapter will follow up with a consideration of how personality develops and changes over the course of one's life.

FOUR WAYS TO STUDY PERSONALITY

Research that seeks to connect personality with behavior uses four basic methods: the single-trait approach, the many-trait approach, the essential-trait approach, and the typological approach.

The **single-trait approach** (see **Figure 6.2**) examines the link between personality and behavior by asking, What do people like *that* do? ("That" refers to a [hopefully] important personality trait.) Some traits have seemed so important that psychologists have devoted a major amount of effort to assessing as many of their implications as possible. For example, extensive research programs have examined self-monitoring and narcissism, to name only two.

The **many-trait approach** (see **Figure 6.3**) works from the opposite direction, beginning with the (implicit) research question, Who does *that*? (where "that" is an important behavior). Researchers attack the behavior of interest with long lists of traits intended to cover a wide range. They determine which traits correlate with the specific behavior, and then seek to explain the pattern of correlations. For example, a researcher might count the number of times that participants use a certain kind of word during an interview, and also measure up to 100 traits in each participant. The researcher can then see which of these traits tend to characterize the participants who often use that kind of word. The goal is to illuminate how personality is reflected in language.

The **essential-trait approach** addresses the difficult question, Which traits are the *most* important? The dictionary includes thousands of traits, and this

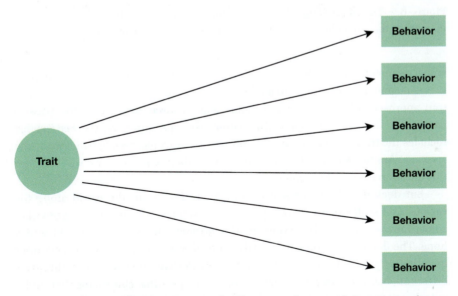

Figure 6.2 The Single-Trait Approach This research approach investigates the behavioral implications of traits of particular interest.

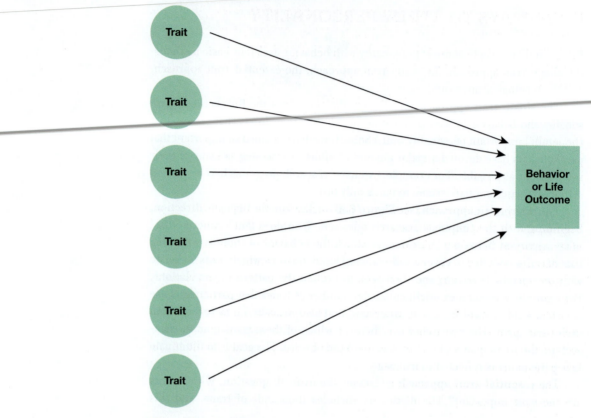

Figure 6.3 The Many-Trait Approach This research approach investigates the many traits that might be associated with a behavior or outcome of particular interest.

embarrassment of riches has led to confusion about which ones really are important enough to be measured and studied. Certainly not all of them! The essential-trait approach, which has made considerable headway over the years, tries to narrow the list to those that really matter. Most prominently, the *Big Five* list includes the traits of *extraversion, neuroticism, conscientiousness, agreeableness,* and *openness.* Are these traits all you need to know about a person? We will consider this question later in the chapter.

But does it *really* make sense to array everybody in the world along the various trait scales that psychologists have developed? Even psychologists have sometimes wondered. The **typological approach** stems from a doubt and a hope. The doubt is whether it is really valid to compare people with each other quantitatively on the same trait dimensions. Perhaps they are so qualitatively different—because they are different types of people—that comparing their individual trait scores makes as little sense as the proverbial comparison between apples and oranges. The hope is that researchers can identify groups of people who resemble each other enough, and are different enough from everybody else, that it makes sense to treat them as if they belong to the same "type." Instead of focusing on traits directly, this approach focuses on the patterns of traits that characterize whole persons, and tries to sort these patterns. One widely used measure of personality types is particularly questionable, as we shall see. But overall, thinking of people in terms of types, while far from ideal, can be useful for some purposes.

THE SINGLE-TRAIT APPROACH

Some of the most influential research in personality has focused on the nature, origins, and consequences of single traits of special interest. Let's begin by considering two of these. Each has been examined in hundreds of studies over several decades. Psychologists view them as important for different reasons. The first trait, self-monitoring, addresses fundamental issues concerning the relationship between one's private inner reality and the external image presented to others. The other trait, narcissism, describes a basic trait of some people who may be charming, attractive, and even charismatic, but also have such a high degree of self-regard and neglect of concern for others that they may cause problems for other people and for themselves. Some psychologists claim that narcissism has become especially prevalent recently. See if you agree.

Self-Monitoring

Mark Snyder, developer of the self-monitoring concept and test, has long been interested in the relationships and discrepancies between the inner and outer selves. For example, a person might drink beer at a party because the situation calls for being a beer drinker, but the same person might be studious, serious, and intelligent in a research seminar because that is the kind of person this academic situation calls for. And yet inside, in her heart of hearts, this individual might still be someone else entirely. Snyder theorized that the degree to which this is true varies across individuals. Some really are different between their inner and outer selves and in how they perform in different settings. Snyder called these individuals "high self-monitors." Others are largely the same outside as they are inside, and do not vary much from one setting to another. Snyder called these individuals "low self-monitors" (M. Snyder, 1974, 1987).

Consider **Try for Yourself 6.1**, which lists 18 items from a personality test that has been used widely for research purposes. Before reading beyond this paragraph, take a moment to respond True or False to these statements as they apply to you, and then calculate your score according to the key at the bottom of the box.

TRY FOR YOURSELF 6.1

Personal Reaction Inventory

Instructions: The statements on this page concern your personal reactions to a number of different situations. No two statements are exactly alike, so consider each statement carefully before answering. If a statement is True or Mostly True as applied to you, circle the T next to the statement. If a statement is False or Usually Not True as applied to you, circle the F next to the statement.

T	F	1. I find it hard to imitate the behavior of other people.
T	F	2. At parties and social gatherings, I do not attempt to do or say things that others will like.
T	F	3. I can only argue for ideas I already believe.
T	F	4. I can make impromptu speeches even on topics about which I have almost no information.
T	F	5. I guess I put on a show to impress or entertain others.
T	F	6. I would probably make a good actor.
T	F	7. In a group of people, I am rarely the center of attention.
T	F	8. In different situations and with different people, I often act like very different persons.
T	F	9. I am not particularly good at making other people like me.
T	F	10. I'm not always the person I appear to be.
T	F	11. I would not change my opinions (or the way I do things) in order to please someone else or win their favor.
T	F	12. I have considered being an entertainer.
T	F	13. I have never been good at games like charades or improvisational acting.
T	F	14. I have trouble changing my behavior to suit different people and different situations.
T	F	15. At a party, I let others keep the jokes and stories going.
T	F	16. I feel a bit awkward in public and do not show up quite as well as I should.
T	F	17. I can look anyone in the eye and tell a lie with a straight face (if for a right end).
T	F	18. I may deceive people by being friendly when I really dislike them.

Note: Score one point for each answer that matches the key.

Key: 1: F, 2: F, 3: F, 4: T, 5: T, 6: T, 7: F, 8: T, 9: F, 10: T, 11: F, 12: T, 13: F, 14: F, 15: F, 16: F, 17: T, 18: T.

A total score of 11 or above implies that the person is probably a high self-monitor; 10 or below implies that one is probably a low self-monitor.

Source: Gangestad & Snyder (1985).

The list of statements you have just responded to is the current standard measure of self-monitoring.[1] In samples of college students, the average score falls between about 10 and 12. A score of 11 or more is interpreted as implying high self-monitoring; 10 or below implies low self-monitoring.

High self-monitors, according to Snyder, carefully survey every situation they enter looking for cues as to the appropriate way to act, and then adjust their behavior accordingly. Low self-monitors tend to be more consistent regardless of the situation, because their behavior is guided more by their inner personality. As a result, one would expect a low self-monitor to be more judgeable, in the sense discussed in Chapter 5, and a high self-monitor to be much less judgeable (Colvin, 1993b).

Snyder has always been careful not to apply value judgments to high or low self-monitoring. One can say good or bad things about either. High self-monitors can reasonably be described as adaptable, flexible, popular, sensitive, and able to fit in wherever they go. They can be described just as reasonably as wishy-washy, two-faced, lacking integrity, and slick. Low self-monitors, for their part, can be regarded as being self-directed, having integrity, and being consistent and honest. Or they can be described as insensitive, inflexible, and stubborn.

One nice thing about the self-monitoring scale is that you probably got the score you wanted. If the description of high self-monitors sounded better to you than the description of low self-monitors, the odds are very good that you are a high self-monitor. If you preferred the description of the low self-monitor, then don't worry, you probably are one. Don't you wish all tests were like this?

Research has demonstrated a number of ways in which high and low self-monitors differ. In one of my own studies (Funder & Harris, 1986), high self-monitors were more likely than low self-monitors to be described by close acquaintances with terms such as the following:

- Skilled in social techniques of imaginative play, pretending, and humor (e.g., is good at the game charades)
- Talkative
- Self-dramatizing, histrionic (exaggerates emotion)
- Initiates humor
- Verbally fluent
- Expressive in face and gestures
- Having social poise and presence

---

[1] The original scale (Snyder, 1974) had 25 items, but it was refined later to this 18-item scale designed to more precisely capture the core construct (Gangestad & Snyder, 1985).

Low self-monitors, by contrast, were more likely to be described as

- Distrustful
- Perfectionist
- Touchy and irritable
- Anxious
- Introspective
- Independent
- Feeling cheated and victimized by life

It is clear from these lists that high self-monitors are described more favorably and are more popular than low self-monitors. However, the difference probably arises because being positively regarded and popular is more important to high self-monitors. The description of low self-monitors might seem more negative, but the low self-monitor probably doesn't care. Other goals, such as independence, are more important.

A second kind of research borrows a leaf from the empiricists' book (recall Chapter 3) by comparing the self-monitoring scores of members of different criterion groups—groups that, according to the theory of self-monitoring, should score differently. For instance, Mark Snyder (1974) administered his scale to professional stage actors. Because their profession involves putting on the persona called for by a script, he expected them to score high on his scale—and they did. He also examined hospitalized mental patients, who typically are hospitalized because their behavior has been seen as inappropriate. Snyder expected them to get low scores on self-monitoring—and they did. (Please note: This does not mean that low self-monitors are mentally ill!)

Snyder also performed some illustrative experiments. He asked his participants to read the following passage into a tape recorder: "I'm going out now; I won't be back all day. If anyone comes by, just tell them I'm not here." Each participant had to read this passage six times, each time trying to project a specific emotion—either happiness, sadness, anger, fear, disgust, or remorse—by using tone of voice, pitch, speed of talking, and so forth. (Try it yourself, right now—unless you are reading at the library.) It turns out to be easier to figure out which emotion is being projected when the reader is a high self-monitor (M. Snyder, 1974).

Studies have demonstrated relationships between self-monitoring scores and numerous other behaviors. Compared to low self-monitors, high self-monitors perform better in job interviews (Osborn, Feild, & Veres, 1998), place themselves in central positions in social networks (Mehra, Kilduff, & Brass, 2001), make more new friends (Sasovova, Mehra, Borgatti, & Schippers, 2010), use more strategies to influence their coworkers (Caldwell & Burger, 1997), are willing to lie in order to get a date (Rowatt, Cunningham, & Druen, 1998), and even masturbate more often (Trivedi & Sabini, 1998). They also respond differently to advertising. High self-monitors will prefer an energy drink if it has an image-oriented name such as Fast Track compared with something more descriptive (and bland) like Energy Drink Enhancer; low self-monitors have the reverse preference (Smidt & DeBono, 2011).

Narcissism

In the ancient Greek myth, a youth named Narcissus fell in love with his own beauty, and pined away to nothing while staring at his reflection in a pool. In modern days, the term *narcissism* refers to excessive self-love, which can be so extreme as to be classified as a personality disorder (see Chapter 17). Short of that, individual differences in narcissism are still important, and have been the subject of a great deal of research and even controversy in recent years (Trzesniewski & Donnellan, 2010; Twenge & Campbell, 2010).

People who score high in narcissism are often charming and make a good first impression (Paulhus, 1998; Robins & Beer, 2001), putting more effort into their hairstyle, clothing, and makeup (Holtzman & Strube, 2010). This can make them appear "sexy," at least at first (Dufner, Rauthmann, Czarna, & Denissen, 2013). But over time they may come to be seen as manipulative, overbearing, entitled, vain, arrogant, and exhibitionistic (Raskin & Terry, 1988; Holtzman & Strube, 2010). When they become the leader of a group, narcissists' arrogant displays of authority may look impressive even as their members stop communicating with each other and the group performs poorly (Nevicka, Ten Velden, De Hoogh, & Van Vianen, 2011). It is not surprising, therefore, that the charm of narcissists tends to wear off over time—they are the kind of people who, the longer you know them, the less you may like them (Paulhus, 1998; Robins & Beer, 2001). They might not even like themselves very much! This is one difference between narcissism and high self-esteem. People with high self-esteem feel good about themselves without necessarily feeling superior to anyone else; narcissists feel superior to others but, somewhat paradoxically, may still not feel good about themselves (Brummelman, Thomaes, & Sedikides, 2016).

Research has discovered a long list of negative behaviors and attributes of people who score high on narcissism. They may become aggressive when their positive view of themselves is threatened (Bushman & Baumeister, 1998; Rhodewalt & Morf, 1998), and when other people reject them they take out their frustration on innocent individuals who weren't even involved (Ang & Yusof, 2005; Twenge & Campbell, 2003). High scorers on narcissism don't handle failure well

(Zeigler-Hill, Myers, & Clark, 2010), they argue and swear a lot (Holtzman, Vazire, & Mehl, 2010), and they are rude behind the wheel (Schreer, 2002). In on-line games such as Minecraft, people who score high in narcissism kill more (virtual) people (Weiler, et al., 2017)!

Why do narcissists act like this? According to one widely accepted theory, narcissists follow an ill-advised strategy for dealing with life in which they seek to defend an unrealistically inflated self-concept through means, such as bragging, that are ultimately unsuccessful (Morf & Rhodewalt, 2001). Although they feel "puffed up," they are extremely sensitive to any sign of being rejected or excluded (Geukes et al., 2017).

Another root cause of narcissistic behavior may be a general failure to control impulses and delay gratification (Vazire & Funder, 2006). Narcissists crave feelings of power, prestige, success, and glory. Rather than take the slow and difficult route toward enjoying these feelings—such as by working hard or being courageous—they take the shortcut of expressing feelings of superiority whenever they feel the need, justified or not. The result, as is so often the case with impulsiveness, is short-term gain but long-term loss. They feel better in the moment, but ultimately alienate others and so undermine the success and admiration that they crave so much.

Is narcissism on the upswing? Maybe so. Some psychologists argue that narcissism has increased in the U.S. population, slowly but surely, over the past few decades (Twenge, 2006; Twenge & Campbell, 2010). As the cause, they point to cultural trends such as awarding trophies to every participant in a race, giving presents to every child at a birthday party, telling everybody that they are "special" and other practices intended to enhance self-esteem. The result, they say, has been the emergence of a "generation me" with too much self-esteem for their own good (Twenge, 2006). Other psychologists respond that the trend, while perhaps real, is too small to be really important (Trzesniewski & Donnellan, 2010) or even that "today's college students are *less* narcissistic than their predecessors and . . . there may never have been an epidemic of narcissism" (Wetzel et al., 2017, p. 13, emphasis added). These contrasting interpretations of the data are difficult to reconcile and I am not going to be able to settle the argument here. So instead, I will ask, what do you think? You can look around at other people and see for yourself. You could also ask your parents whether you and your friends are more narcissistic than they were at your age, but beware: Every generation tends to think the one after them has gotten worse in some way, and I'm afraid my own is no exception.

Where do you score on narcissism? After reading the above, do you dare find out? If you do, see **Try for Yourself 6.2**. But before you add up your score, consider that not all of narcissism is problematic. For one thing, narcissists do tend to be charming and good-looking and make a good (first) impression. For

Instructions: In each of the following pairs of attitudes, please choose the one that you MOST AGREE with. Indicate your answer by writing the letter (A or B) in the space provided to the right of each item. Please do not skip any items.

1. A. I have a natural talent for influencing people.
    B. I am not good at influencing people. 1. ____

2. A. Modesty doesn't become me.
    B. I am essentially a modest person. 2. ____

3. A. I would do almost anything on a dare.
    B. I tend to be a fairly cautious person. 3. ____

4. A. When people compliment me, I sometimes get embarrassed.
    B. I know that I am good because everybody keeps telling me so. 4. ____

5. A. The thought of ruling the world frightens the hell out of me.
    B. If I ruled the world, it would be a better place. 5. ____

6. A. I can usually talk my way out of anything.
    B. I try to accept the consequences of my behavior. 6. ____

7. A. I prefer to blend in with the crowd.
    B. I like to be the center of attention. 7. ____

8. A. I will be a success.
    B. I am not too concerned about success. 8. ____

9. A. I am no better or worse than most people.
    B. I think I am a special person. 9. ____

10. A. I am not sure if I would make a good leader.
    B. I see myself as a good leader. 10. ____

11. A. I am assertive.
    B. I wish I were more assertive. 11. ____

12. A. I like to have authority over other people.
    B. I don't mind following orders. 12. ____

13. A. I find it easy to manipulate people.
    B. I don't like it when I find myself manipulating people. 13. ____

14. A. I insist upon getting the respect that is due me.
    B. I usually get the respect that I deserve. 14. ____

Continued

TRY FOR YOURSELF 6.2

NPI—cont'd

15. A. I don't particularly like to show off my body.

    B. I like to show off my body.   15. ____

16. A. I can read people like a book.

    B. People are sometimes hard to understand.   16. ____

17. A. If I feel competent, I am willing to take responsibility for making decisions.

    B. I like to take responsibility for making decisions.   17. ____

18. A. I just want to be reasonably happy.

    B. I want to amount to something in the eyes of the world.   18. ____

19. A. My body is nothing special.

    B. I like to look at my body.   19. ____

20. A. I try not to be a show off.

    B. I will usually show off if I get the chance.   20. ____

21. A. I always know what I am doing.

    B. Sometimes I am not sure of what I am doing.   21. ____

22. A. I sometimes depend on people to get things done.

    B. I rarely depend on anyone else to get things done.   22. ____

23. A. Sometimes I tell good stories.

    B. Everybody likes to hear my stories.   23. ____

24. A. I expect a great deal from other people.

    B. I like to do things for other people.   24. ____

25. A. I will never be satisfied until I get all that I deserve.

    B. I take my satisfactions as they come.   25. ____

26. A. Compliments embarrass me.

    B. I like to be complimented.   26. ____

27. A. I have a strong will to power.

    B. Power for its own sake doesn't interest me.   27. ____

28. A. I don't care about new fads and fashions.

    B. I like to start new fads and fashions.   28. ____

29. A. I like to look at myself in the mirror.

    B. I am not particularly interested in looking at myself in the mirror.   29. ____

30. A. I really like to be the center of attention.

    B. It makes me uncomfortable to be the center of attention.   30. ____

31. A. I can live my life in any way I want to.

     B. People can't always live their lives in terms of what they want.   31. ____

32. A. Being an authority doesn't mean that much to me.

     B. People always seem to recognize my authority.   32. ____

33. A. I would prefer to be a leader.

     B. It makes little difference to me whether I am a leader or not.   33. ____

34. A. I am going to be a great person.

     B. I hope I am going to be successful.   34. ____

35. A. People sometimes believe what I tell them.

     B. I can make anybody believe anything I want them to.   35. ____

36. A. I am a born leader.

     B. Leadership is a quality that takes a long time to develop.   36. ____

37. A. I wish somebody would someday write my biography.

     B. I don't like people to pry into my life for any reason.   37. ____

38. A. I get upset when people don't notice how I look when I go out in public.

     B. I don't mind blending into the crowd when I go out in public.   38. ____

39. A. I am more capable than other people.

     B. There is a lot that I can learn from other people.   39. ____

40. A. I am much like everybody else.

     B. I am an extraordinary person.   40. ____

Note: Score one point for each answer that matches the key.

1, 2, and 3: A; 4, 5: B; 6: A; 7: B; 8: A; 9 and 10: B; 11, 12, 13, and 14: A; 15: B; 16: A; 17, 18, 19, and 20: B; 21: A; 22, 23: B; 24 and 25: A; 26: B; 27: A; 28: B; 29, 30, and 31: A; 32: B; 33, 34: A; 35: B; 36, 37, 38, and 39: A; 40: B.

The test is intended to measure the trait of "narcissism" (see text). The average score is 15.3 and the standard deviation is 6.8, which means that a score above about 22 is quite high and a score of 29 is extremely high. A score of 8.5 is quite low and a score of less than 2 is extremely low. According to one source, the average score of "celebrities" is 17.8 (Pinsky & Young, 2009).

Source: Adapted from Raskin & Hall (1981) and Raskin & Terry (1988).

another thing, narcissism, like so many concepts in personality psychology, is multifaceted (Ackerman et al., 2011; see also Back et al., 2013). Part of narcissism stems from an attribute that has been named "entitlement/exploitativeness," which is basically the obnoxious, arrogant element. But narcissists may also be high on another subtrait, named "leadership/authority," which is associated with self-confidence, charisma, popularity, and power. Adolescents and young adults (but not older adults) who score high on narcissism report being more satisfied with life (Hill & Roberts, 2012). Even the impulsiveness associated with narcissism

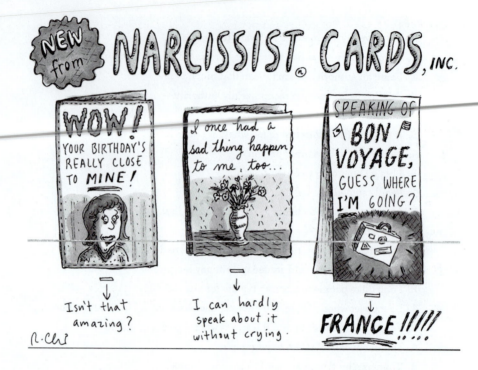

may not be all bad. It can lead to a willingness to take the risks that are inevitably associated with making friends and influencing people (Jones & Paulhus, 2011). Remember Funder's First Law (see Chapter 1), about advantages being disadvantages and vice versa? Narcissism may provide yet another example. But there is a limit. Narcissism in the normal range may have its pros and cons, but, in some individuals (fortunately just a few), it reaches such an extreme that it has to be considered a personality disorder.[2]

THE MANY-TRAIT APPROACH

It can be interesting and useful to explore one trait in depth, as we just saw. However, some personality psychologists—including me—enjoy looking at many traits at once (Sherman & Serfass, 2014). Several lists have been developed for this purpose, including Allport and Odbert's list of 17,953, which is a bit long to be practical (Allport & Odbert, 1936). One more recent effort uses 504 trait adjectives—still an awful lot—organized into 61 clusters (Wood, Nye, & Saucier,

---

[2] Narcissistic personality disorder is considered further in Chapter 17.

2010). For the present, my favorite remains the list of 100 personality traits called the **California Q-Set** (Bem & Funder, 1978; J. Block, 1961, 1978).

The California Q-Set

Maybe *trait* is not quite the right word for the items of the Q-set. The set consists of 100 phrases. Traditionally, they were printed on separate paper cards; now they are usually sorted on a computer screen. Each phrase describes an aspect of personality that might be important for characterizing a particular individual. For example, Item 1 reads, "Is critical, skeptical, not easily impressed"; Item 2 reads, "Is a genuinely dependable and responsible person"; Item 3 reads, "Has a wide range of interests"; and so forth, for the remaining 97 items (see **Table 6.1** for more examples).

Both the way this list of items is used and its origin are rather unusual. Raters express judgments of personality by sorting the items into nine categories ranging from highly uncharacteristic of the person being described (Category 1) to highly characteristic (Category 9). Items neither characteristic nor uncharacteristic are

---

Table 6.1 | SAMPLE ITEMS FROM THE CALIFORNIA Q-SET

1.	Is critical, skeptical, not easily impressed
2.	Is a genuinely dependable and responsible person
3.	Has a wide range of interests
11.	Is protective of those close to him or her
13.	Is thin-skinned; sensitive to criticism or insult
18.	Initiates humor
24.	Prides self on being "objective," rational
26.	Is productive; gets things done
28.	Tends to arouse liking and acceptance
29.	Is turned to for advice and reassurance
43.	Is facially and/or gesturally expressive
51.	Genuinely values intellectual and cognitive matters
54.	Emphasizes being with others; gregarious
58.	Enjoys sensuous experiences—including touch, taste, smell, physical contact
71.	Has high aspiration level for self
75.	Has a clear-cut, internally consistent personality
84.	Is cheerful
98.	Is verbally fluent
100.	Does not vary roles; relates to everyone in the same way

Source: Adapted from J. Block (1961, 1978), pp. 132–136.

Figure 6.4   The California Q-Set in Action To describe an individual, the rater places the items of the Q-set into a symmetrical, forced distribution ranging from "highly uncharacteristic" (Category 1) to "highly characteristic" (Category 9). The rater in this picture is using the original sorting method that employed paper cards.

placed in or near Category 5. The distribution is forced, which means that a predetermined number of items must go into each category. The usual Q-sort[3] distribution is peaked, or "normal," meaning that most items are placed near the center and only a few (just 5 of the 100) can be placed on each end (see **Figures 6.4** and **6.5).**

The rater who does the sorting might be an acquaintance, a researcher, or a psychotherapist; in these cases, the item placements constitute I data. Alternatively, a person might provide judgments of his own personality, in which case the item placements constitute S data. The most important advantage of Q-sorting is that it forces the judge to compare all of the items directly against each other; rather than rating the items one at a time, the judge must decide which items are the most descriptive. Furthermore, the judge is restricted to identifying only a few items as being most important. Nobody can be described as all good or all bad; there simply is not enough room to put all the good traits—or all the bad traits—into Categories 9 or 1. Finer and subtler discriminations must be made.

The items of the California Q-Set were not derived through a formal, empirical procedure. Rather, a team of researchers and clinical practitioners sought to develop a comprehensive set of terms sufficient to describe the people they interacted with every day (J. Block, 1961, 1978). After formulating an initial list, the team met regularly to use the items to describe their clients and research participants. When an item proved useless or vague, they revised or eliminated it. When the set was insufficient to describe some aspect of a particular person, they wrote a new item. The resulting set emerged after years of such revisions and refinements. Later, other investigators further revised the Q-set so that its sometimes-technical phrasing could be understood and used by nonpsychologists; this slightly reworded list is excerpted in Table 6.1 (Bem & Funder, 1978). The 100 items of the California Q-Set have been used to study topics ranging from talking to political beliefs.

Talking

People talk (and write) all day long. Psychologists have begun to investigate the implications of this fact for personality. For example, have you ever noticed that some people often use words such as "absolutely," "exactly," and "sure," while others hardly ever do? Does this imply anything about their personalities?

---

[3] A note on terminology: A *Q-set* is a set of items (such as the 100 items of the California Q-Set) that a rater then sorts into categories in order to describe someone. A *Q-sort* is the resulting arrangement, and *Q-sorting* is the process of turning a Q-set into a Q-sort. In practice, however, these terminological distinctions tend to get lost.

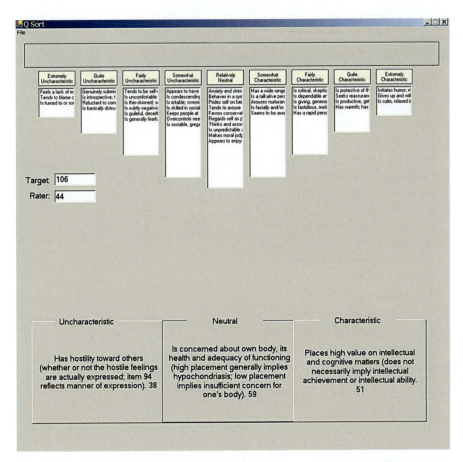

Figure 6.5 Q-Sorting on the Computer The screen here shows a partially complete Q-sort. The rater began by sorting the 100 items into three preliminary categories labeled "uncharacteristic," "neutral," and "characteristic." In the second step, shown here, the rater drags each of the items from the three categories (at the bottom of the screen) into one of the nine categories at the top of the screen. (The program shown in this picture can be downloaded free of charge from http://rap.ucr.edu/qsorter.)

A study in our laboratory used the Q-sort and its "many-trait approach" to address this question (Fast & Funder, 2008). Each of our participants underwent a 1-hour life-history interview, with topics that ranged over past experiences, current activities, and future prospects. The interview was recorded, and then the questions were deleted, leaving just the participants' answers. Then these answers were transcribed into computer files containing the thousands of words used by each participant. Finally, the word files were analyzed by a computer program called "LIWC" (Linguistic Inquiry and Word Count; Pennebaker, Francis, & Booth, 2001). The program calculates the number of words that appear in each of a long list of categories. We also gathered personality ratings of each participant from

Table 6.2	PERSONALITY CORRELATES OF USING "CERTAINTY" WORDS IN A LIFE-HISTORY INTERVIEW

Informants' Q-Item Description	Correlation with Certainty Word Use
Positive correlates	
High intellectual capacity	.26
Verbally fluent	.25
Is turned to for advice and reassurance	.22
Has high aspiration level for self	.21
Concerned w/own body and its physiological functioning	.21
Behaves in a giving manner to others	.20
Behaves in an assertive fashion	.20
Straightforward and candid	.19
Negative correlates	
Is emotionally bland	−.23
Creates and exploits dependency	−.21
Repressive and dissociative tendencies	−.19

Note: All correlations are significant at $p < .01$. Examples of certainty words include "absolutely," "exact," "guarantee," "sure," and "truly."
Source: Adapted from Fast & Funder (2008), p. 340.

people who knew them well (I data; see Chapter 2), using the 100-item Q-sort described above.[4] Of course, these informants had not been present during the life history interview; they could base their ratings only on what they had observed during normal acquaintanceship with the participants.

One category counted by the LIWC program is "certainty words," which include (among others) "absolutely," "exact," "guarantee," "sure," and "truly." Who uses words like these when chatting about their life history? Perhaps these are people who are sure of themselves. Or, they might be people who are acting confident to cover up their insecurity. Since both possibilities seem plausible, we need to look at the data.

So, consider the findings summarized in **Table 6.2**. Not all of the Q-sort personality items were significantly correlated with word use, but many of them were (the table is a partial list). People who used a relatively large number of certainty words were described by their acquaintances as (among other attributes) intelligent, verbally fluent, the kind of person who is turned to for advice, ambitious,

---

[4] As you can tell, this project was a *lot* of work.

and generous. People who used such words relatively rarely were more likely to be described as emotionally bland, exploitative, and "repressive" (which means they tend to avoid recognizing unpleasant facts). And remember: the acquaintances who made these personality ratings were not present at the interview, so if they had ever heard the participant using certainty words, it was in real life, not in the lab.

Do these results tell us anything about the psychological meaning of using certainty words? You can come to your own conclusion. My own answer would be yes, to an extent. It does seem like people who use such words are not simply covering up their own insecurity. Overall, they appear to be smart and well functioning. But not quite all of the traits are consistent with this pattern. Why did people who were "concerned with own body and its physiological functioning" use more certainty words? I have absolutely no idea. So, while the overall pattern seems fairly clear, not everything completely fits. This is a typical result of research using the many-trait approach. Looking at the whole pattern is probably more informative than paying a lot of attention to occasional inconsistencies—which might, after all, just be due to chance.

Political Beliefs

An individual's political beliefs might be the last thing you would expect to be related to the personality she had as a child. Well, you would be wrong. Psychologists Jack and Jeanne Block assessed the personalities of a group of children in nursery school (J. Block & Block, 2006a, 2006b). Almost 20 years later, the same children, now grown up[5], completed a measure of their political beliefs. The measure included questions about abortion, welfare, national health insurance, rights of criminal suspects, and so forth. Each individual earned a score along a dimension from "liberal" to "conservative." This score turned out to have a remarkable set of personality correlates reaching back in time. Children who grew into political conservatives were likely to have been described *almost 20 years earlier* as tending to feel guilty, as anxious in unpredictable environments, and as unable to handle stress well. Those who grew into liberals, by contrast, were more likely to have been described years earlier as resourceful, independent, self-reliant, and confident.

What do these findings mean? One hint may come from the work of a group of psychologists (Adorno, Frenkel-Brunswik, Levinson, & Sanford, 1950) who wrote a book called *The Authoritarian Personality*, a classic of psychological research that culminated in the *California F scale* (F meaning "fascism"). This scale aimed to measure the basic antidemocratic psychological orientation that these researchers believed to be the common foundation of anti-Semitism, racial prejudice, and political *pseudoconservatism*—which they viewed as a pathological mutation of true (and nonpathological) political conservatism.

---

[5] Sort of.

More than 50 years after the concept was introduced, research on authoritarianism and related concepts continues at a steady pace, with more than 4,000 articles and counting.[6] Research since the time of the classic studies has shown that authoritarians tend to be uncooperative and inflexible when playing experimental games, and they are relatively likely to obey an authority figure's commands to harm another person (Elms & Milgram, 1966). They experience fewer positive emotions than nonauthoritarians (Van Hiel & Kossowska, 2006), are likely to oppose equal rights for transsexuals (Tee & Hegarty, 2006), and, if they are Americans, tended to favor the 2003 American military intervention in Iraq (Crowson, DeBacker, & Thoma, 2005). Authoritarians also watch more television (Shanahan, 1995)![7]

Research has explored the idea that authoritarians, deep inside, are afraid, and their attitudes stem from an attempt to lessen this fear. When authoritarians feel their standard of living is declining, that crime is getting worse, and that environmental quality is declining, they become six times more likely[8] to favor restrictions on welfare and eight times more likely to support laws to ban abortions (Rickert, 1998). When society is in turmoil and basic values are threatened, authoritarians become particularly likely to support "strong" candidates for office who make them feel secure, regardless of the candidate's party (McCann, 1990, 1997). Indeed, even communists can be authoritarian. A study conducted in Romania 10 years after the collapse of communist rule found that people who scored high on authoritarianism still believed in communist ideas (such as government ownership of factories), but also supported fascist political parties and candidates whose positions were at the opposite extreme (S. W. Krauss, 2002). The common thread seemed to be that the personalities of these people led them to crave strong leaders. They rather missed their communist dictators, it seemed, and wouldn't have minded substituting strong, fascist dictators instead of seemingly weak, democratic politicians.

The connection between fearfulness and this kind of pseudoconservatism (not actual conservatism) might help explain the connection between childhood personality and adult political beliefs found by the Blocks. As they wrote:

> Timorous conservatives of either gender will feel more comfortable and safer with already structured and predictable—therefore traditional— environments; they will tend to be resistant to change toward what might be self-threatening and forsaking of established modes of behavior; they will be attracted by and will tend to support decisive (if self-appointed) leaders who are presumed to have special and security-enhancing knowledge. (J. Block & Block, 2006a, p. 746)

---

[6] Instead of the classic F scale, much of this research uses an updated measure of "right-wing authoritarianism" (RWA) developed by Canadian psychologist Bob Altemeyer (1981, 1998).

[7] The data didn't say which channel, but do you want to guess?

[8] Compared to nonthreatened authoritarians or nonauthoritarians.

Liberals, by contrast, are motivated more by what the Blocks call "under-control," a desire for a wide range of gratifications soon. They seek and enjoy the good life, which is perhaps why so many of them drive brand-new Subarus and sip excellent Chardonnays.[9] As a result,

> Various justifications, not necessarily narrowly self-serving, will be con-fidently brought forward in support of alternative political principles ori-ented toward achieving a better life for all. Ironically, the sheer variety of changes and improvements suggested by the liberal-minded under-controller may explain the diffuseness, and subsequent ineffectiveness, of liberals in politics where a collective singlemindedness of purpose so often is required. (J. Block & Block, 2006a, p. 746)

Longitudinal research like the Blocks'—wherein the same people are followed and measured repeatedly from childhood to adulthood—is still much too rare (see Chapter 7), and no finding really should be trusted until it's been replicated, as was discussed in Chapter 3. But in the present case, I have some good news to report. A large longitudinal study attempted to replicate the findings just summarized—and largely succeeded. Not only did the new study—with a large sample of 708 children and their parents—obtain similar results, it also shed new light on what might be going on (Fraley, Griffin, Belsky, & Roisman, 2012). It turns out that the children with early emotional difficulties such as described by the Blocks were likely to have parents who themselves scored high on authoritarianism. Thus, the later political beliefs of their children might be associated with these early emotional traits, but could also be a direct result of absorbing the outlook of their parents and perhaps even genetic similarity. Two more recent, even larger studies (with more than 8,700 participants each) conducted in the United Kingdom also confirmed that early childhood personality is associated with later political beliefs (Lewis, 2018). Children described at ages 5 or 7 as anxious, misbe-haved, and hyperactive grew up to be adults who were discontented with the economic and political system.

> Although research on the personality correlates of political beliefs is fascinating, much of it leads to conclusions of the sort that should make you wary.

Although research on the personality correlates of political beliefs is fascinat-ing, much of it leads to conclusions of the sort that should make you wary. Most psychologists are political liberals, and so have a built-in readiness to conclude that conservatives are flawed in some way[10]. Would research done by a conservative psychologist—if you could find one—reach the same conclusion?

---

[9] This is my observation, not the Blocks'.

[10] Personally, I often find that there is something wrong with the people who disagree with me. Don't you?

Psychologist Jonathan Haidt has suggested that, rather than focus on the character flaws of people on one or the other side of an ideological divide, it might be more fruitful to understand how they favor different but equally defensible values (Haidt, 2008). His research shows that liberals and conservatives alike endorse values he calls *harm/care* (kindness, gentleness, nurturance) and *fairness/reciprocity* (justice, rights, and fair dealing). However, conservatives are also likely to strongly favor three other values that liberals regard as less important: *in-group loyalty* (taking care of members of one's own group and staying loyal), *authority/respect* (following the orders of legitimate leaders), and *purity* (living in a clean, moral way). These differences in values help to explain, for example, why conservatives in the United States get upset seeing someone burn an American flag, whereas liberals are more often baffled about why anybody would think it's a big deal.

Haidt's argument provides a useful counterpoint to the usual assumptions of political psychology, which sometimes comes uncomfortably close to treating conservatism as a pathology (Jost, Glaser, Kruglanski, & Sulloway, 2003). But it is not clear how far it can go toward explaining findings such as the childhood predictors and adult personality correlates of adult conservatism. These remain data that need to be accounted for. The next few years promise to be an exciting time at the intersection of politics and personality, both because more data and theory are coming out of psychological research, and because rapidly changing events are altering the context in which we think about politics.

THE ESSENTIAL-TRAIT APPROACH

The 100 personality characteristics in the Q-set are a lot by themselves, and a thorough survey of the literature of personality and clinical psychology would find many more. Recall Allport and Odbert's famous estimate of the number of traits in the dictionary: 17,953. For a long time, psychologists have suspected that this is entirely too many. Several important efforts have been made over the years to dismantle this Tower of Babel by discovering which traits are truly essential.

Reducing the Many to a Few: Theoretical Approaches

More than half a century ago, psychologist Henry Murray (inventor of the Thematic Apperception Test described in Chapter 3) theorized that 20 traits—he called them *needs*—were central to understanding personality (Murray, 1938). His list included needs for aggression, autonomy, exhibition, order, play, sex, and so on. Murray came up with this list theoretically—that is, by thinking about it.

Later, psychologists Jack and Jeanne Block – whose work on childhood antecedents of political beliefs was summarized earlier in this chapter – developed a theory that proposed just two essential characteristics of personality, called "ego resilience" (or psychological adjustment) and "ego control" (or impulse control) (J. Block, 2002; J. H. Block & Block, 1980; Letzring, Block, & Funder, 2005). A fundamental idea behind these constructs is the psychoanalytic—or Freudian (see Chapters 10 and 11)—concept that people constantly experience needs and impulses ranging from sexual drives to the desire to eat doughnuts. *Overcontrolled* people (those high in the ego-control dimension) inhibit these impulses, while *undercontrolled* individuals (low in ego control) are more prone to act on them immediately.

Is it better to be undercontrolled or overcontrolled? It depends: If nice things are safely available, you may as well take advantage of them, but if gratification is risky under the circumstances, self-control might be a better course. People high in the Blocks' other personality dimension, ego resilience, can adjust their level of control from high to low and back again as circumstances warrant. For example, an ego-resilient student might study hard all week (and thus be temporarily overcontrolled), and then cut loose on the weekends (and become temporarily, but appropriately, undercontrolled). As Jack Block once remarked, "undercontrol gets you into trouble, but resilience gets you out."

Reducing the Many to a Few: Factor Analytic Approaches

Other psychologists have tried to identify the essential traits of personality using factor analysis. The most significant early proponent was Raymond Cattell, who pioneered the development of this statistical technique prior to the computer age. As you may recall from Chapter 3, factor analysis involves correlating every measured variable with every other variable. The result is a *correlation matrix*. Correlation matrices can quickly get very large. Consider that a test with only 60 items would develop a correlation matrix with 1,770 non-redundant entries. According to legend, to factor analyze hundreds of items Cattell had to borrow the basketball court at the University of Illinois, the only place on campus with a floor large enough to lay out all of his calculations.[11] Beginning with a large number of traits that he considered important, Cattell concluded that 16 traits were essential. These included "friendliness," "intelligence," "stability," "sensitivity," and "dominance," among others (Cattell & Eber, 1961). However, in later years many psychologists concluded that Cattell's work "was characterized by an *overextraction* of factors" (Wiggins & Trapnell, 1997, p. 743)—that is, 16 is probably too many. Moreover, while Cattell's many statistical contributions continue to be admired,

---

[11] As you might expect, this cumbersome method appears to have led to some serious computational errors—which were not detected until computers came along, years later (Digman & Takemoto-Chock, 1981).

one psychologist wrote, "it is difficult to avoid the conclusion that Cattell's lists of variables and factors primarily represent those traits that he himself considered the most important" (John, 1990, p. 71).

An alternative early factor analytic proposal for the essential traits of personality identified only 3, rather than 16. According to Hans Eysenck, these were *extraversion, neuroticism* (or "unstable emotionality"), and a trait he (rather confusingly) labeled *psychoticism*, which he saw as a blend of aggressiveness, creativity, and impulsiveness (H. J. Eysenck, 1947; S. B. G. Eysenck & Long, 1986). More recently, Auke Tellegen updated this system. His Multidimensional Personality Questionnaire (Tellegen, 1982; for a shorter version see Donnellan, Conger, & Burzette, 2005) is organized around three "superfactors" called *positive emotionality, negative emotionality*, and *constraint*, which are roughly parallel to, but definitely better labeled than, Eysenck's three.

The Big Five and Beyond

DISCOVERY OF THE BIG FIVE At present, the most widely accepted factor analytic solution to the problem of reducing the trait lexicon is also the one that has the deepest historical roots. The search began with a simple but profound idea: If something is important, then people will have invented a word for it. For example, over the course of history people have observed water falling from the sky and found it useful to be able to talk about it; the word *rain* (and its equivalents in every other language) was invented. But that's not all: Water from the sky is so important that people also developed words for different forms, including sleet, drizzle, hail, and snow. As was mentioned in Chapter 4, the Eskimos are famous for having come up with an exceptional number of words to describe snow. The **lexical hypothesis** (Goldberg, 1981) is that the important aspects of human life will be labeled, and that if something is truly important and universal, many words for it will exist in all languages.

This hypothesis provides a unique route for identifying the most important personality traits. Which ones have the largest number of relevant words, and which ones are the most universal across languages? In principle, answering this question might seem straightforward, but psychologists have been struggling with it for more than 80 years (John & Srivastava, 1999). As Gordon Allport observed, after cataloging (with Henry Odbert's help) almost 18,000 personality-descriptive English words, finding the essential needles in that haystack could be the work of a lifetime. He was right. Allport started the project by identifying about 4,500 words (still a lot) that he thought were particularly good descriptors of personality traits. Raymond Cattell (who was mentioned above) selected from that list 35 traits he thought were especially important and focused his analyses on those. Donald Fiske (1949) chose 22 traits from Cattell's list and used them to analyze self-ratings along with ratings by peers and by psychologists. Fiske's analyses found five factors that may have been the first emergence of what is now known as the Big Five.[12] Later, a team of two psychologists examined data from eight different samples, including graduate students and Air Force personnel; they, too, found the same five basic factors (Tupes & Christal, 1961). Since then, the Big Five have been found again and again, using many different lists of traits and a wide range of samples of people (Saucier & Goldberg, 1996).[13]

In recent years, work on the Big Five has become a major focus of personality research. One reason is that when personality tests—not just words in the dictionary—are factor analyzed, a common finding is that they, too, tend to fall into groups defined by the Big Five (McCrae & Costa, 1987). These include the other lists of basic traits discussed earlier—Cattell's 16 traits and Tellegen's 3, among others, can be described in terms of one or more of the Big Five (John & Srivastava, 1999). As a result, the Big Five can be viewed as an integration rather than an opponent of these other systems (Saucier & Goldberg, 2003).

IMPLICATIONS OF THE BIG FIVE Although some researchers have suggested that the Big Five be referred to by Roman numerals I–V (John, 1990), the most common labels are *neuroticism*, *extraversion*, *agreeableness*, *conscientiousness*, and *openness* (or *intellect*); the labels vary somewhat from one investigator to the next. One of the original ideas behind these five basic factors is that they are *orthogonal*, which means that getting a high or low score on any one of them is not supposed to predict whether a person will get a high or low score on any of the others. That property makes this short list of traits useful because, together, they cover a wide swath and summarize much of what any test can measure. For example, we saw in Chapter 4 how the Big Five are useful in compiling lists of outcomes associated with personality, because they can bring a large number of otherwise divergent traits together under a few common labels (see **Table 4.6**). Indeed, one review concluded that Big Five traits could be used to predict outcomes such as career success and health as well or better than traditional predictors such as socioeconomic status and cognitive ability (Roberts et al., 2007).

The Big Five are not quite as simple as they may seem; their commonplace labels hide a good deal of complexity. For one thing, they aren't quite as orthogonal as originally hoped (Digman, 1997). Agreeableness, conscientiousness, and neuroticism (reversed, often called "emotional stability") go together to form one factor sometimes labeled *stability*, and extraversion and openness form a factor called *plasticity*. Psychologist Colin DeYoung suggests that these factors might have a biological basis (DeYoung, 2006, 2010); more will be said about this possibility in

---

[12] Yes, "Big Five" is traditionally capitalized. They're that big.
[13] You can take one of the most widely used measures, the Big Five Inventory (John, Donahue, & Kentle, 1991), online, for free, at www.outofservice.com/bigfive.

Figure 6.6 **The Other Big Five** I always thought the name referred to five basic types of sports, but it seems I was wrong—it refers to the chain's five original stores. Still, do you think there might be five basic types of sports?

Chapter 8. DeYoung's two broader traits look a lot like the two essential traits posited years ago by Jack and Jeanne Block (and discussed earlier in this chapter): Plasticity resembles ego resilience, and stability resembles ego control. And if you want to go even broader, some psychologists have argued that there is really just one underlying trait, which they call the *General Factor of Personality* (van der Linden et al., 2017). The general factor combines all five in the (traditionally) desirable direction: high extraversion, agreeableness, conscientiousness and openness, and low neuroticism. The core of this general factor, these psychologists suggest, is emotional intelligence, the ability to understand and regulate your own emotions and to be able to understand the feelings of others.

Going in the reverse direction, toward more specific traits, each of the Five is divided into six "facets" by some researchers (Costa & McCrae, 1995), into three facets by other researchers (Soto & John, 2017), and into two "aspects" by still other researchers (DeYoung, Quilty, & Peterson, 2007); see **Table 6.3**.[14] As researchers Gerard Saucier and Lewis Goldberg have written, "a broad factor [like one of the Big Five] is not so much one thing as a collection of many things that have something in common" (2003, p. 14). So, although the labels are useful, they are also necessarily oversimplified and potentially misleading (which is precisely why some psychologists have suggested using Roman numerals instead). With that in mind, let's give each of the Big Five a look under the hood.

Extraversion

EYSENCK'S VIEW OF EXTRAVERSION   The pioneering personality psychologist Hans Eysenck was one of the first to theorize about how extraverts might be different from introverts. His theory seems counterintuitive at first. He proposed that introverts react *more* strongly and often more negatively to bright lights, loud noises, strong tastes, and other kinds of sensory stimulation than do extraverts—a general idea that can be traced back to early work by Ivan Pavlov (1927). In a famous experiment, he showed that if you squirted lemon juice into the mouths of

---

[14] Please don't ask me to explain the difference between a "facet" and an "aspect."

Table 6.3 | FACETS AND ASPECTS OF THE BIG FIVE

Big Five Trait	Facets (Costa & McCrae, 1995)	Facets (Soto & John, 2017)	Aspects (DeYoung et al., 2007)
Extraversion	Warmth	Sociability	Enthusiasm
	Gregariousness	Assertiveness	Assertiveness
	Assertiveness	Energy level	
	Activity		
	Excitement seeking		
	Positive emotion		
Neuroticism	Anxiety	Anxiety	Volatility
	Hostility	Depression	Withdrawal
	Depression	Emotional volatility	
	Self-consciousness		
	Impulsiveness		
	Vulnerability to stress		
Agreeableness	Trust	Compassion	Compassion
	Straightforwardness	Respectfulness	Politeness
	Altruism	Trust	
	Compliance		
	Modesty		
	Tender-mindedness		
Conscientiousness	Competence	Organization	Industriousness
	Order	Productiveness	Orderliness
	Dutifulness	Responsibility	
	Achievement striving		
	Self-discipline		
	Deliberation		
Openness to Experience	Fantasy	Intellectual curiosity	Intellect
	Aesthetics	Aesthetic sensitivity	Openness
	Feelings	Creative imagination	
	Actions		
	Ideas		
	Values		

Note. Soto and John (2017) relabeled "Neuroticism" as "Negative emotionality," and "Openness to experience" as "Open-mindedness."

introverts, they salivated more than extroverts (S. B. G. Eysenck & Eysenck, 1967; G. D. Wilson, 1978).[15]

In daily life, according to Eysenck, extraverts and introverts are about equally stimulated when the environment is quiet and calm. But introverts react more quickly and more strongly to loud, bright, or exciting stimuli—or, even, as we just learned, sour tastes (Zuckerman, 1998). These reactions lead them to withdraw—the crowds, noise, excitement, and mouth-puckering lemony tastes are just too much—and exhibit the pattern of behavior we identify as introverted.

But extreme levels of stimulation are exactly what extraverts crave and need (Geen, 1984)—and this need can, according to one writer, even lead to a life of crime. "The vandal is a failed creative artist," who is bored, needs to be constantly stimulated, and "does not have the intellectual or other skills and capacities to amuse or occupy himself" (Apter, 1992, p. 198; Mealey, 1995). Eysenck also argued that a nervous system requiring extra stimulation can make a person dangerous. According to the "general arousal theory of criminality" (H. J. Eysenck & Gudjonsson, 1989, p. 118), such a person seeks out high-risk activities such as crime, drug use, gambling, and promiscuous sex. To prevent these people from becoming dangerous, according to another psychologist, perhaps they should be encouraged to enter stimulating but harmless professions such as stunt person, explorer, skydiving exhibitionist, or radio talk-show host (Mealey, 1995). Personally, I question this advice. Are radio talk-show hosts really harmless?

THE BIG FIVE VIEW OF EXTRAVERSION   The Big Five version of extraversion is somewhat different from Eysenck's, and definitely less dangerous-sounding. It encompasses traits such as "active," "outspoken," "dominant," "forceful," "adventurous," and even "spunky" (John & Srivastava, 1999). Some Big Five researchers describe extraverts as cheerful, upbeat, and optimistic (Costa & McCrae, 1985). Still others characterize them as ambitious, hardworking, and achievement oriented (Hogan, 1983; Tellegen, 1985; Watson & Clark, 1997, p. 769). These characteristics overlap, as you can see, and even though exact interpretations differ, the trait or something much like it shows up in just about every broad-based personality inventory, including Cattell's 16PF, Tellegen's MPQ, Douglas Jackson's Personality Research Form (PRF), Gough's CPI, and the MMPI (D. Watson & Clark, 1997).

Extraversion has a powerful influence on behavior. It actually takes effort for an extravert to act any other way—when forced to act like an introvert, extraverts get tired and revert, when allowed, to acting even more extraverted (Gallagher et al., 2011). They walk more quickly than introverts and, as they get older, this

---

[15] I guess it's OK to try this experiment with your introverted room-mate, but keep a towel nearby.

difference only increases: elderly extraverts walk much more quickly than elderly introverts (Stephan et al., 2017). Extraverts are prone to make moral judgments that hold people responsible for the effects of their actions, even if the effects were unintentional (Cokely & Feltz, 2009). Both male and female extraverts achieve higher social status than introverts (C. Anderson, John, Keltner, & Kring, 2001). Extraverts are consistently rated as more popular (Jensen-Campbell et al., 2002) and more physically attractive than introverts (they also exercise more); this may be why they attend more parties, where they drink more alcohol (Paunonen, 2003). But they had better be careful, because research also shows that extraverts are more likely to be on the receiving end of attempts to steal them away from their steady romantic part-ners (Schmitt & Buss, 2001). Some of these attempts at "mate poaching" (as the researchers call it) occur at parties, where drinking has been known to occur.

> Have you ever sat next to an extremely extraverted stranger on a long plane flight? Then you see the potential problem.

Extraverts may be especially sensitive to rewards (Denissen & Penke, 2008), or simply tend to experience positive emotions more (Watson & Clark, 1997). In daily speech they are more likely to use upbeat words like "adorable" than downbeat words such as "dreadful" (Augustine, Mehl, & Larsen, 2011). They like uncomplicated and relaxing music, especially performed by folksingers who write their own songs (Nave, Minxha, Greenberg, Kosinski, Stillwell, & Renfrow, 2018). Extraverts tend to be happier than introverts. Part of the reason is extra-verts are more sociable and their social activity makes them happy (Eaton & Funder, 2003; Wilt, Noftle, Fleeson, & Spain, 2011). They are also more likely to spend their money, when they have it, on experiences such as food, travel, and other positive experiences, rather than on material things—a priority that has been shown to increase happiness (Howell, Pchelin, & Iyer, 2011). But in addi-tion to that, extraversion may have a direct, perhaps even biological, connection with positive emotions. Even when the amount of social activity was (statisti-cally) held constant, extraversion still correlated with happiness (Lucas, Le, & Dyrenforth, 2008).

However, here goes Funder's First Law again: Even extraversion has its down side. People high in this trait can be argumentative, to need to be in control too much, and to not manage their time effectively (Boudreaux, Piedmont, & Sherman, 2011). Extraverts are also at risk for becoming overweight[16] (Sutin, Ferruci, Zonderman, & Terracciano, 2011). While extraverts can be good salespeople, that's true only to a point. Potential customers find overly extraverted salespeople annoying (Grant, 2013), and have you ever sat next to an extremely extraverted stranger on a long plane flight? Then you see the potential problem here.

---

[16] Even though, as was mentioned above, they tend to exercise more. Go figure.

Neuroticism

Neuroticism is another Big Five trait with wide implications. Persons who score high on this trait tend to deal ineffectively with problems in their lives and react more negatively to stressful events (Bolger & Zuckerman, 1995; Ferguson, 2001). They are particularly sensitive to social threats, such as indications that other people do not accept or support them (Denissen & Penke, 2008).

It turns out that numerous questionnaires intended to assess happiness, well-being, and physical health correlate strongly (and negatively) with neuroticism (sometimes, and less pejoratively, called *negative emotionality*). The higher the level of neuroticism, the more likely people are to report being unhappy, anxious, and even physically sick (McCrae & Costa, 1991; D. Watson & Clark, 1984). This finding implies that many of these instruments, despite their different intentions and titles, may be, to some degree, measuring the same underlying tendency. Some people (those scoring high on neuroticism) complain a lot about nearly everything; others (those scoring low in neuroticism) complain less.

Because it correlates with so many other measures of unhappiness, anxiety, and other indicators of psychological difficulty, neuroticism appears to capture a general tendency toward psychopathology (Barlow, Ellard, Sauer-Zavala, Bullis, & Carl, 2014). In the long run, this tendency may put someone scoring high on neuroticism at higher risk for developing a serious mental illness. In the short run, it can make a person vulnerable in other ways. For example, people scoring high on neuroticism are not especially likely to have people try to "poach" them away from their romantic partners. But if someone does make a move, they are less likely to resist (Schmitt & Buss, 2001). People high on neuroticism also report feeling stressed, taking things too seriously, being unable to handle criticism, and even feeling oppressed by life (Boudreaux et al., 2011).

Not surprisingly, neuroticism is associated with several undesirable life outcomes (Ozer & Benet-Martínez, 2006). People who score high on this trait are more likely to be unhappy, to have problems in their family relationships, to be dissatisfied with their jobs, and even to engage in criminal behavior. This last finding requires a caution concerning how to interpret correlations such as those summarized in this chapter: Most neurotics are not criminals! However, people who score high on measures of neuroticism are *more* likely to engage in criminal behavior than people who score lower. It is this kind of relative likelihood that is reflected by correlations between traits and life outcomes.

Conscientiousness

The trait of conscientiousness comprises being dutiful, careful, rule-abiding and, some evidence shows, ambitious. The trait has even been measured in animals. Surprisingly many studies (876!) have examined facets of this trait in a large number of non-human species. What does a conscientious animal do? According to a major review, conscientiousness in animals reveals itself through behaviors including speed in foraging, care in nest building, careful decision making (in guppies), and willingness (of bees) to do their job to protect the hive (Delgado & Sulloway, 2017).

Returning to what conscientious humans do, evidence to be reviewed in Chapter 16 consistently shows that people who score high in conscientiousness are usually valued employees who can be trusted to show up on time, do as they are told, and not steal anything. But that's not all. Conscientiousness has many implications beyond job performance. For example, people who score high in conscientiousness are careful and considerate drivers, and so get in fewer accidents. Yet they are more likely to carry a lot of car insurance, a behavior that economists consider paradoxical. From a strictly economic point of view, it actually makes more sense for high-risk people to do so. After all, who needs car insurance more than a reckless driver? Perhaps all is explained by conscientiousness: Highly conscientious people both avoid risks and seek to protect themselves just in case, so they are the ones who drive carefully *and* carry lots of insurance (Caplan, 2003).

Moreover, conscientious people live longer, and not just because they drive more carefully—though that surely helps (H. S. Friedman et al., 1993). A major analysis of 194 studies found that highly conscientious people are more likely to avoid many kinds of risky behavior as well as to engage in activities that are good for their health (Bogg & Roberts, 2004). They are less likely to smoke, overeat, or use alcohol to excess. They avoid violence, risky sex, and drug abuse. They are more likely to exercise regularly. More will be said about the implications of conscientiousness for health in Chapter 17.

Despite all these advantages, the trait does have a few downsides: Highly conscientious people are prone to feel guilty when they don't live up to expectations (Fayard, Roberts, Robins, & Watson, 2012), and are especially likely to suffer psychologically if they become unemployed—their satisfaction with life decreases 120 percent more than less conscientious people (Boyce, Wood, & Brown, 2010). Moreover, conscientious people are not necessarily popular (van der Linden, Scholte, Cillessen, te Nijenhuis, & Segers, 2010) and, when they try to work together in a group, their output might not be very creative (Robert & Cheung, 2010). They also tend to be conforming and not rebellious; they can generally be trusted to follow orders. That is not always a good thing, is it?

Agreeableness

This dimension of the Big Five has carried several labels over the years including *conformity*, *friendly compliance*, *likeability*, *warmth*, and even *love* (Graziano & Eisenberg, 1997). And some research has separated agreeableness out into facets called *compassion*, *morality*, *trust*, *affability*, and *modesty* (Crowe, Lynam, & Miller,

2017). Psychologist Robert Hogan (1983) suggests that the core of agreeableness is a tendency to be cooperative, an essential behavior in the small social groups in which humans have lived during most of evolutionary history. Thus, the emergence of the *agreeableness* factor—or whatever you want to call it—reflects how important it is for people to get along and work together. The different aspects of agreeableness sometimes have different implications. People high in *compassion* tend to be politically liberal and egalitarian, whereas people high in the other aspect of agreeableness, *politeness*, are more likely to be conservative and traditional (Hirsh, DeYoung, Xu, & Peterson, 2010).

Acquaintances pay attention to who is and is not agreeable and generally reach consensus about who can be described in this way (Graziano & Eisenberg, 1997). For their part, agreeable people rate other people more positively than disagreeable people do (Wood, Harms, & Vazire, 2010), say nice things more often than mean things (Augustine et al., 2011), smoke less (for some unknown reason), and women tend to score higher than men (Paunonen, 2003).

Agreeableness predicts a large number of life outcomes (Ozer & Benet-Martínez, 2006). People high in this trait are more likely to be involved in religious activities, have a good sense of humor, be psychologically well adjusted, and have a healthy heart. They go out of their way to look at pleasant rather than unpleasant things (Bresin & Robinson, 2014). Agreeable people recover more quickly from disabling accidents or illnesses (Boyce & Wood, 2011). They enjoy more peer acceptance and dating satisfaction, have a large number of social interests, and are unlikely to engage in criminal behavior. Newlywed couples where the wife is high in agreeableness have more frequent sex (Meltzer & McNulty, 2016). Clearly, it is important—and usually beneficial—to be easy to get along with.

Agreeableness can also make children less vulnerable. One study examined children who had "internalizing problems," which meant that other children described them using phrases such as "on the playground, she/he just stands around," "she/he is afraid to do things," "she/he seems unhappy and looks sad often," and "when other kids are playing, she/he watches them but doesn't join in" (Jensen-Campbell et al., 2002, p. 236). In general, this pattern described children who tended to be victims of bullying, but *not* if they were also agreeable. Similarly, children who were physically weak or otherwise lacked social skills managed to avoid being bullied if they were high in agreeableness. Apparently, a friendly and nonconfrontational outlook can help protect you from abuse—but it won't win you social status. For that, extraversion is necessary, too (Anderson et al., 2001). Research has not yet addressed whether these findings apply to college students or working adults. Do you think they would?

Agreeableness has its limits. When agreeable people who are married or in committed relationships are approached by somebody attempting to entice them into an affair, they are more likely to tell him or her to get lost (Schmitt & Buss, 2001). In other words, agreeable people don't agree to absolutely everything.

> Agreeable people don't agree to absolutely everything.

Openness to Experience/Culture/Intellect

Opennness to experience, also sometimes called *culture* or *intellect*, is the most controversial of the Big Five, as is perhaps revealed by the fact that I felt obligated to label this section with three different terms. People scoring high on openness are viewed by others as creative, imaginative, open minded, and clever. They are more prone than most people to be politically liberal, to use drugs, and to play a musical instrument (Ozer & Benet-Martínez, 2006; Paunonen, 2003). They like to listen to opera, jazz, classical, and other kinds of so-called "sophisticated" music (Nave et al., 2018). They appreciate nature, so they are active in environmental causes (Markowitz, Goldberg, Ashton, & Lee, 2012). But, as the prominent Big Five researchers Robert McCrae and Paul Costa have written, "the concept of Openness[17] appears to be unusually difficult to grasp" (1997, p. 826). The difficulty arises in part because some researchers view the trait as reflecting a person's approach to intellectual matters or even her basic level of intelligence, while others see it as a result of the degree to which one has been taught to value aspects of culture such as literature, art, and music. Still others see openness to experience as a basic dimension of personality that underlies creativity and perceptiveness. Another reason this dimension is controversial is that, among the Big Five, it has the spottiest record of replication across different samples and different cultures (John & Srivastava, 1999).

Still, it is interesting. McCrae and Costa (1997) argue that people can score high on openness to experience *without* necessarily being "cultured" in their education and background, and even without being particularly intelligent. Being open minded does not make you right, and can sometimes imply the reverse. College students higher in openness to experience are more likely to believe in UFOs, astrology, and the existence of ghosts (Epstein & Meier, 1989). At the same time, persons high in this trait are described as imaginative, intelligent, original, curious, artistic, inventive, and witty, and they are unlikely to be viewed as simple, shallow, or unintelligent. So, McCrae and Costa (1997) may be correct that you don't have to be intelligent to be open to experience, but people high in openness are generally viewed as intelligent. Their curious and exploring approach to life leads people high in openness to know many things in many domains, but that tendency may actually mislead them into thinking they know more than they really do. People high in openness are prone to "overclaim," that is, to state that they are familiar with facts or even pictures that they actually have not seen before

---

[17] Hard-core adherents of the Big Five approach often capitalize the names of the traits. But I don't.

"Let's go somewhere fun and not really experience it."

(Dunlop, et al, 2017). This might be why they sometimes admit to having an overactive imagination and "being too smart for my own good" (Boudreaux et al., 2011). Finally, people high in openness report more frequent substance abuse and a tendency to feel "inspired"—I won't comment on any possible connection between these last two findings.

Beyond the Big Five

Although the Big Five have proved useful, they also remain controversial in some circles (J. Block, 1995, 2010). A central objection is that there is more to personality than just five traits. Even advocates acknowledge that the list may not encompass attributes such as sensuality, frugality, humor, and cunning (Saucier & Goldberg, 1998). Psychologists Sampo Paunonen and Douglas Jackson performed factor analyses aimed at the part of personality missed by the Big Five, and found 10 additional factors, including seductiveness, manipulativeness, integrity, and religiosity (Paunonen & Jackson, 2000). Studies conducted in several languages suggest that a sixth factor called "honesty-humility" should be added (Ashton & Lee, 2005), and further analyses suggest that several traits Paunonen and Jackson identified as missing from the Big Five can be included under this label (K. Lee, Ogunfowora, & Ashton, 2005). For example, highly religious people tend to score high on honesty-humility, whereas manipulative people score low. On the other hand, the honesty-humility dimension correlates with the agreeableness factor of the Big Five (honest and humble people are more agreeable), so we can look forward to years of debate as to whether the Big Five has to be expanded to a Big Six.[18] Actually, the proposed label is not Big Six, but rather HEXACO, which stands for honesty-humility (H), emotionality (E), extraversion (X), agreeableness (A), conscientiousness (C), and openness (O) (K. Lee & Ashton, 2004).

A further issue concerns the degree to which broad traits at the level of the Big Five (or six) are sufficient for really understanding people. For example, one could summarize narcissism, discussed earlier in this chapter, as a combination of high extraversion, low conscientiousness, low openness, and low agreeableness (and/or low humility), but that summary seems to miss the essence of the construct. Similarly, self-monitoring could be recast as a combination of high extraversion and high agreeableness, but that summary also seems insufficient. And, for one more example, the trait of "ambition" seems to not map neatly onto the Big Five,

---

[18] Won't that be fun.

since it seems to be a combination of parts (but not all of) high conscientiousness and high extraversion, along with a strong desire to lead and be successful, and a high amount of self-control (Jones, Sherman & Hogan, 2016). This is the reason the Big Five are frequently broken down into "facets" or "aspects," as we have seen, but it remains doubtful that even such smaller pieces of the Big Five can be added up to yield all the ways in which personality can differ.

Despite these shortcomings, the Big Five keep popping up no matter what measures are used or which populations are studied, leading some psychologists to consider these traits as the essential "structure" of personality. But, as Costa and McCrae noted,

> The organization of specific traits into broad factors [such as the Big Five] is traditionally called the *structure of personality*, although it refers to the structure of traits in a population, not in an individual. (Costa & McCrae, 1998, pp. 107–108)

In other words, the Big Five are types of traits, not of people. Are there types of people, and can their distinct personality structures be characterized? That is the question we shall consider next.

TYPOLOGICAL APPROACHES TO PERSONALITY

Over the years of successfully applying the three trait approaches, some psychologists have occasionally expressed misgivings about the whole enterprise. First, as just noted, the structure of personality traits across many individuals is not the same thing as the structure of personality as it resides *within* a person, and it seems a little strange to call the former the "structure of personality" (Cervone, 2005). Second, it is at least possible that important differences between people are not just quantitative but qualitative. The trait approach typically assumes that all people can be characterized on a common scale. You might score high on extraversion and I might score low, but at least we are being compared on the same scale. But what if some differences between people are matters not of degree but of kind? If your extraversion is fundamentally different from my shyness, then to summarize this difference by comparing our extraversion scores might be a little like comparing apples to oranges by giving both of them scores in "appleness" and concluding that oranges score lower.

Evaluating Typologies

Of course, it is one thing to raise doubts like these and quite another to say what the essential types of people really are. To typify all individuals, one must "carve nature at its joints" (as Plato reportedly said). Just as an expert turkey carver, by knowing where to cut, can give all the guests a nice, clean piece of breast or a neatly separated drumstick, a scientist must find the exact dividing lines that distinguish one type of person from another in order for these types to be clearly identified. The further challenge is to show that these divisions are not just a matter of degree, that different types of people are qualitatively—rather than quantitatively—distinct. Repeated attempts at this carving did not achieve notable success over the years, leading one reviewer to summarize the literature in the following manner:

> Muhammad Ali was reputed to offer this typology: People come in four types, the pomegranate (hard on the outside, hard on the inside), the walnut (hard-soft), the prune (soft-hard), and the grape (soft-soft). As typologies go, it's not bad—certainly there is no empirical reason to think it any worse than those we may be tempted to take more seriously. (Mendelsohn, Weiss, & Feimer, 1982, p. 1169)

Nonetheless, interest in typological conceptions of personality revived a bit (Kagan, 1994; Robins, John, & Caspi, 1998) after psychologist Avshalom Caspi (1998) reported some surprising progress: Across seven different studies with diverse participants all over the world, three types showed up again and again. One of the types is the *well-adjusted* person, who is adaptable, flexible, resourceful, and interpersonally successful. Then there are two maladjusted types: The *maladjusted overcontrolling* person is too uptight for his own good, denying himself pleasure needlessly, and being difficult to deal with on an interpersonal level. The *maladjusted undercontrolling* person has the reverse problem. She is too impulsive, prone to be involved in activities such as crime and unsafe sex, and tends to wreak general havoc on other people and herself. This is an interesting typology because it suggests that there is one way to be well adjusted, but two ways to have psychological problems.

The types received wide attention by researchers and were found repeatedly in samples of participants in North America and Europe (Alessandri et al., 2014; Asendorpf & van Aken, 1999; Asendorpf, Borkenau, Ostendorf, & van Aken, 2001). One analysis showed that people classified into a particular type were likely to belong to the same type four years later (Specht, Luhmann, & Geiser, 2014). But older people were less likely to belong to the undercontrolled type, and more likely to belong to the well-adjusted, or (as these investigators called it) "resilient" type than younger people.

Other work limits these conclusions in an important way. When thinking about personality types, one should keep two questions in mind. The first is, are different types of people, as identified by the typological approach, qualitatively and not just quantitatively different from each other? That is, are they different from each other in ways that conventional trait measurements cannot capture? The possibility that this is the case—the apples-versus-oranges issue—is a big part of the reason for why psychologists viewed personality types as potentially important. However, the answer to this question turned out to be no. The latest evidence indicates that knowing a person's personality type adds little or nothing to the ability to predict his behavior or life outcomes, beyond what can be done using the traits that define the typology (Costa, Herbst, McCrae, Samuels, & Ozer, 2002; McCrae, Terracciano, Costa, & Ozer, 2006).

A second important limitation of personality types is more technical. On many measures, the type a person is categorized to belong to is determined by a cut-off score. For example, imagine a 25-item test of friendliness in which different people earn scores anywhere between 0 and 25. Scores on almost every measure of anything turn out to be "normally distributed" which simply means that, as in **Figure 6.7,** most people score towards the middle and fewer score extremely high or low. In other words, on most things, most people are pretty average. Now imagine, as is sometimes done, a psychologist wanted to call everybody who scored 12 or above as "Friendly" and everybody who scored 11 or below "Unfriendly." This

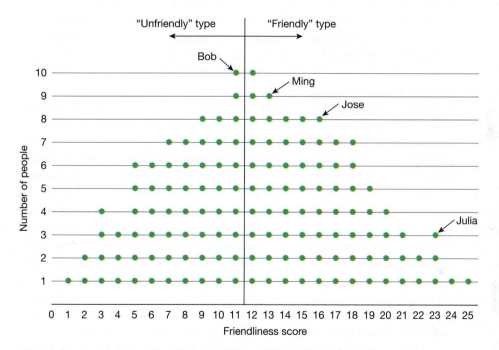

Figure 6.7 Cutoff scores and Type Indicators The figure illustrates one problem with personality typologies when based on cutoff scores. In this hypothetical example, people who score above average are described as belonging to the Friendly type, and those below to the Unfriendly type. But notice that Bob and Ming are only 2 points apart on the measure of friendliness, but classified as different types, whereas Jose and Julia are 7 points apart and classified as the same type!

would be a typological approach, and potentially very misleading, because notice that Bob (who scored 11) and Ming (who scored 13) are categorized as being different types because they fall on different sides of the line, but Jose (who scored 16) and Julia (who scored 23) are categorized as the same type because they are on the same side of the line. But Jose and Julia's scores are much further apart than Bob and Ming's! This is actually a pretty common problem with typological measures, because measures with a "bimodal distribution" — where most scores are either very high or very low, with few in the middle, are quite rare.

The Myers-Briggs Type Indicator

One particular measure of personality types deserves consideration here, if for no other reason than because it is so popular. The Myers-Briggs Type Indicator (MBTI; Myers & McCaulley, 1985) is given to millions of people every year in workplaces, schools, counseling centers, and management workshops (Pittinger, 1993). And not for free. The MBTI is a big business, with certified trainers and a network of marketers selling it as an ideal guide for career guidance and self-development. It's very possible you have already encountered it yourself.

In case you haven't, here is what it is like. The MBTI presents 166 items (only 95 of which are scored[19]) that force the test taker to make choices such as, "Which word in each pair appeals to you more? (a) Sociable (b) Detached." The test is intended to measure which of two opposing tendencies, in four pairs, better characterize you. The four pairs are Extroversion[20] (E) vs. Introversion (I), Sensing (S) vs. Intuition (N), Thinking (T) vs. Feeling (F), and Judgment (J) vs. Perception (P). For example, in the sample item above, the (a) choice points towards Extroversion, and the (b) choice points toward Introversion. The final result places you into one of 16 possible personality types, so you might be described as an ESTJ or and ISTJ or some other combination.

The test's popularity stems, in part, from the seemingly rich and intriguing descriptions that it offers. An ESTJ, for example, is described as someone who reacts to the world rather than what is in her head, focuses on what can be seen rather than on her intuitions, is rational rather than emotional, and makes decisions by thinking and feeling, rather than by sensing and intuiting. The fact that many of the items on the MBTI are vague and difficult to answer seems to give the impression that it offers especially deep insight (Stein & Swan, 2018). Another reason for the test's popularity is probably that there are no bad scores, something that the tests' authors have been quite explicit about. Each type is a "different gift" (Myers, 1980), so nobody is ever unhappy with their test results. That's wonderful, I suppose, but it does not make the MBTI very useful for selection or predicting life outcomes.

---

[19] Nobody seems to know why; the Manual does not explain why almost half the items on the test are ignored (Sipps et al., 1985).
[20] This spelling of "extroversion" is unusual in psychology, but not wrong.

The MBTI has been criticized on other grounds as well (for a summary see Pittinger, 1993). Perhaps the most obvious problem is the same one that was described a few paragraphs ago and illustrated in **Figure 6.7**. The scores on the various scales of the MBTI are distributed normally, not bimodally, which means that two people both classified as E could be more different from each other than two people who are classified as E and I. A second problem is that although MBTI types are described as fundamental aspects of personality, the measurement is not reliable, in the sense described in Chapter 2. Specifically, if you were to be categorized as one type today, and you take the test again in five weeks, there is about a 50% chance you will be categorized as a different type, especially if you are in a different mood (Howes & Carskadon, 1979). Finally, the whole theory of using types for occupational guidance assumes that different MBTI types follow, persist in, or succeed in different lines of work. Yet there is no evidence this is so (Pittinger, 1993). For example, the ESTJ type is sometimes described as well suited for the teaching profession, but about 12 percent of the population are ESTJ's, and so are about 12 percent of all teachers!

So perhaps the MBTI should carry a label, "for entertainment purposes only." Because, indeed, many people seem to find learning their MBTI types to be enjoyable. Then again, many people enjoy reading their horoscopes too.

> Perhaps the MBTI should carry a label, "for entertainment purposes only."

Uses of Personality Types

As we have now seen, there are many reasons to be skeptical of the typological approach to personality in general, and the MBTI in particular. Still, a further question remains: Is it at all useful to think about people in terms of personality types? Despite everything, the answer to this question may still be yes (Asendorpf, 2002; Costa et al., 2002). Each personality type serves as a summary of how a person stands on a large number of traits. The adjusted, overcontrolled, and undercontrolled patterns are rich portraits that make it easy to think about how the traits within each type tend to be found together, and how they interact. In the same way, thinking of people in terms of whether they are "military types," "rebellious student types," or "hassled suburban soccer mom types" brings to mind an array of traits in each case that would be cumbersome, though not impossible, to summarize in terms of ratings on each dimension. Advertisers and political consultants, in particular, often design their campaigns to appeal to specific types of people. For this reason, it has been suggested that types may be useful in the way they summarize "many traits in a single label" (Costa et al., 2002, p. 573) and make it easier to think about psychological dynamics. Even though types may not add much for conventional psychometric measurement and prediction, they may still be useful for education and applications such as advertising.

FROM ASSESSMENT TO UNDERSTANDING

The usefulness of personality assessment goes beyond its ability to predict behavior, performance, and life outcomes. When we learn which personality traits are associated with which behaviors, we can learn about why people do what they do. We have seen how personality assessment can shed light on the mechanisms of self-presentation, the roots of political beliefs, how people use language, and other aspects of human psychology. This kind of increased understanding is the most important goal of science.

WRAPPING IT UP

SUMMARY

- Traits are useful not just for predicting behavior, but also for increasing our understanding of the reasons for behavior. This chapter examined four basic approaches to the study of traits.

The Single-Trait Approach

- The single-trait approach zeros in on one particular trait and its consequences for behavior; this approach has been used to study self-monitoring and narcissism, among many others.

The Many-Trait Approach

- The many-trait approach looks at the relationship between a particular behavior and as many different traits as possible. One test used in this approach, the California Q-Set, assesses 100 different personality characteristics at once. The Q-sort has been used to explore the bases of word use and political ideology, among other topics.

The Essential-Trait Approach

- The essential-trait approach attempts to identify the few traits, out of the thousands of possibilities, that are truly central to understanding all of the others. The most widely accepted essential trait list is the Big Five, which identifies extraversion, neuroticism, conscientiousness, agreeableness, and openness as broad traits that can organize the understanding of personality.

- Some researchers argue that a sixth basic trait, called honesty/humility, should be added to the Big Five.

- While the Big Five are useful for organizing the many findings of personality research, they are probably still not sufficient to describe all the ways in which people are psychologically different from each other.

Typological Approaches to Personality

- The typological approach attempts to capture the ways people might differ in kind, not just in degree. Research has identified three basic types of personality: well adjusted, maladjusted overcontrolled, and maladjusted undercontrolled. However, these types add little, if any, predictive validity to what can be achieved using trait measures.

- A particular problem with personality typologies is that when people are sorted into types based on cutoff scores, a common practice, people classified together as the same type are often more different from each other than people classified as being different types.

- The Myers-Briggs Type Indicator is very popular and widely used, but has seriously shortcomings of reliability and validity, and should probably be used only for entertainment.

From Assessment to Understanding

- Personality assessment is not an end in itself but should be a tool for psychological understanding.

KEY TERMS

single-trait approach, p. 185
many-trait approach, p. 185
essential-trait approach, p. 185
typological approach, p. 186
California Q-Set, p. 197
lexical hypothesis, p. 206

THINK ABOUT IT

1. From the examples in this chapter, which approach do you find yields the most insight: the single-trait, the many-trait, or the essential-trait approach?

2. If you could choose, would you rather be a high or low self-monitor? According to Try for Yourself 6.1, which are you?

3. Do you think people are more narcissistic than they used to be? Try asking your parents (or your professors) this question.

4. Do you know people who abuse drugs? From your experience, what personality traits are associated with drug use? Are these traits a cause of drug abuse, a result of drug abuse, or both?

5. It has been suggested that the study of the personality antecedents for political orientation tends to paint an unfair picture of political conservatives. Do you agree? What other interpretations could be made of the data?

6. Rate yourself or a good friend on the five essential traits of personality (the Big Five). You can use a 1–5 scale or rate your target as "high" or "low" on each. Do these ratings contain useful information? What aspects of personality do they leave out?

7. If you have ever lived in a different country than you do now, or in different parts of the country, have you found that people in different places have different personalities? If so, in what ways? Why do you think this is?

8. Do you think it is possible to be creative (artistic) without being particularly intelligent?

9. A recent study experimented with various slogans for a fictitious product[21] called the Xphone (Hirsh, Kang, & Bodenhausen, 2012). Different slogans worked best depending on the recipient's personality. The best slogans (slightly abbreviated) for people high in each of the Big Five traits were as follows:
   - Extraversion: "With the Xphone, you'll always be where the excitement is."
   - Neuroticism: "Stay safe and secure with the Xphone."
   - Agreeableness: "Xphone helps you take the time for the people you care most about."
   - Conscientiousness: "Organize your life with the Xphone."
   - Openness: "Xphone helps you channel your imagination where it leads you."
   What is it about these slogans that makes them appeal to people with these traits?

---

[21]For now

10. Have you taken the Myers-Briggs Type Inventory? What was your type, or if you haven't taken the test, what do you think your type would be? Would describing yourself as this type be useful? For what purposes?

SUGGESTED RESOURCES

Online

Big Five Personality Test

If you are curious about your own scores on the Big Five personality traits, you can take one widely used test here, for free:

http://www.outofservice.com/bigfive

Summary of Myers-Briggs Critiques

The chapter is pretty critical of the Myers-Briggs Type Indicator. For a summary of even more criticisms, see:

http://www.teamtechnology.co.uk/myers-briggs-criticisms.html

Myers-Briggs Website

And, for balance, here is the website of the MBTI publishers:

http://www.myersbriggs.org/my-mbti-personality-type/mbti-basics/the-16-mbti-types.htm?bhcp=1

Print

Allport, G. W. (1937). *Personality: A psychological interpretation*. New York: Holt, Rinehart, & Winston.

The classic and perhaps still best presentation of how trait psychologists think about personality.

Snyder, M. (1987). *Public appearances, private realities: The psychology of self-monitoring*. New York: Freeman.

A summary, by the test's originator, of the research stimulated by the self-monitoring scale. The book goes beyond test-relevant issues and has much to say about basic topics in social psychology, notably self-presentation.

Twenge, J. M. (2006). *Generation me: Why today's young Americans are more confident, assertive, entitled—and more miserable than ever before*. New York: Free Press.

A highly readable and interesting summary of the argument that narcissism is on the upswing in the United States, and discussion of the implications of this trend. Be aware, however, that the conclusions reached in this book are controversial among psychologists.

Want to earn a better grade on your test?
Go to **INQUIZITIVE** to learn and review this chapter's content, with personalized feedback along the way.

7

PERSONALITY STABILITY, DEVELOPMENT, AND CHANGE

"The more things change, the more they stay the same"[1]
—JEAN-BAPTISTE ALPHONSE KARR

YOU ARE NOT EXACTLY the same as you were five years ago, and you will almost certainly be at least somewhat different five years from now. Yet you will still feel like—and you will be—the same person. The paradox between these two facts lies at the core of the study of personality development. People change their personalities throughout their lives, sometimes in response to dramatic events and sometimes seemingly just because of the passage of time. Yet fundamental traits remain consistent. Indeed, changing personality, on purpose, is difficult. But it's not impossible, as we shall see.

The present chapter begins with a survey of the evidence concerning the stability of personality, the traits that remain relatively unchanged across decades. Notice I said "relatively" unchanged. Relatively tall children tend to become relatively tall adults, even though they and their shorter friends are both growing. Similarly, differences in personality generally are consistent over time, even while everybody is changing from adolescents to adults to senior citizens. Addressing this point, the second part of the chapter summarizes how personality changes systematically, or "develops" across the life span. In most cases, personality becomes both more stable and more "mature" (we will consider what this means) as the individual gets older. Finally, the chapter considers the possibilities for personality change. If you want to affect the way someone's personality develops—or if you want to change your own personality—is this possible? If so, how? And, on balance, is personality change a good thing or bad?

---

[1] Or, if you prefer the original : *"Plus ça change, plus c'est la même chose."*

PERSONALITY STABILITY

People tend to maintain their distinctive patterns of behavior throughout life. A child who is more extraverted than most other children is likely, when she gets older, to be more extraverted than most other adolescents, more extraverted than most other adults, and finally, when the time comes, more extraverted than most fellow residents of the Golden Acres Retirement Home. Likewise, a child who is either more or less neurotic, agreeable, conscientious, or open than his peers is likely to maintain this distinction throughout life, too (Costa & McCrae, 1994). Psychologists call this kind of stability **rank-order consistency.** Like the consistency of personality in general (see Chapter 4), it does not mean people do not change over the years. It just means they tend to maintain the ways in which they are *different* from other people the same age.

Evidence for Stability

The evidence for this kind of stability is widespread and impressive. In one study, personality trait scores from the same people measured 10 years apart correlated between $r = .60$ and $r = .90$, which are high numbers by any standard (Hopwood et al., 2013). In another study, elementary school children described by their teachers as especially "adaptable" were seen (in a videotaped interview) to act in a relatively cheerful and intellectually curious manner when they were middle-aged adults, and children rated as "impulsive" were seen, decades later, to talk more and in a louder voice than most other adults the same age (Nave, Sherman, & Funder, 2010). Even people who experience natural disasters such as earthquakes often turn out to be resilient; despite everything, most manage to maintain their core personality traits (Milojev, Osborne, & Sibley, 2014).

It is also possible to predict adult life outcomes on the basis of personality ratings in childhood. For example, 4- to 6-year-old children rated as more "inhibited" than most of their peers were slower to find a stable romantic partner and slower to find a first job 19 years later, compared to children rated as less inhibited (Asendorpf, Denissen, & van Aken, 2008). In general, children with extreme scores on trait ratings, or those who were rated as especially "difficult," tend to have problems after they grow up (Van den Akker et al., 2013).

Personality disorders are generally stable across the life span—though not as stable as basic personality traits—and being in therapy doesn't seem to make much difference (Ferguson, 2010; Hopwood, et al., 2013; see also Chapter 17). On a more positive note, 8- to 12 year-old children who received high ratings on traits such as "mastery motivation" (the desire to learn from failure) and agreeableness were found, 20 years later, to have greater achievement in school and at work, less antisocial conduct, and better relationships with their romantic partners and friends (Shiner, Masten, & Roberts, 2003).

Causes of Stability

What keeps personality so stable over such long periods of time? There are several causes.

FROM TEMPERAMENT TO PERSONALITY First, and perhaps most obviously, many aspects of the individual that affect his or her personality remain constant for years. Some of these pertain to the individual's physical body, including his or her DNA.[2] The personality that one begins with—which is traditionally called **temperament** in young children—is to some degree determined by the genes inherited from one's parents. Fundamental behavioral and emotional tendencies stem from that very early root, and persist throughout life. However, the effects of these fundamental tendencies change with age, a process called **heterotypic continuity** (Caspi & Roberts, 1999). For example, a shy child at a social gathering might hide behind a parent; a shy adult is unlikely to do that, but still might avoid conversing with strangers. An aggressive child might express disagreement by kicking a playmate; an aggressive adult is more likely to get into a verbal argument than a physical one (though adults get into physical fights too).

According to one analysis, the three basic aspects of childhood temperament are positive emotionality, negative emotionality, and "effortful control" (Vroman, Lo, & Durbin, 2014). Positive emotionality may be the precursor (via heterotypic continuity) of the adult trait of extraversion, negative emotionality the precursor of neuroticism, and effortful control the precursor of conscientiousness and agreeableness (Ahadi & Rothbart, 1994). Much more will be said about the biological and genetic foundations of personality in Chapters 8 and 9.

PHYSICAL AND ENVIRONMENTAL FACTORS Beyond one's genes and internal biology, visible attributes of the body are no doubt important as well. Whether you are physically female or male, tall or short, or meet your culture's conventional definition of attractiveness—these are facts that you can do little or nothing about; they will affect the kind of experiences you have and therefore the kind of person you become, and they will remain the same throughout much or all of your life. Other consistent influences reside in the world that surrounds you. You might be rich or poor, or you might live in a city or in the country, or you might come from a large family or small one. These facts, too, are largely, if not entirely, out of your control, and will continuously affect how you think, feel, and behave—the three elements of the personality triad introduced in Chapter 1.

---

[2] Although, the stability of the effects of DNA is not so simple. Recent work on *epigenetics* has shown that experience can affect how, when, or even whether a gene is expressed. More will be said about epigenetics in Chapter 9.

BIRTH ORDER   One long-lasting fact about you, over which you had no influence whatsoever, is your birth order. But does it really matter whether you were the firstborn in your family, or came along later? Psychologists have argued about this question for years (Rodgers, Cleveland, van den Oord, & Rowe, 2000). Much of the debate centers around a proposal by the psychologist Frank Sulloway, who says that parents tend to lavish the most attention and resources on their firstborn child, who then becomes likely to identify with the parents' values and goals, and may even take on the role of "assistant parent" in raising the siblings who come along later (Sulloway, 2001). The later born child, however, has to find a niche in the family not already occupied by the child (or children) who came before, has fewer responsibilities within the family, and so is more likely to draw on other sources for relationships and values. As a result, firstborns grow up to favor "the establishment," are conventionally ambitious, and support traditional values. Laterborns are more likely to be independent, open-minded, and even rebellious.

While this proposal sounds reasonable, research to establish whether it is actually true has turned out to be difficult. For one thing, it is not enough to simply compare firstborns with laterborns if they come from different families, because families are often dissimilar to each other in many ways that might be important. Unless the researcher is careful, effects that appear to be due to birth order could stem from factors such as family size, family income, or parental genetics. But at least one study that attempted to carefully account for these variables did find that firstborn children were more conscientious than second born children (in families that had at least two), and that the second born children were higher on openness to experience. Both of these findings are consistent with Sulloway's proposal (Healey & Ellis, 2007). A review of the literature written by Sulloway himself concluded that in addition to firstborns scoring higher on conscientiousness, later born children tended to score higher on extraversion, openness to experience, and agreeableness—but neuroticism showed no difference at all (Sulloway, 2010). However, none of the effects were very large—the overall correlation between birth order and conscientiousness, which was the largest one among the Big Five traits, was $r = -.18$.[3]

Another study found no relationship at all between birth order and rebelliousness, contrary to the prediction that laterborns would score higher than firstborns on this trait (Cundiff, 2013). And, perhaps finally, a recent and very large study of several thousand people in about a thousand different families directly contradicted Sulloway's hypothesis, finding no differences whatsoever in the personalities of earlier and later-born individuals (Rohrer, Egloff, & Schmukle, 2017).[4]

---

[3] The negative sign on the correlation reflects that people with lower (earlier) birth order had higher conscientiousness scores.

[4] The single exception was one item where people rated the degree to which they were "eager for knowledge"; first-borns rated themselves slightly higher, on average.

I said "perhaps finally" just now because I actually don't think the idea of birth order being important will go away so easily; people just seem to intuitively believe, or want to believe, that it matters. So I expect the debate to continue. If you have sisters or brothers, you might do a small informal study of the effect of birth order within your own family. In what ways are you different from your older or younger siblings, and why?

EARLY EXPERIENCE Early adverse experiences can have consequences that persist for many years, especially for children who are already sensitive and vulnerable (Slagt, Dubas, Deković, & van Aken, 2016). Adults who remember being rejected by either of their parents, as children, have difficulties in forming relationships throughout their lives (Khaleque & Rohner, 2012). Similarly, the experience of being bullied in childhood (at age 11) can lead to symptoms such as anxiety, paranoid thoughts, and disorganized thinking in late adolescence (at age 16). Children who were already somewhat depressed, anxious, or impulsive have especially bad reactions to experiences such as being kicked, called names, or rejected by their peer group (Singham et al., 2017). Other kinds of stress during childhood, such as growing up in poverty or being maltreated, can produce a lifelong pattern of chronic (biological) inflammation, which can lead to frailty, fatigue, and general ill health (Fagundes & Way, 2014). These outcomes, in turn, create a long-term tendency to have stronger emotional reactions to ordinary, daily stress (Glaser, van Os, Portegijs, & Myin-Germeys, 2006). The effects of early bad experiences can be difficult to undo. Romanian orphans who spent more than 6 months in an orphanage, and then were adopted into prosperous British families when they were 6 years old, nonetheless suffered increased risk of later difficulties relating to their social group, low educational achievement, and unemployment (Sonuga-Barke et al., 2017).

Fortunately, some parents are successful at creating environments for their children that promote good outcomes. Highly educated parents appear to be especially likely to succeed at this. A large study of seven samples that examined a total of more than 60,000 people from the ages of 7 to 95 found that parents with more years of education had children who turned out, as adults, to be more open, extraverted and emotionally stable—but not more conscientious! This finding held for both biological and adopted children, which indicated that it really was the environment that mattered, not just the genetics of the parent (Sutin, Luchetti, Stephan, Robins, & Terracciano, 2017). What the study did not reveal is exactly what the better-educated parents did that produced these favorable outcomes for their children. What do you think it might have been?

A hint might come from another study, which looked at relationships between the childhood family environment and adult self-esteem in 8,711 American participants who were followed from ages 8 to 27. The environments of the children who grew up to feel good about themselves were characterized by cognitively stimulating

Table 7.1	PERSON-ENVIRONMENT TRANSACTIONS THAT CAN MAGNIFY PERSONALITY TRAITS OVER TIME	
Transaction	**Process**	**Examples**
Active person–environment transaction	Person seeks out compatible environments and avoids incompatible ones	Aggressive person goes to bar where fights are frequent; introvert avoids social gatherings
Reactive person–environment transaction	Different people respond differently to the same situation	Extravert finds party enjoyable; introvert finds same party unbearable
Evocative person–environment transaction	Aspect of an individual's personality leads to behavior that changes the situations he or she experiences	Conscientious person tells group "it's time to get to work"; disagreeable person starts argument over minor matter

activities such as being read to, physical comfort, the presence of the father, and all-around prosperity (Orth, 2018). Is this kind of environment more likely when the parents are better educated?[5]

PERSON-ENVIRONMENT TRANSACTIONS One reason personality remains stable over the years is that people respond to, seek out, and even create environments that are compatible with, and may magnify, their personality traits. These processes are called **person-environment transactions**.[6] There are several types (Caspi, Elder, & Bem, 1987; Roberts, Wood, & Caspi, 2008; see **Table 7.1**). As an example of an **active person-environment transaction**, an aggressive person may be attracted to (and be attractive to) similarly aggressive friends, which may put that person into environments where conflict, fights, and even delinquency are common. A more scholarly person, by contrast, may prefer to hang out with fellow denizens of the library, and in that environment develop a strong academic record and perhaps a successful professional life. Of course, such environments are not always completely freely chosen. Someone who gets arrested did not exactly choose the jail environment, but the experience may affect her personality. And even the most studious scholar may find that he failed to be admitted to the college of his choice. So happenstance—luck—plays a role here, too.

The reason people tend to seek out environments compatible with their traits is that they may find other kinds of environments unpleasant. A true extravert might feel miserable sitting quietly on the porch, while a true introvert suffers just

---

[5] Yes, I think so. Stay in school. Your children will thank you someday.

[6] The term "transaction," in this context, means that one psychological factor is affecting the other, and vice versa. The person chooses or changes his or her environment even while the environment is changing the person.

as much at a noisy party (Lucas & Diener, 2001). This kind of pattern of differential response to situations is called a **reactive person-environment transaction.**

People do not just choose and experience their environments; they change them. This process is called an **evocative person-environment transaction.** For example, parents who are emotionally positive and uninhibited tend to be highly responsive to their 3- to 6-year-old children. At the same time, children of this age who are emotionally positive and self-controlled evoke better responses from their parents (Wilson & Durbin, 2012). The path of influence from parent to child is a two-way street; depending on their personalities, each draws out behaviors from the other in a way likely to magnify the effect on the child's development over time.

> People do not just choose their environments; they change them.

Similar transactions occur at every age. The atmosphere of a study group or a work team can change in a moment if just one person says, "Let's stop working so hard and go get some beers," *or* says, "Let's quit fooling around and get something done for a change." The person who does either of these things affects the environment of the people around him, but also—and probably consistently—affects his or her own environment, too. Over time, the second person will inhabit environments that promote achievement; the first person, not so much. Long-term consequences of persistent patterns like this can be significant. People described as "ill-tempered" (low in agreeableness) chronically create situations where people are arguing or fighting with each other and, as a result, are more likely to suffer outcomes such as divorce and unemployment (Ozer & Benet-Martínez, 2006).

CUMULATIVE CONTINUITY AND MATURITY According to one major summary of the literature, the correlation coefficient reflecting consistency of individual differences in personality is .31 across childhood, .54 during the college years, and .74 between the ages of 50 and 70 (Roberts & DelVecchio, 2000).[7] While all three figures indicate impressive stability, it does appear that individual differences in personality become more consistent as one gets older. This conclusion has been called the **cumulative continuity principle.** This principle asserts not only that personality traits are relatively stable across the life span, but also that consistency increases as a person matures (Roberts, Wood, & Caspi, 2008; see also Anusic & Schimmack, 2016, for a replication of this finding). One result is that people's self-views of their own personality come to agree better with ratings by others as they mature between the ages of 14 and 29 (Rohrer et al., 2017). It's easier to agree about what somebody is like when that person behaves consistently, and young adults are more consistent than adolescents are.

> Individual differences in personality become more consistent as one gets older.

---

[7] Within each age range, personality was compared at two times about seven years apart.

When traits do change, they tend to change together—one trait changes, and others do, too (Klimstra, Bleidorn, Asendorpf, van Aken, & Denissen, 2013). The flip side of this finding is that when one trait stays the same, so do the others—and this observation is especially true in older adults (specifically, older than 70). The main reason personality becomes more stable during the transition from child to adult to senior citizen seems to be that one's environment also gets more stable with age (Briley & Tucker-Drob, 2014). Among other factors, older people are more likely to have finally decided where they live, who they live with, and what they do for a living. As the saying goes, they've "settled down."

But it's not just a matter of age—stability stems from *psychological maturity*. From a psychological point of view, "maturity" generally refers to behavioral consistency and also to the specific traits that help a person to fulfill socially important adult roles such as being a spouse, a parent, or a worker. These traits include self-control, interpersonal sensitivity, and emotional stability. Adolescents with relatively mature personalities—in these terms—change less over the next 10 years than do others, the same age, who are less mature (Donnellan et al., 2007). An intriguing and surprisingly hopeful recent finding is that people may be becoming more psychologically mature around the world! You might have heard of the "Flynn effect," which is the apparently robust finding that IQ is increasing slowly but consistently, everywhere (Pietschnig & Voracek, 2015). A recent study proposed that something similar may be happening in the domain of personality, with people around the world increasing gradually but consistently in traits such as self-confidence, sociability, leadership motivation, and achievement striving, among others (Jokela et al., 2017). There do not seem to be many indications that the world is becoming a better place, but maybe this is one.

> An intriguing and surprisingly hopeful recent finding is that people may be becoming more psychologically mature around the world!

THE END OF HISTORY? At what point does personality stop developing? Take a moment and ask yourself a couple of questions. Has your personality changed over the past few years? The answer might depend to some degree on how old you are. Most people about to graduate from college think they changed a lot over the previous 4 or 5 years, and they are usually right (Robins, Noftle, Trzesniewski, & Roberts, 2005). Fewer middle-aged people think they have changed significantly over the previous 6 years—in one study, about 38 percent of the respondents thought they had changed "a little"[8] (Herbst, McCrae, Costa, Feaganes, & Siegler, 2000). But now ask yourself another question: Will my personality be different 10 years from now? According to some research, most people think the answer to

---

[8] Nine percent thought they had changed "a good deal," and 53 percent thought they had "stayed the same."

this question is No (Quoidbach, Gilbert, & Wilson, 2013). From the perspective of the present moment, today looks like "the end of history" and we feel like finished products. We expect to change less in the future than we have in the past, or even not at all. But if we really do think this, it's an illusion. The evidence indicates that personality continues to develop throughout the life span. You won't always be exactly the way you are now—probably.

PERSONALITY DEVELOPMENT

Are older people different, on average, than younger people? This is an entirely different issue than the stability of individual differences just summarized (Roberts, Donnellan, & Hill, 2012). For illustration, imagine that three young children had mean agreeableness scores of 20, 40, and 60 (on whatever test was being used), but when they were measured again later, as young adults, their scores were 40, 60, and 80, respectively. Notice that their rank-order consistency is perfect—the correlation between the two sets of scores is $r = 1.0$. But each individual's agreeableness score has increased by 20 points. So, at the same time, they are showing high rank-order consistency *and* a strong increase in their mean level of the trait. This kind of increase (or, in some cases, decrease) in the mean level of a trait over time is what is meant by **personality development.**

Cross-Sectional Studies

One relatively easy way to chart the course of personality development is with a **cross-sectional study**, which simply surveys people at different ages. One large project gathered self-reported personality tests scores (S data) from the Internet. The results, based on more than *a million* respondents—surely among the largest *N*s in the history of psychological research—found that people at different ages show different mean levels of the Big Five personality traits (Soto, John, Gosling, & Potter, 2011). You probably will not find the findings particularly surprising. According to an international survey, people in 26 different countries agreed with the stereotype that adolescents are relatively impulsive, rebellious, and undisciplined, whereas older adults are less impulsive, less active, less antagonistic, and less open (Chan et al., 2012). Do you agree as well? I hope so, because this worldwide stereotype turns out to be largely correct (see **Figure 7.1**).

Between ages 10 and 20, scores on agreeableness, openness, and conscientiousness all dip during the transition from childhood to adolescence and then recover approaching age 20. Extraversion dips from a high level in childhood—little kids are such extraverts!—and then levels off. Neuroticism seems a bit more complicated, as young women increase notably on this trait during adolescence, while young men decline somewhat—perhaps adolescence is harder on girls than

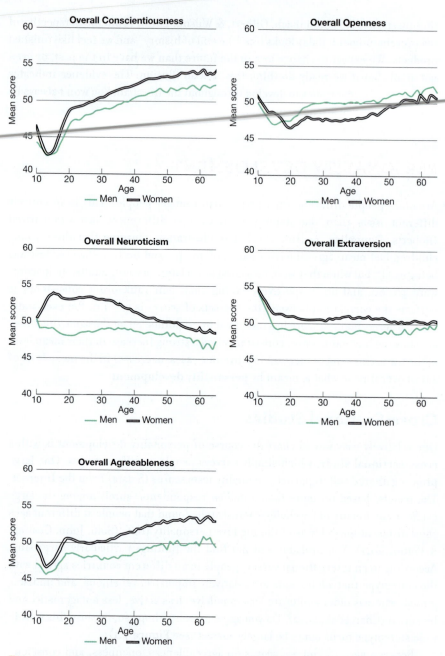

Figure 7.1 Mean Scores on Big Five Personality Traits Between Ages 10 and 60 for Men (M) and Women (F) Personality continues to change across the life span, on average. Trait levels are shown in terms of T-scores, which have a mean of 50 and a standard deviation of 10.

Source: Soto, John, Gosling, & Potter (2011), pp. 339–341.

on boys. After age 20, scores on conscientiousness, agreeableness, and openness begin to increase among men and women, while extraversion stays fairly constant. (At older ages some of these traits begin to decline again, as will be discussed later in the chapter.) The higher level of neuroticism among women begins a slow and steady decline around age 20, whereas men's neuroticism scores stay more constant (and generally lower than women's).

Cohort Effects

As was mentioned, the findings just surveyed came from cross-sectional research, meaning that people of different ages were surveyed simultaneously. But this method, while common, is not the ideal way to study development. When you gather personality ratings of people of different ages, all at the same time, you are necessarily gathering data from people who were born in different years and grew up in different social (and perhaps physical) environments. This fact might make a difference. The possibility is called a **cohort effect.** Some critics, especially worried about cohort effects, have argued that much of psychology is really history, meaning it is no more than the study of a particular group of people in a particular time and place (Gergen, 1973).

Without going that far, it is easy to see that aspects of personality can be affected by the historical period in which one lives. A classic survey of Americans who grew up during the Great Depression of the 1930s found that they developed attitudes toward work and financial security that were noticeably different from the outlooks of those who grew up earlier or later (Elder, 1974). The finding cited earlier in this chapter, that "mature" traits seem to be increasing around the world, is also an example of a cohort effect (Smits et al., 2017). A related study found that (in the Netherlands) extraversion, agreeableness, and conscientiousness all increased slightly between 1982 and 2007, while neuroticism went down (Smits, Dolan, Vorst, Wicherts, & Timmerman, 2011). The reasons for these changes are not clear, but presumably they have something to do with changes in the cultural and social environment. And we already considered, in Chapter 6, the controversy over whether current college-age adults are more narcissistic than earlier generations. Whether this particular difference is real or not, it is important to keep the possibility of cohort effects in mind when evaluating the results of cross-sectional studies.

Longitudinal Studies

A better method for studying development—when possible—is the **longitudinal study**, in which the same people are repeatedly measured over the years from childhood through adulthood. Naturally, longitudinal studies are difficult and they take a long time to do—by definition—but several important ones have been completed fairly recently. Some of these studies followed their participants for 60 years or more! And, fortunately, for the most part their results are turning out to be fairly consistent with the results of the earlier cross-sectional studies. According to one major review, longitudinal data show that, on average, people tend to become more socially dominant, agreeable, conscientious, and emotionally stable (lower on neuroticism) over time (Roberts et al., 2006). Similar (but not quite identical) results were found in a study of more than 10,000 people in New Zealand, which also found that the trait of honesty/humility[9] increased steadily over the adult years (Milojev & Sibley, 2017). Older people are less prone to take risks (Josef et al., 2016), and self-esteem increases slowly but steadily from adolescence to about age 50 (Orth, Robins, & Widaman, 2012).[10] Yet another longitudinal study measured *ego development*, the ability to deal well with the social and physical world and to think for oneself when making moral decisions (Lilgendahl, Helson, & John, 2012; more will be said about ego development in Chapter 11). This trait increased noticeably between the ages of 43 and 61. These findings, and others, illustrate what is sometimes called the **maturity principle** of development, which is that the traits needed to perform adult roles effectively increase with age (Caspi, Roberts, & Shiner, 2005; Roberts et al., 2008). These traits include, most notably, conscientiousness and emotional stability, but also several others as we have just seen.

There might be a limit to the maturity principle, however. The same study that showed an increase in self-esteem up to about age 50 showed a gradual decline thereafter (Orth et al., 2012). And findings from Germany suggest that conscientiousness, extraversion, and agreeableness also decline in old age (past the mid-sixties; Lucas & Donnellan, 2011). Perhaps at that point in life, traits associated with performing typical adult roles become less important. Older people are less concerned with careers, social activity, ambition, or the need to please other people, and become more interested in just relaxing and enjoying life—a possibility that psychologist Herbert Marsh has dubbed the *La Dolce Vita*[11] effect (cited in Lucas & Donnellan, 2011, p. 848; see also Specht, Egloff, & Schmukle, 2011).

But not everybody does this. Some very highly motivated, highly conscientious older adults express their needs for achievement in retirement by volunteering for community service (Mike, Jackson, & Oltmanns, 2014). As one busy retiree once said, "I work for free." People like this seem to live longer (Friedman, Kern, & Reynolds, 2010; more will be said about these findings in Chapter 17).

---

[9] You may recall from Chapter 6 that honesty/humility has been suggested as a sixth basic trait in addition to the Big Five.

[10] This trend is similar among men and women, even though men generally report higher levels of self-esteem at every age (Orth & Robins, 2014).

[11] *La Dolce Vita* is Italian for "the good life." The famous movie with this title is actually a cynical portrayal of a man who fails in his search for love and happiness.

Late old age appears to be particularly challenging, though the data are limited as you might imagine. A rare study of persons between the ages of 80 and 98 found that while neuroticism stayed fairly constant over this period, extraversion became noticeably lower, especially in people who had suffered significant hearing loss (Berg & Johansson, 2013).

"You got better-looking as you got older—up to a point."

A couple of comments can be made about these findings. First, the data refer to mean levels of traits, so they do not apply to everybody—some people actually become less agreeable or less conscientious as they progress through adulthood, and surely at least a few people become *more* extraverted during the years between age 80 and age 98, if they live that long. And other people don't really change much at all. While the average findings just summarized are impressively robust and replicable, there still are big individual differences in both the amount and direction of personality change (Borghuis et al., 2017).

Second, these findings surprised traditional developmental psychologists, who for many years had assumed that personality emerges mostly during childhood and early adolescence, and is stable thereafter. The pioneering psychologist William James (1890) is often quoted as having claimed that personality "sets like plaster" after age 30. The available data indicate he was wrong, in the sense that personality traits continue to change across at least several more decades.

Causes of Personality Development

Some of the causes of personality change over time involve physical development. Intelligence (IQ) and linguistic ability increase steadily throughout childhood and early adolescence, before leveling off at about age 20 or perhaps slightly later. Hormone levels change as well, with dramatic and consequential surges during adolescence, and slow, steady decreases thereafter (see Chapter 8). Other age-related changes are surely also important, as physical strength increases during youth and declines gradually—or not so gradually— in old age. And as was already mentioned, older people who lose their hearing become more introverted.

Another (and less depressing) reason for systematic personality change has to do with the changing social roles at different stages of life. In a classic account, the neo-Freudian theorist Erik Erikson described the varying challenges that a person faces at different ages (Erikson, 1963). These include the need to develop skills in childhood, relationships in adulthood, and an overview and assessment of one's life in old age. This theorizing became the foundation of the field of study later called "life-span development" (Santrock, 2014; see Chapter 11 for more on Erikson).

More recent research has focused particularly on the trait of conscientiousness. In North America, Europe, and Australasia, the time period of about ages 20 to 30 is typically when an individual leaves the parental home, starts a career, finds a spouse, and begins a family. In other areas of the world, such as Bolivia, Brazil, and Venezuela, these transitions start much earlier. Either way, the changes in responsibilities are associated with changes in personality (Bleidorn, Klimstra, Denissen, Rentfrow, Potter, & Gosling, 2013). A first job requires that a person learn to be reliable, punctual, and agreeable to customers, coworkers, and bosses. Building a stable romantic relationship and starting a family require a person to learn to regulate emotional ups and downs. And progression through one's career and as a parent requires an increased inclination to influence the behavior of others (social dominance). Life demands different things of you when you move from being a child, young adult or beginning employee to becoming a parent or the boss, and your personality changes accordingly (Bleidorn, Hopwood, & Lucas, 2018).

The Social Clock

Systematic changes in the demands that are made on a person over the years were studied by the developmental psychologist Ravenna Helson, who described the pattern as a **social clock** (Helson, Mitchell, & Moore, 1984). Just as a so-called "biological clock" limits the time that women (and to some extent, men) can have children, Helson pointed out that a "social clock" places strong pressures on all people to accomplish certain things by certain ages. A person who stays "on time" receives social approval and enjoys the feeling of being in sync with society. But someone who falls behind receives less social approval and may feel out of step.

Helson looked at the consequences of staying in or out of sync with the social clock in a study of students at Mills College, a prestigious women's college in Oakland, California. Looking at students from the 1960s, she followed up and assessed their life satisfaction 20 years later, when they were in their early to mid-forties. She divided the students into three groups. One group had followed what she called the (stereotypical) Feminine Social Clock (FSC), which prescribes that one should start a family by the time one is in one's early to mid-twenties. A second group had followed what she called the Masculine Social Clock (MSC), which prescribes that one should start a career with the potential to achieve status by the time one is 28 or so. Finally, a third group had followed neither schedule (Neither Social Clock, NSC).

Notice that all of the participants in this research were women. At the time Helson did her study, that fact alone was a big change from most prior research, which, you may recall from Chapter 2, sometimes forgot to include women at all! One interesting question addressed by this study, therefore, is whether it is better for women to follow the traditional FSC than the MSC. What Helson found is, in retrospect, not surprising:[12] Women who followed *either* the FSC or the MSC reported being fairly content and satisfied with life 20 years after graduation. It was only those women who did not manage to follow either agenda who reported feeling depressed, alienated, and bitter when they entered their forties.

The Development of Narrative Identity

Beyond starting families and careers, which most people do at some point, another important life task is faced by everybody. This is the task of developing a sense of who you are. According to the psychologist Dan McAdams (2013), every individual develops three aspects of identity one on top of the other (see **Figure 7.2**).

The first step is to learn to see oneself as an *actor*, and the mission is to develop the social skills, traits, and roles that will allow one to begin to take a place in society. This task begins very early, as the young child begins to take on competencies that allow her to separate from her parents and do things independently. She learns to read; she learns to add and subtract; she learns to drive; she learns a profession and the skills of parenthood. This task of acquiring new skills required by new roles continues throughout life.

The second task is to become an *agent*, a person who is guided by goals and values. This process begins at around ages 7–9 and, again, is a lifelong endeavor. When you begin to think of yourself as an agent, you look beyond the present moment, and start to plan for the future and align those plans toward the outcomes that are important to you. You have to pay serious attention choosing a

---

[12] Actually, a lot of findings in psychology seem unsurprising, in retrospect. But that doesn't mean we could have predicted them.

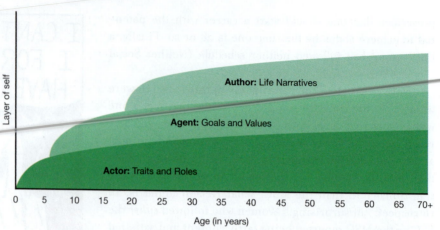

Figure 7.2 McAdams' View of How the Three Layers of the Self Develop Over Time The view of oneself as an actor begins first, followed by developing a sense of how one is an agent, and then also an author of one's own life story. All of these aspects of the self continue to develop throughout life.
Source: McAdams (2013), p. 280.

career, finding a life partner, and developing the values that allow you to make these choices wisely.

The third and final task is to become the *author* of your own autobiography. This process begins in late adolescence, and results in the "narrative" that one can provide when asked, as McAdams often does, to "tell me your life story." The story is continuous; you add chapters as long as you live, and this whole, self-authored "book" comprises your ever-evolving **narrative identity.**

The story that comprises a person's narrative identity is important because it reveals how she views her entire life, up until now, and how its trajectory fits into her goals and dreams. And it turns out that just about everybody has such a story. McAdams reports that in his research, people thoroughly enjoy telling them. The narratives have various themes, consistent with the individual's cultural background and personality. For some people, the story of one's life is about a series of lucky breaks; for others, the theme may be hard luck, success, or tragedy. And the story can change as the result of major life events, such as becoming a parent (Sensevang, Pratt, Alisat, & Sadler, 2017).

People from different cultures may tell different kinds of stories about themselves. One pioneering cross-cultural study found that nonimmigrant European-Canadians, when asked to explain how they are the same person over time, refer to stable aspects of themselves such as their values, their beliefs, their eternal souls, or even their birthmarks! Canadians who had immigrated from Asia, in contrast, were more likely to spin a more complex story in which events in their lives affected their personalities, which in turn affected future events in their lives. For example, being arrested for shoplifting might cause a person to rethink the kind of life one wants to lead, which can lead to changes in how one acts in the future (Dunlop & Walker, 2015).

Most research on narrative identity focuses on its relations with personality. A particular theme that appears fairly often in North American culture, a theme that McAdams calls "agency," organizes the life story around episodes of challenging oneself and then accomplishing goals. Such a story might be the hallmark of a person high in the trait of conscientiousness. Another important theme, called "redemption," typically includes an event that seemed terrible at the time, but in the end turned out for the best. For example, a person might describe how the tragic death of his father led the rest of the family to become closer (McAdams & McClean, 2013). Redemptive stories appear to be a good sign. People who think of their lives in this way are able to change their behavior for better—for example, stop problem drinking—and in general develop healthier habits (Dunlop & Tracy, 2013).

A few years ago I was at a psychology conference where McAdams gave a keynote address in which he presented some of this research. The following speaker was the newly elected president of the society. The new president proceeded to tell the audience a bit of his own life story, including the time he failed to be awarded tenure at his first university job. While this can be a devastating blow to one's academic career, he described how instead it led him to take a different position where he was able to finally do the kind of research he really wanted, which led to many future successes. McAdams sat politely and silently while this story was being related, but I'm fairly sure he was thinking something along the lines of, "That's what I'm talking about."

Goals Across the Life Span

A person's sense of identity is always important, but other goals may change over time (Carstensen & Mikels, 2005). When a person is young, and life seems as if it will go on forever, goals are focused on preparation for the future. On a broad level, they include learning new things, exploring possibilities, and generally expanding one's horizons. More specific goals include completing one's education, finding a spouse, and establishing a career. When old age approaches, priorities change. As the end of life becomes a more salient concern, it may seem less important to start new relationships or to make that extra dollar. Instead, goals of older persons—defined in most research as those around age 70 and up—focus more on what they find emotionally meaningful, especially ties with family and long-time friends. They also—wisely, it would appear—work to regulate their emotional experience, by thinking more about the good things in life and less

> If being with someone is a hassle, older persons are pretty good at avoiding him.

about the things that trouble them. One advantage of old age is that (usually) one no longer must associate in the workplace or social settings with people one does not enjoy. Research by gerontological psychologist Laura Carstensen and her colleagues indicates that older persons take advantage of this freedom. If being with someone is a hassle, they are pretty good at avoiding him (Carstensen, Isaacowitz, & Charles, 1999). This may be the best part of the *La Dolce Vita* effect mentioned earlier.

This shift in goals is not an effect of age, per se; nor is it just a matter of changing social roles. Rather, it appears to result from having a broader or narrower perspective about time. Young people with life-threatening illnesses also appear to shift their goals from exploration to emotional well-being (Carstensen & Fredrickson, 1998), and when older people are asked to imagine they will have at least 20 more years of healthy life than they expected, they exhibit a style of emotional attention otherwise more typical of the young (Fung & Carstensen, 2003). According to the research of Carstensen and her colleagues, the life goals that one sets depend, in part, on how much life one expects to have left.

PERSONALITY CHANGE

Can personality change? In one respect, the answer is clearly "yes." As we have already seen, ample evidence shows that, overall, personality *does* change. Look again at Figure 7.1, which shows personality traits moving around quite a bit, on average, across the years from adolescence to adulthood to old age. But when people ask, "Can personality change?" the inevitable consequences of the passing years are probably not what they have in mind. Instead, what they are asking is: Can personality *be changed*? Can I change my own personality? Or can I change the personality of my child, or my spouse, or anyone, for that matter?

The Desire for Change

According to one survey, almost everybody would like to change at least one of their Big Five traits at least somewhat—the estimates range from 87 percent to 97 percent, depending on the trait. Neuroticism was the trait that the most people wanted to change; fewer wanted to change their agreeableness (Hudson & Roberts, 2014). Another survey asked more than 15,000 college-age people in more than 60 countries a slightly different (and more demanding) question, "Is there an aspect of your personality that you're currently trying to change?" Sixty-one percent said "yes" (Baranski, 2018). Slightly more women reported trying to change (63%) than men (56%). Around the world, the highest percentage of people who were trying to change was in Thailand (81%) and Russia was not far behind (81%). The smallest percentage of "yes" answers was in Israel, where only 29% of the participants reported trying to change anything about themselves. In the United States, the proportion was about 50/50. These differences between women and men and among countries are interesting, but I do not know what they mean.[13] Do you have any ideas?

Not surprisingly, the change people wanted was almost always in the socially desirable direction. People would like to be a bit higher in extraversion, conscientiousness, agreeableness and openness, and lower in neuroticism.[14] Interestingly, these traits match almost exactly what most people desire in their romantic partners: They would prefer mates who are *more* conscientious, extraverted, and agreeable, and lower in neuroticism than they are themselves (Figuredo, Sefcek, & Jones, 2006). I guess most people really are seeking their "better half."

One question that might arise about both of these studies concerns their participants. They were almost all undergraduate college students. Do these results just mean that the personalities of people in this age range (mostly 18–22) are still in the "design stage" (as was noted in Chapter 4), making them more amenable to change than people who are older and more set in their ways? Good question, but the answer appears to be No. A study conducted over the Internet surveyed 594 people from the ages of 18 all the way to 74, and found an almost 0 correlation ($r = .024$ to be exact) between age and the desire to change (Baranski, Morse, & Dunlop, 2017).

In the college student studies, the main reason for wanting to change appeared to be the hope that having a different personality might make life better. The people who most wanted to be more extraverted were those who were dissatisfied with their friendships, emotions, recreational activities, or sex lives. Those who most wanted to be more conscientious were unhappy with how things were going at work or at school (Baranski et al., 2017; see also Hudson & Roberts, 2014).

Maybe there is hope for these people. A small amount of research that suggests personality actually can be changed has been around for decades. In just the past few years, a number of studies and theoretical models have added to this evidence. Current research suggests that four methods have the potential

---

[13] We're working on it.

[14] To be exact, they wanted to be higher in emotional stability, which is the inverse of neuroticism.

to change personality: psychotherapy, general intervention programs aimed at life outcomes, targeted intervention programs aimed at specific traits, and life experiences.

Psychotherapy

Psychotherapy has long been used as a route for attempting to change personality. The pioneering psychologist Carl Rogers proposed that if a "client" (Rogers never used the word "patient") was vulnerable or anxious, it was enough for a therapist to experience and express unconditional positive regard to the client, and desirable change would then occur (Rogers, 1957). To this day, many therapists use techniques inspired by Rogers' approach (see Chapter 12), as well as approaches such as *cognitive-behavioral therapy* that combine developing insight with "homework" practicing more adaptive emotional responses and behaviors. So, does any of this work?

As long ago as 1980, a major literature review concluded that psychotherapy—almost regardless of the specific technique used—can indeed produce long-term behavior change (Smith, Glass, & Miller, 1980). A much more recent review of 207 studies that tracked personality change during psychotherapy concluded that "marked" increases were seen in emotional stability and extraversion over (on average) a 6-month period (Roberts et al., 2017). But psychotherapy might have a downside as well. Another review found that being in therapy was associated with increases in chronic stress, depression, and neuroticism, and decreases in self-esteem and conscientiousness (Chow et al., in press). These are surprising and disturbing findings, to say the least. But they might have arisen because the people undergoing therapy in these latter studies were not necessarily willing participants; the sample included people getting therapy under court order, in a probation process, or even as part of a child custody dispute. Still, the findings serve as a bit of a caution that perhaps psychotherapy isn't always good for everybody.

To an increasing degree in recent years, psychotherapy is conducted in conjunction with the prescription of psychiatric drugs, such as fluoxetine (Prozac). As will be discussed in Chapter 8, fluoxetine and related drugs are not only useful (in some cases) for treating depression, they also have an overall effect, in many people, of making them more extraverted and less anxious. Just one dose of the hallucinogenic drug psilocybin (when taken in a medically controlled setting) can lead to increases in openness to experience that last a year or more (MacLean, Johnson, & Griffiths, 2011). And if you just want to be more extraverted for a little while, alcohol can do it (Winograd, Steinley, Lane, & Sher, 2017). But, of course, all drugs have side effects and that definitely includes alcohol. And, as we just saw, intensive psychotherapy

TRY FOR YOURSELF 7.1

The Change Goals Inventory

Instructions

How much do you want to change yourself? Here are a number of personality traits that you may or may not want to change within yourself. Please rate the extent to which you want to change each trait.

Response Scale

All items are rated using the following response scale (Note: "Am" must be changed to "do" when grammatically required by the item text—e.g., "I want to have an assertive personality"):

Much more than I currently am (+2)

More than I currently am (+1)

I do not want to change in this trait (0)

Less than I currently am (−1)

Much less than I currently am (−2)

Items

1. I want to be talkative.

2. I want to be reserved.

3. I want to be someone who is full of energy.

4. I want to be someone who generates a lot of enthusiasm.

5. I want to be someone who tends to be quiet.

6. I want to have an assertive personality.

7. I want to be sometimes shy, inhibited.

8. I want to be outgoing, sociable.

SCORING: Reverse the scores for items 2, 5, and 7—that is, multiply your answers to each of these items by −1. Then add up the eight scores and divide the total by eight. Compare this average answer to the results in Figure 7.3.

Source: Hudson & Roberts (2014), p. 62.

might have side effects as well. Fortunately, there are several other routes to changing personality.

General Interventions

Many intervention programs have tried to improve the lives of children and adolescents in a wide variety of ways. Typically, they are aimed not at "changing personality" as such, but at important outcomes such as completing education, lessening criminal behavior, and improving prospects for employment. Such programs can be expensive, but if they work, they can be worth the cost. One example was a large-scale attempt to affect the development of a group of 3- to 4-year-old preschool students living in a high-risk, low-income area of a major city (Reynolds, Template, Robertson, & Mann, 2001). The program included intensive instruction in reading and writing, diverse learning experiences in one-to-one and group settings, parenting programs, home visits, and health and nutrition services. The researchers also made sure that the class sizes for these children were small—no more than 17 students for every two teachers.

As you can see, this program was ambitious and expensive. What were the results? A follow-up 15 years later showed some pretty dramatic effects. The children in the program—compared to similar children not enrolled—grew into adolescents and young adults who were more likely to have completed high school (49.7 percent versus 38.5 percent) and less likely to have been arrested (16.9 percent versus 25.1 percent). The program was especially beneficial for boys.

Was it worth it? The answer is almost certainly yes. Just in sheer financial terms, consider the cost of arresting even just one young man and putting him through the court and jail system, and the further costs when later in life he can't find a job or support a family. And, on a human level, such an outcome is a tragedy. Still, it is important to remember that interventions like this do not always succeed. A large-scale program in Finland attempted to develop social skills and employment possibilities in youths who had been arrested between the ages of 15 and 17 (Huttunen, Kerr, & Mällkönen, 2014). The program appeared to make re-arrest less likely for a year or so, but after that its effect wore off. Comparing these two programs raises the following question: Is age 15 too late for this kind of intervention? For a program intended to avert delinquency, maybe earlier is better. More research on this important question is definitely needed.

Targeted Interventions

Intervention programs can also be tailored to address personality traits. For example, we saw earlier that openness to experience is a Big Five trait that tends to decrease somewhat in old age. Can this tendency be changed? A 30-week training program tried to do this with a group of men between the ages of 60 and 94

(Jackson, Hill, Payne, Roberts, & Stine-Morrow, 2012). The program included practice in inductive reasoning, and working on crossword and Sudoku puzzles. The results were that the men who received this training actually increased in openness. This is one of the first studies, if not the first, to show that the trajectory of openness to experience can be changed late in life, without the use of drugs. And this conclusion was supported by a later study of more than 7,000 people in the Netherlands from ages 16 to 95, which found that making "cultural investments" such as going to the opera or visiting museums was positively associated with increases in openness (Schwaba, Luhmann, Denissen, Chung, & Bleidorn, 2017).

One program of research suggests that writing "self-affirmations" can lead to lasting personality change (Cohen & Sherman, 2014). In the usual procedure, people are asked to identify one or more values that are important to them, and then to write a brief essay about when and why these values matter the most. Typical essays talk about relationships with friends and family, but also include values such as humor, kindness, and religion. The sheer act of writing essays like these appears to lead to greater tolerance for stress and a decrease in defensiveness. The reason seems to be that when you remind yourself about what is really important, other hassles don't matter so much.

Another program attempted to reduce the future risk of anxiety disorders in high-risk children, but had the interesting additional result that it seemed to reduce later overall neuroticism (Barlow, Sauer-Zavala, Carl, Bullis, & Ellard, 2014). The intervention focused on the children's parents, teaching them about the general nature of anxiety and also giving them specific tools such as techniques for managing behavior and for thinking about anxiety-provoking topics in less-threatening ways (Rapee, Kennedy, Ingram, Edwards, & Sweeny, 2010). The parents were even given lessons on how to avoid being overprotective. For example, one set of parents was urged not to allow their son to "avoid situations that made him anxious, such as attending parties and new activities. They were also encouraged to give [the child] the opportunity to speak for himself rather than answering for him" (Rapee et al., 2010, p. 1523). The overall result was an impressive reduction in the tendency of high-risk children to develop generally neurotic tendencies, and the difference between the treated and untreated groups actually seemed to increase over a three-year time period. This last result hints that the program might really have succeeded at beginning to produce lasting personality change.

Even the notoriously difficult trait of narcissism (see Chapter 6) may be amenable to change. Narcissists in general do not feel much empathy for the problems of others. However, this tendency was (at least temporarily) changed in one experiment by simply instructing them to "imagine how [the other person] feels. Try to take her perspective . . . imagining how she is feeling about what is happening" (Hepper, Hart, & Sedikides, 2014, p. 1084). Apparently, the problem

> The problem with narcissists isn't that they can't appreciate the feelings of others; it's that they don't want to.

with narcissists isn't that they can't appreciate the feelings of others; it's that they don't want to.

Another trait that might be particularly important to change, if you could, is "self-control." This trait is associated with all sorts of good outcomes both in childhood and adulthood. Children with better self-control do better in school and have fewer altercations with their classmates (Kochanska & Knaack, 2003); adults with better self-control have more stable occupational lives and personal relationships (Kern et al., 2013).

Can self-control be improved? One major literature review surveyed programs aimed at children younger than 10 years of age (the presumption may have been that after that, it's too late). Exercises used to help develop self-control included meditating, relaxing, and learning to think differently about temptations and frustrations. The results showed consistent effects such that in adolescence, children who had received training experienced fewer delinquency and behavior problems (Piquero, Jennings, & Farrington, 2010). There is also recent evidence that you can work to improve your own self-control, even if you are older than 10. Techniques of "mindfulness meditation" appear to be able to increase self-control and compassion, at least in the short term. In one study, individuals who had completed a meditation course were more likely to jump up and offer their seat to a person who approached on crutches, seemingly in pain (Condon, Desbordes, Miller, & DeSteno, 2013); another study showed that similar training made people more altruistic when playing a game where they had a chance to give something to another person (Weng et al., 2013).

Many years ago, while I was a graduate student at Stanford University, I took a course by the distinguished psychologist Albert Bandura titled "Principles of Personality Change." Ironically, given the title, the course wasn't really about personality; it was about how techniques based on social learning theory could be used to change specific problematic behaviors (see Chapter 14). Two behaviors of particular interest were agoraphobia (the fear of going outside) and fear of snakes. Stanford had an experimental clinic that would run occasional newspaper ads offering free treatment and would always be immediately deluged with calls. In particular, Palo Alto, California (where Stanford is located), had a surprising number of housewives who were so afraid of snakes they couldn't go outdoors, thus combining the two phobias. I can personally testify that I lived in Palo Alto for more than four years and never saw a single snake. Yet it turned out to be easier to train these clients not to fear snakes than it was to convince them that in Palo Alto, there really aren't any.

The treatment involved "systematic desensitization," in which clients are induced to perform the feared behavior through small, incremental steps. One day Dr. Bandura told our class about a recent client who graduated to the point of being able to comfortably handle a boa constrictor. After that, she was able to go home and, for the first time, confront her landlord and get her toilet fixed. I recall asking whether that didn't show that the snake phobia treatment had an effect on her trait of assertiveness. My recollection of Dr. Bandura's answer is less clear, but I do recall that he didn't care much for any sort of reference to personality traits. As we saw in Chapter 4, the concept of the "trait" was (and in some quarters still is) a construct some psychologists prefer to avoid. He preferred to talk of things like "generalization

> A client who graduated to the point of being able to comfortably handle a boa constrictor was able to go home and, for the first time, confront her landlord and get her toilet fixed.

gradients" (landlord = snake?).[15] But I thought then, and I think now, that it is simpler, clearer, and just plain correct to think about an effect like this in terms of traits. If you could change a trait, you might be able to change a lot of behaviors all at the same time.

This is exactly the perspective of an intriguing new theory called the "sociogenomic trait intervention model" (Roberts, Hill, & Davis, 2017). According to this model, the first step in personality change is to identify specifically the thoughts, feelings, and behaviors that the person wants to change. Then, the person needs to be challenged to do things outside her comfort zone to act out those changes, over and over, until they become habitual and automatic. Even a behavior as simple as regularly doing one's homework can lead to beneficial personality change (Göllner et al., 2017). It is also important to make sure that the environment the person is in is structured to support the change; family members need to be encouraging, for example.

One demonstration of this process worked with a man who had serious problems with substance abuse, with his job, and in relations with his family (Magidson, Roberts, Collado-Rodriguez, & Lezuez, 2012). The psychologists persuaded him to identify the goals that were important to him and to identify the behaviors that would help him to reach these goals. As a result, he began to show up for work on time, he spent more time socializing with his family, and he began to do these things instead of using substances such as cocaine. In other words, he began to develop an enhanced trait of conscientiousness, which spilled over in a beneficial way to all areas of his life, sort of like the snake phobic who increased her assertiveness and was finally able to confront her landlord.

Surely this is all easier said than done. One successful intervention does not prove that it will work with all people or for all problems. But it does provide an encouraging indication that such interventions are possible, and should spur research to find out more about how to make them work better and for more people.

---

[15] A *generalization gradient*, in behaviorist terminology, reflects the degree to which a response learned to one stimulus is also elicited by other, similar stimuli.

Behaviors and Life Experiences

You don't necessarily need to enter psychotherapy or receive a formal intervention to change your personality. Even something as simple as exercise can make a difference. People who are physically active in midlife can change the way their personality develops in old age (Stephan, Sutin, & Terracciano, 2014). The personalities of exercisers remain more stable, and show less of the typical late-life decline otherwise seen in conscientiousness, extraversion, openness, and agreeableness.

Certain life experiences have the potential to affect personality as well. Starting college is often associated with a drop in self-esteem, but the recovery is fairly quick. By the time of graduation, self-esteem is usually higher than it was at the beginning (Chung et al., 2014). Another study showed that entering college, starting a job, or beginning a new, serious relationship were all associated with increases in conscientiousness (Leikas & Salmela-Aro, 2014). Trying drugs was associated with increased neuroticism, and the onset of a chronic disease was associated with increases in both neuroticism and conscientiousness. What do you think the reason is for this last finding?

An event that happens to many people at some point in their lives is becoming unemployed. Does this have an effect on personality? One recent study, conducted in Germany, found that it does (Boyce, Wood, Daly, & Sedikides, 2015). People who lost their jobs—both men and women—became less agreeable, conscientious, and open to experience over a four-year period. However, if they found another job, their personality traits quickly rebounded to where they used to be.

Some events have lasting results that increase over time. One study looked at the effects of negative life experiences over a 16-year period in a sample of young adults (their mean age was 34) in the Netherlands (Jeronimus, Riese, Sanderman, & Omel, 2014). The negative events included health crises, losing a job or having other problems at work, educational difficulties, financial setbacks, and relationship problems. The perhaps not-surprising finding was that experiences like these tended to increase individuals' scores on neuroticism. The more interesting finding is that the reverse was true as well. In other words, negative experiences lead to an increase in neuroticism, but being higher in neuroticism also makes a person more prone to encounter negative experiences such as the ones just listed. These findings illustrate the long-lasting nature of the person-environment transactions described earlier in this chapter, which can amount to a feedback loop by which life events affect personality, and vice versa, in a spiral that becomes stronger as time goes on.

However, there might be such a thing as too little stress in one's life. One study looked at the number of negative events that had accumulated in participants' lives, and compared that with their ability to handle stress in laboratory tasks such as placing their hands in cold water or being warned they were going to "take an important test of nonverbal intelligence" (Seery et al., 2013, p. 1186). The results showed that people who had accumulated some adverse experiences did better than those who had encountered almost none. However, beyond a certain point the effect of adversity became harmful, a finding consistent with the study, cited earlier in the chapter, that showed a moderate—but not excessive—amount of stress in early life helped buffer reactions to events later in life (Ellis & Thomas, 2008). **Figure 7.3** shows the relationship between lifetime negative experiences and cardiovascular stress responses to the threatened test.

Events that might change personality can happen long after childhood is over. One study looked at older adults (65 and up) who had just finished an extended period of time caring for a spouse with terminal lung cancer. After this grueling ordeal finally ended, the former caregivers experienced increases in interpersonal orientation, sociability, and favorable attitudes toward other people (Hoerger et al., 2014).

Another, more pleasant example of an adult experience that can change personality is travel. Many people have joined institutions such as the Peace Corps

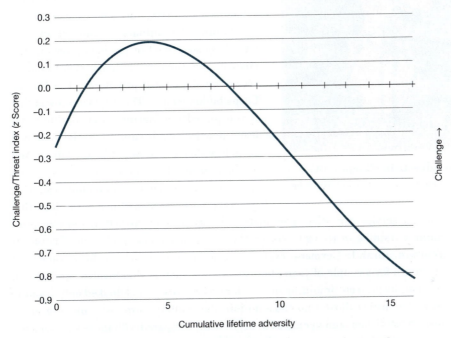

Figure 7.3 Relationship Between Lifetime Adverse Experiences and Cardiovascular Reactivity to Stress The figure shows that the cardiovascular "challenge/threat index," which is interpreted as a resilient response to stress, was highest for people who had experienced a moderate number of negative life experiences—not too few or too many.

Source: Seery et al. (2013), p. 1187.

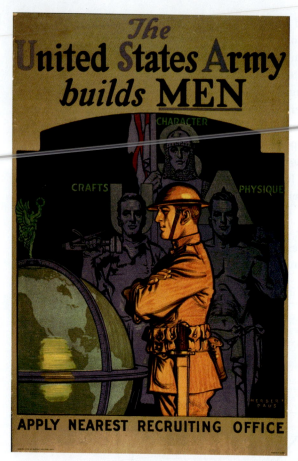

Figure 7.4 **A Classic Advertising Slogan** This is a claim about one way personality can be changed. Is it true?

to see the world[16] and an extended "overseas experience" (OE) is a tradition for young people from New Zealand. What is the long-term? People report, informally, that they feel they learned confidence and social skills from interacting with people from around the world, and recent research would seem to bear them out. Studying abroad for a year, while in high school, has been found to raise self-esteem (Hutteman, Nestler, Wagner, Egloff, & Back, in press). "Sojourners"—college students who lived abroad for a time—showed an increase in openness and agreeableness, and a decrease in neuroticism (Zimmerman & Neyer, 2013). Yet another study showed that the experience of living temporarily in another culture leads to measurable increases in creativity later (Maddux & Galinsky, 2009; see Chapter 13).

Joining the military is another experience long suspected of producing personality change. The American military used to have a recruiting slogan that promised, "The Marine Corps builds men."[17] The implication was that if you joined the Marines, you wouldn't just learn how to fix a bayonet or make your bed so tightly that a coin would bounce on it. You would also develop stereotypically masculine traits such as confidence and dominance.

There may be something to the idea that military service can affect personality. A recent study looked at the effects of military training in young Germans (Jackson, Thoemmes, Jonkmann, Lüdtke, & Trautwin, 2012). In Germany, every young adult is required to perform some kind of service for a couple of years, but can choose whether this involves working on community projects or joining the military. The study—which looked only at young men—found that those who chose to join the military were lower on agreeableness, neuroticism, and openness to begin with, compared with those who selected other options. So they started off different. But the effect of the military experience appeared to be to widen these gaps. Over a five-year period, all participants, on average, increased in agreeableness. This is consistent with the general age

---

[16] Others join the Foreign Legion to forget.
[17] This was before the Marines began recruiting women. The Army used the slogan even earlier (see **Figure 7.4**).

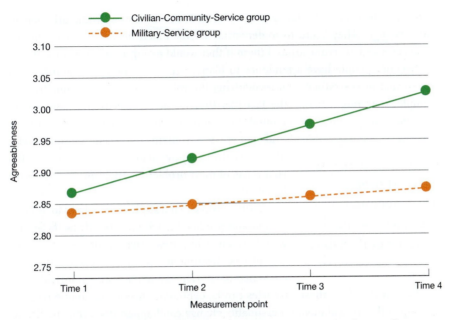

Figure 7.5 Changes in Agreeableness Over Time In a sample of young Germans, agreeableness was first assessed prior to beginning either community or military service (Time 1), and then reassessed at two-year intervals.

Source: Jackson, Thoemmes, Jonkmann, Lüdtke, & Trautwein (2012), p. 274.

trends seen in Figure 7.1. But the Germans who had performed community service increased in agreeableness *more* than did those who received military training, making the difference between them larger as time went on (see **Figure 7.5**).

Overcoming Obstacles to Change

Despite the evidence for the malleability of personality just summarized, it would be a mistake to conclude that change is easy. Several obstacles lie in the way (Hennecke, Bleidorn, Denissen, & Wood, 2014).

First, most people like their personalities pretty much the way they are (Wortman & Wood, 2011). The widespread desire to improve one or more Big Five traits to at least some degree, mentioned earlier, should not be taken to mean that very many people are hoping for wholesale change. Notice that in Figure 7.3, the largest number of people wanted to be "more" extraverted, not "much more." And the kind of change some people need the most probably amounts to more than just small changes on the Big Five. One study that showed that introverts, in particular, often do not realize how much more fun their social lives could be if they just would act more extraverted (Zelinski et al., 2013). But this is difficult for them to do. Acting in a way contrary to one's traits takes effort and can be exhausting (Gallagher, Fleeson, & Hoyle, 2011). As was mentioned earlier, resistance to change can be especially strong in people, such as narcissists, whom others *wish* would change. They seem to underestimate how much better life could be for themselves and everyone around them if they would just quit being so annoying.

Second, people have a tendency to blame negative experiences and failures on external forces rather than recognizing the role of their own personality. For example, they might blame the fact that they frequently get into arguments on the obnoxious people who surround them, rather than recognize the role of their own disagreeableness. This blind spot creates problems for psychotherapists, who often have difficulty persuading their clients that the root cause of their problem is their own maladaptive behavior.

> Change requires learning new skills, going new places, meeting new people, and acting in unaccustomed ways. That can make it uncomfortable.

Third, people generally like their lives to be consistent and predictable (Swann, Rentfrow, & Guinn, 2003). Change requires learning new skills, going new places, meeting new people, and acting in unaccustomed ways. That can make it uncomfortable.[18]

Still, with effort, these obstacles can be overcome. According to one recently developed theoretical model, personality change can happen if several conditions are met (Hennecke et al., 2014; see **Figure 7.6**). First, the person must think that changing some aspect of personality is desirable, and that such change is possible. For example, imagine a person who is in danger of flunking out of college because of her low conscientiousness. To do something about this, she has to recognize the source of problem and want to change—which, for the reasons just summarized, may be difficult or even painful to acknowledge (Allemand & Flückiger, 2017). (In many cases, students who are failing in college are quite creative at finding ways to blame everything except their own behavior for what is happening.) She also must believe that she is capable of changing (Dweck, 2008; see Chapter 14). Second, the person must follow up by beginning to change her relevant behaviors, one by one. She has to work to get her next assignment in on time, attend class regularly, study rather than party on the night before the big exam, and so forth. Over time, if all goes well (and that's asking a lot), such behaviors will become habitual. Finally, in the ideal outcome, she will find that her trait of conscientiousness has stabilized at a higher level than it was at before. She might even clean her room!

Notice how this approach to personality change works in a way contrary to what we might ordinarily expect. Rather than changing personality in order to change behavior, the prescription outlined in Figure 7.7 advises changing behavior first in order to change personality! One recent study suggests that this tactic can indeed be effective, especially if the person develops a plan of the specific behaviors to work on (Hudson & Fraley, 2015). For example, a person trying to become more extraverted might make an effort to "call Andrew and ask him to lunch on

---

[18] Psychoanalytic theory (see Chapters 10 and 11) includes the idea of the "flight from health," which is that patients are so accustomed to their neuroses that they sometimes actively resist improvement.

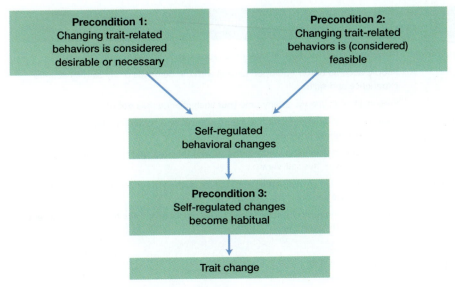

Figure 7.6 Steps to Personality Change According to this theoretical model, the first steps are to want to change, and to believe change is possible. Then one can begin to perform the necessary new behaviors, which, over time, become habitual and lead to lasting personality change.

Source: Hennecke et al. (2014), p. 290.

Tuesday"; someone trying to be less neurotic might set the goal of "if I feel stress, then I will call my mom to talk about it" (Hudson & Fraley, 2015, p. 8). As these actions, and behaviors like them, become habitual, then the patterns become "calcified" (to use the authors' term) into changes in traits that, in turn, produce long-lasting and broad changes in behavior.

PRINCIPLES OF PERSONALITY CONTINUITY AND CHANGE

It should be clear by this point that personality is characterized by stability over the life span, and also by significant change. As we have seen, many processes have been proposed to explain both of these facts. But these processes interact and sometimes even seem to contradict each other, and their sheer number can be overwhelming. The psychologists Brent Roberts, Dustin Wood, and Avshalom Caspi made a significant contribution, therefore, when they proposed a list of seven principles for personality development (Roberts, Wood, & Caspi, 2008).

The principles are not exactly empirical facts, nor are they theoretical statements. They are general claims about the bases of personality development and

Table 7.2 | PRINCIPLES OF PERSONALITY DEVELOPMENT

Cumulative continuity principle	Personality traits increase in rank-order consistency as people get older.
Maturity principle	People become better equipped to deal with the demands of life as they acquire experience and skills.
Plasticity principle	Personality can change at any time (but such change may not be easy).
Role continuity principle	Taking on roles or images such as being a "jock" or a "brain" can lead personality to be consistent over time.
Identity development principle	People seek to develop a stable sense of who they are, and then strive to act consistently with this self-view.
Social investment principle	Changing social roles at different stages of life, such as becoming a spouse, parent, or boss, can cause personality to change.
Correspondsive principle	Person-environment transactions can cause personality traits to remain consistent or even magnify over time.

Source: Adapted from Roberts, Wood, & Caspi (2008), p. 376.

change, and each of them can serve as a guide to future research (see **Table 7.2**). The first is the cumulative continuity principle, which was mentioned earlier in this chapter; it is the proposal that personality becomes more consistent as the individual gets older. The second, also mentioned earlier, is the maturity principle, which proposes that people become better equipped to deal with the demands of life as they acquire experience and skills.

The other principles have not been mentioned by name yet in this chapter, but we have seen examples of how they operate. The *plasticity principle* asserts that personality can change at any time during the life course, though such change may not be easy. The *role continuity principle* presents the idea that people choose "roles" to play that may stay the same over their lives, such as the person who becomes a "jock" or "brain" in high school and continues to enact that role in college and adult life. The *identity development principle* states that people construct a sense of "who am I" as they grow up, and that this self-view becomes an important foundation of behavioral stability as people try to be consistent with their sense of self. This principle is closely related to the process of identity formation described by Dan McAdams and summarized earlier in this chapter. The *social investment principle* describes how people become connected to social structures and institutions, and how this connection affects their psychological development. In particular, people are expected to—and generally do—connect differently to the social world as they progress from child to parent to grandparent, and from student to employee to boss. This principle can be seen to underlay Ravenna Helson's notion of the social clock, described earlier in the chapter. Finally, the *correspondsive principle* relates how life experience tends to magnify the personality traits that already exist, and establish them ever more firmly over time. The person-environment transactions discussed earlier, and listed in Table 7.1, illustrate how this process works.

You may have heard the expression that "as you get older, you just become more like the way you were all along." I don't know if this cliché is literally true, but notice how it does embody notions of both continuity and change over the life course. Perhaps it deserves inclusion as an eighth principle of personality development. What do you think?

IS PERSONALITY CHANGE GOOD OR BAD?

Yes. That is, personality change has both a downside and an upside.

Consider the downside first. A great deal of psychological research over the years has shown that, in general, instability and inconsistency can cause problems (see Chapter 4). Having a disorganized, unsteady personality leads to difficulties in presenting a consistent self to other people, which can make them wary. Recall from Chapter 5 that people tend to like others who are "judgeable," who are easy to understand, predict, and relate to. But when they don't know what to expect or how to predict what a person will do, they are more likely to avoid that person. Instability is also a problem for the individual himself. Feeling that "I don't know who I am" is a prime attribute of *borderline personality disorder* (see Chapter 17), a very severe affliction.

> The theme that emerges from behavior and personality that's constantly changing is this: "It's not working."

Moreover, if one's personality is constantly changing, then it will be difficult to choose consistent goals that can be pursued over the long term. It is possible to become a world-class pianist, a respected scientist, or a successful business owner—but only if you choose this goal, stick to it, and strive towards it over months, years, and even decades. In contrast, the theme that emerges from behavior and personality that's constantly changing is this: "It's not working." Overall, rapid changes in personality are associated with poor mental and physical health (Human, Biesanz, Miller, Chen, Lachman, & Seeman, 2012).

But that's overall. Really, whether personality change is good or bad depends on exactly what changes. As we have already seen, neuroticism tends to decrease over most of the life span and conscientiousness tends to increase, and both of these changes are to the good (Magee, Heaven, & Miller, 2013). Probably the best kind of personality change is the slow, steady sort such as is illustrated in Figure 7.7. If you want to try to change your personality, you don't need to do anything too drastic, sudden, or inconsistent with your previous self. Start with small changes that will accumulate over time and become habitual. Go, just this once, to the class you usually miss, skip that morning doughnut, head to the gym tonight, and then, do it all again tomorrow. Eventually you can become the person you want to be.

But first, ask yourself this: Who *do* I want to be, and how is that person different from the one I am now? Then ask yourself, what can I do, today, to make this change start to happen?

WRAPPING IT UP

SUMMARY

- People change over time, and are also the same persons over time. The paradox between these two facts lies at the core of the study of personality development, which addresses both change and stability.

Personality Stability

- Extensive and impressive evidence demonstrates the stability of personality over long periods of time. Patterns of behavior seen in children are also visible when they are adults, and traits identified early in life have important associations with long-term life outcomes, including academic achievement, occupational success, and satisfying interpersonal relationships.

- Personality is stable over time because the environment that surrounds a person itself tends to be stable, because early experiences can have long-lasting consequences, because people will seek out environments that are compatible with and magnify their personality traits, and because people actively change the environments they enter.

- Personality tends to become *more* stable over time, an effect known as the *cumulative continuity principle.*

Personality Development

- Although individual differences in personality tend to remain consistent over long periods of time, several traits change, on average, as people get older. In particular, conscientiousness tends to increase while neuroticism declines.

- The tendency of socially adaptive traits to increase with age is called the *maturity principle.* However, some adaptive traits may decline late in life.

- Personality changes over the life span because of physical changes to the body, because of the impact of particular events, and because of the different demands that are made on a person at different stages of life.

- The *social clock* describes the accomplishments conventionally expected of people at certain ages. For women, following either the stereotypical feminine or masculine social clocks can lead to long-term life satisfaction, but following neither can lead to problems.

- An important development task for everyone is to develop a life story, or *narrative identity*.

- Goals tend to change over the life span. Younger people look to explore new possibilities and develop skills; older people focus more on maintaining emotional well-being and enjoying relationships.

Personality Change

- Most people would like to change at least one of their Big Five personality traits to at least some degree.

- Increasing evidence indicates that personality can be changed, though it is not easy to do.

- Personality change can potentially be accomplished through psychotherapy, general intervention programs, targeted interventions, or behaviors and life experiences.

- Negative life experiences can lead to increases in neuroticism, but people higher in neuroticism also encounter more negative life experiences.

- People may resist significantly changing their personalities, but it is possible to do if they strongly desire to change and believe change is possible.

Principles of Personality Continuity and Change

- Seven basic principles summarize the bases of personality development and change: the cumulative continuity principle, the maturity principle, the plasticity principle, the role continuity principle, the identity development principle, the social investment principle, and the corresponsive principle.

Is Personality Change Good or Bad?

- In general, erratic and unstable personality change has negative consequences. But increases in traits such as conscientiousness and decreases in traits such as neuroticism can be beneficial.

- Self-change begins with identifying how one wishes to be different, and beginning to steadily do the small behaviors that can eventually bring about the desired change.

KEY TERMS

rank-order consistency, p. 228
temperament, p. 229
heterotypic continuity, p. 229
person-environment transactions, p. 232
active person-environment transaction, p. 232
reactive person-environment transaction, p. 233
evocative person-environment transaction, p. 233
cumulative continuity principle, p. 233
personality development, p. 235
cross-sectional study, p. 235
cohort effect, p. 237
longitudinal study, p. 237
maturity principle, p. 238
social clock, p. 240
narrative identity, p. 242

THINK ABOUT IT

1. How is your personality different than it was five years ago? Has it changed for the better or for the worse? Why?
2. Do you think people can accurately judge whether their own personality has changed? Why might this be difficult to do?
3. Do you expect your personality to change in the next five years? Do you want it to?
4. What kinds of situations do you seek out? What kinds of situations do you tend to avoid? Why? Does the answer have anything to do with your personality?
5. What kind of situations do you tend to avoid? What would happen if you went there anyway? Do you think you might enjoy yourself, or would you be miserable?
6. Psychologists generally define "psychological maturity" as increased conscientiousness and decreased neuroticism. Do you agree with this definition? Does it leave anything out?
7. A major study cited in this chapter (Sutin, Luchetti, Stephan, Robins, & Terracciano, 2017) found that the children of better-educated parents grew up to be more open, extraverted, and emotionally stable. Why do you think this is?
8. Do you have goals for what you want to accomplish at certain ages in the future? Does this plan at all resemble Helson's idea of the "social clock"? How will you feel if you don't accomplish these goals on schedule? How will other people (e.g., your parents) feel?
9. If you told the story of your life, what would be its theme?

10. Why do you think people high in neuroticism seem to encounter more negative life experiences?

11. Do you know anyone whose personality would be better if it could somehow be changed? If you told that to this person (which I don't recommend), would they agree? Why not?

12. According to the survey cited in the text (Hudson & Roberts, 2014) almost everybody would like to change at least one of their Big Five traits at least somewhat. Does this include you?

13. What would it take for someone to want truly to change her own personality? Is a profound event (e.g., a spectacular failure of some kind) necessary, or is vague dissatisfaction with how things are going enough to motivate change?

14. If you wanted to become more conscientious, what could you do today to make that start to happen?

SUGGESTED RESOURCES

Roberts, B. W., Donnellan, M. B., & Hill, P. L. (2012). Personality trait development in adulthood. In I. B. Weiner (Ed.), *Handbook of psychology, 5,* 183–196.

> *This chapter provides a superb overview of the major issues in the study of personality development. It includes a clear presentation of some key methodological points that are necessary to understand and properly interpret the research literature.*

Want to earn a better grade on your test?

Go to **INQUIZITIVE** to learn and review this chapter's content, with personalized feedback along the way.

PART III

THE MIND AND THE BODY
Biological Approaches to Personality

Let's face it: People are animals. From a biological point of view, every human being is a member in good standing of the class *Mammalia*, and the human body, especially its internal anatomy including the brain and nervous system, is similar in many ways to the bodies of other species. One anatomical researcher concluded that one part of the human brain resembles the brain of a reptile, a second part resembles the brain of most mammals, and a third part is uniquely human (the *triune brain* hypothesis; see MacLean, 1990). This description is oversimplified (Buck, 1999; Fridlund, 1994), but the brains and nervous systems of many species do show a striking resemblance.

The resemblance is chemical as well as anatomical. My elderly dog was once put on a thyroid medication that, it turned out, was identical to one prescribed for a relative of mine who was the same age, adjusting for dog years. The only difference was that the human version was about 10 times more expensive. (On the upside, it was covered by Medicare.) The slightly unsettling fact that most medicines prescribed by veterinarians have similar effects on people reminds us that our physiology is not unique. We share with our fellow mammals many of the same or similar chemicals that sustain and regulate the body and, yes, the mind. The familiar antidepressant Prozac (fluoxetine) works just fine on vervet monkeys (Raleigh, 1987; Raleigh, McGuire, Brammer, Pollack, & Yuwiler, 1991), and it was once prescribed to our family cat to help her deal with the stress of two new dogs in the house (it seemed to help, though they never did become friends).

A third area of cross-species similarity is the way so much of human nature and personality seems to be biologically inherited. The family resemblance observed at many holiday gatherings illustrates how traits such as hair and skin color, body size, and perhaps even abilities and behavioral styles are transmitted from one generation to the next. Animal breeders have known for a long time how to accentuate or minimize various behavioral tendencies as well as aspects of appearance through careful selection of parental matches. Not only will the offspring of two poodles surely have curly fur, but they will also probably have gentler dispositions than the offspring of two rottweilers. Evidence summarized in the following chapters suggests that personality traits of humans are, to some degree, inherited as well.

Finally, and most controversially, all of life—plant, animal, and human—is the product of a long process of biological evolution. Evolution is more than just a theory: It is the fundamental principle that organizes biology, systematizes the taxonomy of species, and accounts for their origin. The process of evolution has worked for millions of generations over hundreds of millions of years to produce a wide diversity of species, and it continues today (e.g., in bacteria that quickly evolve immunity to overused antibiotics). The implication of evolution for psychology is that any attribute of any species—including behavioral patterns in humans—may be present because of advantages they offered for the survival and reproduction of members of past generations.

The principle of evolution sometimes evokes opposition because it seems, to some, to violate religious beliefs. As William Jennings Bryan said in 1922, the "evolutionary hypothesis . . . takes from man the breath of the almighty and substitutes the blood of a brute" (Bryan, 1922, 2009). But the underlying issue goes beyond dogma. Bryan reportedly offered $100 to anyone who would sign an affidavit acknowledging having personally descended from an ape. Apparently, he had no takers, which illustrates that people are reluctant to think of themselves as animals. I confess that I was disturbed when I found the same drug in my aunt's medicine chest that, at home, I stored next to the dog food. Besides the possible loss of dignity in thinking of oneself as an almost hairless ape (or a dog who walks upright), the topic of evolution returns us to the statement with which we began this section: Are people really just animals?

The question raises one of the oldest issues in philosophy, one with particular relevance to psychology: the *mind-body problem*. To what degree is the human mind—including behavior, emotion, thought, and experiences ranging from the appreciation of beauty to moral reasoning—a direct product of physical, biological processes? This question has become increasingly acute for psychology because, as recently as a couple of decades ago, so little was known about the biological basis of personality that the issue could be safely ignored. This is no longer possible. Rapidly developing, sophisticated technology is uncovering relationships between structures and processes of the brain and psychological functioning. At the same time, it is becoming apparent that personality traits are, to an important degree, inherited and some aspects of human nature are rooted in our evolutionary history.

These intersections between the study of biology and the study of personality— anatomy, physiology, genetics, and evolution—are the topics of the next two chapters. More will be said near the end of Chapter 9 about the degree to which biology could subsume psychology; in the meantime, I urge you keep the mind-body question in the back of your mind as you read.

To what degree is human psychology—behavior, emotion, thought, and experience—reducible to processes of the body and the brain? It is not difficult to find people willing to argue that the answer is 100 percent (this is the *reductionist* position), and others who maintain that the answer is 0 percent (this is the *humanist* position). As we shall see, both are wrong. In psychology, nothing is ever that simple.

8

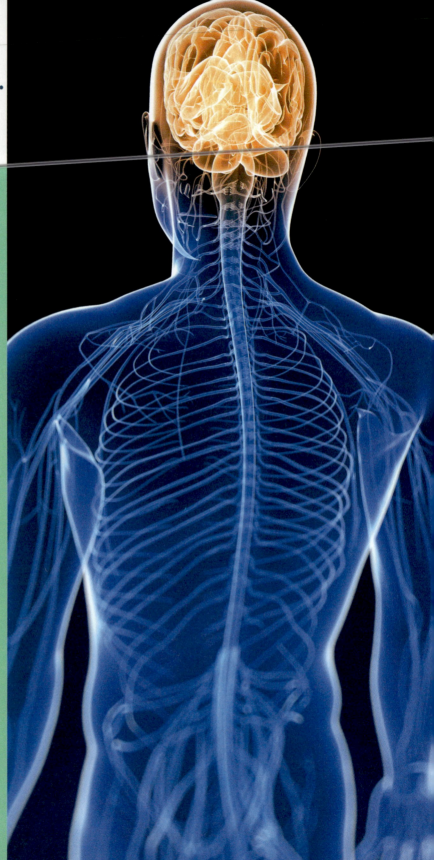

THE ANATOMY AND
PHYSIOLOGY OF
PERSONALITY

FOR A LONG TIME, people have been pretty sure that the brain must be important for the mind and behavior. In the fourth century B.C., the Greek physician Hippocrates maintained that "from the brain and from the brain only arise our pleasures, joys, laughter and jests, as well as our sorrows, pains, secrets, and fears. Through it, in particular, we think, see, hear and distinguish the ugly from the beautiful, the bad from the good, the pleasant from the unpleasant" (Hippocrates, 1923, p. 175). More recently, personality neuroscientist Colin DeYoung observed that all "personality differences are 'biological' . . . in the sense that they must be proximally generated by the brain no matter whether they originated in genes or environment" (DeYoung, 2010, p. 1166). However, realizing that the brain is important and figuring out how it functions are two very different matters.

To appreciate the plight of anyone who would seek to solve this problem, picture the following scenario: Imagine we could travel to ancient Greece and give Hippocrates an MP3 player[1] loaded with a selection of early 21st-century music. As Hippocrates listened to some of Lady Gaga's additions to the musical canon, he would likely be amazed and perplexed. Then, being curious, he might try to figure out how this remarkable device works.

What would he do? He could try dismantling the player, though it is unlikely he would recognize anything he saw inside, and it is even more unlikely he would ever get it back together again afterward. But if he were too cautious to probe the device's innards, his only recourse would be to observe it, listen to it, and fiddle with the controls. Only after the battery ran down might he dare open it up (rechargers being unavailable in ancient Greece). Unfortunately, all he would see would be the interior of a mechanism that no longer functioned.

---

[1] MP3 players are already pretty obsolete, I know, but Hippocrates still would have been impressed.

Part of Hippocrates' problem is that his tools are limited. What if we also used our time transporter to send him a voltmeter and an X-ray machine? Now Hippocrates might have a chance to make some progress, though he would still face many conceptual problems in trying to understand the meaning of X-ray images and voltmeter readings.

Anyone seeking to understand the physical basis of the mind faces a situation every bit as difficult as the imaginary quandary we gave to Hippocrates. Here stands a living, thinking person who possesses a functioning brain that can do amazing things, more amazing than any electronic device, by far. How do you figure out how it works? You could say or do things to the person and note how he replies and what he does. This is a little like Hippocrates pushing the little "play" button and noticing that he hears music. It is a useful start but tells you little about what is going on inside. Still, sometimes observing from the outside is all you can do. You cannot easily open up a person's brain, especially while that person is alive. And even then, all you see is squishy, bloody tissue, the function of which is far from obvious. Again, the problem may lie in the limitations of the available tools. For centuries, people curious about brain function were limited to studying either people who had suffered brain damage or the bodies of people who had died, using tools such as scalpels and magnifying glasses. But a dramatic revolution began about two decades ago with the invention and refinement of tools such as EEG machines, PET scanners, fMRI magnets, and other devices that provide information about the activities of intact, living brains.

> You cannot easily open up a person's brain, especially while that person is alive.

Modern technology allows close examination of two aspects of the brain: its anatomy and its biochemistry. Anatomical researchers examine the functions of different parts of the brain and try to determine the physical location and timing of various brain processes. Researchers of brain biochemistry examine the effects of two fundamental groups of chemicals, neurotransmitters and hormones. The two topics are related; different neurotransmitters and hormones influence different parts of the brain, and different parts of the brain secrete different neurotransmitters and hormones. All of this affects how people feel and what they do, and that is the subject of this chapter.

We will consider two main questions. First, what can the structure of the brain tell us about personality? Just about every part of the brain, from the brain stem (the rear portion that connects to the spinal cord) to the frontal cortex (the portion just behind the forehead) has been found to be related to personality in one way or another. The research literature is vast, complex, sometimes contradictory, and changing rapidly, but a few conclusions are beginning to come through loud and clear, as we shall see.

The second question is, to what degree is personality a matter of chemistry? The brain is filled with blood and many chemicals, including a wide variety of neurotransmitters and hormones, each of which relates to behavior in complex ways. This chapter will consider some of the more important ones, along with a discussion of the drugs used, increasingly often, to affect the chemistry of the brain in order to change how people feel, what they do, and (maybe) even who they are.

This last topic is a reminder that one reason for the fascination with the biology of the brain is the potential to use new knowledge to make things better—to cure mental illness, or at least to lessen anxiety, alleviate depression, and improve quality of life. Not too long ago, surgery was routinely used to change the physical structure of the brain in an attempt to treat mental illness. These days, drugs are commonly used to alter the chemistry of the brain, with the same goal. The history of psychological surgery was not a happy one, as we shall see, and drugs have drawbacks, too. But one thing is clear: As our understanding of the biological bases of emotion, behavior, and personality improves, the potential to use that knowledge to help people improves as well.

THE ANATOMY OF PERSONALITY

The physical basis of personality is the brain and its tentacles, the nerves that reach into every corner of the body right down to the tip of the big toe. Nerve cells, or **neurons**, typically have projections called *dendrites*, which receive stimulation, and *axons*, which pass the message on. The dendrites of *afferent* nerves, which can be extremely long, extend from the central nervous system to every part of the body; messages travel up these dendrites to the brain to report what the body is feeling and doing. At the same time, *efferent* nerves, with extra-long axons, send impulses and instructions from the central nervous system back to the muscles, glands, and other organs. The activity of one neuron may affect the activity of many other neurons, transmitting sensations from the far reaches of the body into the brain; connecting these sensations with feelings, memories, and plans in the brain; and sending behavioral instructions out to the muscles, causing the body to move. *Interneurons*, which have short axons or none at all, organize and regulate transmissions between nerve cells. The biggest bundle of interneurons is the large, wrinkled organ known as the brain[2] (see **Figure 8.1**).

The brain has several parts. In the middle lie small organs such as the *thalamus*, which regulates arousal and serves other functions. The **hypothalamus**—which lies underneath the thalamus near the bottom center of the brain, just

---

[2] Actually, neurons make up only about 10 percent to 15 percent of the cells in the brain. The rest, called *glial cells*, help to nourish and hold together the neurons, and apparently play other roles that are not completely understood.

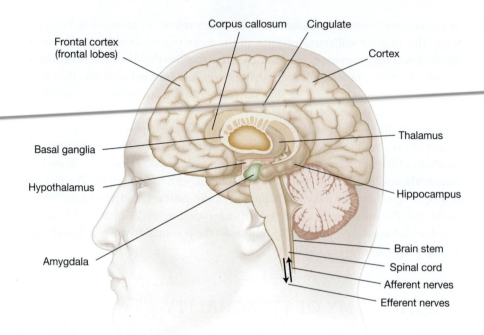

Figure 8.1 Personality and the Brain Some of the major organs of the brain and nervous system that are relevant to personality.

above the roof of the mouth—is particularly important because it is connected to just about everything else. Its nerves extend throughout the brain, and it secretes several **hormones**—biological chemicals that affect the entire body. Behind and to the outer sides of the hypothalamus is wrapped the **amygdala**, which (as we shall see later in the chapter) has an important role in emotion, and near the amygdala lies a tube-shaped structure called the **hippocampus**, which is especially important in processing memories.

Wrapped all around these inner organs is the outer layer of the brain called the **cortex** (or *cerebral cortex*), which itself has six layers that differ in anatomy and function. The outermost layer, the **neocortex**, is the most distinctive part of the human brain. It is more complex—and also more wrinkled—than the cortex in other animals. Another distinctive aspect of the human brain is the large size of the **frontal cortex,** which is the part that (as you might have guessed) lies in front. The frontal cortex, like the rest of the brain, is divided into two lobes on the right and left sides. The two *frontal lobes* appear to be crucial for such uniquely human aspects of cognition as the ability to plan ahead and to anticipate consequences, and for aspects of emotional experience, such as empathy and moral reasoning, that may be uniquely human.

Research Methods for Studying the Brain

Psychologists use three main methods for learning about how the brain works: the study of brain damage, experiments using brain stimulation, and the newest technique, brain imaging.

BRAIN DAMAGE The oldest source of knowledge about the human brain, dating back many centuries, comes from observations of people who have suffered head injuries. If enough injuries are carefully observed, it becomes possible to draw conclusions by keeping track of the specific problems caused by damage to different parts. Sometimes researchers damage brains deliberately; in other words, they perform brain surgery. Parts of the brain are deliberately *lesioned* (destroyed) by being cut off from other brain structures or even removed completely.

Nearly all of this surgical research has been done on animals such as rats, dogs, and (more rarely) monkeys. This is a reasonable place to begin because, as we have already mentioned, the brains of different mammals look alike and function alike in many ways. Indeed, the study of animal personality is a rapidly growing field (Gosling, 2008a).

Personality traits have been assessed in hyenas, dogs, tortoises, and many other animals (Gosling, 1998; Gosling & Vazire, 2002; J. E. King & Figueredo, 1997; Sahagun, 2005). One study closely observed the behavior of chimpanzees and identified a Chimp Big Five of fundamental traits that included reactivity, dominance, openness, extraversion, and agreeableness (Freeman, Brosnan, Hopper, Lambeth, Schapiro, & Gosling, 2013). Another study of macaques found individual differences in traits including friendliness, aggression, and social skill (Adams et al., 2015). Even squid can have different personalities, it appears: Some are bold and some are shy (Sinn, Gosling, & Moltschaniwsky, 2008). So while we should not assume animals and humans to be the same in all respects, knowledge about animal brains is surely relevant to understanding human brains. In addition, a small amount of research addresses the effects of surgery on human brains. We will consider some of that work later in the chapter.

BRAIN STIMULATION A particularly intriguing—but difficult and rare—approach to studying the brain is to stimulate its parts directly with electrodes. For obvious reasons, most of this research, too, is done on animals, and researchers have published detailed atlases of the brains of animals, such as rats, along with descriptions of which muscles in the body respond to stimulation of each region. In the middle of the 20th century, neurosurgeon Wilder Penfield performed brain surgery on conscious human patients and asked what they experienced when he electrically stimulated different parts. Depending on where in the brain he placed his probe, his patients reported visions, sounds, dreams, and memory flashbacks (Penfield & Perot, 1963). More recently, surgeons unexpectedly discovered that stimulating a particular area (the central region of the left *substantia nigra*, deep in the middle of the brain) could produce symptoms of depression (Bejjani et al., 1999). A 65-year-old woman, who had electrodes inserted into her brain in an attempt to control her Parkinson's disease, was electrically stimulated in this area, and researchers described her response:

> Although still alert, the patient leaned to the right, started to cry, and [said] . . . "I'm falling down in my head, I no longer wish to live, to see anything, hear anything, feel anything. . . ." When asked why she was crying and if she felt pain, she responded, "No, I'm fed up with life, I've had enough. . . . I don't want to live any more, I'm disgusted with life. . . . Everything is useless, always feeling worthless, I'm scared in this world." (Bejjani et al., 1999, p. 1477)

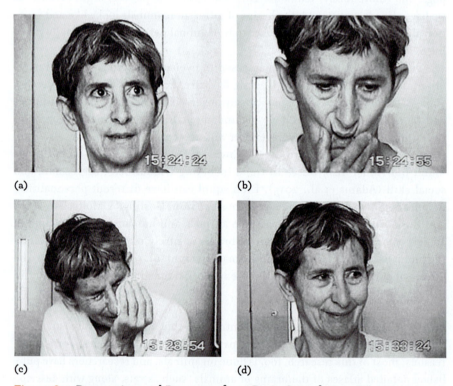

(a)

(b)

(c)

(d)

Figure 8.2 Depression and Recovery from Brain Stimulation The woman in the photographs had electrodes planted in her brain to try to control Parkinson's disease, but stimulating them triggered an acute episode of depression. (a) Her usual expression. (b) Her face 17 seconds after stimulation began. (c) Crying after 4 minutes and 16 seconds of stimulation. (d) Fully recovered and smiling, 1 minute 20 seconds after the stimulation was turned off.

Less than 90 seconds after the stimulation was turned off, her depression went away, and within 5 minutes the patient became cheerful, laughing and joking with the researcher and even "playfully pulling his tie" (see **Figure 8.2**).

While studies like this are understandably rare—and, as in this case, may examine just a single patient—they can add important knowledge (recall the discussion of the case study method in Chapter 2). The areas of the substantia nigra relevant to this case are associated with neurotransmitters such as dopamine, norepinephrine, and serotonin, which other research has shown to be involved in depression (as will be discussed later), so this is an example of one patient adding an important piece of information to the puzzle.

A relatively new method called *transcranial magnetic stimulation (TMS)* uses rapidly changing magnetic fields to temporarily "knock out" (turn off) areas of brain activity (see **Figure 8.3**). In this way, researchers can create a "virtual lesion," cutting off part of the brain without physically having to cut anything, and thereby see whether that part is essential for a psychological task (Fitzgerald, Fountain, & Daskalakis, 2006). For example, if the areas of the brain essential for speech are turned off using TMS, the individual will (temporarily) be unable to talk (Highfield, 2008). Using a related technique,

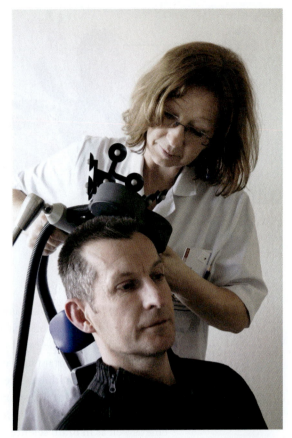

Figure 8.3 Transcranial Magnetic Stimulation This technique uses a magnetic pulse to temporarily "turn off" specific areas of the brain in order to learn more about their functions.

transcranial direct current stimulation (tDCS), researchers have shown that the right frontal lobe (but not the left) is important for making morally relevant decisions, such as whether to punish someone for playing a game unfairly, or whether to play fairly oneself (Knoch et al., 2008; Knoch, Schneider, Schunk, Hohman, & Fehr, 2009). Though just beginning, use of these techniques to study personality looks promising; they may also turn out to be useful for treating brain disorders such as migraine headaches, effects of strokes, hallucinations, and depression.

BRAIN ACTIVITY AND IMAGING A third approach to studying the brain is to observe its function directly—to view what the brain is doing while it is doing it. The oldest technique is **electroencephalography (EEG),** in which electrodes are placed on the scalp to pick up electrical signals generated by the brain activity underneath

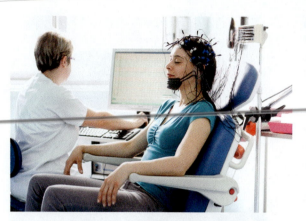

Figure 8.4 Electroencephalography Electrodes placed on the outside of the scalp pick up minute electrical signals from the brain that are displayed as wiggly lines on a screen or printout.

(see **Figure 8.4**). A newer, related technique is **magnetoencephalography (MEG)**, which uses delicate sensors to detect magnetic (as opposed to electrical) indications of brain activity. Both of these techniques are useful for determining *when* the brain is especially active, but they are not very specific as to just *where* in the brain the activity is concentrated. I once heard the analogy that trying to understand brain activity by looking at an EEG is a little like trying to follow a football game by standing outside the stadium and listening to the cheering. It will be easy to tell when something important happens but more difficult to know precisely what it was that happened or where; was it a touchdown, an interception, or something else?

The ability to see what is going on inside the living brain changed dramatically as a result of technological developments near the end of the 20th century. The most important was the rapid increase in the availability and power of computers. Computers are important for a couple of reasons. One is that they allow many different images from multiple angles—X-rays, for example—to be combined into representations of very thin slices (*tomographs*) of the brain, allowing minute structures to be examined. These *computed tomography (CT)* scans are now widely used in medicine as well as in brain science. Another reason is that the construction of images of the brain requires complex data analyses that compare many images to each other.

CT scans can be used with different data sources, including **positron emission tomography (PET)**, which was developed in the late 1980s. A PET scan creates a map of brain activity by following the location of a harmless radioactive tracer injected into the bloodstream. The assumption is that the harder the brain works, the more blood it needs, so by following blood flow, researchers can learn where the brain is most active when doing various sorts of tasks. Some PET studies use radioactive molecules that bind to, or collect at, particular brain structures, allowing studies to focus on specific regions. Another way to image the workings of the brain is **functional magnetic resonance imaging (fMRI)**, which monitors magnetic pulses generated by oxygen in the blood to map where the brain is most active at a given moment. New methods continue to be developed, including *diffusion tensor imaging (DTI)* and *magnetic resonance spectroscopy (MRS)*.[3]

Each of these imaging techniques has its strengths and weaknesses, and there is no one best method. Each of them is continually undergoing further

---

[3] Despite its abbreviation, this technique is not wedded to any of the others.

development and refinement, and their use entails a host of technical challenges. Perhaps the most important one is that all parts of a living brain are always metabolically active to some degree, so a researcher must do more than simply measure what the brain does. For example, the *blood oxygen level dependent (BOLD)* signal measured by fMRI is not an absolute number; rather, it is calculated as a difference in levels of brain activity between experimental conditions, or between different individuals (Zald & Curtis, 2006). A new technique called *perfusion imaging*, which uses something called *arterial spin labeling*, appears to yield more precise measures of blood flow in the brain than do BOLD signals, but it relies on the same experimental logic (Liu & Brown, 2007). To show that a certain brain region is relevant to emotional experience, for example, it is necessary for the researcher to come up with a stimulus that evokes an emotion in the participant (e.g., a photograph of the participant's child) and a stimulus that is as similar as possible without being emotionally affecting (perhaps a picture of a stranger). Then the areas where brain activation differs between the two conditions are mapped. These parts of the brain might be—but very possibly are not—specifically relevant to emotion.

There are a couple of reasons for why the areas that differentially "light up" (as it is often said) in response to emotional stimuli might not be specifically relevant to emotion (Barrett & Wager, 2006). One reason is that the data in most studies allow an inference in only one direction: An area of the brain responds to emotional stimuli. But this does not necessarily mean that a person feels an emotion whenever this area of the brain is active. As was discussed in Chapter 2, correlation is not necessarily causality, and this principle applies to fMRI data as well.

A second complication is that most studies necessarily look at small areas of the brain at a time. Therefore, such studies cannot show which other areas may be active, or whether the area in question becomes active only if another area is (or is not) active at the same time, a phenomenon called *neural context* (McIntosh, 1998). In other words, the function of activity in one part of the brain may depend on what is happening elsewhere (Canli, 2004, p. 1118). I will return to this point later in the chapter.

Yet another challenge is that, as the technology to image brain activity becomes both more powerful and more sensitive, it is also becoming frightfully expensive and increasingly difficult to use. An fMRI scan requires the research participant to lie still inside a cramped cylinder filled with loud buzzing noises (see **Figure 8.5**). The magnetic field generated by the scanner is so strong that, in one terrible

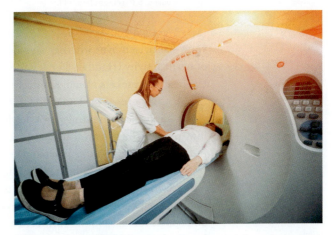

Figure 8.5 An fMRI Scan A research participant being slid into an MRI scanner.

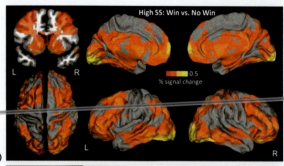

(a)

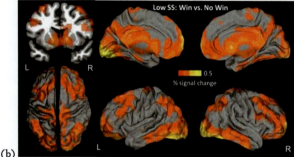

(b)

Figure 8.6 fMRI Data These figures are graphic summaries of data obtained from fMRI scans of adolescents who were high in sensation-seeking (panel a) and low (panel b). The areas in red show where participants' brains responded, on average, more to winning than to losing an experimental game. The two patterns were interpreted as showing that different areas of the brains of high and low sensation-seekers are responsive to reward.

Source: Cservenka, Herting, Seghete, Hudson, & Nagel (2013), p. 188.

accident, a heavy oxygen tank flew across the room at almost 3o feet per second, killing a small boy (Chen, 2001). So the room in which the scanner is housed must be carefully shielded, and the building itself must be specially constructed with, for example, an extra-solid floor (the machine is almost always located in the basement). Despite special construction and expensive shielding, MEG scans, for example, are so sensitive that they can be disrupted by someone elsewhere in the building turning on a light at the wrong moment. Data from these various imaging devices must be carefully analyzed to eliminate as much interference as possible. It's not like snapping a photograph.

Indeed, the images that are published from fMRI and other scans, despite their appearance, are not photographs at all; they are (sometimes beautiful) color-coded data summaries (see **Figure 8.6**). Their construction is the result of a complex set of analyses fraught with statistical difficulties (D. P. McCabe & Castel, 2008). One influential critique suggested that some of the commonly used data analytic techniques are questionable, leading to results that might be misleading at worst and exaggerated at best (Vul, Harris, Winkielman, & Pashler, 2009; Eklund, Nichols, & Knutsson, 2016). As if that weren't bad enough, a controversy has arisen over whether signals such as BOLD actually reflect specific areas of brain activity (Handwerker & Bandettini, 2011; Sirotin & Das, 2009). So even as the research rockets ahead, some of its basic assumptions remain in flux.

At this point, I have to emphasize that neuroimaging research is an exciting, vibrant area that is yielding new knowledge at a rate that is almost impossible to follow. In 2007, 82 research articles that noted "fMRI" as a descriptive key word were published in psychology journals, according to the online reference PsychInfo; by 2009, just two years later, this number had more than tripled, and by 2015 it had grown by a factor of more than 20 (see **Figure 8.7**). As a side effect of this phenomenal acceleration, neuroimaging has suffered inevitable growing pains, and controversies abound (Miller, 2008). However, the rate of growth seems to be leveling off; researchers are starting to solve some long-standing difficulties, and

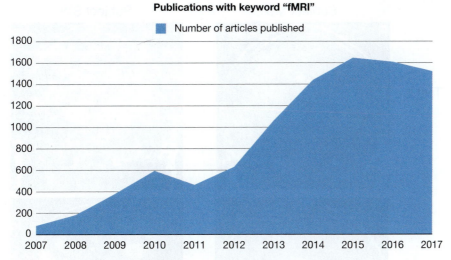

Figure 8.7 Trends in fMRI Research The number of psychological research articles identifying "fMRI" as a keyword has increased dramatically since the year 2007, but seems to have leveled off or even dropped slightly since 2015.
Source: PsychInfo.

results are becoming more reliable (Stanley & Adolphs, 2013, Editorial, 2017). For example, one fMRI study examined the correlates between several emotional traits and brain activation and then—remarkably—did the same thing again, with the same participants, five years later. It is reassuring to see that the individual differences in brain response at the two times of measurement time remained recognizably similar (Wu, Samanez-Larkin, Katovich, & Knutson, 2013; see **Figure 8.8**).

The Amygdala

The **amygdala** is a small structure located near the base of the brain, behind the hypothalamus. It is found in humans and in many other animals, and it appears to link perceptions and thoughts about the world with their emotional meaning (Adolphs, 2001). When the amygdala is surgically removed from rhesus monkeys, they become less aggressive and less fearful, they sometimes try to eat things that are not edible (even feces and urine), and they may exhibit increased and unusual sexual behavior. Research on humans and other animals indicates that the amygdala has important effects on negative emotions such as anger and fear. The amygdala of shy people becomes highly active when they are shown pictures of people that they don't know (Birbaumer et al., 1998), and people with anxiety disorders such as panic attacks and post-traumatic stress disorder (PTSD) tend to have an active amygdala all the time, even at rest (Drevets, 1999). The effect persists throughout life. Adults described as "inhibited" back when they were infants have stronger amygdala

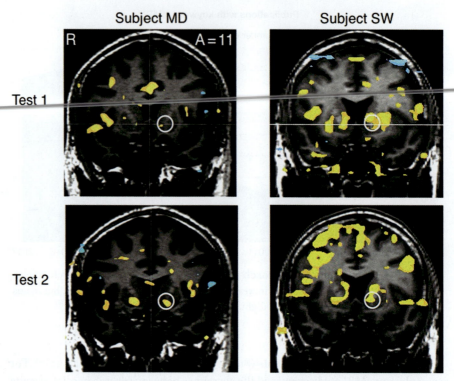

Figure 8.8 **Consistency of fMRI Data Over Time** The top figures show the fMRI-detected brain activity of two participants, labeled MD and SW, when anticipating a large monetary reward. The bottom figures show their responses in a similar experiment five years later. The differences between the two people are noticeable and consistent over time.

Source: Wu et al. (2013), p. 285.

responses to pictures of strangers than do those who were described, many years earlier, as "uninhibited" (Schwartz, Wright, Shin, Kagan, & Rauch, 2003).

The functioning of the amygdala is also related to positive emotions such as social attraction and sexual responsiveness (Barrett, 2006; Klein & Kihlstrom, 1998), as well as reactions to pleasurable stimuli such as photographs of happy scenes (Hamann, Ely, Hoffman, & Kilts, 2002), words describing positive emotions (Hamann & Mao, 2002), and pleasant tastes (Small et al., 2003). From this varied evidence, psychologist Lisa Feldman Barrett concludes that the amygdala plays an important role in computing the degree to which a stimulus, whether a person or a thing, offers impending threat or reward (2006; Barrett & Wager, 2006). After the brain assesses the situation, the amygdala may respond by making the heart beat faster, raising blood pressure, and releasing hormones such as cortisol and epinephrine (Bremner, 2005).

This hypothesis helps to explain the wide variety of personality traits that appears to be relevant to the amygdala and two related structures, the insula and anterior cingulate (both of which are located deep within the middle of the brain). These traits include chronic anxiety, fearfulness, sociability, and sexuality (DeYoung, 2010; Zuckerman, 1991), all of which are related to whether other people are generally seen as attractive or threatening.

The importance of the amygdala and related structures was dramatically illustrated by an incident at the University of Texas on July 31, 1966. A graduate student named Charles Whitman wrote a letter that read, in part,

> I have been a victim of many unusual and irrational thoughts. These thoughts constantly recur, and it requires a tremendous mental effort to concentrate on useful and productive tasks. . . . After my death I wish that an autopsy would be performed on me to see if there is any visible physical disorder. . . . It was after much thought that I decided to kill my wife, Kathy, tonight after I pick her up from work. . . . I love her dearly, and she has been as fine a wife to me as any man could ever hope to have. I cannot rationally pinpoint any specific reason for doing this. (Johnson, 1972, as cited in Buck, 1999, p. 312)

That night, Whitman did murder his wife, and then his mother. The next day he took a high-powered rifle and climbed to the top of a tower at the center of campus and began firing at random, killing 14 more people and wounding 32 before police managed to scramble to the top of the tower and shoot him. The autopsy he wished for found the "visible physical disorder" Whitman suspected. He had a malignant tumor in the right hemisphere of his brain, in the basal ganglia next to the amygdala (see Figures 8.1 and **8.9**).

This finding implies that lower parts of the brain near and including the amygdala may be capable of producing motivations for actions like killing one's wife and mother along with innocent strangers (Buck, 1999). But these motivations, powerful as they are, might arise without the thoughts, or even the emotional experiences (e.g., rage), one might expect to be associated with killing. The rest of his brain did not understand the strange impulses

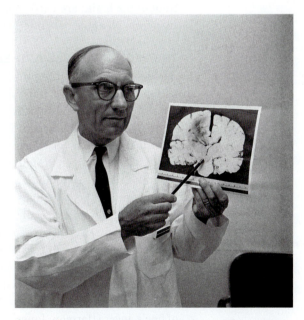

Figure 8.9 Doctor Showing Evidence That Texas Sniper Had a Brain Tumor Charles Whitman himself suspected there was something wrong with his brain because he did not understand the cause of his actions.

produced by his amygdala any more than outside observers did; in that sense, the rest of his brain *was* an outside observer.

Just as the frontal cortex has been viewed as the seat of uniquely human cognitive functions such as thinking and planning, the amygdala and associated structures near the core of the brain have become widely accepted as contributing to motivations and emotions. The case of Charles Whitman adds an important wrinkle to this idea. In order to understand, to experience consciously or "feel" these emotions, other brain structures such as the cerebral cortex may be necessary. The fact that many animals, including reptiles, have an amygdala suggests that the basic foundation of emotional processes is ancient, evolutionarily speaking, and functions similarly across species. But the unique development of the neocortex in humans suggests that other animals might not understand or experience emotions as humans do.

The Frontal Lobes and the Neocortex

The neocortex, which forms the outer layer of the brain, is the brain's most uniquely human part. Spread out flat, it would be about the size of a sheet of newspaper, but to fit inside the skull it is scrunched around the rest of the brain in a way that explains its wrinkled appearance. Psychologists have long accepted the idea that the frontal lobes, the two parts of the neocortex at the left-front and right-front of the brain, are particularly important for higher cognitive functions such as speech, planning, and interpreting the world.

THE FRONTAL LOBES AND EMOTION Although the two lobes look similar, they serve somewhat different functions. EEG studies suggest that the left frontal lobe is more active when a person wants to approach something pleasant, whereas activity in the right frontal lobe is associated with wanting to withdraw from something unpleasant or frightening (Hewig, Hagemann, Seifert, Naumann, & Bartussek, 2004; Shackman, McMenamin, Maxwell, Greischar, & Davidson, 2009). Also, activity in the left side of the frontal lobe is associated with the ability to inhibit responses to unpleasant stimuli, so the left frontal cortex may be able both to promote good feelings and dampen bad ones (D. C. Jackson et al., 2003). This may be why an especially active left brain seems to be associated with emotional stability, whereas an especially active right brain is associated with the Big Five trait of neuroticism (see Chapter 7). However, not all of neuroticism lives on the right side of the brain (DeYoung, 2010). A propensity to get angry, which is part of this trait, seems more associated with left-brain activity—probably because the impulse to attack includes a motivation to approach, rather than avoid, the target of one's anger (Harmon-Jones, 2004).

THE CASE OF PHINEAS GAGE On a difficult day in 1848, a railroad construction supervisor named Phineas Gage stood in the wrong place at the wrong time, near a dynamite explosion that sent a 3-foot iron rod through his left cheek, into the

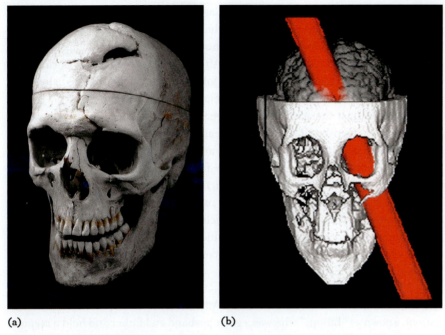

(a) (b)

Figure 8.10 **Phineas Gage** (a) This photograph shows the incredible damage to Phineas Gage's skull. (b) The computer image reconstructs the path of the rod that caused the injury.

frontal lobes of his brain, and out through the top of his head (see **Figure 8.10**). Remarkably, he survived and lived another 15 years. According to some preliminary reports, after he recovered from his injury Gage was just fine. He could speak and move normally, and his memories were intact. Some observers reported that he was perhaps a little less emotional than he used to be (Bigelow, 1850; Harlow, 1849).

These early reports had an unfortunately long-lasting influence: A century later, they reassured some surgeons that it was OK to remove large portions of the human brain in an attempt to "cure" excessive emotionality (Freeman & Watts, 1950). But these impressions were incorrect (Klein & Kihlstrom, 1998). In his final reports, Gage's physician, who seems to have been an astute observer, recorded that although Gage retained some reasonable degree of mental functioning, his personality was noticeably changed—and not for the better (Harlow, 1868, 1869). According to this physician, Gage's behavior became "fitful, irreverent, indulging at times in the grossest profanity (which was not previously his custom), manifesting but little deference for his fellows, impatient of restraint or advice . . . at times pertinaciously obstinate, yet capricious and facillating [*sic*]." Overall, Gage had become "a child in his intellectual capacity and manifestations . . . [yet had] the animal passions of a strong man" (Harlow, as cited in Valenstein, 1986, p. 90).

Indeed, the long-term outcome for Gage was disastrous. His emotional life flattened out—nothing ever made him either very happy or very upset. The rest of his life fell apart. Before the accident, he was one of the most valued employees of the Rutland & Burlington Railroad. Afterward, he was unable to perform his duties and never managed to hold another job. He made one unwise decision after another, and both his professional and personal lives disintegrated.

Gage's was just the most famous of many brain injuries that turned out to be informative. Gunshot wounds to the head and other injuries have shown that people can live despite having remarkable amounts of tissue removed or severed. According to some accounts—similar to the first impressions of Gage—when these accidents involved the frontal lobes, the victims could still function but were less excitable and emotional than prior to the injury (Brickner, 1936). Overall, however, people with frontal-lobe damage—including damage due to brain surgeries such as lobotomies (considered later in this chapter)—appear to suffer from an inability to understand the emotions of others and to appropriately regulate their own impulses and feelings.

THE CASE OF ELLIOTT   Neuroscientist Antonio Damasio reported the case of a patient, known as "Elliott," who was a good husband and father and held a responsible job. When he began to report headaches and an inability to concentrate (Damasio, 1994), his family physician suspected a brain tumor; unfortunately, that turned out to be correct. Elliott had a large tumor right above the nasal cavities, at the midline of the brain. The surgery to remove it also removed a good deal of his cerebral cortex.

After the surgery, Elliott seemed much improved and showed no obvious mental defects. Like Gage, he could move and speak normally, and his memory was unimpaired. Also like Gage, however, he had become peculiarly unemotional—he seemed not to experience strong positive or negative emotions. Over time, it became apparent that something was seriously lacking in his judgment. At a restaurant, he might sit for an hour, unable to decide between different dishes as he weighed the advantages and disadvantages of each. At work, he might begin to sort through papers for a client, and then stop to read one and spend the rest of the day deeply analyzing that single paper instead of completing his main mission. He seemed unable to allocate his time and effort appropriately between important tasks and activities and those that were trivial. He lost his job and, in the end, his family as well.

According to Damasio's analysis, Gage's and Elliott's flattened emotional landscape and their problems with decision making stemmed from the same kind of neural damage. The damage to tissue in the right frontal lobes impaired their ability to use

Emotions enable people to make decisions that maximize good outcomes and minimize bad ones, and to focus on what is really important. Feelings tie the body to the brain.

their emotional reactions in decision making. According to Damasio's **somatic marker hypothesis,** emotions enable people to make decisions that maximize good outcomes and minimize bad ones, and to focus on what is really important. Feelings tie the body to the brain. Without the ability to connect emotions to thinking, Gage and Elliott lost not only an important part of life's experience, but also a crucial component of the ability to make decisions.

COGNITION AND EMOTION One important lesson from research on the brain is that cognition and emotion are inextricably intertwined. And when they become detached, the consequences can be severe.

For example, consider *Capgras syndrome*, named after one of the first doctors to identify it. An early case involved a 53-year-old woman who believed that her husband, daughter, and other important persons in her life had disappeared and been replaced by doubles who were merely impersonating them (Capgras & Reboul-Lachaux, 1923, as cited in Doran, 1990). In a more recent case, a 20-year-old man received a severe blow to the head and subsequently came to believe that his parents and siblings had been shot by Chinese communist spies. The similar-looking people caring for him and worrying about him must be imposters, he concluded (Weston & Whitlock, 1971, as cited in Doran, 1990). In yet another case, a victim of a severe head injury returned home from the hospital to a family who, he insisted, was an entirely different family from the one he had before the accident, although he admitted they looked a lot like his real wife and four children.

*"I make decisions as much with my gut as
I do with my brain. Let's eat."*

A woman believed that her husband, daughter, and other important persons in her life had disappeared and been replaced by doubles who were merely impersonating them.

What all of these Capgras cases had in common was an injury to the right frontal lobe, which a large amount of evidence indicates is particularly important in positive emotional response (Sautter, Briscoe, & Farkas, 1991; Stuss & Levine, 2002). Apparently, when these patients recognize a loved one, they fail to feel any emotional response to this recognition. Imagine, if you can, seeing your parents, your siblings, or your boyfriend or girlfriend and feeling no emotion whatsoever. What would you think? What these patients concluded, it seems, is that these people could not possibly be who they appeared to be, and that the most likely explanation (conjured up by the uninjured left frontal lobe) was that they must have been replaced by identical doubles.

More broadly, cognitive understanding is important for full emotional experience, and emotional experience is crucial for full cognitive understanding. Recognizing someone who is emotionally significant to you is not just a judgment; it is also a feeling, without which the judgment may be meaningless. The connection between cognition and emotion may also help explain why many people who excel at what they do are so involved with their work, not just intellectually but emotionally. I know a superb lawyer who, after a long, detailed, and tedious (to me) explanation of a point of law, apologized by saying, "Sorry, I'm the sort of nerd who finds this fascinating." The best physicists become similarly excited as they talk about black holes, multidimensional space, and string theory. The most successful football coaches care deeply about every step taken by every player during every play. Their emotions motivate their thinking and guide their strategic decision making. This does not mean that people "think with their gut," but it is clear that the gut—emotional experience—is an important part of thinking, and one does not fully work without the other.

> Recognizing someone who is emotionally significant to you is not just a judgment; it is also a feeling, without which the judgment may be meaningless.

The Anterior Cingulate

The *cingulate* is a brain structure in the cortex, just on top of the **corpus callosum** (which connects the two halves of the brain) and extending all the way from the front of the brain to the back. The back of this structure, or *posterior cingulate,*[4] appears to be important for processing information about time and space and in reacting rapidly to threatening situations, while the front, the **anterior cingulate,** appears to be especially important for the experience of normal emotion, in part because it projects inhibitory circuits into the amygdala (Bremner, 2005). This interaction between the cingulate, in the frontal lobes, and lower areas in the brain such as the amygdala, may be critical for controlling emotional responses and impulsive behavior (Ochsner & Gross, 2005). Charles Whitman, the Texas sniper, suffered from a brain tumor interfering with precisely this circuit, which may be what made his emotional experience both incomprehensible to himself and eventually uncontrollable.

---

[4] A number of words commonly used in anatomy refer to directions within the brain. For example, posterior = toward the rear, anterior = toward the front, ventral = lower, lateral = out to the side (or both sides, since the brain, like the body, is mostly symmetrical), and medial = toward the middle. Directions can also be combined; for example, ventromedial = lower but more toward the middle.

Studies have implicated the anterior cingulate in two different personality traits. One fMRI study found that the anterior cingulate responded more strongly to positive and neutral words in extraverts than in introverts (Canli, Amin, Haas, Omura, & Constable, 2004). Another study found that the anterior cingulate in people who scored higher on measures of neuroticism was more active than usual during "oddball" tasks, in which they had to detect stimuli (such as letters) that were different from what they expected (Eisenberger, Lieberman, & Satpute, 2005). Taken together, these studies suggest that the anterior cingulate is not directly responsible for negative emotional responses but *is* important for computing mismatches between expected and actual states of the world. These mismatches sometimes trigger negative emotions (e.g., when getting an unpleasant surprise). When the anterior cingulate is chronically overactive, one result may be neuroticism.

The Lessons of Psychosurgery

At the 1935 World Congress of Neurology, Yale psychologist J. F. Fulton told assembled delegates about two laboratory chimps named Becky and Lucy. They were difficult to handle because they were easily frustrated, and when they were frustrated, they became irritable and bit their keepers. As part of a study on the function of the brain in learning, surgeons removed part of the chimps' frontal lobes. The effects on learning were inconclusive, but researchers noticed something else: Becky and Lucy had become relaxed and mellow chimps, placid instead of vicious, and downright pleasures to work with. According to legend, after Fulton presented these results, a Portuguese neurosurgeon named António Egas Moniz stood up and asked whether such an operation might be helpful for controlling human psychotics. Fulton was so shocked by the question he couldn't answer.

That didn't stop Dr. Moniz. By 1937, two years later, he had performed—on a human!—the first *prefrontal leucotomy*, in which small areas of white matter behind each of the frontal lobes were deliberately damaged. This may have been the first instance of *psychosurgery* done with the specific purpose of altering personality, emotions, or behavior. The idea was that patients with pathological levels of agitation and emotional arousal had overactive frontal lobes, and this operation—aimed at the same area as Gage's iron bar—might make them less emotional, more rational, and calmer, like Becky and Lucy.

Psychosurgery received the ultimate scientific seal of approval in 1949, when Egas Moniz was awarded the Nobel Prize.

It is important to note that Egas Moniz operated only on people with severe emotional problems and may even have done most of them some good. Whatever subtle damage was done to their emotional lives or decision-making capabilities may have been outweighed by their relief from a miserable and uncontrollable

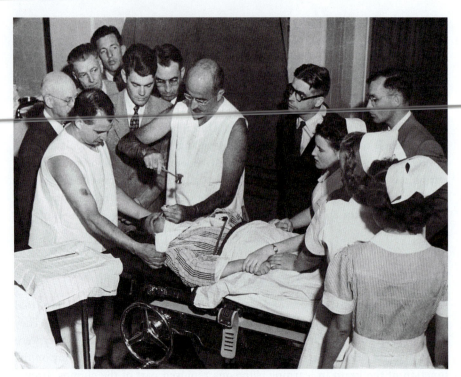

Figure 8.11 Demonstrating the Lobotomy Dr. Walter Freeman shows how to insert an instrument similar to an ice pick under the eyelid to sever nerve connections in the frontal lobe. This picture was taken in 1949 when the technique was becoming increasingly popular. Such operations are rare today.

degree of emotional overexcitement (Damasio, 1994). In any case, the operation quickly became popular around the world, especially in the United States, and it received the ultimate scientific seal of approval in 1949, when Egas Moniz was awarded the Nobel Prize.

But there was a dark side to this popularity. As its use spread, the surgical procedure became increasingly drastic. The standard technique changed from Egas Moniz's relatively modest leucotomy, in which small areas of tissue were damaged, to the more famous *prefrontal lobotomy*, in which whole sectors of the frontal lobes were scooped out. The results were correspondingly more drastic. Some lobotomy patients ended up much worse than either Gage or Elliott and became almost inert, mere shells of the people they were before. One was Rosemary Kennedy, the mentally disabled elder sister of John, Robert, and Edward Kennedy, who was operated on in 1941 in an attempt to control her "mood swings" (Thompson, 1995). She lived in an institution—a convent school in Wisconsin—for most of the next 60 years, until she died in 2005 at the age of 86.

Even the leading American advocates of the lobotomy noted that

> it is almost impossible to call upon a person who has undergone [an] operation on the frontal lobes for advice on any important matter. His reactions to situations are direct, hasty, and dependent upon his emotional set at the moment. (Freeman & Watts, 1950, p. 549)

Notice how this observation is consistent with the cases of Gage and Elliott. Evidence from a number of sources converges to suggest that the frontal lobes are centers of cognitive control, serving to anticipate the future and plan for it. These results also suggest that a particular function of the frontal lobes might be to anticipate future negative outcomes and respond emotionally to the possibility—in other words, worrying. This emotional aspect of forethought seems to be particularly important. Unless you have the appropriate reaction to future possibilities— pleasant anticipation on the one hand, or worrying on the other—you will not be able to plan appropriately or make the right decisions about what to do.

Tens of thousands of lobotomies and other psychosurgeries were performed for more than four decades, but such operations are rare today. The side effects became too obvious to ignore and began to be widely publicized, not just in medical journals and newspapers but also in works such as *One Flew Over the Cuckoo's Nest*.[5] Perhaps a more important factor is that chemical therapies (drugs) were developed to make mentally ill patients manageable, if not cured. Someone like Rosemary Kennedy, who troubled her family with mood swings, would today be tranquilized rather than lobotomized. In other words, her brain would be altered with chemicals rather than with a knife. Somehow this seems less drastic and more acceptable. Is it?

Brain Systems

Most studies of brain function and personality focus on one area of the brain at a time, which is understandable because of the limits of the available technology. However, anatomists have known for a long time that nearly everything in the brain is connected to everything else, which means that systems or circuits within the brain may be more important than discrete areas. One fMRI study examined *persistence*, the ability to complete a task in the face of obstacles and in the absence of immediate reward, a trait similar to conscientiousness in the Big Five model (see Chapter 6). This trait was associated with relatively high levels of brain activity in a

---

[5] *One Flew Over the Cuckoo's Nest*, a novel by Ken Kesey (1962, 1999), was made into a play, as well as into a motion picture (starring Jack Nicholson), about life in a particularly harsh mental hospital and the disastrous effect of a lobotomy on the main character.

complex circuit that included two areas of the frontal cortex and the ventral (lower) part of the *striatum*, which is found in the middle of the brain behind the frontal lobes (Gusnard et al., 2003). Another line of research seeks to identify the set of structures associated with what researchers call the *C-system* (involved in effortful, reflective thinking about the self and others) and the *X-system* (involved in effortless, reflexive social thought). Early studies using fMRI found that the C-system includes, among other areas, the lateral (side) prefrontal cortex, the hippocampus, the medial temporal lobe, and the posterior parietal cortex. The X-system includes the ventromedial prefrontal cortex, the amygdala, and the lateral temporal cortex (Lieberman, Jarcho, & Satpute, 2004).

The importance of systems rather than discrete areas in the brain helps to explain why the results of psychosurgery were so erratic and disappointing, and why the results of the hundreds of accumulating fMRI and other imaging studies can be so difficult to integrate and assimilate. The activities of individual areas may not mean very much in the absence of knowledge about what other areas of the brain are doing at the same time. As noted earlier in the chapter, researchers call this the neural context effect (Canli, 2004; McIntosh, 1998). The effect of context is important to keep in mind; otherwise, brain science is in danger of devolving into a simplistic attempt to map traits and behaviors onto specific locations. Understanding the brain is not easy. Its parts work together and constantly interact with the rest of the body and with the outside world, and research to understand how these systems are coordinated is still in its early stages. In other words, things are just starting to get interesting.

THE BIOCHEMISTRY OF PERSONALITY

I once attended a scientific meeting where I heard eminent psychologist Robert Zajonc cry out, "The brain is not a digital computer, it is a juicy gland!" Indeed, that is what it looks like, and, to an important degree, that is exactly how it functions—through the chemicals it secretes and to which it responds.

Chemical approaches to the study of personality have a long history. The ancient Greek physician Galen (who lived between A.D. 130 and 200, practicing mostly in Rome), building on Hippocrates' earlier proposal, theorized that personality depended on the balance between four *humors*, or fluids, in the body. These humors were blood, black bile, yellow bile (also called choler), and phlegm. A person who had a lot of blood relative to the other three humors, Galen conjectured, tended to be *sanguine* (cheerful), ruddy, and robust. Excess black bile caused a person to be depressed and *melancholy*; excess yellow bile caused a person to be *choleric*, angry, and bitter; and excess phlegm made one *phlegmatic*, cold, and apathetic. These four terms survive in the English language to this day, carrying roughly the same psychological meanings that Galen ascribed to them. Even more remarkably, this fourfold typology has undergone something of a revival among health psychologists who find it useful in connecting personality with disease (H. S. Friedman, 1991, 1992). The choleric, or chronically hostile person, for example, may be at extra risk for heart attack (see Chapter 17). But modern research suggests the basis of this risk is not the person's yellow bile but the stress (and hormonal reactions) caused by a life filled with tension and fights.

Instead of humors, the two important chemicals for behavior are **neurotransmitters** and hormones. Neurotransmitters are critical for communication between neurons. As illustrated in **Figure 8.12,** a bioelectrical impulse causes a release of neurotransmitters at the end of the neuron. These neurotransmitters travel across the **synapse** to the next neuron in line, where they cause a chemical reaction that has either an excitatory or inhibitory effect. In an excitatory effect, the second neuron fires, which causes the release of neurotransmitters at its other end, and so on down the neural network. In an inhibitory effect, the firing of the second neuron is suppressed. Although this process is often portrayed as if neurons link to each other one-to-one, in fact the activity of one neuron might be influenced by excitatory *and* inhibitory inputs—from hundreds, or even thousands, of other neurons. In other words, neural networks are amazingly complicated.

Hormones work somewhat differently. By definition, they are biological substances that affect the body in locations different from where they were produced (Cutler, 1976). After release from central locations, such as the *adrenal glands* (located atop the kidneys) or the hypothalamus, hormones spread throughout the body via the bloodstream. Once a hormone reaches neurons sensitive to it, it either stimulates or inhibits their activity. The difference between neurotransmitters and hormones can be confusing because both affect the transmission of nerve impulses, and some chemicals belong to both categories. For example, norepinephrine functions within the brain as a neurotransmitter, but is also released from the adrenal glands as a hormone in response to stress. Epinephrine also works as a neurotransmitter and hormone, with different associated behaviors. Both substances will be considered in detail later in the chapter.

Many neurotransmitters and hormones have been discovered, and more are still being identified: Researchers have counted about 60 chemicals that transmit information throughout the brain and body (Gazzaniga & Heatherton, 2003). Neurotransmitters and hormones are associated with a variety of neural subsystems and thus have many different effects on behavior. For example, norepinephrine and dopamine work almost exclusively in the **central nervous system**—the brain and spinal cord. By contrast, very little of the neurotransmitter epinephrine is found in the brain; mostly it works in the **peripheral nervous system**, the neuronal networks that extend throughout the body (see **Figure 8.13**). Serotonin has important functions in the brain—it appears to help ward off depression, among other contributions—but even more serotonin is found in the gut, where it apparently plays a role in regulating digestion. Oxytocin also functions in both

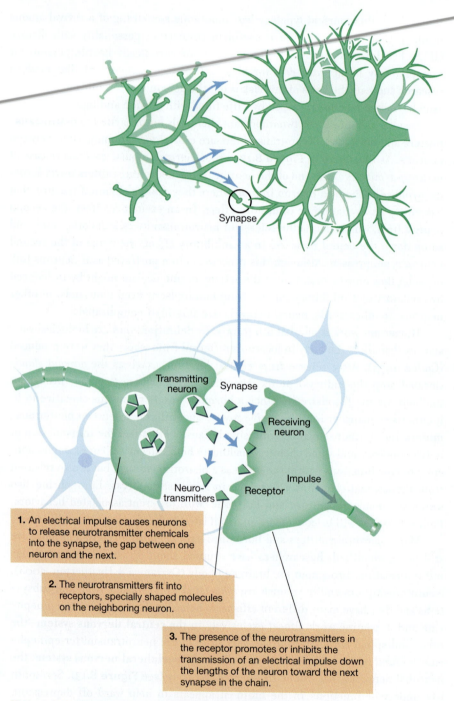

Synapse

Transmitting neuron

Synapse

Receiving neuron

Neuro-transmitters

Receptor

Impulse

1. An electrical impulse causes neurons to release neurotransmitter chemicals into the synapse, the gap between one neuron and the next.

2. The neurotransmitters fit into receptors, specially shaped molecules on the neighboring neuron.

3. The presence of the neurotransmitters in the receptor promotes or inhibits the transmission of an electrical impulse down the lengths of the neuron toward the next synapse in the chain.

Figure 8.12 **Communications Among Neurons** The transmission of impulses throughout the nervous system is mediated by electrical and chemical processes that carry impulses across the synapses between nerve cells.

(a) Central nervous system

(b) Peripheral nervous system

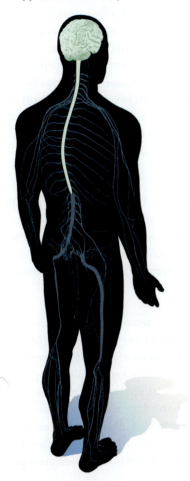
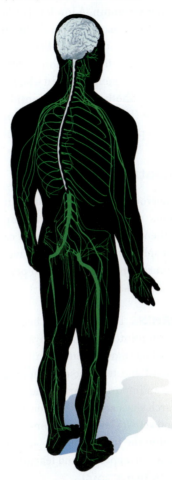

Figure 8.13 Two Nervous Systems (a) The central nervous system includes the brain and spinal cord. (b) The peripheral nervous system includes the nerves that extend throughout the body. Different neurotransmitters and hormones affect the two systems.

the central and peripheral nervous systems. As another complication, some neurotransmitters cause adjacent neurons to fire while, as was mentioned earlier, others inhibit neuronal impulses. For example, the body's natural painkilling system is based on a class of hormones called **endorphins,** which work by inhibiting the neuronal transmission of pain. Endorphins are opiates produced by the body. And they are legal!

The chemicals that make up neurotransmitters are also important, as are the enzymes that break them down into their constituent chemical parts after they have traveled across the synaptic gap. For example, the enzyme monoamine oxidase

(MAO) regulates the breakdown of the neurotransmitters dopamine, norepinephrine, and serotonin. A low level of MAO in the blood, which allows higher levels of these neurotransmitters to build up, is associated with sensation seeking, extraversion, and even criminal behavior (Zuckerman, 1998). On the other hand, a gene that promotes the activation of MAO seems to help prevent the development of delinquency among children who have been maltreated (Caspi et al., 2002; Moffitt, 2005). For another example, antidepressant drugs such as paroxetine (Paxil) and fluoxetine (Prozac) increase the amount of serotonin in the body by inhibiting the chemical process that causes serotonin to break down (Kramer, 1993).

Neurotransmitters

The nervous system is affected in important ways by the availability and the amounts of various neurotransmitters. This availability varies depending on what the individual is doing, and can fluctuate widely over short periods of time. But people also differ in their average levels of certain transmitters, and these differences are associated with particular personality traits, as we shall see in the coming pages.

DOPAMINE Dopamine has been described as the neurotransmitter that turns motivation into action. It plays a key role in mechanisms that allow the brain to control body movements, and it also is involved in systems associated with response to reward and tendencies to approach attractive objects and people. (Dopamine is also an important part of the chemical process that produces norepinephrine.) Research suggests that this neurotransmitter is part of the basis of sociability and general activity level, and a gene associated with response to dopamine seems to be related to the trait of novelty seeking (Ebstein et al., 1996). Dopamine facilitates exploration, approach and learning, and is associated with extraversion and openness (DeYoung, 2015).

A severe lack of dopamine is the basis of Parkinson's disease. A famous case—shown, with artistic license, in the 1990 movie *Awakenings* (loosely based on the book of the same title by neurologist Oliver Sacks, 1983)—concerns a group of patients who developed Parkinson's during World War I as a result of an epidemic of encephalitis. They were given the new drug L-dopa 40 years later, during the 1960s. L-dopa increases the brain's production of dopamine, and for some patients who had been nearly catatonic for years, the results were dramatic. Suddenly, they not only could move around, but also were able, for the first time in years, to experience positive emotions, motivation, sociability, and interest in and awareness of their surroundings.

Sadly, most of these patients' conditions worsened again over time. They went from normal enthusiasm and energy levels into hypermanic excitement, restlessness, and grandiosity. Then they "crashed" into deep depression (Sacks,

1983; Zuckerman, 1991). These effects suggest that *dopaminergic* systems (systems affected by dopamine) also might be related to manic-depressive disorder (now usually referred to as *bipolar disorder*). Perhaps even more important, they suggest that dopamine might be relevant to the personality traits of extraversion, impulsivity, and perhaps others.

Dopamine might affect these traits through its interactions with a part of the brain called the *nucleus accumbens*, which is located in the basal ganglia, an important junction between the cerebral cortex and the brain stem. According to neuropsychologist Jeffrey Gray, dopamine and the nucleus accumbens together form part of what is sometimes called the "Go" system (J. A. Gray, 1981). More formally called the *behavioral activation system (BAS)*, this system produces and reinforces the motivation to seek rewards.[6] Consistent with this view, the left nucleus accumbens is particularly responsive to the experience of reward, such as winning money in an experimental game (Wu et al., 2013).

A related theory focuses on differences in the degree to which people develop neurons that produce and are responsive to dopamine (Depue & Collins, 1999). These individual differences might have a genetic basis, but they also might come from experience: People who have had an abundance of rewarding experiences, especially early in life, may develop more such cells, causing the dopaminergic part of their nervous systems to be well developed and active. As a result, they are motivated to seek out rewards and are capable of enjoying them strongly; they also become assertive, dominant, and outgoing—in a word, extraverts.

Dopamine might have even wider implications. As was mentioned in Chapter 6, one recent theory proposes that two fundamental dimensions of personality—stability and plasticity—organize the traits of the Big Five into two groups. A large amount of evidence suggests that the dopaminergic system is the foundation of plasticity, defined as "a general tendency to explore and engage with possibilities," which combines extraversion with openness to experience (DeYoung, 2010, p. 1170). The behaviors associated with plasticity are, to a large extent, the same ones traditionally viewed as part of BAS. The critical common element appears to be dopamine and its role in the motivation to seek reward (DeYoung, 2010), and even in impulsivity (Buckholtz et al., 2010). As we saw in Chapter 7, extraversion has close ties to positive emotional experience as well as behaviors that seek social rewards such as being talkative, sociable, and cheerful. Openness to experience includes a certain kind of mental playfulness, curiosity, and intellectual risk-taking. Dopamine may play a central role in all of this.

---

[6] In Gray's theory, the BAS is complemented by the "Stop" system, also known as the *behavioral inhibition system (BIS)*, said to be located in the sepal-hippocampal system, which assesses and responds to risk (Corr, Pickering, & Gray, 1997). In some accounts, an overactive BIS is a cause of neuroticism (DeYoung, 2010).

"Of course your daddy loves you. He's on Prozac—he loves everybody."

SEROTONIN **Serotonin** is another important neurotransmitter, one which seems to play a role in the inhibition of behavioral impulses (e.g., stopping oneself from doing something attractive yet unwise or dangerous). This ability can be useful. For example, a predator stalking its prey must inhibit the urge to leap before it is close enough to catch the prey. If you have ever watched a cat wait to pounce on a bird, you might conclude that the typical cat has a lot of serotonin in its system. Serotonin can help keep humans from being too quick to anger, from being oversensitive to the minor insults of daily life, and from worrying too much.

The effects of serotonin and the validity of the serotonin depletion syndrome as a clinical diagnosis are controversial topics. In 2000, the pharmaceutical company Eli Lilly sold $2.7 billion worth of Prozac, a *selective serotonin reuptake inhibitor (SSRI)*,[7] and the entire market for related drugs (including fluoxetine, the generic version of Prozac) may be more than $20 billion per year (Druss, Marcus, Olfson, & Pincus, 2004). By 1999, an estimated 22 million Americans—almost 1 person in 10—had used this drug (Shenk, 1999), and the number is surely even higher today. The physical effect of these drugs seems fairly clear—they raise serotonin levels in the nervous system. The psychological effects, however, are more controversial, as are the implications of those effects.

In his best-selling book, *Listening to Prozac*, psychiatrist Peter Kramer (1993) claimed that Prozac can dramatically improve many people's personalities. It can stop a person from needlessly worrying and being oversensitive to minor stresses, and so provide a newly cheerful outlook on life. Some individuals who take Prozac claim that it makes them more like "themselves": They don't feel like *different* people than they were without the drug; they feel like *better* people. They get more work done and even become more attractive to members of the opposite sex. One particularly interesting study showed that normal people—that is, people with no diagnosable personality disorders in themselves or in any of their close relatives—showed noticeable personality changes when they took paroxetine (the generic equivalent of Paxil), a drug closely related to Prozac. They became more extraverted and obtained lower scores on a neuroticism test (Tang et al., 2009). Another study found that in as little as one week, people taking this drug reported feeling happier and less hostile. One participant commented, "I used to think about good

---

[7] *Transporter* molecules remove up to 90 percent of the serotonin from the synapse; SSRI molecules inhibit this removal, which allows more serotonin to remain available at the synapse.

and bad, but now I don't; I'm in a good mood" (Knutson et al., 1998, p. 377). On the other hand, they also reported side effects such as feeling sleepy and having delayed orgasms! But apparently they didn't mind.

Another researcher concluded from the evidence that SSRIs such as Prozac "are not happy pills, shifting depressed people to normalcy and normal people to bliss" (Farah, 2005, p. 36). Rather, they seem to make negative emotions less severe while leaving positive emotions unaffected. In a similar vein, psychologist Steven Reise (2006) noted that SSRIs might be better classified as "antineurotics" than antidepressants, and that they could be helpful toward the fundamental goal of psychotherapy:

> It is not that bad turns to good, but rather bad doesn't seem so devastating (because an individual has more psychological reserve to deal with the issue). For example, in psychotherapy, low self-esteem does not magically turn into high self-esteem, but rather into an absence of devastating self-concern. Consider a man who is in therapy because of his obsessive concern about his baldness. We do not expect such a man to ever "love baldness," but rather to not see it as such a big issue. (Reise, 2006, p. 6)

Reise's comments are consistent with recent theorizing that gives serotonin a critical role in the broad trait of *stability*, which subsumes the other three traits of the Big Five (DeYoung, 2010, 2015; Allen & DeYoung, 2016). Serotonin's role in inhibiting feelings and impulses helps people to organize their behavior and get work done (conscientiousness), get along with other people even when they are annoying (agreeableness), and, perhaps most importantly, avoid mood swings and emotional overreactions to life events (emotional stability, or low neuroticism). The personality psychologist Colin DeYoung points out that serotonin helps to stabilize information processing in the brain and generally calm things down (DeYoung, 2015); if serotonin had an advertising slogan, it might be "steady as she goes."

> If serotonin had an advertising slogan, it might be "steady as she goes."

Hormones

As we have already seen, some neurotransmitters, such as norepinephrine, also can be considered hormones because they affect nerve cells far from their origins. The status of other chemicals as hormones, especially those produced in a central location, is clearer: Their main function is to act throughout the body, stimulating the activity of neurons in many locations in the brain and body at the same time. Different hormones affect different kinds of nerve cells, and so influence different neural systems. Hormones that are important for behavior are released by the hypothalamus, the **gonads** (testes and ovaries), and the **adrenal cortex** (part of the adrenal gland that sits atop the kidneys).

EPINEPHRINE AND NOREPINEPHRINE Two particularly important hormones are **epinephrine** (also known as *adrenaline*) and **norepinephrine** (*noradrenaline*). Epinephrine and the neurons that respond to it are found throughout the body, while norepinephrine and its neurons work primarily within the brain, especially in the brain stem. The levels of both hormones can rise dramatically and suddenly in response to stress. When they are released into the bloodstream, the heart speeds up, digestion stops, and muscles tense, producing the well-known "adrenaline rush." At the same time, the brain becomes fully alert and concentrated on the matter at hand.[8] This sequence of events has long been called the *fight-or-flight response* (Cannon, 1932; Selye, 1956). The idea is that if the threat—such as a predator or an enemy—is one that you have a realistic chance of overcoming, you will stand and fight. If the situation seems hopeless, you will run away. Either way, the body has prepared you to react.

The fight-or-flight response has been documented in dozens of studies over the years. However, psychologist Shelley Taylor and her colleagues have noted that almost all of these studies—both in animals (usually rats) and in humans—were conducted on males (S. E. Taylor et al., 2000). Why does this matter? According to Taylor and colleagues, the response to threats may be different in men and women. They point out that during the prehistoric era when our species evolved, a man under threat had a relatively simple choice: stand and fight, or run away. For a woman—who might have been pregnant, nursing infants, or caring for children—the choice was not so simple. Either fighting or running away might have put her and the children at unacceptable risk. Instead, it may have made more sense for her to respond differently, to calm everyone down and band people together to fend off the threat—a response Taylor and her colleagues call *tend-and-befriend*. They point out that another hormone in the stress-response cascade is **oxytocin,** which, in females, promotes nurturant and sociable behavior along with relaxation and reduction of fear—the exact opposite of fight-or-flight. One effect of oxytocin may be to decrease anxiety and increase attachment between mothers and their children (McCarthy, 1995). This might be why primates—including human mothers—rarely abandon their infants, even under conditions of grave danger. (More will be said about oxytocin later in this chapter.)

This is a fascinating argument. On a methodological level, it shows the high cost of limiting research subjects to just one gender. Researchers did this not out of malicious intent, but to avoid the complications of accounting for estrous and menstrual cycles when conducting neurobiological assays. But this simplification may have come at the cost of missing a fundamental difference between the sexes. On a substantive level, moving from prehistoric environments to the modern day, Taylor's argument implies that men and women have fundamentally

---

[8] Mark Twain is said to have remarked that "the imminent prospect of hanging focuses a man's mind most wonderfully"—a classic effect of norepinephrine.

different responses to threats and attacks. Men evaluate their strength relative to their opponent and assess their chances of escape. Then they either fight or run away. Women are more likely to seek out their friends and relatives and "circle the wagons," as it were. If you can't always fight or flee, at least there is some safety in numbers.

It is important to remember that this thesis, to the extent that it is correct, refers to the initial and automatic response to threat. It does not imply that further behavior is completely constrained. Men do form alliances, and women sometimes stand and fight. But Taylor and her colleagues suggest that the first instinctive responses of men and women to a threatening situation may be fundamentally different (S. E. Taylor et al., 2000).

TESTOSTERONE Probably the best-known hormones are the gonadal, or sex hormones: **testosterone** (primarily in males) and **estrogen** (primarily in females), although both hormones are present in all humans. It has long been observed that men seem generally to be more aggressive than women (Kagan, 1978; Maccoby & Jacklin, 1974), and men certainly have more testosterone in their bodies. To be exact, normal women have about 40 ng (nanograms) of testosterone in each deciliter of their blood, whereas normal men have 300–1,000 ng per deciliter, approximately a 10 times (or more) greater concentration.

This fact has led some psychologists to hypothesize that testosterone causes aggressive behavior, and many studies have pursued this idea. In one study, male American military veterans were asked about their past behaviors. Those with higher testosterone levels reported more trouble with parents, teachers, and classmates; a history of assaulting others; more use of hard drugs, marijuana, or alcohol; numerous sexual partners; and a "general tendency toward excessive behavior" (Dabbs & Morris, 1990, p. 209). In another study, young men with higher basal testosterone levels were found to be higher on the traits of avoidance, dominance, and loneliness (Turan, Guo, Boggiano, & Bedgood, 2014). When about to play a competitive game, high-testosterone men are more likely to choose a red rather than blue symbol for themselves, apparently because they perceive the color to be more dominant, risky, eye-catching, powerful, and aggressive[9] (Farrelly, Slater, Elliott, Walden, & Wetherell, 2013). When researchers directly observed men competing with each other for the attention of an attractive young woman, the men with higher testosterone were more dominant and "clicked"[10] with her better (Slatcher, Mehta, & Josephs, 2011). On the other hand, and perhaps ironically, fatherhood appears to lower testosterone temporarily, presumably because men

[9] What this finding may imply about the difference between "red states" and "blue states" in the United States—or even about the rivalry between the Los Angeles Dodgers and the Los Angeles Angels baseball teams—I will not speculate.

[10] This is the actual term the researchers used.

need to mellow out in order to be able to help take care of their children (Kuzawa, Gettler, Muller, McDade, & Feranil, 2009). And men's testosterone levels tend to fall after marriage, and rise after divorce (this was a replicated finding that studied 1,113 men aged 30 to 60; Holmboe et al., 2017).

Testosterone might interfere with certain kinds of thinking. One recent study applied either testosterone gel or a placebo (inert substance) to (male) participants' upper bodies, then asked them to solve problems such as the following:

> In a lake, there is a patch of lily pads. Every day, the patch doubles in size. If it takes 48 days for the patch to cover the entire lake, how long would it take for the patch to cover half of the lake?

How did you do? The "impulsive" answer, the one that might come most quickly to mind, is 24 but if you slow down and think about it, you will realize the correct answer is actually 47. It turns out that having extra testosterone in one's system via the gel was enough to make a person more likely to give the quick and wrong answer instead of the slower and right one (Nave, Nadler, Zava, & Camerer, 2017).

Further evidence concerning the effects of testosterone comes from bodybuilders and athletes who take anabolic steroids to promote muscular development (H. G. Pope & Katz, 1994). *Anabolic steroids* are synthetic testosterone; their effects include not only speedier muscle development but also a whole host of troublesome side effects. Steroid users frequently experience erratic and uncontrolled aggressiveness and sexuality. For example, male steroid users may experience erections without stimulation, but they also seem to have a lower overall sex drive and a tendency to impotence and sterility.

When interpreting research on testosterone, a couple of important complications are important to keep in mind. First, although some extreme criminal types (e.g., rapists who also commit other kinds of bodily harm) may be likely to have high levels of testosterone (Rada, Laws, & Kellner, 1976), the reverse is not true: Men with high levels of testosterone are not necessarily aggressive. Furthermore, while the males in many species are more aggressive than females, this is not always the case: Males are not more aggressive than females among gibbons, wolves, rabbits, hamsters, and even laboratory rats (Floody, 1983). And as every mountain hiker knows (or should know), the most dangerous place in the wilderness is between a mother bear and her cubs. If you get in her way, Mama Bear will not "tend and befriend."

Indeed, let's not forget that women have testosterone as well. Most female testosterone is produced by the adrenal cortex (a small amount is also produced in the ovaries), and the hormone can have important behavioral effects. One study showed that female prisoners who had committed unprovoked violent crimes had higher levels of testosterone than women who had been violent after provocation or who had committed nonviolent crimes (Dabbs, Ruback, Frady, Hopper, & Sgoritas, 1988). Lesbian women who take on the "butch" role (dressing and acting in masculine ways) have higher testosterone than either lesbians who take the "femme" role or heterosexual women (Singh, Vidaurri, Zambarano, & Dabbs, 1999). Other research showed that women who produce less testosterone (due to impaired adrenocortical functioning) seem to be less interested in sex. Moreover, the administration of testosterone injections to women can sometimes dramatically increase sexual desire (Zuckerman, 1991). These results suggest that testosterone is a chemical contributor to sexual motivation in women as well as in men.

Also similar to the findings among men, higher levels of testosterone in women are associated with higher levels of self-reported sociability and with impulsivity, lack of inhibition, and lack of conformity. An experimental study which administered testosterone to women found that they became less trusting of their opponent when playing an experimental game, but more inclined to cooperate if the opponent cooperated, too (Boksem et al., 2013). In both sexes, higher testosterone is also associated with holding a blue-collar industrial job as opposed to a white-collar professional job. Among lawyers, the ones who battle cases in court have higher testosterone levels than do those who work in the back room with law books (Dabbs, Alford, & Fielden, 1998).

Despite its reputation (have you ever heard a woman complain of a particular man suffering from "testosterone poisoning"?), the hormone is not all bad. Males with more testosterone are higher in "stable extraversion," that is, sociability, self-acceptance, and dominance. They have more restless energy, spend a lot of time thinking about concrete problems in the immediate present, and become frustrated when they can't get things done (Dabbs, Strong, & Milun, 1997). They smile less, which makes them appear more dominant (Dabbs, 1997); they also report having more sexual experience and more sexual partners, which suggests that maybe they really do "click" with women. But again, sexual activity might itself cause higher testosterone levels (Zuckerman, 1991).

Testosterone also has interesting interactions with personality traits. One study found that, relative to other men with similar traits, high-testosterone men who are also conscientious make better emergency medical service (EMS) providers, and high-testosterone men who are extraverted and active are better firefighters. The researchers concluded that testosterone should be thought of as an energizing factor that "appears to facilitate the behavior of individuals along directions they are already inclined to take" (Fannin & Dabbs, 2003, p. 107).

What can we conclude from all this? It would be an oversimplification to conclude that testosterone causes aggression or sexuality in any direct way. Instead, it seems to play a role in the control and inhibition of aggressiveness and sexuality—including normal assertiveness and perhaps even general activity level—as well

"Fill'er up with testosterone."

as the normal range of sexual function and responsiveness in both sexes. Recall the comment from Dabbs and Morris (1990) that in their study, men with high testosterone levels were prone to "excessive" behavior. In general, the evidence suggests that when this hormone is present in abnormally high proportions, which occurs naturally in certain individuals and artificially in steroid users, aggression and sexuality are not so much enhanced as they are messed up. Both may occur at inappropriate times and fail to occur at appropriate times.

Moreover, testosterone is not just a cause of behavior; it is also an effect. As was mentioned above, sexual activity can increase testosterone levels. Men's levels of testosterone also rise after they get to drive a brand new $150,000 Porsche Carrera; the levels go down if instead they have to drive a 16-year-old Toyota station wagon with 186,000 miles on the odometer (Saad & Vongas, 2009). In a study of World Cup soccer fans watching a playoff match, testosterone was measured from the fans' saliva before and after the game (Bernhardt, Dabbs, Fielden & Lutter, 1998). Afterward, the testosterone levels in fans of the winning team had increased, while the testosterone levels in fans of the losing team had decreased. For possibly the same reason, after a U.S. presidential election, people from the states that supported the winning candidate look at more pornography on the Internet than do people from states who supported the loser (Markey & Markey, 2010). Apparently, they are just responding to their victory-induced testosterone rush.

The connection between victory and testosterone production might help explain why riots so often break out in the winning city after an NBA championship and at colleges that win football championships, while the losing city or college remains quiet as the fans slink silently home (Gettleman, 2002). More importantly, these findings may provide insight into testosterone's regulatory function. You win a fight (Schultheiss et al., 2005). Your testosterone level goes up, and you press your advantage. But if, instead, you lose a fight, your testosterone level goes down, and you leave the field of battle before you suffer further damage or even get killed. In a parallel (and less violent) way, men[11] who achieve prestige in a new group because of their success, skills, and knowledge experience a rise in testosterone, which increases their further efforts to gain even more prestige (Cheng, Kornienko, & Granger, 2018). Testosterone is, therefore, more than a simple or unidirectional cause of behavior; it is an important part of the feedback system that regulates how people[12] respond to winning and losing.

CORTISOL In the earlier discussion of the hormones epinephrine and norepinephrine, I described their role in the fight-or-flight response. Another part of this same response is the glucocorticoid hormone known as **cortisol**. Released into the bloodstream by the adrenal cortex as a response to physical or psychological stress,

---

[11] This effect was found only in men.

[12] Or perhaps only men; the evidence on this point is not completely clear.

cortisol is part of the body's preparation for action as well as an important part of several normal metabolic processes. It can speed the heart rate, raise blood pressure, stimulate muscle strength, metabolize fat, and cause many other effects as well.

Individuals who suffer from severe stress, anxiety, and depression tend to have chronically high levels of cortisol. In this case, the rise in cortisol seems to be an effect of stress and depression rather than a cause; injecting cortisol into people does not produce these feelings (Born, Hitzler, Pietrowsky, Pairschinger, & Fehm, 1988). Infants with high levels of cortisol tend to be timid and vulnerable to developing *social phobias* (irrational fears of other people) later in life (Kagan, Reznick, & Snidman, 1988). Again, however, cortisol production may be stimulated by their fearful reactions rather than the other way around. People high in the trait of narcissism (see Chapter 6) who have to make a videotaped speech and perform mental arithmetic in front of a pair of poker-faced observers apparently *really* don't like it: They respond to this stressful experience with heightened cortisol levels, compared with non-narcissists (Edelstein, Yim, & Quas, 2010). Over time, this kind of reaction can be dangerous. Excess cortisol production stimulated by too much fear and anxiety increases the risk of heart disease and may even, over time, make one's brain smaller (Knutson, Momenan, Rawlings, Fong, & Hommer, 2001).

Low levels of cortisol entail risks, too. Chronically low cortisol levels appear to be associated with post-traumatic stress disorder (PTSD), the collection of psychological problems that can result from experiences such as physical or sexual abuse, or harrowing experiences in war (Meewisse, Reitsma, De Vries, Gersons, & Olff, 2007). Low levels of cortisol may also lead to "sensation seeking" and under-reactivity, such that people become impulsive and disinclined to follow the rules of society (Zuckerman, 1991, 1998). This pattern may arise because they have lost their ability to generate the normal surge in cortisol production in response to danger, causing them to fail to respond normally to danger signals associated with high-risk activities like automobile racing and shoplifting.

OXYTOCIN Recent years have seen a huge increase in research in another hormone, *oxytocin*. Sometimes called the "love hormone," oxytocin appears to play an important role in mother-child bonding, romantic attachment, and sexual response. Oxytocin is released by the hypothalamus and circulates through the body and brain via the bloodstream. It is of special relevance to females because the chemicals from which it is constructed and the neural receptors that respond to it are closely related to estrogen.

The most interesting behavioral correlates of oxytocin have also been observed in women. It is closely related to the stages of reproduction: Its level in the body increases during sexual activity and orgasm (Carmichael, Warburton, Dixen, & Davidson, 1994), childbirth (Takagi, Tanizawa, Otsuki, Haruta, & Yamaji, 1985), and breastfeeding (Matthiesen, Ransio-Arvidson, Nissen, & Uvnas-Moberg, 2001). Women whose levels of oxytocin increase during pregnancy appear to bond better with their children (Levine, Zagoory-Sharon, Feldman, & Weller, 2007).

They are more likely to think fondly about their babies, gaze at them, touch them affectionately, and check on them frequently to make sure they are OK.

One particularly strong effect of oxytocin appears to be to make people less fearful. An fMRI study in which subjects looked at frightening pictures showed that the fear-associated parts of the amygdala responded less if the subjects were given a dose of oxytocin first (Kirsch et al., 2005). Oxytocin also causes people to rate the faces of strangers as more trustworthy and attractive (Theodoridou, Rowe, Penton-Voak, & Rogers, 2009). The hormone also appears increase receptiveness to signs of affection; in one study, romantically involved adults experienced more love for their partners after the partner expressed gratitude towards them, if their oxytocin was already high (Algoe, Kurtz & Grewen, 2017). But findings like this one, and others, should be looked at cautiously. In general, the effects of oxytocin are complicated and depend upon the individual, the situation, and the local environment (Campbell, 2010, Bartz, 2016).

Research on oxytocin has been accumulating so quickly that psychologists have found it difficult to make sense of it all. But a couple of recent theories provide some interesting insights. British psychologist Anne Campbell proposes that a primary function of oxytocin is to help women to accept the "challenges to bodily or psychological integrity" (2010, p. 287) that inevitably arise in vital activities such as sex, childbirth, and breastfeeding, which—as she puts it—can be "seen as invasions of the usual bodily boundaries that define the individual as a discrete organism." On a more general level, Australian psychologists Andrew Kemp and Adam Guastella (2011) propose that oxytocin facilitates all kinds of approach behavior, both positive (e.g., sexual encounters) and negative (attacking someone). Indeed, as I mentioned earlier, there may be no fiercer creature in nature than a mother whose young are threatened.

NOW YOU SEE IT, NOW YOU DON'T I mentioned in Chapter 3 the persistent issue of replication, whether findings of a particular study can be repeated by other researchers and thereby be deemed reliable. Of the findings summarized in this chapter, I'm pretty sure that not all of them would replicate in this sense. Unfortunately, I don't know which ones! I have tried to focus on findings from better studies with larger samples and consistent results, but in a still rapidly developing area of research, such as the relationship between biology and personality, most findings should be regarded as interesting, but tentative.

And a few are turning out not to be true at all. There was some prominence, a few years ago, for reports that men with wider, shorter faces (width-to-height ratio, or *fWHR*), were more violent and antisocial. This finding was ascribed to the influence of androgens (male sex hormones[13]) during prenatal and early childhood development, which made for a good story. But the story turned out to not have a happy ending, because the finding simply went away when it was tested

---

[13] The main male sex hormone is testosterone but there are also others such as dihydrotestosterone and androstenedione. These names may appear next time you attend a spelling bee.

in larger, more representative samples (Kosinski, 2017). Interestingly, this finding might have been so widely accepted in the first place because, according to other research, many people have what is called "*physiognomic belief*—a generic belief that various traits can be inferred from faces ... because the world is an orderly place where people get faces they deserve" (Suzuki, Tsukamoto, & Takahashi, 2017, p. 1).

THE BIG FIVE AND THE BRAIN

If at this point in reading this chapter you are feeling a bit overwhelmed, I can't blame you. The findings involving the relationships between personality and brain anatomy, neurotransmitters, and hormones are complex and rapidly changing. Different researchers have different theories about how personality, behavior, and biology are tied together, and findings are complicated, tentative, and sometimes contradictory. So perhaps the most important thing I can tell you, as we wind up this survey, is that some order is at last beginning to emerge. An important step was taken by personality neuroscientist Colin DeYoung, who has already been cited several times in this chapter. DeYoung proposes that a vast amount of research on the biology of personality—if not quite all of it—can be organized around the Big Five personality traits discussed in Chapter 6.

His integration is summarized very briefly in **Table 8.1**, and some of the specific brain areas associated with the Big Five can be seen in **Figure 8.14.** As was

Table 8.1 | POSSIBLE BIOLOGICAL BASES OF THE BIG FIVE

Metatrait		Stability		Plasticity	
Big Five Trait	**Emotional Stability (inverse of Neuroticism)**	**Agreeableness**	**Conscientiousness**	**Extraversion**	**Openness**
Neurotransmitter	Serotonin	Serotonin	Serotonin	Dopamine	Dopamine
Hormones	Cortisol Norepinephrine			Endorphins	
Brain Structures	Right frontal lobe (withdrawal)	Left dorsolateral prefrontal cortex	Middle frontal gyrus	Medial orbito-frontal cortex	Left prefrontal cortex
	Left frontal lobe (anger)	Superior temporal sulcus		Nucleus accumbens	Posterior medial prefrontal cortex
	Amygdala	Posterior cingulate cortex		Amygdala	
	Insula			Striatum	
	Anterior cingulate				

Source: Based on research summarized by DeYoung (2010).

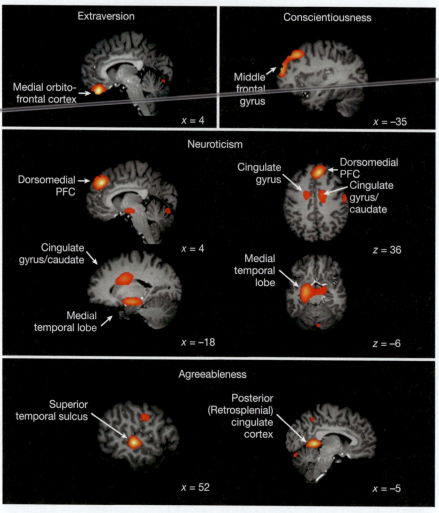

Figure 8.14 Regions of the Brain Associated With Four of the Big Five Four of the Big Five personality traits appear to be related to the size of specific areas of the brain, as summarized in these pictures. Lighter colors indicate places where brain size was more strongly related to personality. The *x* and *z* numbers are three-dimensional coordinates that pinpoint the locations of the brain slices.

Source: DeYoung et al. (2010), p. 825.

mentioned earlier in this chapter and in Chapter 6, DeYoung theorizes that the "metatraits" of stability and plasticity organize the Big Five into two groups. The stability traits include emotional stability (the inverse of neuroticism), agreeableness, and conscientiousness, and are associated with the neurotransmitter serotonin. The plasticity traits include extraversion and openness, and are associated with dopamine. After that, each of the five basic traits has its own unique pattern of associations with hormones and brain structures. Not all of the brain structures listed in the table have been discussed in this chapter—I couldn't cover everything—but the list illustrates how research is accumulating concerning the brain and the Big Five, and provides a map of where research might go next.

BIOLOGY: CAUSE AND EFFECT

When looking deeply into the relationships between brain activity, neural chemicals, and behavior, it is tempting to believe that we are finally getting to the real causes of things. There is also something downright seductive about colorful brain images, such as Figure 8.6, that appear to show the living brain at work (D. P. McCabe & Castel, 2008). Since all behavior must have its origin somewhere in the nervous system, it might seem that once the brain is understood, behavior will be demystified as well. But the relationship between the brain and its environment works in both directions.

As we saw several times in this chapter, biological processes are the effects of behaviors or experiences as often as they are the causes (Roberts & Jackson, 2008). For example, a stressful environment will raise one's cortisol level, as will feeling depressed or anxious, and the result (not the cause) may be a smaller brain! Winning a game (or an election) raises one's testosterone level; likewise, behavior and the social environment affect levels of other hormones and neurotransmitters, as well as the development and functioning of the brain. Measurable brain activity can be changed by drugs; it can also be changed by psychotherapy (Isom & Heller, 1999). So we will not fully understand the nervous system until we understand depression, anxiety, psychotherapy, stressful environments, election outcomes, and why some people win fights while others lose. The workings of the brain help to explain personality and social behavior, but a greater understanding of personality and social behavior is also necessary to better understand the brain.

Remember Hippocrates' MP3 player? Let's imagine, clever fellow that he is, that he actually manages to make progress in understanding how it works. "Ah," he realizes, "the power comes out of the battery and rotates this tiny disk, and then it is amplified through this transistor and comes out in the earbuds." If he figured all of this out, it would be a stunning accomplishment, comparable to modern attempts to understand the workings of the brain. Then, being wise as well as clever, Hippocrates might ask, "And who is this Lady Gaga person? What does this song mean? Who decided to record music like this, and why do people choose to listen to it?" The important questions haven't ended; they've just started.

WRAPPING IT UP

SUMMARY

- Studies of the biology of personality raise the philosophical issue called the mind-body problem, which concerns the degree to which all aspects of human nature can be understood as processes of our physical brains and bodies, making humans no different from any other animal.

The Anatomy of Personality

- Both brain anatomy and neurophysiology are relevant to personality. Knowledge about the brain comes from studies of the effects of brain injury and brain surgery, from measurements of brain activity using relatively old techniques such as electroencephalography (EEG) and newer techniques such as magnetoencephalography (MEG), from studies of direct brain stimulation (including a new technique called transcranial magnetic stimulation, or TMS, and a related technique called transcranial direct current stimulation, or tDCS), and from imaging tools such as positron emission tomography (PET) scans and functional magnetic resonance imaging (fMRI).

- Computerized data analysis can combine data gathered from instruments such as PET and fMRI scanners to provide data summaries, represented as pictures, that identify the brain areas that are most active during various mental tasks and emotional reactions. Researchers have also used these techniques to compare brain activity in people with different personality attributes. The data analyses this research requires are complex and sometimes controversial.

- The amygdala plays a special role in generating emotional response. Based on its computation of whether the environment seems to offer impending threat or reward, the amygdala can respond by making the heart beat faster and raising the blood pressure, among other effects. Traits associated with functioning of the amygdala include chronic anxiety, fearfulness, sociability, and sexuality.

- The frontal lobes are the basis of uniquely human abilities such as language and foresight; they also are important for understanding the self and other people, and for regulating emotion. In fMRI studies, strong activity in this area occurs in people who are prone to negative emotions, but also in people who are consistently cooperative. Cases such as Phineas Gage, Elliott, and victims of Capgras syndrome show how basic emotional responses and cognitive functioning must work together for meaningful experiences and adaptive decision making.

- Psychosurgeries on the frontal lobes, such as lobotomies, may have helped some desperately ill people in the past, but overall they seemed to damage patients' ability to reason and to function, especially in their emotional lives and relations with others.

- Recent fMRI research suggests that personality may be affected more by systems or circuits of different areas of the brain acting in concert than by the relevance of single areas to particular traits.

The Biochemistry of Personality

- The chemical bases of behavior include neurotransmitters and hormones, both of which play a role in communication between and stimulation of the cells of the nervous system.

- The neurotransmitters epinephrine and norepinephrine are an important part of the fight-or-flight response to threatening situations. Some psychologists have recently proposed that tend-and-befriend better characterizes women's instinctive response to a threat.

- Dopamine is important for responding to rewards and may be the basis of "extraversion." Dopamine is an important basis of the behavioral activation system (BAS), hypothesized by Jeffrey Gray.

- Serotonin aids in regulating emotions. Some widely prescribed antidepressant drugs are designed to increase its prevalence in the brain. When its level is raised via selective serotonin reuptake inhibitors (SSRIs) such as Prozac, the result is often a general lessening of neurotic overreactions to negative events.

- The male sex hormone testosterone plays a role in sexuality, aggression, and dominance, especially in people who have not been socialized against physical aggression. Testosterone level is an effect as well as a cause of certain social behaviors; for example, it rises after the experience of victory over an opponent.

- Cortisol is an important part of the fight-or-flight (or tend-and-befriend) response. Excess production may lead to chronic anxiety and even brain damage, whereas a shortage can lead to dangerously impulsive behavior.

- Oxytocin, sometimes called the "love hormone," is associated with sexual response, mother-child bonding, and the lowering of anxiety.

- Despite major progress, research connecting biology with personality is still in its early stages and most of its findings should be considered tentative. A few prominent early findings have already been disconfirmed.

The Big Five and the Brain

- The broad trait of "plasticity" subsumes the Big Five traits of extraversion and openness and appears to be associated with dopamine and related brain structures. The broad trait of "stability" subsumes neuroticism (reversed), agreeableness, and conscientiousness, and appears to be associated with serotonin and related brain structures.

Biology: Cause and Effect

- It is important to remember that biological processes affect personality and social behavior, but personality and behavior, along with the social environment, also affect biological processes. Understanding each is helpful for understanding the others.

KEY TERMS

neurons, p. 269

hypothalamus, p. 269

hormones, p. 270

amygdala, p. 270

hippocampus, p. 270

cortex, p. 270

neocortex, p. 270

frontal cortex, p. 270

electroencephalography (EEG), p. 273

magnetoencephalography (MEG), p. 274

positron emission tomography (PET), p. 274

functional magnetic resonance imaging (fMRI), p. 274

amygdala, p. 277

somatic marker hypothesis, p. 283

corpus callosum, p. 284

anterior cingulate, p. 284

neurotransmitters, p. 289

synapse, p. 289

central nervous system, p. 289

peripheral nervous system, p. 289

endorphins, p. 291

serotonin, p. 294

gonads, p. 295

adrenal cortex, p. 295

epinephrine, p. 296

norepinephrine, p. 296

THINK ABOUT IT

1. Are people just animals? In what ways—if any—are they not?

2. What if Charles Whitman had survived that awful day in Texas? Would it have been fair to prosecute him for murder?

3. Psychosurgery has mostly given way to drug therapy. Is this an improvement? Does it make a difference whether a person's mood, behavior, or personality is changed with drugs, or with surgery?

4. In your experience, do women respond to stress and danger differently than men?

5. Imagine that you are involved in intense negotiations. Your adversary takes a testosterone pill to become more confident and aggressive, and thereby achieves a better outcome than you do. Did your adversary have an unfair advantage? Will you take one of those pills yourself next time?

6. Is it important to know which areas of the brain are associated with which personality traits? Why?

SUGGESTED RESOURCES

Allen, T.A., & DeYoung, C.G. (2015). Personality neuroscience and the five factor model. In Widiger, T.A. (Ed.), *Oxford Handbook of the Five Factor Model*. New York: Oxford University Press.

> *A clearly written and succinct summary of the recent research addressing the biological underpinnings of personality, with an emphasis on the Big Five.*

Damasio, A. R. (1994). *Descartes' error: Emotion, reason, and the human brain*. New York: Putnam.

> *A lively and highly readable summary of one neurologist's view of the relationship between the brain and behavior. It includes several compelling case studies (including that of Elliott, summarized in this chapter) and the author's somatic marker hypothesis, in which he argues that emotions are an indispensable component of rational thought.*

 Want to earn a better grade on your test?
Go to **INQUIZITIVE** to learn and review this chapter's content, with personalized feedback along the way.

9

GENETICS AND EVOLUTION
The Inheritance of Personality

THE NEXT MEMBER OF New York's Rockefeller family will be born rich. Why? The reason, of course, is *inheritance*. The child's parents are already rich, so he or she will join a wealthy family and have all of the advantages (and perhaps disadvantages) that accompany large amounts of money. But why are this child's parents rich? Why are *all* the Rockefellers wealthy? The explanation goes back more than 100 years to the career of John D. Rockefeller, an utterly ruthless and fabulously successful businessman. Using secret buyouts, intimidation, and market manipulation, between 1870 and 1882 he built Standard Oil of Ohio into the Standard Oil Trust, which for years held a near monopoly on the U.S. oil business. After many battles with competitors and the legal system, he retired in 1911 with a fortune beyond imagining. His name became a synonym for wealth.

Now consider a question that might seem unrelated. Where did your personality come from? Why are you so friendly, competitive, or stubborn? Maybe you have chosen to be this way, or maybe it is a result of everything you have experienced in your life, but we need to consider the strong possibility that this answer also concerns inheritance. Are your parents especially friendly, competitive, or stubborn? And are you, as well? If the answer is yes, as it may well be, then a further question arises: Where did this trait come from in the first place? The answer might lie in the careers of some ancestors who lived a very long time ago.

Chapter 7 talked about personality development, the way personality changes and remains the same from childhood to old age. The topic of this chapter goes back even earlier, to the very beginning. Two approaches consider personality's ultimate biological roots (Penke, Dennisen, & Miller, 2007). The first, *behavioral genetics*, addresses how traits are passed from parent to child and shared by biological relatives. The second, *evolutionary psychology*, addresses how patterns of behavior that characterize all humans may have originated in the way these characteristics promoted survival during the early history of the species.

This chapter will consider the inheritance of personality from both perspectives. First, it surveys research on behavioral genetics that examines how personality traits are shared among biological relatives, including recent studies seeking to uncover the molecular genetic basis of personality. The chapter will also examine how inheritance interacts with experience: Two people with the same genes might have very different attributes, depending on the environments in which they are raised, and, as recent research is beginning to show, environments can actually shape how and even whether genes are expressed. Second, the chapter will summarize theorizing on how modern human nature and personality may be results of the evolutionary history going back hundreds of thousands of years. It will also consider controversies over this approach, and the light that evolutionary theory can shed on understanding human nature. The chapter ends by reconsidering the question that began this section of the book: Are people just animals? Or, to put the question another way, is an explanation of the biology of behavior sufficient for explaining human psychology?[1]

BEHAVIORAL GENETICS

People tend to look somewhat like their biological parents, and at family reunions it can be fascinating to see how aunts, uncles, and cousins share a certain resemblance. The similarity may be obvious, but its exact basis can be surprisingly difficult to pin down. Is it a similar shape of the eyes, curl of the hair, characteristic facial expression, or some complex combination of all of these? No matter how the similarity manifests, the reason biological relatives look alike is because they share genes.

Physical appearance is one thing, but now consider some other questions: Is there family resemblance in personality? Did you inherit your traits from your parents? Are you psychologically similar to your brother or sister because you are biologically related? Questions like these motivate the study of behavioral genetics. This field of research examines the way inherited biological material—genes—can influence broad patterns of behavior. A pattern of behavior that is generally consistent across situations is, by definition, a **personality trait** (Plomin, Chipuer, & Loehlin, 1990). Thus, "behavioral" genetics might more accurately be called "trait" genetics, but in this chapter I will stick with the traditional term.

Controversy

The field of behavioral genetics has been controversial from the beginning, in part because of its historic association with a couple of notorious ideas. One is *eugenics*, the belief that humanity could (and should) be improved through selective

---

[1] Spoiler alert: No.

breeding. Over the years, this idea has led to activities ranging from campaigns to keep "inferior" immigrants out of some countries, to attempts to set up sperm banks stocked with deposits from winners of the Nobel Prize. A second controversial idea to emerge from eugenics is cloning, the belief that it might be technologically possible to produce a complete duplicate—psychological as well as physical—of a human being. Both of these ideas have dodgy histories (e.g., Adolf Hitler promoted eugenics), and seem to imply nightmarish future scenarios. A less dramatic, but still worrisome concern is that research on genetic bases of behavior might lead the public to think that outcomes such as intelligence, poverty, criminality, mental illness, and obesity are fixed in one's genes rather than changeable by experience or social circumstances (Dar-Nimrod & Heine, 2011).

Modern behavioral geneticists are quick to distance themselves from ideas like these. They view themselves as basic scientists pursuing knowledge both for its own sake and because understanding genetic influences can help to develop ways to treat behavioral disorders. After all, ignorance never got anyone very far (see the discussion of research ethics in Chapter 3). But a more reassuring observation may be that neither eugenics nor cloning turns out to be very feasible. Because personality is the result of a complex interaction between an individual's genes and the environment, as we shall see, the chances of being able to breed people to specification or to duplicate any individual are, thankfully, slim. Even if you could create an exact genetic clone of yourself, this other person would differ from you in numerous ways.[2] And no modern behavioral geneticist views genetically influenced traits as being inevitably fixed, though some popular accounts might give that impression. The real contribution of behavioral genetics is the way it expands our understanding of the sources of personality development to include its bases in both genes and the environment.

Calculating Heritability

The oldest research method in behavioral genetics is based on a simple idea: If a trait is influenced by genes, people who are genetic relatives ought to be more similar on that trait than people who are not genetic relatives, and the closer their genetic relationship, the more similar they should be. The classic technique focuses on twins. As you probably know, there are two kinds of human twins: identical (also called monozygotic, or MZ) twins and fraternal (dizygotic, or DZ) twins. Monozygotic ("one-egg") twins come from the splitting of a single fertilized egg and therefore are genetically identical.[3] Dizygotic ("two-egg") twins come from

---

[2] Although, as a colleague of mine once remarked, meeting your clone would still be "pretty danged weird."

[3] Actually, that's not quite true (Li et al., 2014), because of *somatic point mutations* that occur as cells divide and multiply throughout the life span. But pretty close.

two eggs fertilized by two different sperm, and so, although born at the same time, they are no more genetically related than any other two full siblings.

All humans are highly similar to each other genetically. More than 99 percent of all human genes are identical from one person to the next. Indeed, 98 percent of these same genes are also found in chimpanzees (Balter, 2002)! Behavioral genetics concentrates on the less than 1 percent of the human genome that commonly varies across individuals. MZ twins are effectively the same in all of these varying genes; DZ twins share about half of them, on average, as is also the case for parents and offspring. Thus, for example, the statement that a mother shares 50 percent of her genetic material with her child really means that she shares 50 percent of the material that varies across individuals. This rather technical point highlights an important fact: Like trait psychology (see Chapters 4 to 7), with which it is closely aligned, behavioral genetics focuses exclusively on individual differences. Inheritance of species-specific traits that all humans share is the focus of evolutionary biology, which is discussed in the second half of this chapter.

> More than 99 percent of all human genes are identical from one person to the next. Indeed, 98 percent of these same genes are also found in chimpanzees.

Behavioral genetic studies have worked hard to find twins of both types (MZ and DZ), and also to seek out the rare twins separated at birth and reared apart. Researchers then measure their personalities, usually with self-report instruments such as those discussed in Chapters 3 and 6. The Eysenck Personality Questionnaire (EPQ), the California Psychological Inventory (CPI), and the NEO-PI, a measure of the Big Five traits (see Chapter 6), are particular favorites. Less frequently, researchers have directly observed twins in laboratory contexts to assess the degree to which they behave similarly (Borkenau, Riemann, Angleitner, & Spinath, 2001).

The next step is to compute the correlation coefficient (see Chapter 3) across the pairs of twins, separately for the MZs and DZs.[4] To the degree that a trait or behavior is influenced by genes, then the trait and behavioral scores of identical (MZ) twins ought to be more highly correlated than the scores of fraternal (DZ) twins. A statistic called the *heritability coefficient* reflects the degree to which variance of the trait in the populations can be attributed to variance in genes (see the hypothetical example in **Table 9.1**). In the case of twins, one simple formula is

$$\text{Heritability quotient} = (r_{MZ} - r_{DZ}) \times 2$$

(that is, twice the difference between the correlation among MZ twins and the correlation among DZ twins). Across many, many traits, the average correlation across MZ twins is about .60, and across DZ twins it is about .40, when adjusted

---

[4] For technical reasons, a related statistic called the *intraclass correlation coefficient* is used.

Table 9.1 | CALCULATING HERITABILITY

	Identical (MZ)		Fraternal (DZ)	
	Score of First Twin	Score of Second Twin	Score of First Twin	Score of Second Twin
Pair 1	54	53	52	49
Pair 2	41	40	41	53
Pair 3	49	51	49	52
...	...	...	...	...
...	...	...	...	...
	$r = .60$		$r = .40$	

Note: Heritability quotient = $(r_{MZ} - r_{DZ}) \times 2$

Calculation: .60 − .40 = .20

.20 × 2 = .40

Conclusion: Heritability = 40%.

for age and gender (Borkenau et al., 2001, p. 661). The difference between these figures is .20; multiply that by 2, and you arrive at a heritability coefficient of .40. This means that, according to twin studies, the average heritability of many traits is about .40, which is interpreted to mean that 40 percent of phenotypic (behavioral) variance is accounted for by genetic variance. The heritabilities of the Big Five traits are a bit higher; according to one comprehensive summary they range from .42, for agreeableness, to .57, for openness (Bouchard, 2004).

Twin studies are simple and elegant, and the calculations are easy because MZ twins share on average twice as many variable genes as do DZ twins. However, these studies are not the only way to estimate heritability. Other kinds of relatives also vary in the degree to which they share genes. Children share 50 percent of their variable genes with each of their biological parents, whereas adopted children (presumably) share no more of their personality-relevant genes with their adoptive parents than they would with any other person chosen at random. Full siblings also share, on average, 50 percent of the genes that vary, whereas half-siblings (who have one parent in common) share only 25 percent, and first cousins 12.5 percent.

Notice that I have been careful to say that these figures are *averages*. For example, the statistic that full siblings share 50 percent of the variable genes is a theoretical average of all siblings, and does not necessarily describe the similarity between any particular pair of brothers and sisters. It is possible, though highly unlikely, that two full siblings could share none of the variable genes at all—or all of them (Johnson, Penke, & Spinath, 2011)—for the same reason that flipping a coin "heads" 12 times in a row is possible, but unlikely. This point illustrates how behavioral genetic analyses and the statistics they produce refer to groups or populations, not individuals. When research concludes that a personality trait is, say, 50 percent heritable, this does not mean that half of the extent to which an individual expresses that trait is determined genetically. Instead, it means that 50 percent of the degree to which the trait varies across the population can be attributed to genetic variation.[5]

For most traits, the estimates of heritability garnered from studies of family resemblance that *don't* include twins average about 20 percent, or half the average heritability estimated from twin studies (Plomin, Chipuer, & Loehlin, 1990)[6]. Why this difference? One likely explanation is that the effects of genes are multiplicative rather than additive. That is, estimates of heritability based on twin studies assume that individual genes and the environment act independently to influence personality, and these influences can simply be added up. If that were true, then because DZ twins share (on average) half of the variable genes that MZ twins do, we could assume they are half as similar in gene expression. But, as will be described later in this chapter, genes can operate differently depending on the other genes that are present. Moreover, genes will express themselves in different ways in different environments and even members of the same family may grow up and live in different social contexts. As a result, while heritability estimates based on twins may be too high, those based on broader family relationships may be too low.

What Heritability Tells You

Admittedly, heritability calculations are rather technical, and before one dives too deeply into the details a more basic question should be asked: Regardless of how you compute it, what does a heritability statistic tell you? Two things.

GENES MATTER First, heritability tells you that genes matter. For years, psychologists presumed that all of personality was determined environmentally; that is, by early experiences and parental practices. Heritability estimates challenge that presumption whenever they turn out to be greater than zero—and they nearly always[7] do (see **Table 9.2**). Indeed, it has been seriously suggested that the first law of behavioral genetics should be "Everything is heritable" (Turkheimer, 1998, p. 785; Turkheimer & Gottesman, 1991). Not all of personality comes from experience; some of it comes from genes. This important realization is, even now, not

---

[5] I know this point is kind of wonky, but it's still important.

[6] A more recent survey gives the numbers as .47 and .22, respectively, but the bottom line is the same: Twin studies yield higher heritability estimates that are roughly double those from family and adoption studies (Vukasović & Bratko, 2015).

[7] Actually, always.

Table 9.2 | HERITABILITY OF SOME PSYCHOLOGICAL TRAITS

Personality

Big Five

Extraversion	.54
Agreeableness (aggression)	.42
Conscientiousness	.49
Neuroticism	.48
Openness	.57

Big Three

Positive emotionality	.50
Negative emotionality	.44
Constraint	.52

Psychiatric illnesses

Schizophrenia	.80
Major depression	.37
Panic disorder	.30-.40
Generalized anxiety disorder	.30
Phobias	.20-.40
Alcoholism	.50-.60
Antisocial behavior (adults)	.41

Social attitudes

Conservatism (age 20 and older)	.45-.65
Right-wing authoritarianism (adults)	.50-.64
Religiousness (adults)	.30-.45

Source: Adapted from Bouchard (2004), p. 150.

accepted by everyone, and its far-reaching implications are still sinking in.

INSIGHT INTO EFFECTS OF THE ENVIRONMENT

A second important contribution of heritability studies is to provide a window into *non*-genetic effects; specifically, how the early environment does—or does not—operate in shaping personality development.

For a long time, many researchers believed that one of the major findings of behavioral genetics was this: Growing up together in the same home does not tend to make children similar to each other. When measured using standard personality questionnaires such as measures of the Big Five,

> Not all of personality comes from experience; some of it comes from genes. This important realization is, even now, not accepted by everyone, and its far-reaching implications are still sinking in.

the traits of adoptive siblings raised in the same family resemble each other with a correlation of only .05. Early writers interpreted this finding to mean that hardly any variation in personality is due to the context shared by siblings who grow up together. Instead, they concluded, the portion of the childhood environments that siblings do *not* share is more important. These include the degree to which children in the same family are treated differently, friendships outside the home, and other outside interests and activities (Loehlin, Willerman, & Horn, 1985, 1989; Rowe, 1994).

Of course, these were just speculations. The research just cited did not specify *which* aspects of a child's environment are important (Turkheimer & Waldron, 2000)—an important omission. It did suggest that whatever the key aspects may be, they do not do much to make family members the same. But other, more recent research tells a somewhat different story.

Several developmental outcomes, including juvenile delinquency, aggression, and even love styles, *have* been found—using standard methods of behavioral genetics—to be affected by growing up in the same household, an influence that behavioral geneticists call the *shared family environment* (Rowe, Rodgers, & Meseck-Bushey, 1992; N. G. Waller & Shaver, 1994). We saw lots of examples of how this works in Chapter 7. A major meta-analysis that summarized the results of many studies concluded that the environment shared by siblings growing up was important in the development of several types of psychopathology during the period between childhood and adolescence, including conduct disorder, rebelliousness, anxiety, and depression (Burt, 2009). The only exception was attention deficit hyperactivity disorder (ADHD), for which the shared family environment did not seem to matter.

To some extent, results vary depending on the methods used (Borkenau, Riemann, Angleitner, & Spinath, 2002). Going beyond self-report questionnaires, one large study gathered ratings of twins' personality traits based on direct observations of 15 different behaviors, including introducing oneself to a stranger, building a paper tower, and singing a song. The result was that "extraversion was the only trait that seemed not to be influenced by shared environment" (Borkenau et al., 2001, p. 655). Every other trait measured in the study *was* affected by the shared environment—which, in most cases, means the family and the neighborhood, especially the family.

As Borkenau and colleagues pointed out, this conclusion has two important implications. First, the widely advertised conclusion that shared family environment is unimportant for personality development was reached too quickly, on the basis of limited data. For many years, behavioral genetics research was based almost exclusively on self-report questionnaires, and these S data show little similarity comparing siblings raised together. But when personality is assessed by directly observing behavior, the picture looks different. The second implication returns us to the message of Chapter 2: Personality research can employ many kinds of data, and they all should be used. Conclusions based on only one kind are at risk; consistent results across several kinds of data are more likely to hold up in the long run.

What Heritability Can't Tell You

Heritability calculations have a couple of important limitations that are often over-looked.

NATURE VERSUS NURTURE First, heritability calculations do not solve the nature-nurture puzzle. Ever since scientists realized that genetics affect behavior, they have longed for a simple calculation that would indicate what percentage of any given trait was due to nature (heredity) and what percentage was due to nurture (upbringing and environment). To some, the heritability coefficient seemed like the answer, since it yields a figure between zero and 100 percent that reflects the percentage of the variation in an observable trait due to variation in genes.

But consider, as an example, the number of arms you have. Take a moment and count them. Was this number determined by nature (your genes) or by nurture (your childhood environment)? We can use some (hypothetical but realistic) twin data to calculate the heritability of this trait. Look again at Table 9.1. For the score of the first identical twin of Pair 1, plug in the number of arms he has, which you can presume to be two. Do the same for the score of the second twin of Pair 1, which presumably also is two. Repeat this process for both twins in all the identical pairs. Then do the same thing for the scores of the fraternal twins. When you are finished, all the numbers in the table will be two. The next step is to calculate the correlation for the identical twins, and the correlation for the fraternal twins. Actually, you cannot do that in either case because the formula to calculate the correlation (not shown in Table 9.1) will require a division by zero, the result of which is undefined in mathematics, and will also make your calculator very unhappy.[8] This fact makes the formula at the bottom of the table a bit awkward to use, but we can presume that the difference between two undefined numbers is zero, which multiplied by two is still zero, and so the heritability of having two arms is zero. Does that mean that the number of arms you have is *not* biologically influenced? Well . . .

What went wrong in this calculation? The problem is that, for the trait "arm quantity," there is practically no variation across individuals; nearly everyone has two. Because heritability is the proportion of variation due to genetic influences, if there is no variation, then the heritability must approach zero.

If you are still following this discussion, you might now appreciate that your calculation of the heritability of number of arms did not go wrong at all. If you look around at people, occasionally you will see someone with one arm. Why? Almost always, it will be because of an accident—an environmental event.[9] The *difference* between people with one arm and those with two arms—the variation in

---

[8] I don't actually know how your calculator will feel. But it will give you an error message.

[9] I once used this example in class and realized, too late, that one of my students actually did have one arm, because of a boating accident. But this unfortunate experience demonstrates the point. The accident was an environmental cause, not a genetic one.

that trait—is produced environmentally and not genetically. That is why the heritability for the number of arms is near zero. Heritability statistics are *not* the nature-nurture ratio; a biologically determined trait can have a zero heritability.

HOW GENES AFFECT PERSONALITY Second, heritability statistics do not really tell you very much about the process by which genes affect personality and behavior. Here is a fact that may astonish you: To a statistically significant degree, television watching is heritable (Plomin, Corley, DeFries, & Fulker, 1990). Does this mean an active gene in your DNA causes you to watch television? Presumably not. Rather, there must be some related propensities—perhaps sensation seeking, or lethargy, or even a craving for blue light—that have genetic components. And these components, interacting somehow with biological development and early experience, cause some people to watch a lot of television. The original research did not examine any of these transactions, however, and more than 35 years later no study has offered so much as a hint as to what the actual inherited propensities related to television watching might be.

> To a statistically significant degree, television watching is heritable.

Divorce is heritable, too: If one or more of your close relatives have been divorced, you are more likely to get divorced than if none of your relatives has been divorced—even if you have never met these relatives (McGue & Lykken, 1992). An impressively large study in Sweden (which included 19,715 adoptees and 82,698 offspring) looked at outcomes of both biological and adopted children of divorced and non-divorced parents, and concluded that people were more likely to have similar marital outcomes to their biological parents than to their adoptive parents (Salvatore, Lönn, Sundquist, Sundquist, & Kendler, 2018). The exact heritability was .13, significantly more than 0.

What does this finding imply about the causes of divorce? Actually, maybe not much (Turkheimer, 1998). It does imply that one or more (very probably more) genetically influenced traits are relevant. The researchers speculated that these might include extreme emotionality and lack of self-control (Salvatore et al., 2018). But as to exactly which traits are involved, or how they influence divorce, their behavioral genetics analyses actually could not say. This has become a familiar story. While it is now well-established that many traits and outcomes are influenced by genes, exactly how this happens remains largely a matter of speculation (Plomin, DeFries, Knopik & Neiderhiser, 2016; Turkheimer, 2016).

Molecular Genetics

The field of behavioral genetics has changed dramatically in recent years as it begins to move away from the study of relatives, such as twins, toward the methods of molecular biology. Research now seeks to unravel the mystery of how specific genes influence life outcomes by diving into the actual DNA.

For example, a complex program of research examines the relationship between traits associated with behavioral and emotional control and a gene called *DRD4*, which affects the development of dopamine receptors. As we saw in Chapter 8, dopamine is part of the brain system that responds to reward, and some psychologists have theorized that a shortage of dopamine, or an inability to respond to it, may lead people to crave extra stimulation to the point of engaging in risky behavior. The *dopaminergic* systems of the brain (the parts of the brain influenced by dopamine) also play broad roles in the control and regulation of behavior and even bodily movement. An early study found that different forms of the *DRD4* gene are associated with variations in sensation seeking, and so concluded that the gene might affect this trait via its effect on dopaminergic systems (Benjamin et al., 1996; see also Blum et al., 1996). The *DRD4* gene is also associated with risk for attention deficit hyperactivity disorder (ADHD), which makes sense given the association between dopamine and regulation of cognition and behavior, as well as the related personality trait of impulsivity (Munafó, Yalcin, Willis-Owen, & Flint, 2008). But there is more to impulsivity than this one gene. *DRD4* apparently has nothing to do with risky behavior among skiers and snowboarders (Thomson, Rajala, Carlson, & Rubert, 2014). Other groups of related genes, not just *DRD4*, are related to dopamine and sensation seeking. Moreover, sensation seeking is also relevant to serotonin and its related genes (Zuckerman, 2012).

Many researchers are working on the genetics associated with serotonin. Recall from Chapter 8 that a shortage of serotonin has been blamed for a number of emotional disorders ranging from depression to anxiety and social phobia, and that drugs (such as SSRIs) that increase the level of serotonin in the brain effectively treat these disorders, at least sometimes. The *5-HTT* gene, associated with a serotonin transporter protein, has two variants, or **alleles**. They are called "short" and "long" based on their chromosomal structure. Several studies have shown that people with the short allele score higher on measures of neuroticism, a broad personality trait that (as we saw in Chapter 6) is relevant to anxiety and overreaction to stress (Canli & Lesch, 2007). Even more interesting, the amygdala in people with the short allele also shows stronger responses—as viewed through fMRI images, PET scans, and other imaging techniques (see Chapter 8)—to viewing fearful and unpleasant stimuli such as pictures of frightened-looking faces, accident victims, mutilated bodies, and polluted scenery (Hariri et al., 2002; Heinz et al., 2004; Munafó, Brown, & Hariri, 2008). In people who suffer from social phobias, the same thing happens if they have to give a public speech (Furmark et al., 2004). This gene also appears to regulate the degree to which the amygdala and the prefrontal cortex work together, which may offer an important clue to the brain structure of depression (Heinz et al., 2004).

A fascinating—and somewhat disconcerting—finding is that the prevalence of the short allele of the *5-HTT* gene may vary across cultural groups. In particular, the allele appears to be present in about 75 percent of Japanese people, more than double its frequency in Caucasians (Kumakiri et al., 1999). What does this

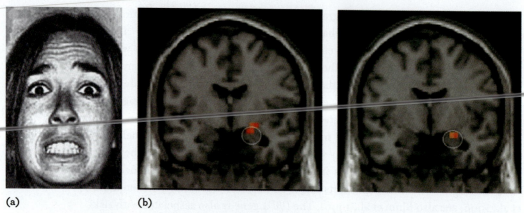

(a)   (b)

Figure 9.1 Genetics and Amygdala Response The amygdala of people who were shown (a) a frightened-looking face and other fear-invoking stimuli responded more strongly if they had (b) the short allele of the *5-HTT* gene (left-hand picture) than if they had the long allele (right-hand picture). Each picture represents data averaged across 14 participants; the circle shows the average location of the amygdala, and the color-coding shows the difference in response between fearful and non-fearful stimuli in terms of T-scores (which are based on the mean difference divided by the standard deviation).

Source: Hariri et al. (2002), p. 401.

finding mean? Some psychologists have speculated that it may be one reason for why Asian cultures emphasize cooperation and avoiding conflict over the kind of individualistic striving said to be characteristic of Western cultures (Chiao & Ambady, 2007). Because of the emotional sensitivity associated with this allele, Asians might tend to find interpersonal conflict more aversive than do Westerners, and so make extra efforts to smooth it over. But we are skating on thin ice here. Attempts to use genetics to account for behavioral differences between cultural groups have a long, nasty, and sometimes tragic history; focusing too much on such differences have led to consequences ranging from unfair discrimination to genocide.

It is also important to remember that, as complex as the findings linking genes to behavior have become, they are still not the whole story. About a quarter of the Japanese population does *not* have the short allele of *5-HTT*, and more than a third of Caucasians *do* have it. Moreover, the effects of *5-HTT* on personality and behavior are fairly small and can't always be replicated (Plomin & Crabbe, 2000). In addition, as has already been mentioned, no single gene accounts for more than a trace of the variation in personality. Thousands of different genes are probably involved in complex traits such as sensation seeking or proneness to anxiety. The chance of finding a single gene that has a simple, direct, and easily understood effect on impulsiveness, anxiety, or any other aspect of personality, therefore, is virtually nil. The real connection between genetics and personality is surely much more complex.

Yet, despite all the complexity, the rate of accumulation of knowledge over the past decade or so has been no less than astonishing. Up until about the year 2000, nearly everything that was known about the interplay of genetics and personality came from studies of genetic relatives such as twins. Since then, serious efforts to explore molecular genetics have yielded tantalizing hints concerning the biological bases of anxiety, impulsiveness, depression, and even criminal behavior. A gene called *COMT* (for catechol-O-methyltransferase) was found to be

"We think it has something to do with your genome."

associated with higher levels of dopamine in the prefrontal cortex and also with extraversion and reasoning ability (Wacker, Mueller, Hennig, & Stemmler, 2012). This finding is especially exciting because it suggests a connection between a gene, a neurotransmitter, a personality trait, and an important aspect of intelligence. The next few years should see further rapid advances, as well as a better understanding of how one's genes transact with experience. We consider this issue next.

Gene-Environment Interactions

It was only natural for the study of behavioral genetics, including molecular genetics of personality, to begin with the study of main effects, of how particular genes or patterns of genes are associated with particular behavioral or personality outcomes. But in the final analysis, genes cannot cause anybody to do anything, any more than you can live in the blueprint of your house. The genotype only provides the design, and so affects the behavioral phenotype indirectly, by influencing biological structure and physiology as they develop within an environment (Turkheimer & Waldron, 2000). The next challenge, therefore, after figuring out how specific aspects of the nervous system are affected by genes, is to understand how their development interacts with environmental experience to affect behavior.

> Genes cannot cause anybody to do anything, any more than you can live in the blueprint of your house.

The environment can even affect heritability itself. For example, when every child gets enough to eat, variance in height will be under the control of genetics. Tall parents will tend to have tall children, and short parents will tend to have short children; the heritability coefficient for height will be close to 1.0. But in an environment where some children are well fed while others go hungry, variance in height will fall more under the control of the environment. Well-fed children will grow near the maximum of their genetic potential while poorly fed children will grow closer to their genetic minimum, and the height of the parents will not matter so much; the heritability coefficient for height will be much closer to 0.

Consider a more psychological trait such as IQ. From the logic just used, we could expect that, in an environment where intellectual stimulation and educational opportunities vary a lot from one child to the next, IQ might be more under the control of the environment. The children who are stimulated and educated will grow up to have intelligence near the top of their genetic potential, while those who are not so lucky will fall far short of what they could achieve, and heritability of IQ will be low. But if we could achieve a society where all children received sufficient stimulation and education, then the differences in IQ that still remained would be due to differences in their genes. In other words, as the intellectual environment improves for everybody, we should expect the heritability of IQ to go up! And that is exactly what has been found. In one major study, the variance in IQ of children from impoverished families was accounted for by their environments, whereas more of the variance in IQ in affluent families was due to genes (Turkheimer, Haley, Waldron, D'Onofrio, & Gottesman, 2003; see **Table 9.3**).

> As the intellectual environment improves for everybody, we should expect the heritability of IQ to go up.

Genes and the environment transact in several other ways (Roberts & Jackson, 2008; Scarr & McCartney, 1983). For example, a boy who is shorter than his peers may be teased in school; the teasing could have long-term effects on his personality. These effects are due, in part, to his genes because height is genetically influenced, but they came about only through an interaction between the genetic expression and the social environment. Without both, there would have been no such effect. Or a girl who inherits a genetically based tendency to be easily angered may tend to create and thereby experience hostile social situations, a process parallel to the *evocative person-environment transaction* introduced in Chapter 7.

Another way genes and environments interact is in how people choose their environments, a process sometimes called "niche picking." It is parallel to the active person-environment transaction described in Chapter 7. People tend to select and even create environments that are compatible with and may magnify

Table 9.3	HERITABILITY OF IQ AS A FUNCTION OF SOCIAL-ECONOMIC STATUS		
Status	DZ correlation	MZ correlation	Heritability
Low	.63	.68	$(.68 - .63) \times 2 = .10$
High	.51	.87	$(.87 - .51) \times 2 = .72$

Source: From data reported by Turkheimer, Haley, Waldron, D'Onofrio, & Gottesman (2003).

their genetically influenced tendencies. A person who inherits a predisposition toward sensation seeking may take dangerous drugs. This practice might harm his health or involve him in the drug culture, either of which could have long-lasting effects on his experience and his personality development. Let's say that from hanging around with criminals, he develops a criminal personality. This outcome was only indirectly due to the inherited trait of sensation seeking; it came about only through the transaction of the inherited trait with the environment he sought out because of that trait.

A more positive example involves the trait of extraversion. Attempts to find genes directly associated with extraversion have generally been unsuccessful (McCrae, Scally, Terracciano, Abecasis, & Costa, 2010). However, people who are physically attractive and strong are relatively likely to be extraverted, probably because these traits make interactions with other people more likely to be frequent and rewarding (Lukaszewski & Roney, 2011). This example not only shows how genes and environments transact, but it also suggests that if one wants to find the genes responsible for extraversion one might be better off studying the bases of attractiveness, strength, and other attributes related to how a person gets along with others.

Genes may even affect how a child is treated by his parents, which can be seen as an extreme example of an evocative person-situation transaction. The usual expectation, as described in Chapter 7, is that parenting affects the development of children's personalities. But the influence can run in the reverse direction, as was also mentioned in Chapter 7. One meta-analysis of 32 studies of twins concluded that boys with genetic tendencies toward poor self-control received less attention from their mothers (Avinun & Knafo, 2014). This tendency only became stronger as the boy got older. It is not true that mothers will put up with anything.

The most basic way in which genes and environments interact is that the same environments that promote good outcomes for some people can promote bad outcomes for others, and vice versa, a process parallel to the *reactive person-environment transaction* described in Chapter 8. A stressful environment may lead a genetically predisposed individual to develop mental illness but leave other individuals unscathed. More generally, the same circumstances might be experienced as stressful, enjoyable, or boring, depending on the genetic predispositions of the individuals involved; these variations in experience can lead to very different behaviors and, over time, to the development of different personality traits.

Two pioneers in exploring the implications of gene-environment interactions are psychologists Avshalom Caspi and Terrie Moffitt. Along with their colleagues, Caspi and Moffitt work closely with a major project that has followed a group of children in New Zealand for decades.[10] One groundbreaking study assessed the degree to which participants experienced difficulties such as unemployment,

---

[10] They are not children anymore, of course.

financial setbacks, housing problems, health challenges, and relationship problems between the ages of 21 and 26, and then whether they experienced depression at the end of this period (Caspi et al., 2003). Building on the results summarized in the preceding section of this chapter, Caspi, Moffitt, and their coworkers found that people who had the short allele for the serotonin-related gene *5-HTT* were more likely to experience depression after these stressful experiences than those without this allele. But—and this is important—there was no difference in outcome between those with the long allele and those with the short allele if they had not suffered any stress. This is a perfect example of a genotype-environment interaction: The genotype is important, but only for people who have experienced a certain kind of environment.

These findings and others like them received a great deal of attention and have been very exciting for the field of behavioral genetics, but recent work has shown the true picture to be more complicated than it seemed at first. Isn't that always how it goes? The provocative result concerning the interaction between the *5-HTT* gene and stressful life environments is not found in every study, and one meta-analysis summarized the literature by saying that it found "no evidence" that the gene "alone or in interaction with stressful life events is associated with an elevated risk of depression in men alone, women alone, or in both sexes combined" (Risch et al., 2009; see also Lester et al., 2017).

This discouraging outcome and other failures to replicate provocative findings have led some researchers to argue that "studies of gene-environment interactions are very unlikely to enhance our understanding" (Zammit, Owen, & Lewis, 2010, p. 65). Yet, this conclusion seems unduly pessimistic. For one thing, giving up on an area of research has yet to yield an increase in knowledge. For another thing, the serious pursuit of genotype-environment interactions is still a very new enterprise—the pioneering findings by Caspi and his colleagues are barely more than 15 years old. As improved methods of studying genes continue to be developed and, perhaps even more importantly, better methods for assessing the environment[11] become available, solid progress may yet be made. After all, it is not really in doubt that the same environment can have different results on people with different genes. The main problem may be that any one gene probably only has a small effect.

For example, consider the trait of neuroticism. As we saw in Chapter 6, this trait is an important risk factor for poor mental and physical health outcomes. Where does this trait come from? According to one theoretical model (see **Figure 9.2**), it is a result of a series of complex transactions (Barlow, Ellard, Sauer-Zavala, Bullis, & Carl, 2014). First, a person may have a general biological vulnerability to stress that is genetically influenced in ways such as discussed above, probably by many different genes. At the same time, the person may have general *psychological*

---

[11] This is a surprisingly neglected topic in behavioral genetics.

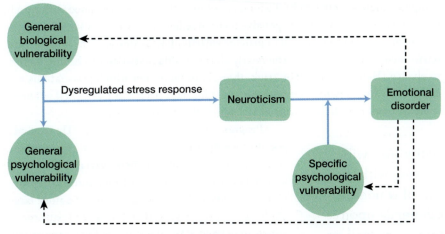

Figure 9.2 A Model of the Sources of Neuroticism According to this theoretical model, general biological and psychological vulnerabilities combine to create an inability to handle stress, which leads to the trait of neuroticism. This trait can interact with specific experiences to create phobias or other vulnerabilities that may, over time, lead to mental illness. Notice that although biological vulnerability is an important factor, it does not lead to either neuroticism or mental illness unless the person also has negative experiences in his or her environment.
Source: Barlow et al. (2014), p. 482.

vulnerability caused by environmental factors such as poor parenting or the lack of a warm, supportive environment during early childhood. These two influences combine to produce a general inability to handle stress well, which is pretty much the definition of neuroticism. What happens next depends, again, on the person's environment. If the person has experiences that seem to teach him, for example, that illness is dangerous—such as having a relative who becomes gravely ill or living in a family that overreacts whenever somebody catches cold—then he may develop a specific phobia to germs or a generally maladaptive response to illness. If he learns that being rejected by other people is a dire threat, perhaps from early negative experiences with peers, he may develop a social phobia. In the end, neuroticism can have any number of negative consequences for mental health, but the specific result will depend not on genes or biology, but on the way these factors interact with experience.

Genome-Wide Association Studies

Another approach to understanding the molecular genetic roots of behavior is the *genome-wide association* (GWA) study. In a GWA study, data concerning hundreds of thousands of genes and patterns of genes in thousands of people are dumped into a computer, together with data about these individuals' personalities. The computer then searches to find which genes or patterns are associated with which traits. This is a difficult and expensive technique because extremely large numbers of people need to be examined to provide sufficient data, and so many analyses are performed that many and maybe nearly all the results that arise will be due merely to chance (Hewitt, 2012). The trick, then, is to figure out which associations are dependably found in different samples of subjects, a trick that has turned out to be more difficult than first assumed (McCrae et al., 2010).

Progress is coming, but it's slow. Three studies of more than 100,000 people each (imagine the research budget!) found genetic variants that were associated with traits related to happiness, depression, and anxiety (Okbay et al., 2016). Another large study—but not as large as that one—found patterns of genes associated with all of the Big Five traits except extraversion. Unfortunately, only the pattern associated with agreeableness was consistent across three separate samples (Terracciano et al., 2010).

> Each major personality trait will turn out to be associated with many different genes, each of which has a small effect that depends upon the effect of other genes as well as the environment.

Discouraged by failures to replicate like this, some researchers have suggested that the attempt to connect traits to genes is doomed at the outset and should be abandoned (Joseph & Ratner, 2012). Sound familiar? Again, this pessimistic argument is almost certainly premature. The most likely outcome, in the long run, is that each major personality trait will turn out to be associated with many different genes, each of which has a small effect that depends upon the effect of other genes as well as the environment. In other words, the ultimate picture is going to be complicated. No big surprise there.

Epigenetics

Even once the genes underlying a particular trait have been identified—and as, we have just seen, that is no easy matter—even more complications remain. Work on **epigenetics** has begun to document how experience, especially early in life, can determine how or even whether a gene is expressed during development (Weaver, 2007). Some of the evidence comes from studies of rats, which differ in the expression of a gene related to their stress response as a function of how much licking and other grooming they received from their mothers when they were young (Weaver et al., 2004). A study of genetically identical mice showed that the ones that explored their environments grew more brain cells than mice that did not, a perfect example of how experience can affect biology (Freund et al., 2013). All of the mice had the genetic potential to grow their brains, but only the ones who bothered to look around took advantage of it. Presumably, they became smarter mice.

Similar epigenetic processes may occur in humans (Roberts, 2017). A very early study that hinted in this direction reported that people from colder areas of

Japan develop fewer sweat glands than people from warmer areas, with the result that they are more susceptible to heat stroke when they travel to a warmer location far from where they grew up (Kawahata & Sakamoto, 1951). More recent evidence indicates that the experience of social stress can activate expression of genes that lead to vulnerabilities to depression, inflammatory diseases, and viral infections (Slavich & Cole, 2013). Perhaps even more impressively, another study found that just acting kindly towards others can reduce the expression of a gene expression profile associated with responses to stressful events (Nelson-Coffey, Fritz, Lyubomirsky & Cole, 2017).[12] As findings like these accumulate—and, hopefully, are replicated—another window will open into how genes and the environment interact, even at the molecular level.

The Future of Behavioral Genetics

Research in behavioral genetics began with studies that calculated heritability coefficients, leading many researchers to think that we were getting close to solving the age-old question of which matters more, heredity or the environment. Since then, evidence has mounted that this is the wrong question to ask. Transactions between genes and the environment can go in both directions and reinforce or even counteract each other. For this reason, one scientist wrote that, when it comes to the nature-versus-nurture controversy, we should probably just "call the whole thing off" (Weaver, 2007, p. 22). He's right. Instead, research in the future must—and surely will—focus on how genes and the environment interact, in daily experience and at the molecular level of gene expression.

> Evidence has mounted that the age-old question of which matters more, heredity or the environment, is the wrong question to ask.

Behavioral genetics sometimes is portrayed as pessimistic because, as was mentioned earlier, it might be taken to imply a sort of doctrine of predestination, that people cannot change what they were born to be (Dar-Nimrod & Heine, 2011). The more we learn about how genetic influence on behavior really works, the clearer it becomes that this view is also wrong. In Chapter 6, I quoted a psychologist who proposed that persons with a genetically influenced determined tendency toward sensation seeking might be deterred from crime by participating in less damaging occupations that satisfy the need for excitement (such as race-car driving or hosting a radio talk show). Frankly, I'm not sure whether this was a serious suggestion. But it makes a point: If we understood an individual's genetic predispositions, we might be able to help her find

---

[12] To be specific, it alters a leukocyte gene expression profile called the Conserved Transcriptional Response to Adversity (CTRA).

an environment where her personality and abilities can lead to good outcomes rather than bad ones.

EVOLUTIONARY PERSONALITY PSYCHOLOGY

Evolutionary theory is the foundation of modern biology. Modern extensions of the theorizing that began with Charles Darwin's *On the Origin of Species* (1859, 1967) are used to compare one species of animal or plant to another, to explain the functional significance of aspects of anatomy and behavior, and to understand how animals function within their environments. Since then, an increasing number of researchers have applied the same kind of theorizing and reasoning to human behavior and even social structure. One landmark book, E. O. Wilson's *Sociobiology: The New Synthesis* (1975), applied evolutionary theory to psychology and sociology. Other earlier efforts, such as Konrad Lorenz's *On Aggression* (1966), also explained human behavior using analogies to animals and their evolution.

Evolution and Behavior

Evolutionary theorizing begins with this recognition: Every human being, including you, is the latest in a long, unbroken chain of winners. In particular, your parents somehow managed to find each other and produce a child who has progressed at least far enough as to be able to read this book. Similarly, all of their parents (your grandparents) successfully survived to adulthood, found mates, and had children who themselves survived to have children. So did their parents, and their parents, and so on back to the misty origins of time.

Consider the magnitude of this family achievement. History has included challenges ranging from volcanic eruptions to epidemics to wars. Many people died, and many of those died young, before they even had a chance to become parents. But this did not happen to any of your ancestors, not one. Without exception, they overcame these challenges with the result that they were able to have, nurture and protect families that survive up to the present day.[13]

> Cultures that worship their ancestors may be on to something.

In other words, your grandparents and great-grandparents knew a few things, and cultures that worship their ancestors may be on to something. The evolutionary approach to personality assumes that human behavioral patterns developed because our long-ago ancestors found them to be helpful or necessary for survival. The more a behavioral tendency has helped individuals to survive and reproduce, the more likely the tendency will be to appear in subsequent generations.

---

[13] So don't you be the one to blow it.

Some specific traits fit this pattern. People higher in extraversion but lower in conscientiousness and openness to experience tend to have more children and grandchildren; higher agreeableness correlates with having more grandchildren but not more children (Berg, Lummaa, Lahdenpera, Rotkirch, & Jokela, 2014). If you were to project these tendencies into the future, you might predict that future humans will be more extraverted and agreeable than they are now, but less conscientious and open to experience. But be patient; the process may take a few thousand years before the results are noticeable.

EVOLUTIONARY MISMATCH However, not all of the results of evolution are as promising as the ones I've just discussed. The human race evolved to its present form in hunter-gatherer societies roaming the African savannah,[14] and the traits that were helpful or even essential for survival there are not necessarily useful in the modern urban world, and may even lead to psychological and physical dysfunction. For example, workplaces take us out of the natural environment, where we evolved to feel safe and comfortable, into fluorescent-lit, windowless offices where stress sometimes increases by the hour. If only a few desks in an office are near a window, people will plot and scheme to get them. Why do you think that is?

The modern environment is a mismatch with human history in other ways, too. Postpartum depression may result from lack of support from the family and community of the kind that our ancestor mothers could take for granted, and our tendency to consume every resource in sight comes from a past where there were too few of us (and we lacked the machines) to destroy our own environment (Li, van Vugt & Colarelli, 2017). Evolution is not the same as progress, and just because a tendency is "natural" does not mean it can't be harmful. Some of our most natural tendencies might be our most dangerous.

> Evolution is not the same as progress, and just because a tendency is "natural" does not mean it can't be harmful.

AGGRESSION AND ALTRUISM The two sides of many human behaviors have been examined through the evolutionary lens. Konrad Lorenz (1966) discussed the possibly necessary—and sometimes harmful—role of the instinct toward aggression. A tendency to be aggressive can help a person to protect territory, property, and mates, and also lead to dominance in the social group and higher status. But the same tendency can also lead to fighting, murder, and the industrial-scale murder called war.

On a happier note, the biologist Richard Dawkins (1976) considered the evolutionary roots of the opposite behavior, altruism. A tendency to aid and protect other people, especially close relatives, might help ensure the survival of one's own genes into succeeding generations, an outcome called *inclusive fitness*. It pays

---

[14] Sometimes called the "environment of evolutionary adaptation" or EEA for short.

*"Whenever Mother's Day rolls around,
I regret having eaten my young."*

to be nice to those around you, especially your relatives, according to this analysis, because if those people who share your genes survive, some of your genes may make it into the next generation through those peoples' children, even if you produce no offspring yourself.

SELF-ESTEEM Evolutionary theory has also been used to explain why self-esteem feels so important. According to the "sociometer theory" developed by psychologist Mark Leary, feelings of self-esteem evolved to monitor the degree to which a person is accepted by others. Humans are highly social, and few outcomes are worse than being shunned by the community. On the African savannah (the EEA) where the human species evolved, ejection from the tribe could mean death. On the reality television program *Survivor*, the dreaded words "The tribe has spoken" touches a deep, instinctual fear.[15] Signs that we are not adequately valued and accepted cause our self-esteem to go down, motivating us to do things that will cause others to think better of us so that we can think better of ourselves. The people who did not develop this motive failed to survive and reproduce (Leary, 1999). We, on the other hand—all of us—are the descendants of people who cared deeply what other people thought about them. And so we do, too.

DEPRESSION Even depression may have evolved because of its survival value. According to one analysis, different kinds of depression[16] have different causes (M. C. Keller & Nesse, 2006). Depression that follows a social loss—such as a breakup with a boyfriend or girlfriend, or bereavement—is characterized by pain, crying, and seeking social support. Depression that follows failure—such as flunking an exam or being fired from a job—is more often characterized by fatigue, pessimism, shame, and guilt.

Psychologists Matthew Keller and Randolph Nesse speculate that, in the history of the species, these reactions may have promoted survival. Pain signals that something has gone wrong and must be fixed. Just as it is important to be able to

---

[15] In the unlikely event you have not seen this program, the host intones the phrase just after a member of the tribe is voted off the island. He then symbolically extinguishes the ex-member's torch (see **Figure 9.3**).

[16] Actually, "depression" is a diagnostic classification that has several specific requirements; the theorizing here is really about "depressive symptoms" such as sadness, crying, social withdrawal, and so on.

Figure 9.3 "The Tribe Has Spoken" These words may touch a deep, evolutionarily based fear of being expelled from one's social group.

feel the pain of a broken leg so you won't try to walk on it, so, too, it may be important to feel emotional pain when something has gone wrong in your social life, because that signals that your chances for reproducing or even surviving may be at risk. This process is similar to Leary's sociometer theory. But Keller and Nesse go further to suggest that crying may often be a useful way of seeking social support, and that fatigue and pessimism can prevent one from wasting energy and resources on fruitless endeavors. One fascinating implication is that in the same way that blocking fever may prolong infections, blocking normal depressive symptoms with antidepressant medication could increase the risk of chronic negative life situations and poorer outcomes, even as the sufferers feel better. Similarly, individuals who lack a capacity for depressive symptoms might be more likely to lose valuable relationships, more likely to persist at unachievable pursuits, less able to learn from mistakes, and less able to recruit friends when things go wrong (M. C. Keller & Nesse, 2006, p. 328). Have you ever told anyone to "go ahead, have a good, long cry"? It might have been good advice. Sometimes we need to feel the pain.

> Have you ever told anyone to "go ahead, have a good, long cry"? It might have been good advice. Sometimes we need to feel the pain.

Individual Differences

Evolutionary psychology has, so far, been more concerned with the origins of general human nature than with individual differences. Indeed, evolutionary influence on human characteristics has sometimes been taken to imply that individual differences should be unimportant, because maladaptive behavioral variations should have been selected out of the gene pool long ago (Tooby & Cosmides, 1990). However, the basic mechanism of evolution *requires* individual differences. Species change only through the selective propagation of the genes of the most successful individuals in earlier generations, which simply cannot happen if everybody is the same. So not only is it fair to expect a "theory of everything" like evolutionary psychology to explain individual differences, such an explanation is essential for the theory to work.

ADAPTATION Diversity is what makes adaptation to changing conditions possible. At the level of the species, a trait that used to be maladaptive or just irrelevant can suddenly become vital for survival. A classic example is the story of the English peppered moth (Majerus, 1998). These moths were mostly white until the Industrial Revolution arrived in the mid-19th century along with factories that spewed coal dust. The white moths stood out in this new environment and became easy prey for birds, but the few individuals in the species who happened to be darker colored were able to survive and propagate. Soon almost all the moths were black. But by the end of the 20th century the air had been substantially cleaned up, and white peppered moths became common again.

The same thing can happen at the level of the individual. Just like white wings are dangerous for a moth who lives amidst coal dust but helpful for a moth who lives in a cleaner environment, a trait that is adaptive in one situation may be harmful in another (Nettle, 2006; Penke et al., 2007). The Big Five personality trait of neuroticism can cause needless anxiety in safe situations, but might promote lifesaving worry in dangerous ones. Similarly, agreeableness can make you popular, but also vulnerable to people intent on cheating you. The end result is that, over hundreds of generations, people continue to be born who are very high or very low on every trait dimension, even while most people continue to have trait scores near the middle.

An individual difference variable that may encompass both kinds of adaptation is called "life history" (or LH for short). The idea is that animals generally exhibit one of two different approaches to reproduction. In one, the animal reproduces multiple times at a young age but does not devote many or any resources to protecting offspring; in the other, the animal does not reproduce until relatively late in life, has fewer offspring, but invests more in each one. Rabbits are an example of the first approach; elephants (and most humans) are examples of the second. The first approach is called "fast-life history" (fast-LH) because it seems best adapted to species that live in dangerous circumstances and typically die young (Ellis, Figueredo, Brumbach, & Schlomer, 2009; Figueredo et al., 2010). The second is called "slow-life history" (slow-LH) because it seems to work better for long-lived species that have a chance for extended protection and nurturing of their offspring.

Early in the history of the human species, the fast-LH strategy may have worked better for reproductive success, but in modern times, in most environments, the slow-LH strategy seems to be more effective. But individuals of both kinds still exist, and may even appear with different frequencies in different environments. Safe, predictable environments promote the appearance of slow-LH individuals who marry late, have few children, and put extensive resources into raising them. Dangerous, unpredictable environments are more likely to produce fast-LH individuals who have children when they are very young but—especially if they are male—may not stay around to help support and raise them. Most current writing on LH tends to describe the slow-LH history as better overall, but there are tradeoffs. In one study, slow-LH individuals were observed to display behavior described as considerate, kind, hardworking, and reliable, but also socially awkward, insecure, and overcontrolling (Sherman, Figueredo, & Funder, 2013). For their part, fast-LH individuals came across as unpredictable, hostile, manipulative, and impulsive; they are also more likely than slow-LH individuals to use swear words, anger words, sexual words, and words related to death (Manson, 2017). But Fast-LH men also are seen as talkative, socially skilled, dominant, and charming, and in everyday speech, they are more likely to talk about work. From an evolutionary perspective, neither LH strategy is "better"; each is adapted to a different set of environmental circumstances.

ACCOUNTING FOR INDIVIDUAL DIFFERENCES Overall, evolutionary psychology accounts for individual differences in three basic ways (D. M. Buss & Greiling, 1999). First, behavioral patterns evolve as reactions to particular environmental experiences. Only under certain conditions does the evolved tendency come "on line," sort of like the way the skin of a Caucasian has a biological tendency to darken if, but only if, it is exposed to the sun. For example, a child who grows up without a father present during the first five years of childhood may respond with an evolved tendency to act as if family life is never stable, which might in turn lead to early sexual maturity and frequent changes of sexual partners, but this same child may reach sexual maturity later if childhood is spent with a reliable father present (Belsky, Steinberg, & Draper, 1991; Sheppard & Sear, 2012). Or, as just related, a person who grows up in an unpredictable and dangerous environment may be stimulated to follow a fast-LH lifestyle; the same person growing up in a safe, predictable environment may do the reverse.

Second, people may have evolved several possible behavioral strategies, but actually use the one that makes the most sense given their other characteristics.

This may be the reason for the finding, cited earlier in this chapter, that physically attractive people are more likely to be extraverts—social activity may be more rewarding for people who are good looking (Lukaszewski & Roney, 2011). Similarly, we may all have innate abilities to be both aggressive and agreeable. But the aggressive style works only if you are big and strong; otherwise, the agreeable style might be a safer course. This may be why big, muscular boys are more likely to become juvenile delinquents (Glueck & Glueck, 1956).

Third, some biologically influenced behaviors may be *frequency dependent*, meaning that they adjust according to how common they are in the population at large. For example, one theory of *psychopathy*—a behavioral style of deception, deceit, and exploitation—is that it is biologically rooted in only a small number of people (Mealey, 1995). If more than a few individuals tried to live this way, nobody would ever believe anybody, and the psychopathic strategy for getting ahead would become evolutionarily impossible to maintain.

These are interesting suggestions, but notice how they all boil down to an argument that human nature has evolved to be flexible. I think that is a very reasonable conclusion, but, at the same time, it tends to undermine the idea that evolution is the root of specific behavioral tendencies—such as self-esteem, depression, mate selection, and jealousy—which has been the whole point of the approach. This is just one reason for why evolutionary psychology is controversial. Psychologists have pointed out several difficulties with an evolutionary approach to human personality, to which we now turn.

> Human nature has evolved to be flexible.

Five Stress Tests for Evolutionary Psychology

Much like Darwin's foundational theory of evolution, the evolutionary approach to human behavior has been controversial almost from the beginning. Its account of sexual behavior and sex differences, in particular, seems almost designed to set some people off, and it certainly does. At least five serious criticisms have been leveled, and each one provides a "stress test" that assesses the degree to which the evolutionary approach to behavior can stand up to challenge. Let's see how it does.

METHODOLOGY The first challenge concerns scientific methodology. It is interesting and even fun to speculate backward in the way that evolutionary theorists do, by wondering about what circumstances or goals in the past might have produced a behavioral pattern we see today. Indeed, such speculation is suspiciously easy, and even sometimes reminiscent of the "just so" stories of Rudyard Kipling, which explained how the whale got its throat, how the camel got its hump, and so forth (Funder, 2007). Evolutionary psychologists sometimes proceed almost in the same way, with the result that they seem ready to explain anything from preferences for salty foods to spousal murder. Remember the sociometer theory of self-esteem summarized a few pages back? It neatly provided an evolutionary reason for why we care what other people think of us. But are other reasons possible as well, or instead?

How can such evolutionary speculations be tested? What sort of experiment could we do to prove or disprove the sociometer theory of self-esteem? Or, how could we test another commonly expressed, evolutionary hypothesis, which is that men really seek multiple sexual partners in order to maximize their genetic propagation (Buss, 2003)? Men who try to maximize their sexual activity aren't necessarily trying to have a lot of children, even if that could be the result. But is that still the underlying aim? Consider the even more radical proposal that males have an evolved instinct toward rape because it furthers reproduction for individuals who could not otherwise find a mate (Thornhill & Palmer, 2000), or that stepparents are prone to child abuse because of the lack of shared genes (Daly & Wilson, 1988). These are provocative suggestions, to say the least, but they also entail problems.

For one, there is something odd about postulating an instinctual basis for behaviors like rape or child abuse when most men are not rapists and most stepparents are not abusive. Primatologist Frans de Waal calls this the "dilemma of the rarely exercised option" (de Waal, 2002, p. 189). Furthermore, it is unwise to assume that every genetically influenced trait or behavior pattern exists because it has an adaptive advantage. Because of the human genome, people walk upright, and because we evolved from four-legged creatures, this design change makes us prone to backache. Apparently, walking upright had enough advantages to counteract the disadvantages, but that does not mean that lower-back pain is an evolved mechanism. In the same way, behavioral patterns such as depression, unfaithfulness, child abuse, and rape—even if they are genetically influenced—may be unfortunate side effects of other, more important adaptations. As de Waal noted, "the natural world is rampant with flawed designs" (2002, p. 188) because evolution always has to build, step-by-step, on what is already there. It doesn't have the luxury of going back and designing a whole new organism from scratch.

> As de Waal noted, "the natural world is rampant with flawed designs" because evolution always has to build, step-by-step, on what is already there.

Evolutionary theorists usually acknowledge that criticisms such as these are fair, to a point, but they also have a reasonable response: For any theoretical proposal in science—not just those in evolutionary psychology—alternative explanations are always possible. Moreover, whole, complex theories are seldom judged on the basis of one crucial, decisive study. Instead, numerous studies test bits and pieces as methods become available. Complex evolutionary theories of behavior are difficult to prove or disprove in their entirety, and some alternative explanations may never be ruled out, but empirical research can address specific predictions. For example, the evolutionary theory of sex differences not only predicts that (on average) men should prefer mates younger than themselves and women should prefer mates who are older, but that this should be true in all cultures (Kenrick & Keefe, 1992). The prediction has been confirmed everywhere it has been tested so far, including India, the United States, Brazil, Kenya, Japan, and Mexico (Dunn, Brinton, & Clark, 2010). This finding does not prove that the reproductive motives described by evolutionary theory cause the age differences, nor does it rule out all possible alternative explanations; but in fairness it must be considered encouraging empirical support.

REPRODUCTIVE INSTINCT   A second challenge is that evolutionary psychology's assumption that everybody is trying to have as many children as possible seems strange in a world where many people choose to limit their own reproduction. For example, how can it make sense to say that a woman who dresses provocatively is seeking an attractive mate who will provide good genes for her children, if at the same time she is on the pill? Evolutionary psychologists have a good response to this objection, too. For evolutionary theorizing about behavior to be correct, it is not necessary for people to consciously try to do what the theory says their behavioral tendencies are ultimately designed to do (Wakefield, 1989). All that is required is for people in the past who followed a certain behavioral pattern to have produced more members of the present generation than did people who did not follow the pattern (Dawkins, 1976).

> Neither sterility nor abstinence runs in anyone's family.

Thus, although you might or might not want children, it cannot be denied that you would not be here unless somebody (your ancestors) had children. (Neither sterility nor abstinence runs in anyone's family.) The same tendencies (e.g., sexual urges) that caused them to produce offspring are also present in you. It is also the case that your sexual urges do increase your chances of reproducing, whether you want them to or not, since birth control methods sometimes fail. According to evolutionary theory, people have tendencies toward sexual behaviors in general because of the effects of similar sexual behaviors on past generations' reproductive outcomes—not necessarily because of any current intention to propagate.

CONSERVATIVE BIAS   A third criticism of the evolutionary approach to behavior is that it embodies a certain conservative bias (Alper, Beckwith, & Miller, 1978; Kircher, 1985). Because it assumes that humans' current behavioral tendencies evolved as a result of the species' past environments, and that these tendencies are biologically rooted, the evolutionary approach seems to imply that the current behavioral order was not only inevitable but also is probably unchangeable and appropriate.[17] This implication can be troubling if you think that male infidelity,

---

[17] Notice that in this context the word "conservative" means tending to favor the status quo, not necessarily any of the various political viewpoints that share this label.

child abuse, and rape are reprehensible (which they are, of course), and believe that human tendencies toward aggression are dangerous and must be changed.

Evolutionary theorists respond that objections like these are irrelevant from a scientific standpoint. They also observe that with this criticism, opponents of evolutionary theories themselves commit the "naturalistic fallacy" of believing that anything shown to be natural must be assumed to be good. But evolutionary theorists do not assume that what is natural is good (Pinker, 1997). As philosopher Daniel Dennett, who writes frequently about evolutionary theory, has stated, "Evolutionary psychologists are absolutely not concerned with the moral justification or condemnation of particular features of the human psyche. They're just concerned with their existence" (cited in Flint, 1995). If an ideological bias does underlie evolutionary psychology, it is more subtle. The basic assumption that our personalities have been selected over the millennia to favor behaviors that promote our individual survival may itself come from the larger culture. As one critic has observed, "In totalitarian regimes, dissidence is treated as a mental illness. In apartheid regimes, interracial contact is treated as unnatural. In free-market regimes, self-interest is treated as hardwired" (Menand, 2002, p. 96).

HUMAN FLEXIBILITY A fourth and more powerful challenge is that evolutionary accounts seem to describe a lot of specific behavior as genetically programmed into the brain, whereas a general lesson of psychology is that humans are extraordinarily flexible creatures with a minimum of instinctive behavior patterns, compared with other species. Indeed, we saw in Chapter 8 that the prefrontal cortex (which is uniquely developed in humans) has the function of planning and thinking beyond simple responses and fixed patterns of behavior. Yet, evolutionary accounts sometimes seem to suggest built-in behavioral patterns that cannot be overcome by conscious, rational thought.

The issue here is not whether the basic theory of evolution is correct; the scientific community settled that question to its satisfaction long ago. Rather, the issue is whether, in the domain of behavior, people evolved general capacities for planning and responding to the environment, or specific behavioral patterns (called *modules*; Öhman & Mineka, 2001). When evolutionary psychology tries to explain behaviors such as mate preference, sex differences in jealousy, and even child abuse and rape, it seems to favor a modular approach (C. R. Harris, 2000). But when it addresses the question of individual differences, evolutionary psychology acknowledges that the evolution of the cerebral cortex has given the human brain the ability to respond flexibly to changing circumstances and even to overcome innate urges. These two kinds of explanation are difficult but perhaps not impossible to reconcile, and debate in the next few years is likely to focus on this issue. What is the human evolutionary heritage? Is it a collection of specific responses triggered almost automatically by particular circumstances? Or is it the ability to plan, foresee, choose, and even override instinctive tendencies?

BIOLOGICAL DETERMINISM OR SOCIAL STRUCTURE? A final criticism of the evolutionary approach to personality is closely related to the idea that people evolved to be flexible. Many behavioral phenomena might be the result not of evolutionary history but of humans responding to changing circumstances, especially social structure. For example, the sex differences discussed earlier may be caused not by biological hard-wiring, but by the current structure of society.

Psychologists Alice Eagly and Wendy Wood have provided an alternative to the evolutionary account of the differences in the criteria used by men and women in choosing mates (Eagly & Wood, 1999; W. Wood & Eagly, 2002). They hypothesize that because of men's greater size and strength, and women's role in childbearing and lactation, societies have developed worldwide in which men and women are assigned different jobs and social roles. Men tend to be warriors, rulers, and controllers of economic resources. Women are more likely to be restricted to staying near the home, gaining power and affluence largely as a function of the men with whom they affiliate. This difference is enough, Eagly and Wood argue, to explain why women value the wealth and power of a man more than his looks, and why the wealth of a woman matters less to a man. The difference comes not from a specific innate module, but from a reasonable and flexible response to the biological and social facts of life (see also Eagly, Eastwick, & Johannesen-Schmidt, 2009).

Figure 9.4 We Have the Power These posters promoted a political campaign for German Prime Minister Angela Merkel. She won the election. As the power differential between the sexes becomes smaller, mating strategies of both men and women may change.

The argument is important for both theoretical and practical reasons. On a theoretical level, it goes to the heart of the question of how much of human nature is evolutionarily determined and biologically inherited. On a practical level, the world is changing. In an industrial culture where physical strength has become less important than it was in the past and alternative child-care arrangements are possible, the traditional division of labor between men and women no longer seems inevitable. But it continues anyway, because societies are slow to change. What happens next?

According to the evolutionary view, the differences between men and women in mate selection and other behaviors are built-in through biological evolution. This view implies that it might be almost impossible to change these differences; at best, any change will occur at the speed of evolution, thus likely requiring thousands of years. According to the contrary societally based view, as the necessity for a gender-based division of labor melts away, societies will change, and sex differences will change (and perhaps lessen) as a result. The process may be slow—it still might take hundreds of years—but will be much quicker than the processes of biological evolution.

It may be happening already. According to one analysis by Eagly and Wood (W. Wood & Eagly, 2002), in modern cultures where women have power relatively equal to men, the sex differences in preference for a wealthy spouse are much smaller than in the cultures where the power difference is intact (see also the findings cited earlier by Zentner & Mitura, 2012). This finding suggests—but it does not prove—that as societies begin to provide equal power to women, some of the sex differences discussed earlier in this chapter may begin to erode. A natural experiment may be underway. In the early 21st-century United States, unlike in past decades, more women are completing college than men. As a result, some women are finding it necessary to "settle" for husbands who make less money than they do, or not marry at all (Taylor et al., 2010; see **Figure 9.5**). This difference reverses the traditional sex roles and, from an evolutionary perspective, may counteract biology as well. How flexible will men and women turn out to be in the face of changing social circumstances? Time will tell.

The Contribution of Evolutionary Theory

Researchers will continue to argue about the details of evolutionary theory as applied to human behavior for a long time to come. But one fact is already beyond argument: Since the introduction of evolutionary thinking into psychology, the field will never be the same (Pinker, 1997). Darwin forced humans to acknowledge that *Homo sapiens* is just another animal—a recognition that encounters resistance even now. Evolutionary psychology goes even further, by placing human thought, motivation, and behavior into a broad natural context.

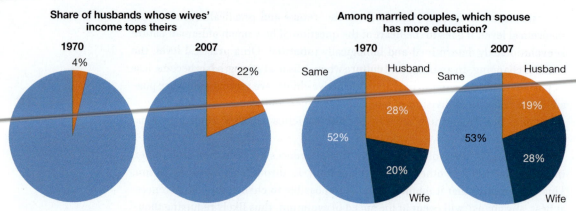

Figure 9.5 **Changes in Educational and Income Differences Between Husbands and Wives** Increasingly often, married women have more education and make more money than their husbands. What does this fact imply for the future of marriage and traditional social roles?

Source: Taylor et al. (2010), p. 1.

Not every aspect of thought or behavior exists because it specifically evolved. But researchers now always have to consider the possibility. Whenever an investigator is trying to explain a brain structure, thought pattern, or behavior, she can no longer avoid asking, Is this explanation plausible from an evolutionary perspective? How might this (brain structure, thought process, or behavior) have promoted survival and reproduction in the past? Does the answer to this question help explain why people today—the descendants of past survivors and reproducers—have it?

INHERITANCE IS THE BEGINNING, NOT THE END

At the end of Chapter 8, I returned to the problem of Hippocrates' music player by noting that once he figured out how it worked, he still would not have begun to answer questions concerning why people like music, how the economics of the music industry works, or why some artists achieve fame and others do not—all of which are important if he wants to fully understand the sounds that come out of that little box.

Let's conclude this discussion of the inheritance of personality by returning to the Rockefellers and the way they routinely transmit large amounts of money from one generation to the next. In the short run, the process is easily explained because each new Rockefeller has wealthy parents. In the longer run, the wealth of the extended clan can be traced to one spectacularly successful ancestor. But let's look at little Baby Rockefeller and ask a few more questions. What will she do with her share of all this inherited wealth? Will she spend it on luxury, give it to charity, use it for a career in politics, or fritter it away on drugs and die broke? Previous Rockefellers have done all of these things. The inheritance is just the beginning; what she does with it depends on the society in which she lives, the way she is raised by her parents, and, yes, on her biological genes. The personality you inherited from your parents and your distant ancestors may work the same way. It determines where you start, but, as we saw in Chapter 8, where you go from there depends on many things, and is ultimately up to you and the world you inhabit and influence.

WILL BIOLOGY REPLACE PSYCHOLOGY?

This chapter and the previous one reviewed the implications for personality of four different areas of biology that apply equally to humans and animals: anatomy, physiology, genetics, and evolution. Each has a lot to say about personality. Indeed, the contributions from each of these fields can be taken to imply that personality is rooted in biology. This implication was anticipated by Gordon Allport's classic definition, which he wrote many years before nearly all of the research just surveyed. Allport wrote that personality is "the dynamic organization within the individual of those *psychophysical systems* that determine his [or her] characteristic behavior or thought" (originally offered in Allport, 1937; also in Allport, 1961, p. 18; my emphasis).

The rapid progress of biological approaches in recent years has led some observers to speculate that, as an independent field of study, psychology is doomed. Because personality is a psychophysical system, once everything is known about brain structure and physiology, there will be nothing left for psychologists to investigate! This point of view is called *biological reductionism*—in the final analysis, it reduces everything about the mind to biology.[18]

Obviously, I have a vested interest in this issue; nevertheless, I will state that I do not think biology is going to replace psychology. It certainly will not do so any time soon. As we have seen, too many huge gaps remain in our knowledge of the nervous system to replace the other approaches to human personality—so far.

But what about—ever? Even in the distant future, I don't think biology will replace psychology, and the reason is fundamental. Biological approaches to psychology, by themselves, tell us much more about biology than about psychology. This biology is extremely interesting, but it does not provide a description of how

---

[18] Just within the past few years, the Departments of Psychology at Dartmouth College, Indiana University, and the University of California at Santa Barbara all changed their names to the "Department of Psychological and Brain Sciences." I wish they hadn't done this. The word "psychology" already includes brain science, and these name changes seem to imply that it doesn't.

people act in their daily social environments, or of the consistencies that can be found in their behaviors (topics that were considered in Part II of this book). A purely biological approach will never describe what psychological conflict feels like, or how such conflict might be revealed through accidental behavior, or what it means to face one's existential anxiety (topics to be considered in Parts IV and V). A purely biological approach does not address how an individual's environment can influence behavior, or explain how an individual interprets that environment or plans a strategy for success (topics to be considered in Part VI). It cannot even say much about what is on your mind at this moment.

For example, the evolutionary process, as it has affected men, gives them a biological tendency to be unfaithful to their mates (according to one theory). But what happens inside the man's head at the moment he is unfaithful? What does he perceive, think, feel, and, above all, want? Evolutionary psychology not only fails to answer this question; it fails to ask it. Similarly, the other biological approaches describe how brain structures, neurochemicals, or genes affect behavior without addressing the psychological processes that connect the brain, neurochemicals, or genes, on the one hand, and behavior on the other.

One theme of this book is that different approaches to personality are not different answers to the same question; rather, they pose different questions. Thus, there is little danger of any one of them completely taking over. The biological approach to personality is becoming more important all the time, and evolutionary theory organizes a huge range of psychological knowledge. But behavioral genetics and evolutionary theory will never supersede the other approaches by showing how behavior is "really" caused by biological mechanisms (de Waal, 2002; Turkheimer, 1998). The greatest promise of the biological approach lies elsewhere, in explaining how biology interacts with social processes to influence what people do.

WRAPPING IT UP

SUMMARY

- Behavioral genetics concerns the degree to which personality is inherited and shared among genetic relatives.

- Evolutionary psychology concerns the ways in which human personality (and other behavioral propensities) may have been inherited from our distant ancestors, and how these propensities have been shaped over the generations by their consequences for survival and reproduction.

Behavioral Genetics

- Behavioral genetics has always been controversial because of its historical association with eugenics (selective breeding), the concept of cloning, and the belief that it implies people's fate is set at birth, but none of these ideas is part of modern thinking on this topic.

- The most commonly used heritability coefficient is calculated as the correlation across pairs of monozygotic twins for that trait, minus the correlation across dizygotic twins, times two: heritability quotient $= (r_{MZ} - r_{DZ}) \times 2$. It is the proportion of population variance that can be attributed to genetic variation, and does not apply to individuals nor to mean levels.

- Heritability statistics computed from the study of monozygotic and dizygotic twins indicate that genetic variance accounts for about 40 percent of the phenotypic variance in many personality traits.

- But genes interact with each other and with the environment rather than simply expressing the sum total of their independent effects.

- Heritability studies confirm that genes are important for personality and can provide insights into the effects of the environment.

- Although many analyses find that aspects of the environment that are shared among children in the same family have only small influences on personality, this appears to depend on how the study is done. More recent studies suggest that the shared family environment affects many important traits, especially when they are measured via behavioral observation rather than self-report.

- While studies of heritability are informative, the heritability statistic is not the "nature-nurture ratio" because traits completely under genetic control often have low or zero heritability.

- Recent research is beginning to map out the complex route by which genes determine biological structures that can affect personality. For example, the *DRD4* gene is associated with dopaminergic systems that may be involved in the trait of extraversion, and the *5-HTT* gene is associated with the neurotransmitter serotonin, which in turn is related to the trait of impulsivity and related patterns of behavior. The amygdala in people with the short-form allele of this gene responds more strongly to unpleasant stimuli; these people are at risk for anxiety disorders or depression.

- While research has begun to document the relationships among genes, brain function, and personality, the situation is even more complex than these relationships: Not only do genes interact with each other, but their effects on development are also critically influenced by the environment.

- Some research has suggested that people with the short allele for the *5-HTT* gene (which affects serotonin) appear to be at risk for depression and antisocial behavior, but only if they experience severe stress or maltreatment in childhood.

- Now that it is established that genes matter for personality and life outcomes, and that almost "everything is heritable," the future of behavioral genetics research lies not in calculating heritability, but in understanding the interactions among genes and between genes and the environment that affect personality traits and life outcomes.

- Not all findings concerning gene-personality correlations or gene-environment interactions are consistently replicated, leading some critics to portray the entire enterprise as misguided. But such a conclusion is surely premature; the field of molecular behavioral genetics is still in its very early stages, and much remains to be learned.

Evolutionary Personality Psychology

- Evolutionary psychology attempts to explain behavioral patterns by analyzing how they may have promoted survival and reproduction in past generations.

- However, some behavioral patterns that were adaptive for our long-ago ancestors may have harmful consequences in the modern environment, including our tendency to use up all resources in sight.

- Evolutionary psychology has considered aggression and altruism in terms of their necessary role for survival and also the potential disadvantages of these behaviors.

- Self-esteem may be a "sociometer," according to Mark Leary's theory, that assesses the degree to which one is accepted by the group. A decline in self-esteem might be an evolved signal that one is in danger of being shunned.

- Depressive symptoms may have evolved as a way to prevent wasting energy on fruitless endeavors and as a means of seeking social support.

- Evolutionary psychology has paid special attention to sex differences in mating behaviors, including differences in what men and women find most attractive in each other and the strategies they use to seek and keep mates. Men seem to be more jealous about sexual than emotional infidelity compared to women, and women show the reverse pattern. However, this is a relative difference: Both kinds of infidelity are unpopular with both sexes.

- Individual differences are important in evolutionary psychology because for a species to remain viable, it must include diversity.

- "Life history" is an individual difference variable related to reproductive strategy. The slow-life history strategy involves having few children later in life and putting resources into nurturing them. The fast-life history strategy involves having many children early in life and putting few if any resources into each. Slow-LH is adapted for environments that are relatively safe and predictable; fast-LH is adapted for dangerous and unpredictable environments. Animal species and humans vary in the degree to which they follow these two strategies.

- Evolutionary processes maintain individual differences in three ways. A trait that is adaptive in one situation may be harmful in another; behavioral patterns have evolved to emerge as functions of environmental experience; and some biologically influenced behaviors are "frequency dependent," meaning that their emergence adjusts according to how common they are in the population at large.

- Controversies over evolutionary psychology provide five "stress tests" for the theory. The key issues are the methodology of evolutionary theorizing; the degree to which people are consciously aware of following evolutionary strategies to promote survival and reproduction; the belief by some that evolutionary explanations imply social change is impossible or must be slow; the question of whether people have evolved specific behavioral "modules" or a broader capacity to respond flexibly to environmental demands; and the question of whether behavioral patterns attributed to evolutionary biology might be better explained by social structure.

- One of the most important contributions of evolutionary theory may be that psychologists are now obligated to consider how the behavioral patterns they uncover may have been adaptive to the species over evolutionary history.

Inheritance Is the Beginning, Not the End

- The biological aspects of personality that you inherited from your parents may determine your psychological starting point, but not your destiny.

Will Biology Replace Psychology?

• Some observers speculate that increases in knowledge will someday allow all psychological processes to be explained in terms of biology, a position called biological reductionism.

• However, biology will never replace psychology because biology does not and cannot, by itself, address many core psychological issues. These issues include the ways people act in their daily social environments, the basis of behavioral consistency, the experience of psychological conflict, the ways people interpret their environments and plan strategies for success, and many others.

KEY TERMS

personality trait, p. 312
alleles, p. 321
epigenetics, p. 328

THINK ABOUT IT

1. What is human nature? To understand human nature, what topics must you address?

2. Do you think your personality was shaped more by how you were raised or by your genes?

3. When scientists learn that a particular brain structure or chemical is associated with a personality trait, how is that knowledge valuable? Does it help us understand the trait better? Does it have practical implications?

4. If you have siblings, was the family environment in which you grew up the same as, or different from, theirs? If different, do these variations account for how you and your siblings turned out?

5. Is there anything useful about acting depressed? Would a person who was unable to experience depression have problems as a result? Can a person learn anything, or benefit in any way, from feeling depressed?

6. Women who are high on agreeableness make more accurate assessments of their "mate value," their attractiveness to the opposite sex. The study that reported this finding did not offer a very clear explanation. Can you come up with one?

7. Do you agree or disagree with evolutionary psychology's conclusions about sex differences? Do you think these differences exist in the way the theory suggests? Could they be explained as well or better by culture?

8. If you are a heterosexual woman, would you be comfortable marrying a man who had less education and made less money than you? (If you are a heterosexual man, would you be comfortable marrying a woman who had more education and made more money than you?) Why? Are these attitudes changing?

9. Do you think psychology will eventually be replaced by biology?

10. Are people just another species of animal? In what ways are people similar to, and different from, "other" animals?

SUGGESTED RESOURCES

Kenrick, D. T. (2011). *Sex, murder, and the meaning of life: A psychologist investigates how evolution, cognition, and complexity are revolutionizing our view of human nature.* New York: Basic Books.

> *A survey of evolutionary psychology and the author's own quirky life story that is both witty and profound. A genuinely fun book.*

Krueger, R. F., & Johnson, W. (2008). Behavioral genetics and personality: A new look at the integration of nature and nurture. In O. P. John, R. W. Robins, & L. A. Pervin (Eds.), *Handbook of personality: Theory and research* (3rd ed.), pp. 287–310. New York: Guilford Press.

> *A relatively brief but thorough review of the current state of knowledge in behavioral genetics, including gene-environment interactions.*

Pinker, S. (1997). *How the mind works.* New York: Norton.

> *A far-ranging, stimulating, and engagingly written survey of cognitive and social psychology from an evolutionary perspective. Pinker provides many creative and startling insights into the way evolutionary history may have shaped the ways in which we think.*

Wilson, E. O. (1975). *Sociobiology: The new synthesis.* Cambridge, MA: Harvard University Press.

> *The book that sparked the revival of interest in using evolutionary theory to explain human behavior.*

Want to earn a better grade on your test?

Go to **INQUIZITIVE** to learn and review this chapter's content, with personalized feedback along the way.

PART IV

THE HIDDEN WORLD OF THE MIND
The Psychoanalytic Approach

Eliot Spitzer was an aggressive and effective crime fighter. As a district attorney, attorney general, and then as governor of New York, he attacked securities fraud, Internet scams, predatory lending, and environmental pollution. A special focus was prostitution, which he called "modern day slavery" (Bernstein, 2008). He agreed with feminist groups that it was unfair to punish only the women while ignoring their customers, and he signed a law that increased the penalty for hiring a prostitute.

On February 13, 2008, Governor Spitzer met "Kirsten,"[1] who worked for an organization called Emperor's Club VIP, in room 871 at the Mayflower Hotel in Washington, DC. She had traveled there with the understanding that he "would be paying for everything—train tickets, cab fare from the hotel and back, minibar or room service, travel time and hotel" (Westfeldt, 2008). Afterward, he paid her $4,300 in cash, which included $1,000 as a deposit toward future services. Sadly for the governor, his attempts to conceal the source of the cash made his bank suspicious, which led to an investigation, and all was revealed in the *New York Times* on March 10, 2008. A week later, he resigned. Governor Spitzer's career was over.[2]

How could something like this happen? How could a dedicated and official opponent of crime and prostitution turn out to be a customer of exactly the same business he so vigorously opposed? His case is not unique. In 2003, William Bennett, conservative pundit, would-be morals teacher, and author of *The Book of Virtues*, was forced to acknowledge a long-standing gambling habit that lost him millions of dollars.[3] In

[1] Presumably, not her real name.
[2] Well, his career as a politician was over. He later got his own cable TV program.
[3] Bennett also wrote *The Children's Book of Virtues*, a guide for morally questing small fry.

2006, a Southern Baptist Church pastor who spoke out against gay marriage and urged homosexuals to reject their "sinful, destructive lifestyle" was arrested for propositioning a plainclothes police officer in an area of Oklahoma City known for "male prostitutes flagging down cars" (Green, 2006). Every few weeks, it seems, the news reveals yet another self-righteous politician or crusading preacher who turns out to be a regular practitioner of the same vices he (it does usually seem to be a he, but there are exceptions) made a career of denouncing. Such strange and paradoxical misbehaviors almost beg for a psychologist to explain them.

It might surprise you, therefore, to learn that most psychologists have surprisingly little to say about cases like these. More than 75 years ago, Henry Murray complained that much of psychology

> is over-concerned with recurrences, with consistency, with what is clearly manifested (the surface of personality), with what is conscious, ordered, and rational. . . . It stops short at the point precisely where a psychology is needed, the point at which it begins to be difficult to understand what is going on. (Murray, 1938, p. 715)

For most of psychology – including pretty much all of the part of personality psychology that this book has covered so far – Murray's complaint remains valid today. However, one approach has sought from the very beginning to explain thoughts and behaviors that are strange and difficult to understand. The approach is psychoanalysis, originally based on the writings of Sigmund Freud.

Psychoanalysis is more than just "Freudian" psychology, however. Freud changed his mind about important matters several times during his career, and many psychologists have continued to translate, interpret, and extend his ideas for nearly a century. Their work addresses the underground part of the mind, the part that is ordinarily hidden and, in some cases, seemingly contradictory, irrational, or absurd.

The next two chapters present a survey of classical, revised, and modern psychoanalysis. Chapter 10 provides a general introduction to Freud and to psychoanalytic thought and its view of the structure and development of the mind. It also says a bit about the workings of the unconscious mind, including how defense mechanisms protect people from feeling more anxiety than they can bear. Chapter 11 brings psychoanalysis into the present day by surveying some prominent neo-Freudian theorists, including Alfred Adler, Carl Jung, and Karen Horney, along with a bit of recent, relevant empirical research and modern psychoanalytic theorizing. Freud is far from dead, we shall find—he lives on in a surprising number of ways.

10

BASICS OF PSYCHOANALYSIS

W**HAT GOES ON IN** the dark, hidden, unconscious recesses of the human mind? The goal of the psychoanalytic approach, initiated by Sigmund Freud and developed by later neo-Freudian theorists, is to answer that question. Psychoanalytic theory is intricate and comes in many versions, but in this chapter I keep things relatively simple. But please note I say *relatively* simple; there is no way to talk seriously about psychoanalysis without delving into some deep and complex matters.

FREUD HIMSELF

In this book, I have tried to avoid the trap of writing about psychologists instead of about psychology. Psychology is much more than "what psychologists do," and there is usually little reason to learn about their personal lives. We must make an exception for Freud. No other psychological approach is at once so influential and so closely identified with a single individual. Freud is one of the most interesting and important people to have lived in the past couple of centuries. So let's take a moment to consider Freud and how he developed his ideas.

Sigmund Freud (1856–1939) was a medical doctor who practiced in Vienna, Austria, from the 1890s until the 1930s. Because he was Jewish, he had to flee his native country after Hitler came to power in the 1930s; he spent the last few years of his life in London. Freud died in a pessimistic frame of mind, convinced that the impending Second World War, following so closely on the heels of the catastrophic First World War, proved that we humans have an aggressive, destructive urge that, in the end, will destroy us all.

Figure 10.1 Sigmund Freud at Work Freud had a home office with a window that overlooked a small garden.

One of Freud's less profound, yet most enduring, cultural legacies is that he is probably the source of the stereotype of what a psychotherapist should look like. He had a beard and small eyeglasses. He favored three-piece suits with a watch chain hanging from the vest. When he spoke English, it was with a Viennese accent. He had a couch in his office—along with some impressive African art that some patients reportedly found distracting.

Freud began his career as a research neurologist. He went to France for a time to study the newly developing field of hypnosis with Jean-Martin Charcot. He gradually moved into the practice of psychiatry, in part so he could make a living and get married. Then, as now, medical practice paid much better than theoretical research. Early in his clinical practice, Freud made a simple but fundamental discovery: When his patients talked about their psychological problems, sometimes that, by itself, was enough to help or even cure them. At first, Freud used hypnosis to get his patients to talk about difficult topics. Later, he turned to the use of *free association*, instructing the patient to say whatever came to mind, for the same purpose. One of Freud's grateful patients dubbed the results of such therapy the "talking cure."

The talking cure was Freud's greatest contribution to psychotherapy. By now, it is ubiquitous. A fundamental assumption of nearly every school of

(a)

(b)

Figure 10.2 **The Outside of Freud's Home at Berggasse 19, Vienna** His office and the apartment where he lived with his family were on the second floor (which Austrians call the first floor). (a) This picture was taken in 1938, shortly after the German army occupied Austria and just before Freud fled to London. If you look closely, you can see that someone has affixed a swastika over the door. (b) This picture was taken by the author during a visit in 2010. Freud's former home is now a museum. The other apartments continue to be occupied by ordinary citizens of Vienna.

psychotherapy—including many whose followers claim they have nothing in common with Freud—is that "talking about it helps."

Freud thought he knew why talking about it helps. One reason is because making thoughts and fears explicit by saying them out loud brings them into the open, where the conscious, rational mind can deal with them. Your crazy thoughts won't make you so crazy once you have thought them through rationally. Another reason is that the psychotherapist can provide emotional support during the patient's difficult task of trying to figure out what is going on. In a letter to Carl Jung, Freud wrote that "psychoanalysis is in essence a cure through love" (cited in Bettelheim, 1982, epigraph), and every psychotherapist keeps a box of tissues handy. Many non-Freudian schools of psychotherapy have adopted these two ideas as well.

Freud attracted numerous disciples whom he encouraged to help spread the ideas of psychoanalysis. Many of them had strong minds of their own, leading to some famous and bitter quarrels. Carl Jung and Alfred Adler were the most prominent of Freud's followers who eventually split from their mentor (see Chapter 11).

Freud's ideas came from the patients he treated and, even more importantly, from his observations of the workings of his own mind. This is something the psychoanalytic approach has in common with the humanistic approach, which is considered later in this book (see Chapter 12). For both psychoanalysts and humanists, the first step in studying psychology is to try to understand your own mind. An essential part of traditional psychoanalytic training is being psychoanalyzed oneself.

Freud's ideas were influenced by the time and place in which he lived and by the patients he saw. Most were well-to-do women, a surprising number of whom reported having been sexually abused by their fathers when they were young. Freud at first believed them and saw this early abuse as a common source of long-lasting trauma. Later he changed his mind, and decided that these memories were fantasies that, for psychological reasons, had come to seem real.[4]

Now that you have met Freud, let us turn to the basics of the theory he developed.

KEY IDEAS OF PSYCHOANALYSIS

An elegant aspect of the psychoanalytic approach is that all of its complexity is built on a small number of key ideas. The four ideas that make up the foundation of psychoanalysis are psychic determinism, internal structure, psychic conflict, and mental energy.

Psychic Determinism

The first and most fundamental assumption of the psychoanalytic approach is **psychic determinism** (Brenner, 1974). Determinism, a basic tenet of science, is the idea that everything that happens has a cause that—in principle, maybe not always in practice—can be identified. The psychic determinism at the root of the psychoanalytic approach is the assumption that everything that happens in a person's mind, and therefore everything that a person thinks and does, also has a specific cause. This idea leaves no room for miracles, free will, or even random accidents. If it did, the entire approach would stall at the starting line. The key faith (and that is really what it is—faith) of a psychoanalyst is that psychology can explain even a prostitute-patronizing anticrime governor, a moralizing compulsive gambler, or a male antihomosexuality crusader who propositions men hanging around outside hotels. All that is needed is diligence, insight, and, of course, the proper psychoanalytic framework.

The nondeterministic alternative would be to say something like, "He just decided to get a prostitute [or go gambling] of his own free will, despite what he said," or, "He's just inconsistent." Those statements might be true, but they

---

[4] Critic Jeffrey Masson (1984) argued that this latter conclusion was a fundamental mistake, because it led psychoanalysts to look inside the mind instead of outside at the world for the origin of psychological problems.

really do not explain anything, and you would never hear either one from a psychoanalyst. Only slightly better would be observations such as, "This governor is a typical politician doing what is popular in order to get elected, but whatever he wants on the side," or, "The author of *The Book of Virtues* is simply a hypocrite." These explanations also might be true, but they still fail to explain how a governor of a major state could be unable to resist behaving in a way that not only contradicted his publicly espoused values, but endangered (and ultimately ended) his political career, and how moral crusading can come out of the same brain as a multimillion-dollar vice. There must be a reason, and psychoanalysts would argue that the reason lies somewhere in the structure and dynamics of personality. The trick is to find it.

Figure 10.3 Freud's Famous Consulting Couch
Freud usually sat in the chair behind the patient because, reportedly, he didn't like being stared at.

From a psychoanalytic perspective, all seeming contradictions of mind and behavior can be resolved, and nothing is ever accidental. There is a reason for why you preached one way and acted another; there is also a reason you forgot that name, dropped that dish, or said a word you did not intend to say. The purpose of psychoanalysis is to dig deep to find those reasons, which usually lie in the hidden part of the mind. The assumption of psychic determinism, therefore, leads directly to the conclusion that many important mental processes are unconscious.[5] Modern research tends to support this conclusion; it appears that only some of what the mind does—perhaps only a small part—is accessible to conscious awareness (Bornstein, 1999b; Kihlstrom, 1990; Shaver & Mikulincer, 2005).

Internal Structure

A second key assumption of psychoanalysis is that the mind has an internal structure made of parts that can function independently of and, in some cases, in conflict with each other. We saw in Chapter 8 that this assumption is consistent with what is now known about brain function, but it is important to remember the distinction between the mind and the brain: The brain is a physical organ, whereas the mind is the psychological result of what the brain and the rest of the body do.

---

[5] Freud believed that the idea of psychic determinism implied unconscious mental processes so directly that to assume one was to assume the other. This is why, following Freud, I do not treat unconscious mental processes as a fifth and separate foundation of psychoanalysis.

Psychoanalytic theory sees the mind as divided into three parts, which will probably sound familiar to you. They are usually given the Latinized labels **id**, **ego**, and **superego.** These terms pertain to the irrational and emotional part of the mind, the rational part of the mind, and the moral part of the mind, respectively.[6]

The independence of these three mental structures can raise interesting problems. The id of the governor of New York compelled him to seek out prostitutes even while his superego condemned the activity. *The Book of Virtues* excoriates a long list of vices that strangely omits gambling. The Oklahoma church official sought out male prostitutes at the same time he publicly denounced homosexuality. In all of these cases, the ego—the rational part of the mind—doesn't seem to have been very effective at its job, which is to manage the crossfire between competing psychological forces.

Modern research in biological and cognitive psychology has not found that the mind is actually divided neatly into three parts. However, both kinds of research do support the idea that the mind includes separate and independent structures that process different thoughts and motivations simultaneously (Gazzaniga, Ivry, & Mangun, 1998; Rumelhart, McClelland, & The PDP Research Group, 1986; Shaver & Mikulincer, 2005). So while the three parts of the mind might not exist exactly as Freud envisioned them, it is plausible to consider the mind as containing many voices, not just one, and that they might not all be saying the same thing. They might even be arguing with each other.

Psychic Conflict and Compromise

Because the mind is divided into distinct and independent parts, it can conflict with itself, as we saw in the cases of the governor, the moralist, and the church official. But psychic conflict is not always so dramatic. Let's assume, for example, that at this moment your id wants ice cream, but your superego thinks you don't deserve it because you haven't studied all week. It might fall to your ego to formulate a compromise: You get to have ice cream *after* you have finished reading this chapter.

The idea of **compromise formation** is a key tenet of modern psychoanalytic thought. The ego's main job, psychoanalysts now believe, is to find a middle course between the competing demands of motivation, morality, and practicality, and also among the many things a person wants at the same time. (Ego psychology will be considered again in Chapter 11.) The result of the compromise is what the individual consciously thinks and actually does (Westen, 1998). If the governor's and the church official's egos had been more effective, they might have been able to find

---

[6] Psychoanalyst Bruno Bettelheim (1982) argued persuasively that these widely used terms mistranslate Freud's original German writing, but it is probably too late to correct that mistake here. Bettelheim's preferred translations for id, ego, and superego are the It, the I, and the Over-I.

some kind of middle ground between their sexual motivations and their morality. The ego of *The Book of Virtues* author failed him by leaving him in the awkward position of campaigning sternly against all modern vices except one. Without reasonable internal compromises, these individuals were left to flail between strong and contradictory impulses—first one way, and then the other—with disastrous results.

Mental Energy

The final key assumption of the psychoanalytic approach is that the apparatus of the mind needs energy to make it go. The kind of energy required is sometimes called mental, or *psychic energy*, also known as **libido,** and only a fixed and finite amount is available at any given moment. Therefore, energy spent doing one thing, such as pushing uncomfortable thoughts out of memory, is unavailable for other purposes, such as having new and creative ideas. The principle of the conservation of energy applies to the mind as it does to the physical world.

This principle seems reasonable, and Freud based it on the Newtonian physics of his day, but some of its implications have not stood the test of time very well. For example, the original formulation assumed that if a psychological impulse was not expressed, it would build up over time, like steam expanding in a boiler. If someone made you angry, then unless you expressed your anger, the associated psychic energy would build up until something snapped. This is an interesting idea that seems in accord with some real-life experience, such as the meek and mild person who allows himself to be pushed around until he bursts forth in murder. However, research suggests that it is usually wrong. Expressing anger typically makes a person more angry, not less, a direct contradiction of the original Freudian idea (Bushman, 2002).

> Expressing anger typically makes a person more angry, not less, a direct contradiction of the original Freudian idea.

There is another reason not to take the energy metaphor too literally. My first teaching job was at a college of engineering and science.[7] One day, my class of future engineers was dozing politely through my lecture on Freud when I mentioned psychic energy. They immediately perked up, and one student, grabbing his notebook, asked eagerly, "Psychic energy—in what units is that measured?" Unfortunately, I replied, psychic energy is not something that Freud ever measured in units of any kind. It was just a metaphor that applied in some respects but not in others—and none too precisely in any case. At that, the students sighed, slouched back into their chairs, and no doubt privately redoubled their determination to become engineers rather than psychologists.

---

[7] I recommend such a bracing experience to all of my psychologist colleagues.

Modern psychoanalytic theory has moved away from Freud's original conception. In current thinking, the assumption is that it is the mind's capacity for processing information, rather than its energy, that is limited (Westen, 1998). This reformulation discards the idea that unexpressed impulses build up over time, but retains the implication that capacity used up by one purpose is not available for anything else. One goal of psychoanalysis is to free up more psychic energy—or computing capacity—for the challenges of daily living, by removing neurotic conflicts one by one.

CONTROVERSY

From the beginning until the present day, the psychoanalytic approach has stirred more controversy than any other approach to psychology. Some people have even viewed it as dangerous. Objections to psychoanalysis change with the times. The Victorians looked at Freud's emphasis on sex and sexual energy, and complained that his theory was "dirty." We supposedly more enlightened folk of the 21st century look at Freud's emphasis on what cannot be seen and cannot be conclusively proved, and complain that his theory is "unscientific." The bases of the criticisms change, but in every age, it seems, a lot of people just don't like psychoanalysis. And many don't like Sigmund Freud either. It is interesting to see how often criticisms of psychoanalysis are mixed with complaints about his ethics, manners, and even personal life (Crews, 1996, 2017; Westen, 1998, pp. 344–45; more will be said about attacks on Freud in Chapter 11).

Freud anticipated these kinds of attacks and sometimes even seemed to revel in them. His response was not exactly self-effacing. He pointed out that Copernicus became unpopular for teaching that the earth is not the center of the universe, and that Darwin was derided for his claim that humans are just another species of animal. Freud's own insights that human nature is largely hidden, and that the motivations that drive many human behaviors are base and irrational, were not ideas he expected would win him many popularity contests. He was right: Psychoanalysis bothers people.

Let's bring this down to a personal level by considering two cautionary tales. They both exemplify the discomfort that psychoanalytic insights can cause, and the dangers of offering such insights unsolicited.

The first takes us way back to the time when I decided to major in psychology. I broke the news to my family in the traditional fashion. Returning home from college for Thanksgiving break, I waited for the inevitable question: "Have you decided on a major yet?" "Psychology," I replied. As many others making this choice have discovered, my family was not exactly thrilled. After a stunned silence, my sister spoke first. "OK," she said, "but so help me, if you ever psych me out, I will never speak to you again!"

Her comment is highly pertinent. Learning about personality psychology, especially the psychoanalytic approach, can produce irresistible urges to analyze the behavior and thoughts of those around us. It's all part of the fun. The advice you should take from my sister's warning, however, is to keep the fun private. People are typically not grateful to be analyzed. Sharing your insights into why your friends "really" did something can start serious trouble. This is true even if your insights are accurate; Freud thought this was true *especially* when your insights are accurate.

> Sharing your insights as to why your friends "really" did something can start serious trouble, especially when your insights are accurate.

My second tale is an example concerning psychoanalysis. When I get to the part of my course when I teach about Freud, I try to do so as an advocate. I make the best, most convincing case for psychoanalytic theory that I can. Who knows what effect this sales job has on my students, but one person I never fail to convince is myself. Thus, for a few weeks each academic year, I turn into a raving Freudian. I become temporarily unable to avoid analyzing every slip, mistake, and accident I see.

I did this once, years ago, on a date. In the course of a casual conversation, my dinner companion related something she had forgotten to do that day. Being deep in the Freudian phase of my syllabus, I immediately offered a complex (and rather clever, I thought) interpretation of the unconscious anxieties and conflicts that probably caused her memory lapse. My insight was not well received. My date vehemently replied that my interpretation was ridiculous, and that in the future I could keep my absurd Freudianisms to myself. Gesturing for emphasis, she knocked a glass of ice water into my lap. Picking up the ice cubes, but still in a Freudian frame of mind, all I could do was acknowledge the vivid, symbolic nature of the warning I had received.[8]

The moral of these two stories is the same: Keep your clever analyses of other people to yourself! If you are wrong, it will make them mad. If you are right, it will make them even madder. As they say at stunt demonstrations: "We are trained professionals. Do not try this at home."

PSYCHOANALYSIS, LIFE, AND DEATH

Behind the many, sometimes contradictory, things that people want, Freud believed two motives are fundamental. The first motive impels toward life, the other toward death. Both motives are always present and competing. In the end, death always wins.

---

[8] We later married anyway.

The life drive is sometimes called *libido*, also referred to as the *sexual drive*, which is what libido means in ordinary conversation.[9] In psychoanalytic writings by Freud and by those who came later, libido receives a great deal of attention. But I think it is also widely misunderstood, perhaps in part because so many people are easily distracted by any reference to sex. In the final analysis, sex is simply life. Sex is necessary for the creation of children, biological interventions aside, and its enjoyment can be an important part of being alive. In this sense, libido is the sexual drive; Freud meant that it had to do with the creation, protection, and enjoyment of life and with creativity, productivity, and growth. This fundamental force exists within every person, Freud believed.[10]

Relatively late in his career, Freud posited a second fundamental motive, a drive toward death. He called it **Thanatos** (Greek for "death"). Although he probably did not mean to claim the existence of a "death wish," he held a fundamental belief in the duality of nature, or the idea that everything contains its own opposite. Freud observed that not only do people engage in a good deal of destructive activity that does not seem rational—wars are a good example—but also, in the end, everybody dies. He introduced the death drive to account for these facts.

This drive, too, is sometimes misunderstood. Freud probably was not as morbid as his idea of a drive toward death makes him sound. I suspect he had in mind something like the concept of *entropy*, the basic force in the universe toward randomness and disorder. Ordered systems tend toward disorder over time, and this trend is inevitable; local, short-term increases in order only result in widespread, long-term increases in disorder.[11] Freud viewed the human mind and life itself in similar terms. We try desperately throughout our lives to make our thoughts and our worlds orderly, and to maintain creativity and growth. Although entropy dooms these efforts to failure in the end, we may have a pretty good ride in the meantime. So Freud's ultimate view of life was far from morbid; it might better be described as tragic.

The opposition of libido and Thanatos derives from another basic idea that arises repeatedly in psychoanalytic thinking: the **doctrine of opposites**. This doctrine states that everything implies, even requires, its opposite: Life requires death, happiness requires sadness, and so forth. One cannot exist without the other.

---

[9] Freudian theory uses the term *libido* in several different, overlapping ways. Libido is the sexual drive. For Freud, this is the same as the life drive, though other psychoanalytic theorists, as we shall see, view the sexual drive as being part, but not all, of the life drive. Either way, the energy generated by this drive is the source of the psychic energy (Freud's term for mental energy) that drives the whole psychological apparatus.

[10] Here, as elsewhere, I am reinterpreting Freud in light of later developments in psychoanalytic thought and modern evidence. I think this rendition is true to the spirit of what Freud thought about libido. However, I also have to admit that Freud frequently talked about libido in a literally sexual sense, and that later psychoanalytic thinkers such as Jung thought Freud overemphasized sexuality at the expense of a broader interpretation of libido as the life drive.

[11] This is why, according to physics, the universe is doomed. In a couple of billion years or so.

An implication of this doctrine is that extremes on any scale may be more similar to each other than either extreme is to the middle. For example, consider pornographers and the leaders of pornography censorship campaigns. The doctrine of opposites would claim that they have more in common with each other than either does with people in the middle, for whom pornography is not much of an issue. There may be something to this idea. Pornographers and censorship crusaders share not only extremism, but also a certain fascination with pornographic material—they agree that it is very important—and they also spend a lot of time looking at it. Those in the middle, by contrast, may have a distaste for pornography, but are not so excited by its existence to make its prohibition a burning issue, or to immerse themselves in it all day long. Or consider an antiprostitution crusader and a regular patron of prostitutes. They could not be more different, right? Remember the sad case of Eliot Spitzer? Or consider what happens when one person stops loving another. Does her new attitude more often move to the middle of the continuum—to "mild liking"—or to the other extreme?

The juxtaposition of the life drive with the death drive is also consistent with the doctrine of opposites. But the death drive came to Freud as a sort of afterthought; he never fully worked it into the fabric of his theory, and most modern analysts do not really believe in it.[12] When I talk about psychic energy in the remainder of this book, therefore, the reference is to life energy, or libido.

PSYCHOSEXUAL DEVELOPMENT: "FOLLOW THE MONEY"

In the film *All the President's Men* (Pakula, 1976), reporter Bob Woodward asks his secret source, Deep Throat, how to get to the bottom of the Watergate scandal embroiling the Nixon White House.[13] Deep Throat replies, "Follow the money." He means that Woodward should find out who controlled a large sum of secret cash at the Committee to Re-Elect the President, a fundraising organization for Nixon, and track how it was spent. This tip allows him and fellow reporter Carl Bernstein to crack the case.

When trying to understand the workings and the development of the human mind, Freud gives us similar advice. His version is, "Follow the energy." Like money, psychic energy is both absolutely necessary

> Like money, psychic energy is both absolutely necessary and absolutely limited, so the story of where it goes tends to be the story of what is really happening.

---

[12] Personally, I find the idea useful. There are some things people do that are pretty hard to explain without it.

[13] Decades later, in 2005, Deep Throat was revealed to have been FBI official Mark Felt.

and absolutely limited, so the story of where it goes tends to be the story of what is really happening.

This principle comes into play in Freud's account of how the mind of an infant gradually develops into the mind of an adult. As we saw in Chapter 7, modern approaches typically view development as a result of the encounter of the physically maturing child and aging adult with the ever-changing tasks of childhood, adulthood, and old age. Freud's approach preceded these, and follows the same basic structure, with one major difference: In Freud's view, *psychosexual development* (as he called it) is the story of how life energy, libido, becomes invested and then redirected over an individual's early years.

A new baby fairly bubbles with life energy, but the energy lacks focus or direction. As the baby develops into a child and then an adult, the energy begins to focus, first on one outlet and then another. The focal points for psychic energy define the stages of psychosexual development. You have probably heard of them: oral, anal, phallic, and genital. Each stage has three aspects: (1) a *physical focus*, where energy is concentrated and gratification is obtained; (2) a *psychological theme*, related both to the physical focus and to the demands on the child from the outside world during development; and (3) an *adult character type* associated with being fixated (to some degree stalled) in that particular stage, rather than fully developing toward the next one. If an individual fails to resolve the issues that arise at a particular stage, the experience will leave psychological scar tissue, and the issues will remain troublesome throughout life.

Table 10.1 | FREUD'S STAGES OF PSYCHOSEXUAL DEVELOPMENT

Stage	Age (approximate)	Physical Focus	Relevant Mental Structure	Psychological Theme	Adult Character Types
Oral	Birth to 18 mos.	Mouth, lips, and tongue	Id	Dependence, passivity	Dependent or overly independent
Anal	18 mos. to 3 1/2 years	Anus and organs of elimination	Ego	Obedience and self-control	Obedient and obsessed with order, or anti-authority and chaotic
Phallic	3 1/2 years to 7 years	Sexual organs	Superego	Gender identity and sexuality	Over- or under-sexualized
(Latency)	7 years to puberty	n/a	n/a	Learning and cognitive development	n/a
Genital	Puberty through adulthood	Sexuality in the context of a mature relationship	Id, ego, and superego are well balanced	Creation and enhancement of life	A mature adult (seldom achieved)

Oral Stage

A newborn baby is essentially helpless. It flails its arms and legs around. It cannot see clearly nor reach out and grab something it wants. It cannot crawl or even turn over. The lack of motor control and physical coordination is almost total.

Almost. There is one thing a newborn baby can do as well as any grown person: suck. This is no small matter. The action is complex; the baby must develop suction with the mouth muscles and bring food into the stomach without cutting off the air supply. In a full-term baby, the necessary neuronal networks and muscles are in working order at birth. (One of the many problems premature babies can have is that this complex mechanism may not yet function well.)

So now ask yourself, how does a new baby have any fun? It can't involve the arms or legs, which don't really work yet. The primary source of pleasure for a new-born, and the one place on his body where the newborn can meaningfully interact with the environment, is right there in the mouth. It stands to reason, therefore, that the mouth will be the first place psychic energy is focused. The **oral stage** of psychosexual development lasts from birth to about 18 months.

Let's consider the three aspects, described earlier, for this stage of develop-ment. The physical focus of the oral stage, as just discussed, is on the mouth, lips, and tongue. Freud sometimes said that for an infant these body parts are sexual organs—another remark that seems almost deliberately designed to be misunder-stood. Freud meant that during this stage the mouth is where the life force and primary feelings of pleasure are concentrated. Eating is an important source of pleasure, but so are sucking on things and exploring the world with one's mouth.

When a baby begins to get control over her hands and arms, and sees some small, interesting object, what is the first thing she does? The baby puts the object in her mouth—often to the distress of the parents. Many parents assume the baby is trying to eat the ball, or the pencil, or the dead cockroach. But that is not the baby's real intention. The baby's hands are simply not developed enough to be of much use for exploration. When you pick up something interesting, you fondle it, turn it around, and feel its texture and its heft. None of this works for a baby because too many fine motor skills are required; putting the object in the mouth can be more informative and interesting, because the mouth is more developed than the hands.

The psychological theme of the oral stage is *dependency*. A baby is utterly, even pathetically, dependent on others for everything he needs to live. The baby is pas-sive in the sense that there is very little he can do for himself, though he may be far from passive in demanding what others should do. The baby's main psychological experience at this stage, therefore, is lying back and having others either provide everything he needs, or not. Either way, there is not much the baby can do about it, besides make plenty of noise. Which babies do know how to do. Another way to make the same point is to observe that, at the oral stage, the baby is all id. That is, the baby wants—full time—to be fed, to be held, to have a dry diaper, to be warm and comfortable, and to be entertained. Wanting stuff is the id's specialty. Actually doing something about those desires is the job of psychological structures that will develop only later, along with the necessary physical competencies.

If a baby's needs at this stage of life are fulfilled to a reasonable degree, then the focus of psychic energy will move along in due course to the next stage. Two things might go wrong, however. One is that the needs might not be fulfilled. The caretakers might be so uncaring, incompetent, or irresponsible that the baby is not fed when hungry, covered when cold, or comforted when upset. If this happens, the baby may develop a basic mistrust of other people and never be able to deal adequately with dependency relationships. The idea of depending on other people—or of being betrayed or abandoned by them—will forever make him upset, although he might not realize why.

A second thing that could happen is that a baby's needs are fulfilled so instantly and automatically that it never occurs to her that the world could respond differently. The increasing demands—and slow service—the world later provides, therefore, come as quite a shock. Such a person may wish to be back at the oral stage, where all that was necessary was to want something and have it immediately appear. Again, any issue that comes up in the baby's later life involving dependency, passivity, and activity might cause anxiety, though again she may be unaware as to just why.

Here we see the doctrine of opposites again. It will resurface many, many times: Any extreme childhood experience or its opposite will, according to Freud, yield equivalently pathological results. The ideal, Freud believed, lies in the middle. He was on to something. One recent study reported that children who grew up to be narcissists (see Chapter 6) tended to have been raised by parents who either were excessively cold *or* showered them with too much admiration (Otway & Vignoles, 2006). In the case of the oral stage, Freud would recommend that a parent make reasonable efforts to fulfill a child's wants and needs but not go overboard by making sure every wish is instantly gratified, nor neglect the child so much that the child starts to doubt whether basic needs will be met.

I find it surprising and a little unfair that Freud gets so little credit for having been such a consistent and profound moderate. He disliked extremes of any kind—in behavior, in child-rearing styles, in personality types, in attitudes—in part because he saw both ends of most scales as equivalently pathological. Freud's ideal was always the golden mean; his adherence to this ideal is one of the most consistent and attractive aspects of his approach.[14]

The adult personality type that Freud thought resulted from extreme childhood experience at this stage is the *oral character*. Both types of oral character

---

[14] We can see a modern version of this idea in the conclusion of most clinical psychologists that personality disorders are extreme positions on the normal range of personality trait variation (L. A. Clark, Livesley, & Morey, 1997; see Chapter 17).

share an obsession, discomfort, and fundamental irrationality about any issue related to dependency and passivity. At one extreme are the supposedly independent souls who refuse help from everyone, who are determined to go it alone no matter what the cost. To these people, no accomplishment means anything unless it is achieved without assistance. At the other extreme are the passive individuals who wait around, seemingly forever, for their ships to come in. They do little to better their situations, yet are continually bewildered— and sometimes angry—about their failure to get what they want. To them, wanting some

"I'm proud of you for making a gurgle."

thing should be enough to make it appear. That is how it works for babies, after all; they feel hunger or some other need, they cry, and somebody takes care of them. It is almost as if, as adults, oral characters expect things to work the same way.

I have a relative who, while in his thirties, was once described as the world's oldest 16-year-old, which is actually an insult to many 16-year-olds. He is an intelligent, likeable person, but for a long time seemed utterly unable to connect what he wanted with what he had to do to get it. At one point, he announced at a family gathering that he had finally formulated a career goal. With some anticipation, we waited to hear what it was. He explained that he had thought about it carefully, worked out all of the figures, and decided that he wanted a job that paid $100,000 a year—after taxes. That would be enough to give him everything he wanted. "And what would the job be?" we asked. He seemed surprised by the question; he had not gotten around to that part.

Some students show a related attitude. At the end of the semester, they plead for a higher grade on the grounds that they need it. Often, they make an eloquent case for why they *really* need it. That should be enough, they seem to feel. The idea that attending class and doing the assignments was the way to earn a higher grade, rather than simply demanding it after the course is over, seems not to have occurred to them. Honestly, maybe it never did.

The reverse kind of oral character, the person who is chronically and pathologically independent, seems to be more rare. Yet, I have seen the same relative whom I just described disdain even the most minor help in preparing a cookout or fixing a car. Perhaps you know people who insist, "I can do it myself," in the midst of utter failure.

Again, the ideal is the middle. A person who has resolved the oral stage accepts help gracefully but is not utterly dependent on it, and understands that people are ultimately responsible for their own outcomes.

Anal Stage

The glory of life at the oral stage is that you do not have to do anything. Because you cannot take care of yourself, you are not expected to. You do and express whatever you feel like, whatever you can, whenever you want. Well and truly, this is too good to last.

Many breast-feeding mothers have had the experience of their baby, sucking away, suddenly trying out his new teeth with a good, strong bite. You can imagine how mom reacts: She yells, "Yow!" or something stronger, and instantly pulls the baby off. And you know how the baby reacts: with outrage, anger, frustration, and maybe even fear, if mom yelled loudly enough. Her reaction comes as a rude shock: What do you mean—I can't bite when I feel like it? Moreover, the baby quickly discovers that until he can muster enough self-control to stop biting, the good stuff will fail to be forthcoming. This experience marks a dark day. Life pretty much goes downhill from then on.

The demands of the world escalate rapidly. The child is expected to do some things for herself—to start to control her emotions, for example. As the child begins to understand language, she is expected to follow orders. She learns the word *no*—a new and alarming concept. And—something that famously got Freud's attention—the child must learn to control her bowels and processes of elimination. Toilet training begins.

From all of this, the child begins to develop a new psychological structure: the ego. The ego's job is to mediate between what the child wants and what is actually possible. It is the rudimentary ego that must figure out that breast feeding will continue only as long as biting ceases. It is through painful lessons like this that the ego typically begins to develop a wide range of capabilities to rationally control the rest of the mind.

The physical focus of the **anal stage** is on the anus and associated organs of elimination. Learning the sensations of "having to go" and dealing with them appropriately are important tasks. Freud and others pointed out that a good deal of everyday language seems to reveal an emotional resonance with the processes and products of elimination. This includes not only many standard insults and expletives with which I suspect you are familiar, but also descriptions of some people, anal characters as it turns out, as "uptight," and the common advice to "let it all out," which suggests relaxing one's self-control and acting "naturally."

But I am going to bend Freud a bit here, to be more consistent with the story of development that was discussed in Chapter 7, and also in the direction of Eriksonian theory, which will be summarized in Chapter 11. I think the classic theory places a misleading degree of emphasis on literal defecation and its supposed physical pleasures. Toilet training is an important period of life and seems to be the source of some powerful symbolic language. But it is just one example among many increasing demands for obedience and self-control that begin around the age of 18 months. As the child develops the capacity for bowel control, the parents, tired of diapers, are eager to have the child use this new skill.[15] But this escalation of expectation applies to many other circumstances as well, from "Get your own drink of water" to "Don't touch that!" The primary psychological theme of the anal stage is *self-control* and its corollary, *obedience*.

There is a lot to learn at the anal stage, and things do not always go smoothly. Typically, a child will try to figure out just how much power the authority figures around him really have to make him do their bidding, as opposed to how much he gets to decide. The child does this by testing the parents, experimenting to find the boundaries of what he can get away with. What happens if the child pulls the cat's tail after being told not to? If the parents say, "No more cookies," what happens if the child sneaks one anyway? In the folklore of parenthood, this testing stage is known as the "terrible twos."

Two things might go wrong at this point. As always in psychoanalytic thinking, the two possible mistakes are polar opposites, and the ideal is in the middle. Unreasonable expectations can be traumatic. If parents insistently make demands that the child is not capable of meeting—for example, that the child always obey, never cry, or hold her bowels longer than physical capability allows—the result can be psychological trauma with long-lasting consequences. And the opposite—never demanding that the child control her urges, neglecting toilet training altogether—can be equally problematic.

As at every stage, the child's developmental task is to figure out what is going on in the world and how to deal with it. At the anal stage, the child must figure out how, and how much, to control himself and how, and how much, to be controlled by those in authority. This is a thorny issue, even for an adult. A child will never work it through sufficiently if the environment is too harsh or too lenient.

Research that followed a sample of children from childhood into late adolescence basically confirmed this Freudian view. Their parents were classified as authoritarian (extremely rigid and obedience oriented), permissive (weak and lacking control), or authoritative (compromising between firm control and their children's freedom). As Freud would have anticipated, it was the authoritative parents—the ones in the middle—whose children fared the best later in life (Baumrind, 1971, 1991).[16]

Psychological mishaps at the anal stage produce the adult *anal character*, whose personality becomes organized around control issues. One way is to become obsessive, compulsive, stingy, orderly, rigid, and subservient to authority. This kind of person tries to control every aspect of her life and often seems equally happy to submit to an authority figure. She cannot tolerate disorganization or ambiguity.

---

[15] Besides the mess, diapers are shockingly expensive.

[16] This finding may be limited to the Western culture with which Freud was most familiar. Authoritative versus authoritarian parenting may have different implications and consequences in an Asian cultural context (Chao, 2001).

Long ago, one of my professors of abnormal psychology said he had a one-item test for detecting an anal character: Go to that person's room, and you will see on the desk a row of pencils or other items in a perfectly straight line. Reach over casually, turn one of the pencils at a 90° angle, and start timing. If within two minutes the person has moved the pencil back, she is an anal character. This test is too facile, of course, but you get the idea.

The other type of anal character is exactly the opposite. This person may have little or no self-control, be unable to do anything on time or because it is necessary, be chaotic and disorganized, and have a compulsive need to defy authority. Freud saw both types of anal characters as psychologically equivalent and further believed that such individuals would more likely flip from one anal extreme to the other than attain the ideal position in the middle.

There is a lame joke dating from the 1970s that expresses this equivalence:

Q: Why did the short-hair cross the road?
A: Because somebody told him to.
Q: Why did the long-hair cross the road?
A: Because somebody told him not to.[17]

Freud's point is similar. If you are rigidly, obsessively organized and obedient, you have a problem. If you are completely disorganized and disobedient because you cannot help it, you also have a problem—in fact, you have the same problem. Self-control and relations with authority should be means to an end, not ends in themselves. The ideal is to determine how and to what degree to organize your life and how you relate to authority, in order to achieve your goals.

Phallic Stage

The next stage of development begins with a realization: Boys and girls are different. According to psychoanalytic theory, this fact begins to sink in at around the age of 3 1/2 to 4 years, and dominates psychosexual development until about age 7.

The specific realization that occurs at the **phallic stage** for both sexes, according to Freud, is that boys have a penis and girls do not—hence the name of the stage.[18] The basic task of the phallic stage is coming to terms with sex differences and all that they imply. According to Freud, boys, having noticed that girls do not

---

[17] This joke relies on a stereotypical image from the late 1960s: Men with short hair were viewed as conservative and subservient to authority, whereas men with long hair were assumed to be radical and disobedient. Today, hairstyles have fewer political implications, thank goodness.

[18] Maybe this is not as specific or universal as Freud thought. I once asked one of my daughters, then not quite 4 years old, what the difference was between boys and girls. "Boys do not have crotches," she instantly replied.

have penises, wonder what happened and if the same thing could happen to them. Girls just wonder what happened.

Hard-core adherents of orthodox psychoanalysis launch into a pretty complicated story at this point. The story is based on the Greek myth of Oedipus, the man who unknowingly killed his father and married his mother. According to the psychoanalytic version of the *Oedipal crisis*, young boys fall physically as well as emotionally in love with their mothers, and because of this they understandably fear their fathers' jealousy. The specific fear is that their fathers might castrate them in retaliation. For girls, this crisis is less intense, but they still suffer grief over the castration they believe has *already* occurred. To resolve this anxiety or grief, each child identifies with the same-sex parent, taking on many of his or her values and ideals, which lessens the child's feelings of rivalry and jealousy that might otherwise reach a critical level.

"Why do you think you cross the road?"

The full story of the Oedipal crisis is rich and fascinating, and the summary just presented (which you may have noticed was exactly four sentences long) fails to do it justice. Nevertheless, I will not say much more about it here, in part because the story is so well told elsewhere. The best rendition in English may be the one provided by Bettelheim (1982). A more important reason for not getting too deeply into the traditional story of the phallic stage is that it has not held up well in light of empirical research (R. R. Sears, 1947). So, I will discuss this point in development in simpler and more modern terms.[19]

It seems obvious that the realization that the sexes differ must be an important milestone in psychosexual development. It also seems natural that with this realization comes the awareness that one parent is male and the other female. I do not think it is far-fetched to think that children wonder about the attraction between their parents, and that they fantasize to some degree about what a relationship with their opposite-sex parent would be like. And, although this may push the envelope a bit, I even think it's plausible that children feel guilty, at some level, about having such fantasies. The fantasies probably seem rather outlandish even to a child, and the child probably suspects, probably correctly, that the same-sex parent would not exactly be thrilled if he or she knew what the child was thinking.

---

[19] Here is yet another place where I am straying from what Freud literally said, and substituting a contemporary rendition that strikes me as both more sensible in light of modern knowledge, and also consistent with the spirit of what Freud meant.

The psychological theme of the phallic stage is *gender identity and sexuality*—the need to figure out what it means to be a boy or girl. For most children, the best, or most obvious, examples are their mothers and fathers. One way to be a girl is to act like mom, and to be a boy, act like dad. This can mean taking on many of the parent's attitudes, values, and ways of relating to the opposite sex. Freud called this process **identification**.[20]

Related psychological themes of the phallic stage include love, fear, and jealousy. The adult consequences of the phallic stage include the development of morality, which Freud saw as a by-product of the process of identification; the values of your same-sex parent provide the beginnings of your own moral outlook. Another adult consequence is the development of sexuality—what kind of person you find attractive, how you handle sexual competition, and the overall role of sexuality in your life. The most important result of the phallic stage is an image of oneself as masculine or feminine, whatever that may entail.

Additional identifications are possible and even likely. A child might take on the values and behaviors of an admired teacher, relative, religious leader, or rock star. In most cases, people identify with those whom they love and admire, but in some circumstances, individuals identify with people they loathe and fear. During World War II, inmates in Nazi death camps reportedly sometimes identified with their guards, making Nazi armbands and uniforms from scraps and giving each other the "Heil Hitler" salute. According to psychoanalyst Bruno Bettelheim, who was an inmate at Dachau and Buchenwald himself, this seemingly strange behavior was an adaptation to deal with their profound and realistic fear of the guards; to become more like the guards was to fear them less (Bettelheim, 1943). I suspect milder forms of this behavior—trying to become more like the people one most fears—are rather common and one basis for the development of the superego. People sometimes identify with a teacher they hate, a coach who intimidates them, an older student who hazes them, or a drill sergeant or an entire branch of the military who gives them little but abuse. In the process, these characters become less fearful while the person becomes a little more like them.

Wherever they come from—and again, the usual source is the parents—the sum of one's identifications makes up the third major psychic structure after the id and ego: the superego. The superego is the part of the mind that passes moral judgment on the other parts, judgments based on a complex mixture of all the different moral lessons learned directly and by example, from everybody one has ever identified with. When successfully developed, the superego provides a conscience

---

[20] The personal lives of many students intersect with the content of a personality course at this point. I have been asked many times, "What happens at this stage if a child is raised by a single parent?" Such questions are not merely hypothetical. I wish I had a good answer. The best I can manage is that these children look elsewhere for salient models of masculinity or femininity, perhaps to relatives, friends, teachers, or (shudder) the mass media.

and a basis for reasonable morality. But as always, the development of the superego is a process that can go too far or not far enough.

An overdeveloped or underdeveloped superego yields the adult type of the *phallic character*. A person who has developed a completely rigid moral code, one that brooks no shades of gray and no exceptions, may be a phallic type. So is someone who lacks a moral code altogether. An extremely promiscuous person might be a phallic type. So, too, might someone who becomes completely asexual. As always, Freud was suspicious of the extremes; the healthy place to be is in the middle.

Genital Stage

After the phallic stage, a child gets a chance to take a developmental breath and concentrate on the important learning tasks of childhood, such as learning to read, the names of plants and birds, arithmetic, and all of the other important stuff taught in elementary school. This *latency* phase is a sort of psychological respite to allow the child to learn much of what he will need in adult life. The rest period ends, with a bang, at puberty.

The **genital stage** of development is fundamentally different from the others in that Freud saw it not as something individuals necessarily pass through, but as something that must be sought. Adulthood is not inevitable; it is an achievement. Sometime after physical puberty, if all goes well, a person develops a mature attitude about sexuality and other aspects of adulthood. Freud is not explicit about when this happens; in some people, apparently, it never happens.

The physical focus of the genital stage is the genitals, but notice how this label differs from that of the phallic stage. *Genital* describes not just a physical organ; the word also refers to the process of reproduction, or giving life. The genitals, at this stage, become not just organs of physical pleasure, but the source of new life and the basis of a new psychological theme.

The focus of the genital stage is the creation and enhancement of life. True maturity, Freud believed, entailed the ability to bring new life into the world and nurture its growth. This new life includes children, but it also can include other kinds of creativity, such as intellectual, artistic, or scientific contributions. The developmental task of the genital stage is to add something constructive to life and to society, and to take on the associated adult responsibilities. In that sense, the psychological theme of the genital stage is *maturity*. And, as I mentioned, not everybody attains it. The *genital character* is psychologically well adjusted and—here comes the familiar word—balanced.

Early in the 20th century, Freud made his only trip to the United States. He was dismayed to find himself trailed by newspaper reporters who found some of his sexual theories titillating, especially after they had finished distorting them. Freud's lifelong aversion to America and anything American seems to have been

> The essence of mental health, Freud said, is the ability "to love and to work."

boosted by this experience. But the trip was not a total loss. At one point, a reporter asked him, "Dr. Freud, what is your definition of mental health?" Freud gave the best answer that anybody has ever come up with, before or since. The essence of **mental health**, he said, is the ability "to love and to work."

The most important word in this definition is "and." Freud thought it was important to love, to have a mate and family to care for and nurture. He also thought it was important to work, to do something useful and constructive for society. The good life, Freud thought, would always contain both. To do just one was to be an incomplete person.

Moving Through Stages

As we have seen, an important task while developing through these stages is building basic psychological structures. At the beginning of the oral stage, the newborn baby is all id—a seething bundle of wants and needs. As the baby moves into the anal stage, experiences of frustration and delay lead part of the mind to differentiate and separate, taking some of its energy to form the ego. The ego has the duty to control and channel the urges of the id. At the phallic stage, the child identifies with important persons, principally her parents, and the sum of these identifications forms the third structure, the superego. The superego is the conscience; it morally judges the person's actions and urges, and sometimes tries to stop them.

Freud once used a different analogy: A mind progressing through the stages of psychosexual development is like an army conquering hostile territory. Periodically, it encounters opposition and, at that point, a battle ensues. To secure the ground afterwards, some troops are left behind. If the battle was particularly bitter, and if the local resistance remains strong, a larger part of the army must stay behind— leaving fewer troops to advance. Moreover, if the main army encounters severe problems later, it is likely to retreat to a stronghold at the site of a former battle.

In this analogy, the individual's store of libido is the army. It encounters "battles" at each of the developmental stages. If the battle of the oral, anal, or phallic stage is not completely won, libidinal energy must be left behind at that point. The result will be **fixation.** The adult will continue to struggle with issues from that stage, and will tend to retreat there under stress. Such retreat is called **regression.** An oral character under stress becomes passive and dependent and may even revert to thumb sucking. An anal character under stress becomes even more rigid or more disorganized than usual. A phallic character under stress may become promiscuous or completely asexual. Victory, in this analogy, means making it through all of these stages to the final (genital) stage, with as much of one's army intact as possible. The more libido available to enjoy the final stage of maturity, the better adjusted the adult will be.

THINKING AND CONSCIOUSNESS

Underneath the progression through these psychosexual stages, the mind is also undergoing a subtle, profound, but incomplete shift between two kinds of thinking: primary process thinking and secondary process thinking. **Secondary process thinking** is what we ordinarily mean by the word *think*. The conscious part of the ego thinks this way; it is rational, practical, and prudent, and it can delay or redirect gratification. It is secondary in two senses. First, it appears only as the ego begins to develop; a newborn has no capacity for secondary process thinking. Second, Freud believed it played a less important role relative to primary process thinking, which he considered more interesting, important, and powerful—throughout life, not just in infancy.

Primary process thinking is the way the unconscious mind operates, and how the infant's as well as the adult's id is said to operate. It is a strange sort of thinking. The fundamental aspect of primary process thinking is that it does not contain the word, or even the idea of, *no*. It is thinking without negatives, qualifications, sense of time, or any of the practicalities, necessities, and dangers of life. It has one goal: the immediate gratification of every desire.

Primary process thinking operates by an odd shorthand that can tie disparate feelings closely together. Your feelings about your family can affect how you feel about your house, for example. Primary process thinking can use displacement to replace one idea or image with another: Your anger toward your father might be replaced by anger at all authority figures, or your anger toward an authority might be transformed into anger at your father. **Condensation** can compress several ideas into one; an image of a house or of a woman might consolidate a complex set of memories, thoughts, and emotions. And through **symbolization,** one thing might stand in for another.

At one point in his career, Freud thought there might be a universal symbolic code of the unconscious mind, in which certain symbols meant the same thing to everybody the world over. He thought people could use these symbols to interpret the meanings of dreams, and some of these are included in the little paperback books on dream analysis you can get at the supermarket. They include translations like

House = human body
Smooth-fronted house = male body
House with ledges and balconies = female body
King and queen = parents
Little animals = children
Children = genitals
Playing with children = (You fill in this one.)
Going on a journey = dying
Clothes = nakedness
Going up stairs = having sex
Bath = birth

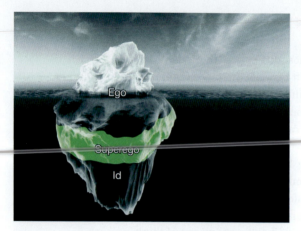

Figure 10.4 Consciousness and the Iceberg
Freud's theory posits that most of what the mind does, including just about all of the operations of the id and superego, occurs out of consciousness. Only a small part of the functioning of the ego routinely enters conscious awareness.

Intriguing as lists like this can be, Freud later dropped the idea of universal symbols. He decided that meanings vary for every individual, and therefore a general dictionary of the unconscious was not useful. The idea of unconscious universal symbols was picked up with a vengeance, however, by Carl Jung (see Chapter 11).

Primary process thinking is a very interesting concept, but one might reasonably ask, if primary process thinking is a property of the unconscious mind, then where is it ever "seen"? Freud thought that it could emerge into consciousness under several limited circumstances. He believed that the conscious thought of very young children operates according to primary process thinking, but because they develop secondary process thinking by the time they can talk, this hypothesis is difficult to verify (actually, it's impossible). He also thought primary process thinking could become conscious during fever delirium and during dreams. This is consistent with the experience that in dreams or delirium, time may run backwards, one person might change into another, images may dissolve into other things, and so on. Freud also thought that psychotics sometimes consciously experience primary process thinking; if you listen to the speech of someone suffering from schizophrenia, you will see where he got this idea.

Freud posited three levels of consciousness in what is sometimes called his *topographic model*[21] (see **Figures 10.4** and **10.5**): The smallest, topmost, and (in Freud's view) least important layer is the **conscious mind**, the part of your mental functioning you can observe when you simply turn your attention inward. A second layer, the **preconscious**, consists of ideas you are not thinking about at the moment, but that you could bring into consciousness easily. For example, how is the weather outside right now? What did you have for breakfast? Where is your car parked? Presumably, none of these things was in your conscious mind until I asked, but you probably had little trouble bringing them into your conscious awareness.

The third, the biggest, and, according to Freud, the most important layer of the mind is the **unconscious**, which includes all of the id, nearly all of the superego, and most of the ego. The unconscious is buried deep; the only way to bring

---

[21] *Topography* refers to elevation; a topographic map is one that shows the elevations of the hills and valleys over an expanse of territory.

it to the surface is by digging. One method of psychological digging that Freud used early in his career was hypnosis. Other clues come from slips of the tongue, accidents, and lapses of memory. All have their causes in mental processes that occur outside of consciousness. Finally, Freud developed the technique of free association, in which a person is encouraged to say whatever comes to mind in relation to some concern or issue. Freud thought the mental wanderings of free association were not random—he never thought anything was random. Therefore, the way a person jumps from one thought to another offers important clues about his unconscious. Another clue to the unconscious is provided by unintentional actions and memory lapses, our next topic.

PARAPRAXES

A **parapraxis** (plural: parapraxes) is another name for what is commonly called a "Freudian slip": a leakage from the unconscious mind manifesting as a mistake, accident, omission, or memory lapse. Remember that Freud was a determinist—he thought everything had a cause. This belief comes into play when considering the causes of accidents and other slips. Freud was never willing to believe that they happened at random.

Forgetting

According to Freud, forgetting something is a manifestation of an unconscious conflict revealing itself in your behavior. The slip, or parapraxis, is the failure to recall something you

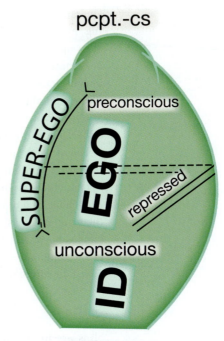

Figure 10.5 Freud's Own Diagram Showing the Relationship between Consciousness and the Id, Ego, and Superego The conscious mind is denoted by pcpt.-cs (which stands for "perception-conscious"). Freud wrote about this diagram, "It is certainly hard to say today how far the drawing is correct. In one respect it is undoubtedly not. The space occupied by the unconscious id ought to have been incomparably greater than that of the ego or the preconscious. I must ask you to correct it in your thoughts."

needed to remember, which can result in embarrassment or worse. These consequences make the lapse a parapraxis; in the service of suppressing something in your unconscious mind, your slip messes up something in your life. To avoid thinking about something painful or anxiety producing, you fail to remember it. You make a date and then have second thoughts, so you forget you made it. Although you might have saved yourself some immediate anxiety, when you run into your erstwhile date the next day in the cafeteria, you will have a significant social problem. Many college students manage to forget the times that exams are held and term papers are due. Failing to remember may make the students less anxious in the short run but can produce serious difficulties in the long run. Occasionally, a student will make an appointment with me to discuss a difficulty he or she is having in class. I know the odds are no better than 50 percent that the student will show up at the appointed time. The explanation is always the same: "I forgot."

These examples are fairly obvious. But Freud insisted that *all* lapses reveal unconscious conflicts. Now the going gets a little tougher: What about when you forget something for no reason? No such thing, according to Freud. The psychoanalytic faith declares that, with sufficient psychotherapy using free association, a therapist can eventually figure out the cause of any memory lapse. The system of causal roots may be quite complex: You may have forgotten to do something because it reminds you of something else, which through primary process thinking has come to symbolize yet a third thing, which makes you anxious. In one case, a psychoanalyst reported that a patient forgot the name of an acquaintance who had the same name as a personal enemy. Moreover, the acquaintance was physically handicapped, which reminded the patient of the harm he wished to do the enemy of the same name. To defend against the superego-induced guilt this wish produced, he forgot the name of his perfectly innocent acquaintance (Brenner, 1974).

Slips

Slips are unintended actions caused by the leakage of suppressed thoughts or impulses. Many of them happen in speech and can be as simple as a failure to suppress what one privately wishes to say. In one of the first courses on psychoanalysis I took in college, the professor was mentioning the students who visited during his office hours. "When infants come to see me . . . ," he said, then he stopped, stammered, and his face turned bright red. His students did not fail to understand this revelation of what he really thought of them.

Saying the name of a former boyfriend or girlfriend at important and delicate moments with one's current boyfriend or girlfriend is a common and extremely embarrassing slip. Explanations are often demanded: "Why did you say her name?" "I just made a mistake—it didn't mean anything!" One's current significant other is no more likely to believe this reply than would Sigmund Freud himself.

Slips can occur in action as well as in speech. Accidentally breaking something can be a leakage of hostility against the person who owns the object, who gave you the object, or whom the object (for some reason) symbolizes. A more pleasant example is the standard interpretation of somebody accidentally leaving something at your house after a visit: It means the object's owner hopes to come back.

As already noted, the person who commits these slips of speech or action may deny that the slip meant anything. Not only does psychoanalysis not accept such a denial, but the louder and more vehement it is, the more a Freudian will suspect a powerful and important impulse.

But what about accidents that happen when a person is tired, not paying attention, in a hurry, or excited? These, too, are not accidents, according to Freud. Fatigue, inattention, or excitement might make slips more likely, but they do not cause them. Freud compared the role of such factors to the way darkness helps a robber. A dark street might make a burglary more likely, but dark streets do not cause burglaries; a burglar is still required. Similarly, fatigue, inattention, and other factors might make it easier for a suppressed impulse to leak into behavior, but they are not the cause of the impulse.

Does this mean that there really are no accidents? Freud believed so. Any failure to do something you ordinarily can do—such as drive a car safely—must be due to the leakage of a suppressed impulse. Some examples that fit this description have been quite prominent. In the Winter Olympics a few years ago, a skier on the way to an important downhill race broke her leg when she crashed into a member of the ski patrol. This was an accident, of course, but it is also reasonable to ask how often an Olympic-level skier crashes into somebody else. How often does any skier crash into a member of the ski patrol? And, of all mornings of this skier's life, why did the accident happen on this morning? One is led to wonder if this skier did not want to show up for her race, and why.

An even more dramatic incident at the 1988 Olympics involved speed skater Dan Jansen, whose sister died of leukemia just five hours before he was scheduled to compete in the 500-meter event. Jansen was favored for the gold medal, and his sister had insisted he go to the Olympics even though the family knew she didn't have long to live. Ten seconds into the race, Jansen fell down. Four days later, in his second event, the 1,000-meter race, he fell again. A psychoanalytic perspective questions whether Jansen might have been ambivalent about coming home bedecked in gold medals at such a time. Had he fully wanted to succeed, it seems unlikely that he would have fallen down in the two most important athletic events of his life.[22]

While there may not be many, or any, Freudians in the typical university psychology department, sometimes you can find them in—of all places—the physical education department. They may not think of themselves in such terms, but coaches are often practicing Freudians. They worry about instilling in their athletes the right mental attitude, a will to win. When a basketball player at the free-throw line in a big game misses a shot she can make 20 times in a row in practice, any good coach knows the solution is not more free-throw practice; something about the athlete's attitude needs work. If the player had fully wanted to make the basket, the ball would have gone in. Ask any coach which team will win any given game, and the coach will reply, "The team that wants it more." Freud would say, "Exactly right."

The next time you fail to perform to your ability in sports, in academics, at work, or wherever, take a moment to ask yourself: Did I really, wholeheartedly, want to succeed? If not, why not?

> They may not think of themselves in such terms, but coaches are often practicing Freudians.

---

[22] The sports world breathed a sigh of relief when, in the 1994 Olympics, Jansen took the gold medal in the 1,000-meter race and set a world record.

ANXIETY AND DEFENSE

Anxiety is unpleasant. Its intensity can range from a vague and uneasy sense that not all is right with the world, to desperate and debilitating terror—the classic anxiety attack. Anxiety can be generated by stresses from the outside world, and also by conflicts within the mind itself—the kind of anxiety Freud found most interesting. Either way, the anxiety might be too intense to bear. To help prevent this from happening, the ego employs an impressive array of **defense mechanismsc** (see **Table 10.2**).

Each defense mechanism serves the function of shielding us from reality, at least temporarily. **Denial** simply involves refusing to believe the bad news or other knowledge that might make one anxious. It's what you see when a student, learning for the first time about a bad grade, shouts "no!" **Repression** is more complex, and might involve failing to acknowledge anything that might remind a person of the unwanted thought and, as was described above, can lead to forgetting names, events, obligations, and appointments. **Reaction formation** defends one's peace of mind by creating the *opposite* idea, as when somebody worried

Table 10.2 | SOME COMMON DEFENSE MECHANISMS

Defense Mechanism	Function	Example
Denial	Prevent perception of source of anxiety	"No! That's not possible!"
Repression	Prevent recall of anything that might remind one of the source of anxiety	"I forgot."
Reaction formation	Protect against a forbidden thought or impulse by instigating the opposite	"Pornography is the biggest menace to humanity there is!"
Projection	Attribute an unwanted impulse or attribute in oneself to other people	"I'm surrounded by morons!"
Rationalization	Create a seemingly logical reason for doing something shameful	"You have to be cruel to be kind."
Intellectualization	Translate a threatening situation into cold, intellectual terms	"After a prolonged period of discomfort, the patient expired."
Displacement	Redirect forbidden impulse onto a safer target	Professor dart boards
Sublimation	Convert base impulse into a noble cause	High art, other occupational choices

about his own moral fiber decides to write a book telling other people how to be virtuous. **Projection** can work almost the same way, by developing the idea that something one fears is true about oneself is instead true about other people, such as when somebody who fears he is unintelligent believes that he is "surrounded by idiots," or someone who is a habitual liar describes many other people as "dishonest." **Rationalization** allows a person to come up with a rational explanation for doing what she wants without acknowledging the real motivation, such as when she convinces herself that she "has to be cruel to

be kind." Similarly, **intellectualization** translates anxiety-producing thoughts into concepts or jargon that put emotions at a distance, such as a doctor who talks about a patient who "expired" or experiences "discomfort," or a general who reports on "sustaining losses" in combat. **Displacement** involves moving the object of one's emotions from a dangerous target to a safe one, such as when one has a disappointment at work and kicks the wall instead of the boss. Finally, **sublimation** provides a safe outlet for otherwise problematical desires, such as when somebody who wants to cut people open becomes a surgeon, someone who likes to argue becomes a lawyer, or somebody who wants to know secrets about other people that are none of his business becomes a psychologist. All of these mechanisms can provide relief from anxiety in the short run, but (except for sublimation), in the long run, they run the risk of making a person dangerously detached from reality.

PSYCHOANALYSIS AS A THERAPY AND AS A ROUTE TOWARD UNDERSTANDING

Freud believed that the problems that make most people anxious and unhappy have their roots in unconscious conflicts. The way to resolve these conflicts is to bring them into the open through dream analysis, analysis of slips and lapses, and free association. Once an unconscious conflict is brought into consciousness, the rational part of the ego is able to deal with it, and the conflict will no longer pose a problem. In the long run of therapy, Freud believed that insight into the hidden parts of the mind would allow the patient full, rational self-control. In other words, despite his focus on irrational mental processes, Freud believed in the ultimate power of reason.

Of course, the process is a bit more complicated than that. Unconscious conflicts must be dealt with not just logically but emotionally, which takes time and can be painful. It can even be dangerous. As psychoanalytic psychologist Robert Bornstein pointed out,

> Some patients with a history of severe sexual or physical abuse do not have the psychological resources available to cope adequately with explicit memories of these experiences. For these patients, therapeutic work should focus primarily on bolstering defenses and coping mechanisms. Only when these resources have been strengthened can insight be used productively within and outside of therapy. (Bornstein, 1999b, p. 169)

The prospect of losing one's neuroses can be surprisingly disconcerting. Many people avoid dealing with their unconscious anxieties for this reason; psychoanalysts call the phenomenon of running away from the solution to one's psychological problems the "flight from health." It is very common; it may be what is going on when you hear someone say, "I don't want to talk about it."

> Psychoanalysts call the phenomenon of running away from the solution to one's psychological problems the "flight from health"; it may be what is going on when you hear someone say, "I don't want to talk about it."

To comfort, guide, and support the patient through this difficult healing process, Freud believed, the therapist and patient must form an emotional bond, called the *therapeutic alliance*. This alliance gets its power through **transference**, the tendency to bring ways of thinking, feeling, and behaving that developed toward one important person into a later relationship with a different person. One might relate to a teacher in the same way one learned years earlier to relate to one's father. Transference is particularly important in psychotherapy, because the emotional relationship the patient develops with the therapist is built on the model of that patient's past relationships with other important people. The therapist has reactions to the patient as well, both positive and negative, called *countertransference*.

The development of transference and countertransference in therapy is important, but it can also cause problems. Freud may have been the first psychotherapist to note that sexual attraction sometimes arises between patients and psychotherapists. He was adamant that it was the duty of the therapist to resist this attraction. The patient must become emotionally invested for the therapy to work, Freud believed, and perhaps the therapist must as well, but the therapist must, at all costs, avoid acting on those emotions. This warning applies to negative reactions as well. Therapists working with difficult patients, such as those characterized by narcissistic personality disorder (see Chapter 17), describe feeling resentful, regretful, frightened, and manipulated (Betan, Heim, Conklin, & Westen, 2005). They feel they are "walking on eggshells" (p. 893), and even dread checking their phone messages! Obviously, to even hope to be helpful to patients like this, therapists must struggle to control their own emotions.

Psychoanalysis often is criticized for its allegedly low or even zero demonstrable cure rate, and for the fact that treatment can last for many years and perhaps never end. But recent research gave it a major and, to some observers, surprising boost. A thorough summary of 23 studies involving 1,053 patients concluded that long-term psychoanalytic therapy was more effective than shorter forms of treatment, especially for what were called "complex mental disorders." Indeed, patients who participated in long-term psychoanalysis fared better than 96 percent of the patients treated by other means (Leichsenring & Rabung, 2008).

This impressive finding does not mean that psychoanalysis always works, or that it is appropriate for everybody. As one psychiatrist wrote,

> Thanks to decades of clinical study, analysts are able to assess which patients are able to do better with medication or . . . [other forms of] therapy and which are likely to benefit more from analysis. Within the group for whom analysis is suitable, patients often make gains unachievable with other treatments. (J. D. Miller, 2009, p. 6)

Despite this recent attempt at resolution, the argument over the efficacy of psychoanalytic psychotherapy continues. Late in his own career, Freud began to see the whole issue as beside the point:

> After forty-one years of medical activities, my self-knowledge tells me that I have not been a physician in the proper sense. . . . [My real interests are] the events of the history of man, the mutual influences between man's nature, the development of culture, and those residues of prehistoric events of which religion is the foremost representation . . . studies which originate with psychoanalysis but go way beyond it. (Cited by Bettelheim, 1982, p. 48; bracketed phrasing is mine)

In the end, Freud was surprisingly uninterested in psychoanalysis as a medical or therapeutic technique, an attitude that some modern psychotherapists share (Bader, 1994). Instead, he saw its real importance as a tool for understanding human nature and culture.

PSYCHOANALYTIC THEORY: A CRITIQUE

Throughout this chapter, I have tried to sell you Freud. Psychoanalytic theory is dramatic and insightful, it is comprehensive, and it even has a certain elegant beauty. Having said that, I still must warn you against taking Freud too seriously.

When a student asks me, "What happens to sexual development if a boy is raised by his mother in a single-parent family?" (recall footnote 20) I really want to reply, "Hey! Don't take this stuff so seriously! Freud has a neat theory, and it's fun to play around with, but don't start using it to evaluate your life." Psychoanalytic theory is far from being received truth. So, having praised Freud, let me now bury him for a bit. Psychoanalytic theory has at least five important shortcomings.

Excessive Complexity

First of all, Freud's theory is highly complex, to put it mildly. A basic principle of science, sometimes called *Occam's razor*, is that less is more: All things being equal, the simplest explanation is the best. Suppose you want to explain why boys take on many of the values and attitudes of their fathers. One possibility is that they look for guides in the world around them and choose the most obvious and prominent. Freud's theory, however, says that boys sexually desire their mothers, but they worry that their fathers will be jealous and castrate them in punishment, so they identify with their fathers in order to vicariously enjoy the mother and lessen the threat from the father. This is intriguing, and maybe it is even correct, but is it the simplest possible explanation? No way. Even modern theorists sympathetic to psychoanalysis have moved away from this complicated story (Westen, 1998).

Case Study Method

A second tenet of science is that data must be public. The bases of one's conclusions must be laid out so that other scientists can evaluate the evidence together (recall the discussion of "open science" in Chapter 3). Classic psychoanalytic theory never did this, and the neo-Freudians and object relations theorists (considered in Chapter 11) have generally followed suit. Their theorizing is based on analysts' (including Freud's) introspections and on insights drawn from single therapeutic cases, which are (as a matter of ethics and law) confidential. Freud himself complained that proof of his theory lay in the details of case studies that he could never reveal because of the need to protect his patients' privacy. The fact that this *case study method* is uncheckable means that it may be biased. This bias may arise out of what psychoanalysts and their patients (such as Freud's turn-of-the-century Viennese patients) are like. Or perhaps the theorist misremembers or misreports what happens. No one can ever be sure. Psychoanalytic theory's traditionally dismissive attitude toward requests for empirical proof could be summarized by the slogan "take it or leave it."

Vague Definitions

Another conventional scientific standard is the *operational definition*. A scientific concept should be defined in terms of the operations or procedures by which it can be identified and measured. Psychoanalytic theory rarely does this. Take the idea of psychic energy. I mentioned that a bright student once asked me what units it was measured in. There are no units, of course, and it is not entirely clear what Freud meant by the term: Was he being literal, or did he intend "energy" as just a metaphor? Exactly how much psychic energy—what percentage, say—needs to be left behind at the oral stage to develop an oral character? As repressions accumulate, at what point will one run out of energy for daily living? Psychoanalytic theory does not even come close to providing specific answers to these questions.

Untestability

Freud's theory is also untestable. A scientific theory should be *disconfirmable*; that is, it should imply a set of observations or results that, if found, would show it to be false. This is the difference between religion and science. There is no conceivable set of observations or results that would prove that God does not exist. God might always just be hiding. Therefore, the existence of God is not a scientific issue. In the same way, there is no set of observations that psychoanalytic theory cannot explain—after the fact. Because no experiment can prove the theory wrong, it is unscientific. Some people have argued that perhaps it should be considered a religion![23]

Still, no single experiment is sufficient to prove or disprove any complex theory. The theory of evolution (see Chapter 9) is not testable in this manner, for example, even though scientists almost universally accept it. So the real question is not whether psychoanalysis is testable in a strict sense, but whether the theory leads to hypotheses that can be tested individually. In the case of psychoanalysis, the best answer is, sometimes yes and sometimes no.

Sexism

Psychoanalytic theory is sexist; even modern writers who are highly sympathetic to Freud admit it (e.g., Gay, 1988). Freud considers men the norm and bases his theories on their psychology. He then considers women, when he considers them at all, as aberrations or deviations from the male model. The side effects of being a woman, in psychoanalytic theory, include having less self-esteem, less creativity, and less moral fiber. Much of a woman's life, according to Freud, is based on her struggle to come to terms with the tragedy that she is not a man. If that's not sexist, then I don't know what is.

> Much of a woman's life, according to Freud, is based on her struggle to come to terms with the tragedy that she is not male.

---

[23] Early in his career, Freud frequently expressed his desire that psychoanalytic theory be considered scientific. As he grew older, this criterion became less important to him (Bettelheim, 1982). However, he would have been horrified at the idea of psychoanalysis as a religion.

WHY STUDY FREUD?

So, with all these acknowledged problems, why study Freud? Several reasons. One is that Freud and the tradition he initiated acknowledge, and indeed focus on, ideas that are underemphasized or even ignored elsewhere. Freud was right that people have conflicting motives and that sorting them out can be a source of confusion and anxiety. He was right that sex and aggression are powerful and mysterious forces in psychological life. And he was right that childhood experiences shape adult personality and behavior, and that a child's relationships with his or her parents in particular form a template that is a basis of relationships throughout life. As I hope you have noticed while reading this chapter, psychoanalytic theory is full of insights, big and small, that the rest of psychology has tended to neglect, and sometimes completely overlook.

Moreover, psychoanalysis continues to profoundly influence psychology and modern conceptions of the mind, even though few modern research psychologists—including those who teach personality psychology—consider themselves Freudians. For example, you might have noticed a certain general resemblance between the currently accepted story of personality development, summarized in Chapter 7, and Freud's theory. When you note this resemblance you should note, also, that Freud's theory came first.

More obviously, Freud continues to influence the practice of psychotherapy. One survey indicated that about 75 percent of practicing psychotherapists rely, to some degree, on psychoanalytic ideas (K. S. Pope, Tabachnick, & Keith-Spiegel, 1987). For example, even many psychotherapists who consider themselves non-Freudians practice the "talking cure" (the idea that talking about a problem helps), free association (encouraging the client to say whatever comes to mind), and transference (building an emotional relationship with the client to promote healing). According to legend, Freud also originated the practice of billing clients for their missed appointments!

Moreover, many of Freud's ideas have entered popular culture and provide a common—and helpful—part of how people think and talk about each other, in ways they might not always recognize as Freudian. For instance, suppose you give somebody an expensive present. The next time you visit him, the present is nowhere in sight. "Whatever happened to . . . ?" you ask. "Oh," your friend replies nonchalantly, "It broke, so I threw it away." How does his response make you feel? If it makes you feel bad, and of course it does, one reason might be that you have made a Freudian interpretation of your friend's behavior (he has unconscious hostility toward you) without quite realizing that you have done so.

Sometimes, everyday thought is even more explicitly Freudian. Have you ever heard somebody hypothesize that "She only goes out with that older guy because he's a father figure" or "He's all messed up because of the way his parents treated him when he was little" or "He never dates because his entire soul goes into programming his computer" or "She's got too much invested in him [psychologically] to break up with him now"? These are all Freudian interpretations.

So, it is probably the case that you knew a good deal of psychoanalytic theory even before you read this chapter. As a result, Freud's ideas do not always seem as original as they should. There is an old joke about the person who went to see one of Shakespeare's plays but walked out halfway through. "It was full of clichés," he complained. Of course, much of Shakespeare is full of clichés because so many of his lines ("To be or not to be") have made it into every-

Figure 10.6 Freud Lives On More than 75 years after his death, books about Freud and his works—both pro and con—continue to appear on a regular basis.

day speech. Some of Freud's most original ideas might sound mundane after all these years for the same reason.

A further consideration is that Freudian thought has undergone something of a revival within research psychology (see Chapter 11), and in 2006, more than 50 years after his death, Freud even appeared on the cover of *Newsweek*. Psychologists continue to do research and write articles on defense mechanisms (see Cramer & Davidson, 1998), transference (Andersen & Berk, 1998), unconscious thought (Bornstein, 1999b; Kihlstrom, 1990), and other classically Freudian topics (Westen, 1998; Westen, Gabbard, & Ortigo, 2008). Some of these research-ers vehemently deny that they are Freudians themselves, even when researching topics that seem psychoanalytic. Do they protest too much?

Perhaps the most important way in which Freud continues to be influential is that his theory remains the only complete theory of personality ever proposed. Freud knew what he wanted to explain: aggression, love, sexuality, development, energy, conflict, neurosis, dreams, humor, accidents—and the list goes on. His theory offers an account for *all* these aspects of psychology. Regardless of whether he is right about every one of them, or even none of them, the theory does map out all the important questions for personality psychology. In science, the most important thing is not answering questions but figuring out the right questions to ask. In this regard, Freud's theory of personality is a triumph that may stand for all time.

WRAPPING IT UP

SUMMARY

- Unlike many approaches to personality, the psychoanalytic approach concentrates on the cases where the cause of behavior is mysterious and hidden.

Freud Himself

- Freud was a practicing psychotherapist who developed his ideas from the cases he saw as well as from introspection and his broad knowledge of literature, art, and culture. One of his grateful patients dubbed his technique "the talking cure."

Key Ideas of Psychoanalysis

- Psychoanalytic theory is based on a small number of key ideas, including psychic determinism, the mind's three-part internal structure (id, ego, and superego), psychic conflict, and mental energy.

Controversy

- Psychoanalysis has been controversial throughout its history, although the nature of the controversy has changed with the times. Freud was one of the geniuses of the 20th century.

Psychoanalysis, Life, and Death

- Freud's psychoanalytic theory posits two fundamental motives: a life force (libido) and a drive toward death and destruction (Thanatos).

- Libido produces psychic energy, and the story of psychosexual development is the story of how this energy is focused in different areas over the course of four stages of life.

Psychosexual Development: "Follow the Money"

- Each developmental stage has a physical focus, a psychological theme, and an adult character type that results if that stage of development does not go well. The main theme for the oral stage is dependency; for the anal stage, it is obedience and self-control; for the phallic stage, it is gender identity and sexuality; and for the genital stage, it is maturity, in which one ideally learns to balance "love and work."

- The different structures of the mind form during progression through these developmental stages. The newborn baby is "all id." The ego develops during the anal stage, as a result of experiences with frustration and delay, and the superego develops during the phallic stage, as a result of identifications with significant people, especially the parents.

- Fixation occurs when an individual gets, to some degree, psychologically "stuck" in a stage of development; regression is movement backward from a more advanced psychological stage to an earlier one.

Thinking and Consciousness

- Primary process thinking, assumed by Freud to be present in babies and in the unconscious part of the adult mind, is unconscious thought characterized by displacement, symbolism, and an irrational drive toward immediate gratification.

- Secondary process thinking, which develops as the child moves toward adulthood, is ordinary, rational, conscious thought.

- The three layers of consciousness are the conscious mind, the preconscious, and the unconscious. Freud thought the conscious mind was by far the smallest of the three.

Parapraxes

- Forbidden impulses and unconscious thoughts can be revealed through *parapraxes*, or "Freudian slips." These include memory lapses and unintentional actions.

Anxiety and Defense

- Anxiety can originate in the real world or in inner psychic conflict, such as produced by an impulse of the id that the ego and superego try to combat.

- The ego uses several defense mechanisms to protect against the conscious experience of excessive anxiety and associated emotions such as shame and guilt. These defense mechanisms include denial, repression, reaction formation, projection, rationalization, intellectualization, displacement, and sublimation.

- Use of these defenses can reduce anxiety in the short run, but in the long run can produce problems in understanding and dealing with reality.

Psychoanalysis as a Therapy and as a Route Toward Understanding

- Psychoanalytic therapy is performed through techniques such as dream analysis and free association in the context of a therapeutic alliance between patient and therapist. The goal is to bring the unconscious thoughts that are the source of an individual's problems into the open, so the conscious, rational mind can deal with them.

- Although psychoanalysis has become notorious for its length and allegedly low cure rate, recent research has provided surprising support for its efficacy. Freud himself might not have cared much; he once wrote that he was interested in psychoanalysis more as a tool for understanding human nature than as a medical technique.

Psychoanalytic Theory: A Critique

- Psychoanalytic theory has been criticized for its excessive complexity, its reliance on the case study method rather than on experimentation, the poor definitions of some of its concepts, its untestability, and its sexism.

Why Study Freud?

- Nonetheless, psychoanalysis is important because of its contributions to psychotherapy (in the form of "talk therapy," for example), its effect on popular culture, the increasing amount of research it has generated in recent years, and because it is a complete theory of personality that raises questions other areas of psychology do not address.

KEY TERMS

psychic determinism, p. 356
id, p. 358
ego, p. 358
superego, p. 358
compromise formation, p. 358
libido, p. 359
Thanatos, p. 362
doctrine of opposites, p. 362
oral stage, p. 365
anal stage, p. 368
phallic stage, p. 370

THINK ABOUT IT

1. Do you hear Freudian ideas used in the ways people talk about each other? Can you think of any examples beyond those presented in this chapter?

2. Has anything happened recently in the news or in your life that seems best explained from a psychoanalytic perspective?

3. Have you heard about Freud or psychoanalytic ideas in any other courses you have taken? Which ones?

4. When your instructors in other psychology courses have mentioned Freud, have they expressed a favorable or hostile attitude? On what grounds? How about your instructors in other fields, such as English?

5. Do you think toilet training is a big deal for children? Does the way it is handled have important consequences for psychosexual development?

6. Research in political science shows that most young adults belong to the same political party as their parents. How would Freud explain this? Do you think this explanation is correct, and can you think of other possible reasons?

7. Can you think of any oral, anal, phallic, or genital characters among the people you know? Without naming names, what are they like? How do you think they got this way?

8. Do you think dreams reveal anything about the mind of the dreamer? Have you ever learned something about yourself by analyzing a dream?

9. If you had a psychological problem, would you go to a psychoanalyst? Why or why not?

10. Can you be anxious about something without knowing what it is? Or does that strike you as a nonsensical idea?

11. What examples of the various defense mechanisms—in your own behavior or that of others—can you come up with?

12. Do you think Freudian psychoanalysis should be considered scientific? Does the answer to this question matter?

13. Colleagues of the author have suggested, more than once, that the chapters on Freud and psychoanalysis should be deleted because the theory is wrong and out of date. Do you agree?

SUGGESTED RESOURCES

Bettelheim, B. (1988). *A good enough parent*. New York: Vintage.

> *A fascinating look at child rearing from a psychoanalytic point of view, by one of the more important psychoanalysts of the latter part of the 20th century. It is never blindly orthodox and is filled with nuggets of wisdom that would interest any parent.*

Gay, P. (1988). *Freud: A life for our time*. New York: Norton.

> *A masterful, thorough, well-written biography of Freud that recounts not just his life, but the development of psychoanalytic thought. The author is clearly sympathetic to Freud and psychoanalysis, but brings a modern perspective.*

Gay, P. (1989). *The Freud reader*. New York: Norton.

> *An excellent collection of Freud's original writings, including some unusual selections, including personal letters, translated specially for this volume.*

Horney, K. (1942). *Self-analysis*. New York: Norton.

Horney, K. (1950). *Neurosis and human growth.* New York: Norton.

Two books by an important female psychoanalytic theorist. They make fascinating reading for their insights into human nature, especially concerning the unrealistic ways people think about themselves and their goals. These are self-help books, but intellectually they are much richer than typical offerings in this category.

Want to earn a better grade on your test?

Go to **INQUIZITIVE** to learn and review this chapter's content, with personalized feedback along the way.

Interpreting Freud

Latter-Day Issues and Theorists
- Common Themes of Neo-Freudian Thought
- Inferiority and Compensation: Adler
- The Collective Unconscious, Persona, and Personality: Jung
- Feminine Psychology and Basic Anxiety: Horney
- Psychosocial Development: Erikson
- Object Relations Theory: Klein and Winnicott
- Where Have All the Neo-Freudian Theorists Gone?

Current Psychoanalytic Research
- Testing Psychoanalytic Hypotheses

Psychoanalysis in Perspective

Wrapping It Up
- Summary
- Key Terms
- Think About It
- Suggested Resources

PSYCHOANALYSIS AFTER FREUD

Neo-Freudians, Object Relations, and Current Research

S IGMUND FREUD DIED IN 1939. His theory of the human mind lives on, however. Academic research psychology—the kind done at universities by psychology professors—largely neglects Freudian theory and psychoanalysis, but more than a few modern psychologists continue to maintain Freud's legacy in one way or another. Some reinterpret his theory or extend it into new domains; others test some of his ideas with empirical research, while still others keep Freud alive just by continuing to argue about him.

Indeed, more than 75 years after his death, a surprising number of psychiatrists, psychologists, professors of English, and even Sanskrit scholars devote entire careers to the seemingly never-ending project of debunking Freud. The goal of many is to prove that he was wrong about absolutely everything from the very beginning (e.g., Crews, 1996, 2017). For example, a book by flamboyant psychoanalyst (and Sanskrit scholar) Jeffrey Masson (1984) stirred the popular media by dredging up material about some of Freud's more questionable friends and using it to attack Freud's whole theory.[1] Similar works appear on a regular basis.[2] As one reporter wrote, "To innocently type [Freud's] name into a search engine is to unleash a torrent of denunciation. . . . Merely being wrong—as even his partisans admit he probably was about a lot of things—seems inadequate to explain the calumny he has engendered" (J. Adler, 2006, p. 44).

---

[1] Masson also received extensive publicity when he sued *The New Yorker* magazine, which he claimed libeled him in a personality profile. He lost the case.

[2] See, for example, Sulloway (1979) or Crews (1998, 2017). The 1998 book is a compilation of attacks on Freud that, according to the book jacket, "decisively [forge] the case against the man and his creation . . . [and] reveal the fumbles and deceptions that led to the 'discovery' of psychoanalysis." That wasn't enough for Professor Crews; almost 20 years later he published another book that, in the words of one reviewer, came "back to stab the corpse again" (Crews, 2017; Prochnick, 2017, p. 20).On the other side of the ledger, Robinson (1993) summarizes the arguments of some of Freud's main critics and offers a defense.

Indeed, the most remarkable aspect of many of these efforts is their vehemence and personal tone. They don't merely suggest that the modern evidence concerning some of Freud's ideas is weak. They go much further, arguing that Freud was a liar, a cheat, and a fraud; that he was mean to his family; and that he never had an original idea in his life. They stop just short of arguing that his books should be pulled from the library shelves and burned in the public square. Are attacks like these a proportionate response, or might a deeper explanation be lurking? As psychiatrist Glenn Gabbard commented, "The unconscious is terribly threatening. It suggests we are moved by forces we cannot see or control, and this is a severe wound to our narcissism" (cited in J. Adler, 2006, p. 44). Psychoanalytically inclined psychologist Drew Westen adds that "any theory that is entirely comfortable to discuss is probably missing something very important about what it means to be human" (Westen et al., 2008, p. 86).

A more constructive development has been the work by clinical practitioners and theorists who—amid varying degrees of acknowledgment of or expressed opposition to the "Big Guy"—have introduced a number of refinements. Some are minor adjustments in summaries of Freud's work to help it make sense in a modern context. I did plenty of adjusting of my own in the previous chapter. Other amendments are more drastic. Carl Jung set up his own version of psychoanalysis, adding some mystical ideas far removed from the way Freud thought. But Jung's spiritual angle—influential as it has been with some people—is unusual.

The theme of most post-Freudian psychoanalysts is to move away from his emphasis on built-in sexual and aggressive instincts, toward a focus on the interpersonal aspects of life. A special concern is the way that early attachments, especially with parents, affect perceptions of, and relations with, other people. The important insight taken from Freud is that our relationships with other people depend upon our mental images of them, and these images sometimes do not much resemble the way they actually are. These partially accurate mental images are called *objects*, and the modern school of psychoanalysis that deals with their origin and implications is called *object relations theory*. A close relative of object relations theory is *attachment theory* which, as will be discussed in Chapter 16, focuses specifically on how attachments to significant other people, called *attachment figures*, and our images of such attachments can be a buffer in times of stress (Bowlby, 1988; Shaver & Mikulincer, 2005).

This chapter aims to bring Freud into the present day by summarizing some of the ways his theory has been reinterpreted and altered since his death, focusing on a few prominent neo-Freudian theorists. Then I will summarize some modern empirical research that has tried to test various psychoanalytic ideas, and conclude by placing psychoanalytic theory—old and new—into perspective, considering some of its shortcomings and accomplishments.

INTERPRETING FREUD

Modern writers who work to make sense of Freud may shade their summaries in various ways that try to maintain the spirit, if not the letter, of Freudian law. I did this in Chapter 10 when I described how a child trying to understand gender roles might look to a role model, such as the same-sex parent, for guidance. The dynamic process is different from the one Freud originally had in mind, but the result is still that boys usually identify with their fathers and girls with their mothers.

Only a fuzzy boundary separates interpreting a theory versus revising it. Freud wrote hundreds of articles and dozens of books over more than six decades, and he changed his mind about important issues more than once. So it is no small or insignificant activity to interpret what he said or meant to say, to determine the overall meaning of his work, or to decide the best way to summarize it. A particular challenge is to interpret Freud's theory in a way that sounds reasonable today, because that will require some changes. The original theory is, after all, nearly a century old.

Many psychologists and historians have attempted this task, with widely varying results. Peter Gay's (1988) monumental biography of Freud includes a thorough and insightful survey of the development of Freud's theory and a firm defense of it. Charles Brenner's (1974) useful outline of psychoanalytic concepts merges Freud's ideas with Brenner's own insights and updates. The preceding chapter of this book likewise constitutes more of a sympathetic interpretation than a literal retelling of Freud. I merged what Freud said with what I think he meant to say or should have said, and even mixed in some ideas contributed by later thinkers in the Freudian tradition.

For example, I altered the traditional story of the Oedipal crisis because I don't think the original makes much sense in light of more recent research about socialization. Thus, my version changes (some would say distorts) Freud's original theory. I also reinterpreted libido by describing it as the "life drive," rather than having it be all about sex. Again, this changes—in fact it directly contradicts—some of Freud's writings, but I prefer to interpret them in terms of what makes sense to me today. I even messed with Freud's description of the stages of personality development. Influenced by the great neo-Freudian theorist Erik Erikson (1963) and modern theories of life-span development outlined in Chapter 7, the summary in Chapter 10 describes how each stage is associated not just with physical maturation and bodily sensations but also with the changing demands of the social world.

Figure 11.1 Literal Freud vs. Interpretations of Freud Many scholars have put in years of effort trying to explain what Freud "really" meant; others strive to stay faithful to his original writings.

The more you become tempted to "fix" Freud by mixing in other thinkers and ideas and inserting your own ideas, the more you become an active developer of psychoanalytic theory yourself. It was Anna Freud, not her father, who wrote the definitive survey of the defense mechanisms, some of which were described in Chapter 10. It is probably safe to say Sigmund Freud would approve (he apparently approved of everything his favorite daughter did), since she did not deviate from the spirit of his theories. Many other thinkers have continued to write about psychoanalysis, attempting to stay true to Freud's theory while extending it.

LATTER-DAY ISSUES AND THEORISTS

The theorists who, in later years, continued to develop **neo-Freudian psychology** are an impressive crew. They include Anna Freud, Carl Jung, Alfred Adler, Erik Erikson, Karen Horney, Bruno Bettelheim, Harry Stack Sullivan, Melanie Klein, D. W. Winnicott, Henry Murray, and John Bowlby. You probably have heard of several of them; Erikson, Jung, and Adler number among the major intellectual figures of the 20th century, and the others are not far behind. But it is also an important fact that every individual just named is deceased. Although some neo-Freudians are still around, their golden age has passed.

Most neo-Freudians used the same research methods as Freud himself. They saw patients, looked into themselves, read widely in history and literature, and drew conclusions. These practices are shared by some of Freud's most vehement critics, such as Jung (an early dissenter) and Jeffrey Masson (a recent dissenter), as well as disciples such as Bruno Bettelheim and Anna Freud.

This approach allows psychoanalysts of every stripe to cover a lot of theoretical ground. It also invokes a style of argument that more conventionally scientific psychologists find frustrating. When Jung argued with Freud, for instance, he would basically say that his cases and introspection showed conclusion A, and Freud would reply no, his own cases and introspection led clearly to conclusion B, to which Jung would reply that anybody can see it's really A . . . and so forth. Anyone looking for an experiment to settle the matter would search in vain; even if somebody were clever enough to come up with one, neither Freud nor Jung—nor any of the classic neo-Freudians—would allow a mere experiment to settle such profound matters.

Common Themes of Neo-Freudian Thought

Most neo-Freudians differ from Freud in three major respects. First, they view sex as less important than Freud did by reinterpreting libido as a general motivation toward life and creativity. You have already seen such a reinterpretation in the preceding chapter. I view this change of emphasis as a permissible modern reinterpretation; other theorists view this issue as an example of how Freud was simply wrong.[3] Freud's emphasis on sexuality—even in children—has been from the beginning one of the most unsettling and controversial aspects of his theory. Thus, it is not surprising that later theorists have been tempted to clean up psychoanalysis in this respect. Freud believed that those who deemphasized the psychological role of sex did so because of their own anxieties. Their defenses made them unable to face directly the importance of sex and caused them to seek the important bases of behavior elsewhere. This kind of argument is not easily settled: If I say you are wrong about something because of your sexual hang-ups, how can you reply except, perhaps, to say the same about me?

In a second deviation, some neo-Freudians put less emphasis on unconscious mental processes and more emphasis on conscious thought than the Big Guy did. Modern ego psychologists focus on the processes driving the perception and conscious comprehension of reality (Hartmann, 1964; G. S. Klein, 1970; Loevinger, 1976; Rapaport, 1960). **Ego psychology** looks less like classic psychoanalysis and more like current mainstream psychology (especially the cognitive process approaches considered in Chapter 14), because instead of focusing on sexuality, psychic conflict, and the unconscious, ego psychologists focus on perception, memory, learning, and rational, conscious thinking. According to Jane Loevinger's influential version, the ego's function is to make sense of everything a person experiences (Loevinger, 1987). Moreover, Loevinger's story of development is essentially the story of the development of the ego itself. Early in life, the ego struggles to understand how the individual is separate from the world and from the mother; later, the ego grapples with such issues as how to relate to society, achieve personal autonomy, and appreciate the autonomy of others. According to Loevinger's test of "ego development," most people never get much further than learning society's basic rules and appreciating that some of those rules have exceptions (Holt, 1980). Very few become truly independent individuals who appreciate and support the independence of others.

A third common neo-Freudian deviation puts less emphasis on instinctual drives and mental life as the source of psychological difficulties, and focuses instead on interpersonal relationships. By modern psychotherapeutic standards, Freud was surprisingly uninterested in the daily lives of his patients. Whereas a modern therapist would want to know the details of a patient's interactions with his spouse, Freud would be more interested in his childhood relationship with his mother. Adler and Erikson both emphasized the way psychological problems arise from day-to-day difficulties relating with other people and with society, and object relations theorists believe that people replay certain key patterns in their relationships throughout their lives.

---

[3] Orthodox Freudians would insist that this is a place where my *summary* is wrong.

Inferiority and Compensation: Adler

Alfred Adler (1870–1937) was the first major disciple to end up at odds with the master. Like many others at the time and since, Adler thought that Freud focused too much on sex as the ultimate motivator and organizer of thought and behavior. Of equal or greater importance, Adler thought, was what he called *social interest*, or the desire to relate positively and productively with other people (A. Adler, 1939).

> People intuitively understand that someone secure in his masculinity does not need to prove it through his choice of vehicle, manner of driving, or any other superficial means.

Adler said individuals are motivated to attain equality with or superiority over other people to compensate for whatever, in childhood, they felt was their weakest aspect. This idea, called **organ inferiority**, implies that someone who felt physically weak as a child will strive for physical strength as an adult, that one who feels stupid will grow into an adult obsessed with being smarter than everyone else, and so on. It matters little whether the child actually *was* physically weak or relatively unintelligent, only how the child *felt*.

A particular kind of compensation for the past is seen in the desire of an adult to act and become powerful, because of feeling inadequate or inferior as a child. Adler called this kind of overcompensating behavior the **masculine protest**. He applied this term to both men and women, but believed the issue to be particularly acute for men. Society tells young boys that males are supposed to be the powerful and dominant gender—and yet, who is the most powerful person during the first years of *their* lives? Mom, obviously. Adler believed this early experience caused some young men to develop a powerful yearning to prove their dominance, power, and masculinity. One way to do this in modern society is to buy a pickup truck that can be entered only via a ladder, loudly rev the engine, and race up and down the highway, terrifying passersby. However, this kind of behavior always rings a little false. I think most people intuitively understand that someone secure in his masculinity does not need to prove it through his choice of vehicle, manner of driving, or any other superficial means. The masculine protest, therefore, is a *compensation* in response to feelings of inferiority.

Adler's larger point is that everyone felt inferior as a child, probably in many ways, and the quest to overcome these feelings continues to influence behavior as an adult. This quest can help explain behaviors that otherwise do not seem to make sense—such as driving an implausibly large vehicle to the supermarket—but

"Dear, do you think you may have become too comfortable with your masculinity?"

also much more. Needs for power, love, and achievement all have roots in early experience. An individual's compensations for perceived childhood inferiorities coalesce into a particular mode of behavior, which Adler called that individual's "style of life." Two familiar terms with roots in Adlerian thought are *inferiority complex* and *lifestyle*.

The Collective Unconscious, Persona, and Personality: Jung

The next major rebel from psychoanalysis was Carl Jung (1875–1961). (See Jung, 1971a, for a collection of his writings.) His feud with Freud was more dramatic and bitter than Adler's because Freud had such high hopes for Jung, one of his earliest disciples. For many years, Jung and Freud were close friends as well as colleagues; they exchanged numerous letters and even traveled to America together. Freud declared Jung his "crown prince," and anointed him the first president of the International Psychoanalytic Association.

But over the years, Jung's theories departed more and more from Freud's, to the point that the two men just couldn't get along any longer. Perhaps Jung's deviation that most irritated Freud was his increasing interest in mystical and spiritual matters. Freud, a devout atheist, found Jung's ideas concerning an inner rhythm of the universe ("synchronicity"), transcendental experiences, and a collective unconscious rather hard to take. These ideas became extremely important to Jung, however, and they are a major reason for why he remains famous.

Jung's best-known idea is the **collective unconscious**. Jung believed that as a result of the history of the human species, all people share inborn "racial" (by which he meant human) memories and ideas, most of which reside in the unconscious. Some of these are basic images, called **archetypes**, which Jung believed go to the core of how people think about the world, both consciously and unconsciously. They include "the earth mother," "the hero," "the devil," and "the supreme being." Versions of these archetypes, sometimes disguised with symbols, show up repeatedly in dreams, fantasies, cultural mythologies, and even modern literature. (Indeed, a school of literary criticism active to this day seeks Jungian archetypes in novels, plays, and cinema.) This seems like an odd idea, but there may be something to it. The snake – another of Jung's archetypes – shows up frequently in cultures' foundational stories, such as the Bible, almost always in a sinister role—and research suggests that the human fear of snakes may be innate (Öhman & Mineka, 2003).

Another of Jung's lasting ideas is the **persona**, his term for the social mask one wears in public. He pointed out that, to some degree, everyone's persona is false, because everyone keeps some aspects of their real selves private, or at least fails to advertise all aspects of the self equally. This idea survives in modern social psychology and sociology (e.g., Goffman, 1959); it also influenced object relations theory, considered later in this chapter. The danger, according to Jung, is that an individual might come to identify more with the persona than with the real self. She may become obsessed with presenting a certain image instead of expressing who she really is and what she really feels, and thus become shallow with no deeper purpose than social success. Such people become creatures of society instead of individuals true to themselves.

Another influential Jungian concept is the anima and animus. The **anima** is the idea, or prototype, of the female, as held in the mind of a male. The **animus** is the idealized image of the male as held in the mind of a female. These two images cause everyone to have some aspects of the opposite sex in their psychological makeup: A man's anima is the root of his "feminine side"; a woman's animus is the basis of her "masculine side." These concepts also shape responses to the opposite sex: A man understands (or misunderstands) women through the psychological lens of his anima; a woman likewise understands or misunderstands men according to her animus. This can lead to real problems if the idealized woman or man in one's mind matches poorly with the real women or men in one's life. This is a common problem, Jung believed, and daily experience would seem to support him on this.

Another key Jungian idea is his distinction between people who are psychologically turned inward (introverts) and those who are oriented toward the external world and other people (extraverts). As we saw in the chapters of Part II, the dimension of extraversion-introversion is one of the Big Five personality traits and has been found in a wide range of psychometric research programs.

Yet another useful Jungian idea is his classification of four basic ways of thinking: rational thinking, feeling, sensing, and intuiting. As Jung wrote,

> Sensation establishes what is actually present, [rational] thinking enables us to recognize its meaning, feeling tells us its value, and intuition points to possibilities as to whence it came and whither it is going in a given situation. (Jung, 1971b/1931, p. 540)

Jung believed that everybody uses all four kinds of thinking, but that people vary in which kind predominates. An engineer might emphasize rational thinking, while an artist emphasizes feeling, a detective emphasizes sensation, and a religious person emphasizes intuition. A modern personality test, the *Myers-Briggs Type Indicator* (*MBTI*; Myers, 1962), is sometimes used to determine which kind of thinking an individual uses most. Guidance counselors and personnel departments frequently use this test but, as was summarized in Chapter 6, the test is rather infamous among modern personality psychologists for not being very valid.

Jung believed that, ideally, one would achieve a balance among all four types of thinking, although he acknowledged that such an achievement is rare. The distinction between Jung and Freud could be summed up in Jungian terms by saying that Freud emphasized rational thinking, whereas Jung had a more intuitive style.

Feminine Psychology and Basic Anxiety: Horney

Karen Horney (1885–1952) did not begin publishing about psychoanalysis until late in Freud's career, and, unlike Adler and Jung, she never feuded with the master. She is one of the three most influential women in the history of psychoanalysis (the other two being Freud's brilliant and devoted daughter Anna and the object relations theorist Melanie Klein). Some of Horney's books are among the best and most readable introductions to psychoanalytic thought (see Horney, 1937, 1950). She also wrote about self-analysis, which she believed could help people through psychological difficulties when professional psychoanalysis was impractical or unavailable (Horney, 1942).

Horney deviated from Freud over an aspect of his theory that many people—especially women—have found objectionable. She disagreed with Freud's portrayal of women as obsessed by "penis envy" and the desire to be male. As mentioned in Chapter 10, in some of his writing, Freud seems to view women as damaged creatures—men without penises—instead of as whole persons in their own right. Horney found this view implausible and objectionable. If some women wish to be men, she theorized, it is probably because they see men as being freer than women to pursue their own interests and ambitions. Although women might lack confidence and overemphasize their love relationships with men as a source of fulfillment, this is due to the structure of society rather than the structure of bodies.[4]

Horney's other contributions fit better into the conventional Freudian mode. She emphasized that adult behavior is often based on efforts to overcome the basic anxiety acquired in childhood: the fear of being alone and helpless in a hostile world. Attempts to avoid such anxiety can cause what Horney called *neurotic needs*, needs that people feel but that are neither realistic nor truly desirable. These include the needs to find a life partner who will solve all of one's problems (love-related and otherwise), to be loved by everybody, to dominate everybody, and to be independent of everybody. Not only are these needs unrealistic, they are mutually contradictory. But people often unconsciously try to pursue all of them anyway, which can lead to self-defeating behavior and relationship problems.

---

[4] As a counter to this observation, the psychoanalytic writer Drew Westen noted that children think in concrete terms and so might be especially prone to symbolize the relative social advantages of men and women in this literal and physical way. Before he became a psychologist, a coworker who knew nothing of psychoanalytic theory "told him that her 6-year-old daughter had cried the night before in the bathtub because her younger brother, with whom she was bathing, had 'one of those things' and she did not. The author has always wondered about the impact of the mother's tongue-in-cheek reply: 'Don't worry, you'll get one someday'" (Westen et al., 2008, p. 65).

Psychosocial Development: Erikson

Erik Erikson (1902–1994) always claimed to be a faithful Freudian, but his innovations in psychoanalytic theory make him Freud's most important revisionist (see Erikson, 1963, 1968). For example, he pointed out persuasively that not all conflicts take place in the unconscious mind—many conflicts are conscious. A person might have to choose between two (or more) activities, careers, or even lovers. These conflicts can be painful and consequential, as well as completely conscious.

Erikson believed that certain basic conflicts arise at various stages of life. This insight led Erikson to develop his own version of Freud's theory of psychological development, in which Erikson emphasized not the physical focus of libido, but the conflicts experienced at each stage and their possible outcomes. For that reason, his theory of development is referred to as a *psychosocial*, as opposed to Freud's *psychosexual*, approach (see **Table 11.1**). Erikson's psychosocial approach heavily influenced the way I interpreted Freud's psychoanalytic view of development in Chapter 10. Erikson's theory covers not just childhood, but psychological change throughout life. In that way, his theory anticipated the study of life-span development, which was considered in detail in Chapter 8.

The first stage, according to Erikson, is *basic trust versus mistrust*. This corresponds to Freud's oral stage of very early childhood, when the utterly dependent child learns whether needs and wants will be met, ignored, or overindulged. Given the appropriate ratio of satisfaction and temporary frustration, the child develops *hope* (which in Erikson's terminology refers to a positive but not arrogant attitude toward life) and confidence—but not overconfidence—that basic needs will be met.

The next stage, corresponding to Freud's anal stage, is that of *autonomy versus shame and doubt*. As the child begins to control bowels and other bodily functions, learns language, and begins to receive orders from adult authorities, an inevitable

Table 11.1 | COMPARISON OF FREUD'S AND ERIKSON'S SEQUENCE OF PERSONALITY DEVELOPMENT

Approximate Age	Freudian Stage	Eriksonian Issue
0–2 years	Oral	Trust vs. mistrust
3–4 years	Anal	Autonomy vs. shame and doubt
4–7 years	Phallic	Initiative vs. guilt
8–12 years	Latency	Industry vs. inferiority
13+ years	Genital (evolves over adulthood)	Identity vs. identity confusion
		Intimacy vs. isolation
		Generativity vs. stagnation
		Integrity vs. despair

conflict arises: Who's in charge here? On the one hand, adults pressure the child to obey, but on the other hand, that child wants control of his own life. Ideally, these wills can strike a balance, but either may win out, leading in some cases to the anal character described in Chapter 10.

Erikson's third stage, corresponding to Freud's phallic stage, is that of *initiative versus guilt*. The child begins to anticipate and fantasize about life as an adult. These fantasies inevitably include sexual ones, as well as various tactics and plans to get ahead in life. Such fantasies are good for a child, Erikson believed, but if adults do not respond to them well, these thoughts can lead the child to feel guilty and to back off from taking initiative in her development toward adulthood. Ideally, the child will develop a sense of right and wrong that is derived from adult teachings but is also true to the child's developing sense of self. This development leads to a principled adult morality, in which moral rules are applied with flexibility and wisdom, rather than a merely conformist pseudomorality in which rigid rules are followed blindly and without exception. You may have noticed that this stage reinterprets Freud's phallic stage without the full Oedipal crisis (see Chapter 10).

The fourth stage is *industry versus inferiority*, during which one should develop the skills and attitudes to succeed in the world of work or otherwise contribute to society. At this time, the child must begin to control his exuberant imagination and unfocused energy and get on with tasks of developing competence, workmanship, and a way of organizing life tasks. This stage corresponds roughly to Freud's latency period.

At Erikson's fifth stage, development deviates more widely from the path laid out by Freud. The Freudian account basically stops with the genital stage, which is reached at some unspecified time after puberty, if at all. In Erikson's view, however, development continues throughout life. The next crisis involves *identity versus identity confusion*, as the adolescent strives to figure out who he is and what is and is not important. At this stage, individuals choose values and goals that are consistent, personally meaningful, and useful. Close on the heels of the identity conflict comes the competition between *intimacy versus isolation*. The task here, in young adulthood, is to find an intimate life partner to share important experiences and further development, rather than becoming isolated and lonely.

As one enters middle age, Erikson said, the next conflict is *generativity versus stagnation*. As a person's position in life becomes firmly set, does she settle into passive comfort, or begin to turn her concerns to the next generation? The challenge here is to avoid the temptation to simply cash in one's savings and go fishing, and instead to raise and nurture children and generally to do what one can to ensure the progress of the next generation. I am reminded here of the modern phenomenon of prosperous American retirees who vote overwhelmingly against taxes to support schools. Which choice do you think these people have made between generativity and stagnation?

The final crisis in life occurs late in old age, as one begins to face the prospect of death. The choice here is between *integrity versus despair*. Does the person regret earlier mistakes and feel that, basically, he blew it? Or from experience, has the person developed wisdom? The test is: After 70, 80, or 90 years of life, does the person have anything of interest and value to say to the next generation? Or not?

In sum, a person progresses in Erikson's scheme not according to physical or genital maturation, but according to the developmental tasks required at different phases of life. This idea is consistent with the analyses of changes in the Big Five personality traits over the life span reviewed in Chapter 7 (e.g., Roberts et al., 2006). It anticipated modern views of personality development, which now unanimously accept that psychological growth is not limited to little children; it is an ongoing task and opportunity throughout life, up to and including old age.

Object Relations Theory: Klein and Winnicott

The most important part of life, the principal source of its pleasure and pain, is probably the relationships one develops. In psychoanalytic terms, emotionally important people are called *objects*, and the analysis of interpersonal relationships is called **object relations theory** (J. R. Greenberg & Mitchell, 1983; M. Klein, 1964; Winnicott, 1958, 1965). The key insight of the object relations approach is that we can only relate to other people via the images of them we hold in our minds, and these images do not always match reality. Not surprisingly, mismatch causes problems.

> We can only relate to other people via the images of them we hold in our minds, and these images do not always match reality.

Object relations theory is the most active area of psychoanalytic thinking at present and has generated a huge literature. A search for "object relations" on the PsychInfo database yields more than 8,000 articles. The core ideas go back (naturally) to Freud, who thought the superego was built from childhood identifications with important people, and who also thought that people repeat important psychological patterns in new relationships through the mechanism of *transference*. Anna Freud pushed this idea further by examining children's relationships with their parents. Other important object relations theorists include Melanie Klein and D. W. Winnicott. The work of many other theorists, including the neo-Freudians summarized earlier, is also relevant to object relations, to the extent that these theorists address problems of interpersonal relations (J. R. Greenberg & Mitchell, 1983).

Object relations theory comes in many forms, but almost every version includes four principal themes. The first is that every relationship has elements of satisfaction and frustration, or pleasure and pain. Melanie Klein theorized that the first important object (literally) in the infant's life is the mother's breast. The infant quickly discovers that this object is a source of great delight, providing nutrition, warmth, and comfort. So the baby adores the breast. At the same time, the breast can be frustrating—it is not always available and not always full. So the baby hates the breast. The baby's demands are not reasonable—remember the description of the id's primary process thinking in Chapter 10. The baby wants everything *now*, and when the breast cannot or does not provide, the baby is angry.[5]

This dichotomy leads to the second theme of object relations: the mix of love and hate. Just like the original object, the breast, significant people are sources of both pleasure and frustration. They may give us love, support, and even sexual satisfaction. So we love them. At the same time, they may express annoyance with us, criticize us, and frustrate us. So we hate them. This sad situation is inevitable, in the view of object relations theory. You cannot satisfy someone without also frustrating her sometimes. So love will never be completely unmixed with resentment.

The third major theme of object relations is the distinction between the parts of the love object and the whole person. To the baby, the mother *is* the breast, at least at first. This is what interests and attracts the baby, not the mother as a person. It is a complex and difficult process, perhaps never completed, for the baby to come to appreciate the mother for more than just what she provides. In the same way, other people in our lives have parts and wholes. One might enjoy a partner's sense of humor, intellect, body, or money. To what degree is this equivalent to loving the partner himself? From an object relations perspective, it is not equivalent at all. Using a person's attributes for one's own enjoyment is very different from loving the whole person. Here, object relations theory intersects with common sense. To love someone's physique or wallet is not the same thing as loving the person, and to move beyond appreciating superficial aspects of people to relating to them as whole persons is a difficult and perhaps rarely accomplished feat.

The fourth major theme of object relations is that, to some degree, the psyche of the baby (and the adult) is aware of and disturbed by these contradictory feelings. The baby worships the mother's breast, but, according to Klein, the baby also feels anger (because there is never enough), envy (because the baby desires the breast's power for herself), fear (because the baby dreads losing the breast), and guilt (if the baby harms the breast, she could lose it). It may not be particularly plausible to attribute all of these complex reactions to a baby, but the overall theme does strike a chord.

Let's say you are fortunate enough to form a relationship with a truly attractive and desirable person. That's great. The downside may be a set of Kleinian reactions that are more or less unconscious. The very delight in the person's company may make you frustrated and even angry that he or she is not always available. You may envy the power this person has over you, precisely because of his or her attractiveness. You may fear losing him or her, and the fear is greater the more

---

[5] Such an immature attitude, right?

"I wish I'd started therapy at your age."

desirable he or she seems. And finally, you may feel secret guilt over all of these negative reactions, because if you expressed them, the person would probably be annoyed, and might even leave you. No wonder relationships can get so messed up.

Melanie Klein developed her theories based, in large part, on her work with children; she was one of the earliest psychoanalysts (along with Anna Freud) to attempt psychoanalytic treatment with the very young. Freud himself dealt almost exclusively with adults' childhood memories rather than working with actual children. One of Klein's innovations in child therapy, still widely used, was to use play for communication and diagnosis (M. Klein, 1955/1986). She provided a range of toys, and then observed which ones the child played with, and how; she believed play allowed the symbolic expression of emotions such as hate, anger, love, and fear. From watching children "play pretend" about their parents, for example, she observed how they divide, or *split*, their important love objects into two parts, one good and one bad. The good part of the object pleases them; the bad part frustrates them. Children wish to destroy the bad part because they fear being destroyed *by* it (Klein called this the *paranoid position*), and they wish to worship and protect the good part because they fear losing it (Klein called this the *depressive position*).

The phenomenon of splitting applies to other love objects as well. The problem, of course, is that people are not neatly divided into good and bad parts; they are indivisible wholes. So both desires—to destroy and to worship—are contradictory and irrational. This situation can lead to some common neurotic defenses. For example, to defend against the (more or less hidden) desire to destroy (the bad part of) a parent, one may idealize him or her. Have you ever heard someone describe her father in terms that were literally too good to be true? Klein believed, in true Freudian fashion, that such idealization is a symptom of underlying hostility being defended against at all costs. She might not be able to accept that her father has flaws, because to do so would expose her anger at those flaws and threaten a loss of his love or the memory of that love. In addition, to the extent that she has identified with her father, he has become a part of her, so to criticize him is to attack herself. She therefore constructs an image of him as having been perfect. People do this with descriptions of their parents, their boyfriends and girlfriends, and even their children. The distortions may be obvious to everyone but the person constructing these images.

Pediatrician D. W. Winnicott started his career in child psychology heavily influenced by Klein, but he soon developed his own important additions to object relations theory. One of his ideas that has come into everyday use was his description of what he called the *niffle* (Winnicott, 1996). The term came from a young patient named Tom, who at age 5 was hospitalized away from his family and took comfort from sleeping with his "niffle," a small piece of cloth to which he developed an emotional attachment. Tragically, the niffle got lost during the journey home. The loss so upset Tom that he became hostile, stubborn, and annoying to the point that his parents took him to Winnicott for therapy. From this experience, Winnicott formed the idea of the *transitional object*, which may be a special blanket, stuffed animal, or niffle that the child uses to bridge the gap between private fantasy and reality. The child endows the object with special, almost magical emotional meaning, so it can comfort the child when adult company (or, as Klein would surely say, the breast) is not available. Over time, the object loses its special meaning as the child becomes better able to handle the world without this kind of support.

Objects like these are transitional in two senses. First, they help the child make the change from the time when adults are constantly caring for him, to the time when he must face the world alone. Second, they exist in an interesting transitional state between fantasy and reality. The objects are always real in that there actually *is* a teddy bear, or a blanket, or whatever the niffle is. (For one of my daughters, the niffle was a toy dinosaur.) But the child gives it a special magic which, importantly, nobody in the family questions. Houses have been turned upside down more than once looking for lost niffles, and for good reason. Objects like this are important, and their use is not limited to children. Adults have sentimental attachments to many things that represent important people in their lives. The most obvious examples are the family pictures many people perch on their desks or living room mantels, and carry in their wallets. The purpose of these pictures and other sentimental keepsakes is to compensate in some small way for the fact that we cannot have our loved ones with us all the time, or forever.[6]

Another idea Winnicott added to object relations theory was the notion of the *false self*, which children—and later, adults—learn to put on to please other people. Notice the similarity of this idea to Jung's notion of the persona. Winnicott believed that, to some degree, putting on a false self is normal and even necessary; ordinary social etiquette and politeness generally require refraining from saying exactly what you think at all times in order to smooth interpersonal relationships. He

---

[6] When people are asked what they would grab first if their house were on fire, family pictures and emotionally important mementos are always high on the list.

worried more about some particularly charming children who, he feared, learned to put on a false act in a desperate attempt to cheer up their depressed mothers, at a high cost to the children's own psychological integrity. Winnicott observed that the false self serves to protect the true self by keeping it invisible: No one can exploit, harm, or even touch the true self if it is hidden behind a big enough false front. The ultimate maneuver of the false self is suicide: If there seems to be no hope that the true self can ever emerge, succeed, and be accepted, then the false self prevents its exposure permanently.

The purpose of psychotherapy, from the perspective of object relations, is to help minimize discrepancies between the true and false selves and, in the classic Freudian tradition, to help the rational resources of the mind work through irrational defenses. The goal is for the client to see the important people in her life as they are, not as the client wishes them to be. Likewise, the client may need help to see these people as whole individuals with a mixture of virtues, vices, and traits in between, rather than splitting them into images of Jekyll-and-Hyde twins who are all good on one side, and all bad on the other. Overcoming these illusions is not easy. On some level, everybody would prefer their important people to be perfect and devoted, and everyone may be on some level outraged that even the most beloved people in our lives fall short of perfection and sometimes disappoint us. Object relations theory retains this idea from Freud: Rationality can win over all. If we think clearly and brush away enough of the neurotic cobwebs, we can do what makes sense and relate to others as real people.

Where Have All the Neo-Freudian Theorists Gone?

As I mentioned earlier, they all seem to be dead. In the publishing business, the chapters in personality textbooks that survey Freud and the neo-Freudians—Chapters 10 and 11 in this book—are sometimes sardonically called the "tour of the graveyard." Certainly no one of the stature of Jung, Adler, Horney, or Erikson, or even Klein or Winnicott, is actively developing psychoanalytic theory today. Although these thinkers contributed important ideas that continue to be influential, their general approach based on informal observation, clinical experience, and personal insight is the wave of the past. The wave of the near future is conducting experimental and correlational research scientifically to confirm, disprove, or alter specific psychoanalytic ideas using the kinds of evidence that modern psychology generally employs.

CURRENT PSYCHOANALYTIC RESEARCH

Almost all conventional psychological research—that is, experimental and correlational studies with publicly reported data—is conducted by academic psychologists at universities or research institutes. The relations between research psychologists and their colleagues who practice clinical psychoanalysis have ranged from uneasy to downright hostile. This situation has only gotten worse over the years. In the 1950s, Freudian ideas were influential throughout psychology, but psychoanalysis gradually faded from view due to several trends, including the rise of behaviorism (see Chapter 14), the increased separation of academic psychology from clinical practice, and the appeal of one-shot laboratory studies over difficult, complex theoretical efforts (Shaver & Mikulincer, 2005). As a result, most university psychology departments that train researchers today have no Freudians on the faculty, so there is a remarkable amount of ignorance about psychoanalysis even among psychology PhDs. Where would they even learn about it? As psychologists Philip Shaver and Mario Mikulincer (2005) observed, "Many students specializing in personality psychology hardly know who Freud was, and most have never read his work" (p. 23). Even when academic psychologists encounter psychoanalytic research that meets their empirical standards, they often seem unwilling to believe the evidence showing aspects of psychoanalytic thought to have value.

For their part, many psychoanalysts are equally guilty of narrow-mindedness (Bachrach, Galatzer-Levy, Skolnikoff, & Waldron, 1991; Westen, 1998). They often show little interest in conventional scientific research, preferring to exchange anecdotal evidence: "I had a patient once who . . ." Freud himself thought that psychodynamic processes could be detected only through clinical case study; most modern psychoanalysts likewise seem to regard experimental and correlational research as irrelevant. For example, one psychoanalyst wrote the following about experimental research:

> I have been singularly uninterested in, if not contemptuous of, anything that the "number crunchers" had to say. . . . The phrase "meaningful statistical data" was, to me, an oxymoron of hilarious proportions. (Tansey, 1992, p. 539)

The result of this mutual myopia between psychoanalytic psychologists and non-psychoanalytic psychologists is that each group mostly ignores the other, and when they do interact, they typically attack or lecture without listening to the other side.

This sorry situation may be changing, however. A few brave psychologists are pursuing research relevant to psychoanalysis, and many more are doing so without realizing the relationship between their work and neo-Freudian ideas. Westen (1998), one of the most important of these modern researchers, has pointed out that while few psychologists research Freud or psychoanalysis directly, many of them pursue work that can be considered relevant to these topics. Westen observes that any research is at least "a little" psychoanalytic, whether knowingly or not, to the extent that it includes any of the following:

1. An examination of independent mental processes that occur simultaneously in the same mind and can conflict with one another
2. Unconscious mental processes

3. Compromises among mental processes negotiated outside of consciousness
4. Self-defensive thought and self-deception
5. The influence of the past on current functioning, especially childhood patterns that endure into adulthood
6. Sexual or aggressive wishes as they influence thought, feeling, and behavior

While very little experimental or correlational research includes all of these concerns, a great deal is relevant to one or more of them. The more of these issues the research includes, the more psychoanalytic that research becomes—whether the researchers know it or not. Westen's observation is extremely important because it implies that conventional experimental and correlational research may not be as irrelevant to psychoanalysis as psychologists on both sides of the fence have long assumed.

Testing Psychoanalytic Hypotheses

Using Westen's definition, it seems that many studies in the psychological literature address psychoanalytic hypotheses. Most did not explicitly set out to test psychoanalysis—and sometimes the articles do not even mention it—but they document and support ideas that began with Freud and other versions of psychoanalysis.

PERCEPTUAL DEFENSE Recall from Chapter 10 that psychoanalytic theory claims the ego tries to prevent stimuli that the superego finds overly threatening from even entering awareness. Psychologists have attempted to test this hypothesis.

In one classic, early experiment, words were presented extremely briefly to participants by use of a machine called a *tachistoscope*, which flashes them on a screen. Some words were neutral, such as apple, child, and dance. Others were sexually charged, such as penis, rape, and whore. Over successive trials, words of both types were presented for increasing durations, beginning with flashes so brief nobody could perceive them and continuing until the long exposures made the words obvious. Researchers measured participants' detection of the words in two ways. One was simply to ask, "Can you read that?" after each presentation. The minimum exposure time required to perceive each word was recorded. The second way was to measure the participants' sweat-gland activity; when they began to sweat in response to a word such as rape, participants were assumed to have detected it.

The interesting finding was that these two ways of measuring perception did not exactly coincide. In particular, when emotionally charged words were shown very briefly, participants might say, "I can't read that word," even while their sweat glands were reacting (see **Figure 11.2**). They also had to look longer at these so-called "critical" words before they would acknowledge recognizing them (see **Figure 11.3**). The authors interpreted these findings to mean that some unconscious part of the mind could read the words, even while the conscious part could not (McGinnies, 1949).

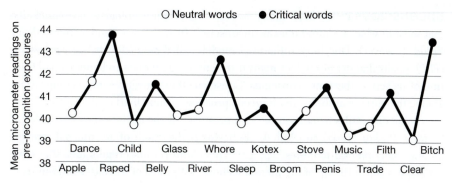

Figure 11.2 Emotional Reactions to "Critical" Words A classic (1949) study found that people reacted relatively emotionally to certain words, even when the words were presented so quickly that the people claimed they couldn't read them.
Source: McGinnies (1949), p. 246

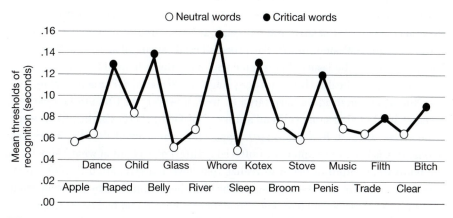

Figure 11.3 Slower Recognition of "Critical" Words These data from 1949 show that people needed to see certain words longer before they reported being able to recognize them.
Source: McGinnies (1949), p. 247

Although, over the years, many investigators have obtained results more or less like those just described, interpretations have been controversial. One obvious possibility is that subjects can read the word penis just fine—they are just too embarrassed to tell the investigator. It is difficult and perhaps impossible to be 100 percent sure. Taken as a whole, however, the evidence does seem persuasive that the mind has mechanisms that not only selectively attend to certain stimuli, but also actively screen out other stimuli that could cause too much anxiety (Erdelyi, 1974, 1985; Weinberger & Davidson, 1994).

UNCONSCIOUS THOUGHT Many modern cognitive psychologists have concluded that most of what the mind does is unconscious (usually they avoid acknowledging Freud, however). One long-influential model, called *parallel distributed processing (PDP)*, posits that the mind does many different things at once and only a small fraction of its activity becomes conscious. Conscious thought represents a compromise among the outputs of these simultaneous processes (Rumelhart et al., 1986).

Behavior results from a similar compromise. As the evolutionary psychologist Stephen Pinker (1997) concluded, "Behavior is the result of an internal struggle among many mental modules" (p. 42). This claim recalls Freud's idea that consciousness is just the tip of the mental iceberg, with most of its causes hidden from view (Sohlberg & Birgegard, 2003).

DEFENSE AND CATHARSIS Modern research also supports other psychoanalytic ideas. For example, new techniques can assess the degree to which people's speech reveals their use of psychoanalytic defense mechanisms (Feldman-Barrett, Williams, & Fong, 2002). The traits of the anal personality—stinginess, orderliness, rigidity, and so on—correlate with each other just as Freud theorized, and the traits of the oral character also seem to intercorrelate as Freud predicted, though perhaps to a weaker degree (Westen, 1990). The process Freud called *catharsis*, which involves freely expressing the issues that trouble you, has proven helpful for psychological and even physical health (Erdelyi, 1994; Hughes, Uhlmann, & Pennebaker, 1994).[7]

Not all Freudian ideas have fared so well, however. As I mentioned earlier, research has failed to support Freud's story of the Oedipal crisis at the phallic stage (Kihlstrom, 1994; R. R. Sears, 1947). Apparently, this part of Freud's theory was wrong; this is why, in Chapter 10, I offered a different account of what happens at the point when children begin to realize that boys and girls are different. Some psychologists claim that the psychoanalytic ideas best supported by research, such as the unconscious, would have been thought of even if Freud had never lived, and that most of his unique ideas, such as the Oedipal crisis, have been proven wrong. These psychologists conclude that Freud contributed nothing to modern human psychology (Kihlstrom, 1994).

This view seems unduly harsh to me. The edifice of Freudian theory has influenced modern thinking and psychology in many, many ways. Indeed, it is difficult to imagine what modern psychology would look like without Freud. Moreover, the completeness and persuasiveness of the original Freudian accounts of human nature, along with some of the neo-Freudian revisions and a bit of modern interpretation, convince me that Freudian theory offers a great deal of insight into the complex nature of ourselves and others.

---

[7] Other aspects of the idea of catharsis, specifically the prediction that expressing aggressive impulses will "vent"—and therefore lessen—aggressive drive, have not been supported by empirical research (Bushman, 2002).

PSYCHOANALYSIS IN PERSPECTIVE

It is not easy to come to an overall evaluation of psychoanalytic thought, because it comes into so many varieties and has been expressed in different ways by psychoanalytic thinkers who disagreed with each other on key points. So, when evaluating psychoanalysis, I think it might be wise to focus more on its general themes than on specific theoretical positions. As one writer recently observed:

> The idea that large parts of our mental life remain obscure or even entirely mysterious to us; that we benefit from attending to the influence of these depths upon our surface self, our behaviors, language, dreams, and fantasies; that we can sometimes be consumed by our childhood familial roles and even find ourselves re-enacting them as adults; that our sexuality might be as ambiguous and multifaceted as our compendious emotional beings and individual histories—these core conceits, in the forms they circulate among us, are indebted to Freud's writings. (Prochnick, 2017, p. 20)

It is also possible that to fully and fairly evaluate psychoanalysis, one must go beyond the published evidence. The distinguished 20th-century psychological methodologist, Paul Meehl, observed that in his experience nobody was ever really convinced that psychoanalysis was valid or useful just from reading about it. He said it was necessary to experience being psychoanalyzed, and even to conduct psychoanalyses oneself. In his career, he did both, and ended up concluding that psychoanalysis had a lot to offer toward deep understanding of the human mind. At the same time, he admitted that formal experimental research did not come close to providing enough evidence to really support this conclusion (Meehl, 1989).

As you decide for yourself what to think, I would suggest you keep this point in mind: The criterion for evaluating the psychoanalytic approach (as well as each of the other approaches) is not whether it is right or wrong—it has been said that all theories are wrong in the end—or even whether it is scientific. Instead, evaluate it by asking: Does the approach raise questions you did not previously consider, and offer insight into things you did not understand as well before? On those questions, I suspect, psychoanalytic theory will earn better than a passing grade.

WRAPPING IT UP

SUMMARY

Interpreting Freud

- Freud died more than half a century ago, but his theory lives on and continues to stimulate controversy and argument.

Latter-Day Issues and Theorists

- Many modern writers have altered Freud's ideas in various degrees through their summaries and interpretations.

- In addition, neo-Freudian theorists proposed their own versions of psychoanalysis. Most of these revised theories include less emphasis on sex and more emphasis on ego functioning and interpersonal relations.

- Alfred Adler wrote about adult strivings to overcome early childhood feelings of inferiority.

- Carl Jung proposed ideas concerning the collective unconscious; the outer, social version of the self called the persona; the concepts of animus and anima; the distinction between extraversion and introversion; and four basic types of thinking.

- Karen Horney developed a neo-Freudian theory of feminine psychology and also described the nature of basic anxiety and associated neurotic needs.

- Erik Erikson developed a detailed description of the stages of psychosocial development during which children and adults must come to terms with their changing life circumstances. Unlike Freud, Erikson extended his account of development through adulthood and old age.

- The object relations theorists, notably Melanie Klein and D. W. Winnicott, described the complex relationships people have with important emotional objects; they also observed that these relationships mix pleasure and pain, and love and hate. It is difficult to relate to other people as whole and complex human beings, and people often feel guilty about their mixed emotions and need to defend against them.

Current Psychoanalytic Research

- Modern psychologists interested in psychoanalysis are bringing rigorous research methodology to bear on some of the hundreds of hypotheses that could be derived from psychoanalytic theory. Evidence has supported some of these hypotheses, such as the existence of unconscious mental processes and phenomena like repression and transference.

Psychoanalysis in Perspective

- Research confirms five basic principles that are consistent with psychoanalytic thought, but, in the end, psychoanalysis might best be evaluated not in terms of the answers it has offered, but in terms of the questions it continues to raise.

KEY TERMS

neo-Freudian psychology, p. 398
ego psychology, p. 399
organ inferiority, p. 400
masculine protest, p. 400
collective unconscious, p. 401
archetypes, p. 401
persona, p. 401
anima, p. 402
animus, p. 402
object relations theory, p. 406

THINK ABOUT IT

1. Why does Freudian theory make some people so angry? Is this reaction justified? For example, Freudian theory is undeniably sexist. Is this a legitimate cause for anger?

2. Does psychoanalysis overestimate the importance of sex? How far-reaching are the effects of sex on human life?

3. Why might one buy a vehicle such as a Humvee? Is it possible that buyers might not know all of their reasons for wanting such a vehicle? Have you seen advertisements that seem to target hidden motives for buying things — in particular, large trucks or powerful automobiles?

4. Have you noticed that the same character types tend to show up in books, movies, and television programs? What are some examples? Could Jung's idea of a collective unconscious have anything to do with this?

5. Are people the age of your parents (or professors) still growing and changing? In what ways? Do you see psychological differences, for example, between people the age of your parents and people the age of your grandparents?

6. Must love always be mixed somewhat with frustration and resentment (as object relations theorists claim)?

7. Do you know anybody who brought a transitional object with them to college? (Did you?) What purpose does it serve? Would the person (or you) be upset if the object was lost? Why?

8. Is it possible to prove psychoanalytic ideas right or wrong using experiments?

9. Every time this textbook is revised, somebody advises the author to delete the chapters on Freud and psychoanalysis because they are not scientific nor relevant to modern research. Obviously, I haven't taken this advice yet, but should I, next time?

SUGGESTED RESOURCES

Online

Meehl, P.E. (1989) *Philosophical Psychology* (lectures 11 and 12). University of Minnesota. http://meehl.umn.edu/recordings/philosophical-psychology-1989

> *The late Paul Meehl was one of the most respected psychometricians and methodologists in personality psychology in the 20th century. The lectures in his graduate course on the philosophy of methodology are fascinating and, thanks to the University of Minnesota, on-line for free viewing. I recommend all of them, but of special interest for this chapter are lectures 11 and 12, where he makes an argument for taking Freud seriously despite the lack of formal experimental evidence for the theory.*

Print

Block, J. (2002). *Personality as an affect-processing system: Toward an integrative theory*. Mahwah, NJ: Erlbaum.

> *A brilliant summary of a model of personality that integrates fundamental tenets of psychoanalytic thought with the state of the art in modern personality research.*

Crews, F. (2017). *Freud: The making of an illusion.* New York: Metropolitan Books/ Henry Holt.

> *The latest of this author's several books attacking Freud. The argument is that Freud was an unoriginal, unethical, deceptive fraud. If you want to see a pure distillation of the anti-Freud viewpoint, this is the place to go. One skeptical reviewer of this book observed that "it seems fair to ask what keeps driving him [the author] back to stab the corpse again" (Prochnik, 2017, p 20).*

Shaver, P. R., & Mikulincer, M. (2005). Attachment theory and research: Resurrection of the psychodynamic approach to personality. *Journal of Research in Personality, 39*, 22–45.

> *A fairly brief but remarkably thorough summary of the argument that attachment theory can integrate psychoanalysis with a wide range of modern research in cognitive, social, developmental, and personality psychology. The article includes clear summaries of important recent experiments that are beginning to make psychoanalytic ideas increasingly susceptible to empirical investigation.*

Westen, D. (1998). The scientific legacy of Sigmund Freud: Toward a psycho-dynamically informed psychological science. *Psychological Bulletin, 124*, 333–371.

> *A thorough and highly readable summary of some of the modern research evidence that supports many of Freud's key ideas.*

Want to earn a better grade on your test?

Go to **INQUIZITIVE** to learn and review this chapter's content, with personalized feedback along the way.

PART V

EXPERIENCE AND AWARENESS
Humanistic and Cross-Cultural Psychology

Individuals have different points of view. Fans of opposing teams, watching the same game, may come away with drastically different impressions of who fouled whom and which side the referees favored (Hastorf & Cantril, 1954). Or, of more consequence, one person may see a woman exercising a free choice about what to do with her own body and whether to start a family, while another person, observing exactly the same behavior, may see the murder of an unborn child.

Humanistic psychology, the main topic of Chapter 12, is based on the premise that to understand a person you must understand her unique view of reality. It focuses on phenomenology, which comprises everything a person hears, feels, and thinks, lies near the center of human experience, and may even be the basis of free will. The other approaches to personality tend to regard people, at least implicitly, almost like things that can be dispassionately examined under the psychological microscope. Humanistic psychology emphasizes that the object of the psychologist's scrutiny is a fellow human who can and does scrutinize right back.

Because humanistic psychologists emphasize the part of psychology that is uniquely human, they pay particular attention to an issue that other psychologists generally ignore: the meaning of life. One view is that people are essentially selfish and life is intrinsically meaningless. A more cheerful perspective suggests that people are basically good and achieve meaning by rising above selfish concerns, serving others, and making the world a better place. Over the years, humanistic psychology has evolved toward an increased emphasis on the latter, optimistic view—to the extent that many of its modern proponents travel under the banner of "positive psychology."

A prime concern is one particular aspect of phenomenology: happiness. Among the insights from positive psychology is that two people in the same objective circumstances may vary greatly in how happy they are, which goes back to the fundamental phenomenological principle that reality is what you make it.

Phenomenological considerations also raise this interesting question: If everybody's view of the world is different, which one is right? Or, in the midst of shifting perceptions, where is reality? The question turns out to be unanswerable, but it is critical nonetheless. Asking this question acknowledges that none of us has an exclusive ownership of truth, and other points of view—even those that seem drastically different, foreign, or strange—may have an equal claim to validity.

This latter insight is the basis of the cross-cultural study of personality, the topic of Chapter 13. Not only do different individuals have different views of reality, but different cultures do, too. A behavior seen as polite by a Japanese person may seem frustratingly inefficient to a North American, and the same action considered ordinary by a Dane may seem dangerously irresponsible to a New Yorker. In recent years, psychologists have paid increasing attention to the degree to which theories of personality forged in Western cultures do or do not apply to people around the world. Cross-cultural psychologists also address a further key question raised by the phenomenological approach to personality: If different cultures have different worldviews, what happens to values? Who is to judge what is right and what is wrong?

The following two chapters, therefore, address the same phenomenological premise— that the way you experience the world is the most important psychological fact about you. Chapter 12 examines this premise at the individual level, and Chapter 13 examines the same idea at the cultural level. Both approaches pose the challenge of trying to see the world the same way as someone else—whether a close friend or a member of a different culture. From a humanistic, phenomenological perspective, this is the only way to understand a person.

12

HUMANISTIC PSYCHOLOGY, POSITIVE PSYCHOLOGY, AND THE SCIENCE OF HAPPINESS

The story is told of how Watergate burglar G. Gordon Liddy liked to impress people by holding his hand steadily above a lit candle as his flesh burned. "How can you do that? Doesn't it hurt?" he was asked. "Of course it hurts. The trick," he replied, "is not to care."[1]

PSYCHOLOGY IS A FUNNY kind of science, because the object of its scrutiny is also the one doing the scrutinizing. Psychologists typically do the best they can to ignore this embarrassing complication. Instead, they try to think about people and the human mind as interesting phenomena that can be examined in the same dispassionate, objective, and precise way that one might examine a rock, a mollusk, or a molecule. Psychologists are eager to have the prestige of "real" scientists and, as I mentioned back in Chapter 2, are sometimes accused of suffering from "physics envy." I actually don't think that most psychologists envy physicists,[2] but many do believe that the best way to understand the human mind is by emulating the physical and biological sciences and their principles of public data, objective analysis, repeatability, and so on.

---

[1] I heard this existential fable from Lily Tomlin, who told it during a performance of *The Search for Signs of Intelligent Life in the Universe*, a play by Jane Wagner. Ms. Tomlin seems reliable on other matters, so perhaps this story is true.
[2] It looks like too much work.

The contradiction built into this approach was caricatured by humanistic psychologist George Kelly:

> I, being a psychologist, and therefore a scientist, am performing this experiment in order to improve the prediction and control of certain human phenomena; but my subject, being merely a human organism, is obviously propelled by inexorable drives welling up within him, or else he is in gluttonous pursuit of sustenance and shelter. (Kelly, 1955, p. 5)

The goal of **humanistic psychology** is to overcome this paradox by acknowledging and addressing the ways in which psychology is unique. The classic humanistic psychologists vehemently disagreed with the idea that the study of the mind is just another science, or that it could or should resemble physics or chemistry. As an object of study, they argued, the mind is not just different from things such as molecules or atoms; it is fundamentally different.

It is fundamentally different because the human mind is aware. It knows it is being studied and has opinions about itself that affect the way it is studied. This fact has two implications. First, psychology needs to address this unique phenomenon of awareness rather than brush it under the rug. Second, and even more important, self-awareness brings to the fore many uniquely human phenomena that do not arise when the object of study is a rock, a molecule, or even another animal. These phenomena include willpower, mindfulness, imagination, self-criticism, aspirations, creativity, virtues, happiness, and, above all, free will. Self-awareness lies at the center of all of these phenomena, and yet the rest of psychology tends to ignore them (Maddi & Costa, 1972; Seligman & Csikszentmihalyi, 2000). That is where humanistic psychologists come in. Their job, as they see it, is to ask questions about awareness, free will, happiness, and the many related aspects of the mind that are uniquely human and that give life meaning (see **Table 12.1**). But what is self-awareness? What is free will? What is happiness? And, most difficult of all, what is the meaning of life?[3] These weighty questions, raised by the original humanistic psychologists and their modern-day successors, are among the topics of this chapter.

PHENOMENOLOGY: AWARENESS IS EVERYTHING

The central insight of humanistic psychology is that one's conscious experience of the world, also called a person's **phenomenology**, is psychologically more important than the world itself. And that summary may be an understatement. Proponents of phenomenological approaches to psychology sometimes assume

---

[3] 42.

Table 12.1	EIGHT ELEMENTS OF HUMANISTIC PSYCHOLOGY
Element	**Definition**
Humanistic	Study of humans, not animals
Holistic	Human system is greater than sum of its parts
Historic	Whole person from birth to death
Phenomenological	Focus on interior, experiential, and existential aspects of personality
Real life	Person in nature, society, and culture—not just the experimental lab
Positivity	Joy, fruitful activities, virtuous actions and attributes
Will	Choices, decisions, voluntary actions
Value	A philosophy of life that describes what is desirable

Note: The table summarizes eight essential elements of humanistic psychology, described at a talk given by Henry Murray in 1964, as reconstructed by Taylor (2000, p. 37).

that immediate, conscious experience is all that matters. Everything that has happened to you in the past, everything that is true about you now, and anything that might happen in the future can influence you only by affecting your thoughts and feelings at this moment. Indeed, from a phenomenological viewpoint, the only place and time in which you exist is in your consciousness, right here, right now. The past, the future, other people, and other places are no more than ideas and, in a sense, illusions. The sense is this: A broader reality might exist, but only the part of it that you perceive—or invent—matters or ever will matter to you. Your hand might be on fire, but the trick, as G. Gordon Liddy observed, is not to care. More importantly, the realization that only your present experience matters is the basis of free will. The past is gone and the future is not here yet. You are here now and can *choose* what to think, feel, and do.

> From a phenomenological viewpoint, the only place and time in which you exist is in your consciousness, right here, right now. The past, the future, other people, and other places are no more than ideas and, in a sense, illusions.

This may all sound rather New Age, but phenomenological analysis is not a recent idea. The Talmud says, "We do not see things as they are. We see them as we are." Epictetus, a Greek Stoic philosopher who lived 2,000 years ago, said, "It is not things in themselves that trouble us, but our opinions of things." Likewise, Marcus Aurelius, the Roman emperor and general who seems to have been one of G. Gordon Liddy's role models, wrote, "If you are distressed by anything external, the pain is not due to the thing itself, but to your estimate of it; and this you have the power to revoke at any moment." More recently, but still more than half a century ago, Carl Rogers (1951, p. 484) wrote, "I do not react to some absolute reality, but to my perception of this reality. It is this perception which for me is reality" (see McAdams, 1990).

Your particular experience of the world is called your **construal**. Your construal, which might be different from anybody else's, forms the basis of how you live your life, including the goals you pursue and the obstacles and opportunities you perceive. How would you view a chance to travel? It would open exciting possibilities and might, at the same time, raise significant risks. How about starting a new relationship? This could be the first step toward an emotionally fulfilling life or, viewed another way, a possible path toward rejection and despair. Research shows that situational construals are related to both personality and gender (Sherman, Nave, & Funder, 2013). Narcissists (see Chapter 6) are relatively likely to construe the situations they experience as putting them at the focus of attention, and people high in openness to experience (also see Chapter 6) are especially likely to construe situations as including intellectual and artistic stimulation. Men are more likely than women to perceive a potential for threat or blame; women are more likely to perceive the need for people to be supportive but also are more likely to perceive a need to be assertive.

While these relations with personality and gender appear to be reliable, the correlations with situational construal are not large, and there is still plenty of room for other influences including, possibly, free choice. Indeed, humanist psychologists believe, it is by choosing your construal of the world—deciding how to interpret your experience—that you can achieve free will (Boss, 1963). And it is by leaving this choice to other people or to society that you lose your autonomy and, in a sense, your soul. (I will say more about this later.)

These observations imply that psychology has a special duty to study how people perceive, understand, and experience reality. In 19th-century Leipzig, Germany, Wilhelm Wundt founded one of the first psychological laboratories. The primary method he followed was **introspection**, in which his research assistants tried to observe their own perceptions and thought processes (Wundt, 1894). But the roots of psychology's interest in phenomenology go back even further, to the existential philosophers.

EXISTENTIALISM

Existentialism is a broad philosophical movement that began in Europe in the mid-1800s. Søren Kierkegaard, the Danish theologian, was one of its early proponents, as were Friedrich Nietzsche, Martin Heidegger, and more recently Ludwig Binswanger, Medard Boss, and Jean-Paul Sartre.

Existentialism arose as a reaction against European rationalism, science, and the Industrial Revolution. The existentialists thought that by the late 19th century, rationality had gone too far in its attempt to account for everything. In particular, they thought science, technology, and rational philosophy had lost touch with human experience. This point of view began to catch on among European philosophers after World War II, which through its previously unimaginable carnage seemed to have disproved much of what they previously had assumed was true about progress, civilization, human nature, and even the meaning of life. The purpose of existential philosophy was to regain contact with the basic experiences of being alive and aware.

Existential analysis begins with the concrete and specific experience of a human being *existing* at a particular moment in time and space. An excellent example is you, right now. (I mean, then, back when you read the words "right now," although that is already past, so maybe we should concentrate on right *now*, instead. Oops, too late.) The point is, your experience of existence happens one infinitesimally small moment at a time, which is then gone and followed by another.

The key existential questions are: What is the nature of existence? How does it feel? And what does it mean?

The Three Parts of Experience

According to existential psychologist Ludwig Binswanger, if you look deeply into your own mind, you will find that the conscious experience of being alive has three components (Binswanger, 1958).

The first component is biological experience, or **Umwelt**, which consists of the sensations you feel by virtue of being a biological organism. Umwelt includes pleasure, pain, heat, cold, and all the bodily sensations. Poke your finger with a pin: The experience is Umwelt.

The second component is social experience, or **Mitwelt**, which consists of what you think and feel as a social being. Your emotions and thoughts about other people and the emotions and thoughts directed at you make up Mitwelt. Think about someone you love, fear, or admire. The experience is Mitwelt.

The third component is inner, psychological experience, or **Eigenwelt**. In a sense, this is the experience of experience itself. It consists of how you feel and think when you try to understand yourself, your own mind, and your own existence. Eigenwelt includes introspection (and we can presume that Binswanger himself felt it strongly when trying to figure out the components of experience). Try to watch your own mind having the experience of a pinprick, or the experience of love, or even the experience of thinking about this paragraph. It's a little bewildering, isn't it? When you observe your own mind and feelings in this way, the (often confusing) experience is Eigenwelt.

"Thrown-ness" and Angst

An important basis of your experience is your **thrown-ness**—Heidegger used the German word *Geworfenheit*. This term refers to the time, place, and circumstances into which you happened to be born (Heidegger, 1927/1962). Your experience obviously is affected by whether you were "thrown" into a medieval slave society, or a 17th-century Native American society, or an early 21st-century industrialized society.

From an existential perspective, this last way of being thrown—yours—is particularly difficult. Existence in modern society is difficult because the world seems to have no overarching meaning or purpose. Religion plays a relatively small role compared with the past. Its modern substitutes—science, art, and philosophy—have failed to provide an alternative worldview that can tell you the two things you most need to know:

1. Why am I here?
2. What should I be doing?

According to existential philosophy, there are no answers to these two concerns beyond those you invent for yourself.

Difficulty in answering these questions leads to anxiety about the meaning of life and whether you are spending yours the right way. After all, life is short, and you get only one—waste it, and you waste everything. The unpleasant feelings caused by contemplating these concerns is called *existential anxiety*, or **Angst**. According to Sartre (1965), Angst can be analyzed into three separate sensations: anguish, forlornness, and despair.

Every conscious human feels *anguish* because choices, though inevitable, are never perfect. A choice to do good in one way can lead to bad outcomes in other ways. For example, deciding to aid one person may leave others to suffer. Such trade-offs are inescapable, according to Sartre, so the resulting anguish is inescapable, too.

Furthermore, nothing and no one—no god, no unquestionable set of rules or values—can guide your choices or let you off the hook for what you have decided. Your choices are yours alone. (Sartre also says that even if there is a god who tells you what to do, you still must decide whether to do what God says—so you remain alone in your choice.) Furthermore, there is no escape from this existential solitude: So there you are, *forlorn*, alone with your choices.

Finally, any aware person realizes that many outcomes are beyond control, including some of the most important elements of life. If you acknowledge this momentous and regrettable fact, you also will feel *despair* at your inability to change crucial aspects of the world. This inability, according to Sartre, only redoubles your responsibility to affect those aspects of the world that you can influence.

Bad Faith

What should you do about Angst and all of these other unpleasant-sounding experiences? According to existentialists such as Sartre, you must face them directly. It is a moral imperative, they believe, to face your own mortality and the apparent meaninglessness of life, and to seek purpose for your existence nonetheless. This is your existential responsibility, which requires existential courage, or what Sartre called *optimistic toughness* (1965, p. 49).

Of course, there is a way out, at least temporarily, that requires neither courage nor toughness: avoid the problem altogether. Quit worrying about what life means, get a good job, buy a big car, and advance your social status. Do as you are told by society, convention, your peer group, political propaganda, religious dogma, and advertising. Lead the unexamined life. Existentialists call this head-in-the-sand approach *living in bad faith*. Although ignoring existential issues in this way is very common, the existentialists point out that it has three problems.

The first problem, they say, is that to ignore the troubling facts of existence is to live a cowardly lie; it is immoral and amounts to selling your soul for comfort. You only get one short life, and you are giving up its very meaning if you refuse to examine the substance of your experience. Existentially speaking, you might as well be a rock.

In his novel *Cat's Cradle*, Kurt Vonnegut (1963) proposed that a human being is really no more than a pile of lucky mud. (After all, the human body is chemically not much different from the dirt it walks on, except that it is about 70 percent water). The only difference, says Vonnegut, is that this mass of person-shaped mud is up and walking around. More important, it has awareness, so it can look around and experience the world. The other mud, that stuff underfoot, does not get to do that. It just lies there, ignorant of all the interesting things happening above.

And that is Vonnegut's good news. The bad news is that this luck cannot last. Sooner or later (at death), the chemicals that make up the body begin to break down and turn back into earth. The Bible says people come from the earth and return to it; that is Vonnegut's point as well.

Therefore, it is imperative not to waste this brief period of lucky awareness. As long as you are alive-and-aware mud, and not just regular mud, you must experience as much of the world as possible, as vividly as possible. In particular, you need to be aware of your luck and know it won't last—this is your only chance. The tragedy, from an existential perspective, is that many people never do this. They lead unexamined lives, never realizing how fortunate they are to be alive and aware, and they eventually lose their awareness forever without realizing how special it was.

A second, more pragmatic problem with living in bad faith is that, even if you manage to ignore troubling existential issues by surrounding yourself with material comforts, you still will not be happy. Indeed, research shows that most people would rather live a meaningful life than be wealthy (L. A. King & Napa, 1998), and that experiences promote happiness more than possessions do (Van Boven, 2005).

The person who chooses the material path, therefore, might occasionally suffer a tantalizing, frustrating glimpse of the more satisfying life that could have been if she had made different choices. These dark moments of the soul may pass quickly, but until one owns up to existential responsibility and thinks seriously about what is really important, such moments will continue to sneak up.

The third problem with the ostrich approach to existential issues is that it is impossible, because choosing not to worry about the meaning of life and surrendering your choices to external authorities is still a choice. As Sartre (1965) put it, "What is not possible is not to choose . . . If I do not choose, I am still choosing" (p. 54). Thus, there is no exit from the existential dilemma, even if you can fool yourself into thinking that there is.

Authentic Existence

The existentialists' preferred alternative to bad faith is to courageously come to terms with the facts: You are mortal, your life is short, and you are master of your own destiny within those limits. This approach, called *authentic existence* (Binswanger, 1963) entails being honest, insightful, and morally correct.

Authentic existence will not relieve you from loneliness and unhappiness; a courageous examination of conscious experience reveals the awful truth that every person is alone and doomed. Life has no meaning beyond what you give it, which means that any apparent meaning it might seem to have is an illusion. The essence

RECIPES FROM THE
JEAN-PAUL SARTRE COOKBOOK

Free Will Soup

Fill a pot with water. Then add anything you want, or add nothing, or pour the water out. It's up to you.

Angsty Tuna Salad

Get out all the stuff to make a nice tuna salad. But maybe you want a grilled cheese. How do you know?

Any Cake At All

Buy a mix, make a cake, take it out of the oven, frost it, look at it, look at yourself. What is this all about?

of human experience is this discovery: The human being is the only animal that understands it must die.

This is pretty stern stuff. Psychologists have noted that the terror inspired by the prospect of death can cause people to distort reality in many different ways in order to feel better (Pyszczynski et al., 1997), and may be the basis of culture itself as "humans must balance a propensity for life with an awareness of the inevitability of death" (Matsumoto, 2006, pp. 35–36). In other words, existentialism is not for wimps (McAdams, 1990). It takes moral courage to cast aside defense mechanisms and the veneer of culture, and peer into the void of mortality and meaninglessness. When existentialist philosopher Friedrich Nietzsche did this, he decided the most honorable response was to rise above it all and become a *superman*. Nietzsche's superman did not wear a cape and tights, however. Instead, his ideal person sought to triumph over the apparent meaninglessness of life by developing the existential strength to face what must be faced. It turns out this is easier said than done. Nietszche never managed to become a superman himself; he went insane and died in an asylum.

Jean-Paul Sartre tried to be both more realistic and a little more optimistic. He sometimes expressed annoyance with people who considered existentialism gloomy, although one wonders what else he could expect, given his claim that the basic elements of existence are anguish, forlornness, and despair. Sartre lightened this load a little with his claim that only through existential analysis can people regain awareness of their freedom. He wrote that existential theory "is the only one which gives man dignity, the only one which does not reduce him to an object" (Sartre, 1965, p. 51). He believed that the existential challenge is to do all you can to better the human condition, even in the face of life's uncertainties.

A similar lesson was offered by existential philosopher Viktor Frankl (1959/1992), who advised that you can become stronger in the face of difficult circumstances if, instead of asking, "What do I want from life?" you can move to asking, "What does life want from me?" Frankl's advice has some empirical support. One study found that people who endorsed such statements as "I strive to make this world a better place" and "I accept my limitations" felt more hope and less depression over the following two months (Mascaro & Rosen, 2005). They also were more likely to report that they had "found a really significant meaning for leading my life." This finding offers a place where philosophy, psychology, and the teachings of many religious traditions come together: Sometimes the best thing you can do for yourself is to do something for somebody else.

"What is this endless series of meaningless experiences trying to teach me?"

The Eastern Alternative

The core view of the existentialists summarized so far in this chapter seems rather gloomy, given the way it harps on individual isolation, mortality, and the difficulty of finding meaning in life. Whatever you think of this philosophy, notice that it is fundamentally European, Western, and focused on the individual. We will consider other cultural differences between Eastern and Western points of view in Chapter 13, but for now just notice how existentialism begins with the experience of the single individual at a single moment in time. All else, it claims, is illusion. The fundamental reality is your own experience at this moment—the past, the future, and the experiences of other people are forever closed off.

From the perspective of the Eastern religions that influence most of the people on earth (such as in China, India, and Japan) and that are often associated with collectivist cultures, this analysis has everything backwards. Consider Zen Buddhism (see Mosig, 1989, 1999; Rahula, 1974). The key idea of Buddhism is **anatta**, or "nonself," the idea that the independent, singular self you sense inside your mind is merely an illusion. French philosopher René Descartes believed that the existence of his own singular self was the one thing he could be sure of; Buddhism teaches that he was overconfident. What feels like your "self" is merely a temporary composite of many things—including your physiology, environment, social setting, and society—all of which are constantly changing. There is no unchanging soul at the center of all this, just a momentary coming together of all these influences that, in the next moment, is gone, only to be replaced by another. The writer Gertrude Stein once said of Oakland, California, "There's no there there."[4] That's what the Buddha says about the self.

> René Descartes believed that the existence of his own singular self was the one thing he could be sure of; Buddhism teaches that he was overconfident.

Furthermore, Buddhism teaches that this illusion of having a separate and independent self is harmful. The illusion leads to feelings of isolation—such as tormented the existentialists—and an excessive concern with "me" and that which is "mine." The true nature of reality is that everything and everyone are interconnected now, and not only in this moment but also across time. It is not true, according to Buddhism, that all you have is your own experience, now. Rather, there is nothing special about your experience or about the moment labeled "the present." All consciousness and all of time have equal claim to existence and are equally important, and time flows not from past to present to future, but from present to present to present (Yozan Mosig, personal communication, November 6, 2000). In a similar fashion, a single person is just one of many. Your existence

---

[4] This was a very mean and unfair thing for her to say. Oakland is a lovely city that offers fine views of San Francisco.

is no more or less real or important than anyone else's. The more important fact is that all people are interconnected.

This viewpoint might seem to diminish the importance of the self, but, in a way, it enhances it. The Buddhist view implies that instead of being forever alone and powerless, you are an integral and interconnected part of the universe and it is part of you, just as the present moment is made of equal parts past and future. Moreover, you are immortal in the sense that you are part of something larger than yourself that will last forever.

If you can begin to grasp these ideas, your selfish thoughts and fears about the future will fall away. You will understand the idea of **anicca**, that all things must pass and it is best to accept this fact instead of repressing or fighting it. The current moment is not particularly important; all moments in the past and future have equal status. The well-being of others matters just as much as your own, because the boundaries between you and them are illusory. These ideas are difficult to grasp, especially for persons raised in Western cultures, and true understanding can be the work of a lifetime. If you do achieve it, you are said to be *enlightened*. Enlightenment is manifested by caring for others the same as for yourself, which leads to universal compassion; according to Buddhism, this is the essence of wisdom and leads to a serene, selfless state called **nirvana**. This definitely sounds better than anguish, forlornness, and despair.

OPTIMISTIC HUMANISM: ROGERS AND MASLOW

America has a reputation—partially deserved—of being a cultural melting pot. So, perhaps it was only natural that two American psychologists would mix European existential philosophy, the less isolated Eastern view of the self, and a stereotypically American can-do attitude to yield an optimistic philosophy of life. Beginning in the early 1940s, Carl Rogers and Abraham Maslow developed related approaches to humanistic psychology. They began with the standard existential assumptions that phenomenology is central and that people have free will, and then added another crucial idea—that people are basically good: They seek to relate closely with one another, and they have an innate need to improve themselves and the world. It is important to bear in mind that this optimistic view is an added *assumption*; Rogers, Maslow, and other humanists believe it but can offer no proof. What kind of evidence would be relevant? All theories begin with assumptions, though, and this one is not particularly extreme. So let us take a closer look at humanistic psychology and see where it leads.

Self-Actualization: Rogers

Carl Rogers changed the tone and much of the message of the classic existential and phenomenological analysis when he proposed that "the organism [by which he means any person] has one basic tendency and striving—to actualize, maintain, and enhance the experiencing organism [itself]" (Rogers, 1951, p. 487). According to Rogers's theory, a person can be understood only from the perspective of her *phenomenal field*, which is the entire panorama of conscious experience. This is where everything comes together—unconscious conflicts, environmental influences, memories, hopes, and so on. These contents of the mind combine in different ways at every moment, and the combinations give rise to ongoing conscious experience. So far, this resembles the standard phenomenological fare we considered earlier.

Rogers added a new aspect, however, when he posited that people have a basic need to *actualize*, that is, to maintain and enhance life. (This need has much in common with Freud's notion of libido as it was interpreted in Chapter 10.) The goal of existence is to satisfy this need. This assumption led Rogers to differ sharply with traditional existentialists who believed that existence has no intrinsic goal.

The Hierarchy of Needs: Maslow

Abraham Maslow developed his theory (1943, 1987) about the same time as Rogers and ended up being almost as influential. Maslow's theory of humanistic psychology begins with the same basic assumption as Rogers's: A person's ultimate need or motive is to self-actualize. However, Maslow claimed that this motive becomes active only if the person's more basic needs are met first. According to Maslow, human motivation is characterized by a *hierarchy of needs* (see **Figure 12.1**). First, a person requires food, water, safety, and the other essentials of survival. When those are in hand, the person then seeks sex, meaningful relationships, prestige, and money. Only when those desires are satisfied does the person turn to the quest for self-actualization. In other words, someone starving to death is not particularly concerned with the higher aspects of existence. In this belief, Maslow is also at odds with traditional existentialists, who would insist that even an individual who is starving has free choice in what to concern himself with.

Maslow's theory is surprisingly practical because it is relevant to topics such as career choice and employee motivation. Consider your own ambitions: What kind of career are you seeking? My parents grew up during the Great Depression of the 1930s and remained acutely aware of the dangers of being unemployed, homeless, and even starving—not that

Figure 12.1 Maslow's Hierarchy of Needs As an individual's needs lower in the pyramid are fulfilled, the higher needs become more important.

any of this ever happened to them, but they had lived through an era during which these outcomes were a real possibility for an unusually large number of Americans. As a result, like others of their generation, they put a premium on finding a career path that was, above everything else, safe. Making a lot of money was not the issue; rather, choosing a field where "you can always get a job," as they repeatedly said, was the way to ensure survival and stability. My father dreamed of being an architect. For most of his career, he worked as an accountant.

You can imagine their reaction when I declared a psychology major![5] But the reason I felt free to do this was precisely because of my parents' success: The issues of homelessness and survival they faced never seemed quite real to me. I took that level of security for granted, which, in Maslow's terms, freed me to move up the hierarchy of needs and choose a field based on its possibilities for self-expression.

At the university where I teach, a large number of students are children of first- or second-generation immigrants; many are from Asia or Latin America. Their situation is not so different from mine at their age. Their parents took risks to come to America in search of opportunity and financial security. And, like my parents, many of my students' parents do not quite understand why their children would choose a major as seemingly impractical as psychology. But again, when a child of immigrant parents chooses a career because of its opportunities for self-expression rather than financial security, this is evidence that her parents have succeeded. She takes security for granted and is therefore willing to take risks to accomplish more.

Maslow's theory is also relevant to employee motivation (see also Chapter 16). The most expensive part of any organization's budget is its payroll. So it is crucial that employees apply their initiative and imagination to the organization's goals. Smart managers understand two things: (a) Employees will not show initiative and imagination unless they feel secure, and (b) employees who feel secure want something besides more money—they want to express themselves through their work by identifying with the organization's goals and contributing to them. At this writing, one of the most successful companies in the United States is Southwest Airlines (and it is one of very few airlines that has not at some point flirted with bankruptcy). It has never laid off an employee. And while it does not pay as much as some of its competitors, it goes to extraordinary lengths to make each employee feel like a valuable part of the organization, with everything from regular company parties to open meetings with management where employees at any level can make suggestions to the boss.

The hierarchy of needs can also be used to explain how people in different cultures may have different bases of happiness. According to one study of 39 nations (including more than 54,000 survey participants), people in poorer nations

---

[5] My father was almost as upset as my sister was (see Chapter 10).

were happier when they had more money, whereas people in richer nations were happier when their home life was going well (Oishi, Diener, Lucas, & Suh, 1999). To be exact, according to a meta-analysis that summarized many different studies, in poorer countries the average correlation (see Chapter 3) between well-being and economic status was $r = .28$, and in richer countries the average was only $r = .10$ (Howell & Howell, 2008). These findings demonstrate one of Maslow's key points: Money is most important when you have very little. After a certain point, it becomes less important to happiness (though we often seek it anyway); our emotional needs and, in particular, our relationships with others grow to matter more.

An update to Maslow's 70-year-old theory comes from the direction of evolutionary psychology. Evolutionary psychologist Douglas Kenrick and his colleagues proposed a revised hierarchy of human motives (Kenrick, Griskevicius, Neuberg, & Schaller, 2010; see **Figure 12.2**). As I hope you recall from Chapter 9, the ultimate evolutionary imperative of every organism, including people, is to reproduce and keep the species going. In Kenrick's pyramid, this is the ultimate goal, on the top, but a person has to get there in stages, just as in Maslow's. First, one has to fulfill immediate physiological needs for survival, then protect oneself, find allies and friends, seek status, find a mate, keep a mate, and raise children—in that order. All of these activities continue throughout life, of course, but first things do

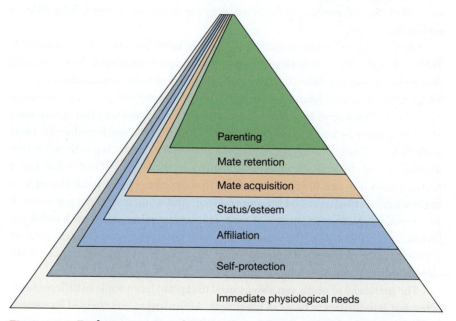

Figure 12.2 Evolutionary-Based Hierarchy of Human Motives This pyramid shows the sequence of the development of motives according to recent evolutionary theorizing.

Source: Kenrick et al. (2010), p. 293.

have to come first. The updated pyramid makes more sense, from an evolutionary point of view, than Maslow's original one, but I wonder what Maslow would have thought about it. My guess is he would have seen it as missing the whole point of humanistic psychology: People are *not* animals, and must be understood in a completely different way.

The Fully Functioning Person

Maslow and Rogers believed that the best way to live is to become more clearly aware of reality and of yourself. If you can perceive the world accurately and without neurotic distortion, and if you take responsibility for your choices, then you become what Rogers called a *fully functioning person*, who lives what the existentialists would call an authentic existence—except that the fully functioning person is happy. A fully functioning person faces the world without fear, self-doubt, or neurotic defenses. Doing this becomes possible only if you have experienced *unconditional positive regard* from the important people in your life, especially during childhood. Maslow disagreed slightly; he believed that anybody from any background could become a fully functioning person. However, if you feel that other people value you only if you are smart, successful, attractive, or good, then according to Rogers, you will develop *conditions of worth*.

Conditions of worth are the idea that we are taught, almost from the cradle, that we are good and valuable people only *if* we fulfill certain criteria. In current society, these criteria include being young, healthy, good-looking, and prosperous. Now look through the photographs that adorn just about any college textbook. Who is usually portrayed in these photos? People who are young, healthy, good-looking, and prosperous. Posed in attractive settings, most of them look like professional models, probably because they *are* professional models. One could call this genre of pictures—and it is a genre in its own right—"Happy Laughing Undergraduates" (see **Figure 12.3**). How do pictures like these affect people who don't fit this ideal—which is, by the way, just about all of us? If nothing else, they advertise the usual conditions of worth and, in most cases, serve as subtle reminders that we don't quite measure up.

Conditions of worth limit your freedom to act and think. If you believe you are valuable only if certain things about you are true, then you may distort your perception of reality so you can believe them even if they are not true. If you think you are valuable only if your behavior conforms to certain rules and expectations, you may lose your ability to choose what to do. Both of these limitations violate the existential imperatives to see the world as it is, choose freely, and take complete responsibility for all of your actions.

A person who has experienced unconditional positive regard from parents and other important people, and has managed to avoid being overly influenced by media portrayals of unrealistic perfection, does not develop such conditions of

Figure 12.3 **Happy Laughing Undergraduates** This is a typical textbook illustration. What message does it send?

worth. This achievement can lead to a life free from existential anxiety, because the person will be confident of her value. She will not need to follow rules, because her sense of innate goodness leads her to make the right choices. A fully functioning person lives a life rich in emotion and self-discovery, and is reflective, spontaneous, flexible, adaptable, confident, trusting, creative, self-reliant, ethical, open-minded—you get the idea. She is also "more understanding of others and more accepting of others as separate individuals" (Rogers, 1951, p. 520).

Psychotherapy

The goal of Rogerian psychotherapy, and humanistic psychotherapy in general, is to help the client become a fully functioning person. To achieve this goal, the therapist develops a genuine and caring relationship with the client and provides unconditional positive regard (Levine, 2006). This technique is sometimes caricatured: The patient says something like, "I would really like to kill you with a knife," and the therapist—reluctant to impose conditions of worth—replies, "You feel you want to kill me with a knife. Uh-huh."

This portrayal is probably unfair—Rogers once stated he would stop a murderer—but it captures the basic idea that, in his view, the therapist's job is (1) to help the client perceive his own thoughts and feelings without the therapist seeking to change them in any way, and (2) to make the client feel appreciated no matter what he thinks, says, or does. This process allows insight and the removal of conditions of worth, the theory goes, and helps the client become a fully functioning person.

Rogerian psychotherapy requires enormous amounts of time and, from the therapist, the patience (and perhaps the courage) of a saint. What is the result of this kind of therapy? Although research on the effects of psychotherapy is extraordinarily difficult to conduct, Rogers and his followers tried to document some of them.

In a typical study, each individual in a group of people about to begin psychotherapy and in a group of people uninterested in therapy was asked to describe first himself and then the ideal person he would like to be. (Often these descriptions were rendered using the Q-sort technique described in Chapter 6.) The results showed that these two descriptions diverged more among people who felt they needed therapy. When the therapy group repeated this procedure after completing a program of Rogerian treatment, their real and ideal selves aligned more closely—although still not as closely as those of the people who never sought therapy (Butler & Haigh, 1954).

Results like these—and they have been reported frequently over the years—show that Rogerian psychotherapy makes people feel they are becoming more like their ideal selves, and this result seems to be about equally due to changes in clients' ideal views as to changes in their self-views. That is, the clients not only change what they think they themselves are like, but also change how they wish to be (Rudikoff, 1954). This may or may not be a good thing, depending.

On the up side, the ideal self that one is trying to live up to be might be a malevolent product of one's conditions of worth. If you feel miserable because you are not living in accord with society's prescriptions for financial success, sexual orientation, or physical attractiveness, for example, then changing your ideal self so you can better accept who you really are is surely a good thing. The former NFL player David Kopay, who came out as gay after leaving football, wrote eloquently about his struggle with the huge gap between who he was and who his traditional, conservative upbringing had taught him that he should be (Kopay, 1977). Through self-reflection and therapy, he was finally able to accept his real self and arrive in a much better place.

On the down side, although Kopay's story is compelling, describing oneself as highly similar to one's idea of a perfect person is not always a good measure of psychological adjustment. One study found that people afflicted with paranoid schizophrenia considered themselves close to ideal, and concluded that to employ a high correlation between the self and ideal-self conceptions "as a sole criterion of adjustment" would lead to the inappropriate categorization of many people, particularly those afflicted with paranoid schizophrenia, as well adjusted (I. Friedman, 1955, p. 614). There is more to mental health than believing you are the way you would most like to be (Wylie, 1974). Narcissists seem pretty pleased with themselves, after all (see Chapter 6).

> Describing oneself as highly similar to one's idea of a perfect person is not always a good measure of psychological adjustment....Paranoid schizophrenics consider themselves close to ideal and narcissists seem pretty pleased with themselves.

Despite this ambiguity about the outcome, Rogerian psychotherapy has contributed the influential idea that any psychotherapist's first job is to listen to the client. Although not all therapists would respond "uh-huh" to statements like those mentioned earlier, the Rogerian example has influenced many therapists to be more patient in listening and more hesitant to impose their own values.

PERSONAL CONSTRUCTS: KELLY

Another important phenomenological psychologist, George Kelly, also thought that a person's individual experience of the world was the most important part of her psychology. As we have seen, individual construals can be general (for example, Bob sees the world as an evil place) or specific (Maria sees parties as boring, or even, Maria saw last Saturday's party as boring). Kelly's unique contribution was to emphasize how one's *cognitive* (thinking) system assembles one's various construals of the world into individually held theories called *personal constructs*. These constructs, in turn, then help determine how new experiences are construed. Accordingly, Kelly's theory (1955) of personality is called *personal construct theory*.

Sources of Constructs

Kelly viewed constructs as *bipolar dimensions* (scales ranging between one concept and its opposite, such as "good-bad") along which people or objects can be arranged. These constructs can include paired opposites of all sorts: for example, the idea of good versus bad (as just mentioned), large versus small, weak versus strong, or conservative versus liberal. If weak versus strong is one of your constructs, you might tend to see everything and everybody in terms of individual strength. Each person's cognitive system is made of a unique set of constructs.

An individual's personal construct system can be assessed in many ways, but Kelly favored a method called the Role Construct Repertory Test, or the Rep test for short. The Rep test asks you to identify three people who are or have been important in your life. Then it asks you to describe how any two of them seem similar to each other and different from the third. Then you follow the same process with three important ideas, three traits you admire, and so on. In each case, the question is the same: How are two of these similar to each other and different from the third?

Kelly believed that the ways you discriminate among these objects, people, and ideas reveal the constructs through which you view the world. For example, if you frequently state that two of the objects are strong whereas the third is weak (or vice versa), then strong versus weak is probably one of your personal constructs.

Research by those publishing after Kelly has shown that particular constructs are more readily brought to mind in certain individuals. These have been called *chronically accessible constructs* (Bargh, Lombardi, & Higgins, 1988). For example, the idea of devastating failure might be chronically accessible to one person, so that, in everything he undertakes or even considers undertaking, the idea that it will all turn into a catastrophe is never far from his mind. For another person, the idea of interpersonal power might be chronically accessible, so that every relationship she observes or enters brings up the question, "Who is in charge here?" which frames her view of these relationships.

Where do these constructs come from? Kelly believed that they come from—but are not determined by—past experience. What does that mean? Kelly relied heavily on the metaphor that every person is, in a sense, a scientist: someone who obtains data and devises a theory to explain the data. But data never determine the scientist's theory; any pattern of data could fit at least two, and perhaps an infinite number, of alternative theories. (This observation comes from elementary philosophy of science.) Therefore, the scientist always *chooses* which theory to use. To be sure, science has developed rules, such as the *principle of parsimony* (also known as "Occam's razor"): The idea that all other things being equal, the simplest theory is the best. But these canons do not ensure the right choice—sometimes a more complex theory is accurate. To choose which theory to believe, the scientist makes a judgment call from among those that fit the data.

> No matter what has happened to you, you *could* have chosen to draw different conclusions about what it means. In fact, you still can.

Kelly believed that the data you use to develop an interpretation, or theory, of what the world is like comes from the sum of your experiences and perceptions. The theory is your personal construct system, which becomes the framework for your perceptions and thoughts about the world. This system is determined not by your past experience but by your—freely chosen—interpretation of past experience. No matter what has happened to you, you *could* have chosen to draw different conclusions about what it means. In fact, you still can.

For example, suppose you had a miserable childhood; perhaps you were even abused. You could draw from this history a personal construct system that tells you the world is unalterably evil and abusive. That conclusion would fit the data of your life experience. Alternatively, you could conclude that no matter what life throws at you, you will survive. That conclusion—since you did survive—also fits the data. Therefore, your conclusion and your worldview are up to you. To pick another example, suppose you are about to

go on a job interview. This situation could be viewed in several different ways, all of which are, to some degree, accurate: an opportunity to show off your talents, a normal conversation, an exhausting ordeal, or a terrifying risk of utter humiliation and career destruction. Which construal will you pick? Your performance at the interview may depend on it.

A corollary of personal construct theory, which Kelly called the **sociality corollary**, holds that understanding another person means understanding her personal construct system; you must be able to look at the world through that person's eyes. Actions that appear incomprehensible or even evil can make sense, Kelly believed, if you can see them from the point of view of the person who chose them. In addition, he believed that the primary duty of a psychotherapist is to lead the client to self-understanding, and he designed the Rep test as a tool to help psychotherapists do that.

Constructs and Reality

The basic lesson of Kelly's theory is that, depending on one's personal constructs, any pattern of experience can lead to numerous—perhaps infinite—construals. That means you choose the construals you use; they are not forced on you, since others are equally possible. Kelly called this view *constructive alternativism*.

The implications are far-reaching. Kelly's theory draws on a part of the philosophy of science that scientists themselves sometimes forget. *Scientific paradigms* are frameworks for construing the meaning of data. The basic approaches to personality considered in this book are paradigms in that sense. Each is sensible, I believe, and each is consistent with the data it regards as important, but each also represents a choice by the researcher to focus on some aspects of human psychology and ignore others. The trait paradigm, combined with the biological approach, dominates current research in personality psychology, is the one within which I do my own research, and (naturally) is my personal favorite. But I think it is important that this book also includes treatments of the psychoanalytic, humanistic and behavioral approaches to personality because there are certain topics that only they address. And who knows, one of them might take over the dominant position someday.[6]

The same lessons apply to many other systems of constructs, or paradigms. Almost everybody—scientist and layperson alike—has developed systems of belief that drive how they understand politics, morality, economics, and many other matters. These belief systems are useful and necessary, but a narrow-minded devotion

---

[6] This does not mean that each paradigm can or should be applied simultaneously, which generally would lead to incoherence. Rather, the psychologist needs to apply the appropriate paradigm for the question at hand while keeping the rest in reserve, lest the question of interest change.

to just one can make a person forget (or worse, deny) that other ways of constructing reality—other belief systems—are equally plausible.

Let me tell you about one of my favorite examples. According to common sense, the cost of something is the amount of resources required to get it or make it. A different view is taught in business schools: The cost of something is the difference between what it brings you and what you could have gained by spending your resources on something else. The difference between these two amounts is not your ordinary cost, but your *opportunity cost*.

These two definitions of cost derive from different construals of the goal of economic life. The first construes the goal as doing what you want as long as you can pay for it. This is sometimes called a *satisficing goal*. The second maintains that you must maximize your gain, and that unless you make as much money as possible, you have failed. This is an *optimizing goal*. Both goals are reasonable, and neither is intrinsically right or wrong. Yet, business schools often teach that the second goal is sophisticated and correct, whereas the first is hopelessly naïve or just plain wrong.

The consequences can be real and concrete. A few years ago, the *Boston Globe* published an article about a mom-and-pop grocery store located on the ground floor of a building in Boston's Beacon Hill area, which had developed into a fashionable neighborhood. The grocer, who had been running the store for decades, was being evicted. The longtime owner of the building discovered that he could command higher rent from a clothing boutique. When neighbors protested, the landlord replied, apparently with a straight face, "I couldn't afford to keep that grocery store there any longer with property values so high."

He may have believed what he said, but from another point of view the landlord's statement was absurd: As long as he could afford to keep the building, he could afford to keep the store. He never claimed the grocer paid him less than the owner needed in order to pay for the building or to live well himself. Rather, he focused on the fact that by evicting the grocer he could make more money, and thought of the difference between what he *was* making and what he *could* make as a "cost" that he could not "afford."

This viewpoint is the inverse of a silly commercial that ran on television a few years ago. The theme of the commercial was, "What will you do with all the money you save (by buying our car)?" In one ad, a happy woman declared that with the money she saved, she was "going to Hawaii!" I have news for this person: Nobody ever went to Hawaii with the money they saved by buying a car. The news for the Boston landlord is that nobody ever went broke from opportunity costs. You can *choose* to think about situations this way, but you are kidding yourself if you think you are getting rich by spending less money than you could, or becoming poor by not collecting as much money as possible.

The Boston landlord and the car buyer in the commercial each absorbed a particular construct about money—and thought of that construct as real. But from the perspective of another construct system, the landlord's behavior was immoral,[7] and the car buyer's was simply ridiculous. The choice of how to think about issues like these can have far-reaching psychological consequences. One study contrasted *maximizers*, the people who believe one should always seek to get as much as one possibly can, with *satisficers*, the ones who believe that some outcomes, short of the maximum, are "good enough." Compared with maximizers, satisficers enjoy more happiness, optimism, and life satisfaction, while maximizers are prone to perfectionism, depression, and regret (B. Schwartz et al., 2002).

The moral of this story is that you should probably question the construals of reality taught in business school, in science classes, or anywhere else, including in this book. Other construals are always possible, and you have the ability, the right, and (Sartre would say) perhaps the duty to choose your own. How you choose to see the world will affect everything in your life.

Early in his career, Kelly learned something else fascinating about construals. He started out as a psychoanalyst practicing in Kansas when he began to doubt some of the exotic Freudian interpretations he was offering to his plainspoken patients. As a little experiment, Kelly began offering deliberately random or odd interpretations just to see how his patients would react. To his astonishment, Kelly reported that even these purposely bizarre interpretations seemed to be helpful! He concluded that the important aspect of psychotherapy was not the content of the intervention, but the therapist's role in getting the patient to think about reality in a different way (Kelly, 1969). Once the patient can do this, he can choose which construals work best and make the most sense, and then be on the way to recovery.

POSITIVE PSYCHOLOGY

Abraham Maslow is often quoted as having said that health means more than simply the absence of disease (Simonton & Baumeister, 2005). This idea, along with humanistic psychology's traditional emphasis on growth, development, and the achievement of one's potential (Levine, 2006), has enjoyed a 21st century resurgence with the advent of the *positive psychology movement* (Gable & Haidt, 2005). The aim of this field of theorizing and research is to correct what its proponents see as a long-standing overemphasis within psychology on psychopathology and malfunction. Instead, positive psychology focuses on phenomena such as "positive subjective experience, positive individual traits, and positive institutions" in order to "improve quality of life and prevent the pathologies that arise when life is barren and meaningless" (Seligman & Csikszentmihalyi, 2000, p. 5).

---

[7] I have received more than a few emails from readers who disagree with my interpretation and defend the concept of opportunity costs. Thank you for paying attention! But my point is not that my construction is necessarily correct, just that different constructions are possible.

Sound familiar? It should: It's the theme of just about every humanistic theory reviewed in this chapter so far.

The reemergence of this theme signals a remarkable turning point in the history of psychology. For a period of several decades—from about the 1970s until just after the turn of the 21st century—humanistic psychology seemed to be dying, though a few lonely voices continued to argue for its importance (e.g., Rychlak, 1988). Their pleas have finally been answered, though perhaps not in the way they would have expected—or wanted.

Positive psychology is the rebirth of humanistic psychology. As we have seen in this chapter, the humanists consistently maintained that traditional psychology, because it treats people almost as inanimate objects of study, tends to ignore uniquely human capacities for creativity, love, wisdom, and free will. Perhaps most crucial, traditional psychology ignores the meaning of life. Positive psychologists place this issue front and center (Baumeister & Vohs, 2002), arguing that a satisfying and meaningful life involves happiness and that true happiness comes from overcoming important challenges (Ryff & Singer, 2003). This idea is not unlike Sartre's conception of optimistic toughness and Deci and Ryan's idea of eudaimonic happiness.

However, positive psychology does more than just revive old-fashioned humanism or put a positive spin on existential philosophy. Positive psychologists also investigate the traits, processes, and social institutions that promote a happy and meaningful life and have found that—Sartre notwithstanding—most people do find their lives meaningful (Heintzelman & King, 2014).

Virtues

A central distinctive feature of positive psychology is its focus on human strengths instead of faults. Recall from Chapters 10 and 11 how Sigmund Freud and the psychoanalytic viewpoint emphasized psychological conflict and the neuroses it produces. More generally, it would be fair to say that psychology focuses more on preventing or curing bad outcomes, such as mental illness, than on promoting good outcomes, such as optimal achievement and health. Positive psychology aims to fix that by identifying and promoting character strengths. A very thick book, published by the American Psychological Association, catalogs and analyzes a long list of "virtues" (C. Peterson & Seligman, 2004).

This topic raises a sticky question, though: What are virtues? After all, one person's virtue might be another person's vice; you may recall that the author of an earlier *Book of Virtues* decided that gambling was OK, apparently just because he enjoyed it (see Chapter 10). Determining how people *should* behave seems to

Table 12.2	CORE VIRTUES IDENTIFIED BY POSITIVE PSYCHOLOGY	
Virtue	**Description**
Courage	Emotional strengths that involve the exercise of will to accomplish goals in the face of opposition; examples include bravery, perseverance, and honesty.
Justice	Strengths that underlie healthy community life; examples include fairness, leadership, and teamwork.
Humanity	Strengths that involve protecting and taking care of others; examples include love and kindness.
Temperance	Strengths that protect against excess; examples include forgiveness, humility, prudence, and self-control.
Wisdom	Strengths that entail the acquisition and use of knowledge; examples include creativity, curiosity, judgment, and perspective.
Transcendence	Strengths that give meaning to life by connecting to the larger universe; examples include gratitude, hope, and spirituality.

Source: Adapted from Dahlsgaard, Peterson, & Seligman (2005), Table 1, p. 205.

involve making value judgments that go beyond science. One way that researchers have approached this problem is by trying to discern which attributes have been viewed as virtues in all cultures, at all times. A particularly ambitious project surveyed the key writings of Confucianism, Taoism, Buddhism, Hinduism, ancient Greek philosophy, Christianity, Judaism, and Islam[8] (Dahlsgaard, Peterson, & Seligman, 2005). The authors identified six *core virtues*: courage, justice, humanity (compassion), temperance, wisdom, and transcendence (see **Table 12.2**). Of these, the most clearly universal appeared to be justice and humanity, because these values were explicitly mentioned as important in all eight of the cultural traditions examined (see **Table 12.3**). Temperance, wisdom, and transcendence were *implied* to be good in the writings of those cultures that did not explicitly identify them as virtues. The only virtue that showed a notable lack of consensus was courage, which was not viewed as particularly important by Confucianism, Taoism, or Buddhism.

What makes these attributes virtues? The authors of this study speculate that their universality suggests they are evolutionarily based (see Chapter 9), because "each allows a crucial survival problem to be solved" (Dahlsgaard et al., 2005, p. 212). Specifically, each virtue counteracts a tendency that could threaten the survival of individuals and cultures. Justice prevents anarchy and chaos; humanity prevents cruelty; wisdom prevents stupidity. And, as the authors note, "We would not need to posit the virtue of courage if people were not (sometimes) swayed from

---

[8]Apparently, Scientology was not included.

| Table 12.3 | AGREEMENT ABOUT VIRTUES ACROSS CULTURAL TRADITIONS |

Tradition	Courage	Justice	Humanity	Temperance	Wisdom	Transcendence
Confucianism		E	E	T	E	T
Taoism		E	E	E	E	T
Buddhism		E	E	E	T	E
Hinduism	E	E	E	E	E	E
Athenian philosophy	E	E	E	E	E	T
Christianity	E	E	E	E	E	E
Judaism	E	E	E	E	E	E
Islam	E	E	E	E	E	E

Note: Traditions that *explicitly* endorse a virtue are identified with E; those that *implicitly* endorse the virtue are identified with T.

Source: Adapted from Dahlsgaard, Peterson, & Seligman (2005), Table 2, p. 211.

doing the right thing by fear or the virtue of temperance if people were not sometimes reckless" (Dahlsgaard et al., 2005, p. 212). This point is important, because if everybody had these virtues, there would be no need to teach them, or even to label them. The key virtues identify six ways in which people try to make themselves better. Some individuals succeed more than others, and probably nobody ever quite manages to achieve all six virtues perfectly.

Positive Experience: Mindfulness, Flow, and Awe

The heart of the phenomenological approach is the conscious awareness of being alive. From this point of view, your moment-to-moment experience is what really matters; the main question is how to make the most of it. Research identified with positive psychology has come up with two answers to this question. And they are nearly opposite! One is to be **mindful** as much as possible, to be explicitly aware of and in control of every moment of your experience. And the other is to experience **flow**, a state of consciousness where you lose track of time and self by becoming completely absorbed in what you are doing. There is definitely something to be said for each recommendation, but let's briefly consider mindfulness first.

MINDFULNESS It is possible, and probably common, to pass through life without paying much attention to what is going on around you. But when you are in a state of *mindfulness*, you are alert and aware of your every thought, every sensation, and every experience. The idea of mindfulness has a long history, with its origins in Buddhist philosophy. Modern enthusiasts who study mindfulness—and some psychologists are indeed enthusiastic about its benefits—claim that it can be helpful in reducing stress, enhancing creativity, improving memory, and freeing oneself from disturbing, recurring thoughts (see Hoffman et al., 2010; Siegel, 2007; Jha, 2010; Chambers et al., 2008). One study reported that people who are mindful can avoid overreacting to bad events in their lives and thereby avoid becoming excessively angry or depressed (Feltman, Robinson, & Ode, 2009; see **Try for Yourself 12.1**).

TRY FOR YOURSELF 12.1

Are You Mindful?

Instructions: Below is a collection of statements about your everyday experience. Using the 1–6 scale below, please indicate how frequently or infrequently you currently have each experience. Please answer according to what *really reflects* your experience rather than what you think your experience should be.

1. I could be experiencing some emotion and not be conscious of it until sometime later.

1	2	3	4	5	6
Almost Always	Very Frequently	Somewhat Frequently	Somewhat Infrequently	Very Infrequently	Almost Never

2. I break or spill things because of carelessness, not paying attention, or thinking of something else.

1	2	3	4	5	6
Almost Always	Very Frequently	Somewhat Frequently	Somewhat Infrequently	Very Infrequently	Almost Never

3. I find it difficult to stay focused on what's happening in the present.

1	2	3	4	5	6
Almost Always	Very Frequently	Somewhat Frequently	Somewhat Infrequently	Very Infrequently	Almost Never

4. I tend to walk quickly to get where I'm going without paying attention to what I experience along the way.

1	2	3	4	5	6
Almost Always	Very Frequently	Somewhat Frequently	Somewhat Infrequently	Very Infrequently	Almost Never

5. I tend not to notice feelings of physical tension or discomfort until they really grab my attention.

1	2	3	4	5	6
Almost Always	Very Frequently	Somewhat Frequently	Somewhat Infrequently	Very Infrequently	Almost Never

6. I forget a person's name almost as soon as I've been told it for the first time.

1	2	3	4	5	6
Almost Always	Very Frequently	Somewhat Frequently	Somewhat Infrequently	Very Infrequently	Almost Never

7. It seems I am "running on automatic" without much awareness of what I'm doing.

1	2	3	4	5	6
Almost Always	Very Frequently	Somewhat Frequently	Somewhat Infrequently	Very Infrequently	Almost Never

8. I rush through activities without being really attentive to them.

1	2	3	4	5	6
Almost Always	Very Frequently	Somewhat Frequently	Somewhat Infrequently	Very Infrequently	Almost Never

9. I get so focused on the goal I want to achieve that I lose touch with what I am doing right now to get there.

1	2	3	4	5	6
Almost Always	Very Frequently	Somewhat Frequently	Somewhat Infrequently	Very Infrequently	Almost Never

10. I do jobs or tasks automatically, without being aware of what I am doing.

1	2	3	4	5	6
Almost Always	Very Frequently	Somewhat Frequently	Somewhat Infrequently	Very Infrequently	Almost Never

11. I find myself listening to someone with one ear, doing something else at the same time.

1	2	3	4	5	6
Almost Always	Very Frequently	Somewhat Frequently	Somewhat Infrequently	Very Infrequently	Almost Never

12. I drive places on "automatic pilot" and then wonder why I went there.

1	2	3	4	5	6
Almost Always	Very Frequently	Somewhat Frequently	Somewhat Infrequently	Very Infrequently	Almost Never

13. I find myself preoccupied with the future or the past.

1	2	3	4	5	6
Almost Always	Very Frequently	Somewhat Frequently	Somewhat Infrequently	Very Infrequently	Almost Never

Continued

TRY FOR YOURSELF 12.1

Are You Mindful?—cont'd

14. I find myself doing things without paying attention.

1	2	3	4	5	6
Almost Always	Very Frequently	Somewhat Frequently	Somewhat Infrequently	Very Infrequently	Almost Never

15. I snack without being aware that I'm eating.

1	2	3	4	5	6
Almost Always	Very Frequently	Somewhat Frequently	Somewhat Infrequently	Very Infrequently	Almost Never

Scoring: Add up the total of the numbers circled and divide by 15. A higher score means that you are more "mindful." In a sample of 313 students at the University of Rochester, the average score was 3.72.

Source: Brown & Ryan (2003).

All of this sounds very good, and no doubt it sometimes is, but it is also impossible to be mindful all the time. Indeed, it seems like it would be exhausting! The philosopher Alfred North Whitehead wrote long ago that

> Operations of thought [by which he meant mindfulness] are like cavalry charges in a battle. They are strictly limited in number, they require fresh horses, and must only be made at decisive moments. (Whitehead, 1911, p. 61).

Like just about anything else in life, therefore, mindfulness can be overdone, but the evidence is persuasive that it can sometimes be useful, especially for interrupting harmful, habitual habits of thought (Davis & Hayes, 2011). "Mindfulness meditation," in particular, can help people who are suffering from depression and anxiety to accept themselves as they are and break habits of negative thinking that hold them back.

FLOW While theorizing about mindfulness addresses the benefits of paying close attention to everything, there also seem to be advantages, at least sometimes, to letting momentary experience drop away. The psychologist Mihalyi Csikszentmihalyi[9]

---

[9] Pronounced "chick-*sent*-me-high," with the emphasis on the second syllable.

investigated the experiences of artists, athletes, and writers as they did what they enjoyed most. He concluded that the best way a person can spend time is in *autotelic* activities, those that are enjoyable for their own sake. The subjective experience of an autotelic activity—the enjoyment itself—is what Csikszentmihalyi calls *flow*.

Flow is characterized by tremendous concentration, total lack of distractibility, and thoughts concerning only the activity at hand. One's mood is elevated slightly (although not to the point of anything like ecstasy), and time seems to pass very quickly. This is what is experienced—when all goes well—by a writer writing, a painter painting, a gardener gardening, or a baseball player waiting for the next pitch. Flow has been reported by surgeons, dancers, and chess players in the midst of intense matches. Computers induce flow in many people. Perhaps you have seen an individual playing video games far into the night, seemingly oblivious to any distraction or to the passage of time itself. That person is likely experiencing flow. I often experience flow when lecturing to a class and sometimes while writing. To me, a 50-minute class feels as if it ends about a minute and a half after it begins. (I know it does not feel this way to my students.) Losing track of time is one sign of experiencing flow.

According to Csikszentmihalyi, flow arises when the challenges an activity presents are well matched with your skills. If an activity is too difficult or too confusing, you will experience anxiety, worry, and frustration. If the activity is too easy, you will experience boredom and (again) anxiety. But when skills and challenges are balanced, you experience flow. Achieving flow also entails staying away from television. Csikszentmihalyi found that watching television disrupts and prevents flow for long periods of time. Some people find that spending time on the Internet can induce flow, but it depends on what you do there. Certain immersive games may put a person in flow, as was mentioned above, but the typical experience in online shopping does not. Online shopping is usually not challenging enough to induce flow, which suggests that if web marketers were clever enough to turn the shopping experience into an immersive game, they could increase their sales immensely (Hoffman & Novak, 2009).

Csikszentmihalyi thinks that the secret for enhancing your quality of life is to spend as much time in flow as possible. Achieving flow entails becoming good at something you find worthwhile and enjoyable. This seems like a decent prescription for happiness, come to think of it, whether you are a phenomenologist or not.

On the other hand, flow does not work for everybody. According to one study, only people high in *locus of control*, who believe they can control their own life outcomes, benefit from activities meant to promote flow (J. Keller & Blomann, 2008). Even in the best of circumstances, flow seems to describe a rather solitary kind of happiness. In that respect Csikszentmihalyi is a true existentialist, perhaps not dwelling on forlornness like Sartre, but still regarding experience as something that happens alone. (Csikszentmihalyi does describe flow as it can occur during sex, but even here he emphasizes the experience of one individual.) The drawback with flow is that somebody experiencing it can be difficult to interact with; she may not hear you, may seem distracted, and in general may be poor company. Interrupt somebody engrossed in a novel or a video game, and you will see what I mean.

Another potential problem with flow is precisely the same as its main advantage: When in this state, a person loses track of what is going on around him or her and gives up conscious control of thoughts and activities. In other words, it is close to the opposite of mindfulness. So, which is it? Should you try to be mindful all the time, or in flow as much as possible? All I can suggest is a wishy-washy compromise. Be mindful about when you are in flow. Enjoy it, but take back conscious control once in a while to make sure you are doing what you really want to do, thinking about what you really want to think about, and not simply following the paths of habit.

AWE A particular experience that might have beneficial effects, according to recent research, is feelings of awe. According to the researchers' definition, awe arises when "individuals encounter an entity that is vast and challenges their worldview" (Stellar et al., 2018, p. 258). People who are prone to experience awe are rated by their friends as more humble, and experiments that attempt to induce awe find that it leads to a more balanced view of one's strengths and weaknesses, and makes a person more humble overall. Awe has the potential to be the antidote to troublesome traits such as entitlement, arrogance and narcissism, so it does sound like something we could use more of. Religions seem to have known this for a long time. Have you ever visited a medieval European cathedral? Many of them have high ceilings, brilliant stain-glass windows and tall towers that are surely meant to be, and often are, awe-inspiring.

Figure 12.4 Awe-inspiring architecture The interior of the cathedral inside Prague Castle might be enough to make even a narcissist feel humble for a minute.

HAPPINESS

Everyone, except perhaps the most hard-core existentialist, wants to be happy, and a key purpose of the positive psychology movement summarized above is to help people achieve this desirable state.

Defining Happiness

The first step is to be clear about what happiness is. According to prominent researchers, it has three components: (1) overall satisfaction with life, (2) satisfaction with how things are going in particular life domains (e.g., relationships, career), and (3) generally high levels of positive emotion and low levels of negative emotion (Kesebir & Diener, 2008). While these three components seem straightforward, the meaning of happiness may change with age. A study of more than 12 million personal blogs found that younger writers—teenagers and people in their twenties—tended to associate reports of happy feelings with words that expressed excited emotions, such as "ecstatic" and "giddy." Older writers, in their forties or fifties, were more likely to report feeling happy at the same time they also used words that expressed peaceful emotions such as "content," "satisfied," and "relaxed" (Mogilner, Kamvar, & Aaker, 2011).

Another way that the definition of happiness can vary comes from the difference between **hedonic** well-being (pleasure seeking) and **eudaimonic** well-being (seeking a meaningful life). According to the modern humanistic psychologists Richard Ryan and Edward Deci, this distinction is crucial (see Ryan & Deci, 2000; Ryan, Huta, & Deci, 2008). In particular, their *Self-determination Theory* (sometimes abbreviated as SDT) states that the more one seeks hedonically to maximize pleasure and minimize pain to the exclusion of other goals, the more one risks living a life "bereft of depth, meaning and community" based on "selfishness, materialism, objectified sexuality and ecological destructiveness" (Ryan et al., 2008, p. 141). Eudaimonia, by contrast, entails finding and seeking goals that are valuable in their own right (*intrinsic goals*) rather than being means to an end (*extrinsic goals*). John-Paul Sartre would probably agree.

But maybe happiness is just happiness. A study that specifically looked for differences between people high in hedonic and eudaimonic well-being found very few, probably because people high in one tend to be high in the other (Nave, Sherman, & Funder, 2008). On reflection, this conclusion is not so surprising. All other things being equal, shouldn't living a meaningful life make a person feel good?

Sources of Happiness

Current research suggests that overall happiness has three primary sources (see **Figure 12.5**). To a (perhaps) surprisingly large extent, one's happiness is determined by an individual set point, and so it is moderately stable over time (Fujita & Diener, 2005). This set point appears to be genetically influenced (Lykken & Tellegen, 1996) and based, in part, on the heritable traits of extraversion (which is good for happiness) and neuroticism (which is bad for it) (E. Diener & Lucas, 1999). Recent research suggests that some people have a tendency to react more strongly to stressful events that is caused by a certain pattern of connections

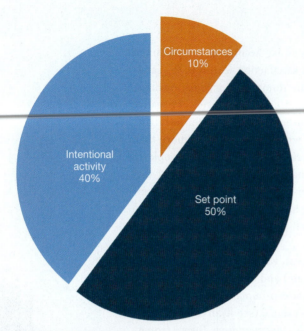

Figure 12.5 Sources of Happiness The three main contributors to happiness, according to current research. The exact percentages should not be taken too seriously; the point of this chart, sometimes called the "happiness pie," is that all three sources are important.
Source: Adapted from Lyubomirsky, Sheldon, & Schkade (2005), p. 115.

between parts of the amygdala and parts of the prefrontal cortex (see Chapter 9), with the result that they feel a "tonically elevated, indiscriminate negative affect" (Schackman et al., 2016, p. 1275). In other words, they feel bad almost all the time. One study found that even day-to-day mood is remarkably stable over a period of two years (Hudson, Lucas, & Donnellan, 2017). Don't you know people who seem to stay cheerful, and others who seem to be almost always gloomy, regardless of what is actually going on in their lives? It really might be, at least in part, because of the way their brains are wired.

Another, though apparently smaller, influence on happiness is objective life circumstances. One of these is age. According to a study of online blogs, the expression (and presumably feeling) of happiness increases steadily after age 13, peaking between about ages 50 and 60, and declining fairly rapidly thereafter (Dodds & Danforth, 2010; see **Figure 12.6**). In addition, having more education, being married, and earning more money are all associated with happiness. Other people will tend to infer that we are happy to the extent that we are healthy and successful in our family life and academic activities, and they will usually be right (Schneider & Schimmack, 2010). But we have to be careful how we interpret findings like these. One study found that while richer people are generally happier, this did not seem to be because more wealth causes more happiness, but rather because the same stable personality traits associated with wealth are also associated with being happy (Luhman, Schimmack, & Eid, 2011). The same may be true about education, marriage, and other circumstances associated with happiness—they may tend to go together, but not necessarily because one causes the other.

In any event, if we put these two influences—genetics and life circumstances—together, nearly half of the variability in individual happiness still remains unexplained (Lykken & Tellegen, 1996; Lyubomirsky, Sheldon, et al., 2005). The implication of this finding is that a third factor is important: An individual's happiness is significantly influenced by what he does, such as "looking on the bright side," "making time for things that matter," and, "working on an important life goal" (Lyubomirsky, Sheldon, et al., 2005, p. 123; see also Carstensen & Mikels, 2005). It also helps to look upon life as being "long and easy" rather than "short and hard." Not surprisingly, people who hold the latter attitude are not very happy (Norton, Anik, Aknin, & Dunn, 2011). But here's an alarming finding: One study looked at the relationship between children's happiness and the amount of fast food and soft drinks they consumed (Chang & Nayga, 2010). It turned out that consuming fast food and sodas made the children happier, even though it also caused them to be more obese![10] No wonder well-intentioned programs to get children to eat healthier food have such a hard time making an impact.

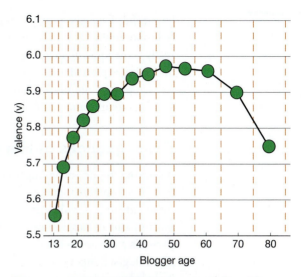

Figure 12.6 Age and Happiness in Online Blogs
The average happiness (positive valence) of the words people use in their online blogs increases with age until it peaks between about ages 50 and 60, and declines thereafter.
Source: Dodds & Danforth (2010), p. 451.

Another way to improve your happiness is by spending your money on experiences rather than things (Howell & Hill, 2009). Experiences, such as a vacation taken with a loved one or a movie enjoyed with a friend, improve not only your own individual happiness but also the happiness of the other people involved and the quality of your long-term relationship with them. Things, on the other hand, are just things. So in the long run, according to research, experiences are a better investment. They are also more fun to anticipate than are material purchases. Looking forward to a concert or a trip is more fun, one study found, than looking forward to buying a new computer (Kumar, Killingsworth, & Gilovich, 2014).

Another, rather surprising way to seek happiness is through political ideology. According to one study, thinking like a political conservative can lead a person to experience negative emotions less, whereas thinking like a liberal can lead a person to experience positive emotions more (Choma, Busseri, & Sadava, 2009). I don't have to reveal any bias here because you can take your pick—both approaches, apparently, will make you happier in the end. People also seek happiness by protecting their health, working hard for occupational success, and building successful relationships.

Some studies have tested various interventions to increase happiness, with moderate success. For example, listing things that you are thankful for (also known as "counting your blessings"), expressing gratitude to someone who has had a beneficial influence on your life, and doing kind acts for others can all, under some circumstances, make you happier (Lyubomirsky & Layous, 2013). But

---

[10] They're not called "happy meals" for nothing.

be careful. Even seemingly benign activities like these sometimes backfire (Fritz & Lyubomirsky, 2017). If you try to think of things to be thankful for but can't really come up with anything, or you do so many favors for someone that you end up feeling exploited, or even if you just try too hard to be happy, the result can be less happiness, not more. In the end, attempts to be happier should be tailored to specific circumstances and the needs and attitudes of the individual.

Consequences of Happiness

According to one intriguing analysis, happiness may not be just a result of good health, occupational success, and supportive relationships, but a cause of all of these outcomes (Lyubomirsky, King, & Diener, 2005). The adaptive function of positive affect—happiness—is to signal to the individual "that life is going well, the person's goals are being met, and resources are adequate" (p. 804). According to psychologist Sonja Lyubomirsky and her colleagues, the results of feeling this way include becoming more confident, optimistic, likeable, sociable, and energetic.

Is there such a thing as too much happiness? Psychologist June Gruber and her colleagues suggest four potential dark sides (Gruber, Mauss, & Tamir, 2011). First, happiness that is too intense can lead to a failure to recognize risky situations or to pouring excessive energy into unproductive pursuits. Second, happiness that is felt at the wrong time—such as when things really are going badly—can short-circuit efforts to make things better. Third, directly "trying to be happy" can be counterproductive, if one then becomes disappointed that one has failed to become happy enough. It is better, these authors argue, to pursue activities and accomplishments that will yield results that will make you happy in the long run, even if not necessarily right now. Finally, there are types of happiness that cause problems for the person or those around them, such as the hubristic or arrogant kind of happiness that might be felt by narcissists (Chapter 6). This kind of happiness may feel good in the moment, but can be harmful to others and lead to the individual's downfall in the end.

So it apparently is good to be unhappy sometimes. College students who experience occasional bouts of unhappiness actually seem to have better academic success than those who are happy almost all the time. Why do you think this is? My own guess is that students need to buckle down and study once in a while, which isn't necessarily the immediate route to happiness, but which leads to greater success in the not-very-long run (Barker, Howard, Galambos & Wrosch, 2016).

Still, if not taken to extreme, happiness is associated with effectiveness in a broad range of domains. Happier people make better decisions, have higher levels of professional accomplishment, and even solve anagrams better (Kesebir & Diener, 2008). Resident advisors in dormitories who felt more positive emotions were rated by their residents as being more effective (DeLuga & Mason, 2000), and cricket players who were happier had higher batting averages (Totterdell,

2000)! Happy employees give better customer service (George, 1995), and happier farmers in Malaysia make more money (Howell, Howell, & Schwabe, 2006). Happy people have more friends they can rely on (G. R. Lee & Ishii-Kuntz, 1987) and enjoy more social support (Pinquart & Sörenson, 2000). Not surprisingly, happiness is associated with less drug use.

The analysis of all these findings is complex because, as has already been noted, the causal arrow runs in both directions. The psychologist Chris Soto conducted a remarkable longitudinal study of 16,367 Australians and found that higher levels of happiness were associated with higher levels of the traits of extraversion, agreeableness, and conscientiousness, which is not surprising, but his study also found that people who became happier also increased, later, in all of these traits (Soto, 2015). You can see how this might work. An extravert might have more friends, which would make her happy. And, over time, having more friends could make her even more extraverted. Overall, analyses by Lyubomirsky, Soto, and others convincingly show that happiness promotes behaviors and problem-solving skills that in themselves can lead to good outcomes, which means that happiness can become a self-perpetuating, virtuous cycle. The analysis also implies that happy times can be useful occasions to "broaden and build" (Fredrickson, 2001). To unhappy people, something seems to be wrong, so they are motivated to undo the damage and protect themselves. Happy people, by contrast, can use their well-being as the foundation for creating and maintaining better life circumstances for themselves and others. In this light, happiness is not just an outcome. It's an opportunity.

> Happiness is not just an outcome. It's an opportunity.

HUMANISTIC AND POSITIVE PSYCHOLOGY IN THE 21ˢᵗ CENTURY

Positive psychology seems inherently optimistic (notice its name), which seems to have caused some grumpy old-school humanistic psychologists to resent its popularity. One recently wrote that positive psychology falls short because "trial and despair appear to be as integral to well-being as optimism and positive self-appraisals" (Schneider, 2014, p. 92). Which raises an interesting question: Should we try to always expect the best? Perhaps not surprisingly, optimistic individuals are less fearful, more willing to take risks, and are usually relatively happy (C. Peterson & Steen, 2002). On the other hand, optimism may lead one to take foolish risks or fail to anticipate problems before they arise. For that reason, psychologist Julie Norem has made the interesting argument that the study of pessimism should also be considered a part of positive psychology (Norem & Chang, 2002).

Despite the recent flurry of empirical and theoretical activity, the rebirth of humanism remains incomplete. Positive psychology has not yet had much to say about existential anxiety, for example, nor does it address the difficult dilemmas that arise from free will. It usually addresses experience in the form of "subjective well-being," which is basically the degree to which one "feels good"—a limited phenomenological analysis compared with the earlier work of existentialists and humanists—and is just beginning to focus on the difference between hedonic and eudaimonic sources of well-being.

But let's be fair. Positive psychology, by that name, is still new—its most important articles and books have all appeared since the year 2000. As Sartre mordantly observed, the dilemmas of free will and mortality cannot be wished away, even if we try to ignore them, so positive psychology likely will address these issues before long. In the meantime, it offers a powerful corrective to psychology's emphasis on the negative side of mental life.

The Mystery of Experience

At the root of the existential and humanistic approach to psychology is phenomenology, the moment-to-moment experience of every aware person. This emphasis on phenomenology allows humanistic analysis to make three unique contributions. It reminds us of the mystery of experience, it teaches that the only way to truly understand another person is to comprehend that person's unique view of reality, and it focuses attention on the nature of optimal experience and happiness.

....

Conscious experience is both an obvious fact and a basic mystery.

....

The essential fact that phenomenologists going back to Wundt have always grasped, which all other basic paradigms neglect, is that conscious experience is both an obvious fact and a basic mystery. It cannot be explained by science or even described very well in words. Though we cannot quite describe what it is to be aware and alive, every one of us knows what it is.

Science and psychology usually choose not to address how something so familiar can be so difficult to understand; they just ignore it, which is fine, to a point. The point is reached when science and psychology seem to assume that conscious awareness is not important or even proceed as if it does not exist. Nearly as bad, psychology sometimes treats conscious experience as simply an interesting form of information processing, no different from the kind done by a computer (Rychlak, 1988). Some theories proposed by cognitive psychologists claim that consciousness is a higher-order cognitive process that organizes thoughts and allows flexible decision making. These theories hold that beyond these functions, consciousness is just a feeling (Dennett, 1994; Dennett & Weiner, 1991; Ornstein, 1977).

Of course, to say consciousness is "just a feeling" bypasses the main question: What does it mean to be able to consciously experience feeling? In fact, conscious

awareness is not in the least similar to the kind of information processing computers perform, even if it fulfills some of the same functions. Awareness is a human
experience, and science can neither credibly deny its existence nor explain just
what it is or where it comes from. It is only natural, therefore, that phenomenological analysis sometimes expands into speculations that are not only philosophical but also religious and spiritual.

Understanding Others

A corollary of the phenomenological view at the heart of humanistic psychology is
that to understand another person, you must understand that person's construals
(Kelly, 1955). You can only comprehend someone's mind to the extent that you
can imagine life from her perspective. The adage "Do not judge me until you have
walked a mile in my shoes" expresses the general idea.

This principle discourages judgmental attitudes about other people. It implies
that if you could see the world through their eyes, you would realize that their
actions and attitudes are the natural consequences of their understanding of reality. Furthermore, there is no way to prove your view of reality right and the views
of others wrong. Thus, it is a mistake to assume that others interpret the world the
same way you do, or that there is only one correct perspective. Others' opinions,
no matter how strange, must be considered as valid as your own.[11]

One direct consequence of this phenomenological principle is a far-reaching
cultural and even moral relativism. You cannot judge the actions and beliefs of other
people through your own moral code. For, when all is said and done, there is no
objective reality—or, if there is, there is no way for anyone to know it. Furthermore,
it is generally misguided to judge the values and practices of other cultures from
the perspective of your own. Although there may be widespread agreement about a
handful of core virtues, separate cultures still see the world very differently, and to
understand other cultures, just as to understand other individuals, we must seek
to understand the world from an alternative point of view. The attempt to apply
personality psychology across different cultures is the topic of the next chapter.

---

[11] Extremists such as Thomas Szasz (1960, 1974) have sometimes argued that this is even true about the
people usually considered mentally ill; they merely have an alternative and equally valid construal of
reality. But this is an extreme position.

WRAPPING IT UP

SUMMARY

- Humanistic psychology concentrates on the ways that studying humans differs from studying objects or animals, including such issues as experience, awareness, and free will.

- Although recent research shows that the way people construe the situations they experience is related to personality and gender, humanistic psychologists emphasize the degree to which every situation has good and bad elements and the freedom of people to choose which ones to emphasize in their construals.

Phenomenology: Awareness Is Everything

- The phenomenological perspective implies that the present moment of experience is all that matters, which means that individuals have free will and that the only way to understand another person is to understand that person's construal, or experience of the world.

Existentialism

- The philosophical school called existentialism breaks experience into three types: experience of the external world, social experience, and introspective experience-of-experiencing. Existentialism also claims that existence has no meaning beyond what each person gives it.

- Existential philosophers such as Sartre concluded that a failure to face life's lack of inherent meaning constitutes living in bad faith.

Optimistic Humanism: Rogers and Maslow

- Modern humanist psychologists added to this existential analysis the assumption that people are basically good and inherently motivated to self-actualize.

- Rogers and Maslow asserted that a person who faces experience directly can become a fully functioning person. Rogers believed this outcome could only occur for individuals who had received unconditional positive regard from the important people in their lives. Maslow believed that higher needs such as self-actualization could come to the fore only after more basic needs related to survival and security became satisfied. A new version of Maslow's hierarchy of needs has been derived from evolutionary theory, placing parenthood at the top.

Personal Constructs: Kelly

- Kelly's personal construct theory says that each person's experience of the world is organized by a unique set of personal constructs. These personal constructs, which stem from, and help determine, one's construals of experience, resemble scientific paradigms.

Positive Psychology

- Positive psychology represents a rebirth of humanistic psychology, focusing on the traits and psychological processes that promote well-being and give life meaning.

- An important contribution of positive psychology is its attempt to catalog universal human virtues, which research suggests include justice, humanity, temperance, wisdom, and transcendence. A sixth core virtue, courage, appears to be somewhat less universal.

- Research in positive psychology has examined and advocated for mindfulness, the state of being fully and consciously aware of one's environment and experiences. Mindfulness has been shown to have beneficial effects, particularly in stress reduction.

- In contrast, Csikszentmihalyi's theory of flow says that the best state of experience is when one loses awareness of the moment because challenges and capabilities are balanced, attention is focused, and time passes quickly.

Happiness

- Happiness can be defined as the achievement of hedonic means (seeking pleasure and comfort) or eudaimonic means (seeking to fulfill one's potential). Research suggests that while these two kinds of happiness are theoretically different, within people they tend to occur together.

- Happiness is determined by genetics, life circumstances, and intentional activities.

- Activities to increase happiness include counting one's blessings, expressing gratitude, and doing good deeds for others. However, these activities should be tailored to circumstances and the preferences of the individual.

- Happiness has positive effects on health, occupational success, and supportive relationships, and these outcomes in turn affect happiness. But it is possible to be too happy.

Humanistic and Positive Psychology in the 21st Century

- The two main and lasting contributions of humanistic psychology's phenomenological approach are the attempt to address the mystery of human experience and its emphasis on nonjudgmental understanding of individuals and cultures.

KEY TERMS

humanistic psychology, p. 424

phenomenology, p. 424

construal, p. 426

introspection, p. 426

Existentialism, p. 426

Umwelt, p. 427

Mitwelt, p. 427

Eigenwelt, p. 427

thrown-ness, p. 427

Angst, p. 428

anatta, p. 432

anicca, p. 433

nirvana, p. 433

sociality corollary, p. 442

mindful, p. 447

flow, p. 447

hedonic, p. 453

eudaimonic, p. 453

THINK ABOUT IT

1. Do people have free will, or are they driven by their past experiences, unconscious motivations, and personality traits? If free will exists, what does this mean, and how is it possible?

2. What does it feel like to be alive and aware? Can consciousness be described in words? How could you tell whether a computer had this feeling? Can psychology further our understanding of this experience? How?

3. How can a person decide between right and wrong? Is there some authority to help sort it out? How do you know whether to heed this authority?

4. Sartre believed that God does not exist, but said that, even if God *did* exist, it wouldn't matter. What did Sartre mean?

5. How do you think Rogers and Maslow could start with existentialist ideas and develop such optimistic-sounding psychologies?

6. The evolutionarily based hierarchy of needs by Kenrick and his colleagues places "parenting" at the top of the pyramid. Is parenthood the ultimate goal of human existence? Can you find anything like "self-actualization" in Kenrick's pyramid?

7. If a psychotherapist is treating a murderer or a child molester, do you think the therapist should give the client unconditional positive regard? Why, or why not?

8. Why are you in college? Are your goals hedonic or eudaimonic? Why do you think most students are in college?

9. Can pessimism be useful? Or should we strive to be optimistic all the time?

10. Can stress be good for you? Or should we seek to avoid stress as much as possible?

11. Is it important for psychology to emphasize human strengths as well as weaknesses? What good would that do?

12. The strongest cross-cultural agreement about virtues seems to concern justice and humanity. Does this mean these are the most important virtues? Courage seems to inspire slightly less agreement. Does this mean it is less important? How can we decide which virtues are the most important?

13. When trying to identify core virtues or to explain the meaning of life, where does psychology leave off and religion—or other cultural teachings—begin?

14. Is it possible to be too happy? Is trying to be happy a good way to spend your day?

15. What things, activities, or experiences make you the most happy? Are these the same things, activities or experiences that make other people happy? Why do different people seek happiness in different ways?

16. We each know we are aware and consciously experiencing the world, yet psychology finds this fact difficult to study. Why? What kinds of investigations might lead to a helpful or convincing explanation of human consciousness?

SUGGESTED RESOURCES

Lyubomirsky, S. (2008). *The how of happiness: A scientific approach to getting the life you want.* New York: Penguin Press.

A clear and succinct summary of the latest research on how to become a happier person.

Maslow, A. H. (1987). *Motivation and personality* (3rd ed.). New York: Harper.

One of the most accessible—and briefest—thorough presentations of American humanistic psychology by one of its two most important figures (the other being Carl Rogers). Maslow's writing is passionate and persuasive.

Sartre, J. P. (1965). The humanism of existentialism. In W. Baskin (Ed.), *Essays in existentialism* (pp. 31–62). Secaucus, NJ: Citadel.

A surprisingly readable and interesting exposition of existentialism from one of its important philosophers.

Want to earn a better grade on your test?

Go to **INQUIZITIVE** to learn and review this chapter's content, with personalized feedback along the way.

CULTURAL VARIATION IN EXPERIENCE, BEHAVIOR, AND PERSONALITY

HE ONLY WAY TO understand a person is to appreciate his distinct view of reality. We saw the phenomenologists make a pretty good case along these lines in Chapter 12. Construals of reality vary not just between individuals but also around the world. Behavior that seems the epitome of politeness in one culture may be viewed as rude in another. Ideas can take on drastically different meanings according to the cultural context. And, perhaps most important, cultures sometimes differ in some of their basic values.

Few areas of psychology are more challenging than cross-cultural research, because the job often entails grappling with concepts that are both unfamiliar and complex. For example, the psychiatrist Takeo Doi reports that the term *amae* is central for understanding personality in Japanese culture. *Amae* literally means something like "sweet," but in a family context the word implies indulgence and dependence, of the sort that may exist between a parent and child. This pattern of benevolent dependence is expected to continue into adult relationships, so that people treat each other thoughtfully and considerately, while appreciating how they depend on each other (Doi, 1973; Tseng, 2003). But it is difficult even to translate *amae* into English, much less to fully comprehend its implications. Does the concept have any meaning outside of Japan? Or is it so embedded in the Japanese way of seeing things that it cannot be exported? Questions like these may be impossible to fully answer, but the business of **cross-cultural psychology**[1] is to attempt to address them anyway. The present chapter will survey some of the

---

[1] A note on terms: Cross-cultural psychology generally refers to research that compares cultures with one another. A variant sometimes called *cultural psychology*, rooted in anthropology, seeks to understand individual cultures in their own terms and avoids making comparisons.

research that is beginning to work through the implications of cultural diversity for personality psychology.

CULTURE AND PSYCHOLOGY

Personality psychology focuses on psychological differences between individuals. Culture comes into play for two reasons. First, individuals may differ from each other to some extent because they belong to different cultural groups. According to one study, people in China are on average more emotionally reserved, introverted, fond of tranquility, and considerate than Americans (Cheung & Song, 1989). Second, members of some groups may differ from *each other* in distinctive ways. Doi described a Japanese mother who complained that her son was not as *amae* as he should be, a complaint you would probably not hear from an American parent. An important challenge for personality psychology is to understand ways that particular personality differences vary from one culture to another, or distinguish among individuals within different cultures.

Cross-Cultural Universals Versus Specificity

To what extent are people from different cultures psychologically similar or different? Are their differences variations on a theme, or are they entirely different symphonies? To put the question one more way, does human nature have a common core? Or are people from separate cultures so fundamentally different that they cannot be meaningfully compared? Anthropologists have grappled with these issues for many years, and psychologists are relative newcomers to the fray. While both fields include plenty of proponents for both the "universal human nature" and "cultural specificity" positions, this is one of those eternal issues, like the nature-versus-nurture question (Chapter 9) or the consistency debate (Chapter 4), that seems bound never to be entirely settled.

> Are people from separate cultures so fundamentally different that they cannot be meaningfully compared?

In what follows, we will see plenty of evidence that culture has an important influence on how people are different from each other, as well as indications that there may be a common core to human nature. Furthermore, while cross-cultural psychology has traditionally emphasized how people in separate cultures are different, in the past few years an increasing amount of research has focused on how people around the world are psychologically similar, and turned more attention to the ways people differ *within* cultures. An important challenge for the future will be to figure out how universal psychological processes, such as personality and emotion, play out in diverse cultural contexts (Tsai, Knutson, & Fung, 2006). We will return to these issues near the end of the chapter.

What Is Culture?

The term *culture* refers to psychological attributes of groups. According to one writer, these include "customs, habits, beliefs and values that shape emotions, behavior and life patterns" (Tseng, 2003, p. 1). Differences between cultural groups develop as a child learns the culture into which she is born (a process called **enculturation**), and as a person who moves from one country to another gradually picks up the culture of her new home (a process called **acculturation**). Culture may include language, modes of thinking, and perhaps even fundamental views of reality.

The concept of the cultural group is difficult to pin down precisely. Any group of people who are identifiably distinct can be a candidate. Traditionally, cultural groups have been defined in terms of ethnicity, nationality, and language, but important cultural differences can be found within national and linguistic borders as well as across them. Studies have compared North Americans with Asians, Japanese with Chinese, Spanish speakers with English speakers, inhabitants of different U.S. cities, and even residents of Manhattan with residents of Queens (Kusserow, 1999).

Psychologists are members of cultures, too. Every psychologist speaks a language and lives in a geographic area that inevitably influences her outlook. It is even possible that being a psychologist makes one a member of a certain "culture."

THE IMPORTANCE OF CROSS-CULTURAL DIFFERENCES

Psychologists have pretty much ignored cross-cultural issues until relatively recently, and many still do. Most of this neglect is fairly benign. Rather than worry about cross-cultural variation at every step, especially in the absence of much relevant data, most psychologists just try to describe and explain the phenomenon at hand as it applies to the people they can study most easily. Freud did not worry too much about cross-cultural concerns; he found middle-class Viennese women plenty complicated enough. Likewise, the European and North American psychologists measuring individual differences and exploring perception, cognition, and the laws of behavioral change have proceeded primarily within the Western cultural context. Research even within these limits has proven sufficiently interesting and difficult that most researchers have not attempted to carry it across cultural borders.

This attitude of benign neglect is rapidly becoming less tenable as research expands and accelerates. Even the Surgeon General of the United States has officially announced that "culture counts" for understanding mental health disorders, interventions, and risk factors (Public Health Service, 2001). Psychologists are interested in cross-cultural differences for three good reasons. Understanding cultural differences is important for increasing international understanding, for assessing the degree to which psychology applies to people around the world, and for appreciating the possible varieties of human experience.

Cross-Cultural Understanding

Different cultural attitudes, values, and behavioral styles frequently cause misunderstandings. The consequences can range from trivial to serious.

Near the trivial end of the spectrum, cross-cultural psychologist Harry Triandis described a mix-up with an Indian hotel caused by the difference between the American practice of marking an X next to the part of a form that *does* apply, and the Indian practice of marking an X at the part that does *not* apply. He received a postcard with an X next to "We have no rooms available," and thought he did not have a hotel reservation, when he actually did (Triandis, 1994). This episode was surely inconvenient, but no major tragedy.[2]

More consequential differences include the preference of businesspeople in Thailand who try to preserve the dignity of everybody involved in a negotiation, or the tradition in Japan of getting to know a potential customer or vendor on a personal level before drawing up a contract. The Japanese practice permits controversial issues that might arise during a meeting to be settled beforehand, in private (L. Miller, 1999). When these styles encounter the relatively brash, direct, and sometimes even insensitive American way of doing business, the result is more conflict and probably less profit than would have been possible with a little more mutual understanding.

In 1994, an American teenager living with his parents in Singapore learned a lesson about cross-cultural differences the hard way. He was convicted of spray-painting some parked cars, which in the United States probably would have been considered an act of petty vandalism (albeit an extremely annoying one), punished by probation or a small fine. In Singapore, such misbehavior is taken more seriously. He was sentenced to pay restitution, spend a few months in jail, and—most surprising from an American perspective—to be hit several times with a bamboo cane, which can split open the skin and cause permanent scarring. The sentence caused an international uproar about whether this was an appropriate punishment or not.[3]

Behaviors that are ordinary in other cultures can also stir up a storm if they are practiced in the United States. In 1997, a Danish mother visiting New York went into a restaurant and left her 14-month-old daughter sleeping in a stroller parked outside. Alarmed New Yorkers saw the "abandoned" baby and called the police, who arrested the mother and placed the child in temporary foster care.

---

[2] Another, only slightly less trivial example: On a visit to Poland I once encountered two restroom doors, one labeled with a circle and the other with a triangle. Which was which? I guessed wrong.

[3] Although, I'm guessing, he never spray-painted a parked car again.

Yet, apparently, this is a common practice in Denmark (see **Figure 13.1**). As one Danish writer commented,

> In Denmark, people have an almost religious conviction that fresh air, preferably cold air, is good for children. All Danish babies nap outside, even in freezing weather—tucked warmly under their plump goose-down comforters. . . . In Denmark, [this mother's] behavior would have been considered perfectly normal. (Dyssegaard, 1997/2004, p. 370)

Cross-cultural misunderstandings occur within as well as across international borders. In some inner cities of North America, a subculture of violence and fear has made it important to always receive proper "respect." Anything that threatens such respect can make one seem vulnerable or can even literally threaten one's life, so tokens such as stylish clothing, a fear-producing appearance, and even an advertised willingness to kill become highly valued (E. Anderson, 1994). Nonverbal expressions take on added meanings, too. For example, to gaze for more than a second or so at a person from this subculture may be taken as a sign of disrespect and provoke a violent response. Similarly, research has suggested that the American South has its own "culture of honor" that is different from the rest of the United States; it includes such behaviors as elaborate displays of mutual respect (such as calling people "sir" and "ma'am") and the obligation to respond forcefully to any insult (D. Cohen, Nisbett, Bowdle, & Schwartz, 1996). Honor cultures will be considered in more detail later in this chapter.

Figure 13.1 Nothing to Get Excited About A few days after a Danish mother visiting New York was arrested for leaving her baby parked on the sidewalk, this photograph was taken outside of the Café Sommersko in Copenhagen.

Generalizability of Theory and Research

Sigmund Freud's theories were largely based on his own introspections and his experience treating upper-middle-class women who lived in turn-of-the-20th-century Vienna. It is not particularly original to observe that his view of humanity may have been skewed by the limits of this database.[4] The problem is not unique to Freud, of course. As was discussed in Chapter 2, a basic worry about the

---

[4] An early tradition in cross-cultural psychology involved trying to interpret different cultures in psychoanalytic terms. For example, Gorer (1943) claimed that Japanese people are anal-compulsive because they subject their children to early and severe toilet training. Theorizing by modern cultural psychologists is very different and seldom Freudian.

generalizability of research findings concerns the degree to which the results of modern empirical research apply to humanity at large. About 80 percent of the participants in psychology studies come from countries that are Western, Educated, Industrialized, Rich, and Democratic—"WEIRD" for short—although only 12 percent of the world's population live there (Henrich et al., 2010).

The issue may be particularly acute for personality psychology, because a great deal of evidence indicates that culture affects the ways personality is expressed and emotion is experienced. The only way to incorporate this fact in psychological research is to include not only people besides college students, but also people from around the world.

The situation has improved a bit in recent years. The principal psychology journals increasingly report research from psychologists in many different countries, including Australia, New Zealand, many countries in Europe—Germany and the Netherlands are particularly active in personality psychology—and a growing number of Asian countries, including Japan, China, Korea, India, and Singapore. As psychology becomes more international, it will become more generalizable, and a better science.

Varieties of Human Experience

A third and more deeply theoretical issue also drives interest in cross-cultural psychology. A moment's reflection is sufficient to realize that the way you see and construe the world is, to a considerable degree, a product of your experience and cultural background. An intriguing possibility to consider is how the world might look if you were from some other culture. Things that are now invisible might become clear, and things you see and take for granted might become invisible. You might even, in a real sense, become a different person.

For example, an indigenous resident of a South American rain-forest community might look at a tree and immediately see the uses for its bark and sap. That same individual might look at an automobile or a computer and have no idea what it's for. A native of Western culture would immediately see the transportation and informational possibilities in the car and the computer, but would probably detect little potential on beholding a teak. A ride around the block might be sufficient to acquaint a visitor from the rain forest with the possibilities of cars; imparting an understanding of computers might be a bit more difficult. And if a Westerner visited the rain forest, there might be artifacts or objects the local residents would find equally difficult to explain. In a similar way, an American might look at a house and never notice which way its door points. To a Chinese person raised in the tradition of *feng shui*, this would be one of the first things noticed and would lead to some immediate conclusions concerning the dangers and possibilities that might exist within the house.[5]

---

[5]If the American happens to live in California, the difference in perception might not be so wide. For several years, the real estate section of the *Los Angeles Times* included a "Feng Shui" column with advice on how to align one's home with unseen forces of the universe.

The Importance of Cross-Cultural Differences   **471**

Observations like these raise a profound phenomenological question: Does the human experience of life vary fundamentally around the world? Do people raised and living in different cultural environments see the same colors, feel the same emotions, desire the same goals, or organize their thoughts in comparable ways? The cultural anthropologist and psychologist Richard Shweder called these aspects of psychology *experience-near constructs*, and proposed that they are the most fitting subject matter for cultural psychology (Shweder & Sullivan, 1993). In a somewhat more accessible phrase, Triandis (1994) claimed, "Culture imposes a set of lenses for seeing the world" (p. 13). If that description is valid—and it probably is—then the natural next question is, How different are these cultural lenses and do they lead to views of the world that are fundamentally incomparable?

In its ultimate form, the question is probably unanswerable. As we saw in Chapter 12, we can never know the experience of another individual in our own culture for certain, much less enter fully into the experience of a member of a different culture. But it's useful to try. The experience of living abroad can make you a more creative person, especially if you make an effort to truly adapt to—rather than merely visit—the unfamiliar culture (Maddux & Galinsky, 2009). What does it mean to be more creative? The study used measures of insight, association ideas, and generation of new ideas. One task asked participants to draw pictures of aliens from another galaxy (see **Figure 13.2**). People who had lived abroad drew more creative aliens! Of course, we should always remember that correlation is not causality (see Chapter 2). It's possible that living abroad makes you more creative, but perhaps also more creative people are also more willing to spend extended periods of time abroad. Either way, travel and creativity seem to go together.

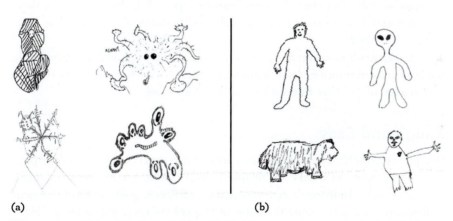

(a)   (b)

Figure 13.2 **Living Abroad and Creativity** In one study, people who had lived abroad and adapted to the new culture were found to be more creative than those who had stayed at home or never experienced more than a brief visit abroad. One measure asked participants to draw an alien they might see if they visited another galaxy. The drawings in panel (a) were judged to be more creative than those in panel (b).

CHARACTERISTICS OF CULTURES

As psychologists turn their attention to culture, the first question that arises is a difficult one: How can one culture be compared with another? Comparison has been attempted in many ways relevant to personality, including the ways in which cultures shape behavior, emotional experience, thoughts, and one's sense of connection with the larger world.

Etics and Emics

The basic assumption underlying cultural comparison is that any idea or concept has aspects that are the same across cultures and aspects particular to a specific culture (J. W. Berry, 1969). The universal components of an idea are called **etics**, and the particular aspects are called **emics**.[6] For example, all cultures have some conception of duty, in the sense that a person should be responsible for doing what she is supposed to do. But beyond this basic etic, different cultures impose their own ideas about what the duty actually is. A dutiful person in New Delhi will probably behave differently from a dutiful person in New York (McCrae & Costa, 1995). At the same time, a renegade in New Delhi and one in New York will both break rules, but they will break different rules.

Some concepts might just be too emic to compare across cultures. Hong Kong psychologist Fanny Cheung and her colleagues suggest that some of these include the Buddhist concept of the selfless-self (which was mentioned in Chapter 12), *renqing* (relationship reciprocity) and *yuan* (predestined relationship) in Taiwan, and *chemyon* (social face) in Korea, along with the Japanese concept of *amae* that you have already read about (Cheung, van de Vijver, & Leong, 2011). Are these concepts understandable outside the cultures in which they arose? The issue remains unsettled.

The more common and much older practice is to try to find etic concepts that *can* be compared across cultures. Many such concepts have been investigated. Let's look at a few of the more interesting and important ones.

Tough and Easy

One pioneering effort more than half a century ago concluded that some cultures are "tough," whereas others are relatively "easy" (Arsenian & Arsenian, 1948). In easy cultures, individuals can pursue many different goals and at least some of them are relatively simple to attain; in tougher cultures, only a few goals are viewed as valuable and few ways are available to achieve them. Another early system

---

[6] The words derive from linguistic terms that refer to *phonetics* (the universal sounds of language) and *phonemics* (the sounds of a specific language) (Tseng, 2003).

Figure 13.3 Easy and Tough Cultures According to one classification, it is less stressful to live in the Ifalik culture (on the left) than the Tupinambá culture (on the right).

suggested that the overall stressfulness of cultures could be indexed by the degree to which they were characterized by suicide, homicide, "drunken brawling," and a tendency to view important events as influenced by witchcraft (Naroll, 1959). According to this classification, the Ifalik culture is much less stressful than the Tupinambá culture, in case you are planning a vacation.[7]

Achievement and Affiliation

David McClelland (1961) theorized that a central aspect of any culture was the degree to which it emphasizes the need to achieve, which he assessed by examining stories traditionally told to children. In some cultures, such as in the United States, children are told many stories along the lines of "The Little Engine That Could," reflecting a high cultural need for achievement. Other cultures tell more stories that reflect needs for love or, to use McClelland's term, *affiliation*. Cultures whose stories manifest a high need for achievement, according to McClelland, show more rapid industrial growth than those whose stories focus less on achievement, and data including measures such as the amount of electrical production have tended to bear him out: more achievement stories, more electricity. As always, though, the correlational nature of these data makes the direction of causality unclear. Does telling achievement-oriented stories to children make them more likely to grow up to build prosperous, industrialized, electricity-using cultures? Or do prosperous cultures create an environment in which children's authors just naturally think up stories about achievement?

---

[7] To answer your next question, the Ifalik live on islands in Micronesia, in the Pacific Ocean, and the Tupinambá hail from the Atlantic coast of Brazil.

Complexity

Are some cultures more complicated than others? Triandis (1997) wrote of the difference in *complexity* between "modern, industrial, affluent cultures [and] the simpler cultures, such as the hunters and gatherers, or the residents of a monastery" (p. 444). This difference seems plausible, but let's be careful. How do we know that modern industrial societies are more complex than hunter-gatherer cultures? Such seemingly simple cultures have their own rich patterns of interpersonal relationships and political struggles, although they may not be visible to an outsider. Things might become pretty complicated, for example, when it comes time to choose a new chief. It also is reasonable to wonder whether monastery life looks as simple from the inside as it does from the outside. While some cultures might be more complex than others, it is not easy to be sure which those are.

Tightness and Looseness

Triandis also proposed that the *tightness-looseness* dimension contrasts cultures that tolerate very little deviation from proper behavior (tight cultures) with those that allow fairly large deviations from cultural norms (loose cultures). He hypothesized that ethnically homogeneous and densely populated societies tend to be culturally tighter than societies that are more diverse or where people are more spread out. This is because in order to strictly enforce norms, people must be similar enough to agree on those norms, and also because strict norms of behavior are more necessary when people must live close together. For example, cultures that developed in places such as Hong Kong would tend to be tighter than cultures in places such as Australia.

The United States, historically a diverse and geographically spread out society, is a classic example of a loose culture. But the degree of looseness varies. Having lived in both places, I can testify that east-central Illinois is a much tighter culture than Berkeley, California. Berkeley is more densely populated than downstate Illinois, but it is also more diverse. This observation suggests that diversity may override density in determining tightness and looseness.

Boston, where I have also lived, is an even more interesting case. Tightness and looseness can vary by block. Homogeneous, ethnic Italian and Irish neighborhoods (the North End and South Boston, respectively), where cultural mores are quite tight, abut more diverse neighborhoods (e.g., Back Bay), where standards are much looser. Again, diversity seems key. All of these neighborhoods are about equally crowded. But whereas South Boston and the North End are populated mostly by people born and raised there and are each dominated by a particular ethnic group, nearly everybody I met in Back Bay seemed to be from somewhere else—usually California![8]

---

[8] On a recent visit, I discovered that Back Bay even has a Trader Joe's now.

So, is population density less important than diversity in determining whether a culture is tight or loose? Not so fast. Consider Singapore, a fairly tight culture, if you recall the incident of the spray-painting teenager.[9] It is ethnically diverse to an amazing degree—much more so than Boston or even California. It is densely populated, however, and its tight organization appears to be an important part of what makes the country function efficiently on a daily basis.

An interesting way to index the tightness of a culture is to examine left- and right-handedness. Worldwide, about 10 percent of the population is left-handed (Hardyck & Petrinovich, 1977). But this figure might be an underestimate of the true propensity, because almost all cultures (including American and European) prefer that people be right-handed. The degree of pressure to be right-handed appears to vary. One cross-cultural survey found that about 10 percent to 12 percent of Eskimos and Australian Aborigines were left-handed, indicating little if any coercion in those two relatively loose cultures. In Western European samples, the rate was about 6 percent, and in Hong Kong, the rate was near 1 percent, suggesting that those cultures are much tighter. Interestingly, the percentage of "lefties" among women enrolled at the University of Hong Kong was zero, suggesting that they are subjected to particularly strong cultural pressures (Dawson, 1974).

Head Versus Heart

As was mentioned earlier, cultural boundaries can be determined in many ways, including even one's city of residence. Anyone who has traveled around the United States knows that its many cities can be quite different from each other. According to psychologists Nansook Park and Christopher Peterson (2010), one important difference is that some cities emphasize "strengths of the heart" such as fairness, mercy, gratitude, hope, love, and religiosity. Others emphasize "strengths of the head" such as artistic excellence, creativity, curiosity, critical thinking, and learning. Using a self-report survey administered to more than 600,000 Americans over the Internet, Park and Peterson computed head and heart scores for a large number of U.S. cities.

Some of the results were what might have been expected, and others seem a bit surprising. The highest "head" cities were San Francisco, Los Angeles, Oakland (CA), and Albuquerque (NM). Do any of these surprise you? The highest "heart" cities were El Paso (TX), Mesa (AZ), Miami, and Virginia Beach (VA) (see **Figure 13.4**). The city in the United States with the lowest "heart" score is Boston. As I've mentioned, I lived there for several years. The verdict seems a little harsh, but I can see where it comes from.[10]

---

[9] It is also a country where, during the final approach to the airport, smiling flight attendants hand out little cards reminding passengers that the penalty for drug smuggling is death.

[10] For example, have you ever had to deal with Boston drivers? Merciless.

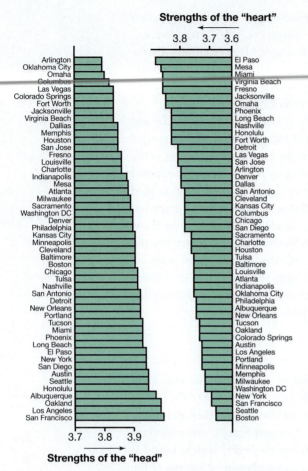

Strengths of the "heart"

3.8   3.7   3.6

(left column)	(right column)
Arlington	El Paso
Oklahoma City	Mesa
Omaha	Miami
Columbus	Virginia Beach
Las Vegas	Fresno
Colorado Springs	Jacksonville
Fort Worth	Omaha
Jacksonville	Phoenix
Virginia Beach	Long Beach
Dallas	Nashville
Memphis	Honolulu
Houston	Fort Worth
San Jose	Detroit
Fresno	Las Vegas
Louisville	San Jose
Charlotte	Arlington
Indianapolis	Denver
Mesa	Dallas
Atlanta	San Antonio
Milwaukee	Cleveland
Sacramento	Kansas City
Washington DC	Columbus
Denver	Chicago
Philadelphia	San Diego
Kansas City	Sacramento
Minneapolis	Charlotte
Cleveland	Houston
Baltimore	Tulsa
Boston	Baltimore
Chicago	Louisville
Tulsa	Atlanta
Nashville	Indianapolis
San Antonio	Oklahoma City
Detroit	Philadelphia
New Orleans	Albuquerque
Portland	New Orleans
Tucson	Tucson
Miami	Oakland
Phoenix	Colorado Springs
Long Beach	Austin
El Paso	Los Angeles
New York	Portland
San Diego	Minneapolis
Austin	Memphis
Seattle	Milwaukee
Honolulu	Washington DC
Albuquerque	New York
Oakland	San Francisco
Los Angeles	Seattle
San Francisco	Boston

3.7   3.8   3.9

Strengths of the "head"

Figure 13.4 Strengths of the Head and the Heart in U.S. Cities The ratings were based on self-reports administered to more than 600,000 U.S. residents via the Internet.

Source: Park & Peterson (2010), Figure 1, p. 541.

Findings like these immediately raise two questions. The first is, why does it matter? Do attributes like these, on the level of whole cities, have any broader implications? The answer appears to be yes. Almost all of the cities in Figure 13.4 were assessed as to their "creativity," on the basis of such criteria as the number of scientists, engineers, professors, and artists who lived there, the number of patents granted per capita, the presence of high-tech industry, and the city's overall level of openness and tolerance (Florida, 2002). Cities that scored high on creativity, defined in this way, tended to have better job growth, lower unemployment, and diverse immigration patterns. And these same cities tended to be the ones with higher strengths of the head, and lower strengths of the heart. They also were more likely to have voted for the Democratic presidential nominee in the 2008 election.

The second question is, why would cities vary on dimensions like this? Psychologist Peter Rentfrow and his colleagues (Rentfrow, Gosling, & Potter, 2008) offer three possible answers. First, different kinds of people are attracted to different cities, leading to *selective migration.* Artists and scientists may prefer to live in Boston or Los Angeles over Oklahoma City or Omaha, for example. Second, social influence can affect a person's values. If you live around people who mostly strongly support—or oppose—gay marriage, for instance, over time these opinions may have an effect on your own beliefs. Third, ecological factors may influence cultural differences between cities (or other geographical areas). For example, a lack of winter sunlight can lead to depression (Kasper, Wehr, Bartko, Gaist, & Rosenthal, 1989), and high temperatures are associated with higher rates of violence (Anderson, 1989). Do either of these factors help explain the differences between U.S. cities in Figure 13.4? In this particular case, I don't see that they do, but I have to admit that I got pretty gloomy by the end of the winter in heartless Boston.

Collectivism and Individualism

One of the most profound ways cultures may differ from each other is the way they view the relationship between the individual and society, and one of the most-studied dimensions of culture seeks to capture this difference. Many studies array cultures along the dimension of collectivism-individualism, which compares the Western view of the individual, which is probably familiar to most readers of this book, with a viewpoint more consistent with the Buddhist philosophy summarized in Chapter 12.

THE SELF AND OTHERS According to psychologists who study this dimension, in collectivist cultures, with Japan used as the typical example, the needs of the group (the "collective") are more important than the rights of individuals (Markus & Kitayama, 1991). Indeed, the boundary between the individual self and the others in one's group is relatively fuzzy. For example, the Japanese word for "self," *jibun*, refers to "one's portion of the shared life space." Japanese also exhibit a general desire to sink inconspicuously into the group; a Japanese proverb says, "The nail that stands out gets pounded down" (Markus & Kitayama, 1991, pp. 224, 228).[11]

In individualist cultures, such as the United States, the single person is more important. People are viewed as separate from each other, and independence and prominence are important virtues. The willingness to stand up for one's rights is all-important, and an American proverb teaches, "The squeaky wheel gets the grease" (Markus & Kitayama, 1991, p. 224). As we saw in Chapter 12, an individualist view also leads to phenomena such as existential anxiety, the concern over whether one is living life in the right way. Because the philosophy of individualism isolates people from each other, members of individualist cultures may be particularly vulnerable to problems such as loneliness and depression (Tseng, 2003).

Japan, China, and India are the most frequently discussed examples of collectivist cultures, and the United States seems like the most obvious—or glaring—example of an individualist culture. A survey of employees of IBM (which has offices all over the world) found that natives of Taiwan, Peru, Pakistan, Colombia, and Venezuela were more collectivist and less individualist in outlook than natives of Australia, Britain, Canada, the Netherlands, and the United States (Hofstede, 1984). Within the United States, Hispanics, Asians, and African Americans are more collectivist than Anglos (Triandis, 1994). Also within the United States, women are more collectivist than men (Lykes, 1985).

---

[11] New Zealand, which is also more collectivist than the United States, has a saying that tall poppies are cut first.

PERSONALITY AND COLLECTIVISM Researchers have developed long lists of behavioral and attitudinal differences. The most far-reaching suggestion is that personality itself might have a different meaning—or even no meaning at all—in collectivist, especially Asian, societies (Markus & Kitayama, 1998). One indication is the number of trait words in Eastern and Western languages. English has about 2,800 trait words that are used in everyday speech (Norman, 1967),[12] whereas Chinese has about 557 (Yang & Lee, 1971). This is a noticeably smaller number, and has led some psychologists to suspect that personality in the Western sense is less meaningful in Eastern contexts (Shweder & Bourne, 1982, 1984). However, 557 is still quite a few, and every language studied so far has at least some trait words. So it is almost certainly going too far to say that personality traits have no meaning in collectivist cultures—and wrong to the point of being troubling to claim that members of collectivist cultures have "no personalities" (more will be said on this point shortly).

One does not have to go to such an extreme to notice many differences between individualist and collectivist cultures that are real, interesting, and important. For example, more autobiographies are written in individualist countries, and more histories of the group are written in collectivist countries (Triandis, 1997). In collectivist countries, satisfaction with life is based on the harmony of one's relationships with others; in individualist countries, self-esteem is more important (Kwan, Bond, & Singelis, 1997). People from collectivist cultures carefully observe social hierarchies. In India, a person who is even one day older is supposed to receive respect from a younger friend (Triandis, 1997). People in individualist cultures are less attentive to differences in status. In the United States, many students call their professors by their first names; this does not happen in China, Japan, or India. However, everybody wants to be distinctive, even members of collectivist cultures. They just go about it differently. In individualist cultures, it has been proposed that people become distinctive by showing that they are independent and different from everyone else. In collectivist cultures, people are more likely to try to stand out by attaining prominent social positions such as becoming leaders, teachers, or intellectual authorities (Becker et al., 2012).

SELF-REGARD The individualist's need for positive self-regard may be felt less acutely by a member of a collectivist culture (Heine, Lehman, Markus, & Kitayama, 1999). Specifically, research has found that Japanese people may not have the pervasive need to think well of themselves that is so characteristic of North Americans, and the theoretical explanation is that they tie their individual well-being to that of a larger group. Consistent with this theory, studies have found Japanese and American students respond differently to success, failure, and negative

---

[12] Most of the 17,953 traits on Allport and Odbert's famous list (see the introductory text for Part II) are rarely used in ordinary conversation. When is the last time you heard someone described as *vulnific*?

self-relevant information. For example, Canadian college students who heard they had failed a test of creativity quickly searched for ways to think well of themselves in other contexts, whereas Japanese students showed no sign of this response (Heine, Kitayama, & Lehman, 2001). In another study, Canadians who failed an experimental task persisted less on a second task and denigrated its importance. Japanese participants had the opposite reaction, working harder and viewing the task as something important they should strive to do better (Heine, Kitayama, Lehman, Takata et al., 2001). Apparently, this is because they have learned the Confucian view that failure always opens an opportunity for learning.

SOCIABILITY, EMOTION, AND MOTIVATION Collectivist cultures are more sociable. For example, Mexicans spend more time in social interaction than Americans (Ramírez-Esparza, Mehl, Álvarez-Bermúdez, & Pennebaker, 2008). Skiing in groups and social bathing are more common in collectivist cultures; members of individualist cultures prefer to do these activities alone (Brandt, 1974). In general, members of individualist cultures spend less time with more people; members of collectivist cultures spend more time with fewer people (L. Wheeler, Reise, & Bond, 1989). The cocktail party, where one is supposed to circulate and meet as many people as possible, is a Western invention. While Easterners may be relatively standoffish and shy at such gatherings, they also tend to have a few close relationships, not casually entered into, that are more intimate than usual Western friendships.

Members of individualist and collectivist cultures may experience emotion differently. People in individualist countries report experiencing more self-focused emotions (such as anger), compared with people in collectivist countries, who are more likely to report experiencing other-focused emotions (such as sympathy) (Markus & Kitayama, 1991). Furthermore, Japanese students reported more pleasant emotional lives when they felt they were fitting well into their group; for American students, individual concerns were just as important (Mesquita & Karasawa, 2002). Arranged marriages are relatively common in collectivist cultures, whereas members of individualist cultures are expected to marry for (self-directed) love. The downside of this romantic, individualist approach is that, when a married couple falls out of love, they may get divorced and cause their family to disintegrate. In collectivist cultures, this is less likely (Tseng, 2003). In general, emotional experience in collectivist cultures appears to be more grounded in assessments of social worth, to reflect the nature of social reality rather than private, inner experience, and, perhaps most importantly, to depend on relationships rather than the individual alone (Mesquita, 2001).

> Arranged marriages are relatively common in collectivist cultures, whereas members of individualist cultures are expected to marry for love.

People in individualist and collectivist cultures also may have different fundamental motivations. According to one theory, a primary danger in collectivist society is "losing face," or respect by one's social group. While respect by others can be lost quickly, it can be increased or regained only slowly, so it makes sense to become risk-averse and attentive to the possibility of loss. In individualist cultures, the focus is more on individual achievement that stands apart from the group, so doing better for oneself is more important than the risk of losing face. In an attempt to test part of this theory, one study found that North Americans (Canadians) were more sensitive to information that indicated the presence or absence of possibilities for pleasure or reward, whereas Asians (in this case, Japanese) were more sensitive to information relevant to risk or loss (Hamamura, Meijer, Heine, Kamaya, & Hori, 2009). For example, when asked to memorize a long list of life events, North Americans were more likely to remember "gorgeous weather for hiking" (representing the presence of a positive outcome), and Japanese were more likely to remember "doing better than expected on a test" (the absence of a negative outcome). Similarly, North Americans were more likely to remember "a favorite class was cancelled" (absence of a positive outcome), and Japanese were more likely to remember "stuck in a traffic jam" (presence of a negative outcome) (Hamamura et al., 2009, p. 457).

This difference in motivation can have advantages. Because of their need to stand out, members of individualist cultures may *self-enhance* (describing themselves as better than they really are), whereas members of collectivist cultures, free of this need, may describe themselves more accurately. One study examined the *holier-than-thou phenomenon*, in which people describe themselves as being more likely than they really are to perform acts such as donating money or avoiding being rude (Balcetis, Dunning, & Miller, 2008). Members of individualistic cultures (English and German participants) were more likely to describe themselves as better ("holier") than they really were, than were members of collectivist cultures (Spanish and Chinese American participants). Interestingly, this bias applied only to perceptions of self: Collectivists and individualists were both fairly accurate in predicting the future virtuous behavior of their acquaintances.

BEHAVIORAL CONSISTENCY Another basic cross-cultural issue is the matter of *self-determination*. The individualist view of the self assumes that the causes of behavior lie within the person. As a result, an individual is expected to behave consistently from one situation to the next. Indeed, in American culture, behavioral consistency is associated with mental health (Donahue, Robins, Roberts, & John, 1993; Sherman et al., 2010). The more socially embedded member of a collectivist culture, by contrast, might be expected to change his behavior more as a function of the particular immediate situation (Markus, Mullally, & Kitayama, 1997). As a result, a member of a collectivist culture might feel less pressure to behave consistently and less conflicted about inconsistent behavior. This difference is apparently the basis of the finding that, among Koreans, unlike among Americans, behavioral consistency is not associated with measures of mental health (Suh, 2002).

Some research suggests that, compared to members of individualist cultures, the behavior and experience of members of collectivist cultures are less consistent from one situation to the next. Koreans describe themselves as less consistent than Americans do, and different acquaintances of a Korean tend to agree less in their descriptions of his or her personality than do acquaintances of an American (Suh, 2002; see also Albright, Malloy, Dong, Kenny, & Fang, 1997). Self-descriptions of personality fluctuate more over time in Japan than in the United States (Chopik & Kitayama, 2017), and emotional experience also seems to vary across situations more for Japanese persons than for Americans (Oishi, Diener, Scollon, & Biswas-Diener, 2004).

This last study adds an important qualification. As was explained in Chapter 4, consistency can be conceptualized and analyzed in two ways. One way focuses on the degree to which an individual varies his behavior or experience from one situation to the next—absolute consistency. The other focuses on the degree to which an individual maintains his differences from other people across situations—relative consistency. For example, even a brave and confident person might be more nervous in a burning house than in a normal classroom (low absolute consistency), but still might be the most confident person present in both situations. The study by Oishi et al. (2004) found that the Japanese had more inconsistent emotional experiences than Americans in an absolute sense; their emotions changed more from one situation to the next. But they had equally consistent emotional experiences in a relative sense, because a Japanese person who was happier than others in one situation also tended to be happier than most in other situations. This finding implies that while members of collectivist cultures may be more inconsistent in an absolute sense than members of individualistic cultures, individual differences and associated personality traits appear to be equally important in both contexts (see also Church, Anderson-Harumi, et al., 2008; Church, Katigbak, et al., 2008).

There is also some reason to wonder whether cultural comparisons of behavioral variability based on self-report are entirely accurate. One study showed that on standard questionnaires, black South Africans (who tend to be more collectivist) rated their behavior as more variable than did white South Africans (who tend to be more individualistic). However, behavior as described in daily diaries and direct observations of behavior (including video observations across 12 laboratory situations!) showed that the behavior of both groups was equally consistent and equally predictable from personality measures (Fetvadjiev et al., 2017). This study highlights the importance of assessing the effect of personality through multiple methods (recall the four types of data discussed in Chapter 2), as well as helping to confirm that personality really does matter, everywhere in the world.

VERTICALITY AND COMPASSION The collectivism-individualism dimension has become a staple of cross-cultural psychology. But as research has accumulated, the picture of this difference between cultures has become more complicated. For one complication, Harry Triandis has suggested that individualistic or collectivist societies can both be further categorized as either vertical or horizontal (Triandis & Gelfand, 1998; see **Table 13.1**). *Vertical societies* assume that individual people are importantly different from each other, whereas *horizontal societies* tend to view all persons as essentially equal. Thus, a collectivist-vertical society might enforce strong authority on its members (e.g., China), while a collectivist-horizontal society might have weaker authority but a strong ethic that enforces equality and sharing (e.g., Israel). An individualist-vertical society would have strong authority but also give individuals the freedom (and the obligation) to support themselves in a market economy (e.g., France), whereas an individualist-horizontal society would value individual freedom but also assume that meeting everyone's needs is a shared obligation (e.g., Norway).

Cultures also differ from each other in other ways that do not map well onto collectivism-individualism. One study compared *self-compassion*, defined as "holding painful emotions in mindful awareness while feelings of care and kindness are extended to the self" (Neff, Pisitsungkagarn, & Hsieh, 2008, p. 267), between the United States, Thailand, and Taiwan. While self-compassion might seem like a quintessentially collectivist idea, the study found that, while the highest levels were in Thailand, the lowest levels were in Taiwan—both ostensibly

Table 13.1	VERTICAL AND HORIZONTAL TYPES OF COLLECTIVISM AND INDIVIDUALISM	
Dimension	**Collectivism**	**Individualism**
Vertical	Self different from others	Self different from others
	Communal sharing	Market economy
	Authority ranking	Authority ranking
	Low freedom	High freedom
	Low equality	Low equality
	e.g., China	*e.g., France*
Horizontal	Self same as others	Self same as others
	Communal sharing	Market economy
	Low freedom	High freedom
	High equality	High equality
	e.g., Israel	*e.g., Norway*

Source: The examples of countries in this table were chosen by Triandis and Gelfand. Table adapted from Triandis & Gelfand (1998), Table 1, p. 119.

collectivist societies—and individualist United States fell in the middle. The authors speculated that the basis of the difference might stem from the predominance of Buddhist philosophy in Thailand compared with Confucianism in Taiwan. This finding also serves as a reminder that Asia—the largest continent on Earth—is too diverse to be considered a single culture. It contains many cultures that differ from each other in important ways.

CAUTIONS ABOUT COLLECTIVISM/INDIVIDUALISM: THE JAPANESE CASE

The collectivism-individualism distinction has been used to compare many cultures, as you have seen, but the most common comparison is between Japan and the United States (Markus & Kitayama, 1991). So it may be surprising to learn that this comparison has been called into question. According to Japanese psychologist Yohtaro Takano, the oft-cited study by Hofstede (1984) failed to measure individualism correctly due to an error in interpreting a factor analysis (Heine, Lehman, Peng, & Greenholtz, 2002; Takano & Osaka, 1999). Even more surprising, a review of 16 other studies found that 11 of them reported Japanese and Americans to be about the same on this dimension and the remaining five actually found the Japanese scored higher on individualism than Americans (Takano & Osaka, 1999)! A further study tested the implication of individualism-collectivism theory that Japanese would conform more to group judgments in a replication of the classic Asch (1956) conformity experiment.[13] The rate of conformity in Japan was about the same (23 percent) as in the United States (25 percent; Takano, 2012; Takano & Sogon, 2008). Another recent study showed that the behaviors associated with aspects of situations were remarkably similar between Japan and the United States. For example, when a person is being criticized, people in Japan and the United States both report that they act irritated, express hostility, and feel anything but cheerful (Funder et al., 2012).

So where does the view of Japan as being so different from the United States come from? Takano and Osaka suggest it might be a cultural myth. They write,

> During the period between the opening of Japan in 1854 and the beginning of the Pacific War, quite a few Western observers noted that the Japanese lacked individuality. . . . In particular, Percival Lowell, who is known for interpreting the pattern on Mars' surface as canals, devoted a whole volume . . . to advocating the view that the Japanese were "impersonal." These observers prepared the basis for the common view. (Takano & Osaka, 1999, p. 311)

---

[13] In this famous study, subjects were asked to judge the length of lines after several accomplices of the experimenter made judgments that were obviously false. A surprising number of subjects (37 percent) conformed to the false judgments. However, note that—unlike the way this study is sometimes summarized—the proportion of conformers was less than half.

This common view, they suggest, led to anecdotes and biased selection of cultural phrases being used as a basis for thinking Japanese are particularly collectivistic, without a firm empirical basis otherwise. Other kinds of bias might have come into play as well.

> "Japanese collectivism" was stressed by Americans and "American individualism" by Japanese during World War II. "Japanese collectivism" (specifically, "Japanese collective economy") was again stressed amidst "Japan bashing" at the time of the 1980s trade conflict between the US and Japan. (Takano, 2012, p. 410)

The implications of Takano's argument are sobering. He highlights the way that a central aspect of collectivism-individualism theory can lead to members of collectivist cultures being seen as basically "all alike" and even as lacking personalities altogether, an attitude that edges uncomfortably close to dehumanization. The Japanese case should remind us that not all initial cultural comparisons will be supported by the evidence that accumulates over time, and that we should be careful that comparisons between cultures not lead us to forget the wide variety of distinctive individuals who inhabit every culture on Earth.

IS THE WORLD BECOMING MORE INDIVIDUALISTIC?   A difference that exists at one moment in history might change or even reverse over time. Evidence that cultural differences are not set in stone comes from a recent study of 78 countries that found that, on average, individualism scores have increased on average about 12 percent since 1960. This change occurred in all but a few countries—exceptions included Armenia, Malaysia, Mali, and Uruguay, which lagged in economic development during this period. The authors concluded that individualism increases, relative to collectivism, in countries that experience higher incomes, more education, and a shift in occupations from rural and farm settings to cities and offices. With the shift in individualism also come shifts in values, with these same countries showing increased tendencies to value friends as much as family, wanting children to be more independent of the family, and valuing free expression more and traditional practices less (Santos, Varnum & Grossman, 2017). The moral of the story is that the world is always changing. For the better or worse? That's a matter of opinion, isn't it?

Honor, Face, and Dignity

Collectivism-individualism theory basically divides the world into two parts, whereas a newer approach divides it into three. Psychologists Angela Leung and Dov Cohen (2011) suggest that cultures differ on three dimensions they call *honor*, *face*, and *dignity*.

Western cultures in general, and the United States in particular, are said to be dignity cultures. The key idea is that individuals are valuable in their own right and this value does not come from what other people think of them. This attitude leads to catchphrases such as "sticks and stones may break my bones, but words will never hurt me" and advertising slogans that exhort people to "think different." Internal strength and sturdiness allows one to be true to oneself, which means living up to one's own values and not necessarily the values of anyone else. This kind of culture fits well with and tends to emerge in market economies that are based on equal exchanges of goods and services among free individuals.

Cultures of honor are said to emerge in environments where the forces of civilization—such as laws and police—are weak or nonexistent and people must protect themselves, their families, and their own property. As was mentioned earlier, one example is the historic American South—which continues to influence modern culture in the southern United States. Another example is Latin America. An insult is an important event in such cultures, because to tolerate it could signal weakness and put one's person and property at risk. A strong social norm demands retaliation, regardless of the cost. Turning the other cheek is not an option. Instead, one needs to signal that one is ready to use violence if necessary, such as by owning and displaying guns. Members of honor cultures are highly sensitive to threats to their reputations, which may be why U.S. states that are part of this culture have higher rates of suicide, and individuals who endorse "honor" values are at higher risk for depression, no matter where they live (Osterman & Brown, 2011).

Finally, cultures of face emerge in societies that have stable hierarchies based on cooperation, such as Japan or China. People in such a culture are motivated to protect each others' social image by being careful not to insult, overtly criticize, or even disagree with each other in public. Authority figures are respected and obeyed, and controversy is avoided. Such behaviors protect the centrally important "3 H's" of hierarchy, humility, and harmony (Leung & Cohen, 2011, p. 510).

DIGNITY   **HONOR**   **FACE**

Of course, all cultures have elements of all three values in them, and individuals within cultures vary in the degree to which they accept the dominant cultural perspective. Leung and Cohen (2011) report a series of experiments in which people from the three cultures returned favors (a dignity behavior), repaid insults in kind (an honor behavior), or refrained from cheating (a face behavior). Not only did members of the three cultures vary in these behaviors as expected, but individuals *within* each group who more strongly accepted the cultural norm were more likely to behave in the culturally typical way. These findings underline yet again a theme that is emerging as increasingly important in the study of cultural differences: Individual differences within a society are every bit as important, if not more important, than the differences between them.

CULTURAL ASSESSMENT AND PERSONALITY ASSESSMENT

Many concepts used to assess differences among cultures can also be used to assess differences among individuals. We just saw this with the concepts of dignity, honor, and face. The three dimensions Triandis uses to describe cultures can also be used to describe persons. The cultural complexity dimension is analogous to the personality trait of *cognitive complexity*; cultural tightness resembles the traits of conscientiousness and *intolerance for ambiguity*; the collectivist-individualist distinction is analogous to a dimension of personal values that focuses on whether one believes that the individual is more important than the group (*ideocentrism*), or vice versa (*allocentrism*). Psychologists have also used more familiar personality-trait concepts to understand cross-cultural differences.

Researchers have done this in two ways. The first is to try to characterize cultural differences by assessing the degree to which average levels of specific traits vary between cultures. The second is to dive a bit more deeply into the cultures being compared by assessing the degree to which the traits that characterize people in one culture can meaningfully characterize people in another.

Comparing the Same Traits Across Cultures

As an example of the first approach, psychologists have translated the MMPI (see Chapter 5) into Chinese and found that, compared with Americans, Chinese people on average score higher on emotional reserve, introversion, considerateness, social caution, and self-restraint (Cheung & Song, 1989). At present, the most common way to compare the personalities of different cultures is using the Big Five (see Chapter 6). A study using translations of the NEO Personality Inventory (see Chapter 3) assessed extraversion in a large number of "Old World" nations, producing the map shown in **Figure 13.5**. Another study using the same inventory

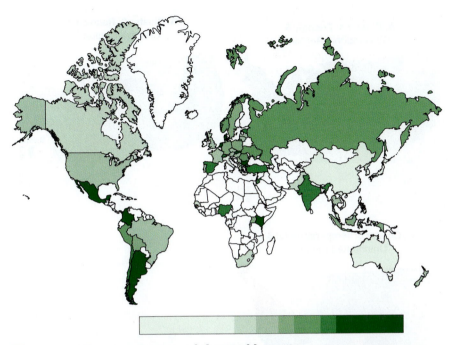

Figure 13.5. Extraversion around the World This figure shows average scores on Extraversion in 63 countries; darker colors are higher scores. The most extraverted countries in this study were Mexico, Hungary, and Bulgaria; the least extraverted were Singapore, Japan, and Hong Kong.

Source: Gardiner, G., Baranski, E., & Funder, D. (2018, July). Reliability of country personality traits: New evidence from the International Situations Project. Paper presented at European Association of Personality, Zadar, Croatia.

compared ethnic Chinese living in Canada with those in Hong Kong. Those who lived in Canada described themselves (S data) as being more open, cheerful, and agreeable, and these differences with people in Hong Kong increased the longer they lived in Canada—which suggests they arose because of the cultural environment (McCrae, Yik, Trapnell, Bond, & Paulhus, 1998).

Single nations can contain different subcultures. One study compared personality differences across areas of Russia (Allik et al., 2009). One notable finding: People who lived farther from Moscow were less trusting. Research has also documented ethnically based differences within the population sometimes described simply as "European Americans." One fascinating study compared American-born, second-generation-or-later descendants of immigrants from Scandinavia, with similarly distant descendants of Irish immigrants. When videotaped recounting times in their lives when they felt happiness or love, Irish Americans smiled more than did Scandinavian Americans, consistent with the customs of their different ancestral cultures (Tsai & Chentsova-Dutton, 2003).

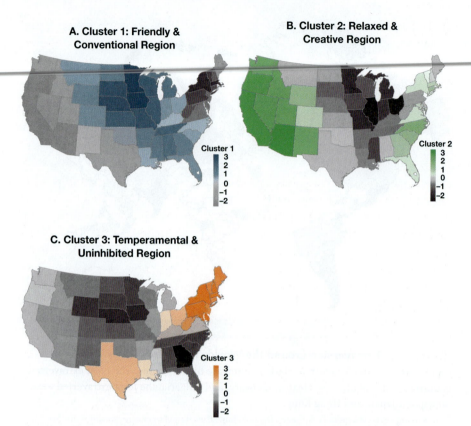

Figure 13.6 The Different Types of People Who Live in Different Parts of the United States The figure shows the statistical "hotspots" that reflect correlations between the average personality scores of states and the personality profiles of the three different types.

Source: Rentfrow et al. (2013), p. 1006.

Another study looked at clusters of traits that vary across the United States (Rentfrow et al., 2013). Based on personality tests taken online by more than a million participants,[14] the researchers identified three types of people. One they called *friendly and conventional,* characterized by traits such as sociable, considerate, dutiful, and traditional. This type of person was especially common in the American Midwest and South (see **Figure 13.6**). A second type they called *relaxed and creative,* characterized by traits such as open-minded, tolerant, individualistic, and emotionally stable (scoring low on neuroticism). These people were predominantly found on the American West Coast, in the Rocky Mountain states, and

---

[14] To be exact, the data came from five different samples that totaled 1,596,704 participants.

in the Sun Belt. The third type they labeled *temperamental and uninhibited*. These people received high scores on traits such as impulsive, irritable, inquisitive, passionate, and competitive. They also scored relatively high on neuroticism. Such people were found in the mid-Atlantic and northeastern states. As was mentioned earlier, such differences can occur for several reasons, including the tendency of people to migrate to areas of the country where they feel like they "fit in," the possibility that people are influenced in their personality development by the people they interact with all day long in the area where they live, and even the effects of climate on mood.

Cultural differences in personality are not just interesting; they can be consequential. Countries where people are more conscientious, on average, are also places where fewer people are atheists and where there is less alcoholism, smoking, and corruption (Mõttus, Allik, & Realo, 2010). On the other hand, these countries also tend to have less democracy, lower life expectancy, and less robust economies. The countries that scored highest and lowest on conscientiousness may surprise you (or maybe not): India, Malaysia, and Croatia had the most conscientious people. Japan, Belgium, and Sweden scored lowest. The reasons for these results are complex, but seem to stem from the fact that conscientiousness is a multifaceted trait (as are all of the Big Five). It subsumes narrower traits such as competence, order, dutifulness, achievement striving, self-discipline, and deliberation, and each of these facets is distinct and has its own consequences. This means that as a tool for cultural comparison, the Big Five traits by themselves might be too broad. It can be useful to look at individual differences a bit more specifically.

For example, another trait that varies around the world is self-esteem. According to one study, residents of Canada have higher self-esteem than those in any other country in the world, followed by Israel, Estonia, and Serbia. Residents of Japan have the lowest self-esteem, and those in Hong Kong and Bangladesh are not much higher. This fact may be significant, because one recent study found that the lower a country's average level of self-esteem, the higher the suicide rate (Chatard, Selimbegović, & Konan, 2009). In this sense, cultural differences in personality might be a matter of life and death.

A further complication when comparing personality around the world is that the same outcome may be associated with different traits. Consider, for example, the tendency of people to be religious. In secular countries where organized religion is relatively weak, highly religious people tend to be low on openness to experience. But in countries where the role of religion is strong, highly religious people are more likely to be agreeable and conscientious (Gebaur et al., 2014). These are people who get along well with others and tend to follow social norms, whatever they may be.

What about gender differences? Psychologists addressed this question by administering the NEO Personality Inventory, or translations of it, in 26 cultures to 23,031 individuals (Costa, Terracciano, & McCrae, 2001). They found that, in almost all cultures, women scored higher than men in neuroticism, agreeableness, warmth, and openness to feelings; men scored higher than women in assertiveness and openness to ideas. Surprisingly, these gender differences were actually larger in so-called developed societies such as Belgium, France, and the United States than in less-developed areas such as Zimbabwe and Malaysia.

Different Traits for Different Cultures?

The findings summarized above are interesting, but their meaning is not always clear, because they depend on a not-so-hidden assumption—that the same traits can be used to describe people in different cultures. This assumption is probably all right if one wishes to compare Michigan with New York, but becomes more tenuous when comparing, say, China and the United States. Psychologists have put major effort into investigating the degree to which the same traits are relevant and have the same meaning across cultures. The results are mixed.

An influential program of research has shown that the Big Five traits of personality can be found in observers' personality ratings in more than 50 cultures (McCrae, Terracciano, & 78 members of the Personality Profiles of Cultures Project, 2005). But other studies have found many variations from one culture to the next. For example, one study concluded that measures of the Big Five could be effectively translated into Spanish, but that such translations also missed particular aspects of Spanish personality, such as humor, good nature, and unconventionality (Benet-Martínez & John, 1998, 2000). In the Levant (Jordan, Lebanon, Syria, and the West Bank), a study of Arabic trait words found seven factors, not five—the two extra factors were integrity and humility (Zeinoun, Daouk-Őyry, Choueiri & van de Vijver, 2017). Another study found that openness to experience did not emerge as an important trait in Chinese personality assessment (Cheung, Cheung, Zhang, Leung, Leong, & Yeh, 2008). Building on findings like these, some researchers have argued that only three of the Big Five—conscientiousness, extraversion, and agreeableness—should be considered truly universal (De Raad & Peabody, 2005).

Translating personality-trait terms from one language to another is hazardous because translations are always at least a little bit inexact. Some quantitatively sophisticated psychologists are attempting to improve the degree to which personality tests are comparable from one culture and language to the next, by using a statistical technique called *item response theory (IRT)*. IRT analyses go deep into personality inventories by looking not just at mean scores, but at patterns in how participants respond to specific items. One such study found that, in a scale used to measure satisfaction with life, four of the five items yielded different patterns of response between Chinese and American participants (Oishi, 2006). Another study found that, while Germans appeared to score higher than Minnesotans in aggression and absorption, and Minnesotans higher in well-being, control, and traditionalism, these findings might be due simply to differences in patterns of item response (W. Johnson, Spinath, Krueger, Angleitner, & Riemann, 2008). Still another study found that the NEO Personality Inventory, widely used in cultural comparison, had different patterns of response in the United States, the Philippines, and Mexico (Church et al., 2011). These recent findings serve as a caution that, when comparing mean trait scores between cultures, there may be more (or less) than meets the eye.

To move beyond such problems, an increasing number of psychologists around the world are developing trait scales *endogenously* (from the inside), to see if personality-trait constructs that emerge in one culture also emerge in another. This approach is much more difficult because the nature of the research requires the work of psychologists who are native to each culture, and many areas of the world do not have the traditions or means to train and support homegrown psychologists. Nonetheless, progress is being made.

One study examined personality traits in China. It began by listing the trait words found in a Chinese dictionary and then asking a total of 751 Chinese participants to rate themselves or one another using those traits. The researchers found that the traits could be summarized by seven factors that they labeled "extraversion," "conscientiousness," "unselfishness," "harmfulness,"[15] "gentle temper," "intellect," and "dependency/fragility" (Zhou, Saucier, Gao, & Liu, 2009). As you can see, only three or four of these seem similar to any of the Big Five: extraversion, conscientiousness, intellect (which resembles openness), and perhaps harmfulness (as the opposite of agreeableness). A parallel study, conducted in Spain, also found seven factors in Castilian Spanish (Benet-Martínez & Waller, 1997). The Spanish personality factors were labeled "positive valence," "negative valence," "conscientiousness," "openness," "agreeableness," "pleasantness" (referring to emotional experience), and "engagement" (or "passion"). Chinese and Spanish may both have seven basic personality traits, but, to read these lists, they are not the same seven.

Thinking

One of the most intriguing and challenging questions facing cross-cultural psychology concerns the degree to which people from different cultures think differently. On one level, it seems safe to infer that because behavioral traits differ across cultures, as we have just seen, the thinking associated with behavior must be different too. On another level, it is difficult to specify the ways in which thought processes in one culture may differ from those in another, so research attempting to do this opens an exciting new frontier in psychology that has important and controversial implications.

---

[15] They also used the label "noxious violativeness," which sounds dreadful.

HOLISTIC PERCEPTION AND THE SELF For example, one line of research suggests that East Asians think more *holistically* than Americans, explaining events in context rather than in isolation, and seeking to integrate divergent points of view rather than set one against another (Nisbett, Peng, Choi, & Norenzayan, 2001). In particular, this difference appears to characterize how they think about the self. According to one study, Japanese and Chinese people are more willing than Americans to describe themselves in contradictory terms (e.g., as friendly but shy), and also use more holistic phrases such as "I am someone insignificant in the universe" or "I am a living form" (Spencer-Rogers, Boucher, Mori, Wang, & Peng, 2009, p. 32). Methods of neuroscience (discussed in Chapter 8) are also beginning to be applied to cross-cultural differences (Kitayama & Park, 2010). One study showed that areas of the prefrontal cortex that are generally activated when one thinks about one's self are also activated when Chinese—but not Americans—think about their mothers! This finding was interpreted to mean that the self is a broader concept for Chinese, because it includes important other people (Zhu, Zhang, Fan, & Han, 2007).

These differences may be related to the collectivism-individualism distinction discussed earlier, in which collectivists feel more a part of their social environment than individualists do. The difference may reach down to the perceptual level. In one study, Japanese participants either watched animated underwater scenes or looked at photographs of wildlife; in both cases, they remembered more information about the wider context than did American participants, and were better able to recognize specific objects when they saw them in their original settings (Masuda & Nisbett, 2001). These results suggest that an American observer may look at a scene and see a specific object or person, whereas the Japanese observer is more likely to see and remember the larger context.

INDEPENDENT THINKING A controversial area of cross-cultural research concerns the degree to which Asians, compared with Americans, characteristically formulate and express independent and original points of view. Various psychologists and educators have observed that Asian students seem drawn to fields that require rote study and memorization rather than independent thinking, and that they are less willing than European Americans to speak up in class discussion (Mahbubani, 2002). One Vietnamese American writer lamented that this occurs because

> self-expression is largely discouraged across Asia. . . . Asia is by and large a continent where the ego is suppressed. The self exists in the context of families and clans . . . [while] America still values the maverick, the inventor, the loudmouth class clown, the individual with a vision. (Lam, 2003, p. M6)

Other observers have offered a different interpretation. One study showed that thinking for Asian Americans is disrupted by trying to talk at the same time, whereas this effect was not found in Americans of European descent (Kim, 2002). Thus, a quiet Asian American student may be silent because she is thinking! The Confucian philosophy of learning prescribes that the first thing a student should do is learn the basic facts of a field, then analyze, and finally innovate. Early in her learning career, a student is not supposed to formulate independent opinions; that should come only later, after she has sufficient knowledge (Tweed & Lehman, 2002). Another writer has observed that

> Asians are respectful not because they are afraid of their teachers or because they have no questions, but because they are brought up with the idea that humility ensures better learning. They are taught to listen attentively and to question only after they have understood others. (J. Li, 2003, pp. 146–147)

Values

The most difficult issues in cross-cultural psychology concern values. People feel deeply about matters of right and wrong, and may be not merely surprised but also upset and angry when they find that other people do not share their views. Sometimes, wars start. Thus, a particular challenge is to try to understand how even seemingly obvious and basic values can vary across cultures, and to formulate an appropriate response to these differences.

THE SEARCH FOR UNIVERSAL VALUES Cross-cultural research on values has followed two tracks. One track seeks values that are universal to all cultures. This is similar in intent to the research summarized in the previous chapter (Chapter 12) that tried to identify traits that all cultures see as virtues. Finding universal values would have two implications. First, we might infer that a value held in all cultures is in some sense a "real" value that goes beyond cultural judgment, a value we can be confident should be valued. (Do you agree with this inference?) Second, if we could find a set of common values, we might be able to use these to settle disputes between cultures by developing compromises based on the areas of universal agreement.

An influential study by cross-cultural psychologists Shalom Schwartz and Lilach Sagiv (1995) identified 10 values as candidates. The 10 possibly universal values are power, achievement, hedonism, stimulation, self-direction, understanding, benevolence, tradition, conformity, and security. Another way to look at these values is to see them as goals that everybody, everywhere, wants to achieve. Schwartz and Sagiv theorize that these values can be organized in terms of two dimensions. One is the *openness to change–conservatism* dimension, and the other they called the *self-transcendence–self-enhancement* dimension. For example, stimulation is high on openness to change and low on conservatism, whereas conformity, tradition, and security are the reverse. Likewise, achievement is high on self-enhancement and low on self-transcendence, while benevolence is the reverse (see **Figure 13.7**). Ratings of these values followed this two-part structure, more or less, in countries including Israel, Japan, and Australia. The hope of this ongoing research is to develop not just a universal list of values, but an understanding of how these values relate to each other and apply to decisions, behaviors, and cultural priorities.

CULTURAL DIFFERENCES IN VALUES While Schwartz and Sagiv's research seeks to identify a universal structure of values, they acknowledge that cultural differences are still important. The second track in cross-cultural research on

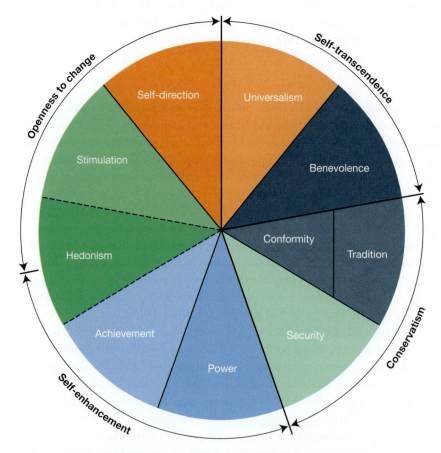

Figure 13.7 Theoretical Structure of Values Suggested to Be Universal The ten terms in this figure all refer to values that, it has been theorized, people in all cultures are motivated to live by. They are arranged here in terms of their relevance to two dimensions: openness to change versus conservatism, and self-transcendence versus self-enhancement.

Source: Schwartz & Sagiv (1995), Figure 1, p. 96.

values strives to illuminate these differences. A long-standing interest of many researchers has been the differences between collectivist and individualist cultures in their styles of moral reasoning (J. G. Miller, Bersoff, & Harwood, 1990). While the individualist cultural ethos emphasizes liberty, freedom of choice, rights, and individual needs, some theorists claim, the collectivist cultural ethos emphasizes obligations, reciprocity, and duties to the group (Iyengar & Lepper, 1999; J. G. Miller & Bersoff, 1992). The collectivist style of moral reasoning imposes a group norm; the individualist style emphasizes independent and individual choice.

We can see this distinction even within North American culture. For example, although individualism is often viewed as a Western cultural attribute, the Roman Catholic Church—a Western institution if ever there was one—is profoundly collectivist in outlook. Individualism is really a Protestant, northwestern European idea, whereas collectivism is more Catholic and southeastern European (Sabini, 1995). Martin Luther broke with the Catholic Church over the right of individuals to interpret the scriptures. The Catholic view was—and still is—that any interpretation must come from the Church itself.

We can hear echoes of this ancient argument, as well as of the distinction between individualism and collectivism, in the modern debate over abortion. The individualist point of view, endorsed by many (though not all) Protestant and Jewish denominations, is that abortion is a matter of individual moral responsibility and choice. One might deplore abortion and regard it as a tragic occurrence but still endorse the idea that it is the pregnant woman who is most centrally involved, and in the end it all comes down to her individual, free decision. Those who endorse the right to safe, legal abortions do not like to be called "pro-abortion"; they prefer the term "pro-choice."

The very different, collectivist point of view, strongly espoused by the Catholic Church and some of the more conservative Protestant denominations, is that abortion is morally wrong, period. The unborn fetus is already a person—a member in good standing of the collective, if you will. To abort that fetus is to kill a member of the collective, something no individual member—not even the fetus's mother—has a right to do. Indeed, it is the duty of the collective, institutionalized in the church or the state, to prohibit any such act. The matter does not come down to personal choice at all. It comes down to a collectively determined issue of right and wrong.

> From either a collectivist or individualist perspective on the abortion debate, the other point of view is simply wrong.

No wonder this debate shows no signs of subsiding, and no wonder, too, that grounds for reasonable compromise seem nonexistent. In the abortion debate, we see a head-on collision between two fundamentally different ways of addressing moral issues. Elements of both views coexist, uneasily, in North American culture, but one of them cannot be mapped onto the other. From either a collectivist or individualist perspective on the abortion debate, the other point of view is simply wrong.

THE ORIGINS OF CULTURAL DIFFERENCES

We have now surveyed ample evidence that the average personalities of people in different cultures are often different, that people differ in *how* they differ in different cultures (i.e., the same traits may not apply in all cultures), and that cultures can hold profoundly divergent basic values. So this may be a good time to step back and ask two questions that, while not often addressed, have been lurking in the background all along: *Why* are cultures so different? And what determines the specific, distinctive psychology that a particular culture develops?

Avoiding the Issue

One approach to cultural psychology, influential until fairly recently, regarded these questions as essentially unanswerable. The philosophy of **deconstructionism** holds that reality has no meaning apart from what humans invent, or "construct." This philosophy is an important part of the modern study of literature, and has also permeated some areas of anthropology (e.g., Shweder & Sullivan, 1990). Translated into cultural psychology, deconstructionism implies that any answer to why a culture is the way it is would itself have to be based on the assumptions of another culture (J. G. Miller, 1999). This is another way of saying that no meaningful answer is possible. If you recall Funder's Third Law—about something beating nothing two times out of three—you will not be surprised to learn that I do not have much patience with the deconstructionist approach. Differences between cultures are real, and to ask why they exist is to ask a good question.

The Ecological Approach

The most reasonable answer would seem to be that different cultures developed, over a long period of time, in different circumstances, and with the need to deal with different problems. Triandis (1994) proposed a straightforward model that can be diagrammed as

Ecology $\longrightarrow$ Culture $\longrightarrow$ Socialization $\longrightarrow$ Personality $\longrightarrow$ Behavior

In this model, behavior comes from personality, which comes from implicit and explicit teaching during childhood (socialization is another name for enculturation in this context), which is a product of the culture. The first term in Triandis's model is *ecology*, by which he means the physical layout and resources of the land where the culture originated, together with the distinctive tasks and challenges this culture has faced.

A somewhat different ecological model was offered by Oishi and Graham (2010). This model can be diagrammed as

$$\text{Ecology}$$
$$\nearrow \nwarrow$$
$$\text{Culture} \longleftrightarrow \text{Mind and Behavior}$$

In this model, everything affects everything else. Ecology changes the culture, but culture also changes the ecology. Ecology changes the mind, but the mind changes the ecology, too. Perhaps most importantly, culture and the minds of the people who live in a culture change each other over time as well.

For example, the collectivist nature of Chinese culture might be traceable to the need, thousands of years ago, to develop complex agricultural projects and water systems that required the coordination of many people. To succeed at these tasks, a culture had to develop in which people were willing to surrender some degree of self-interest in order to serve the common good. In terms of the systems diagrammed above, the ecology changed both how people related to each other and the overall culture. At the same time, the success of this change allowed the building of huge irrigation systems and terraced farms that changed the overall ecology and Chinese civilization in profound ways.

In the same historical period, people who lived in hunting and gathering societies, where individual effort is more important, did not develop the same collectivist outlook or complex social system as did the Chinese. While it takes thousands of people to build a water system, a hunting party that becomes too large will not catch anything. This difference, we could speculate (and honestly, that's all we are doing), may be one reason China developed a collectivist culture while Germany developed an individualist one. A related line of speculation explains that North Americans value independence and personal achievement more than do Europeans (British and Germans) because North America was settled largely by voluntary immigrants who faced the task of developing a whole, new, seemingly

"I don't know how it started, either. All I know is that it's part of our corporate culture."

empty continent[16]. The necessity to complete this *cultural task* led a distinctively American culture to emerge from its European roots (Kitayama, Park, Sevincer, Karasawa, & Uskul, 2009).

On an even broader scale, biologist Jared Diamond has argued that European countries became dominant colonial powers around the world because of an accident of geography. Ancient Europe had native plants that were easily turned into reliable, food-giving crops and animals that were readily domesticated to provide food and transportation. Another, ironic "advantage" is that at the same time Europeans began to travel around the world, at home they often lived close together in filthy cities. Those who survived developed wide immunity to diseases that were fatal to other peoples, such as Native Americans, who lived in cleaner environments (Diamond, 1999). The arrival of Europeans often marked the beginning of a devastating epidemic.

Disease can affect cultural development in other ways. One study examined the degree to which cultures differ in their average levels of extraversion, openness, and sociosexuality (which, as explained in Chapter 5, is the willingness to engage in sexual relationships in the absence of a long-term relationship) (Schaller & Murray, 2008). The average level of these traits tends to be lower, it turns out, in countries that historically have suffered from high levels of infectious disease. (Many of these countries lie near the equator,[17] where the warm climate apparently facilitates disease transmission.) Why? The authors of the study speculate that extraverted behavior, open behavior, and—perhaps most of all—"sociosexual" behavior, all increase interpersonal contact and the risk of catching an infectious disease. As a result, people who are more introverted and less open and sociosexual have better chances for survival, making their type more common as members of the culture over time. In a related finding, cultures from areas with historically high levels of pathogens also tend to promote conformity, presumably because this leads to behaviors—such as cleanliness and orderliness—that help to prevent the spread of disease (Murray, Trudeau, & Schaller, 2011). Such cultures also have fewer left-handed people! This does not mean that being left-handed spreads disease; rather, it implies, as was mentioned earlier, that the suppression of natural left-handedness is an indicator of the degree to which a culture enforces tight adherence to its rules.

Even small differences in ecology can lead to cultural differences in personality. Truk and Tahiti, small islands in the South Pacific with cultures dependent on fishing, have evolved different patterns of gender roles and aggressive behavior

---

[16] As Americans are prone to forget, there were people living there already.

[17] Of course, the equator runs through several continents. Countries historically high in infectious disease include Nigeria, Zambia, Greece, Italy, India, China, Indonesia, Venezuela, and Brazil. Some of the lowest historic rates were in South Africa, Sweden, Norway, and Germany (Gangestad & Buss, 1993).

(Gilmore, 1990). In Truk, catching fish requires venturing out to sea, which is hazardous. The result is a culture in which the men who must do this learn to be brave, violent, and physical; they are also dominating of women. In Tahiti, fish can be caught easily in the home lagoon, which is not dangerous at all. The men in this culture tend to be gentle, to ignore insults, to be very slow to fight, and also to be respectful of women. Apparently, this is all because of where the fish are!

It is also possible to explain the development of subcultures as a function of particular conditions experienced by groups within larger cultures. As I mentioned earlier, extreme poverty and decades of racial discrimination have led some ethnic subcultures within the United States to develop styles of self-presentation (young males seeking to appear tough and threatening) and self-definition (through identification with gangs and other sources of social support and physical protection) that strongly contrast with the mainstream culture (E. Anderson, 1994). The culture of honor in the American South may have its roots in the agrarian past of that region, where land and possessions had to be personally protected, or else lost (D. Cohen et al., 1996). Other aspects of minority subcultures in the United States and Canada stem from distinct ethnic heritages rooted in Asia, Africa, Latin America, and Europe, which have been more or less imported to the North American continent.

Genetics and Culture

Almost all psychologists who study cultural differences assume the differences are mostly learned, not innate. Genetic differences may also play a role, but if they do, the role is complicated. One relatively large study (with 398 participants) found that Americans and Asian-born Asians differed in the trait of "interdependence" (with Asians being on average higher), but only among individuals who carried certain alleles of the DRD4 receptor gene (Kitayama, King, Yoon, Tompson, Huff & Liberzon, 2014; see Chapter 9). Notice that the finding was not that the two groups had different genes, but that the groups appeared different only when individuals who shared this gene were compared. The best interpretation appears to be that people with this gene are different in their interdependence depending on which culture they grow up in, whereas the interdependence of individuals without this gene are not so strongly affected by their cultural upbringing. As I said, it's complicated.

More generally, genetic differences are unlikely to be the primary basis of cross-cultural differences because, according to DNA analyses, individuals within a given ethnic or racial group are only slightly more similar to each other than they are to individuals from different groups (American Anthropological Association, 1998). Another reason genetics cannot fully explain cultural differences is because cultural groups are not just ethnic or linguistic but can also be defined on the basis of history, geography, religion, philosophy, or even politics.

Moreover, the distinction between culture determining personality, and personality determining culture, is not clear-cut. Take, for example, the hypothesis that societies that must develop large-scale projects requiring many participants—such as ancient China—tend to develop collectivist cultures. The same pressures that push the culture in a collectivist direction may also push individuals in the same direction: Collectivists thrive, have more children, and their genes (e.g., a gene that predisposes one to avoid interpersonal conflict) become more widely represented in the gene pool over generations. This gradual change in genetics might, in turn, help to entrench the cultural differences even more deeply. A child born into such a culture—or someone who migrates to it—might or might not have the relevant gene, but will absorb the relevant cultural teachings. So, does culture produce personality or is it the other way around? This question might, in the end, be a lot like the classic query concerning chickens and eggs. It's not only hard to say which one came first, it's also not very meaningful.

CHALLENGES AND NEW DIRECTIONS FOR CROSS-CULTURAL RESEARCH

Cross-cultural psychology raises several issues that make research especially challenging, and which are likely to receive increasing attention in the future. How do we avoid having our view of other cultures colored by our own cultural background? Does focusing exclusively on cultural differences lead us to exaggerate them? How can different cultures' values be reconciled? What is the right way to think about areas of the world—or even individuals—with more than one culture? Now that we have almost finished our survey of recent research, it is time to consider these questions.

Ethnocentrism

Any observation of another culture almost certainly will be colored by the observer's cultural background, no matter how hard he tries to avoid it. A truly objective point of view, free from any cultural bias, is difficult to attain, and some anthropologists argue that it is impossible. As Triandis (1994) pointed out, researchers are most in danger of committing *ethnocentrism* (judging another culture from the point of view of your own) when the "real" nature of the situation seems most obvious. It never occurred to the Danish mother visiting New York that parking her baby outside was a problem, and, more importantly, when profound values clash, it can be a real challenge to appreciate how the opposing point of view might have some validity.

The Exaggeration of Cultural Differences

Cross-cultural research sometimes exaggerates differences by acting almost as if all members of a given culture are alike (Gjerde, 2004). Researchers often imply that everybody in India, Japan, or China acts or thinks in the same way; some even claim that Indians, Japanese, and Chinese all have the same, "Eastern" view of the world. Given the size and diversity of these populations, such blanket characterizations are almost certainly wrong (Matsumoto, 2004; Oishi, 2004). Indeed, one recent analysis found that the average differences in personality traits across countries were about 8 times smaller than the differences between any two individuals randomly selected from these countries (Allik, et al., 2017). As one writer observed,

> For instance, we say, the Japanese culture is serene (although many Japanese are not; just look at my sisters!), or the American culture is fast-paced (although many Americans are laid-back; just look at the students in my personality course!). (Oishi, 2004, p. 69)

Cultural differences tend to be exaggerated for at least three reasons. One is that cross-cultural psychology has long been in the business of finding differences. After all, if cultures were predominantly similar, then cross-cultural psychology would not have much to do. At the same time, even cross-cultural psychologists harbor stereotypes, which may increase their tendency to exaggerate the differences they perceive (Oishi, 2004; Oyserman et al., 2002; Takano, 2012).

A second reason is statistical, and it concerns some of the issues raised in Chapter 3. Many studies of cultural differences use significance tests rather than examining effect sizes. If the cultural groups studied are large, as they often are, then statistically significant results—differences that would be unlikely if only chance were operating—are easy to find. Once found, they will be published and may be described as important. Yet, the actual size of the differences may be very small. A related problem is that many analyses of cultures look for differences at the aggregate or general level, which examines an average across a large cultural context. For example, studies have showed that advertising is often different from one culture to the next (e.g., Han & Shavitt, 1994). But advertising targets the largest possible number of people at once and reflects general cultural views rather than individual perspectives. At the level of the individual, differences between cultures may be smaller (Oishi, 2004; Oyserman et al., 2002).

A third reason is the psychological phenomenon that social psychologists call the **outgroup homogeneity bias** (e.g., Linville & Jones, 1980; Lorenzi-Cioldi, 1993; B. Park & Rothbart, 1982). One's own group naturally seems to contain individuals who differ widely from each other. But members of groups to which one does not belong seem to be "all the same." For example, students at one college often have stereotypes about what students at another, nearby college are like. But they are well aware that the students at their own college are very different from one another. Many of us can easily describe stamp collectors, Californians, and members of the National Rifle Association—unless we happen to belong to one of those groups, in which case we may feel they are too diverse to characterize in any simple way. Even cross-cultural psychologists and anthropologists—who, of all people, should know better—sometimes fall into this bias trap. They may describe members of another culture (but never their own culture!) as if everybody in it were essentially the same. But just as Western culture contains both individualists and collectivists, the same is true about China, India, or anyplace else. Somebody who says "Nobody in India has a sense of the self as being separate" is making the same mistake as somebody who assumes that everybody in the world senses the self as being separate.

Interestingly, to emphasize the variations between individuals within a culture is an individualist view. To emphasize variations between whole cultures is a collectivist view. Which view is yours?

Cultures and Values

Unless one is careful, cross-cultural psychology can sometimes lead to *cultural relativism*. As we saw in Chapter 12, cultural relativism is the phenomenologically based idea that all views of reality are equally valid, and that it is presumptuous and ethnocentric to judge any of them as good or bad.

This is a point of view that seems fine until we begin to consider some examples. In some areas of Africa and Asia, female genitals are mutilated as part of a cultural tradition intended to preserve purity and thereby improve girls' chances for marriage. Typically, elderly village women use a razor blade or piece of glass, under unhygienic conditions and without anesthesia, to remove the clitoris or the clitoris and labia minora of a young girl. Each year, this procedure is performed on about 2 million girls between the ages of 4 and 15. Opposition expressed by the World Health Organization and some international human rights groups has sometimes been denounced as ethnocentric (Associated Press, 1994). For another example, in Afghanistan, women who are raped may be considered adulterers, and, in some cases, are only released from prison if they agree to marry their rapists (King, 2011)! Does our different cultural perspective truly mean that we have no grounds for condemning traditions like these?

Steven Spielberg's movie *Schindler's List* describes the career of Oskar Schindler, who, by the standards of the dominant culture of his day (the Nazi culture), was a misfit and an outlaw. One of the fascinating things about this movie is the way it shows that Schindler was far from a perfect person. He is portrayed as disorganized, deceitful, impulsive, and not very good at calculating risks. Yet, it is precisely these traits that allowed him to engage in behavior—a complex and dangerous scheme to save thousands of Jewish lives over several years—that today is regarded as heroic. Being a misfit in one's culture is not always a bad thing.

The dangers of cultural relativism have been compellingly described by psychologists Jack and Jeanne Block and their colleagues:

> If the absolute definition [of psychological adjustment and of right and wrong] risks the danger of a parochial arrogance, the relative definition may be advocating the value of valuelessness. . . . To the extent that relativism implies one culture is as good as another . . . relativism provides a rationale for tolerance that is also a rationale for perpetuation of what is, rather than what might be. (J. Block, Block, Siegelman, & von der Lippe, 1971, p. 328)

This issue is what makes the search for universal values, discussed earlier in this chapter, so important. Every culture is likely to have its own values, but perhaps we can all agree about a few.

Subcultures and Multiculturalism

At the beginning of this chapter we saw how the term *culture* was surprisingly difficult to pin down. Some cultural groupings are both obvious and oversimplified, such as the difference between East and West (which neatly divides the globe in two), or (almost the same thing) collectivism and individualism. Another way to group people is on the basis of language or in terms of geography, such as political boundaries or one's continent of residence. All of these groupings have proved useful as bases of psychological comparison, but it is important to bear in mind that they are also imprecise and, to some extent, arbitrary. Members of the same cultural group by one definition may belong to different groups by another definition.

Another complication to cultural grouping, especially in nations of immigrants such as the United States and Canada, is the existence of *multicultural* individuals. For example, California includes many young people raised in Spanish-speaking households among extended and powerful Mexican American family groups, who also attend English-speaking schools, watch U.S. television, and participate in other thoroughly "Americanized" aspects of U.S. culture. The same is true of many Asian Americans and first-generation children of immigrants from many different lands, not to mention the many children whose two parents come from different ethnic or cultural groups. When confronted by the typical university form that demands, "State your ethnicity," what are they supposed to put down?

Perhaps some of them should check "all of the above" (or at least more than one option). One study showed that bicultural Chinese Americans can switch quickly between Chinese and American ways of looking at the world, sometimes without being aware of doing so (Benet-Martínez, Leu, Lee, & Morris, 2002). Another study suggested that bilingual individuals may, in some sense, have "two personalities" (Ramírez-Esparza, Gosling, Benet-Martínez, Potter, & Pennebaker, 2006). Americans who spoke only English, and bilinguals taking the personality test in English, scored higher in extraversion, agreeableness, and conscientiousness. Mexicans who spoke only Spanish and bilinguals taking the test in Spanish scored higher in neuroticism; results for openness were mixed (for related work with Chinese/English bilinguals, see Chen & Bond, 2010).

By some estimates, about half the world's population is bilingual (Grosjean, 1982), so many individuals may have two personalities, in this sense. But such biculturalism does not always come easy. Some people integrate multiple cultural identities to gain the maximum benefit from each, while others experience conflict and even stress (Haritatos & Benet-Martínez, 2002). The concept of *bicultural identity integration (BII)* has been introduced to measure and explain this difference (Benet-Martínez et al., 2002). Individuals who score high on BII see themselves as members of a combined or emergent joint culture that integrates aspects of both source cultures. For example, they might see themselves as "Mexican American" in a way that is neither Mexican nor American but comfortably combines aspects of both cultures' traditions and languages. Individuals who score low on BII, by contrast, experience conflict between their two cultures and feel stress from being unsure which one they really belong to. Research has further refined this picture, suggesting that BII has two aspects: the degree to which bicultural individuals see their two cultures as distinct from each other (as opposed to overlapping), and the degree to which they see their two cultures as being in conflict as opposed to in harmony (Benet-Martínez & Haritatos, 2005).

The study of multicultural individuals is important on both theoretical and practical grounds. On a theoretical level, the concept of two personalities within one individual is truly fascinating. An old Czech proverb says, "Learn a new language and get a new soul" (quoted in Ramírez-Esparza et al., 2006, p. 2), and psychology is just beginning to explore the ways this proverb may be correct. On a practical level, many areas of the world, including the United States, Canada, and many countries in Europe, are experiencing increased waves of immigration, and a major challenge in the coming years will be accommodating these multicultural citizens into the larger society in a way that minimizes stress and conflict within as well as between people. Personality psychology may be a useful tool for figuring out how to do this.

THE UNIVERSAL HUMAN CONDITION

According to the existential philosopher Sartre, discussed in Chapter 12, one fact applies across all individuals and all cultures. That fact comprises the "*a priori* limits which outline man's fundamental situation in the universe." In the same passage, Sartre wrote,

> Historical situations vary; a man may be born a slave in a pagan society or a feudal lord or a proletarian. What does not vary is the necessity for him to exist in the world, to be at work there, to be there in the midst of other people, and to be a mortal there. . . . In this sense we may say that there is a universality of man. (Sartre, 1965, pp. 52–53)

Despite cross-cultural psychology's traditional emphasis on differences between cultures, the pendulum is beginning to swing the other way, with an increasing number of psychologists emphasizing the degree to which people all over the world are psychologically similar (e.g., Matsumoto, 2004; McCrae, 2004; Oishi, 2004).

For one thing, differences between cultural rules for appropriate behavior might mask similar motivations. For example, it is easy to observe that the Chinese generally appear less extraverted than Americans. They talk less often and more quietly, among other differences. However, Chinese culture tends to restrain feelings and considers their public display inappropriate. Thus, it is possible that an extraverted American might laugh twice as much as, and appear to have stronger feelings than, an equivalently extraverted Chinese when the two feel the same way (McCrae et al., 1996). In a similar fashion, the same sensations that Americans report as emotional experiences are interpreted by members of many other cultures in a more physical manner. An American might report "feeling depressed," and a Chinese might report "feelings of discomfort in the heart" (Zheng, Xu, & Shen, 1986). Other research suggests that culture may influence more how a person *wants* to feel rather than how she *does* feel. For example, Asians may hope to feel positive low-arousal emotions such as calm, whereas European Americans prefer positive high-arousal emotions such as enthusiasm. Yet, when asked about their actual experience, they report feeling about the same (Tsai et al., 2006). And everybody, it seems, wants to please their parents. In one recent study, European American and Asian American college students both reported more life satisfaction to the degree that they felt they had fulfilled their parents' expectations—even though the contents (and intensity) of those expectations were quite different (Oishi & Sullivan, 2005).

We saw, in Chapter 4, that psychologists debated for years whether personality traits or situations were more important determinants of behavior. The eventual conclusion was that both are important, and because each affects the other—they interact, in other words—it's not really meaningful to say which one matters more. Cross-cultural psychology has begun to explore the degree to which persons and situations are similar or different around the world, and the conclusion appears to be that both are more similar than might have been expected. A study of the aspects of situational experience in 20 countries found that experiences were largely similar no matter where you went, and the typical situation was "mildly pleasant" (Guillaume et al., 2016, p. 493). In a related study of 21 countries, behavior was pretty consistent around the world as well—the typical behavior at 7 pm, around the world, was a positive and relaxed activity (Baranski et al., 2017).

In a similar vein, I once heard psychologist Brian Little relate an unpublished result from a cross-cultural research project. He was interested in the goals or "personal projects" people pursue (see Chapter 14), and the degree to which they might vary cross-culturally. Little teaches at a university in Canada, and it was easy for him to ask his students to describe their current personal projects. At considerable expense and difficulty, he managed to have a group of Chinese students in China surveyed on a similar question. The researchers took great pains to translate the question into Chinese, then back-translate[18] it into English to make sure it accurately crossed the cultural divide, and they expended the same efforts translating the students' answers. Almost uniformly, the results disappointed anyone expecting large differences. The goals—get good grades, shop for tonight's dinner, find a new girlfriend—seemed more universal than culturally specific. Then, to his great excitement, Little read one particular Chinese student's response: One of her current projects, she reported, was to "work on my guilt."

Little reported his initial reaction as: Wow, what a profoundly different, non-Western type of goal. What interesting insight a goal like *working on one's guilt* provides into the fundamentally contrasting, collectivist Chinese worldview. And, not least of all, what a publication this will make! Then, good scientist that he is, Little did some checking. The statement turned out to be a misprint. The Chinese student enjoyed making homemade blankets, so she was trying to find time to work on her *quilt*.

Sometimes, cross-cultural differences in personality have a way of disappearing just when you think you have found them.

---

[18] In *back translation*, the researcher takes a phrase in one language, gets it translated into a second language, and then translated by a different translator back into the first (original) language. Finally, a native speaker of the original language judges whether the original and back-translated statements mean the same thing—as they should, if the two translations were correct.

WRAPPING IT UP

SUMMARY

- If, as the phenomenologists claim, a person's construal of the world is all-important, a logical next question concerns the variations in such construals of reality across cultures.

Culture and Psychology

- Individuals from different cultures may be psychologically different from one another, and members of particular cultural groups may differ from each other in distinctive ways.

- The process by which a child picks up the culture into which she is born is called enculturation; the process by which someone who moves into a culture picks up its mores is called acculturation.

The Importance of Cross-Cultural Differences

- It is important to examine psychological differences between cultures because misunderstandings can lead to conflict and even war, because theory and data developed in one culture might not be applicable in another, and because understanding how other peoples view reality can expand our understanding of the world.

Characteristics of Cultures

- The comparative approach of most modern cultural psychologists contrasts etics, elements common to all cultures, with emics, elements that make cultures different.

- Cultures have been compared on emic dimensions including toughness (vs. easiness), achievement and affiliation, complexity, tightness-looseness, emphasis on the head versus heart, collectivism-individualism, and the degrees to which they emphasize dignity, honor, or face.

- People in collectivist cultures are said to regard society and relations with others as more important, relative to individual experience and gain, compared with people in individualistic cultures. The usual assumption that Asian cultures are more collectivist than European or American cultures is probably too broad, given all the exceptions (e.g., Mexican culture is more collectivist than North American culture).

- A large amount of research has contrasted collectivist and individualist cultures on behavior, values, and views of the self. As cultures around the world become more industrialized, individualism seems to be increasing.

- Dignity cultures emphasize the importance of the individual; honor cultures emphasize self-protection and rituals of respect; and face cultures emphasize harmony and the maintenance of stable hierarchies.

Cultural Assessment and Personality Assessment

- Trait analyses have assessed the average differences between members of separate cultural groups across various personality traits, and also have evaluated the degree to which the traits that characterize people in one culture can accurately characterize people in another.

- Analyses of thinking styles have addressed hypotheses such as the idea that members of collectivist cultures think more holistically and are less prone to self-expression than members of individualist cultures.

- A few values may be universal. One analysis suggests 10 potentially global values that can be organized in terms of two dimensions: openness to change versus conservatism, and transcendence versus self-enhancement.

- Despite the evidence for a few universal values, cultural differences are still important. Collectivist cultures place group values (such as harmony) ahead of individual values (such as freedom); individualist cultures do the reverse.

The Origins of Cultural Differences

- Deconstructionists avoid the question of where cultural differences originate, but the ecological comparative approach holds that cultural differences originate in the diverse ecologies to which groups around the world must adapt. Such ecological differences may also produce small but consequential genetic differences.

Challenges and New Directions for Cross-Cultural Research

- Ethnocentrism is a constant hazard in doing cross-cultural research because one's cultural context inevitably affects one's point of view. The other extreme—cultural relativism—is also a hazard. Though difficult, it is important to find ways to make basic moral judgments while avoiding ethnocentrism.

- Cultural differences may be exaggerated in some cases, because cultural psychologists are in the business of explaining differences, because researchers can be prone to stereotyping, and because analyses of statistical significance may describe small differences as important.

- In particular, the outgroup homogeneity bias may lead to exaggerated views of the degree to which people in another culture are "all the same." Individuals differ within as well as between cultures.

- Cultures often contain subcultures; many individuals are multicultural, and in that sense may even have more than one personality. Their challenge is to successfully integrate the different cultures within themselves rather than feel conflicted by them.

- Although cross-cultural psychology has traditionally emphasized differences between cultures, some recent work is emphasizing psychological processes that all persons have in common.

The Universal Human Condition

- Cross-cultural psychology has traditionally emphasized differences between cultures, but some recent work is emphasizing psychological processes that all persons have in common.

- The universal human condition, regardless of culture, was identified by Sartre: Everybody everywhere must exist, work, relate to other people, and ultimately die.

KEY TERMS

cross-cultural psychology, p. 465
enculturation, p. 467
acculturation, p. 467
etics, p. 472
emics, p. 472
deconstructionism, p. 496
outgroup homogeneity bias, p. 501

THINK ABOUT IT

1. Have you ever lived in a different culture or known someone from a culture other than your own? Do people in that other culture view things differently? How fundamental are these differences?

2. If you wanted to understand another culture, such as one that resides on a small island in the South Pacific, what would you have to do? How could you be sure your interpretation of that culture was correct?

3. Is the city you live in a "city of the head" or a "city of the heart"? Which kind of city would you prefer?

4. What are the pros and cons of living in an individualist culture? A collectivist culture? Which do you think you would prefer? Is your preference a result of cultural conditioning?

5. Which do you think is more important: the differences between cultures or the differences among individuals within cultures?

6. Do you know several members of a culture different from your own? To what degree and in what ways are they alike? How are they different from each other?

7. If a trait is considered to be a virtue in all cultures, does this mean we can be certain the trait is truly virtuous? What other criteria could we use to decide whether a trait is good or bad?

8. Consider the example presented in the text of the practice of female genital mutilation. Can we judge this practice as wrong? On what grounds, if any, can we judge the practices of another culture as moral or immoral?

9. Can a person be a member of two (or more) cultures at once? To approach this issue another way: Given the definition of culture in this chapter, is it possible to be a member of just one culture?

10. How many cultures do you belong to? Is one of them more important to you than the others?

SUGGESTED RESOURCES

Kurylo, A. (Ed.). (2012). *Intercultural communication: Representation and construction of culture*. Thousand Oaks, CA: Sage.

> A diverse collection of articles on culture differences, some of which present unconventional viewpoints (e.g., the chapter by Yohtaro Takano).

Triandis, H. C. (1994). *Culture and social behavior*. New York: McGraw-Hill.

> A readable introduction to comparative cross-cultural psychology, now a little out of date.

Tseng, W.-S. (2003). *Clinician's guide to cultural psychiatry*. San Diego: Academic Press.

> *A very thorough and well-written survey of cross-cultural psychiatry that includes specific case studies. Although it focuses on mental disorders as they vary across cultures, the book includes many insights on the psychology of specific cultures and the difficulties of cross-cultural comparison.*

Personality and Culture (video), Society for Personality and Social Psychology

> *Professor Shige Oishi, a leading cross-cultural researcher, summarizes current research on how personality varies across cultures, including relationships between personality and well-being—which are different around the world. Click on "Personality and Culture" at the website* http://spsp.org/resources/multimedia/experts/insight.

Want to earn a better grade on your test?

Go to **INQUIZITIVE** to learn and review this chapter's content, with personalized feedback along the way.

PART VI

WHAT PERSONALITY DOES

Learning, Motivation, Emotion, and the Self

One day long ago, in the very first psychology class I ever took, the professor decided to teach us about the power of reward. He produced a basket of slips of paper. Printed on each slip were the words, "Good for one extra point on the next exam." Did we want them? Indeed we did. He began a class discussion about what we would be willing to do for an extra point or two, and how our desire for higher grades could be used to manipulate our behavior. From time to time, he would suddenly bestow one of the precious little slips on a student. But it wasn't clear why. He might call out "Wrong!" in response to a comment, and then give the student a slip of paper. He might say "Right!" and give nothing. Slowly, we began to catch on. First one student, then another, realized that he handed out an extra point to anyone who said the word *reinforcement*. Suddenly, a critical mass of awareness was achieved, and we were all screaming, "Reinforcement! Reinforcement! Reinforcement!" Game over.

This little demonstration conveyed three lessons. First, behaviors that are rewarded—reinforced, in behaviorist terminology—become more likely to occur. I think we were beginning to say "reinforcement" increasingly often even before we quite realized what the deal was. Second, this fact offers a powerful tool for influencing what people do. His little slips of paper were enough to make a room full of legal adults scream the same word over and over—a pretty weird behavior actually. The third lesson was more subtle. There was a moment, an obvious moment, when everyone in the class suddenly realized what was going on (when we began to yell "reinforcement!" in unison). This observation shows that awareness is important. People don't just respond to what is rewarded; they respond to what they *expect* will be rewarded.

The fact that people base their behavior on their expectations has several important implications. First, it means that behavior can change suddenly—as soon as someone "gets it," or thinks she gets it, her behavior may change immediately and drastically. Second, it means that people might sometimes change their behavior for the wrong reason. We respond to what we think will be rewarded, and expectations and reality are not always the same. Third, it implies that our behavior might change not just because we have been rewarded, but because we have seen other people rewarded. As soon as my classmates realized that other students were getting those extra points just for saying "reinforcement," they immediately began to do it themselves. Fourth, it means that to understand human behavior, it is not enough to map out the ways people are rewarded and punished. We must also try to understand how people think.

In one 50-minute class demonstration, my first psychology professor recreated the 50-year evolution of behaviorism, social learning theory, and cognitive conceptualizations of personality. This evolution began early in the 20th century with proud and confident behaviorist decrees that the basic facts of behavior were simple, and that anybody could be made to do anything or even be anyone through reward and punishment. Then the picture became more complex, as psychologists began to demonstrate that people also learn from watching *other* people get rewarded and punished, and that the rewards and punishments we expect are not always the ones we receive. These recognitions led to the development of social learning theory. Finally, by late in the century, social learning theory had evolved into theories by psychologists such as Julian Rotter, Albert Bandura, Walter Mischel, Carol Dweck and others that focused on mental, or *cognitive*, phenomena such as perceptions, thoughts, goals, plans, and the self.

The theme underlying all of this research is that you have learned to be the person you are, and that the psychological processes that build your personality include your responses to reward and punishment as well as perceiving, thinking, and feeling. Through the rewards and punishments that have come your way, and the distinctive manner in which you have interpreted the experiences of your life, the world has taught you, and you have taught yourself, how to be yourself. The topic of the next two chapters is how this works.

Chapter 14 reviews the basic principles of behaviorism and how it increasingly came to emphasize cognitive processes as it evolved into several versions of social learning theory, while still remaining true to its theoretical roots. Then it describes the processes of perception, thought, motivation, and emotion, and some of the theorizing that ties cognition to personality. Chapter 15 focuses on the "self," which consists of the different kinds of knowledge that you have—or think you have—about who you are.

14

PERSONALITY PROCESSES: LEARNING, MOTIVATION, EMOTION, AND THINKING

Give me a dozen healthy infants, well-formed, and my own specified world to bring them up in and I'll guarantee to take any one at random and train him to become any type of specialist I might select—doctor, lawyer, artist, merchant, chief and yes, even beggarman and thief, regardless of his talents, penchants, tendencies, vocations, and race of his ancestors.

—J. B. WATSON[1]

CONSIDER TWO SIMPLE IDEAS. First, two stimuli—events, things, or people—repeatedly experienced together will eventually elicit the same response. For example, if someone puffs air into your eye at the same time he presses a buzzer, before too long the sound of the buzzer will be enough to make you blink. Second, behaviors followed by pleasant outcomes tend to be repeated, and behaviors followed by unpleasant outcomes tend to be dropped. For example, if your hard work is rewarded, you may try even harder; if your hard work goes unappreciated, you may figure, why bother?

Both of these ideas can be reduced to a single, even simpler idea: Behavior changes as a result of experience. Whether you blink at the sound of a buzzer, or work hard, or do any number of other things depends on what has happened to you in the past. This process—the change of behavior as a function of experience—is called **learning**,[2] and the learning-based approaches to personality attempt to explain all of the phenomena considered so far in this book in terms of this process.

---

[1] J. B. Watson (1930), p. 65.
[2] Notice that this is a technical, narrow definition of "learning," because it refers only to behavior change and does not include knowledge and understanding.

Learning-based approaches to personality come in two varieties: behaviorism and the social learning theories. By carefully applying one simple idea, learning, to more and more complex situations, psychologists in these two related traditions built theories of the basis of personality and behavior and an effective technology for behavioral change. Behavioral psychologists study how a person's behavior is a direct result of her environment, particularly the rewards and punishments that environment contains. The implication is that anybody else in the same situation would do exactly the same thing. As you may recall, the protagonists of the person-situation controversy reviewed in Chapter 4 debated which were more important determinants of behavior—persons or situations. Behaviorists would definitely vote for the situation.

Despite its early success, some researchers eventually grew dissatisfied with behaviorism's rigidity and with the number of psychological phenomena it ignores, especially thinking, motivation, and emotion, and expanded it into broader social learning theories. Over time, these theories expanded their reach even further and were relabeled "cognitive social learning theory." The result is a broad approach to personality that conceptualizes personality not just as something one *has,* such as one's traits, but as something one does: learning, thinking, and feeling.

BEHAVIORISM

Psychology—the study of the psyche, after all—is often regarded as an attempt to "get inside the head." The personality researchers considered so far in this book—the psychoanalysts, humanists, and even most trait theorists and biological psychologists—put great efforts into understanding the unseen recesses of the mind. However, early behaviorists such as John Watson and B. F. Skinner believed that the best vantage point for understanding a person is actually from the outside, because that is where the visible causes of behavior are to be found. They were wary of any kind of theorizing that might imply that anything important lay inside the mind, where you couldn't see it. This theme continues to influence their modern intellectual descendants such as Walter Mischel, who wrote, "If I have learned any lesson from my life as a scientist in psychology, it is that whatever way one chooses to define 'personality' it surely is not a de-contextualized 'entity within the mind'" (2009, p. 289).

The behaviorists never developed an official slogan, but I will happily make one up for them: "We can only know what we can see, and we can see everything we need to know." Consider the two parts of this slogan separately. First, the behaviorist believes that all knowledge worth having comes from direct, public observation. Private introspection is invalid because nobody can verify it. Attempting to tap other people's thoughts, via psychoanalysis for example, is similarly suspect. The whole idea of theorizing about something we can't see—any entity within the mind—is a dubious business at best. The only valid way to know about somebody is to watch what he does—the person's behavior. That is why the approach is called **behaviorism**.

This idea implies that your personality is simply the sum total of everything you do. Nothing else. Personality does *not* include traits, unconscious conflicts, psychodynamic processes, conscious experiences, or anything else that cannot be directly observed. Close on the heels of the importance of observing behavior comes a further tenet that the causes of behavior can be observed as directly as behavior itself. This is because the causes are not hidden in the mind; they can be found in the individual's environment. In this context, *environment* refers not to the trees and rivers of nature, but to the rewards and punishments in the physical and social world. The goal of behaviorism is a **functional analysis** that maps out exactly how behavior is a product of the environmental situation.

The fundamental tenet of behaviorism is that everything you do, and therefore everything you are, is learned through experience. Behaviorism traditionally identifies three types of learning: habituation, classical (or respondent) conditioning, and operant conditioning.

> "If I have learned any lesson from my life as a scientist in psychology, it is that whatever way one chooses to define 'personality' it surely is not a de-contextualized 'entity within the mind.'" – Walter Mischel

Habituation

Sneak up behind someone and bang a gong. The person will probably jump, perhaps high in the air. Then bang it again. The second jump will not be as high. Then bang it again. The third jump (assuming the person has not snatched the gong away from you by now) will be still lower. Eventually, the sound of the gong will produce almost no response at all.

This kind of learning is called **habituation**. It is the simplest way behavior changes as a result of experience. A crayfish, which has only a few neurons, can do it. Habituation even happens in single neurons and single-celled animals such as amoebas. If you repeatedly electrically stimulate a neuron or poke a crayfish, the response diminishes with each repetition until it almost disappears.

Despite its simplicity, habituation can have important consequences. Images projected in the international popular culture seem to be increasingly violent. Video games feature exploding bodies and sprays of blood. Movies display levels of mayhem and gore that, at one time, would have been considered unthinkable. What effect does being exposed to such images, again and again, have on people? According to some research, it might make them "comfortably numb," and not in a good way (Bushman & Anderson, 2009, p. 273). Repeated exposure to violent video games can make an individual's personality more aggressive and less empathic (C. A. Anderson et al., 2010).

Even the impact of major life events can lessen over time (Brickman, Coates, & Janoff-Bulman, 1978). People who win millions of dollars in a lottery have a pretty exciting day, but, over the long run, end up not much happier than they were before. They become habituated to their millionaire status—it becomes the "new normal." The reverse effect sometimes happens with people who become paraplegic in accidents. They may habituate even to this momentous change and regain more happiness than they might have thought possible. This is why, according to research on *affective forecasting*, people tend to overestimate the emotional impact of future events, both good and bad. Winning that big promotion won't make you as happy as you expect, over time, but flunking that test won't make you as miserable as you anticipate either (T. D. Wilson & Gilbert, 2005). It seems, to a degree, you can get used to almost anything, eventually.

Classical Conditioning

You moved away 10 years ago and have not been back since, but one day you find yourself near the old neighborhood, so you drop by. As you walk down the street you used to travel every day, long-forgotten images and feelings flood your mind. It can be a strange sensation, a little like traveling back in time. You might feel emotions you cannot label but know you have not felt in years; you might surprise yourself with the strength of your reaction to a familiar mailbox or your old front door; you might even, in some inexpressible way, feel 10 years younger! What is going on here? You are experiencing the results of **classical conditioning**.

HOW CLASSICAL CONDITIONING WORKS Classical conditioning is usually described in a very different context from the previous example, often involving animals—traditionally dogs. The nearly legendary story of classical conditioning involves Russian scientist Ivan Pavlov, who was originally interested in the physiology of digestion. (He won a Nobel Prize for his work on that subject in 1904.) His subjects were dogs, which he hooked up to an apparatus that measured their salivation as they were fed.

Pavlov ran into some unexpected complications. He wanted to study how dogs salivated while eating, but inconveniently they often started salivating *before* they were fed. They might salivate at the sight of the assistant who brought their food, or at the sound of the streetcar that passed outside at their usual feeding time or, he discovered by experimenting, at the clang of a bell rung just before the food arrived. Importantly, the response was learned most quickly and reliably when the bell was rung not simultaneously with feeding, but slightly before. (If rung too early, the bell also lost its effectiveness.) Pavlov realized that this finding means conditioning is more than a simple pairing of stimuli; it involves teaching the animal that one stimulus (the bell) is a warning or signal of the other (the food). Events become associated not merely because they occurred together, but because the *meaning* of one event has changed the meaning of another. The bell used to be just a sound. Now it means "food is coming."

Classical conditioning can work in a negative direction as well. If you encounter a particular food under unpleasant circumstances—for example, when you are sick, or if the food itself is dirty or smelly—you may avoid it forever after (Rozin & Zellner, 1985). Or if you become convinced that smoking cigarettes is deadly or eating meat is immoral, you may come to find cigarettes or meat physically disgusting (Rozin, 1999; Rozin, Markwith, & Stoess, 1997). This progression is even more likely if you start calling cigarettes "cancer sticks" and meat "flesh."

LEARNED HELPLESSNESS So far, we have considered what happens when a person learns that one stimulus is associated with another. What about the cases where one stimulus is not associated with another—where both seem to happen randomly? This might seem like a nonsensical question, but random events also teach an important lesson: The world is unpredictable. If bad things happen without any stimulus to provide advance warning, you learn this: You are never safe (Gleitman, 1995). The result can be chronic anxiety.

The feeling of anxiety due to unpredictability can lead to a behavioral pattern called **learned helplessness** (Maier & Seligman, 1976; C. Peterson, Maier, & Seligman, 1993). Experiments with animals such as rats and dogs, and later with humans, suggest that receiving random rewards and punishments can lead to the belief that nothing one does really matters. In turn, this belief can lead to depression (W. R. Miller & Seligman, 1975). One long-recognized symptom of depression is the "why bother?" syndrome, where everything—including, in extreme cases, even getting out of bed—simply seems like too much trouble. The learned helplessness hypothesis is that this syndrome results from a history of unpredictable rewards and punishments, leading the person to act as if nothing she does will make any difference.

S-R CONCEPTION OF PERSONALITY Early American behaviorists such as John Watson derived their understanding of personality directly from Pavlov's ideas. They assumed that the essential activity of life was to learn a vast array of responses to specific environmental stimuli, and that an individual's personality consists of a repertoire of learned *stimulus-response (S-R)* associations. Because everyone has a different learning history, each person's patterns will be idiosyncratic, so the S-R pattern for a given person need not have any particular structure or coherence. It will depend simply on what he has happened to learn. For example, if one has learned to be dominant at home but meek at work, a business meeting might trigger a subservient response and a home situation might trigger dominance. This conception of personality is not without its influence today, as we shall see, but it is an old version of behaviorism. Skinner greatly enriched and expanded this basic behaviorism by formulating the idea of operant conditioning.

Figure 14.1 Thorndike's Puzzle Box Pioneering psychologist Edward Thorndike put cats in this box and observed how long it took them to escape. A food treat was nearby. The cats learned quickly.

Operant Conditioning

Early in the 20th century, even before Pavlov began his work with dogs, American psychologist Edward Thorndike was putting hungry cats in a device he called the "puzzle box" (**Figure 14.1**). The cats could escape only by doing some specific, simple act, such as pulling on a wire or pressing a bar. The box would then spring open, allowing the cat to jump out and find a bit of food nearby. Then Thorndike would put the cat back in the box, to try again (Thorndike, 1911). The cats escaped more and more quickly. At first it took them almost 3 minutes to figure out how to get out; after 25 trials or so, the cats were happily eating their treats within 15 seconds.

TECHNIQUES OF OPERANT CONDITIONING: SKINNER B.F. Skinner (1938) noticed an important difference between Pavlov's dogs and Thorndike's cats. For the dogs, their salivating did not affect their situation. It was a response that happened to be followed by food. But when Thorndike's cats pushed the lever that opened their cage, something different did happen. A closed door sprang open, allowing them to escape.

Skinner called the first kind of learning **respondent conditioning**, meaning that the conditioned response is essentially passive with no impact of its own. The second kind of learning, which he found much more interesting, he called **operant conditioning**: The animal learns to *operate* on its world in such a way as to change it to that animal's advantage. If an animal—or a person—performs a behavior, and the behavior is followed by a good result—a **reinforcement**—the behavior becomes more likely. If the behavior is followed by a punishment, it becomes less likely.

Despite Skinner's emphasis on how reinforcement derives from the organism's effect on its environment, the results of operant conditioning are not necessarily logical. It can increase the frequency of any behavior, regardless of its real connection with the consequences that follow. As a little joke, I once rubbed a $10 bill on a colleague's grant proposal "for luck." It was funded. For months thereafter, everyone in my department came by to have me rub money on their grants.[3]

---

[3] They don't do this anymore. After a while, the magic stopped working.

Skinner worked hard to develop practical techniques for changing behavior that can produce impressive results with both animals and humans. Consider *shaping*. A sculptor shapes a piece of clay or marble into a statue by gradually shaving here and there until a square block comes to resemble a person or an animal. The process happens in small steps, but the result can be amazing. Behavior can be shaped in a similar manner. Begin by rewarding a pigeon for hitting a bar; this behavior becomes more frequent. Then raise the criterion for reward: Now the pigeon must step forward and back and then hit the bar. (Because a pigeon is constantly emitting different behaviors, sooner or later it will do this.) This behavior, too, gradually becomes more frequent. Then raise the reward criterion again. Before too long, the pigeon may be doing a complete tango, and ready to appear on *Dancing with the Stars*.[4]

Figure 14.2 A Skinner Box Psychologist B.F. Skinner performed famous experiments on learning by placing pigeons inside this box.

According to legend—advertised as true when told to me but probably apocryphal—Skinner's students at Harvard University decided to try out his principles on their esteemed instructor. One day, as Skinner began the class, they looked bored and shuffled their feet. The first time he happened to step away from the podium, they all perked up. When he stepped back, they returned to an apathetic slouch. After Skinner had learned to lecture from a step away, the students raised the criterion. Now they did not look alert until he was two steps away from the podium. By the end of the semester, B. F. Skinner was delivering his lectures from the doorway, with one foot in the hall, running occasionally to the podium to glance at his notes, and then back to the doorway to continue. Here comes the punch line. A colleague happened by the class one day. Later, he asked Skinner why he lectured from the doorway, instead of from the podium. Skinner replied, "Don't you know, the light is much better in the doorway."

Another example, which I know is true because I was there, concerns my old college roommate, Rick. A psychology major before I was (and now a successful firefighter in Idaho—who says you can't have a valuable career with a BA in psychology?), Rick was given the assignment of shaping behavior in a real-life context. He chose the dorm lounge where, every night at 6:00 P.M., most of the residents gathered to watch *Star Trek*. Rick was an electronics buff as well as a psychology major. He

---

[4] Not really.

"Oh, not bad. The light comes on, I press the bar, they write me a check. How about you?"

attached a wire to the innards of the television, ran the wire under the carpet to the back of the room, and there connected the wire to a button. When he pressed the button, the television picture became scrambled and unwatchable.

Now he was ready to strike. That evening, as the crowd gathered, he silently selected his victim; that person, he decided, was going to stand by the television with one hand on top, the other hand raised straight up in the air, and one foot lifted off the floor. It was easy enough. As the program began to get interesting, Rick pushed the button and scrambled the picture. Various people leapt up to fix things, but the picture cleared only when his victim stood. It scrambled again when she sat down. After she was standing, he raised the criterion. Now she had to stand closer, and then even closer to the television to clear the picture. Well before 7:00 P.M., Rick's victim was standing by the television with one hand on top, the other one up in the air, and one foot off the floor.

After *Star Trek* ended, Rick approached his victim and asked innocently why she had been standing like that. "Oh, don't you know," she replied, "the body acts like a natural antenna."

THE CAUSES OF BEHAVIOR A number of lessons can be derived from these stories including, perhaps, the moral that neither psychologists nor their students are to be trusted (see the discussion of ethics in Chapter 3). A deeper moral is that people may do things for very simple reasons of which they may be unaware. They even make up elaborate rationales for their actions that have little or nothing to do with the real causes (Nisbett & Wilson, 1977).

But let's not get too carried away. The human mind has many processes that occasionally produce errors but usually lead to correct outcomes (Funder, 1987). One can perhaps fool somebody into doing something without knowing why. But under most circumstances, it is a good bet that we know the reason we do certain things. In part, this is because rewards are not usually so hidden. The paycheck that causes many people to go to work is an effective and obvious reinforcement.

SOCIAL LEARNING THEORY

Behaviorism boasts high standards of scientific rigor and many practical applications. However, even in its early days, some psychologists suspected it did not tell the whole story. One of these was German psychologist Wolfgang Köhler, who studied chimpanzees. He would set up puzzles for them, such as hanging a banana

Figure 14.3 **Köhler's Clever Chimps** Chimps studied by German psychologist Wolfgang Köhler figured out many ways to reach a hanging banana, including stacking boxes and using a stick to pole-vault.

out of reach, and then watch his chimps figure out what to do. Some of their solutions were so clever—such as stacking boxes or using a stick to pole-vault up to the banana (see **Figure 14.3**)—that Köhler concluded the chimps had done more than learn from reward. They actually came to understand their situation—to develop *insight*. His evidence was that once the chimps realized what behavior would get them a banana, they used the tactic immediately, not gradually (Gleitman, 1995; Köhler, 1925). This sudden change in behavior resembles that of my classmates, years ago, when they realized they could get points just for saying "reinforcement."

Years later, this idea of insight opened the door for the introduction of social learning theory and for some of the cognitively oriented research that followed. Social learning theory arose to correct several shortcomings of orthodox behaviorism.

Shortcomings of Behaviorism

The most obvious shortcoming is that behaviorism ignores thinking, motivation, and emotion. Behaviorists have sometimes tried to make a virtue of these omissions. The writings of Skinner and his followers typically deny that thinking is important and sometimes have tried to deny it exists. Behaviorists would certainly never conduct research on it. Social learning theorists, by contrast, claim that the ways people think, plan, perceive, and believe are important parts of learning, and that research must address these processes.

Second, classic behaviorism, to a surprisingly large extent, is based on research using animals. Thorndike favored cats, Pavlov used dogs, and much of Skinner's own work was done with rats and pigeons. Behaviorists study animals because they hope to formulate laws of learning that are relevant to all species. This is a laudable goal, but, in fact, not all species are the same. Notice how Köhler, who studied chimps, came to conclusions about the role of insight that were different from those of his colleagues who studied rats, pigeons, and even dogs and cats. Humans are an even more special case. In general, according to social learning theorists, behaviorists have concentrated too much on elements of learning that are important for animals, such as reinforcement, and not enough on aspects that are more important for humans, such as solving a problem by thinking about it.

A third shortcoming of classic behaviorism is that it ignores the social dimension of learning. The typical rat or pigeon in the Skinner box is lonely in there. It cannot interact with, learn from, or influence any other animal. In real life, however, learning tends to be social. We learn by watching others—something a pigeon isolated in a box is in no position to do even if it were capable. Social learning theorists, as their label implies, are highly sensitive to this issue.

A fourth shortcoming of classic behaviorism is that it treats the animal or person as essentially passive. How does a rat or pigeon get into a Skinner box in the first place? Easy—the experimenter put it there. Once inside, the *contingencies* of the box—its rules for what will and will not be rewarded—are ironclad and may even be automated. The pigeon did not seek out the box, but there it is, and unless it pushes the bar, there will be no food pellets. For humans, the situation is different. To an important (if not unlimited) degree, we not only choose our environments, but also change these environments as a result of what we do in them.

Imagine if rats were allowed to choose among several Skinner boxes, and then could change the reinforcement contingencies inside. For humans, real life is rather like that. A party might bring out certain behaviors you would not do otherwise, but you can choose whether to go to the party in the first place. Moreover, once you are there, the party changes as a result of your presence. These processes—which were introduced in Chapter 7 as *person-environment* transactions—complicate any analysis of how the environment affects behavior. Unlike classical behaviorists, modern social learning theorists welcome and study these complications.

Three major theories of personality have expanded behaviorism. It seems somewhat ironic—and it is confusing—that although the three theories are different in important ways, all were named *social learning theory* by their inventors.

The earliest was developed during the 1940s and 1950s by Yale psychologists John Dollard and Neal Miller. Among other goals, their theory tried to reconcile aspects of then-popular psychoanalytic theory with behaviorism by positing, for example, that people instinctively respond to frustration by becoming aggressive. A second version, by Julian Rotter, focused on how people decided what to do based on their understanding of the likely consequences of their actions. You are more likely to seek out a particular job, for example, to the extent that (a) it pays well and (b) you think you can get it. Moreover, the more you think your actions will determine the consequences in your life—the degree to which you have what is called internal *locus of control*—the more motivated you will be to try to make a difference. However, the most famous and influential version of social learning theory is the one by Albert Bandura.

SELF-EFFICACY　　Like Rotter's theory, Bandura's theory gives a central role to the expectation that one can accomplish something successfully, which he calls **self-efficacy**. For example, you might have the expectation that you will someday be able to finish reading this book. As I type these words, I am trying to maintain my own expectation that I can finish writing this book. In either case, our beliefs about our own capabilities are likely to affect whether we persist. Since you are holding this book in your hands, we can presume that my self-efficacy held up. How is yours doing?

Self-efficacy can interact with, or be determined by, other kinds of self-judgments. For example, if you think you are extremely attractive, you are more likely to attempt to date someone who interests you than you would be if you saw yourself as unattractive. In other words, your **self-concept** (see Chapter 15) affects your efficacy expectation in this domain. Of course, both of these—your self-concept and your efficacy expectation—can be independent of how attractive you really are. A person's actual physical attractiveness might matter less than people sometimes believe; individuals who merely think they are attractive often do surprisingly well, it seems (see the discussion of expectancies in Chapter 5).

Bandura emphasized that the goal of psychotherapy should be to improve self-efficacy. If you achieve a better match between what you think you can accomplish and what you really can accomplish, your life will be more rational and productive. Moreover, efficacies can create capacities. A snake phobic who is persuaded, by whatever means, that he can handle a snake subsequently will be able to do so. The real target of therapy, therefore, is not behavior, but beliefs. Change the belief, and behavioral change will follow.

> Change the belief, and the behavior will follow.

A psychotherapist in Bandura's mold will use all sorts of tactics to accomplish this goal, including verbal persuasion ("You can do it!") and *modeling*, which means allowing the client to watch somebody else (the model) accomplish the desired behavior. Therapy for snake phobics may begin with watching somebody else cheerfully handle a snake. But the most powerful technique is to actually have the client perform the behavior. The goal of therapy, therefore, is to build to the point where the client can pick up and cuddle with a snake (or at least, not panic at the thought that a snake might be nearby). This is the most effective way to convince the client that such a thing is possible.

Bandura's prescription for self-change follows the same pattern. If you are reluctant to do something you know you should do, force yourself to do it. It will be less difficult next time. A small example: Suppose you know you should exercise more but do not think you are really the type. Take control of your life and go exercise anyway. This experience, if you can keep it up, will change your view of yourself, allowing exercise to become a natural part of your day rather than something strange that you must force yourself to do. In its brilliant way, Madison Avenue created a commercial for an athletic shoe that boiled this principle down to three words: "JUST DO IT."

OBSERVATIONAL LEARNING   One of the most influential aspects of Bandura's theory has been its emphasis on **observational learning**, that is, learning a behavior by watching someone else. It is very different from what happens inside a Skinner box. At one time, psychologists believed that only humans could learn from observation, but research has since indicated otherwise. Learning by songbirds is a frequently cited example. Some bird species seem to learn their songs simply by listening to adult birds, without any rewards or punishments. Apparently, some animals do learn by observation, and not always the animals we would expect. Pigeons can learn from watching other pigeons (Zentall, Sutton, & Sherburne, 1996), but apes (orangutans) are not good at learning from other apes (Call & Tomasello, 1995). Humans, however, learn nearly everything by observation.

Bandura famously demonstrated this process with his "Bobo doll" studies (see **Figure 14.4**). A Bobo doll is a large plastic clown on a round weighted base that bounces back when it is hit. Bandura showed that a child who watches an adult hit the doll is likely to later hit the doll as well, especially if the child sees the adult rewarded for the aggressive behavior (Bandura, Ross, & Ross, 1963). The implications for the probable effects of television and other popular media seem obvious. A person—particularly a child—who day after day watches violence glamorized and rewarded may become more likely to engage in such behavior.

Observational learning also can be used for positive purposes. A role model can provide useful and desirable behaviors to emulate. A student who wants to perform better in school, or an employee who wants to do better at work, would be well-advised to observe closely successful students and employees—and then do what they do.

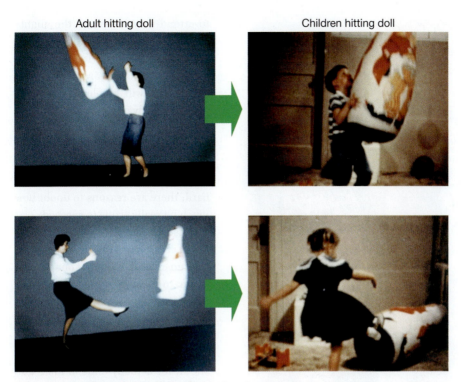

Adult hitting doll　　　　　　　Children hitting doll

Figure 14.4 **The Bobo Doll Study** In this classic study, children were more likely to beat up a Bobo doll if they had seen adults do so.

MOTIVATION

What do you want? And how will you try to get it? These are the key questions of motivation, one of the oldest topics in psychology. Most of the early personality theories characterized people as having overriding, general motivations that drive everything. Freud's original theory of psychoanalysis was based on sexual motives, and later versions included aggressive motives as well (Chapter 10). Humanistic theorists such as Rogers and Maslow (Chapter 12) proposed that the driving force in human thought and behavior is the goal of self-actualization. Even behaviorism assumes that "organisms" want something, and that getting what they want reinforces their behavior.

Current research addresses motivation through the study of goals and strategies. **Goals** are the ends that one desires, and **strategies** are the means the individual uses to achieve his goals. This is how goals drive behavior. They influence what you attend to, think about, and do (H. Grant & Dweck, 1999). If you are hungry (and thereby have the goal of eating and the motivation of hunger), you will be primed

GIFTS FROM THE HOUSE OF LOW GOALS

to attend very closely to the slightest whiff of cooking, think about where there might be food, and seek groceries. If you desire a successful career, you will be alert for opportunities to advance, think about how to get ahead, and work hard. By the same token, if a person is not alert to opportunities, does not think about how to get ahead, and does not work hard, there are reasons to doubt how much he really wants to succeed.

Esteemed clinical psychologist David Shapiro (1965, 2000) has written extensively about people who claim to have particular goals but make little or no moves toward fulfilling them. He describes a woman who continuously complains about an unsatisfactory relationship that she never actually ends; a man who states emphatically that he doesn't *"want to drink,"* but continues to be a heavy drinker; and another woman who claims she "really wants" to move to a new city, but never searches for an apartment, looks for a job, or calls movers (Shapiro, 2000, p. 75).

Self-contradictions like this are surprisingly common. Many people express desires to get better grades, be promoted, improve their social life, or even leave their spouses, and yet never make the first move toward initiating these events. To know what people want, Shapiro implies, it's not always very informative to listen to what they say. Instead, watch what they do.

Goals

Much of life—it could be argued, all of life—consists of efforts to achieve goals. A goal can take many different forms. It might be a specific project: I want to finish this paper by Thursday; I want to mow the lawn. Or it can be more general: I want to be a better person; I want to help the environment; I want to contribute to world peace. Specific goals are usually, though not always, immediate—they represent something that is intended to be accomplished soon. General goals tend to be long-term, because it takes a long time to be a better person, help the environment, or contribute to world peace.

SHORT-TERM GOALS AND LONG-TERM GOALS Goals can be arranged hierarchically. You might have the general goal of impressing your neighbors. To reach that long-term goal, you seek to have a beautiful yard. Toward that shorter-term goal, you mow your lawn. Or perhaps you want to be financially secure. To reach that general goal, you must get a good job. Toward that goal, you must graduate from college. Toward that goal, you must pass this course. Toward *that* goal, you must finish this book. Toward that goal, you have to read all the way to the bottom of this page (and then the one after).

Keeping your eye on a general, long-term goal can help you to choose wisely and to organize more specific, short-term goals. You have probably heard the old story about the two medieval workers who were asked what they were doing. One said, "I'm laying bricks." The other said, "I am building a cathedral." Of course, they were actually doing the same thing. The first worker focused on his specific activity, while the second focused on the ultimate purpose of that activity. When goal structures are well organized, life can be lived fairly smoothly and with clear purpose. If you know your general goals, then everything you do on a daily basis can be organized to help reach them.

Many people are not so fortunate, however. When a person has few or no general, long-term goals, or spends time in activities that do not serve general, personally relevant goals, then life is chaotic and disorganized, and nothing important seems to get done. Moreover, if you lack general goals or any clear connection between your daily activities and your general goals, your life may seem to lack meaning and your overall motivation may suffer. Indeed, you may become depressed.

But the relationship between general and specific goals must not be too one-sided. The potential disadvantage of a general, cathedral-type goal is that you might become too inflexible to accomplish important short-term goals, such as fixing the leaky roof on your hut. If your general goal is to promote world peace, you might forget to be kind to your friends. So, it is useful to be able to shift flexibly between long-term and short-term goals (Vallacher & Wegner, 1987).

It is also important to realize that the only way to achieve a long-term goal is to focus on the short-term goals you can achieve every day. President John F. Kennedy liked to tell the story of the French Marshall Lyautey, who asked his gardener to plant a tree for some shade. The gardener replied that the tree was slow-growing, and wouldn't provide any shade for 100 years. The Marshall answered, "In that case, there is no time to lose; plant it this afternoon!" (United Nations Environment Programme, 2009).

IDIOGRAPHIC GOALS *Idiographic goals* are those that are unique to the individuals who pursue them. Various researchers have conceptualized idiographic goals in somewhat different terms.

Current Concerns   Psychologist Eric Klinger (1987) proposed that daily life is characterized by what he called current concerns. A *current concern* is an ongoing motivation that persists in the mind until the goal is either attained or abandoned. Examples include visiting a friend, keeping a dental appointment, losing weight, saving money, and finding a job. At any given moment, you can probably list around half a dozen current concerns that frequently come to mind (Klinger, 1977). Some of these can make you emotionally aroused when you think about them consciously, and you will find many of them drifting into your daydreams (Gold & Reilly, 1985; Nikula, Klinger, & Larson-Gutman, 1993). According to one study, the more a current concern is valued, committed to, and under threat, the more frequently a person thinks about it (Klinger, Barta, & Maxeiner, 1981). Moreover, when words relating to a person's current concerns are briefly presented on a computer screen, her thought processes are momentarily disrupted (Young, 1988). Concerns range from narrow to broad, and a given concern may last from a few seconds to a lifetime. Once the concern is resolved—when that person finally calls you back, or that problem is finally fixed—you typically forget it quickly.

Personal Projects   Another kind of idiographic goal is psychologist Brian Little's idea of the personal project (Little, 1989). Whereas a current concern is something people think about, *personal projects* are what people do. They are made up of the efforts people put into such goals as "going to the prom with Brad," "finding a part-time job," "shopping for the holidays," or, as you may recall from Chapter 13, "working on my quilt" (Little, 1983). This idea is similar to *life tasks*, conceptualized by Nancy Cantor and her colleagues as the organizing goals people pursue at particular times of their lives. For example, a college student who has recently moved away from home for the first time might be pursuing the life task of attaining independence (Cantor & Kihlstrom, 1987). Later in life, this task will cease to be so important, and others will rise to the fore.

Personal Strivings   A somewhat broader kind of idiographic goal is Robert Emmons's (1996) idea of *personal strivings*, which are long-term goals that can organize broad areas of a person's life. For example, a person may be "trying to appear attractive to the opposite sex," "trying to be a good listener to friends," or "trying to be better than others."

   The personal strivings that a person reports can provide useful insights into what she is like. One of Emmons's research participants, who called herself "Crocodile Dundee,"[5] said her personal strivings included "always appear cool," "always amuse others," "always keep physically fit," and "dress fashionably"

---

[5] Emmons asked his participants to give themselves pseudonyms so they could be anonymously identified for follow-up studies.

(Emmons, 1989, p. 38). Another participant, who called herself "0372," expressed the personal strivings to "please others," "tell the truth," and "be productive in work." It turned out that Crocodile Dundee scored high on a test of the personality trait of narcissism, which measures the tendency to be self-centered and confident sometimes to the point of arrogance (see Chapter 6). The person called 0372, as her relatively modest nickname perhaps suggests, scored low on this dimension.

Strivings can also be a source of difficulty, as people commonly report two or more strivings that are inconsistent with each other. I mentioned in Chapter 6 that the goal to "get ahead" (of others) and the goal to "get along" (with others) are often in conflict. If you strive to rise to the top, it is difficult to have everyone—such as the people you defeat—continue to like you. On the other hand, if you focus only on making people like you, you are unlikely to get ahead. One study found that people whose strivings are in conflict tend to experience more psychological distress and even more physical illness than those whose strivings are compatible (Emmons & King, 1988).

Properties and Limitations of Idiographic Goals All of these concepts—current concerns, personal projects, life tasks, and personal strivings—have several elements in common. First, idiographic goals are held consciously at least some of the time. Indeed, typically they are measured by asking participants to list their concerns, projects, tasks, or strivings. Second, they describe thoughts and behaviors aimed at fairly specific outcomes. Third, they are changeable over time—one day's important personal project might be forgotten and irrelevant a few weeks later. Finally, an individual's various concerns, projects, tasks, or goals are assumed to function independently: Having the goal to be better looking, for example, might not have any implications for other goals you might also have.

This last-named limitation is important (H. Grant & Dweck, 1999). Concerns, projects, tasks, or goals (by whatever label) can organize thought and behavior, but they are not themselves coherently organized. For example, people typically present their strivings in a simple, unordered list (Emmons, 1989). To some researchers, this seems an unsatisfactory state of affairs. Can the many different goals that people might pursue be categorized to refine our understanding of what people seek in life?

NOMOTHETIC GOALS The attempt to answer this question leads researchers to seek *nomothetic goals*, which refer to the relatively small number of essential motivations that almost everyone pursues. Researchers in this area hope to bring order to the domain of goals, much as the Big Five organizes thousands of personality traits (see Chapter 6).

The Big Three, or Five, or Two According to psychologist David McClelland (1985) and his colleagues, three primary motivations drive human behavior: the need for achievement, the need for affiliation (or intimacy), and the need for power. Research into these motives usually assesses whether they emerge as themes in stories people tell in response to the pictures that comprise the Thematic Apperception Test (TAT; see Chapter 3).

Achievement motivation is a tendency to direct one's thoughts and behavior toward striving for excellence. People high in this motive set standards for themselves and then work hard to attain them. *Affiliation motivation* is the tendency to direct thoughts and behavior toward finding and maintaining close, warm emotional relationships. People high in affiliation motivation seek the close company of others for its own sake, not as a means to any end (McAdams, 1980). *Power motivation* is the tendency to direct thoughts and behavior toward feeling strong and influencing others. People high in power motivation put great efforts into seeking prestige and status, prefer friends low in power motivation (whom presumably they can dominate), and are relatively promiscuous in their sexual behavior (Winter & Stewart, 1978).

What proportion of the goals that people follow can be organized around themes of achievement, intimacy, and power? At present, research offers only a general answer. Many goals fall into one of these categories, but not all. For example, according to one survey, five—not three—categories of goals emerged repeatedly in a number of studies (Emmons, 1997): (1) enjoyment, (2) self-assertion, (3) esteem, (4) interpersonal success, and (5) avoidance of negative affect. You can see for yourself where these five goals overlap with McClelland's three. According to another analysis, many goals generated by a group of college students could be boiled down to two types: goals related to work (in this case, academic work) and those related to social interaction (e.g., friendships, romantic relationships) (Kaiser & Ozer, 1999). This last finding is particularly interesting because it is reminiscent of Freud's formulation of the complete life, which was "to love and to work" (see Chapter 10).

JUDGMENT GOALS AND DEVELOPMENT GOALS Carol Dweck and her colleagues claim that two other kinds of goals are also important (see H. Grant & Dweck, 1999). One kind she calls *judgment goals*. Judgment, in this context, refers to seeking to judge or validate an attribute in oneself. For example, you might have the goal of convincing yourself that you are smart, beautiful, or popular. The other kind she calls *development goals*. A development goal is the desire to actually improve oneself, to become smarter, more beautiful, or more popular.

At first glance, these goals might seem highly similar. Don't people want both to see themselves as smart and to be smart, for example? Indeed, Dweck notes that both kinds of goals "are natural and important in our everyday lives" (H. Grant & Dweck, 1999, p. 350). But the balance between them differs from one person to another, and may even change within an individual from one situation to the next or across time. And, if you think about it for a moment, it is not difficult to find situations in which these two types of goals lead to different outcomes.

For example, consider the plight of a teacher trying to correct a student. Have you ever been in this situation? Let's say you are trying to help a high school student learn algebra. You look at his work, find a mistake, and point it out. You take a piece of paper and patiently begin to explain the right way to solve the problem. You are surprised when the student interrupts you. "This problem is unfair and too hard," he says, "and algebra is stupid. And what makes you so smart anyway?"

Why is the student responding so negatively? According to Dweck's perspective, he is pursuing a judgment goal instead of a development goal. He is anxious to demonstrate that he is smart and competent. He is so anxious to do this that when he makes a mistake, he belittles the test, the teacher, and perhaps the whole topic. This attitude has its uses, to be sure. If he can convince himself that the test is unfair, the teacher no smarter than he is, and the topic pointless, he will feel better about having failed algebra. But he will still have failed algebra—and with that attitude, he will never pass.

Contrast this with the student who listens carefully to what you have to say, eagerly tries out the new technique you have taught, and immediately asks you to correct his new work. This student, according to Dweck, is following a development goal. At this moment, he is less interested in proving that he is smart than in becoming smarter. So he uses his "failure" on this particular problem to learn how to do better next time. This student may have no greater intrinsic mathematical ability than the first student, but his chances of success are much greater.

Let's bring this a little closer to home. Think about the most recent exam on which you scored lower than you had hoped. What was your reaction? Did you argue that the test was unfair, the teaching bad, and the topic pointless? Or did you try to find out what you could do differently to score better next time? Your response may identify the degree to which you are pursuing judgment goals as opposed to developmental goals, and also may predict how successful you will be.[6]

> Think about the most recent exam on which you scored lower than you had hoped. What was your reaction?

From the perspective of Dweck's theory, these two kinds of goals are important in many areas of life because they produce different reactions to failure, and everybody fails sometimes. A person with a development goal will respond to failure with what Dweck calls a *mastery-oriented pattern*, in which she tries even harder the next time. The student might get a poor grade on her paper but be eager to learn from the experience how to do a better job on her next paper. In contrast, a person with a judgment goal responds to failure with what Dweck calls the *helpless pattern*: Rather than try harder, this individual simply concludes, "I can't do it," and gives up. Of course, that only guarantees more failure in the future.

---

[6] Sometimes the test really *is* unfair, the teaching poor, and the topic pointless. Still, you can expect your outcome to improve only if you focus on how to do better next time.

Theory of the world	Goal	Response to failure
Entity →	Judgment →	Helplessness
Incremental →	Development →	Mastery

Figure 14.5 **Dweck's Motivational Theory** Carol Dweck's theory describes the relationships between views of the world, goals, and behavioral responses.

Entity and Incremental Theories Where do these dramatic differences in goals and behavior come from? Dweck believes they originate in different kinds of implicit theories about the nature of the world—personal constructs, if you will (see Chapter 12). Some people hold what Dweck calls **entity theories**, and believe that personal qualities such as intelligence and ability are unchangeable, leading them to respond helplessly to any indication that they do not have what it takes. Other people hold **incremental theories**, believing that intelligence and ability can change with time and experience. Their goals, therefore, involve not only proving their competence but increasing it. **Figure 14.5** diagrams these relationships. One young boy in Dweck's research, following a failure to solve an experimental puzzle, "pulled up his chair, rubbed his hands together, smacked his lips, and exclaimed, 'I love a challenge!'" (Dweck & Leggett, 1988, p. 258).

Being an incremental theorist may not be helpful in all circumstances, however. As we've seen, entity theorists tend to blame failure on lack of ability, whereas incremental theorists blame it on lack of effort. So, what happens when, after failure, these two kinds of people are asked to tackle a *different* task, one that uses different abilities? According to a recent study, the incremental theorist may continue to ruminate about his prior lack of effort that led to failure, harming his performance on the new task (Park & Kim, 2015). But the entity theorist is untroubled, because his previously demonstrated lack of ability is no longer relevant. As a result, in this case, the entity theorist may actually perform better than the incremental theorist. After being turned down for a date, the entity theorist might find it harder to ask somebody else out than would an incremental theorist. But if instead a new task immediately comes up at work, the entity theorist might do better than the incremental theorist, still distracted about why he didn't try harder to get that date.

Research and Measurement Most of the research on Dweck's theory has focused on academic goals or simulations of such goals. For example, the responses of children to their failure to solve word puzzles have been examined repeatedly. Dweck and her students have consistently found that children who are incremental theorists, as just described, do better in the face of failure than do entity theorists (C. I. Diener & Dweck, 1978; Goetz & Dweck, 1980). The kind of theorist one is also affects relations with others. "Entity theorists" are prone to seek vengeance after being bullied, apparently because they don't think the bully can ever change (Yeager, Trzesniewski, Tirri, Nokelainen, & Dweck, 2011).

How are these young "theorists" identified? In the time-honored method of trait psychology, they complete a self-report questionnaire (S data). For example, participants choose between options such as

1. Smartness is something you can increase as much as you want to, or
2. You can learn new things, but how smart you are stays pretty much the same.

If you choose the first option, you are an incremental theorist; if you choose the second, you are an entity theorist (Dweck & Leggett, 1988, p. 263). Another method is to give subjects a questionnaire that describes a series of hypothetical social situations involving rejection. For example, a participant might be asked, "Suppose you move to a new neighborhood. A girl you meet does not like you very much. Why would this happen to you?" If the participant responds that the likely reason is his own social incompetence, then the participant is assumed to be an entity theorist (Goetz & Dweck, 1980, p. 248).

The goals that children pursue also can be manipulated experimentally. In one study, fourth- and fifth-grade children were asked to participate in a "pen-pal tryout" (Erdley et al., 1997). Each child wrote a letter to a potential pen pal, and were told that the letters would be rated to decide who could join the pen-pal club. Every child was initially told that the rater was "not sure whether to have you in the club" and was asked to write another letter. After that, all children were told they could join.

The experimental manipulation came before the children wrote the first letter. Half were told, "We'd like to see how good you are at making friends," which was intended to set up a judgment goal. The other half were told, "This is a chance to practice and improve how you make friends," to set up a development goal. The second letter (written after the initial failure) was then rated by independent coders, who found that letters written by children in the first (judgment) condition were shorter and of lesser quality than those written by children in the second (development) condition. Apparently, the first group of children came to believe they were socially inadequate and might as well give up; the second group saw a chance to improve.

This finding led to three conclusions. First, the kind of goal that a person pursues—judgment or development—can have important implications for how she responds to failure. (And, again, we all fail sometimes.) A judgment goal can lead to helplessness and withdrawal; a development goal can lead to renewed and improved effort.

Second, this effect seems to occur in social as well as academic (and presumably work-related) realms. If a person fails an exam, or fails to close a deal at work, or fails to get a prospective date to say yes, she has two options. One—if the person pursues a judgment goal—is to decide she is inadequate, inept, or unattractive, and to simply give up. Another option—if the person pursues a development goal—is to try to learn from the failure and figure out what to do differently next time. Yet another option, as we have seen, is simply to move on to a new activity where the lack of ability that led to failure is no longer relevant. This is sometimes a wise thing to do.

The third implication is that the type of goal someone pursues can be determined from within or from without. Most of Dweck's research has assumed that people are either entity theorists or incremental theorists, and that they characteristically pursue judgment or development goals. But other research, including the pen-pal study by Erdley and colleagues, suggests that sometimes a person's goal can be determined by the way people around the person structure the task. This final point has obvious and important implications for teaching: Teachers should be sure that their students see class as a place to learn and improve, not merely a place to succeed or fail. The study by Park and Kim suggests, further, that if a student persistently fails at one kind of task the teacher might be wise to find another where the student *can* shine. Nobody is good at everything. But hopefully everybody is good at something.

Strategies

How do you get what you want? Let's say you are hungry and decide you want to get a hamburger at McDonald's.[7] Once there, you will follow what cognitive psychologists call the McDonald's script (Schank, 1996). Your knowledge of what to do at McDonald's is not based on any particular visit; it is an abstraction derived from the usual pattern. You follow this script without thinking about it. You won't sit down at a table and expect a waiter to take your order. You will stand in line, instead. The "how to get food at McDonald's" script can be thought of as a strategy. It is a sequence of activities that progress toward a goal; in this case, to acquire food. However, it is not a very interesting strategy. From the perspective of personality psychology, the more important strategies are the broad ones that pursue important goals in life and organize a wide range of activities.

We have already seen a couple of examples of such broad strategies. The authoritarian personality (described in Chapter 6) responds to situations involving authority relationships with a style of behavior that is obsequious to those of higher rank and contemptuous to those of lower rank. In another example, some people are said to be oriented toward *assessment*, meaning that they focus on how well they do things and the ways in which other people do (or could) evaluate their performance. Other people are more focused on *locomotion*, which means that they tend to avoid distractions and focus on getting the job done. Not surprisingly, evaluators are more prone to procrastinate than are locomotors (Pierro et al., 2011).

DEFENSIVE PESSIMISM One of the most interesting personality strategies is the difference between optimists and pessimists. At a general level, the optimistic

---

[7] I do not mean to imply a position concerning the nutritional wisdom of this choice.

strategy is to assume that the best will happen. This assumption can produce a positive outlook and motivate goal-seeking behavior that is maintained by the cheerful assumption that if you do your part, all will be well. The pessimistic strategy assumes the reverse: The worst is likely to happen. This assumption produces a negative outlook on life but can also motivate goal-seeking behavior, driven by attempts to avoid almost certain doom.

Psychologist Julie Norem examined the difference between people who employ these contrasting strategies (Norem, 1989, 2002) and developed a test to identify them, which you saw in Chapter 3. One early study focused on the strategies college students use in dealing with their academic work. Optimistic students deal with anxiety about exams by expecting to do their best. Others expect the worst, which gives them the chance to be pleasantly surprised when the worst does not happen— Norem calls these individuals *defensive pessimists*. Interestingly, Norem found that both kinds of student seem to succeed about equally in coping with anxiety and performing well on exams (although, admittedly, the optimists seem to enjoy life more). The two strategies represent different routes to a common goal. Indeed, if a researcher examined only the outcomes and not the strategies by which they are attained, the important difference between these two kinds of people would be masked.

Optimistic and pessimistic strategies also apply outside academic life. Several years ago, a friend of mine was waiting anxiously for his wife to have a baby. The pregnancy had been difficult, and the delivery was expected to be complicated. Many people would deal with this situation by hoping for the best, convincing themselves that the mother was a strong person who would do fine, that the doctors could take care of everything, and so on. My friend did just the reverse. An extremely defensive pessimist, he acted as if he expected nothing but the worst from the very beginning. The night before the baby was born, he cornered the attending physician and demanded, "What is the worst that could possibly happen?" Understandably, the physician was taken aback, but under continued prodding he finally acknowledged that, well, the worst that could happen would be for the mother to die and for the baby to be born dead. My friend seemed strangely satisfied with this answer.

The next day, all did not go smoothly, but neither did the worst transpire. My friend seemed to maintain equilibrium through his constant awareness that things were not as bad as they could be. And when, in the end, mother and baby came through fine, he seemed to have gotten through the trauma not much worse for the wear. Apparently, his insistence on focusing on the negative was just an exaggerated version of the strategy pursued by Norem's defensive pessimists. He reduced the anxiety that bad news might produce by imagining, in advance, the very worst possible news. Then, even as unpleasant news arrived, he could always compare it against this worst-case scenario and feel relieved. I am not sure that this is a wise strategy, but perhaps it works for some people.

Two important questions arise in connection with these different strategies. The first is, how general are optimistic and pessimistic strategies? Does someone who employs an optimistic strategy in the academic domain also act optimistically in social situations? Evidence suggests that the answer is yes, sort of. Correlations between the degree to which one uses an optimistic or pessimistic strategy in one context and the same strategy in another context range from about .30 to .40 (Norem & Chang, 2001). This means that these styles are generally consistent (see Chapter 3 on interpreting correlations). The friend whose reaction to his wife's childbirth I described earlier tends to evince gloomy and pessimistic attitudes about all aspects of his life—not just genuine crises. But a consistency correlation in the range of .30 to .40 leaves plenty of room for people to use an optimistic strategy in one domain and a pessimistic strategy in another. Some people are optimists in their personal relationships but pessimists in their academic life, for example.

The second question is, Which is better, optimism or pessimism? Cultural values in the United States certainly appear to value an optimistic outlook, and the research summarized near the end of this chapter suggests that happiness has many good consequences, but pessimism has its virtues, too. An optimistic, self-enhancing style may help motivate individual achievement but interfere with emotional intimacy and interpersonal sensitivity. Pessimism may prove more adaptive than optimism in cultures that emphasize these more collectivist values (Norem, 2002; also, see Chapter 13). Furthermore, too much optimism can be dangerous, leading to carelessness and needless risk taking (Norem & Chang, 2002). According to one study of 11,000 German adults, a pessimistic attitude about growing older is associated with lower illness and long life, which might reflect the benefits of being realistic about what to expect from old age (Lang, Weiss, Gerstorf, & Wagner, 2013). Finally, the general fact—and it does seem to be a fact—that optimists are generally happier than pessimists does not necessarily mean that pessimists would be happier if they changed their strategy. Both optimists and defensive pessimists may have found viable strategies, and trying to change them is not necessarily a good idea. Indeed, Norem's research has shown that some pessimists perform worse if they are forced to think optimistically because it deprives them of the negative thinking they use to manage anxiety.

EMOTION

Emotions lie close to the core of the experience of being alive, and are important for many other reasons. As one research review concluded, "When emotional processing is compromised, most things social go awry" (Niedenthal & Brauer, 2012, p. 259). Disrupted emotions can "lead to the loss of social support, disintegration of groups, and failure of economic viability" (p. 261), and the inability to control emotion is a central aspect of many personality disorders (see Chapter 17; Gross & Jazaieri, 2014). From the perspective of cognitive psychology, emotions can be considered a kind of **procedural knowledge**, similar to skills such as bike riding, singing, or shooting basketballs, which cannot be learned or fully expressed through words, but only through action and experience.[8] As is true about inner experience in general, you cannot fully understand emotions by reading about them, nor can you really describe emotions in words. But everybody knows what they are.

Consider anger. A person's heart rate accelerates, and his blood pressure rises; he may get red in the face and clench his fist and jaw. His thoughts are taken over by the way the object of his anger mistreated or threatened him, and he makes plans to get even or lashes out without thinking. He may not recognize that everything he is doing is part of the emotion. That is, he will not necessarily say to himself, "Boy, am I angry." But that is what all of the other activities of his body and mind amount to.

Thus, an emotion is a set of mental and physical procedures. It is something you do, not merely a set of concepts or a passive experience (Ekman & Davidson, 1994), and therefore it qualifies as a personality process. Personality psychologists have attempted to describe emotional experience (despite the difficulty just noted), outlined relationships between different emotions, explored individual differences in emotional life, and studied the implications of the emotional experience of happiness.

Emotional Experience

The usual psychological account of emotional experience describes it as a series of stages (R. S. Miller, 1999). Above, I described the stages of experiencing anger. The very different emotion of joy follows the same steps. First, the person perceives that something great has happened—she just got admitted to medical school! She might smile, laugh, and literally "jump for joy." Then she might begin to consider ways to expand on or share her happiness, such as calling her parents. The basic stages of emotion, then, are *appraisal*, when a stimulus is judged as emotionally relevant; *physical responses*, such as changes in pulse, blood pressure, and bodily tension; *facial expressions*, such as smiles or snarls, paired with *nonverbal behaviors* such as jumping or fist clenching; and finally, the invocation of *motives* to spread one's joy or to harm someone.

This basic template is reasonable and seems to describe accurately many emotional experiences, but it can be slightly misleading: The stages do not have to happen separately or in a particular order. Psychologist Robert Zajonc suggested that appraisal does not have to come first; the physical and even behavioral changes associated with emotion can begin *before* the individual understands why (Zajonc, 1980). For example, a person might feel attraction to someone associated with a

---

[8] The other kind, *declarative knowledge*, consists of the facts one can talk about, or "declare."

prior good experience, before explicitly recognizing that person. This is because, as Zajonc famously said, "preferences need no inferences" (1980, p. 151). The comment turned out to be controversial (see Lazarus, 1984), and triggered several years of debate over whether emotion could occur prior to, or in the absence of, knowledge about the emotion's stimulus. The argument was never settled, but the discussions clarified that emotional experience does not happen in a clear-cut set of separate steps; the different aspects of emotion can occur out of order, simultaneously, or so close together in time that the sequence does not really matter. It is also clear that emotional experience is a complex mixture of thoughts, physical sensations, and motivations.

Another complication is that emotions can have at least three different sources. First, and most obviously, emotions can be triggered by immediate stimuli. Somebody does something obnoxious, and you become mad; someone does something kind, and you feel gratitude. Second, as discussed earlier in this chapter, emotional experiences can be classically conditioned to almost anything. A house where you have had many happy experiences may feel pleasant to enter even when nobody is home. An office where you have had too many arguments may, in a similar fashion, become an unpleasant place to be. If properly conditioned, neutral stimuli such as ringing bells can make a human—or a dog—feel nervous, happy, or, as you may recall, hungry. A third source of emotions is a person's own memories or thoughts. A college football player named Nobel Doss dropped an easy pass during a major game in the 1940s and reported more than 60 years later that he still felt shame when he remembered it, every day (Leary, 2006). Humans can experience just about any emotion by thinking about past or potential events.

Varieties of Emotions

As far as I know, nobody has ever tried to count all the words in the dictionary that describe emotions[9], but it would not surprise me if there are almost as many as the 17,953 terms for personality traits. But just as in the domains of traits and motives, it seems doubtful that all the terms for emotions are strictly necessary, and we can also ask whether one culture's terms for emotion mean the same thing—or mean anything at all—in a different culture (see Chapter 13). Psychologist Paul Ekman (1992) has argued that a few core emotions have substantially the same meaning and means of expression around the world; these include happiness, sadness, anger, fear, surprise, and disgust. For example, when people anywhere in the world are happy, they generally pull the corners of their mouths upward and crinkle the skin around their eyes—in other words, they smile. A classic study by Ekman and his colleagues showed that natives of an isolated region of New Guinea

---

[9] You are welcome to be the first.

could accurately identify the emotions portrayed in photographs of Americans' faces (Ekman, Sorenson, & Friesen, 1969).

Evolutionary theory (Chapter 9) suggests that some emotions may be universal because they are necessary for survival. It may be almost as important to be able to communicate and perceive these emotions accurately. For example, anger might be a response built in to protect us from those who would trespass on our land, steal our food, or abscond with our mates. Feeling the emotion can motivate a person to do something about these insults, but, even better, communicating anger might be enough to prevent them from happening in the first place. Shake your fist, and the trespasser might simply go away. On the other side of the transaction, realizing that one's actions are seriously angering someone might also have important survival value.

Another way to categorize emotions is to try to find the essential words for emotions in a given language, much as the thousands of words in the trait lexicon were pared down to the Big Five (Chapter 6). One study began with a list of 590 emotional terms—not many by trait standards, but still quite a few—and a team of judges evaluated their similarity and overlap. The result was a "big three" of emotions: Almost all the terms were negative, positive, or neutral. Analyses also yielded a tree of subcategories in which *bad-awful* emotions included pain and sadness, and *good-wonderful* emotions included happiness and joy (Averill, 1997; Storm & Storm, 1987).

Perhaps the differences among emotions are not as clear-cut or sharp as these categorical schemes suggest. The difference between happiness and joy might be just a matter of degree. Could the same thing be true of the difference between happiness and sadness? If so, then perhaps all emotions can be plotted and compared on a circumplex model like **Figure 14.6**. The model assumes that all emotions vary along two dimensions, from aroused to unaroused, and from negative to positive (Averill, 1997; J. A. Russell, 1983). Thus, "defiant" is both aroused and somewhat negative, while "envious" is more negative but less aroused. The model can also be rotated by 45 degrees, which does not change the relationships among the emotions but redefines the model's key dimensions as excited versus bored, and alarmed versus serene (D. Watson & Tellegen, 1985).

Circumplex models such as Figure 14.6 are more useful for comparing emotions to each other than they are for explaining particular emotions. For that, it seems necessary to examine them one at a time, to describe the bases and implications of each in detail. For example, **Table 14.1** summarizes a functional analysis of five basic emotions. For each one, it describes a typical stimulus for the emotion and its associated response, along with the emotion's possible adaptive function—what it's good for. For example, if you have harmed someone else in a way that violates the generally accepted moral code, you might feel guilt, apologize, and receive forgiveness from the wronged individual and reacceptance by the larger social group (Keltner, 1995).

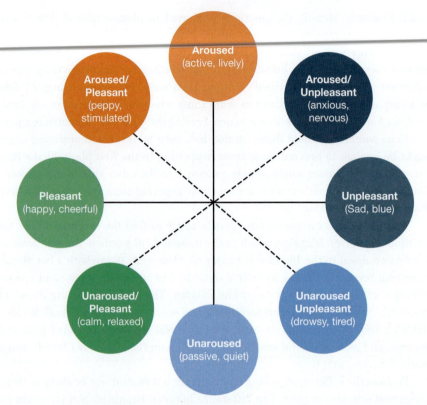

Figure 14.6 An Emotions Circumplex This circumplex diagram arranges emotions in terms of two dimensions, the degree to which they are positive or negative, and aroused or unaroused.
Source: Badr, Hoda et. al. (2006), p. 461–75.

Table 14.1 | STIMULI, RESPONSES, AND FUNCTIONS OF SOME BASIC EMOTIONS

Emotion	Typical Stimulus	Typical Responses	Adaptive Function
Anger	Threat, trespass	Threaten, attack	Protect territory, resources, or mates
Guilt	Harm to others that violates social code	Apologize, make amends	Obtain forgiveness from the offended party and reentry to the social group
Anxiety	Possibility of harm, danger	Worry, flee	Anticipate danger, escape harm
Sadness	Loss	Sad facial expressions, crying	Receive support from others, disengage from loss
Hope	Possibility of future gain	Continue effort, maintain commitment	Perseverance in the face of obstacles

Source: Adapted, in part, from Smith & Lazarus (1990), Table 23.2, p. 619.

Individual Differences in Emotional Life

General descriptions of emotions can be interesting and useful, but, in the end, emotional experience is personal. No two people ever feel things exactly the same way, and these individual differences are core aspects of personality. People differ in the emotions they experience, the emotions they *want* to experience, how strongly they experience emotions, how frequently their emotions change, and how well they understand and control their emotions.

EMOTIONAL EXPERIENCE, INTENSITY AND CHANGE The fundamental trait of extraversion—the first and broadest of the Big Five (Chapter 6)—appears to be based on a strong, consistent, and stable tendency to experience positive and energizing emotions (Eaton & Funder, 2001; D. Watson & Clark, 1997). In rare cases, people can be so extraverted that they seem out of control and are perceived as manic (Watson & Naragon-Gainey, 2014). But for the most part extraverts simply feel good, and they are peppy. That's why they act the way they do and tend to be liked by others. By contrast, one major study found that ill-tempered boys often grew up to be grouchy men who held low-status jobs from which they were frequently fired. Their wives divorced them, too (Caspi, Elder, & Bem, 1987). Thus, individual differences in positive and negative emotions can affect behavior and have important consequences.

People also differ in their attitudes about the emotions they prefer to experience or avoid (Harmon-Jones, Harmon-Jones, Amodio, & Gable, 2011). Extraverts *want* to feel happy and energized, so they seek out social situations that will make them feel that way. Other people seem to actually find that feeling anger is enjoyable,[10] so they seek out or create opportunities to get mad. And some people dislike feeling fear most of all, so they try to stay away from situations that contain any kind of threat and, I'm guessing, won't stand in line for the Super Scream roller coaster.

Separately from whether emotions are positive or negative, some people seem to experience them more strongly than others. People high in *affect intensity* (Larsen & Diener, 1987) experience both more intense joy and more powerful sadness. In some cases, they overreact. I once heard psychologist Ed Diener, one of the originators of this construct, describe a young woman in one of his classes at the University of Illinois who had scored very high on the Affect Intensity Measure (AIM; Larsen & Diener, 1987). She missed the final exam in his course. When he inquired why, it turned out she had been reading one of the Chicago newspapers that morning and saw an ad for a really excellent sale at a department store. She jumped in the car to go shopping, so excited that she forgot that (1) Chicago is 130 miles from Champaign-Urbana, and (2) the final exam started in two hours.

Not all the consequences of affect intensity are negative, but, in general, it does seem to be a risk factor for various bad outcomes. Women are generally

---

[10] Try to avoid people like this.

higher than men in affect intensity, which may explain why they are more prone to depression (Fujita, Diener, & Sandvik, 1991). Even intense positive emotions can have costs (E. Diener, Colvin, Pavot, & Allman, 1991), including the possibility that experiencing one event as extremely positive can make other events seem less positive. If last night's party was the "best party ever," how good can tomorrow night's party possibly be? Another cost is that, paradoxically, people often perceive events as positive because they are rebounding from negative events. For example, one young woman in the study wrote that an especially happy time in her life was the night she met her boyfriend. Just before that, she wrote, "It was a no-win situation as far as guys went. Things were not working with me and the guys I was dating" (E. Diener et al., 1991, p. 498). In general, as Diener and his coauthors note, the price one pays for a strong positive experience might be a certain degree of suffering first. This might be related to the positive outcomes associated with having a "redemptive" life story, where one sees oneself as having overcome obstacles so that everything turned out for the best (see Chapter 7). Evidence also suggests that, although positive emotions in general are good for one's health, emotions that are *extremely* positive may lead to physiological arousal that can harm the heart and the immune system (Pressman & Cohen, 2005).

Rapidly changing emotions can cause other problems. In one study, participants reported their emotions four times a day for eight days. Those whose emotions showed the highest rate of change described themselves, and were described by people who knew them, as generally fearful and hostile (Eaton & Funder, 2001). Perhaps they lack a strong emotional core and, as a result, are buffeted more than most by the ever-changing circumstances of everyday life. Or, possibly, wide and frequent emotional swings cause stress for both the person who experiences them and the others who have to deal with the person. Probably, it's both.

EMOTIONAL INTELLIGENCE I mentioned at the beginning of this section that emotions might be a kind of procedural knowledge. People vary in how much of this knowledge they have and can use, and these differences are important. The construct of **emotional intelligence** includes accurately perceiving emotions in oneself and others, and controlling and regulating one's own emotions (Mayer, 2014; Salovey,

Hsee, & Mayer, 1993). At the low end of the emotional intelligence scale are people sometimes characterized as *alexithymic*, who have so little emotional awareness that they are virtually unable to think about or talk about their own feelings (Haviland & Reise, 1996; G. J. Taylor & Bagby, 2000). People high in emotional intelligence are more emotionally expressive, have better personal relationships, and tend to be optimistic (Goleman, 1995).

People high in emotional intelligence also can regulate their emotions with strategies such as focusing on the positive, planning ahead for big events, and remembering to take long, deep breaths and count to 10 to stave off the desire to scream at someone. Such strategies allow a person to use rational thinking to control both how she feels and how she responds to the way she feels—a process called **cognitive control**. This kind of self-control can help a person to not overreact to stressful experiences, and to resist temptation. Research is beginning to identify the brain structures that make cognitive control possible (Ochsner & Gross, 2005; see also Chapter 8); people may vary in their ability because of differences in structures such as the prefrontal cortex.

COGNITIVE THEORIES OF PERSONALITY: CAPS AND BEATS

The cognitive perspective has provided new insights into motivation, goal-setting, planning, and emotion. Two theorists have sought to integrate these insights into the more basic learning theories that came before. Walter Mischel—yes, the very same person who triggered the person-situation controversy by claiming that personality traits are not important and that situations are much more powerful determinants of behavior (see Chapter 4)—has offered a theory of the *cognitive-affective personality system (CAPS)* (Michel, 1999). More recently, the Stanford psychologist Carol Dweck has presented a theory that integrates Beliefs, Emotions, and Action Tendencies (BEATS).

CAPS

Mischel theorizes that the most important aspect of the many systems of personality and cognition is their interaction. His Cognitive-Affective Personality System (CAPS) is "a stable system that mediates how the individual selects, construes, and processes social information and generates social behaviors" (Mischel & Shoda, 1995, p. 246). An example Mischel addressed many times in his research concerned a child trying to delay gratification. Most experiments of this sort present a child with two rewards, such as marshmallows and pretzels. The child is told that he can have the less preferred reward immediately, but can have the better reward if able to wait for a few minutes. Mischel was interested in the strategies the child might use to get through the waiting period.

One strategy he suggested to the waiting children was to mentally transform the object that presumably was being so eagerly awaited. For example, if a child's preferred treat was the marshmallow, she might hardly be able to wait while imagining its "chewy, sweet, soft taste." If instead she thought about the marshmallow as a cloud, it became easy to wait much longer. If a child preferred the pretzel, tolerance for waiting would end quickly if the child concentrated on its "crunchy, salty taste." But thinking about the pretzel as a brown log made the waiting easier.

Mischel drew from this research not only some pointers on how to help children delay gratification, but also a deeper moral that fits right into the point of view of the phenomenologists:

> The results [of the research just described] clearly show that what is in the children's heads—not what is physically in front of them—determines their ability to delay. (Mischel, 1973, p. 260)

Another key aspect of Mischel's theory of personality is the idea of what he calls *if . . . then contingencies*. Learning history and cognitive processes combine in each individual to yield a repertoire of actions triggered by particular stimulus situations. For example, one person, when insulted, might simply walk away. Another, with a different *if . . . then* pattern, might respond with a punch in the nose (Shoda, 1999). Every individual's pattern of contingencies is unique, and comprises his *behavioral signature* (Mischel, 1999, p. 44). Notice the similarity between this description and Watson's original *S-R* conception of personality, summarized earlier in this chapter.

Mischel's goal was for *if . . . then* contingencies to replace personality traits— for which he still had no great love, even after all these years—as the essential units for understanding personality differences. The main advantage of the *if . . . then* idea is its specificity. A trait such as dominance, for example, provides only general guidance for predicting what a dominant person might do. Reconceptualizing the trait in *if . . . then* terms might allow the specific prediction that if a person joins a business meeting, then she will quickly take charge. The *if . . . then* idea is also more sensitive to the way people change their behavior across situations. Perhaps the same person who dominates a meeting relates very differently to her family. A trait notion of dominance, in contrast, assumes that a person who is dominant in one situation is likely to display the trait in other situations as well. Research shows this to be generally true (see Chapter 4), but the *if . . . then* theory describes the exceptions, and focuses more specifically on discerning which situations would probably elicit dominant behavior.

Mischel's *if . . . then* contingencies have the potential to integrate trait conceptions of personality with social learning conceptions and cognitive conceptions, by redescribing traits as specific behavior patterns. For example, if a friendly person meets a stranger, then he will probably engage in conversation. If a shy person is at a social gathering, then he will probably be sensitive to any sign of rejection. And so on. For all their demonstrated usefulness, personality traits are sometimes too broad and vague to provide the most useful way to think about behavior. Integrating traits with the *if . . . then* idea offers a promising field for future research (Moeller, Robinson, & Bresin, 2010; Yang et al., 2011).

BEATS

An even more ambitious version of cognitive social learning theory was recently offered by the psychologist Carol Dweck (Dweck, 2017). Her theory is organized around the idea that personality emerges from an individual's mental representations of the beliefs, emotions, and action tendencies (BEATS) that are relevant to his or her most important goals. Specifically, people have a total of seven fundamental needs. At the most basic level, everybody needs trust, control, and respect from others and from oneself (self-esteem). These basic needs combine to produce three "emergent" needs for predictability, acceptance, and competence. And when all of these are put together, the final need emerges for "self-coherence," or a feeling of meaning in life (see **Figure 14.7**).

Her theory has a little bit of everything. It begins by assuming, like many theories of personality, that people have basic motivations that drive everything they do. These needs lead people to create goals, which are often different from

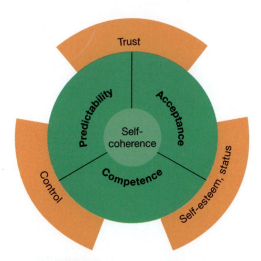

Figure 14.7 Dweck's BEATS Model of Personality The diagram shows how basic needs for trust, control, and status combine into needs for predictability, acceptance, and competence, culminating in a need for self-coherence, or meaning in life.

one person to another. The goals create beliefs about the world, feelings about the world, and tendencies to act in different ways in the world (the BEATS). The result, for each individual, is a collection of consistent patterns of thought, emotion, and behavior. In other words, personality traits. In this way, Dweck has come closer than any other theorist to bridging the gap between cognitive behavioral theory, on the one hand, and traditional trait theory, on the other.

PERSONALITY AS A VERB

Philosopher and architect R. Buckminster Fuller once wrote,

> . . . I don't know what I am. I know that I am not a category. I am not a thing—a noun. I seem to be a verb, an evolutionary process—an integral function of the universe. (Fuller, 1970, p. 1)

Fuller refers to being "a verb," but the psychological inner life he is discussing encompasses several verbs, including *thinking*, *wanting*, and *feeling*. Anybody who is alive is doing all of these. The personality processes of learning, motivation, and emotion that were the subjects of this chapter are also what psychologist Nancy Cantor meant when she argued that personality is not something that an individual merely "has"; it is something a person "does" (Cantor, 1990). In that sense, "personality" is a verb.

WRAPPING IT UP

SUMMARY

Behaviorism

- Behaviorism's key tenet is that all of behavior stems from the rewards and punishments in past and present environments.

- The three basic principles of learning are habituation, classical conditioning, and operant conditioning.

- Habituation causes a stimulus to produce smaller effects with repetition. In humans, it might lessen the impact of important life events—good and bad— over time.

- Classical conditioning pairs experiences with stimuli, and affects emotions, feelings, and physiological responses. If negative experiences appear to occur randomly the result can be "learned helplessness," the feeling that life is unpredictable and uncontrollable.

- The S-R conception of personality, based on classical conditioning, describes it as a repertoire of arbitrary stimulus-response associations.

- Operant conditioning causes rewarded behavior to be more likely to occur, and can produce complex patterns of behavior in animals and humans.

Social Learning Theory

- Social Learning Theory arose in response to four limitations of behaviorism: (1) It ignores motivation, thought, and emotion. (2) It is primarily based on animals. (3) It ignores the social aspect of learning. (4) It treats the organism (animal or person) as passive.

- Dollard and Rotter's social learning theory tried to combine behaviorism with aspects of psychoanalytic theory. Rotter's social learning theory emphasizes how expectancies of reward can be more important determinants of behavior than reward itself.

- Bandura's social learning theory, the most impactful today, focuses on how individuals' expectancies about their own behavioral capacities affect what they will attempt to do. His theory also develops a detailed analysis of observational learning, in which a person learns by watching the behaviors and outcomes of others, and reciprocal determinism.

Motivation

- Motivation can be studied by examining goals and strategies.

- Goals can be specific and short-term, or general and long-term, and they can be arranged hierarchically. Ideally, one should be able to shift flexibly between the two kinds of goals.

- Idiographic goals are unique to each individual and may include current concerns (Klinger), personal projects (Little), and personal strivings (Emmons).

- Nomothetic goals are common to all people; several studies have proposed different sets of these, including one with three primary goals (achievement, affiliation, and power), one with five goals (enjoyment, self-assertion, esteem, interpersonal success, and avoiding negative affect), and one supporting Freud's big two (love and work).

- Dweck's theory of motivation says that all people are theorists who hold differing views about the changeability of intelligence and ability. Entity theorists see intelligence and ability as unchanging while incremental theorists believe they can be improved. As a result, entity theorists pursue judgment goals and respond to failure with helplessness. Incremental theorists pursue development goals and respond to failure with mastery.

- Many and perhaps all personality traits can be conceptualized in terms of the strategies that people follow; for example, the agreeable person follows the strategy of avoiding arguments and being friendly to everyone.

- According to Norem, defensive pessimists follow the motivational strategy of imagining the worst outcomes and then seeking to avoid them. The strategy seems to work for some people.

Emotion

- Emotions are a form of procedural knowledge; everyone knows what they are, but they are difficult to put into words and can only be fully learned and expressed through action and experience.

- Emotional experience includes stages of appraisal, physical response, nonverbal behaviors, and motivation. These stages may occur nearly simultaneously or in various orders.

- A circumplex model of emotion contrasts the degrees to which emotions are aroused versus unaroused and negative versus positive; another widely used rotation of this model contrasts emotions on the dimensions of excited versus bored and alarmed versus serene.

- People differ in the degree to which they are prone to particular emotions; the intensity of their emotional experience; the frequency with which their emotions change; and their understanding of, and ability to control, their emotions (emotional intelligence).

Cognitive Theories of Personality: CAPS and BEATS

- Mischel's theory of the Cognitive-affective Personality System (CAPS) culminates in an *if . . . then* model of personality that describes how a person responds distinctively to each situation he encounters.

- Dweck's theory addresses individuals' mental representations of Beliefs, Emotions, and Action Tendencies (BEATS), and describes how basic motivations produce individual needs and an overall desire for "self-coherence," or meaning in life.

Personality as a Verb

- Personality is something an individual "does" as well as something the individual "has," so, in that sense, personality is a verb.

KEY TERMS

learning, p. 515
behaviorism, p. 517
functional analysis, p. 517
habituation, p. 517
classical conditioning, p. 518
learned helplessness, p. 519
respondent conditioning, p. 520
operant conditioning, p. 520
reinforcement, p. 520
self-efficacy, p. 525
self-concept, p. 525
observational learning, p. 526
goals, p. 527
strategies, p. 527

THINK ABOUT IT

1. Does what you do depend on rewards and punishments? What else does it depend on?

2. What might psychology look like today if behaviorism had never been invented?

3. An important reason for the rise of the social learning theories was that orthodox behaviorism paid too little attention to the ways that people think and solve problems. But what about animals? Does your household dog or cat, for example, merely respond to rewards and punishments or does your pet think and solve problems? How could this be demonstrated?

4. Does the concept of *personality processes* constitute a "basic approach" like the trait, biological, psychodynamic, humanistic, and learning approaches considered in earlier chapters? Is it an amalgamation of these other approaches, or is it something else entirely?

5. Is your behavior generally part of a strategy to obtain a long-term goal? Would it be better if more of your behaviors were?

6. Do you think most college students have what Dweck would call judgment goals or development goals?

7. Can you really understand the emotions of another person? Do you ever find your own emotions difficult to understand?

SUGGESTED RESOURCES

Bandura, A. (1977). *Social learning theory*. Englewood Cliffs, NJ: Prentice-Hall.

Miller, N. E., & Dollard, J. (1947). *Social learning and imitation*. New Haven, CT: Yale University Press.

Rotter, J. B. (1954). *Social learning and clinical psychology*. Englewood Cliffs, NJ: Prentice-Hall.

Although many people identify Bandura as the originator of social learning theory, his version is actually the third of three major versions, summarized in the books above. Of these three, Rotter's may be the most interesting to read because of its direct applications and clinical examples.

Mayer, J. (2014). *Personal intelligence: The power of personality and how it shapes our lives.* New York: Scientific American/Farrar, Straus & Giroux.

> *One of the pioneers of the study of emotional intelligence explains how our natural "intelligence" about personality can help us to understand ourselves better and relate better to other people. This is a lively book full of compelling examples.*

Norem, J. (2001). *The positive power of negative thinking: Using defensive pessimism to manage anxiety and perform at your peak.* New York: Basic Books.

> *A highly readable introduction to Julie Norem's defense of the benefits of a pessimistic outlook on life. The book summarizes a wide range of research and is full of useful advice.*

Skinner, B. F. (1938). *The behavior of organisms: An experimental analysis.* New York: Macmillan.

> *Nearly every college library has a copy of this book (either the original 1938 version or one of the reprints), and it is worth a firsthand look. It is still the best comprehensive survey of the thinking of this prominent behaviorist, and helps to explain why he became so famous; the book is clearly written and full of clever insights.*

Want to earn a better grade on your test?

Go to **INQUIZITIVE** to learn and review this chapter's content, with personalized feedback along the way.

15

THE SELF: WHAT YOU KNOW ABOUT YOU

Tell me something about yourself.
—INTERVIEW QUESTION

A FEW YEARS AGO, I worked on a study that gathered a large amount of information on almost 200 undergraduate participants. It began with a life-history interview, which we videotaped. The very first question in the interview is quoted above, and the interviewer asked it straight out of the blue. How would you reply? Some participants replied simply by telling us their names, hometowns, and majors. Some described favorite activities or life goals. But the most common response by far was a quick look of panic and an answer along the lines of "um . . . er . . . well . . ." You might think we would know our "selves" better than we know anybody or anything else, but for most people this basic question turns out to be surprisingly difficult.

THE *I* AND THE *ME*

As William James (1890) noted many years ago, "the self" can have two different meanings, which he called the *I* and the *me*. The *me* is a sort of object, which can be observed and described. The *I* is the rather mysterious entity that does the observing and describing. (Some philosophers and psychologists call the *I* the **ontological self**, and the *me* the **epistemological self**.) When you describe yourself as "friendly," you are describing your *me*. But when you try to describe how you feel deep down inside about knowing you are friendly, you are trying to talk about your *I*, which is not easy to do. To put this another way, the *me* is the collection of statements you could make about yourself ranging from "I am friendly"[1] to "I am 6 feet tall." The *I* is more like the little person in the head (sometimes called the *homunculus*), or even the soul, which experiences your life and makes your decisions (Klein, 2012). Although the theoretical distinction is important, the *I* and the *me* are often confused in practice. As the eminent psychologist Ernest Hilgard once observed,

> the self-evident character of self-awareness is in fact most illusive. You presently find yourself as between the two mirrors of a barbershop, with each image viewing each other, so that as the self takes a look at itself taking a look at itself, it soon gets all confused as to the self that is doing the looking and the self which is being looked at. (Hilgard, 1949, p. 377)

The self that is doing the looking, as Hilgard said, is the *I*, and the self that is being looked at is the *me*. The existential-phenomenological psychologists discussed in Chapter 12 attempted to address the nature and mystery of the experience of the *I*. And the *I* is relevant to personality, because people differ in their degree of self-awareness (Robins, Tracy, & Trzesniewski, 2008).

Beyond that observation, psychologists have not succeeded in saying much that is useful or interesting about the *I*. Indeed, psychologist Stan Klein (2012) suggests that the *I* may not even be accessible to conventional scientific investigation. I will return to the implications of the *I* at the end of this chapter, but recent research has much more to say about the *me*, the part of the self that we and the people who know us can talk about, describe, and put into action. What you know about you, and what I know about me, the *epistemological self*, is the main topic of this chapter.

THE CONTENTS AND PURPOSES OF THE SELF

William James believed that our *me* includes everything we hold dear, and so includes not just our personality traits, but also our body, home, possessions, and even family members. He observed that if someone were to harm any of these, we would be upset and angry. Someone who hits your child might as well punch you in the face; your reaction will be the same (or worse), and we also do not take kindly to people who damage or even criticize our homes, cars, or stamp collections.

The central aspect of the self, however, is surely our psychological nature: our abilities and, especially, our personalities. If you see yourself as kind, for example, this is important for several reasons. The self-image and your need to maintain it may influence your behavior (e.g., how you respond to a homeless person asking

---

[1] English grammar confuses the issue here, because in James's terms, we really should say, "Me am friendly" (which sounds like something Tarzan would say).

for spare change), and it organizes a vast array of memories as well as your impressions and judgments of other people.

This organization of knowledge is one of the important functions of the self. In fact, psychologist Richard Robins and his colleagues (2008) propose that the self has four important jobs. The first is *self-regulation*, the ability to restrain impulses and maintain focus on long-term goals. The second purpose is as an *information-processing filter*, guiding us to pay attention to and remember the information that really matters to us, as well as to keep it organized. To some degree, this job involves gathering accurate information about our traits and abilities, but it also sometimes

Figure 15.1 Self-Observation Trying to observe yourself as you think about yourself is like looking into a mirror that is in front of another mirror.

involves a bit of distortion of self-knowledge in order to put on a better face for others and allow us to feel more positively about ourselves. If we can see ourselves as at least a little bit better than we really are, we can be more confident and effective when dealing with other people (von Hippel & Trivers, 2011). The third purpose of the self is to help us relate to other people. We understand others through the lens of our own experience, such as empathizing with someone's distress by imagining how we would feel. The final purpose of the self is *identity*, to remind us of where we fit in. We each hold a unique position in our family, our community, and in the social hierarchy that is part of every civilization. As we saw in Chapter 7, part of our identity is the "life story" we tell ourselves, about ourselves (McAdams & McLean, 2013). Self-knowledge provides an internal marker on the map that says, "You are here."

> Self-knowledge provides an internal marker on the map that says, "You are here."

Self-knowledge can be divided into two types, both of which serve all four purposes. **Declarative knowledge** consists of the facts and impressions that we consciously know and can describe. It is self-knowledge we can "declare." For example, a person who knows that she is friendly can easily say so, and thus "friendliness" will be part of her declarative self-knowledge. *Procedural knowledge*, as described in the previous chapter, is expressed through actions rather than words. For example, a shy person might habitually avoid other people and social interaction whenever possible, and this habit may be so ingrained that he does not consciously realize how characteristic this behavior is. Intriguingly, however, as we shall see later in this chapter, this shy person *might* be aware of his tendencies on some deeper, unconscious level. In both cases, these unconscious aspects of shyness would be considered part of his procedural self. Procedural self-knowledge includes patterns of social skills, styles of relating to others that comprise the *relational self*, and the unconscious self-knowledge that resides in the *implicit self*.

THE DECLARATIVE SELF

The **declarative self** comprises two kinds of knowledge or opinions you have about your own personality traits. First is your overall opinion about whether you are good or bad, worthy or unworthy, or somewhere in between. This opinion is called **self-esteem**. The second kind of opinion is more detailed and contains everything you know, or think you know, about your traits and abilities. Sometimes this supposed self-knowledge is correct, sometimes it is wrong, and sometimes it is somewhere in between.

Self-Esteem

In one of its most truly Californian acts, in 1987 the California legislature set up a task force to enhance the self-esteem of the state's residents. Perhaps this law was not as flaky as it sounds (though, decades later, the self-esteem of Californians has not noticeably improved). A large amount of research suggests that low self-esteem—feeling you are bad or unworthy—is correlated with outcomes such as dissatisfaction with life, hopelessness, and depression (Crocker & Wolfe, 2001; Orth, Robins, & Roberts, 2008), as well as loneliness (Cutrona, 1982) and delinquency (Donnellan, Trzesniewski, Robins, Moffitt, & Caspi, 2005; Trzesniewski et al., 2006). Declines in self-esteem also appear to cause outcomes including depression, lower satisfaction with relationships, and lower satisfaction with one's career (Orth et al., 2012). As we saw in Chapter 13, countries whose people have lower self-esteem, on average, also have higher suicide rates (Chatard et al., 2009). This last finding is ironic, in a way, because research also shows that people with low self-esteem have a greater fear of death (Schmeichel et al., 2009). Psychologists have thought for a long time that low self-esteem is bad, and for good reason.

HIGH AND LOW SELF-ESTEEM The advantages of high self-esteem are pretty much the reverse of the disadvantages just summarized. In particular, it seems often to be good for relationships if not quite always. One interesting study found that people with high self-esteem who are also high in the trait of agreeableness were more likely to disclose their emotional distress, when they felt it, to their relationship partners (McCarthy, Wood & Holmes, 2017). This was because they trusted their partners more and, in return, received better social support. But this advantage for high self-esteem only was found for those who also were agreeable—high self-esteem people who were disagreeable didn't trust their partners enough to share what was going on in their emotional lives. The result was bad for their relationships.

Low self-esteem, by itself, might literally be a danger signal. According to psychologist Mark Leary's sociometer theory described in Chapter 9, the desire to maintain high self-esteem may have evolutionary roots. Your self-esteem suffers when you have failed in the eyes of your social group (Denissen, Penke, Schmitt, & van Aken, 2008; Leary, 1999). This drop in self-esteem may be a warning about possible rejection or even social ostracism—which, for our distant ancestors, could literally be fatal—and motivate you to restore your reputation. High self-esteem, by contrast, is a reflection of success and acceptance. It certainly feels good.

Attempts to bolster self-esteem can backfire. Many self-help books urge people to chant phrases to themselves such as "I am a lovable person," "I'm powerful, I'm strong, and nothing in this world can stop me," and other so-called "affirmations" of the self. Early-20th-century French pharmacist Émile Coué told his patients to repeat "Every day, in every way, I am getting better and better."[2] Psychologist Joanne Wood and her colleagues argue that statements like these can be dangerous, because if the person who says them finds them to be too extreme to be plausible, a boomerang effect may actually cause the person to feel worse (J. V. Wood, Perunovic, & Lee, 2009). For example, if you say "I am a lovable person," but you don't really believe it, repeating the phrase may make your (perceived) unlovability just that much more prominent in your mind.

Besides, it is not good for self-esteem to get *too* high. If a person fails to recognize the ways that other people dislike or have lost respect for her, she may risk exploitation or social ostracism. People who *self-enhance*—who think they are better than the other people who know them think they are—can run into problems in relations with others, mental health, and adjustment (Kurt & Paulhus, 2008; Kwan, John, Robins, & Kuang, 2008).[3] In terms of the sociometer analogy, if your gas gauge breaks with the needle stuck on "full," you may happily think you don't need to fill your tank, but later you will find yourself stranded on the highway.

In other words, it is possible to love oneself too much (Funder, 2011). Overly high self-esteem can lead to behavior that is arrogant, abusive, and even criminal (Baumeister, Smart, & Boden, 1996; Colvin, Block, & Funder, 1995). The trait of narcissism, which was described in Chapter 6, can become so extreme in some people that it becomes classified as a personality disorder (see Chapter 17), which harms both the narcissist and, sometimes even more so, the people with whom

---

[2] Or, if you prefer the original French, *tous les jours à tous points de vue je vais de mieux en mieux*. This is a famous phrase, but I found the exact quote in Wikipedia (where else?): http://en.wikipedia.org/wiki/%C3%89mile_Cou%C3%A9#cite_note-britannica-0.

[3] The awkward phrasing of this sentence is deliberate. People who describe themselves as better than *they* describe others are not necessarily maladjusted; sometimes—in fact, often—they really *are* better than others in certain respects. What turns out to cause problems is to see yourself as better than do other people who know you well. On the flip side, psychologist Virginia Kwan and her colleagues maintain that to see yourself as others see you is the meaning of *self-insight*. (See Kwan et al., 2008, and Kurt & Paulhus, 2008, for extended discussions.)

he comes in contact. Narcissism is associated with high self-esteem that is brittle and unstable because it is unrealistic (Vazire & Funder, 2006; Zeigler-Hill, 2006), and unstable self-esteem may be even worse than low self-esteem (Kernis, Lakey, & Heppner, 2008).

The bottom line is that promoting psychological health is more complex than simply trying to make everybody feel better about themselves (Swann, Chang-Schneider, & McClarty, 2007). The best way to raise self-esteem is through accomplishments that increase it legitimately (DuBois & Flay, 2004; Haney & Durlak, 1998). Make some friends; get a job done; help another person in need. You will feel better about yourself, and deservedly so.

GENDER DIFFERENCES IN SELF-ESTEEM On average, men have higher self-esteem than women. This finding holds for whites, Hispanics, and Asian Americans—but not African Americans or immigrants to the United States. Perhaps surprisingly, the self-esteem advantage for men is bigger in places, such as the United States and Western Europe, where the values of equality and freedom are emphasized. The gender difference increased from the 1970s through the 1990s, but has declined a bit in the years since then. So what's going on?

According to one analysis, the gender difference in self-esteem develops— or could have developed—through three historical stages (Zuckerman & Hall, 2016). At the first stage, traditional sex discrimination is widespread and accepted without question. Women and men live in separate social worlds and, when assessing their own well-being, compare themselves to other women or to other men (respectively). Thus, women and men would be expected to have similar levels of self-esteem. At the second stage, as a society modernizes and gender barriers begin to soften or break down, and social movements toward gender equality begin to appear, women increasingly become aware of their disadvantaged position. Gender differences in self-esteem emerge and grow (Baumeister & Leary, 1995). But there is hope, at a final stage (which these theorists call "Progress"), when the move toward gender equality moves forward as people start to realize that their disadvantages are not personal but societal (Crocker & Major, 1989). Instead of blaming oneself, one learns to blame the system. The end result is that women's self-esteem can rise, and the gender difference will fade away.

This theory is highly speculative, of course, but even if its optimistic prediction is not correct, it has an interesting moral. How you feel about yourself is not completely a result of your own abilities, accomplishments, virtues, or even psychological health. Your self-worth is to some extent telegraphed to you by society, which might teach you that you are inferior (or superior) not only because of your gender, but also because of your wealth (or lack thereof), race, attractiveness, or other attribute beyond your control. Remember from Chapter 12 how humanistic psychologists such as Carl Rogers decried "conditions of worth." That seems to be the problem to be overcome here, as well.

The Self-Schema

Some psychologists theorize that the declarative self resides in a cognitive (mental) structure called the **self-schema** (Markus, 1977), which includes all of one's ideas about the self, organized into a coherent system. When a trait psychologist asks someone to complete a personality questionnaire, the person presumably answers these questions by reaching into her memory system for the relevant information. This memory system is the self-schema, and the act of responding to the questionnaire amounts to reporting what the self-schema contains. That is why this kind of questionnaire is said to gather S data (Chapter 2); I hope you recall that S stands for *self*-report. But there is more than one way to get at the self-schema.

The self-schema can be identified using S data, B data, or both (see Chapter 2). For example, one early study identified college students who were "schematic for" (had self-schemas pertaining to) the traits of dependence and sociability by simply asking them to rate themselves on a series of scales (Markus, 1977). If these S data indicated that a student rated himself as extremely sociable and that he also rated his sociability important, he was deemed schematic for that trait. Otherwise, he was deemed "aschematic." A later study employed the widely used California Psychological Inventory (CPI; Gough, 1968) to gather self-ratings on the traits of responsibility and sociability (Fuhrman & Funder, 1995). When these S data indicated an exceptionally high score on responsibility, the participant was deemed schematic for that trait.

Both of these studies also gathered B data. In this case, the B data were reaction times. Participants read words such as *friendly* or *responsible* on a computer screen, and then responded by pressing keys labeled "me" or "not me" as quickly as they could. Schematics responded to relevant traits more quickly than did aschematics, regardless of whether they were identified using Markus's rating scales or the CPI (Fuhrman & Funder, 1995; Markus, 1977; see **Figure 15.2**).

This research has two important implications. A methodological implication is that the phenomena studied by cognitively oriented personality psychologists, of the sort discussed in this and the previous chapter, and those studied by the trait psychologists, discussed in Chapters 4 through 7, might not be as different as is sometimes presumed (Rieger et al., 2017). Being assessed as schematic for a given trait and attaining a high score on that trait using a conventional personality inventory such as the CPI seem to have the same implications for response time and other indications of cognitive processing—and they may well be the very same thing.

A second implication is that one's self-view—conceptualized as a schema or a trait, take your pick—may have important consequences for how one processes information. As cognitive personality psychologist Nancy Cantor (1990) pointed out, being schematic for a personality trait such as sociability, responsibility, or shyness amounts to being an "expert" about that trait. Research elsewhere in cognitive psychology has shown that experts in any domain—chess or mechanical

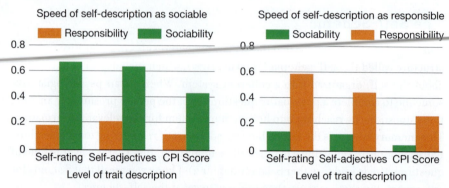

Figure 15.2 Correlations Between Being "Schematic" on a Trait and Reaction Time The figure displays the correlation (*r* on a 0 to 1 scale) between three measures of being "schematic" on sociability and responsibility, and the speed of responding "me" to these terms. The three measures were self-rating, self-descriptive adjectives, and the individual's score on the relevant scale of the California Psychological Inventory (CPI). As the results show, the higher a person's schematicity score (in any of the three measures), the faster was his or her response to the relevant trait descriptor. Notice that responses to both terms were measured in relation to both traits, to make sure that it wasn't simply the case that sociable or responsible people respond more quickly overall. Source: Fuhrman & Funder (1995), p. 967.

engineering, for example—easily remember information relevant to their domain of expertise, tend to see the world in terms dictated by their expertise, and have a ready and almost automatic plan of action that can be invoked in relevant situations (Chase & Simon, 1973; Larkin, McDermott, Simon, & Simon, 1980). This kind of expertise has some obvious advantages—it can help a person to be a better chess player or engineer—but it also can limit that person's view of the world. An expert may view things too rigidly, or fail to test possibilities beyond the limits of her expertise. In the same way, your expertise about yourself can help you remember a lot of information about yourself and process this information quickly, but it also may keep you from seeing beyond the boundaries of your own self-image.

The self-schema embodies knowledge based on past experience, but not on any particular past experience. For example, perhaps you have behaved kindly many times and in many situations, and as a result have come to view yourself as a kind person. What would happen if you somehow forgot about all of the occasions on which you were kind, if they were literally erased from your memory? Would your self-view change?

This question might seem unanswerable, but it actually has been addressed by two remarkable case studies. In one case, a college student sustained a head injury that caused her temporarily to lose all memory of everything she had done during the past year (S. B. Klein, Loftus, & Kihlstrom, 1996). Yet, she was able to describe her own personality almost perfectly, in a way that agreed with the perceptions of

TRY FOR YOURSELF 15.1

Are You Schematic?

Instructions: Mark the point on each scale that best describes you:

Independent	1 2 3 4 5 6 7 8 9 10 11	Dependent

How important to you is your description on this scale?

Unimportant	1 2 3 4 5 6 7 8 9 10 11	Important

Individualist	1 2 3 4 5 6 7 8 9 10 11	Conformist

How important to you is your description on this scale?

Unimportant	1 2 3 4 5 6 7 8 9 10 11	Important

Leader	1 2 3 4 5 6 7 8 9 10 11	Follower

How important to you is your description on this scale?

Unimportant	1 2 3 4 5 6 7 8 9 10 11	Important

Interpreting Scores:

- If you rated yourself from points 1–4 on at least two of the three trait scales, and rated the same traits from points 8–11 on the importance scales, you are "schematic" for the trait of "independence."
- If you rated yourself from points 8–11 on at least two of the three trait scales, and rated the same traits from points 8–11 on the importance scales, you are "schematic" for the trait of "dependence."

Source: Markus (1977), p. 66.

her parents and boyfriend. More remarkably, she could describe herself in ways that reflected how she had changed during the past year (which happened to be her first year of college), even without any memory of events that happened during the year.[4] A second case study was even more striking. As a result of a heart attack that cut off oxygen to his brain, a 78-year-old man lost almost all memory of specific events of his life. Yet, he still had general knowledge of himself (e.g., "I usually try to be kind") that agreed with the impressions of others who knew him

---

[4] The case had a happy ending. Three weeks after the accident, the student recovered all of her memories except for a brief period immediately after her fall.

well (S. B. Klein, Rozendal, & Cosmides, 2002). These cases suggest that the answer to the question asked at the end of the preceding paragraph—would your self-view change if you lost memory of your past?—is no. Once formed, your impression of what you are like does not depend on your memory for specific things you have done, and these two bases of self-knowledge may exist independently in separate sectors of the brain (Klein & Lax, 2010; Lieberman et al., 2004). Your self, in that sense, has a life of its own.

Self-Reference and Memory

Another indication that the self has deep roots is how it affects memory. An old theory suggested that if you repeated something over and over in your mind, such *rehearsal* was sufficient to move the information into **long-term memory (LTM)**, or permanent memory storage. Later research showed that this idea is not quite correct. The best way to get information into LTM, it turns out, is not just to repeat it, but to really think about it (a process called *elaboration*). The longer and more complex the processing that a piece of information receives, the more likely it is to get transferred into LTM (Craik & Tulving, 1975; Craik & Watkins, 1973).

This principle of cognitive psychology yields some useful advice about how to study. A common strategy is rote repetition. Everyone has seen college students in the library with their yellow highlighters, marking passages in the textbook they think may pertain to the exam. To study, they reread everything highlighted; if they have time, they do it again and even again. This strategy is not very effective. A much better approach is to take each of these highlighted passages, pause, and consider several questions. Do I agree with this statement? Why? Is it useful? Does it contradict anything else I know from experience or have learned in this course? Answering these questions will make you much more likely to remember the statements you have read. Moreover, it's less boring than just trying to memorize everything.

A particularly good way to remember something, research has shown, is to think about some specific way that it relates to one's self (C. Symons & Johnson, 1997). For example, if you must memorize a long list of adjectives, it can be effective to ask yourself whether each of them describes you. The reason appears to be that the mental structure of self-knowledge, the self-schema, is rich, well developed, and often used. Any information tied to this schema in memory remains accessible for a long time. Ask, "What does this have to do with me?" The answer doesn't really matter; the important part is to think about how the information *might* be self-relevant (even if it isn't). The enhancement of LTM that comes from thinking of how information relates to the self is called the **self-reference effect**, and a particular area of the

> A particularly good way to remember something is to think about some specific way that it relates to one's self.

frontal cortex of the brain might be specialized to process this kind of information (Heatherton, Macrae, & Kelley, 2004).

The self-reference effect explains why your most personally meaningful memories are the ones that stick with you the longest. These may include tragic events, major milestones (such as graduation day, your wedding day, and the day your child—especially your first child—is born), and other events that stand out for some reason. Try this right now: Think of a memory from your early childhood. Why has this event stayed in your mind all of these years? It must mean something special to you—what?

We saw in Chapter 13 that the concept of the self may have different implications in collectivist cultures, such as China, than in individualist cultures, such as the United States. It is reasonable to suspect, therefore, that the self-reference effect might also work differently in the two places. One study indicates that it does (Qi & Zhu, 2002). In Chinese culture, information thought about in terms of the self is indeed remembered better than most other kinds of information, but information thought about in terms of one's mother or father showed the same effect, leading the authors to conclude that "the self-concept might include the concepts of father and mother in Chinese people, supporting the independent/dependent self-concept model in Eastern culture" (Qi & Zhu, 2002, p. 275).

Self-Efficacy

Because the (conscious) self-schema contains our ideas about our characteristics and capabilities (Markus & Nurius, 1986), it affects what we do. If we think we are sociable, we are more likely to seek out the company of others. If we think we are academically capable, we are more likely to go to college. Recall Bandura's ideas of self-efficacy from Chapter 14: Our opinions about our capabilities set the limits of what we will attempt. For example, perhaps you had a friend in high school who was just as smart and hardworking as you. For whatever reason, however, your friend thought that he couldn't possibly succeed in college. You might have tried to argue otherwise: "Of course you can do it—if I can, you can too!" But in the face of a negative self-attitude, such arguments are usually ineffective. So you went to college, and your friend did not. In a year or two, you will graduate, and your friend will still be pumping gas or flipping burgers.[5] The difference was not one of ability or drive—it was in the self.

This example shows how important and sometimes devastating one's self-concept can be. It also shows the dangers in persuading people that they cannot do certain things. For example, many young girls pick up the message from society that girls cannot—or should not—excel at math (Hilton & Berglund, 1974; Stipek & Gralinski, 1991). The result? Here's a personal example: I used to teach at a

---

[5] I am presuming that with your college education, you will find a better job than these.

"Really, only you can tell yourself to giddyup."

prestigious engineering college. More than 90 percent of the students were male—hardly a result of chance or, I am sure, of sex differences in ability.[6] Similarly, members of certain racial groups and economic classes are taught, usually implicitly but powerfully by the media and other sources, that "their kind" do not go to college or otherwise better themselves. So sometimes these individuals give up, or they find other ways—not necessarily constructive— to feel that they have succeeded. This is why people are not merely being sensitive when they object to stereotyped media portrayals of particular ethnic groups as lazy, unsuccessful, or even criminal, and why there was so much outrage a few years ago when a talking Barbie doll was sold that said, "Math class is tough!" These portrayals can have important consequences, especially for children.

Possible Selves

The person that you are—is that the only person you could be? Probably not. For this reason, some psychologists have studied *possible selves*, the images we have or can construct of the other ways we might be. The possible self you envision for your future may affect your goals in life.

For instance, David Buss (1989) showed that women, more than men, preferred mates who were older than themselves and had the ability to provide for them. As we saw in Chapter 9, Buss interpreted this result as indicating that women have evolved to seek mates who can protect and provide for them and their children, whereas men have different priorities. A later study questioned this interpretation, in an interesting way (Eagly, Eastwick, & Johannesen-Schmidt, 2009). Women *and* men were asked to imagine themselves—a possible future self—as a "married person with children who is either a homemaker or a provider" (2009, p. 403). Then they were asked what kind of mate would be best for them. People of either gender who imagined themselves as homemakers, compared with those who imagined themselves as providers, preferred a mate who was older and could provide for them! This finding implies that the different mate preferences of women and men might stem, to some degree, from the selves they expect to be possible in the future, which itself is a function of society—not necessarily from a built-in biological tendency.

---

[6] However, that was back in the 1980s. I just looked up the current statistics and at the same college the gender ratio between women and men is 48/52. Progress!

Most work on possible selves has focused on our images of the people we wish we were. People report desiring future selves that fulfill their needs for self-esteem, competence, and meaning. But they don't want their future selves to change too much. Another desired attribute of the future self is *continuity*—maintaining the same identity over time (Vignoles, Manzi, Regalia, Scabini, & Jemmolo, 2008). And, as was mentioned in Chapter 7, people acknowledge having changed in the past, but neither expect nor usually want their personality to change much in the future.

Self-Discrepancy Theory

According to *self-discrepancy theory*, you have not one but two kinds of desired selves, and the difference between them and your actual self determines how you feel (Higgins, Bond, Klein, & Strauman, 1986; Higgins, Roney, Crowe, & Hymes, 1994). One is the *ideal self*, which is your view of what you could be at your best. A second is your *ought self*, which is your view of what you should—as opposed to what you would like to—be. Although they both represent hypothetical optimums, the ideal and ought selves typically differ. For example, your ideal self might include an image of yourself as being so good-looking that people have to pause and stare as you walk by. Your ought self might include an image of somebody who never, ever tells a lie.

Both of these nonactual selves are probably unrealistic. Let's face facts: You are probably neither that good-looking nor that honest. But the discrepancies between the actual self and these two potential selves have different consequences, according to the theory. To the extent that you fail to attain your ideal self, you become depressed. To the extent that you fail to attain your ought self, you become anxious.[7]

Why do these reactions differ? According to theorist Tory Higgins (1997), the two nonactual selves represent different foci to life. The ideal self is reward based and resembles the Go system hypothesized by Jeffrey Gray (see Chapter 8). To some extent, you focus your life on the pursuit of pleasures and rewards. Your ideal self represents the goal state of that focus—the state where you finally attain all of the rewards you seek. The other focus is punishment based and resembles Gray's Stop system. It emphasizes avoiding punishments and other bad outcomes. Your ought self represents the goal state based on that focus—where no punishments or other bad events will occur.

Of course, everybody has both kinds of goals, just as in Gray's theory everybody has a Stop system and a Go system. And nobody achieves either final state described by the ideal or the ought self. But Higgins's point is that individuals

---

[7] Neo-Freudian theorist Karen Horney (see Chapter 11) also wrote extensively about the neurotic consequences of trying to live up to an unrealistic ideal self-image (Horney, 1950).

balance these goals differently. If you primarily pursue reward—focused on the ideal self—failures to attain your goal will make you sad. If you primarily avoid punishment—focused on the ought self—failures to attain your goal will make you anxious. In other words, the root of depression is disappointment. The root of anxiety is fear.

> The root of depression is disappointment. The root of anxiety is fear.

THE PROCEDURAL SELF

We saw in the previous chapter that personality is not just something you have; it is also something you do. The unique aspects of what you do comprise the **procedural self**, and your knowledge of this self typically takes the form of procedural knowledge.

Procedural knowledge, as you recall, consists of ways of doing things, or procedures, which is why it is also called "knowing how."[8] It is knowledge of a special sort—you are not conscious of the knowledge itself and generally cannot, if asked, explain it to anyone else very well. (In some cases, you may reply with a statement such as, "Here, let me show you.") Examples include the ability to read, to ride a bicycle, to close a business deal, to analyze a set of data, or to ask someone out on a date. For the most part—by which I mean about 98 percent of the time—you learn these skills by doing them and sometimes by watching them.

A classic example is bike riding. I can tell you how to ride a bike: Sit on the seat, grab the handlebars, pump the pedals around and around, and maintain balance so you will not fall off. I could say more, but it would never be sufficient for teaching you how to ride a bicycle, or even to let you know what bike riding is really like. You can learn how to ride a bicycle only by doing it and getting practice and feedback. Social skills are like this, too. Despite the prevalence of books with titles like *How to Sell Anything to Anyone* or even *How to Pick Up Girls*, social skills must be acquired through practice.

> Despite the prevalence of books with titles like *How to Sell Anything to Anyone* or even *How to Pick Up Girls,* social skills must be acquired through practice.

The procedural self is made up of the behaviors through which you express who you think you are, generally without knowing you are doing so (Cantor, 1990; Langer, 1992, 1994). Like riding a bicycle, the working of the procedural self is automatic and not very accessible to conscious awareness.

---

[8] Or, simply, "knowhow."

Relational Selves

An aspect of the procedural self that has received particular research attention is the *relational self-schema*, said to be based on past experiences that direct how we relate with each of the important people in our lives (Baldwin, 1999).

As mentioned in Chapter 2, you have probably developed some specific patterns in the way you interact with your parents. You may even forget these patterns exist until you visit home after a long absence. Before you know it, you are falling into the same old, well-rehearsed childhood routine. This is rarely a pleasant experience, so a common response is to try to oppose old patterns by relating to the family as differently as possible from how you did before (Andersen & Chen, 2002). We all know what this can include: odd clothes, tattoos, body piercings, an unsuitable boyfriend or girlfriend, or maybe just a spectacularly bad attitude. All of these behaviors announce, "I'm not the child I used to be." This is only natural, but pause a moment, and have a kind thought for the baffled and dismayed parents.

Despite this example, most of our patterns of relating to other people are deeply ingrained and difficult to change. Even the multiply pierced and thoroughly inked adolescent may run to Mommy when feeling sick or insecure. One reason these patterns persist is that their roots reach so deep. Attachment theory (Mikulincer & Shaver, 2003; Sroufe et al., 1993; see Chapter 16) and newer, relational self-theory (Andersen & Chen, 2002) agree that many scripts for relating to others are set early in life. Later, through transference (see Chapter 11), we may find ourselves responding to new people much like important people they seem to resemble from our past (Andersen & Baum, 1994; Zhang & Hazan, 2002). For example, if you were intimidated by your father and tried at all costs to avoid making him angry, you might find yourself responding to your male boss the same way. Or, if your early romantic relationships did not turn out well, you might find yourself, in a self-perpetuating manner, approaching new relationships implicitly expecting betrayal and disappointment.

Implicit Selves

In many cases, these self-relevant behavioral patterns are not readily accessible to consciousness. Unlike the self-schema, which is generally assumed to be consciously accessible and which can be measured on straightforward questionnaires (S data; see Chapter 2), relational selves and other implicit aspects of the self-concept may work unconsciously and powerfully (Greenwald et al., 2002). In that case, how can they be measured? Psychologist Anthony Greenwald and his colleagues have invented an ingenious method called the IAT, or Implicit Association Test.

The IAT is a measure of reaction time, in which participants are asked to push one of two buttons as quickly as possible, depending on which of four concepts is displayed to them. To understand how this works, imagine that, as a research participant, you are shown a series of playing cards and asked to push button A if a heart or diamond is displayed, or button B if a spade or club is displayed. This should be easy, because hearts and diamonds are both red, and spades and clubs are both black, and you can use either attribute to decide correctly. Now imagine being asked to push button A if a heart or spade is displayed, or button B if a club or diamond is displayed. For most people, this would be more difficult because color no longer helps.[9] The idea is that when two closely associated categories (heart–red) share the same button, responding will be easy and quick. If two categories that are less associated or that conflict with each other share the button (heart–black), then responding will be more difficult and slower. Greenwald creatively used this principle to measure the strength of associations in an individual's cognitive system of which the individual might not be conscious (Greenwald & Farnham, 2000).

In a study of *implicit self-esteem*, the four concepts were "good," "bad," "me," and "not me." Before the study started, the experimenter obtained 18 self-descriptive words from each subject ("me") and 18 words each participant considered not self-descriptive ("not me"). The experimenter also assembled separate lists of pleasant ("good") words (diamond, health, sunrise) and unpleasant ("bad") words (agony, filth, poison). Now the study could begin. In the first part, the participant was asked to push button A if a "me" word or a "good" word was displayed, and B

---

[9] Greenwald and his colleagues point out that for an experienced bridge player, this might also be easy, because hearts and spades are the higher-ranking suits.

if a "not me" word or a "bad" word was displayed. In the second part, the pairings were switched. Now the participant pushed button A if a "me" word or "bad" word was displayed, and button B if a "not me" word or a "good" word was displayed.[10]

The logic is that, for someone with high self-esteem, reactions should be easier and quicker in the first part of the study than the second: See something self-relevant or good, push A—that's easy. But the second part should be harder, and slower: See something self-relevant or bad, that requires one to slow down and think a bit. The reason is that, for someone with high self-esteem, "good" and "me" are implicitly associated in the cognitive unconscious, as are "bad" and "not me." Now, what about someone with low self-esteem? For them, the me/good and not-me/bad associations might be weaker or even reversed. If this is true, then the difference in a participant's reaction time between the two parts of the experiment might measure that person's "implicit" self-esteem—someone with higher self-esteem should react more quickly in the first part relative to the second part; reaction times for someone with lower self-esteem should have a smaller difference, or even show the reverse effect.

It worked! It turned out implicit self-esteem—and other implicit attributes of the self such as stereotypes and attitudes—could be measured in this way. The measure was reliable, predicted responses to success and failure, and, perhaps most interesting of all, related only weakly to more traditional S-data measures of declarative self-esteem. Further research suggests that when one's implicit self-esteem is lower than one's declarative self-esteem, this can indicate the kind of fragile self-view associated with narcissism (Zeigler-Hill, 2006).

The IAT has also been used to measure implicit shyness (Asendorpf, Banse, & Mücke, 2002). The same study also gathered more conventional S data, self-ratings of shyness like the ones gathered by the Stanford Shyness Survey (Zimbardo, 1977). Finally, the participants were videotaped as they chatted with an attractive stranger of the opposite sex, a task selected as one that just might induce shyness in some people.

The fascinating result is that aspects of shyness that participants consciously controlled, such as how long they spoke, could be predicted by the S-data shyness scores. (Self-described shy people spoke less.) However, more spontaneous indicators of shyness, such as facial expressions and tense body posture, were predicted better by the IAT measure. This result suggests that, although people's awareness of their own shyness is only partially conscious, their deeper, underlying knowledge not only can be measured, but can also be used to predict behavior.

A further study extended the study of the implicit self to the Big Five personality traits (summarized in Chapter 6). Conventional self-reports (S data) of all

---

[10] The procedure also includes other kinds of counterbalancing to make sure, for example, that the A and B buttons are used equally for the various possible combinations of stimuli.

five of these traits predicted overt behavior, as would be expected. Interestingly, IAT measures of two of the five traits—neuroticism and extraversion—also predicted behavior, and the predictability from the IAT for these two traits was over and above what could be achieved from self-report (Back, Schmukle, & Egloff, 2009). Apparently, some aspects of an individual's neuroticism and even extraversion remain unknown to the conscious mind. But this did not seem to be true for conscientiousness, agreeableness, or openness. Implicit measures of these traits failed to predict overt behavior. What do you suppose is the difference?[11]

Taken as a whole, these findings show that we may have attitudes and feelings about many things, including ourselves, of which we are not entirely conscious, but which nonetheless can influence our emotions and behaviors, perhaps without our even knowing why. To the extent this is true—and it does seem to be true to some extent—then some of the cognitive patterns that guide our behavior are deeply embedded indeed.

Acquiring and Changing Procedural Knowledge

Can the procedural self—or selves—be changed? The answer is yes, but implicit knowledge and associated behavioral patterns consist of procedural knowledge, not declarative knowledge, so changing them requires more than advice, lectures, or even well-meaning, conscious intentions to change. Procedural knowledge can be acquired or changed only by doing, specifically through practice and feedback.

A number of colleges now have courses on "How to Think," where instructors explain the rules of logic, describe tactics for organizing thinking, teach brainstorming methods, and so on. I am not a big fan of these courses because I believe every college course ought to teach you how to think—by giving you something to think *about*.[12] You then formulate ideas and get feedback on them (such as the instructor or a fellow student saying, "Good!" or "Very interesting!"). You learn to think with practice and feedback, the same way you learn any other kind of procedural knowledge.

Similarly, an athletic coach motivates practice and provides useful feedback. Teachers of singing, dancing, violin playing, and other forms of procedural knowledge play the same role as coaches. And, in some cases, a psychotherapist trying to help you change your behavior patterns may work the same way. First, the therapist must motivate his clients to practice their desired behavior change. (Improve your relationship with your mother by not contradicting her every time she says something you disagree with; practice this restraint as often as possible.) Second, the therapist must provide feedback on how the clients are doing.

---

[11] Frankly, I have no idea.

[12] The "Think About It" questions at the end of every chapter of this book are intended to do precisely that. You are looking at those, right?

This teaching method points to a big difference between declarative and pro-cedural knowledge. The first can be taught by reading or listening to lectures; the second, only through practice and feedback. The first requires a teacher who is good at what is being taught; you cannot learn Russian history from somebody who does not know the topic. But you can learn to sing from somebody whose own voice is hoarse, or learn to bat from a middle-aged coach with slow reflexes and a beer gut. You might even get some help developing your personality from a therapist who has not yet worked out all of his own personal problems.

Which brings us back to how one acquires, and might be able to change, procedural knowledge about social behavior and the self. A style of respond-ing to authority figures with fear, or of expecting and remembering repeated social rejection, has roots in bitter experience and was not created in a day. Undoing these learning experiences is not easy, therefore; verbal exhorta-tion and even willpower are unlikely to be enough. The person, perhaps with help (professional or otherwise), must have the courage to change the relevant behavior and slowly but (hopefully) surely, begin to accumulate countervail-ing experiences that eventually generate a new behavioral style and outlook on life. With enough practice, you might even be able to change your personality (see Chapter 7).

And let us not forget that not all patterns of transference, or of characteristic perception and behavior, are maladaptive. A child fortunate enough to grow up in a supportive and encouraging environment may develop a resilient attitude that will help her to bounce back from defeat, rejection, or whatever other disappointments life might have in store. Whether it be explicit or implicit, a strong and consistent self-concept that is not easily changed could be useful.

HOW MANY SELVES?

According to some theorists, you have not one declarative and procedural self, but many selves. For example, according to one theory, the particular subset of selves that is active in working memory and has conscious and unconscious effects on behavior at any given moment depends on where you are and whom you are with (Markus & Kunda, 1986). In this way, your experience of yourself may shift from moment to moment. You might feel (and act) like a student, then like a parent, and then like a hard worker, as the situation and the people in it continue to change.

This view of the continuously changing self is called the *working self-concept* (Markus & Kunda, 1986). A particularly important influence on your working self-concept at a particular moment is the person you are with (Andersen & Chen, 2002; Ogilvie & Ashmore, 1991). You may have a different image of yourself—and act differently—when you are with your parents than when you are with your boy-friend or girlfriend. You may also find that, with some people, you become tense

"I know what I said ten minutes ago. That was the old me talking."

and irritable, and even turn into someone you do not particularly like. With other people, you find yourself relaxed and charming, becoming someone you wish you could be all the time. (You should try to spend as much time as possible with this second kind of person.) The theory behind the working self-concept claims that you are characterized by not one but many selves. In different situations with different people, different selves come into play.

One's different selves might even have competing goals. One common example is the idea of the *future self*, the person you will be five years—or five minutes—from now. Does that future-you have the same interests as you do right now? Your present self might want to have another cookie, skip today's workout, or knock off studying. But your future self might be sorry you did these things. I know someone who likes to say "that's not a problem for me, that's a problem for Future Amy!" This is an attitude that might work well in the short run; not so well in the long run. Not surprisingly, one study shows that people with greater "future self-continuity"—who are prone to see their present and future selves as the same person—do better in college because they have better self-control as they direct behavior to their long-term goals (Adelman et al., 2017).

Another problem with the idea of multiple me's is that a unitary and coherent sense of self is traditionally viewed as a hallmark of mental health, at least in Western contexts (see Chapter 13). People who feel they are acting in concert with who they really are feel "authentic" and comfortable with themselves (Kernis & Goldman, 2006). Acting in a way that is in accordance with one's personality traits, called *congruence*, has been found to be associated with better psychological adjustment (Sherman, Nave, & Funder, 2012). And when one's goals are concordant with one's self-image, the result is more happiness and better goal attainment (Sheldon, 2002).

In contrast, not knowing who you are, or feeling that your identity is constantly in flux, can, at the extremes, be a symptom of mental illnesses such as borderline personality disorder (see Chapter 17). An erratic self-view may result from traumatic experiences such as sexual abuse (Westen, 1992). People undergoing major transitions, such as the changes that occur during adolescence, suffer in part because they begin to lose their sense of having a single self that feels real in all the situations they encounter. In general, too much *self-concept differentiation*, defined as seeing oneself as having different personalities in different contexts, is associated with poor psychological adjustment, especially in individualist cultures such as the United States (Bleidorn & Ködding, 2013). By contrast, as was noted in Chapter 5, people who are consistent and easy to judge not only tend to present the same self in every situation, but they are also evaluated by others as stable, well organized, and psychologically healthy (Colvin, 1993b).

The idea of multiple selves has also been criticized on philosophical grounds. One of the most important of the cognitive social learning personality theorists discussed in Chapter 14, Albert Bandura (1999), argues that psychologists should reject "the fractionation of human agency into multiple selves" (p. 194) for two reasons. First, he notes, "a theory of personality cast in terms of multiple selves plunges one into deep philosophical waters" (p. 194). It seems to require one self that decides which self is appropriate for a given situation, and perhaps another self beyond that to decide which self should decide which self is currently relevant. Another difficulty with the idea of multiple selves is that it raises the following, perhaps unanswerable, question:

> Once one starts fractionating the self, where does one stop? For example, an athletic self can be split into an envisioned tennis self and a golfing self. These separable selves would, in turn, have their subselves. Thus, a golfing self can be subdivided into different facets of the athletic ability to include a driving self, a fairway self, a sand-trapped self, and a putting self. How does one decide where to stop fractionating selves? (Bandura, 1999, p. 194)

Bandura's point is that there is no way to decide. Although we may seem like different people in different situations or different company, each of us is, in the end, one person. It is both more parsimonious and philosophically coherent, he believes, to assume that one self interprets experience and decides what to do next.

THE *REALLY* REAL SELF

As Bandura observed, beneath all of the real, ideal, ought, and relational selves, it still feels like deep down, a single self must be running the whole show, and the idea that people have a "real self" separate from superficial appearances seems to be present in all cultures (Strohminger, Knobe & Newman, 2017). But how is this possible? All day long, and throughout our lives, we move from situation to situation, from one relationship partner to another, and through different stages of learning and aging. The fact that we inevitably act like different people as a function of these changes is the basis of the idea that people have variable or even multiple selves. So what stays the same?

Years ago, my grandmother, then in her late 80s, told a little story that has stuck with me ever since. She recalled being a teenager around the turn of the (20th) century riding the El (elevated) train in Chicago. One day, she watched an "old lady" (who was probably much younger than she was when she told the story) shuffle slowly on board. "I remember wondering," she said, "what must it feel like to be that *old*?" "Well," she continued cheerfully, "now I know. It feels just the same. Except, you're older."

I don't think my grandmother ever read anything by William James—she never even went to high school—but I do think she and James had the same view of the core, unchanging self. External appearances, attitudes, and behaviors change across situations and over time, but the one who does the experiencing is still in there someplace, watching (and perhaps directing) everything (Klein, 2012). As we saw in Chapter 7, the sense of being the same person persists across the entire life span, and as we have seen in this chapter, can remain intact despite brain damage, memory loss, and even schizophrenia (Klein, Altinyazar, & Metz, 2013). As James wrote, "the *I* is unaltered as the *me* is changed" (1890, p. 378).

Is the "I" in this sense simply a passive bystander—an "epiphenomenon," as the philosophers would call it—that seems to exist but cannot actually influence anything? Or is this inner, hidden, and unchanging observer the *really* real self, perhaps even the "soul," and the basis of free will? This question is probably too deep—and may be too unscientific—for a psychology book. But it is worth thinking about.

WRAPPING IT UP

SUMMARY

The I *and the* Me

- According to William James, the self includes the *me*, the object of self-knowledge, and the *I*, the mysterious entity that does the knowing. Psychology has much more to say about the *me* than the *I*.

The Contents and Purposes of the Self

- In terms of the *me*, the self comprises everything we know, or think we know, about what we are like, including both declarative and procedural self-knowledge.

- Psychologists have proposed that the self has four purposes: self-regulation, information filtering, understanding others, and maintaining identity.

The Declarative Self

- The declarative self includes self-esteem, one's opinion of one's own worth. Self-esteem can cause problems when it is too low *or* too high because, according to Leary's sociometer theory, it serves as a useful gauge of one's social standing.

- Psychologists theorize that the wide range of knowledge one has about one's psychological attributes is located in a cognitive structure called the *self-schema*. The self-schema can be assessed via S data (questionnaires, including traditional personality questionnaires such as the CPI) or B data (reaction-time studies).

- Case studies of brain-damaged individuals suggest that one's sense of self and personality can remain intact even when all the specific memories that created it are lost.

- A good way to remember something is to consider what it has to do with one's self; this effect on memory is called the self-reference effect.

- Your view of your own capabilities—your self-efficacy—influences what you will attempt to do.

- Discrepancies between one's real self and ideal self can lead to depression, whereas discrepancies between one's real self and ought self can lead to anxiety.

The Procedural Self

- Aspects of the procedural self are not typically available to conscious awareness, but they can still drive behavior by means of deeply ingrained styles of thinking, feeling, and relating to others.

- One theory about the procedural self is the notion of relational selves, the habitual ways one interacts with different kinds of people.

- Implicit selves—notions of what we are like that affect our behavior but of which we may not be consciously aware—can be measured through an instrument called the Implicit Association Test (IAT). The IAT is used to assess "implicit self-esteem," and can predict behavior over and above overt self-report for shyness and the traits of extraversion, neuroticism, and perhaps others.

- The procedural self—or selves—can probably be changed slowly, through practice and feedback, as with other procedural knowledge.

How Many Selves?

- While many theorists suggest that individuals have changing or even multiple selves, a constant sense of self is a hallmark of psychological health. Social learning theorist Albert Bandura has pointed out that the idea of multiple selves raises philosophical difficulties.

The Really Real Self

- The inner observer that William James called the *I* appears to be the part of the self that remains constant across situations and throughout life.

KEY TERMS

ontological self, p. 555
epistemological self, p. 555
declarative knowledge, p. 557
declarative self, p. 558
self-esteem, p. 558
self-schema, p. 561
long-term memory (LTM), p. 564
self-reference effect, p. 564
procedural self, p. 568

THINK ABOUT IT

1. Is what William James called the *I* something that psychologists can study? How do we know whether it even exists?

2. Do you know anyone who has too little or too much self-esteem? How do you think this came about? Is it due to how this person was raised, to societal influences, or to some other factor?

3. How well do you think most people know themselves? What aspects of oneself are the hardest to know?

4. Do your beliefs about yourself affect what you do? Can these beliefs be changed? How?

5. The workings of the implicit self are described in this chapter in terms of relational selves, self-esteem, shyness, and self-consciousness. In what other areas do you think the implicit self might be important?

6. Can the self—its declarative part or its procedural part—be changed? Has your view of yourself ever changed? How did that come about? What kinds of experiences can change a person's self-image?

7. A 79-year-old once commented to his son that he has always felt 12 years old (Klein, 2012). What do you think he meant? Is this comment true for you?

8. Is James's idea of the *I* the same as what psychologists now call the procedural self, or is the *I* something deeper and more mysterious?

SUGGESTED RESOURCES

Klein, S. B. (2014). *The two selves: Their metaphysical commitments and functional independence.* New York and Oxford: Oxford University Press.

> *An unconventional, even radical view of the psychological self, written by a prolific and influential researcher. The book includes summaries of several fascinating case studies of persons with brain damage. If you are interested in what the present chapter calls the "really real self," this book is for you.*

Wilson, T. D. (2002). *Strangers to ourselves: Discovering the adaptive unconscious.* Cambridge, MA: Harvard University Press.

> *A lively survey of a wide range of research that explains why knowing ourselves is more difficult than we might think, and the book includes pointers on how to know yourself better.*

Want to earn a better grade on your test?

Go to **INQUIZITIVE** to learn and review this chapter's content, with personalized feedback along the way.

PART VII

APPLICATIONS OF PERSONALITY PSYCHOLOGY

Personality psychology is best known for its theories, which are sometimes even capitalized as Personality Theories. As you have seen throughout this book, the big names[1] of the field—Allport, Bandura, Freud, Maslow, Rogers, Skinner, and all the rest—are identified with theoretical points of view that organize ways of thinking about people. The insights afforded by these points of view sometimes have implications for understanding oneself and others, and can in that way be useful.

But personality psychology is even more directly useful than that, as the next three chapters shall demonstrate. The trait approach in particular, but also the behavioral, cognitive, and even psychodynamic approaches can all be used—and even better, combined—to achieve practical purposes. These purposes include having better relationships and a more successful business or career. These are exactly the goals Freud was talking about when he said the definition of mental health was the ability to love and to work (Chapter 10). Applications of personality psychology to these two goals is the topic of Chapter 16.

Since its inception, personality psychology has also been closely associated with another practical aim: the alleviation of mental illness and the promotion of psychological health. Many of the pioneering figures in personality psychology, including Henry Murray, Carl Rogers, Abraham Maslow and, of course, Sigmund Freud, were all clinical practitioners who saw and treated patients (or, if you prefer, "clients") almost every day throughout their careers. The research of the dominant

[1] Sometimes capitalized as Big Names.

trait approach and the concerns of clinical psychology drifted apart during the late 20th century, but are becoming increasingly integrated as the 21st century moves forward. In particular, psychologists are increasingly becoming aware of the close connections between the study of so-called "normal" personality traits, and the nature of personality disorders.

Personality disorders, recent research is making clear, are best thought of as extremes on the range of the personality traits that everybody has. Making this recognition (almost) official, the latest *Diagnostic and Statistical Manual* (DSM-5) of the American Psychiatric Association recognizes the continuity between the normal and abnormal. Chapter 17 summarizes the nature of the major recognized disorders of personality and the insights that modern personality psychology is increasingly providing into the diagnosis, understanding and, hopefully, alleviation of these afflictions.

The relevance of personality to psychological health is fairly obvious, but recent research is also showing increasingly that it is relevant to physical health. Even the ultimate health outcome—longevity—turns out to be predictable, to a surprising degree, from personality traits. The association between personality and physical health is the other major topic of Chapter 17.

The book concludes with a brief, 18th chapter that asks, after reading a book about personality psychology that is more than 600 pages long, what can a person reasonably be expected to have learned and remember? In the chapter I will try to answer that question, and point out a few hopefully lasting lessons that might just be useful in your own life.

16

Relationships

RELATIONSHIPS AND BUSINESS

PSYCHOLOGICAL DIFFERENCES BETWEEN PEOPLE—personality traits—are important for many outcomes in life, as we have already seen (mostly in Chapter 4 and Chapter 6). Two particular contexts for the importance of personality deserve extra attention: relationships and business. Our relationships with our friends, family, and romantic partners form the core of our life experience. To be alone and lonely is one of the worst things that can happen to a person; supportive and emotionally fulfilling interpersonal relationships can be the source of life's most significant joys. But not all of life is about surviving and enjoying our relationships; we also need to make a living, and perhaps just as significantly, we seek to make an impact on the world. For many and perhaps most people, both of these goals are sought through the workplace and the career (or careers) that one follows through life. Personality psychology has a lot to say about who is most likely to succeed and why, who is most (and least) fit to lead and why, and how to choose one's own occupational path.

As we will see in this chapter, the trait approach has the most to contribute to the understanding of relationships and business. But as we shall also see, other areas of personality contribute as well, including the humanistic, evolutionary, and even psychoanalytic perspectives. I have said many times in this book that personality is a puzzle and each basic approach provides a piece. Now I hope to show you that if you put the pieces together, the result can be useful.

RELATIONSHIPS

First, consider relationships. As everyone knows, relationships can be an important source of support, security, amusement, and pleasure. But they can also make you crazy, which is often what people really mean when they say, "Life is complicated."

A simple fact is that some people have more successful relationships than others, and this difference in social outcomes is closely connected to personality traits and processes. In what follows, I will begin by considering the traits that are associated with success and failure for relationships in general, and then look more closely at two specific kinds: sexual relationships and attachment relationships.

Deal-makers: Traits that Promote Good Relationships

You might recall from Chapter 4 that people who score high in the Big Five traits of extraversion and agreeableness tend to have more and better relationships with other people (Ozer & Benet-Martínez, 2006). In other words, some traits are social "deal-makers." Extraverts are socially active; they meet more people and do more activities with them than do introverts. Agreeable people are easy to get along with; they not only avoid getting into disputes with others, they are also skilled at preventing and defusing conflicts when they arise (Graziano & Eisenberg, 1997).

One study looked specifically at the traits associated with being liked by others. In a sample of students who lived in fraternities and sororities at the University of Illinois, being rated higher on "communal" traits (traits relevant to relating well to others) is what it takes. Specifically, people are more prone to like others whom they see as "warm" and "trustful," and less inclined to like those who seem "devious," "moody," or "irritable" (Wortman & Wood, 2011). Research also has shown that broad traits such as extraversion, sociability, and (low) shyness predict how many friends you are likely to have overall and the degree to which, in general, you will find yourself in agreement or conflict with them (Asendorpf & Wilpers, 1998; Reis, Capobianco, & Tsai, 2002). Three other personality variables—a low level of negative emotionality, a high level of positive emotionality, and good self-control ("constraint")—tend to predict the degree to which people have successful relationships regardless of whom the relationship is with (Robins, Caspi, & Moffitt, 2002).

These findings were generally confirmed in a more recent study that attempted to predict which couples would hit it off in a speed-dating encounter. People looking for relationships were paired for a series of 4-minute interactions with 12 opposite-sex partners each, and rated their degree of interest in and attraction to the partner at the conclusion of each mini-"date" (Joel, Eastwick & Finkel, 2017). The participants all completed lengthy personality questionnaires and then sophisticated machine-learning algorithms tried to use those data to predict which specific couples would feel the spark.

Simply put, the machine and its algorithms failed. Whatever the secret is for love at first sight, it did not seem to lie in the degree to which the dating partners' personalities were compatible with each other. On the other hand, the study did identify several traits that were important for successful (4-minute) dates regardless of who was partnered. People who described themselves as "picky" were less likely to report being attracted to their partners,[2] while those who rated themselves as "warm" were more likely to say they felt some heat. And these same warm participants, along with those who rated themselves highly on extraversion, were more likely to have partners who reported being interested in them.

As the authors concluded, trying to predict who will be attracted to whom is a bit like trying to predict an earthquake. Geologists know where earthquakes are more and less likely to occur (i.e., near fault lines) but are almost completely unable to predict exactly when they will occur, within a range of a couple of hundred years or so. Similarly, psychologists know a fair amount about who, in general, is more and less likely to successfully initiate romantic relationships, but "the dynamic and chaos-like processes that initiate (romantic attraction) require considerable additional scientific inquiry before prediction is realistic" (Joel et al., 2017, p. 1487). In other words, love is complicated. Who knew.

> People who described themselves as "picky" were less likely to report being attracted to their partners, while those who rated themselves as "warm" were more likely to say they felt some heat.

Deal-breakers: Traits that Prevent or Undermine Relationships

To some degree, the traits that predict who will have relationships that are not successful or even fail to develop them in the first place, are simply the inverse of the positive traits already considered. Introverts and disagreeable people, specifically, are less likely to enjoy social and dating success. But one study found that some traits are especially significant, being "deal-breakers" that are almost enough by themselves to sabotage romantic relationships. These traits include being untrustworthy and having anger issues (Jonason et al., 2015). This finding makes sense, because probably the two worst things that can destroy a relationship are cheating on or otherwise deceiving one's partner, and being emotionally or physically abusive. A relationship with someone who does either of these things—or both!—probably *should* end.

DISPOSITIONAL CONTEMPT Consider what it would be like to be in a relationship—of any kind—with a person who scores high on the recently-studied trait of "dispositional contempt" (Schriber et al., 2017). People earn a high score on this trait by agreeing to items on the Dispositional Contempt Scale (DCS) such as "I often feel contempt for others" and "I often feel like others are wasting my time." (See **Try for Yourself 16.1**.) Not surprisingly, high scorers on this scale can come across as cold, arrogant, disagreeable, and even racist—but they also seem emotionally fragile and insecure. Men score somewhat higher on this trait than women, and older people score a bit lower than younger people.

---

[2] Apparently they really were picky.

TRY FOR YOURSELF 16.1

The DCS Scale

Instructions. Below are a series of statements that may or may not relate to you. Please read each statement carefully, considering each one by one, and indicate the extent to which each describes you by using the response options. There are no right or wrong answers. Please answer honestly, as we are interested in how you actually think, feel, and behave.

1. I tend to disregard people who fall short of my standards.

   Strongly Disagree   Strongly Agree
       1   2   3   4   5

2. I often lose respect for others.

   Strongly Disagree   Strongly Agree
       1   2   3   4   5

3. Feeling disdain for others comes naturally to me.

   Strongly Disagree   Strongly Agree
       1   2   3   4   5

4. I tend to accept people regardless of their flaws.

   Strongly Disagree   Strongly Agree
       1   2   3   4   5

5. I would never try to make someone feel worthless.

   Strongly Disagree   Strongly Agree
       1   2   3   4   5

6. I often feel like others are wasting my time.

   Strongly Disagree   Strongly Agree
       1   2   3   4   5

7. I hardly ever think others are inferior to me.

   Strongly Disagree   Strongly Agree
       1   2   3   4   5

8. All in all, I am repelled by others' faults.

   Strongly Disagree   Strongly Agree
       1   2   3   4   5

9. Others tend to give me reasons to look down on them.

   Strongly Disagree   Strongly Agree
       1   2   3   4   5

TRY FOR YOURSELF 16.1

The DCS Scale—cont'd

10. I often feel contempt for others.

Strongly Disagree   Strongly Agree

1   2   3   4   5

Scoring: Add up your scores on items 1, 2, 3, 6, 8, 9, and 10. "Reverse score" items 4, 5, and 7; for these items convert 1 = 5, 2 = 4, 3 = 3, 4 = 2, and 5 = 1. Add the total of the reversed scores to the total for the other items. Divide this total by 10 to compute the average.

Interpretation and Norms: The scale is a measure of "dispositional contempt." In an on-line sample of 283 people, the average score for men was 2.73 and the average score for women was 2.34.

Source: Schriber, R. A.; Chung, J. M.; Sorensen, K. S.; Robins, Richard W. (2017). *Journal of Personality and Social Psychology, 113*, 280–309. (p. 287)

Scoring high on this trait seems pretty bad for relationships. In the study that introduced the DCS, high scorers reported dissatisfaction with their partners and the feeling appeared to be mutual (Shriber et al., 2017). The unlucky romantic partners of contemptuous people reported feeling less committed to them and less satisfied with their relationships; you have to wonder why they were in the relationship at all.

Is there an upside to this trait? Remember that Funder's First Law (Chapter 1) claims that advantages are often also disadvantages and vice versa. Could that possibly apply here? Consider how it could. Perhaps people who score high on the DCS are just those who are not naïve, readily fooled, or easily impressed. While this attitude might make relationships more difficult—and that indeed is what the evidence suggests—for people high on this trait perhaps the trade-off seems worth it.

REJECTION SENSITIVITY Another trait that is associated with relationship problems, without exactly being a deal-breaker, is a disposition called *rejection sensitivity* (Downey & Feldman, 1996; Downey, Freitas, Michaelis, & Khouri, 1998). When a person afflicted with this syndrome discusses a relationship problem with a romantic partner, the slightest expression of irritation or disinterest may lead him to conclude that he is being rejected, leading to an anxious or even panicked response. Often, the partner then rejects the person (wouldn't you?). In this way, the attribute of rejection sensitivity can produce the very outcome the person fears most.

Rejection sensitivity only comes into play when relevant stimuli are present. Specifically, it can be triggered by any indication—even an ambiguous one—that rejection may be imminent. But in the absence of such indications (perhaps, early in a relationship, when both partners are still being nice all the time), the very same person may be exceptionally caring and supportive. Depending on the circumstances, then, the same person might be "hurtful and kind, caring and uncaring, abusive and gentle" (Mischel, 1999, p. 51).

This observation raises a question: Which person is "real"—the kind, caring, and gentle one the partner sees at the beginning of the relationship, or the hurtful, uncaring, and abusive one who appears later? The answer is both, because behavior patterns stem from the same underlying system, and though they might seem inconsistent, in fact they are meaningfully coherent.

Compatibility

An intuitively appealing idea is that the secret to a good relationship is compatibility. In other words, it's not that some traits are deal-makers or deal-breakers, it's that everybody can find the right partner as long as they are compatible. In particular, a widespread assumption is that people who are more similar to each other will have better relationships. Many dating websites—and even would-be matchmaker friends—proceed on this assumption. Is it right? Yes and no.

The answer is "yes" because around the world, the average person is fairly agreeable, well-adjusted, and mildly extraverted (Guillaume et al., 2018). Most people are about average—that's the definition of average!—so two people who are both pretty normal will probably have a good chance of getting along. And think about the person who is *not* normal in this statistical sense. The non-normal person is not only likely to be relatively disagreeable, neurotic and introverted, he or she will also tend—for statistical reasons alone—not to resemble any particular potential partner with whom he or she is compared.

So, the answer to the question above is also "no" because, as was seen in the study by Joel et al. (2017) cited above, certain traits just go with certain outcomes. Disagreeable people – who are also statistically unusual – tend to have relationship problems. Pairing them with similarly disagreeable people—or, to consider another trait, pairing one person who suffers from rejection sensitivity with another person who has the same problem—seems unlikely to lead anywhere good.

When considering a potential relationship partner, the essential question to ask is probably not "does this person have a personality that is similar to mine?" A better question is simpler: "Is the person normal?" In the end, for most people, the two questions amount to pretty much the same thing.[3]

---

[3] This is why dating websites that match you to "similar people" might actually provide useful information even though their numbers are really telling you how similar your potential partner is to the average person.

Sexual Relationships

Sexual relationships are obviously an important part of life, but while psychologists have extensively studied romantic relationships, they have had surprisingly little to say about sexual attraction and activity itself. This might be because, as the pioneering psychologist Henry Murray noted long ago, psychology "is over-concerned . . . with what is clearly manifested, with what is conscious, ordered and rational" (1938, p. 715). Sexuality is surely anything but conscious, ordered, and rational! Another reason for the neglect of the topic might be that it is considered too sensitive, or too embarrassing, or even too politically dangerous to study. Politicians have been known to attack or even mock scientific studies that attempt to survey and understand sexual behavior.

Two areas of personality psychology have paid attention to sexual behavior. One is psychoanalysis, which, as we saw in Chapters 10 and 11, uses "libido" as a core concept. The other approach that gives a lot of attention to sexual behavior is evolutionary psychology, which is only natural because, as was explained in Chapter 9, reproduction is the key mechanism of evolution.

MATING BEHAVIOR In particular, evolutionary psychologists have paid special attention to differences in sexual behavior between men and women. Their research has focused on **mate selection** and attraction—what one looks for in the opposite sex—and **mating strategies**—how one handles heterosexual relationships.

Attraction   When seeking someone of the opposite sex with whom to form a relationship, is an average heterosexual more likely to be interested in his or her (1) physical attractiveness or (2) financial security? Across a wide variety of cultures, including those in early 21st-century North America, men are more likely than women to place higher value on physical attractiveness (D. M. Buss, 1989). In these same cultures, by contrast, women are more likely to value economic security. Indeed, there is some evidence that men and women consider attractiveness and resources, respectively, as essential, not just nice (N. P. Li, Bailey, Kenrick, & Linsenmeier, 2002).

In addition, as was mentioned in Chapter 9, heterosexual men are likely to desire (and typically do find) mates several years younger than themselves (the average age difference is about three years, and increases as men get older), whereas women prefer mates who are somewhat older than themselves. This difference can be documented through marriage statistics and even personal ads. When age is mentioned, men advertising for women usually specify an age younger than their own, whereas women do the reverse. The dichotomy between attractiveness and resources mentioned earlier also can be found in the personals: Men are more likely to describe themselves as financially secure than as physically attractive, whereas women are more likely to describe their physical charms than their financial ones (Kenrick & Keefe, 1992). Presumably, individuals of each sex sense what the other is looking for and so try to maximize their own appeal.

The evolutionary explanation of these and other differences is that men and women seek essentially the same thing: the greatest likelihood of having healthy offspring who will survive to reproduce. But each sex contributes to and pursues this goal differently, and thus the optimal mate for each sex is different. Women bear and nurse children, so their youth and physical health are essential. Attractiveness, according to the evolutionary explanation, is simply a display, or cue, that informs a man that a woman is indeed young, healthy, and fit to bear his children (D. M. Buss & Barnes, 1986; D. Symons, 1979).

In contrast, a man's biological contribution to reproduction is relatively minimal. Viable sperm can be produced by males of a wide range of ages, physical conditions, and appearances. For women, what is essential in a mate is his capacity to provide resources conducive to her children thriving until their own reproductive years. Thus, since a woman seeks a mate to optimize her children's circumstances, she will seek someone with resources (and perhaps attitudes) that will support a family, whereas a man will seek a mate who will provide his children with the optimal degree of physical health.

We can see already that these explanations gloss over some complications. For example, a woman who lacks sufficient body fat will stop menstruating and therefore be unable to conceive children, yet many women considered by men to be highly physically attractive are thin, nearly to the point of anorexia. In previous eras, larger (and better fed) women were considered ideal.[4] Moreover, the degree to which we consider someone attractive can be influenced by how much we like them, as well as vice versa. One study found that when people are told someone is honest, they come to like them more and, as a result, rate them as more physically attractive (Paunonen, 2006). In this and other ways, so-called physical attractiveness is more than just physical.

Likewise, men's looks are more important to many women than the standard evolutionary explanation seems to allow. In other species, male displays of large manes or huge fans of plumage appear to be signs of health that attract females, so visible attributes clearly matter. It is not clear why the situation would be so different in humans. However, it must be admitted that physical attractiveness does not seem to be as important to women as to men. The question is why this is. In addition to whatever evolutionary basis the difference has, culture seems to matter. In countries where men and women have smaller gender gaps in earnings and

---

[4] However, women generally overestimate the degree of thinness that men find most attractive. Conversely, men overestimate the degree of muscularity that women find most attractive (Frederick & Haselton, 2007). Perhaps because of this, pictures of men in men's magazines are more muscular than pictures of men in women's magazines (Frederick, Fessler, & Haselton, 2005). Conversely, we might expect pictures of women in women's magazines to show thinner women than pictures of women in men's magazines, but I have not seen a study that documents this.

opportunities, the sex difference in mate preference is also smaller (Zentner & Mitura, 2012). Specifically, women and men are more likely to have similar preferences in Finland, the Philippines, and Germany than in Mexico, South Korea, and Turkey. This finding suggests that differences in mate preference may reflect practical considerations in the current context rather than just instinctive, evolved biases. If you don't need a guy for his money, you might as well choose a good-looking one.

Mating Strategies Beyond the stage of initial attraction, men and women also differ in the strategies they follow in establishing and maintaining relationships. According to the evolutionary account, men want more sexual partners than women do, and are less faithful to and picky about the women with whom they will mate. In a famous (or infamous) study, attractive male and female research assistants walked up to fellow students of the opposite sex and asked them to go to bed with them. Most men accepted; not a single woman did (Clark & Hatfield, 1989). But a follow-up study clarified what was going on (Conley et al., 2011). The women thought that any man who would approach them like that was probably a creep[5]. A little more finesse might have been more effective.

More generally, men appear to be prone to certain kinds of wishful thinking in which they are quick to conclude that women are sexually interested in them, even when they are not (Haselton, 2002). Women, in contrast, are more selective about their mating partners and, having mated, seem to have greater desires for monogamy and stable relationships.

These differences also can be explained in terms of reproductive success. A male may succeed in having the greatest number of children who reproduce to subsequent generations—which, evolutionarily speaking, is the only outcome that matters—by having as many children by as many women as possible. In a reproductive sense, it may be a waste of his time to stay with one woman and one set of children; if he leaves them, they will probably survive somehow and he can spend his limited reproductive time trying to impregnate somebody else. A woman, however, is more likely to have viable offspring if she can convince the father to stay to support and protect her and the family they create. In that case, her children will survive, thrive, and eventually propagate her genes.

Men and women are not different in all respects, however (Hyde, 2005). For example, once a stable relationship is formed, both have interests in maintaining it. As will be discussed later in this chapter, people "attach" to their romantic partners in much the same way that parents and children do, and the same evolved psychological mechanism might underlie both kinds of attachment[6] (Fraley & Shaver, 2000; Hazan & Diamond, 2000). Relationship maintenance might also

---

[5] They had a point.

[6] Have you noticed how many love songs include the word "baby"?

be the reason that both men and women who are in steady dating relationships find opposite-sex strangers less attractive than do those who are not in such relationships (Simpson, Gangestad, & Lerma, 1990). It is adaptive to find prospective partners attractive if you still need one, but once you are in a relationship the attractiveness of others—and your response to that attraction—could end up threatening what you already have.

Jealousy   A related difference between men and women is the way they experience sexual jealousy. One study asked participants to respond to the following vignette (D. M. Buss, Larsen, Westen, & Semmelroth, 1992, p. 252):

> Please think of a serious committed relationship that you have had in the past, that you currently have, or that you would like to have. Imagine that the person with whom you've become seriously involved became interested in someone else. What would distress or upset you more? (Circle only one.)
> (a) Imagining your partner forming a deep emotional attachment to that person, or
> (b) Imagining your partner enjoying passionate sexual intercourse with that person.

In this study, 60 percent of the men chose option b, whereas 82 percent of the women chose option a. In a follow-up study, the question was changed slightly (D. M. Buss et al., 1992, p. 252):

> What would upset you more?
> (a) Imagining your partner trying different sexual positions with that other person, or
> (b) Imagining your partner falling in love with that other person.

This time, 45 percent of the men chose option a, whereas only 12 percent of the women chose option a. In other words, option b was chosen by 55 percent of the men and 88 percent of the women. Notice that this question does not produce a complete reversal between the sexes; most members of each sex find their partner falling in love with someone else more threatening than their partner having intercourse with him or her. But the difference is much stronger among women than men.

Why is this? Evolutionarily speaking, a man's greatest worry—especially for a man who has decided to stay with one woman and support her family—is that he might not be the biological father of the children he supports. This fact makes sexual infidelity by his mate his greatest danger and her greatest betrayal, from a biological point of view. For a woman, however, the greatest danger is that her mate will develop an emotional bond with some other woman and so withdraw support—or, almost as bad, that her mate will share their family's resources with some other woman and her children. This makes emotional infidelity a greater threat than mere sexual infidelity, from the woman's biological point of view.

Related evolutionary logic can even explain some seeming paradoxes or exceptions to these general tendencies. For example, why are some women attracted to men who are obviously unstable? Consider the situation described by many country-and-western songs. Some women prefer men who may be highly physically attractive (and/or own motorcycles) even when such men have no intention of forming a serious relationship and are just "roaming around." I have no idea how common this situation is, but from an evolutionary standpoint it should never happen, right?

Wrong. The theory is rescued here by what has been called the "sexy son hypothesis" (Gangestad, 1989). This hypothesis proposes that a few women consistently—and many women occasionally—follow an atypical reproductive strategy (Gangestad & Simpson, 1990). Instead of maximizing the reproductive viability of their offspring by mating with a stable (but perhaps unexciting) male, they instead take their chances with an unstable but attractive one. The theory is that if they produce a boy, even if the father then leaves, the son will be just like his dad. When he grows up, this "sexy son" will spread numerous children (who of course will also be the woman's grandchildren) across the landscape, in the same ruthless, irresponsible, but effective manner as his father.

Some evidence does support this hypothesis, if not prove it. Women report more interest in having sex with someone other than their primary partner when the "other man" is significantly more attractive than their regular partner and they are themselves near ovulation (Pillsworth & Haselton, 2006). Moreover, women's short-term sexual partners tend to be more muscular than men with whom they have longer-term relationships (though it turns out to be important that they not be *too* muscular; Frederick & Haselton, 2007). But male attractiveness is more than just a matter of muscles: Women in their fertile period also find creative men especially attractive (Haselton & Miller, 2006). It might be in order to attract these attractive, muscular, creative men that women tend to dress more provocatively when they are in the middle of their cycle (Durante, Li, & Haselton, 2008).

You might not be surprised to learn that these findings have turned out to be controversial. Researchers have attempted to replicate (see Chapter 3) some of the key findings in this area that relate women's sexual preferences to their menstrual cycle, with mixed results (Harris, 2011; DeBruine, Jones, Frederick, Haselton, Penton-Voak & Perrett, 2010). So while the results summarized above are certainly interesting and even provocative, more research is needed before they can be regarded as firmly established.

SOCIOSEXUALITY Evolutionary psychologists have also paid close attention to a trait that researchers call "sociosexuality" which, as was mentioned in Chapter 5, is defined as the willingness to engage in sexual relations in the absence of a serious relationship (Penke & Asendorpf, 2008; Simpson & Gangestad, 1991) (see **Try for Yourself 16.2**). Men generally score higher than women in this trait, as you might expect, but it has other implications as well. For example, both men and women who are "unrestricted"—who score high on sociosexuality —are

TRY FOR YOURSELF 16.2

The Sociosexuality Scale

Instructions: Please respond honestly to the following questions:

1. With how many different partners have you had sex within the past 12 months?

☐	☐	☐	☐	☐
0	1	2 to 3	4 to 7	8 or more

2. With how many different partners have you had sexual intercourse on one and only one occasion?

☐	☐	☐	☐	☐
0	1	2 to 3	4 to 7	8 or more

3. With how many different partners have you had sexual intercourse without having an interest in a long-term committed relationship with this person?

☐	☐	☐	☐	☐
0	1	2 to 3	4 to 7	8 or more

4. Sex without love is OK.

1 ☐	2 ☐	3 ☐	4 ☐	5 ☐
Totally disagree				Totally agree

5. I can imagine myself being comfortable and enjoying "casual" sex with different partners.

1 ☐	2 ☐	3 ☐	4 ☐	5 ☐
Totally disagree				Totally agree

6. I do not want to have sex with a person until I am sure that we will have a long-term, serious relationship.

1 ☐	2 ☐	3 ☐	4 ☐	5 ☐
Totally disagree				Totally agree

TRY FOR YOURSELF 16.2

The Sociosexuality Scale—cont'd

7. How often do you have fantasies about having sex with someone you are *not* in a committed romantic relationship with?

1 ☐   2 ☐   3 ☐   4 ☐   5 ☐

Never   Very seldom   About once a month   About once a week   Nearly every day

8. How often do you experience sexual arousal when you are in contact with someone you are not in a committed romantic relationship with?

1 ☐   2 ☐   3 ☐   4 ☐   5 ☐

Never   Very seldom   About once a month   About once a week   Nearly every day

9. In everyday life, how often do you have spontaneous fantasies about having sex with someone you have just met?

1 ☐   2 ☐   3 ☐   4 ☐   5 ☐

Never   Very seldom   About once a month   About once a week   Nearly every day

Scoring: Score each response from 1 to 5, with the lowest response (on the left) scoring 1 and the highest (on the right) scoring 5. Divide the total by 9.

Norms: For men: average = 3.08, high = 3.77 or above, low = 2.32 or less. For women: average = 2.65, high = 3.42 or above, low = 1.88 or less. (Compared to an online sample of 511 male and 1,203 female German-speaking college students. High scores are one standard deviation above average or more; low scores are one standard deviation below average or more. For other norms and instructions on scoring subscales, see http://www.larspenke.eu/en/research/soi-r.html.)

Note: This scale, by Lars Penke and Jens Asendorpf, is a refinement of the original version by Simpson and Gangestad (1991).

Source: Penke & Asendorpf (2008).

especially interested in the physical attractiveness and social prestige of potential partners. This desire for multiple, casual sexual partners also appears to be particularly common in men characterized by traits sometimes called "the Dark Triad": narcissism, psychopathy, and Machiavellianism[7] (Jonason, Li, Webster, &

---

[7] Machiavellianism is a selfish, manipulative and amoral style of interpersonal behavior (the name comes from the 15th-century writer Niccoló Machiavelli, who advised a prince that, realistically, this was the only way to prosper) (Jones & Paulhus, 2009).

Schmitt, 2009). Men and women who are more "restricted"—who score lower—are more interested in partners' personal qualities and their potential to be good parents (Simpson & Gangestad, 1992).

Another implication of this trait was illustrated by a speed dating study in which men and women had a series of brief conversations with a number of potential partners and then, afterwards, nominated who they were interested in getting to know better (Back, Penke, Schmukle, & Asendorpf, 2011). They also tried to guess who had chosen them. Men higher in sociosexuality were more accurate in these guesses. They knew their "mate value" in the sense that they had a realistic view about whether many or few women had chosen them, and which ones.

Apparently, a man who desires to have sexual relations with numerous women, if he is going to be successful, must develop an accurate eye for who might be interested. You can also see, from **Figure 16.1**, that men higher in sociosexuality actually were chosen more often than men lower in this trait. For women, by contrast, this trait was not associated with how accurately they assessed their own mate value, nor with how often they were chosen. Instead, women's accuracy was predicted by their agreeableness—a finding that is harder to explain.

Other studies have found that men higher in sociosexuality are especially likely to engage in "conspicuous consumption"—buying and displaying expensive objects, such as designer watches and expensive cars—to try to attract women for short-term encounters (Sundie et al., 2011). To some degree, this is effective. Women rated a man described as driving a Porsche Boxster as a more desirable date—but not a better possible marriage partner—than a man who drove a Honda. You can almost hear what the women were thinking: "A date with this guy might be fun, but who would want to be married to somebody who wastes money like that?" Other results suggest that women understand exactly what these high-sociosexuality men are up to. They know that someone who flashes wealth in a dating context is more likely to be interested in a short-term fling than a long-term relationship.

SEXUAL ORIENTATION AND HOMOSEXUALITY For many people, sexual attraction is primarily to individuals of their own rather than the other sex, and many more people are attracted to at least some individuals of the same sex, at least some of the time. The famous Kinsey surveys of sexual behavior, published in the early 1950s, estimated that the sexual behavior of about 5 percent of men was exclusively homosexual, and about 10 percent had at least one extended period of homosexual experience at some point in their lives (Kinsey, Gebhard, & Pomeroy, 1948; Kinsey, Pomeroy, Martin, & Gebhard, 1953). They estimated a slightly lower percentage of exclusively homosexual behavior among women (3%), but a larger number of women who had at least one same-sex sexual experience (13%). Reliable data are difficult to get, and many writers have suspected that Kinsey's estimates were low because of social taboos against revealing sexual preference, which were strong in the 1950s

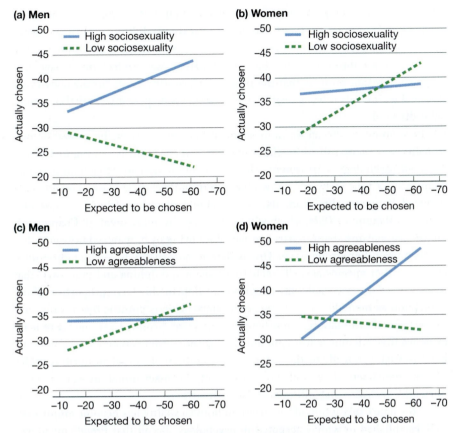

Figure 16.1 Sociosexuality, Agreeableness, and the Accuracy of Perception of Mate Value The figures show the mean proportion of the times participants' partners in a speed-dating study said they wanted to get to know them better, as a function of the mean proportion of times the participants thought they were interested. Men who were higher in the trait of sociosexuality were more accurate; among women, accuracy was associated with agreeableness.

Source: Back, Penke, Schmukle, & Asendorpf (2011), p. 987.

and which, to be honest, have not completely disappeared today.[8] But it seems safe to say that homosexual orientations and experiences are far from rare.

Sigmund Freud's views on homosexuality were in one way ahead of his time, because he viewed "why are some people attracted to members of their own sex" as the wrong question to ask. He pointed out that the psychologically more

---

[8] Kinsey did not consider other aspects of sexual identification, such as transsexuals or people who have fluid gender identities. However, he did conceptualize sexual orientation as a continuum with lots of people in the middle, rather than using a strict heterosexual/homosexual dichotomy.

useful question is, "why is anybody attracted to anybody?" According to his theory of psychosexual development (see Chapter 10), very young children experience erotic gratification though various areas of their body as they mature, and only through socialization are they eventually taught the "correct" ways to feel and behave. But Freud's important point is that the inherent possibility exists for anybody to be attracted to anybody or even anything. Socialization shapes which way this potential is directed.

In another way Freud was a prisoner of his time, because he viewed homosexuality as a mental disorder that came from mistakes in parenting and which deserved psychological treatment. This was a common view throughout psychiatry until at least the early 1970s, when the American Psychiatric Association officially removed homosexuality from its list of mental disorders (the *Diagnostic and Statistical Manual*, or *DSM*, which will be discussed in more detail in Chapter 17). This decision came about in part because of lobbying by human rights groups, but also had two other strong bases. One is that homosexuality is so common—and it exists in other species as well, including baboons, dolphins and penguins—that to say it is a "disease" suddenly diagnoses an implausibly large proportion of the population as mentally ill. Another, even more obvious point is that people with various sexual orientations enjoy happy, productive, healthy lives and there is no evidence this outcome is less common among those groups than among "normal" heterosexuals. Indeed, to the extent that members of sexual minorities suffer adverse outcomes, it is probably because of the discrimination against non-normative sexuality that still exists in some quarters.

No single explanation of the origin of homosexuality has become empirically well-established or widely accepted in psychology. Recall that Freud considered this the wrong question to ask in the first place. But this has not stopped people from speculating. Suggestions have included biological theories, environmental theories, and even evolutionary theories. Biological researchers have announced, and then retracted, discoveries of a "gay gene" on more than one occasion, and aspects of brain structure have also been implicated. I am not citing them here because although I think it is highly plausible that homosexuality (like all sexuality) has a genetic and biological basis, I haven't seen a convincing account of just how. Similarly, environmental explanations have included psychoanalytically inspired descriptions of boys who fall so in love with their mothers that they can't betray them with another woman (really!), and the psychologist Daryl Bem's "exotic becomes erotic" theory that a child gradually develops sexual attraction to the gender that he or she does *not* interact with in childhood (Bem, 1996). A previous edition of this book considered Bem's theory in detail but the empirical evidence for this interesting idea does not seem to have held up very well (Peplau, Garnets, Spalding, Conley & Veniegas, 1998). Even evolutionary theorists have weighed in with some ideas about how homosexuality could have led to adaptive fitness for some members of our species (Baragh, 2012). For example, it's possible that gay and lesbian individuals take better care of the children of other family members[9], which promotes the success of their broader gene pool, or that other adaptive traits might be associated with the same genes that influence homosexuality. If genes that promoted intelligence or good health happened to be connected to genes that promote homosexuality, for example, then that outcome could become evolutionarily advantageous, despite the obvious paradox. Let me conclude this long paragraph by noting that *all* of the suggestions in it are highly speculative. There are bits of supporting and disconfirming evidence about each of them, but the final answer is far from settled. I can predict this, though: It will be complicated.

For now, the best way to think about homosexuality is probably to go back to Freud and not think of it as a special case at all. Sexuality is one of the most powerful and at the same time mysterious forces in human life. It comes in many varieties, and it can be a source of joys and traumas and everything in between. And let us not forget, please, that for humans, sexuality is just part of the larger picture of how we relate to each other. That larger context includes love and attachment.

> The best way to think about homosexuality is probably not to think about it as a special case at all.

Love and Attachment

People have characteristic styles of relating to other people, almost no matter who (or what gender) the other person is. This observation has blossomed into a large body of research on **attachment theory**, which focuses on patterns of relationships with others that are consistently repeated with different partners throughout life. Attachment is clearly a trait; the consistency of attachment styles has been demonstrated in several laboratory studies (Andersen & Baum, 1994; Andersen & Berk, 1998). The psychological concept of attachment can be traced to pioneering writings by the English psychoanalyst John Bowlby (1969/1982), who was heavily influenced by Freud and the object relations theorists who followed Freud (see Chapters 10 and 11). In turn, Bowlby has inspired a wide-ranging program of research led by psychologists Philip Shaver and Mario Mikulincer, who use the basic concept of attachment to integrate modern research psychology with older psychoanalytic thinking (Mikulincer & Shaver, 2003; Shaver & Mikulincer, 2005; Waters, Kondo-Ikemura, Posada, & Richters, 1991).

According to Bowlby, the basis of love is attachment, and attachment begins in infancy, usually in relations with the mother.[10] Bowlby hypothesized that,

---

[9] This idea is sometimes called the "gay uncle hypothesis."
[10] Notice how his description resembles some of the theorizing by evolutionary biologists that was described in Chapter 9.

in the risky environment in which the human species developed over thousands of years, humans (indeed, all primates) evolved a strong fear of being alone, especially in unusual, dark, or dangerous places, and especially when tired, injured, or sick. This fear motivates us to desire protection from someone, preferably someone with an interest in our survival and well-being. In other words, when we are afraid, we want to be near someone who loves us. This desire is especially strong in infancy and early childhood, but it never truly goes away; it forms the basis of many of our most important interpersonal relationships (Bowlby, 1969/1982).

The desire for protection leads us to develop what Bowlby called *attachments*. The child forms the first attachment with the primary caregiver, usually the mother. The term *primary* implies that a child generally has other caregivers as well, and all of those relationships are important. If everything goes well, the child's attachments provide both a safe haven from danger and a secure base from which to explore in happier times.

Unfortunately, everything does not always go well. As a result of the child's interactions with the primary and other caregivers, and the degree to which his basic needs are met, he develops expectations about attachment relationships and what they should provide. These expectations are represented in the mind as vivid images of how others can be expected to react (*working models of others*), as well as how he expects himself to feel and behave (the child's *working model of the self*).

Bowlby pointed out that a child draws two lessons from her early experiences with adult caregivers. First, the child develops a belief about whether the people to whom she becomes attached—her *attachment figures*—will generally be reliable. Second, and perhaps more important, she develops a belief about whether she is the kind of person to whom attachment figures are likely to respond in a helpful way. In other words, if a child does not receive the necessary amount of love and care, the child might conclude that he or she is not lovable or worth caring about. This inference is not logical, of course: Just because a negligent caregiver fails to love and nurture the child does not mean the child is not lovable.

> Just because a negligent caregiver fails to love and nurture the child does not mean the child is not lovable.

American psychologist Mary Ainsworth tried to make the consequences of these expectations and conclusions concrete and visible. She invented an experimental procedure called the *strange situation*, in which a child is briefly separated from, and then reunited with, his mother. Ainsworth believed that the child's reactions, both to the separation and to the reunion, could be quite informative—in particular, one could determine the type of attachment relationship the child had developed (Ainsworth, Blehar, Waters, & Wall, 1978). From her research, Ainsworth classified children into three types, depending on the kinds of expectations they had about their primary caregivers and how they reacted to the strange situation.

Anxious-ambivalent children come from home situations where their caregivers' behaviors are "inconsistent, hit-or-miss, or chaotic" (Sroufe, Carlson, & Shulman, 1993, p. 320). In the strange situation, these children are vigilant about the mother's presence and grow very upset when she disappears for even a few minutes. In school, they are often victimized by other children and unsuccessfully attempt to cling to teachers and peers in a way that only drives these people away—and leads to further hurt feelings, anger, and insecurity.

Avoidant children come from homes where they have been rebuffed repeatedly in their attempts to enjoy contact or reassurance. Their mothers tend to dislike hugs and other bodily contact (Main, 1990). In the strange situation, they do not appear distressed, but their heart rate reveals tension and anxiety (Sroufe & Waters, 1977). When the mother returns from the brief separation, they simply ignore her. In school settings, these children are often hostile and defiant, alienating teachers and peers. As they grow older, they develop an angry self-reliance and a cold, distant attitude toward other people.

The luckiest ones, *secure* children, manage to develop a confident faith in themselves and their caregivers. When the mother returns after the separation, they greet her happily, with open arms. They are easily soothed when upset, and they actively explore their environment, returning frequently to the primary caregiver for comfort and encouragement. They are sure of the caregiver's support and do not worry about it. This positive attitude carries over into their other relationships.

One remarkable aspect of these attachment styles is their self-fulfilling nature (Shaver & Clark, 1994). The anxious, clingy child annoys people and drives them away; the avoidant child makes people angry; the secure child is likeable and attracts both caregivers and friends. Thus, a child's developing attachment style affects outcomes throughout life.

Further research has examined what happens to children with different attachment styles as they grow into adults and try to develop various elements of a mature life including satisfying romantic relationships. Psychologists have developed at least 21 different methods[11] to assess *adult attachment style*, the grown-up version of the childhood pattern just described. One of the simplest methods is to ask people the following question:

Which of these descriptions best describes your feelings?

1. I am somewhat uncomfortable being close to others; I find it difficult to trust them completely, difficult to allow myself to depend on them. I am nervous when anyone gets too close, and often, love partners want me to be more intimate than I feel comfortable being.

---

[11] That is definitely too many.

2. I find that others are reluctant to get as close as I would like. I often worry that my partner doesn't really love me or won't want to stay with me. I want to get very close to my partner, and this sometimes scares people away.

3. I find it relatively easy to get close to others and am comfortable depending on them. I don't often worry about being abandoned or about someone getting too close to me. (Hazan & Shaver, 1987, p. 515)

According to this measure, if you checked Item 1, you are avoidant; if you checked Item 2, you are anxious-ambivalent; and if you checked Item 3, you are secure. Simple as that. When this survey was published in a Denver newspaper, 55 percent of the respondents described themselves as secure, 25 percent as avoidant, and 20 percent as anxious—the same percentages found in American infants observed by Ainsworth in the strange situation (Campos, Barrett, Lamb, Goldsmith, & Stenberg, 1983).

Studies that examined attachment styles in more detail found that avoidant individuals are relatively uninterested in romantic relationships; they are also more likely than secure individuals to have their relationships break up and grieve less after a relationship ends, even though they admit to being lonely (Shaver & Clark, 1994). They like to work alone, and they sometimes use work as an excuse to detach from emotional relationships. They describe their parents as having been rejecting and cold, or else describe them in vaguely positive ways ("nice") without being able to provide specific examples. (For example, when asked, "What did your mother do that was *particularly* nice?" they are typically stuck.) Avoidant individuals under stress withdraw from their romantic partners, and instead tend to cope by ignoring stress or denying it exists. For example, avoidant individuals who were victims of sexual abuse in childhood tend to be unable to remember the experience 14 years later (Edelstein et al., 2005). They do not often share personal information, and they dislike people who do.

Anxious-ambivalent adults, in contrast, are obsessed with their romantic partners—they think about them all the time and have trouble allowing them to have their own lives. They suffer from extreme jealousy, report a high rate of relationship failures (not surprisingly), and sometimes exhibit a cycle of breaking up and getting back together with the same partner. Anxious-ambivalent adults tend to have low and unstable self-esteem, and they like to work with other people but typically feel unappreciated by coworkers. They are highly emotional under stress and have to work hard to control their emotions. They describe their parents as having been intrusive, unfair, and inconsistent.

Insecurely attached people (either of the first two styles listed above) suffer other consequences as well. When they are children, according to one major recent review, they are less able to control their impulses and modulate their emotions (Pallini et al., 2018). When they become adults, according to another major review, the relationship problems caused by their insecure attachment style leads them to be more likely to become involved in dangerous drug use (Fairbairn et al., 2018).

You will be relieved to learn that secure adults tend to enjoy long, stable romantic relationships characterized by deep trust and friendship. They have high self-esteem as well as high regard for others. Under stress, they seek out others, particularly their romantic partners, for emotional support. They also offer loyal support to their romantic partners when they need it. They describe their parents in positive but realistic terms, which they are able to back up with specific examples. In sum, they are people who are easy to be with (Shaver & Clark, 1994).

Secure individuals can deal directly with reality because their attachment experience has been positive and reliable. They have always had a safe refuge from danger and a secure base from which to explore the world. This idealized description does not mean that secure people never cry, become angry, or worry about abandonment. But they do not need to distort reality to deal with their sadness, anger, or insecurity.

According to attachment theory, these patterns are learned in early childhood and reinforced in an increasingly self-fulfilling manner across young adulthood. This pattern of transference can persist across a person's life span, affecting her approach to work as well as relationships (Hazan & Shaver, 1990). If an individual learns an avoidant or anxious-ambivalent style, change is difficult but perhaps not impossible. Psychotherapists who use attachment theory try to teach these people the origins of their relationship styles, the way these styles lead to self-defeating outcomes, and more constructive ways to relate to others (Shaver & Clark, 1994).

Recent years have seen an explosion of research on attachment (Dozier, Stovall, & Albus, 1999; Shaver & Mikulincer, 2005). As seems to always happen when an area of research starts to become more active, later results are showing that some early conclusions were a little too simple. For example, one recent study shows that even securely attached individuals are not immune from relationship problems. If their feelings of attachment fluctuate too much from one day to the next, even if on average their feelings are good, their relationship satisfaction will become just as bad over time as that of someone who is anxiously attached (see **Figure 16.2**). I suspect one reason for this finding is that we prefer other people, and especially our relationship partners, to be predictable. A relationship with an insecurely attached person can be difficult because it's a bit nerve-wracking to not know what is coming next.

Some of the research progress is more technical. For example, researchers are moving beyond the three-category classification of attachment just described to a two-dimensional model on which people vary according to their degree of *anxiety* about relationships, and their degree of *avoidance* of relationships. Only a person low on both dimensions would be considered securely attached. A person high in attachment anxiety characteristically worries that his emotionally significant

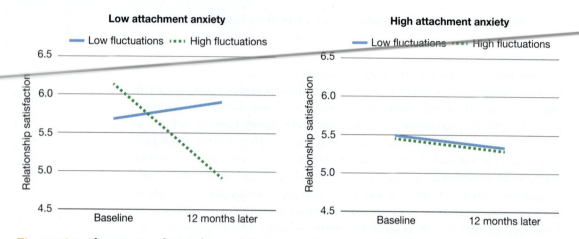

Figure 16.2 **Changes in relationship satisfaction as a function of attachment anxiety and fluctuation** The figure on the left shows that even among securely attached people (with low attachment anxiety), those who fluctuated in their feelings from one day to the next experienced a decline in relationship satisfaction over time, whereas those with more steady feelings actually increased a bit. The figure on the right shows that people high in attachment anxiety had slight declines in relationship satisfaction over the same period of time, but the degree of fluctuation in their feelings didn't really matter, probably because their feelings were negative at the outset.

Source: Girme, Y.U., et al. (2018). The ebbs and flows of attachment: Within-person variation in attachment undermine secure individuals' relationship wellbeing across time. *Journal of Personality and Social Psychology, 114,* 397-421. (p. 408)

other people will not be available at times of need, and deals with it by maintaining extreme vigilance, watching for signs of rejection almost to the point of paranoia. A person high in attachment avoidance has learned to distrust other people and so strives to maintain independence and emotional distance and tries to convince himself that close emotional relationships are unimportant.[12] According to one recent experiment, someone high in both avoidance *and* anxiety will tend to avoid paying attention to any signs of emotion from another person, such as angry *or* happy facial expressions (Dewitte & De Houwer, 2008).

Other research uses increasingly ingenious methods to demonstrate how attachment styles are invoked unconsciously. In one study, participants looked at a computer screen that showed either a neutral word (*hat*) or a threatening word (*failure*) *subliminally*, meaning too fast for them to read consciously, though presumably they still perceive the word on some level (Mikulincer, Gillath, & Shaver, 2002, Study I).[13] Then the participants were asked to indicate on the keyboard, as

---

[12] Paul Simon wrote a song that has the refrain "I am a rock, I am an island." If you know the song, this would be a good time to hum it to yourself.

[13] This study was conducted in Israel, and the words were in Hebrew.

quickly as possible, whether each string in a series of letter strings consisted of words or nonwords—and they were told that proper names counted as words. Some of the words presented to them were names of people to whom the participants were emotionally attached (according to a questionnaire they completed earlier), while other names were of people with whom they were acquainted but to whom they were not emotionally attached. The results showed that people recognized the names of attachment figures more quickly in the threat condition than in the neutral condition; this was not true for other acquaintances. The conclusion of the study was that when people feel threatened, even by the subliminal presentation of a word with unpleasant connotations, they respond by thinking of the people to whom they are emotionally attached. In other words, we go to our attachment figures when we feel under threat, and if they are not physically present, we go to them in our minds.

WORK AND BUSINESS

Personality, more than any other branch of psychology, has a long history of being applied in business contexts. Personality is relevant to the business world for three reasons: (1) Some people make better employees than others. (2) Some people make better bosses (leaders) than others. And, (3) some people fit better to some occupations than others. Thus, the three basic topics in the field of personality and business are occupational success, leadership, and occupational choice.

Occupational Success

What do employers look for when selecting new employees? According to one survey in which more than 3,000 employers ranked the importance of 86 possible employee qualities, seven out of the top eight involved conscientiousness, integrity, trustworthiness, and similar qualities (the eighth was general mental ability) (Michigan Department of Education, 1989). When deciding whether to hire you, any prospective employer will try to gauge these traits. As job interview workshops repeatedly advise, employers pay close attention to how you are groomed, how you are dressed, and whether you are on time. (Showing up late or in ragged jeans is not recommended.)

Sometimes employers go beyond these casual observations by administering formal personality assessments. Some of these are called *integrity tests*, but they typically measure a wide range of qualities, including responsibility, long-term job commitment, consistency, moral reasoning, friendliness, work ethic, dependability, cheerfulness, energy level, and even-temperedness (O'Bannon, Goldinger, & Appleby, 1989). The qualities measured by these tests are partially described by the Big Five traits of *agreeableness* and *emotional stability* (the inverse of neuroticism) that were described in Chapter 6. But the trait most closely associated with integrity tests is *conscientiousness* (Ones, Viswesvaran, & Schmidt, 1993, 1995), which is another one of the Big Five traits, and the one most closely associated with occupational success. The tests don't seem to do particularly well at their originally intended purpose, predicting employee theft, having a mean validity of .13 (about 57 percent accuracy as defined earlier; see Chapter 3). In fairness, this figure may underestimate the tests' validity because theft is difficult to detect, so the criteria used in these studies may have been less than perfect. Still, Ones and coworkers concluded that so-called integrity tests are better viewed as broad measures of personality traits related to job performance, especially conscientiousness, than merely tests of honesty.

CONSCIENTIOUSNESS AND JOB PERFORMANCE How well does conscientiousness predict job performance? To some extent, the answer depends on what you mean by job performance. In many studies in industrial psychology, the criterion of interest is supervisors' ratings, typically offered about a year after the person is hired. This criterion might seem subjective—and it is—but, from a supervisor's point of view, it is exactly what she wants: a test that can peer into the future. In other words, if I hire this person, a year from now will I be glad or sorry I did? Ones and coworkers reviewed more than 700 studies that used a total of 576,460 subjects in assessing the validity of 43 different tests for predicting supervisors' ratings of job performance. The validity was equivalent to a correlation of .41. Recall the discussion of the Binomial Effect Size Display (BESD) in Chapter 3, and the example in Chapter 4: If an employer's predictions of future job performance, made without using one of these tests, are accurate 50 percent of the time (e.g., if half of the candidates are qualified, but she makes hiring decisions by flipping a coin), her predictions if she uses the test instead will have an accuracy rate of greater than 70 percent. As we saw in Chapter 4, given the costs of training (and, when necessary, firing) employees, this difference could add up to a lot of money.

A more specific criterion of job performance is absenteeism. Obviously, if someone does not show up for work, he is not doing a very good job. Another, later meta-analysis by the same researchers examined 28 studies with a total sample of 13,972 participants, and found the overall correlation between "integrity" test scores and absenteeism to be equivalent to a correlation of .33[14] (Ones, Viswesvaran, & Schmidt, 2003). To use the BESD yet again, this means that high scorers on this test would be in the more reliable half of employees about two thirds (or 67 percent) of the time.

Regardless of the exact criterion used, according to large review of the literature (which included 117 studies), "conscientiousness showed consistent

---

[14] Actually, of course, the correlation is negative, -.33. People with higher integrity scores have less absenteeism.

relations with all job performance criteria for all occupational groups" (Mount & Barrick, 1998, p. 849). This finding held for both genders and even after controlling for age and years of education (Costa, 1996).

One reason that these relations are so pervasive was noted by the industrial psychologists Walter Borman and Louis Penner, who pointed out that certain aspects of good performance are general across almost all jobs. One of these is a behavioral pattern they call "citizenship performance," in which the employee tries in various ways to promote the goals of the organization. This might include behaviors such as helping to teach new employees their jobs, alleviating conflicts in the workplace, being aware of problems and opportunities as they arise and trying to respond to them, and having the kind of positive attitude that makes everything go better. This pattern of behavior is predicted by such traits as conscientiousness and is a boon to organizational performance, regardless of whether the work setting is a store, a factory, or an office (Borman & Penner, 2001).

Conscientiousness is important not just for one's own occupational success, but for the success of one's spouse! One recent study found that people whose spouses—male or female, it didn't matter—were high in conscientiousness were themselves more likely to enjoy success on the job (Solomon & Jackson, 2014). This might be because conscientious spouses keep things running smoothly at home and so it's easier to concentrate at work, or because a conscientious spouse is a role model of sorts. If your spouse is working hard, it might be harder to sit around all day in front of the TV yourself. Another possibility is that conscientious people choose each other as spouses. Love might not, after all, be completely blind.

The pervasive relationship between conscientiousness and job performance has other implications as well. One surprising implication is that personality assessment could help alleviate the effects of bias in testing. It is well known that African Americans, as a group, score lower than white Americans on many so-called aptitude tests used by businesses to select employees. (Although a few psychologists believe this difference to be genetic, more believe it to be a by-product of discrimination in educational and social environments; see Sternberg, 1995.) The results of such tests can damage employment prospects and financial well-being, and lead to illegal and unwise discrimination. Tests of integrity, conscientiousness, and most other personality tests, however, typically do *not* show racial or ethnic differences (Sackett et al., 1989). Thus, if more employers could be persuaded to use personality tests instead of, or in addition to, ability tests, racial imbalance in hiring

> If more employers could be persuaded to use personality tests instead of, or in addition to, ability tests, racial imbalance in hiring could be addressed without affecting productivity.

could be addressed without affecting productivity (Ones et al., 1993). The same lesson applies to college admissions. Conscientious students do very well in college, and the trait is a better predictor of academic success than either SAT scores or high school grade-point averages (Wagerman & Funder, 2007).

People with higher conscientiousness tend to accumulate more years in school even though the trait is uncorrelated with IQ (Barrick & Mount, 1991). This might be because, for example, highly conscientious 5th and 8th graders put more effort into their homework (Göllner et al., 2017). These findings imply that years of education can be used as a *marker variable*, or signal of conscientiousness. An employer might be wise to hire someone with more schooling, not necessarily because of what he has learned, but because a person who has completed—and survived!—many years of education is likely to be highly conscientious (Caplan, 2003, p. 399).

PERSONALITY AND ECONOMIC SUCCESS Employers value good job performance by their workers, but from the workers' perspective, perhaps a more relevant criterion for success is how far they advance in their careers and how much money they make. You probably won't be surprised to learn that personality matters for these outcomes, as well.

In everyday speech, we sometimes refer to successful people as having "drive," the combination of industriousness, impulse-control, and orderliness that is an important foundation of conscientiousness (Costantini & Perugini, 2016). Another term you might have heard of is "grit," the attitude toward life that is advertised (in best-selling books and TED talks) as leading toward success in school and work (Duckworth et al., 2007; Duckworth, 2016). Well, grit and conscientiousness are pretty much the same thing, even at the level of genetics (Rimfeld, Kovas, Dale & Plomin, 2016).

By any name, the kind of drive associated with this trait can help you get ahead. For example, highly conscientious employees seek out opportunities to learn about the company, and to acquire skills and knowledge that go beyond their present job (F.L. Schmidt & Hunter, 1992). As a result, guess who gets promoted? Similarly, highly conscientious individuals tend to do well in interviews, not just because they present themselves well, but because they spend more time seeking information and

"I've been up all night drinking to prepare for this interview."

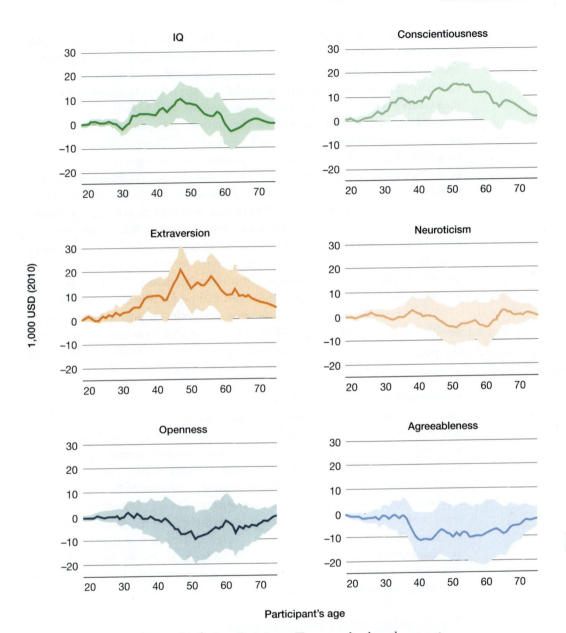

Figure 16.3 Personality and Lifetime Earnings These graphs show the ages at which IQ and the Big Five traits have the greatest effect on earnings (in men). At ages when the line is above zero the trait is associated with making more money; when the line is below zero the trait is associated with making less money. The graphs clearly show that in several cases personality matters even more than IQ, but the effect of IQ might be underestimated because all of the participants in the Terman study, from which these data came, were selected to have high IQs.

getting prepared (Caldwell & Burger, 1998). They do so well in advance—highly conscientious people don't procrastinate (D. C. Watson, 2001). And any student who has ever been assigned to a group project knows that one member—the most conscientious one—will probably wait a while for the others to do something, and then (sadly but effectively) end up doing most of the work herself.

Several traits associated with career success, not just conscientiousness, can start to be detected as early as 8 years of age! Using data from a classic longitudinal study of personality development (Terman, 1925), a modern labor economist found that parents' and teachers' personality ratings at age 8, when combined with self-ratings at age 30, predicted how much money the child would grow up to earn between ages 40 and 60.[15] The traits associated with making more money were conscientiousness (not surprisingly), but also extraversion, along with *low* agreeableness (Gensowski, 2017). It's easy to see why conscientious people, who, as we have seen, generally do a good job, and extraverted people, who tend to be popular, would enjoy career success and make more money. But why low agreeableness? The author of the study speculated that people who are highly agreeable might be less successful at manipulating people in office politics and also "less aggressive in wage bargaining" (p. 9). In other words, if you are too agreeable to insist on a raise, it could cost you.

> If you are too agreeable to insist on a raise, it could cost you.

PERSONALITY AND ECONOMICS In sum, personality is relevant to occupational success in many ways and for many reasons. It makes sense, therefore, that understanding personality is becoming increasingly important for the study of economics. Traditionally, economists interested in what they call "human capital formation" (the development of knowledge and skills) focused on cognitive abilities, such as IQ. More recently, some pioneering economists, including Nobel laureate James Heckman, have come to recognize that personality traits such as motivation, persistence, and self-control matter at least as much if not more (Borghans, Duckworth, Heckman, & ter Weel, 2008; Borghans, Golsteyn, Heckman, & Humphries, 2011; see also Roberts, Kuncel, Shiner, Caspi, & Goldberg, 2007). As this fact becomes more widely known and better understood in future research, the fields of personality psychology and economics will inch a little closer to each other.

Leadership and Management

If personality of employees is important, then the personality of their bosses is surely even more important, because the actions of a manager or leader affect the behavior and outcomes of many other people and even the company or organization

---

[15] These findings pertained mostly to men, perhaps because women in the study (which was begun in the 1920s) had fewer opportunities to exploit their talents for career success.

itself. In any organizational context, good management entails getting other people to do things, and the best managers accomplish this through persuasion, counseling, and suggestion rather than through commands, criticisms, and coercion (Blickle et al., 2013). Some people have more talent for doing this than others do.

A major literature review by Judge et al. (2002) combined the results of 73 studies of personality and leadership performance, which looked at a total of more than 25,000 high- and low-level managers in almost 5,000 organizations, and measured leadership performance in many different ways. The results were strong and consistent. Four of the Big Five personality traits were associated with better leadership. The best predictor of management performance was emotional stability (the inverse of neuroticism). In other words, managers who were calm and not anxious or depressed made better leaders (the overall r was .33). The other predictors of management success were conscientiousness (r = .29), extraversion (r = .27) and openness (r = .21). Agreeableness didn't seem to have much to do with being a good manager (r = .07), perhaps for the same reason it wasn't found to help occupational success in the study cited earlier in this chapter (Gensowski, 2017). Managers have to manage after all, and being too agreeable might undermine one's authority.

Most research on leadership tries to identify who makes the best leaders, but some recent work has focused on the worst-case scenarios, the people who should *not* but often do attain powerful positions. The *dark triad* of the traits of narcissism, Machiavellianism, and psychopathy, mentioned earlier in this chapter in the context of sexual behavior, is also important for understanding leadership styles. People high in the dark triad traits sometimes have an advantage in gaining power because of their ruthlessness and cunning, and these traits might even be good for helping them to achieve their organizations' goals in some circumstances.[16] But they are not pleasant to work for, to say the least. One study assessed their leadership styles as "selfish, impulsive, exploitative and toxic" (Furtner, Mann & Rauthmann, 2017, p. 75).

Organizational leaders do more than boss people around, of course. One important function of leaders in many organizations is financial decision making. What should a company invest in, how should it raise money, and how should it strategize for the future are all questions that many managers must answer in their daily work. There is not yet much psychological research about how managers make financial decisions, but one intriguing study suggests that personality might be relevant here, too, providing a specific example of cross-situational consistency in the economic realm. The study compared the degree to which corporate CEOs "leveraged" (borrowed a lot of money) when running their companies, with how much they leveraged when buying their personal homes. It turned out that the same people who do risky borrowing in their corporate life tend to do the same thing in their

---

[16] Like, maybe, when the organization has evil goals?

personal life (Cronqvist, Makhija, & Yonker, 2011). An implication of this finding might be that if you are trying to decide whether to trust your broker, you might want to find out, first, whether she has tapped out her own credit cards![17]

Occupational Choice

Success is more than a matter of having the right traits; also important is the fit between a person's traits and the kind of occupation she pursues.

Humanistic psychology (Chapter 12) is not usually thought of as a field of applied science, but Maslow's hierarchy of needs is often used in the analysis of occupational choice and employee motivation. Recall from Chapter 12 that once basic needs are fulfilled, people seek higher forms of satisfaction, such as attaining prestige and making the world a better place. Thus, when trying to motivate employees, a wise manager knows that paying a sufficient salary is only part of what is needed. The best employees will use their full talents and energies when they see their jobs as respected and impactful. Everybody wants to make a difference, and the workplace is an opportunity to do that. The hierarchy of needs also illustrates the kinds of jobs people will seek in the first place. If they can, most people will seek an occupation where they can do more than make a living.[18]

Trait psychology (Chapters 4–7) has even more to say about occupational choice. According to one recent study, the "fit" between personality and job is important, because "economic success depends not only on having a 'successful personality' but also, in part, on finding the best niche for one's personality" (Denissen et al., 2017, p. xx). For example, extraversion is a poor fit for being a bookkeeper, but a good fit for being an actor. Agreeableness is a poor fit for "armed forces," but a good fit for "religious professional," and so forth. The most important implication of this finding is that it matters, a lot, what occupation you choose to pursue in life. A good fit can lead to great outcomes; a poor fit can lead to failure and unhappiness.

One highly influential approach to matching people with jobs is the typology introduced by the industrial psychologist John Holland (1996).[19] The six types are Realistic (e.g., being an engineer), Investigative (scientist), Artistic (artist, musician), Social (teacher, therapist), Enterprising (entrepreneur, business owner),

---

[17] I wish you enough prosperity someday to have to worry about whether to trust your broker. And in case you really make it into the 1%, remember that psychopathic hedge fund managers make bad investments (ten Brinke, Kish & Keltner, 2018), so watch out for them too.

[18] Although, make no mistake, the ability to make a living is important. Underpaying employees is not a way to bring out their best.

[19] His typology is different from—and superior to—the Myers-Briggs typology discussed and criticized in Chapter 6, because it classifies a person as being more or less similar to each type rather than being only one particular type, because its results are more stable over time, and because its empirical research support is more persuasive.

and Conventional (accountant).[20] When a person follows a career that better matches his or her "Holland type" they will enjoy better job satisfaction, longer employment, and better performance (along with all the rewards that come from that) (Assouline & Meir, 1987; Van Iddekinge et al., 2011).

PERSONALITY AND LIFE

How people feel about and behave with their relationship partners, and the way people develop their skills, choose their careers, and handle their obligations and opportunities at work are critically important determinants of how life turns out. Personality traits affect all of these outcomes, because they comprise the psychological aspects of a person that she carries along throughout life, from one relationship, job, and situation to the next. As I mentioned earlier, personality is the baggage you always have with you. This is why in the *long run*—not always in the short run—it affects so many outcomes.

---

[20] Which type do you most resemble? You can take a quick test for free at https://openpsychometrics .org/tests/RIASEC/

WRAPPING IT UP

SUMMARY

Personality Traits and Life Outcomes

- Personality has an important impact on relationships and occupational success.

Relationships

- Communal traits such as warmth and trustfulness, and other traits such as low negative emotionality and high positive emotionality, are all associated with good relationship outcomes.

- Predicting from personality traits who will specifically be compatible with whom is surprisingly difficult.

- Deal-breakers, traits that undermine or prevent relationships, include being untrustworthy, having anger issues, and feeling "dispositional contempt" for other people.

- Another trait associated with relationship problems, but less of a total deal-breaker, is rejection sensitivity, in which a person is overly reactive to any indication that one's partner might be losing interest.

- While compatibility is often touted as the secret to relationship success, the real key might be that most people are average, well-adjusted, and agreeable, and people who resemble that average are likely to be able to have good relationships with each other.

- Some individual differences in sexual behavior are described by the trait of sociosexuality, which is defined as the willingness to engage in sexual relations in the absence of a serious relationship.

- Homosexual orientation and experiences are common. The real puzzle, as Freud pointed out, is not what causes homosexuality, but what are the roots of sexuality in general. Many biological, environmental, and evolutionary explanations have been offered, but none yet has achieved firm empirical support or wide acceptance.

- Attachment theory, which has its roots in psychoanalytic thinking, describes the style of emotional relationships in adult life that is based on early experiences with caregivers such as one's mother and family.

- A child who grows up in a home experienced as safe and supportive can grow up to be securely attached and enjoy good adult relationships, whereas a child who grows up in a chaotic home may turn out to have an anxious-ambivalent attachment style, and a child who grows up in a home that is emotionally cold may turn out to have an avoidant attachment style. Both of these latter styles are associated with difficult relationship issues in adult life.

Work and Business

- When seeking employees, most employers are looking for traits such as conscientiousness, integrity, and trustworthiness, and often use personality tests to find people with these traits.

- Conscientiousness is a particularly important trait for occupational success, being associated with a wide range of outcomes including (low) absenteeism, high performance ratings by supervisors, and exhibiting "citizenship performance" behaviors that promote organizational goals.

- Specific types of personalities might be best suited for certain jobs.

- One influential scheme for organizing this connection is Holland's occupational typology, which includes six types: Realistic (e.g., being an engineer), Investigative (scientist), Artistic (artist, musician), Social (teacher, therapist), Enterprising (entrepreneur, business owner), and Conventional (accountant).

- More successful leaders and managers tend to be high in emotional stability (low neuroticism), and also high in conscientiousness, extraversion, and openness. Agreeableness is not strongly related to management success.

- The dark triad traits of narcissism, Machiavellianism, and psychopathy can sometimes be helpful for attaining leadership roles, but leaders high in these traits can be disastrous to work for.

- The relationship between financial decision-making and personality is not yet well-studied, but one recent finding suggests that managers who take risks in their personal finances also take more risks when managing their companies.

Personality and Life

- Personality affects so many life outcomes because it influences the small behaviors we perform every day, all day long, and the effects add up over time.

KEY TERMS

mate selection, p. 589
mating strategies, p. 589
attachment theory, p. 599

THINK ABOUT IT

1. What traits do you think are the most important to seek out in relationship partners, and what traits are most important to avoid? Do your answers match the findings of research summarized in this chapter? Why might your personal answers and the results of research sometimes be different?

2. Are certain traits really "deal-breakers"? What kind of person would you absolutely, positively want to avoid? Why?

3. How did you score on the trait of Dispositional Contempt (Try for Yourself 16.1)? Perhaps you or someone you know got a high score. Is there, as suggested in the text, a possible upside to this trait?

4. What kinds of upbringing or experiences do you think might make a person grow up to be high or low in sociosexuality? Note that there is no right or wrong answer here because there is yet little research on the origins of this trait. So feel free to speculate!

5. Attachment theory makes strong claims about how styles of adult relationships have their origins in the early family environment. How plausible do you find these claims? Can you think of other influences that might affect attachment style?

6. Have you ever applied for a job? What kinds of information do you think the person doing the hiring used to make his or her decisions? Was this information valid, do you think?

7. Take the test (see Suggested Readings and Resources) to assess your Holland Occupational Type. Did the results seem accurate? Do they match what you are hoping to do in your own career?

8. If you were hiring employees for a new company you were starting, what would you look for? Would their personalities matter? How and why?

9. Think of the best boss you've ever had (or heard of). What made that person good at their job?

10. Now think of the worst boss and answer the same question. What are the essential differences between good and bad bosses? Is being popular with one's employees essential? What other attributes might be necessary?

11. What kind of organization would find it useful to have a leader that is high in the dark triad traits of narcissism, Machiavellianism, and psychopathy? What would its goals be? Would you want to work for an organization like this?

SUGGESTED RESOURCES

Online

Holland Occupational Themes, https://openpsychometrics.org/tests/RIASEC/

> *This website offers an online version of a test to assess which of Holland's occupational types you match most closely. See if you agree with its results! (The same website also offers several other tests you can take for free.)*

Sociosexuality Website, *http://www.larspenke.eu/en/research/soi-r.html*

> *This website offers a number of resources concerning the theory and measurement of sociosexuality, including background readings and the test translated into 25 languages!*

Print

Christiansen, N.D., & Tett, R.P. (2013). *Handbook of Personality at Work.* New York: Routledge.

> *A collection of chapters by different authors on how personality psychology is relevant to the workplace and occupational success. Everything you'd want to know on the topic is in here someplace.*

Friedman, H. S., & Kern, M. L. (2014). Personality, well-being, and health. *Annual Review of Psychology, 65,* 719–742.

> *This chapter is a well-written, up-to-date (as of 2014) summary of what psychological research has learned about the connections between personality and physical health. It includes a sophisticated explanation of the many methodological pitfalls of research in this area, and some wise recommendations for designing interventions intended to improve health.*

Mikulincer, M., & Shaver, P.R. (2003). The attachment behavioral system in adulthood: Activation, psychodynamics, and interpersonal processes. *Advances in Experimental Social Psychology, 35,* 53-152.

> *A thorough and readable introduction to attachment theory and its importance for relationships. A good place to go if you want to know more about the topic than is presented in this chapter.*

Want to earn a better grade on your test?

Go to **INQUIZITIVE** to learn and review this chapter's content, with personalized feedback along the way.

17

MENTAL AND PHYSICAL HEALTH

I**F THIS BOOK—AND** the study of personality—has a single, unifying theme, it is this: People are different. Every individual thinks, feels, and acts in distinctive ways. The entire field of personality psychology is an effort to specify how and explain why. The trait approach (Chapters 4 through 7) addresses individual differences more explicitly than any other, but, as you have seen, biological research (Chapters 8 and 9), psychoanalytic approaches (Chapters 10 and 11), humanistic interpretations (Chapter 12), cultural psychology (Chapter 13), and even learning theories and descriptions of cognitive processes (Chapters 14 and 15) all seek to outline the ways in which people are different from each other and to explain the causes and implications of these differences.

It is good that people are different. Life would certainly be less interesting and perhaps even lose much of its meaning if everyone thought, felt, and acted the same. Moreover, as we saw in Chapter 9, individual differences allow people to survive and thrive in different environments and under different circumstances, and are crucial for the process of evolution. And, as we saw in the previous chapter, understanding individual differences can be useful for attaining success in relationships and business.

Other consequences of personality specifically involve mental and physical health. Concerning mental health, aspects of personality can become so extreme as to cause serious problems. When this happens, psychologists begin to speak of personality disorders, the topic of the first part of this chapter. Personality also has important implications for physical health, up to and including how long a person lives. As the writer Augesten Burroughs once observed, "If you have good health, you have everything. When you do not have your health, nothing else matters at all." Personality matters for this outcome, too. Some traits go along with good health and others with risk, although the reasons for these associations are complicated. The relationship between personality and physical health is the topic of the second part of this chapter.

PERSONALITY DISORDERS

In general, personality disorders are configurations of traits considered "socially undesirable," which means, very simply, that most people don't like them. Patterns such as social awkwardness, suspiciousness, arrogance, whininess, and just plain strangeness, when taken to extremes, begin to shade into the range that might reasonably be characterized as a disorder. But it is difficult to specify the point beyond which normal variation in a personality trait becomes pathological. In fact, finding an *exact* point may well be impossible.

> It is difficult to specify the point beyond which normal variation in a personality trait becomes pathological. In fact, finding an *exact* point may well be impossible.

But this ambiguity does not mean personality disorders are not real and important. They can create severe problems for the affected individual or others who know that person, and it is rather likely that you could name a few people to whom this applies. Indeed, one survey estimates that about 15 percent of all adult Americans have at least one personality disorder (B. F. Grant et al., 2004), and there is no reason to think that the prevalence varies much elsewhere in the world.

THE *DIAGNOSTIC AND STATISTICAL MANUAL (DSM)*

As long ago as the early 1800s, the pioneering French psychiatrist Philippe Pinel identified what he called *manie sans delire* (madness without distortion of reality), and for many years psychiatrists and psychologists discussed and sometimes attempted to treat people who, while not exactly insane, had unusual personalities that got them into trouble. In 1952, the American Psychiatric Association imposed some order on this discussion by publishing the first edition of the *DSM*, the *Diagnostic and Statistical Manual*, which included a list and description of what were seen as the major disorders of personality, along with other psychological afflictions. Over subsequent editions it grew and grew, and its most recent versions top out at nearly 1,000 pages.

Controversy over the *DSM*

The *DSM* has acquired the status of a bible for psychiatrists and clinical psychologists, but its current state is embarrassingly chaotic. Until recently, a massive book called the *DSM-IV-TR*[1] (American Psychiatric Association, 2000) reigned supreme,

---

[1] TR stands for "text revision"; the *DSM-IV-TR* was a relatively minor revision meant to be a transitional publication between the *DSM-IV* and the long-delayed *DSM-5* (see footnote 2). In what follows, I will sometimes refer to the *DSM-IV-TR* as simply the *DSM-IV*.

but over more than a decade of use it became widely acknowledged that a major revision—including some streamlining—was long overdue. The process of revision began with much hope, but ultimately was less productive than expected because of political infighting. Major battles broke out on various fronts. One of the most contentious stemmed from a controversy over how to define personality disorders (Krueger & Markson, 2014).

Basically, the battle was between an "old guard" of experienced clinicians who had become comfortable with a long-established standard list of disorders, and a more scientifically oriented group of mostly academic researchers who insisted on a classification system based on empirical data rather than clinical experience. The outcome finally published in the new, improved *DSM-5*[2] (American Psychiatric Association, 2013) was an uneasy compromise. The traditional system is still presented in the part of the manual that provides the definitive list of mental disorders. The new system appears, too, but in a separate section near the back of the book. The *DSM-5* attempts to reconcile this inconsistency with the rather astonishing statement that "it is hoped that both versions will serve clinical practice and research initiatives, respectively" (p. 645). The word "respectively" seems to imply that clinical practice does not need to be scientifically based; I hope that isn't really what the writers meant.

In any case, the long-term outcome seems clear. The new system will eventually completely replace the old, in the *DSM-6* (whenever that appears) or maybe *DSM-7*. The old guard will die away sooner or later, as old guards inevitably do. For now, we are left in the awkward position of talking about personality disorders in two ways, (a) a time-honored, traditional way still followed by many clinical practitioners, and (b) a newer way that is more scientifically grounded. Although great efforts have been made to reconcile the two systems, as will be described later, we still have little choice but to consider both.

Purposes of the *DSM*

The succeeding editions of the *DSM* have two purposes. The first is to make psychological diagnosis more objective. Two clinical psychologists or psychiatrists cannot even talk about a client or a patient[3], much less come to a mutual

---

[2] You may have noticed that the numbering between the two editions went from IV to 5. This was done so that subsequent editions could be numbered in the same way as versions of software, with minor revisions being designated as 5.1, 5.2 and so on until a major revision, someday, produces *DSM-6*.
[3] Clinical psychologists are more likely to talk about "clients" and psychiatrists about "patients."

understanding, unless they have a common vocabulary. The hope of the *DSM* is that a specific list of criteria for diagnosis will make discussions and analysis clearer and more useful. This goal of objectivity is even more important for research. If a scientist believes that she has developed a promising treatment or a medication for a disorder, then there is no way to test the treatment or medication without some way to identify who has the disorder in the first place.

The second purpose for the *DSM* may sound trivial, but it is not. The *DSM* gives the psychiatrist or clinical psychologist something to write on the insurance billing form! Go ahead and chuckle, but I am not joking. Insurance providers will not reimburse for the treatment of something that is not specified. Your primary care physician is not permitted to write on your chart that you came in because you were "sick." A more descriptive label is required. So, too, if psychological treatment is going to be paid for—which is the same as saying, if it is to be offered at all—then categories of psychological disorders must be specified. The *DSM* can be and has been criticized on many grounds, but lack of comprehensiveness is not usually among them. The 943 pages of the *DSM-IV-TR* provided a label and a numerical code for a long list of just about everything that could conceivably go wrong with a person, psychologically speaking. I already mentioned that one goal of the revision was to streamline this list but the outcome was not especially successful. The *DSM-5* is (exactly) 945 pages long.

DEFINING PERSONALITY DISORDERS

The person who has a personality disorder may see it not as a disorder at all, but a basic part of who he or she is.

Personality disorders have five general characteristics. They are (1) unusual and, (2) by definition, tend to cause problems. In addition, most but not quite all personality disorders (3) affect social relations and (4) are stable over time. Finally, (5) in some cases, the person who has a personality disorder may see it not as a disorder at all, but a basic part of who he or she is.

Unusually Extreme and Problematic

The two defining features of personality disorders were described by the pioneering psychiatrist Kurt Schneider (1923). The first is that a person exhibits an *unusually extreme* degree of one or more attributes of personality. It is important that the variation be not only extreme but also unusual, particularly considering the individual's cultural context. Thus, cutting somebody off in traffic on a Southern California freeway is an extreme behavior—it can be life-threatening for everyone involved—but it probably does not qualify as a symptom of personality disorder because it is (sadly) much too common. On a deeper level, clinical practice is just beginning to come to terms with the implications of cultural variation (see Chapter 13) for understanding abnormal psychology. Patterns of shy, self-effacing behavior (which is more the norm in interdependent or collectivistic cultures) or loud, aggressive behavior (which is more the norm in individualistic cultures) that otherwise could be viewed as symptoms of personality disorders might, in fact, be typical in context. Similarly, a parenting practice that is normal within one culture may seem harsh, and even draw the attention of the child protection authorities, if the neighbors notice it in a different cultural context. Recall the Danish mother, described in Chapter 13, who left her baby in a stroller parked outside a New York City restaurant and was arrested. Should she seek psychological treatment?[4]

As we saw in Chapter 10, Freud firmly believed that the extremes on any dimension are pathological and that sanity always lies somewhere in the middle. This idea may offer a way to separate out what is extreme in a pathological way from something that is extreme only in relation to the practices of a particular culture. Extremism requires the denial of reality. We see this frequently in politics, where in order to occupy an extreme position it is necessary to deny any possibility that people who disagree with you could possibly be correct in any way. Similarly, extreme styles of behavior may stem from denying the reality that some people are trustworthy, that other people are worthy of respect, or even that oneself is actually, potentially loveable. So perhaps we can revise this first criterion a bit, to recognize that the extreme behavior is a sign of disorder if it stems, on some level, from a denial or distortion of reality.

The second fundamental criterion for a personality disorder is that the associated extreme behavioral pattern causes major problems for the person *or* for others. A personality disorder typically—not always—causes some degree of suffering for the person who has it, which may include anxiety, depression, and confusion. But in the case of several disorders, many and perhaps most of the associated problems are suffered not so much by the affected person, but by those—such as spouses, employers, and (former) friends—who must deal with the results

---

[4] No.

(Heim & Westen, 2005; Yudofsky, 2005). For example, an acquaintance with antisocial personality disorder may blithely steal your money, and while this is a problem for you, it is not really a problem for the acquaintance—unless he gets caught.

Social, Stable, and Ego-Syntonic

Personality disorders have three other characteristics, which, although not as fundamental as the two just discussed, are generally viewed as part of the pattern. First, personality disorders are *social*; they manifest in interactions with other people. Alone on a desert island, it would be difficult to exhibit anything symptomatic of a personality disorder. After all, how can you be inflexible in your relations with a palm tree? How can you misperceive the intentions of a coconut? Other people are required for the full expression of many psychological symptoms.

> How can you misperceive the intentions of a coconut?

Second, personality disorders are, by the usual definition, *stable*. They may first become visible in adolescence or even childhood and persist throughout life (DeClercq, 2018). Change can occur, but generally the time scale is years rather than weeks or months (Zanarini, 2008), and improvement, when it happens, is generally associated with increases in psychological maturity (Wright, Pincus, & Lenzenweger, 2011). Personality disorders are about as stable as personality itself which, as we saw in Chapter 7, is pretty stable (Durbin & Klein, 2006; Ferguson, 2010). This stability contrasts with more serious psychiatric disorders, which may come and go through acute phases and stages of remission much like other medical conditions. Less extreme maladaptive patterns of thought, feeling, and behavior that turn out to be temporary—the familiar combination of anxiety and hostility sometimes exhibited in adolescence, for example—also are generally not considered personality disorders. Because personality disorders are stable, they are (pretty much by definition) difficult to change through therapeutic intervention or any other means (Ferguson, 2010).

Third, and relatedly, personality disorders can be **ego-syntonic**, which means the people who have them do not think anything is wrong. People who suffer from other kinds of mental disorder generally experience their symptoms of confusion, depression, or anxiety as **ego-dystonic** afflictions of which they would like to be cured. For a surprising number of people with personality disorders, in contrast, their symptoms feel like normal and valued aspects of who they are, and they even may rate disorder-related traits as likable (Lamkin, Maples-Keller & Miller, 2018)!

Individuals with the attributes of the antisocial or narcissistic personality disorders, in particular, typically do not think they have a problem. They are more likely to see a disorder in the people who have problems with *them*. And the problems they cause for others may be as serious, or even more serious, than the problems they cause for themselves (Yudofsky, 2005).

This last characteristic implies, again, that therapists who treat personality disorders have a tough hill to climb. My university operates an assistance program that is intended, among other purposes, to help employees who have psychological problems that interfere with their work. When I was chair of my department, I went to a presentation by the director of this program. He begged any supervisor making a referral to *please* call him first and let him know why. He was having difficulties because employees would suddenly appear at his office. He would ask them what the problem was, and they would reply, "I don't know; everything is fine; for some reason I was sent here." Individuals with personality disorders say things like that surprisingly often, even while causing havoc for themselves and the people around them.

THE MAJOR PERSONALITY DISORDERS

The traditional section of *DSM-5* (like the previous *DSM-IV*) lists 10 major disorders that describe patterns of personality so extreme that they can cause serious problems. They are organized into three *clusters* that are named, not particularly helpfully, Clusters A, B, and C. Cluster A disorders are characterized by odd or eccentric patterns of thinking, including the *schizotypal*, *schizoid*, and *paranoid* personality disorders. Cluster B includes impulsive and erratic patterns of behavior, including the *histrionic*, *narcissistic*, *antisocial*, and *borderline* personality disorders. These are the disorders that tend to be most stable—that change the least—over time (Durbin & Klein, 2006). Finally, Cluster C comprises disorders characterized by anxious and avoidant emotional styles, including the *dependent*, *avoidant*, and *obsessive-compulsive* personality disorders.

A more useful way to think about personality disorders is in terms of the basic beliefs, attitudes and behaviors associated with each one. The pioneering psychologist Aaron Beck and his colleagues (Beck, Freeman, & Davis, 2004) view most of the disorders as characterized by (1) a fundamentally wrong idea that the person has somehow made the foundation of how he or she views the world, and (2) a strategy or style of behavior for dealing with the world that results from this wrong idea. For example, people suffering from dependent personality disorder hold the basic belief that "I am helpless" and as a result attempt to attach themselves to people they think will take care of them. Two of the disorders are explained a little differently because borderline personality disorder is characterized more by chaotic thinking than by any particular thought and, similarly, schizotypal disorder is associated with peculiar thinking in general rather than any specific idea. A summary of how this approach explains each of the 10 classic disorders is shown in **Table 17.1**. Cognitive-behavioral therapy is largely based on this system; its goal is to work with the client to change the mistaken core belief

Table 17.1	BELIEFS, THOUGHT PATTERNS AND BEHAVIORAL STYLES ASSOCIATED WITH THE TRADITIONAL PERSONALITY DISORDERS	
Personality Disorder	**Belief or Thought Pattern**	**Behavioral Strategy or Style**
Dependent	"I am helpless"	Attachment
Avoidant	"I may get hurt"	Avoidance
Paranoid	"People are dangerous"	Wariness
Narcissistic	"I am special"	Self-aggrandizement
Histrionic	"I need to impress"	Dramatics
Obsessive-compulsive	"I must not err"	Perfectionism
Antisocial	"Others are to be taken"	Attack
Schizoid	"I need plenty of space"	Isolation
Borderline	Confused thinking and chaotic emotions	Disorganized and unpredictable behavior
Schizotypal	Peculiar thoughts	Odd actions

Source: Adapted from: Beck, A.T., Freeman, A., & Davis, D. (2004). *Cognitive Therapy of Personality Disorders (2nd edition).* New York: Guilford Press. Table 2.1, p. 21.

or thinking style and thereby improve the pattern of behavior that is causing so many problems.

In the newer, research-based section of the *DSM-5*, four of the classic disorders have been deleted, along with the clustering scheme. In the views of the researchers who prepared the new list, four previously listed disorders have not proved to be sufficiently coherent, common, or distinct from the other disorders to be useful diagnoses. These are (or were) the *schizoid* (asocial), *histrionic* (overly expressive), *dependent* (overly reliant on others), and *paranoid* (overly suspicious) personality disorders.

In the sections that follow, I summarize the six remaining disorders that survived this cut. But I still draw on their traditional descriptions, because they are not incompatible with the new descriptions and include more information and vivid detail. The chapter then summarizes the way in which personality disorders can be organized according to relevant personality traits, describes some of the changes in the new approach to psychological diagnosis, and, finally, concludes the discussion by considering the meaning and implications of labeling people with personality disorders.

Schizotypal Personality Disorder

Some people are idiosyncratic; they experience odd thoughts, have seemingly strange ideas, and behave unconventionally. They may have superstitious beliefs; they may actively avoid black cats or believe they have ESP or the ability to see the future. They may wear odd and unkempt clothing, and espouse unique ideologies or "theories of everything." They may also experience discomfort in relating to other people—their odd actions might be somewhat off-putting, for one thing—and have particular difficulty in close relationships. None of these characteristics is especially rare and, taken one at a time, may not pose serious problems. But when the pattern becomes extreme, the individual may be characterized as having **schizotypal personality disorder.**

At its extreme, this disorder can dangerously approach *schizophrenia*, a serious psychotic condition characterized by major distortions of reality, jumbled thinking, and even hallucinations; indeed, some psychologists believe that schizotypal personality disorder should be grouped with it, rather than with the personality disorders.[5] According to the *DSM-5*, schizotypal personality disorder has a prevalence ranging around the world from about 0.6 percent (in a Norwegian sample) to 3.9 percent or 4.6 percent (in two different U.S. surveys). The disorder appears to be slightly more common in men, and tends to be stable throughout life.

Narcissistic Personality Disorder

Narcissism is a special case of a personality trait that shades over into a personality disorder. We saw in Chapter 6 that while people high in this trait are sometimes annoying in the long run, they often make an excellent first impression and come across as extraverted, confident, and even charismatic. Indeed, their exaggerated self-esteem can, within limits, be useful (von Hippel & Trivers, 2011). The personality disorder goes beyond these limits and is much darker, associated not only with a wide range of exploitative and damaging behaviors, but also emotional instability and an unpleasant emotional life (J. D. Miller & Campbell, 2008).

The individual with **narcissistic personality disorder (NPD)** believes, sometimes against all evidence, that she is a superior being, and expects recognition for this, walking around all day with visions of unlimited wealth, absolute power, flawless beauty, or perfect love. She does not just expect the admiration of others; she needs it; so she may maneuver to evoke it. The tactics are not necessarily subtle. The narcissist may say things like, "Don't you love my dress?" or "How about my great new car?" or simply brag about her accomplishments, wealth, friends, or appearance. She does not seem to have a clue about how obvious these contrivances generally are, and happily accepts the most transparent kinds of flattery. Tell the person with NPD that her clothes, car, accomplishments, or haircut are the greatest you have ever seen. She will agree; you will not be suspected of insincerity.

---

[5] The film *A Beautiful Mind*, starring Russell Crowe, told the true story—with Hollywood's usual degree of poetic license—of famous mathematician John Nash, who suffered from full-blown schizophrenia, including complex hallucinations of an imaginary best friend and a top-secret relationship with a spy agency.

The person with NPD expects special treatment. Rules apply to other people, as does the need to stand in line, wait one's turn, or be judged by consistent standards. Because of this sense of entitlement, he feels justified in taking advantage of others. After all, the purpose is merely to get what he deserves anyway. He may blithely lie, cheat, or simply leave the hard work to be done by other people. If your roommate has NPD, he will expect you to wash the dirty dishes. He has more important things to do. You don't.

This exploitation is accompanied by a lack of empathy, because he is the only person on Earth who really matters. He assumes that everything about him must be of great interest, and may offer lengthy and inappropriately detailed monologues about his activities or feelings. At the same time, the person with NPD can be shockingly inconsiderate of the feelings of others.

People with NPD are not generally difficult to spot. Their arrogance gives them away. They belittle others and brag about themselves. They are rude to service people, seeming to revel in their small (and temporary) degree of social superiority over waiters and cashiers. They are boastful about small (or nonexistent) accomplishments, and sarcastic and condescending about the virtues or accomplishments of anybody else.

There is something pitiable about people with NPD and the related pattern of traits known as "entitlement" (Grubbs & Exline, 2016). Although they feel they are especially deserving of everything they want, this very feeling can make them vulnerable to disappointment, ego threat, and a sense that people aren't treating them the way they deserve. This experience, in turn, can make them angry and emotionally upset.

But at the same time, people with NPD can be dangerous. The very characteristics that can make them attractive at first sight are the ones that cause the most problems in the long run[6] (Back, Schmukle, & Egloff, 2010; Paulhus, 1998). As one experienced therapist writes,

> Sadly, the combination of burning ambition and a willingness to distort the truth in people with narcissistic personality disorder can lead them to acquire substantial power and high position. These individuals harm many innocent people along the route to their personal aggrandizement. (Yudofsky, 2005, p. 126)

A fascinating, recently declassified psychological study of Adolf Hitler, commissioned by the OSS (the precursor to the CIA) during World War II and written by the pioneering personality psychologist Henry Murray (mentioned in Chapters 4 and 6), describes Hitler as a textbook case of narcissistic personality disorder

---

[6] Recall (from Chapter 16) that narcissism is part of the "dark triad" of traits often identified as particularly dangerous in leaders.

(Murray, 1943). (Interestingly, this study was written before the formal identification of this disorder in the first *DSM*.) Apparently, being a narcissist is not a bar to becoming powerful, and other infamous figures such as Mussolini and Stalin have also been characterized by this syndrome. The sense of self-importance and lack of empathy, coupled with impressive political skills, seems to have made these individuals utterly ruthless—and successful—in their drive for power. The results were disastrous for everyone around them (and ultimately, in the cases of Hitler and Mussolini, for themselves).[7]

Narcissistic personality disorder is infamous among clinical psychologists for being difficult if not impossible to treat because, more than any other personality disorder, it's ego-syntonic. People with NPD actually have some insight that they come across as arrogant and that people like them less over time (Carlson, Vazire, & Oltmanns, 2011); they still prefer to remain the way they are. Others may wish them to change; they have little or no desire to do so.

Estimates of the prevalence of this disorder are all over the map. The *DSM-5* quotes a range somewhere between 0 percent of the population (which seems low to me) and 6.2 percent (which seems awfully high).

Antisocial Personality Disorder

Some people are less honest than others, but when deceit and manipulation become core aspects of an individual's way of dealing with the world, he may be diagnosed with **antisocial personality disorder.** This dangerous pattern includes behaviors such as vandalism, harassment, theft, and a wide variety of illegal activities such as burglary and drug dealing. People with this disorder are impulsive and engage in risky behaviors such as reckless driving, drug abuse, and dangerous sexual practices. They typically are irritable, aggressive, and irresponsible. The damage they do to others bothers them not one whit; they rationalize (see Chapter 10) that life is unfair; the world is full of suckers; and if you don't take what you want whenever you can, then you are a sucker, too. Children unlucky enough to come under the care of someone with this disorder are at high risk for neglect or abuse. A wide variety of negative outcomes may accompany this disorder, including unemployment, divorce, drug addiction, imprisonment, murder, and suicide.

Antisocial personality disorder is sometimes confused with the trait of psychopathy, which was mentioned in Chapter 9 (Mealey, 1995), but it's importantly different (Hare, 1996). Psychopaths are emotionally cold, they disregard social norms, and they are manipulative and often cunning. Most psychopaths meet the criteria for antisocial personality disorder, but the reverse is not true. Antisocial and even criminal behaviors have many sources; psychopathy is only one of them, in some people.

---

[7] All three caused the deaths of millions of innocent people. Hitler committed suicide, and Mussolini was shot and then his body was hanged in the town square. But Stalin died peacefully in bed.

Figure 17.1 **Ted Bundy** This sadistic killer was an extreme example of antisocial personality disorder. His "normal," unthreatening physical appearance helped him to lure his victims.

When combined with psychopathy, antisocial personality disorder can be especially dangerous. Serial killer Ted Bundy used his clean-cut good looks and well-developed social skills, combined with a fake cast on his arm, to persuade young women near college campuses to help him load a sofa into his van. After his victim climbed inside he would slam the door and drive off to a secluded spot where he could abuse, torture, and eventually kill her. In general, people like this have an eye for people who are "nonsuspicious, kindly, and generous" (Yudofsky, 2005, p. 219), and are ruthless about exploiting them. It can be difficult to protect yourself from antisocial psychopaths, but one experienced therapist recommends that you "pay attention to your feelings," especially feelings like *"At first I felt uncomfortable, but I couldn't quite figure out why"* (Yudofsky, 2005, p. 220, italics in original). In other words, listen to your gut.

The *DSM-5*'s summary includes an interesting discussion of the apparent association of antisocial personality disorder with low economic status and urban settings—in other words, it's largely (but not solely) a disorder of the poor and criminal. This observation raises several questions. Is it possible that, when separated from psychopathy, antisocial personality disorder merely describes a behavioral style that is adaptive or even necessary in certain settings? If so, should it still be considered a psychological disorder? Should a person with this disorder who commits a crime be considered not really a criminal but only ill? I will return to this issue near the end of the chapter, but this is a good time to begin thinking seriously about the disadvantages, as well as advantages, of having a psychological label for every pattern of socially undesirable behavior.

Estimates of the prevalence of this disorder range from 0.2 percent to 3.3 percent, and I sincerely hope the lower number is more accurate. By all accounts, antisocial personality disorder is much more common in men than in women.

Borderline Personality Disorder

From day to day with different people, and over time with the same people, most individuals feel and act pretty consistently. This fundamental fact was discussed in detail (and debated, to some extent) in Chapter 4. Predictability makes it possible to deal with others in a reasonable way, and gives each of us a sense of individual identity. But some people are less consistent than others, and have thoughts, emotions, and behaviors that are in flux and unpredictable even to them. When this pattern becomes extreme, a person may be diagnosed with **borderline personality disorder,** which is the most severe one on the list. It is characterized by unstable and confused behavior, a poor sense of identity, and patterns of self-harm that range from self-defeating behaviors to self-mutilation to suicide. Their chaotic thoughts, emotions, and behaviors make persons suffering from this disorder very difficult for others to "read"—they would be considered very low on the dimension of judgability considered in Chapter 5 (Flury, Ickes, & Schweinle, 2008).

Borderline personality disorder (BPD) entails so many problems for the affected person that nobody doubts that it is, at the very least, on the "border-line" with severe psychopathology.[8] Its hallmark is emotional instability. The person's mood can change rapidly from one moment to the next, and he may seem on the verge of going to pieces (Gunderson, 1984). The foundation of the disorder, according to some writers, is a sort of "emotional hemophilia," in which a reaction, once stimulated, cannot be stanched—the individual emotionally "bleeds to death" (Kreisman & Straus, 1989, p. 8). Another prominent researcher writes that an individual with this disorder is "the psychological equivalent of [a] third-degree burn patient [with] . . . no emotional skin. Even the slightest touch or movement can cause immense suffering" (Linehan, 1993, p. 69).

According to the *DSM-5*, suicide attempts are common among people with BPD, and eventually 8 percent to 10 percent do kill themselves (American Psychiatric Association, 2013, p. 664). If this statistic is even close to correct, then BPD is a dangerous affliction indeed, comparable to the most threatening physical diseases. Even among nonsuicidal people with BPD, self-mutilation is common and may include compulsively "cutting"[9] (with fingernails or knives) parts of the body including the hands, arms, and even genitals. The reasons for this behavior are far from clear; possibilities range from the rather psychoanalytic-sounding speculation that people with BPD feel guilty and are punishing themselves, to the idea that they are so emotionally disconnected that they must hurt themselves to know they are alive. It might also be a means of socially bonding with friends with similar disorders, communicating distress, or even demonstrating strength (especially in prison populations) (Hooley & Franklin, 2017). Perhaps the most plausible explanation comes from the description of the inner life of persons with this disorder as characterized by "emotional cascades," which are "vicious cycles of intense rumination and negative affect" that lead to extreme suffering (Selby, Anestis, Bender, & Joiner, 2009, p. 375). Behaviors such as using fingernail clippers to pull off

---

[8] Some writers claim that this is why it's called "borderline," because it lies between the less serious *neuroses* and the more serious *psychoses,* but the actual origin of the term is obscure.

[9] I put this word in quotes because it's almost a technical term; tell a clinical psychologist that someone is "cutting" (or is a "cutter"), and he or she will immediately understand what you are talking about.

slices of skin (Cloud, 2008) may interrupt the process. Several studies support the conclusion that the main reason people engage in gruesome self-harm is "to alleviate negative emotions" (Klonsky, 2011, p. 1981; see also Klonsky & Muehlenkamp, 2007). Consider what this means: The feelings people with BPD are seeking to avoid must hurt even worse.

A major and immediate challenge for a therapist working with someone suffering from BPD is to stop this cycle of self-harm. One suggestion—a serious suggestion!—is to teach patients other means of distraction from their emotional state, such as Sudoku. Other possibly useful therapeutic approaches include drawing the patient's attention to the physical pain and social disapproval that results from cutting, and discouraging communities of BPD patients from communicating with each other about how and when they harm themselves (Hooley & Franklin, 2017).

Many people with BPD literally do not know who they are. They may have great difficulty understanding how they appear to others, and be confused about their values, career goals, and even sexual identity. They do not understand their own actions—cutters, for example, can say almost nothing meaningful about why they do it—and those with BPD may try to be social chameleons, avoiding behavioral choices and fading into the background by doing what everybody else seems to be doing. Recall from Chapter 15 that one function of the self is to provide a marker on an internal map that says "you are here." People with BPD have lost the map.

The interpersonal relationships of people with BPD are confusing, chaotic, noisy, unpredictable, and unstable. In part, this is because they are prone to *splitting*, a term you may recall from object relations theory (described in Chapter 11) that refers to the tendency to view other people as either all good or all bad. Thus, a new relationship may be perceived as perfect, the best ever. Then, the first disappointment leads the person to conclude that the new partner is hopelessly thoughtless and cruel. These two extreme views, as Freud would have noted, have the same underlying dynamic. In both cases, the person with BPD is unable to handle the complex reality that people have a mix of good and bad characteristics, so she oversimplifies by jumping to one extreme evaluation or the other.

All of the personality disorders are rather mixed bags of indicators, and BPD may be the most mixed of all. It is difficult to find a coherent, common thread among its characteristics, which may be why the label "borderline" is so descriptively unhelpful. Some psychologists, indeed, have suggested that this category is too diffuse and should be abandoned. But although other disorders were eliminated in the new system in the *DSM-5*, as we have seen, this one remains. The confusing and mixed-up nature of BPD may be the whole point. The pattern of emotion and behavior of someone with this disorder is to have no pattern. The personality itself is confused and disorganized, and the results can be disastrous and even fatal.

> The pattern of emotion and behavior of someone with borderline personality disorder is to have no pattern.

A huge amount of research attention has been paid to BPD in recent years, and some progress has been made. New theories have been proposed about its origins. One theory is that BPD arises when a genetic risk factor combines with an early family environment that fails to teach children how to understand and regulate their emotions. Children are put at risk when their "expressions of emotion are . . . rejected by the family and life's problems are oversimplified" (Crowell, Beauchaine, & Linehan, 2009, p. 504). Another promising suggestion is that the disorder stems from problems with the *endogenous opioid system*, which regulates the body's natural painkillers (the endorphins described in Chapter 8). "Frantic efforts to avoid abandonment, frequent and risky sexual contacts, and attention-seeking behavior"—all hallmarks of BPD—may be attempts to stimulate this system and thereby feel better (Bandelow, Schmahl, Falkai, & Wedekind, 2010, p. 623).

The most encouraging development is in therapies that might actually help. A technique called *dialectical behavioral therapy* (Linehan, 1993) teaches skills for emotional self-control. In individual and group sessions, the therapist and client closely examine past episodes of inappropriate emotional reactions and analyze how similar situations could be handled better next time. In a sense, it's basic training in how to deal with emotions—a skill people with this disorder somehow never learned.

The *DSM-5* estimates that about 2 percent of the population has this disorder, and about 75 percent of those diagnosed are women.

Avoidant Personality Disorder

Everybody feels inadequate sometimes. Sometimes we do things we shouldn't, sometimes we fail at what we attempt, and sometimes we are rejected. Moreover, none of these experiences is pleasant, and everybody seeks to avoid them. Fear of failure or rejection can lead to patterns of behavior such as shyness, and, in moderation, such patterns are both common and normal. When taken to an extreme, the result may be **avoidant personality disorder**. The fundamental problem experienced by individuals with this disorder is that their fear of failure, criticism, or rejection may lead them to avoid normal activities of school, work, and interactions with others. They expect the absolute worst: criticism, contempt, and rejection. They cannot join a group activity or have a relationship without constant reassurance that they will be uncritically accepted, and they may actively inhibit any emotional expression because they fear being mocked and rejected. As a result, others cannot get close to them, and their interpersonal world is constricted. It is safer to stay at home with the blinds pulled and the phone turned off.

This withdrawal from contact with others is very sad because, according to clinical psychologists who have studied people with this disorder, they really have deep cravings for affection and social acceptance, and they may spend much of their solitary time fantasizing about how much fun it would be to have friends or a lover. They may have trouble in their careers as well, because they try to avoid the meetings and social functions that are important for success in the business world.

A recent survey estimates that about 2.4 percent of the population suffer (and here the word *suffer* does seem appropriate) from this disorder, and its prevalence appears to be about the same in women as in men. In some people, the disorder may begin as severe shyness in childhood and gradually improve as they grow into later adulthood.

Obsessive-Compulsive Personality Disorder

It can be nice when the world is orderly and structured, and everybody follows the rules. Some people feel this need for order and structure more strongly than others (just peek into some of your professors' offices if you want to see how widely this trait can vary). Within the normal range, being an orderly, structured person is generally a good thing, and this book relates many examples of the advantages of being highly conscientious, which (as we shall see later in this chapter) include good health and long life. But even this trait can go too far (Carter, Guan, Maples, Williamson, & Miller, 2015). The problematic extreme is called **obsessive-compulsive personality disorder (OCPD)**. People with OCPD are bound by rituals and rules, can be severely judgmental of others, and are often miserly and stubborn. The individual who has OCPD resembles, in many ways, the type of person that Freud called the anal character (Chapter 10). Above all else, the person with OCPD lacks a sense of proportion, the big picture that allows one to judge when rules fail to apply to a given situation or when a particular detail just doesn't matter very much.

People with OCPD are often stereotypical workaholics. They cannot take a weekend or even an evening off because they "have so much to do." And yet, strangely, they seldom seem to get much done. It does seem that the amount of time people spend working correlates only loosely with how much they accomplish, and while people with OCPD may work long hours, they often don't have much to show for it.

People with OCPD may be compulsively unable to throw anything away, even things that have no possible use or sentimental value. They become anxious about discarding anything because they cannot escape feeling that they might need it someday, no matter how absurd the prospect is. There are famous cases of people with OCPD collecting huge piles of newspapers that fill their homes, unable to throw away even the sports section from 11 years ago, because they haven't had a chance to read it yet.

"Is the Itsy Bitsy Spider obsessive-compulsive?"

This idea of the person with OCPD as a packrat is an interesting characteristic, in part because it seems to contradict some of the others, such as being compulsively neat and clean. This is where Freud comes in, though not through the pages of the *DSM*, which never mentions him, not in any of its editions. You may recall (from Chapter 10) that Freud believed opposites in character and behavior were always equivalent at a deep level, and the anal character is a good example. Anal characters might be compulsively neat *or* compulsively messy; the underlying dynamics in both cases are the same. The heaps of junk that fill the houses of some people with OCPD, and the sterile, bare, sparkling surfaces in the nearly empty houses of other people with OCPD may result from the same underlying psychological dynamics.

A major barrier to treatment is that, although people with OCPD are compulsively driven and may suffer from extreme anxiety if things do not go exactly their way, in some cases OCPD may be ego-syntonic. It is true that people with this disorder are—relatively speaking—less impaired in their daily functioning than are people with some of the other personality disorders (Skodol et al., 2002). Indeed, strange as it may sound, some people with OCPD claim they *like* being that way, and, to a degree, the traits associated with OCPD can be useful. There is something to be said for a surgeon, an accountant, or a data analyst who checks everything several times, whether it is really necessary or not. Certain kinds of mistakes become less likely. On the other hand, some of the compulsions that often go with OCPD—such as obsessive worrying about things that don't really matter or are highly unlikely to happen, needing to turn back home several times to check whether the stove was left on, and bodily tics and habits such as compulsively picking at one's scalp—are unpleasant symptoms most people would be happy to get rid of.

Indeed, OCPD is sometimes confused with the similarly labeled *obsessive-compulsive disorder (OCD)*. OCD is a severe anxiety disorder characterized by compulsive behaviors that can range from repetitive hand-washing to bizarre rituals of speech or action (e.g., needing to touch every surface with which one comes into contact exactly 11 times before moving on). People suffering from OCD often have fearful obsessions and need the rituals to quell them. OCPD is different because it generally does not include such specific compulsions, but it can be more far-reaching because it may affect all areas of a person's life. Interestingly, OCD may actually be more treatable than OCPD (Foa, 2004), in part because people with OCD generally are aware that their fears, unwanted thoughts and uncontrollable actions are unreasonable and would like to get rid of them, whereas people with OCPD are more likely to believe that "their way is the 'right and best' way" (Van Noppen, 2010, p. 1).

According to *DSM-5*, estimates of the prevalence of OCPD range from 2.1 percent to 7.9 percent, making it one of the more common personality disorders. Some studies suggest that antidepressant drugs such as fluoxetine and other specific serotonin reuptake inhibitors (SSRIs) of the sort discussed in Chapter 8 can effectively treat OCPD (Piccinelli, Pini, Bellantuono, & Wilkinson, 1995). This finding hints at the nature of OCPD and the degree to which it may be fundamentally driven by anxiety, depression, and general unhappiness.

ORGANIZING AND DIAGNOSING DISORDERS WITH THE *DSM-5*

The personality disorders just described appear in both the old and new approaches included in the *DSM-5*. However, an updated method for organizing the disorders has been added, and this new scheme is almost certainly the wave of the future. It varies from the traditional approach in a couple of major ways. First, the list of discrete disorders is shorter by almost half; as we have seen, the new list maintains only the antisocial, avoidant, borderline, narcissistic, obsessive-compulsive, and schizotypal disorders; everything else is categorized as a "personality disorder—trait specified." But second and more importantly, it tries to move beyond placing disorders into discrete categories, such as the unhelpful "clusters" of the old version, and to instead recognize that psychological maladjustment is more a matter of degree than of kind (Clark & Watson, 1999a; Krueger & Eaton, 2010).

The Bad Five

The new system in the *DSM-5* organizes personality disorders in terms of five major domains of traits that are more than reminiscent of the Big Five that we have seen many times in this book. They could be (but aren't) called the "Bad Five." Like the original Big Five, each of these trait domains also has facets that generally, but not always, go together (see **Table 17.2**). The traits are

1. **Negative Affectivity,** a tendency to feel negative emotions such as anxiety, depression, and suspicion
2. **Detachment,** a tendency to withdraw from and to avoid emotional contacts with other people
3. **Antagonism,** including deceitfulness, grandiosity, callousness, and manipulativeness; you may recognize some of the hallmarks of narcissism here.
4. **Disinhibition,** characterized by careless and impulsive behavior (the opposite of this trait, compulsivity, involves a kind of rigid overcontrol and perfectionism that can be almost equally maladaptive)
5. **Psychoticism,** a tendency to have bizarre thoughts or experiences, and to exhibit eccentric behavior

Table 17.2	THE "BAD FIVE" PERSONALITY TRAITS AND THEIR FACETS

Trait (vs. its opposite)	Facets
Negative Affectivity (vs. Emotional Stability)	Emotional lability (changeability)
	Anxiousness
	Separation insecurity (fear at being apart from significant others)
	Submissiveness
	Hostility
	Perseveration (persistence at ineffective behaviors)
	Depressivity (feeling down and miserable)
	Suspiciousness
	Restricted emotionality
Detachment (vs. Extraversion)	Withdrawal
	Intimacy avoidance
	Anhedonia (inability to experience pleasure)
	Depressivity (feeling down and miserable)
	Restricted emotionality
	Suspiciousness
Antagonism (vs. Agreeableness)	Manipulativeness
	Deceitfulness
	Grandiosity
	Attention seeking
	Callousness
	Hostility
Disinhibition (vs. Conscientiousness)	Irresponsibility
	Impulsivity
	Distractibility
	Risk taking
	Carelessness (vs. rigid perfectionism)
Psychoticism (vs. Lucidity)	Unusual beliefs and experiences
	Eccentricity
	Odd or unusual thought processes

Source: Adapted from *DSM-5* (American Psychiatric Association, 2013), pp. 779–780.

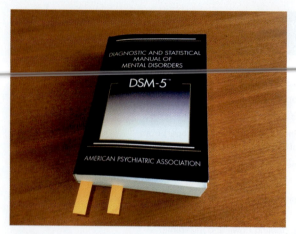

Figure 17.2 The *DSM-5* The bookmarks indicate the location of the two different conflicting sections on personality disorder.

Notice how negative affectivity is akin to neuroticism in the Big Five; detachment is the extreme low end of extraversion; antagonism is the extreme low end of agreeableness; disinhibition is the extreme low end of conscientiousness; and psychoticism is the extreme high end of some aspects of openness to experience. This correspondence highlights the view, becoming ever more widespread in clinical and personality psychology, that the differences between normal and abnormal personality are not sharp or distinct, but lie along a continuum (further implications will be considered later in this chapter).

Diagnosis

The new section of the *DSM-5* also describes a new way to go about psychological diagnosis. Rather than counting up the number of indicators that are present or absent and making a yes or no diagnostic decision, which was the old system, a clinical psychologist or psychiatrist is advised to take the following steps:

1. Assess whether or not the client's "personality functioning" is seriously impaired and, if so, rate the degree of dysfunction.
2. Assess whether or not at least one of the six defined types of personality disorder is present.
3. Assess the degree to which the client is characterized by each of the five maladaptive personality traits.

This three-step assessment is intended to provide a specific description of the client's psychological difficulty and the degree to which he is experiencing problems, but avoids sorting him into a single diagnostic bin. Clinical psychologists currently are hotly debating whether this will actually work in daily practice,[10] and we probably won't know until it begins to be tried on a large scale. Many front-line clinicians are already happy with the new system (Morey, Skodol, & Oldham, 2014). The U.S. government is definitely on the side of a more progressive approach. The National Institute of Mental Health, which funds a vast amount of research on psychopathology, has announced that new grant proposals should

---

[10] Among other worries, practicing clinicians are concerned about how this change will affect the way they bill for service.

avoid the traditional categories and use a more dimensional approach, with a particular focus on biological aspects of mental disorder (Kruger, Hopwood, Wright, & Markson, 2014). Money talks, so this statement will be influential. Stay tuned.

PERSONALITY AND DISORDER

Amidst much debate, clinical psychology, psychiatry, and the successive editions of the *DSM* have displayed an increasing amount of insight and imagination as they formulate descriptions of many psychological disorders. This very success and the resulting proliferation of diagnoses raise issues concerning the pitfalls of describing so many behaviors as pathological, the nature of mental health, the pros and cons of labeling in general, and the fine line between normal and abnormal personality.

Pathologizing

Personality disorders describe bad ways to be. Does this mean that bad people have personality disorders, by definition? For example, some psychologists have proposed that "pathological bias," such as extreme racism, homophobia, or other strong feelings about certain groups, should be defined as a personality disorder. One writer has noted that if this proposal succeeds, "perpetrators of hate crimes could become candidates for treatment, and physicians would become arbiters on how to distinguish 'ordinary prejudice' from pathological bias" (Vedantam, 2005, p. A01). Many personality disorders include patterns of socially undesirable, illegal, or immoral behavior. If certain people lie, cheat, steal, or even murder, should we refrain from punishing or perhaps even judging them because they suffer from antisocial personality disorder (which remains in the new system, by the way), and therefore are not accountable for those actions?

If you think I am going to answer this question, you are in for a disappointment. The issue is an eternal conundrum in the foggy area where psychology meets moral reasoning, and has been a long-standing dilemma in philosophy, religion, and law. No resolution is in sight. Some people are sure that the answer to this question is Yes, because it is absurd, pointless, and wrong to punish someone for having a psychological disorder. Others are sure the answer is No, because some behaviors should be punished regardless of their psychological (or even physical) cause. The truth, as always, lies somewhere in between—and, also as always, resists quick summary and easy understanding.

A further pitfall in pathologizing behaviors—describing them as the result of mental illness—is that it is entirely too easy. Critics of the old *DSM-IV* enjoyed pointing out that it included a label for everything from compulsive gambling to coffee nerves (Davis, 1997). It described so many behavioral patterns as

> If everything is a mental illness,
> then nothing is a mental illness.

forms of mental illness that it threatened to under-mine the meaning of the concept altogether. If everything is a mental illness, then nothing is a mental illness.

Mental Health

No matter how long and detailed a list of disorders might be, it does not tell us much about the nature of mental health. This omission is precisely what motivates the positive psychology movement, focused on human strengths and virtues, that was discussed in Chapter 12. Positive psychology aims to move beyond an exclusive focus on fixing what's wrong with people and instead promote meaningful and happy living. One way to define the healthy personality is in terms of the Big Five personality traits and their facets. In one large study, a group of experts agreed that the ideally psychologically healthy person has high levels of openness to feelings, positive emotions, and straightforwardness (non-pretentious and honest). At the same time, the ideally healthy person has low levels of depression and anxiety (neuroticism). In a sample of more than 3,000 individuals, people described in this way were found to be psychologically well-adjusted, optimistic, and self-controlled. They weren't aggressive, mean, or exploitative, and they handled stress well (Bleidorn et al., 2019). This is useful to know, because improving mental health requires an understanding of normal and adaptive personality, not just mental illness and personality disorders.[11]

Labeling

Labels are always a little bit misleading, and sometimes they are seriously misleading. For example, it is important to avoid simply describing people we don't like as having personality disorders, tempting though that may be. Such a description has a very good chance of being unfair. It can shut off rather than promote further understanding, because once a person has been labeled as mentally ill, we may no longer feel that we have to take seriously her feelings, outlook, and even rights, or to empathize with her point of view. A label is not an explanation, and the conclusion that someone has a personality disorder raises more questions than it answers.

On the other hand, the labels *can* be useful. If you come across someone who exhibits one or more of the characteristics of a personality disorder, it might be wise to consider whether he or she might show some of the other symptoms as well. For example, if someone acts in a grandiose and arrogant manner (a sign of narcissistic personality disorder), it might pay to be wary of the possibility he could seek to take advantage of you. If somebody gives signs of being just a little too

---

[11] This seemingly obvious point is not accepted by everybody. The National Institute of Mental Health in the United States has had directors (including the current one, as of this writing) who believe, despite the name of their institute, that the research it supports should focus solely on alleviating mental illness.

impressed by the rule book and unable to adjust for the changing circumstances of real life (signs of obsessive-compulsive personality disorder), I would advise that you avoid at all costs putting her in charge of anything, or putting yourself in a position to take orders from her. And if someone you care about exhibits the emotional instability characteristic of borderline personality disorder, you might want to watch for indications that he might harm himself via drug addiction, eating disorders, cutting, or even suicide.

It might even be advisable to watch for signs of these disorders in yourself (although, as I discuss shortly, some of these attributes might sometimes be advantageous). If you catch yourself acting arrogantly, or following rules without regard to their purpose, or even harming yourself, this could be a warning to prevent further movement in a potentially dangerous direction. Thus, no matter how uncomfortable we may be about labeling people, it is still worthwhile to learn the basic characteristics of the major personality disorders (Yudofsky, 2005).

Finally, it must be acknowledged that, in the end, labels are absolutely necessary. There is simply no escaping them. When a psychiatrist or clinical psychologist records impressions of a patient, she must write *something*, so the more precise the labels, the better. Research, or even serious discussion, about mental illness would be completely impossible without words—labels—to refer to the different varieties that exist. Remember Funder's Third Law (Chapter 2), that something usually beats nothing: No matter how flawed they may be—and they are flawed—the labels in the *DSM-5* and its subsequent editions will persist until and unless something better comes along.

Normal and Abnormal

Although the issue used to be highly controversial, the modern research literature on personality disorders has come close to consensus about one conclusion: There is no sharp dividing line between psychopathology and normal variation (Boudreaux, 2016; L. A. Clark & Watson, 1999a; Furr & Funder, 1998; Hong & Paunonen, 2011; Krueger & Eaton, 2010; Krueger & Tackett, 2003; B. P. O'Connor, 2002; Trull & Durrett, 2005). Normal personality traits are associated with a wide range of psychopathologies (Kotov et al., 2010), and the special tests designed to measure abnormal personality may do no better a job, for this purpose, than the instruments designed for the normal range, such as those surveyed in Chapter 3 (Walton, Roberts, Krueger, Blonigen, & Hicks, 2008). One recent study found that judgments of several personality disorder-related traits made by friends and acquaintances converged nicely with self-reports of the Big Five traits related to the same disorders, as well as with behavior observed directly in the laboratory (Kaurin, Sauerberger & Funder, 2018).

One implication of the continuum between normality and abnormality is that you may have recognized people you know, and even yourself, in parts of the descriptions of personality disorders. Your acquaintances, or even you, may indeed check the stove twice before leaving the house, experience deep hurt when other people don't recognize an accomplishment, or have strange ideas sometimes. But it is important to remember that having a mild degree of a few characteristics does *not* imply that someone has a personality disorder.

Moreover, it is possible to think of each personality disorder as an exaggerated version of a trait that in the normal range can have some advantages (Oldham & Morris, 1995). For example, consider the person who is lovably unusual and idiosyncratic, has original, creative ideas, and generally marches to a different drummer: These fine tendencies overlap with elements of schizotypal personality disorder. An individual who is self-confident and proud has attributes that overlap with narcissistic personality, and so on.

An individual's personality is a complete package that cannot be separated tidily into good and bad parts.[12] Indeed, elements of some of the personality disorders may be cherished aspects of yourself! Remember Funder's First Law (Chapter 1) about great strengths often being great weaknesses, and vice versa? Perhaps your creative spark and original outlook are among the best things about you; it's just that occasionally this causes you to come off as a bit strange. Maybe you are valued for your perfectionism and attention to detail; only once in a while does this tendency go too far and annoy people. Your weaknesses may be part of your strengths; only when the characteristics are numerous, consistent, severe, and problematic should we speak about personality disorders.

There may be a little—just a little—of the personality disorders in all of us, and even people suffering from severe personality disorders probably have at least some sane, useful, and adaptive traits. This brings us back to the issue of normal behavioral variation and psychopathology. There is a difference, but the dividing line is neither sharp nor easy to find.

PHYSICAL HEALTH

The implications of personality for physical health may be even more important than its implications for mental health. After all, nobody ever died of a personality disorder—at least, not directly. But several aspects of personality have important relationships with illness, with healthy functioning, and with that ultimate health outcome, longevity.

Connections between Personality and Health

It is harder to do good research on the connections between personality and health than it might seem at first. One challenge is gathering good data. While assessing personality is not so difficult, thanks to the well-developed technology of testing

---

[12] Recall that the inability to appreciate this fact underlines the phenomenon of "splitting," which was discussed during the presentation of object relations theory in Chapter 11.

described in Chapter 3, assessing health is a different matter. Many studies use S-data measures in which people simply report how healthy they are or how good they feel. All the shortcomings of S data summarized in Chapter 2 apply. People may not really know or admit how healthy or unhealthy they are, or be unwilling to answer health questions truthfully on a questionnaire. Even worse, some of the questions on some personality tests also appear on health questionnaires! It is not uncommon to measure neuroticism, for example, with items such as "I feel bad all the time." Items like this also show up on health questionnaires, so some studies showing neuroticism to be related to health have results that are questionable, at best (Friedman & Kern, 2014).

An alternative, as we saw back in Chapter 2, is L data such as medical records. Some studies of personality and health use these records, but they are protected by layers of privacy laws and can be difficult to obtain. As a partial solution to this problem, at least one major study of personality and health focused on obtaining death certificates (Friedman & Martin, 2011). One nice thing about death certificates is that they are, in most jurisdictions, treated as public records. Another advantage is that death is an ultimate measure of physical well-being. As two experienced researchers noted, a person who has been issued a death certificate is, without question, "currently in terrible 'health'" (Friedman & Kern, 2014, p. 721).

One recent research program combined a focus on longevity with personality assessments that moved beyond self-reports, being based on peer ratings. In other words (the words of the researchers), the study examined whether "your friends know how long you will live" (Jackson et al., 2015). It turns out they do, to some extent. Between 1935 and 1938, the study gathered friends' ratings of the personalities of 600 people who were then in their mid-twenties, and checked to see who was still alive in 2013, more than 75 years later. The friends' ratings predicted longevity better than self-ratings did. Men rated by their friends as more conscientious and open to experience tended to live longer, as did women who had been rated, years earlier, as more emotionally stable and agreeable.

> A person who has been issued a death certificate is, without question, currently in terrible "health."

These are interesting findings, but what do they mean? A further challenge is explaining the connections between personality and health that data like these reveal. Correlations between personality traits and self-reports of "feeling good" may reflect how personality affects mood rather than physical health. Correlations between personality traits and *biomarkers*, biological indicators related to health outcomes, may not actually reveal connections between personality and health. For example, personality traits have been related to cortisol levels (see Chapter 8), indicators of immune function, and vagal tone (a measure of activity of the parasympathetic nervous system; see Chapter 8), but the connections between these traits and actual health outcomes—such as functioning well in life and simply staying alive—are often less clear. Researchers have also found intriguing connections between personality traits and specific diseases, but these connections, too, are difficult to explain. For example, one major study found that in later life low conscientiousness was associated with a greater risk of stroke, high blood pressure, diabetes and arthritis; neuroticism was associated with lung disease, heart disease, and arthritis; and low openness was associated with stroke, heart disease, high blood pressure and arthritis (Weston, Hill, & Jackson, 2015). But why? It is undeniably important when personality traits turn out to predict how long a person lives and even specific diseases, but that does not mean it's easy to figure out what's going on.

At least two possible pathways between personality and health always need to be considered. One is biological: A personality trait may predispose an individual to certain physical reactions that have short- or long-term health consequences. For example, neuroticism may lead to repeated experiences of stress, which cause corticosteroids to be released into the bloodstream so often that there is excessive wear and tear on the heart. The other is behavioral: A personality trait may predispose an individual to certain behaviors that have health consequences. For example, a conscientious person may refrain from smoking, drive carefully, and even be careful to stay inside during thunderstorms (Friedman & Kern, 2014). All of these behaviors will make the person likely to stay healthier and live longer.

These are important points to keep in mind as we home in on the implications for health of three aspects of personality: The Type A personality, emotionality (negative and positive), and conscientiousness.

The Type A Personality

The modern age of research on personality and health was initiated by a cardiologist named Meyer Friedman,[13] who noticed that some of his heart patients seemed jittery, overreactive, and hyper-competitive. With colleague Ray Rosenman, he published a pioneering report claiming that blood and cardiovascular indications of risk for heart disease were correlated with a behavioral style of being obsessively ambitious to the point of being a "workaholic," and sometimes hostile as well (Friedman & Rosenman, 1959). This person became labeled the *Type A Personality*

---

[13] No relation to Howard Friedman, another prominent researcher on personality and health who has already been cited in this chapter.

said to be on the way to a heart attack—everyone else was a *Type B.* In later work, Friedman and Rosenman claimed that they could detect a Type A simply by listening to his[14] speech patterns, which were described as loud, rapid, and "explosive" (Friedman, Brown, & Rosenman, 1969, p. 829).

However, the idea of the Type A personality has faded from prominence over the years. It turns out that there is little evidence that a behavioral style aimed at striving to achieve is associated with health risk; if anything, as we shall see below, the reverse seems to be true. Support for the idea that being Type A in any way causes heart disease is inconsistent at best (Kuper, Marmot, & Hemingway, 2002), and, to make things even more confusing, the two most widely used questionnaire measures of the syndrome (the Jenkins Activity Survey and the Framingham scale) don't correlate very highly with each other and may even measure different traits (Langeluddecke & Tennant, 1986). It is also notable that findings have fluctuated over the years. Early studies tended to be supportive; later research was more discouraging. By the beginning of the 1990s, even advocates of the original concept noticed that more recent studies didn't seem to be finding that Type A and heart disease were strongly related (Miller, Turner, Tindale, Posavac, & Dugoni, 1991). After that, research on Type A dropped off precipitously and eventually pretty much stopped altogether (see **Figure 17.3**).

There probably was a small kernel of truth in the Type A portrait, but it had nothing to do with ambition or hard work. Instead, it seems to have involved hostility (Williams, 2001). Early researchers who used an interview (rather than a questionnaire) to identify Type A individuals discovered that some interviewees were hostile to the whole idea of being interviewed. They answered questions sarcastically and made comments like, "I don't have time for this" but such comments had more to do with irritability and impatience than with actually having a lot of work to do. People like that may indeed be at risk. The chronic experience of repeated hostile encounters can stress the physical system via corticosteroid response and other mechanisms, and the result over time can be both coronary disease and earlier mortality (Barefoot, Dahlstrom, & Williams, 1983). One study found that the experience of "cynical distrust"—of the sort exhibited by the people who didn't like being interviewed—was associated with blood indicators of inflammation, which is a risk factor for atherosclerosis (Ranjit et al., 2007). So chronic hostility does appear to be bad for your health, while the other, more distinctive aspects of Type A—in particular, ambition and hard work—are not.

> There probably was a small kernel of truth in the Type A portrait, but it had nothing to do with ambition or hard work. Instead, it seems to have involved hostility.

[14] Research on the Type A personality for the most part focused on white, middle-class men, and this particular study had only male subjects.

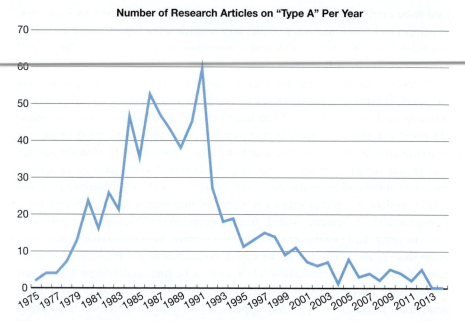

Number of Research Articles on "Type A" Per Year

Figure 17.3 **The Rise and Fall of "Type A" Research** The chart shows the number of psychology journal articles that had "Type A" in the title and mentioned the word "heart" anywhere in the text. Research peaked in 1991, but by 2013 the number of published articles was 0. (There have been 1-3 articles per year since then, most of them critical of the concept).
Source: PsychInfo.

How did the idea of the Type A personality stay popular as long as it did? One astonishing reason may be that, for years, research on the topic was subsidized by the tobacco industry! According to a review of documents made available through settlement of a major court case,[15] both the Philip Morris and R.J. Reynolds companies provided major funding for research on Type A (Petticrew, Lee, & McKee, 2012) and considered it a "crown jewel" of their efforts to convince people that smoking isn't bad for you.[16] The reason for their interest was that tobacco companies wanted to argue that smokers were likely to be Type A personalities, and so research on smoking and health had a "third variable problem" of the sort that was described in Chapter 2: It was smokers' personalities, not their smoking, that led to their heart disease and early death. Through the 1960s and even into the

[15] The archive of papers is called the "Legacy Tobacco Documents Library" and it is maintained by the University of California, San Francisco. Everything is online at http://legacy.library.ucsf.edu.
[16] You can read the memo for yourself at http://legacy.library.ucsf.edu/tid/ygw44e00/pdf. It's fascinating.

1970s some people thought this was a persuasive argument; almost needless to say, hardly anybody does anymore. Smoking really is bad for you. Count on it. But so is being angry all the time.

Emotionality

Research has addressed the relationship between both negative and positive emotions and health. "Negative emotionality"—the general tendency to experience negative feelings—is to some extent the reverse of extraversion, which you will recall from Chapter 6 is associated with the experience of positive emotions. Negative emotionality is also an important component of neuroticism. By any label, a vast amount of research shows that negative emotionality is associated with poor physical health. Indeed, one of the influences that led researchers to turn away from an emphasis on Type A and hyperactive overachieving was a classic paper that reported essentially the opposite result, that depression and withdrawal from life were risk factors for heart disease (Booth-Kewley & Friedman, 1987). Many related studies reporting similar findings followed, and the research topic grew into a popular sensation. Some prominent writers even claimed that watching funny movies or having a positive attitude can cure serious illnesses, including heart disease and even cancer (Cousins, 1979).

However, the idea that there is a direct connection between emotions and health may be one of those ideas that feels right, intuitively, but is mostly wrong. Much of the research suffers from the problem, noted earlier, in which self-reports of emotion overlap with self-reports of physical well-being. Studies also have reported contradictory results. One study of 997 Catholic priests, nuns, and brothers found neuroticism was associated with general poor health (e.g., Wilson, Mendes de Leon, Bienias, Evans, & Bennett, 2004). But another study of 597 Medicare participants between the ages of 66 and 102 found that neuroticism actually had a long-term positive relationship with health (Weiss & Costa, 2005). The reason for this latter finding, the researchers suggested, was that "impulsivity," which is a facet of neuroticism, might actually be an indication of robust good health in older adults. On the other hand, the overall relationship between neuroticism and poor health, when it is found, may to a large degree be simply due to the fact that people high in this trait are more likely to be smokers (Mroczek, Spiro, & Turiano, 2009). But even that is not the whole story. Smokers who are high in "negative affect" are prone to contract lung cancer earlier in life (Augustine, Larsen, Walker, & Fisher, 2008).

An even more widespread complication in this research is that, to the extent there is a relationship between negative emotionality and poor health, either one may be the cause of the other. People who experience serious illness naturally feel negative emotions about this fact, and may indeed be physically suffering. One large study tried to disentangle the process by following a group of people over time and calculating *cross-lagged correlations* between emotional experience and health (Gana et al., 2013). A cross-lagged correlation looks at relationships between variables across time to assess whether changes in one variable precede or follow changes in the other. The results of their analysis showed that better health led to more positive emotional experience, and poor health led to negative emotions, but that no effect in the other direction could be found. According to this study, at least, while being sick leads to negative emotions, experiencing negative emotions does not necessarily make you sick. Other researchers noted the classic finding, mentioned above, that depression is associated with heart disease and so did a meta-analysis to review the evidence as to whether treating depression would improve heart health (Rutledge, Redwine, Linke, & Mills, 2013). The answer was mixed; mental health treatment appeared to lower CHD (coronary heart disease) "events," but had no effect on the overall death rate.

The most important way that negative emotions are connected to physical health may be the way they affect behaviors that lead to stress. One large study of almost a thousand middle-aged residents of the St. Louis area found that people high on neuroticism (negative) emotionality were more likely to experience what the researchers called "dependent stress life events." These are negative life events that occur at least in part because of the person's own behavior, such as divorce, unemployment, and financial problems. The occurrence of such events was more common in people high in neuroticism, as well as people who were impulsive and disagreeable. And the experience of these events, in turn, was associated with the onset of new health problems (Iacovino, Bogdan, & Oltmanns, 2015). These results suggest that personality traits can lead to poor health indirectly, by influencing behaviors that lead to stressful outcomes, rather than by being direct causes of illness.

Through this behavioral route, neuroticism can sometimes actually be beneficial to health! According to one large study in the United Kingdom, people high in neuroticism actually lived somewhat longer, apparently because their tendency to worry and feel vulnerable led them to pay more attention to their health and to seek medical help more quickly (Gale et al., 2017). This positive effect of neuroticism might be particularly important in men, because neuroticism appears to decrease mortality risk in old age for men, even as it increases risk for women (Friedman, Kern & Reynolds, 2010).

What about positive emotions, such as optimism? While excess optimism can lead one to ignore health risks and take unwise chances, as we saw in Chapter 14, a certain amount of optimism can encourage healthy behaviors and enhance resilience in the face of difficulties (Carver, Scheier, & Segestrom, 2010). When faced with a health challenge, optimistic people seek more information and are more likely to do helpful things such as exercise and watch their diet, compared to pessimists. In other words, "people who expect good things to happen take active steps to make sure good things *do* happen" (Carver et al., 2010, p. 883).

Overall, the relationship between emotionality and health is complicated. Some aspects of negative emotion probably just exacerbate feelings that are bad already; other aspects can serve as a warning that motivates a person to change her behavior or avoid risks. When it comes to positive emotions, popular claims that simply having an upbeat attitude can improve health are (sadly) false (Coyne & Tennen, 2010). Such claims are also potentially dangerous, because they sometimes come close to blaming victims of disease for their fate (Friedman & Kern, 2014). It's hard to imagine anything much more frustrating and unfair than suffering from a serious disease, and then being told you could become healthier if you would just cheer up. Needless to say (I hope), it's not nearly that simple.

> It's hard to imagine anything more frustrating and unfair than suffering from a serious disease, and being told you would be healthier if you would just cheer up.

To the extent that positive emotions have an effect, it is probably that they motivate people to seek information and change their behaviors in beneficial ways. Other conclusions are harder to draw. The many possible pathways between emotions and health remain open for exploration.

Conscientiousness

Fortunately, the relationship between one personality trait and health is crystal-clear. Conscientiousness is good for you. It really is. Highly conscientious people don't just live longer, as was noted in Chapters 4 and 6; they also enjoy a whole range of positive outcomes that include quality as well as length of life. One reason for the relationship to health is that highly conscientious people may handle stress better; specifically, they react less strongly and less negatively to the difficult challenges of daily life (Leger et al., 2016, see **Figure 17.4**).

> Highly conscientious people don't just live longer; they also enjoy a whole range of positive outcomes that include quality as well as length of life.

Another reason for the connection between conscientiousness and health is that people high on this trait do things every day that make good health more likely. A recent meta-analysis summarized studies that, in total, looked at 76,150 participants, 3,947 of whom had died (Jokela et al., 2013). Conscientiousness was the only trait that consistently identified who would live rather than die during the period of the study. The reason seemed to be that people low in that trait exhibited low persistence, poor self-control, and a lack of long-term planning to do things to protect their health. By contrast, according to another study, people high in conscientiousness are less likely to be smokers, heavy drinkers, or obese (Turiano, Chapman, Gruenewald, & Mroczek, 2015). Similarly, an Internet survey with 460,172 respondents found that people lower in conscientiousness had poorer (self-reported) health, higher body-mass index (BMI, a measure

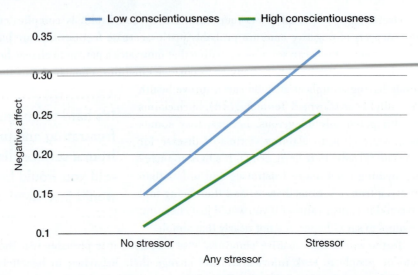

Figure 17.4 Conscientiousness and the Relationship between Stress and Negative Emotions This shows that people low in conscientiousness (blue line) experience generally stronger negative emotions than people high in conscientiousness (green line); the difference is larger on stressful days. (But notice that the difference between the slopes of the two lines, while "statistically significant," is not very large.) **Source:** Leger et al., 2016, p. 921.

of unhealthy vs. healthy weight), and more substance abuse (Atherton, Robins, Rentfrow, & Lamb, 2014).

Not all of the health-promoting behavioral patterns associated with conscientiousness are directly related to health. For example, being unemployed is bad for your health, in part because it may lead to lack of access to health care, poor nutrition, or even homelessness. Even in the short term, losing a job can cause stress that leads to adverse health consequences if the individual does not find reemployment within a year (Strully, 2009). But, statistically speaking, conscientious people are relatively likely to be employed and unlikely to be fired, as was summarized in Chapter 16. Thus, the employment-related behavioral styles associated with conscientiousness have consequences for health.

Notice how the lessons from research on conscientiousness, like the research on depression, are almost exactly opposite those initially drawn from studies of the Type A personality. The original Type A stereotype nearly seemed to imply that hard work is bad and ambition, dangerous. But research has repeatedly shown not only that occupational success and striving are related to health, but also that people who stay active into old age live the longest. Indeed, some studies show that early retirement may make early death more likely, even if the researcher adjusts for the possibility that people who are unhealthy seek to quit their jobs earlier (Bamia, Trichopoulou, & Trichopoulos, 2008; Carlsson, Andersson, Michaëlson, Vågerö, & Ahlbom, 2012).

So the best advice for a ripe old age just might be: Keep working, especially if you can find something enjoyable and creative to do (Turiano, Spiro, & Mroczek, 2012).

Prospects for Improving Health

Many prescriptions for improving health through psychological means have focused on changing personality. If we could just make people less anxiously driven, more emotionally positive, and more conscientious, perhaps we could make them healthier. Although seeking to strive less in life turns out likely to be bad medicine, increases in positive emotionality and conscientiousness might be helpful, although far from easy to accomplish. As we saw in Chapter 7, this kind of personality change might be possible, but it is certainly not easy.

Until we figure out how to change major traits of personality, more direct routes for improving health, informed by psychological research, remain highly feasible. For example, one study provided strong evidence that an important reason that conscientious people live longer is simply that that they smoke less. This finding implies it might be more practical to focus interventions on stopping smoking than on increasing conscientiousness, per se. The other health-enhancing behaviors associated with conscientiousness also offer promising targets for intervention, ranging from improving habits such as exercise, to promoting engagement in work and being active and productive into old age. Of course, if we really could do something effective to increase conscientiousness, we might, just might, be able to affect all of these behaviors at once. That would be awesome.

THE HEALTHY PERSONALITY

The ideal "healthy personality" has two aspects. One concerns mental health, and the other concerns physical health. The new, improved section of the *DSM-5* defines the psychologically "optimally functioning individual" as someone who

> . . . has a complex, fully elaborated, and well-integrated psychological world that includes a mostly positive, volitional, and adaptive self-concept; a rich, broad, and appropriately regulated emotional life; and the capacity to behave as a productive member of society with reciprocal and fulfilling interpersonal relationships." (American Psychiatric Association, 2013, p. 771).

On the physical side of things, researchers Howard Friedman and Margaret Kern (2014) list six indicators of health that include

1. Having the ability to do the things one wants to do
2. Feeling good

3. Having supportive social relationships and being able to support others
4. Being productive and getting things done
5. Having good memory capacity and being able to make good decisions
6. Staying alive

Both of these definitions are pretty good, but you may recall that Sigmund Freud said essentially the same thing in fewer words. Health, he said, is the ability to love and to work.

WRAPPING IT UP

SUMMARY

- People are different, and these differences have important implications for mental and physical health.

Personality Disorders

- Personality disorders are configurations of traits that cause serious problems for the people who have them and the others who must deal with those people.

The Diagnostic and Statistical Manual (DSM)

- The *Diagnostic and Statistical Manual* of the American Psychiatric Association describes a wide variety of mental problems, including personality disorders.

- The new edition of the Manual, *DSM-5*, includes both an older, traditional and a new, more scientific approach to the personality disorders.

- The purposes of every edition of the *DSM* have been to make psychological diagnosis more objective and to provide useful categories for various purposes ranging from scientific research to billing.

Defining Personality Disorders

- All personality disorders have two essential characteristics: (1) They are unusually extreme in a way that generally entails a distortion of reality, and (2) they cause problems for the self or others.

- Most, if not all, personality disorders are also social and stable. In addition, some disorders are ego-syntonic, which means they are not experienced as problems by the people diagnosed with the disorder.

The Major Personality Disorders

- The traditional section of the *DSM-5* lists 10 major personality disorders divided into three categories: Cluster A, the odd/eccentric disorders, include schizotypal, schizoid, and paranoid personality disorder. Cluster B, the impulsive/erratic disorders, include histrionic, narcissistic, antisocial, and borderline personality disorders. Cluster C, the anxious/avoidant disorders, include dependent, avoidant, and obsessive-compulsive personality disorders.

- A useful system used by Aaron Beck and his colleagues conceptualizes personality disorders as incorrect beliefs or problematic ways of thinking which result in maladaptive patterns of behavior.

- The new section of the *DSM-5* retains only six disorders as having a sound scientific basis; the schizoid, histrionic, dependent, and paranoid disorders have been removed from the list. The ones retained are the schizotypal, narcissistic, antisocial, borderline, avoidant, and obsessive-compulsive personality disorders.

Organizing and Diagnosing Disorders with the DSM-5

- The new approach of the *DSM-5* not only reduces the list of disorders to six, it also moves away from discrete categories of disorders to describing them along continuous trait dimensions.

- The "Bad Five" personality traits of the new *DSM-5*, analogous to the Big Five traits for describing normal personality, are negative affectivity, detachment, antagonism, disinhibition, and psychoticism.

- The three steps to diagnosis of personality disorder are (1) assess the degree of the client's function, (2) assess whether one of the six recognized disorders is present, and (3) assess the degree to which the client is characterized by each of the "Bad Five."

Personality and Disorder

- Pathologizing undesirable behavior can raise difficult moral issues, and also risks describing so many patterns as mental illnesses that the concept of illness begins to lose its meaning.

- A list of psychological disorders does not imply a definition of mental health.

- Labeling disorders carries serious risks, but also has helpful applications and may be inevitable.

- The line between normal personality variation and personality disorder is fine and uncertain. Indeed, some personality disorders can be seen as exaggerations of traits that, in moderation, are desirable.

Physical Health

CONNECTIONS BETWEEN PERSONALITY AND HEALTH

- Personality has important implications for physical as well as mental health.

- Much research on personality and health uses self-report (S data) to measure both personality and health outcomes, which can make results difficult to interpret.

- L data used in research on personality and health can include medical records and even death certificates.

- Personality may have direct, biological associations with health, but a more important pathway is probably the way personality affects behaviors that affect health, such as smoking.

THE TYPE A PERSONALITY

- Early research on personality and health identified Type A personality as a pattern of nervous and compulsive seeking for achievement, combined with hostility, that promoted heart disease.

- Later research has tended to disconfirm early indications that Type A behaviors are unhealthy overall, and research on the topic has nearly stopped. However, chronic hostility does appear to have negative health consequences.

EMOTIONALITY

- Negative emotions may be a consequence as much or more than a cause of poor health, and in some cases can actually motivate people to monitor and protect their health more carefully.

- Positive emotions such as optimism do not lead directly to better health, but may help a person to seek information and change behavior in beneficial ways.

CONSCIENTIOUSNESS

- The evidence about conscientiousness and health is clear. More conscientious people tend to be healthier and live longer, mostly because they perform behaviors that promote their health (e.g., drive carefully, stop smoking) and because their overall success at life promotes a healthy environment.

PROSPECTS FOR IMPROVING HEALTH

- Although there is some indication that changing personality to improve health might be possible, in the short run a more promising route to improving health may be to target the behaviors that promote and harm health that personality research has identified.

The Healthy Personality

- The healthy personality, both mentally and physically, belongs to someone who is capable of love and work.

KEY TERMS

THINK ABOUT IT

1. It is generally assumed to be good to be tolerant of individual differences and to accept people as they are. Is this wise in the case of someone with a personality disorder? Does the answer to this question depend on which disorder the person has? What else might the answer depend on?

2. Answer the following question in your own mind (if discussed out loud or in writing, be sure to protect the privacy of everyone involved). Do you know anyone who seems to have a personality disorder? What can be, or is being done, for this person? What is the best way for you to interact with this person?

3. Do any of the personality disorders entail characteristics that you think it might be good to watch out for—in oneself or others—even in people who are mentally healthy? Which characteristics in which disorders might be particularly important?

4. Experienced clinicians often report that, when first dealing with someone with a personality disorder, they intuitively feel that something is "not quite right." Have you had this kind of intuition about a person? Did it turn out to be correct?

5. If someone with a personality disorder commits a crime, what is the right way for society to respond? Does the answer depend on whether the person has a *severe* mental illness? If so, how would you define a severe mental illness? Do any of the personality disorders qualify? If not, what does?

6. Are any of the personality disorders, or aspects of them, ever good to have?

7. What are the characteristics of a healthy personality? Put another way, how would you describe the most psychologically healthy person you know? What is he or she like?

8. Are all bad behaviors symptoms of personality disorders? How can we distinguish between a behavior that is maladaptive or obnoxious, and one that is a sign of mental illness?

9. Do you know anyone you would describe as a classic Type A personality? Is this person generally healthy?

10. Can you think of any ways in which experiencing negative emotions might actually be good for your health?

11. Conscientious people seem to be described as "good" in just about every way possible, including occupational success and physical health. Has this description gone too far? Is it possible to be overly conscientious?

12. What is the essence of mental health? What is the essence of physical health? Are these different or the same?

SUGGESTED RESOURCES

Online

Legacy Tobacco Documents Library, http://legacy.library.ucsf.edu.

> *A fascinating, searchable collection of 14 million documents that reveal how tobacco companies advertise and market their products while trying to conceal the health risks. The site is maintained by the University of California, San Francisco.*

Personality and Health (video), Society for Personality and Social Psychology

> *Researcher Olivia Atherton describes methods, findings, and challenges in current research on the relationship between personality and health. Click on "Personality and Health" at the website http://spsp.org/resources/multimedia/experts/insight.*

Print

American Psychiatric Association (2013). *Diagnostic and statistical manual of mental disorders: DSM-5*. Washington, DC: American Psychiatric Association.

> *The latest edition of this standard reference book is surprisingly readable and interesting. It describes more ways to go psychologically wrong than you would have thought possible, and includes detailed commentary and specific examples. The book is a bit conflicted, though, because, as discussed in the chapter, it includes two different approaches to the personality disorders. You might find it interesting to compare the traditional approach described on pp. 645–684 and the "new improved" approach on pp. 761–781.*

Murray, H. A. (1943). *Analysis of the personality of Adolf Hitler, with predictions of his future behavior and suggestions for dealing with him now and after Germany's surrender.* Washington, DC: Office of Strategic Services.

> *During World War II, the U.S. Office of Strategic Services (now the CIA) commissioned psychologist Henry Murray (whose photograph you saw in Chapter 4) to write an analysis of the personality of Adolf Hitler. The classified report is now available. It is a fascinating mixture of insight and what at least one critic has called "psychobabble" (Carey, 2005), and includes the prediction—correct, as it turned out—that at the end of the war Hitler would retreat to his bunker and commit suicide. The report is available online at http://ebooks.library.cornell.edu/n/nur/analysis.php.*

Yudofsky, S. C. (2005). *Fatal flaws: Navigating destructive relationships with people with disorders of personality and character.* Washington, DC: American Psychiatric Publishing.

> *This well-written book, by an experienced and knowledgeable therapist, surveys the 10 traditional personality disorders and provides sage—and potentially lifesaving—advice on how to deal with people who have them. He describes a large number of actual cases, carefully explains what therapy can and cannot do, and describes how people with these disorders affect everybody around them. It all makes for fascinating and useful reading.*

Want to earn a better grade on your test?

Go to **INQUIZITIVE** to learn and review this chapter's content, with personalized feedback along the way.

18

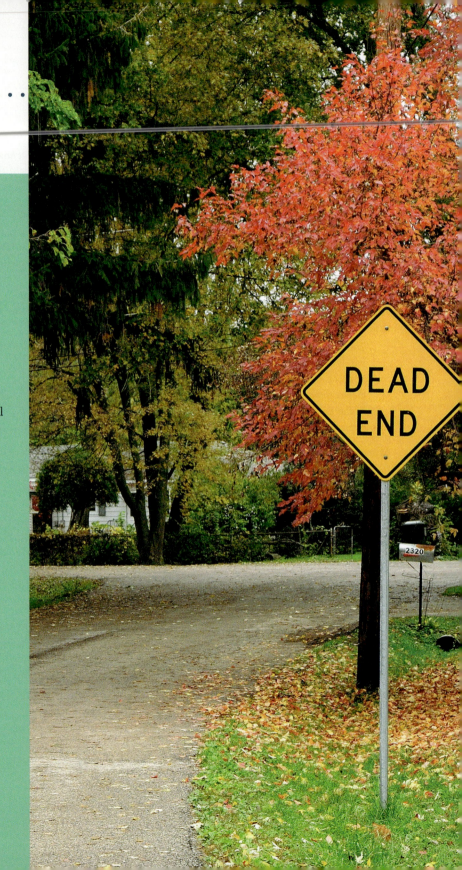

WHAT HAVE WE LEARNED?

PERSONALITY IS MY FAVORITE topic in psychology because it includes most[1] of what makes the subject interesting. It is where the other strands of psychology come together into a complete account of what people think, how they feel, and what they do. This is the psychological triad I mentioned in Chapter 1. In the following 16 chapters, we saw that research can lead to theories that are deep and complex, empirical methodologies that are sophisticated and rigorous, and long lists of findings that are intricate and sometimes seem to be contradictory. A student using this book for a class certainly finds a lot to memorize!

This complexity, rigor and even memorization are all well and good, but they also run the risk of overlooking or forgetting why all of this theorizing and research was done in the first place. After trekking through the deep thicket of a theoretical derivation or a set of research results and coming out on the other side, or, perhaps even more so, after slogging through more than 650 pages of a textbook, it is time to take a moment to ask this: "What do I now know about people that I didn't know before?"

The answers provided in this book came from several directions. Personality psychologists follow different basic approaches, each of which addresses some questions very well while, at the same time, ignoring others. Here, as we finish our journey, I will say a little more about why personality psychology has so many different approaches, and conclude by identifying some of the general lessons that I hope you remember.

---

[1] OK, all.

WHICH APPROACH IS RIGHT?

This book began with the observation that the field of personality seeks to study the whole person and everything that is important about an individual's psychology. A problem with this goal immediately arises, however: It's overwhelming—in fact, it's impossible. We cannot really account for everything at once; we must limit ourselves to a certain perspective and to the questions and variables that seem most important. The only alternative to such self-limitation is hopeless confusion.

For this reason, each basic approach to personality focuses on a limited number of key concerns and pretty much ignores everything else. The trait approach (Part II) focuses on individual differences, the personality traits that make every individual psychologically unique. The biological approach (Part III) concentrates on the architecture and function of the nervous system, and on the heritability and evolutionary history of behavioral patterns. The psychoanalytic approach (Part IV) focuses on the unconscious mind and the complicated effects of motivations and conflicts of which we may not even be aware. The humanistic approach (Part V) focuses on moment-to-moment conscious awareness, and the way experiencing life one moment at a time might give us free will and the ability to choose how we see things; this approach also leads to an appreciation of the way cultural differences create diverse construals of reality. The learning and cognitive approaches, which focus on personality processes (Part VI) address on how rewards and punishments in the environment shape behavior, and how motivation, emotion, and the cluster of memories and attitudes called "the self" are important contributors to every individual's personality.

After a semester of presenting these approaches in sequence, anybody who has taught personality psychology has had the following experience. A bright but confused student comes up and asks, "All these different approaches – which one is right?" By now, you can understand why professors often flounder around trying to answer. The competing approaches to personality psychology cannot be meaningfully compared as to which one is "right," or even the most right, because they are not different answers to the same question. Rather, they are different questions. Each approach lives or dies not by being right or wrong—because in the end, all theories are wrong—but by usefully accounting for a limited

"It's dull now, but at the end they smash their instruments and set fire to the chairs."

set of known facts, by being useful, and by clarifying important facets of human nature.[2]

A better criterion is this: Does the approach offer a way to seek an answer to a question you feel is worthwhile? The trait approach asks about individual differences; the psychoanalytic approach asks about the unconscious; the biological approach asks about physical mechanisms; the humanistic approach asks about consciousness, free will, and individual and cultural construals of reality; the learning and cognitive approaches ask about behavioral change, along with the processes of thinking and feeling that underlie behavioral coherence. What do you need or want to know about? The answer tells you which approach to use. And, as we saw in the discussion of the personality's implications for relationships, business, and mental and physical health (Part VII), real-life concerns often require us to draw upon several approaches. Although the different approaches to personality are often portrayed as competitors, none of them is enough to account for everything; all of them are necessary.

> The competing approaches to personality are not different answers to the same question. Rather, they are different questions.

WHAT HAVE WE LEARNED?

One of my colleagues has a cartoon on his office door that depicts a student frantically cramming for exams. "It's not *what* you know," the caption reads, "it's *when* you know it." The implicit message is that most of what one learns in a college course, or reads in a 650-page book, is forgotten soon after finals week. That view is not cynical; it's realistic. What, then, will you retain from taking a personality course or reading this book? One lasting benefit may be that you became a little smarter. This is more likely to have happened if you thought about the material, whether you agreed or disagreed with my point of view, especially if you received feedback from your instructor and fellow students. In particular, I hope you thought about how this material

"What does he know, and how long will he know it?"

---

[2] Statistician G. E. P. Box once commented, "All models are wrong but some are useful" (Box, 1979, p. 202).

pertains to you because, as you will recall[3] from Chapter 15, that is the most effective way to learn it—as well as being the most interesting thing you can do with psychological knowledge.

Another realistic possibility after taking a course, and reading a long book such as this, is that after the final exam you will retain not specific details of theories and experiments, surely, but knowledge about a few general themes that emerged again and again. So, here's a brief survey of what I hope you really do remember.

Research Methods Are Useful

I mentioned back at the start of Part I that research methods are not a particularly popular topic with most students, and that's a shame. Knowing about them is critical for understanding research in personality psychology or any other topic, and also just might get you a job!

Let me tell you a little story. Until recently, I taught Personality Psychology in a movie theater located at a shopping center the university owns. (The on-campus classrooms were all taken.) A Starbuck's is a few doors away[4]. The coffee shop was not always there. When the shopping center first opened, Riverside, California, did not yet have a Starbucks (if you can imagine!) and the university was eager to host the very first one. But Starbucks management declined. They had done a data analysis. They got out a census map and drew a one-mile circle around the possible spot. Then they calculated the average annual income of the people who live in that circle. If that value was not above a certain number (which is secret, by the way), they wouldn't open. But when the shopping center was being built, its only neighbors were a couple of gas stations, a few not-so-nice motels, some deteriorating apartment buildings mostly housing students, and a major highway. So the income number came in much too low. The university responded by offering Starbucks free rent for a year. That's different, their management said, so the store opened after all. It did the second-largest opening-day business in the chain's history. In fact, it did so well that soon thereafter a second and larger Starbucks was opened only about 100 yards away. But that turned to be a bit much, even for Starbucks. As I write this, we are back to just the original location (see **Figure 18.1**), which continues to thrive.[5]

The point of this story is that everything hinged critically on research methods. Starbucks had a numerical method for calculating sales potential, but it didn't turn out to be *valid* in the sense that was discussed in Chapter 2—it didn't provide a correct prediction of sales. Further decisions were also based on numbers, of the sort you learned in your statistics and methods classes. What is the mean sales per

---

[3] Right?

[4] In a perfect world, every lecture hall would have a ready source of caffeine nearby.

[5] However, Riverside now has 17 other Starbucks elsewhere in town.

Figure 18.1 Is This a Good Location for a Starbucks? Research methods are the only way to find the answer.

day per square foot? What is the correlation between the average income within a mile of a shop and its sales? Are the average sales figures in two different locations significantly different from each other? What is the effect size of this difference? Is it large enough to have important financial implications?

Understanding the research methods summarized in Chapter 2, and the techniques for evaluating effect size described in Chapter 3, puts you in a position to answer all of these questions. Whether you know it or not, if you are a psychology major, you probably are a statistical expert. If you know how to calculate and interpret a mean and standard deviation, you are already much more statistically sophisticated than most people. If you can calculate, understand, and explain a correlation coefficient, you are practically a professional!

Consider the typical assignment in a psychology class on research methods. (1) Formulate a research question. (2) Gather relevant information, in the form of numbers (data). (3) Crunch these numbers in some way; calculate means, standard deviations, correlations, and so forth. (4) Write a report that clearly explains what these numbers mean, in a way that answers the question you started with. If you can do all

If you can calculate, understand, and explain a correlation coefficient, you are practically a professional statistician.

this, you will not only get an A in Research Methods, but Starbucks wants to hire you—in the corporate office, not as a barista. These skills are necessary for any business in the world, and surprisingly few people have them. Don't sell back your research methods textbook.[6] It may come in handy one day.

Cross-Situational Consistency and Aggregation

People remain who they are regardless of the situation. We saw in Chapter 4 that psychologists still argue about "behavioral consistency," but the evidence is clear and comes from all directions. Someone who dominates a business meeting will probably dominate a party; someone who is pessimistic about his career will probably also be pessimistic about the outcome of his wife's childbirth; and someone who has "issues" about her father is likely to bring them to bear in many of her other relationships with men. These examples come from three different basic approaches. Research in the trait paradigm has demonstrated the consistency of dominance. Research in the cognitive paradigm has demonstrated the consistency of pessimism. And both the psychoanalytic and cognitive paradigms have demonstrated transference of consistent patterns of how one handles relationships.

Let's consider consistency another way. If you move by yourself thousands of miles away, which some students do after college graduation, you will find yourself in a completely new environment where nobody knows you or has any expectations for what you will do. You will nonetheless continue to be who you are; your personality will determine how you respond to the new challenges you face and how you relate to the new people you meet. In fact, it's not unlikely that before long, you will develop a pattern of behavior and personality relationships not very different from the one you left behind! Your personality is the baggage you always have with you.

Still, the consistency of personality is limited in two ways. First, behavior changes from one situation to the next. The most talkative person at a party will almost surely become less talkative in class. The consistency of his personality implies only that he will probably still be more talkative than everybody else in class, not that he will be equally talkative in both situations (Oishi et al., 2004). In the same way, a talkative child is likely to grow into a (relatively) talkative adult, but only in the sense that he or she will probably continue to be more talkative than other people his or her own age (Chapter 7). Behavior and emotion change over time, but individuals maintain their differences. This idea is not obvious at first glance, and not even all psychologists quite grasp it, but it is important.

A second limitation is that behavioral consistency is not strong enough to predict a single action in a single situation with any great fidelity. Recall the personality correlation coefficient of around .30 to .40 (Chapter 4), which means a

---

[6] Or this one either, please.

behavioral prediction is likely to be right about two times out of three. This is a useful level of accuracy, but it includes a lot of errors. Behavioral consistency only becomes truly worthy of the name when you predict the average or aggregate of several behaviors. Will your roommate greet you cheerfully when you come home next Tuesday at 4:30 P.M.? Who knows? But if she is a cheerful person, you can confidently predict that, in the 30 times you arrive home next month, her greeting will be more pleasant on average than that of your other, crabbier roommate.

Personality Growth and Change

While, as just mentioned, personality is consistent over long periods of the lifespan in the sense of maintaining individual differences, there are also clear patterns of personality change from childhood to adulthood to old age. On average—with many exceptions of course—people become gradually higher on conscientiousness and lower on neuroticism as they get older, with smaller trends to increase in openness and agreeableness. Some of this change may be the result of physical maturation, but a more important influence is probably the changing tasks and demands of different stages of life, and the attitudes and skills that they require a person to develop. Parenthood, marriage, or that first job, may require you to become a different person.

Can you change your personality? As we saw in Chapter 7, it seems to be possible, although it is far from easy. One opportunity arises when you change environments and your social group and, in that way, get a fresh start, but even then, discarding long-ingrained ways of behavior can be a struggle. If there is something you want to change about your personality – and recall this is true for over half the people in the word – the best and perhaps only way to do it is slowly and consistently. Find a behavior that reflects the desired "new you" and practice it every day; add more behaviors over time. But be patient. You've heard the expression "old habits die hard"; it's true.

The Biological Roots of Personality

As we saw in Chapters 8 and 9, biological research relevant to personality is accelerating so fast that it's hard to keep up. Proponents of the other approaches (such as the learning and cognitive approaches) no longer try to deny—as they once did—that biology matters for personality. Consistent patterns of behavior are rooted in anatomical structures such as the brain's frontal lobes and the amygdala, and in chemicals such as neurotransmitters and hormones, which, in turn, stem from the DNA people inherit from their parents, and from their ancestors over the course of evolutionary history. Philosopher John Locke claimed the human mind started out at birth like a blank slate, or *tabula rasa*. Nice idea, but he was wrong. Behaviorist John Watson believed he could take any baby and with the proper training produce a "doctor, lawyer, beggar man, or thief." Another nice idea, but he was wrong, too.

Biologically based research on psychology is technologically impressive. The sophisticated—and expensive!—equipment required to analyze hormonal levels or DNA structures, or to produce amazing color pictures that seem to show the brain in action, can be dazzling, even somewhat intimidating. It is important to remember, therefore, that this research is still near its beginning. What we don't know vastly exceeds what we do know, and—as in all maturing fields of research—the growth of knowledge clarifies, above all else, just how complex everything is. Genetic structures, neurotransmitters, hormones, and regions of the brain all have important relationships with behavior and personality, but the connections are not simple because everything interacts with everything else. Genes influence each other, the effect of one neurotransmitter or hormone depends on levels of others, and the densely interconnected regions of the brain act together in complicated patterns. And that is just the beginning. The whole neurological system constantly interacts with the external world, including all of the continually changing aspects of the environment and other people. Your biology affects how you feel and what you do, but events in your life, your relationships, and what you feel and what you do all affect your biology as well. The fact that psychology is beginning to appreciate this interaction is an important sign of progress.

The Unconscious Mind

The unconscious mind is no longer an exotic, implausible idea kept alive by Freudian diehards. It has re-entered the mainstream. We saw evidence throughout this book that the unconscious part of the mind—the part we cannot describe or explain in words, and that can occasionally surprise or even mystify us—is important in many ways.

Recall just a few examples. Biological research has shown that the connections between the emotional and more rational areas of the brain can be damaged or severed to the point that people have thoughts that make no sense, emotions they cannot explain, or behaviors they cannot control. Psychoanalytic theory provides many examples of how people fend off perceptions and thoughts they find too troublesome to experience directly. The cognitive approach to personality has demonstrated how some aspects of the self are known only implicitly, not explicitly or consciously.

Free Will and Responsibility

Because psychology tries 99 percent of the time to seem like a "real," deterministic science, it usually ignores the idea of free will and the related concept of responsibility. We saw theorists as diverse as Sigmund Freud and B. F. Skinner unite behind the idea that behavioral freedom is an illusion. The most valuable contribution of humanistic psychology (Chapter 12) has been a reasonable way to think about free will. Behavior is determined only up to a point, after which choices become possible and even necessary. Indeed, as Sartre pointed out, the only choice you can't make is the choice not to choose. The secret of psychological success may be recognizing the choice points in life and responsibly making the most of them.

The Nature of Happiness

Another contribution from the humanists and the related positive psychology movement is the reminder that happiness comes at least as much from the inside as from the outside. It matters less whether you are a millionaire, research shows, than how you choose to think about whatever you do have (it helps to be grateful). Moreover, the goal of life is not to achieve a state of zero stress—a totally stress-free life would be boring and meaningless. A healthy life involves seeking out difficult but reasonable and meaningful challenges, and, when they are accomplished, seeking more. This kind of constant striving is both a cause and a result of happiness. As was discussed in Chapter 12, the experience of happiness is more than a passive end state. It is an opportunity to broaden and build the foundations for a better life for yourself and for others.

Culture and Personality

Psychologists have renewed their attention to psychological differences between cultures, and to the different ways people differ from each other *within* cultures. But recent research also increasingly appreciates what we as humans have in common—not just our common mortal fate, as Sartre observed, but basic psychological processes, such as the need to follow rules or wanting to please our parents. Moreover, areas of the world often described as single "cultures"—including Asia, Europe, and North America—have important diversity within them, and individuals can and often do belong to more than one culture at the same time. So it is important not to let a fascination with cross-cultural differences lead us back into stereotyping—that would be ironic, wouldn't it?

Choosing and Changing Situations

Rewarded behaviors become more likely, and punished behaviors become less likely (*duh*). This is true for creatures from amoebas to humans. The edifices of behaviorism and social learning theories (Chapter 14) are based on this key idea, but the most important thing to remember is that rewards and punishments are not just imposed. Often, you can select which ones you will be subject to. Imagine a rat being allowed to choose his favorite Skinner box. Now think of someone choosing (or not) to enroll in medical school, or take a job with a law firm, or enlist in the military. What will be the consequences of the rewards and punishments in each of those environments? The most important choice points in life entail selecting an environment and its associated rewards and punishments. These choices include where to go to school, what career to enter, and whether or whom to marry. Much of who you turn out to be will depend on these decisions.

And there is more. Once you enter an environment, it changes just because you are there, and what you do will cause even further changes. If you ever find yourself in an unsatisfactory situation—a hostile work environment, an exploitative relationship—then ask yourself, "Is any aspect of this situation the result of something I am doing?" Maybe the answer is no. In that case, leave. But maybe the answer is yes. In that case, see what you can do to change things.

Construals

It is not things that matter, but our opinions of things. This Talmudic insight not only is a theme of existential philosophy and humanistic psychology, but also lies at the core of the psychoanalytic, cross-cultural, and cognitive approaches to personality. Psychoanalysis emphasizes how unrealistic or fantasized views of reality can cause neurotic, self-defeating behavior. From a humanistic perspective, choosing a point of view is the core existential obligation. The only way to understand another person is to try to understand his personal and cultural perspective. Research on the personality processes of motivation, emotion, and thinking also illuminate the origins and consequences of individuals' differing views of reality.

Indeed, it could be argued that the totality of psychology boils down to the moment of construal. All of your past experiences, biological processes, needs, ambitions, and perceptions combine to yield your view of reality, right now. Then, you decide what to do.

The Fine, Uncertain, and Important Line Between Normal and Abnormal

Personality psychology is in the business of understanding and even celebrating differences among people, but sometimes those differences go too far. A pattern of personality that is both unusual and problematic may be labeled a *personality disorder*, and such labeling is at once useful, probably inevitable, and also dangerous. Terminology helps us to talk about and understand such phenomena as borderline, avoidant, and other commonly recognized personality disorders, and there really is no way to avoid using labels to describe something so important. But labeling can also be dangerous, because it runs the risk of pathologizing so many undesirable patterns that the concept of mental illness begins to disappear. Furthermore, once somebody is labeled, other people—even psychologists—may come to view the person only as the label and not as an individual. Another complication is that probably everybody has personality characteristics that, at their most extreme, would be labeled disorders, yet in the normal range, these aspects may be desirable—even essential—to a person's identity. As I said way back in Chapter 1, great strengths are often great weaknesses and vice versa. I'm not sure they should be separated. Plus, it doesn't matter what I think, because our weaknesses and strengths *can't* be separated: Personality is a package deal.

Personality, Behavior, and Health

We saw in Chapter 17 that personality has important implications for physical health, which raises the question of whether it is possible to change personality in order to improve health. Maybe so, but we saw in Chapter 7 that changing personality, while perhaps possible, is far from easy. For now, it might be more useful to learn the lessons of research on personality and health that identify healthy and unhealthy behaviors. Hostile people get into more fights, which is bad for their health because fights are dangerous and probably stress the heart as well. People high on neuroticism may withdraw from life and fail to take care of themselves. People high on conscientiousness live longer because they usually don't smoke, drink to excess, drive recklessly, or go for long strolls in the open during thunderstorms (Chapter 17). They do exercise and stay active in general. If you want to be healthy and live a long time, pay attention to these findings.

THE QUEST FOR UNDERSTANDING

Remember S, I, L, and B data (Chapter 2)? To learn about a person we have no alternative but to watch what he or she does and listen to what he or she says. In the end, these behaviors form the basis of all our conclusions about personality, whether our approach is based on a trait, biological, psychoanalytic, behaviorist, cognitive, or even humanistic perspective. By the same token, the only way to find out whether we are right in thinking we understand an individual's personality is to try to explain (and sometimes predict) what the person does or says. Again, this is true no matter which basic approach we follow.

Our minds are forever sealed off from each other. We cannot directly know another person's thoughts or feelings; we can only watch what she does or listen to what she says. From there, we can try to infer what is going on inside. And that inference, in turn, helps us begin to grasp what each other thinks, feels, and wants. So personality psychology is, in the final analysis, a quest for mutual understanding.

WRAPPING IT UP

SUMMARY

Which Approach Is Right?

- Each approach to personality explains some aspects of individuals, while not explaining other aspects or ignoring them entirely. Thus, the choice between approaches depends not on which one is right, but on what we wish to know.

What Have We Learned?

- It is unreasonable to expect to remember the details in a long book such as this, but certain recurring themes are important to retain. These include the usefulness of research methods; the nature of behavioral consistency; the stability and development of personality over the lifespan; the biological roots of personality; the workings of the unconscious mind; the issues of free will and responsibility; the sources of happiness that come from within the mind as well as from the circumstances of life; the nature of psychological differences within as well as across cultures; the importance of construals; the fine line between normal and abnormal personality; and the robust findings concerning the behaviors that are most likely to keep us healthy.

The Quest for Understanding

- In the final analysis, personality psychology attempts to turn our observations of ourselves and each other into mutual understanding.

THINK ABOUT IT

1. Is personality psychology really a science, and how can you tell? Is its scientific status important?
2. What is your favorite approach to personality among those covered in this book? What is your least favorite approach? Why?
3. Will the different approaches to personality someday be combined into one big, integrated approach? What would that approach look like?
4. How is personality psychology relevant to (a) your own daily life, (b) understanding and solving social problems, and (c) understanding human nature?
5. Think about a course you took a year or two ago. What do you remember from it? If the answer is "not much," does that mean you did not benefit from the course?
6. Do you ever encounter situations in your daily life where you find your knowledge about research methods useful? Do you ever see situations where other people would do better if they knew a couple of basic things about research methods?

7. What do you think you will remember, if anything, from this book and this course 20 years from now?
8. What do we know when we know a person?

SUGGESTED RESOURCES

Online

Funderstorms: www.funderstorms.wordpress.com

> *In case you suffer from separation anxiety as you finish reading this book, you can always continue to read the author's blog. Topics include current issues in personality psychology, research methodology, and random musings.*

Print

Corr, P. J., & Matthews, G. (2009). *The Cambridge handbook of personality psychology*. Cambridge University Press.

> *This book, with 46 chapters, has the same basic design as the handbook by John et al. (2008) listed below; but the chapters are shorter and more of the contributors are European. Comparing these two books provides an interesting glimpse of the somewhat different approaches to personality psychology in North America and Europe.*

John, O. P., Robins, R. W., & Pervin, L. A. (2008). *Handbook of personality: Theory and research* (3rd ed.). New York: Guilford Press.

> *This book is a collection of 32 chapters written by active researchers (mostly Americans) on the many topics in personality psychology. It would be an excellent next step for a reader who, having finished this book, wants a more detailed and technical survey of the field.*

Want to earn a better grade on your test?

Go to **INQUIZITIVE** to learn and review this chapter's content, with personalized feedback along the way.

CREDITS

Falko/dpa/Alamy; **p. 76** left: Bettmann/Corbism via Getty Images, center: Photograph from Architect of the Capitol, AOC no. 73009-24/Library of Congress, right: Bettman/Corbis via Getty Images; **p. 81**: Siewert Falko/dpa/Alamy; **p. 84**: Barbara Smaller/The New Yorker Collection/The Cartoon Bank; **p. 94**: The Los Angeles Times **p. 95**: Morgan Funder; **p. 98**: Leo Cullum/The New Yorker Collection/The Cartoon Bank; **p. 99**: Steve Dietl/©IFC Films/Courtesy Everett Collection.

Try for Yourself 3.2 (p. 81): Optimism-Pessimism Test adapted from J.K. Norem & B.J. Prayson, Validation of a New Defensive Pessimism Questionnaire-Short Form. Poster presented at the bi-annual meeting of the Association for Research in Personality, St. Louis, MO. June 2015. Reprinted by permission of J.K. Norem.

CHAPTER 4

Photos: p. 110: Mark Nolan/Getty Images; **p. 113:** Mike Twohy/The New Yorker Collection/The Cartoon Bank; **p. 116:** Danny Shanahan/The New Yorker Collection/The Cartoon Bank; **p. 119** left: Peter Hvizdak/The Image Works, right: U.S. Air Force photo by Master Sgt. Lance S. Cheung; **p. 120:** Mark Nolan/Getty Images; **p. 124:** Department of Defense; **p. 127** left and right: From the film Obedience ©1965 by Stanley Milgram. ©Renewed 1993 by Alexandra Milgram. Distributed by Alexander Street Press; **p. 139:** AP Photo/Jeff Widener; **p. 140** left: HUP Murray, Henry A. (3), olvwork188005. Harvard University Archives; right: Kris Snibbe/Harvard News Office Gazette.

Try for Yourself 4.1 (p. 120): Copyright © 1995 by the American Psychological Association. Reproduced with permission. Appendix from "Preference for consistency: The development of a valid measure and the discovery of surprising behavioral implications." Cialdini, Robert B., et. al. *Journal of Personality and Social Psychology*, Vol. 69(2), Aug. 1995, 318-328. No further reproduction or distribution is permitted without written permission from the American Psychological Association.

Line Art: Fig. 4.4 (p.132): Copyright © 2012 by the American Psychological Association. Reproduced with permission. Figure 1 from "Persons, situations, and behaviors: Consistency and variability of different behaviors in four interpersonal situations." Leikas, Sointu; Lönnqvist, Jan-Erik; Verkasalo, Markku. *Journal of Personality and Social Psychology*, Vol 103(6), Dec 2012, 1007-1022. http://dx.doi.org/10.1037/a0030385. The use of APA information does not imply endorsement by APA.

CHAPTER 5

Photos: p. 146: Jim West/Alamy; **p. 154:** David Funder; **p. 155:** Figure 1B from Todorov, Mandisodza, Goren, & Hall (2005), Inferences of Competence from Faces Predict Election Outcomes, *SCIENCE*, p. 1624. Reprinted with permission from AAAS; **pp. 158** and **159:** Penton-Voak, I.S., Pound, N., Little, A.C., & Perrett, D.I. (2006). Personality judgments from natural and composite facial images: More evidence for a 'kernel of truth' in social perception.

CHAPTER 7

CHAPTER 8

A. Countway Library of Medicine, right: Figure 5 from H. Damasio, T. Grabowski, R. Frank, A.M. Galaburda & A. R. Damasio (1994) The Return of Phineas Gage: clues about the brain from a famous patient, Science, 264, 1102-1105. Dornsife Neuroscience Imaging Center and Brain and Creativity Institute, University of Southern California; **p. 283**: Peter Steiner/The New Yorker Collection/The Cartoon Bank; **p. 286**: Bettmann/Corbis via Getty Images; **p. 294**: Leo Cullum/The New Yorker Collection/The Cartoon Bank; **p. 299**: Robert Mankoff/Cartoonstock; **p. 304**: DeYoung, C.G., Hirsch, J.B., Shane, M.S., Papademetris, X., Rajeevan, N., & Gray, J.R. (2010). Testing predictions from personality neuroscience: Brain structure and the Big Five. *Psychological Science*, 21, 820-828, p. 825. Copyright © 2010, Association for Psychological Science. Reprinted by permission of Sage Publications.

CHAPTER 9

Photos: **p. 310**: Attila Kisbenedek/AFP/Getty Images; **p. 322**: Figure 1 from Hariri et al. "Serotonin Transporter Genetic Variation and the Response of the Human Amygdala" 19 July 2002 Vol 297 Science Copyright © 2002, American Association for the Advancement of Science; **p. 323**: Robert Mankoff/Cartoonstock; **p. 332**: Edward Frascino/The New Yorker Collection/The Cartoon Bank; **p. 333**: Monty Brinton/CBS/Getty Images; **p. 340**: Alex Grimm/Getty Images.

Line Art: **Fig. 9.2 (p. 327)**: Figure 1 from D.H. Barlow et. al., "The origins of neuroticism." *Perspectives on Psychological Science* 9(5): pp. 481-496. Copyright © 2014 by Association for Psychological Science. Reprinted by permission of SAGE Publications; **Fig. 9.5 (p. 342)**: Figure from Fry, Richard and D'Vera Cohn in Taylor, et. al., "Women, Men and the New Economics of Marriage," Pew Research Center, Washington, D.C. (January 19, 2010). http://www.pewsocialtrends.org/2010/01/19/women-men-and-the-new-economics-of-marriage/. Reprinted with permission.

CHAPTER 10

Photos: **p. 352**: Colin Anderson/Digital Vision/Getty Images; **p. 354**: Chronicle/Alamy Stock Photo; **p. 355** left: Bourgeron-Rue des Archives/Granger, NYC—All rights reserved, right: David Funder; **p. 357**: Bjanka Kadic/Alamy; **p. 367**: Bruce Eric Kaplan The New Yorker Collection/The Cartoon Bank; **p. 371**: Arnie Levin/The New Yorker Collection/The Cartoon Bank; **p. 381**: Sam Marlow/The New Yorker Collection/The Cartoon Bank; **p. 387**: Kathy deWitt/Alamy.

CHAPTER 11

Photos: **p. 394**: R Creation/amana images/Getty Images; **p. 397**: David Funder; **p. 400**: Robert Mankoff/Cartoonstock; **p. 408**: Victoria Roberts/The New Yorker Collection/The Cartoon Bank; **p. 409**: Bill Woodman/The New Yorker Collection/The Cartoon Bank;

PART V

Photos: **p. 421**: Morgan Funder.

CHAPTER 12

Photos: **p. 422**: Owen Franken/Corbis via Getty Images; **p. 430**: Roz Chast/The New Yorker Collection/The Cartoon Bank; **p. 431**: Bruce Eric Kaplan The New Yorker Collection/The Cartoon Bank; **p. 438**: Montgomery Martin/Alamy Stock Photo; **p. 441**: Morgan Funder; **pp. 448, 449, and 450**: Owen Franken/Corbis via Getty Images; **p. 452**: David Funder.

Try for Yourself 12.1 (pp. 448–450): Copyright © 2003 by the American Psychological Association. Reproduced with permission. Table 2 from "The benefits of being present: Mindfulness and its role in psychological well-being." Brown, Kirk Warren; Ryan, Richard M. *Journal of Personality and Social Psychology*, Vol 84(4), Apr 2003, 822-848. http://dx.doi.org/10.1037/0022-3514.84.4.822. No further reproduction or distribution is permitted without written permission from the American Psychological Association.

Line Art: **Fig. 12.2 (p. 436)**: Figure 2 from Kenrick, et al., "Renovating the pyramid of needs: Contemporary extensions built upon ancient foundations," *Perspectives on Psychological Science* 5(3): pp. 292-314. Copyright © 2010 by Association for Psychological Science. Reprinted by Permission of SAGE Publications; **Fig 12.6 (p. 455)**: Figure 9A from Dodds, P.S. & C. M. Danforth, "Measuring the happiness of large-scale written expression: Songs, blogs, and presidents." *Journal of Happiness Studies* 11(4): 441-456, August 2010, Copyright © 2009 by Peter Sheridan Dodds and Christopher M. Danforth. Reprinted with kind permission of Springer Science + Business Media.

CHAPTER 13

Photos: **p. 464**: Bill Bachmann/Design Pics/Getty Images; **p. 469**: AP Photo/Bjoern Kaehler; **p. 471**: Maddux, W. W., & Galinsky, A. D. (2009). Cultural borders and mental barriers: The relationship between living abroad and creativity. *Journal of Personality and Social Psychology*, 96(5), 1047-1061; **p. 473** left: Anne Bråtveit, right: Lunae Parracho/Reuters/Newscom; **p. 485**: Morgan Funder; **p. 497**: Mick Stevens/The New Yorker Collection/The Cartoon Bank.

Line Art: **Fig. 13.5 (p. 487)**: Figure adapted with permission from Gardiner, G., Baranski, E., & Funder, D. (2018, July). Reliabilitiy of country personality traits: New evidence from the International Situations Project. Paper presented at European Association of Personality, Zadar, Croatia; **Fig. 13.6 (p. 488)**: Copyright © 2013 by the American Psychological Association. Reproduced with permission. Figure 2 from "Divided we stand: Three psychological regions of the United States and their political, economic, social, and health correlates." Rentfrow, Peter J.; Gosling, Samuel D.; Jokela, Markus; Stillwell, David J.; Kosinski, Michal; Potter, Jeff. *Journal of Personality and Social Psychology*, Vol 105(6), Dec 2013, 996-1012. http://dx.doi.org/10.1037/a0034434 The use of APA information does not imply endorsement by APA; **Fig. 13.7 (p. 494)**: Figure 1 from Schwartz & Sagiv, "Identifying culture-specifics in the content and structure of values," *Journal of Cross-Cultural Psychology* 26(1): pp. 92-116. Copyright © 1995 by SAGE Publications. Reprinted by Permission of SAGE Publications.

CHAPTER 14

CHAPTER 15

CHAPTER 16

Try for Yourself 16.2 **(pp. 594–595)**: Copyright © 2008 by the American Psychological Association. Reproduced with permission. Table from "Beyond global sociosexual orientations: A more differentiated look at sociosexuality and its effects on courtship and romantic relationships." Penke, Lars; Asendorpf, Jens B. *Journal of Personality and Social Psychology*, Vol 95(5), Nov 2008, 1113-1135. http://dx.doi.org/10.1037/0022-3514.95.5.1113. No further reproduction or distribution is permitted without written permission from the American Psychological Association

Line Art: Fig. 16.1 (p. 591): Figure 1 from Back, Penke, Schmukle & Asendorpf, "Knowing your own mate value: Sex-specific personality effects on the accuracy of expected mate choices." *Psychological Science* 22(8): pp. 984-989. Copyright © 2011 by Association for Psychological Science. Reprinted by Permission of SAGE Publications; **Fig. 16.2 (p. 604)**: Copyright © 2018 by the American Psychological Association. Reproduced with permission. Figure 2 from "The ebbs and flows of attachment: Within-person variation in attachment undermine secure individuals' relationship wellbeing across time." Girme, Yuthika U., et. al., *Journal of Personality and Social Psychology*, Vol. 114(3), 397-421.10.1037/pspi0000115. The use of APA information does not imply endorsement by APA; **Fig. 16.3 (p. 609)**: Figure reprinted by permission of the author from Gensowski, M. "Personality, IQ, and Lifetime Earnings" IZA Discussion Paper No. 8235, June 2014, p. 19. See also, Gensowski, M. (2018). Personality, IQ, and Lifetime Earnings. *Labour Economics*, 51, 170-183.

CHAPTER 17

Photos: p. 618: James Porto/Getty Images; **pp. 621 and 622**: Morgan Funder; **p. 630**: AP Photo; **p. 634**: Michael Shaw/The New Yorker Collection/The Cartoon Bank; **p. 638**: David Funder; **p. 643**: Morgan Funder.

Line Art: Fig. 17.4 (p. 650): Copyright © 2016 by the American Psychological Association. Reproduced with permission. Figure 1 from "Personality and stressor-related affect." Leger, K.A. et. al. *Journal of Personality and Social Psychology*, Vol 111(6), Dec. 2016, 917-928. 10.1037/pspp0000083. The use of APA information does not imply endorsement by APA.

CHAPTER 18

Photos: p. 658: Chuck Eckert/Alamy; **p. 660**: J.B. Handelsman/The New Yorker Collection/The Cartoon Bank; **p. 661**: Frank Cotham/The New Yorker Collection/The Cartoon Bank; **p. 663**: David Funder.

REFERENCES

Abelson, R., Cohen, J., & Rosenthal, R. (Chairs). (1996). *Initial report of the task force on statistical inference.* Washington, DC: Board of Scientific Affairs, American Psychological Association.

Ackerman, R. A., Witt, E. A., Donnellan, M. B., Trzesniewski, K. H., Robins, R. W., & Kashy, D. A. (2011). What does the Narcissistic Personality Inventory really measure? *Assessment, 18,* 67–87.

Adams, C. (2001, Feb. 2). Are there nine Eskimo words for snow? *The Straight Dope.* Retrieved from www.straightdope.com/columns/010202.html

Adelman, R.M., Herrmann, S.D., Bodford, J.E., Barbour, J.E., Graudejus, O., Okun, M.A. & Kwan, V.S.Y. (2017). Feeling closer to the future self and doing better: Temporal psychological mechanisms underlying academic performance. *Journal of Personality, 85,* 398–408.

Ader, R., & Cohen, N. (1993). Psychoneuroimmunology: Conditioning and stress. *Annual Review of Psychology, 44,* 53–85.

Adler, A. (1939). *Social interest.* New York: Putnam.

Adler, J. (2006, March 27). Freud in our midst. *Newsweek, 197,* 42–49.

Adolphs, R. (2001). The neurobiology of social cognition. *Current Opinion in Neurobiology, 11,* 231–239.

Adorno, T. W., Frenkel-Brunswik, E., Levinson, D., & Sanford, N. (1950). *The authoritarian personality.* New York: Harper & Row.

Ahadi, S., & Diener, E. (1989). Multiple determinants and effect size. *Journal of Personality and Social Psychology, 56,* 398–406.

Ahadi, S., & Rothbart, M. K. (1994). Temperament, development and the Big Five. In C. F. Halverson, Jr., G. A. Kohnstamm, & R. P. Martin (Eds.), *The developing structure of temperament and personality from infancy to adulthood* (pp. 189–207). Hillsdale, NJ: Erlbaum.

Ainsworth, M. D. S., Blehar, M. C., Waters, E., & Wall, S. (1978). *Patterns of attachment: Assessed in the strange situation and at home.* Hillsdale, NJ: Erlbaum.

Albright, L., Kenny, D. A., & Malloy, T. E. (1988). Consensus in personality judgments at zero acquaintance. *Journal of Personality and Social Psychology, 55,* 387–395.

Albright, L., Malloy, T. E., Dong, Q., Kenny, D. A., & Fang, X. (1997). Cross-cultural consensus in personality judgments. *Journal of Personality and Social Psychology, 72,* 558–569.

Alessandri, G., Vecchione, M., Donnellan, B. M., Eisenberg, N., Caprara, G. V., & Cieciuch, J. (2014). On the cross-cultural replicability of the resilient, undercontrolled and overcontrolled personality types. *Journal of Personality, 82,* 340–353

Algoe, S.B., Kurtz, L.E., & Grewen, K. (2017). Oxytocin and social bonds: The role of oxytocin in perceptions of romantic partners' bonding behavior. *Psychological Science,* published online 10/2/17.

Allemand, M., & Flückiger, C. (2017). Changing personality traits: Some considerations from psychotherapy process-outcome research for intervention efforts on intentional personality change. *Journal of Psychotherapy Integration, 27,* 476–494.

Alley, T. R. (1988). Physiognomy and social perception. In T. R. Alley (Ed.), *Social and applied aspects of perceiving faces* (pp. 167–186). Hillsdale, NJ: Erlbaum.

Alliek, J., Church, A., Ortiz, T. Fernando, A., Rossier, J., Hřebíčková, M., et al. (2017). *Journal of Cross-cultural Psychology, 48,* 402–420.

Allik, J., Mõttus, R., Realo, A., Pullmann, H., Trifonova, A., McCrae, R. R., & 56 Members of the Russian Character and Personality Survey. (2009). Personality traits of Russians from the observers' perspective. *European Journal of Personality, 23,* 567–588.

Allport, G. W. (1937). *Personality: A psychological interpretation.* New York: Holt, Rinehart.

Allport, G. W. (1958). What units shall we employ? In G. Lindzey (Ed.), *Assessment of human motives* (pp. 239–260). New York: Holt, Rinehart.

Allport, G. W. (1961). *Pattern and growth in personality.* New York: Holt, Rinehart.

Allport, G. W. (1965). *Letters from Jenny.* New York: Harcourt, Brace.

Allport, G. W., & Odbert, H. S. (1936). Trait-names: A psycho-lexical study. *Psychological Monographs: General and Applied, 47* (1, Whole No. 211), 171–220.

Allport, G. W., & Vernon, P. E. (1933). *Studies in expressive movement.* New York: Macmillan.

Alonso-Zaldivar, R. (2002, December 11). Jet crash probe is concluded. *Los Angeles Times,* p. B1.

Alper, J., Beckwith, J., & Miller, L. G. (1978). Sociobiology is a political issue. In A. L. Caplan (Ed.), *The sociobiology debate: Readings on ethical and scientific issues* (pp. 476–488). New York: Harper & Row.

Altemeyer, B. (1981). *Right-wing authoritarianism.* Winnipeg: University of Manitoba Press.

Altemeyer, B. (1998). The other "authoritarian personality." *Advances in Experimental Social Psychology, 30,* 47–92.

Ambady, N., Hallahan, M., & Rosenthal, R. (1995). On judging and being judged accurately in zero-acquaintance situations. *Journal of Personality and Social Psychology, 69,* 518–529.

American Psychiatric Association. (2000). *Diagnostic and statistical manual of mental disorders: DSM-IV-TR* (4th ed., text revision). Washington, DC: American Psychiatric Association.

American Psychiatric Association. (2013). *Diagnostic and statistical manual of mental disorders: DSM-5* (5th ed.). Washington, DC: American Psychiatric Association.

American Psychological Association. (2010). *Publication manual of the American Psychological Association* (6th ed.). Washington, DC: American Psychological Association.

Anastasi, A. (1982). *Psychological testing.* New York: Macmillan.

Andersen, S. M. (1984). Self-knowledge and social inference: II. The diagnosticity of cognitive/affective and behavioral data. *Journal of Personality and Social Psychology, 46,* 294–307.

Andersen, S. M., & Baum, A. (1994). Transference in interpersonal relations: Inferences and affect based on significant-other representations. *Journal of Personality, 62,* 459–497.

Andersen, S. M., & Berk, M. S. (1998). The social-cognitive model of transference: Experiencing past relationships in the present. *Current Directions in Psychological Science, 7,* 109–115.

Andersen, S. M., & Chen, S. (2002). The relational self: An interpersonal social-cognitive theory. *Psychological Review, 109,* 619–645.

Andersen, S. M., & Thorpe, J. S. (2009). An IF-THEN theory of personality: Significant others and the relational self. *Journal of Research in Personality, 43,* 163–170.

Anderson, C. A. (1989). Temperature and aggression: Ubiquitous effects of heat on occurrence of human violence. *Psychological Bulletin, 106,* 74–96.

Anderson, C. A., Buckley, K. E., & Carnagey, N. L. (2008). Creating your own hostile environment: A laboratory examination of trait aggressiveness and the violence escalation cycle. *Personality and Social Psychology Bulletin, 34,* 462–473.

Anderson, C. A., Shibuya, A., Ihori, N., Swing, E. L., Bushman, B. J., Sakamoto, A., et al. (2010). Violent video game effects on aggression, empathy, and prosocial behavior in Eastern and Western countries: A meta-analytic review. *Psychological Bulletin, 136,* 151–173.

Anderson, C., John, O. P., Keltner, D., & Kring, A. M. (2001). Who attains social status? Effects of personality and physical attractiveness in social groups. *Journal of Personality and Social Psychology, 81,* 116–132.

Anderson, E. (1994, May). The code of the streets. *Atlantic Monthly, 273,* 80–94.

Anderson, Z. (2015). Elderly priming effects on reaction time, grip strength, and driving proficiency. *Carnegie Mellon University Research Showcase.* Retrieved from http://repository.cmu.edu/cgi/viewcontent.cgi?article=1227&context=hsshonors

Ang, R. P., & Yusof, N. (2005). The relationship between aggression, narcissism, and self-esteem in Asian children and adolescents. *Current Psychology, 24,* 113–122.

Anusic, I., & Schimmack, U. (2016). Stability and change of personality traits, self-esteem, and well-being: Introducing the meta-analytic stability and change model of retest correlations. *Journal of Personality and Social Psychology, 110*(5), 766–781.

Appelbaum, M., Cooper, H., Kline, R.B., Mayo-Wilson, E., Nezu, A.M., & Rao, S.M. (2018). Journal article reporting standards for quantitative research in psychology: The APA Publications and Communications Board task force report. *American Psychologist, 73,* 3–25.

Apter, M. J. (1992). *The dangerous edge: The psychology of excitement.* New York: Free Press.

Archer, J. (2000). Sex differences in aggression between heterosexual partners: A meta-analytic review. *Psychological Bulletin, 126,* 651–680.

Aronson, E. (1972). *The social animal.* San Francisco: Freeman.

Arsenian, J., & Arsenian, J. M. (1948). Tough and easy cultures: A conceptual analysis. *Psychiatry, 11,* 377–385.

Asch, S. E. (1956). Studies of independence and conformity: I. A minority of one against a unanimous group. *Psychological Monographs, 70*(9, Whole No. 416).

Asendorpf, J. B. (2002). The puzzle of personality types [Editorial]. *European Journal of Personality, 16,* 51–55.

Asendorpf, J. B., & van Aken, M. A. G. (1991). Correlates of the temporal consistency of personality patterns in childhood. *Journal of Personality, 59,* 689–703.

Asendorpf, J. B., & van Aken, M. A. G. (1999). Resilient, overcontrolled, and undercontrolled personality prototypes in childhood: Replicability, predictive power, and the trait-type issue. *Journal of Personality and Social Psychology, 77,* 815–832.

Asendorpf, J. B., Banse, R., & Mücke, D. (2002). Double dissociation between implicit and explicit personality self-concept: The case of shy behavior. *Journal of Personality and Social Psychology, 83,* 380–393.

Asendorpf, J. B., Borkenau, P., Ostendorf, F., & van Aken, M. A. G. (2001). Carving personality description at its joints: Confirmation of three replicable personality prototypes for both children and adults. *European Journal of Personality, 15,* 169–198.

Asendorpf, J. B., Conner, M., De Fruyt, F., De Houwer, J., Denissen, J. J. A., Fiedler, K., et al. (2013). Recommendations for increasing replicability in psychology. *European Journal of Personality, 27*(2), 108–119.

Asendorpf, J. B., Denissen, J. J. A., & van Aken, M. A. G. (2008). Inhibited and aggressive preschool children at 23 years of age: Personality and social transitions into adulthood. *Developmental Psychology, 44,* 997–1011.

Ashton, M. C., & Lee, K. (2005). Honesty-humility, the Big Five, and the Five-Factor Model. *Journal of Personality, 73,* 1321–1353.

Associated Press. (1994, May 5). African emigrants spread practice. Retrieved online from Prodigy service.

Assouline, M., & Meir, E. I. (1987). Meta-analysis of the relationship between congruence and well-being measures. *Journal of Vocational Behavior, 31,* 319–332.

Atherton, O. E., Robins, R. E., Rentfrow, P. J., & Lamb, M. E. (2014). Personality correlates of risky health outcomes: Findings from a large internet study. *Journal of Research in Personality, 50,* 56–60.

Augustine, A. A., Larsen, R. J., Walker, M. S., & Fisher, E. B. (2008). Personality predictors of the time course for lung cancer onset. *Journal of Research in Personality, 42,* 1448–1455.

Augustine, A. A., Mehl, M. R., & Larsen, R. J. (2011). A positivity bias in written and spoken English and its moderation by personality and gender. *Social Psychological and Personality Science, 2,* 508–515.

Averill, J. R. (1997). The emotions: An integrative approach. In R. Hogan, J. Johnson, & S. Briggs (Eds.), *Handbook of personality psychology* (pp. 513–541). San Diego, CA: Academic Press.

Avinun, R., & Knafo, A. (2014). Parenting as a reaction evoked by children's genotype: A meta-analysis of children-as-twin studies. *Personality and Social Psychology Review, 18,* 87–102.

Azrin, N. H., & Holz, W. C. (1966). Punishment. In W. K. Honig (Ed.), *Operant behavior: Areas of research and application* (pp. 380–447). East Norwalk, CT: Appleton-Century-Crofts.

Bachrach, H. M., Galatzer-Levy, R., Skolnikoff, A., & Waldron, S. (1991). On the efficacy of psychoanalysis. *Journal of the American Psychoanalytic Association, 39*, 871–916.

Back, M. D., Küffner, A. C. P., Dufner, M., Gerlach, T. M., Rauthmann, J. F., & Denissen, J. J. A. (2013). Narcissistic admiration and rivalry: Disentangling the bright and dark sides of narcissism. *Journal of Personality and Social Psychology, 105*, 1013–1037.

Back, M. D., Penke, L., Schmukle, S. C., & Asendorpf, J. B. (2011). Knowing your own mate value: Sex-specific personality effects on the accuracy of expected mate choices. *Psychological Science, 22*, 984–989.

Back, M. D., Schmukle, S. C., & Egloff, B. (2009). Predicting actual behavior from the explicit and implicit self-concept of personality. *Journal of Personality and Social Psychology, 97*, 533–548.

Back, M. D., Schmukle, S. C., & Egloff, B. (2010). Why are narcissists so charming at first sight? Decoding the narcissism-popularity link at zero acquaintance. *Journal of Personality and Social Psychology, 98*, 132–145.

Back, M. D., Stopfer, J. M., Vazire, S., Gaddis, S., Schmukle, S. C., Egloff, B., et al. (2010). Facebook profiles reflect actual personality, not self-idealization. *Psychological Science, 21*, 372–374.

Bader, M. J. (1994). The tendency to neglect therapeutic aims in psychoanalysis. *Psychoanalytic Quarterly, 63*, 246–270.

Bakan, D. (1966). *The duality of human existence.* Chicago: Rand McNally.

Balcetis, E., Dunning, D., & Miller, R. L. (2008). Do collectivists know themselves better than individualists? Cross-cultural studies of the holier-than-thou phenomenon. *Journal of Personality and Social Psychology, 95*, 1252–1267.

Baldwin, M. W. (1999). Relational schemas: Research into social-cognitive aspects of interpersonal experience. In D. Cervone & Y. Shoda (Eds.), *The coherence of personality: Social-cognitive bases of consistency, variability, and organization* (pp. 127–154). New York: Guilford Press.

Ball, J. D., Archer, R. P., & Imhof, E. A. (1994). Time requirements of psychological testing: A survey of practitioners. *Journal of Personality Assessment, 63*, 239–247.

Balter, M. (2002). What made humans modern? *Science, 295*, 1219–1225.

Bamia, C., Trichopoulou, A., & Trichopoulos, D. (2008). Age at retirement and mortality in a general population sample. The Greek EPIC study. *American Journal of Epidemiology, 167*, 561–569.

Bandelow, B., Schmahl, C., Falkai, P., & Wedekind, D. (2010). Borderline personality disorder: A dysregulation of the endogenous opioid system? *Psychological Review, 117*, 623–636.

Bandura, A. (1971). *Social learning theory.* New York: General Learning Press.

Bandura, A. (1977). *Social learning theory.* Englewood Cliffs, NJ: Prentice-Hall.

Bandura, A. (1978). The self system in reciprocal determinism. *American Psychologist, 33*, 344–358.

Bandura, A. (1989). Human agency in social cognitive theory. *American Psychologist, 44*, 1175–1184.

Bandura, A. (1999). Social cognitive theory of personality. In D. Cervone & Y. Shoda (Eds.), *The coherence of personality: Social-cognitive bases of consistency, variability, and organization* (pp. 185–241). New York: Guilford Press.

Bandura, A., Ross, D., & Ross, S. A. (1963). Imitation of film-mediated aggressive models. *Journal of Abnormal and Social Psychology, 66*, 3–11.

Baragh, D. P. (2012). *Homo mysteriousus: Evolutionary puzzles of human nature.* New York and Oxford: Oxford University Press.

Baranski, E. N. (2018). *Volitional personality change across 58 countries.* Unpublished doctoral dissertation, University of California, Riverside.

Baranski, E. N., Gardiner, G., Guillaume, E., Aveyard, M., Bastian, B., Bronin, Il, Ivanova, C., . . . Funder, D. C. (2017). Comparisons of daily behavior across 21 countries. *Social Psychological and Personality Science, 8*, 252–266.

Baranski, E. N., Morse, P. J., & Dunlop, W. L. (2017). Lay conceptions of volitional personality change: From strategies pursued to stories told. *Journal of Personality, 85*, 285–299.

Baranski, E. N., Morse, P. J., & Dunlop, W. L. (2014). *Internet survey of desires to change personality.* Unpublished data, University of California, Riverside.

Barefoot, J. C., Dahlstrom, G. W., & Williams, R. B. (1983). Hostility, CHD incidence, and total mortality: A 25-year follow-up study of 255 physicians. *Psychosomatic Medicine, 45*, 59–63.

Bargh, J. A., Bond, R. N., Lombardi, W. J., & Tota, M. E. (1986). The additive nature of chronic and temporary sources of construct accessibility. *Journal of Personality and Social Psychology, 50*, 869–878.

Bargh, J. A., Lombardi, W. J., & Higgins, E. T. (1988). Automaticity of chronically accessible constructs in person × situation effects on person perception: It's just a matter of time. *Journal of Personality and Social Psychology, 55*, 599–605.

Bargh, J.A., Chen, M., & Burrows, L. (1996). Automaticity of social behavior: Direct effects of trait construct and stereotype activation in on action. *Journal of Personality and Social Psychology, 71*, 230–244.

Barker, E. T., Howard, A. L., Galambos, N. L., & Wrosch, C. (2016). Tracking affect and academic success across university: Happy students benefit from bouts of negative mood. *Developmental Psychology, 52*(12), 2022–2030.

Bartz, J.A. (2016). Oxytocin and the pharmacological dissection of affiliation. *Current Directions in Psychological Science, 25*, 104–110.

Barlow, D. H., Ellard, K. K., Sauer-Zavala, S., Bullis, J. R., & Carl, J. R. (2014). The origins of neuroticism. *Perspectives on Psychological Science, 9*, 481–496.

Barlow, D. H., Sauer-Zavala, S., Carl, J. R., Bullis, J. R., & Ellard, K. K. (2014). The nature, diagnosis, and treatment of neuroticism: Back to the future. *Clinical Psychological Science, 2*(3), 344–365.

Barrett, L. F. (2006). Are emotions natural kinds? *Perspectives on Psychological Science, 1*, 28–58.

Barrett, L. F., & Wager, T. D. (2006). The structure of emotion: Evidence from neuroimaging studies. *Current Directions in Psychological Science, 15*, 79–83.

Barrick, M. R., & Mount, M. K. (1991). The Big Five personality dimensions and job performance: A meta-analysis. *Personnel Psychology, 44*, 1–26.

Baumeister, R. F., & Tice, D. M. (1988). Metatraits. *Journal of Personality, 56*, 571–598.

Baumeister, R. F., & Vohs, K. D. (2002). The pursuit of meaningfulness in life. In C. R. Snyder & S. J. Lopez (Eds.), *Handbook of positive psychology* (pp. 608–618). New York: Oxford University Press.

Baumeister, R. F., Smart, L., & Boden, J. M. (1996). Relation of threatened egotism to violence and aggression: The dark side of high self-esteem. *Psychological Review, 103*, 5–33.

Baumeister, R.F., & Leary, M.R. (1995). The need to belong: Desire for interpersonal attachments as a fundamental human motivation. *Psychological Bulleting, 117*, 497–529.

Baumeister, R.F., Vohs, K.D., & Funder, D.C. (2007). Psychology as the science of self-reports and finger movements. Whatever happened to actual behavior? *Perspectives on Psychological Science, 2*, 396–403.

Baumrind, D. (1971). Current patterns of parental authority. *Developmental Psychology, 4*, 1–103.

Baumrind, D. (1985). Research using intentional deception: Ethical issues revisited. *American Psychologist, 40*, 165–174.

Baumrind, D. (1991). The influence of parenting style on adolescent competence and substance use. *Journal of Early Adolescence, 11*, 56–95.

Becker, M., Vignoles, V. L., Owe, E., Brown, R., Smith, P. B, Easterbrook, M., et al. (2012). Culture and the distinctiveness motive: Constructing identity in individualistic and collectivist contexts. *Journal of Personality and Social Psychology, 102*, 833–855.

Bégue, L., Beauvois, J-L., Courbet, D., Oberlé, D., Lepage, J., & Duke, A.A. (2015). Personality predicts obedience in a Milgram paradigm. *Journal of Personality, 83*, 299–306.

Bejjani, B.-P., Damier, P., Arnulf, I., Thivard, L., Bonnet, A-M., Dormonet, D., et al. (1999). Transient acute depression induced by high-frequency deep-brain stimulating. *New England Journal of Medicine, 340*, 1476–1480.

Bellamy, G. T. (1975). The Pygmalion effect: What teacher behaviors mediate it? *Psychology in the Schools, 12*, 454–461.

Belsky, J., Steinberg, L., & Draper, P. (1991). Childhood experience, interpersonal development, and reproductive strategy: An evolutionary theory of socialization. *Child Development, 62*, 647–670.

Bem, D. J. (1972). Self-perception theory. In L. Berkowitz (Ed.), *Advances in experimental social psychology* (Vol. 6, pp. 1–62). New York: Academic Press.

Bem, D.J. (1996). Exotic becomes erotic: A developmental theory of sexual orientation. *Psychological Review, 103*, 320–355.

Bem, D. J., & Allen, A. (1974). On predicting some of the people some of the time: The search for cross-situational consistencies in behavior. *Psychological Review, 81*, 506–520.

Bem, D. J., & Funder, D. C. (1978). Predicting more of the people more of the time: Assessing the personality of situations. *Psychological Review, 85*, 485–501.

Bem, D.J. (2011). Feeling the future: Experimental evidence for anomalous retroactive influences on cognition and affect. *Journal of Personality and Social Psychology, 100*, 407–425.

Benet-Martínez, V., & Haritatos, J. (2005). Bicultural identity integration (BII): Components and psychosocial antecedents. *Journal of Personality, 73*, 1015–1050.

Benet-Martínez, V., & John, O. P. (1998). Los Cinco Grandes across cultures and ethnic groups: Multitrait-multimethod analyses of the Big Five in Spanish and English. *Journal of Personality and Social Psychology, 75*, 729–750.

Benet-Martínez, V., & John, O. P. (2000). Toward the development of quasi-indigenous personality constructs: Measuring Los Cinco Grandes in Spain with indigenous Castilian markers. *American Behavioral Scientist, 44*, 141–157.

Benet-Martínez, V., & Waller, N. G. (1997). Further evidence for the cross-cultural generality of the Big Seven Factor model: Indigenous and imported Spanish personality constructs. *Journal of Personality, 65*, 567–598.

Benet-Martínez, V., Leu, J., Lee, F., & Morris, M. (2002). Negotiating biculturalism: Cultural frame switching in biculturals with oppositional versus compatible cultural identities. *Journal of Cross-Cultural Psychology, 33*, 492–516.

Benjamin, D. J., Berger, J., Johannesson, M., Nosek, B. A., Wagenmakers, E., . . . Johnson, V. (2017). Redefine statistical significance. Retrieved from psyarxiv.com/mky9j.

Benjamin, J., Li, L., Patterson, C., Greenberg, B. D., Murphy, D. L., & Hamer, D. H. (1996). Population and familial association between the D4 dopamine receptor gene and measures of novelty seeking. *Nature Genetics, 12*, 81–84.

Bentham, J. (1988). *The principles of morals and legislation.* Amherst, NY: Prometheus Books. (Originally published 1781).

Berg, A. I., & Johansson, B. (2013). Personality change in the oldest-old: Is it a matter of compromised health and functioning? *Journal of Personality, 82*, 25–31.

Berg, V., Lummaa, V., Lahdenpera, M., Rotkirch, A., & Jokela, M. (2014). Personality and long-term reproductive success measured by the number of grandchildren. *Evolution and Human Behavior, 35*, 533–539

Bergeman, C. S., Chipuer, H. M., Plomin, R., Pedersen, N. L., McClearn, G. E., Nesselroade, J. R., et al. (1993). Genetic and environmental effects on openness to experience, agreeableness, and conscientiousness: An adoption/twin study. *Journal of Personality, 61*, 159–179.

Berke, R. L. (1998, September 27). The good leader: In presidents, virtues can be flaws (and vice versa). *New York Times.*

Bernhardt, P. C., Dabbs, J. M., Jr., Fielden, J. A., & Lutter, C. D. (1998). Testosterone changes during vicarious experiences of winning and losing among fans at sporting events. *Physiology and Behavior, 65*, 59–62.

Bernstein, N. (2008, March 12). Foes of sex trade are stung by the fall of an ally. *New York Times*. Retrieved from http://www.nytimes.com/2008/03/12/nyregion/12prostitute.html?_r=1.

Berry, D. S., & Pennebaker, J. W. (1993). Nonverbal and verbal emotional expression and health. *Psychotherapy and Psychosomatics, 59*, 11–19.

Berry, D. S., & Wero, J. F. (1993). Accuracy in face perception: A view from ecological psychology. *Journal of Personality, 61*, 497–520.

Berry, J. W. (1969). On cross-cultural comparability. *International Journal of Psychology, 4*, 119–128.

Betan, E., Heim, A. K., Conklin, C. Z., & Westen, D. (2005). Countertransference phenomena and personality psychology in clinical practice: An empirical investigation. *American Journal of Psychiatry, 162*, 890–898.

Bettelheim, B. (1943). Individual and mass behavior in extreme situations. *Journal of Abnormal and Social Psychology, 38*, 417–452.

Bettelheim, B. (1982). *Freud and man's soul*. New York: Vintage.

Bettelheim, B. (1988). *A good enough parent*. New York: Vintage.

Bhattacharjee, Y. (2013, April 28). The mind of a con man (Diederik Stapel). New York Times Magazine.

Biernat, M. (1989). Motives and values to achieve: Different constructs with different effects. *Journal of Personality, 57*, 69–95.

Biesanz, J. C., & Human, L. J. (2010). The cost of forming more accurate impressions: Accuracy-motivated perceivers see the personality of others more distinctively but less normatively than perceivers without an explicit goal. *Psychological Science, 21*, 589–594.

Biesanz, J. C., Human, L. J., Paquin, A., Chan, M., Parisotto, K. L., Sarracino, J., et al. (2011). Do we know when our impressions of others are valid? Evidence for realistic accuracy awareness in first impressions of personality. *Social Psychological and Personality Science, 2*, 452–459.

Biesanz, J. C., West, S. G., & Millevoi, A. (2007). What do you learn about someone over time? The relationship between length of acquaintance and consensus and self-other agreement in judgments of personality. *Journal of Personality and Social Psychology, 92*, 119–135.

Bigelow, H. J. (1850). Dr. Harlow's case of recovery from the passage of an iron bar through the head. *American Journal of Medical Sciences, 16*(39), 13–22.

Binswanger, L. (1958). The case of Ellen West. In R. May, E. Angel, & H. F. Ellenberger (Eds.), *Existence* (pp. 237–364). New York: Basic Books.

Binswanger, L. (1963). *Being-in-the-world: Selected papers of Ludwig Binswanger*. New York: Basic Books.

Birbaumer, N., Grodd, W., Diedrich, O., Klose, U., Erb, M., & Lotze, M. (1998). fMRI reveals amygdala activation to human faces in social phobics. *Neuroreport, 9*, 1223–1226.

Blackman, M. C. (2002a). The employment interview via the telephone: Are we sacrificing accurate personality judgments for cost efficiency? *Journal of Research in Personality, 36*, 208–223.

Blackman, M. C. (2002b). Personality judgment and the utility of the unstructured employment interview. *Basic and Applied Social Psychology, 24*, 241–250.

Blackman, M. C., & Funder, D. C. (1998). The effect of information on consensus and accuracy in personality judgment. *Journal of Experimental Social Psychology, 34*, 164–181.

Blanton, H., & Jaccard, J. (2006). Arbitrary metrics in psychology. *American Psychologist, 61*, 27–41.

Bleidorn, W. (2012). Hitting the road to adulthood: Short-term personality development during a major life transition. *Personality and Social Psychology Bulletin, 38*, 1594–1608.

Bleidorn, W., Hopwood, C. J., Ackerman, R. A., Witt, E. A., Kandler, C., Riemann, R., . . . Donnellan, M. B. (2019). The healthy personality from a basic trait perspective. *Journal of Personality and Social Psychology*. Advance online publication.

Bleidorn, W., Hopwood, C. J., & Lucas, R. E. (2018). Life events and personality trait change. *Journal of Personality, 86*, 83–96.

Bleidorn, W., Klimstra, T. A., Denissen, J. A., Rentfrow, P. J., Potter, J., & Gosling, S. (2013). Personality maturation around the world: A cross-cultural examination of social investment theory. *Psychological Science, 24*, 2530–2540.

Blickle, G., Kane-Frieder, R. E., Oerder, K.,Wihler, A., von Below, A., Schütte, N., . . . Ferris, G. R. (2013a). Leader behaviors as mediators of the leader characteristics—follower satisfaction relationship. *Group & Organization Management, 38,* 601–628.

Block, J. (1961). *The Q-sort method in psychological assessment and psychiatric research.* Springfield, IL: Thomas.

Block, J. (1977). Advancing the science of psychology: Paradigmatic shift or improving the quality of research? In D. Magnusson & N. S. Endler (Eds.), *Personality at the crossroads: Current issues in interactional psychology* (pp. 37–64). Hillsdale, NJ: Erlbaum.

Block, J. (1978). *The Q-sort method in personality assessment and psychiatric research.* Palo Alto, CA: Consulting Psychologists Press. (Originally published 1961)

Block, J. (1989). Critique of the act frequency approach to personality. *Journal of Personality and Social Psychology, 56,* 234–245.

Block, J. (1993). Studying personality the long way. In D. C. Funder, R. D. Parke, C. Tomlinson-Keasey, & K. Widaman (Eds.), *Studying lives through time: Personality and development* (pp. 9–41). Washington, DC: American Psychological Association.

Block, J. (1995). A contrarian view of the five-factor approach to personality description. *Psychological Bulletin, 117,* 187–215.

Block, J. (2002). *Personality as an affect-processing system: Toward an integrative theory.* Mahwah, NJ: Erlbaum.

Block, J. (2008). *The Q-sort in character appraisal: Encoding subjective impressions of persons quantitatively.* Washington, DC: American Psychological Association.

Block, J. (2010). The five-factor framing of personality and beyond: Some ruminations. *Psychological Inquiry, 21*(1), 2–25.

Block, J. H., & Block, J. (1980). The role of ego-control and ego-resiliency in the organization of behavior. In W. A. Collins (Ed.), *Development of cognition, affect, and social relations: The Minnesota symposia on child psychology* (Vol. 13, pp. 39–101). Hillsdale, NJ: Erlbaum.

Block, J., & Block, J. H. (2006a). Nursery school personality and political orientation two decades later. *Journal of Research in Personality, 40,* 734–749.

Block, J., & Block, J. H. (2006b). Venturing a 30-year longitudinal study. *American Psychologist, 61,* 315–327.

Block, J., Block, J. H., Siegelman, E., & von der Lippe, A. (1971). Optimal psychological adjustment: Response to Miller's and Bronfenbrenner's discussions. *Journal of Consulting and Clinical Psychology, 36,* 325–328.

Block, J., Gjerde, P. F., & Block, J. H. (1991). Personality antecedents of depressive tendencies in 18-year-olds: A prospective study. *Journal of Personality and Social Psychology, 60,* 726–738.

Blum, K., Cull, J. G., Braverman, E. R., & Comings, D. E. (1996). Reward deficiency syndrome. *American Scientist, 84,* 132–146.

Bogg, T., & Roberts, B. W. (2004). Conscientiousness and health-related behaviors: A meta-analysis of the leading behavioral contributors to mortality. *Psychological Bulletin, 130,* 887–919.

Boksem, M. A. S., Mehta, P. H., van den Bergh, B., van Son, V., Trautmann, S. T., Roelofs, K., . . . Sanfey, A. G. (2013). Testosterone inhibits trust promotes reciprocity. *Psychological Science, 24,* 2306–2314.

Bolger, N., & Zuckerman, A. (1995). A framework for studying personality in the stress process. *Journal of Personality and Social Psychology, 69,* 890–902.

Bollich, K.L., Rogers, K.H., & Vazire, S. (2015). Knowing more than we can tell: People are aware of their biased self-perceptions. *Personality and Social Psychology Bulletin, 41,* 918–929.

Bond, M. H. (1979). Dimensions of personality used in perceiving peers: Cross-cultural comparisons of Hong Kong, Japanese, American, and Filipino university students. *International Journal of Psychology, 14,* 47–56.

Bond, M. H., Nakazato, H., & Shiraishi, D. (1975). Universality and distinctiveness in dimensions of Japanese person perception. *Journal of Cross-Cultural Psychology, 6,* 346–357.

Booth-Kewley, S., & Friedman, H. S. (1987). Psychological predictors of heart disease: A quantitative review. *Psychological Bulletin, 101,* 343–362.

Borghans, L., Duckworth, A. L., Heckman, J. J., & ter Weel, B. (2008). The economics and psychology of personality traits. *Journal of Human Resources, 43,* 972–1059.

Borghans, L., Golsteyn, B. H. H., Heckman, J. J., & Humphries, J. E. (2011). *Identification problems in personality psychology.* Working paper 16917. Cambridge, MA: National Bureau of Economic Research.

Borghuis, J., Deniseen, J.J.A., Obserski, D., Sijtsma, K., Meeus, W.H.J., Branje, S., . . . Bleidorn, W. (2017). Big Five personality stability, change, and coedevelopment across adolescence and early adulthood. *Journal of Personality and Social Psychology, 113,* 641–657.

Borkenau, P., & Liebler, A. (1993). Consensus and self-other agreement for trait inferences from minimal information. *Journal of Personality, 61,* 477–496.

Borkenau, P., Riemann, R., Angleitner, A., & Spinath, F. M. (2001). Genetic and environmental influences on observed personality: Evidence from the German observational study of adult twins. *Journal of Personality and Social Psychology, 80,* 655–668.

Borkenau, P., Riemann, R., Angleitner, A., & Spinath, F. M. (2002). Assessment issues in behavior-genetic research in personality. *Psychology: The Journal of the Hellenic Psychological Society, 9,* 212–225.

Borman, W. C., & Penner, L. A. (2001). Citizenship performance: Its nature, antecedents and motives. In B. W. Roberts & R. Hogan (Eds.), *Personality psychology in the workplace* (pp. 45–61). Washington, DC: American Psychological Association.

Borman, W. C., Hanson, W., & Hedge, J. (1997). Personnel selection. *Annual Review of Psychology, 48,* 299–337.

Born, J., Hitzler, V., Pietrowsky, R., Pairschinger, P., & Fehm, H. L. (1988). Influences of cortisol on auditory evoked potentials and mood in humans. *Neuropsychobiology, 20,* 145–151.

Bornstein, R. F. (1999a). Criterion validity of objective and projective dependency tests: A meta-analytic assessment of behavioral prediction. *Psychological Assessment, 11,* 48–57.

Bornstein, R. F. (1999b). Source amnesia, misattribution, and the power of unconscious perceptions and memories. *Psychoanalytic Psychology, 16,* 155–178.

Borsboom, D., Mellenbergh, G. J., & van Heerden, J. (2004). The concept of validity. *Psychological Review, 111,* 1061–1071.

Boss, M. (1963). *Psychoanalysis and daseinsanalysis.* New York: Basic Books.

Bouchard, T. J., Jr. (2004). Genetic influence on human psychological traits: A survey. *Current Directions in Psychological Science, 13,* 148–151.

Boudreaux, M. J. (2016). Personality-related problems and the five-factor model of personality. *Personality Disorders: Theory, Research, and Treatment, 7*(4), 372–383.

Boudreaux, M. J., Piedmont, R. C., Sherman, M. F., & Ozer, D. J. (2012). Identifying personality-related problems in living: The multi-context problems checklist. *Journal of Personality Assessment, 95,* 62–73.

Boudreaux, M. J., Piedmont, R. L., & Sherman, M. F. (2011, June). *Identifying personality-related problems in living: The multi-context problems checklist.* Paper presented at the Biannual Meetings of the Association for Research in Personality, Riverside, CA.

Bower, G. H., & Hilgard, E. R. (1981). *Theories of learning* (5th ed.). Englewood Cliffs, NJ: Prentice-Hall.

Bowers, K. S. (1973). Situationism in psychology: An analysis and critique. *Psychological Review, 80,* 307–336.

Bowlby, J. (1982). *Attachment and loss: Vol. 1. Attachment* (2nd ed.). New York: Basic Books. (Originally published 1969).

Bowlby, J. (1988). *A secure base: Clinical applications of attachment theory.* London: Routledge.

Bowling, N.A., Huang, J.L., Bragg, C.B., Khazaon, S., Liu, M., & Blackmore, C.E. (2016). Who cares and who is careless? Insufficient effort responding as a reflection of respondent personality. *Journal of Personality and Social Psychology, 111,* 218–229.

Box, G. E. P. (1979). Robustness in the strategy of scientific model building. In R. Launer & G. Wilkinson (Eds.), *Robustness in statistics* (pp. 201–236). New York: Academic Press.

Boyce, C. J., & Wood, A. M. (2011). Personality prior to disability determines adaptation: Agreeable individuals recover lost life satisfaction faster and more completely. *Psychological Science, 22,* 1397–1402.

Boyce, C. J., Wood, A. M., & Brown, G. D. A. (2010). The dark side of conscientiousness: Conscientious people experience greater drops in life satisfaction following unemployment. *Journal of Research in Personality, 44,* 535–539.

Boyce, C. J., Wood, A. M., Daly, M., & Sedikides, C. (in press). Personality change following unemployment. *Journal of Applied Psychology.*

Boyce, C.J., Wood, A.M., Daly, M., & Sedikides, C. (2015). Personality change following unemployment. *Journal of Applied Psychology, 100,* 991–1011.

Boyle, C., & Shapiro, R. (2010, April 7). Rescue of baby Bridget wasn't on brave Frenchman Julien Duret's New York City vacation itinerary. *New York Daily News.* Retrieved from http://www.nydailynews.com/new-york/rescue-baby-bridget-wasn-brave-frenchman-julien-duret-new-york-city-vacation-itinerary-article-1.165621

Brandt, V. S. (1974). Skiing cross-culturally. *Current Anthropology, 15,* 64–66.

Braun, C. (1976). Teacher expectation: Sociopsychological dynamics. *Review of Educational Research, 46,* 185–213.

Bremner, J. D. (2005). *Brain imaging handbook.* New York: Norton.

Brenner, C. (1974). *An elementary textbook of psychoanalysis.* Garden City, NY: Doubleday/Anchor.

Bresin, K., & Robinson, M. D. (2014). You are what you see and choose: Agreeableness and situation selection. *Journal of Personality.* Advance online publication. doi: 10.1111/jopy.12121.

Brickman, P., Coates, D., & Janoff-Bulman, R. (1978). Lottery winners and accident victims: Is happiness relative? *Journal of Personality and Social Psychology, 36,* 917–927.

Brickner, R. M. (1936). *The intellectual functions of the frontal lobes.* New York: Macmillan.

Briggs, S. R., & Cheek, J. M. (1986). The role of factor analysis in the development and evaluation of personality scales. *Journal of Personality, 54,* 106–148.

Briley, D. A., & Tucker-Drob, E. M. (2014). Genetic and environmental continuity in personality development: A meta-analysis. *Psychological Bulletin, 140,* 1301–1331.

Brown, K. W., & Ryan, R. M. (2003). The benefits of being present: Mindfulness and its role in psychological well-being. *Journal of Personality and Social Psychology, 84,* 822–848.

Brown, N.A., Blake, A.B., & Sherman, R.A. (2017). A snapshot of the life as lived: Wearable cameras in social and personality psychological science. *Social Psychological and Personality Science, 8,* 592–600.

Brown, R. (1996). *Against my better judgment: An intimate memoir of an eminent gay psychologist.* New York: Harrington Park Press.

Brown, W. (1910). Some experimental results in the correlation of mental abilities. *British Journal of Psychology, 3,* 296–302.

Brummelman, E., Thomaes, & Sedikides, C. (2016). Separating narcissism from self-esteem. *Current Directions in Psychological Science, 25,* 8–13.

Brunstein, J. C., & Maier, G. W. (2005). Implicit and self-attributed motives to achieve: Two separate but interacting needs. *Journal of Personality and Social Psychology, 89,* 205–222.

Bryan, W. J. (1922/2009). *The menace of evolution.* Retrieved from http://www.law.umkc.edu/faculty/projects/ftrials/scopes/scopes.htm

Buck, R. (1999). The biological affects: A typology. *Psychological Review, 106,* 301–336.

Buckholtz, J. W., Treadway, M. T., Cowan, R. L., Woodward, N. D., Li, R., Ansari, M. S., et al. (2010). Dopaminergic network differences in human impulsivity. *Science, 329,* 532.

Buffardi, L. E., & Campbell, W. K. (2008). Narcissism and social networking sites. *Personality and Social Psychology Bulletin, 34,* 1303–1314.

Burt, S. A. (2009). Rethinking environmental contributions to child and adolescent psychopathology: A meta-analysis of shared environmental influences. *Psychological Bulletin, 135,* 608–637.

Burwen, L. S., & Campbell, D. T. (1957). The generality of attitudes toward authority and nonauthority figures. *Journal of Abnormal and Social Psychology, 54,* 24–31.

Bushman, B. J. (2002). Does venting anger feed or extinguish the flame? Catharsis, rumination, distraction, anger and aggressive responding. *Personality and Social Psychology Bulletin, 28*, 724–731.

Bushman, B. J., & Anderson, C. A. (2009). Comfortably numb: Desensitizing effects of violent media on helping others. *Psychological Science, 20*, 273–277.

Bushman, B. J., & Baumeister, R. F. (1998). Threatened egotism, narcissism, self-esteem, and direct and displaced aggression: Does self-love or self-hate lead to violence? *Journal of Personality and Social Psychology, 75*, 219–229.

Buss, A. R. (1979). The trait-situation controversy and the concept of interaction. *Personality and Social Psychology Bulletin, 6*, 196–201.

Buss, D. M. (1989). Sex differences in human mate preferences: Evolutionary hypotheses tested in 37 cultures. *Behavioral and Brain Sciences, 12*, 1–49.

Buss, D. M., & Barnes, M. F. (1986). Preferences in human mate selection. *Journal of Personality and Social Psychology, 50*, 559–570.

Buss, D. M., & Greiling, H. (1999). Adaptive individual differences. *Journal of Personality, 67*, 209–243.

Buss, D. M., Larsen, R. J., Westen, D., & Semmelroth, J. (1992). Sex differences in jealousy: Evolution, physiology and psychology. *Psychological Science, 3*, 251–255.

Buss, D.M. (2003). *The evolution of desire.* New York: Basic Books.

Butcher, J. N. (1999). *A beginner's guide to the MMPI-2.* Washington, DC: American Psychological Association.

Butler, J. M., & Haigh, G. V. (1954). Changes in the relation between self-concepts and ideal concepts consequent upon client-centered counseling. In C. R. Rogers & R. F. Dymond (Eds.), *Psychotherapy and personality change: Co-ordinated studies in the client-centered approach* (pp. 55–75). University of Chicago Press.

Bykov, K. M. (1957). *The cerebral cortex and the internal organs* (W. H. Gantt, Trans.). New York: Chemical Publishing.

Byrne, D. (1961). The repression-sensitization scale: Rationale, reliability, and validity. *Journal of Personality, 29*, 334–349.

Caldwell, D. F., & Burger, J. M. (1997). Personality and social influence strategies in the workplace. *Personality and Social Psychology Bulletin, 23*, 1003–1012.

Caldwell, D. F., & Burger, J. M. (1998). Personality characteristics of job applicants and success in screening interviews. *Personnel Psychology, 51*, 119–136.

Call, J., & Tomasello, M. (1995). The use of social information in the problem-solving of orangutans and human children. *Journal of Comparative Psychology, 109*, 308–320.

Camara, W. J., Nathan, J. S., & Puente, A. E. (2000). Psychological test usage: Implications in professional psychology. *Professional Psychology: Research and Practice, 31*, 141–154.

Campbell, A. (2010). Oxytocin and human social behavior. *Personality and Social Psychology Review, 14*, 281–295.

Campos, J. J., Barrett, K., Lamb, M. E., Goldsmith, H. H., & Stenberg, C. (1983). Socioemotional development. In M. M. Haith & J. J. Campos (Eds.), *Handbook of child psychology: Vol. 2. Infancy and developmental psychobiology* (pp. 783–916). New York: Wiley.

Canli, T. (2004). Function brain mapping of extraversion and neuroticism: Learning from individual differences in emotion processing. *Journal of Personality, 72*, 1105–1132.

Canli, T., & Lesch, K. (2007). Long story short: The serotonin transporter in emotion regulation and social cognition. *Nature Neuroscience, 10*, 1103–1109.

Canli, T., Amin, Z., Haas, B., Omura, K., & Constable, R. T. (2004). A double dissociation between mood states and personality traits in the anterior cingulate. *Behavioral Neuroscience, 118*, 897–904.

Canli, T., Sivers, H., Whitfield, S. L., Gotlib, I. H., & Gabrieli, J. D. (2002). Amygdala response to happy faces as a function of extraversion. *Science, 296*, 2191.

Cannon, W. B. (1932). *The wisdom of the body.* New York: Norton.

Cantor, N. (1990). From thought to behavior: "Having" and "doing" in the study of personality and cognition. *American Psychologist, 45*, 735–750.

Cantor, N., & Kihlstrom, J. F. (1987). *Personality and social intelligence*. Englewood Cliffs, NJ: Prentice-Hall.

Capgras, J., & Reboul-Lachaux, J. (1923). L'illusion des "sosies" dans un delire systèmisé chronique [The illusion of doubles as a chronically systematized delusion]. *Bulletin de la Société Clinique de Médecine Mentale, 11*, 6–16.

Caplan, B. (2003). Stigler-Becker versus Myers-Briggs: Why preference-blind explanations are scientifically meaningful and empirically important. *Journal of Economic Behavior and Organization, 50*, 391–405.

Carlson, E. N. (2013). Overcoming the barriers to self-knowledge: Mindfulness as a path to seeing yourself as you really are. *Perspectives on Psychological Science, 8*, 173–186.

Carlson, E. N., & Furr, R. M. (2009). Evidence of differential meta-accuracy: People understand the different impressions they make. *Psychological Science, 20*, 1033–1039.

Carlson, E. N., Vazire, S., & Furr, R. M. (2011). Meta-insight: Do people really know how others see them? *Journal of Personality and Social Psychology, 101*, 831–846.

Carlson, E. N., Vazire, S., & Oltmanns, T. F. (2011). You probably think this paper's about you: Narcissists' perceptions of their personality and reputation. *Journal of Personality and Social Psychology, 101*, 185–201.

Carlsson, S., Andersson, T., Michaëlsson, K., Vågerö, D., & Ahlbom, A. (2012). Late retirement is not associated with increased mortality. Results based on all Swedish retirements 1991–2007. *European Journal of Epidemiology, 27*, 483–486.

Carmichael, M. S., Warburton, V. L., Dixen, J., & Davidson, J. M. (1994). Relationships among cardiovascular, muscular, and oxytocin responses during human sexual activity. *Archives of Sexual Behavior, 23*, 59–79.

Carney, D. R., Colvin, C. R., & Hall, J. A. (2007). A thin slice perspective on the accuracy of first impressions. *Journal of Research in Personality, 41*, 1054–1072.

Carstensen, L. L., & Fredrickson, B. L. (1998). Influence of HIV status and age on cognitive representations of others. *Health Psychology, 17*, 494–503.

Carstensen, L. L., & Mikels, J. A. (2005). At the intersection of emotion and cognition: Aging and the positivity effect. *Current Directions in Psychological Science, 14*, 117–121.

Carstensen, L. L., Isaacowitz, D. M., & Charles, S. T. (1999). Taking time seriously: A theory of socioemotional selectivity. *American Psychologist, 54*, 165–181.

Carter, N.T., Guan, L., Maples, R.L., & Miller, J.D. (2015). The downsides of extreme conscientiousness for psychological wellbeing: The role of obsessive compulsive tendencies. *Journal of Personality*. Advance online publication. doi: 10.1111/jopy.12177.

Carver, C. S., & Scheier, M. F. (1995). The role of optimism versus pessimism in the experience of the self. In A. Oosterwegel & R. A. Wicklund (Eds.), *The self in European and North American culture: Development and processes* (pp. 193–204). Dordrecht, Netherlands: Kluwer Academic Press.

Carver, C. S., Scheier, M. F., & Segerstrom, S. C. (2010). Optimism. *Clinical Psychology Review, 30*, 878–889.

Cases, W., Seif, I., Grimsby, J., Gaspar, P., Chen, K., Pournin, S., et al. (1995). Aggressive behavior and altered amounts of brain serotonin and norepinephrine in mice lacking MAOA. *Science, 268*, 1763–1766.

Caspi, A. (1998). Personality development across the life course. In N. Eisenberg (Ed.), *Handbook of child psychology: Vol. 3. Social, emotional, and personality development* (5th ed., pp. 311–388). New York: Wiley.

Caspi, A., & Roberts, B. W. (1999). Personality continuity and change across the life course. In L. A. Pervin & O. John (Eds.), *Handbook of personality: Theory and research* (pp. 300–326). New York: Guilford.

Caspi, A., Elder, G. H., & Bem, D. J. (1987). Moving against the world: Life course patterns of explosive children. *Developmental Psychology, 23*, 308–313.

Caspi, A., McClay, J., Moffitt, T. E., Mill, J., Martin, J., Craig, I., et al. (2002, August 2). Role of genotype in the cycle of violence in maltreated children. *Science, 297*, 851–854.

Caspi, A., Roberts, B. W., & Shiner, R. L. (2005). Personality development: Stability and change. *Annual Review of Psychology, 56*, 453–484.

Caspi, A., Sugden, K., Moffitt, T. E., Taylor, A., Craig, I. W., Harrington, H., et al. (2003, July 18). Influence of life stress on depression: Moderation by a polymorphism in the *5-HTT* gene. *Science, 301,* 386–389.

Cattell, R. B. (1950). *Personality: A systematic, theoretical and factual study.* New York: McGraw-Hill.

Cattell, R. B. (1952). *Factor analysis.* New York: Harper & Row.

Cattell, R. B. (1957). *Personality and motivation structure and measurement.* New York: World Book.

Cattell, R. B. (1965). *The scientific analysis of personality.* Baltimore: Penguin Books.

Cattell, R. B., & Eber, H. W. (1961). *The Sixteen Personality Factor Questionnaire* (3rd ed.). Champaign, IL: Institute for Personality and Ability Testing.

Cervone, D. (2005). Personality architecture: Within-person structures and processes. *Annual Review of Psychology, 56,* 423–452.

Chaiken, S., & Trope, Y. (Eds.). (1999). *Dual-process models in social psychology.* New York: Guilford Press.

Chambers, R., Lo, B. C. Y., & Allen, N. B. (2008). The impact of intensive mindfulness training on attentional control, cognitive style, and affect. *Cognitive Therapy and Research, 32,* 303–322.

Chan, M., Rogers, K. H., Parisotto, K. L., & Biesanz, J. C. (2011). Forming first impressions: The role of gender and normative accuracy in personality perception. *Journal of Research in Personality, 45,* 117–120.

Chan, W., McCrae, R. R., DeFruyt, F., Jussim, L., Löckenhoff, C. E., DeBolle, M., et al. (2012). Stereotypes of age differences in personality traits: Universal and accurate? *Journal of Personality and Social Psychology, 103,* 1050–1066.

Chang, H-H., & Nayga, R. M. (2010). Childhood obesity and unhappiness: The influence of soft drinks and fast food consumption. *Journal of Happiness Studies, 11,* 261–275.

Chao, R. (2001). Extending research on the consequences of parenting style for Chinese Americans and European Americans. *Child Development, 72,* 1832–1843.

Chaplin, W. F. (1991). The next generation of moderator research in personality psychology. *Journal of Personality, 59,* 143–178.

Chaplin, W. F., & Goldberg, L. R. (1984). A failure to replicate the Bem and Allen study of individual differences in cross-situational consistency. *Journal of Personality and Social Psychology, 47,* 1074–1090.

Chaplin, W. F., Phillips, J. B., Brown, J. D., Clanton, N. R., & Stein, J. L. (2000). Handshaking, gender, personality, and first impressions. *Journal of Personality and Social Psychology, 79,* 110–117.

Chase, W. G., & Simon, H. A. (1973). The mind's eye in chess. In W. G. Chase (Ed.), *Visual information processing* (pp. 215–281). New York: Academic Press.

Chatard, A., Selimbegovi, L., & Konan, P. N. (2009). Self-esteem and suicide rates in 55 nations. *European Journal of Personality, 23,* 19–32.

Cheek, J. M. (1990). Shyness, self-esteem, and self-consciousness. In H. Leitenberg (Ed.), *Handbook of social and evaluation anxiety* (pp. 47–82). New York: Plenum Press.

Chen, D. W. (2001, July 31). Boy, 6, dies of skull injury during MRI. *New York Times.* Retrieved from http://query.nytimes.com/gst/fullpage.html?sec=health&res=9400EEDC1E3DF932A05754C0A9679b C8 B63

Chen, S. X., & Bond, M. H. (2010). Two languages, two personalities? Examining language effects on the expression of personality in a bilingual context. *Personality and Social Psychology Bulletin, 36,* 1514–1528.

Cheng, J. T., Kornienko, O., & Granger, D. A. (2018). Prestige in a large-scale social group predicts longitudinal changes in testosterone. *Journal of Personality and Social Psychology, 114*(6), 924–944.

Cheung, F. M., & Song, W. (1989). A review of the clinical applications of the Chinese MMPI. *Psychological Assessment, 1,* 230–237.

Cheung, F. M., Cheung, S. F., Zhang, J., Leung, K., Leong, F., & Yeh, K. H. (2008). Relevance of openness as a personality dimension in Chinese culture: Aspects of its cultural relevance. *Journal of Cross-Cultural Psychology, 39,* 81–108.

Cheung, F. M., Leung, K., Fan, R. M., Song, W. S., Zhang, J. X., & Zhang, J. P. (1996). Development of the Chinese Personality Assessment Inventory. *Journal of Cross-Cultural Psychology, 27,* 181–199.

Cheung, F. M., Van de Vijver, F. J. R., & Leong, F. T. L. (2011). Toward a new approach to the study of personality in culture. *American Psychologist, 66,* 593–603.

Chiao, J. Y., & Ambady, N. (2007). Cultural neuroscience: Parsing universality and diversity across levels of analysis. In S. Kitayama & D. Cohen (Eds.), *Handbook of cultural psychology* (pp. 237–254). New York: Guilford Press.

Choma, B. L., Busseri, M. A., & Sadava, S. W. (2009). Liberal and conservative ideologies: Different routes to happiness? *Journal of Research in Personality, 43,* 502–505.

Chopik, W.J., & Kitayama, S. (2017). Personality change across the life span: Insights from a cross-cultural, longitudinal study. *Journal of Personality.* Published online 29 July 2017.

Chow, P.I., Wagner, J., Lüdke, L., Trautwein, U., & Roberts, B.W. (in press). Therapy experience in naturalistic observational studies is associated with negative changes in personality. *Journal of Research in Personality.*

Christiansen, N. D., Wolcott-Burnam, S., Janovics, J. E., Burns, G. N., & Quirk, S. W. (2005). The good judge revisited: Individual differences in the accuracy of personality judgments. *Human Performance, 18,* 123–149.

Chung, J. M., Robins, R. W., Trzesniewski, K. H., Noftle, E. E., Roberts, B. W., & Widaman, K. F. (2014). Continuity and change in self-esteem during emerging adulthood. *Journal of Personality and Social Psychology, 106,* 469–483.

Church, A. T., Alvarez, J. M., Mai, N. T. Q., French, B. F., Katigbak, M. S., & Ortiz, F. A. (2011). Are cross-cultural comparisons of personality profiles meaningful? Differential item and facet functioning in the Revised NEO Personality Inventory. *Journal of Personality and Social Psychology, 101,* 1068–1089.

Church, A. T., Anderson-Harumi, C. A., del Prado, A. M., Curtis, G. J., Tanaka-Matsumi, J., Medina, J. L. V., et al. (2008). Culture, cross-role consistency, and adjustment: Testing trait and cultural psychology perspectives. *Journal of Personality and Social Psychology, 95,* 739–755.

Church, A. T., Katigbak, M. S., Reyes, J. A. S., Salanga, M. G. C., Miramontez, L. A., & Adams, N. B. (2008). Prediction and cross-situational consistency across cultures: Testing trait and cultural perspectives. *Journal of Research in Personality, 42,* 1199–1215.

Clark, H. H., & Clark, E. V. (1977). *Psychology and language: An introduction to psycholinguistics.* New York: Harcourt, Brace.

Clark, J. M., & Paivio, A. (1989). Observational and theoretical terms in psychology: A cognitive perspective on scientific language. *American Psychologist, 44,* 500–512.

Clark, L. A., & Watson, D. (1999a). Personality, disorder, and personality disorder: Toward a more rational conceptualization. *Journal of Personality Disorders, 13,* 142–151.

Clark, L. A., Livesley, W. J., & Morey, L. (1997). Personality disorder assessment: The challenge of construct validity. *Journal of Personality Disorders, 11,* 205–231.

Clark, R. D., & Hatfield, E. (1989). Gender differences in receptivity to sexual offers. *Journal of Psychology and Human Sexuality, 2,* 39–55.

Cloud, J. (2008, January 8). The mystery of borderline personality disorder. *Time.* Retrieved from http://www.time.com/time/printout/0,8816,1870491,00.html

Cochran, R.N., vanDellen, M.R., & Haas, B.W. (2018, March). *Personality judgment accuracy: The associations between time, social context, and personality on the accuracy of personality judgments.* Poster presented at the meetings of the Society for Personality and Social Psychology, Atlanta.

Cohen, D., Nisbett, R. E., Bowdle, B. F., & Schwartz, N. (1996). Insult, aggression and the southern culture of honor: An "experimental ethnography." *Journal of Personality and Social Psychology, 70,* 945–960.

Cohen, G. L., & Sherman, D. K. (2014). The psychology of change: Self-affirmation and social psychological intervention. *Annual Review of Psychology, 65,* 333–371.

Cohen, J. (1994). The earth is round (*p* <.05). *American Psychologist, 49,* 997–1003.

Cokely, E. T., & Feltz, A. (2009). Individual differences, judgment biases, and theory-of-mind: Deconstructing the intentional action side effect asymmetry. *Journal of Research in Personality, 43*, 18–24.

Colman, D.E., Letzring, T.D., & Biesanz, J.C. (2017). Seeing and feeling your way to accurate personality judgments: The moderating role of perceiver empathic tendencies. *Social Psychological and Personality Science.* Published online, April 27, 2017.

Colvin, C. R. (1993a). Childhood antecedents of young-adult judgability. *Journal of Personality, 61*, 611–635.

Colvin, C. R. (1993b). "Judgable" people: Personality, behavior, and competing explanations. *Journal of Personality and Social Psychology, 64*, 861–873.

Colvin, C. R., & Bundick, M. J. (2001). In search of the good judge of personality: Some methodological and theoretical concerns. In J. A. Hall & F. J. Bernieri (Eds.), *Interpersonal sensitivity: Theory and measurement* (pp. 47–65). Mahwah, NJ: Erlbaum.

Colvin, C. R., & Funder, D. C. (1991). Predicting personality and behavior: A boundary on the acquaintanceship effect. *Journal of Personality and Social Psychology, 60*, 884–894.

Colvin, C. R., Block, J., & Funder, D. C. (1995). Overly positive self-evaluations and personality: Negative implications for mental health. *Journal of Personality and Social Psychology, 68*, 1152–1162.

Condon, P., Desbordes, G., Miller, W., & DeSteno, D. (2013). Meditation increases compassionate responses to suffering. *Psychological Science, 24*, 2125–2127.

Conley, T. D., Moors, A. C., Matsick, J. L., Ziegler, A., & Valentine, B. A. (2011). Women, men and the bedroom: Methodological and conceptual insights that narrow, reframe and eliminate gender differences in sexuality. *Psychological Science, 20*, 296–300.

Connelly, B. S., & Ones, D. S. (2010). Another perspective on personality: Meta-analytic integration of observers' accuracy and predictive validity. *Psychological Bulletin, 136*, 1092–1122.

Cook, T. D., & Campbell, D. T. (Eds.). (1979). *The design and analysis of quasi-experiments for field settings.* Chicago: Rand-McNally.

Corr, P. J., & Matthews, G. (Eds.). (2009). *The Cambridge handbook of personality psychology.* Cambridge University Press.

Corr, P. J., Pickering, A. D., & Gray, J. A. (1997). Personality, punishment and procedural learning: A test of J. A. Gray's anxiety theory. *Journal of Personality and Social Psychology, 73*, 337–344.

Costa, P. T., & McCrae, R. R. (1995). Domains and facets: Hierarchical personality assessment using the Revised NEO Personality Inventory. *Journal of Personality Assessment, 64*, 21–50.

Costa, P. T., Jr. (1996). Work and personality: Use of the NEO-PI-R in industrial/organizational psychology. *Applied Psychology: An International Review, 45*, 225–241.

Costa, P. T., Jr., & McCrae, R. R. (1985). *The NEO Personality Inventory manual.* Odessa, FL: Psychological Assessment Resources.

Costa, P. T., Jr., & McCrae, R. R. (1994). Set like plaster? Evidence for the stability of adult personality. In T. Heatherton & J. Weinberger (Eds.), *Can personality change?* (pp. 21–40). Washington, DC: American Psychological Association.

Costa, P. T., Jr., & McCrae, R. R. (1997). Stability and change in personality assessment: The Revised NEO Personality Inventory in the year 2000. *Journal of Personality Assessment, 68*, 86–94.

Costa, P. T., Jr., & McCrae, R. R. (1998). Trait theories in personality. In D. F. Barone, M. Hersen, & V. B. Van Hasselt (Eds.), *Advanced personality* (pp. 103–121). New York: Plenum Press.

Costa, P. T., Jr., Herbst, J. H., McCrae, R. R., Samuels, J., & Ozer, D. J. (2002). The replicability and utility of three personality types. *European Journal of Personality, 16*, 573–588.

Costa, P. T., Terracciano, A., & McCrae, R. R. (2001). Gender differences in personality traits across cultures: Robust and surprising findings. *Journal of Personality and Social Psychology, 81*, 322–331.

Costantini, G., & Perugini, M. (2016). The network of conscientiousness. *Journal of Research in Personality, 65*, 68–88.

Cousins, N. (1979). *Anatomy of an illness*. New York: Norton.

Coyne, J. C., & Tennen, H. (2010). Positive psychology in cancer care. Bad science, exaggerated claims, and unproven medicine. *Annals of Behavioral Medicine, 39*, 16–26.

Craik, F. I. M., & Tulving, E. (1975). Depth of processing and the retention of words in episodic memory. *Journal of Experimental Psychology: General, 104*, 268–294.

Craik, F. I. M., & Watkins, M. J. (1973). The role of rehearsal in short-term memory. *Journal of Verbal Learning and Verbal Behavior, 12*, 599–607.

Craik, K. H. (2009). *Reputation: A network interpretation*. New York and Oxford: Oxford University Press.

Cramer, P., & Davidson, K. (Eds.). (1998). Defense mechanisms in contemporary personality research [Special Issue]. *Journal of Personality, 66*(6).

Crews, F. (1996). The verdict on Freud. *Psychological Science, 7*, 63–68.

Crews, F. (2017). *Freud: The making of an illusion*. New York: Metropolitan Books/Henry Holt.

Crews, F. (Ed.). (1998). *Unauthorized Freud: Doubters confront a legend*. New York: Viking Press.

Crocker, J., & Major, B. (1989). Social stigma and self-esteem: The self-protecting properties of stigma. *Psychological Review, 96*, 608–630.

Crocker, J., & Wolfe, C. T. (2001). Contingencies of self-worth. *Psychological Review, 108*, 593–623.

Cronbach, L. J. (1951). Coefficient alpha and the internal structure of tests. *Psychometrika, 16*, 297–334.

Cronbach, L. J. (1955). Processes affecting scores on "understanding of others" and "assumed similarity." *Psychological Bulletin, 52*, 177–193.

Cronbach, L. J., & Meehl, P. E. (1955). Construct validity in psychological tests. *Psychological Bulletin, 52*, 281–302.

Cronbach, L. J., Gleser, G. C., Nanda, H., & Rajaratnam, N. (1972). *The dependability of behavioral measurements: Theory of generalizability for scores and profiles*. New York: Wiley.

Cronqvist, H., Makhiga, A. K., & Yonker, S. E. (2011). Behavioral consistency in corporate finance: CEO personal and corporate leverage. *Journal of Financial Economics, 103*, 20–40.

Crowe, M. L., Lynam, D. R., & Miller, J. D. (2017). Uncovering the structure of Agreeableness from self-report measures. *Journal of Personality*. Published online 26 October 2017.

Crowell, S. E., Beauchaine, T. P., & Linehan, M. M. (2009). A biosocial developmental model of borderline personality: Elaborating and extending Linehan's theory. *Psychological Bulletin, 135*, 495–510.

Crowson, H. M., DeBacker, T. K., & Thoma, S. J. (2005). Does authoritarianism predict post-9/11 attitudes? *Personality and Individual Differences, 39*, 1273–1283.

Cservenka, A., Herting, M. M., Seghete, K. L. M., Hudson, K. A., & Nagel, B. J. (2013). High and low sensation seeking adolescents show distinct patterns of brain activity during reward processing. *NeuroImage, 66*, 184–193.

Csikszentmihalyi, M., & Csikszentmihalyi, I. S. (Eds.). (1988). *Optimal experience: Psychological studies of flow in consciousness*. New York: Cambridge University Press.

Csikszentmihalyi, M., & Larson, R. (1992). Validity and reliability of the Experience Sampling Method. In M. V. deVries (Ed.), *The experience of psychopathology: Investigating mental disorders in their natural settings* (pp. 43–57). Cambridge University Press.

Cumming, G. (2012). *Understanding the new statistics: Effect sizes, confidence intervals and meta-analysis*. New York: Taylor & Francis.

Cumming, G. (2014). The new statistics: Why and how. *Psychological Science, 25*, 7–29.

Cundiff, P. R. (2013). Ordered delinquency: The "effects" of birth order on delinquency. *Personality and Social Psychology Bulletin, 39*, 1017–1029.

Cutrona, C. E. (1982). Transition to college: Loneliness and the process of social adjustment. In L. A. Peplau & D. Perlman (Eds.), *Loneliness: A sourcebook of current theory, research, and therapy* (pp. 291–309). New York: Wiley.

Dabbs, J. M., Jr. (1997). Testosterone, smiling, and facial appearance. *Journal of Nonverbal Behavior, 21*, 45–55.

Dabbs, J. M., Jr., & Morris, R. (1990). Testosterone, social class, and antisocial behavior in a sample of 4,462 men. *Psychological Science, 1*, 209–211.

Dabbs, J. M., Jr., Alford, E. C., & Fielden, J. A. (1998). Trial lawyers and testosterone: Blue-collar talent in a white-collar world. *Journal of Applied Psychology, 28,* 84–94.

Dabbs, J. M., Jr., Ruback, R. B., Frady, R. L., Hopper, C. H., & Sgoritas, D. S. (1988). Saliva testosterone and criminal violence among women. *Personality and Individual Differences, 9,* 269–275.

Dabbs, J. M., Jr., Strong, R., & Milun, R. (1997). Exploring the mind of testosterone: A beeper study. *Journal of Research in Personality, 31,* 577–587.

Dahlsgaard, K., Peterson, C., & Seligman, M. E. P. (2005). Shared virtue: The convergence of valued human strengths across culture and history. *Review of General Psychology, 9,* 203–213.

Daly, M., & Wilson, M. (1988). Evolutionary social-psychology and family homicide. *Science, 242,* 519–524.

Damasio, A. R. (1994). *Descartes' error: Emotion, reason, and the human brain.* New York: Putnam.

Darley, J. M., & Batson, C. D. (1967). "From Jerusalem to Jericho": A study of situational and dispositional variables in helping behavior. *Journal of Personality and Social Psychology, 27,* 100–108.

Darley, J. M., & Fazio, R. (1980). Expectancy confirmation processes arising in the social interaction sequence. *American Psychologist, 35,* 867–881.

Darley, J. M., & Latané, B. (1968). Bystander intervention in emergencies: Diffusion of responsibility. *Journal of Personality and Social Psychology, 28,* 377–383.

Dar-Nimrod, I., & Heine, S. J. (2011). Genetic essentialism: On the deceptive determinism of DNA. *Psychological Bulletin, 137,* 800–818.

Darwin, C. (1967). *On the origin of the species by means of natural selection, or the preservation of favoured races in the struggle for life.* New York: Modern Library. (Originally published 1859).

Davis, D.M., & Hayes, J.A. (2011). What are the benefits of mindfulness? A practice review of psychotherapy-related research. *Psychotherapy, 48,* 198–208.

Davis, L. J. (1997, February). The encyclopedia of insanity: A psychiatric handbook lists a madness for everyone. *Harper's,* pp. 61–66.

Dawkins, R. (1976). *The selfish gene.* New York: Oxford University Press.

Dawson, J. L. M. (1974). Ecology, social pressures toward conformity, and left-handedness: A bio-social psychological approach. In J. L. M. Dawson & K. W. J. Lonner (Eds.), *Readings in cross-cultural psychology* (pp. 124–149). University of Hong Kong Press.

De Clercq, B. (2018). Integrating developmental aspects in current thinking about personality pathology. *Current Opinions in Psychology, 21,* 69–73.

De Raad, B., & Peabody, D. (2005). Cross-culturally recurrent personality factors: Analyses of three factors. *European Journal of Personality, 19,* 451–474.

De Waal, F. B. M. (2002). Evolutionary psychology: The wheat and the chaff. *Current Directions in Psychological Science, 11,* 187–191.

DeBruine, L., Jones, B. C., Frederick, D. A., Haselton, M. G., Penton-Voak, I. S., & Perrett, D. I. (2010). Evidence for menstrual cycle shifts in women's preference for masculinity. *Evolutionary Psychology, 8(4),* 768–775.

Delgado, M.M., & Sulloway, F.J. (2017). Attributes of conscientiousness throughout the animal kingdom: An empirical and evolutionary overview. *Psychological Bulletin, 143,* 823–867.

DeLuga, R. J., & Mason, S. (2000). Relationship of resident assistant conscientiousness, extraversion and positive affect with rated performance. *Journal of Research in Personality, 34,* 225–235.

Denissen, J. J. A., & Penke, L. (2008). Neuroticism predicts reactions to cues of social inclusion. *European Journal of Personality, 22,* 497–517.

Denissen, J. J. A., Penke, L., Schmitt, D. P., & Van Aken, M. A. G. (2008). Self-esteem reactions to social interactions: Evidence for sociometer mechanisms across days, peoples and nations. *Journal of Personality and Social Psychology, 95,* 181–196.

Denissen, J.J.A., Bleidorn, W., Hennecke, M., Luhmann, M., Orth, U., Specht, J., & Zimmerman, J. (2017). Uncovering the power of personality to shape income. *Psychological Science.* (published online, November 20, 2017).

Dennett, D. C., & Weiner, P. (1991). *Consciousness explained.* Boston: Little, Brown.

DePaulo, B. M., Dull, W. R., Greenberg, J. M., & Swaim, G. W. (1989). Are shy people reluctant to ask for help? *Journal of Personality and Social Psychology, 56,* 834–844.

Depue, R. A., & Collins, P. F. (1999). Neurobiology of the structure of personality: Dopamine, facilitation of incentive motivation, and extraversion. *Behavioral and Brain Sciences, 22,* 491–569.

Derby, S. P. (1994, November 2). Eskimo words for snow derby. *The AFU and Urban Legend Archive.* Retrieved from www.urbanlegends.com/language/eskimo_words_for_snow_derby.html

Dewitte, M., & De Houwer, J. (2008). Adult attachment and attention to positive and negative emotional face expressions. *Journal of Research in Personality, 42,* 498–505.

DeYoung, C. G. (2006). Higher order factors of the Big Five in a multi-informant sample. *Journal of Personality and Social Psychology, 91,* 1138–1151.

DeYoung, C. G. (2010). Personality neuroscience and the biology of traits. *Social and Personality Psychology Compass, 4,* 1165–1180.

DeYoung, C. G., Hirsh, J. B., Shane, M. S., Papademetris, X., Rajeevan, N., & Gray, J. R. (2010). Testing predictions from personality neuroscience: Brain structure and the Big Five. *Psychological Science, 21,* 820–828.

DeYoung, C. G., Quilty, L. C., & Peterson, J. B. (2007). Between facets and domains: 10 aspects of the Big Five. *Journal of Personality and Social Psychology, 93,* 880–896.

Diamond, J. (1999). *Guns, germs and steel: The fates of human societies.* New York: Norton.

Diener, C. I., & Dweck, C. S. (1978). An analysis of learned helplessness: Continuous changes in performance, strategy and achievement cognitions following failure. *Journal of Personality and Social Psychology, 36,* 451–462.

Diener, E., & Lucas, R. E. (1999). Personality and subjective well-being. In D. Kahneman, E. Diener, & N. Schwarz (Eds.), *Well-being: The foundations of hedonic psychology* (pp. 213–229). New York: Russell Sage.

Diener, E., Colvin, C. R., Pavot, W. G., & Allman, A. (1991). The psychic costs of intense positive affect. *Journal of Personality and Social Psychology, 61,* 492–503.

Diener, E., Lucas, R. E., & Oishi, S. (2002). Subjective well-being: The science and happiness of life satisfaction. In C. L. M. Keyes & J. Haidt (Eds.), *Flourishing: Positive psychology and the life well-lived* (pp. 463–473). Washington, DC: American Psychological Association.

Dienes, Z. (2011). Bayesian versus orthodox statistics: Which side are you on? *Perspectives on Psychological Science, 6,* 274–290.

Digman, J. M. (1997). Higher-order factors of the Big Five. *Journal of Personality and Social Psychology, 73,* 1246–1256.

Digman, J. M., & Takemoto-Chock, N. K. (1981). Factors in the natural language of personality: Re-analysis and comparison of six major studies. *Multivariate Behavioral Research, 16,* 149–170.

Dodds, P. S., & Danforth, C. M. (2010). Measuring the happiness of large-scale written expression: Songs, blogs, and presidents. *Journal of Happiness Studies, 11,* 441–456.

Dodge, K. A. (1993). Social-cognitive mechanisms in the development of conduct disorder and depression. *Annual Review of Psychology, 44,* 559–584.

Dodge, K. A., & Frame, C. L. (1982). Social cognitive biases and deficits in aggressive boys. *Child Development, 53,* 620–635.

Doi, T. (1973). Amae: A key concept for understanding Japanese personality structure. In R. J. Smith & R. K. Beardsley (Eds.), *Japanese culture: Its development and characteristics* (pp. 132–139). Chicago: Aldine.

Donahue, E. M., Robins, R. W., Roberts, R. W., & John, O. P. (1993). The divided self: Concurrent and longitudinal effects of psychological adjustment and social roles on self-concept differentiation. *Journal of Personality and Social Psychology, 64,* 834–846.

Donnellan, M. B., Conger, R. D., & Burzette, B. G. (2005). Criterion-related validity, self-other agreement, and longitudinal analyses of the Iowa personality questionnaire: A short alternative to the MPQ. *Journal of Research in Personality, 39,* 458–485.

Donnellan, M. B., Conger, R. D., & Burzette, R. G. (2007). Personality development from late adolescence to young adulthood: Differential stability, normative maturity, and evidence for the maturity-stability hypothesis. *Journal of Personality, 75*(2), 237–263.

Donnellan, M. B., Trzesniewski, K. H., Robins, R. W., Moffitt, T. E., & Caspi, A. (2005). Low self-esteem is related to aggression, antisocial behavior, and delinquency. *Psychological Science, 16*, 328–335.

Donnellan, M.B., & Lucas, R.E. (2018). Introduction to the special issue: A replication project in personality psychology. *Journal of Research in Personality, 72*, 1–4.

Doran, J. M. (1990). The Capgras syndrome: Neurological/neuropsychological perspectives. *Neuropsychology, 4*, 29–42.

Downey, G., & Feldman, S. I. (1996). Implications of rejection sensitivity for intimate relationships. *Journal of Personality and Social Psychology, 70*, 1327–1343.

Dozier, M., Stovall, K. C., & Albus, K. E. (1999). Attachment and psychopathology in adulthood. In J. Cassidy & P. R. Shaver (Eds.), *Handbook of attachment: Theory, research, and clinical applications* (pp. 497–519). New York: Guilford Press.

Drevets, W. C. (1999). Prefrontal cortical-amygdalar metabolism in major depression. *Annals of the New York Academy of Sciences, 877*, 614–637.

Druss, B. G., Marcus, S. C., Olfson, M., & Pincus, H. A. (2004). Listening to generic Prozac: Winners, losers and sideliners. *Health Affairs, 23*, 210–216.

Dubois, D. L., & Flay, B. R. (2004). The healthy pursuit of self-esteem: Comment on an alternative to the Crocker and Park (2004) formulation. *Psychological Bulletin, 130*, 415–420.

Duckworth, A. (2016). *Grit: The power of passion and perseverance.* New York: Scribner.

Duckworth, A., Peterson, C. Matthews, M.D., & Kelly, D.R. (2007). *Journal of Personality and Social Psychology, 92*, 1087–1101.

Dufner, M., Rauthmann, J. F., Czarna, A. Z., & Denissen, J. J. A. (2013). Are narcissists sexy? Zeroing in on the effect of narcissism on short-term mate appeal. *Personality and Social Psychology Bulletin, 39*, 870–882.

Dunlop, P. D., Bourdage, J. S., de Vries, R. E., Hilbig, B. E., Zettler, I., & Ludeke, S. G. (2017). Openness to (reporting) experiences that one never had: Overclaiming as an outcome of the knowledge accumulated through a proclivity for cognitive and aesthetic exploration. *Journal of Personality and Social Psychology, 113*(5), 810–834.

Dunlop, W. L., & Tracy, J. L. (2013). Sobering stories: Narratives of self-redemption predict behavioral change and improved health among recovering alcoholics. *Journal of Personality and Social Psychology, 104*, 576–590.

Dunlop, W. L., & Walker, L. J. (2013). The personality profile of brave exemplars: A person-centered analysis. *Journal of Research in Personality, 47*, 380–384.

Dunlop, W. L., & Walker, L. J. (2015). Cross-cultural variability in self-continuity warranting strategies. *Journal of Language and Social Psychology, 34*, 300–315.

Dunlop, W. L., & Walker, L. J. (in press). Cross-cultural variability in self-continuity warranting strategies. *Journal of Language and Social Psychology.*

Dunn, M. J., Brinton, S., & Clark, L. (2010). Universal sex differences in online advertisers age preference: Comparing data from 14 cultures and 2 religious groups. *Evolution and Human Behavior, 31*, 383–393.

Durante, K. M, Li, N. P., & Haselton, M. G. (2008). Changes in women's choice of dress across the ovulatory cycle: Naturalistic and laboratory task-based evidence. *Personality and Social Psychology Bulletin, 34*, 1451–1460.

Durbin, C. E., & Klein, D. N. (2006). Ten-year stability of personality disorders among outpatients with mood disorders. *Journal of Abnormal Psychology, 115*, 75–84.

Dweck, C. S. (2008). Can personality be changed? The role of beliefs in personality and change. *Current Directions in Psychological Science, 17*, 391–394.

Dweck, C. S., & Leggett, E. L. (1988). A social-cognitive approach to personality and motivation. *Psychological Review, 95*, 256–273.

Dweck, C.S. (2017). From needs to goals and representations: Foundations for a unified theory of motivation, personality, and development. *Psychological Review, 124*, 689–719.

Dworkin, B. R. (1993). *Learning and physiological regulation.* University of Chicago Press.

Dyssegaard, E. K. (2004). The Danes call it fresh air. In D. C. Funder & D. J. Ozer (Eds.), *Pieces of the personality puzzle: Readings in theory and research* (3rd ed., pp. 369–370). New York: Norton. (Originally published May 17, 1997, in the *New York Times*).

Eagly, A. H., & Wood, W. (1999). The origins of sex differences in human behavior: Evolved dispositions versus social roles. *American Psychologist, 54,* 408–423.

Eagly, A. H., Eastwick, P. W., & Johannesen-Schmidt, M. C. (2009). Possible selves in marital roles: The impact of the anticipated division of labor on the mate preferences of women and men. *Personality and Social Psychology Bulletin, 35,* 403–414.

Eaton, L. G., & Funder, D. C. (2001). Emotional experience in daily life: Valence, variability and rate of change. *Emotion, 1,* 413–421.

Eaton, L. G., & Funder, D. C. (2003). The creation and consequences of the social world: An interactional analysis of extraversion. *European Journal of Personality, 17,* 375–395.

Ebstein, R. P., Novick, O., Umansky, R., Priel, B., Osher, Y., Blaine, D., et al. (1996). Dopamine D4 receptor (D4DR) exon III polymorphism associated with the human personality trait of novelty seeking. *Nature Genetics, 12,* 78–80.

Edelstein, R. S., Ghetti, S., Quas, J. A., Goodman, G. S., Alexander, K. W., Redlich, A. D., et al. (2005). Individual differences in emotional memory: Adult attachment and long-term memory for child sexual abuse. *Personality and Social Psychology Bulletin, 31,* 1537–1548.

Edelstein, R. S., Yim, I. S., & Quas, J. A. (2010). Narcissism predicts heightened cortisol reactivity to a psychosocial stressor in men. *Journal of Research in Personality, 44,* 565–572.

Eisenberger, N. I., Lieberman, M. D., & Satpute, A. B. (2005). Personality from a controlled processing perspective: An fMRI study of neuroticism, extraversion, and self-consciousness. *Cognitive, Affective, and Behavioral Neuroscience, 5,* 169–181.

Ekman, P. (1992). Are there basic emotions? *Psychological Review, 99,* 550–553.

Ekman, P., & Davidson, R. J. (Eds.). (1994). *The nature of emotion: Fundamental questions.* New York: Oxford University Press.

Ekman, P., Sorenson, E. R., & Friesen, W. V. (1969). Pan-cultural elements in facial displays of emotion. *Science, 164,* 86–88.

Elder, G. (1974). *Children of the Great Depression.* University of Chicago Press.

Ellis, B. J., & Thomas, W. T. (2008). Biological sensitivity to context. *Current Directions in Psychological Science, 17,* 183–187.

Ellis, B. J., Figueredo, A. J., Brumbach, B. H., & Schlomer, G. L. (2009). Fundamental dimensions of environmental risk: The impact of harsh versus unpredictable environments on the evolution and development of life history strategies. *Human Nature, 20,* 204–268.

Elms, A. C., & Milgram, S. (1966). Personality characteristics associated with obedience and defiance toward authoritative command. *Journal of Experimental Research in Personality, 1,* 282–289.

Emmons, R. A. (1989). Exploring the relations between motives and traits: The case of narcissism. In D. M. Buss & N. Cantor (Eds.), *Personality psychology: Recent trends and emerging directions* (pp. 32–44). New York: Springer-Verlag.

Emmons, R. A. (1996). Striving and feeling: Personal goals and subjective well-being. In P. M. Gollwitzer & J. A. Bargh (Eds.), *The psychology of action: Linking cognition and motivation to behavior* (pp. 314–337). New York: Guilford Press.

Emmons, R. A. (1997). Motives and life goals. In R. Hogan, J. Johnson, & S. Briggs (Eds.), *Handbook of personality psychology* (pp. 485–512). San Diego, CA: Academic Press.

Emmons, R. A., & King, L. A. (1988). Conflict among personal strivings: Immediate and long-term implications for psychological and physical well-being. *Journal of Personality and Social Psychology, 54,* 1040–1048.

Emmons, R. A., & McAdams, D. P. (1991). Personal strivings and motive dispositions: Exploring the links. *Personality and Social Psychology Bulletin, 17,* 648–654.

Epstein, S. (1973). The self-concept revisited, or a theory of a theory. *American Psychologist, 28,* 404–416.

Epstein, S. (1979). The stability of behavior: I. On predicting most of the people much of the time. *Journal of Personality and Social Psychology, 37,* 1097–1126.

Epstein, S. (1980). The stability of behavior: II. Implications for psychological research. *American Psychologist, 35,* 790–806.

Epstein, S. (1994). Integration of the cognitive and the psychodynamic unconscious. *American Psychologist, 49,* 709–724.

Epstein, S. (2003). Cognitive-experiential self-theory of personality. In T. Millon & M. J. Lerner (Ed.), *Handbook of psychology: Personality and social psychology* (pp. 159–184). New York: Wiley.

Epstein, S., & Meier, P. (1989). Constructive thinking: A broad coping variable with specific components. *Journal of Personality and Social Psychology, 57,* 332–350.

Epstein, S., Lipson, A., Holstein, C., & Huh, E. (1992). Irrational reactions to negative outcomes: Evidence for two conceptual systems. *Journal of Personality and Social Psychology, 62,* 328–339.

Erdelyi, M. H. (1974). A "new look" at the New Look in perception. *Psychological Review, 81,* 1–25.

Erdelyi, M. H. (1985). *Psychoanalysis: Freud's cognitive psychology.* San Francisco: Freeman.

Erdelyi, M. H. (1994). Commentary: Integrating a dissociation-prone psychology. *Journal of Personality, 62,* 669–680.

Erdley, C. A., Cain, K. M., Loomis, C. C., Dumas-Hines, F., & Dweck, C. S. (1997). The relations among children's social goals, implicit personality theories, and responses to social failure. *Developmental Psychology, 33,* 263–272.

Erikson, E. (1963). *Childhood and society.* New York: Norton.

Erikson, E. (1968). *Identity: Youth and crisis.* New York: Norton.

Exner, J. E., Jr. (1993). *The Rorschach: A comprehensive system: Vol. 1. Basic foundations* (3rd ed.). New York: Wiley.

Eysenck, H. J. (1947). *Dimensions of personality.* London: Routledge.

Eysenck, H. J. (1976). *Sex and personality.* Austin: University of Texas Press.

Eysenck, H. J., & Beech, H. R. (1971). Counter conditioning and related methods. In A. E. Bergin & S. Garfield (Eds.), *Handbook of psychotherapy and behavior change* (pp. 543–611). New York: Wiley.

Eysenck, H. J., & Gudjonsson, G. H. (1989). *The causes and cures of criminality.* New York: Plenum Press.

Eysenck, S. B. G., & Eysenck, H. J. (1967). Salivary response to lemon juice as a measure of introversion. *Perceptual and Motor Skills, 24,* 1047–1053.

Eysenck, S. B. G., & Long, F. Y. (1986). A cross-cultural comparison of personality in adults and children: Singapore and England. *Journal of Personality and Social Psychology, 58,* 281–291.

Fagundes, C. P., & Way, B. (2014). Early-life stress and adult inflammation. *Current Directions in Psychological Science, 23,* 277–283.

Fahrenberg, J., Myrtek, M., Pawlik, K., & Perrez, M. (2007). Ambulatory assessment: Monitoring behavior in daily life settings. *European Journal of Psychological Assessment, 23,* 206–213.

Fairbairn, C. E., Briley, D. A., Kang, D., Fraley, R. C., Hankin, B. L., & Ariss, T. (2018). A meta-analysis of longitudinal associations between substance use and interpersonal attachment security. *Psychological Bulletin, 144*(5), 532–555.

Farah, M. J. (2005). Neuroethics: The practical and the philosophical. *Trends in Cognitive Science, 9,* 34–40.

Farrelly, D., Slater, R., Elliott, H. R., Walden, H. R., & Wetherell, M. A. (2013). Competitors who choose to be red have higher testosterone levels. *Psychological Science, 24,* 2122–2124.

Fast, L. A., & Funder, D. C. (2008). Personality as manifest in word use: Correlations with self-report, acquaintance-report, and behavior. *Journal of Personality and Social Psychology, 94,* 334–346.

Fast, L. A., Reimer, H. M., & Funder, D. C. (2008). The social behavior and reputation of attributionally complex. *Journal of Research in Personality, 42,* 208–222.

Fayard, J. V., Roberts, B. W., Robins, R. W., & Watson, D. (2012). Uncovering the affective core of conscientiousness: The role of self-conscious emotions. *Journal of Personality, 80*, 1–32.

Feldman-Barrett, L., & Barrett, D. J. (2001). An introduction to computerized experience sampling in psychology. *Social Science Computer Review, 19*, 175–185.

Feldman-Barrett, L., Williams, N. L., & Fong, G. T. (2002). Defensive verbal behavior assessment. *Personality and Social Psychology Bulletin, 28*, 776–788.

Feltman, R., Robinson, M. D., & Ode, S. (2009). Mindfulness as a moderator of neuroticism-outcome relations: A self-regulation perspective. *Journal of Research in Personality, 43*, 953–961.

Fenz, W. D., & Epstein, S. (1967). Gradients of physiological arousal of experienced and novice parachutists as a function of an approaching jump. *Psychosomatic Medicine, 29*, 33–51.

Ferguson, C. J. (2010). A meta-analysis of normal and disordered personality across the life span. *Journal of Personality and Social Psychology, 98*, 659–667.

Ferguson, E. (2001). Personality and coping traits: A joint factor analysis. *British Journal of Health Psychology, 6*, 311–325.

Festinger, L., & Carlsmith, J. M. (1959). Cognitive consequences of forced compliance. *Journal of Abnormal and Social Psychology, 58*, 203–210.

Fetvadjiev, V. H., Meiring, D., van de Vijver, F. J. R., Nel, J. A., Sekaja, L., & Laher, S. (2017). Personality and Behavior Prediction and Consistency Across Cultures: A Multimethod Study of Blacks and Whites in South Africa. *Journal of Personality and Social Psychology, 114*, 465–481.

Figueredo, A. J., Sefcek, J. A., & Jones, D. N. (2006). The ideal romantic partner personality. *Personality and Individual Differences, 41*, 431–441.

Figueredo, A. J., Wolf, P. S. A., Gladden, P. R., Olderbak, S. G., Andrzejczak, D. J., & Jacobs, W. J. (2010). Ecological approaches to personality. In D. M. Buss & P. H. Hawley (Eds.), *The evolution of personality and individual differences* (pp. 210–239). New York, NY: Oxford University Press.

Fischer, H., Tillfors, M., Furmark, T., & Fredrikson, M. (2001). Dispositional pessimism and amygdala activity: A PET study in healthy volunteers. *Neuroreport, 12*, 1635–1638.

Fishbein, M., & Ajzen, I. (1974). Attitudes toward objects as predictors of single and multiple behavioral criteria. *Psychological Review, 81*, 59–74.

Fisher, J. (2004). War, situations, opportunity can make heroic figures out of Eve. *Clarksburg Exponent Telegram*. Retrieved from http://www.cpubco.com/cgibin/LiveIQue.acgi$rec=14128cbg CurrentLocalNews?cbg CurrentLocalNews

Fisher, R.A. (1966). *The design of experiments* (8th ed). New York: Hafner Publishing Company.

Fiske, D. W. (1949). Consistency of the factorial structures of personality ratings from different sources. *Journal of Abnormal and Social Psychology, 44*, 329–344.

Fitzgerald, P. B., Fountain, S., & Daskalakis, Z. J. (2006). A comprehensive review of the effects of rTMS on motor cortical excitability and inhibition. *Clinical Neurophysiology, 117*, 2584–2596.

Fleeson, W. (2001). Toward a structure- and process-integrated view of personality: Traits as density distributions of states. *Journal of Personality and Social Psychology, 80*, 1011–1027.

Fleeson, W. (2004). Moving personality beyond the person-situation debate: The challenge and the opportunity of within-person variability. *Current Directions in Psychological Science, 13*, 83–87.

Fleeson, W., & Law, M. K. (2015). Trait enactments as density distributions: The role of actors, situations, and observers in explaining stability and variability. *Journal of Personality and Social Psychology, 109*(6), 1090–1104.

Flint, A. (1995, October 25). Stone age weighs us down today. *Press-Enterprise* (Riverside, CA), p. D1.

Floody, O. R. (1983). Hormones and aggression in female mammals. In B. B. Svare (Ed.), *Hormones and aggressive behavior* (pp. 39–89). New York: Plenum Press.

Florida, R. (2002). *The rise of the creative class.* New York: Perseus Books.

Florida, R. (2008, May 4). Where do all the neurotics live? *Boston Globe*. Retrieved from http://www.boston.com/bostonglobe/ideas/articles/2008/05/04/where_do_all_the_neurotics_live

Flury, J. M., Ickes, W., & Schweinle, W. (2008). The borderline empathy effect: Do high BPD individuals have greater empathic ability? Or are they just more difficult to read? *Journal of Research in Personality, 42,* 312–332.

Foa, E. B. (2004). *Mastery of obsessive-compulsive disorder: A cognitive-behavioral approach therapist guide.* New York: Oxford University Press.

Foley, D., Eaves, L., Wormley, B., Silberg, J., Maes, H., Hewitt, J., et al. (2004). Childhood adversity, MAOA genotype, and risk for conduct disorder. *Archives of General Psychiatry, 61,* 738–744.

Fong, K., & Mar, R. A. (2015). What does my avatar say about me? Inferring personality from avatars. *Personality and Social Psychology Bulletin, 41,* 237–249.

Fraley, R. C., & Shaver, P. R. (2000). Adult romantic relationships: Theoretical developments, emerging controversies, and unanswered questions. *Review of General Psychology, 4,* 132–154.

Fraley, R. C., Griffin, B. N., Belsky, J., & Roisman, G. I. (2012). Developmental antecedents of political ideology: A longitudinal investigation from birth to age 18 years. *Psychological Science, 23,* 1425–1431.

Frank, L. K. (1939). Projective methods for the study of personality. *Journal of Psychology, 8,* 389–413.

Frankl, V. E. (1992). *Man's search for meaning: Foundations and applications of logotherapy.* Boston: Beacon Press. (Originally published 1959).

Frederick, D. A., & Haselton, M. G. (2007). Why is muscularity sexy? Tests of the fitness indicator hypothesis. *Personality and Social Psychology Bulletin, 33,* 1167–1183.

Frederick, D. A., Fessler, D. M. T., & Haselton, M. G. (2005). Do representations of male muscularity differ in men's and women's magazines? *Body Image, 2,* 81–86.

Fredrickson, B. L. (2001). The role of positive emotions in positive psychology: The broaden-and-build theory of positive emotions. *American Psychologist, 56,* 218–226.

Freeberg, N. E. (1969). Relevance of rater-ratee acquaintance in the validity and reliability of ratings. *Journal of Applied Psychology, 53,* 518–524.

Freeman, H. D., Brosnan, S. F., Hopper, L. M., Lambeth, S. P., Schapiro, S. J., & Gosling, S. D. (2013). Developing a comprehensive and comparative questionnaire for measuring personality in chimpanzees using a simultaneous top-down/bottom-up design. *American Journal of Primatology, 75,* 1042–1053.

Freeman, W., & Watts, J. W. (1950). *Psychosurgery: In the treatment of mental disorders and intractable pain* (2nd ed.). Springfield, IL: Thomas.

Freund, J., Brondmaier, A. M., Lewejohann, L., Kirste, I., Kritzler, M., Krüger, A., Sachser, N., Lindenberger, U., & Kempermann, G. (2013). Emergence of individuality in genetically identical mice. *Science, 340,* 756–759.

Fridlund, A. J. (1994). *Human facial expression.* San Diego: Academic Press.

Friedman, H. S. (1992). Disease-prone and self-healing personalities. *Hospital and Community Psychiatry, 43,* 1177–1179.

Friedman, H. S. (Ed.). (1991). *Hostility, coping, and health.* Washington, DC: American Psychological Association.

Friedman, H. S., & Kern, M. L. (2014). Personality, well-being, and health. *Annual Review of Psychology, 65,* 719–742.

Friedman, H. S., & Martin, L. R. (2011). *The Longevity Project: Surprising discoveries for health and long life from the landmark eight-decade study.* New York: Hudson St. Press.

Friedman, H. S., Kern, M. L., & Reynolds, C. A. (2010). Personality and health, subjective well-being, and longevity. *Journal of Personality, 78,* 179–216.

Friedman, H. S., Tucker, J. S., Tomlinson-Keasey, C., Schwartz, J. E., Wingard, D. L., & Criqui, M. H. (1993). Does childhood personality predict longevity? *Journal of Personality and Social Psychology, 65,* 176–185.

Friedman, H.S., Kern., M.L., & Reynolds, C.A. (2010). Personality, subjective well-being, and longevity. *Journal of Personality, 78,* 179–216

Friedman, I. (1955). Phenomenal, ideal, and projected conception of self. *Journal of Abnormal and Social Psychology, 51,* 611–614.

Friedman, M., & Rosenman, R. (1959). Association of specific overt behavioral pattern with blood and cardiovascular findings. *Journal of the American Medical Association, 169,* 1286–1296.

Friedman, M., Brown, A. E., & Rosenman, R. H. (1969). Voice analysis test for detection of behavior pattern. *Journal of the American Medical Association, 208,* 828–836.

Fritz, M.M., & Lyubomirsky, S. (2017). Whither happiness? When, how and why might positive activities undermine well-being. In J.P. Forgas & R.F. Baumeister (Eds.), *The social psychology of living well.* New York: Psychology Press.

Fuhrman, R. W., & Funder, D. C. (1995). Convergence between self and peer in the response-time processing of trait-relevant information. *Journal of Personality and Social Psychology, 69,* 961–974.

Fujita, F., & Diener, E. (2005). Life satisfaction set point: Stability and change. *Journal of Personality and Social Psychology, 88,* 158–164.

Fujita, F., Diener, E., & Sandvik, E. (1991). Gender differences in negative affect and well-being: The case for emotional intensity. *Journal of Personality and Social Psychology, 61,* 427–434.

Fuller, R. B. (1970). *I seem to be a verb.* New York: Bantam Books.

Funder, D. C. (1982). On the accuracy of dispositional versus situational attributions. *Social Cognition, 3,* 205–222.

Funder, D. C. (1987). Errors and mistakes: Evaluating the accuracy of social judgment. *Psychological Bulletin, 101,* 75–90.

Funder, D. C. (1991). Global traits: A neo-Allportian approach to personality. *Psychological Science, 2,* 31–39.

Funder, D. C. (1993). Judgments as data for personality and developmental psychology: Error vs. accuracy. In D. C. Funder, R. D. Parke, C. Tomlinson-Keasey, & K. Widaman (Eds.), *Studying lives through time: Personality and development* (pp. 121–146). Washington, DC: American Psychological Association.

Funder, D. C. (1995). On the accuracy of personality judgment: A realistic approach. *Psychological Review, 102,* 652–670.

Funder, D. C. (1998b). Why does personality psychology exist? *Psychological Inquiry, 9,* 150–152.

Funder, D. C. (1999). *Personality judgment: A realistic approach to person perception.* San Diego, CA: Academic Press.

Funder, D. C. (2001). Personality. *Annual Review of Psychology, 52,* 197–221.

Funder, D. C. (2003). Towards a social psychology of person judgments: Implications for person perception accuracy and self-knowledge. In J. Forgas, K. Williams, & W. von Hippel (Eds.), *Social judgments: Implicit and explicit processes. Sydney Symposium on Social Psychology* (pp. 115–133). New York: Cambridge University Press.

Funder, D. C. (2006). Towards a resolution of the personality triad: Persons, situations, and behaviors. *Journal of Research in Personality, 40,* 21–34.

Funder, D. C. (2007). Beyond just-so stories towards a psychology of situations: Evolutionary accounts of individual differences require independent assessment of personality and situational variables. *European Journal of Personality, 21,* 599–601.

Funder, D. C. (2008). Persons, situations and person-situation interactions. In O. P. John, R. Robins, & L. Pervin (Eds.), *Handbook of Personality* (3rd ed., pp. 568–580). New York: Guilford Press.

Funder, D. C. (2011). Directions and beliefs of self-presentational bias. *Behavioral and Brain Sciences, 34,* 23.

Funder, D. C., & Colvin, C. R. (1988). Friends and strangers: Acquaintanceship, agreement, and the accuracy of personality judgment. *Journal of Personality and Social Psychology, 55,* 149–158.

Funder, D. C., & Colvin, C. R. (1991). Explorations in behavioral consistency: Properties of persons, situations, and behaviors. *Journal of Personality and Social Psychology, 60,* 773–794.

Funder, D. C., & Dobroth, K. M. (1987). Differences between traits: Properties associated with inter-judge agreement. *Journal of Personality and Social Psychology, 52,* 409–418.

Funder, D. C., & Harris, M. J. (1986). On the several facets of personality assessment: The case of social acuity. *Journal of Personality, 54,* 528–550.

Funder, D. C., & Ozer, D. J. (1983). Behavior as a function of the situation. *Journal of Personality and Social Psychology, 44*, 107–112.

Funder, D. C., & Sneed, C. D. (1993). Behavioral manifestations of personality: An ecological approach to judgmental accuracy. *Journal of Personality and Social Psychology, 64*, 479–490.

Funder, D. C., & West, S. G. (1993). Consensus, self-other agreement, and accuracy in personality judgment: An introduction. *Journal of Personality, 61*, 457–476.

Funder, D. C., Furr, R. M., & Colvin, C. R. (2000). The Riverside behavioral Q-sort: A tool for the description of social behavior. *Journal of Personality, 68*, 450–489.

Funder, D. C., Guillaume, E., Kumagai, S., Kawamoto, S., & Sato, T. (2012). The person-situation debate and the assessment of situations. *Japanese Journal of Personality, 21*, 1–11.

Funder, D. C., Levine, J. M., Mackie, D. M., Morf, C. C., Sansone, C., Vazire, S., et al. (2014). Improving the dependability of research in personality and social psychology: Recommendations for research and educational practice. *Personality and Social Psychology Review, 18*, 3–12.

Funder, D.C. (2016). Taking situations seriously: The situation construal model and the Riverside Situational Q-sort. *Current Directions in Psychological Science, 25*(3), 203–208.

Funder, D.C. (2017, July 26). Thresholds. *Funderstorms* (blog post). Retrieved from https://funderstorms.wordpress.com/2017/07/26/thresholds

Funder, D.C. Baranski, E., & Gardiner, G. (2018). *Data from the International Situations Project.* Ms. In preparation, University of California, Riverside.

Fung, H. H., & Carstensen, L. L. (2003). Sending memorable messages to the old: Age differences in preferences and memory for advertisements. *Journal of Personality and Social Psychology, 85*, 163–178.

Furmark, T., Tillfors, M., Garpenstrand, H., Maarteinsdottir, I., Långstrom, B., Oreland, L., et al. (2004). Serotonin transporter polymorphism related to amygdala excitability and symptom severity in patients with social phobia. *Neuroscience Letters, 362*, 189–192.

Furnham, A. (2001). Self-estimates of intelligence: Culture and gender differences in self and other estimates of both general (g) and multiple intelligences. *Personality and Individual Differences, 31*, 1381–1405.

Furr, R. M. 2009. Personality psychology as a truly behavioral science. *European Journal of Personality, 23*, 369–401.

Furr, R. M., & Funder, D. C. (1998). A multi-modal analysis of personal negativity. *Journal of Personality and Social Psychology, 74*, 1580–1591.

Furr, R. M., & Funder, D. C. (2004). Situational similarity and behavioral consistency: Subjective, objective, variable-centered, and person-centered approaches. *Journal of Research in Personality, 38*, 421–447.

Furr, R. M., & Funder, D. C. (2007). Behavioral observation. In R. Robins, C. Fraley, & R. Krueger (Eds.), *Handbook of research methods in personality psychology* (pp. 273–291). New York: Guilford Press.

Furtner, M.R., Maran, T., & Rauthmann, J.F. (2017). Dark leadership: The role of leaders' dark triad personality traits. In M. Clark & C. Gruber (Eds.), *Leader Development Deconstructed, Annals of Theoretical Psychology* (pp. 75–99). Cham, Switzerland: Springer International.

Gable, S. L., & Haidt, J. (2005). What (and why) is positive psychology? *Review of General Psychology, 9*, 103–110.

Gale, G.R., Čukić, I., Batty, G.D., McIntosh, A.M., Weiss, A., & Deary, I.J. (2017). When is higher neuroticism protective against death? Findings from UK Biobank. *Psychological Science, 28*(9), 1345–1357.

Gallagher, P., Fleeson, W., & Hoyle, R. (2011). A self-regulatory mechanism for personality trait stability: Contra-trait effort. *Social Psychological and Personality Science, 2*, 335–342.

Gana, K., Bailly, N., Saada, Y., Joulain, M., Trouillet, R., Hervé, C., & Alaphilippe, D. (2013). Relationship between life satisfaction and physical health in older adults: A longitudinal test of cross-lagged and simultaneous effects. *Health Psychology, 32*(8), 896–904.

Gangestad, S. W. (1989). The evolutionary history of genetic variation: An emerging issue in the behavioral genetic study of personality. In D. Buss & N. Cantor (Eds.), *Personality psychology: Recent trends and emerging directions* (pp. 320–332). New York: Springer-Verlag.

Gangestad, S. W., & Buss, D. M. (1993). Pathogen preferences and human mate preferences. *Ethology and Sociobiology, 14,* 89–96.

Gangestad, S. W., & Simpson, J. A. (1990). Toward an evolutionary history of female sociosexual variation. *Journal of Personality, 58,* 69–96.

Gangestad, S. W., & Snyder, M. (1985). "To carve nature at its joints": On the existence of discrete classes in personality. *Psychological Review, 92,* 317–349.

Gangestad, S. W., Simpson, J. A., DiGeronimo, K., & Biek, M. (1992). Differential accuracy in person perception across traits: Examination of a functional hypothesis. *Journal of Personality and Social Psychology, 62,* 688–698.

Garb, H. N., Florio, C. M., & Grove, W. M. (1998). The validity of the Rorschach and the Minnesota Multiphasic Personality Inventory: Results from meta-analyses. *Psychological Science, 9,* 402–404.

Garb, H. N., Florio, C. M., & Grove, W. M. (1999). The Rorschach controversy: Reply to Parker, Hunsley, and Hanson. *Psychological Science, 10,* 293–294.

Garb, H. N., Wood, J. M., Nezworski, M. T., Grove, W. M., & Stejskal, W. J. (2001). Toward a resolution of the Rorschach controversy. *Psychological Assessment, 13,* 433–448.

Gay, P. (1988). *Freud: A life for our time.* New York: Norton.

Gay, P. (Ed.). (1989). *The Freud reader.* New York: Norton.

Gazzaniga, M. S., & Heatherton, T. F. (2003). *Psychological science: Mind, brain, and behavior.* New York: Norton.

Gazzaniga, M. S., Ivry, R. B., & Mangun G. R. (1998). *Cognitive neuroscience: The biology of the mind.* New York: Norton.

Gebaur, J. E., Bleidorn, W., Gosling, S. D., Rentfrow, P. D., Lamb, M. E., & Potter, J. (2014). Cross-culture variation in Big Five relationships with religiosity: A sociocultural perspective. *Journal of Personality and Social Psychology, 107,* 1064–1091.

Geen, R. G. (1984). Preferred stimulation levels in introverts and extraverts: Effects on arousal and performance. *Journal of Personality and Social Psychology, 46,* 1303–1312.

George, J. M. (1995). Leader positive mood and group performance: The case of customer service. *Journal of Applied Social Psychology, 25,* 778–795.

Gergen, K. (1973). Social psychology as history. *Journal of Personality and Social Psychology, 26,* 309–320.

Gettleman, J. (2002, December 1). A fall tradition: Rooting and rioting for the home team. *New York Times Week in Review,* p. 2.

Geukes, K., Nestler, S., Hutteman, R., Dufner, M., Küfner, A. C. P., Egloff, B., . . . Back, M. D. (2017). Puffed-up but shaky selves: State self-esteem level and variability in narcissists. *Journal of Personality and Social Psychology, 112*(5), 769–786.

Gigerenzer, G., Hoffrage, U., & Kleinbolting, H. (1991). Probabilistic mental models: A Brunswikian theory of confidence. *Psychological Review, 98,* 506–528.

Gilbert, D. T., & Malone, P. S. (1995). The correspondence bias. *Psychological Bulletin, 117,* 21–38.

Gilmore, D. D. (1990). *Manhood in the making.* New Haven, CT: Yale University Press.

Girme, Y.U., et al. (2018). The ebbs and flows of attachment: Within-person variation in attachment undermine secure individuals' relationship wellbeing across time. *Journal of Personality and Social Psychology, 114,* 397–421.

Gjerde, P. F. (2004). Culture, power, and experience: Toward a person-centered cultural psychology. *Human Development, 47,* 138–157.

Glaser, J.-P., van Os, J., Portegijs, P. J., & Myin-Germeys, I. (2006). Childhood trauma and emotional reactivity to daily life stress in adult frequent attenders of general practitioners. *Journal of Psychosomatic Research, 61,* 229–236.

Gleitman, H. (1995). *Psychology* (4th ed.). New York: Norton.

Glueck, S., & Glueck, E. (1956). *Physique and delinquency.* New York: Harper & Bros.

Goetz, T. E., & Dweck, C. S. (1980). Learned helplessness in social situations. *Journal of Personality and Social Psychology, 39,* 246–255.

Goffman, E. (1959). *The presentation of self in everyday life.* Garden City, NY: Doubleday/Anchor.

Gold, S. R., & Reilly, J. P. (1985). Daydreaming, current concerns and personality. *Imagination, Cognition and Personality, 5,* 117–125.

Goldberg, L. R. (1981). Language and individual differences: The search for universals in personality lexicons. In L. Wheeler (Ed.), *Review of personality and social psychology* (Vol. 2, pp. 141–165). Beverly Hills, CA: Sage.

Goldberg, L. R. (1990). An alternative "description of personality": The Big-Five factor structure. *Journal of Personality and Social Psychology, 59*, 1216–1229.

Goldberg, L. R. (1992). The social psychology of personality. *Psychological Inquiry, 3*, 89–94.

Goldman, W., & Lewis, P. (1977). Beautiful is good: Evidence that the physically attractive are more socially skillful. *Journal of Experimental Social Psychology, 13*, 125–130.

Goleman, D. (1995). *Emotional intelligence.* New York: Bantam Books.

Göllner, R., Damian, R.I., Rose, N., Spengler, M., Trautwein, U., Nagengast, B., & Roberts, B.W. (2017). Is doing your homework associated with becoming more conscientiousness? *Journal of Research in Personality, 71*, 1–12.

Gosling, S. (2008a). Personality in non-human animals. *Personality and Social Psychology Compass, 2*, 985–1001.

Gosling, S. (2008b). *Snoop: What your stuff says about you.* New York: Basic Books.

Gosling, S. D. (1998). Personality dimensions in spotted hyenas (*Crocuta crocuta*). *Journal of Comparative Psychology, 112*, 107–118.

Gosling, S. D., & John, O. P. (1999). Personality dimensions in nonhuman animals: A cross-species review. *Current Directions in Psychological Science, 8*, 69–75.

Gosling, S. D., & Vazire, S. (2002). Are we barking up the right tree? Evaluating a comparative approach to personality. *Journal of Research in Personality, 36*, 607–614.

Gosling, S. D., Augustine, A. A., Vazire, S., Holtzman, N., & Gaddis, S. (2011). Manifestations of personality in online social networks: Self-reported Facebook-related behaviors and observable public profile information. *Cyberpsychology, Behavior, and Social Networking, 14*, 483–488.

Gosling, S. D., Ko, S. J., Mannarelli, T., & Morris, M. E. (2002). A room with a cue: Personality judgments based on offices and bedrooms. *Journal of Personality and Social Psychology, 82*, 379–398.

Gosling, S. D., Vazire, S., Srivastava, S., & John, O. P. (2004). Should we trust Web-based studies? A comparative analysis of six preconceptions about internet questionnaires. *American Psychologist, 59*, 93–104.

Gough, H. G. (1968). An interpreter's syllabus for the California Psychological Inventory. In P. McReynolds (Ed.), *Advances in psychological assessment* (Vol. 1, pp. 55–79). Palo Alto, CA: Science and Behavior Books.

Gough, H. G. (1995). Career assessment and the California Psychological Inventory. *Journal of Career Assessment, 3*, 101–122.

Grant, A. M. (2013). Rethinking the extraverted sales ideal: The ambivert advantage. *Psychological Science, 24*, 1024–1030.

Grant, B. F., Hasin, D. S., Stinson, F. S., Dawson, D. A., Chou, S. P., Ruan, W. J., et al. (2004). Prevalence, correlates and disability of personality disorders in the United States: Results from the National Epidemiologic Survey on Alcohol and Related Conditions. *Journal of Clinical Psychiatry, 65*, 948–958.

Grant, H., & Dweck, C. S. (1999). A goal analysis of personality and personality coherence. In D. Cervone & Y. Shoda (Eds.), *The coherence of personality: Social-cognitive bases of consistency, variability, and organization* (pp. 345–371). New York: Guilford Press.

Gray, J. A. (1981). A critique of Eysenck's theory of personality. In H. J. Eysenck (Ed.), *A model for personality* (pp. 246–276). New York: Springer-Verlag.

Graziano, W. G., & Eisenberg, N. (1997). Agreeableness: A dimension of personality. In R. Hogan, J. Johnson, & S. Briggs (Eds.), *Handbook of personality psychology* (pp. 795–824). San Diego: Academic Press.

Graziano, W., & Bryant, W. H. (1998). Self-monitoring and the self-attribution of positive emotions. *Journal of Personality and Social Psychology, 74*, 250–261.

Green, R. (2006, January 5). Tulsa pastor arrested on lewdness accusation. *Dallas Voice.* Retrieved from http://www.dallasvoice.com/artman/publish/article_324.php

Greenberg, J. R., & Mitchell, S. A. (1983). *Object relations in psychoanalytic theory.* Cambridge, MA: Harvard University Press.

Greenberg, J., & Folger, R. (1988). *Controversial issues in social research methods.* New York: Springer-Verlag.

Greenwald, A. G., & Farnham, S. D. (2000). Using the implicit association test to measure self-esteem and the self-concept. *Journal of Personality and Social Psychology, 79,* 1022–1028.

Greenwald, A. G., Banaji, M. R., Rudman, L. A., Farnham, S. D., Nosek, B. A., & Mellott, D. S. (2002). A unified theory of implicit attitudes, stereotypes, self-esteem, and self-concept. *Psychological Review, 109,* 3–25.

Greenwald, A. G., McGhee, D. E., & Schwartz, J. L. K. (1998). Measuring individual differences in implicit cognition. The implicit association test. *Journal of Personality and Social Psychology, 74,* 1464–1480.

Griffith, R. L., & Peterson, M. (Eds.). (2006). *A closer examination of applicant faking behavior.* Greenwich, CT: Information Age Publishing.

Grissom, R. J., & Kim, J. J. (2012). *Effect sizes for research: Univariate and multivariate applications.* New York: Taylor & Francis.

Grosjean, F. (1982). *Life with two languages.* Cambridge, MA: Harvard University Press.

Gross, J. J., & Jazaieri, H. (2014). Emotion, emotion regulation, and psychopathology: An affective science perspective. *Clinical Psychological Science, 2,* 387–401.

Grubbs, J. B., & Exline, J. J. (2016). Trait entitlement: A cognitive-personality source of vulnerability to psychological distress. *Psychological Bulletin, 142*(11), 1204–1226.

Gruber, J., Mauss, I. B., & Tamir, M. (2011). A dark side of happiness? How, when and why happiness is not always good. *Perspectives on Psychological Science, 6,* 222–233.

Guadagno, R. E., & Cialdini, R. B. (2010). Preference for consistency and social influence: A review of current research findings. *Social Influence, 5*(3), 152–163.

Guarnaccia, V., Dill, C. A., Sabatino, S., & Southwick, S. (2001). Scoring accuracy using the Comprehensive System for the Rorschach. *Journal of Personality Assessment, 77,* 464–474.

Guilford, J. P., & Zimmerman, W. S. (1956). Fourteen dimensions of temperament. *Psychological Monographs, 70*(10, Whole No. 417).

Guillaume, E., Baranski, E., Todd, E., Bastian, B., Bronin, I., Ivanova, C., . . . Funder, D.C. (2015). The world at 7:00: Comparing the experience of situations across 20 countries. *Journal of Personality, 84,* 493–509.

Guillaume, E., Gardiner, G., Stauner, N., Bae, J., Han, G., Moon, J., . . . Funder, D.C. (2018). *Assessing personality across 13 countries using the California Adult Q-sort.* Manuscript in preparation, University of California, Riverside.

Gusnard, D. A., Ollinger, J. M., Schulman, G. L., Cloninger, C. R., Price, J. L., Van Essen, D. C., et al. (2003). Persistence and brain circuitry. *Proceedings of the National Academy of Sciences, 100,* 3479–3484.

Guthrie, G. M., & Bennett, A. B. (1971). Cultural differences in implicit personality theory. *International Journal of Psychology, 6,* 305–312.

Haas, B. W., Omura, K., Constable, R. T., & Canli, T. (2007). Emotional conflict and neuroticism: Personality-dependent activation in the amygdala and subgenual anterior cingulate. *Behavioral Neuroscience, 121,* 249–256.

Haidt, J. (2008, September 9). What makes people vote Republican? *Edge.* Retrieved from http://www.edge.org/3rd_culture/haidt08/haidt08_index.html

Haig, B. D. (2005). An abductive theory of scientific method. *Psychological Methods, 10,* 371–388.

Hall, J. A., Andrzejewski, S. A., Yopchick, J. E. (2009). Psychosocial correlates of interpersonal sensitivity: A meta-analysis. Journal of Nonverbal Behavior, 33, 149–180.

Hall, J. A., Gunnery, S. D., Horgan, T. G. (2016). Gender differences in interpersonal accuracy. In Hall, J. A., Schmid Mast, M., West, T. V. (Eds.), *The social psychology of perceiving others accurately* (pp. 309–327). Cambridge, England: Cambridge University Press.

Hamamura, T., Meijer, Z., Heine, S. J., Kamaya, K., & Hori, I. (2009). Approach-avoidance motivation and information processing: A cross-cultural analysis. *Personality and Social Psychology Bulletin, 35,* 454–462.

Hamann, S. B., & Mao, H. (2002). Positive and negative emotional verbal stimuli elicit activity in the left amygdala. *Neuroreport, 13,* 15–19.

Hamann, S. B., Ely, T. D., Hoffman, J. M., & Kilts, C. D. (2002). Ecstasy and agony: Activation of the human amygdala in positive and negative emotion. *Psychological Sciences, 13,* 135–141.

Hammond, K. R. (1996). *Human judgment and social policy: Irreducible uncertainty, inevitable error, unavoidable injustice.* New York: Oxford University Press.

Hampson, S. E. (2012). Personality processes: Mechanisms by which personality traits "get outside the skin." *Annual Review of Psychology, 63,* 315–339.

Han, S.-P., & Shavitt, S. (1994). Persuasion and culture: Advertising appeals in individualistic and collectivist societies. *Journal of Experimental Social Psychology, 30,* 326–350.

Handwerker, D. A., & Bandettini, P. A. (2011). Hemodynamic signals not predicted? No so: A comment on Sirotin and Das (2009). *NeuroImage, 55,* 1409–1412.

Haney, C., Banks, W. C., & Zimbardo, P. G. (1973). A study of prisoners and guards in a simulated prison. *Naval Research Review, 30,* 4–17.

Haney, P., & Durlak, J. A. (1998). Changing self-esteem in children and adolescents: A meta-analytic review. *Journal of Clinical Child Psychology, 27,* 423–433.

Hanson, F. A. (1993). *Testing testing: Social consequences of the examined life.* Berkeley: University of California Press.

Hardyck, C., & Petrinovich, L. F. (1977). Left-handedness. *Psychological Bulletin, 84,* 385–404.

Hariri, A. R., Mattay, V. S., Tessitore, A., Kolachana, B., Fera, F., Goldman, D., et al. (2002). Serotonin transporter genetic variation and the response of the human amygdala. *Science, 297,* 400–403.

Haritatos, J., & Benet-Martínez, V. (2002). Bicultural identities: The interface of cultural, personality, and socio-cognitive processes. *Journal of Research in Personality, 36,* 598–606.

Harlow, J. M. (1849). Medical miscellany [Letter to the editor]. *Boston Medical and Surgical Journal, 39,* 389–393.

Harlow, J. M. (1868). Recovery from the passage of an iron bar though the head. *Publications of the Massachusetts Medical Society, 2,* 327–347.

Harlow, J. M. (1869). *Recovery from the passage of an iron bar through the head.* Boston: Clapp.

Harmon-Jones, E. (2004). Contributions from research on anger and cognitive dissonance to understanding the motivational functions of asymmetrical front brain activity. *Biological Psychology, 67,* 51–76.

Harmon-Jones, E., Harmon-Jones, C., Amodio, D. M., & Gable, P. A. (2011). Attitudes toward emotions. *Journal of Personality and Social Psychology, 101,* 1332–1350.

Harris, C.R. (2011). Menstrual cycle and facial preferences reconsidered. *Sex Roles, 64,* 669–681.

Harris, C. R. (2000). Psychophysiological responses to imagined infidelity: The specific innate modular view of jealousy reconsidered. *Journal of Personality and Social Psychology, 78,* 1082–1091.

Harris, M. J., & Rosenthal, R. (1985). Mediation of interpersonal expectancy effects: 31 Meta-analyses. *Psychological Bulletin, 97,* 363–386.

Hartmann, H. (1964). *Essays on ego psychology: Selected problems in psychoanalytic theory.* New York: International Universities Press.

Haselton, M. G. (2002). The sexual overperception bias: Evidence of a systematic bias in men from a survey of naturally occurring events. *Journal of Research in Personality, 37,* 34–47.

Haselton, M. G., & Miller, G. F. (2006). Women's fertility across the cycle increases the short term attractiveness of creative intelligence. *Human Nature, 17,* 50–73.

Hassin, R., & Trope, Y. (2000). Facing faces: Studies on the cognitive aspects of physiognomy. *Journal of Personality and Social Psychology, 78,* 837–852.

Hastie, R., & Rasinski, K. A. (1988). The concept of accuracy in social judgment. In D. Bar-Tal & A. W. Kruglanski (Eds.), *The social psychology of knowledge* (pp. 193–208). Cambridge University Press.

Hastorf, A. H., & Cantril, H. (1954). They saw a game: A case study. *Journal of Abnormal and Social Psychology, 49,* 129–134.

Hathaway, S. R., & Meehl, P. E. (1951). *An atlas for the clinical use of the MMPI.* Minneapolis: University of Minnesota Press.

Haviland, M. G., & Reise, S. P. (1996). A California Q-set alexithymia prototype and its relationship to ego-control and ego-resiliency. *Journal of Psychosomatic Research, 41,* 597–607.

Hazan, C., & Diamond, L. M. (2000). The place of attachment in human mating. *Review of General Psychology, 4,* 186–204.

Hazan, C., & Shaver, P. (1987). Romantic love conceptualized as an attachment process. *Journal of Personality and Social Psychology, 52,* 511–524.

Hazan, C., & Shaver, P. (1990). Love and work: An attachment-theoretical perspective. *Journal of Personality and Social Psychology, 59,* 270–280.

Healey, M. D., & Ellis, B. J. (2007). Birth order, conscientiousness and openness to experience: Tests of the family-niche model of personality using a within-family methodology. *Evolution and Human Behavior, 28,* 55–59.

Heatherton, T. F., Macrae, C. N., & Kelley, W. M. (2004). What the social brain sciences can tell us about the self. *Current Directions in Psychological Science, 13,* 190–193.

Heffernan, M. E., & Fraley, R. C. (2013). Do early care-giving experiences shape what people find attractive in adulthood? Evidence from a study on parental age. *Journal of Research in Personality, 47,* 364–368.

Heidegger, M. (1962). *Being and time.* New York: Harper & Row. (Originally published 1927).

Heim, A., & Westen, D. (2005). Theories of personality and personality disorders. In J. M. Oldham, A. E. Skodol, & D. S. Bender (Eds.), *The American Psychiatric Publishing textbook of personality disorders* (pp. 17–33). Arlington, VA: American Psychiatric Publishing.

Heine, S. J., Kitayama, S., & Lehman, D. R. (2001). Cultural differences in self-evaluation: Japanese readily accept negative self-relevant information. *Journal of Cross-Cultural Psychology, 32,* 434–443.

Heine, S. J., Lehman, D. R., Markus, H. R., & Kitayama, S. (1999). Is there a universal need for positive self-regard? *Psychological Review, 106,* 766–794.

Heine, S. J., Lehman, D. R., Peng, K., & Greenholtz, J. (2002). What's wrong with cross-cultural comparisons of subjective Likert scales? *Journal of Personality and Social Psychology, 82,* 903–918.

Heintzelman, S. J., & King, L. A. (2014). Life is pretty meaningful. *American Psychologist, 69,* 561–574.

Helson, R., Mitchell, V., & Moore, G. (1984). Personality and patterns of adherence and nonadherence to the social clock. *Journal of Personality and Social Psychology, 46,* 1079–1096.

Hemenway, D., Solnick, S., & Carter, J. (1994). Child-rearing violence. *Child Abuse and Neglect, 18,* 1011–1020.

Hennecke, M., Bleidorn, W., Denissen, J. J. A., & Wood, D. (2014). A three-part framework for self-regulated personality development across adulthood. *European Journal of Personality, 28,* 289–299.

Henrich, J., Heine, S., & Norenzayan, A. (2010). The weirdest people in the world? *Behavioral and Brain Sciences, 33,* 61–83.

Hepper, E. G., Hart, C. M., & Sedikides, C. (2014). Moving narcissus: Can narcissists be empathic? *Personality and Social Psychology Bulletin, 40,* 1079–1091.

Herbst, J. H., McCrae, R. R., Costa, P. T., Jr., Feaganes, J. R., & Siegler, I. C. (2000). Self-perceptions of stability and change in personality at midlife: The UNC alumni heart study. *Assessment, 7,* 379–388.

Hewig, J., Hagemann, D., Seifert, J., Naumann, E., & Bartussek, D. (2004). On the selective relation of frontal cortical asymmetry and anger-out versus anger-control. *Journal of Personality and Social Psychology, 87,* 926–939.

Hewitt, J. K. (2012). Editorial policy on candidate gene association and candidate gene-by-environment interaction studies of complex traits. *Behavioral Genetics, 42,* 1–2.

Higgins, E. T. (1997). Beyond pleasure and pain. *American Psychologist, 52,* 1280–1300.

Higgins, E. T. (1999). Persons and situations: Unique explanatory principles or variability in general principles? In D. Cervone & Y. Shoda (Eds.), *The coherence of personality: Social-cognitive bases of consistency, variability, and organization* (pp. 61–93). New York: Guilford Press.

Higgins, E. T., Bond, R., Klein, R., & Strauman, T. J. (1986). Self-discrepancies and emotional vulnerability: How magnitude, accessibility, and type of discrepancy influence affect. *Journal of Personality and Social Psychology, 51,* 5–15.

Higgins, E. T., Rholes, W. S., & Jones, C. R. (1977). Category accessibility and impression formation. *Journal of Experimental Social Psychology, 13*, 141–154.

Higgins, E. T., Roney, C. J. R., Crowe, E., & Hymes, C. (1994). Ideal versus ought predilections for approach and avoidance: Distinct self-regulatory systems. *Journal of Personality and Social Psychology, 66*, 276–286.

Highfield, R. (2008, May 17). How a magnet turned off my speech. *The Telegraph*. Retrieved from http://www.telegraph.co.uk/scienceandtechnology/science/sciencenews/3342331/How-a-magnet-turned-off-my-speech.html

Highhouse, S. (2008). Stubborn reliance on intuition and subjectivity in employee selection. *Industrial and Organizational Psychology, 1*, 333–342.

Hilgard, E. R. (1949). Human motives and the concept of the self. *American Psychologist, 4*, 374–382.

Hill, P. L., & Roberts, B. W. (2012). Narcissism, well-being, and observer-rated personality across the lifespan. *Social Psychological and Personality Science, 3*, 216–223.

Hiller, J. B., Rosenthal, R., Bornstein, R. F., Berry, D. T. R., & Brunell-Neuleib, S. (1999). A comparative meta-analysis of Rorschach and MMPI validity. *Psychological Assessment, 11*, 278–296.

Hilton, T. L., & Berglund, G. W. (1974). Sex differences in mathematics achievement: A longitudinal study. *Journal of Educational Research, 67*, 231–237.

Hippocrates. (1923). *Works* (W. H. S. Jones, Trans.; Vol. 2). New York: Putnam.

Hirschmüller, S., Egloff, B., Schmukle, S. C., Nestler, S., & Back, M. D. (2015). Accurate judgments of personality at zero acquaintance: A question of relevance. *Journal of Personality, 108*, 767–783.

Hirsh, J. B., DeYoung, C. G., Xu, X., & Peterson, J. B. (2010). Compassionate liberals and polite conservatives: Associations of agreeableness with political ideology and moral values. *Personality and Social Psychology Bulletin, 36*, 655–664.

Hoerger, M., Chapman, B. D., Prigerson, H. G., Fagerlin, A., Mohile, S. G., Epstein, R. M., et al. (2014). Personality changes pre- to post-loss in spousal caregivers of patients with terminal lung cancer. *Social Psychological and Personality Science, 5*, 722–729.

Hoffman, D. L., & Novak, T. P. (2009). Flow online: Lessons learned and future prospects. *Journal of Interactive Marketing, 23*, 23–34.

Hoffman, S. G., Sawyer, A. T., Witt, A. A., & Oh, D. (2010). The effect of mindfulness-based therapy on anxiety and depression: A meta-analytic review. *Journal of Consulting and Clinical Psychology, 78*, 169–183.

Hofstede, G. (1984). The cultural relativity of the quality of life concept. *Academy of Management Review, 9*, 389–398.

Hofstee, W. K. B. (1994). Who should own the definition of personality? *European Journal of Personality, 8*, 149–162.

Hofstee, W. K. B., & Ten Berge, J. M. F. (2004). Personality in proportion: A bipolar proportional scale for personality assessments and its consequences for trait structure. *Journal of Personality Assessment, 83*, 120–127.

Hogan, J., Barrett, P., & Hogan, R. (2007). Personality measurement, faking, and employment selection. *Journal of Applied Psychology, 93*, 1270–1285.

Hogan, R. (1969). Development of an empathy scale. *Journal of Consulting and Clinical Psychology, 33*, 307–316.

Hogan, R. (1998). Reinventing personality. *Journal of Social and Clinical Psychology, 17*, 1–10.

Hogan, R. T. (1983). A socioanalytic theory of personality. In M. Page (Ed.), *Nebraska Symposium on Motivation: Personality—Current theory and research* (pp. 55–89). Lincoln: University of Nebraska Press.

Hogan, R., & Blickle, G. (2018). Socioanalytic theory: Basic concepts, supporting evidence, and practical implications. In V. Ziegler-Hill & T.K. Shackelford (Eds)., *The SAGE handbook of personality and individual differences: Volume 1. The science of personality and individual differences*. London: Sage.

Holland, J. L. (1996). Exploring careers with a typology. *American Psychologist, 51*, 397–406.

Holt, R. R. (1980). Loevinger's measure of ego development: Reliability and national norms for male and female short forms. *Journal of Personality and Social Psychology, 39*, 909–920.

Holtzman, N. S., & Strube, M. J. (2010). Narcissism and attractiveness. *Journal of Research in Personality, 44*, 133–136.

Holtzman, N. S., Vazire, S., & Mehl, M. R. (2010). Sounds like a narcissist: Behavioral manifestations of narcissism in everyday life. *Journal of Research in Personality, 44,* 478–484.

Hong, R. Y., & Paunonen, S. V. (2011). Personality vulnerabilities to psychopathology: Relations between trait structure and affective-cognitive processes. *Journal of Personality, 79,* 527–561.

Hong, Y., Benet-Martínez, V., Chiu, C., & Morris, M. W. (2003). Boundaries of cultural influence: Construct activation as a mechanism for cultural differences in social perception. *Journal of Cross-Cultural Psychology, 34,* 453–464.

Hong, Y., Morris, M., Chiu, C. Y., & Benet-Martínez, V. (2000). Multicultural minds: A dynamic constructivist approach to culture and cognition. *American Psychologist, 55,* 709–720.

Hooley, J.M., & Franklin, J.C. (2017). Why do people hurt themselves? A new conceptual model of nonsuicidal self injury. *Clinical Psychological Science.* Published online December 28, 2017.

Hopwood, C. J., Morey, L. C., Donnellan, M. B., Samuel, D. B., Grilo, C. M., McGlashan, T. H., et al. (2013). Ten-year rank-order stability of personality traits and disorders in a clinical sample. *Journal of Personality, 81,* 335–344.

Horney, K. (1937). *The neurotic personality of our time.* New York: Norton.

Horney, K. (1942). *Self-analysis.* New York: Norton.

Horney, K. (1950). *Neurosis and human growth.* New York: Norton.

Howell, C. J., Howell, R. T., & Schwabe, K. A. (2006). Does wealth enhance life satisfaction for people who are materially deprived? Exploring the association among the Orang Asli of Peninsular Malaysia. *Social Indicators Research, 76,* 499–524.

Howell, R. T., & Hill, G. (2009). The mediators of experiential purchases: Determining the impact of psychological needs satisfaction and social comparison. *The Journal of Positive Psychology, 4,* 511–522.

Howell, R. T., & Howell, C. J. (2008). The relation of economic status to subjective well-being in developing countries: A meta-analysis. *Psychological Bulletin, 134,* 536–560.

Howell, R. T., Pchelin, P., & Iyer, R. (2011). The preference for experiences over possessions: Measurement and construct validity of the Experiential Buying Tendency Scale. *Journal of Positive Psychology, 7,* 57–71.

Howes, R.J., & Carskadon, T.G. (1979). Test-retest reliabilities of the Myers-Briggs Type Indicator as a function of mood changes. *Research in Psychological Type, 2,* 67–72.

Hudson, N. W., & Roberts, B. W. (2014). Goals to change personality traits: Concurrent links between personality traits, daily behavior, and goals to change oneself. *Journal of Research in Personality, 53,* 68–83.

Hudson, N.W., & Fraley, R.C. (2015). Volitional personality trait change: Can people choose to change their personality traits? *Journal of Personality and Social Psychology.* Advance online publication. doi: 10.1037/pspp0000021.

Hudson, N.W., Lucas, R.E., & Donnellan, M.B. (2017). Day-to-day affect is surprisingly stable: A 2-year longitudinal study of well-being. *Social Psychological and Personality Science, 8,* 45–54.

Hughes, C. F., Uhlmann, C., & Pennebaker, J. W. (1994). The body's response to emotional trauma: Linking verbal text with autonomic activity. *Journal of Personality, 62,* 565–586.

Human, L. J., & Biesanz, J. C. (2011a). Target adjustment and self-other agreement: Utilizing trait observability to disentangle judgeability and self-knowledge. *Journal of Personality and Social Psychology, 101,* 202–216.

Human, L. J., & Biesanz, J. C. (2011b). Through the looking glass clearly: Accuracy and assumed similarity in well-adjusted individuals' first impressions. *Journal of Personality and Social Psychology, 100,* 349–364.

Human, L. J., & Biesanz, J. C. (2013). Targeting the good target: An integrative review of the characteristics and consequences of being accurately perceived. *Personality and Social Psychology Review, 17,* 248–272.

Human, L. J., Biesanz, J. C., Finseth, S. M., Pierce, B., & Le, M. (2014). To thine own self be true: Psychological adjustment promotes judgeability via personality-behavior congruence. *Journal of Personality and Social Psychology, 106,* 286–303.

Human, L. J., Biesanz, J. C., Miller, G. E., Chen, E., Lachman, M. E., & Seeman, T. E. (2012). Is change bad? Personality change is associated with poorer psychological health and greater metabolic syndrome in midlife. *Journal of Personality, 81*, 324–334.

Human, L. J., Sandstrom, G. M., Giesanz, J. C., & Dunn, E. W. (2012). Accurate first impressions leave a lasting impression: The long-term effects of distinctive self-other agreement on relationship development. *Social and Personality Psychology Science, 4*, 395–402.

Human, L.J., & Mendes, W.B. (2018). Cardiac vagal flexibility and accuracy personality impressions: Examining a physiological correlate of the good judge. *Journal of Personality.* Published online, 23 February 2018.

Hunter, J. E. (1997). Needed: A ban on the significance test. *Psychological Science, 8*, 3–7.

Hutteman, R., Nestler, S., Wagner, J., Egloff, B., & Back, M.D. (2015). Wherever I may roam: Processes of self-esteem development from adolescence to emerging adulthood in the context of international student exchange. *Journal of Personality and Social Psychology.* Advance online publication. doi:10.1037/pspp0000015.

Huttunen, K., Kerr, S. P., & Mällkönen, V. (2014). The effect of rehabilitative punishments on juvenile crime and labor market outcomes. *Institute for the Study of Labor Discussion Paper Series,* No. 8403.

Hyde, J. B. (2005). The gender similarities hypothesis. *American Psychologist, 60*, 581–592.

Iacovino, J.M., Bogdan, R., & Oltmanns, T.F. (2015). Personality predicts health declines through stressful events during late mid-life. *Journal of Personality,* in press. DOI: 10.1111/jopy.12179.

Inzlicht, M., Legault, L., & Teper, R. (2014). Exploring the mechanisms of self-control improvement. *Current Directions in Psychological Science, 23*, 302–307.

Ionnadis, J.P.A. (2005). Why most published research findings are false. *PLOS-MEDICINE.* Retrieved from http://journals.plos.org/plosmedicine/article?id=10.1371/journal.pmed.0020124

Isom, J., & Heller, W. (1999). Neurobiology of extraversion: Pieces of the puzzle still missing. *Behavioral and Brain Sciences, 22*, 524.

Iyengar, S. S., & Lepper, M. R. (1999). Rethinking the value of choice: A cultural perspective on intrinsic motivation. *Journal of Personality and Social Psychology, 76*, 349–366.

Jackson, D. C., Mueller, C. J., Dolski, I., Dalton, K. M., Nitschke, J. B., Urry, H. L., et al. (2003). Now you feel it, now you don't: Frontal EEG asymmetry and individual differences in emotion regulation. *Psychological Science, 14*, 612–617.

Jackson, D. N. (1971). The dynamics of structured personality tests: 1971. *Psychological Review, 78*, 229–248.

Jackson, J. J., Hill, P. L., Payne, B. R., Roberts, B. W., & Stine-Morrow, E. A. L. (2012). Can an old dog learn (and want to experience) new tricks? Cognitive training increases openness to experience in older adults. *Psychological and Aging, 27*, 286–292.

Jackson, J. J., Thoemmes, F., Jonkmann, K., Lüdtke, O., & Trautwein, V. (2012). Military training and personality trait development: Does the military make the man, or does the man make the military? *Psychological Science, 23*, 270–277.

Jahoda, M. (1958). *Current concepts of positive mental health.* New York: Basic Books.

James, W. (1890). *Principles of psychology* (Vol. 1). London: Macmillan.

Jensen-Campbell, L. A., Adams, R., Perry, D. G., Workman, K. A., Furdella, J. Q., & Egan, S. K. (2002). Agreeableness, extraversion, and peer relations in early adolescence: Winning friends and deflecting aggression. *Journal of Research in Personality, 36*, 224–251.

Jeronimus, B. F., Riese, H., Sanderman, R., & Omel, J. (2014). Mutual reinforcement between neuroticism and life experiences: A five-wave, 16-year study to test reciprocal causation. *Journal of Personality and Social Psychology, 107*, 751–764.

Jha, A. P., Stanley, E. A., Kiyonaga, A., Wong, L., & Gelfand, L. (2010). Examining the protective effects of mindfulness training on working memory capacity and affective experience. *Emotion, 10*, 54–64.

Joel, S., Eastwick, P.W., 7 Finkel, E.J. (2017). Is romantic desire predictable? Machine learning applied to initial romantic attraction. *Psychological Science, 28*, 1478–1489.

John, O. P. (1990). The "Big Five" factor taxonomy: Dimensions of personality in the natural language and in questionnaires. In L. Pervin (Ed.), *Handbook of personality: Theory and research* (pp. 261–271). New York: Guilford Press.

John, O. P., & Srivastava, S. (1999). The Big-Five trait taxonomy: History, measurement, and theoretical perspectives. In L. Pervin & O. John (Eds.), *Handbook of personality: Theory and research* (2nd ed., pp. 102–138). New York: Guilford Press.

John, O. P., Donahue, E. M., & Kentle, R. L. (1991). *The Big Five Inventory.* University of California, Berkeley, Institute of Personality and Social Research.

John, O. P., Robins, R. W., & Pervin, L. A. (2008). *Handbook of personality: Theory and research* (3rd ed.). New York: Guilford Press.

Johnson, J. A. (1981). The "self-disclosure" and "self-presentation" views of item response dynamics and personality scale validity. *Journal of Personality and Social Psychology, 40,* 761–769.

Johnson, J. A. (2006). Ego-syntonicity in responses to items in the California Psychological Inventory. *Journal of Research in Personality, 40,* 73–83.

Johnson, W., Penke, L, & Spinath, F. M. (2011). Heritability in the era of molecular genetics: Some thoughts for understanding genetic influences on behavioural traits. *European Journal of Personality, 25,* 254–266.

Johnson, W., Spinath, F., Krueger, R. F., Angleitner, A., & Riemann, R. (2008). Personality in Germany and Minnesota: An IRT-based comparison of MPQ self-reports. *Journal of Personality, 76,* 665–706.

Jokela, M., Batty, G. D., Nyberg, S. T., Virtanen, M., Nabi, H., Singh-Manoux, A., & Kivimäki, M. (2013). Personality and all-cause mortality: Individual-participant meta-analysis of 3947 deaths in 76,150 adults. *American Journal of Epidemiology, 179,* 791–792.

Jokela, M., Pekkarinen, Sarvimaki, M., Tervio, & Uusitalo, R. (2017). Secular rise in economically valuable personality traits. *Proceedings of the National Academy of Science, 114,* 6527–6532.

Jonason, P. K., Li, N. P., Webster, G. D., & Schmitt, D. P. (2009). The Dark Triad: Facilitating a short-term mating strategy in men. *European Journal of Personality, 23,* 5–18.

Jonason, P.K., Garcia, J.R., Webster, G.D., Li, N.P., & Fisher, H.E. (2015). Relationship dealbreakers: Traits people avoid in potential mates. *Personality and Social Psychology Bulletin.* Published online September 5, 2015.

Jones, A.B., Sherman, R.A., & Hogan, R. (2016). Where is ambition in factor models of personality? *Personality and Individual Differences.*

Jones, D. N., & Paulhus, D. L. (2011). The role of impulsivity in the Dark Triad of personality. *Journal of Research in Personality, 51,* 679–682.

Jones, D. N., & Paulhus, D. L. (2017). Duplicity among the dark triad: Three faces of deceit. *Journal of Personality and Social Psychology, 113,* 329–342.

Jones, D. N., Paulhus, D. L. (2009). Machiavellianism. In Leary, M. R., & Hoyle (Eds.), *R. H. Handbook of Individual Differences in Social Behavior.* New York/London: The Guilford Press. pp. 257–273.

Jones, E. E., & Nisbett, R. E. (1971). *The actor and the observer: Divergent perceptions of the causes of behavior.* Morristown, NJ: General Learning Press.

Jones, T. (2003, February 1). On eve of 800th win, Knight's antics still fan flames of debate. *Columbus Dispatch*, Sports, p. 6E.

Josef, A. K., Richter, D., Samanez-Larkin, G. R., Wagner, G. G., Hertwig, R., & Mata, R. (2016). Stability and change in risk-taking propensity across the adult life span. *Journal of Personality and Social Psychology, 111*(3), 430–450.

Joseph, J., & Ratner, C. (2012). The fruitless search for genes in psychiatry and psychology: Time to re-examine a paradigm. In S. Krimsky & J. Gruber (Eds.), *Genetic explanations: Sense and nonsense* (pp. 94–106). Cambridge: Harvard University Press.

Jost, J. T., Glaser, J., Kruglanski, A. W., & Sulloway, F. J. (2003). Political conservatism as motivated social cognition. *Psychological Review, 129,* 339–375.

Jourard, S. M. (1971). *Self-disclosure: An experimental analysis of the transparent self.* New York: Wiley.

Judge, T. A., Bono, J. E., Ilies, R., & Gerhardt, M. (2002). Personality and leadership. *Journal of Applied Psychology, 87,* 765–80.

Jung, C. G. (1971a). *The portable Jung* (J. Campbell, Ed.). New York: Viking.

Jung, C. G. (1971b). A psychological theory of types. In H. Read, M. Fordham, & G. Adler (Eds.), *Collected works of C. G. Jung* (Vol. 20, pp. 524–541). Princeton University Press. (Originally published 1931 in German).

Jussim, L. (1991). Social perception and social reality: A reflection-construction model. *Psychological Review, 98*, 54–73.

Jussim, L., & Eccles, J. (1992). Teacher expectations II: Construction and reflection of student achievement. *Journal of Personality and Social Psychology, 63*, 947–961.

Kagan, J. (1978). Sex differences in the human infant. In T. E. McGill, D. A. Dewsbury, & B. D. Sachs (Eds.), *Sex and behavior* (pp. 305–316). New York: Plenum Press.

Kagan, J. (1994). *Galen's prophecy: Temperament in human nature.* New York: Basic Books.

Kagan, J., Reznick, J. S., & Snidman, N. (1988). Biological bases of childhood shyness. *Science, 240*, 167–171.

Kahneman, D. (2011). *Thinking: Fast and slow.* New York: Farrar, Straus & Giroux.

Kaiser, R. T., & Ozer, D. J. (1999). *The structure of personal goals and their relation to personality traits.* Unpublished manuscript, University of California, Riverside.

Kasser, T., & Ryan, R. M. (1993). A dark side of the American dream: Correlates of financial success as a central life aspiration. *Journal of Personality and Social Psychology, 65*, 410–422.

Kasser, T., & Ryan, R. M. (1996). Further examining the American dream: Differential correlates of intrinsic and extrinsic goals. *Personality and Social Psychology Bulletin, 22*, 280–287.

Kaurin, A., Sauerberger, K., & Funder, D.C. (2018). Associations between informant ratings of personality disorder traits, self-reports of personality, and directly observed behavior. *Journal of Personality, 86*, 1078–1011.

Kawahata, A., & Sakamoto, H. (1951). Some observations on sweating of the Aino. *The Japanese Journal of Physiology, 2*, 166–169.

Kazdin, A. E., & Bootzin, R. R. (1972). The token economy: An evaluative review. *Journal of Applied Behavior Analysis, 5*, 343–372.

Keller, J., & Blomann, F. (2008). Locus of control and the flow experience: An experimental analysis. *European Journal of Personality, 22*, 589–607.

Keller, M. C., & Nesse, R. M. (2006). The evolutionary significance of depressive symptoms: Different adverse situations lead to different depressive symptom patterns. *Journal of Personality and Social Psychology, 91*, 316–330.

Kelly, G. A. (1955). *The psychology of personal constructs* (Vols. 1 and 2). New York: Norton.

Kelly, G. A. (1969). The autobiography of a theory. In B. Maher (Ed.), *Clinical psychology and personality: Selected papers of George Kelly* (pp. 46–65). New York: Wiley.

Keltner, D. (1995). Signs of appeasement: Evidence for the distinct displays of embarrassment, amusement, and shame. *Journal of Personality and Social Psychology, 68*, 441–454.

Kemp, A. H., & Guastella, A. J. (2011). The role of oxytocin in human affect: A novel hypothesis. *Current Directions in Psychological Science, 20*, 222–231.

Kenny, D. A. (1994). *Interpersonal relations: A social relations analysis.* New York: Guilford Press.

Kenrick, D. T. (2011). *Sex, murder, and the meaning of life: A psychologist investigates how evolution, cognition and complexity are revolutionizing our view of human nature.* New York: Basic Books.

Kenrick, D. T., & Funder, D. C. (1988). Profiting from controversy: Lessons from the person-situation debate. *American Psychologist, 43*, 23–34.

Kenrick, D. T., & Keefe, R. C. (1992). Age preferences in mates reflect sex differences in human reproductive strategies. *Behavioral and Brain Sciences, 15*, 75–133.

Kenrick, D. T., Griskevicius, V., Neuberg, S. L., & Schaller, M. (2010). Renovating the pyramid of needs: Contemporary extensions built upon ancient foundations. *Perspectives on Psychological Science, 5*, 292–314.

Kern, M. L., Duckworth, A. L., Urzúa, S. S., Loeber, R., Stouthamer-Loeber, M., & Lynam, D. R. (2013). Do as you're told! Facets of agreeableness and early adult outcomes for inner-city boys. *Journal of Research in Personality, 47*, 795–799.

Kern, M. L., Park, G., Eichstaedt, J. C., Schwartz, H. A., Sap, M., Smith, L. K., & Ungar, L. H. (2016). Gaining insights from social media language: Methodologies and challenges. *Psychological Methods, 21*(4), 507–525.

Kernis, M. H., & Goldman, B. M. (2006). A multicomponent conceptualization of authenticity: Theory and research. In M. P. Zanna (Ed.), *Advances in Experimental Social Psychology* (Vol. 38, pp. 283–357). San Diego, CA: Elsevier Academic Press.

Kernis, M. H., Lakey, C. E., & Heppner, W. L. (2008). Secure versus fragile high self-esteem as a predictor of verbal defensiveness: Converging findings across three different markers. *Journal of Personality, 76,* 477–512.

Kesebir, P., & Diener, E. (2008). In pursuit of happiness: Empirical answers to philosophical questions. *Perspectives on Psychological Science, 3,* 117–125.

Kesey, K. (1999). *One flew over the cuckoo's nest.* New York: Penguin Books. (Original work published 1962).

Keyes, C. L. M., & Haidt, J. (Eds.). (2003). *Flourishing: Positive psychology and the life well-lived.* Washington, DC: American Psychological Association.

Khaleque, A., & Rohner, R. P. (2012). Transnational relations between perceived parental acceptance and personality dispositions of children and adults: A meta-analytic review. *Personality and Social Psychology Review, 16,* 103–115.

Kihlstrom, J. F. (1990). The psychological unconscious. In L. Pervin (Ed.), *Handbook of personality: Theory and research* (pp. 445–464). New York: Guilford Press.

Kihlstrom, J. F. (1994). Psychodynamics and social cognition: Notes on the fusion of psychoanalysis and psychology. *Journal of Personality, 62,* 681–696.

Kim, H. S. (2002). We talk, therefore we think? A cultural analysis of the effect of talking on thinking. *Journal of Personality and Social Psychology, 83,* 828–842.

King, J. E., & Figueredo, A. (1997). The five-factor model plus dominance in chimpanzee personality. *Journal of Research in Personality, 31,* 257–271.

King, L. (2011, Dec. 3). Afghan rape victim freed, with a catch. *Los Angeles Times,* p. A9.

King, L. A., & Napa, C. K. (1998). What makes a life good? *Journal of Personality and Social Psychology, 75,* 156–165.

King, M. G., & Husband, A. J. (1991). Altered immunity through behavioral conditioning. In J. G. Carlson & A. R. Seifert (Eds.), *International perspectives in behavioral psychophysiology and medicine* (pp. 197–204). New York: Plenum Press.

Kinsey, A.C., Pomeroy, W.B., & Martin, C.E. (1948). *Sexual behavior in the human male.* Philadelphia: Saunders.

Kinsey, A.C., Pomeroy, W.B., Martin. E.C., & Gebhard, P. (1953) *Sexual behavior in the human female.* Philadelphia: Saunders.

Kircher, P. (1985). *Vaulting ambition: Sociobiology and the quest for human nature.* Cambridge, MA: MIT Press.

Kirsch, P., Esslinger, C., Chen, Q., Mier, D., Lis, S., Siddahanti, S., et al., (2005). Oxytocin modulates neural circuitry for social cognition and fear in humans. *Journal of Neuroscience, 25,* 11489–11493.

Kitayama, S., & Park, J. (2010). Cultural neuroscience of the self: Understanding the social grounding of the brain. *Social Cognitive and Affective Neuroscience, 5,* 111–129.

Kitayama, S., King, A., Yoon, C., Tompson, S., Huff, S., & Liberzon, I. (2014). The dopamine receptor gene (DRD4) moderates cultural difference in independent versus interdependent social orientation. *Psychological Science, 25,* 1169–1177.

Kitayama, S., Park, H., Sevincer, A. T., Karasawa, M., & Uskul, A. K. (2009). A cultural task analysis of implicit independence: Comparing North America, Western Europe, and East Asia. *Journal of Personality and Social Psychology, 97,* 236–255.

Klein, G. S. (1970). *Perception, motives, and personality.* New York: Knopf.

Klein, M. (1964). *Contributions to psychoanalysis, 1921–1945.* New York: McGraw-Hill.

Klein, M. (1986). The psycho-analytic play technique: Its history and significance. In J. Mitchell (Ed.), *The selected Melanie Klein* (pp. 35–54). New York: Free Press. (Originally published 1955).

Klein, S. B. (2012). The two selves: The self of conscious experience and its brain. In M. R. Leary & J. P. Tagney (Eds.), *Handbook of self and identity* (2nd ed., pp. 617–637). New York: Guilford Press.

Klein, S. B., & Kihlstrom, J. F. (1998). On bridging the gap between social-personality psychology and neuropsychology. *Personality and Social Psychology Bulletin, 2,* 228–242.

Klein, S. B., & Lax, M. L. (2010). The unanticipated resilience of trait self-knowledge in the face of neural damage. *Memory, 18,* 918–948.

Klein, S. B., Altinyazar, V., & Metz, M. A. (2013). Facets of self in schizophrenia: The reliability and accuracy of trait self-knowledge. *Clinical Psychological Science, 1,* 276–289.

Klein, S. B., Loftus, J., & Kihlstrom, J. F. (1996). Self-knowledge of an amnesic patient: Toward a neuropsychology of personality and social psychology. *Journal of Experimental Psychology: General, 125,* 250–260.

Klein, S. B., Rozendal, K., & Cosmides, L. (2002). A social-cognitive neuroscience analysis of the self. *Social Cognition, 20,* 105–135.

Klimstra, T. A., Bleidorn, W., Asendorpf, J. B., van Aken, M. A. G., & Denissen, J. J. A. (2013). Correlated change of the Big Five traits across the lifespan: A search for determinants. *Journal of Personality and Social Psychology, 47,* 768–777.

Klinger, E. (1977). *Meaning and void: Inner experience and the incentives in people's lives.* Minneapolis: University of Minnesota Press.

Klinger, E. (1987). The interview questionnaire technique: Reliability and validity of a mixed idiographic-nomothetic measure of motivation. In J. N. Butcher and C. D. Spielberger (Eds.), *Advances in personality assessment* (pp. 31–48). Hillsdale, NJ: Erlbaum.

Klinger, E., Barta, S. G., & Maxeiner, M. E. (1981). Current concerns: Assessing therapeutically relevant motivation. In P. C. Kendall & S. Hollon (Eds.), *Assessment strategies for cognitive-behavioral interventions* (pp. 161–195). New York: Academic Press.

Klopfer, B., & Davidson, H. H. (1962). *The Rorschach technique: An introductory manual.* New York: Harcourt, Brace.

Kluckhohn, C., & Murray, H. A. (1961). Personality formation: The determinants. In C. Kluckhohn, H. A. Murray, & D. M. Schneider (Eds.), *Personality in nature, society, and culture* (2nd ed., pp. 53–67). New York: Knopf.

Knoch, D., Nitsche, M. A., Fischbacher, U., Eisenegger, C., Pascual-Leone, A., & Fehr, E. (2008). Studying the neurobiology of social interaction with transcranial direct current stimulation: The example of punishing unfairness. *Cerebral Cortex, 18,* 1987–1990.

Knoch, D., Schneider, F., Schunk, D., Hohman, M., & Fehr, E. (2009). Disrupting the prefrontal cortex diminishes the human ability to build a good reputation. *Proceedings of the National Academy of Sciences of the United States of America, 106,* 20895–20899.

Knutson, B., Momenan, R., Rawlings, R. R., Fong, G. W., & Hommer, D. (2001). Negative association of neuroticism with brain volume ratio in healthy humans. *Biological Psychiatry, 50,* 685–690.

Knutson, B., Wolkowitz, O. M., Cole, S. W., Chan, T., Moore, E. A., Johnson, R. C., et al. (1998). Selective alteration of personality and social behavior by serotonergic intervention. *American Journal of Psychiatry, 155,* 373–379.

Kochanska, G., & Knaack, A. (2003). Effortful control as a personality characteristic of young children: Antecedents, correlates, and consequences. *Journal of Personality, 71,* 1087–1112.

Köhler, W. (1925). *The mentality of apes* (E. Winter, Trans.). New York: Harcourt, Brace.

Kolar, D. W. (1996). *Individual differences in the ability to accurately judge the personality characteristics of others.* Unpublished doctoral dissertation, University of California, Riverside.

Kolar, D. W., Funder, D. C., & Colvin, C. R. (1996). Comparing the accuracy of personality judgments by the self and knowledgeable others. *Journal of Personality, 64,* 311–317.

Konrath, S. H., O'Brien, E. H., & Hisng, C. (2011). Changes in dispositional empathy in American college students over time: A meta-analysis. *Personality and Social Psychology Review, 15,* 180–198.

Kopay, D. (1977). *The David Kopay Story: An extraordinary self-revelation.* Westminster, MD: Arbor House.

Kosinski, M. (2017). Facial width-to-height ratio does not predict self-reported behavioral tendencies. *Psychological Science,* published online October 4, 2017.

Kotov, R., Gamez, W., Schmidt, F., & Watson, D. (2010). Linking "big" personality traits to anxiety, depressive, and substance use disorders: A meta-analysis. *Psychological Bulletin, 136,* 768–821.

Kramer, P. D. (1993). *Listening to Prozac.* New York: Viking.

Krauss, S. W. (2002). Romanian authoritarianism 10 years after communism. *Personality and Social Psychology Bulletin, 28,* 1255–1264.

Krauss, S., & Wassner, C. (2002, July). *How significance tests should be presented to avoid the typical misinterpretations.* Paper presented at the Sixth International Conference on Teaching Statistics, Cape Town, South Africa.

Kreisman, J., & Straus, H. (1989). *I hate you—don't leave me! Understanding the borderline personality.* New York: HarperCollins/Avon Books.

Krueger, J.I., & Heck, P.R. (2018). Testing significance testing. *Collabra: Psychology, 4,* 1–13.

Krueger, R. F., & Eaton, N. R. (2010). Personality traits and the classification of mental disorders: Toward a more complete integration in *DSM-5* and an empirical model of psychopathology. *Personality Disorders: Theory, Research, and Treatment, 1,* 97–118.

Krueger, R. F., & Johnson, W. (2008). Behavioral genetics and personality: A new look at the integration of nature and nurture. In O. P. John, R. W. Robins, & L. A. Pervin (Eds.), *Handbook of personality: Theory and research* (3rd ed., pp. 287–310). New York: Guilford Press.

Krueger, R. F., & Markon, K. E. (2014). The role of the DSM-5 personality trait model in moving toward a quantitative and empirically based approach to classifying personality and psychopathology. *Annual Review of Clinical Psychology, 10,* 7.1–7.25.

Krueger, R. F., & Tackett, J. L. (2003). Personality and psychopathology: Working toward the bigger picture. *Journal of Personality Disorders, 17,* 109–128.

Kruglanski, A. W. (1989). The psychology of being "right": The problem of accuracy in social perception and cognition. *Psychological Bulletin, 106,* 395–409.

Küfner, A. C. P., Back, M. D., Nestler, S., & Egloff, B. (2010). Tell me a story and I will tell you who you are! Lens model analyses of personality and creative writing. *Journal of Research in Personality, 44,* 427–435.

Kumakiri, C., Kodama, K., Shimizu, E., Yamanouchi, N., Okada, S., Noda, S., et al. (1999). Study of the association between the serotonin transporter gene regulatory region polymorphism and personality traits in a Japanese population. *Neuroscience Letters, 263,* 205–207.

Kumar, A., Killingsworth, M. A., & Gilovich, T. (2014). Waiting for Merlot: Anticipatory consumption of experiential and material purchases. *Psychological Science, 25,* 1924–1931.

Kuper, H., Marmot, M., & Hemingway, H. (2002). Systematic review of prospective cohort studies of psychosocial factors in the etiology and prognosis of coronary heart disease. *Seminars in Vascular Medicine, 2,* 267–314.

Kurt, A., & Paulhus, D. L. (2008). Moderators of the adaptiveness of self-enhancement: Operationalization, motivational domain, adjustment facet, and evaluator. *Journal of Research in Personality, 42,* 839–853.

Kusserow, A. (1999). De-homogenizing American individualism: Socializing hard and soft individualism in Manhattan and Queens. *Ethos, 27,* 210–234.

Kuzawa, C. W., Gettler, L. T., Muller, M. N., McDade, T. W., & Feranil, A. B. (2009). Fatherhood, pairbonding and testosterone in the Philippines. *Hormones and Behavior, 56,* 429–435.

Kwan, V. S. Y., Bond, M. H., & Singelis, T. M. (1997). Pancultural explanations for life satisfaction: Adding relationship harmony to self-esteem. *Journal of Personality and Social Psychology, 73,* 1038–1051.

Kwan, V. S. Y., John, O. P., Robins, R. W., & Kuang, L. L. (2008). Conceptualizing and assessing self-enhancement bias: A componential approach. *Journal of Personality and Social Psychology, 94,* 1062–1077.

Lally, S. J. (2001). Should human figure drawings be admitted into court? *Journal of Personality Assessment, 76,* 135–149.

Lam, A. (2003, June 15). Let the I's have it: Think for yourselves, a writer from Vietnam tells Asian American students. *Los Angeles Times,* p. M6.

Lamkin, J., Maples-Keller, J.L., & Miller, J.D. (2018). How likable are personality disorder and general personality traits to those who possess them? *Journal of Personality, 86,* 173–185.

Landy, F. J., & Guion, R. M. (1970). Development of scales for the measurement of work motivation. *Organizational Behavior and Human Performance, 5*, 93–103.

Lang, F. R., Weiss, D., Gerstorf, D., & Wagner, G. G. (2013). Forecasting life satisfaction across adulthood: Benefits of seeing a dark future? *Psychology and Aging, 28*, 249–261.

Langeluddecke, P., & Tennant, C. (1986). Psychological correlates of the type A behaviour pattern in coronary angiography patients. *British Journal of Medical Psychology, 59*, 141–148.

Langer, E. J. (1992). Matters of mind: Mindfulness/mindlessness in perspective. *Consciousness and Cognition, 1*, 289–305.

Langer, E. J. (1994). The illusion of calculated decisions. In R. C. Schank & E. Langer (Eds.), *Beliefs, reasoning, and decision making: Psycho-logic in honor of Bob Abelson* (pp. 33–53). Hillsdale, NJ: Erlbaum.

Larkin, J. H., McDermott, J., Simon, D. P., & Simon, H. A. (1980). Models of competence in solving physics problems. *Cognitive Science, 4*, 317–345.

Larsen, R. J., & Diener, E. (1987). Affect intensity as an individual difference characteristic: A review. *Journal of Research in Personality, 21*, 1–39.

Lau, R. R. (1988). Beliefs about control and health behavior. In D. S. Gochman (Ed.), *Health behavior: Emerging research perspectives* (pp. 43–63). New York: Plenum Press.

Lazarus, R. S. (1984). On the primacy of cognition. *American Psychologist, 39*, 124–129.

Leary, M. R. (1999). Making sense of self-esteem. *Current Directions in Psychological Science, 8*, 32–35.

Leary, M. R. (2006, January). *How and why did the self get tangled up in emotion?* Paper presented at the SPSP Emotions Pre-Conference, Palm Springs, CA.

Lee, G. R., & Ishii-Kuntz, M. (1987). Social interaction, loneliness, and emotional well-being among the elderly. *Research on Aging, 9*, 459–482.

Lee, K., & Ashton, M. C. (2004). Psychometric properties of the HEXACO personality inventory. *Multivariate Behavioral Research, 39*, 329–358.

Lee, K., Ogunfowora, B., & Ashton, M. C. (2005). Personality traits beyond the Big Five: Are they within the HEXACO space? *Journal of Personality, 73*, 1437–1463.

Leger, K. A., Charles, S. T., Turiano, N. A., & Almeida, D. M. (2016). Personality and stressor-related affect. *Journal of Personality and Social Psychology, 111*, 917–928.

Leichsenring, F., & Rabung, S. (2008). Effectiveness of long-term psychodynamic psychotherapy. *Journal of the American Medical Association, 300*, 1551–1565.

Leikas, S. Lönnqvist, J-E., & Verkasalo, M. (2012). Persons, situations, and behaviors: Consistency and variability of different behaviors in four interpersonal situations. *Journal of Personality and Social Psychology, 103*, 1007–1022.

Leikas, S., & Salmela-Aro, K. (2015). Personality trait changes among young Finns: The role of life events and transitions. *Journal of Personality, 83*, 117–126.

Leising, D., Erbs, J., & Fritz, U. (2010). The letter of recommendation effect in informant ratings of personality. *Journal of Personality and Social Psychology, 98*, 668–682.

Leising, D., Scharloth, J., Lohse, O., & Wood D. (2014). What types of terms do people use when describing an individual's personality? *Psychological Science, 25*, 1787–1794.

Lester, K. J., et al, (2017) Collaborative meta-analysis finds no evidence of a strong interaction between stress and 5-HTTLPR genotype contributing to the development of depression. *Molecular Psychiatry, 774*, 494–515.

Letzring, T. D. (2015). Observer judgmental accuracy of personality: Benefits related to being a good (normative) judge. *Journal of Research in Personality, 54*, 51–60.

Letzring, T. D. (2008). The good judge of personality: Characteristics, behaviors, and observer accuracy. *Journal of Research in Personality, 42*, 914–932.

Letzring, T. D., & Funder, D. C. (2006, January). *Relations between judge's personality and types of realistic accuracy.* Paper presented at the annual meetings of the Society for Personality and Social Psychology, Palm Springs, CA.

Letzring, T. D., & Human, L. J. (2014). An examination of information quality as a moderator of accurate personality judgment. *Journal of Personality, 82*, 440–451.

Letzring, T. D., Block, J., & Funder, D. C. (2005). Ego-control and ego-resiliency: Generalization of self-report scales based on personality descriptions from acquaintances, clinicians, and the self. *Journal of Research in Personality, 39*, 395–422.

Letzring, T. D., Wells, S., & Funder, D. C. (2006). Quantity and quality of available information affect the realistic accuracy of personality judgment. *Journal of Personality and Social Psychology, 91*, 111–123.

Letzring, T.D. (2015). Observer judgmental accuracy: Benefits related to being a good (normative) judge. *Journal of Research in Personality, 54*, 51–60.

Leung, A. K-Y., & Cohen, D. (2011). Within- and between-culture variation: Individual differences and the cultural logics of honor, face, and dignity cultures. *Journal of Personality and Social Psychology, 100*, 507–526.

Levine, A., Zagoory-Sharon, O., Feldman, R., & Weller, A. (2007). Oxytocin during pregnancy and early postpartum: Individual patterns and maternal-fetal attachment. *Peptides, 28*, 1162–1169.

Levine, M. (2006). *Humanism in psychology.* Unpublished manuscript, Kenyon College, Gambier, OH.

Lewis, G.J., (2018). Early-childhood conduct problems predict economic and political discontent in adulthood: Evidence from two large, longitudinal UK cohorts. *Psychological Science.* Published online February 16, 2018.

Li, J. (2003). The core of Confucian learning. *American Psychologist, 58*, 146–147.

Li, N. P., Bailey, J. M., Kenrick, D. T., & Linsenmeier, J. A. W. (2002). The necessities and luxuries of mate preferences: Testing the tradeoffs. *Journal of Personality and Social Psychology, 82*, 947–955.

Li, N.P., van Vugt, M., & Colarelli, S.M. (2017). The evolutionary mismatch hypothesis: Implications for psychological science. *Current Directions in Psychological Science, 27*, 38–44.

Li, R., Montpetit, A., Rosseau, M., Wu, S. Y. M., Greenwood, C. M. T., Spector, T. D., Pollak, M., . . . Richards, J. B. (2014). Somatic point mutations occurring early in development: A monozygotic twin study. *Journal of Medical Genetics, 51*, 28–34.

Lieberman, M. D., Jarcho, J. M., & Satpute, A. B. (2004). Evidence-based and intuition-based self-knowledge: An fMRI study. *Journal of Personality and Social Psychology, 87*, 421–435.

Lieder, F., Griffiths, T. L., & Hsu, M. (2018). Overrepresentation of extreme events in decision making reflects rational use of cognitive resources. *Psychological Review, 125*(1), 1–32.

Lilgendahl, J. P., Helson, R., & John, O. P. (2012). Does ego development increase during midlife? The effects of openness and accommodative processing of difficult events. *Journal of Personality, 81*, 403–416.

Lilienfeld, S. O. (1999). Projective measures of personality and psychopathology: How well do they work? *Skeptical Inquirer, 23*(5), 32–39.

Lilienfeld, S. O., Wood, J. M., & Garb, H. N. (2000). The scientific status of projective techniques. *Psychological Science in the Public Interest, 1*, 27–66.

Linehan, M. M. (1993). *Cognitive behavioral therapy of borderline personality disorder.* New York: Guilford Press.

Linville, P., & Jones, E. E. (1980). Polarized appraisals of out-group members. *Journal of Personality and Social Psychology, 38*, 689–703.

Little, B. R. (1983). Personal projects: A rationale and method for investigation. *Environment and Behavior, 15*, 273–309.

Little, B. R. (1989). Personal projects analysis: Trivial pursuits, magnificent obsessions, and the search for coherence. In D. M. Buss & N. Cantor (Eds.), *Personality psychology: Recent trends and emerging directions* (pp. 15–31). New York: Springer-Verlag.

Liu, T. T., & Brown, G. G. (2007). Measurement of cerebral perfusion with arterial spin labeling: Part I. Methods. *Journal of the International Neurophysiological Society, 13*, 517–525.

Lodi-Smith, J., & Roberts, B. W. (2010). Getting to know me: Social role experiences and age differences in self-concept clarity during adulthood. *Journal of Personality, 78*, 1383–1410.

Loehlin, J. C., Willerman, L., & Horn, J. M. (1985). Personality resemblances in adoptive families when the children are late-adolescent or adult. *Journal of Personality and Social Psychology, 48,* 376–392.

Loehlin, J. C., Willerman, L., & Horn, J. M. (1989). Personality resemblance in adoptive families: A 10-year follow-up. *Journal of Personality and Social Psychology, 53,* 961–969.

Loevinger, J. (1976). *Ego development: Conceptions and theories.* San Francisco: Jossey-Bass.

Loevinger, J. (1987). *Paradigms of personality.* New York: Freeman.

Loftus, G. R. (1996). Psychology will be a much better science when we change the way we analyze data. *Current Directions in Psychological Science, 5,* 161–170.

Lorenz, K. (1966). *On aggression.* New York: Harcourt, Brace.

Lorenzi-Cioldi, F. (1993). They all look alike, but so do we . . . sometimes: Perceptions of in-group and out-group homogeneity as a function of sex and context. *British Journal of Social Psychology, 32,* 111–124.

Lucas, R. E., & Diener, E. (2001). Understanding extraverts' enjoyment of social situations: The importance of pleasantness. *Journal of Personality and Social Psychology, 81,* 343–356.

Lucas, R. E., & Donnellan, M. B. (2011). Personality development across the life span: Longitudinal analyses with a national sample from Germany. *Journal of Personality and Social Psychology, 101,* 847–861.

Lucas, R. E., Le, K., & Dyrenforth, P. S. (2008). Explaining the extraversion/positive affect relation: Sociability cannot account for extraverts' greater happiness. *Journal of Personality, 76,* 385–414.

Luhmann, M., Schimmack, U., & Eid, M. (2011). Stability and variability in the relationship between subjective well-being and income. *Journal of Research in Personality, 45,* 186–197.

Lukaszewski, A. W., & Roney, J. R. (2011). The origins of extraversion: Joint effects of facultative calibration and genetic polymorphism. *Personality and Social Psychology Bulletin, 37,* 409–421.

Lykes, M. B. (1985). Gender and individualistic vs. collectivist bases for notions about the self. *Journal of Personality, 53,* 356–383.

Lykken, D., & Tellegen, A. (1996). Happiness is a stochastic phenomenon. *Psychological Science, 7,* 186–189.

Lyubomirsky, S. (2001). Why are some people happier than others? The role of cognitive and motivational processes in well-being. *American Psychologist, 56,* 239–249.

Lyubomirsky, S. (2008). *The how of happiness: A scientific approach to getting the life you want.* New York: Penguin Press.

Lyubomirsky, S., & Layous, K. (2013). How do simply positive actions increase well-being? *Current Directions in Psychological Science, 22,* 57–62.

Lyubomirsky, S., King, L., & Diener, E. (2005). The benefits of frequent positive affect: Does happiness lead to success? *Psychological Bulletin, 131,* 803–855.

Lyubomirsky, S., Sheldon, K. M., & Schkade, D. (2005). Pursuing happiness: The architecture of sustainable change. *Review of General Psychology, 9,* 111–131.

Maccoby, E. E., & Jacklin, C. N. (1974). *The psychology of sex differences.* Stanford University Press.

Machover, K. (1949). *Personality projection in the drawing of the human figure.* Springfield, IL: Thomas.

MacLean, K. A., Johnson, M. W., & Griffiths, R. R. (2011). Mystical experiences occasioned by the hallucinogen psilocybin lead to increases in the personality domain of openness. *Journal of Psychopharmacology, 25,* 1453–1451.

MacLean, P. D. (1990). *The triune brain in evolution: Role in paleocerebral functions.* New York: Plenum Press.

Maddi, S. R., & Costa, P. T. (1972). *Humanism in personology: Allport, Maslow, and Murphy.* Chicago: Aldine/Atherton.

Maddux, W. W., & Galinsky, A. D. (2009). Cultural borders and mental barriers: The relationship between living abroad and creativity. *Journal of Personality and Social Psychology, 96,* 1047–1061.

Madon, S., Guyll, M., Spoth, R., & Willard, J. (2004). Self-fulfilling prophecies: The synergistic accumulative effect of parents' beliefs on children's drinking behavior. *Psychological Science, 15,* 837–845.

Magee, C. A., Heaven, C. L., & Miller, L. M. (2013). Personality change predicts self-reported mental and physical health. *Journal of Personality, 81,* 324–334.

Magidson, J. F., Roberts, B. W., Collado-Rodriguez, A., & Lejuez, C. W. (2012). Theory-driven intervention for changing personality: Expectancy value theory, behavioral activation, and conscientiousness. *Developmental Psychology, 50*, 1442–1450.

Mahbubani, K. (2002). *Can Asians think? Understanding the divide between East and West* (Rev. ed.: expanded for North America). S. Royalton, VT: Steerforth Press.

Maier, S. F., & Seligman, M. E. (1976). Learned helplessness: Theory and evidence. *Journal of Experimental Psychology: General, 105*, 3–46.

Main, M. (1990). Parental aversion to infant-initiated contact is correlated with the parent's own rejection during childhood: The effects of experience on signals of security with respect to attachment. In K. E. Barnard & T. B. Brazelton (Eds.), *Touch: The foundation of experience* (pp. 461–495). Madison, CT: International Universities Press.

Maio, G. R., & Esses, V. M. (2001). The need for affect: Individual differences in the motivation to approach or avoid emotions. *Journal of Personality, 69*, 583–615.

Majerus, M. E. N. (1998). *Melanism: Evolution in action.* New York: Oxford University Press.

Maniaci, M. R., & Rogge, R. D. (2014). Caring about carelessness: Participant inattention and its effects on research. *Journal of Research in Personality, 48*, 61–83.

Manson, J.H. (2017). Life history strategy and everyday word use. *Evolutionary Psychological Science.* doi: 10.1007/s40806-017-0119-3

Markey, P. M., & Markey, C. N. (2010). Changes in pornography-seeking behaviors following political elections: An examination of the challenge hypothesis. *Evolution and Human Behavior, 31*, 442–446.

Markey, P. M., Markey, C. N., Tinsley, B. J., & Ericksen, A. J. (2002). A preliminary validation of preadolescents' self-reports using the five-factor model of personality. *Journal of Research in Personality, 36*, 173–181.

Markowitz, E. M., Goldberg, L. R., Ashton, M. C., & Lee, K. (2012). Profiling the "pro-environmental individual": A personality perspective. *Journal of Personality, 80*, 81–111.

Markus, H. R. (1977). Self-schemata and processing information about the self. *Journal of Personality and Social Psychology, 35*, 63–78.

Markus, H. R., & Kitayama, S. (1991). Culture and the self: Implications for cognition, emotion, and motivation. *Psychological Review, 98*, 224–253.

Markus, H. R., & Kitayama, S. (1998). The cultural psychology of personality. *Journal of Cross-Cultural Psychology, 29*, 63–87.

Markus, H. R., & Nurius, P. (1986). Possible selves. *American Psychologist, 41*, 954–969.

Markus, H. R., Mullally, P. R., & Kitayama, S. (1997). Selfways: Diversity in modes of cultural participation. In U. Neisser & D. Jopling (Eds.), *The conceptual self in context: Culture, experience, self-understanding* (pp. 13–60). New York: Cambridge University Press.

Mascaro, N., & Rosen, D. H. (2005). Existential meaning's role in the enhancement of hope and prevention of depressive symptoms. *Journal of Personality, 73*, 985–1014.

Maslow, A. H. (1943). A theory of human motivation. *Psychological Review, 50*, 370–396.

Maslow, A. H. (1987). *Motivation and personality* (3rd ed.). New York: Harper & Row.

Masson, J. M. (1984). *The assault on truth: Freud's suppression of the seduction theory.* New York: Farrar, Straus and Giroux.

Mast, M. S., & Hall, J. A. (2018). The impact of interpersonal accuracy on behavioral outcomes. *Current Directions in Psychological Science.* Published on-line August 18, 2018.

Masuda, T., & Nisbett, R. E. (2001). Attending holistically versus analytically: Comparing the context sensitivity of Japanese and Americans. *Journal of Personality and Social Psychology, 81*, 922–934.

Matsumoto, D. (2004). Paul Ekman and the legacy of universals. *Journal of Research in Personality, 38*, 45–51.

Matsumoto, D. (2006). Culture and cultural worldviews: Do verbal descriptions about culture reflect anything other than verbal descriptions of culture? *Culture and Psychology, 12*, 33–62.

Matsumoto, D., Nakagawa, S., & Estrada, A. (2009). The role of dispositional traits in accounting for country and ethnic differences in adjustment. *Journal of Personality, 77*, 177–211.

Matthiesen, A. S., Ransio-Arvidson, A. B., Nissen, E., & Uvnas-Moberg, K. (2001). Postpartum maternal oxytocin release by newborns: Effects of infant hand massage and suckling. *Birth, 28*, 13–19.

Mayer, J. D. (1998). A systems framework for the field of personality. *Psychological Inquiry, 9*, 118–144.

Mayer, J. D. (2005). A tale of two visions: Can a new view of personality help integrate psychology? *American Psychologist, 60*, 294–307.

Mayer, J. D., Lin, S. C., & Korogodsky, M. (2011). Exploring the universality of personality judgments: Evidence from the Great Transformation (1000 BCE–200 BCE). *Review of General Psychology, 15*, 65–76.

McAdams, D. P. (1980). A thematic coding system for the intimacy motive. *Journal of Research in Personality, 14*, 413–432.

McAdams, D. P. (1984). Scoring manual for the intimacy motive. *Psychological Documents, 14* (Ms. no. 2613), 1.

McAdams, D. P. (1990). *The person.* San Diego, CA: Harcourt, Brace.

McAdams, D. P. (2013). The psychological self as actor, agent and author. *Perspectives on Psychological Science, 8*, 272–295.

McAdams, D. P., & McLean, K. C. (2013). Narrative identity. *Current Directions in Psychological Science, 22*, 233–238.

McAdams, D. P., Anyidoho, N. A., Brown, C., Huang, Y. T., Kaplan, B., & Machado, M. A. (2004). Traits and stories: Links between dispositional and narrative features of personality. *Journal of Personality, 72*, 761–784.

McCabe, D. P., & Castel, A. D. (2008). Seeing is believing: The effect of brain images on judgments of scientific reasoning. *Cognition, 107*, 343–352.

McCann, S. J. (1990). Authoritarianism and preference for the presidential candidate perceived to be higher on the power motive. *Perceptual and Motor Skills, 70*, 577–578.

McCann, S. J. (1997). Threatening times, "strong" presidential popular vote winners, and the victory margin. *Journal of Personality and Social Psychology, 73*, 160–170.

McCarthy, M. M. (1995). Estrogen modulation of oxytocin and its relation to behavior. In R. Ivell & J. Russell (Eds.), *Oxytocin: Cellular and molecular approaches in medicine and research* (pp. 235–242). New York: Plenum Press.

McCarthy, M.H., Wood, J.V., & Holmes, J.G. (2017). Dispositional pathways to trust: Self-esteem and agreeableness interact to predict trust and negative emotional disclosure. *Journal of Personality and Social Psychology, 113*, 95–116.

McDonald, J.S., & Letzring, T.D. (2016). Judging personal values and personality traits: Accuracy and its relation to visibility. *Journal of Research in Personality, 65*, 140–151.

McClelland, D. C. (1961). *The achieving society.* Princeton, NJ: Van Nostrand.

McClelland, D. C. (1972). Opinions predict opinions: So what else is new? *Journal of Consulting and Clinical Psychology, 38*, 325–326.

McClelland, D. C. (1975, January). Love and power: The psychological signals of war. *Psychology Today, 8*, 44–48.

McClelland, D. C. (1984). *Motives, personality, and society.* New York: Praeger.

McClelland, D. C. (1985). How motives, skills, and values determine what people do. *American Psychologist, 40*, 812–825.

McClelland, D. C., & Boyatzis, R. E. (1982). Leadership motive pattern and long-term success in management. *Journal of Applied Psychology, 67*, 737–743.

McClelland, D. C., Koestner, R., & Weinberger, J. (1989). How do self-attributed and implicit motives differ? *Psychological Review, 96*, 690–702.

McCrae, R. R. (1982). Consensual validation of personality traits: Evidence from self-reports and ratings. *Journal of Personality and Social Psychology, 43*, 293–303.

McCrae, R. R. (1994). The counterpoint of personality assessment: Self-reports and observer ratings. *Assessment, 1*, 159–172.

McCrae, R. R. (2002). The maturation of personality psychology: Adult personality development and psychological well-being. *Journal of Research in Personality, 36,* 307–317.

McCrae, R. R. (2004). Human nature and culture: A trait perspective. *Journal of Research in Personality, 38,* 3–14.

McCrae, R. R., & Costa, P. T., Jr. (1987). Validation of the five-factor model of personality across instruments and observers. *Journal of Personality and Social Psychology, 52,* 81–90.

McCrae, R. R., & Costa, P. T., Jr. (1991). Adding Liebe und Arbeit: The full five-factor model and well-being. *Personality and Social Psychology Bulletin, 17,* 227–232.

McCrae, R. R., & Costa, P. T., Jr. (1995). Trait explanations in personality psychology. *European Journal of Personality, 9,* 231–252.

McCrae, R. R., & Costa, P. T., Jr. (1997). Conceptions and correlates of openness to experience. In R. Hogan, J. Johnson, & S. Briggs (Eds.), *Handbook of personality psychology* (pp. 825–847). San Diego: Academic Press.

McCrae, R. R., Costa, P. T., Jr., & Yik, M. S. M. (1996). Universal aspects of Chinese personality structure. In M. H. Bond (Ed.), *The handbook of Chinese psychology* (pp. 189–207). Hong Kong: Oxford University Press.

McCrae, R. R., Scally, M., Terracciano, A., Abecasis, G., & Costa, P. T., Jr. (2010). An alternative to the search for single polymorphisms: Toward molecular personality scales for the five-factor model. *Journal of Personality and Social Psychology, 99,* 1014–1024.

McCrae, R. R., Terracciano, A., & 78 members of the Personality Profiles of Cultures Project. (2005). Universal features of personality trait terms from the observer's perspective: Data from 50 cultures. *Journal of Personality and Social Psychology, 88,* 547–561.

McCrae, R. R., Terracciano, A., Costa, P. T., Jr., & Ozer, D. J. (2006). Person-factors in the California Adult Q-Set: Closing the door on personality trait types? *European Journal of Personality, 20,* 29–44.

McCrae, R. R., Yik, M. S. M., Trapnell, P. D., Bond, M. H., & Paulhus, D. L. (1998). Interpreting personality profiles across cultures: Bilingual, acculturation, and peer rating studies of Chinese undergraduates. *Journal of Personality and Social Psychology, 74,* 1041–1055.

McGinnies, E. (1949). Emotionality and perceptual defense. *Psychological Review, 56,* 244–251.

McGrath, R. E. (2008). The Rorschach in the context of performance-based personality assessment. *Journal of Personality Assessment, 90*(5), 465–475.

McGue, M., & Lykken, D. T. (1992). Genetic influence on risk of divorce. *Psychological Science, 3,* 368–373.

McIntosh, A. R. (1998). Understanding neural interactions in learning and memory using functional neuroimaging. *Annals of the New York Academy of Sciences, 855,* 556–571.

McKay, J. R., O'Farrell, T. J., Maisto, S. A., Connors, G. J., & Funder, D. C. (1989). Biases in relapse attributions made by alcoholics and their wives. *Addictive Behaviors, 14,* 513–522.

McLarney-Vesotski, A., Bernieri, F., & Rempala, D. (2011). An experimental examination of the "good judge." *Journal of Research in Personality, 45,* 398–400.

Mealey, L. (1995). The sociobiology of sociopathy: An integrated evolutionary model. *Behavioral and Brain Sciences, 18,* 523–599.

Meehl, P.E. (1989) *Philosophical Psychology* (lectures 11 and 12). University of Minnesota. Retrieved from http://meehl.umn.edu/recordings/philosophical-psychology-1989

Meewisse, M., Reitsma, J. B., De Vries, G.-J., Gersons, B. P. R., & Olff, M. (2007). Cortisol and post-traumatic stress disorder in adults: Systematic review and meta-analysis. *British Journal of Psychiatry, 191,* 367–392.

Mehl, M. R., Pennebaker, J. W., Crow, D. M., Dabbs, J., & Price, J. H. (2001). The electronically activated recorder (EAR): A device for sampling naturalistic daily activities and conversations. *Behavior Research Methods, Instruments, and Computers, 33,* 517–523.

Mehl, M.R. (2017). The electronically activated recorder (EAR): A method for the naturalistic observation of daily social behavior. *Current Directions in Psychological Science, 26,* 184–190.

Mehra, A., Kilduff, M., & Brass, D. J. (2001). The social networks of high and low self-monitors: Implications for workplace performance. *Administrative Science Quarterly, 46*, 121–146.

Meltzer, A.L. & McNulty, J.K. (2016). Who is having more and better sex? The Big Five as predictors of sex in marriage. *Journal of Research in Personality, 63*, 62–66.

Menand, L. (2002, November 25). What comes naturally: Does evolution explain who we are? *New Yorker*, pp. 96–101.

Mendelsohn, G. A., Weiss, D. S., & Feimer, N. R. (1982). Conceptual and empirical analysis of the typological implications of patterns of socialization and femininity. *Journal of Personality and Social Psychology, 42*, 1157–1170.

Mesquita, B. (2001). Emotions in collectivist and individualist contexts. *Journal of Personality and Social Psychology, 80*, 68–74.

Mesquita, B., & Karasawa, M. (2002). Different emotional lives. *Cognition and Emotion, 16*, 127–141.

Metzner, R. J. (1994, March 14). Prozac is medicine, not a miracle. *Los Angeles Times*, p. B7.

Meyer, G. J., Finn, S. E., Eyde, L. D., Kay, G. G., Moreland, K. L., Dies, R. R., et al. (2001). Psychological testing and psychological assessment: A review of evidence and issues. *American Psychologist, 56*, 128–165.

Michigan Department of Education. (1989). *The Michigan employability survey*. Lansing, MI: Author.

Mike, A., Jackson, J. J., & Oltmanns, T. F. (2014). The conscientious retiree: The relationship between conscientiousness, retirement, and volunteering. *Journal of Research in Personality, 52*, 68–77.

Mikulincer, M., & Shaver, P. R. (2003). The attachment behavioral system in adulthood: Activation, psychodynamics, and interpersonal processes. *Advances in Experimental Social Psychology, 35*, 53–152.

Mikulincer, M., Gillath, O., & Shaver, P. R. (2002). Activation of the attachment system in adulthood: Threat-related primes increase the accessibility of mental representations of attachment figures. *Journal of Personality and Social Psychology, 83*, 881–895.

Milgram, S. (1975). *Obedience to authority*. New York: Harper & Row.

Miller, G. (2008). Growing pains for fMRI. *Science, 320*, 1412–1414.

Miller, G. A. (1956). The magical number seven plus or minus two: Some limits on our capacity for processing information. *Psychological Review, 63*, 81–97.

Miller, J. D. (2009, January 11). American therapy [Letter to the editor]. *New York Times Book Review*, p. 6.

Miller, J. D., & Campbell, W. K. (2008). Comparing clinical and social-personality conceptualizations of narcissism. *Journal of Personality, 76*, 449–476.

Miller, J. G. (1999). Cultural psychology: Implications for basic psychological theory. *Psychological Science, 10*, 85–91.

Miller, J. G., & Bersoff, D. M. (1992). Culture and moral judgment: How are conflicts between justice and interpersonal responsibilities resolved? *Journal of Personality and Social Psychology, 62*, 541–554.

Miller, J. G., Bersoff, D. M., & Harwood, R. L. (1990). Perceptions of social responsibilities in India and in the United States: Moral imperatives or personal decisions? *Journal of Personality and Social Psychology, 58*, 33–47.

Miller, L. (1999). Stereotype legacy: Culture and person in Japanese/American business interactions. In Y.-T. Lee, C. R. McCauley, & J. G. Draguns (Eds.), *Personality and person perception across cultures* (pp. 213–232). Mahwah, NJ: Erlbaum.

Miller, N. E., & Dollard, J. (1947). *Social learning and imitation*. New Haven, CT: Yale University Press.

Miller, R. S. (1999). Emotion. In V. J. Derlaga, B. A., Winstead, & W. H. Jones (Eds.), *Personality: Contemporary theory and research* (pp. 366–385). Chicago: Nelson-Hall.

Miller, T. Q., Turner, C. W., Tindale, R. S., Posavac, E. J., & Dugoni, B. L. (1991). Reasons for the trend toward null findings in research on Type A behavior. *Psychological Bulletin, 110*, 469–485.

Miller, W. R., & Seligman, M. E. (1975). Depression and learned helplessness in man. *Journal of Abnormal Psychology, 84*, 228–238.

Milojev, P., & Sibley, C.G. (2017). Normative personality trait development in adulthood: A 6-year cohort-sequential growth model. *Journal of Personality and Social Psychology, 112*, 510–526.

Milojev, P., Osborne, D., & Sibley, C. G. (2014). Personality resilience following a natural disaster. *Social Psychological and Personality Science, 5,* 760–768.

Mischel, W. (1968). *Personality and assessment.* New York: Wiley.

Mischel, W. (1973). Toward a cognitive social learning reconceptualization of personality. *Psychological Review, 80,* 252–283.

Mischel, W. (1999). Personality coherence and dispositions in a cognitive-affective personality system (CAPS) approach. In D. Cervone & Y. Shoda (Eds.), *The coherence of personality: Social-cognitive bases of consistency, variability, and organization* (pp. 37–60). New York: Guilford Press.

Mischel, W. (2009). From *Personality and Assessment* (1968) to personality science, 2009. *Journal of Research in Personality, 43,* 282–290.

Mischel, W., & Shoda, Y. (1995). A cognitive-affective system theory of personality: Reconceptualizing situations, dispositions, dynamics, and invariance in personality structure. *Psychological Review, 102,* 246–268.

Moeller, S. K., Robinson, M. D., & Bresin, K. (2010). Integrating trait and social-cognitive views of personality: Neuroticism, implicit stress priming, and neuroticism-outcome relationships. *Personality and Social Psychology Bulletin, 36,* 677–689.

Moeller, S. K., Robinson, M. D., & Zabelina, D. L. (2008). Personality dominance and preferential use of the vertical dimension of space. *Psychological Science, 19,* 355–361.

Moffitt, T. E. (1991). *An approach to organizing the task of selecting measures for longitudinal research* (Tech. Rep.). University of Wisconsin, Madison.

Moffitt, T. E. (2005). The new look of behavioral genetics in developmental psychopathology: Gene-environment interplay in antisocial behaviors. *Psychological Bulletin, 131,* 533–554.

Mogilner, C., Kamvar, S. D., & Aaker, J. (2011). The shifting meaning of happiness. *Social Psychological and Personality Science, 2,* 395–402.

Montag, I., & Levin, J. (1994). The five-factor personality model in applied settings. *European Journal of Personality, 8,* 1–11.

Morf, C. C., & Rhodewalt, F. (2001). Unraveling the paradoxes of narcissism: A dynamic self-regulatory processing model. *Psychological Inquiry, 12,* 177–196.

Morgan, C. D., & Murray, H. A. (1935). A method for investigating fantasies: The Thematic Apperception Test. *Archives of Neurology and Psychiatry, 34,* 289–306.

Morsella, E. (2005). The function of phenomenal states: Supramodular interaction theory. *Psychological Review, 112,* 1000–1021.

Mosig, Y. D. (1989). Wisdom and compassion: What the Buddha taught. *Theoretical and Philosophical Psychology, 9,* 27–36.

Mosig, Y. D. (1999). Zen Buddhism. In B. Engler, *Personality theories* (5th ed., pp. 456–481). Boston: Houghton Mifflin.

Motta, M. (2011). A critique of the Myers Briggs type Indicator. *Recruiter.* Retrieved from https://www.recruiter.com/i/critique-of-the-myers-briggs-type-indicator-critique

Mõttus, R., Allik, J., & Realo, A. (2010). An attempt to validate national mean scores on conscientiousness: No necessarily paradoxical findings. *Journal of Research in Personality, 44,* 630–640.

Mount, M. K., & Barrick, M. R. (1998). Five reasons why the "Big Five" article has been frequently cited. *Personnel Psychology, 51,* 849–857.

Mroczek, D. K., Spiro, A. I., II, & Turiano, N. A. (2009). Do health behaviors explain the effect of neuroticism on mortality? Longitudinal findings from the VA normative aging study. *Journal of Research in Personality, 43*(4), 653–659.

Munafó, M. R., Brown, S. M., & Hariri, A. R. (2008). Serotonin transporter (5-HTTLPR) genotype and amygdala activation: A meta-analysis. *Biological Psychiatry, 63,* 852–857.

Munafó, M. R., Yalcin, B., Willis-Owen, S. A., & Flint, J. (2008). Association of the dopamine D4 receptor (*DRD4*) gene and approach-related personality traits: Meta-analysis and new data. *Biological Psychiatry, 63,* 197–206.

Murray, D. R., Trudeau, R., & Schaller, M. (2011). On the origins of cultural differences in conformity: Four tests of the pathogen prevalence hypothesis. *Personality and Social Psychology Bulletin, 37,* 318–329.

Murray, H. A. (1938). *Explorations in personality.* New York: Oxford University Press.

Murray, H. A. (1943). *Analysis of the personality of Adolf Hitler, with predictions of his future behavior and suggestions for dealing with him now and after Germany's surrender.* Washington, DC: Office of Strategic Services.

Myers, I. B. (1962). *The Myers-Briggs Type Indicator.* Princeton, NJ: Educational Testing Service.

Myers, I.B. (1980). *Gifts differing: Understanding personality type.* Palo Alto: Davies-Black Publishing.

Myers, I.B., & McCaulley, M.H. (1985). *Manual: A guide to the development and use of the Myers-Briggs Type Indicator.* Palo Alto, CA: Consulting Psychologists Press.

Naroll, R. (1959). A tentative index of culture-stress. *International Journal of Social Psychiatry, 5,* 107–116.

Nave, C. S., Sherman, R. A., & Funder, D. C. (2008). Beyond self-report in the study of hedonic and eudaimonic well-being: Correlations with acquaintance reports, clinician judgments and directly observed social behavior. *Journal of Research in Personality, 42,* 643–659.

Nave, C. S., Sherman, R. A., & Funder, D. C. (2010). On the contextual independence of personality: Teachers' assessments predict directly observed behavior after four decades. *Social Psychological and Personality Science, 1,* 327–334.

Nave, G., Minxha, J., Greenberg, D.M., Kosinski, M., Stillwll, D., & Rentfrow, J. (2018). Musical preferences predict personality: Evidence from active listening and Facebook likes. *Psychological Science,* published online March 27, 2018.

Neff, K. D., Pisitsungkagarn, K., & Hsieh, Y.-P. (2008). Self-compassion and self-construal in the United States, Thailand, and Taiwan. *Journal of Cross-Cultural Psychology, 39,* 267–285.

Nelson-Coffey, S.K., Fritz, M., Lyubomirsky, S., & Cole, S. (2017). Kindness in the blood: A randomized controlled trial of the gene regulatory impact of prosocial behavior. *Psychoneuroendocrinology, 81,* 8–13.

Nestle, J., Howell, C., & Wilchins, R. A. (Eds.). (2002). *GenderQueer: Voices from beyond the sexual binary.* Los Angeles: Alyson Books.

Nettle, D. (2006). The evolution of personality variation in humans and other animals. *American Psychologist, 61,* 622–631.

Nevicka, B., Ten Velden, F. S., De Hoogh, A. H. B., & Van Vianen, A. E. M. (2011). Reality at odds with perception: Narcissistic leaders and group performance. *Psychological Science, 22,* 1259–1264.

Nickerson, R. S. (2000). Null hypothesis significance testing: A review of an old and continuing controversy. *Psychological Methods, 5,* 241–301.

Niedenthal, P. M., & Brauer, M. (2012). Social functionality of human emotion. *Annual Review of Psychology, 63,* 259–285.

Nikula, R., Klinger, E., & Larson-Gutman, M. K. (1993). Current concerns and electrodermal reactivity: Responses to words and thoughts. *Journal of Personality, 61,* 63–84.

Nisbett, R. E. (1980). The trait construct in lay and professional psychology. In L. Festinger (Ed.), *Retrospections on social psychology* (pp. 109–130). New York: Oxford University Press.

Nisbett, R. E., & Wilson, T. D. (1977). Telling more than we can know: Verbal reports on mental processes. *Psychological Review, 84,* 231–259.

Nisbett, R. E., Peng, K., Choi, I., & Norenzayan, A. (2001). Culture and systems of thought: Holistic versus analytic cognition. *Psychological Review, 108,* 291–310.

Norem, J. (2001). *The positive power of negative thinking: Using defensive pessimism to manage anxiety and perform at your peak.* New York: Basic Books.

Norem, J. K. (1989). Cognitive strategies as personality: Effectiveness, specificity, flexibility, and change. In D. M. Buss & N. Cantor (Eds.), *Personality psychology: Recent trends and emerging directions* (pp. 45–60). New York: Springer-Verlag.

Norem, J. K. (2002). Defensive self-deception and social adaptation among optimists. *Journal of Research in Personality, 36,* 549–555.

Norem, J. K., & Cantor, N. (1986). Defensive pessimism: "Harnessing" anxiety as motivation. *Journal of Personality and Social Psychology, 51*, 1211.

Norem, J. K., & Chang, E. C. (2001). A very full glass: Adding complexity to our thinking about the implications and applications of optimism and pessimism research. In E. C. Chang (Ed.), *Optimism and pessimism: Implications for theory, research, and practice* (pp. 347–367). Washington DC: American Psychological Association.

Norem, J. K., & Chang, E. C. (2002). The positive psychology of negative thinking. *Journal of Clinical Psychology, 58*, 993–1001.

Norem, J. K., & Prayson, B.J. (2015, June). Validation of a new Defensive Pessimism Questionnaire-Short Form. Poster presented at the bi-annual meeting of the Association for Research in Personality, St. Louis, MO.

Norman, W. T. (1967). *2800 personality trait descriptors: Normative operating characteristics for a university population*. Ann Arbor, MI: University of Michigan.

Norton, M. I., Anik, L., Aknin, L. B., & Dunn, E. W. (2011). Is life nasty, brutish and short? Philosophies of life and well-being. *Social Psychological and Personality Science, 2*, 570–575.

O'Bannon, R. M., Goldinger, L. A., & Appleby, G. S. (1989). *Honesty and integrity testing*. Atlanta, GA: Applied Information Resources.

O'Connor, B. P. (2002). The search for dimensional structure differences between normality and abnormality: A statistical review of published data on personality and psychopathology. *Journal of Personality and Social Psychology, 83*, 962–982.

Ochsner, K. N., & Gross, J. J. (2005). The cognitive control of emotion. *Trends in Cognitive Sciences, 9*, 242–249.

Ogilvie, D. M., & Ashmore, R. D. (1991). Self-with-other representation as a unit of analysis in self-concept research. In R. C. Curtis (Ed.), *The relational self* (pp. 282–314). New York: Guilford Press.

Öhman, A., & Mineka, S. (2001). Fears, phobias, and preparedness: Toward an evolved module of fear and fear learning. *Psychological Review, 108*, 483–522.

Öhman, A., & Mineka, S. (2003). The malicious serpent: Snakes as a prototypical stimulus for an evolved module of fear. *Current Directions in Psychological Science, 12*, 5–9.

Oishi, S. (2004). Personality in culture: A neo-Allportian view. *Journal of Research in Personality, 38*, 68–74.

Oishi, S. (2006). The concept of life satisfaction across cultures: An IRT analysis. *Journal of Research in Personality, 40*, 411–423.

Oishi, S., & Graham, J. (2010). Social ecology: Lost and found in psychological science. *Perspectives in Psychological Science, 5*, 356–377.

Oishi, S., & Sullivan, H. W. (2005). The mediating role of parental expectations in culture and well-being. *Journal of Personality, 73*, 1267–1294.

Oishi, S., Diener, E., Lucas, R. E., & Suh, E. M. (1999). Cross-cultural variations in predictors of life satisfaction: Perspectives from needs and values. *Personality and Social Psychology Bulletin, 25*, 980–990.

Oishi, S., Diener, E., Scollon, C. N., & Biswas-Diener, R. (2004). Cross-situational consistency of affective experiences across cultures. *Journal of Personality and Social Psychology, 86*, 460–472.

Oldham, J. M., & Morris, L. B. (1995). *The new personality self-portrait*. New York: Bantam Books.

Oltmanns, T. F., & Turkheimer, E. (2009). Person perception and personality pathology. *Current Directions in Psychological Science, 18*, 32–36.

Ones, D. S., Viswesvaran, C., & Schmidt, F. L. (1993). Comprehensive meta-analysis of integrity test validities: Findings and implications for personnel selection and theories of job performance. *Journal of Applied Psychology, 78*, 679–703.

Ones, D. S., Viswesvaran, C., & Schmidt, F. L. (1995). Integrity tests: Overlooked facts, resolved issues, and remaining questions. *American Psychologist, 50*, 456–457.

Ones, D. S., Viswesvaran, C., & Schmidt, F. L. (2003). Personality and absenteeism: A meta-analysis of integrity tests. *European Journal of Personality, 17*(Suppl.: Personality and industrial, work, and organizational applications), S19–S38.

Open Science Collaboration (2015). Estimating the reproducibility of psychological science. *Science, 349*, 943.

Ornstein, R. E. (1977). *The psychology of consciousness* (2nd ed.). New York: Harcourt, Brace.

Orth, U. (2018). The family environment in early childhood as a long-term effect on self-esteem: A longitudinal study from birth to age 27 years. *Journal of Personality and Social Psychology, 114*, 637–655.

Orth, U., & Robins, R. W. (2014). The development of self-esteem. *Current Directions in Psychological Science, 23*, 381–387.

Orth, U., Robins, R. W., & Roberts, B. W. (2008). Low self-esteem prospectively predicts depression in adolescence and young adulthood. *Journal of Personality and Social Psychology, 95*, 695–708.

Orth, V., Robins, R. W., & Widaman, K. F. (2012). Life-span development and its effects on important life outcomes. *Journal of Personality and Social Psychology, 102*, 1271–1288.

Osborn, S. M., Feild, H. S., & Veres, J. G. (1998). Introversion-extraversion, self-monitoring and applicant performance in a situational panel interview: A field study. *Journal of Business and Psychology, 13*, 143–156.

Ostendorf, F., & Angleitner, A. (1994, July). *Psychometric properties of the German translation of the NEO Personality Inventory (NEO-PI-R).* Paper presented at the Seventh Conference of the European Association for Personality Psychology, Madrid, Spain.

Osterman, L. L., & Brown, R. P. (2011). Culture of honor and violence against the self. *Personality and Social Psychology Bulletin, 37*, 1611–1623.

Otway, L. J., & Vignoles, V. J. (2006). Narcissism and childhood recollection: A quantitative test of psychoanalytic predictions. *Personality and Social Psychology Bulletin, 32*, 104–116.

Oyserman, D., Coon, H. M., & Kemmelmeir, M. (2002). Rethinking individualism and collectivism: Evaluation of theoretical assumptions and meta-analysis. *Psychological Bulletin, 128*, 3–72.

Ozer, D. J. (1985). Correlation and the coefficient of determination. *Psychological Bulletin, 97*, 307–315.

Ozer, D. J., & Benet-Martínez, V. (2006). Personality and the prediction of consequential outcomes. *Annual Review of Psychology, 57*, 401–421.

Pagan, J. L., Eaton, N. R., Turkheimer, E., & Oltmanns, T. F. (2006). Peer-reported personality problems of research nonparticipants: Are our samples biased? *Personality and Individual Differences, 41*, 1131–1142.

Pakula, A. J. [Director], & Goldman, W. [Writer]. (1976). *All the president's men* [Motion picture]. United States: Warner Bros.

Pallini, S., Chirumbolo, A., Morelli, M., Baiocco, R., Laghi, F., & Eisenberg, N. (2018). The relation of attachment security status to effortful self-regulation: A meta-analysis. *Psychological Bulletin, 144*(5), 501–531.

Park, B., & Rothbart, M. (1982). Perceptions of out-group homogeneity and levels of social categorization: Memory for the subordinate attributes of in-group and out-group members. *Journal of Personality and Social Psychology, 42*, 1051–1068.

Park, D., & Kim, S. (2015). Time to move on? When entity theorists perform better than incremental theorists. *Personality and Social Psychology Bulletin, 41*, 736–748.

Park, G., Lubinski, D., & Benbow, C. P. (2007). Contrasting intellectual patterns predict creativity in the arts and sciences: Tracking intellectually precocious youth over 25 years. *Psychological Science, 18*, 948–952.

Park, N., & Peterson, C. (2010). Does it matter where we live? The urban psychology of character strengths. *American Psychologist, 65*, 535–547.

Park, S. W., & Colvin, C. R. (2014). Narcissism and discrepancy between self and friends' perceptions of personality. *Journal of Personality, 82*, 278–286.

Passini, F. T., & Norman, W. T. (1966). A universal conception of personality structure? *Journal of Personality and Social Psychology, 4*, 44–49.

Paulhus, D. L. (1998). Interpersonal and intrapsychic adaptiveness of trait self-enhancement: A mixed blessing? *Journal of Personality and Social Psychology, 74*, 1197–1208.

Paunonen, S. V. (2003). Big Five factors of personality and replicated predictions of behavior. *Journal of Personality and Social Psychology, 84*, 411–422.

Paunonen, S. V. (2006). You are honest, therefore I like you and find you attractive. *Journal of Research in Personality, 40,* 237–249.

Paunonen, S. V., & Jackson, D. N. (2000). What is beyond the Big Five? *Journal of Personality, 68,* 821–835.

Paunonen, S. V., & Kam, C. (2014). The accuracy of roommate ratings of behaviors versus beliefs. *Journal of Research in Personality, 52,* 55–67.

Pavlov, I. P. (1927). Conditioned reflexes: An investigation of the physiological activity of the cerebral cortex. *Classics in the history of psychology* (G. V. Anrep, Trans.). Retrieved from psychclassics.yorku.ca/Pavlov/lecture23.htm

Penfield, W., & Perot, P. (1963). The brain's record of auditory and visual experience. *Brain, 86,* 595–596.

Penke, L., & Asendorpf, J. B. (2008). Beyond global sociosexual orientations: A more differentiated look at sociosexuality and its effects on courtship and romantic relationships. *Journal of Personality and Social Psychology, 95,* 1113–1135.

Penke, L., Denissen, J. J. A., & Miller, G. F. (2007). The evolutionary genetics of personality. *European Journal of Personality, 21,* 549–587.

Pennebaker, J. W. (1992). Inhibition as the linchpin of health. In H. S. Friedman (Ed.), *Hostility, coping, and health* (pp. 127–139). Washington, DC: American Psychological Association.

Pennebaker, J. W., Francis, M. E., & Booth, R. J. (2001). *Linguistic inquiry and word count (LIWC): LIWC2001.* Mahwah, NJ: Erlbaum.

Penton-Voak, I. S., Pound, N., Little, A. C., & Perrett, D. I. (2006). Personality judgments from natural and composite facial images: More evidence for a "kernel of truth" in social perception. *Social Cognition, 24,* 607–640.

Peplau, L.A., Garnets, L.D., Spalding, L.R., Conley, T.D., & Veniegas, R.C. (1998). A critique of Bem's 'Exotic becomes erotic' theory of sexual orientation. *Psychological Review, 105,* 387–394.

Peterson, C., & Seligman, M. E. P. (Eds.). (2004). *Character strengths and virtues: A handbook and classification.* Washington, DC: American Psychological Association.

Peterson, C., & Steen, T. A. (2002). Optimistic explanatory style. In C. R. Snyder & S. J. Lopez (Eds.), *Handbook of positive psychology* (pp. 244–256). London: Oxford University Press.

Peterson, C., Maier, S. F., & Seligman, M. E. (1993). *Learned helplessness: A theory for the age of personal control.* London: Oxford University Press.

Petticrew, M. P., Lee, K., & McKee, M. (2012). Type A behavior pattern and coronary heart disease: Philip Morris's "crown jewel." *American Journal of Public Health, 102,* 2018–2025.

Piccinelli, M., Pini, S., Bellantuono, C., & Wilkinson, G. (1995). Efficacy of drug treatment in obsessive-compulsive disorder: A meta-analytic review. *British Journal of Psychiatry, 166,* 424–443.

Piedmont, R. L., & Chae, J. H. (1997). Cross-cultural generalizability of the five-factor model of personality. *Journal of Cross-Cultural Psychology, 28,* 131–155.

Pierro, A., Giacomantonio, M., Pica, G., Kruglanski, A. W., & Higgins, E. T. (2011). On the psychology of time in action: Regulatory mode orientations and procrastination. *Journal of Personality and Social Psychology, 101,* 1317–1331.

Pietschnig J., & Voracek, M. (2015). One century of global IQ gains: A formal meta-analysis of the Flynn effect (1909–2013). *Perspectives on Psychological Science, 10,* 282–306.

Pillsworth, E. G., & Haselton, M. G. (2006). Male sexual attractiveness predicts differential ovulatory shifts in female extra-pair attraction and male mate retention. *Evolution and Human Behavior, 27,* 247–258.

Pinker, S. (1997). *How the mind works.* New York: Norton.

Pinquart, M., & Sörensen, S. (2000). Influences of socioeconomic status, social network, and competence on subjective well-being in later life: A meta-analysis. *Psychology and Aging, 15,* 187–224.

Pinsky, D., & Young, S. M. (2009). *The mirror effect.* New York: HarperCollins.

Piquero, A. R., Jennings, W. G., & Farrington, D. P. (2010). On the malleability of self-control: Theoretical and policy implications regarding a general theory of crime. *Justice Quarterly, 27,* 803–834.

Pittinger, D.J. (1993). Measuring the MBTI . . . and coming up short. *Journal of Career Planning and Employment, 54*, 48–52.

Plomin, R., & Crabbe, J. (2000). DNA. *Psychological Bulletin, 126*, 806–828.

Plomin, R., Chipuer, H. M., & Loehlin, J. C. (1990). Behavioral genetics and personality. In L. Pervin (Ed.), *Handbook of personality: Theory and research* (pp. 225–243). New York: Guilford Press.

Plomin, R., Corley, R., DeFries, J. C., & Fulker, D. W. (1990). Individual differences in television viewing in early childhood: Nature as well as nurture. *Psychological Science, 1*, 371–377.

Plomin, R., DeFries, J.C., Knopik, V.S., & Neiderhiser, J.M. (2016). Top 10 replicated findings from behavioral genetics. *Perspectives on Psychological Science, 11*, 3–23.

Pope, H. G., & Katz, D. L. (1994). Psychiatric and medical effects of anabolic-androgen steroid use: A controlled study of 160 athletes. *Archives of General Psychiatry, 51*, 375–382.

Pope, K. S., Tabachnick, B., & Keith-Spiegel, P. (1987). Ethics of practice: The beliefs and behaviors of psychologists as therapists. *American Psychologist, 42*, 993–1006.

Powell, D.M., & Bourdage, J.S. (2016). The detection of personality traits in employment interviews: Can "good judges" be trained? *Personality and Individual Differences, 94*, 194–199.

Pressman, S. D., & Cohen, S. (2005). Does positive affect influence health? *Psychological Bulletin, 131*, 925–971.

Price, R. H., & Bouffard, D. L. (1974). Behavioral appropriateness and situational constraint as dimensions of social behavior. *Journal of Personality and Social Psychology, 30*, 579–586.

Prochnik, G. (2017). Our Freudian complex. *New York Times Book Review*, August 20, pp. 1,20.

Public Health Service. (1991). *Application for Public Health Service grant* (PHS 398; OMB Publication No. 0925-0001). Washington, DC: U.S. Government Printing Office.

Public Health Service. (2001). *Mental health: Culture, race, and ethnicity. A supplement to mental health: A report of the Surgeon General*. Washington, DC: U.S. Government Printing Office.

Pullum, G. K. (1991). *The great Eskimo vocabulary hoax, and other irreverent essays on the study of language*. University of Chicago Press.

Pyszczynski, T., Greenberg, J., & Solomon, S. (1997). Why do we need what we need? A terror management perspective on the roots of human social motivation. *Psychological Inquiry, 8*, 1–20.

Qi, J., & Zhu, Y. (2002). The self-reference effect of Chinese college students. *Psychological Science (China), 25*, 275–278.

Quartier, V., & Rossier, J. (2008). A study of personality in children aged 8–12 years: Comparing self- and parents' ratings. *European Journal of Personality, 22*, 575–588.

Quoidbach, J., Gilbert, D. T., & Wilson, T. D. (2013). The "end of history" illusion. *Science, 339*, 96–98.

Rabiner, D. L., Lenhart, L., & Lochman, J. E. (1990). Automatic versus reflective social problem solving in relation to sociometric status. *Developmental Psychology, 26*, 1010–1016.

Rada, R. T., Laws, D. R., & Kellner, R. (1976). Plasma testosterone levels in the rapist. *Psychosomatic Medicine, 38*, 257–268.

Rahula, W. (1974). *What the Buddha taught*. New York: Grove Press.

Raleigh, M. J. (1987). Differential behavioral effects of tryptophan and 5-hydroxy-tryptophan in vervet monkeys: Influences of catecholaminergic systems. *Psychopharmacology, 93*, 44–50.

Raleigh, M. J., McGuire, M. T., Brammer, G. L., Pollack, D. B., & Yuwiler, A. (1991). Serotonergic mechanisms promote dominance acquisition in adult male vervet monkeys. *Brain Research, 559*, 181–190.

Ramírez-Esparza, N., Gosling, S. D., Benet-Martínez, V., Potter, J. P., & Pennebaker, J. W. (2006). Do bilinguals have two personalities? A special case of cultural frame switching. *Journal of Research in Personality, 40*, 99–120.

Ramírez-Esparza, N., Mehl, M. R., Álvarez-Bermúdez, J., & Pennebaker, J. W. (2008). Are Mexicans less sociable than Americans? Insights from a naturalistic observation study. *Journal of Research in Personality, 43*, 1–7.

Ranjit, N., Diez-Roux, A. V., Shea, S., Cushman, M., Seeman, T., Jackson, S. A., & Ni, H. (2007). Psychosocial factors and inflammation in the multi-ethnic study of atherosclerosis. *Archives of Internal Medicine, 167*, 174–181.

Rapaport, D. (1960). *The structure of psychoanalytic theory: A systematizing attempt.* New York: International Universities Press.

Rapee, R. M., Kennedy, S. J., Ingram, M., Edwards, S. L., & Sweeney, L. (2010). Altering the trajectory of anxiety in at-risk young children. *American Journal of Psychiatry, 167*, 1518–1525.

Raskin, R., & Hall, C. S. (1981). The Narcissistic Personality Inventory: Alternative form reliability and further evidence of construct validity. *Journal of Personality Assessment, 45*, 159–162.

Raskin, R., & Terry, H. (1988). A principal-components analysis of the Narcissistic Personality Inventory and further evidence of its construct validity. *Journal of Personality and Social Psychology, 54*, 890–902.

Rational Wiki (2018). Extraordinary claims require extraordinary evidence. Retrieved from https://rationalwiki.org/wiki/Extraordinary_claims_require_extraordinary_evidence

Raymund, P., Garcia, J. M., Restubog, L. D., & Denson, T. F. (2010). The moderating role of prior exposure to aggressive home culture in the relationship between negative reciprocity beliefs and aggression. *Journal of Research in Personality, 44*, 380–385.

Reis, H. T., Capobianco, A., & Tsai, F. (2002). Finding the person in personal relationships. *Journal of Personality, 70*, 813–850.

Reise, S. (2006). *Notes on psychology lectures.* Unpublished manuscript, University of California, Los Angeles.

Rentfrow, P. J., & Gosling, S. D. (2003). The do re mi's of everyday life: The structure and personality correlates of music preferences. *Journal of Personality and Social Psychology, 84*, 1236–1256.

Rentfrow, P. J., & Gosling, S. D. (2006). Message in a ballad: The role of music preferences in interpersonal perception. *Psychological Science, 17*, 236–242.

Rentfrow, P. J., Goldberg, L. R., & Levitin, D. J. (2011). The structure of musical preferences: A five-factor model. *Journal of Personality and Social Psychology, 100*, 1139–1157.

Rentfrow, P. J., Gosling, S. D., Jokela, M., Stillwell, D. J., Kosinski, M., & Potter, J. (2013). Divided we stand: Three psychological regions of the United States and their political, economic, social and health correlates. *Journal of Personality and Social Psychology, 105*, 996–1012.

Revelle, W., & Oehlberg, K. (2008). Integrating experimental and observational personality research: The contributions of Hans Eysenck. *Journal of Personality, 76*, 1387–1414.

Revelle, W., Amaral, P., & Turriff, S. (1976). Introversion-extraversion, time stress, and caffeine: The effect on verbal performance. *Science, 192*, 149–150.

Revelle, W., Humphreys, M. S., Simon, L., & Gilliland, K. (1980). Interactive effect of personality, time of day, and caffeine: Test of the arousal model. *Journal of Experimental Psychology: General, 109*, 1–31.

Reynolds, A. J., Template, J. A., Robertson, D. L., & Mann, E. A. (2001). Long-term effects of an early childhood intervention on educational achievement and juvenile arrest: A 15-year follow-up of low income children in public schools. *Journal of the American Medical Association, 285*, 2339–2346.

Rhodewalt, F., & Morf, C. C. (1998). On self-aggrandizement and anger: A temporal analysis of narcissism and affective reactions to success and failure. *Journal of Personality and Social Psychology, 74*, 672–685.

Richard, F. D., Bond, C. F., Jr., & Stokes-Zoota, J. J. (2003). One hundred years of social psychology quantitatively described. *Review of General Psychology, 7*, 331–363.

Rickert, E. J. (1998). Authoritarianism and economic threat: Implications for political behavior. *Political Psychology, 19*, 707–720.

Rieger, S., Göllner, R., Spengler, M., Trautwein, U., Nagengast, B., & Roberts, B.W. (2017). Social cognitive constructs are just as stable as the Big Five between grades 5 and 8. *AERA Open, 3,* 1–9.

Rimfeld, K., Kovas, Y., Dale, P. S., & Plomin, R. (2016). True grit and genetics: Predicting academic achievement from personality. *Journal of Personality and Social Psychology, 111*(5), 780–789.

Risch, N., Herrell, R., Lehner, T., Liang, K-Y., Eaves, L., Hoh, J., et al. (2009). Interaction between the serotonin transporter gene (*5-HTTLPR*), stressful life events, and risk of depression. *Journal of the American Medical Association, 301,* 2462–2492.

Robbins, M.L. (2017). Practical suggestions for legal and ethical concerns with social environment sampling methods. *Social Psychological and Personality Science, 8,* 573–580.

Robert, C., & Cheung, Y. H. (2010). An examination of the relationship between conscientiousness and group performance on a creative task. *Journal of Research in Personality, 44,* 222–231.

Roberts, B. W., & DelVecchio, W. F. (2000). The rank-order consistency of personality traits from childhood to old age: A quantitative review of longitudinal studies. *Psychological Bulletin, 126,* 3–25.

Roberts, B. W., & Jackson, J. J. (2008). Sociogenomic personality psychology. *Journal of Personality, 76,* 1523–1544.

Roberts, B. W., & Pomerantz, E. M. (2004). On traits, situations and their integration: A developmental perspective. *Personality and Social Psychology Review, 8,* 402–416.

Roberts, B. W., Caspi, A., & Moffitt, T. (2001). The kids are alright: Growth and stability in personality development from adolescence to adulthood. *Journal of Personality and Social Psychology, 81,* 670–683.

Roberts, B. W., Donnellan, M. B., & Hill, P. L. (2012). Personality trait development in adulthood. In I. B. Weiner (Ed.), *Handbook of Psychology, 5,* 183–196.

Roberts, B. W., Kuncel, N. R., Shiner, R., Caspi, A., & Goldberg, L. R. (2007). The power of personality: The comparative validity of personality traits, socioeconomic status, and cognitive ability for predicting important life outcomes. *Perspectives on Psychological Science, 2*(4), 313–345.

Roberts, B. W., Walton, K. E., & Viechtbauer, W. (2006). Patterns of mean-level change in personality traits across the life course: A meta-analysis of longitudinal studies. *Psychological Bulletin, 132,* 1–25.

Roberts, B. W., Wood, D., & Caspi, A. (2008). The development of personality traits in adulthood. In O. P. John, R. W. Robins, & L. A. Pervin (Eds.), *Handbook of personality: Theory and research* (3rd ed., pp. 375–398). New York: Guilford Press.

Roberts, B.W. (2017). A revised sociogenomic model of personality traits. *Journal of Personality.* Published online, 6 July 2017.

Roberts, B.W., Hill, P.L., & Davis, J.P. (2017). How to change conscientiousness: The sociogenomic trait intervention model. *Personality Disorders: Theory, Research and Treatment, 8,* 199–205.

Roberts, B.W., Luo, J., Briley, D.A., Chow, P.I., Su, R. & Hill, P.L. (2017). A systematic review of personality trait change through intervention. *Psychological Bulletin, 143,* 117–141.

Robins, R. W., & Beer, J. S. (2001). Positive illusions about the self: Short-term benefits and long-term costs. *Journal of Personality and Social Psychology, 80,* 340–352.

Robins, R. W., Caspi, A., & Moffitt, T. (2002). It's not just who you're with, it's who you are: Personality and relationship experiences across multiple relationships. *Journal of Personality, 70,* 925–964.

Robins, R. W., John, O. P., & Caspi, A. (1998). The typological approach to studying personality. In R. B. Cairns & L. R. Bergman (Eds.), *Methods and models for studying the individual* (pp. 135–160). Thousand Oaks, CA: Sage.

Robins, R. W., Noftle, E. E., Trzesniewski, K. H., & Roberts, B. W. (2005). Do people know how their personality has changed? Correlates of perceived and actual personality change in young adulthood. *Journal of Personality, 73,* 489–522.

Robins, R. W., Tracy, J. L., & Trzesniewski, K. H. (2008). Naturalizing the self. In O. P. John, R. W. Robins, & L. A. Pervin (Eds.), *Handbook of personality: Theory and research* (3rd ed., pp. 421–447). New York: Guilford Press.

Robinson, M. D., Zabelina, D. L., Ode, S., & Moeller, S. K. (2008). The vertical nature of dominance-submission: Individual differences in vertical attention. *Journal of Research in Personality, 42,* 933–948.

Robinson, P. (1993). *Freud and his critics.* Berkeley: University of California Press.

Rodgers, J. L., Cleveland, H. H., van den Oord, E., & Rowe, D. C. (2000). Resolving the debate over birth order, family size, and intelligence. *American Psychologist, 55,* 599–612.

Rogers, C. R. (1951). *Client-centered therapy: Its current practice, implications, and theory.* Boston: Houghton Mifflin.

Rogers, C. R. (1961). *On becoming a person.* Boston: Houghton Mifflin.

Rogers, C.R. (1957). The necessary and sufficient conditions of therapeutic personality change. *Journal of Consulting Psychology, 21,* 95–103.

Rogers, K.H., Le, M.T., Buckels, E.E., Kim, M., & Biesanz, J.C. (2018). Dispositional malevolence and impression formation: Dark Tetrad associations with accuracy and positivity in first impressions. *Journal of Personality.* Published online 19 February 2018.

Rohrer, J. M., Egloff, B., & Schmukle, S. C. (2017). Probing Birth-Order Effects on Narrow Traits Using Specification-Curve Analysis. *Psychological science, 28*(12), 1821–1832.

Rohrer, J.M., Egloff, B., Kosinski, M., Stillwell, D., & Schmukle, S.C. (2017). In your eyes only? Discrepancies and agreement between self- and other-reports of personality from age 14 to 29. *Journal of Personality and Social Psychology.* Published online February 17, 2017.

Rorer, L. G. (1990). Personality assessment: A conceptual survey. In L. Pervin (Ed.), *Handbook of personality: Theory and research* (pp. 693–720). New York: Guilford Press.

Rorschach, H. (1921). *Psychodiagnostik.* Bern, Switzerland: Huber.

Rosenthal, R. (1973b). The mediation of Pygmalion effects: A four-factor "theory." *Papua New Guinea Journal of Education, 9,* 1–12.

Rosenthal, R. (1973c). *On the social psychology of the self-fulfilling prophecy: Further evidence for Pygmalion effects and their mediating mechanisms* (Module No. 53). New York: MSS Modular Publications.

Rosenthal, R. (Ed.). (1980). *Quantitative analysis of research domains. New directions for methodology of social and behavioral science* (no. 5). San Francisco: Jossey-Bass.

Rosenthal, R., & Jacobson, L. (1968). *Pygmalion in the classroom: Teacher expectation and pupils' intellectual development.* New York: Holt, Rinehart.

Rosenthal, R., & Rubin, D. B. (1978). Interpersonal expectancy effects: The first 345 studies. *Behavioral and Brain Sciences, 1,* 377–415.

Rosenthal, R., & Rubin, D. B. (1982). A simple, general purpose display of magnitude of experimental effect. *Journal of Educational Psychology, 74,* 166–169.

Rosenthal, R., Hiller, J. B., Bornstein, R. F., Berry, D. T. R., & Brunell-Neuleib, S. (2001). Meta-analytic methods, the Rorschach, and the MMPI. *Psychological Assessment, 13,* 449–451.

Rosolack, T. K., & Hampson, S. E. (1991). A new typology of health behaviors for personality-health predictions: The case of locus of control. *European Journal of Personality, 5,* 151–168.

Ross, L., & Nisbett, R. E. (1991). *The person and the situation: Perspectives of social psychology.* New York: McGraw-Hill.

Ross, L., Greene, D., & House, P. (1977). The false consensus phenomenon: An attributional bias in self-perception and social perception processes. *Journal of Experimental Social Psychology, 13,* 279–301.

Ross, L., Lepper, M. R., & Hubbard, M. (1975). Perseverance in self perception and social perception: Biased attribution processes in the debriefing paradigm. *Journal of Personality and Social Psychology, 32,* 880–892.

Rosse, J. G., Stecher, M. D., Miller, J. L., & Levin, R. A. (1998). The impact of response distortion on preemployment personality testing and hiring decisions. *Journal of Applied Psychology, 83,* 634–644.

Rotter, J. B. (1954). *Social learning and clinical psychology.* Englewood Cliffs, NJ: Prentice-Hall.

Rotter, J. B. (1982). *The development and applications of social learning theory: Selected papers.* New York: Praeger.

Rowatt, W. C., Cunningham, M. R., & Druen, P. B. (1998). Deception to get a date. *Personality and Social Psychology Bulletin, 24,* 1228–1242.

Rowe, D. C. (1994). *The limits of family influence: Genes, experience, and behavior.* New York: Guilford Press.

Rowe, D. C., Rodgers, J. L., & Meseck-Bushey, S. (1992). Sibling delinquency and the family environment: Shared and unshared influences. *Child Development, 63,* 59–67.

Rozeboom, W. W. (1960). The fallacy of the null-hypothesis significance test. *Psychological Bulletin, 57,* 416–428.

Rozin, P. (1999). The process of moralization. *Psychological Science, 10,* 218–221.

Rozin, P., & Zellner, D. (1985). The role of Pavlovian conditioning in the acquisition of food likes and dislikes. *Annals of the New York Academy of Sciences, 443,* 189–202.

Rozin, P., Markwith, M., & Stoess, C. (1997). Moralization and becoming a vegetarian: The transformation of preferences into values and the recruitment of disgust. *Psychological Science, 8,* 67–73.

Rudikoff, E. C. (1954). A comparative study of the changes in the concepts of the self, the ordinary person, and the ideal in eight cases. In C. R. Rogers & R. F. Dymond (Eds.), *Psychotherapy and personality change: Co-ordinated studies in the client-centered approach* (pp. 85–98). University of Chicago Press.

Rule, N. O., & Ambady, N. (2008a). Brief exposures: Male sexual orientation is accurately perceived at 50 ms. *Journal of Experimental Social Psychology, 44,* 1100–1105.

Rule, N. O., & Ambady, N. (2008b). The face of success: Inferences from chief executive officers' appearance predict company profits. *Psychological Science, 19,* 109–111.

Rumelhart, D. E., McClelland, J. L., & The PDP Research Group. (1986). *Parallel distributed processing: Explorations in the microstructure of cognition: Vol. 1. Foundations.* Cambridge, MA: MIT Press.

Russell, J. A. (1983). Pancultural aspects of the human conceptual organization of emotions. *Journal of Personality and Social Psychology, 45,* 1281–1288.

Russell, S. S., & Zickar, M. J. (2005). An examination of differential item and test functioning across personality judgments. *Journal of Research in Personality, 39,* 354–368.

Rutledge, T., Redwine, L. S., Linke, S. E., & Mills, P. J. (2013). A meta-analysis of mental health treatments and cardiac rehabilitation for improving clinical outcomes and depression among patients with coronary heart disease. *Psychosomatic Medicine, 75,* 335–349.

Ryan, R. M., & Deci, E. L. (2000). Self-determination theory and the facilitation of intrinsic motivation, social development, and well-being. *American Psychologist, 55,* 68–78.

Ryan, R. M., Huta, V., & Deci, E. L. (2008). Living well: A self-determination theory perspective on eudaimonia. *Journal of Happiness Studies, 9,* 139–170.

Rychlak, J. F. (1988). *The psychology of rigorous humanism* (2nd ed.). New York University Press.

Ryff, C. D., & Singer, B. (2003). Flourishing under fire: Resilience as a prototype of challenged thriving. In C. L. M. Keyes & J. Haidt (Eds.), *Flourishing: Positive psychology and the life well-lived* (pp. 15–36). Washington, DC: American Psychological Association.

Saad, G., & Vongas, J. G. (2009). The effects of conspicuous consumption on men's testosterone levels. *Organizational Behavior and Human Decision Processes, 110,* 80–92.

Sabini, J. (1995). *Social psychology* (2nd ed.). New York: Norton.

Sackett, P. R., Burris, L. R., & Callahan, C. (1989). Integrity testing for personnel selection: An update. *Personnel Psychology, 42,* 491–529.

Sacks, O. W. (1983). *Awakenings.* New York: Dutton.

Sahagun, L. (2005, November 28). Far more than creatures of habit. *Los Angeles Times,* p. B1.

Salovey, P., Hsee, C. K., & Mayer, J. D. (1993). Emotional intelligence and the self-regulation of affect. In D. M. Wegner & J. W. Pennebaker (Eds.), *Handbook of mental control* (pp. 258–277). Englewood Cliffs, NJ: Prentice-Hall.

Salvatore, J.E., Lönn, S.L., Sundquist, J., Sundquist, K., & Kendler, K.S. (2018). Genetics, the rearing environment, and the intergenerational transmission of divorce: A Swedish national adoption study. *Psychological Science*. Published online January 18, 2018.

Santos, H.C., Varnum, M.I.W., & Grossman, I. (2017). Global increases in individualism. *Psychological Science, 28,* 1228–1239.

Santrock, J. W. (2014). *A topical approach to life-span development* (7th ed.). New York: McGraw-Hill.

Santrock, J. W. (2014). *Life-span development* (14th ed.). New York: McGraw-Hill.

Sartre, J. P. (1965). The humanism of existentialism. In W. Baskin (Ed.), *Essays in existentialism* (pp. 31–62). Secaucus, NJ: Citadel Press.

Sasovova, Z., Mehra, A., Borgatti, S. P., & Schippers, M. C. (2010). Network churn: The effects of self-monitoring personality on brokerage dynamics. *Administrative Science Quarterly, 55,* 639–670.

Saucier, G., & Goldberg, L. R. (1996). Evidence for the Big Five in analyses of familiar English personality adjectives. *European Journal of Personality, 10,* 61–77.

Saucier, G., & Goldberg, L. R. (1998). What is beyond the Big Five? *Journal of Personality, 66,* 495–524.

Saucier, G., & Goldberg, L. R. (2003). The structure of personality attributes. In M. R. Barrick & A. M. Ryan (Eds.), *Personality and work: Reconsidering the role of personality in organizations* (pp. 1–29). San Francisco: Jossey-Bass.

Sauerberger, K.S., & Funder, D.C. (2017). Behavioral change and consistency across contexts. *Journal of Research in Personality, 69,* 264–272.

Sautter, S. W., Briscoe, L., & Farkas, K. (1991). A neuropsychological profile of Capgras syndrome. *Neuropsychology, 5,* 139–150.

Scarr, S., & McCartney, K. (1983). How people make their own environments: A theory of genotype-environment interactions. *Child Development, 54,* 424–435.

Schaller, M., & Murray, D. R. (2008). Pathogens, personality, and culture: Disease prevalence predicts worldwide variability in sociosexuality, extraversion, and openness to experience. *Journal of Personality and Social Psychology, 95,* 212–221.

Schank, R. C. (1996). Goal-based scenarios: Case-based reasoning meets learning by doing. In D. Leake (Ed.), *Case-based reasoning: Experiences, lessons and future directions* (pp. 295–347). Cambridge, MA: AAAI Press/MIT Press.

Scherer, K. R. (1978). Personality inference from voice quality: The loud voice of extraversion. *European Journal of Social Psychology, 8,* 467–487.

Schmeichel, B. J., Gailliot, M. T., Filardo, E., McGregor, I., Gitter, S., & Baumeister, R. F. (2009). Terror management theory and self-esteem revisited: The roles of implicit and explicit self-esteem in mortality salience effects. *Journal of Personality and Social Psychology, 96,* 1077–1087.

Schmidt, D. B., Lubinski, D., & Benbow, C. P. (1998). Validity of assessing educational-vocational preference dimensions among intellectually talented 13-year-olds. *Journal of Counseling Psychology, 45,* 436–453.

Schmidt, F. L. (1996). Statistical significance testing and cumulative knowledge in psychology: Implications for training of researchers. *Psychological Methods, 1,* 115–129.

Schmidt, F. L., & Hunter, J. E. (1992). Development of a causal model of processes determining job performance. *Current Directions in Psychological Science, 1,* 89–92.

Schmitt, D. P., & Buss, D. M. (2001). Human mate poaching: Tactics and temptations for infiltrating existing mateships. *Journal of Personality and Social Psychology, 80,* 894–917.

Schmitt, D. P., Realo, A., Voracek, M., & Allik, J. (2008). Why can't a man be more like a woman? Sex differences in Big Five personality traits across cultures. *Journal of Personality and Social Psychology, 94,* 168–182.

Schneider, K. (1923). *Die psychopathischen Persönlichkeiten* [Psychopathic Personalities]. Vienna: Deuticke.

Schneider, K. J. (2014). Humanistic and positive psychology need each other and to advance, our field needs both. *American Psychologist, 69*, 92.

Schneider, L., & Schimmack, U. (2010). Examining sources of self-other agreement in life-satisfaction judgments. *Journal of Research in Personality, 44*, 207–212.

Schreer, G. E. (2002). Narcissism and aggression: Is inflated self-esteem related to aggressive driving? *North American Journal of Psychology, 4*, 333–341.

Schriber, R.A., Chung, J.M., Sorensen, K.S., & Robins, R.W. (2017) Dispositional contempt: A first look at the contemptuous person. *Journal of Personality and Social Psychology, 113*, 280–309.

Schuerger, J. M., Zarrella, K. L., & Hotz, A. S. (1989). Factors that influence the temporal stability of personality by questionnaire. *Journal of Personality and Social Psychology, 56*, 777–783.

Schultheiss, O. C. (2008). Implicit motives. In O. P. John, R. W. Robins, & L. A. Pervin (Eds.), *Handbook of personality* (3rd ed., pp. 603–633). New York: Guilford Press.

Schultheiss, O. C., Wirth, M. M., Torges, C. M., Pang, J. S., Vallacorta, M. A., & Welsh, K. M. (2005). Effects of implicit power motivation on men's and women's implicit learning and testosterone changes after social victory or defeat. *Journal of Personality and Social Psychology, 88*, 174–188.

Schwaba, T., Luhmann, M., Denissen, J. J. A., Chung, J. M., & Bleidorn, W. (2017). Openness to Experience and Culture-Openness Transactions Across the Lifespan. *Journal of Personality and Social Psychology*. Advance online publication, May 31, 2017.

Schwartz, B., Ward, A., Monterosso, J., Lyubomirsky, S., White, K., & Lehman, D. R. (2002). Maximizing versus satisficing: Happiness is a matter of choice. *Journal of Personality and Social Psychology, 83*, 1178–1197.

Schwartz, C. E., Wright, C. I., Shin, L. M., Kagan, J., & Rauch, S. L. (2003). Inhibited and uninhibited infants "grown up": Adult amygdalar response to novelty. *Science, 300*, 1952–1953.

Schwartz, S. H., & Sagiv, L. (1995). Identifying culture-specifics in the content and structure of values. *Journal of Cross-Cultural Psychology, 26*, 92–116.

Sears, D. O. (1986). College sophomores in the laboratory: Influences of a narrow data base on social psychology's view of human nature. *Journal of Personality and Social Psychology, 51*, 515–530.

Sears, R. R. (1947). *Survey of objective studies of psychoanalytic concepts.* New York: Social Science Research Council.

Selby, E. A., Anestis, M. D., Bender, T. W., & Joiner, T. E., Jr. (2009). An exploration of the emotional cascade model in borderline personality disorder. *Journal of Abnormal Psychology, 118*, 375–387.

Seligman, M. E. P. (1968). Chronic fear produced by unpredictable electric shock. *Journal of Comparative and Physiological Psychology, 66*, 402–411.

Seligman, M. E. P., & Csikszentmihalyi, M. (2000). Positive psychology: An introduction. *American Psychologist, 55*, 5–14.

Selye, H. (1956). *The stress of life.* New York: McGraw-Hill.

Sensavang, S., Pratt, M.W., Alisat, S., & Sadler, P. (2017). The life story from age 26 to 32: Rank-order stability and mean-level change. *Journal of Personality.* Published online 10 October 2017.

Shackman, A. J., McMenamin, B. W., Maxwell, J. S., Greischar, L. L., & Davidson, R. L. (2009). Right dorsolateral prefrontal cortical activity and behavioral inhibition. *Psychological Science, 20*, 1500–1506.

Shackman, A. J., Tromp, D. P. M., Stockbridge, M. D., Kaplan, C. M., Tillman, R. M., & Fox, A. S. (2016). Dispositional negativity: An integrative psychological and neurobiological perspective. *Psychological Bulletin, 142*(12), 1275–1314.

Shanahan, J. (1995). Television viewing and adolescent authoritarianism. *Journal of Adolescence, 18*, 271–288.

Shapiro, D. (1965). *Neurotic styles.* New York: Basic Books.

Shapiro, D. (2000). *Dynamics of character: Self-regulation in psychopathology.* New York: Basic Books.

Sharpe, D., Adair, J. G., & Roese, N. J. (1992). Twenty years of deception research: A decline in subjects' trust? *Personality and Social Psychology Bulletin, 18*, 585–590.

Shaver, P. R., & Clark, C. L. (1994). The psychodynamics of adult romantic attachment. In J. M. Masling & R. F. Bornstein (Eds.), *Empirical perspectives on object relations theory* (pp. 105–156). Washington, DC: American Psychological Association.

Shaver, P. R., & Mikulincer, M. (2005). Attachment theory and research: Resurrection of the psychodynamic approach to personality. *Journal of Research in Personality, 39*, 22–45.

Sheldon, K. M. (2002). The self-concordance model of healthy goal striving: When personal goals correctly represent the person. In E. Deci & R. Ryan (Eds.), *Handbook of self-determination research* (pp. 65–86). Rochester, NY: University of Rochester Press.

Shenk, J. W. (1999, May). America's altered states. *Harper's, 298*, 38–52.

Sheppard, P., & Sear, R. (2012). Father absence predicts age at sexual maturity and reproductive timing in British men. *Biology Letters, 12*, 237–240.

Sherman, R. A., & Funder, D. C. (2009). Evaluating correlations in studies of personality and behavior: Beyond the number of significant findings to be expected by chance. *Journal of Research in Personality, 43*, 1053–1063.

Sherman, R. A., & Serfass, D. G. (2015). The comprehensive approach to analyzing multivariate constructs. *Journal of Research in Personality, 54*, 40–50.

Sherman, R. A., Nave, C. S., & Funder, D. C. (2009). The apparent objectivity of behavior is illusory (comment). *European Journal of Personality, 23*, 430–433.

Sherman, R. A., Nave, C. S., & Funder, D. C. (2010). Situational similarity and personality predict behavioral consistency. *Journal of Personality and Social Psychology, 99*, 330–343.

Sherman, R. A., Nave, C. S., & Funder, D. C. (2012). Properties of persons and situations related to overall and distinctive personality-behavior congruence. *Journal of Research in Personality, 46*, 87–101.

Sherman, R. A., Nave, C. S., & Funder, D. C. (2013). Situational construal is related to personality and gender. *Journal of Research in Personality, 47*, 1–14.

Sherman, R. A., Rauthmann, J. F., Brown, N. A., Serfass, D. G., & Jones, A. B. (2015). The independent effects of personality and situations on real-time expressions of behavior and emotion. *Journal of Personality and Social Psychology, 109*(5), 872–888.

Sherman, R. Q., Figueredo, A. J., & Funder, D. C. (2013). The behavioral correlates of overall and distinctive life history strategy. *Journal of Personality and Social Psychology, 105*, 873–888.

Shiner, R. L., Masten, A. S., & Roberts, J. M. (2003). Childhood personality foreshadows adult personality and life outcomes two decades later. *Journal of Personality, 71*, 1145–1170.

Shoda, Y. (1999). Behavioral expressions of a personality system: Generation and perception of behavioral signatures. In D. Cervone and Y. Shoda (Eds.), *The coherence of personality: Social-cognitive bases of consistency, variability, and organization* (pp. 155–181). New York: Guilford Press.

Shrout, P.E., & Rodgers, J.L. (2018). Psychology, science and knowledge construction: Broadening perspectives from the replication crisis. *Annual Review of Psychology, 69*, 487–510.

Shweder, R. A., & Bourne, E. J. (1982). Does the concept of person vary cross-culturally? In A. J. Marsella & G. M. White (Eds.), *Cultural conceptions of mental health and therapy* (pp. 97–137). London: Reidel.

Shweder, R. A., & Bourne, E. J. (1984). Does the concept of person vary cross-culturally? In R. A. Shweder & R. LeVine (Eds.), *Culture theory* (pp. 158–199). Cambridge, UK: Cambridge University Press.

Shweder, R. A., & Sullivan, M. A. (1990). The semiotic subject of cultural psychology. In L. A. Pervin (Ed.), *Handbook of personality: Theory and research* (pp. 399–416). New York: Guilford Press.

Shweder, R. A., & Sullivan, M. A. (1993). Cultural psychology: Who needs it? *Annual Review of Psychology, 44*, 497–523.

Siegel, D. J. (2007a). Mindfulness training and neural integration: Differentiation of distinct streams of awareness and the cultivation of well-being. *Social Cognitive and Affective Neuroscience, 2*, 259–263.

Siegel, S. (1984). Pavlovian conditioning and heroin overdose: Reports by overdose victims. *Bulletin of the Psychonomic Society, 22,* 428–430.

Siegel, S., & Ellsworth, D. W. (1986). Pavlovian conditioning and death from apparent overdose of medically prescribed morphine: A case report. *Bulletin of the Psychonomic Society, 24,* 278–280.

Silverstein, S. (1993, July 10). Target to pay $2 million in testing case. *Los Angeles Times,* pp. D1–D2.

Simmons, J.P., Nelson, L.D., & Simonsohn, U. (2011). False-positive psychology: Undisclosed flexibility in data collection and analysis allows presenting anything as significant. *Psychological Science, 22,* 1359–1366.

Simonton, D. K., & Baumeister, R. F. (2005). Positive psychology at the summit. *Review of General Psychology, 9,* 99–102.

Simpson, J. A., & Gangestad, S. W. (1991). Individual differences in sociosexuality: Evidence for convergent and discriminant validity. *Journal of Personality and Social Psychology, 60,* 870–883.

Simpson, J. A., & Gangestad, S. W. (1992). Sociosexuality and romantic partner choice. *Journal of Personality, 60,* 31–51.

Simpson, J. A., Gangestad, S. W., & Lerma, M. (1990). Perception of physical attractiveness: Mechanisms involved in the maintenance of romantic relationships. *Journal of Personality and Social Psychology, 59,* 1192–1201.

Singh, D., Vidaurri, M., Zambarano, R. J., & Dabbs, J. M., Jr. (1999). Lesbian erotic role identification: Behavioral, morphological, and hormonal correlates. *Journal of Personality and Social Psychology, 76,* 1035–1049.

Singham, T., Viding, E., Schoeler, T., Arseneault, L., Ronald, A., Cecil, C.M., . . . & Pingault, J-B. (2017). Concurrent and longitudinal contribution of exposure to bullying in childhood and mental health: The role of vulnerability and resilience. *JAMA:Psychiatry,* published online October 4.

Sinn, D. L., Gosling, S. D., & Moltschaniwskyj, N. A. (2008). Development of shy/bold behavior in the squid: Context-specific phenotypes associated with developmental plasticity. *Animal Behaviour, 75,* 433–442.

Sipps, G.J., Alexander, R.A., & Friedt, L. (1985). Item analysis of the Myers-Briggs Type Indicator. *Educational and Psychological Measurement, 45,* 789–796.

Sirotin, Y. B., & Das, A. (2009). Anticipatory haemodynamic signals in sensory cortex not predicted by local neuronal activity. *Nature, 457,* 475–480.

Skinner, B. F. (1938). *The behavior of organisms: An experimental analysis.* New York: Macmillan.

Skinner, B. F. (1948). *Walden Two.* New York: Macmillan.

Skinner, B. F. (1971). *Beyond freedom and dignity.* New York: Knopf.

Skodol, A. E., Gunderson, J. G., McGlashan, T. H., Dyck, I. R., Stout, R. L., Bender, D. S., et al. (2002). Functional impairment in patients with schizotypal, borderline, avoidant, or obsessive-compulsive personality disorder. *American Journal of Psychiatry, 159,* 276–283.

Slagt, M., Dubas, J. S., Deković, M., & van Aken, M. A. G. (2016). Differences in sensitivity to parenting depending on child temperament: A meta-analysis. *Psychological Bulletin, 142*(10), 1068–1110.

Slatcher, R. B., Mehta, P. H., & Josephs, R. A. (2011). Testosterone and self-reported dominance interact to influence human mating behavior. *Social Psychological and Personality Science, 2,* 531–539.

Slavich, G. M., & Cole, S. W. (2013). The emerging field of human social genomics. *Clinical Psychological Science, 1,* 331–348.

Small, D. M., Gregory, M. D., Mak, Y. E., Gitelman, D., Mesulam, M. M., & Parrish, T. (2003). Dissociation of neural representation of intensity and affective valuation in human gestation. *Neuron, 39,* 701–711.

Smidt, K. E., & DeBono, K. G. (2011). On the effects of product name on product evaluation: An individual difference perspective. *Social Influence, 6,* 131–141.

Smith, C. P. (Ed.). (1992). *Motivation and personality: Handbook of thematic content analysis.* New York: Cambridge University Press.

Smith, E. R., & Branscombe, N. R. (1987). Procedurally mediated social inferences: The case of category accessibility effects. *Journal of Experimental Social Psychology, 23,* 361–382.

Smith, M. L., Glass, G. V., & Miller, T. I. (1980). *The benefits of psychotherapy.* Baltimore: Johns Hopkins University Press.

Smith, R. E., Shoda, Y., Cumming, S. P., & Smoll, F. L. (2009). Behavioral signatures at the ballpark: Intra-individual consistency of adults' situation-behavior patterns and their interpersonal consequences. *Journal of Research in Personality, 43,* 187–195.

Smith, S. S., & Richardson, D. (1983). Amelioration of deception and harm in psychological research: The important role of debriefing. *Journal of Personality and Social Psychology, 44,* 1075–1082.

Smits, A. M., Dolan, C. V., Vorst, H. C. M., Wicherts, J. M., & Timmerman, M. E. (2011). Cohort differences in Big Five personality factors over a period of 25 years. *Journal of Personality and Social Psychology, 100,* 1124–1138.

Snyder, M. (1974). The self-monitoring of expressive behavior. *Journal of Personality and Social Psychology, 30,* 526–537.

Snyder, M. (1987). *Public appearances, private realities: The psychology of self-monitoring.* New York: Freeman.

Snyder, M., & Ickes, W. (1985). Personality and social behavior. In G. Lindzey & E. Aronson (Eds.), *Handbook of social psychology* (3rd ed., Vol. 2, pp. 883–948). Reading, MA: Addison-Wesley.

Snyder, M., & Monson, T. C. (1975). Persons, situations, and the control of social behavior. *Journal of Personality and Social Psychology, 32,* 637–644.

Snyder, M., & Swann, W. B. (1978). Behavioral confirmation in social interaction: From social perception to social reality. *Journal of Experimental Social Psychology, 14,* 148–162.

Snyder, M., Tanke, E. D., & Berscheid, E. (1977). Social perception and interpersonal behavior: On the self-fulfilling nature of social stereotypes. *Journal of Personality and Social Psychology, 35,* 656–666.

Sohlberg, S., & Birgegard, A. (2003). Persistent complex subliminal activation effects: First experimental observations. *Journal of Personality and Social Psychology, 85,* 302–316.

Solomon, B. C., & Jackson, J. J. (2014). The long reach of one's spouse: Spousal personality influences occupational success. *Psychological Science, 25,* 2189–2198.

Solomon, B. C., & Vazire, S. (2014). You are so beautiful . . . to me: Seeing beyond bias and achieving accuracy in romantic relationships. *Journal of Personality and Social Psychology, 107,* 516–528.

Somer, O., & Goldberg, L. R. (1999). The structure of Turkish trait-descriptive adjectives. *Journal of Personality and Social Psychology, 76,* 431–450.

Sonuga-Barke, E.J.S., Kumsta, R., Knights, N., Golm, D., Rutter, M., Maughan, B., Schlotz, W., & Kreppner, J. (2017). Child-to-adult neurodevelopmental and mental health trajectories after early life deprivation: the young adult follow-up of the longitudinal English and Romanian adoptees study. *Lancet, 389,* 1539–1548.

Soto, C. J., & John, O. P. (2017). The next Big Five Inventory (BFI-2): Developing and assessing a hierarchical model with 15 facets to enhance bandwidth, fidelity, and predictive power. *Journal of Personality and Social Psychology, 113,* 117–143.

Soto, C. J., John, O. P., Gosling, S. D., & Potter, J. (2011). Age differences in personality traits from 10 to 65: Big Five domains and facets in a large cross-sectional sample. *Journal of Personality and Social Psychology, 100,* 330–348.

Soto, C.J. (2015). Is happiness good for your personality? Concurrent and prospective relations of the Big Five with subjective well-being. *Journal of Personality, 83,* 45–55.

Spain, J. (1994). *Personality and daily life experience: Evaluating the accuracy of personality judgments.* Unpublished doctoral dissertation, University of California, Riverside.

Spain, J., Eaton, L. G., & Funder, D. C. (2000). Perspectives on personality: The relative accuracy of self vs. others for the prediction of behavior and emotion. *Journal of Personality, 68,* 837–867.

Spearman, C. (1910). Correlation calculated from faulty data. *British Journal of Psychology, 3,* 271–295.

Specht, J., Egloff, B., & Schmukle, S. C. (2011). Stability and change across the life course: The impact of age and major life events on mean-level and rank-order stability of the Big Five. *Journal of Personality and Social Psychology, 101,* 862–882.

Specht, J., Luhmann, M., & Geiser, C. (2014). On the consistency of personality types across adulthood: Latent profile analyses in two large-scale panel studies. *Journal of Personality and Social Psychology, 107,* 540–556.

Spencer-Rogers, J., Boucher, H. C., Mori, S. C., Wang, L., & Peng, K. (2009). The dialectical self-concept: Contradiction, change, and holism in East Asian cultures. *Personality and Social Psychology Bulletin, 35,* 29–44.

Spengler, M., Roberts, B.W., Lüdtke, O., Martin, R., & Brunner, M. (2015). The kind of student you were in elementary school predicts mortality. DOI: 10.1111/jopy.12180.

Sroufe, L. A., & Waters, E. (1977). Heart rate as a convergent measure in clinical and developmental research. *Merrill-Palmer Quarterly, 23,* 3–27.

Sroufe, L. A., Carlson, E., & Shulman, S. (1993). Individuals in relationships: Development from infancy through adolescence. In D. C. Funder, R. D. Parke, C. Tomlinson-Keasey, & K. Widaman (Eds.), *Studying lives through time* (pp. 315–342). Washington, DC: American Psychological Association.

Srull, T. K., & Wyer, R. S., Jr. (1980). Category accessibility and social perception: Some implications for the study of person memory and interpersonal judgments. *Journal of Personality and Social Psychology, 38,* 841–856.

Stanley, D. A., & Adolphs, R. (2013). Toward a neural basis for social behavior. *Neuron, 80,* 816–826.

Stanovich, K. E. (1991). Cognitive science meets beginning reading. *Psychological Science, 2,* 70–81.

Stein, R., & Swan, A.B. (2018). Deeply confusing: Conflating difficulty with deep revelation on personality assessment. *Social Psychological and Personality Science.* Published online April, 2018.

Stellar, J. E., Gordon, A., Anderson, C. L., Piff, P. K., McNeil, G. D., & Keltner, D. (2018). Awe and humility. *Journal of Personality and Social Psychology, 114*(2), 258269.

Stephan, Y., Sutin, A. R., & Terracciano, A. (2014). Physical activity and personality development across adulthood and old age: Evidence from two longitudinal studies. *Journal of Research in Personality, 49,* 1–7.

Stephan, Y., Sutin, A.R., Bovier-Lapierre, G., & Terracciano, A. (2017). Personality and walking speed across adulthood: Prospective evidence from five samples. *Social Psychological and Personality Science.* (published online August 28, 2017).

Sternberg, R. J. (1995). For whom the bell curve tolls. [Review of the book *The Bell Curve.*] *Psychological Science, 6,* 257–261.

Stipek, D. J., & Gralinski, J. H. (1991). Gender differences in children's achievement-related beliefs and emotional response to success and failure in mathematics. *Journal of Educational Psychology, 83,* 361–371.

Storm, C., & Storm, T. (1987). A taxonomic study of the vocabulary of emotions. *Journal of Personality and Social Psychology, 53,* 805–816.

Strack, F., & Deutsch, R. (2004). Reflective and impulsive determinants of social behavior. *Personality and Social Psychology Review, 8,* 220–247.

Strohminger, N., Knobe, J., & Newman, G. (2017). The true self: A psychological concept distinct from the self. *Perspectives in Psychological Science, 12,* 551–560.

Strong, E. K., Jr. (1959). *Strong Vocational Interest Blank.* Palo Alto, CA: Consulting Psychologists Press.

Strully, K. W. (2009). Job loss and health in the U.S. labor market. *Demography, 46,* 221–246.

Stuss, D. T., & Levine, B. (2002). Adult clinical neuropsychology: Lessons from studies of the frontal lobes. *Annual Review of Psychology, 53,* 401–433.

Suh, E. M. (2002). Culture, identity consistency, and subjective well-being. *Journal of Personality and Social Psychology, 83,* 1378–1391.

Sulloway, F. J. (1979). *Freud: Biologist of the mind.* New York: Basic Books.

Sulloway, F. J. (2001). Birth order, sibling competition and human behavior. In H. R. Holcomb III (Ed.), *Conceptual challenges in evolutionary psychology: Innovative research strategies* (pp. 39–83). Boston: Kluwer.

Sulloway, F. J. (2010). Why siblings are like Darwin's finches: Birth order, sibling competition and adaptive divergence within the family. In D. M. Buss & P. H. Hawley (Eds.), *Evolution and individual differences* (pp. 86–119). New York: Oxford University Press.

Sundberg, N. D. (1977). *The assessment of persons.* Englewood Cliffs, NJ: Prentice-Hall.

Sundie, J. M., Kenrick, D. T., Griskevicius, V., Tybur, J. M., Vohs, K. D., & Beal, D. J. (2011). Peacocks, porches and Thorstein Veblen: Conspicuous consumption as a sexual signaling system. *Journal of Personality and Social Psychology, 100,* 664–680.

Sutin, A. R., Ferrucci, L., Zonderman, A. B., & Terracciano, A. (2011). Personality and obesity across the adult life span. *Journal of Personality and Social Psychology, 101,* 579–592.

Sutin, A. R., Luchetti, M., Stephan, Y., Robins, R. W., & Terracciano, A. (2017). Parental educational attainment and adult offspring personality: An intergenerational life span approach to the origin of adult personality traits. *Journal of Personality and Social Psychology, 113*(1), 144–166.

Suzuki, A., Tsukamoto, S., & Takahashi, Y. (2017). Faces tell everything in a just and biologically determined world: Lay theories behind face reading. *Social Psychological and Personality Science.* Published online, October 13, 2017.

Swann, W. B., & Ely, R. J. (1984). A battle of wills: Self-verification versus behavioral confirmation. *Journal of Personality and Social Psychology, 46,* 1287–1302.

Swann, W. B., Jr., Chang-Schneider, C. C., & McClarty, K. L. (2007). Do our self-views matter? Self-concept and self-esteem in everyday life. *American Psychologist, 62,* 84–94.

Swann, W. B., Rentfrow, P. J., & Guinn, J. S. (2003). Self-verification: The search for coherence. In M. Leary & J. Tagney (Eds.), *Handbook of self and identity* (pp. 367–383). New York: Guilford.

Sweeney, A. M., & Moyer, A. (2014, August 4). Self-Affirmation and responses to health messages: A Meta-analysis on intentions and behavior. *Health Psychology.* Advanced online publication. http://dx.doi.org/10.1037/hea0000110.

Symons, C., & Johnson, B. T. (1997). The self-reference effect in memory: A meta-analysis. *Psychological Bulletin, 121,* 371–394.

Symons, D. (1979). *The evolution of human sexuality.* New York: Oxford University Press.

Szasz, T. S. (1960). The myth of mental illness. *American Psychologist, 15,* 113–118.

Szasz, T. S. (1974). *The myth of mental illness: Foundations of a theory of personal conduct* (Rev. ed.). New York: Harper & Row.

Taft, R. (1955). The ability to judge people. *Psychological Bulletin, 52,* 1–23.

Takagi, T., Tanizawa, O., Otsuki, Y., Haruta, M., & Yamaji, K. (1985). Oxytocin in the cerebrospinal fluid of pregnant and non-pregnant subjects. *Hormone and Metabolism Research, 17,* 308–310.

Takano, Y. (2012). Japanese culture explored through experimental design. In A. Kurylo (Ed.), *Intercultural communication: Representation and construction of culture* (pp. 405–411). Thousand Oaks, CA: Sage.

Takano, Y., & Osaka, E. (1999). An unsupported common view: Comparing Japan and the U.S. on individualism/collectivism. *Asian Journal of Social Psychology, 2,* 311–341.

Takano, Y., & Sogon, S. (2008). Are Japanese more collectivistic than Americans? Examining conformity in in-groups and the reference-group effect. *Journal of Cross-Cultural Psychology, 39,* 237–250.

Tanaka, J. W., & Farah, M. J. (1993). Parts and wholes in face recognition. *Quarterly Journal of Experimental Psychology A: Human Experimental Psychology, 46A,* 225–245.

Tang, T. Z., DeRubeis, R. J., Hollon, S. D., Amsterdam, J., Shelton, R., & Schalet, B. (2009). Personality change during depression treatment: A placebo-controlled trial. *Archives of General Psychiatry, 66,* 1322–1330.

Tansey, M. J. (1992). Countertransference theory, quantitative research, and the problem of therapist-patient sexual abuse. In J. W. Barron, M. N. Eagle, & D. L. Wolitzky (Eds.), *Interface of psychoanalysis and psychology* (pp. 539–557). Washington, DC: American Psychological Association.

Taylor, E. (2000). "What is man, psychologist, that thou art so unmindful of him?": Henry A. Murray on the historical relation between classical personality theory and humanistic psychology. *Journal of Humanistic Psychology, 40,* 29–42.

Taylor, G. J., & Bagby, R. M. (2000). An overview of the alexithymia construct. In R. Bar-On & J. D. A. Parker (Eds.), *The handbook of emotional intelligence* (pp. 41–67). San Francisco: Jossey-Bass.

Taylor, P., Fry, R., Cohn, D., Wang, W., Velasco, G., & Dockterman, D. (2010). *Women, men, and the new economics of marriage.* Washington, DC: Pew Research Center.

Taylor, S. E., Klein, L. C., Lewis, B. P., Gruenewald, T. L., Gurung, R. A. R., & Updegraff, J. A. (2000). Biobehavioral responses to stress in females: Tend-and-befriend, not fight-or-flight. *Psychological Review, 107,* 411–429.

Tee, N., & Hegarty, P. (2006). Predicting opposition to the civil rights of trans persons in the United Kingdom. *Journal of Community and Applied Social Psychology, 16,* 70–80.

Tellegen, A. (1982). *Brief manual for the Multidimensional Personality Questionnaire.* Unpublished manuscript, University of Minnesota, Minneapolis.

Tellegen, A. (1985). Structures of mood and personality and their relevance to assessing anxiety, with an emphasis on self-report. In A. H. Tuma & J. D. Maser (Eds.), *Anxiety and the anxiety disorders* (pp. 681–706). Hillsdale, NJ: Erlbaum.

ten Brinke, L., Kish, A., & Keltner, D. (2018). Hedge fund managers with psychopathic tendencies make for worse investors. *Personality and Social Psychology Bulletin, 44,* 214–223

Tennen, H., Affleck, G., & Armeli, S. (Eds.). (2005). Personality and daily experience revisited [Special Issue]. *Journal of Personality, 73,* 1465–1774.

Terman, Lewis M. (1925). *Mental and Physical Traits of a Thousand Gifted Children.* Genetic Studies of Genius Volume 1. Stanford (CA): Stanford University Press.

Terracciano, A., Sanna, S., Uda, M., Deiana, B., Usala, G., Busonero, F., et al. (2010). Genome-wide association scan for five major dimensions of personality. *Molecular Psychiatry, 15,* 647–656.

Theodoridou, A., Rowe, A. C., Penton-Voak, I. S., & Rogers, P. J. (2009). Oxytocin and social perception: Oxytocin increases perceived facial trustworthiness and attractiveness. *Hormones and Behavior, 56,* 128–132.

Thomas, C., Turkheimer, E., & Oltmanns, T. F. (2003). Factorial structure of pathological personality as evaluated by peers. *Journal of Abnormal Psychology, 112,* 81–91.

Thompson, C. (1995, July 19). Kennedy secretary writes of Rosemary. *Press-Enterprise,* p. A2.

Thomson, C. J., Rajala, A. K., Carlson, S. R., & Rupert, J. L. (2014). Variants in the dopamine-4-receptor gene promoter are not associated with sensation seeking in skiers. PLoS ONE 9(4): e93521. doi:10.1371/journal.pone.0093521

Thorndike, E. L. (1911). *Animal intelligence.* New York: Macmillan.

Thornhill, R., & Palmer, C. T. (2000). *A natural history of rape: Biological bases of sexual coercion.* Cambridge, MA: MIT Press.

Todorov, A., Mandisodza, A. N., Goren, A., & Hall, C. C. (2005). Inferences of competence from faces predict election outcomes. *Science, 308,* 1623–1626.

Tomer, R., & Aharon-Peretz, J. (2004). Novelty seeking and harm avoidance in Parkinson's disease: Effects of asymmetric dopamine deficiency. *Journal of Neurology, Neurosurgery, and Psychiatry, 75,* 972–975.

Tooby, J., & Cosmides, L. (1990). On the universality of human nature and the uniqueness of the individual: The role of genetics and adaptation. *Journal of Personality, 58,* 17–67.

Tooke, W. S., & Ickes, W. (1988). A measure of adherence to conventional morality. *Journal of Social and Clinical Psychology, 6,* 310–334.

Totterdell, P. (2000). Catching moods and hitting runs: Mood linkage and subjective performance in professional sports teams. *Journal of Applied Psychology, 85*, 848–859.

Triandis, H. C. (1994). *Culture and social behavior.* New York: McGraw-Hill.

Triandis, H. C. (1997). Cross-cultural perspectives on personality. In R. Hogan, J. Johnson, & S. Briggs (Eds.), *Handbook of personality psychology* (pp. 439–464). San Diego: Academic Press.

Triandis, H. C., & Gelfand, M. J. (1998). Converging measurement of horizontal and vertical individualism and collectivism. *Journal of Personality and Social Psychology, 74*, 118–128.

Trivedi, N., & Sabini, J. (1998). Volunteer bias, sexuality, and personality. *Archives of Sexual Behavior, 27*, 181–195.

Trull, T. J., & Durrett, C. A. (2005). Categorical and dimensional models of personality disorder. *Annual Review of Clinical Psychology, 1*, 355–380.

Trzesniewski, K. H., & Donnellan, M. B. (2010). Rethinking "generation me": A study of cohort effects from 1976–2006. *Perspectives on Psychological Science, 5*, 58–75.

Trzesniewski, K. H., Donnellan, M. B., Moffitt, T. E., Robins, R. W., Poulton, R., & Caspi, A. (2006). Low self-esteem during adolescence predicts poor health, criminal behavior, and limited economic prospects during adulthood. *Developmental Psychology, 42*, 381–390.

Tsai, J. L., & Chentsova-Dutton, Y. (2003). Variation among European Americans in emotional facial expression. *Journal of Cross-Cultural Psychology, 34*, 650–657.

Tsai, J. L., Knutson, B., & Fung, H. H. (2006). Cultural variation in affect valuation. *Journal of Personality and Social Psychology, 90*, 288–307.

Tseng, W.-S. (2003). *Clinician's guide to cultural psychiatry.* San Diego: Academic Press.

Tupes, E. C., & Christal, R. C. (1961). *Recurrent personality factors based on trait ratings* (Tech. Rep.). San Antonio, TX: USAF, Lackland Air Force Base.

Turan, B. Guo, J., Boggiano, M. M., & Bedgood, D. (2014). Dominant, cold, avoidant, and lonely: Basal testosterone as a biological marker for an interpersonal style. *Journal of Research in Personality, 50*, 84–89.

Turiano, N. A., Chapman, B. P., Gruenewald, T. L., & Mroczek, D. K. (2015). Personality and the leading behavioral contributors of mortality. *Health Psychology, 34*(1), 51.

Turiano, N. A., Hill, P. L., Roberts, B. W., Spiro, A. I., II, & Mroczek, D. K. (2012). Smoking mediates the effect of conscientiousness on mortality: The veterans affairs normative aging study. *Journal of Research in Personality, 46*(6), 719–724.

Turiano, N. A., Spiro, A. S. III, & Mroczek, D. K. (2012). Openness to experience and mortality in men: Analysis of trait and facets. *Journal of Aging and Health, 24*, 654–672.

Turkheimer, E. (1998). Heritability and biological explanation. *Psychological Review, 105*, 782–791.

Turkheimer, E. (2016). Weak genetic explanation 20 years later: Reply to Plomin et al. (2016). *Perspectives on Psychological Science, 11*, 24–28.

Turkheimer, E., & Gottesman, I. I. (1991). Is H_2 = 0 a null hypothesis anymore? *Behavioral and Brain Sciences, 14*, 410–411.

Turkheimer, E., & Waldron, M. (2000). Nonshared environment: A theoretical, methodological, and quantitative review. *Psychological Bulletin, 126*, 78–108.

Turkheimer, E., Haley, A., Waldron, M., D'Onofrio, B., & Gottesman, I. I. (2003). Socioeconomic status modifies heritability of IQ in young children. *Psychological Science, 14*, 623–628.

Tversky, A., & Kahneman, D. (1973). Availability: A heuristic for judging frequency and probability. *Cognitive Psychology, 5*, 207–232.

Tversky, A., & Kahneman, D. (1983). Extensional versus intuitive reasoning: The conjunction fallacy in probability judgment. *Psychological Review, 90*, 1124–1131.

Tweed, R. G., & Lehman, D. R. (2002). Learning considered in a cultural context: Confucian and Socratic approaches. *American Psychologist, 57*, 89–99.

Twenge, J. M. (2006). *Generation me: Why today's young Americans are more confident, assertive, entitled—and more miserable than ever before.* New York: Free Press.

Twenge, J. M., & Campbell, W. K. (2003). "Isn't it fun to get the respect that we're going to deserve?" Narcissism, social rejection, and aggression. *Personality and Social Psychology Bulletin, 29,* 261–272.

Twenge, J. M., & Campbell, W. K. (2010). Birth cohort differences in the Monitoring the Future Dataset and elsewhere: Further evidence for Generation Me—Commentary on Trzesniewski & Donnellan (2010). *Perspectives on Psychological Science, 5,* 81–88.

Twenge, J. M., Konrath, S., Foster, J. D., Campbell, W. K., & Bushman, B. J. (2008). Egos inflating over time: A cross-temporal meta-analysis of the Narcissistic Personality Inventory. *Journal of Personality, 76,* 875–902.

United Nations Environment Programme. (2009). *The billion tree campaign.* Retrieved from http://www.unep.org/billiontreecampaign/Treeandhumanity/index.asp

Uttal, W. R. (2002). Précis of *The new phrenology: The limits of localizing cognitive processes in the brain. Brain and Mind, 3,* 221–228.

Valenstein, E. S. (1986). *Great and desperate cure: The rise and decline of psychosurgery and other radical treatments for mental illness.* New York: Basic Books.

Vallacher, R., & Wegner, D. (1987). What do people think they're doing? Action identification and human behavior. *Psychological Review, 94,* 3–15.

Van Boven, L. (2005). Experientialism, materialism, and the pursuit of happiness. *Review of General Psychology, 9,* 132–142.

Van den Akker, A. L., Prinzie, P., Dekovi, M., De Haan, A. D., Asscher, J. J., & Widiger, T. (2013). The development of personality extremity from childhood to adolescence: Relations to internalizing and externalizing problems. *Journal of Personality and Social Psychology, 105,* 1038–1048.

van der Linden, D., Pekaar, K.A., Bakker, A.B., Schermer, J.A., Veron, P.A., Dunkel, C.S., & Petrides, K.V. (2017). Overlap between the general factor of personality and emotional intelligence: A meta–analysis. *Psychological Bulletin, 143,* 36–52.

Van der Linden, D., Scholte, R. H. J., Cillessen, A. H. N., te Nijenhuis, J., & Segers, E. (2010). Classroom ratings of likeability and popularity are related to the Big Five and the general factor of personality. *Journal of Research in Personality, 44,* 669–672.

Van Hiel, A., & Kossowska, M. (2006). Having few positive emotions, or too many negative feelings? Emotions as moderating variables of authoritarianism effects on racism. *Personality and Individual Differences, 40,* 919–930.

Van Iddekinge, C. H., Roth, P. L., Putka, D. J., & Lanivich, S. E. (2011). Are you interested? A meta-analysis of the relations between vocational interests and employee performance and turnover. *Journal of Applied Psychology, 96,* 1167–1194.

Vazire, S. (2006). Informant reports: A cheap, fast, and easy method of personality assessment. *Journal of Research in Personality, 40,* 472–481.

Vazire, S. (2010). Who knows what about a person? The self-other knowledge asymmetry (SOKA) model. *Journal of Personality and Social Psychology, 98,* 281–300.

Vazire, S., & Carlson, E. N. (2011). Others sometimes know us better than we know ourselves. *Current Directions in Psychological Science, 20,* 104–108.

Vazire, S., & Funder, D. C. (2006). Impulsivity and the self-defeating behavior of narcissists. *Personality and Social Psychological Review, 10,* 154–165.

Vazire, S., & Mehl, M. R. (2008). Knowing me, knowing you: The accuracy and unique predictive validity of self-ratings and other-ratings of daily behavior. *Journal of Personality and Social Psychology, 95,* 1202–1216.

Vedantam, S. (2005, December 10). Psychiatry ponders whether extreme bias can be an illness [Electronic version]. *Washington Post,* p. A01.

Vignoles, V. L, Manzi, C., Regalia, C., Scabini, E., & Jemmolo, S. (2008). Identity motives underlying desired and feared possible future selves. *Journal of Personality, 76,* 1165–1200.

Vogt, D. S., & Colvin, C. R. (2003). Interpersonal orientation and the accuracy of personality judgment. *Journal of Personality, 71,* 267–295.

Vogt, D. S., & Colvin, C. R. (2005). Assessment of accurate self-knowledge. *Journal of Personality Assessment, 84*, 239–251.

Von Hippel, W., & Trivers, R. (2011). The evolution and psychology of self-deception. *Behavioral and Brain Sciences, 34*, 1–16.

Vonnegut, K., Jr. (1963). *Cat's cradle.* New York: Holt, Rinehart.

Vonnegut, K., Jr. (1966). *Mother night.* New York: Delacorte Press.

Vroman, L. N., Lo, S. L., & Durbin, E. (2014). Structure and convergent validity of children's temperament traits as assessed by experimenter ratings of child behavior. *Journal of Research in Personality, 52*, 6–12.

Vukasović, T., & Bratko, D. (2015). Heritability of personality: A meta-analysis of behavior genetic studies. *Psychological Bulletin, 141*(4), 769–785.

Vul, E., Harris, C., Winkielman, P., & Pashler, H. (2009). Puzzlingly high correlations in fMRI studies of emotion, personality, and social cognition [formerly titled "Voodoo correlations in social neuroscience"]. *Perspectives on Psychological Science, 4*, 274–290.

Wacker, J., Mueller, E. M., Hennig, J., & Stemmler, G. (2012). How to consistently link extraversion and intelligence to the catecho-O-methyltransferase (COMT) gene: On defining and measuring psychological phenotypes in neurogenetic research. *Journal of Personality and Social Psychology, 102*, 427–444.

Wagenmakers, E.J., Wetzels, R., Borsboom, D., & van der Maas, H. (2011). Why psychologists must change the way they analyze their data: The case of psi. *Journal of Personality and Social Psychology, 100*, 426–432.

Wagerman, S. A., & Funder, D. C. (2007). Acquaintance reports of personality and academic achievement: A case for conscientiousness. *Journal of Research in Personality, 41*, 221–229.

Wagerman, S. A., & Funder, D. C. (2009). Personality psychology of situations. In P. J. Corr and G. Matthews (Eds.), *Cambridge handbook of personality* (pp. 27–42). Cambridge: Cambridge University Press.

Wakefield, J. C. (1989). Levels of explanation in personality theory. In D. Buss & N. Cantor (Eds.), *Personality psychology: Recent trends and emerging directions* (pp. 333–346). New York: Springer-Verlag.

Waller, D. (1993, April 12). A tour through "hell week." *Newsweek*, p. 33.

Waller, N. G., & Shaver, P. R. (1994). The importance of nongenetic influences on romantic love styles: A twin-family study. *Psychological Science, 5*, 268–274.

Walton, K. E., Roberts, B. W., Krueger, R. F., Blonigen, D. M., & Hicks, B. M. (2008). Capturing abnormal personality with normal personality inventories: An item response theory approach. *Journal of Personality, 76*, 1623–1648.

Waters, E., Kondo-Ikemura, K., Posada, G., & Richters, J. E. (1991). Learning to love: Mechanisms and milestones. In M. R. Gunnar & L. A. Sroufe (Eds.), *Self processes and development* (pp. 217–255). Hillsdale, NJ: Erlbaum.

Watkins, C. E., Campbell, V. L., Nieberding, R., & Hallmark, R. (1995). Contemporary practice of psychological assessment by clinical psychologists. *Professional Psychology: Research and Practice, 26*, 54–60.

Watson, D. (1989). Strangers' ratings of five robust personality factors: Evidence of a surprising convergence with self-report. *Journal of Personality and Social Psychology, 57*, 120–128.

Watson, D. C. (2001). Procrastination and the five-factor model: A facet level analysis. *Personality and Individual Differences, 30*, 149–158.

Watson, D., & Clark, L. A. (1984). Negative affectivity: The disposition to experience aversive emotional states. *Psychological Bulletin, 96*, 465–490.

Watson, D., & Clark, L. A. (1997). Extraversion and its positive emotional core. In R. Hogan, J. Johnson, &S. Briggs (Eds.), *Handbook of personality psychology* (pp. 767–793). San Diego: Academic Press.

Watson, D., & Naragon-Gainey, K. (2014). Personality, emotion and the emotional disorders. *Clinical Psychological Science, 2*, 422–442.

Watson, D., & Tellegen, A. (1985). Toward a consensual structure of mood. *Psychological Bulletin, 98*, 219–235.

Watson, J. B. (1930). *Behaviorism* (Rev. ed.). New York: Norton.

Watts, A. L., Lilienfeld, S. O., Smith, S. F., Miller, J. D., Campbell, W. K., Waldman, I. D., . . . Faschingbauer, T. J. (2013). The double-edged sword of grandiose narcissism: Implications for successful and unsuccessful leadership among US Presidents. *Psychological Science, 24*, 2379–2389.

Weaver, I. C. G. (2007). Epigenetic programming by maternal behavior and pharmacological intervention—Nature vs. Nurture: Let's call the whole thing off. *Epigenetics, 2*, 22–28.

Weaver, I. C. G., Cervoni, N., Champagne, F. A., D'Alessio, A. C., Sharma, S., Seckl, J. R., et al. (2004). Epigenetic programming by maternal behavior. *Nature Neuroscience, 7*, 847–854.

Weiler, P., McCain, J.L., McLane, W.L., & Campbell, W.K. (2017). Personality and Minecraft: An exploratory study of the Big Five and narcissism. Unpublished ms.

Weinberg, R. S., Gould, D., & Jackson, A. (1979). Expectations and performance: An empirical test of Bandura's self-efficacy theory. *Journal of Sport Psychology, 1*, 320–331.

Weinberger, D. A., & Davidson, M. N. (1994). Styles of inhibiting emotional expression: Distinguishing repressive coping from impression management. *Journal of Personality, 62*, 587–613.

Weiss, J. M. (1970). Somatic effects of predictable and unpredictable shock. *Psychosomatic Medicine, 32*, 397–408.

Weiss, J. M. (1977). Psychological and behavioral influences on gastrointestinal lesions in animal models. In J. D. Maser & M. E. P. Seligman (Eds.), *Psychopathology: Experimental models* (pp. 232–269). San Francisco: Freeman.

Weng, H. Y., Fox, A. S., Shackman, A. J., Stodola, D. E., Caldwell, J. Z., Olson, M. C., et al. (2013). Compassion training alters altruism and neural responses to suffering. *Psychological Science, 24*, 1171–1180.

Westen, D. (1990). Psychoanalytic approaches to personality. In L. Pervin (Ed.), *Handbook of personality: Theory and research* (pp. 21–65). New York: Guilford Press.

Westen, D. (1992). The cognitive self and the psychoanalytic self: Can we put ourselves together? *Psychological Inquiry, 3*, 1–13.

Westen, D. (1998). The scientific legacy of Sigmund Freud: Toward a psychodynamically informed psychological science. *Psychological Bulletin, 124*, 333–371.

Westen, D., Gabbard, G. O., & Ortigo, K. M. (2008). Psychoanalytic approaches to personality. In O. P. John, R. W. Robins, & L. A. Pervin (Eds.), *Handbook of personality: Theory and research* (3rd ed., pp. 61–113). New York: Guilford Press.

Westfeldt, A. (2008, March 10). NY Governor linked to prostitution ring. *Associated Press.*

Weston, M. J., & Whitlock, F. A. (1971). The Capgras syndrome following head injury. *British Journal of Psychiatry, 119*, 25–31.

Weston, S.J., Hill, P.J., & Jackson, J.J. (2015). Personality traits predict the onset of disease. *Social Psychological and Personality Science, 6*, 309–317.

Wetzel, E., Brown, A., Hill, P.L., Chung, J.M., Robins, R.W., & Roberts, B.W. (2017). The narcissism epidemic is dead; Long live the narcissism epidemic. *Psychological Science, 28*, 1833–1847.

Wheeler, L., Reise, H. T., & Bond, M. H. (1989). Collectivism-individualism in everyday social life: The Middle Kingdom and the melting pot. *Journal of Personality and Social Psychology, 57*, 79–86.

Whitehead, A.N. (1911). *An Introduction to Mathematics.* New York: Henry Holt and Company.

Whorf, B. L. (1956). Science and linguistics. In J. B. Carroll (Ed.), *Language, thought, and reality* (pp. 207–219). Cambridge, MA: MIT Press.

Widom, C. S. (1989). The cycle of violence. *Science, 244*, 160–166.

Wiggins, J. S. (1973). *Personality and prediction: Principles of personality assessment.* Reading, MA: Addison-Wesley.

Wiggins, J. S., & Trapnell, P. D. (1997). Personality structure: The return of the Big Five. In R. Hogan, J. Johnson, & S. Briggs (Eds.), *Handbook of personality psychology* (pp. 737–765). San Diego: Academic Press.

Wilkinson, L., & The Task Force on Statistical Inference, APA Board of Scientific Affairs (1999). Statistical methods in psychology journals. *American Psychologist, 54*, 594–604.

Williams, R. B. (2001). Hostility: Effects on health and the potential for successful behavioral approaches to prevention and treatment. In A. Baum, T. A. Revenson, & J. E. Singer (Eds.), *Handbook of Health Psychology* (pp. 661–668). Mahwah, NJ: Erlbaum.

Wilson, E. O. (1975). *Sociobiology: The new synthesis.* Cambridge, MA: Harvard University Press.

Wilson, G. D. (1978). Introversion/extraversion. In H. London and J. E. Exner (Eds.), *Dimensions of personality* (pp. 51–56). New York: Wiley.

Wilson, R. S., Mendes de Leon, C. F., Bienias, J. L., Evans, D. A., & Bennett, D. A. (2004). Personality and mortality in old age. *Journal of Gerontology. B. Psychological Science and Social Science, 59*, 110–116.

Wilson, S., & Durbin, C. E. (2012). Dyadic parent-child interaction during early childhood: Contributions of parent and child personality traits. *Journal of Personality, 80*, 1313–1338.

Wilson, T. D. (2002). *Strangers to ourselves: Discovering the adaptive unconscious.* Cambridge, MA: Harvard University Press.

Wilson, T. D., & Gilbert, D. T. (2005). Affecting forecasting: Knowing what to want. *Current Directions in Psychological Science, 14*, 131–134.

Wilt, J., Noftle, E. E., Fleeson, W., & Spain, J. S. (2011). The dynamic role of personality states in mediating the relationship between extraversion and positive affect. *Journal of Personality, 80*, 1205–1236.

Winnicott, D. W. (1958). *Through paediatrics to psychoanalysis.* London: Hogarth Press.

Winnicott, D. W. (1965). *The maturational process and the facilitating environment.* London: Hogarth Press.

Winnicott, D. W. (1996). The niffle. In R. Shepherd, J. Johns, & H. T. Robinson (Eds.), *Thinking about children* (pp. 104–110). Reading, MA: Addison-Wesley.

Winograd, R.P., Steinley, D., Lane, S.P, & Sher, K.J. (2017). An experimental investigation of drunk personality using self and observer reports. *Clinical Psychological Science, 5*, 439–456.

Winter, D. G. (1991). Measuring personality at a distance: Development of an integrated system for scoring motives in running text. In D. J. Ozer, J. M. Healy, & A. J. Stewart (Eds.), *Perspectives in personality* (Vol. 3, pp. 59–89). London: Jennifer Kingsley.

Winter, D. G. (2002). The motivational dimensions of leadership: Power, achievement, and affiliation. In R. E. Riggio, S. E. Murphy, & F. J. Pirozzolo (Eds.), *Multiple intelligences and leadership* (pp. 119–138). Mahwah, NJ: Erlbaum.

Winter, D. G., & Stewart, A. J. (1978). The power motive. In H. London & J. E. Exner, Jr. (Eds.), *Dimensions of personality* (pp. 391–448). New York: Wiley.

Winter, D. G., John, O. P., Stewart, A. J., Klohnen, E. C., & Duncan, L. E. (1998). Traits and motives: Toward an integration of two traditions in personality research. *Psychological Review, 105*, 230–250.

Woike, B. A. (1995). Most-memorable experiences: Evidence for a link between implicit and explicit motives and social cognitive processes in everyday life. *Journal of Personality and Social Psychology, 68*, 1081–1091.

Woike, B. A., & Aronoff, J. (1992). Antecedents of complex social cognitions. *Journal of Personality and Social Psychology, 63*, 97–104.

Wood, D., Harms, P., & Vazire, S. (2010). Perceiver effects as projective tests: What your perceptions of others say about you. *Journal of Personality and Social Psychology, 99*, 174–190.

Wood, D., Nye, C. D., & Saucier, G. (2010). Identification and measurement of a more comprehensive set of person-descriptive trait markers from the English lexicon. *Journal of Research in Personality, 44*, 258–272.

Wood, J. M., Nezworski, M. T., & Garb, H. N. (2003). What's right with Rorschach? *Scientific Review of Mental Health Practice, 2*, 142–146.

Wood, J. V., Perunovic, E., & Lee, J. W. (2009). Positive self-statements: Power for some, peril for others. *Psychological Science, 20*, 860–866.

Wood, W., & Eagly, A. H. (2002). A cross-cultural analysis of the behavior of women and men: Implications for the origins of sex differences. *Psychological Bulletin, 128*, 699–727.

Woodworth, R. S. (1917). *Personal data sheet*. Chicago: Stoelting.

Wortman, J., & Wood, D. (2011). The personality traits of liked people. *Journal of Research in Personality, 45,* 519–528.

Wright, A. G. C., Pincus, A. L., & Lenzenweger, M. F. (2011). Development of personality and the remission and onset of personality pathology. *Journal of Personality and Social Psychology, 101,* 1351–1358.

Wu, C. C., Samenez-Larkin, G. R., Katovich, K., & Knutson, B. (2013). Affective traits link to reliable neural markers of incentive anticipation. *NeuroImage, 84,* 279–284.

Wundt, W. (1894). *Lectures on human and animal psychology* (J. E. Creighton & E. B. Titchener, Trans.). New York: Macmillan.

Wylie, R. E. (1974). *The self concept* (Vols. 1 and 2). Lincoln: University of Nebraska Press.

Yang, K. S., & Bond, M. H. (1990). Exploring implicit personality theories with indigenous or imported constructs: The Chinese case. *Journal of Personality and Social Psychology, 58,* 1087–1095.

Yang, K. S., & Lee, P. H. (1971). Likeability, meaningfulness, and familiarity of 557 Chinese adjectives for personality trait description [in Chinese]. *Acta Psychologica Taiwanica, 13,* 36–37.

Yang, Y., Read, S. J., Zhang, J., Denson, T. F., Xu, Y., & Pedersen, W. C. (2011). *From traits to situations, behaviors, and explanations: Integrating the trait and social cognitive perspectives on psychology.* Unpublished manuscript, China Europe International Business School, Shanghai.

Yeager, D. S., Trzesniewski, K. H., Tirri, K., Nokelainen, P., & Dweck, C. S. (2011). Adolescents' implicit theories predict desire for vengeance after peer conflicts: Correlational and experimental evidence. *Developmental Psychology, 47,* 1090–1107.

Young, J. (1988). *The role of selective attention in the attitude-behavior relationship.* Unpublished doctoral dissertation, University of Minnesota, Minneapolis.

Youyou, Wu, Stillwell, D, Schwartz, A.A., & Kosinski, M. (2017). Birds of a feather do flock together: Behavior-based personality assessment methods reveals personality similarity among couples and friends. *Psychological Science,* published online January 6, 2017.

Yudofsky, S. C. (2005). *Fatal flaws: Navigating destructive relationships with people with disorders of personality and character.* Washington, DC: American Psychiatric Publishing.

Zajonc, R. B. (1980). Feeling and thinking: Preferences need no inferences. *American Psychologist, 35,* 151–175.

Zald, D. H., & Curtis, C. (2006). Brain imaging and related methods. In M. Eid & E. Diener (Eds.), *Handbook of multimethod measurement in psychology* (pp. 173–187). Washington, DC: American Psychological Association.

Zammit, S., Owen, M. J., & Lewis, G. (2010). Misconceptions about gene-environment interactions in psychiatry. *Evidence Based Mental Health, 13,* 65–68.

Zanarini, M. C. (2008). Reasons for change in borderline personality disorder (and other Axis II disorders). *Psychiatric Clinics of North America, 31,* 505–515.

Zeigler-Hill, V. (2006). Discrepancies between implicit and explicit self-esteem: Implications for narcissism and self-esteem instability. *Journal of Personality, 74,* 119–143.

Zeigler-Hill, V., Myers, E. M., & Clark, C. B. (2010). Narcissism and self-esteem reactivity: The role of negative achievement events. *Journal of Research in Personality, 44,* 285–292.

Zeinoun, P., Daouk-Öyry, L., Choueiri, L, & van de Vijver, F.J.R. (2017). A mixed-methods study of personality conceptions in the Levant: Jordan, Lebanon, Syria and the West Bank. *Journal of Personality and Social Psychology, 113,* 453–465.

Zelenski, J. M., Whelan, D. C., Nealis, L. J., Besner, C. M., Santoro, M. S., & Wynn, J. E. (2013). Personality and affecting forecasting: Trait introverts underpredict the hedonic benefits of acting extraverted. *Journal of Personality and Social Psychology, 104,* 1092–1108.

Zelli, A., Cervone, D., & Huesmann, L. R. (1996). Behavioral experience and social inference: Individual differences in aggressive experience and spontaneous versus deliberate trait inference. *Social Cognition, 14,* 165–190.

Zelli, A., Huesmann, L. R., & Cervone, D. (1995). Social inference and individual differences in aggression: Evidence for spontaneous judgments of hostility. *Aggressive Behavior, 21,* 405–417.

Zentall, T. R., Sutton, J. E., & Sherburne, L. M. (1996). True imitative learning in pigeons. *Psychological Science, 7,* 343–346.

Zentner, M., & Mitura, K. (2012). Stepping out of the caveman's shadow: Nations' gender gap predicts degree of sex differentiation in mate preferences. *Psychological Science, 23,* 1176–1185.

Zhang, F., & Hazan, C. (2002). Working models of attachment and person perception processes. *Personal Relationships, 9,* 225–235.

Zheng, Y., Xu, L., & Shen, Q. (1986). Styles of verbal expression of emotional and physical experience: A study of depressed patients and normal controls in China. *Culture, Medicine, and Psychiatry, 10,* 231–243.

Zhou, X., Saucier, G., Gao, D., & Liu, J. (2009). The factor structure of Chinese personality terms. *Journal of Personality, 77,* 363–400.

Zhu, Y., Zhang, L., Fan, J., & Han, S. (2007). Neural basis of cultural influence on self representation. *NeuroImage, 34,* 1310–1317.

Zickar, M. J. (2001). Using personality inventories to identify thugs and agitators: Applied psychology's contribution to the war against labor. *Journal of Vocational Behavior, 59,* 149–164.

Zimbardo, P. G. (1977). *Shyness: What it is. What to do about it.* Reading, MA: Addison-Wesley.

Zimmerman, J., & Neyer, F. J. (2013). Do we become a different person when we hit the road? Personality development of sojourners. *Journal of Personality and Social Psychology, 105,* 515–530.

Zuckerman, M. (1991). *Psychobiology of personality.* New York: Cambridge University Press.

Zuckerman, M. (1998). Psychobiological theories of personality. In D. F. Barone, M. Hersen, & V. B. Van Hasselt (Eds.), *Advanced personality* (pp. 123–154). New York: Plenum Press.

Zuckerman, M. (2012). Biological bases of personality. In I. B. Weiner (Ed.), *Handbook of Psychology* (2nd ed., Vol. 5, pp. 27–42). New York: Wiley.

Zuckerman, M., Koestner, R., DeBoy, T., Garcia, K. T., Maresca, B. C., & Sartoris, J. M. (1988). To predict some of the people some of the time: A reexamination of the moderator variable approach in personality theory. *Journal of Personality and Social Psychology, 54,* 1006–1019.

Zuckerman, M., Li, C., & Hall, J. A. (2016). When men and women differ in self-esteem and when they don't: A meta-analysis. *Journal of Research in Personality, 64,* 34–51.

Zweigenhaft, R. L. (2008). A do re mi encore: A closer look at the personality correlates of music preferences. *Journal of Individual Differences, 29,* 45–55.

GLOSSARY

acculturation The process of social influence by which a person partially or fully acquires a new cultural outlook, either by having contact with or living in a culture different from his or her culture of origin.

active person-environment transaction The process by which people seek out situations that are compatible with their personalities, or avoid situations that they perceive as incompatible.

adrenal cortex The outer layer of the adrenal gland, atop the kidneys, that secretes several behaviorally important hormones.

aggregation The combining together of different measurements, such as by averaging them.

allele A particular variant, or form, of a gene; most genes have two or more alleles.

amygdala A structure located near the base of the brain that is believed to play a role in emotion, especially negative emotions such as anger and fear.

anal stage In psychoanalytic theory, the stage of psychosexual development, from about 18 months to 3 or 4 years of age, in which the physical focus of the libido is located in the anus and associated eliminative organs.

anatta In Zen Buddhism, the fundamental idea of "nonself"—that the single, isolated self is an illusion.

Angst In existential philosophy, the anxiety that stems from doubts about the meaning and purpose of life; also called *existential anxiety*.

anicca In Zen Buddhism, the recognition that all things are temporary and, therefore, it is best to avoid attachments to them.

anima In Jung's version of psychoanalysis, the idea of the typical female as held in the mind of a male.

animus In Jung's version of psychoanalysis, the idea of the typical male as held in the mind of a female.

antagonism One of five trait domains associated with personality disorders in the *DSM-5*, it is characterized by deceitfulness, grandiosity, callousness, and manipulativeness.

anterior cingulate The front part of the cingulate, a brain structure that runs from the front to the back of the brain in the middle, just above the corpus callosum. The anterior cingulate is believed to be important for the experience of normal emotion and self-control.

antisocial personality disorder An extreme pattern of deceitful, manipulative, and sometimes dangerous behavior.

archetypes In Jung's version of psychoanalysis, the fundamental images of people that are contained in the collective unconscious, including (among others) "the earth mother," "the hero," "the devil," and "the supreme being."

associationism The idea that all complex ideas are combinations of two or more simple ideas.

attachment theory A theoretical perspective that draws on psychoanalytic thought to describe the development and importance of human attachments to emotionally significant other people.

avoidant personality disorder An extreme pattern of feelings of inadequacy accompanied by fear of social contact.

basic approach (to personality) A theoretical view of personality that focuses on some phenomena and ignores others. The basic approaches are trait, biological, psychoanalytic, phenomenological, learning, and cognitive (the last two being closely related).

B data Behavioral data, or direct observations of another's behavior that are translated directly or nearly directly into numerical form. B data can be gathered in natural or contrived (experimental) settings.

behavioral confirmation The self-fulfilling prophecy tendency for a person to become the kind of person others expect him or her to be; also called the *expectancy effect*.

behavioral prediction The degree to which a judgment or measurement can predict the behavior of the person in question.

behaviorism (or behaviorist approach) The theoretical view of personality that focuses on overt behavior and the ways in which it can be affected by rewards and punishments in the environment. A modern variant is the social learning approach, which adds a concern with how behavior is affected by observation, self-evaluation, and social interaction; also called the *learning approach*.

Binomial Effect Size Display (BESD) A method for displaying and understanding more clearly the magnitude of an effect reported as a correlation, by translating the value of *r* into a 2×2 table comparing predicted with obtained results.

biological approach The view of personality that focuses on the way behavior and personality are influenced by neuroanatomy, biochemistry, genetics, and evolution.

borderline personality disorder An extreme and sometimes dangerous pattern of emotional instability, emotional emptiness, confused identity, and tendencies toward self-harm.

California Q-Set A set of 100 descriptive items (e.g., "is critical, skeptical, not easily impressed") that comprehensively covers the personality domain.

case method Studying a particular phenomenon or individual in depth both to understand the particular case and to discover general lessons or scientific laws.

central nervous system The brain and spinal cord.

chronic accessibility The tendency of an idea or concept to come easily to mind for a particular individual.

chunk Any piece of information that can be thought of as a unit. A chunk can vary with learning and experience. The capacity of short-term memory is seven chunks, plus or minus two.

classical conditioning The kind of learning in which an unconditioned response (such as salivating) that is naturally elicited by one stimulus (such as food) becomes elicited also by a new, conditioned stimulus (such as a bell).

cognitive Pertaining to basic mental processes of perception, memory, and thought.

cognitive control Using rational thinking to regulate one's emotions and to control how one reacts to emotional feelings.

cohort effect The tendency for a research finding to be limited to one group, or cohort, of people, such as people all living during a particular era or in a particular location.

collective unconscious In Jung's version of psychoanalysis, the proposition that all people share certain unconscious ideas because of the history of the human species.

compromise formation In modern psychoanalytic thought, the main job of the ego, which is to find a compromise among the different structures of the mind and the many different things the individual wants all at the same time. What the individual actually thinks and does is the result of this compromise.

condensation In psychoanalytic theory, the method of primary process thinking in which several ideas are compressed into one.

conscious mind The part of the mind's activities of which one is aware.

construal An individual's particular experience of the world or way of interpreting reality.

construct An idea about a psychological attribute that goes beyond what might be assessed through any particular method of assessment.

constructivism The philosophical view that reality, as a concrete entity, does not exist and that only ideas ("constructions") of reality exist.

construct validation The strategy of establishing the validity of a measure by comparing it with a wide range of other measures.

content validity The degree to which an assessment instrument, such as a questionnaire, includes content obviously relevant to what it is intended to predict.

convergent validation The process of assembling diverse pieces of information that converge on a common conclusion.

corpus callosum The thick bundle of nerve fibers connecting the right and left halves of the brain.

correlational method A research technique that establishes the relationship (not necessarily causal) between two variables, traditionally denoted x and y, by measuring both variables in a sample of participants.

correlation coefficient A number between −1 and +1 that reflects the degree to which one variable, traditionally called y, is a linear function of another, traditionally called x. A negative correlation means that as x goes up, y goes down; a positive correlation means that as x goes up, so does y; a zero correlation means that x and y are unrelated.

cortex The outside portion of an organ (see *adrenal cortex*); in the context of this book, the cortex refers to the outer layers of the brain.

cortisol A collective term for the glucocorticoid hormones, which are released into the bloodstream by the adrenal cortex as a response to physical or psychological stress.

critical realism The philosophical view that the absence of perfect, infallible criteria for determining the truth does not imply that all interpretations of reality are equally valid; instead, one can use empirical evidence to determine which views of reality are more or less likely to be valid.

cross-cultural psychology Psychological research and theorizing that attempts to account for the psychological differences between and within different cultural groups.

cross-sectional study A study of personality development in which people of different ages are assessed at the same time.

cumulative continuity principle The idea that personality becomes more stable and unchanging as a person gets older.

declarative knowledge Information held in memory that is able to be verbalized; sometimes called *knowing that*.

declarative self An individual's (conscious) opinions about his or her own personality traits and other relevant attributes.

deconstructionism A philosophy that argues reality does not exist apart from human perceptions, or constructions, of it.

defense mechanisms In psychoanalytic theory, the mechanisms of the ego that serve to protect an individual from experiencing anxiety produced by conflicts with the id, superego, or reality.

denial In psychoanalytic theory, the defense mechanism that allows the mind to deny that a current source of anxiety exists.

detachment One of five trait domains associated with personality disorders in the *DSM-5*, it is characterized by a tendency to withdraw from and avoid emotional contacts with other people.

disinhibition One of five trait domains associated with personality disorders in the *DSM-5*, it is characterized by a lack of self-control and impulsive behavior.

displacement In psychoanalytic theory, the defense mechanism that redirects an impulse from a dangerous target to a safe one.

doctrine of opposites In psychoanalytic theory, the idea that everything implies or contains its opposite.

dopamine A neurotransmitter in the brain that plays an important role in positive emotions and response to reward.

drive In learning theories, a state of psychological tension, the reduction of which feels good.

duck test If it looks like a duck, sounds like a duck, and acts like a duck, it probably *is* a duck.

effect size A number that reflects the degree to which one variable affects, or is related to, another variable.

efficacy expectation In Bandura's social learning theory, one's belief that one can perform a given goal-directed behavior.

ego In psychoanalytic theory, the relatively rational part of the mind that balances the competing claims of the id, the superego, and reality.

ego control In Jack Block's personality theory, the psychological tendency to inhibit the behavioral expression of motivation and emotional impulse. At the extremes, people may be either undercontrolled or overcontrolled.

ego-dystonic Refers to troubling thoughts, feelings, beliefs, or behaviors that one experiences as alien or foreign and would like to be rid of.

ego psychology The modern school of psychoanalytic thought that believes the most important aspect of mental functioning is the way the ego mediates between, and formulates compromises among, the impulses of the id and the superego.

ego resiliency In Jack Block's personality theory, the ability to vary one's level of ego control in order to respond appropriately to opportunities and situational circumstances.

ego-syntonic Refers to thoughts, feelings, beliefs, or behaviors that one accepts as part of oneself and does not want to be cured of, even if others find them difficult to deal with.

Eigenwelt In Binswanger's phenomenological analysis, the experience of experience itself; the result of introspection.

electroencephalography (EEG) A technique for measuring the brain's electrical activity by placing electrode sensors on the outside of the skull.

emics The locally relevant components of an idea; in cross-cultural psychology, aspects of a phenomenon that are specific to a particular culture.

emotional intelligence The ability to perceive emotions accurately in oneself and others and to control and use one's own emotions constructively.

empiricism The idea that everything a person knows comes from experience.

enculturation The process of socialization through which an individual acquires his or her native culture, mainly early in life.

endorphins The body's own pain-killing chemicals, which operate by blocking the transmission of pain messages to the brain.

entity theory In Dweck's theory of motivation, an individual's belief that abilities are fixed and unchangeable.

epigenetics Nongenetic influences on a gene's expression, such as stress, nutrition, and so forth.

epinephrine A neurotransmitter in the brain and also a hormone that is released by the adrenal gland as part of the body's response to stress; also called *adrenaline*.

epistemological self Knowledge of one's own personality traits, experiences, and other attributes; also called the *me*, as opposed to the I or ontological self.

essential-trait approach The research strategy that attempts to narrow the list of thousands of trait terms into a shorter list of the ones that really matter.

estrogen The female sex hormone.

etics The universal components of an idea; in cross-cultural psychology, aspects of a phenomenon that all cultures have in common.

eudaimonia Seeking happiness through developing one's full potential, helping others, and building community.

evocative person-environment transaction The process by which a people may change situations they encounter through behaviors that express their personality.

existentialism The approach to philosophy that focuses on conscious experience (phenomenology), free will, the meaning of life, and other basic questions of existence.

expectancy In Rotter's social learning theory, the degree to which an individual believes a behavior will probably attain its goal.

expectancy effect The tendency for someone to become the kind of person others expect him or her to be; also known as a *self-fulfilling prophecy* and *behavioral confirmation*.

expectancy value theory Rotter's theory of how the value and perceived attainability of a goal combine to affect the probability of a goal-seeking behavior.

experimental method A research technique that establishes the causal relationship between an independent variable (x) and dependent variable (y) by randomly assigning participants to experimental groups characterized by differing levels of x, and measuring the average behavior (y) that results in each group.

face validity The degree to which an assessment instrument, such as a questionnaire, on its face appears to measure what it is intended to measure. For example, a face-valid measure of sociability might ask about attendance at parties.

factor analysis A statistical technique for finding clusters of related traits, tests, or items.

fixation In psychoanalytic theory, leaving a disproportionate share of one's libido behind at an earlier stage of development.

flow The totally absorbing experience of engaging in an activity that is valuable for its own sake. In flow, mood is slightly elevated and time seems to pass quickly.

frontal cortex The front part of the cortex of the brain. Divided left and right into the two frontal lobes, this part of the brain is associated with cognitive functioning such as planning, foresight, and understanding.

functional analysis In behaviorism, a description of how a behavior is a function of the environment of the person or animal that performs it.

functional magnetic resonance imaging (fMRI) A technique for imaging brain activity by using a powerful magnet to help detect blood flow in the brain.

Funder's First Law Great strengths are usually great weaknesses, and surprisingly often the opposite is true as well.

Funder's Second Law There are no perfect indicators of personality; there are only clues, and clues are always ambiguous.

Funder's Third Law Something beats nothing, two times out of three.

generalizability The degree to which a measurement can be found under diverse circumstances, such as time, context, participant population, and so on. In modern psychometrics, this term includes both reliability and validity.

genital stage In psychoanalytic theory, the final stage of psychosexual development, in which the physical focus of the libido is on the genitals, with an emphasis on heterosexual relationships. The stage begins at about puberty, but is only fully attained when and if the individual achieves psychological maturity.

goal In learning and cognitive approaches to personality, a desired end state that serves to direct perception, thought, and behavior.

gonads The glands, testes in men and ovaries in women, that (among other effects) produce the sex hormones testosterone and estrogen, respectively.

habituation The decrease in response to a stimulus on repeated applications; this is the simplest kind of learning.

hedonia Seeking happiness through the pursuit of pleasure and comfort.

hedonism The idea that people are motivated to seek pleasure and avoid pain.

heterotypic continuity The reflection of the consistency of fundamental differences in personality that changes with age; e.g., the emotionally fragile child will act differently than the emotionally fragile adult, but the underlying trait is the same.

hippocampus A complex structure deep within the brain, behind the hypothalamus, that plays an important role in memory processes.

hormone A biological chemical that affects parts of the body some distance from where it is produced.

humanistic psychology The approach to personality that emphasizes aspects of psychology that are distinctly human. Closely related to the phenomenological approach and existentialism.

hypothalamus A complex structure near the lower center of the brain that has direct connections to many other parts of the brain and is involved in the production of psychologically important hormones; thought to be important for mood and motivation.

id In psychoanalytic theory, the repository of the drives, the emotions, and the primitive, unconscious part of the mind that wants everything *now*.

I data Informants' data, or judgments made by knowledgeable informants about general attributes of an individual's personality.

identification In psychoanalytic theory, taking on the values and worldview of another person (e.g., a parent).

incremental theory In Dweck's theory of motivation, an individual's belief that abilities can increase with experience and practice.

intellectualization In psychoanalytic theory, the defense mechanism by which thoughts that otherwise would cause anxiety are translated into cool, analytic, non-arousing terms.

interactionism The principle that aspects of personality and of situations work together to determine behavior; neither has an effect by itself, nor is one more important than the other.

interjudge agreement The degree to which two or more people making judgments about the same person provide the same description of that person's personality.

introspection The task of observing one's own mental processes.

judgability The extent to which an individual's personality can be judged accurately by others.

judgments Data that derive, in the final analysis, from someone using his or her common sense and observations to rate personality or behavior.

L data Life data, or more-or-less easily verifiable, concrete, real-life outcomes, which are of possible psychological significance.

learned helplessness A belief that nothing one does matters, derived from an experience of random or unpredictable reward and punishment, and theorized to be a basis of depression.

learning In behaviorism, a change in behavior as a result of experience.

learning approach The theoretical view that focuses on how behavior changes as a function of rewards and punishments; also called *behaviorism*.

lexical hypothesis The idea that, if people find something is important, they will develop a word for it, and therefore the major personality traits will have synonymous terms in many different languages.

libido In psychoanalytic theory, the drive toward the creation, nurturing, and enhancement of life (including but not limited to sex), or the energy stemming from this drive; also called *psychic energy*.

long-term memory (LTM) The final stage of information processing, in which a nearly unlimited amount of information can be permanently stored in an organized manner; this information may not always be accessible, however, depending on how it was stored and how it is looked for.

longitudinal study A study of personality development in which the same people are assessed repeatedly over extended periods of time, sometimes many years.

magnetoencephalography (MEG) A technique for using delicate magnetic sensors on the outside of the skull to detect brain activity.

many-trait approach The research strategy that focuses on a particular behavior and investigates its correlates with as many different personality traits as possible in order to explain the basis of the behavior and to illuminate the workings of personality.

masculine protest In Adler's version of psychoanalysis, the idea that a particular urge in adulthood is an attempt to compensate for one's powerlessness felt in childhood.

mate selection What a person looks for in the opposite sex.

mating strategies How individuals handle heterosexual relationships.

maturity principle The idea that traits associated with effective functioning increase with age.

measurement error The variation of a number around its true mean due to uncontrolled, essentially random influences; also called *error variance*.

mental health According to Freud's definition, the ability to both love and work.

mindful(ness) In positive psychology, the idea that one should be consciously aware of and in control of every moment of your subjective experience.

Mitwelt In Binswanger's phenomenological analysis, social experience such as feelings and thoughts about others and oneself in relation to them.

moderator variable A variable that affects the relationship between two other variables.

narcissism A personality trait that, in the normal range, is associated with high self-regard and a pattern of extraverted and confident behavior that can make an excellent first impression but become annoying in the long run. At the extreme, this trait can be characterized as a personality disorder.

narcissistic personality disorder An extreme pattern of arrogant, exploitative behavior combined with a notable lack of empathy.

narrative identity The story one tells oneself about who one is.

negative affectivity One of five trait domains associated with personality disorders in the *DSM-5*, it is characterized by a tendency to feel negative emotions such as anxiety, depression and suspicion.

neocortex The outer layer of the cortex of the brain, regarded as uniquely human.

neo-Freudian psychology A general term for the psychoanalytically oriented work of many theorists and researchers who are influenced by Freud's theory.

neuron A cell of the nervous system that receives and transmits information; also called *nerve cell*.

neurotransmitters The chemicals that allow one neuron to affect, or communicate with, another.

nirvana In Zen Buddhism, the serene state of selfless being that is the result of having achieved enlightenment.

norepinephrine An important neurotransmitter in the brain that is associated with responses to stress; also called *noradrenaline*.

objective test A personality test that consists of a list of questions to be answered by the subject as True or False, Yes or No, or along a numeric scale (e.g., 1 to 7).

object relations theory The psychoanalytic study of interpersonal relations, including the unconscious images and feelings associated with the important people ("objects") in a person's life.

observational learning Learning a behavior by watching someone else do it.

obsessive-compulsive personality disorder (OCPD) An extreme pattern of rigidly conscientious behavior, including an anxious and inflexible adherence to rules and rituals, perfectionism, and a stubborn resistance to change.

ontological self The somewhat mysterious inner self of thinking, observation, and experience; also called the *I*, as opposed to the me or epistemological self.

open science A set of emerging principles intended to improve the transparency of scientific research and that encourage fully reporting all methods and variables used in a study, reporting studies that failed as well as succeeded, and sharing data among scientists.

operant conditioning Skinner's term for the process of learning in which an organism's behavior is shaped by the effect of the behavior on the environment.

oral stage In psychoanalytic theory, the stage of psychosexual development, from birth to about 18 months of age, during which the physical focus of the libido is located in the mouth, lips, and tongue.

organ inferiority In Adler's version of psychoanalysis, the idea that people are motivated to succeed in adulthood in order to compensate for whatever they felt, in childhood, was their weakest aspect.

outgroup homogeneity bias The sociopsychological phenomenon by which members of a group to which one does not belong seem more alike than do members of a group to which one does belong.

oxytocin A hormone that may have specific effects in women of emotional attachment and calming.

p-Hacking Analyzing data in various ways until one finds the desired result.

parapraxis An unintentional utterance or action caused by a leakage from the unconscious parts of the mind; also called *Freudian slip*.

perceptual defense The process of failing to perceive stimuli that an individual might find disturbing or threatening.

peripheral nervous system The system of nerves running throughout the body, not including the brain and spinal cord.

persona In Jung's version of psychoanalysis, the social mask one wears in public dealings.

person-environment transactions The processes by which people respond to, seek out, and create environments that are compatible with, and may magnify, their personality traits.

personality An individual's characteristic patterns of thought, emotion, and behavior, together with the psychological mechanisms behind those patterns.

personality development Change in personality over time, including the development of adult personality from its origins in infancy and childhood, and changes in personality over the life span.

personality disorder A pattern of thought, feeling, and behavior that goes beyond the normal range of and causes problems for the affected individual or for others.

personality processes The mental activities of personality, including perception, thought, motivation, and emotion.

personality trait A pattern of thought, emotion, or behavior that is relatively consistent over time and across situations.

phallic stage In psychoanalytic theory, the stage of psychosexual development from about 4 to 7 years of age in which the physical focus of the libido is the penis (for boys) and its absence (for girls).

phenomenological approach The theoretical view of personality that emphasizes experience, free will, and the meaning of life. Closely related to humanistic psychology and existentialism.

phenomenology The study of conscious experience. Often, conscious experience itself is referred to as an individual's phenomenology.

p-level In statistical data analysis, the probability that the obtained correlation or difference between experimental conditions would be expected by chance.

positron emission tomography (PET) A technique for creating images of brain activity by injecting a radioactive tracer into the blood and then, using a scanner, finding where in the brain the blood is being metabolized.

preconscious Thoughts and ideas that temporarily reside just out of consciousness but which can be brought to mind quickly and easily.

predictive validity The degree to which one measure can be used to predict another.

primary process thinking In psychoanalytic theory, the term for the strange and primitive style of unconscious thinking manifested by the id.

priming Activation of a concept or idea by repeatedly perceiving it or thinking about it. The usual result is that this concept or idea comes to mind more quickly and easily in new situations.

procedural knowledge What a person knows but cannot really talk about; sometimes called *knowing how*.

procedural self Patterns of behavior that are characteristic of an individual.

projection In psychoanalytic theory, the defense mechanism of attributing to somebody else a thought or impulse one fears in oneself.

psychic determinism The assumption that everything psychological has a cause that is, in principle, identifiable.

psychic energy In psychoanalytic theory, the energy that allows the psychological system to function; also called *libido*.

psychoanalytic approach The theoretical view of personality, based on the writings of Sigmund Freud, that emphasizes the unconscious processes of the mind.

psychological triad The three essential topics of psychology: how people think, how they feel, and how they behave.

psychometrics The technology of psychological measurement.

psychoticism One of five trait domains associated with personality disorders in the *DSM-5*, it is characterized by a tendency to have bizarre thoughts or experiences, and to exhibit eccentric behavior.

publication bias The tendency of scientific journals preferentially to publish studies with strong results.

punishment An aversive consequence that follows an act in order to stop the act and prevent its repetition.

questionable research practices (QRP's) Research practices that, while not exactly deceptive, can increase the chances of obtaining the result the researcher desires. Such practices including deleting unusual responses, adjusting results to remove the influence of seemingly extraneous factors, and neglecting to report variables or experimental conditions that fail to yield expected results. Such practices are not always wrong, but they should always be questioned.

rank-order consistency The maintenance of individual differences in behavior or personality over time or across situations.

rationalization In psychoanalytic theory, the defense mechanism that produces a seemingly logical rationale for an impulse or thought that otherwise would cause anxiety.

reaction formation In psychoanalytic theory, the defense mechanism that keeps an anxiety-producing impulse or thought in check by producing its opposite.

reactive person-environment transaction The process by which people with different personalities may react differently to the same situation.

reciprocal determinism Bandura's term for the way people affect their environments even while their environments affect them.

regression In psychoanalytic theory, retreating to an earlier, more immature stage of psychosexual development, usually because of stress but sometimes in the service of play and creativity.

reinforcement In operant conditioning, a reward that, when applied following a behavior, increases the frequency of that behavior. In classical conditioning, this refers to the pairing of an unconditioned stimulus (such as food) with a conditioned stimulus (such as a bell).

reliability In measurement, the tendency of an instrument to provide the same comparative information on repeated occasions.

replication Doing a study again to see if the results hold up. Replications are especially persuasive when done by different researchers in different labs than the original study.

repression In psychoanalytic theory, the defense mechanism that banishes the past from current awareness.

research Exploration of the unknown; finding out something that nobody knew before one discovered it.

respondent conditioning Skinner's term for classical conditioning.

response Anything a person or animal does as a result of a stimulus.

Rorschach test A projective test that asks subjects to interpret blots of ink.

scatter plot A diagram that shows the relationship between two variables by displaying points on a two-dimensional plot. Usually the two variables are denoted x and y, each point represents a pair of scores, and the x variable is plotted on the horizontal axis while the y variable is plotted on the vertical axis.

schizotypal personality disorder An extreme pattern of odd beliefs and behaviors, and of difficulties relating to others.

S data Self-judgments, or ratings that people provide of their own personality attributes or behavior.

secondary process thinking In psychoanalytic theory, the term for rational and conscious processes of ordinary thought.

self-concept A person's knowledge and opinions about herself.

self-efficacy One's beliefs about the degree to which one will be able to accomplish a goal if one tries.

self-esteem The degree to which a person thinks he or she is good or bad, worthy or unworthy.

self-reference effect The enhancement of long-term memory that comes from thinking about how information being memorized relates to the self.

self-schema The cognitive structure hypothesized to contain a person's self-knowledge and to direct self-relevant thought.

self-verification The process by which people try to bring others to treat them in a manner that confirms their self-conceptions.

serotonin A neurotransmitter within the brain that plays an important role in the regulation of emotion and motivation.

short-term memory (STM) The stage of information processing in which the person is consciously aware of a small amount of information (about seven chunks) as long as that information continues to be actively processed.

single-trait approach The research strategy of focusing on one particular trait of interest and learning as much as possible about its behavioral correlates, developmental antecedents, and life consequences.

situationism The belief, held by some psychologists, that behavior is primarily determined by the immediate situation and that personality traits are not very important.

social clock The traditional expectations of society for when a person is expected to have achieved certain goals such as starting a family or getting settled into a career.

sociality corollary In Kelly's personal construct theory, the principle that understanding another person requires understanding that person's unique view of reality.

somatic marker hypothesis Neurologist Antonio Damasio's idea that the bodily (somatic), emotional component of thought is a necessary part of problem solving and decision making.

Spearman-Brown formula In psychometrics, a mathematical formula that predicts the degree to which the reliability of a test can be improved by adding more items.

state A temporary psychological event, such as an emotion, thought, or perception.

stimulus Anything in the environment that impinges on the nervous system.

strategy A sequence of activities directed toward a goal.

structured interview A clinical interview with a predetermined and consistent list of questions designed to produce objective ratings of personality disorders, personality traits, or other psychological attributes.

sublimation In psychoanalytic theory, the defense mechanism that turns otherwise dangerous or anxiety-producing impulses toward constructive ends.

superego In psychoanalytic theory, the part of the mind that consists of the conscience and the individual's system of internalized rules of conduct, or morality.

symbolization In psychoanalytic theory, the process of primary process thinking in which one thing stands for another.

synapse The space between two neurons across which impulses are carried by neurotransmitters.

temperament The term often used for the "personality" of very young, pre-verbal children. Aspects of temperament include basic attributes such as activity level, emotional reactivity, and cheerfulness.

testosterone The male sex hormone.

Thanatos In psychoanalytic theory, another term for the drive toward death, destruction, and decay.

Thematic Apperception Test (TAT) A projective test that asks subjects to make up stories about pictures.

thrown-ness In Heidegger's existential analysis, the era, location, and situation into which a person happens to be born.

trait A relatively stable and long-lasting attribute of personality.

trait approach The theoretical view of personality that focuses on individual differences in personality and behavior, and the psychological processes behind them.

transcranial magnetic stimulation (TMS) A brain research technique that uses rapidly changing magnetic fields to temporarily *knock out* (turn off) an area of brain activity to create a *virtual lesion*, allowing investigation as to whether that area is essential for a psychological task.

transference In psychoanalytic theory, the tendency to bring ways of thinking, feeling, and behavior that developed toward one important person into later relationships with different persons.

Type I error In research, the mistake of thinking that one variable has an effect on, or relationship with, another variable, when really it does not.

Type II error In research, the mistake of thinking that one variable does not have an effect on or relationship with another, when really it does.

typological approach The research strategy that focuses on identifying types of individuals. Each type is characterized by a particular pattern of traits.

Umwelt In Binswanger's phenomenological analysis, biological experience such as the sensations a person feels of being a live animal.

unconscious (mind) Those areas and processes of the mind of which a person is not aware.

utilitarianism The idea that the best society is the one that creates the most happiness for the largest number of people.

validity The degree to which a measurement actually reflects what it is intended to measure.

NAME INDEX

Aaker, J., 453
Abecasis, G., 325
Abelson, R., 88
Ackerman, R. A., 195
Adams, C., 133n10
Adelman, R. M., 574
Adler, J., 396
Adolphs, R., 277
Adorno, T. W., 201
Affleck, G., 40
Ahadi, S., 229
Ahlbom, A., 650
Ainsworth, M. D. S., 600
Ajzen, I., 121
Aknin, L. B., 455
Albright, L., 156, 481
Albus, K. E., 603
Alessandri, G., 218
Alford, E. C., 299
Algoe, S. B., 302
Alisat, S., 242
Allemand, M., 256
Allen, A., 114, 119
Allen, T. A., 295, 309
Alley, T. R., 156
Allik, J., 487, 489, 501
Allman, A., 544
Allport, G. W., 51, 55, 67, 108, 113,
    119, 121, 164, 196, 206, 225
Alonso-Zaldivar, R., 54
Alper, J., 338
Altemeyer, B., 202n6
Altinyazar, V., 576
Álvarez-Bermúdez, J., 479
Ambady, N., 156, 160, 164, 322
Amin, Z., 285
Amodio, D. M., 543

Anastasi, A., 74
Andersen, S. M., 170, 387, 569, 570,
    573, 599
Anderson-Harumi, C. A., 481
Anderson, C., 211, 214
Anderson, C. A., 137, 475, 517
Anderson, Z., 95, 96
Andersson, T., 650
Andrzejewski, S. A., 161
Ang, R. P., 191
Angleitner, A., 318, 491
Anestis, M. D., 631
Anik, L., 455
Anusic, I., 233
Appelbaum, M., 102
Appleby, G. S., 605
Apter, M. J., 210
Archer, R. P., 74
Armeli, S., 40
Aronoff, J., 76
Aronson, E., 124
Arsenian, J., 472
Arsenian, J. M., 472
Asch, S. E., 483
Asendorpf, J. B., 93, 114, 218, 221,
    228, 234, 571, 594, 595, 596, 597f
Ashmore, R. D., 573
Ashton, M. C., 215, 216
Assouline, M., 613
Atherton, O. E., 650
Augustine, A. A., 41, 211, 214, 647
Averill, J. R., 541
Avinun, R., 325

Bachrach, H. M., 411
Back, M. D., 41, 158, 170, 195, 254,
    572, 596, 597f, 628

Bader, M. J., 383
Bagby, R. M., 545
Bailey, J. M., 589
Bakan, D., 160
Balcetis, E., 480
Baldwin, M. W., 569
Ball, J. D., 74
Balter, M., 314
Bamia, C., 650
Bandelow, B., 633
Bandettini, P. A., 276
Bandura, A., 526, 552, 575
Banks, W. C., 99
Banse, R., 571
Baragh, D. P., 598
Baranski, E. N., 245, 487f, 506
Barefoot, J. C., 645
Bargh, J. A., 95, 441
Barker, E. T., 456
Barlow, D. H., 212, 249, 326
Barnes, M. F., 590
Barrett, D. J., 40
Barrett, K., 602
Barrett, L. F., 275, 278
Barrett, P., 28
Barrick, M. R., 607, 608
Barta, S. G., 530
Bartussek, D., 280
Bartz, J. A., 302
Batson, C. D., 126, 126t
Baum, A., 570, 599
Baumeister, R. F., 29, 44, 114, 191,
    444, 445, 559, 560
Baumrind, D., 100, 369
Beauchaine, T. P., 633
Becker, M., 478
Beckwith, J., 338

SUBJECT INDEX

Note: Page numbers followed by *f, t,* or *b* refer to figures, tables, and boxes, respectively. Page number in **bold** refer to glossary terms.